Alphabetical List of Authors

Chimamanda Ngozi
  Adichie
Ai
Sherman Alexie
Julia Alvarez
Matthew Arnold
Margaret Atwood
Agha Shahid Ali
W. H. Auden
Jimmy Santiago Baca
James Baldwin
Toni Cade Bambara
Jim Barnes
Wendell Berry
Elizabeth Bishop
William Blake
Eavan Boland
T. Coraghessan Boyle
Anne Bradstreet
Gwendolyn Brooks
Olga Broumas
Elizabeth Barrett
  Browning
Robert Browning
Robert Burns
Raymond Carver
Willa Cather
Lorna Dee Cervantes
Anton Chekhov
Marilyn Chin
Kate Chopin
Sandra Cisneros
Lucille Clifton
Judith Ortiz Cofer
Samuel Taylor
  Coleridge
Billy Collins
Countee Cullen
E. E. Cummings
Toi Derricotte
Junot Díaz
Emily Dickinson
John Donne
Mark Doty
Rita Dove
Paul Laurence
  Dunbar
Robert Duncan
Cornelius Eady
T. S. Eliot
Ralph Ellison
Anita Endrezze
Martín Espada

William Faulkner
F. Scott Fitzgerald
Carolyn Forché
Robert Francis
Robert Frost
Richard Garcia
Gabriel García
  Márquez
Charlotte Perkins
  Gilman
Allen Ginsberg
Susan Glaspell
Ray González
George Gordon, Lord
  Byron
Thomas Gray
Marilyn Hacker
Kimiko Hahn
Lorraine Hansberry
Thomas Hardy
Joy Harjo
Michael S. Harper
Robert Hass
Nathaniel Hawthorne
Robert Hayden
Terrance Hayes
Samuel Hazo
Seamus Heaney
Ernest Hemingway
George Herbert
Victor Hernández
  Cruz
Robert Herrick
Bob Hicok
Conrad Hilberry
Jane Hirshfield
Tony Hoagland
Linda Hogan
Garrett Kaoru Hongo
Gerard Manley
  Hopkins
A. E. Housman
Langston Hughes
Zora Neale Hurston
Henrik Ibsen
David Ives
Shirley Jackson
Randall Jarrell
Honorée Fanonne
  Jeffers
Sarah Orne Jewett
Ha Jin
Richard Jones

Ben Jonson
A. Van Jordan
Allison Joseph
James Joyce
Franz Kafka
John Keats
Jane Kenyon
Jamaica Kincaid
Galway Kinnell
Etheridge Knight
Yusef Komunyakaa
Ted Kooser
Maxine Kumin
Stanley Kunitz
Jhumpa Lahiri
D. H. Lawrence
Li-Young Lee
Denise Levertov
Philip Levine
Larry Levis
Audre Lorde
Richard Lovelace
Robert Lowell
Katherine Mansfield
Christopher Marlowe
Andrew Marvell
Heather McHugh
Claude McKay
Herman Melville
John Milton
Marianne Moore
Thylias Moss
Marilyn Nelson
Lorine Niedecker
John Frederick Nims
Lynn Nottage
Naomi Shihab Nye
Joyce Carol Oates
Tim O'Brien
Flannery O'Connor
Frank O'Hara
Sharon Olds
Mary Oliver
Tillie Olsen
Simon J. Ortiz
Wilfred Owen
Linda Pastan
Marge Piercy
Robert Pinsky
Sylvia Plath
Edgar Allan Poe
Alexander Pope
Ezra Pound

Dudley Randall
John Crowe Ransom
Adrienne Rich
Alberto Ríos
Edwin Arlington
  Robinson
Theodore Roethke
Mary Ruefle
Anne Sexton
William Shakespeare
Percy Bysshe Shelley
Leslie Marmon Silko
Charles Simic
Gary Snyder
Cathy Song
Sophocles
Gary Soto
Edmund Spenser
William Stafford
Gerald Stern
Wallace Stevens
Mark Strand
Virgil Suárez
Sekou Sundiata
Jonathan Swift
Amy Tan
James Tate
Alfred, Lord
  Tennyson
Dylan Thomas
Jean Toomer
Natasha Trethewey
Quincy Troupe
John Updike
Alice Walker
James Welch
Eudora Welty
Walt Whitman
Richard Wilbur
Nancy Willard
Tennessee Williams
William Carlos
  Williams
August Wilson
William Wordsworth
Charles Wright
James Wright
Lady Mary Wroth
Sir Thomas Wyatt
William Butler Yeats
Al Young
Ray A. Young Bear
Paul Zimmer

Literature
A Portable Anthology

Literature
A Portable Anthology
Third Edition

Edited by

JANET E. GARDNER

BEVERLY LAWN
Adelphi University

JACK RIDL
Hope College

PETER SCHAKEL
Hope College

Bedford/St. Martin's   BOSTON ◆ NEW YORK

For Bedford/St. Martin's

Executive Editor: Stephen A. Scipione
Developmental Editor: Deja Earley
Production Editor: Kendra LeFleur
Production Supervisor: Samuel Jones
Marketing Manager: Stacey Propps
Editorial Assistant: Regina Tavani
Production Assistant: Elise Keller
Copy Editor: Linda McLatchie
Indexer: Jake Kawatski
Permissions Manager: Kalina K. Ingham
Senior Art Director: Anna Palchik
Text Design: Sandra Rigney and Janis Owens
Cover Design: Donna Lee Dennison
Cover Photo: Mason Swinging—Ashland, OR—2005. © Cole Thompson.
Composition: Jouve
Printing and Binding: RR Donnelley and Sons

President, Bedford/St. Martin's: Denise B. Wydra
Presidents, Macmillan Higher Education: Joan E. Feinberg and Tom Scotty
Editor in Chief: Karen S. Henry
Director of Marketing: Karen R. Soeltz
Director of Production: Susan W. Brown
Associate Director, Editorial Production: Elise S. Kaiser
Managing Editor: Elizabeth M. Schaaf

Library of Congress Control Number: 2012932569

Manufactured in the United States of America.

7 6 5 4 3 2
f e d c b a

For information, write: Bedford/St. Martin's, 75 Arlington Street, Boston, MA 02116 (617-399-4000)

ISBN 978-1-4576-0650-2

Acknowledgments

Acknowledgments and copyrights appear at the back of the book on pages 1363–70, which constitute an extension of the copyright page. It is a violation of the law to reproduce these selections by any means whatsoever without the written permission of the copyright holder.

Preface for Instructors

The third edition of *Literature: A Portable Anthology* presents, in a compact and highly affordable format, an ample and flexible choice of fiction, poetry, and drama for introductory literature courses. Arranged chronologically by genre, the stories, poems, and plays are complemented by editorial matter that offers enough help for students learning to think, read, and write about literature, without interfering with their enjoyment of the literary works.

In these pages students will discover:

- 40 engaging and significant stories, from classic authors such as Edgar Allan Poe, William Faulkner, and Flannery O'Connor to contemporary writers such as Jhumpa Lahiri, Junot Diaz, and Sherman Alexie.
- A judicious and varied selection of 200 poems—not only an abundant selection of many classic and frequently assigned works by canonical writers such as William Blake, Langston Hughes, and Elizabeth Bishop, but also the most diverse selection of contemporary American poetry in an anthology of this scope, including poems by Li-Young Lee, Naomi Shihab Nye, and Natasha Trethewey, among many others.
- A teaching canon of 9 plays—from Sophocles' classical tragedy *Oedipus Rex* to modern masterpieces such as Tennessee Williams's *The Glass Menagerie* to deeply admired contemporary works such as August Wilson's *Fences*. The selection represents not only important works in the Western dramatic tradition but also a core of plays most frequently assigned and popular in the classroom.

At the back of the book, in addition to biographical notes on every author and a glossary of literary terms, students will find a section devoted to helping them read literature closely and write about it effectively. Written by Janet E. Gardner and also available as a separate supplementary volume (*Reading and Writing about Literature: A Portable Guide*), this section explains how to think critically, read analytically, and write a variety of commonly assigned papers about literature, from

summaries to research papers, with several sample student papers included as models.

New to the third edition

The choice of literary selections has been significantly revised and updated. The third edition includes:

- A more contemporary and diverse selection of fiction. Of the 15 new
  stories, several are by classic authors such as Anton Chekhov and
  Zora Neale Hurston, but most are of our day, including recent gems
  by Ha Jin, T. Coraghessan Boyle, and Chimamanda Ngozi Adichie.
- Several canonical poets represented in greater depth, and a fresh-
  ened selection of contemporary poems. The 55 new poems include
  more classic selections from the work of Emily Dickinson and
  Robert Frost as well as recent pieces by younger poets such as
  Marilyn Chin, Terrance Hayes, and Martín Espada.
- Three new plays: a classroom favorite, William Shakespeare's
  Othello; a modern classic, Lorraine Hansberry's *A Raisin in the Sun*;
  and an award-winning contemporary play, Lynn Nottage's *POOF!*

Additionally, the writing instruction at the back of the book has been
updated and expanded. Along with more detailed advice on critical reading and common writing assignments, Part Four now includes new examples of literature annotated to model close-reading for students, including T. S. Eliot's long poem "The Love Song of J. Alfred Prufrock,"
new student papers, and overall a more thorough and illuminating instruction on the literary elements and the writing process.

YOU GET MORE RESOURCES FOR *LITERATURE: A PORTABLE ANTHOLOGY.*

Literature: A Portable Anthology doesn't stop with a book. Online, you'll
find both free and affordable premium resources to help students get
even more out of the book and your course. You'll also find convenient
instructor resources, and even a nationwide community of teachers.
To learn more about or order any of the following products, contact
your Bedford/St. Martin's sales representative, e-mail sales support
(sales_support@bfwpub.com), or visit the Web site at **bedfordstmartins
.com/literatureportable/catalog.**

Literature: A Portable Anthology **now comes with videos.**

Bring today's best writers into your classroom. *VideoCentral: Literature*, our growing library of more than 50 video interviews with today's writers, includes Ha Jin on how he uses humor, Chitra Banerjee Divakaruni on how she writes from experience, and T. Coraghessan Boyle on how he works with language and style. Biographical notes and questions make each video an assignable module. See **bedfordstmartins.com/videolit/catalog**.

This resource can be packaged at a discount with new student editions of this book. An activation code is required and must be purchased. To order *VideoCentral: Literature* with this print text, use **ISBN 978-1-4576-3118-4**.

Visit *Re:Writing for Literature*
bedfordstmartins.com/rewritinglit

Supplement your print text with our free and open resources for literature (no codes required) and flexible premium content.

Get free online help for your students. *Re:Writing for Literature* provides close-reading help, reference materials, and support for working with sources.

- *VirtuaLit* tutorials for close-reading (fiction, poetry, and drama)
- *AuthorLinks* and biographies for 800 authors
- Glossary of literary terms
- MLA-style student papers
- Help for finding and citing sources, including access to Diana Hacker's *Research and Documentation Online*

Get teaching ideas you can use today.

Are you looking for professional resources for teaching literature and writing? How about some help with planning classroom activities?

TeachingCentral. We've gathered all of our print and online professional resources in one place. You'll find landmark reference works, sourcebooks on pedagogical issues, award-winning collections, and practical advice for the classroom—all free for instructors and available at **bedfordstmartins .com/teachingcentral**.

LitBits *Blog: Ideas for Teaching Literature and Creative Writing.* Our new *LitBits* blog—hosted by a growing team of instructors, poets, novelists, and scholars—offers a fresh, regularly updated collection of ideas and assignments. You'll find simple ways to teach with new media, to excite your students with activities, and to join an ongoing conversation about teaching. Go to **bedfordstmartins.com/litbits/catalog** and **bedfordstmartins.com/litbits**.

ACKNOWLEDGMENTS

For their helpful responses to a questionnaire about their experiences using previous editions of the book, the editors are grateful to Tony Ardizzone, Indiana University; Robert Bailey, South Suburban College; Raquel Baker, The University of Iowa; Ann Bomberger, Gannon University; David Bradford, Brevard Community College; Alexis Cattivera, University of California, Davis; Kerry L. Ceszyk, University of Colorado; Robert Timothy Davis, University of West Florida; James A. Dervin, Winston-Salem State University; Jason M. Dew, Georgia Perimeter College; Jeff Doty, University of Iowa; Michael Felker, South Plains College; Jacqueline Foertsch, University of North Texas; Kelley D. McKay Fuemmeler, Missouri Valley College; Armida Gilbert, Georgia Perimeter College; Gael Grossman, Jamestown Community College; Molly Hiro, University of Portland; Cynthia Howell, Black Hills State University; Gladys Huggins, Winston-Salem State University; Elizabeth JK James, Red Rocks Community College; Ana Johnson, Miami Dade College, Kendall Campus; Susan Johnston, University of Regina; Gerald Kenney, Valencia Community College; John Kerrigan, Rockhurst University; Tracey Lander-Garrett, Borough of Manhattan Community College; Walter Lowe, Green River Community College; Carol McFrederick, Florida International University; Katharina Mendoza, University of Iowa; Janet Minc, The University of Akron: Wayne College; Ann H. Moser, Virginia Western Community College; Kristen Muir, Madison Area Technical College; David Mulry, Schreiner University; Lisa Neville, SUNY Tompkins Cortland Community College; Marc Pietrzykowski, Niagara County Community College; Larry Poe, Fisher College; Jeffrey Rubinstein, Hillsborough Community College; Suzanne Scanlon, Columbia College, Chicago; Carl Seiple, Kutztown University; Allison Smith, Middle Tennessee State University; Michael P. Steier, University of Delaware; Michael Tomanek, Minnesota State University; Linda Trombley, University of Southern Maine; Rick Van Noy, Radford University; Dawn Winters, Western Kentucky University; Jerome L. Wyant, Mount Saint Mary College; Margaret Enright Wye, Rockhurst University; Peter T. Zoller, Wichita State University; and Genevieve Zuidervaart, Golden West College.
    The editors would like to thank Joan E. Feinberg, Co-President of

Macmillan Higher Education; Denise Wydra, President of Bedford/ St. Martin's; and Karen S. Henry, Editor in Chief, English. Senior Executive Editor Steve Scipione and Developmental Editor Deja Earley were instrumental in shaping the third edition. We appreciate Margaret Gorenstein's work in clearing permissions and Stacey Propp's marketing expertise, and we especially appreciate those who turned the manuscript into a book: Elizabeth Schaaf, Elise Kaiser, and our hardworking Production Editor, Kendra LeFleur.

Beverly Lawn prepared the materials for the fiction section, Jack Ridl and Peter Schakel for the poetry section, and Janet E. Gardner for the Reading and Writing about Literature section. Beverly Lawn particularly thanks her husband, Robert Lawn, and her daughters, Hilary Cantilina and Pamela Lawn-Williams, for their help. Jack Ridl and Peter Schakel are grateful to Hope College colleagues who provided help with earlier editions — Susan Atefat Peckham, Marla Lunderberg, William Pannapacker, and Charles Huttar, and especially Jesse Montaño for his continued assistance. Janet Gardner deeply thanks Stephanie Tucker, Parmita Kapadia, Sarah Johnson, and Patrick McCorkle for their contributions and support, and Joanne Diaz for her revision efforts on the Reading and Writing about Literature section.

Brief Contents

Contents

PART TWO. 200 POEMS   447

PART THREE. 9 PLAYS   705

PART FOUR. READING AND WRITING ABOUT

LITERATURE   1129

PART ONE

40 Stories

NATHANIEL HAWTHORNE   [1804–1864]

Young Goodman Brown

Young Goodman Brown came forth at sunset into the street at Salem village; but put his head back, after crossing the threshold, to exchange a parting kiss with his young wife. And Faith, as the wife was aptly named, thrust her own pretty head into the street, letting the wind play with the pink ribbons of her cap while she called to Goodman Brown.

"Dearest heart," whispered she, softly and rather sadly, when her lips were close to his ear, "prithee put off your journey until sunrise and sleep in your own bed to-night. A lone woman is troubled with such dreams and such thoughts that she's afeared of herself sometimes. Pray tarry with me this night, dear husband, of all nights in the year."

"My love and my Faith," replied young Goodman Brown, "of all nights in the year, this one night must I tarry away from thee. My journey, as thou callest it, forth and back again, must needs be done 'twixt now and sunrise. What, my sweet, pretty wife, dost thou doubt me already, and we but three months married?"

"Then God bless you!" said Faith, with the pink ribbons, "and may you find all well when you come back."

"Amen!" cried Goodman Brown. "Say thy prayers, dear Faith, and go to bed at dusk, and no harm will come to thee."

So they parted; and the young man pursued his way until, being about to turn the corner by the meeting-house, he looked back and saw the head of Faith still peeping after him with a melancholy air, in spite of her pink ribbons.

"Poor little Faith!" thought he, for his heart smote him. "What a wretch am I to leave her on such an errand! She talks of dreams, too. Methought as she spoke there was trouble in her face, as if a dream had warned her what work is to be done to-night. But no, no; 't would kill her to think it. Well, she's a blessed angel on earth, and after this one night I'll cling to her skirts and follow her to heaven."

With this excellent resolve for the future, Goodman Brown felt himself justified in making more haste on his present evil purpose. He had taken a dreary road, darkened by all the gloomiest trees of the forest, which barely stood aside to let the narrow path creep through, and closed immediately behind. It was all as lonely as could be; and there is this

3

peculiarity in such a solitude, that the traveller knows not who may be concealed by the innumerable trunks and the thick boughs overhead; so that with lonely footsteps he may yet be passing through an unseen multitude.

"There may be a devilish Indian behind every tree," said Goodman Brown to himself; and he glanced fearfully behind him as he added, "What if the devil himself should be at my very elbow!"

His head being turned back, he passed a crook of the road, and, looking forward again, beheld the figure of a man, in grave and decent attire, seated at the foot of an old tree. He arose at Goodman Brown's approach and walked onward side by side with him.

"You are late, Goodman Brown," said he. "The clock of the Old South was striking as I came through Boston, and that is full fifteen minutes agone."

"Faith kept me back a while," replied the young man, with a tremor in his voice, caused by the sudden appearance of his companion, though not wholly unexpected.

It was now deep dusk in the forest, and deepest in that part of it where these two were journeying. As nearly as could be discerned, the second traveller was about fifty years old, apparently in the same rank of life as Goodman Brown, and bearing a considerable resemblance to him, though perhaps more in expression than features. Still they might have been taken for father and son. And yet, though the elder person was as simply clad as the younger, and as simple in manner too, he had an indescribable air of one who knew the world, and who would not have felt abashed at the governor's dinner table or in King William's court, were it possible that his affairs should call him thither. But the only thing about him that could be fixed upon as remarkable was his staff, which bore the likeness of a great black snake, so curiously wrought that it might almost be seen to twist and wriggle itself like a living serpent. This, of course, must have been an ocular deception, assisted by the uncertain light.

"Come, Goodman Brown," cried his fellow-traveller, "this is a dull pace for the beginning of a journey. Take my staff, if you are so soon weary."

"Friend," said the other, exchanging his slow pace for a full stop, "having kept covenant by meeting thee here, it is my purpose now to return whence I came. I have scruples touching the matter thou wot'st of."

"Sayest thou so?" replied he of the serpent, smiling apart. "Let us walk on, nevertheless, reasoning as we go; and if I convince thee not thou shalt turn back. We are but a little way in the forest yet."

"Too far! too far!" exclaimed the goodman, unconsciously resuming his walk. "My father never went into the woods on such an errand, nor his father before him. We have been a race of honest men and good Christians since the days of the martyrs; and shall I be the first of the name of Brown that ever took this path and kept"—

"Such company, thou wouldst say," observed the elder person, interpreting his pause. "Well said, Goodman Brown! I have been as well acquainted with your family as with ever a one among the Puritans; and that's no trifle to say. I helped your grandfather, the constable, when he lashed the Quaker woman so smartly through the streets of Salem; and it was I that brought your father a pitch-pine knot, kindled at my own hearth, to set fire to an Indian village, in King Philip's war.° They were my good friends, both; and many a pleasant walk have we had along this path, and returned merrily after midnight. I would fain be friends with you for their sake."

"If it be as thou sayest," replied Goodman Brown, "I marvel they never spoke of these matters; or, verily, I marvel not, seeing that the least rumor of the sort would have driven them from New England. We are a people of prayer, and good works to boot, and abide no such wickedness."

"Wickedness or not," said the traveller with the twisted staff, "I have a very general acquaintance here in New England. The deacons of many a church have drunk the communion wine with me; the selectmen of divers towns make me their chairman; and a majority of the Great and General Court are firm supporters of my interest. The governor and I, too—But these are state secrets."

"Can this be so?" cried Goodman Brown, with a stare of amazement at his undisturbed companion. "Howbeit, I have nothing to do with the governor and council; they have their own ways, and are no rule for a simple husbandman like me. But, were I to go on with thee, how should I meet the eye of that good old man, our minister, at Salem village? Oh, his voice would make me tremble both Sabbath day and lecture day."

Thus far the elder traveller had listened with due gravity; but now burst into a fit of irrepressible mirth, shaking himself so violently that his snake-like staff actually seemed to wriggle in sympathy.

"Ha! ha! ha!" shouted he again and again; then composing himself, "Well, go on, Goodman Brown, go on; but, prithee, don't kill me with laughing."

"Well, then, to end the matter at once," said Goodman Brown, considerably nettled, "there is my wife, Faith. It would break her dear little heart; and I'd rather break my own."

"Nay, if that be the case," answered the other, "e'en go thy ways, Goodman Brown. I would not for twenty old women like the one hobbling before us that Faith should come to any harm."

As he spoke he pointed his staff at a female figure on the path, in whom Goodman Brown recognized a very pious and exemplary dame, who had taught him his catechism in youth, and was still his moral and spiritual adviser, jointly with the minister and Deacon Gookin.

King Philip: Wampanoag chief, waged war against the New England colonists (1675–76).

"A marvel, truly that Goody Cloyse should be so far in the wilderness at nightfall," said he. "But with your leave, friend, I shall take a cut through the woods until we have left this Christian woman behind. Being a stranger to you, she might ask whom I was consorting with and whither I was going."

"Be it so," said his fellow-traveller. "Betake you to the woods, and let me keep the path."

Accordingly the young man turned aside, but took care to watch his companion, who advanced softly along the road until he had come within a staff's length of the old dame. She, meanwhile, was making the best of her way, with singular speed for so aged a woman, and mumbling some indistinct words—a prayer, doubtless—as she went. The traveller put forth his staff and touched her withered neck with what seemed the serpent's tail.

"The devil!" screamed the pious old lady.

"Then Goody Cloyse knows her old friend?" observed the traveller, confronting her and leaning on his writhing stick.

"Ah, forsooth, and is it your worship indeed?" cried the good dame. "Yea, truly is it, and in the very image of my old gossip, Goodman Brown, the grandfather of the silly fellow that now is. But—would your worship believe it?—my broomstick hath strangely disappeared, stolen, as I suspect, by that unhanged witch, Goody Cory, and that, too, when I was all anointed with the juice of smallage, and cinquefoil, and wolf's bane"°—

"Mingled with fine wheat and the fat of a new-born babe," said the shape of old Goodman Brown.

"Ah, your worship knows the recipe," cried the old lady, cackling aloud. "So, as I was saying, being all ready for the meeting, and no horse to ride on, I made up my mind to foot it; for they tell me there is a nice young man to be taken into communion to-night. But now your good worship will lend me your arm, and we shall be there in a twinkling."

"That can hardly be," answered her friend. "I may not spare you my arm, Goody Cloyse; but here is my staff, if you will."

So saying, he threw it down at her feet, where, perhaps, it assumed life, being one of the rods which its owner had formerly lent to the Egyptian magi. Of this fact, however, Goodman Brown could not take cognizance. He had cast up his eyes in astonishment, and, looking down again, beheld neither Goody Cloyse nor the serpentine staff, but his fellow-traveller alone, who waited for him as calmly as if nothing had happened.

Smallage, cinquefoil, and wolf's bane: Three plants sometimes associated with witchcraft. Smallage refers to varieties of parsley and celery; cinquefoil to plants with compound leaves, each having five leaflets; wolf's bane to plants with dull green leaves and yellow foliage, sometimes called winter wheat or aconite.

"That old woman taught me my catechism," said the young man; and there was a world of meaning in this simple comment.

They continued to walk onward, while the elder traveller exhorted his companion to make good speed and persevere in the path, discoursing so aptly that his arguments seemed rather to spring up in the bosom of his auditor than to be suggested by himself. As they went, he plucked a branch of maple to serve for a walking stick, and began to strip it of the twigs and little boughs, which were wet with evening dew. The moment his fingers touched them they became strangely withered and dried up as with a week's sunshine. Thus the pair proceeded, at a good free pace, until suddenly, in a gloomy hollow of the road, Goodman Brown sat himself down on the stump of a tree and refused to go any farther.

"Friend," he said, stubbornly, "my mind is made up. Not another step will I budge on this errand. What if a wretched old woman do choose to go to the devil when I thought she was going to heaven: is that any reason why I should quit my dear Faith and go after her?"

"You will think better of this by and by," said his acquaintance, composedly. "Sit here and rest yourself a while; and when you feel like moving again, there is my staff to help you along."

Without more words, he threw his companion the maple stick, and was as speedily out of sight as if he had vanished into the deepening gloom. The young man sat a few moments by the roadside, applauding himself greatly, and thinking with how clear a conscience he should meet the minister in his morning walk, nor shrink from the eye of good old Deacon Gookin. And what calm sleep would be his that very night, which was to have been spent so wickedly, but so purely and sweetly now, in the arms of Faith! Amidst these pleasant and praiseworthy meditations, Goodman Brown heard the tramp of horses along the road, and deemed it advisable to conceal himself within the verge of the forest, conscious of the guilty purpose that had brought him thither, though now so happily turned from it.

On came the hoof tramps and the voices of the riders, two grave old voices, conversing soberly as they drew near. These mingled sounds appeared to pass along the road, within a few yards of the young man's hiding-place; but, owing doubtless to the depth of the gloom at that particular spot, neither the travellers nor their steeds were visible. Though their figures brushed the small boughs by the wayside, it could not be seen that they intercepted, even for a moment, the faint gleam from the strip of bright sky athwart which they must have passed. Goodman Brown alternately crouched and stood on tiptoe, pulling aside the branches and thrusting forth his head as far as he durst without discerning so much as a shadow. It vexed him the more, because he could have sworn, were such a thing possible, that he recognized the voices of the minister and

Deacon Gookin, jogging along quietly, as they were wont to do, when bound to some ordination or ecclesiastical council. While yet within hearing, one of the riders stopped to pluck a switch.

"Of the two, reverend sir," said the voice like the deacon's, "I had rather miss an ordination dinner than to-night's meeting. They tell me that some of our community are to be here from Falmouth and beyond, and others from Connecticut and Rhode Island, besides several of the Indian powwows, who, after their fashion, know almost as much deviltry as the best of us. Moreover, there is a goodly young woman to be taken into communion."

"Mighty well, Deacon Gookin!" replied the solemn old tones of the minister. "Spur up, or we shall be late. Nothing can be done, you know, until I get on the ground."

The hoofs clattered again; and the voices, talking so strangely in the empty air, passed on through the forest, where no church had ever been gathered or solitary Christian prayed. Whither, then, could these holy men be journeying so deep into the heathen wilderness? Young Goodman Brown caught hold of a tree for support, being ready to sink down on the ground, faint and overburdened with the heavy sickness of his heart. He looked up to the sky, doubting whether there really was a heaven above him. Yet there was the blue arch, and the stars brightening in it.

"With heaven above and Faith below, I will yet stand firm against the devil!" cried Goodman Brown.

While he still gazed upward into the deep arch of the firmament and had lifted his hands to pray, a cloud, though no wind was stirring, hurried across the zenith and hid the brightening stars. The blue sky was still visible, except directly overhead, where this black mass of cloud was sweeping swiftly northward. Aloft in the air, as if from the depths of the cloud, came a confused and doubtful sound of voices. Once the listener fancied that he could distinguish the accents of towns-people of his own, men and women, both pious and ungodly, many of whom he had met at the communion table, and had seen others rioting at the tavern. The next moment, so indistinct were the sounds, he doubted whether he had heard aught but the murmur of the old forest, whispering without a wind. Then came a stronger swell of those familiar tones, heard daily in the sunshine at Salem village, but never until now from a cloud of night. There was one voice, of a young woman, uttering lamentations, yet with an uncertain sorrow, and entreating for some favor, which, perhaps, it would grieve her to obtain; and all the unseen multitude, both saints and sinners, seemed to encourage her onward.

"Faith!" shouted Goodman Brown, in a voice of agony and desperation; and the echoes of the forest mocked him, crying, "Faith! Faith!" as if bewildered wretches were seeking her all through the wilderness.

The cry of grief, rage, and terror was yet piercing the night, when the unhappy husband held his breath for a response. There was a scream, drowned immediately in a louder murmur of voices, fading into far-off laughter, as the dark cloud swept away, leaving the clear and silent sky above Goodman Brown. But something fluttered lightly down through the air and caught on the branch of a tree. The young man seized it, and beheld a pink ribbon.

"My Faith is gone!" cried he after one stupefied moment. "There is no good on earth; and sin is but a name. Come, devil; for to thee is this world given."

And, maddened with despair, so that he laughed loud and long, did Goodman Brown grasp his staff and set forth again, at such a rate that he seemed to fly along the forest path rather than to walk or run. The road grew wilder and drearier and more faintly traced, and vanished at length, leaving him in the heart of the dark wilderness, still rushing onward with the instinct that guides mortal man to evil. The whole forest was peopled with frightful sounds—the creaking of the trees, the howling of wild beasts, and the yell of Indians; while sometimes the wind tolled like a distant church bell, and sometimes gave a broad roar around the traveller, as if all Nature were laughing him to scorn. But he was himself the chief horror of the scene, and shrank not from its other horrors.

"Ha! ha! ha!" roared Goodman Brown when the wind laughed at him. "Let us hear which will laugh loudest. Think not to frighten me with your deviltry. Come witch, come wizard, come Indian powwow, come devil himself, and here comes Goodman Brown. You may as well fear him as he fear you."

In truth, all through the haunted forest there could be nothing more frightful than the figure of Goodman Brown. On he flew among the black pines, brandishing his staff with frenzied gestures, now giving vent to an inspiration of horrid blasphemy, and now shouting forth such laughter as set all the echoes of the forest laughing like demons around him. The fiend in his own shape is less hideous than when he rages in the breast of man. Thus sped the demoniac on his course, until, quivering among the trees, he saw a red light before him, as when the felled trunks and branches of a clearing have been set on fire, and throw up their lurid blaze against the sky, at the hour of midnight. He paused, in a lull of the tempest that had driven him onward, and heard the swell of what seemed a hymn, rolling solemnly from a distance with the weight of many voices. He knew the tune; it was a familiar one in the choir of the village meeting-house. The verse died heavily away, and was lengthened by a chorus, not of human voices, but of all the sounds of the benighted wilderness pealing in awful harmony together. Goodman Brown cried out, and his cry was lost to his own ear by its unison with the cry of the desert.

In the interval of silence he stole forward until the light glared full upon his eyes. At one extremity of an open space, hemmed in by the dark wall of the forest, arose a rock, bearing some rude, natural resemblance either to an altar or a pulpit, and surrounded by four blazing pines, their tops aflame, their stems untouched, like candles at an evening meeting. The mass of foliage that had overgrown the summit of the rock was all on fire, blazing high into the night and fitfully illuminating the whole field. Each pendent twig and leafy festoon was in a blaze. As the red light arose and fell, a numerous congregation alternately shone forth, then disappeared in shadow, and again grew, as it were, out of the darkness, peopling the heart of the solitary woods at once.

"A grave and dark-clad company," quoth Goodman Brown.

In truth they were such. Among them, quivering to and fro between gloom and splendor, appeared faces that would be seen next day at the council board of the province, and others which, Sabbath after Sabbath, looked devoutly heavenward, and benignantly over the crowded pews, from the holiest pulpits in the land. Some affirm that the lady of the governor was there. At least there were high dames well known to her, and wives of honored husbands, and widows, a great multitude, and ancient maidens, all of excellent repute, and fair young girls, who trembled lest their mothers should espy them. Either the sudden gleams of light flashing over the obscure field bedazzled Goodman Brown, or he recognized a score of the church members of Salem village famous for their especial sanctity. Good old Deacon Gookin had arrived, and waited at the skirts of that venerable saint, his revered pastor. But, irreverently consorting with these grave, reputable, and pious people, these elders of the church, these chaste dames and dewy virgins, there were men of dissolute lives and women of spotted fame, wretches given over to all mean and filthy vice, and suspected even of horrid crimes. It was strange to see that the good shrank not from the wicked, nor were the sinners abashed by the saints. Scattered also among their pale-faced enemies were the Indian priests, or powwows, who had often scared their native forest with more hideous incantations than any known to English witchcraft.

"But where is Faith?" thought Goodman Brown; and, as hope came into his heart, he trembled.

Another verse of the hymn arose, a slow and mournful strain, such as the pious love, but joined to words which expressed all that our nature can conceive of sin, and darkly hinted at far more. Unfathomable to mere mortals is the lore of fiends. Verse after verse was sung; and still the chorus of the desert swelled between like the deepest tone of a mighty organ; and with the final peal of that dreadful anthem there came a sound, as if the roaring wind, the rushing streams, the howling beasts, and every other voice of the unconcerted wilderness were mingling and according with the voice of guilty man in homage to the prince of all. The four blazing pines threw up a loftier flame, and obscurely discovered shapes and visages of horror on the smoke wreaths above the impious assembly. At the same moment the fire on the rock shot redly forth and formed a flowing arch above its base, where now appeared a figure. With reverence be it spoken, the figure bore no slight similitude, both in garb and manner, to some grave divine of the New England churches.

"Bring forth the converts!" cried a voice that echoed through the field and rolled into the forest.

At the word, Goodman Brown stepped forth from the shadow of the trees and approached the congregation, with whom he felt a loathful brotherhood by the sympathy of all that was wicked in his heart. He could have well-nigh sworn that the shape of his own dead father beckoned him to advance, looking downward from a smoke wreath, while a woman, with dim features of despair, threw out her hand to warn him back. Was it his mother? But he had no power to retreat one step, nor to resist, even in thought, when the minister and good old Deacon Gookin seized his arms and led him to the blazing rock. Thither came also the slender form of a veiled female, led between Goody Cloyse, that pious teacher of the catechism, and Martha Carrier, who had received the devil's promise to be queen of hell. A rampant hag was she. And there stood the proselytes beneath the canopy of fire.

"Welcome, my children," said the dark figure, "to the communion of your race. Ye have found thus young your nature and your destiny. My children, look behind you!"

They turned; and flashing forth, as it were, in a sheet of flame, the fiend worshippers were seen; the smile of welcome gleamed darkly on every visage.

"There," resumed the sable form, "are all whom ye have reverenced from youth. Ye deemed them holier than yourselves and shrank from your own sin, contrasting it with their lives of righteousness and prayerful aspirations heavenward. Yet here are they all in my worshipping assembly. This night it shall be granted you to know their secret deeds: how hoary-bearded elders of the church have whispered wanton words to the young maids of their households; how many a woman, eager for widows' weeds, has given her husband a drink at bedtime and let him sleep his last sleep in her bosom; how beardless youths have made haste to inherit their fathers' wealth; and how fair damsels—blush not, sweet ones—have dug little graves in the garden, and bidden me, the sole guest, to an infant's funeral. By the sympathy of your human hearts for sin ye shall scent out all the places—whether in church, bedchamber, street, field, or forest—where crime has been committed, and shall exult to behold the whole earth one stain of guilt, one mighty blood spot. Far more than this. It shall be yours to penetrate, in every bosom, the deep mystery of sin, the fountain of all wicked arts, and which inexhaustibly supplies more evil impulses than human power—than my power at its utmost—can make manifest in deeds. And now, my children, look upon each other."

They did so; and, by the blaze of the hell-kindled torches, the wretched man beheld his Faith, and the wife her husband, trembling before that unhallowed altar.

"Lo, there ye stand, my children," said the figure, in a deep and solemn tone, almost sad with its despairing awfulness, as if his once angelic nature could yet mourn for our miserable race. "Depending upon one another's hearts, ye had still hoped that virtue were not all a dream. Now are ye undeceived. Evil is the nature of mankind. Evil must be your only happiness. Welcome again, my children, to the communion of your race."

"Welcome," repeated the fiend worshippers, in one cry of despair and triumph.

And there they stood, the only pair, as it seemed, who were yet hesitating on the verge of wickedness in this dark world. A basin was hallowed, naturally, in the rock. Did it contain water, reddened by the lurid light? or was it blood? or, perchance, a liquid flame? Herein did the shape of evil dip his hand and prepare to lay the mark of baptism upon their foreheads, that they might be partakers of the mystery of sin, more conscious of the secret guilt of others, both in deed and thought, than they could now be of their own. The husband cast one look at his pale wife, and Faith at him. What polluted wretches would the next glance show them to each other, shuddering alike at what they disclosed and what they saw!

"Faith! Faith!" cried the husband, "look up to heaven, and resist the wicked one."

Whether Faith obeyed he knew not. Hardly had he spoken when he found himself amid calm night and solitude, listening to a roar of the wind which died heavily away through the forest. He staggered against the rock, and felt it chill and damp; while a hanging twig, that had been all on fire, besprinkled his cheek with the coldest dew.

The next morning young Goodman Brown came slowly into the street of Salem village, staring around him like a bewildered man. The good old minister was taking a walk along the graveyard to get an appetite for breakfast and meditate his sermon, and bestowed a blessing, as he passed, on Goodman Brown. He shrank from the venerable saint as if to avoid an anathema. Old Deacon Gookin was at domestic worship, and the holy words of his prayer were heard through the open window. "What God doth the wizard pray to?" quoth Goodman Brown. Goody Cloyse, that excellent old Christian, stood in the early sunshine at her own lattice, catechizing a little girl who had brought her a pint of morning's milk. Goodman Brown snatched away the child as from the grasp of the fiend himself. Turning the corner by the meeting-house, he spied the head of Faith, with the pink ribbons, gazing anxiously forth, and bursting into such joy at sight of him that she skipped along the street and almost kissed her husband before the whole village. But Goodman Brown looked sternly and sadly into her face, and passed on without a greeting.

Had Goodman Brown fallen asleep in the forest and only dreamed a wild dream of a witch-meeting?

Be it so if you will; but, alas! it was a dream of evil omen for young Goodman Brown. A stern, a sad, a darkly meditative, a distrustful, if not a desperate man did he become from the night of that fearful dream. On the Sabbath day, when the congregation were singing a holy psalm, he could not listen because an anthem of sin rushed loudly upon his ear and drowned all the blessed strain. When the minister spoke from the pulpit with power and fervid eloquence, and, with his hand on the open Bible, of the sacred truths of our religion, and of saint-like lives and triumphant deaths, and of future bliss or misery unutterable, then did Goodman Brown turn pale, dreading lest the roof should thunder down upon the gray blasphemer and his hearers. Often, awaking suddenly at midnight, he shrank from the bosom of Faith; and at morning or eventide, when the family knelt down at prayer, he scowled and muttered to himself, and gazed sternly at his wife, and turned away. And when he had lived long, and was borne to his grave a hoary corpse, followed by Faith, an aged woman, and children and grandchildren, a goodly procession, besides neighbors not a few, they carved no hopeful verse upon his tombstone, for his dying hour was gloom.

[1835]

EDGAR ALLAN POE   [1809–1849]

The Cask of Amontillado

The thousand injuries of Fortunato I had borne as I best could; but when he ventured upon insult, I vowed revenge. You, who so well know the nature of my soul, will not suppose, however, that I gave utterance to a threat. *At length* I would be avenged; this was a point definitely settled — but the very definitiveness with which it was resolved precluded the idea of risk. I must not only punish, but punish with impunity. A wrong is unredressed when retribution overtakes its redresser. It is equally unredressed when the avenger fails to make himself felt as such to him who has done the wrong.

It must be understood, that neither by word nor deed had I given Fortunato cause to doubt my good-will. I continued, as was my wont, to smile in his face, and he did not perceive that my smile *now* was at the thought of his immolation.

He had a weak point — this Fortunato — although in other regards he was a man to be respected and even feared. He prided himself on his connoisseurship in wine. Few Italians have the true virtuoso spirit. For the most part their enthusiasm is adopted to suit the time and opportunity — to practise imposture upon the British and Austrian *millionaires*. In painting and gemmary Fortunato, like his countrymen, was a quack — but in the matter of old wines he was sincere. In this respect I did not differ from him materially: I was skilful in the Italian vintages myself, and bought largely whenever I could.

It was about dusk, one evening during the supreme madness of the carnival season, that I encountered my friend. He accosted me with excessive warmth, for he had been drinking much. The man wore motley. He had on a tight-fitting parti-striped dress, and his head was surmounted by the conical cap and bells. I was so pleased to see him, that I thought I should never have done wringing his hand.

I said to him: "My dear Fortunato, you are luckily met. How remarkably well you are looking to-day! But I have received a pipe° of what passes for Amontillado, and I have my doubts."

"How?" said he. "Amontillado? A pipe? Impossible! And in the middle of the carnival!"

Pipe: A large cask.

"I have my doubts," I replied; "and I was silly enough to pay the full Amontillado price without consulting you in the matter. You were not to be found, and I was fearful of losing a bargain."

"Amontillado!"

"I have my doubts."

"Amontillado!"

"And I must satisfy them."

"Amontillado!"

"As you are engaged, I am on my way to Luchesi. If any one has a critical turn, it is he. He will tell me——"

"Luchesi cannot tell Amontillado from Sherry."

"And yet some fools will have it that his taste is a match for your own."

"Come, let us go."

"Whither?"

"To your vaults."

"My friend, no; I will not impose upon your good nature. I perceive you have an engagement. Luchesi——"

"I have no engagement;—come."

"My friend, no. It is not the engagement, but the severe cold with which I perceive you are afflicted. The vaults are insufferably damp. They are encrusted with nitre."°

"Let us go, nevertheless. The cold is merely nothing. Amontillado! You have been imposed upon. And as for Luchesi, he cannot distinguish Sherry from Amontillado."

Thus speaking, Fortunato possessed himself of my arm. Putting on a mask of black silk, and drawing a *roquelaire*° closely about my person, I suffered him to hurry me to my palazzo.

There were no attendants at home; they had absconded to make merry in honor of the time. I had told them that I should not return until the morning, and had given them explicit orders not to stir from the house. These orders were sufficient, I well knew, to insure their immediate disappearance, one and all, as soon as my back was turned.

I took from their sconces two flambeaux, and giving one to Fortunato, bowed him through several suites of rooms to the archway that led into the vaults. I passed down a long and winding staircase, requesting him to be cautious as he followed. We came at length to the foot of the descent, and stood together on the damp ground of the catacombs of the Montresors.

The gait of my friend was unsteady, and the bells upon his cap jingled as he strode.

Nitre: Potassium nitrate, or saltpeter; believed at the end of the eighteenth century to be an element in air and plants.
Roquelaire: A cloak.

"The pipe?" said he.

"It is farther on," said I; "but observe the white web-work which gleams from these cavern walls."

He turned toward me, and looked into my eyes with two filmy orbs that distilled the rheum of intoxication.

"Nitre?" he asked, at length.

"Nitre," I replied. "How long have you had that cough?"

"Ugh! ugh! ugh!—ugh! ugh! ugh!—ugh! ugh! ugh!—ugh! ugh! ugh! ugh! ugh! ugh!"

My poor friend found it impossible to reply for many minutes.

"It is nothing," he said, at last.

"Come," I said, with decision, "we will go back; your health is precious. You are rich, respected, admired, beloved; you are happy, as once I was. You are a man to be missed. For me it is no matter. We will go back; you will be ill, and I cannot be responsible. Besides, there is Luchesi—"

"Enough," he said; "the cough is a mere nothing; it will not kill me. I shall not die of a cough."

"True—true," I replied; "and, indeed, I had no intention of alarming you unnecessarily; but you should use all proper caution. A draught of this Medoc will defend us from the damps."

Here I knocked off the neck of a bottle which I drew from a long row of its fellows that lay upon the mould.

"Drink," I said, presenting him the wine.

He raised it to his lips with a leer. He paused and nodded to me familiarly, while his bells jingled.

"I drink," he said, "to the buried that repose around us."

"And I to your long life."

He again took my arm, and we proceeded.

"These vaults," he said, "are extensive."

"The Montresors," I replied, "were a great and numerous family."

"I forget your arms."

"A huge human foot d'or,° in a field azure; the foot crushes a serpent rampant whose fangs are imbedded in the heel."

"And the motto?"

"*Nemo me impune lacessit.*"°

"Good!" he said.

The wine sparkled in his eyes and the bells jingled. My own fancy grew warm with the Medoc. We had passed through walls of piled bones, with casks and puncheons intermingling into the inmost recesses of the cata-

D'or: Of gold.
Nemo me impune lacessit: "No one wounds me with impunity"; the motto of the Scottish royal arms.

combs. I paused again, and this time I made bold to seize Fortunato by an arm above the elbow.

"The nitre!" I said; "see, it increases. It hangs like moss upon the vaults. We are below the river's bed. The drops of moisture trickle among the bones. Come, we will go back ere it is too late. Your cough——"

"It is nothing," he said; "let us go on. But first, another draught of the Medoc."

I broke and reached him a flagon of De Grâve. He emptied it at a breath. His eyes flashed with a fierce light. He laughed and threw the bottle upward with a gesticulation I did not understand.

I looked at him in surprise. He repeated the movement—a grotesque one.

"You do not comprehend?" he said.

"Not I," I replied.

"Then you are not of the brotherhood."

"How?"

"You are not of the masons."

"Yes, yes," I said; "yes, yes."

"You? Impossible! A mason?"

"A mason," I replied.

"A sign," he said.

"It is this," I answered, producing a trowel from beneath the folds of my *roquelaire*.

"You jest," he exclaimed, recoiling a few paces. "But let us proceed to the Amontillado."

"Be it so," I said, replacing the tool beneath the cloak, and again offering him my arm. He leaned upon it heavily. We continued our route in search of the Amontillado. We passed through a range of low arches, descended, passed on, and descending again, arrived at a deep crypt, in which the foulness of the air caused our flambeaux rather to glow than flame.

At the most remote end of the crypt there appeared another less spacious. Its walls had been lined with human remains, piled to the vault overhead, in the fashion of the great catacombs of Paris. Three sides of this interior crypt were still ornamented in this manner. From the fourth the bones had been thrown down, and lay promiscuously upon the earth, forming at one point a mound of some size. Within the wall thus exposed by the displacing of the bones, we perceived a still interior recess, in depth about four feet, in width three, in height six or seven. It seemed to have been constructed for no especial use within itself, but formed merely the interval between two of the colossal supports of the roof of the catacombs, and was backed by one of their circumscribing walls of solid granite.

It was in vain that Fortunato, uplifting his dull torch, endeavored to pry into the depth of the recess. Its termination the feeble light did not enable us to see.

"Proceed," I said; "herein is the Amontillado. As for Luchesi——"

"He is an ignoramus," interrupted my friend, as he stepped unsteadily forward, while I followed immediately at his heels. In an instant he had reached the extremity of the niche, and finding his progress arrested by the rock, stood stupidly bewildered. A moment more and I had fettered him to the granite. In its surface were two iron staples, distant from each other about two feet, horizontally. From one of these depended a short chain, from the other a padlock. Throwing the links about his waist, it was but the work of a few seconds to secure it. He was too much astounded to resist. Withdrawing the key I stepped back from the recess.

"Pass your hand," I said, "over the wall; you cannot help feeling the nitre. Indeed it is *very* damp. Once more let me *implore* you to return. No? Then I must positively leave you. But I must first render you all the little attentions in my power."

"The Amontillado!" ejaculated my friend, not yet recovered from his astonishment.

"True," I replied; "the Amontillado."

As I said these words I busied myself among the pile of bones of which I have before spoken. Throwing them aside, I soon uncovered a quantity of building stone and mortar. With these materials and with the aid of my trowel, I began vigorously to wall up the entrance of the niche.

I had scarcely laid the first tier of the masonry when I discovered that the intoxication of Fortunato had in a great measure worn off. The earliest indication I had of this was a low moaning cry from the depth of the recess. It was *not* the cry of a drunken man. There was then a long and obstinate silence. I laid the second tier, and the third, and the fourth; and then I heard the furious vibrations of the chain. The noise lasted for several minutes, during which, that I might hearken to it with the more satisfaction, I ceased my labors and sat down upon the bones. When at last the clanking subsided, I resumed the trowel, and finished without interruption the fifth, the sixth, and the seventh tier. The wall was now nearly upon a level with my breast. I again paused, and holding the flambeaux over the masonwork, threw a few feeble rays upon the figure within.

A succession of loud and shrill screams, bursting suddenly from the throat of the chained form, seemed to thrust me violently back. For a brief moment I hesitated—I trembled. Unsheathing my rapier, I began to grope with it about the recess; but the thought of an instant reassured me. I placed my hand upon the solid fabric of the catacombs, and felt satisfied. I reapproached the wall. I replied to the yells of him who clamored. I reechoed—I aided—I surpassed them in volume and in strength. I did this, and the clamorer grew still.

It was now midnight, and my task was drawing to a close. I had completed the eighth, the ninth, and the tenth tier. I had finished a portion of the last and the eleventh; there remained but a single stone to be fitted and plastered in. I struggled with its weight; I placed it partially in its destined position. But now there came from out the niche a low laugh that erected the hairs upon my head. It was succeeded by a sad voice, which I had difficulty in recognizing as that of the noble Fortunato. The voice said—

"Ha! ha! ha!—he! he!—a very good joke indeed—an excellent jest. We will have many a rich laugh about it at the palazzo—he! he! he!—over our wine—he! he! he!"

"The Amontillado!" I said.

"He! he! he!—he! he! he!—yes, the Amontillado. But is it not getting late? Will not they be awaiting us at the palazzo, the Lady Fortunato and the rest? Let us be gone."

"Yes," I said, "let us be gone."

"For the love of God, Montresor!"

"Yes," I said, "for the love of God!"

But to these words I hearkened in vain for a reply. I grew impatient. I called aloud:

"Fortunato!"

No answer. I called again:

"Fortunato!"

No answer still, I thrust a torch through the remaining aperture and let it fall within. There came forth in return only a jingling of the bells. My heart grew sick—on account of the dampness of the catacombs. I hastened to make an end of my labor. I forced the last stone into its position; I plastered it up. Against the new masonry I reerected the old rampart of bones. For the half of a century no mortal has disturbed them. *In pace requiescat!*°

[1846]

In pace requiescat: May he rest in peace (Latin).

HERMAN MELVILLE [1819–1891]

Bartleby, the Scrivener

A Story of Wall Street

I am a rather elderly man. The nature of my avocations, for the last thirty years, has brought me into more than ordinary contact with what would seem an interesting and somewhat singular set of men, of whom, as yet, nothing, that I know of, has ever been written—I mean, the law-copyists, or scriveners. I have known very many of them, professionally and privately, and, if I pleased, could relate divers histories, at which good-natured gentlemen might smile, and sentimental souls might weep. But I waive the biographies of all other scriveners, for a few passages in the life of Bartleby, who was a scrivener, the strangest I ever saw, or heard of. While, of other law-copyists, I might write the complete life, of Bartleby nothing of that sort can be done. I believe that no materials exist, for a full and satisfactory biography of this man. It is an irreparable loss to literature. Bartleby was one of those beings of whom nothing is ascertainable, except from the original sources, and, in his case, those are very small. What my own astonished eyes saw of Bartleby, *that* is all I know of him, except, indeed, one vague report, which will appear in the sequel.

Ere introducing the scrivener, as he first appeared to me, it is fit I make some mention of myself, my *employés*, my business, my chambers, and general surroundings, because some such description is indispensable to an adequate understanding of the chief character about to be presented. Imprimis:° I am a man who, from his youth upwards, has been filled with a profound conviction that the easiest way of life is the best. Hence, though I belong to a profession proverbially energetic and nervous, even to turbulence, at times, yet nothing of that sort have I ever suffered to invade my peace. I am one of those unambitious lawyers who never address a jury, or in any way draw down public applause; but, in the cool tranquillity of a snug retreat, do a snug business among rich men's bonds, and mortgages, and title-deeds. All who know me, consider me an eminently *safe* man. The late John Jacob Astor, a personage little given to poetic enthusiasm, had no hesitation in pronouncing my first grand point to be prudence; my next, method. I do not speak it in vanity, but

Imprimis: In the first place (Latin).

20

simply record the fact, that I was not unemployed in my profession by the late John Jacob Astor; a name which, I admit, I love to repeat; for it hath a rounded and orbicular sound to it, and rings like unto bullion. I will freely add, that I was not insensible to the late John Jacob Astor's good opinion.

Some time prior to the period at which this little history begins, my avocations had been largely increased. The good old office, now extinct in the State of New York, of a Master in Chancery,° had been conferred upon me. It was not a very arduous office, but very pleasantly remunerative. I seldom lose my temper; much more seldom indulge in dangerous indignation at wrongs and outrages; but I must be permitted to be rash here and declare, that I consider the sudden and violent abrogation of the office of Master in Chancery, by the new Constitution, as a——premature act; inasmuch as I had counted upon a life-lease of the profits, whereas I only received those of a few short years. But this is by the way.

My chambers were up stairs, at No.—Wall Street. At one end, they looked upon the white wall of the interior of a spacious skylight shaft, penetrating the building from top to bottom.

This view might have been considered rather tame than otherwise, deficient in what landscape painters call "life." But, if so, the view from the other end of my chambers offered, at least, a contrast, if nothing more. In that direction, my windows commanded an unobstructed view of a lofty brick wall, black by age and everlasting shade; which wall required no spy-glass to bring out its lurking beauties, but, for the benefit of all near-sighted spectators, was pushed up to within ten feet of my window-panes. Owing to the great height of the surrounding buildings, and my chambers being on the second floor, the interval between this wall and mine not a little resembled a huge square cistern.

At the period just preceding the advent of Bartleby, I had two persons as copyists in my employment, and a promising lad as an office-boy. First, Turkey; second, Nippers; third, Ginger Nut. These may seem names, the like of which are not usually found in the Directory. In truth, they were nicknames, mutually conferred upon each other by my three clerks, and were deemed expressive of their respective persons or characters. Turkey was a short, pursy Englishman, of about my own age—that is, somewhere not far from sixty. In the morning, one might say, his face was of a fine florid hue, but after twelve o'clock, meridian—his dinner hour—it blazed like a grate full of Christmas coals; and continued blazing—but, as it were, with a gradual wane—till six o'clock, P.M., or thereabouts; after which, I saw no more of the proprietor of the face, which, gaining its meridian with

Master in Chancery: Courts of equity officer whose duty is to assist the chancellor or judge in remedying injustices of the law.

the sun, seemed to set with it, to rise, culminate, and decline the following day, with the like regularity and undiminished glory. There are many singular coincidences I have known in the course of my life, not the least among which was the fact, that, exactly when Turkey displayed his fullest beams from his red and radiant countenance, just then, too, at that critical moment, began the daily period when I considered his business capacities as seriously disturbed for the remainder of the twenty-four hours. Not that he was absolutely idle, or averse to business then; far from it. The difficulty was, he was apt to be altogether too energetic. There was a strange, inflamed, flurried, flighty recklessness of activity about him. He would be incautious in dipping his pen into his inkstand. All his blots upon my documents were dropped there after twelve o'clock, meridian. Indeed, not only would he be reckless, and sadly given to making blots in the afternoon, but, some days, he went further, and was rather noisy. At such times, too, his face flamed with augmented blazonry, as if cannel coal had been heaped on anthracite.° He made an unpleasant racket with his chair; spilled his sand-box;° in mending his pens, impatiently split them all to pieces, and threw them on the floor in a sudden passion; stood up, and leaned over his table, boxing his papers about in a most indecorous manner, very sad to behold in an elderly man like him. Nevertheless, as he was in many ways a most valuable person to me, and all the time before twelve o'clock, meridian, was the quickest, steadiest creature, too, accomplishing a great deal of work in a style not easily to be matched—for these reasons, I was willing to overlook his eccentricities, though, indeed, occasionally, I remonstrated with him. I did this very gently, however, because, though the civilest, nay, the blandest and most reverential of men in the morning, yet, in the afternoon, he was disposed, upon provocation, to be slightly rash with his tongue—in fact, insolent. Now, valuing his morning services as I did, and resolved not to lose them—yet, at the same time, made uncomfortable by his inflamed ways after twelve o'clock—and being a man of peace, unwilling by my admonitions to call forth unseemly retorts from him, I took upon me, one Saturday noon (he was always worse on Saturdays) to hint to him, very kindly, that, perhaps, now that he was growing old, it might be well to abridge his labors; in short, he need not come to my chambers after twelve o'clock, but, dinner over, had best go home to his lodgings, and rest himself till tea-time. But no; he insisted upon his afternoon devotions. His countenance became intolerably fervid, as he oratorically assured me—gesticulating with a long ruler at the other end of the room—that if his services in the morning were useful, how indispensable, then, in the afternoon?

Anthracite: A variety of hard coal.
Sand-box: As used here, a box with a perforated top, holding sand to sprinkle on ink to blot it.

"With submission, sir," said Turkey, on this occasion, "I consider my-self your right-hand man. In the morning I but marshal and deploy my columns; but in the afternoon I put myself at their head, and gallantly charge the foe, thus"—and he made a violent thrust with the ruler.

"But the blots, Turkey," intimated I.

"True; but, with submission, sir, behold these hairs! I am getting old. Surely, sir, a blot or two of a warm afternoon is not to be severely urged against gray hairs. Old age—even if it blot the page—is honorable. With submission, sir, we *both* are getting old."

This appeal to my fellow-feeling was hardly to be resisted. At all events, I saw that go he would not. So, I made up my mind to let him stay, resolv-ing, nevertheless, to see to it that, during the afternoon, he had to do with my less important papers.

Nippers, the second on my list, was a whiskered, sallow, and, upon the whole, rather piratical-looking young man, of about five-and-twenty. I always deemed him the victim of two evil powers—ambition and indi-gestion. The ambition was evinced by a certain impatience of the duties of a mere copyist, an unwarrantable usurpation of strictly professional affairs such as the original drawing up of legal documents. The indiges-tion seemed betokened in an occasional nervous testiness and grinning irritability, causing the teeth to audibly grind together over mistakes committed in copying; unnecessary maledictions, hissed, rather than spoken, in the heat of business; and especially by a continual discontent with the height of the table where he worked. Though of a very ingenious mechanical turn, Nippers could never get this table to suit him. He put chips under it, blocks of various sorts, bits of pasteboard, and at last went so far as to attempt an exquisite adjustment, by final pieces of folded blotting paper. But no invention would answer. If, for the sake of easing his back, he brought the table-lid at a sharp angle well up towards his chin, and wrote there like a man using the steep roof of a Dutch house for his desk, then he declared that it stopped the circulation in his arms. If now he lowered the table to his waistbands, and stooped over it in writing, then there was a sore aching in his back. In short, the truth of the matter was, Nippers knew not what he wanted. Or, if he wanted any-thing, it was to be rid of a scrivener's table altogether. Among the mani-festations of his diseased ambition was a fondness he had for receiving visits from certain ambiguous-looking fellows in seedy coats, whom he called his clients. Indeed, I was aware that not only was he, at times, considerable of a ward-politician, but he occasionally did a little busi-ness at the justices' courts, and was not unknown on the steps of the Tombs.° I have good reason to believe, however, that one individual who called upon him at my chambers, and who, with a grand air, he insisted

The Tombs: Nickname of the Manhattan House of Detention.

was his client, was no other than a dun, and the alleged title-deed, a bill. But, with all his failings, and the annoyances he caused me, Nippers, like his compatriot Turkey, was a very useful man to me; wrote a neat, swift hand; and, when he chose, was not deficient in a gentlemanly sort of deportment. Added to this, he always dressed in a gentlemanly sort of way; and so, incidentally, reflected credit upon my chambers. Whereas, with respect to Turkey, I had much ado to keep him from being a reproach to me. His clothes were apt to look oily, and smell of eating-houses. He wore his pantaloons very loose and baggy in summer. His coats were execrable, his hat not to be handled. But while the hat was a thing of indifference to me, inasmuch as his natural civility and deference, as a dependent Englishman, always led him to doff it the moment he entered the room, yet his coat was another matter. Concerning his coats, I reasoned with him; but with no effect. The truth was, I suppose, that a man with so small an income could not afford to sport such a lustrous face and a lustrous coat at one and the same time. As Nippers once observed, Turkey's money went chiefly for red ink. One winter day, I presented Turkey with a highly respectable-looking coat of my own—a padded gray coat, of a most comfortable warmth, and which buttoned straight up from the knee to the neck. I thought Turkey would appreciate the favor, and abate his rashness and obstreperousness of afternoons. But no; I verily believe that buttoning himself up in so downy and blanket-like a coat had a pernicious effect upon him upon the same principle that too much oats are bad for horses. In fact, precisely as a rash, restive horse is said to feel his oats, so Turkey felt his coat. It made him insolent. He was a man whom prosperity harmed.

Though, concerning the self-indulgent habits of Turkey, I had my own private surmises, yet, touching Nippers, I was well persuaded that, whatever might be his faults in other respects, he was, at least, a temperate young man. But, indeed, nature herself seemed to have been his vintner, and, at his birth, charged him so thoroughly with an irritable, brandy-like disposition, that all subsequent potations were needless. When I consider how, amid the stillness of my chambers, Nippers would sometimes impatiently rise from his seat, and stooping over his table, spread his arms wide apart, seize the whole desk, and move it, and jerk it, with a grim, grinding motion on the floor, as if the table were a perverse voluntary agent, intent on thwarting and vexing him, I plainly perceive that, for Nippers, brandy-and-water were altogether superfluous.

It was fortunate for me that, owing to its peculiar cause—indigestion—the irritability and consequent nervousness of Nippers were mainly observable in the morning, while in the afternoon he was comparatively mild. So that, Turkey's paroxysms only coming on about twelve o'clock, I never had to do with their eccentricities at one time. Their fits relieved each other, like guards. When Nippers' was on, Turkey's was off; and *vice versa*. This was a good natural arrangement, under the circumstances.

Ginger Nut, the third on my list, was a lad, some twelve years old. His father was a carman, ambitious of seeing his son on the bench instead of a cart, before he died. So he sent him to my office, as student at law, errand-boy, cleaner, and sweeper, at the rate of one dollar a week. He had a little desk to himself, but he did not use it much. Upon inspection, the drawer exhibited a great array of the shells of various sorts of nuts. Indeed, to this quick-witted youth, the whole noble science of the law was contained in a nutshell. Not the least among the employments of Ginger Nut, as well as one which he discharged with the most alacrity, was his duty as cake and apple purveyor for Turkey and Nippers. Copying lawpapers being proverbially a dry, husky sort of business, my two scriveners were fain to moisten their mouths very often with Spitzenbergs,° to be had at the numerous stalls nigh the Custom House and Post Office. Also, they sent Ginger Nut very frequently for that peculiar cake—small, flat, round, and very spicy—after which he had been named by them. Of a cold morning, when business was but dull, Turkey would gobble up scores of these cakes, as if they were mere wafers—indeed, they sell them at the rate of six or eight for a penny—the scrape of his pen blending with the crunching of the crisp particles in his mouth. Of all the fiery afternoon blunders and flurried rashness of Turkey, was his once moistening a ginger-cake between his lips, and clapping it on to a mortgage, for a seal. I came within an ace of dismissing him then. But he mollified me by making an oriental bow, and saying—

"With submission, sir, it was generous of me to find you in stationery on my own account."

Now my original business—that of a conveyancer and title hunter, and drawer-up of recondite documents of all sorts—was considerably increased by receiving the Master's office. There was now great work for scriveners. Not only must I push the clerks already with me, but I must have additional help.

In answer to my advertisement, a motionless young man one morning stood upon my office threshold, the door being open, for it was summer. I can see that figure now—pallidly neat, pitiably respectable, incurably forlorn! It was Bartleby.

After a few words touching his qualifications, I engaged him, glad to have among my corps of copyists a man of so singularly sedate an aspect, which I thought might operate beneficially upon the flighty temper of Turkey, and the fiery one of Nippers.

Spitzenbergs: A type of apple.

I should have stated before that ground-glass folding-doors divided my premises into two parts, one of which was occupied by my scriveners, the other by myself. According to my humor, I threw open these doors, or closed them. I resolved to assign Bartleby a corner by the folding-doors, but on my side of them, so as to have this quiet man within easy call, in case any trifling thing was to be done. I placed his desk close up to a small side-window in that part of the room, a window which originally had afforded a lateral view of certain grimy brickyards and bricks, but which, owing to subsequent erections, commanded at present no view at all, though it gave some light. Within three feet of the panes was a wall, and the light came down from far above, between two lofty buildings, as from a very small opening in a dome. Still further to a satisfactory arrangement, I procured a high green folding screen, which might entirely isolate Bartleby from my sight, though not remove him from my voice. And thus, in a manner, privacy and society were conjoined.

At first, Bartleby did an extraordinary quantity of writing. As if long famishing for something to copy, he seemed to gorge himself on my documents. There was no pause for digestion. He ran a day and night line, copying by sun-light and by candle-light. I should have been quite delighted with his application, had he been cheerfully industrious. But he wrote on silently, palely, mechanically.

It is, of course, an indispensable part of a scrivener's business to verify the accuracy of his copy, word by word. Where there are two or more scriveners in an office, they assist each other in this examination, one reading from the copy, the other holding the original. It is a very dull, wearisome, and lethargic affair. I can readily imagine that, to some sanguine temperaments, it would be altogether intolerable. For example, I cannot credit that the mettlesome poet, Byron, would have contentedly sat down with Bartleby to examine a law document of, say five hundred pages, closely written in a crimpy hand.

Now and then, in the haste of business, it had been my habit to assist in comparing some brief document myself, calling Turkey or Nippers for this purpose. One object I had, in placing Bartleby so handy to me behind the screen, was, to avail myself of his services on such trivial occasions. It was on the third day, I think, of his being with me, and before any necessity had arisen for having his own writing examined, that, being much hurried to complete a small affair I had in hand, I abruptly called to Bartleby. In my haste and natural expectancy of instant compliance, I sat with my head bent over the original on my desk, and my right hand sideways, and somewhat nervously extended with the copy, so that, immediately upon emerging from his retreat, Bartleby might snatch it and proceed to business without the least delay.

In this very attitude did I sit when I called to him, rapidly stating what it was I wanted him to do—namely, to examine a small paper with me. Imagine my surprise, nay, my consternation, when, without moving from his privacy, Bartleby, in a singularly mild, firm voice, replied, "I would prefer not to."

I sat awhile in perfect silence, rallying my stunned faculties. Immediately it occurred to me that my ears had deceived me, or Bartleby had entirely misunderstood my meaning. I repeated my request in the clearest tone I could assume; but in quite as clear a one came the previous reply, "I would prefer not to."

"Prefer not to," echoed I, rising in high excitement, and crossing the room with a stride. "What do you mean? Are you moonstruck? I want you to help me compare this sheet here—take it," and I thrust it towards him.

"I would prefer not to," said he.

I looked at him steadfastly. His face was leanly composed; his gray eye dimly calm. Not a wrinkle of agitation rippled him. Had there been the least uneasiness, anger, impatience, or impertinence in his manner; in other words, had there been anything ordinarily human about him, doubtless I should have violently dismissed him from the premises. But as it was, I should have as soon thought of turning my pale plaster-of-paris bust of Cicero out of doors. I stood gazing at him awhile, as he went on with his own writing, and then reseated myself at my desk. This is very strange, thought I. What had one best do? But my business hurried me. I concluded to forget the matter for the present, reserving it for my future leisure. So, calling Nippers from the other room, the paper was speedily examined.

A few days after this, Bartleby concluded four lengthy documents, being quadruplicates of a week's testimony taken before me in my High Court of Chancery. It became necessary to examine them. It was an important suit, and great accuracy was imperative. Having all things arranged, I called Turkey, Nippers, and Ginger Nut, from the next room, meaning to place the four copies in the hands of my four clerks, while I should read from the original. Accordingly, Turkey, Nippers, and Ginger Nut had taken their seats in a row, each with his document in his hand, when I called to Bartleby to join this interesting group.

"Bartleby! quick, I am waiting."

I heard a slow scrape of his chair legs on the uncarpeted floor, and soon he appeared standing at the entrance of his hermitage.

"What is wanted?" said he, mildly.

"The copies, the copies," said I, hurriedly. "We are going to examine them. There"—and I held towards him the fourth quadruplicate.

"I would prefer not to," he said, and gently disappeared behind the screen.

For a few moments I was turned into a pillar of salt,° standing at the head of my seated column of clerks. Recovering myself, I advanced towards the screen, and demanded the reason for such extraordinary conduct.

"*Why* do you refuse?"

"I would prefer not to."

With any other man I should have flown outright into a dreadful passion, scorned all further words, and thrust him ignominiously from my presence. But there was something about Bartleby that not only strangely disarmed me, but, in a wonderful manner, touched and disconcerted me. I began to reason with him.

"These are your own copies we are about to examine. It is labor saving to you, because one examination will answer for your four papers. It is common usage. Every copyist is bound to help examine his copy. Is it not so? Will you not speak? Answer!"

"I prefer not to," he replied in a flute-like tone. It seemed to me that, while I had been addressing him, he carefully revolved every statement that I made; fully comprehended the meaning; could not gainsay the irresistible conclusion; but, at the same time, some paramount consideration prevailed with him to reply as he did.

"You are decided, then, not to comply with my request—a request made according to common usage and common sense?"

He briefly gave me to understand, that on that point my judgment was sound. Yes: his decision was irreversible.

It is not seldom the case that, when a man is browbeaten in some unprecedented and violently unreasonable way, he begins to stagger in his own plainest faith. He begins, as it were, vaguely to surmise that, wonderful as it may be, all the justice and all the reason is on the other side. Accordingly, if any disinterested persons are present, he turns to them for some reinforcement for his own faltering mind.

"Turkey," said I, "what do you think of this? Am I not right?"

"With submission, sir," said Turkey, in his blandest tone, "I think that you are."

"Nippers," said I, "what do *you* think of it?"

"I think I should kick him out of the office."

(The reader of nice perceptions will have perceived that, it being morning, Turkey's answer is couched in polite and tranquil terms, but Nippers replies in ill-tempered ones. Or, to repeat a previous sentence, Nippers' ugly mood was on duty, and Turkey's off.)

Turned into a pillar of salt: A reference to the biblical book of Genesis, 19.26, meaning, in this context, "paralyzed."

"Ginger Nut," said I, willing to enlist the smallest suffrage in my behalf, "what do *you* think of it?"

"I think, sir, he's a little *luny*," replied Ginger Nut, with a grin.

"You hear what they say," said I, turning towards the screen, "come forth and do your duty."

But he vouchsafed no reply. I pondered a moment in sore perplexity. But once more business hurried me. I determined again to postpone the consideration of this dilemma to my future leisure. With a little trouble we made out to examine the papers without Bartleby, though at every page or two Turkey deferentially dropped his opinion, that this proceeding was quite out of the common; while Nippers, twitching in his chair with a dyspeptic nervousness, ground out, between his set teeth, occasional hissing maledictions against the stubborn oaf behind the screen. And for his (Nippers') part, this was the first and the last time he would do another man's business without pay.

Meanwhile Bartleby sat in his hermitage, oblivious to everything but his own peculiar business there.

Some days passed, the scrivener being employed upon another lengthy work. His late remarkable conduct led me to regard his ways narrowly. I observed that he never went to dinner; indeed, that he never went anywhere. As yet I had never, of my personal knowledge, known him to be outside of my office. He was a perpetual sentry in the corner. At about eleven o'clock though, in the morning, I noticed that Ginger Nut would advance towards the opening in Bartleby's screen, as if silently beckoned thither by a gesture invisible to me where I sat. The boy would then leave the office, jingling a few pence, and reappear with a handful of gingernuts, which he delivered in the hermitage, receiving two of the cakes for his trouble.

He lives, then, on ginger-nuts, thought I; never eats a dinner, properly speaking; he must be a vegetarian, then, but no; he never eats even vegetables, he eats nothing but ginger-nuts. My mind then ran on in reveries concerning the probable effects upon the human constitution of living entirely on ginger-nuts. Ginger-nuts are so called, because they contain ginger as one of their peculiar constituents, and the final flavoring one. Now, what was ginger? A hot, spicy thing. Was Bartleby hot and spicy? Not at all. Ginger, then, had no effect upon Bartleby. Probably he preferred it should have none.

Nothing so aggravates an earnest person as a passive resistance. If the individual so resisted be of a not inhumane temper, and the resisting one perfectly harmless in his passivity, then, in the better moods of the former, he will endeavor charitably to construe to his imagination what proves impossible to be solved by his judgment. Even so, for the most part, I regarded Bartleby and his ways. Poor fellow! thought I, he means no mischief; it is plain he intends no insolence; his aspect sufficiently evinces that his eccentricities are involuntary. He is useful to me. I can get along with him. If I turn him away, the chances are he will fall in with some less indulgent employer, and then he will be rudely treated, and perhaps driven forth miserably to starve. Yes. Here I can cheaply purchase a delicious self-approval. To befriend Bartleby; to humor him in his strange wilfulness, will cost me little or nothing, while I lay up in my soul what will eventually prove a sweet morsel for my conscience. But this mood was not invariable with me. The passiveness of Bartleby sometimes irritated me. I felt strangely goaded on to encounter him in new opposition—to elicit some angry spark from him answerable to my own. But, indeed, I might as well have essayed to strike fire with my knuckles against a bit of Windsor soap. But one afternoon the evil impulse in me mastered me, and the following little scene ensued:

"Bartleby," said I, "when those papers are all copied, I will compare them with you."

"I would prefer not to."

"How? Surely you do not mean to persist in that mulish vagary?"

No answer.

I threw open the folding-doors nearby, and turning upon Turkey and Nippers, exclaimed:

"Bartleby a second time says, he won't examine his papers. What do you think of it, Turkey?"

It was afternoon, be it remembered. Turkey sat glowing like a brass boiler; his bald head steaming; his hands reeling among his blotted papers.

"Think of it?" roared Turkey. "I think I'll just step behind his screen, and black his eyes for him!"

So saying, Turkey rose to his feet and threw his arms into a pugilistic position. He was hurrying away to make good his promise, when I detained him, alarmed at the effect of incautiously rousing Turkey's combativeness after dinner.

"Sit down, Turkey," said I, "and hear what Nippers has to say. What do you think of it, Nippers? Would I not be justified in immediately dismissing Bartleby?"

"Excuse me, that is for you to decide, sir. I think his conduct quite unusual, and, indeed, unjust, as regards Turkey and myself. But it may only be a passing whim."

"Ah," exclaimed I, "you have strangely changed your mind, then—you speak very gently of him now."

"All beer," cried Turkey; "gentleness is effects of beer—Nippers and I dined together to-day. You see how gentle *I* am, sir. Shall I go and black his eyes?"

"You refer to Bartleby, I suppose. No, not to-day, Turkey," I replied; "pray, put up your fists."

I closed the doors, and again advanced towards Bartleby. I felt additional incentives tempting me to my fate. I burned to be rebelled against again. I remembered that Bartleby never left the office.

"Bartleby," said I, "Ginger Nut is away; just step around to the Post Office, won't you?" (it was but a three minutes' walk) "and see if there is anything for me."

"I would prefer not to."

"You *will* not?"

"I *prefer* not."

I staggered to my desk, and sat there in a deep study. My blind inveteracy returned. Was there any other thing in which I could procure myself to be ignominiously repulsed by this lean, penniless wight? my hired clerk? What added thing is there, perfectly reasonable, that he will be sure to refuse to do?

"Bartleby!"

No answer.

"Bartleby," in a louder tone.

No answer.

"Bartleby," I roared.

Like a very ghost, agreeably to the laws of magical invocation, at the third summons, he appeared at the entrance of his hermitage.

"Go to the next room, and tell Nippers to come to me."

"I would prefer not to," he respectfully and slowly said, and mildly disappeared.

"Very good, Bartleby," said I, in a quiet sort of serenely-severe self-possessed tone, intimating the unalterable purpose of some terrible retribution very close at hand. At the moment I half intended something of the kind. But upon the whole, as it was drawing towards my dinner-hour, I thought it best to put on my hat and walk home for the day, suffering much from perplexity and distress of mind.

Shall I acknowledge it? The conclusion of this whole business was, that it soon became a fixed fact of my chambers, that a pale young scrivener, by the name of Bartleby, had a desk there; that he copied for me at the usual rate of four cents a folio (one hundred words); but he was permanently exempt from examining the work done by him, that duty being transferred to Turkey and Nippers, out of compliment, doubtless, to their superior acuteness; moreover, said Bartleby was never, on any account, to be dispatched on the most trivial errand of any sort; and that even if entreated to take upon him such a matter, it was generally understood that he would "prefer not to"—in other words, that he would refuse point blank.

As days passed on, I became considerably reconciled to Bartleby. His steadiness, his freedom from all dissipation, his incessant industry (except when he chose to throw himself into a standing revery behind his screen), his great stillness, his unalterableness of demeanor under all circumstances, made him a valuable acquisition. One prime thing was this—*he was always there*—first in the morning, continually through the day, and the last at night. I had a singular confidence in his honesty. I felt my most precious papers perfectly safe in his hands. Sometimes, to be sure, I could not, for the very soul of me, avoid falling into sudden spasmodic passions with him. For it was exceeding difficult to bear in mind all the time those strange peculiarities, privileges, and unheard-of exemptions, forming the tacit stipulations on Bartleby's part under which he remained in my office. Now and then, in the eagerness of dispatching pressing business, I would inadvertently summon Bartleby, in a short, rapid tone, to put his finger, say, on the incipient tie of a bit of red tape with which I was about compressing some papers. Of course, from behind the screen the usual answer, "I prefer not to," was sure to come; and then, how could a human creature, with the common infirmities of our nature, refrain from bitterly exclaiming upon such perverseness—such unreasonableness? However, every added repulse of this sort which I received only tended to lessen the probability of my repeating the inadvertence.

Here it must be said, that, according to the custom of most legal gentlemen occupying chambers in densely populated law buildings, there were several keys to my door. One was kept by a woman residing in the attic, which person weekly scrubbed and daily swept and dusted my apartments. Another was kept by Turkey for convenience sake. The third I sometimes carried in my own pocket. The fourth I knew not who had.

Now, one Sunday morning I happened to go to Trinity Church, to hear a celebrated preacher, and finding myself rather early on the ground I thought I would walk round to my chambers for a while. Luckily I had my key with me; but upon applying it to the lock, I found it resisted by something inserted from the inside. Quite surprised, I called out; when to my consternation a key was turned from within; and thrusting his lean visage at me, and holding the door ajar, the apparition of Bartleby appeared, in his shirt-sleeves, and otherwise in a strangely tattered *deshabille*,° saying quietly that he was sorry, but he was deeply engaged just then, and preferred not admitting me at present. In a brief word or two, he moreover added, that perhaps I had better walk round the block two

Deshabille: Careless style of dress (French).

or three times, and by that time he would probably have concluded his affairs.

Now, the utterly unsurmised appearance of Bartleby, tenanting my law-chambers of a Sunday morning, with his cadaverously gentlemanly *nonchalance*, yet withal firm and self-possessed, had such a strange effect upon me, that incontinently I slunk away from my own door, and did as desired. But not without sundry twinges of impotent rebellion against the mild effrontery of this unaccountable scrivener. Indeed, it was his wonderful mildness chiefly, which not only disarmed me, but unmanned me, as it were. For I consider that one, for the time, is sort of unmanned when he tranquilly permits his hired clerk to dictate to him, and order him away from his own premises. Furthermore, I was full of uneasiness as to what Bartleby could possibly be doing in my office in his shirt-sleeves, and in an otherwise dismantled condition on a Sunday morning. Was anything amiss going on? Nay, that was out of the question. It was not to be thought of for a moment that Bartleby was an immoral person. But what could he be doing there?—copying? Nay again, whatever might be his eccentricities, Bartleby was an eminently decorous person. He would be the last man to sit down to his desk in any state approaching to nudity. Besides, it was Sunday; and there was something about Bartleby that forbade the supposition that he would by any secular occupation violate the proprieties of the day.

Nevertheless, my mind was not pacified; and full of a restless curiosity, at last I returned to the door. Without hindrance I inserted my key, opened it, and entered. Bartleby was not to be seen. I looked round anxiously, peeped behind his screen; but it was very plain that he was gone. Upon more closely examining the place, I surmised that for an indefinite period Bartleby must have ate, dressed, and slept in my office, and that too without plate, mirror, or bed. The cushioned seat of a rickety old sofa in one corner bore the faint impress of a lean, reclining form. Rolled away under his desk, I found a blanket; under the empty grate, a blacking box and brush; on a chair, a tin basin, with soap and a ragged towel; in a newspaper a few crumbs of ginger-nuts and a morsel of cheese. Yes, thought I, it is evident enough that Bartleby has been making his home here, keeping bachelor's hall all by himself. Immediately then the thought came sweeping across me, what miserable friendlessness and loneliness are here revealed! His poverty is great; but his solitude, how horrible! Think of it. Of a Sunday, Wall Street is deserted as Petra;° and every night of every day it is an emptiness. This building, too, which of week-days hums with industry and life, at nightfall echoes with sheer vacancy, and

Petra: A Middle Eastern city, deserted for more than ten centuries until its rediscovery by explorers in 1812.

all through Sunday is forlorn. And here Bartleby makes his home; sole spectator of a solitude which he has seen all populous—a sort of innocent and transformed Marius° brooding among the ruins of Carthage!

For the first time in my life a feeling of overpowering stinging melancholy seized me. Before, I had never experienced aught but a not unpleasing sadness. The bond of a common humanity now drew me irresistibly to gloom. A fraternal melancholy! For both I and Bartleby were sons of Adam. I remembered the bright silks and sparkling faces I had seen that day, in gala trim, swan-like sailing down the Mississippi of Broadway; and I contrasted them with the pallid copyist, and thought to myself, Ah, happiness courts the light, so we deem the world is gay; but misery hides aloof, so we deem that misery there is none. These sad fancyings—chimeras, doubtless, of a sick and silly brain—led on to other and more special thoughts, concerning the eccentricities of Bartleby. Presentiments of strange discoveries hovered round me. The scrivener's pale form appeared to me laid out, among uncaring strangers, in its shivering winding-sheet.

Suddenly I was attracted by Bartleby's closed desk, the key in open sight left in the lock.

I mean no mischief, seek the gratification of no heartless curiosity, thought I; besides, the desk is mine, and its contents, too, so I will make bold to look within. Everything was methodically arranged, the papers smoothly placed. The pigeon-holes were deep, and removing the files of documents, I groped into their recesses. Presently I felt something there, and dragged it out. It was an old bandanna handkerchief, heavy and knotted. I opened it, and saw it was a saving's bank.

I now recalled all the quiet mysteries which I had noted in the man. I remembered that he never spoke but to answer; that, though at intervals he had considerable time to himself, yet I had never seen him reading—no, not even a newspaper; that for long periods he would stand looking out, at his pale window behind the screen, upon the dead brick wall; I was quite sure he never visited any refectory or eating-house; while his pale face clearly indicated that he never drank beer like Turkey; or tea and coffee even, like other men; that he never went anywhere in particular that I could learn; never went out for a walk, unless, indeed, that was the case at present; that he had declined telling who he was, or whence he came, or whether he had any relatives in the world; that though so thin and pale, he never complained of ill-health. And more than all, I remembered a certain unconscious air of pallid—how shall I call it?—of pallid haughtiness, say, or rather an austere reserve about

Marius: Gaius Marius (157?–86 B.C.), Roman general and consul who was banished and fled to Africa, scene of his greatest military triumphs.

him, which has positively awed me into my tame compliance with his eccentricities, when I had feared to ask him to do the slightest incidental thing for me, even though I might know, from his long-continued motionlessness, that behind his screen he must be standing in one of those dead-wall reveries of his.

Revolving all these things, and coupling them with the recently discovered fact, that he made my office his constant abiding place and home, and not forgetful of his morbid moodiness; revolving all these things, a prudential feeling began to steal over me. My first emotions had been those of pure melancholy and sincerest pity; but just in proportion as the forlornness of Bartleby grew and grew to my imagination, did that same melancholy merge into fear, that pity into repulsion. So true it is, and so terrible, too, that up to a certain point the thought or sight of misery enlists our best affections; but, in certain special cases, beyond that point it does not. They err who would assert that invariably this is owing to the inherent selfishness of the human heart. It rather proceeds from a certain hopelessness of remedying excessive and organic ill. To a sensitive being, pity is not seldom pain. And when at last it is perceived that such pity cannot lead to effectual succor, common sense bids the soul be rid of it. What I saw that morning persuaded me that the scrivener was the victim of innate and incurable disorder. I might give alms to his body; but his body did not pain him; it was his soul that suffered, and his soul I could not reach.

I did not accomplish the purpose of going to Trinity Church that morning. Somehow, the things I had seen disqualified me for the time from church-going. I walked homeward, thinking what I would do with Bartleby. Finally, I resolved upon this—I would put certain calm questions to him the next morning, touching his history, etc., and if he declined to answer them openly and unreservedly (and I supposed he would prefer not), then to give him a twenty dollar bill over and above whatever I might owe him, and tell him his services were no longer required; but that if in any other way I could assist him, I would be happy to do so, especially if he desired to return to his native place, wherever that might be, I would willingly help to defray the expenses. Moreover, if, after reaching home, he found himself at any time in want of aid, a letter from him would be sure of a reply.

The next morning came.

"Bartleby," said I, gently calling to him behind his screen.

No reply.

"Bartleby," said I, in a still gentler tone, "come here; I am not going to ask you to do anything you would prefer not to do—I simply wish to speak to you."

Upon this he noiselessly slid into view.

"Will you tell me, Bartleby, where you were born?"

"I would prefer not to."

"Will you tell me *anything* about yourself?"

"I would prefer not to."

"But what reasonable objection can you have to speak to me? I feel friendly towards you."

He did not look at me while I spoke, but kept his glance fixed upon my bust of Cicero, which, as I then sat, was directly behind me, some six inches above my head.

"What is your answer, Bartleby?" said I, after waiting a considerable time for a reply, during which his countenance remained immovable, only there was the faintest conceivable tremor of the white attenuated mouth.

"At present I prefer to give no answer," he said, and retired into his hermitage.

It was rather weak in me I confess, but his manner, on this occasion, nettled me. Not only did there seem to lurk in it a certain calm disdain, but his perverseness seemed ungrateful, considering the undeniable good usage and indulgence he had received from me.

Again I sat ruminating what I should do. Mortified as I was at his behavior, and resolved as I had been to dismiss him when I entered my office, nevertheless I strangely felt something superstitious knocking at my heart, and forbidding me to carry out my purpose, and denouncing me for a villain if I dared to breathe one bitter word against this forlornest of mankind. At last, familiarly drawing my chair behind his screen, I sat down and said: "Bartleby, never mind, then, about revealing your history; but let me entreat you, as a friend, to comply as far as may be with the usages of this office. Say now, you will help to examine papers tomorrow or next day: in short, say now, that in a day or two you will begin to be a little reasonable:—say so, Bartleby."

"At present I would prefer not to be a little reasonable," was his mildly cadaverous reply.

Just then the folding-doors opened, and Nippers approached. He seemed suffering from an unusually bad night's rest, induced by severer indigestion than common. He overheard those final words of Bartleby.

"*Prefer not*, eh?" gritted Nippers—"I'd *prefer* him, if I were you, sir," addressing me—"I'd *prefer* him; I'd give him preferences, the stubborn mule! What is it, sir, pray, that he *prefers* not to do now?"

Bartleby moved not a limb.

"Mr. Nippers," said I, "I'd prefer that you would withdraw for the present."

Somehow, of late, I had got into the way of involuntarily using this word "prefer" upon all sorts of not exactly suitable occasions. And I trembled to think that my contact with the scrivener had already and seriously affected me in a mental way. And what further and deeper aberration might it not yet produce? This apprehension had not been without efficacy in determining me to summary measures.

As Nippers, looking very sour and sulky, was departing, Turkey blandly and deferentially approached.

"With submission, sir," said he, "yesterday I was thinking about Bartleby here, and I think that if he would but prefer to take a quart of good ale every day, it would do much towards mending him, and enabling him to assist in examining his papers."

"So you have got the word, too," said I, slightly excited.

"With submission, what word, sir?" asked Turkey, respectfully crowding himself into the contracted space behind the screen, and by so doing, making me jostle the scrivener. "What word, sir?"

"I would prefer to be left alone here," said Bartleby, as if offended at being mobbed in his privacy.

"*That's* the word, Turkey," said I—"*that's* it."

"Oh, *prefer*? oh yes—queer word. I never use it myself. But, sir, as I was saying, if he would but prefer—"

"Turkey," interrupted I, "you will please withdraw."

"Oh certainly, sir, if you prefer that I should."

As he opened the folding-door to retire, Nippers at his desk caught a glimpse of me, and asked whether I would prefer to have a certain paper copied on blue paper or white. He did not in the least roguishly accent the word "prefer." It was plain that it involuntarily rolled from his tongue. I thought to myself, surely I must get rid of a demented man, who already has in some degree turned the tongues, if not the heads of myself and clerks. But I thought it prudent not to break the dismission at once.

The next day I noticed that Bartleby did nothing but stand at his window in his dead-wall revery. Upon asking him why he did not write, he said that he had decided upon doing no more writing.

"Why, how now? what next?" exclaimed I, "do no more writing?"

"No more."

"And what is the reason?"

"Do you not see the reason for yourself?" he indifferently replied.

I looked steadfastly at him, and perceived that his eyes looked dull and glazed. Instantly it occurred to me, that his unexampled diligence in copying by his dim window for the first few weeks of his stay with me might have temporarily impaired his vision.

I was touched. I said something in condolence with him. I hinted that of course he did wisely in abstaining from writing for a while; and urged him to embrace that opportunity of taking wholesome exercise in the open air. This, however, he did not do. A few days after this, my other clerks being absent, and being in a great hurry to dispatch certain letters by the mail, I thought that, having nothing else earthly to do, Bartleby would surely be less inflexible than usual, and carry these letters to the Post Office. But he blankly declined. So, much to my inconvenience, I went myself.

Still added days went by. Whether Bartleby's eyes improved or not, I could not say. To all appearance, I thought they did. But when I asked him if they did he vouchsafed no answer. At all events, he would do no copying. At last, in replying to my urgings, he informed me that he had permanently given up copying.

"What!" exclaimed I; "suppose your eyes should get entirely well— better than ever before—would you not copy then?"

"I have given up copying," he answered, and slid aside.

He remained as ever, a fixture in my chamber. Nay—if that were possible—he became still more of a fixture than before. What was to be done? He would do nothing in the office; why should he stay there? In plain fact, he had now become a millstone to me, not only useless as a necklace, but afflictive to bear. Yet I was sorry for him. I speak less than truth when I say that, on his own account, he occasioned me uneasiness. If he would but have named a single relative or friend, I would instantly have written, and urged their taking the poor fellow away to some convenient retreat. But he seemed alone, absolutely alone in the universe. A bit of wreck in the mid-Atlantic. At length, necessities connected with my business tyrannized over all other considerations. Decently as I could, I told Bartleby that in six days' time he must unconditionally leave the office. I warned him to take measures, in the interval, for procuring some other abode. I offered to assist him in this endeavor, if he himself would but take the first step towards a removal. "And when you finally quit me, Bartleby," added I, "I shall see that you go not away entirely unprovided. Six days from this hour, remember."

At the expiration of that period, I peeped behind the screen, and lo! Bartleby was there.

I buttoned up my coat, balanced myself; advanced slowly towards him, touched his shoulder, and said, "The time has come; you must quit this place; I am sorry for you; here is money; but you must go."

"I would prefer not," he replied, with his back still towards me.

"You *must*."

He remained silent.

Now I had an unbounded confidence in this man's common honesty. He had frequently restored to me sixpences and shillings carelessly dropped upon the floor, for I am apt to be very reckless in such shirt-button affairs. The proceeding, then, which followed will not be deemed extraordinary.

"Bartleby," said I, "I owe you twelve dollars on account; here are thirty-two; the odd twenty are yours—Will you take it?" and I handed the bills towards him.

But he made no motion.

"I will leave them here, then," putting them under a weight on the table. Then taking my hat and cane and going to the door, I tranquilly turned and added—"After you have removed your things from these offices, Bartleby, you will of course lock the door—since every one is now gone for the day but you—and if you please, slip your key underneath the mat, so that I may have it in the morning. I shall not see you again; so good-bye to you. If, hereafter, in your new place of abode, I can be of any service to you, do not fail to advise me by letter. Good-bye, Bartleby, and fare you well."

But he answered not a word; like the last column of some ruined temple, he remained standing mute and solitary in the middle of the otherwise deserted room.

As I walked home in a pensive mood, my vanity got the better of my pity. I could not but highly plume myself on my masterly management in getting rid of Bartleby. Masterly I call it, and such it must appear to any dispassionate thinker. The beauty of my procedure seemed to consist in its perfect quietness. There was no vulgar bullying, no bravado of any sort, no choleric hectoring, and striding to and fro across the apartment, jerking out vehement commands for Bartleby to bundle himself off with his beggarly traps. Nothing of the kind. Without loudly bidding Bartleby depart—as an inferior genius might have done—I *assumed* the ground that depart he must; and upon that assumption built all I had to say. The more I thought over my procedure, the more I was charmed with it. Nevertheless, next morning, upon awakening, I had my doubts—I had somehow slept off the fumes of vanity. One of the coolest and wisest hours a man has, is just after he awakes in the morning. My procedure seemed as sagacious as ever—but only in theory. How it would prove in practice—there was the rub. It was truly a beautiful thought to have assumed Bartleby's departure; but, after all, that assumption was simply my own, and none of Bartleby's. The great point was, not whether I had assumed that he would quit me, but whether he would prefer to do so. He was more a man of preferences than assumptions.

After breakfast, I walked down town, arguing the probabilities *pro* and *con*. One moment I thought it would prove a miserable failure, and Bartleby would be found all alive at my office as usual; the next moment it seemed certain that I should find his chair empty. And so I kept veering about. At the corner of Broadway and Canal Street, I saw quite an excited group of people standing in earnest conversation.

"I'll take odds he doesn't," said a voice as I passed.

"Doesn't go?—done!" said I, "put up your money."

I was instinctively putting my hand in my pocket to produce my own, when I remembered that this was an election day. The words I had over-heard bore no reference to Bartleby, but to the success or non-success of some candidate for the mayoralty. In my intent frame of mind, I had, as it were, imagined that all Broadway shared in my excitement, and were debating the same question with me. I passed on, very thankful that the uproar of the street screened my momentary absent-mindedness.

As I had intended, I was earlier than usual at my office door. I stood listening for a moment. All was still. He must be gone. I tried the knob. The door was locked. Yes, my procedure had worked to a charm; he indeed must be vanished. Yet a certain melancholy mixed with this: I was almost sorry for my brilliant success. I was fumbling under the door mat for the key, which Bartleby was to have left there for me, when accidentally my knee knocked against a panel, producing a summoning sound, and in response a voice came to me from within—"Not yet; I am occupied."

It was Bartleby.

I was thunderstruck. For an instant I stood like the man who, pipe in mouth, was killed one cloudless afternoon long ago in Virginia, by sum-mer lightning; at his own warm open window he was killed, and re-mained leaning out there upon the dreamy afternoon, till someone touched him, when he fell.

"Not gone!" I murmured at last. But again obeying that wondrous as-cendancy which the inscrutable scrivener had over me, and from which ascendancy, for all my chafing, I could not completely escape, I slowly went down stairs and out into the street, and while walking round the block, considered what I should next do in this unheard-of perplexity. Turn the man out by an actual thrusting I could not; to drive him away by calling him hard names would not do; calling in the police was an unpleasant idea; and yet, permit him to enjoy his cadaverous triumph over me—this, too, I could not think of. What was to be done? or, if noth-ing could be done, was there anything further that I could *assume* in the matter? Yes, as before I had prospectively assumed that Bartleby would depart, so now I might retrospectively assume that departed he was. In the legitimate carrying out of this assumption, I might enter my office in a great hurry, and pretending not to see Bartleby at all, walk straight against him as if he were air. Such a proceeding would in a singular de-gree have the appearance of a home-thrust. It was hardly possible that Bartleby could withstand such an application of the doctrine of assump-tion. But upon second thoughts the success of the plan seemed rather dubious. I resolved to argue the matter over with him again.

"Bartleby," said I, entering the office, with a quietly severe expression,

"I am seriously displeased. I am pained, Bartleby. I had thought better of you. I had imagined you of such a gentlemanly organization, that in any delicate dilemma a slight hint would suffice—in short, an assumption. But it appears I am deceived. Why," I added, unaffectedly starting, "you have not even touched that money yet," pointing to it, just where I had left it the evening previous.

He answered nothing.

"Will you, or will you not, quit me?" I now demanded in a sudden passion, advancing close to him.

"I would prefer *not* to quit you," he replied, gently emphasizing the *not*.

"What earthly right have you to stay here? Do you pay any rent? Do you pay my taxes? Or is this property yours?"

He answered nothing.

"Are you ready to go on and write now? Are your eyes recovered? Could you copy a small paper for me this morning? or help examine a few lines? or step round to the Post Office? In a word, will you do anything at all, to give a coloring to your refusal to depart the premises?"

He silently retired into his hermitage.

I was now in such a state of nervous resentment that I thought it but prudent to check myself at present from further demonstrations. Bartleby and I were alone. I remembered the tragedy of the unfortunate Adams and the still more unfortunate Colt in the solitary office of the latter; and how poor Colt,° being dreadfully incensed by Adams, and imprudently permitting himself to get wildly excited, was at unawares hurried into his fatal act—an act which certainly no man could possibly deplore more than the actor himself. Often it had occurred to me in my ponderings upon the subject that had that altercation taken place in the public street, or at a private residence, it would not have terminated as it did. It was the circumstance of being alone in a solitary office, up stairs, of a building entirely unhallowed by humanizing domestic associations—an uncarpeted office, doubtless, of a dusty, haggard sort of appearance—this it must have been, which greatly helped to enhance the irritable desperation of the hapless Colt.

But when this old Adam of resentment rose in me and tempted me concerning Bartleby, I grappled him and threw him. How? Why, simply by recalling the divine injunction: "A new commandment give I unto you, that ye love one another."° Yes, this it was that saved me. Aside from higher considerations, charity often operates as a vastly wise and prudent

Colt: John C. Colt, who murdered the printer Samuel Adams in a fit of rage in January 1842, committed suicide a half hour before he was to be hanged for the crime.
"A new commandment . . .": John 13.34 and 15.17.

principle—a great safeguard to its possessor. Men have committed murder for jealousy's sake, and anger's sake, and hatred's sake, and selfishness' sake, and spiritual pride's sake; but no man, that ever I heard of, ever committed a diabolical murder for sweet charity's sake. Mere self-interest, then, if no better motive can be enlisted, should, especially with high-tempered men, prompt all beings to charity and philanthropy. At any rate, upon the occasion in question, I strove to drown my exasperated feelings towards the scrivener by benevolently construing his conduct. Poor fellow, poor fellow! thought I, he don't mean anything; and besides, he has seen hard times, and ought to be indulged.

I endeavored, also, immediately to occupy myself, and at the same time to comfort my despondency. I tried to fancy, that in the course of the morning, at such time as might prove agreeable to him, Bartleby, of his own free accord, would emerge from his hermitage and take up some decided line of march in the direction of the door. But no. Half-past twelve o'clock came; Turkey began to glow in the face, overturn his inkstand, and become generally obstreperous; Nippers abated down into quietude and courtesy; Ginger Nut munched his noon apple; and Bartleby remained standing at his window in one of his profoundest dead-wall reveries. Will it be credited? Ought I to acknowledge it? That afternoon I left the office without saying one further word to him.

Some days now passed, during which, at leisure intervals I looked a little into "Edwards on the Will," and "Priestley on Necessity."° Under the circumstances, those books induced a salutary feeling. Gradually I slid into the persuasion that these troubles of mine, touching the scrivener, had been all predestined from eternity, and Bartleby was billeted upon me for some mysterious purpose of an all-wise Providence, which it was not for a mere mortal like me to fathom. Yes, Bartleby, stay there behind your screen, thought I; I shall persecute you no more; you are harmless and noiseless as any of these old chairs; in short, I never feel so private as when I know you are here. At last I see it, I feel it; I penetrate to the predestined purpose of my life. I am content. Others may have loftier parts to enact; but my mission in this world, Bartleby, is to furnish you with office-room for such period as you may see fit to remain.

I believe that this wise and blessed frame of mind would have continued with me, had it not been for the unsolicited and uncharitable remarks obtruded upon me by my professional friends who visited the rooms. But thus it often is, that the constant friction of illiberal minds

Edwards . . . Priestley: Jonathan Edwards (1703–1758), American theologian and author of the Calvinist *Freedom of the Will* (1754), and Joseph Priestley (1733–1803), English scientist, clergyman, and author of *The Doctrine of Philosophical Necessity* (1777).

wears out at last the best resolves of the more generous. Though to be sure, when I reflected upon it, it was not strange that people entering my office should be struck by the peculiar aspect of the unaccountable Bartleby, and so be tempted to throw out some sinister observations concerning him. Sometimes an attorney, having business with me, and calling at my office, and finding no one but the scrivener there, would undertake to obtain some sort of precise information from him touching my whereabouts; but without heeding his idle talk, Bartleby would remain standing immovable in the middle of the room. So after contemplating him in that position for a time, the attorney would depart, no wiser than he came.

Also, when a reference was going on, and the room full of lawyers and witnesses, and business driving fast, some deeply-occupied legal gentleman present, seeing Bartleby wholly unemployed, would request him to run round to his (the legal gentleman's) office and fetch some papers for him. Thereupon, Bartleby would tranquilly decline, and yet remain idle as before. Then the lawyer would give a great stare, and turn to me. And what could I say? At last I was made aware that all through the circle of my professional acquaintance, a whisper of wonder was running round, having reference to the strange creature I kept at my office. This worried me very much. And as the idea came upon me of his possibly turning out a long-lived man, and keeping occupying my chambers, and denying my authority; and perplexing my visitors; and scandalizing my professional reputation; and casting a general gloom over the premises; keeping soul and body together to the last upon his savings (for doubtless he spent but half a dime a day), and in the end perhaps outlive me, and claim possession of my office by right of his perpetual occupancy: as all these dark anticipations crowded upon me more and more, and my friends continually intruded their relentless remarks upon the apparition in my room, a great change was wrought in me. I resolved to gather all my faculties together, and forever rid me of this intolerable incubus.

Ere revolving any complicated project, however, adapted to this end, I first simply suggested to Bartleby the propriety of his permanent departure. In a calm and serious tone, I commended the idea to his careful and mature consideration. But, having taken three days to meditate upon it, he apprised me, that his original determination remained the same; in short, that he still preferred to abide with me.

What shall I do? I now said to myself, buttoning up my coat to the last button. What shall I do? what ought I to do? what does conscience say I *should* do with this man, or, rather, ghost. Rid myself of him, I must; go, he shall. But how? You will not thrust him, the poor, pale, passive mortal—you will not thrust such a helpless creature out of your door? you will not dishonor yourself by such cruelty? No, I will not, I cannot do that. Rather would I let him live and die here, and then mason up his remains in the wall. What, then, will you do? For all your coaxing, he will not budge. Bribes he leaves under your own paper-weight on your table; in short, it is quite plain that he prefers to cling to you.

Then something severe, something unusual must be done. What! surely you will not have him collared by a constable, and commit his innocent pallor to the common jail? And upon what ground could you procure such a thing to be done?—a vagrant, is he? What! he a vagrant, a wanderer, who refuses to budge? It is because he will not be a vagrant, then, that you seek to count him *as* a vagrant. That is too absurd. No visible means of support: there I have him. Wrong again: for indubitably he *does* support himself, and that is the only unanswerable proof that any man can show of his possessing the means so to do. No more, then. Since he will not quit me, I must quit him. I will change my offices; I will move elsewhere, and give him fair notice, that if I find him on my new premises I will then proceed against him as a common trespasser.

Acting accordingly, next day I thus addressed him: "I find these chambers too far from the City Hall; the air is unwholesome. In a word, I propose to remove my offices next week, and shall no longer require your services. I tell you this now, in order that you may seek another place."

He made no reply, and nothing more was said.

On the appointed day I engaged carts and men, proceeded to my chambers, and, having but little furniture, everything was removed in a few hours. Throughout, the scrivener remained standing behind the screen, which I directed to be removed the last thing. It was withdrawn; and, being folded up like a huge folio, left him the motionless occupant of a naked room. I stood in the entry watching him a moment, while something from within me upbraided me.

I re-entered, with my hand in my pocket—and—and my heart in my mouth.

"Good-bye, Bartleby; I am going—good-bye, and God some way bless you; and take that," slipping something in his hand. But it dropped upon the floor, and then—strange to say—I tore myself from him whom I had so longed to be rid of.

Established in my new quarters, for a day or two I kept the door locked, and started at every footfall in the passages. When I returned to my rooms, after any little absence, I would pause at the threshold for an instant, and attentively listen, ere applying my key. But these fears were needless. Bartleby never came nigh me.

I thought all was going well, when a perturbed-looking stranger visited me, inquiring whether I was the person who had recently occupied rooms at No.— Wall Street.

Full of forebodings, I replied that I was.

"Then, sir," said the stranger, who proved a lawyer, "you are responsible for the man you left there. He refuses to do any copying; he refuses to do anything; he says he prefers not to; and he refuses to quit the premises."

"I am very sorry, sir," said I, with assumed tranquillity, but an inward tremor, "but, really, the man you allude to is nothing to me—he is no relation or apprentice of mine, that you should hold me responsible for him."

"In mercy's name, who is he?"

"I certainly cannot inform you. I know nothing about him. Formerly I employed him as a copyist; but he has done nothing for me now for some time past."

"I shall settle him, then—good morning, sir."

Several days passed, and I heard nothing more; and, though I often felt a charitable prompting to call at the place and see poor Bartleby, yet a certain squeamishness, of I know not what, withheld me.

All is over with him, by this time, thought I, at last, when, through another week, no further intelligence reached me. But, coming to my room the day after, I found several persons waiting at my door in a high state of nervous excitement.

"That's the man—here he comes," cried the foremost one, whom I recognized as the lawyer who had previously called upon me alone.

"You must take him away, sir, at once," cried a portly person among them, advancing upon me, and whom I knew to be the landlord of No.— Wall Street. "These gentlemen, my tenants, cannot stand it any longer; Mr. B———" pointing to the lawyer, "has turned him out of his room, and he now persists in haunting the building generally, sitting upon the banisters of the stairs by day, and sleeping in the entry by night. Everybody is concerned; clients are leaving the offices; some fears are entertained of a mob; something you must do, and that without delay."

Aghast at this torrent, I fell back before it, and would fain have locked myself in my new quarters. In vain I persisted that Bartleby was nothing to me—no more than to any one else. In vain—I was the last person known to have anything to do with him, and they held me to the terrible account. Fearful, then, of being exposed in the papers (as one person present obscurely threatened), I considered the matter, and, at length, said, that if the lawyer would give me a confidential interview with the scrivener, in his (the lawyer's) own room, I would, that afternoon, strive my best to rid them of the nuisance they complained of.

Going up stairs to my old haunt, there was Bartleby silently sitting upon the banister at the landing.

"What are you doing here, Bartleby?" said I.

"Sitting upon the banister," he mildly replied.

I motioned him into the lawyer's room, who then left us.

"Bartleby," said I, "are you aware that you are the cause of great tribulation to me, by persisting in occupying the entry after being dismissed from the office?"

No answer.

"Now one of two things must take place. Either you must do something, or something must be done to you. Now what sort of business would you like to engage in? Would you like to re-engage in copying for some one?"

"No; I would prefer not to make any change."

"Would you like a clerkship in a dry-goods store?"

"There is too much confinement about that. No, I would not like a clerkship; but I am not particular."

"Too much confinement," I cried, "why, you keep yourself confined all the time!"

"I would prefer not to take a clerkship," he rejoined, as if to settle that little item at once.

"How would a bar-tender's business suit you? There is no trying of the eye-sight in that."

"I would not like it at all; though, as I said before, I am not particular."

His unwonted wordiness inspirited me. I returned to the charge.

"Well, then, would you like to travel through the country collecting bills for the merchants? That would improve your health."

"No, I would prefer to be doing something else."

"How, then, would going as a companion to Europe, to entertain some young gentleman with your conversation—how would that suit you?"

"Not at all. It does not strike me that there is anything definite about that. I like to be stationary. But I am not particular."

"Stationary you shall be, then," I cried, now losing all patience, and, for the first time in all my exasperating connections with him, fairly flying into a passion. "If you do not go away from these premises before night, I shall feel bound—indeed, I *am* bound—to—to—to quit the premises myself!" I rather absurdly concluded, knowing not with what possible threat to try to frighten his immobility into compliance. Despairing of all further efforts, I was precipitately leaving him, when a final thought occurred to me—one which had not been wholly unindulged before.

"Bartleby," said I, in the kindest tone I could assume under such exciting circumstances, "will you go home with me now not to my office, but my dwelling—and remain there till we can conclude upon some convenient arrangement for you at our leisure? Come, let us start now, right away."

"No: at present I would prefer not to make any change at all."

I answered nothing; but, effectually dodging every one by the suddenness and rapidity of my flight, rushed from the building, ran up Wall Street towards Broadway, and, jumping into the first omnibus, was soon removed from pursuit. As soon as tranquillity returned, I distinctly perceived that I had now done all that I possibly could, both in respect to the demands of the landlord and his tenants, and with regard to my own desire and sense of duty, to benefit Bartleby, and shield him from rude persecution. I now strove to be entirely care-free and quiescent; and my conscience justified me in the attempt; though, indeed, it was not so successful as I could have wished. So fearful was I of being again hunted out by the incensed landlord and his exasperated tenants, that, surrendering my business to Nippers, for a few days, I drove about the upper part of the town and through the suburbs, in my rockaway;° crossed over to Jersey City and Hoboken, and paid fugitive visits to Manhattanville and Astoria. In fact, I almost lived in my rockaway for the time.

When again I entered my office, lo, a note from the landlord lay upon the desk. I opened it with trembling hands. It informed me that the writer had sent to the police, and had Bartleby removed to the Tombs as a vagrant. Moreover, since I knew more about him than any one else, he wished me to appear at that place, and make a suitable statement of the facts. These tidings had a conflicting effect upon me. At first I was indignant; but, at last, almost approved. The landlord's energetic, summary disposition, had led him to adopt a procedure which I do not think I would have decided upon myself; and yet, as a last resort, under such peculiar circumstances, it seemed the only plan.

As I afterwards learned, the poor scrivener, when told that he must be conducted to the Tombs, offered not the slightest obstacle, but, in his pale, unmoving way, silently acquiesced.

Some of the compassionate and curious bystanders joined the party; and headed by one of the constables arm-in-arm with Bartleby, the silent procession filed its way through all the noise, and heat, and joy of the roaring thoroughfares at noon.

The same day I received the note, I went to the Tombs, or, to speak more properly, the Halls of Justice. Seeking the right officer, I stated the purpose of my call, and was informed that the individual I described was, indeed, within. I then assured the functionary that Bartleby was a perfectly honest man, and greatly to be compassionated, however unaccountably eccentric. I narrated all I knew, and closed by suggesting the idea of letting him remain in as indulgent confinement as possible, till something less harsh might be done—though, indeed, I hardly knew

Rockaway: A four-wheeled carriage with two or three seats, open sides, and a standing top.

what. At all events, if nothing else could be decided upon, the alms-house must receive him. I then begged to have an interview.

Being under no disgraceful charge, and quite serene and harmless in all his ways, they had permitted him freely to wander about the prison, and, especially, in the inclosed grass-platted yards thereof. And so I found him there, standing all alone in the quietest of the yards, his face towards a high wall, while all around, from the narrow slits of the jail windows, I thought I saw peering out upon him the eyes of murderers and thieves.

"Bartleby!"

"I know you," he said, without looking round—"and I want nothing to say to you."

"It was not I that brought you here, Bartleby," said I, keenly pained at his implied suspicion. "And to you, this should not be so vile a place. Nothing reproachful attaches to you by being here. And see, it is not so sad a place as one might think. Look, there is the sky, and here is the grass."

"I know where I am," he replied, but would say nothing more, and so I left him.

As I entered the corridor again, a broad meat-like man, in an apron, accosted me, and, jerking his thumb over my shoulder, said, "Is that your friend?"

"Yes."

"Does he want to starve? If he does, let him live on the prison fare, that's all."

"Who are you?" asked I, not knowing what to make of such an unofficially speaking person in such a place.

"I am the grub-man. Such gentlemen as have friends here, hire me to provide them with something good to eat."

"Is this so?" said I, turning to the turnkey.

He said it was.

"Well, then," said I, slipping some silver into the grub-man's hands (for so they called him), "I want you to give particular attention to my friend there; let him have the best dinner you can get. And you must be as polite to him as possible."

"Introduce me, will you?" said the grub-man, looking at me with an expression which seemed to say he was all impatience for an opportunity to give a specimen of his breeding.

Thinking it would prove of benefit to the scrivener, I acquiesced; and, asking the grub-man his name, went up with him to Bartleby.

"Bartleby, this is a friend; you will find him very useful to you."

"Your sarvant, sir, your sarvant," said the grub-man, making a low salutation behind his apron. "Hope you find it pleasant here, sir; nice grounds—cool apartments—hope you'll stay with us some time—try to make it agreeable. What will you have for dinner to-day?"

"I prefer not to dine to-day," said Bartleby, turning away. "It would disagree with me; I am unused to dinners." So saying, he slowly moved to the other side of the inclosure, and took up a position fronting the dead-wall.

"How's this?" said the grub-man, addressing me with a stare of astonishment. "He's odd, ain't he?"

"I think he is a little deranged," said I, sadly.

"Deranged? deranged is it? Well, now, upon my word, I thought that friend of yourn was a gentleman forger; they are always pale and genteel-like, them forgers. I can't help pity 'em—can't help it, sir. Did you know Monroe Edwards?" he added, touchingly, and paused. Then, laying his hand piteously on my shoulder, sighed, "he died of consumption at Sing-Sing. So you weren't acquainted with Monroe?"

"No, I was never socially acquainted with any forgers. But I cannot stop longer. Look to my friend yonder. You will not lose by it. I will see you again."

Some few days after this, I again obtained admission to the Tombs, and went through the corridors in quest of Bartleby; but without finding him.

"I saw him coming from his cell not long ago," said a turnkey, "may be he's gone to loiter in the yards."

So I went in that direction.

"Are you looking for the silent man?" said another turnkey, passing me. "Yonder he lies—sleeping in the yard there. 'Tis not twenty minutes since I saw him lie down."

The yard was entirely quiet. It was not accessible to the common prisoners. The surrounding walls, of amazing thickness, kept off all sounds behind them. The Egyptian character of the masonry weighed upon me with its gloom. But a soft imprisoned turf grew under foot. The heart of the eternal pyramids, it seemed, wherein, by some strange magic, through the clefts, grass-seed, dropped by birds, had sprung.

Strangely huddled at the base of the wall, his knees drawn up, and lying on his side, his head touching the cold stones, I saw the wasted Bartleby. But nothing stirred. I paused; then went close up to him; stooped over, and saw that his dim eyes were open; otherwise he seemed profoundly sleeping. Something prompted me to touch him. I felt his hand, when a tingling shiver ran up my arm and down my spine to my feet.

The round face of the grub-man peered upon me now. "His dinner is ready. Won't he dine to-day, either? Or does he live without dining?"

"Lives without dining," said I, and closed the eyes.

"Eh!—He's asleep, ain't he?"

"With kings and counselors,"° murmured I.

There would seem little need for proceeding further in this history. Imagination will readily supply the meagre recital of poor Bartleby's interment. But, ere parting with the reader, let me say, that if this little narrative has sufficiently interested him, to awaken curiosity as to who Bartleby was, and what manner of life he led prior to the present narrator's making his acquaintance, I can only reply, that in such curiosity I fully share, but am wholly unable to gratify it. Yet here I hardly know whether I should divulge one little item of rumor, which came to my ear a few months after the scrivener's decease. Upon what basis it rested, I could never ascertain; and hence, how true it is I cannot now tell. But, inasmuch as this vague report has not been without a certain suggestive interest to me, however sad, it may prove the same with some others; and so I will briefly mention it. The report was this: that Bartleby had been a subordinate clerk in the Dead Letter Office at Washington, from which he had been suddenly removed by a change in the administration. When I think over this rumor, hardly can I express the emotions which seize me. Dead letters! does it not sound like dead men? Conceive a man by nature and misfortune prone to a pallid hopelessness, can any business seem more fitted to heighten it than that of continually handling these dead letters, and assorting them for the flames? For by the cartload they are annually burned. Sometimes from out the folded paper the pale clerk takes a ring—the finger it was meant for, perhaps, moulders in the grave; a bank-note sent in swiftest charity—he whom it would relieve, nor eats nor hungers any more; pardon for those who died despairing; hope for those who died unhoping; good tidings for those who died stifled by unrelieved calamities. On errands of life, these letters speed to death.

Ah, Bartleby! Ah, humanity!

[1853]

With kings and counselors: A reference to the biblical book of Job, 3:13–14: "then had I been at rest with kings and counselors of the earth, which built desolate places for themselves."

SARAH ORNE JEWETT   [1849–1909]

A White Heron

I

The woods were already filled with shadows one June evening, just before eight o'clock, though a bright sunset still glimmered faintly among
the trunks of the trees. A little girl was driving home her cow, a plodding,
dilatory, provoking creature in her behavior, but a valued companion for
all that. They were going away from the western light, and striking deep
into the dark woods, but their feet were familiar with the path, and it was
no matter whether their eyes could see it or not.

There was hardly a night the summer through when the old cow could
be found waiting at the pasture bars; on the contrary, it was her greatest
pleasure to hide herself away among the high huckleberry bushes, and
though she wore a loud bell she had made the discovery that if one stood
perfectly still it would not ring. So Sylvia had to hunt for her until she
found her and call Co'! Co'! with never an answering Moo, until her
childish patience was quite spent. If the creature had not given good
milk and plenty of it, the case would have seemed very different to her
owners. Besides, Sylvia had all the time there was, and very little use to
make of it. Sometimes in pleasant weather it was a consolation to look
upon the cow's pranks as an intelligent attempt to play hide and seek,
and as the child had no playmates she lent herself to this amusement
with a good deal of zest. Though this chase had been so long that the
wary animal herself had given an unusual signal of her whereabouts,
Sylvia had only laughed when she came upon Mistress Moolly at the
swampside, and urged her affectionately homeward with a twig of birch
leaves. The old cow was not inclined to wander farther, she even turned
in the right direction for once as they left the pasture, and stepped along
the road at a good pace. She was quite ready to be milked now, and seldom stopped to browse. Sylvia wondered what her grandmother would
say because they were so late. It was a great while since she had left
home at half past five o'clock, but everybody knew the difficulty of making this errand a short one. Mrs. Tilley had chased the horned torment
too many summer evenings herself to blame any one else for lingering,
and was only thankful as she waited that she had Sylvia, nowadays, to

give such valuable assistance. The good woman suspected that Sylvia loitered occasionally on her own account; there never was such a child for straying about out-of-doors since the world was made! Everybody said that it was a good change for a little maid who had tried to grow for eight years in a crowded manufacturing town, but, as for Sylvia herself, it seemed as if she never had been alive at all before she came to live at the farm. She thought often with wistful compassion of a wretched dry geranium that belonged to a town neighbor.

"'Afraid of folks,'" old Mrs. Tilley said to herself, with a smile, after she had made the unlikely choice of Sylvia from her daughter's houseful of children, and was returning to the farm. "'Afraid of folks,' they said! I guess she won't be troubled no great with 'em up to the old place!" When they reached the door of the lonely house and stopped to unlock it, and the cat came to purr loudly, and rub against them, a deserted pussy, indeed, but fat with young robins, Sylvia whispered that this was a beautiful place to live in, and she never should wish to go home.

The companions followed the shady wood-road, the cow taking slow steps, and the child very fast ones. The cow stopped long at the brook to drink, as if the pasture were not half a swamp, and Sylvia stood still and waited, letting her bare feet cool themselves in the shoal water, while the great twilight moths struck softly against her. She waded on through the brook as the cow moved away, and listened to the thrushes with a heart that beat fast with pleasure. There was a stirring in the great boughs overhead. They were full of little birds and beasts that seemed to be wide-awake, and going about their world, or else saying good-night to each other in sleepy twitters. Sylvia herself felt sleepy as she walked along. However, it was not much farther to the house, and the air was soft and sweet. She was not often in the woods so late as this, and it made her feel as if she were a part of the gray shadows and the moving leaves. She was just thinking how long it seemed since she first came to the farm a year ago, and wondering if everything went on in the noisy town just the same as when she was there; the thought of the great red-faced boy who used to chase and frighten her made her hurry along the path to escape from the shadow of the trees.

Suddenly this little woods-girl is horror-stricken to hear a clear whistle not very far away. Not a bird's whistle, which would have a sort of friendliness, but a boy's whistle, determined, and somewhat aggressive. Sylvia left the cow to whatever sad fate might await her, and stepped discreetly aside into the bushes, but she was just too late. The enemy had discovered her, and called out in a very cheerful and persuasive tone, "Halloa, little girl, how far is it to the road?" and trembling Sylvia answered almost inaudibly, "A good ways."

She did not dare to look boldly at the tall young man, who carried a gun over his shoulder, but she came out of her bush and again followed the cow, while he walked alongside.

"I have been hunting for some birds," the stranger said kindly, "and I have lost my way, and need a friend very much. Don't be afraid," he added gallantly. "Speak up and tell me what your name is, and whether you think I can spend the night at your house, and go out gunning early in the morning."

Sylvia was more alarmed than before. Would not her grandmother consider her much to blame? But who could have foreseen such an accident as this? It did not appear to be her fault, and she hung her head as if the stem of it were broken, but managed to answer, "Sylvy," with much effort when her companion again asked her name.

Mrs. Tilley was standing in the doorway when the trio came into view. The cow gave a loud moo by way of explanation.

"Yes, you'd better speak up for yourself, you old trial! Where'd she tucked herself away this time, Sylvy?" Sylvia kept an awed silence; she knew by instinct that her grandmother did not comprehend the gravity of the situation. She must be mistaking the stranger for one of the farmer-lads of the region.

The young man stood his gun beside the door, and dropped a heavy game-bag beside it; then he bade Mrs. Tilley good-evening, and repeated his wayfarer's story, and asked if he could have a night's lodging.

"Put me anywhere you like," he said. "I must be off early in the morning, before day; but I am very hungry, indeed. You can give me some milk at any rate, that's plain."

"Dear sakes, yes," responded the hostess, whose long slumbering hospitality seemed to be easily awakened. "You might fare better if you went out on the main road a mile or so, but you're welcome to what we've got. I'll milk right off, and you make yourself at home. You can sleep on husks or feathers," she proffered graciously. "I raised them all myself. There's good pasturing for geese just below here towards the ma'sh. Now step round and set a plate for the gentleman, Sylvy!" And Sylvia promptly stepped. She was glad to have something to do, and she was hungry herself.

It was a surprise to find so clean and comfortable a little dwelling in this New England wilderness. The young man had known the horrors of its most primitive housekeeping, and the dreary squalor of that level of society which does not rebel at the companionship of hens. This was the best thrift of an old-fashioned farmstead, though on such a small scale that it seemed like a hermitage. He listened eagerly to the old woman's quaint talk, he watched Sylvia's pale face and shining gray eyes with ever growing enthusiasm, and insisted that this was the best supper he had eaten for a month; then, afterward, the new-made friends sat down in the doorway together while the moon came up.

Soon it would be berry-time, and Sylvia was a great help at picking. The cow was a good milker, though a plaguy thing to keep track of, the hostess gossiped frankly, adding presently that she had buried four children, so that Sylvia's mother, and a son (who might be dead) in California were all the children she had left. "Dan, my boy, was a great hand to go gunning," she explained sadly. "I never wanted for pa'tridges or gray squer'ls while he was to home. He's been a great wand'rer, I expect, and he's no hand to write letters. There, I don't blame him, I'd ha' seen the world myself if it had been so I could.

"Sylvia takes after him," the grandmother continued affectionately, after a minute's pause. "There ain't a foot o' ground she don't know her way over, and the wild creatur's counts her one o' themselves. Squer'ls she'll tame to come an' feed right out o' her hands, and all sorts o' birds. Last winter she got the jay-birds to bangeing here, and I believe she'd 'a' scanted herself of her own meals to have plenty to throw out amongst 'em, if I hadn't kep' watch. Anything but crows, I tell her, I'm willin' to help support,—though Dan he went an' tamed one o' them that did seem to have reason same as folks. It was round here a good spell after he went away. Dan an' his father they didn't hitch,—but he never held up his head ag'in after Dan had dared him an' gone off."

The guest did not notice this hint of family sorrows in his eager interest in something else.

"So Sylvy knows all about birds, does she?" he exclaimed, as he looked round at the little girl who sat, very demure but increasingly sleepy, in the moonlight. "I am making a collection of birds myself. I have been at it ever since I was a boy." (Mrs. Tilley smiled.) "There are two or three very rare ones I have been hunting for these five years. I mean to get them on my own ground if they can be found."

"Do you cage 'em up?" asked Mrs. Tilley doubtfully, in response to this enthusiastic announcement.

"Oh, no, they're stuffed and preserved, dozens and dozens of them," said the ornithologist, "and I have shot or snared every one myself. I caught a glimpse of a white heron three miles from here on Saturday, and I have followed it in this direction. They have never been found in this district at all. The little white heron, it is," and he turned again to look at Sylvia with the hope of discovering that the rare bird was one of her acquaintances.

But Sylvia was watching a hop-toad in the narrow footpath.

"You would know the heron if you saw it," the stranger continued eagerly. "A queer tall white bird with soft feathers and long thin legs. And it would have a nest perhaps in the top of a high tree, made of sticks, something like a hawk's nest."

Sylvia's heart gave a wild beat; she knew that strange white bird, and had once stolen softly near where it stood in some bright green swamp grass, away over at the other side of the woods. There was an open place where the sunshine always seemed strangely yellow and hot, where tall, nodding rushes grew, and her grandmother had warned her that she might sink in the soft black mud underneath and never be heard of more. Not far beyond were the salt marshes and beyond those was the sea, the sea which Sylvia wondered and dreamed about, but never had looked upon, though its great voice could often be heard above the noise of the woods on stormy nights.

"I can't think of anything I should like so much as to find that heron's nest," the handsome stranger was saying. "I would give ten dollars to anybody who could show it to me," he added desperately, "and I mean to spend my whole vacation hunting for it if need be. Perhaps it was only migrating, or had been chased out of its own region by some bird of prey."

Mrs. Tilley gave amazed attention to all this, but Sylvia still watched the toad, not divining, as she might have done at some calmer time, that the creature wished to get to its hole under the doorstep, and was much hindered by the unusual spectators at that hour of the evening. No amount of thought, that night, could decide how many wished-for treasures the ten dollars, so lightly spoken of, would buy.

The next day the young sportsman hovered about the woods, and Sylvia kept him company, having lost her first fear of the friendly lad, who proved to be most kind and sympathetic. He told her many things about the birds and what they knew and where they lived and what they did with themselves. And he gave her a jack-knife, which she thought as great a treasure as if she were a desert-islander. All day long he did not once make her troubled or afraid except when he brought down some unsuspecting singing creature from its bough. Sylvia would have liked him vastly better without his gun; she could not understand why he killed the very birds he seemed to like so much. But as the day waned, Sylvia still watched the young man with loving admiration. She had never seen anybody so charming and delightful; the woman's heart, asleep in the child, was vaguely thrilled by a dream of love. Some premonition of that great power stirred and swayed these young foresters who traversed the solemn woodlands with soft-footed silent care. They stopped to listen to a bird's song; they pressed forward again eagerly, parting the branches—speaking to each other rarely and in whispers; the young man going first and Sylvia following, fascinated, a few steps behind, with her gray eyes dark with excitement.

She grieved because the longed-for white heron was elusive, but she did not lead the guest, she only followed, and there was no such thing as speaking first. The sound of her own unquestioned voice would have terrified her—it was hard enough to answer yes or no when there was need of that. At last evening began to fall, and they drove the cow home together, and Sylvia smiled with pleasure when they came to the place where she heard the whistle and was afraid only the night before.

II

Half a mile from home, at the farther edge of the woods, where the land was highest, a great pine-tree stood, the last of its generation. Whether it was left for a boundary mark, or for what reason, no one could say; the woodchoppers who had felled its mates were dead and gone long ago, and a whole forest of sturdy trees, pines and oaks and maples, had grown again. But the stately head of this old pine towered above them all and made a landmark for sea and shore miles and miles away. Sylvia knew it well. She had always believed that whoever climbed to the top of it could see the ocean; and the little girl had often laid her hand on the great rough trunk and looked up wistfully at those dark boughs that the wind always stirred, no matter how hot and still the air might be below. Now she thought of the tree with a new excitement, for why, if one climbed it at break of day, could not one see all the world, and easily discover whence the white heron flew, and mark the place, and find the hidden nest?

What a spirit of adventure, what wild ambition! What fancied triumph and delight and glory for the later morning when she could make known the secret! It was almost too real and too great for the childish heart to bear.

All night the door of the little house stood open, and the whippoorwills came and sang upon the very step. The young sportsman and his old hostess were sound asleep, but Sylvia's great design kept her broad awake and watching. She forgot to think of sleep. The short summer night seemed as long as the winter darkness, and at last when the whippoorwills ceased, and she was afraid the morning would after all come too soon, she stole out of the house and followed the pasture path through the woods, hastening toward the open ground beyond, listening with a sense of comfort and companionship to the drowsy twitter of a half-awakened bird, whose perch she had jarred in passing. Alas, if the great wave of human interest which flooded for the first time this dull little life should sweep away the satisfactions of an existence heart to heart with nature and the dumb life of the forest!

There was the huge tree asleep yet in the paling moonlight, and small and hopeful Sylvia began with utmost bravery to mount to the top of it, with tingling, eager blood coursing the channels of her whole frame, with her bare feet and fingers, that pinched and held like bird's claws to the monstrous ladder reaching up, up, almost to the sky itself. First she must mount the white oak tree that grew alongside, where she was almost lost among the dark branches and the green leaves heavy and wet with dew; a bird fluttered off its nest, and a red squirrel ran to and fro and scolded pettishly at the harmless housebreaker. Sylvia felt her way easily. She had often climbed there, and knew that higher still one of the oak's upper branches chafed against the pine trunk, just where its lower boughs were set close together. There, when she made the dangerous pass from one tree to the other, the great enterprise would really begin.

She crept out along the swaying oak limb at last, and took the daring step across into the old pine-tree. The way was harder than she thought; she must reach far and hold fast, the sharp dry twigs caught and held her and scratched her like angry talons, the pitch made her thin little fingers clumsy and stiff as she went round and round the tree's great stem, higher and higher upward. The sparrows and robins in the woods below were beginning to wake and twitter to the dawn, yet it seemed much lighter there aloft in the pine-tree, and the child knew that she must hurry if her project were to be of any use.

The tree seemed to lengthen itself out as she went up, and to reach farther and farther upward. It was like a great main-mast to the voyaging earth; it must truly have been amazed that morning through all its ponderous frame as it felt this determined spark of human spirit creeping and climbing from higher branch to branch. Who knows how steadily the least twigs held themselves to advantage this light, weak creature on her way! The old pine must have loved his new dependent. More than all the hawks, and bats, and moths, and even the sweet-voiced thrushes, was the brave, beating heart of the solitary gray-eyed child. And the tree stood still and held away the winds that June morning while the dawn grew bright in the east.

Sylvia's face was like a pale star, if one had seen it from the ground, when the last thorny bough was past, and she stood trembling and tired but wholly triumphant, high in the tree-top. Yes, there was the sea with the dawning sun making a golden dazzle over it, and toward that glorious east flew two hawks with slow-moving pinions. How low they looked in the air from that height when before one had only seen them far up, and dark against the blue sky. Their gray feathers were as soft as moths; they seemed only a little way from the tree, and Sylvia felt as if she too could go flying away among the clouds. Westward, the woodlands and farms reached miles and miles into the distance; here and there were church steeples, and white villages; truly it was a vast and awesome world.

The birds sang louder and louder. At last the sun came up bewilderingly bright. Sylvia could see the white sails of ships out at sea, and the clouds that were purple and rose-colored and yellow at first began to fade away. Where was the white heron's nest in the sea of green branches, and was this wonderful sight and pageant of the world the only reward for having climbed to such a giddy height? Now look down again, Sylvia, where the green marsh is set among the shining birches and dark hemlocks; there where you saw the white heron once you will see him again; look, look! a white spot of him like a single floating feather comes up from the dead hemlock and grows larger, and rises, and comes close at last, and goes by the landmark pine with steady sweep of wing and outstretched slender neck and crested head. And wait! wait! do not move a foot or a finger, little girl, do not send an arrow of light and consciousness from your two eager eyes, for the heron has perched on a pine bough not far beyond yours, and cries back to his mate on the nest, and plumes his feathers for the new day!

The child gives a long sigh a minute later when a company of shouting cat-birds comes also to the tree, and vexed by their fluttering and lawlessness the solemn heron goes away. She knows his secret now, the wild, light, slender bird that floats and wavers, and goes back like an arrow presently to his home in the green world beneath. Then Sylvia, well satisfied, makes her perilous way down again, not daring to look far below the branch she stands on, ready to cry sometimes because her fingers ache and her lamed feet slip. Wondering over and over again what the stranger would say to her, and what he would think when she told him how to find his way straight to the heron's nest.

"Sylvy, Sylvy!" called the busy old grandmother again and again, but nobody answered, and the small husk bed was empty, and Sylvia had disappeared.

The guest waked from a dream, and remembering his day's pleasure hurried to dress himself that it might sooner begin. He was sure from the way the shy little girl looked once or twice yesterday that she had at least seen the white heron, and now she must really be persuaded to tell. Here she comes now, paler than ever, and her worn old frock is torn and tattered, and smeared with pine pitch. The grandmother and the sportsman stand in the door together and question her, and the splendid moment had come to speak of the dead hemlock-tree by the green marsh.

But Sylvia does not speak after all, though the old grandmother fretfully rebukes her, and the young man's kind appealing eyes are looking straight in her own. He can make them rich with money; he has prom-

ised it, and they are poor now. He is so well worth making happy, and he
waits to hear the story she can tell.

No, she must keep silence! What is it that suddenly forbids her and
makes her dumb? Has she been nine years growing, and now, when the
great world for the first time puts out a hand to her, must she thrust it
aside for a bird's sake? The murmur of the pine's green branches is in her
ears, she remembers how the white heron came flying through the golden
air and how they watched the sea and the morning together, and Sylvia
cannot speak; she cannot tell the heron's secret and give its life away.

Dear loyalty, that suffered a sharp pang as the guest went away disappointed later in the day, that could have served and followed him and
loved him as a dog loves! Many a night Sylvia heard the echo of his
whistle haunting the pasture path as she came home with the loitering
cow. She forgot even her sorrow at the sharp report of his gun and the
piteous sight of thrushes and sparrows dropping silent to the ground,
their songs hushed and their pretty feathers stained and wet with blood.
Were the birds better friends than their hunter might have been,—who
can tell? Whatever treasures were lost to her, woodlands and summertime, remember! Bring your gifts and graces and tell your secrets to this
lonely country child!

[1886]

KATE CHOPIN   [1851–1904]

The Story of an Hour

[handwritten: Dramatic point of view]

[handwritten: her life is free for an hour and then it's over]

Knowing that Mrs. Mallard was afflicted with a heart trouble, great care
was taken to break to her as gently as possible the news of her husband's
death.

It was her sister Josephine who told her, in broken sentences; veiled
hints that revealed in half concealing. Her husband's friend Richards was
there, too, near her. It was he who had been in the newspaper office when
intelligence of the railroad disaster was received, with Brently Mallard's
name leading the list of "killed." He had only taken the time to assure
himself of its truth by a second telegram, and had hastened to forestall
any less careful, less tender friend in bearing the sad message.

She did not hear the story as many women have heard the same, with

[handwritten: not prepared to live in a different way]

a paralyzed inability to accept its significance. She wept at once, with sudden, wild abandonment, in her sister's arms. When the storm of grief had spent itself she went away to her room alone. She would have no one follow her.

There stood, facing the open window, a comfortable, roomy armchair. Into this she sank, pressed down by a physical exhaustion that haunted her body and seemed to reach into her soul.

She could see in the open square before her house the tops of trees that were all aquiver with the new spring life. The delicious breath of rain was in the air. In the street below a peddler was crying his wares. The notes of a distant song which some one was singing reached her faintly, and countless sparrows were twittering in the eaves.

There were patches of blue sky showing here and there through the clouds that had met and piled one above the other in the west facing her window.

She sat with her head thrown back upon the cushion of the chair, quite motionless, except when a sob came up into her throat and shook her, as a child who had cried itself to sleep continues to sob in its dreams.

She was young, with a fair, calm face, whose lines bespoke repression and even a certain strength. But now there was a dull stare in her eyes, whose gaze was fixed away off yonder on one of those patches of blue sky. It was not a glance of reflection, but rather indicated a suspension of intelligent thought.

There was something coming to her and she was waiting for it, fearfully. What was it? She did not know; it was too subtle and elusive to name. But she felt it, creeping out of the sky, reaching toward her through the sounds, the scents, the color that filled the air.

Now her bosom rose and fell tumultuously. She was beginning to recognize this thing that was approaching to possess her, and she was striving to beat it back with her will—as powerless as her two white slender hands would have been.

When she abandoned herself a little whispered word escaped her slightly parted lips. She said it over and over under her breath: "free, free, free!" The vacant stare and the look of terror that had followed it went from her eyes. They stayed keen and bright. Her pulses beat fast, and the coursing blood warmed and relaxed every inch of her body.

She did not stop to ask if it were or were not a monstrous joy that held her. A clear and exalted perception enabled her to dismiss the suggestion as trivial.

She knew that she would weep again when she saw the kind, tender hands folded in death; the face that had never looked save with love upon her, fixed and gray and dead. But she saw beyond that bitter moment a long procession of years to come that would belong to her absolutely. And she opened and spread her arms out to them in welcome.

There would be no one to live for her during those coming years: she would live for herself. There would be no powerful will bending hers in that blind persistence with which men and women believe they have a right to impose a private will upon a fellow-creature. A kind intention or a cruel intention made the act seem no less a crime as she looked upon it in that brief moment of illumination.

And yet she had loved him—sometimes. Often she had not. What did it matter! What could love, the unsolved mystery, count for in face of this possession of self-assertion which she suddenly recognized as the strongest impulse of her being!

"Free! Body and soul free!" she kept whispering.

Josephine was kneeling before the closed door with her lips to the keyhole, imploring for admission. "Louise, open the door! I beg; open the door—you will make yourself ill. What are you doing, Louise? For heaven's sake open the door."

"Go away. I am not making myself ill." No; she was drinking in a very elixir of life through that open window.

Her fancy was running riot along those days ahead of her. Spring days, and summer days, and all sorts of days that would be her own. She breathed a quick prayer that life might be long. It was only yesterday she had thought with a shudder that life might be long.

She arose at length and opened the door to her sister's importunities. There was a feverish triumph in her eyes, and she carried herself unwittingly like a goddess of Victory. She clasped her sister's waist, and together they descended the stairs. Richards stood waiting for them at the bottom.

Some one was opening the front door with a latchkey. It was Brently Mallard who entered, a little travel-stained, composedly carrying his gripsack and umbrella. He had been far from the scene of accident, and did not even know there had been one. He stood amazed at Josephine's piercing cry; at Richards' quick motion to screen him from the view of his wife.

But Richards was too late.

When the doctors came they said she had died of heart disease—of joy that kills.

[1894]

ANTON CHEKHOV [1860–1904]

The Lady with the Dog

TRANSLATED BY CONSTANCE GARNETT, 1899

I

It was said that a new person had appeared on the sea-front: a lady with a little dog. Dmitri Dmitritch Gurov, who had by then been a fortnight at Yalta, and so was fairly at home there, had begun to take an interest in new arrivals. Sitting in Verney's pavilion, he saw, walking on the sea-front, a fair-haired young lady of medium height, wearing a *béret*; a white Pomeranian dog was running behind her.

And afterwards he met her in the public gardens and in the square several times a day. She was walking alone, always wearing the same *béret*, and always with the same white dog; no one knew who she was, and every one called her simply "the lady with the dog."

"If she is here alone without a husband or friends, it wouldn't be amiss to make her acquaintance," Gurov reflected.

He was under forty, but he had a daughter already twelve years old, and two sons at school. He had been married young, when he was a student in his second year, and by now his wife seemed half as old again as he. She was a tall, erect woman with dark eyebrows, staid and dignified, and, as she said of herself, intellectual. She read a great deal, used phonetic spelling, called her husband, not Dmitri, but Dimitri, and he secretly considered her unintelligent, narrow, inelegant, was afraid of her, and did not like to be at home. He had begun being unfaithful to her long ago—had been unfaithful to her often, and, probably on that account, almost always spoke ill of women, and when they were talked about in his presence, used to call them "the lower race."

It seemed to him that he had been so schooled by bitter experience that he might call them what he liked, and yet he could not get on for two days together without "the lower race." In the society of men he was bored and not himself, with them he was cold and uncommunicative; but when he was in the company of women he felt free, and knew what to say to them and how to behave; and he was at ease with them even when he was silent. In his appearance, in his character, in his whole na-

62

ture, there was something attractive and elusive which allured women and disposed them in his favour; he knew that, and some force seemed to draw him, too, to them.

Experience often repeated, truly bitter experience, had taught him long ago that with decent people, especially Moscow people—always slow to move and irresolute—every intimacy, which at first so agreeably diversifies life and appears a light and charming adventure, inevitably grows into a regular problem of extreme intricacy, and in the long run the situation becomes unbearable. But at every fresh meeting with an interesting woman this experience seemed to slip out of his memory, and he was eager for life, and everything seemed simple and amusing.

One evening he was dining in the gardens, and the lady in the *béret* came up slowly to take the next table. Her expression, her gait, her dress, and the way she did her hair told him that she was a lady, that she was married, that she was in Yalta for the first time and alone, and that she was dull there. . . . The stories told of the immorality in such places as Yalta are to a great extent untrue; he despised them, and knew that such stories were for the most part made up by persons who would themselves have been glad to sin if they had been able; but when the lady sat down at the next table three paces from him, he remembered these tales of easy conquests, of trips to the mountains, and the tempting thought of a swift, fleeting love affair, a romance with an unknown woman, whose name he did not know, suddenly took possession of him.

He beckoned coaxingly to the Pomeranian, and when the dog came up to him he shook his finger at it. The Pomeranian growled: Gurov shook his finger at it again.

The lady looked at him and at once dropped her eyes.

"He doesn't bite," she said, and blushed.

"May I give him a bone?" he asked; and when she nodded he asked courteously, "Have you been long in Yalta?"

"Five days."

"And I have already dragged out a fortnight here."

There was a brief silence.

"Time goes fast, and yet it is so dull here!" she said, not looking at him.

"That's only the fashion to say it is dull here. A provincial will live in Belyov or Zhidra and not be dull, and when he comes here it's 'Oh, the dullness! Oh, the dust!' One would think he came from Grenada."

She laughed. Then both continued eating in silence, like strangers, but after dinner they walked side by side; and there sprang up between them the light jesting conversation of people who are free and satisfied, to whom it does not matter where they go or what they talk about. They walked and talked of the strange light on the sea: the water was of a soft warm lilac hue, and there was a golden streak from the moon upon it.

They talked of how sultry it was after a hot day. Gurov told her that he came from Moscow, that he had taken his degree in Arts, but had a post in a bank; that he had trained as an opera-singer, but had given it up, that he owned two houses in Moscow. . . . And from her he learnt that she had grown up in Petersburg, but had lived in S—— since her marriage two years before, that she was staying another month in Yalta, and that her husband, who needed a holiday too, might perhaps come and fetch her. She was not sure whether her husband had a post in a Crown Department or under the Provincial Council—and was amused by her own ignorance. And Gurov learnt, too, that she was called Anna Sergeyevna.

Afterwards he thought about her in his room at the hotel—thought she would certainly meet him next day; it would be sure to happen. As he got into bed he thought how lately she had been a girl at school, doing lessons like his own daughter; he recalled the diffidence, the angularity, that was still manifest in her laugh and her manner of talking with a stranger. This must have been the first time in her life she had been alone in surroundings in which she was followed, looked at, and spoken to merely from a secret motive which she could hardly fail to guess. He recalled her slender, delicate neck, her lovely grey eyes.

"There's something pathetic about her, anyway," he thought, and fell asleep.

II

A week had passed since they had made acquaintance. It was a holiday. It was sultry indoors, while in the street the wind whirled the dust round and round, and blew people's hats off. It was a thirsty day, and Gurov often went into the pavilion, and pressed Anna Sergeyevna to have syrup and water or an ice. One did not know what to do with oneself.

In the evening when the wind had dropped a little, they went out on the groyne° to see the steamer come in. There were a great many people walking about the harbor; they had gathered to welcome some one, bringing bouquets. And two peculiarities of a well-dressed Yalta crowd were very conspicuous: the elderly ladies were dressed like young ones, and there were great numbers of generals.

Owing to the roughness of the sea, the steamer arrived late, after the sun had set, and it was a long time turning about before it reached the groyne. Anna Sergeyevna looked through her lorgnette at the steamer and the passengers as though looking for acquaintances, and when she turned to Gurov her eyes were shining. She talked a great deal and asked

Groyne: A wall or jetty built out from a shore to control erosion.

disconnected questions, forgetting next moment what she had asked; then she dropped her lorgnette in the crush.

The festive crowd began to disperse; it was too dark to see people's faces. The wind had completely dropped, but Gurov and Anna Sergeyevna still stood as though waiting to see some one else come from the steamer. Anna Sergeyevna was silent now, and sniffed the flowers without looking at Gurov.

"The weather is better this evening," he said. "Where shall we go now? Shall we drive somewhere?"

She made no answer.

Then he looked at her intently, and all at once put his arm round her and kissed her on the lips, and breathed in the moisture and the fragrance of the flowers; and he immediately looked round him, anxiously wondering whether any one had seen them.

"Let us go to your hotel," he said softly. And both walked quickly.

The room was close and smelt of the scent she had bought at the Japanese shop. Gurov looked at her and thought: "What different people one meets in the world!" From the past he preserved memories of careless, good-natured women, who loved cheerfully and were grateful to him for the happiness he gave them, however brief it might be; and of women like his wife who loved without any genuine feeling, with superfluous phrases, affectedly, hysterically, with an expression that suggested that it was not love nor passion, but something more significant; and of two or three others, very beautiful, cold women, on whose faces he had caught a glimpse of a rapacious expression—an obstinate desire to snatch from life more than it could give, and these were capricious, unreflecting, domineering, unintelligent women not in their first youth, and when Gurov grew cold to them their beauty excited his hatred, and the lace on their linen seemed to him like scales.

But in this case there was still the diffidence, the angularity of inexperienced youth, an awkward feeling; and there was a sense of consternation as though some one had suddenly knocked at the door. The attitude of Anna Sergeyevna—"the lady with the dog"—to what had happened was somehow peculiar, very grave, as though it were her fall—so it seemed, and it was strange and inappropriate. Her face dropped and faded, and on both sides of it her long hair hung down mournfully; she mused in a dejected attitude like "the woman who was a sinner" in an old-fashioned picture.

"It's wrong," she said. "You will be the first to despise me now."

There was a water-melon on the table. Gurov cut himself a slice and began eating it without haste. There followed at least half an hour of silence.

Anna Sergeyevna was touching; there was about her the purity of a

good, simple woman who had seen little of life. The solitary candle burning on the table threw a faint light on her face, yet it was clear that she
was very unhappy.

"How could I despise you?" asked Gurov. "You don't know what you
are saying."

"God forgive me," she said, and her eyes filled with tears. "It's awful."

"You seem to feel you need to be forgiven."

"Forgiven? No. I am a bad, low woman; I despise myself and don't attempt to justify myself. It's not my husband but myself I have deceived.
And not just now; I have been deceiving myself for a long time. My husband may be a good, honest man, but he is a flunkey! I don't know what
he does there, what his work is, but I know he is a flunkey! I was twenty
when I was married to him. I have been tormented by curiosity; I wanted
something better. 'There must be a different sort of life,' I said to myself.
I wanted to live! To live, to live! . . . I was fired by curiosity . . . you don't
understand it, but, I swear to God, I could not control myself; something
happened to me: I could not be restrained. I told my husband I was ill,
and came here. . . . And here I have been walking about as though I were
dazed, like a mad creature; . . . and now I have become a vulgar, contemptible woman whom any one may despise."

Gurov felt bored already, listening to her. He was irritated by the naïve
tone, by this remose, so unexpected and inopportune; but for the tears in
her eyes, he might have thought she was jesting or playing a part.

"I don't understand," he said softly. "What is it you want?"

She hid her face on his breast and pressed close to him.

"Believe me, believe me, I beseech you . . ." she said. "I love a pure,
honest life, and sin is loathsome to me. I don't know what I am doing.
Simple people say: 'The Evil One has beguiled me.' And I may say of myself now that the Evil One has beguiled me."

"Hush, hush! . . ." he muttered.

He looked at her fixed, scared eyes, kissed her, talked softly and affectionately, and by degrees she was comforted, and her gaiety returned;
they both began laughing.

Afterwards when they went out there was not a soul on the sea-front.
The town with its cypresses had quite a deathlike air, but the sea still
broke noisily on the shore; a single barge was rocking on the waves, and
a lantern was blinking sleepily on it.

They found a cab and drove to Oreanda.

"I found out your surname in the hall just now: it was written on the
board—Von Diderits," said Gurov. "Is your husband a German?"

"No; I believe his grandfather was a German, but he is an Orthodox
Russian himself."

At Oreanda they sat on a seat not far from the church, looked down at the sea, and were silent. Yalta was hardly visible through the morning mist; white clouds stood motionless on the mountain-tops. The leaves did not stir on the trees, grasshoppers chirruped, and the monotonous hollow sound of the sea rising up from below, spoke of the peace, of the eternal sleep awaiting us. So it must have sounded when there was no Yalta, no Oreanda here; so it sounds now, and it will sound as indifferently and monotonously when we are all no more. And in this constancy, in this complete indifference to the life and death of each of us, there lies hid, perhaps, a pledge of our eternal salvation, of the unceasing movement of life upon earth, of unceasing progress towards perfection. Sitting beside a young woman who in the dawn seemed so lovely, soothed and spellbound in these magical surroundings—the sea, mountains, clouds, the open sky—Gurov thought how in reality everything is beautiful in this world when one reflects: everything except what we think or do ourselves when we forget our human dignity and the higher aims of our existence.

A man walked up to them—probably a keeper—looked at them and walked away. And this detail seemed mysterious and beautiful, too. They saw a steamer come from Theodosia, with its lights out in the glow of dawn.

"There is dew on the grass," said Anna Sergeyevna, after a silence.

"Yes. It's time to go home."

They went back to the town.

Then they met every day at twelve o'clock on the sea-front, lunched and dined together, went for walks, admired the sea. She complained that she slept badly, that her heart throbbed violently; asked the same questions, troubled now by jealousy and now by the fear that he did not respect her sufficiently. And often in the square or gardens, when there was no one near them, he suddenly drew her to him and kissed her passionately. Complete idleness, these kisses in broad daylight while he looked round in dread of some one's seeing them, the heat, the smell of the sea, and the continual passing to and fro before him of idle, well-dressed, well-fed people, made a new man of him; he told Anna Sergeyevna how beautiful she was, how fascinating. He was impatiently passionate, he would not move a step away from her, while she was often pensive and continually urged him to confess that he did not respect her, did not love her in the least, and thought of her as nothing but a common woman. Rather late almost every evening they drove somewhere out of town, to Oreanda or to the waterfall; and the expedition was always a success, the scenery invariably impressed them as grand and beautiful.

They were expecting her husband to come, but a letter came from him, saying that there was something wrong with his eyes, and he entreated his wife to come home as quickly as possible. Anna Sergeyevna made haste to go.

"It's a good thing I am going away," she said to Gurov. "It's the finger of destiny!"

She went by coach and he went with her. They were driving the whole day. When she had got into a compartment of the express, and when the second bell had rung, she said:

"Let me look at you once more ... look at you once again. That's right."

She did not shed tears, but was so sad that she seemed ill, and her face was quivering.

"I shall remember you ... think of you," she said. "God be with you; be happy. Don't remember evil against me. We are parting forever—it must be so, for we ought never to have met. Well, God be with you."

The train moved off rapidly, its lights soon vanished from sight, and a minute later there was no sound of it, as though everything had conspired together to end as quickly as possible that sweet delirium, that madness. Left alone on the platform, and gazing into the dark distance, Gurov listened to the chirrup of the grasshoppers and the hum of the telegraph wires, feeling as though he had only just waked up. And he thought, musing, that there had been another episode or adventure in his life, and it, too, was at an end, and nothing was left of it but a memory. . . . He was moved, sad, and conscious of a slight remorse. This young woman whom he would never meet again had not been happy with him; he was genuinely warm and affectionate with her, but yet in his manner, his tone, and his caresses there had been a shade of light irony, the coarse condescension of a happy man who was, besides, almost twice her age. All the time she had called him kind, exceptional, lofty; obviously he had seemed to her different from what he really was, so he had unintentionally deceived her. . . .

Here at the station was already a scent of autumn; it was a cold evening.

"It's time for me to go north," thought Gurov as he left the platform. "High time!"

III

At home in Moscow everything was in its winter routine; the stoves were heated, and in the morning it was still dark when the children were having breakfast and getting ready for school, and the nurse would light the lamp for a short time. The frosts had begun already. When the first snow has fallen, on the first day of sledge-driving it is pleasant to see the white earth, the white roofs, to draw soft, delicious breath, and the season brings back the days of one's youth. The old limes and birches, white with hoar-frost, have a good-natured expression; they are nearer to one's heart than cypresses and palms, and near them one doesn't want to be thinking of the sea and the mountains.

Gurov was Moscow born; he arrived in Moscow on a fine frosty day, and when he put on his fur coat and warm gloves, and walked along Petrovka, and when on Saturday evening he heard the ringing of the bells, his recent trip and the places he had seen lost all charm for him. Little by little he became absorbed in Moscow life, greedily read three newspapers a day, and declared he did not read the Moscow papers on principle! He already felt a longing to go to restaurants, clubs, dinner-parties, anniversary celebrations, and he felt flattered at entertaining distinguished lawyers and artists, and at playing cards with a professor at the doctors' club. He could already eat a whole plateful of salt fish and cabbage. . . .

In another month, he fancied, the image of Anna Sergeyevna would be shrouded in a mist in his memory, and only from time to time would visit him in his dreams with a touching smile as others did. But more than a month passed, real winter had come, and everything was still clear in his memory as though he had parted with Anna Sergeyevna only the day before. And his memories glowed more and more vividly. When in the evening stillness he heard from his study the voices of his children, preparing their lessons, or when he listened to a song or the organ at the restaurant, or the storm howled in the chimney, suddenly everything would rise up in his memory: what had happened on the groyne, and the early morning with the mist on the mountains, and the steamer coming from Theodosia, and the kisses. He would pace a long time about his room, remembering it all and smiling; then his memories passed into dreams, and in his fancy the past was mingled with what was to come. Anna Sergeyevna did not visit him in dreams, but followed him about everywhere like a shadow and haunted him. When he shut his eyes he saw her as though she were living before him, and she seemed to him lovelier, younger, tenderer than she was; and he imagined himself finer than he had been in Yalta. In the evenings she peeped out at him from the bookcase, from the fireplace, from the corner—he heard her breathing, the caressing rustle of her dress. In the street he watched the women, looking for some one like her.

He was tormented by an intense desire to confide his memories to some one. But in his home it was impossible to talk of his love, and he had no one outside; he could not talk to his tenants nor to any one at the bank. And what had he to talk of? Had he been in love, then? Had there been anything beautiful, poetical, or edifying or simply interesting in his relations with Anna Sergeyevna? And there was nothing for him but to talk vaguely of love, of woman, and no one guessed what it meant; only his wife twitched her black eyebrows, and said: "The part of a lady-killer does not suit you at all, Dimitri."

One evening, coming out of the doctors' club with an official with whom he had been playing cards, he could not resist saying:

"If only you knew what a fascinating woman I made the acquaintance of in Yalta!"

The official got into his sledge and was driving away, but turned suddenly and shouted:

"Dmitri Dmitritch!"

"What?"

"You were right this evening: the sturgeon was a bit too strong!"

These words, so ordinary, for some reason moved Gurov to indignation, and struck him as degrading and unclean. What savage manners, what people! What senseless nights, what uninteresting, uneventful days! The rage for card-playing, the gluttony, the drunkenness, the continual talk always about the same thing. Useless pursuits and conversations always about the same things absorb the better part of one's time, the better part of one's strength, and in the end there is left a life grovelling and curtailed, worthless and trivial, and there is no escaping or getting away from it—just as though one were in a madhouse or a prison.

Gurov did not sleep all night, and was filled with indignation. And he had a headache all next day. And the next night he slept badly; he sat up in bed, thinking, or paced up and down his room. He was sick of his children, sick of the bank; he had no desire to go anywhere or to talk of anything.

In the holidays in December he prepared for a journey, and told his wife he was going to Petersburg to do something in the interests of a young friend—and he set off for S——. What for? He did not very well know himself. He wanted to see Anna Sergeyevna and to talk with her—to arrange a meeting, if possible.

He reached S—— in the morning, and took the best room at the hotel, in which the floor was covered with grey army cloth, and on the table was an inkstand, grey with dust and adorned with a figure on horseback, with its hat in its hand and its head broken off. The hotel porter gave him the necessary information; Von Diderits lived in a house of his own in Old Gontcharny Street—it was not far from the hotel: he was rich and lived in good style, and had his own horses; every one in the town knew him. The porter pronounced the name "Dridirits."

Gurov went without haste to Old Gontcharny Street and found the house. Just opposite the house stretched a long grey fence adorned with nails.

"One would run away from a fence like that," thought Gurov, looking from the fence to the windows of the house and back again.

He considered: to-day was a holiday, and the husband would probably be at home. And in any case it would be tactless to go into the house and upset her. If he were to send her a note it might fall into her husband's hands, and then it might ruin everything. The best thing was to trust to chance. And he kept walking up and down the street by the fence, waiting for the chance. He saw a beggar go in at the gate and dogs fly at him; then an hour later he heard a piano, and the sounds were faint and indistinct. Probably it was Anna Sergeyevna playing. The front door suddenly opened, and an old woman came out, followed by the familiar white Pomeranian. Gurov was on the point of calling to the dog, but his heart began beating violently, and in his excitement he could not remember the dog's name.

He walked up and down, and loathed the grey fence more and more, and by now he thought irritably that Anna Sergeyevna had forgotten him, and was perhaps already amusing herself with some one else, and that that was very natural in a young woman who had nothing to look at from morning till night but that confounded fence. He went back to his hotel room and sat for a long while on the sofa, not knowing what to do, then he had dinner and a long nap.

"How stupid and worrying it is!" he thought when he woke and looked at the dark windows: it was already evening. "Here I've had a good sleep for some reason. What shall I do in the night?"

He sat on the bed, which was covered by a cheap grey blanket, such as one sees in hospitals, and he taunted himself in his vexation:

"So much for the lady with the dog . . . so much for the adventure. . . . You're in a nice fix. . . ."

That morning at the station a poster in large letters had caught his eye. *The Geisha* was to be performed for the first time. He thought of this and went to the theatre.

"It's quite possible she may go to the first performance," he thought.

The theatre was full. As in all provincial theatres, there was a fog above the chandelier, the gallery was noisy and restless; in the front row the local dandies were standing up before the beginning of the performance, with their hands behind them; in the Governor's box the Governor's daughter, wearing a boa, was sitting in the front seat, while the Governor himself lurked modestly behind the curtain with only his hands visible; the orchestra was a long time tuning up; the stage curtain swayed. All the time the audience were coming in and taking their seats Gurov looked at them eagerly.

Anna Sergeyevna, too, came in. She sat down in the third row, and when Gurov looked at her his heart contracted, and he understood clearly that for him there was in the whole world no creature so near, so precious, and so important to him; she, this little woman, in no way remarkable, lost in a provincial crowd, with a vulgar lorgnette in her hand, filled his whole life now, was his sorrow and his joy, the one happiness that he now desired for himself, and to the sounds of the inferior orchestra, of the wretched provincial violins, he thought how lovely she was. He thought and dreamed.

A young man with small side-whiskers, tall and stooping, came in with Anna Sergeyevna and sat down beside her; he bent his head at every step and seemed to be continually bowing. Most likely this was the husband whom at Yalta, in a rush of bitter feeling, she had called a flunkey. And there really was in his long figure, his side-whiskers, and the small bald patch on his head, something of the flunkey's obsequiousness; his smile was sugary, and in his buttonhole there was some badge of distinction like the number on a waiter.

During the first interval the husband went away to smoke; she remained alone in her stall. Gurov, who was sitting in the stalls, too, went up to her and said in a trembling voice, with a forced smile:

"Good-evening."

She glanced at him and turned pale, then glanced again with horror, unable to believe her eyes, and tightly gripped the fan and the lorgnette in her hands, evidently struggling with herself not to faint. Both were silent. She was sitting, he was standing, frightened by her confusion and not venturing to sit down beside her. The violins and the flute began tuning up. He felt suddenly frightened; it seemed as though all the people in the boxes were looking at them. She got up and went quickly to the door; he followed her, and both walked senselessly along passages, and up and down stairs, and figures in legal, scholastic, and civil service uniforms, all wearing badges, flitted before their eyes. They caught glimpses of ladies, of fur coats hanging on pegs; the draughts blew on them, bringing a smell of stale tobacco. And Gurov, whose heart was beating violently, thought:

"Oh, heavens! Why are these people here and this orchestra! . . ."

And at that instant he recalled how when he had seen Anna Sergeyevna off at the station he had thought that everything was over and they would never meet again. But how far they were still from the end!

On the narrow, gloomy staircase over which was written "To the Amphitheatre," she stopped.

"How you have frightened me!" she said, breathing hard, still pale and overwhelmed. "Oh, how you have frightened me! I am half dead. Why have you come? Why?"

"But do understand, Anna, do understand . . ." he said hastily in a low voice. "I entreat you to understand. . . ."

She looked at him with dread, with entreaty, with love; she looked at him intently, to keep his features more distinctly in her memory.

"I am so unhappy," she went on, not heeding him. "I have thought of nothing but you all the time; I live only in the thought of you. And I wanted to forget, to forget you; but why, oh, why, have you come?"

On the landing above them two schoolboys were smoking and looking down, but that was nothing to Gurov; he drew Anna Sergeyevna to him, and began kissing her face, her cheeks, and her hands.

"What are you doing, what are you doing!" she cried in horror, pushing him away. "We are mad. Go away to-day; go away at once. . . . I beseech you by all that is sacred, I implore you. . . . There are people coming this way!"

Some one was coming up the stairs.

"You must go away," Anna Sergeyevna went on in a whisper. "Do you hear, Dmitri Dmitritch? I will come and see you in Moscow. I have never been happy; I am miserable now, and I never, never shall be happy, never! Don't make me suffer still more! I swear I'll come to Moscow. But now let us part. My precious, good, dear one, we must part!"

She pressed his hand and began rapidly going downstairs, looking round at him, and from her eyes he could see that she really was unhappy. Gurov stood for a little while, listened, then, when all sound had died away, he found his coat and left the theatre.

IV

And Anna Sergeyevna began coming to see him in Moscow. Once in two or three months she left S——, telling her husband that she was going to consult a doctor about an internal complaint—and her husband believed her, and did not believe her. In Moscow she stayed at the Slaviansky Bazaar hotel, and at once sent a man in a red cap to Gurov. Gurov went to see her, and no one in Moscow knew of it.

Once he was going to see her in this way on a winter morning (the messenger had come the evening before when he was out). With him walked his daughter, whom he wanted to take to school: it was on the way. Snow was falling in big wet flakes.

"It's three degrees above freezing-point, and yet it is snowing," said Gurov to his daughter. "The thaw is only on the surface of the earth; there is quite a different temperature at a greater height in the atmosphere."

"And why are there no thunderstorms in the winter, father?"

He explained that, too. He talked, thinking all the while that he was going to see *her*, and no living soul knew of it, and probably never would know. He had two lives: one, open, seen and known by all who cared to know, full of relative truth and of relative falsehood, exactly like the lives of his friends and acquaintances; and another life running its course in secret. And through some strange, perhaps accidental, conjunction of circumstances, everything that was essential, of interest and of value to him, everything in which he was sincere and did not deceive himself, everything that made the kernel of his life, was hidden from other people; and all that was false in him, the sheath in which he hid himself to conceal the truth—such, for instance, as his work in the bank, his discussions at the club, his "lower race," his presence with his wife at anniversary festivities—all that was open. And he judged of others by himself, not believing in what he saw, and always believing that every man had his real, most interesting life under the cover of secrecy and under the cover of night. All personal life rested on secrecy, and possibly it was partly on that account that civilised man was so nervously anxious that personal privacy should be respected.

After leaving his daughter at school, Gurov went on to the Slaviansky Bazaar. He took off his fur coat below, went upstairs, and softly knocked at the door. Anna Sergeyevna, wearing his favourite grey dress, exhausted by the journey and the suspense, had been expecting him since the evening before. She was pale; she looked at him, and did not smile, and he had hardly come in when she fell on his breast. Their kiss was slow and prolonged, as though they had not met for two years.

"Well, how are you getting on there?" he asked. "What news?"

"Wait; I'll tell you directly. . . . I can't talk."

She could not speak; she was crying. She turned away from him, and pressed her handkerchief to her eyes.

"Let her have her cry out. I'll sit down and wait," he thought, and he sat down in an arm-chair.

Then he rang and asked for tea to be brought him, and while he drank his tea she remained standing at the window with her back to him. She was crying from emotion, from the miserable consciousness that their life was so hard for them; they could only meet in secret, hiding themselves from people, like thieves! Was not their life shattered?

"Come, do stop!" he said.

It was evident to him that this love of theirs would not soon be over, that he could not see the end of it. Anna Sergeyevna grew more and more attached to him. She adored him, and it was unthinkable to say to her that it was bound to have an end some day; besides, she would not have believed it!

He went up to her and took her by the shoulders to say something affectionate and cheering, and at that moment he saw himself in the looking-glass.

His hair was already beginning to turn grey. And it seemed strange to him that he had grown so much older, so much plainer during the last few years. The shoulders on which his hands rested were warm and quivering. He felt compassion for this life, still so warm and lovely, but probably already not far from beginning to fade and wither like his own. Why did she love him so much? He always seemed to women different from what he was, and they loved in him not himself, but the man created by their imagination, whom they had been eagerly seeking all their lives; and afterwards, when they noticed their mistake, they loved him all the same. And not one of them had been happy with him. Time passed, he had made their acquaintance, got on with them, parted, but he had never once loved; it was anything you like, but not love.

And only now when his head was grey he had fallen properly, really in love—for the first time in his life.

Anna Sergeyevna and he loved each other like people very close and akin, like husband and wife, like tender friends; it seemed to them that fate itself had meant them for one another, and they could not understand why he had a wife and she a husband; and it was as though they were a pair of birds of passage, caught and forced to live in different cages. They forgave each other for what they were ashamed of in their past, they forgave everything in the present, and felt that this love of theirs had changed them both.

In moments of depression in the past he had comforted himself with any arguments that came into his mind, but now he no longer cared for arguments; he felt profound compassion, he wanted to be sincere and tender. . . .

"Don't cry, my darling," he said. "You've had your cry; that's enough. . . . Let us talk now, let us think of some plan."

Then they spent a long while taking counsel together, talked of how to avoid the necessity for secrecy, for deception, for living in different towns and not seeing each other for long at a time. How could they be free from this intolerable bondage?

"How? How?" he asked, clutching his head. "How?"

And it seemed as though in a little while the solution would be found, and then a new and splendid life would begin; and it was clear to both of them that they had still a long, long road before them, and that the most complicated and difficult part of it was only just beginning.

[1899]

CHARLOTTE PERKINS GILMAN   [1860–1935]

The Yellow Wallpaper

It is very seldom that mere ordinary people like John and myself secure ancestral halls for the summer.

A colonial mansion, a hereditary estate, I would say a haunted house and reach the height of romantic felicity—but that would be asking too much of fate!

Still I will proudly declare that there is something queer about it.

Else, why should it be let so cheaply? And why have stood so long untenanted?

John laughs at me, of course, but one expects that in marriage.

John is practical in the extreme. He has no patience with faith, an intense horror of superstition, and he scoffs openly at any talk of things not to be felt and seen and put down in figures.

John is a physician, and *perhaps*—(I would not say it to a living soul, of course, but this is dead paper and a great relief to my mind)—*perhaps* that is one reason I do not get well faster.

You see, he does not believe I am sick!

And what can one do?

If a physician of high standing, and one's own husband, assures friends and relatives that there is really nothing the matter with one but temporary nervous depression—a slight hysterical tendency—what is one to do?

My brother is also a physician, and also of high standing, and he says the same thing.

So I take phosphates or phosphites—whichever it is, and tonics, and journeys, and air, and exercise, and am absolutely forbidden to "work" until I am well again.

Personally, I disagree with their ideas.

Personally, I believe that congenial work, with excitement and change, would do me good.

But what is one to do?

I did write for a while in spite of them; but it *does* exhaust me a good deal—having to be so sly about it, or else meet with heavy opposition.

I sometimes fancy that in my condition if I had less opposition and more society and stimulus—but John says the very worst thing I can do is to think about my condition, and I confess it always makes me feel bad.

So I will let it alone and talk about the house.

The most beautiful place! It is quite alone, standing well back from the road, quite three miles from the village. It makes me think of English places that you read about, for there are hedges and walls and gates that lock, and lots of separate little houses for the gardeners and people.

There is a *delicious* garden! I never saw such a garden—large and shady, full of box-bordered paths, and lined with long grape-covered arbors with seats under them.

There were greenhouses, too, but they are all broken now.

There was some legal trouble, I believe, something about the heirs and co-heirs; anyhow, the place has been empty for years.

That spoils my ghostliness, I am afraid, but I don't care—there is something strange about the house—I can feel it.

I even said so to John one moonlight evening, but he said what I felt was a *draught*, and shut the window.

I get unreasonably angry with John sometimes. I'm sure I never used to be so sensitive. I think it is due to this nervous condition.

But John says if I feel so, I shall neglect proper self-control; so I take pains to control myself—before him, at least, and that makes me very tired.

I don't like our room a bit. I wanted one downstairs that opened on the piazza and had roses all over the window, and such pretty old-fashioned chintz hangings! but John would not hear of it.

He said there was only one window and not room for two beds, and no near room for him if he took another.

He is very careful and loving, and hardly lets me stir without special direction.

I have a schedule prescription for each hour in the day; he takes all care from me, and so I feel basely ungrateful not to value it more.

He said we came here solely on my account, that I was to have perfect rest and all the air I could get. "Your exercise depends on your strength, my dear," said he, "and your food somewhat on your appetite; but air you can absorb all the time." So we took the nursery at the top of the house.

It is a big, airy room, the whole floor nearly, with windows that look all ways, and air and sunshine galore. It was nursery first and then play-room and gymnasium, I should judge; for the windows are barred for little children, and there are rings and things in the walls.

The paint and paper look as if a boys' school had used it. It is stripped off—the paper—in great patches all around the head of my bed, about as far as I can reach, and in a great place on the other side of the room low down. I never saw a worse paper in my life.

One of those sprawling flamboyant patterns committing every artistic sin.

It is dull enough to confuse the eye in following, pronounced enough to constantly irritate and provoke study, and when you follow the lame uncertain curves for a little distance they suddenly commit suicide—plunge off at outrageous angles, destroy themselves in unheard of contradictions.

The color is repellant, almost revolting; a smouldering unclean yellow, strangely faded by the slow-turning sunlight.

It is a dull yet lurid orange in some places, a sickly sulphur tint in others.

No wonder the children hated it! I should hate it myself if I had to live in this room long.

There comes John, and I must put this away,—he hates to have me write a word.

We have been here two weeks, and I haven't felt like writing before, since that first day.

I am sitting by the window now, up in this atrocious nursery, and there is nothing to hinder my writing as much as I please, save lack of strength.

John is away all day, and even some nights when his cases are serious.

I am glad my case is not serious!

But these nervous troubles are dreadfully depressing.

John does not know how much I really suffer. He knows there is no *reason* to suffer, and that satisfies him.

Of course it is only nervousness. It does weigh on me so not to do my duty in any way!

I meant to be such a help to John, such a real rest and comfort, and here I am a comparative burden already!

Nobody would believe what an effort it is to do what little I am able,—to dress and entertain, and order things.

It is fortunate Mary is so good with the baby. Such a dear baby!

And yet I *cannot* be with him, it makes me so nervous.

I suppose John never was nervous in his life. He laughs at me so about this wallpaper!

At first he meant to repaper the room, but afterward he said that I was letting it get the better of me, and that nothing was worse for a nervous patient than to give way to such fancies.

He said that after the wallpaper was changed it would be the heavy bedstead, and then the barred windows, and then that gate at the head of the stairs, and so on.

"You know the place is doing you good," he said, "and really, dear, I don't care to renovate the house just for a three months' rental."

"Then do let us go downstairs," I said, "there are such pretty rooms there."

Then he took me in his arms and called me a blessed little goose, and said he would go down cellar, if I wished, and have it white-washed into the bargain.

But he is right enough about the beds and windows and things.

It is an airy and comfortable room as anyone need wish, and, of course, I would not be so silly as to make him uncomfortable just for a whim.

I'm really getting quite fond of the big room, all but that horrid paper.

Out of one window I can see the garden, those mysterious deep-shaded arbors, the riotous old-fashioned flowers, and bushes and gnarly trees.

Out of another I get a lovely view of the bay and a little private wharf belonging to the estate. There is a beautiful shaded lane that runs down there from the house. I always fancy I see people walking in these numerous paths and arbors, but John has cautioned me not to give way to fancy in the least. He says that with my imaginative power and habit of story-making, a nervous weakness like mine is sure to lead to all manner of excited fancies, and that I ought to use my will and good sense to check the tendency. So I try.

I think sometimes that if I were only well enough to write a little it would relieve the press of ideas and rest me.

But I find I get pretty tired when I try.

It is so discouraging not to have any advice and companionship about my work. When I get really well, John says we will ask Cousin Henry and Julia down for a long visit; but he says he would as soon put fireworks in my pillow-case as to let me have those stimulating people about now.

I wish I could get well faster.

But I must not think about that. This paper looks to me as if it *knew* what a vicious influence it had!

There is a recurrent spot where the pattern lolls like a broken neck and two bulbous eyes stare at you upside down.

I get positively angry with the impertinence of it and the everlastingness. Up and down and sideways they crawl, and those absurd, unblinking eyes are everywhere. There is one place where two breadths didn't match, and the eyes go all up and down the line, one a little higher than the other.

I never saw so much expression in an inanimate thing before, and we all know how much expression they have! I used to lie awake as a child and get more entertainment and terror out of blank walls and plain furniture than most children could find in a toy-store.

I remember what a kindly wink the knobs of our big, old bureau used to have, and there was one chair that always seemed like a strong friend.

I used to feel that if any of the other things looked too fierce I could always hop into that chair and be safe.

The furniture in this room is no worse than inharmonious, however, for we had to bring it all from downstairs. I suppose when this was used as a playroom they had to take the nursery things out, and no wonder! I never saw such ravages as the children have made here.

The wallpaper, as I said before, is torn off in spots, and it sticketh closer than a brother—they must have had perseverance as well as hatred.

Then the floor is scratched and gouged and splintered, the plaster itself is dug out here and there, and this great heavy bed, which is all we found in the room, looks as if it had been through the wars.

But I don't mind it a bit—only the paper.

There comes John's sister. Such a dear girl as she is, and so careful of me! I must not let her find me writing.

She is a perfect and enthusiastic housekeeper, and hopes for no better profession. I verily believe she thinks it is the writing which made me sick!

But I can write when she is out, and see her a long way off from these windows.

There is one that commands the road, a lovely shaded winding road, and one that just looks off over the country. A lovely country, too, full of great elms and velvet meadows.

This wallpaper has a kind of sub-pattern in a different shade, a particularly irritating one, for you can only see it in certain lights, and not clearly then.

But in the places where it isn't faded and where the sun is just so—I can see a strange, provoking, formless sort of figure, that seems to skulk about behind that silly and conspicuous front design.

There's sister on the stairs!

Well, the Fourth of July is over! The people are all gone and I am tired out. John thought it might do me good to see a little company, so we just had mother and Nellie and the children down for a week.

Of course I didn't do a thing. Jennie sees to everything now.

But it tired me all the same.

John says if I don't pick up faster he shall send me to Weir Mitchell° in the fall.

But I don't want to go there at all. I had a friend who was in his hands once, and she says he is just like John and my brother, only more so!

Weir Mitchell: Dr. S. Weir Mitchell (1829–1914) was an American neurologist and author who advocated "rest cures" for nervous illnesses.

Besides, it is such an undertaking to go so far.

I don't feel as if it was worthwhile to turn my hand over for anything, and I'm getting dreadfully fretful and querulous.

I cry at nothing, and cry most of the time.

Of course I don't when John is here, or anybody else, but when I am alone.

And I am alone a good deal just now. John is kept in town very often by serious cases, and Jennie is good and lets me alone when I want her to.

So I walk a little in the garden or down that lovely lane, sit on the porch under the roses, and lie down up here a good deal.

I'm getting really fond of the room in spite of the wallpaper. Perhaps *because* of the wallpaper.

It dwells in my mind so!

I lie here on this great immovable bed—it is nailed down, I believe—and follow that pattern about by the hour. It is as good as gymnastics, I assure you. I start, we'll say, at the bottom, down in the corner over there where it has not been touched, and I determine for the thousandth time that I *will* follow that pointless pattern to some sort of a conclusion.

I know a little of the principle of design, and I know this thing was not arranged on any laws of radiation, or alternation, or repetition, or symmetry, or anything else that I ever heard of.

It is repeated, of course, by the breadths, but not otherwise.

Looked at in one way each breadth stands alone, the bloated curves and flourishes—a kind of "debased Romanesque" with *delirium tremens*—go waddling up and down in isolated columns of fatuity.

But, on the other hand, they connect diagonally, and the sprawling outlines run off in great slanting waves of optic horror, like a lot of wallowing sea-weeds in full chase.

The whole thing goes horizontally, too, at least it seems so, and I exhaust myself in trying to distinguish the order of its going in that direction.

They have used a horizontal breadth for a frieze, and that adds wonderfully to the confusion.

There is one end of the room where it is almost intact, and there, when the crosslights fade and the low sun shines directly upon it, I can almost fancy radiation after all,—the interminable grotesques seem to form around a common centre and rush off in headlong plunges of equal distraction.

It makes me tired to follow it. I will take a nap I guess.

I don't know why I should write this.

I don't want to.

I don't feel able.

And I know John would think it absurd. But I *must* say what I feel and think in some way—it is such a relief!

But the effort is getting to be greater than the relief.

Half the time now I am awfully lazy, and lie down ever so much.

John says I mustn't lose my strength, and has me take cod liver oil and lots of tonics and things, to say nothing of ale and wine and rare meat.

Dear John! He loves me very dearly, and hates to have me sick. I tried to have a real earnest reasonable talk with him the other day, and tell him how I wish he would let me go and make a visit to Cousin Henry and Julia.

But he said I wasn't able to go, nor able to stand it after I got there; and I did not make out a very good case for myself, for I was crying before I had finished.

It is getting to be a great effort for me to think straight. Just this nervous weakness I suppose.

And dear John gathered me up in his arms, and just carried me upstairs and laid me on the bed, and sat by me and read to me till it tired my head.

He said I was his darling and his comfort and all he had, and that I must take care of myself for his sake, and keep well.

He says no one but myself can help me out of it, that I must use my will and self-control and not let any silly fancies run away with me.

There's one comfort, the baby is well and happy, and does not have to occupy this nursery with the horrid wallpaper.

If we had not used it, that blessed child would have! What a fortunate escape! Why, I wouldn't have a child of mine, an impressionable little thing, live in such a room for worlds.

I never thought of it before, but it is lucky that John kept me here after all, I can stand it so much easier than a baby, you see.

Of course I never mention it to them any more—I am too wise, but I keep watch of it all the same.

There are things in the wallpaper that nobody knows but me, or ever will.

Behind that outside pattern the dim shapes get clearer every day.

It is always the same shape, only very numerous.

And it is like a woman stooping down and creeping about behind that pattern. I don't like it a bit. I wonder—I begin to think—I wish John would take me away from here!

It is so hard to talk with John about my case, because he is so wise, and because he loves me so.

But I tried it last night.

It was moonlight. The moon shines in all around just as the sun does.

I hate to see it sometimes, it creeps so slowly, and always comes in by one window or another.

John was asleep and I hated to waken him, so I kept still and watched the moonlight on that undulating wallpaper till I felt creepy.

The faint figure behind seemed to shake the pattern, just as if she wanted to get out.

I got up softly and went to feel and see if the paper *did* move, and when I came back John was awake.

"What is it, little girl?" he said. "Don't go walking about like that — you'll get cold."

I thought it was a good time to talk, so I told him that I really was not gaining here, and that I wished he would take me away.

"Why, darling!" said he, "our lease will be up in three weeks, and I can't see how to leave before.

"The repairs are not done at home, and I cannot possibly leave town just now. Of course if you were in any danger, I could and would, but you really are better, dear, whether you can see it or not. I am a doctor, dear, and I know. You are gaining flesh and color, your appetite is better, I feel really much easier about you."

"I don't weigh a bit more," said I, "nor as much; and my appetite may be better in the evening when you are here but it is worse in the morning when you are away!"

"Bless her little heart!" said he with a big hug, "she shall be as sick as she pleases! But now let's improve the shining hours by going to sleep, and talk about it in the morning!"

"And you won't go away?" I asked gloomily.

"Why, how can I, dear? It is only three weeks more and then we will take a nice little trip of a few days while Jennie is getting the house ready. Really dear you are better!"

"Better in body perhaps —" I began, and stopped short, for he sat up straight and looked at me with such a stern, reproachful look that I could not say another word.

"My darling," said he, "I beg you, for my sake and for our child's sake, as well as for your own, that you will never for one instant let that idea enter your mind! There is nothing so dangerous, so fascinating, to a temperament like yours. It is a false and foolish fancy. Can you trust me as a physician when I tell you so?"

So of course I said no more on that score, and we went to sleep before long. He thought I was asleep first, but I wasn't, and lay there for hours trying to decide whether that front pattern and the back pattern really did move together or separately.

On a pattern like this, by daylight, there is a lack of sequence, a defiance of law, that is a constant irritant to a normal mind.

The color is hideous enough, and unreliable enough, and infuriating enough, but the pattern is torturing.

You think you have mastered it, but just as you get well underway in following, it turns a back-somersault and there you are. It slaps you in the face, knocks you down, and tramples upon you. It is like a bad dream.

The outside pattern is a florid arabesque, reminding one of a fungus. If you can imagine a toadstool in joints, an interminable string of toad-stools, budding and sprouting in endless convolutions—why, that is something like it.

That is, sometimes!

There is one marked peculiarity about this paper, a thing nobody seems to notice but myself, and that is that it changes as the light changes.

When the sun shoots in through the east window—I always watch for that first long, straight ray—it changes so quickly that I never can quite believe it.

That is why I watch it always.

By moonlight—the moon shines in all night when there is a moon—I wouldn't know it was the same paper.

At night in any kind of light, in twilight, candlelight, lamplight, and worst of all by moonlight, it becomes bars! The outside pattern I mean, and the woman behind it is as plain as can be.

I didn't realize for a long time what the thing was that showed behind, that dim sub-pattern, but now I am quite sure it is a woman.

By daylight she is subdued, quiet. I fancy it is the pattern that keeps her so still. It is so puzzling. It keeps me quiet by the hour.

I lie down ever so much now. John says it is good for me, and to sleep all I can.

Indeed he started the habit by making me lie down for an hour after each meal.

It is a very bad habit I am convinced, for you see I don't sleep.

And that cultivates deceit, for I don't tell them I'm awake—O, no!

The fact is I am getting a little afraid of John.

He seems very queer sometimes, and even Jennie has an inexplicable look.

It strikes me occasionally, just as a scientific hypothesis,—that perhaps it is the paper!

I have watched John when he did not know I was looking, and come into the room suddenly on the most innocent excuses, and I've caught him several times *looking at the paper*! And Jennie too. I caught Jennie with her hand on it once.

She didn't know I was in the room, and when I asked her in a quiet, a very quiet voice, with the most restrained manner possible, what she was doing with the paper—she turned around as if she had been caught stealing, and looked quite angry—asked me why I should frighten her so!

Then she said that the paper stained everything it touched, that she had found yellow smooches on all my clothes and John's, and she wished we would be more careful!

Did not that sound innocent? But I know she was studying that pattern, and I am determined that nobody shall find it out but myself!

Life is very much more exciting now than it used to be. You see I have something more to expect, to look forward to, to watch. I really do eat better, and am more quiet than I was.

John is so pleased to see me improve! He laughed a little the other day, and said I seemed to be flourishing in spite of my wallpaper.

I turned it off with a laugh. I had no intention of telling him it was *because* of the wallpaper—he would make fun of me. He might even want to take me away.

I don't want to leave now until I have found it out. There is a week more, and I think that will be enough.

I'm feeling ever so much better! I don't sleep much at night, for it is so interesting to watch developments; but I sleep a good deal in the daytime.

In the daytime it is tiresome and perplexing.

There are always new shoots on the fungus, and new shades of yellow all over it. I cannot keep count of them, though I have tried conscientiously.

It is the strangest yellow, that wallpaper! It makes me think of all the yellow things I ever saw—not beautiful ones like buttercups, but old foul, bad yellow things.

But there is something else about that paper—the smell! I noticed it the moment we came into the room, but with so much air and sun it was not bad. Now we have had a week of fog and rain, and whether the windows are open or not, the smell is here.

It creeps all over the house.

I find it hovering in the dining-room, skulking in the parlor, hiding in the hall, lying in wait for me on the stairs.

It gets into my hair.

Even when I go to ride, if I turn my head suddenly and surprise it—there is that smell!

Such a peculiar odor, too! I have spent hours in trying to analyze it, to find what it smelled like.

It is not bad—at first, and very gentle, but quite the subtlest, most enduring odor I ever met.

In this damp weather it is awful, I wake up in the night and find it hanging over me.

It used to disturb me at first. I thought seriously of burning the house—to reach the smell.

But now I am used to it. The only thing I can think of that it is like is the *color* of the paper! A yellow smell.

There is a very funny mark on this wall, low down, near the mopboard. A streak that runs round the room. It goes behind every piece of furniture, except the bed, a long, straight, even *smooch*, as if it had been rubbed over and over.

I wonder how it was done and who did it, and what they did it for. Round and round and round—round and round and round—it makes me dizzy!

I really have discovered something at last.

Through watching so much at night, when it changes so, I have finally found out.

The front pattern *does* move—and no wonder! The woman behind shakes it!

Sometimes I think there are a great many women behind, and sometimes only one, and she crawls around fast, and her crawling shakes it all over.

Then in the very bright spots she keeps still, and in the very shady spots she just takes hold of the bars and shakes them hard.

And she is all the time trying to climb through. But nobody could climb through that pattern—it strangles so; I think that is why it has so many heads.

They get through, and then the pattern strangles them off and turns them upside down, and makes their eyes white!

If those heads were covered or taken off it would not be half so bad.

I think that woman gets out in the daytime!

And I'll tell you why—privately—I've seen her!

I can see her out of every one of my windows!

It is the same woman, I know, for she is always creeping, and most women do not creep by daylight.

I see her in that long shaded lane, creeping up and down. I see her in those dark grape arbors, creeping all around the garden.

I see her on that long road under the trees, creeping along, and when a carriage comes she hides under the blackberry vines.

I don't blame her a bit. It must be very humiliating to be caught creeping by daylight!

I always lock the door when I creep by daylight. I can't do it at night, for I know John would suspect something at once.

And John is so queer now, that I don't want to irritate him. I wish he would take another room! Besides, I don't want anybody to get that woman out at night but myself.

I often wonder if I could see her out of all the windows at once.

But, turn as fast as I can, I can only see out of one at one time.

And though I always see her, she *may* be able to creep faster than I can turn!

I have watched her sometimes away off in the open country, creeping as fast as a cloud shadow in a high wind.

If only that top pattern could be gotten off from the under one! I mean to try it, little by little.

I have found out another funny thing, but I shan't tell it this time! It does not do to trust people too much.

There are only two more days to get this paper off, and I believe John is beginning to notice. I don't like the look in his eyes.

And I heard him ask Jennie a lot of professional questions, about me. She had a very good report to give.

She said I slept a good deal in the daytime.

John knows I don't sleep very well at night, for all I'm so quiet!

He asked me all sorts of questions too, and pretended to be very loving and kind.

As if I couldn't see through him!

Still, I don't wonder he acts so, sleeping under this paper for three months.

It only interests me, but I feel sure John and Jennie are secretly affected by it.

Hurrah! This is the last day, but it is enough. John to stay in town over night, and won't be out until this evening.

Jennie wanted to sleep with me—the sly thing! But I told her I should undoubtedly rest better for a night all alone.

That was clever, for really I wasn't alone a bit! As soon as it was moonlight and that poor thing began to crawl and shake the pattern, I got up and ran to help her.

I pulled and she shook, I shook and she pulled, and before morning we had peeled off yards of that paper.

A strip about as high as my head and half around the room.

And then when the sun came and that awful pattern began to laugh at me, I declared I would finish it to-day!

We go away to-morrow, and they are moving all my furniture down again to leave things as they were before.

Jennie looked at the wall in amazement, but I told her merrily that I did it out of pure spite at the vicious thing.

She laughed and said she wouldn't mind doing it herself, but I must not get tired.

How she betrayed herself that time!

But I am here, and no person touches this paper but me,—not *alive*!

She tried to get me out of the room—it was too patent! But I said it was so quiet and empty and clean now that I believed I would lie down again and sleep all I could, and not to wake me even for dinner—I would call when I woke.

So now she is gone, and the servants are gone, and the things are gone, and there is nothing left but that great bedstead nailed down, with the canvas mattress we found on it.

We shall sleep downstairs to-night, and take the boat home to-morrow.

I quite enjoy the room, now it is bare again.

How those children did tear about here!

This bedstead is fairly gnawed!

But I must get to work.

I have locked the door and thrown the key down into the front path.

I don't want to go out, and I don't want to have anybody come in, till John comes.

I want to astonish him.

I've got a rope up here that even Jennie did not find. If that woman does get out, and tries to get away, I can tie her!

But I forgot I could not reach far without anything to stand on!

This bed will *not* move!

I tried to lift and push it until I was lame, and then I got so angry I bit off a little piece at one corner—but it hurt my teeth.

Then I peeled off all the paper I could reach standing on the floor. It sticks horribly and the pattern just enjoys it! All those strangled heads and bulbous eyes and waddling fungus growths just shriek with derision!

I am getting angry enough to do something desperate. To jump out of the window would be admirable exercise, but the bars are too strong even to try.

Besides I wouldn't do it. Of course not. I know well enough that a step like that is improper and might be misconstrued.

I don't like to *look* out of the windows even—there are so many of those creeping women, and they creep so fast.

I wonder if they all come out of that wallpaper as I did?

But I am securely fastened now by my well-hidden rope—you don't get *me* out in the road there!

I suppose I shall have to get back behind the pattern when it comes night, and that is hard!

It is so pleasant to be out in this great room and creep around as I please!

I don't want to go outside. I won't, even if Jennie asks me to.

For outside you have to creep on the ground, and everything is green instead of yellow.

But here I can creep smoothly on the floor, and my shoulder just fits in that long smooch around the wall, so I cannot lose my way.

Why, there's John at the door!

It is no use, young man, you can't open it!

How he does call and pound!

Now he's crying for an axe.

It would be a shame to break down that beautiful door!

"John dear!" said I in the gentlest voice, "the key is down by the front steps, under a plantain leaf!"

That silenced him for a few moments.

Then he said—very quietly indeed, "Open the door, my darling!"

"I can't," said I. "The key is down by the front door under a plantain leaf!"

And then I said it again, several times, very gently and slowly, and said it so often that he had to go and see, and he got it of course, and came in. He stopped short by the door.

"What is the matter?" he cried. "For God's sake, what are you doing!"

I kept on creeping just the same, but I looked at him over my shoulder.

"I've got out at last," said I, "in spite of you and Jane. And I've pulled off most of the paper, so you can't put me back!"

Now why should that man have fainted? But he did, and right across my path by the wall, so that I had to creep over him every time!

[1892]

WILLA CATHER [1873–1947]

Paul's Case

It was Paul's afternoon to appear before the faculty of the Pittsburgh High School to account for his various misdemeanors. He had been suspended a week ago, and his father had called at the Principal's office and confessed his perplexity about his son. Paul entered the faculty room suave and smiling. His clothes were a trifle outgrown and the tan velvet on the collar of his open overcoat was frayed and worn; but for all that there was something of the dandy about him, and he wore an opal pin in his neatly knotted black four-in-hand, and a red carnation in his buttonhole. This latter adornment the faculty somehow felt was not properly significant of the contrite spirit befitting a boy under the ban of suspension.

Paul was tall for his age and very thin, with high, cramped shoulders and a narrow chest. His eyes were remarkable for a certain hysterical brilliancy and he continually used them in a conscious, theatrical sort of way, peculiarly offensive in a boy. The pupils were abnormally large, as though he were addicted to belladonna,° but there was a glassy glitter about them which that drug does not produce.

When questioned by the Principal as to why he was there, Paul stated, politely enough, that he wanted to come back to school. This was a lie, but Paul was quite accustomed to lying; found it, indeed, indispensable for overcoming friction. His teachers were asked to state their respective charges against him, which they did with such a rancor and aggrievedness as evinced that this was not a usual case. Disorder and impertinence were among the offenses named, yet each of his instructors felt that it was scarcely possible to put into words the real cause of the trouble, which lay in a sort of hysterically defiant manner of the boy's; in the contempt which they all knew he felt for them, and which he seemingly made not the least effort to conceal. Once, when he had been making a synopsis of a paragraph at the blackboard, his English teacher had stepped to his side and attempted to guide his hand. Paul had started back with a shudder and thrust his hands violently behind him. The astonished woman could scarcely have been more hurt and embarrassed

---

Belladonna: A drug containing atropine, derived from the leaves and root of the poisonous Deadly Nightshade.

had he struck at her. The insult was so involuntary and definitely personal as to be unforgettable. In one way and another, he had made all his teachers, men and women alike, conscious of the same feeling of physical aversion. In one class he habitually sat with his hand shading his eyes; in another he always looked out of the window during the recitation; in another he made a running commentary on the lecture, with humorous intention.

His teachers felt this afternoon that his whole attitude was symbolized by his shrug and his flippantly red carnation flower, and they fell upon him without mercy, his English teacher leading the pack. He stood through it smiling, his pale lips parted over his white teeth. (His lips were continually twitching, and he had a habit of raising his eyebrows that was contemptuous and irritating to the last degree.) Older boys than Paul had broken down and shed tears under that baptism of fire, but his set smile did not once desert him, and his only sign of discomfort was the nervous trembling of the fingers that toyed with the buttons of his overcoat, and an occasional jerking of the other hand that held his hat. Paul was always smiling, always glancing about him, seeming to feel that people might be watching him and trying to detect something. This conscious expression, since it was as far as possible from boyish mirthfulness, was usually attributed to insolence or "smartness."

As the inquisition proceeded, one of his instructors repeated an impertinent remark of the boy's, and the Principal asked him whether he thought that a courteous speech to make to a woman. Paul shrugged his shoulders slightly and his eyebrows twitched.

"I don't know," he replied. "I didn't mean to be polite or impolite, either. I guess it's a sort of way I have of saying things regardless."

The Principal, who was a sympathetic man, asked him whether he didn't think that a way it would be well to get rid of. Paul grinned and said he guessed so. When he was told that he could go, he bowed gracefully and went out. His bow was but a repetition of the scandalous red carnation.

His teachers were in despair, and his drawing master voiced the feeling of them all when he declared there was something about the boy which none of them understood. He added: "I don't really believe that smile of his comes altogether from insolence; there's something sort of haunted about it. The boy is not strong, for one thing. I happen to know that he was born in Colorado, only a few months before his mother died out there of a long illness. There is something wrong about the fellow."

The drawing master had come to realize that, in looking at Paul, one saw only his white teeth and the forced animation of his eyes. One warm afternoon the boy had gone to sleep at his drawing-board, and his master had noted with amazement what a white, blue-veined face it was; drawn and wrinkled like an old man's about the eyes, the lips twitching even in his sleep, and stiff with a nervous tension that drew them back from his teeth.

His teachers left the building dissatisfied and unhappy; humiliated to have felt so vindictive toward a mere boy, to have uttered this feeling in cutting terms, and to have set each other on, as it were, in the gruesome game of intemperate reproach. Some of them remembered having seen a miserable street cat set at bay by a ring of tormentors.

As for Paul, he ran down the hill whistling the Soldiers' Chorus from *Faust*, looking wildly behind him now and then to see whether some of his teachers were not there to writhe under this light-heartedness. As it was now late in the afternoon and Paul was on duty that evening as usher at Carnegie Hall, he decided that he would not go home to supper. When he reached the concert hall the doors were not yet open and, as it was chilly outside, he decided to go up into the picture gallery—always deserted at this hour—where there were some of Raffelli's gay studies of Paris streets and an airy blue Venetian scene or two that always exhilarated him. He was delighted to find no one in the gallery but the old guard, who sat in one corner, a newspaper on his knee, a black patch over one eye and the other closed. Paul possessed himself of the place and walked confidently up and down, whistling under his breath. After a while he sat down before a blue Rico and lost himself. When he bethought him to look at his watch, it was after seven o'clock, and he rose with a start and ran downstairs, making a face at Augustus, peering out from the cast-room, and an evil gesture at the Venus of Milo as he passed her on the stairway.

When Paul reached the ushers' dressing-room half-a-dozen boys were there already, and he began excitedly to tumble into his uniform. It was one of the few that at all approached fitting, and Paul thought it very becoming—though he knew that the tight, straight coat accentuated his narrow chest, about which he was exceedingly sensitive. He was always considerably excited while he dressed, twanging all over to the tuning of the strings and the preliminary flourishes of the horns in the music-room; but tonight he seemed quite beside himself, and he teased and plagued the boys until, telling him that he was crazy, they put him down on the floor and sat on him.

Somewhat calmed by his suppression, Paul dashed out to the front of the house to seat the early comers. He was a model usher; gracious and smiling he ran up and down the aisles; nothing was too much trouble for him; he carried messages and brought programmes as though it were his greatest pleasure in life, and all the people in his section thought him a charming boy, feeling that he remembered and admired them. As the house filled, he grew more and more vivacious and animated, and the color came to his cheeks and lips. It was very much as though this were a great reception and Paul were the host. Just as the musicians came out to take their places, his English teacher arrived with checks for the seats which a prominent manufacturer had taken for the season. She betrayed some embarrassment when she handed Paul the tickets, and a *hauteur* which subsequently made her feel very foolish. Paul was startled for a moment, and had the feeling of wanting to put her out; what business had she here among all these fine people and gay colors? He looked her over and decided that she was not appropriately dressed and must be a fool to sit downstairs in such togs. The tickets had probably been sent her out of kindness, he reflected as he put down a seat for her, and she had about as much right to sit there as he had.

When the symphony began Paul sank into one of the rear seats with a long sigh of relief, and lost himself as he had done before the Rico. It was not that symphonies, as such, meant anything in particular to Paul, but the first sigh of the instruments seemed to free some hilarious and potent spirit within him; something that struggled there like the Genius in the bottle found by the Arab fisherman. He felt a sudden zest of life; the lights danced before his eyes and the concert hall blazed into unimaginable splendor. When the soprano soloist came on, Paul forgot even the nastiness of his teacher's being there and gave himself up to the peculiar stimulus such personages always had for him. The soloist chanced to be a German woman, by no means in her first youth, and the mother of many children; but she wore an elaborate gown and a tiara, and above all she had that indefinable air of achievement, that world-shine upon her, which, in Paul's eyes, made her a veritable queen of Romance.

After a concert was over Paul was always irritable and wretched until he got to sleep, and tonight he was even more than usually restless. He had the feeling of not being able to let down, of its being impossible to give up this delicious excitement which was the only thing that could be called living at all. During the last number he withdrew and, after hastily changing his clothes in the dressing-room, slipped out to the side door where the soprano's carriage stood. Here he began pacing rapidly up and down the walk, waiting to see her come out.

Over yonder the Schenley, in its vacant stretch, loomed big and square through the fine rain, the windows of its twelve stories glowing like those of a lighted cardboard house under a Christmas tree. All the actors and singers of the better class stayed there when they were in the city, and a number of the big manufacturers of the place lived there in the winter. Paul had often hung about the hotel, watching the people go in and out, longing to enter and leave school-masters and dull care behind him forever.

At last the singer came out, accompanied by the conductor, who helped her into her carriage and closed the door with a cordial *auf wiedersehen* which set Paul to wondering whether she were not an old sweetheart of his. Paul followed the carriage over to the hotel, walking so rapidly as not to be far from the entrance when the singer alighted and disappeared behind the swinging glass doors that were opened by a negro in a tall hat and a long coat. In the moment that the door was ajar it seemed to Paul that he, too, entered. He seemed to feel himself go after her up the steps, into the warm, lighted building, into an exotic, a tropical world of shiny, glistening surfaces and basking ease. He reflected upon the mysterious dishes that were brought into the dining-room, the green bottles in buckets of ice, as he had seen them in the supper party pictures of the *Sunday World* supplement. A quick gust of wind brought the rain down with sudden vehemence, and Paul was startled to find that he was still outside in the slush of the gravel driveway; that his boots were letting in the water and his scanty overcoat was clinging wet about him; that the lights in front of the concert hall were out, and that the rain was driving in sheets between him and the orange glow of the windows above him. There it was, what he wanted—tangibly before him, like the fairy world of a Christmas pantomime, but mocking spirits stood guard at the doors, and, as the rain beat in his face, Paul wondered whether he were destined always to shiver in the black night outside, looking up at it.

He turned and walked reluctantly toward the car tracks. The end had to come sometime; his father in his night-clothes at the top of the stairs, explanations that did not explain, hastily improvised fictions that were forever tripping him up, his upstairs room and its horrible yellow wallpaper, the creaking bureau with the greasy plush collar-box, and over his painted wooden bed the pictures of George Washington and John Calvin, and the framed motto, "Feed my Lambs," which had been worked in red worsted by his mother.

Half an hour later, Paul alighted from his car and went slowly down one of the side streets off the main thoroughfare. It was a highly respectable street, where all the houses were exactly alike, and where businessmen of moderate means begot and reared large families of children, all of whom went to Sabbath-school and learned the shorter catechism, and were interested in arithmetic; all of whom were as exactly alike as their homes, and of a piece of the monotony in which they lived. Paul never went up Cordelia Street without a shudder of loathing. His home was next to the house of the Cumberland minister. He approached it tonight with the nerveless sense of defeat, the hopeless feeling of sinking back forever into ugliness and commonness that he had always had when he came home. The moment he turned into Cordelia Street he felt the waters close above his head. After each of these orgies of living, he experienced all the physical depression which follows a debauch; the loathing of respectable beds, of common food, of a house penetrated by kitchen odors; a shuddering repulsion for the flavorless, colorless mass of every-day existence; a morbid desire for cool things and soft lights and fresh flowers.

The nearer he approached the house, the more absolutely unequal Paul felt to the sight of it all; his ugly sleeping chamber; the cold bathroom with the grimy zinc tub, the cracked mirror, the dripping spiggots; his father, at the top of the stairs, his hairy legs sticking out from his night-shirt, his feet thrust into carpet slippers. He was so much later than usual that there would certainly be inquiries and reproaches. Paul stopped short before the door. He felt that he could not be accosted by his father tonight; that he could not toss again on that miserable bed. He would not go in. He would tell his father that he had no car fare, and it was raining so hard he had gone home with one of the boys and stayed all night.

Meanwhile, he was wet and cold. He went around to the back of the house and tried one of the basement windows, found it open, raised it cautiously, and scrambled down the cellar wall to the floor. There he stood, holding his breath, terrified by the noise he had made, but the floor above him was silent, and there was no creak on the stairs. He found a soap-box, and carried it over to the soft ring of light that streamed from the furnace door, and sat down. He was horribly afraid of rats, so he did not try to sleep, but sat looking distrustfully at the dark, still terrified lest he might have awakened his father. In such reactions, after one of the experiences which made days and nights out of the dreary blanks of the calendar, when his senses were deadened, Paul's head was always singularly clear. Suppose his father had heard him getting in at the window and had come down and shot him for a burglar? Then, again, suppose his father had come down, pistol in hand, and he had cried out in time to save himself, and his father had been horrified to think how nearly he had killed him? Then, again, suppose a day should come when his father would remember that night, and wish there had been no warning cry to stay his hand? With this last supposition Paul entertained himself until daybreak.

The following Sunday was fine; the sodden November chill was broken by the last flash of autumnal summer. In the morning Paul had to go to church and Sabbath-school, as always. On seasonable Sunday afternoons the burghers of Cordelia Street always sat out on their front "stoops," and talked to their neighbors on the next stoop, or called to those across the street in neighborly fashion. The men usually sat on gay cushions placed upon the steps that led down to the sidewalk, while the women, in their Sunday "waists,"° sat in rockers on the cramped porches,

Waist: An article of women's clothing that spans from the neck to the waist; a blouse.

pretending to be greatly at their ease. The children played in the streets; there were so many of them that the place resembled the recreation grounds of a kindergarten. The men on the steps—all in their shirt sleeves, their vests unbuttoned—sat with their legs well apart, their stomachs comfortably protruding, and talked of the prices of things, or told anecdotes of the sagacity of their various chiefs and overlords. They occasionally looked over the multitude of squabbling children, listened affectionately to their high-pitched, nasal voices, smiling to see their own proclivities reproduced in their offspring, and interspersed their legends of the iron kings° with remarks about their sons' progress at school, their grades in arithmetic, and the amounts they had saved in their toy banks.

On this last Sunday of November, Paul sat all the afternoon on the lowest step of his "stoop," staring into the street, while his sisters, in their rockers, were talking to the minister's daughters next door about how many shirt-waists they had made in the last week, and how many waffles some one had eaten at the last church supper. When the weather was warm, and his father was in a particularly jovial frame of mind, the girls made lemonade, which was always brought out in a red-glass pitcher, ornamented with forget-me-nots in blue enamel. This the girls thought very fine, and the neighbors always joked about the suspicious color of the pitcher.

Today Paul's father sat on the top step, talking to a young man who shifted a restless baby from knee to knee. He happened to be the young man who was daily held up to Paul as a model, and after whom it was his father's dearest hope that he would pattern. This young man was of a ruddy complexion, with a compressed, red mouth, and faded, near-sighted eyes, over which he wore thick spectacles, with gold bows that curved about his ears. He was clerk to one of the magnates of a great steel corporation, and was looked upon in Cordelia Street as a young man with a future. There was a story that, some five years ago—he was now barely twenty-six—he had been a trifle dissipated but in order to curb his appetites and save the loss of time and strength that a sowing of wild oats might have entailed, he had taken his chief's advice, oft reiterated to his employees, and at twenty-one had married the first woman whom he could persuade to share his fortunes. She happened to be an angular school-mistress, much older than he, who also wore thick glasses, and who had now borne him four children, all near-sighted, like herself.

The young man was relating how his chief, now cruising in the Mediterranean, kept in touch with all the details of the business, arranging his

Iron kings: Businessmen who prospered from investments in iron and steel manufacturing.

office hours on his yacht just as though he were at home, and "knocking off work enough to keep two stenographers busy." His father told, in turn, the plan his corporation was considering, of putting in an electric railway plant at Cairo. Paul snapped his teeth; he had an awful apprehension that they might spoil it all before he got there. Yet he rather liked to hear these legends of the iron kings, that were told and retold on Sundays and holidays; these stories of palaces in Venice, yachts on the Mediterranean, and high play at Monte Carlo appealed to his fancy, and he was interested in the triumphs of these cash boys who had become famous, though he had no mind for the cash-boy stage.

After supper was over, and he had helped to dry the dishes, Paul nervously asked his father whether he could go to George's to get some help in his geometry, and still more nervously asked for car fare. This latter request he had to repeat, as his father, on principle, did not like to hear requests for money, whether much or little. He asked Paul whether he could not go to some boy who lived nearer, and told him that he ought not to leave his school work until Sunday; but he gave him the dime. He was not a poor man, but he had a worthy ambition to come up in the world. His only reason for allowing Paul to usher was, that he thought a boy ought to be earning a little.

Paul bounded upstairs, scrubbed the greasy odor of the dish-water from his hands with the ill-smelling soap he hated, and then shook over his fingers a few drops of violet water from the bottle he kept hidden in his drawer. He left the house with his geometry conspicuously under his arm, and the moment he got out of Cordelia Street and boarded a downtown car, he shook off the lethargy of two deadening days, and began to live again.

The leading juvenile of the permanent stock company which played at one of the downtown theatres was an acquaintance of Paul's, and the boy had been invited to drop in at the Sunday-night rehearsals whenever he could. For more than a year Paul had spent every available moment loitering about Charley Edwards' dressing-room. He had won a place among Edwards' following not only because the young actor, who could not afford to employ a dresser, often found him useful, but because he recognized in Paul something akin to what churchmen term "vocation."

It was at the theatre and at Carnegie Hall that Paul really lived; the rest was but a sleep and a forgetting. This was Paul's fairy tale, and it had for him all the allurement of a secret love. The moment he inhaled the gassy, painty, dusty odor behind the scenes, he breathed like a prisoner set free, and felt within him the possibility of doing or saying splendid, brilliant, poetic things. The moment the cracked orchestra beat out the overture from *Martha*, or jerked at the serenade from *Rigoletto*, all stupid and ugly things slid from him, and his senses were deliciously, yet delicately fired.

Perhaps it was because, in Paul's world, the natural nearly always wore the guise of ugliness, that a certain element of artificiality seemed to him necessary in beauty. Perhaps it was because his experience of life elsewhere was so full of Sabbath-school picnics, petty economies, wholesome advice as to how to succeed in life, and the unescapable odors of cooking, that he found this existence so alluring, these smartly-clad men and women so attractive, that he was so moved by these starry apple orchards that bloomed perennially under the lime-light.

It would be difficult to put it strongly enough how convincingly the stage entrance of that theatre was for Paul the actual portal of Romance. Certainly none of the company ever suspected it, least of all Charley Edwards. It was very like the old stories that used to float about London of fabulously rich Jews, who had subterranean halls there, with palms, and fountains, and soft lamps and richly apparelled women who never saw the disenchanting light of London day. So, in the midst of that smoke-palled city, enamored of figures and grimy toil, Paul had his secret temple, his wishing carpet, his bit of blue-and-white Mediterranean shore bathed in perpetual sunshine.

Several of Paul's teachers had a theory that his imagination had been perverted by garish fiction, but the truth was that he scarcely ever read at all. The books at home were not such as would either tempt or corrupt a youthful mind, and as for reading the novels that some of his friends urged upon him—well, he got what he wanted much more quickly from music; any sort of music, from an orchestra to a barrel organ. He needed only the spark, the indescribable thrill that made his imagination master of his senses, and he could make plots and pictures enough of his own. It was equally true that he was not stage struck—not, at any rate, in the usual acceptation of that expression. He had no desire to become an actor, any more than he had to become a musician. He felt no necessity to do any of these things; what he wanted was to see, to be in the atmosphere, float on the wave of it, to be carried out, blue league after blue league, away from everything.

After a night behind the scenes, Paul found the school-room more than ever repulsive; the bare floors and naked walls; the prosy men who never wore frock coats, or violets in their buttonholes; the women with their dull gowns, shrill voices, and pitiful seriousness about prepositions that govern the dative. He could not bear to have the other pupils think, for a moment, that he took these people seriously; he must convey to them that he considered it all trivial, and was there only by way of a jest, anyway. He had autographed pictures of all the members of the stock company which he showed his classmates, telling them the most incredible stories of his familiarity with these people, of his acquaintance with the soloists who came to Carnegie Hall, his suppers with them and the flowers he sent them. When these stories lost their effect, and his audience grew listless, he became desperate and would bid all the boys good-bye, announcing that he was going to travel for a while; going to Naples, to Venice, to Egypt. Then, next Monday, he would slip back, conscious and nervously smiling; his sister was ill, and he should have to defer his voyage until spring.

Matters went steadily worse with Paul at school. In the itch to let his instructors know how heartily he despised them and their homilies, and how thoroughly he was appreciated elsewhere, he mentioned once or twice that he had no time to fool with theorems; adding—with a twitch of the eyebrows and a touch of that nervous bravado which so perplexed them—that he was helping the people down at the stock company; they were old friends of his.

The upshot of the matter was that the Principal went to Paul's father, and Paul was taken out of school and put to work. The manager at Carnegie Hall was told to get another usher in his stead; the door-keeper at the theatre was warned not to admit him to the house; and Charley Edwards remorsefully promised the boy's father not to see him again.

The members of the stock company were vastly amused when some of Paul's stories reached them—especially the women. They were hard-working women, most of them supporting indigent husbands or brothers, and they laughed rather bitterly at having stirred the boy to such fervid and florid inventions. They agreed with the faculty and with his father that Paul's was a bad case.

The east-bound train was ploughing through a January snowstorm; the dull dawn was beginning to show grey when the engine whistled a mile out of Newark. Paul started up from the seat where he had lain curled in uneasy slumber, rubbed the breath-misted window glass with his hand, and peered out. The snow was whirling in curling eddies above the white bottom lands, and the drifts lay already deep in the fields and along the fences, while here and there the long dead grass and dried weed stalks protruded black above it. Lights shone from the scattered houses, and a gang of laborers who stood beside the track waved their lanterns.

Paul had slept very little, and he felt grimy and uncomfortable. He had made the all-night journey in a day coach, partly because he was ashamed, dressed as he was, to go into a Pullman, and partly because he was afraid of being seen there by some Pittsburgh businessman, who might have noticed him in Denny & Carson's office. When the whistle awoke him, he clutched quickly at his breast pocket, glancing about him with an uncertain smile. But the little, clay-bespattered Italians were still sleeping, the slatternly women across the aisle were in open-mouthed oblivion, and even the crumby, crying babies were for the nonce stilled. Paul settled back to struggle with his impatience as best he could.

When he arrived at the Jersey City station, he hurried through his breakfast, manifestly ill at ease and keeping a sharp eye about him. After he reached the Twenty-third Street station, he consulted a cabman, and had himself driven to a men's furnishing establishment that was just opening for the day. He spent upward of two hours there, buying with endless reconsidering and great care. His new street suit he put on in the fitting-room; the frock coat and dress clothes he had bundled into the cab with his linen. Then he drove to a hatter's and a shoe house. His next errand was at Tiffany's, where he selected his silver and a new scarf-pin. He would not wait to have his silver marked, he said. Lastly, he stopped at a trunk shop on Broadway, and had his purchases packed into various travelling bags.

It was a little after one o'clock when he drove up to the Waldorf, and after settling with the cabman, went into the office. He registered from Washington; said his mother and father had been abroad, and that he had come down to await the arrival of their steamer. He told his story plausibly and had no trouble, since he volunteered to pay for them in advance, in engaging his rooms; a sleeping-room, sitting-room, and bath.

Not once, but a hundred times Paul had planned this entry into New York. He had gone over every detail of it with Charley Edwards, and in his scrap book at home there were pages of description about New York hotels, cut from the Sunday papers. When he was shown to his sitting-room on the eighth floor, he saw at a glance that everything was as it should be; there was but one detail in his mental picture that the place did not realize, so he rang for the bell boy and sent him down for flowers. He moved about nervously until the boy returned, putting away his new linen and fingering it delightedly as he did so. When the flowers came, he put them hastily into water, and then tumbled into a hot bath. Presently he came out of his white bath-room, resplendent in his new silk under-wear, and playing with the tassels of his red robe. The snow was whirling so fiercely outside his windows that he could scarcely see across the street, but within the air was deliciously soft and fragrant. He put the violets and jonquils on the taboret beside the couch, and threw himself down, with a long sigh, covering himself with a Roman blanket. He was thoroughly tired; he had been in such haste, he had stood up to such a strain, covered so much ground in the last twenty-four hours, that he wanted to think how it had all come about. Lulled by the sound of the wind, the warm air, and the cool fragrance of the flowers, he sank into deep, drowsy retrospection.

It had been wonderfully simple; when they had shut him out of the theatre and concert hall, when they had taken away his bone, the whole thing was virtually determined. The rest was a mere matter of opportunity. The only thing that at all surprised him was his own courage—for he realized well enough that he had always been tormented by fear, a sort of apprehensive dread that, of late years, as the meshes of the lies he had told closed about him, had been pulling the muscles of his body tighter and tighter. Until now, he could not remember the time when he had not been dreading something. Even when he was a little boy, it was always there—behind him, or before, or on either side. There had always been the shadowed corner, the dark place into which he dared not look, but from which something seemed always to be watching him—and Paul had done things that were not pretty to watch, he knew.

But now he had a curious sense of relief, as though he had at last thrown down the gauntlet to the thing in the corner.

Yet it was but a day since he had been sulking in the traces; but yesterday afternoon that he had been sent to the bank with Denny & Carson's deposit, as usual—but this time he was instructed to leave the book to be balanced. There was above two thousand dollars in checks, and nearly a thousand in the bank notes which he had taken from the book and quietly transferred to his pocket. At the bank he had made out a new deposit slip. His nerves had been steady enough to permit of his returning to the office, where he had finished his work and asked for a full day's holiday tomorrow, Saturday, giving a perfectly reasonable pretext. The bank book, he knew, would not be returned before Monday or Tuesday, and his father would be out of town for the next week. From the time he slipped the bank notes into his pocket until he boarded the night train for New York, he had not known a moment's hesitation. It was not the first time Paul had steered through treacherous waters.

How astonishingly easy it had all been; here he was, the thing done; and this time there would be no awakening, no figure at the top of the stairs. He watched the snow flakes whirling by his window until he fell asleep.

When he awoke, it was three o'clock in the afternoon. He bounded up with a start; half of one of his precious days gone already! He spent more than an hour in dressing, watching every stage of his toilet carefully in the mirror. Everything was quite perfect; he was exactly the kind of boy he had always wanted to be.

When he went downstairs, Paul took a carriage and drove up Fifth Avenue toward the Park. The snow had somewhat abated; carriages and tradesmen's wagons were hurrying soundlessly to and fro in the winter twilight; boys in woollen mufflers were shovelling off the doorsteps; the avenue stages made fine spots of color against the white street. Here and there on the corners were stands, with whole flower gardens blooming under glass cases, against the sides of which the snow flakes stuck and melted; violets, roses, carnations, lilies of the valley—somewhat vastly more lovely and alluring that they blossomed thus unnaturally in the snow. The Park itself was a wonderful stage winterpiece.

When he returned, the pause of the twilight had ceased, and the tune of the streets had changed. The snow was falling faster, lights streamed from the hotels that reared their dozen stories fearlessly up into the storm, defying the raging Atlantic winds. A long, black stream of carriages poured down the avenue, intersected here and there by other streams, tending horizontally. There were a score of cabs about the entrance of his hotel, and his driver had to wait. Boys in livery were running in and out of the awning stretched across the sidewalk, up and down the red velvet carpet laid from the door to the street. Above, about, within it all was the rumble and roar, the hurry and toss of thousands of human beings as hot for pleasure as himself, and on every side of him towered the glaring affirmation of the omnipotence of wealth.

The boy set his teeth and drew his shoulders together in a spasm of realization: the plot of all dramas, the text of all romances, the nerve-stuff of all sensations was whirling about him like the snow flakes. He burnt like a faggot in a tempest.°

When Paul went down to dinner, the music of the orchestra came floating up the elevator shaft to greet him. His head whirled as he stepped into the thronged corridor, and he sank back into one of the chairs against the wall to get his breath. The lights, the chatter, the perfumes, the bewildering medley of color—he had, for a moment, the feeling of not being able to stand it. But only for a moment; these were his own people, he told himself. He went slowly about the corridors, through the writing-rooms, smoking-rooms, reception-rooms, as though he were exploring the chambers of an enchanted palace, built and peopled for him alone.

When he reached the dining-room he sat down at a table near a window. The flowers, the white linen, the many-colored wine glasses, the gay toilettes of the women, the low popping of corks, the undulating repetitions of the *Blue Danube* from the orchestra, all flooded Paul's dream with bewildering radiance. When the roseate tinge of his champagne was added—that cold, precious, bubbling stuff that creamed and foamed in his glass—Paul wondered that there were honest men in the world at

---

Faggot in a tempest: If we take "faggot" to mean a bundle of sticks, its common non-slang meaning, the simile does not make much sense. Given Paul's unconventional appearance and temperament, other standard meanings seem to apply. In the Middle Ages, "faggot" sometimes referred to an unattractive or old woman, sometimes to a homosexual or other person considered heretic and burned on a pile of sticks.

all. This was what all the world was fighting for, he reflected; this was what all the struggle was about. He doubted the reality of his past. Had he ever known a place called Cordelia Street, a place where fagged-looking businessmen got on the early car; mere rivets in a machine they seemed to Paul—sickening men, with combings of children's hair always hanging to their coats, and the smell of cooking in their clothes. Cordelia Street—Ah! that belonged to another time and country; had he not always been thus, had he not sat here night after night, from as far back as he could remember, looking pensively over just such shimmering textures, and slowly twirling the stem of a glass like this one between his thumb and middle finger? He rather thought he had.

He was not in the least abashed or lonely. He had no especial desire to meet or to know any of these people; all he demanded was the right to look on and conjecture, to watch the pageant. The mere stage properties were all he contended for. Nor was he lonely later in the evening, in his loge at the Metropolitan. He was now entirely rid of his nervous misgivings, of his forced aggressiveness, of the imperative desire to show himself different from his surroundings. He felt now that his surroundings explained him. Nobody questioned the purple; he had only to wear it passively. He had only to glance down at his attire to reassure himself that here it would be impossible for anyone to humiliate him.

He found it hard to leave his beautiful sitting-room to go to bed that night, and sat long watching the raging storm from his turret window. When he went to sleep it was with the lights turned on in his bedroom; partly because of his old timidity, and partly so that, if he should wake in the night, there would be no wretched moment of doubt, no horrible suspicion of yellow wallpaper, or of Washington or Calvin above his bed.

Sunday morning the city was practically snow-bound. Paul breakfasted late, and in the afternoon he fell in with a wild San Francisco boy, a freshman at Yale, who said he had run down for a "little flyer" over Sunday. The young man offered to show Paul the night side of the town, and the two boys went out together after dinner, not returning to the hotel until seven o'clock the next morning. They had started out in the confiding warmth of a champagne friendship, but their parting in the elevator was singularly cool. The freshman pulled himself together to make his train, and Paul went to bed. He awoke at two o'clock in the afternoon, very thirsty and dizzy, and rang for ice-water, coffee, and the Pittsburgh papers.

On the part of the hotel management, Paul excited no suspicion. There was this to be said for him, that he wore his spoils with dignity and in no way made himself conspicuous. Even under the glow of his wine he was never boisterous, though he found the stuff like a magician's wand for wonder-building. His chief greediness lay in his ears and eyes, and his excesses were not offensive ones. His dearest pleasures were the grey winter twilights in his sitting-room; his quiet enjoyment of his flowers, his clothes, his wide divan, his cigarette, and his sense of power. He could not remember a time when he had felt so at peace with himself. The mere release from the necessity of petty lying, lying every day and every day, restored his self-respect. He had never lied for pleasure, even at school; but to be noticed and admired, to assert his difference from other Cordelia Street boys; and he felt a good deal more manly, more honest, even, now that he had no need for boastful pretensions, now that he could, as his actor friends used to say, "dress the part." It was characteristic that remorse did not occur to him. His golden days went by without a shadow, and he made each as perfect as he could.

On the eighth day after his arrival in New York, he found the whole affair exploited in the Pittsburgh papers, exploited with a wealth of detail which indicated that local news of a sensational nature was at a low ebb. The firm of Denny & Carson announced that the boy's father had refunded the full amount of the theft, and that they had no intention of prosecuting. The Cumberland minister had been interviewed, and expressed his hope of yet reclaiming the motherless lad, and his Sabbath-school teacher declared that she would spare no effort to that end. The rumor had reached Pittsburgh that the boy had been seen in a New York hotel, and his father had gone East to find him and bring him home.

Paul had just come in to dress for dinner; he sank into a chair, weak to the knees, and clasped his head in his hands. It was to be worse than jail, even; the tepid waters of Cordelia Street were to close over him finally and forever. The grey monotony stretched before him in hopeless, unrelieved years; Sabbath-school, Young People's Meeting, the yellow-papered room, the damp dish-towels; it all rushed back upon him with a sickening vividness. He had the old feeling that the orchestra had suddenly stopped, the sinking sensation that the play was over. The sweat broke out on his face, and he sprang to his feet, looked about him with his white, conscious smile, and winked at himself in the mirror. With something of the old childish belief in miracles with which he had so often gone to class, all his lessons unlearned, Paul dressed and dashed whistling down the corridor to the elevator.

He had no sooner entered the dining-room and caught the measure of the music than his remembrance was lightened by his old elastic power of claiming the moment, mounting with it, and finding it all sufficient. The glare and glitter about him, the mere scenic accessories had again, and for the last time, their old potency. He would show himself that he was game, he would finish the thing splendidly. He doubted, more than ever, the existence of Cordelia Street, and for the first time he drank his wine recklessly. Was he not, after all, one of those fortunate beings born to the purple, was he not still himself and in his own place? He drummed a nervous accompaniment to the Pagliacci music and looked about him, telling himself over and over that it had paid.

He reflected drowsily, to the swell of the music and the chill sweetness of his wine, that he might have done it more wisely. He might have caught an outboard steamer and been well out of their clutches before now. But the other side of the world had seemed too far away and too uncertain then; he could not have waited for it; his need had been too sharp. If he had to choose over again, he would do the same thing tomorrow. He looked affectionately about the dining-room, now gilded with a soft mist. Ah, it had paid indeed!

Paul was awakened next morning by a painful throbbing in his head and feet. He had thrown himself across the bed without undressing, and had slept with his shoes on. His limbs and hands were lead heavy, and his tongue and throat were parched and burnt. There came upon him one of those fateful attacks of clear-headedness that never occurred except when he was physically exhausted and his nerves hung loose. He lay still and closed his eyes and let the tide of things wash over him.

His father was in New York; "stopping at some joint or other," he told himself. The memory of successive summers on the front stoop fell upon him like a weight of black water. He had not a hundred dollars left; and he knew now, more than ever, that money was everything, the wall that stood between all he loathed and all he wanted. The thing was winding itself up; he had thought of that on his first glorious day in New York, and had even provided a way to snap the thread. It lay on his dressing-table now; he had got it out last night when he came blindly up from dinner, but the shiny metal hurt his eyes, and he disliked the looks of it.

He rose and moved about with a painful effort, succumbing now and again to attacks of nausea. It was the old depression exaggerated; all the world had become Cordelia Street. Yet somehow he was not afraid of anything, was absolutely calm; perhaps because he had looked into the dark corner at last and knew. It was bad enough, what he saw there, but somehow not so bad as his long fear of it had been. He saw everything clearly now. He had a feeling that he had made the best of it, that he had lived the sort of life he was meant to live, and for half an hour he sat staring at the revolver. But he told himself that was not the way, so he went downstairs and took a cab to the ferry.

When Paul arrived at Newark, he got off the train and took another cab, directing the driver to follow the Pennsylvania tracks out of the town. The snow lay heavy on the roadways and had drifted deep in the open fields. Only here and there the dead grass or dried weed stalks projected, singularly black, above it. Once well into the country, Paul dismissed the carriage and walked, floundering along the tracks, his mind a medley of irrelevant things. He seemed to hold in his brain an actual picture of everything he had seen that morning. He remembered every feature of both his drivers, of the toothless old woman from whom he had bought the red flowers in his coat, the agent from whom he had got his ticket, and all of his fellow-passengers on the ferry. His mind, unable to cope with vital matters near at hand, worked feverishly and deftly at sorting and grouping these images. They made for him a part of the ugliness of the world, of the ache in his head, and the bitter burning on his tongue. He stopped and put a handful of snow into his mouth as he walked, but that, too, seemed hot. When he reached a little hillside, where the tracks ran through a cut some twenty feet below him, he stopped and sat down.

The carnations in his coat were drooping with the cold, he noticed; their red glory all over. It occurred to him that all the flowers he had seen in the glass cases that first night must have gone the same way, long before this. It was only one splendid breath they had, in spite of their brave mockery at the winter outside the glass; and it was a losing game in the end, it seemed, this revolt against the homilies by which the world is run. Paul took one of the blossoms carefully from his coat and scooped a little hole in the snow, where he covered it up. Then he dozed a while, from his weak condition, seemingly insensible to the cold.

The sound of an approaching train awoke him, and he started to his feet, remembering only his resolution, and afraid lest he should be too late. He stood watching the approaching locomotive, his teeth chattering, his lips drawn away from them in a frightened smile; once or twice he glanced nervously sidewise, as though he were being watched. When the right moment came, he jumped. As he fell, the folly of his haste occurred to him with merciless clearness, the vastness of what he had left undone. There flashed through his brain, clearer than ever before, the blue of Adriatic water, the yellow of Algerian sands.

He felt something strike his chest, and that his body was being thrown swiftly through the air, on and on, immeasurably far and fast, while his limbs were gently relaxed. Then, because the picture making mechanism was crushed, the disturbing visions flashed into black, and Paul dropped back into the immense design of things.

[1905]

JAMES JOYCE [1882–1941]

Araby

North Richmond Street, being blind, was a quiet street except at the hour when the Christian Brothers' School set the boys free. An uninhabited house of two storeys stood at the blind end, detached from its neighbours in a square ground. The other houses of the street, conscious of decent lives within them, gazed at one another with brown imperturbable faces.

The former tenant of our house, a priest, had died in the back drawing-room. Air, musty from having been long enclosed, hung in all the rooms, and the waste room behind the kitchen was littered with old useless papers. Among these I found a few paper-covered books, the pages of which were curled and damp: *The Abbot*, by Walter Scott, *The Devout Communicant*, and *The Memoirs of Vidocq*. I liked the last best because its leaves were yellow. The wild garden behind the house contained a central apple-tree and a few straggling bushes under one of which I found the late tenant's rusty bicycle-pump. He had been a very charitable priest; in his will he had left all his money to institutions and the furniture of his house to his sister.

When the short days of winter came dusk fell before we had well eaten our dinners. When we met in the street the houses had grown sombre. The space of sky above us was the colour of ever-changing violet and towards it the lamps of the street lifted their feeble lanterns. The cold air stung us and we played till our bodies glowed. Our shouts echoed in the silent street. The career of our play brought us through the dark muddy lanes behind the houses where we ran the gauntlet of the rough tribes from the cottages, to the back doors of the dark dripping gardens where odours arose from the ashpits, to the dark odorous stables where a coachman smoothed and combed the horse or shook music from the buckled harness. When we returned to the street light from the kitchen windows had filled the areas. If my uncle was seen turning the corner we hid in the shadow until we had seen him safely housed. Or if Mangan's sister came out on the doorstep to call her brother in to his tea we watched her from our shadow peer up and down the street. We waited to see whether she would remain or go in and, if she remained, we left our shadow and walked up to Mangan's steps resignedly. She was waiting for us, her figure defined by the light from the half-opened door. Her brother always teased her before he obeyed and I stood by the railings looking at her. Her dress swung as she moved her body and the soft rope of her hair tossed from side to side.

Every morning I lay on the floor in the front parlour watching her door. The blind was pulled down to within an inch of the sash so that I could not be seen. When she came out on the doorstep my heart leaped. I ran to the hall, seized my books, and followed her. I kept her brown figure always in my eye and, when we came near the point at which our ways diverged, I quickened my pace and passed her. This happened morning after morning. I had never spoken to her, except for a few casual words, and yet her name was like a summons to all my foolish blood.

Her image accompanied me even in places the most hostile to romance. On Saturday evenings when my aunt went marketing I had to go to carry some of the parcels. We walked through the flaring streets, jostled by drunken men and bargaining women, amid the curses of labourers, the shrill litanies of shop-boys who stood on guard by the barrel of pigs' cheeks, the nasal chanting of street-singers, who sang a *come-all-you* about O'Donovan Rossa,° or a ballad about the troubles in our native land. These noises converged in a single sensation of life for me: I imagined that I bore my chalice safely through a throng of foes. Her name sprang to my lips at moments in strange prayers and praises which I myself did not understand. My eyes were often full of tears (I could not tell why) and at times a flood from my heart seemed to pour itself out into my bosom. I thought little of the future. I did not know whether I would ever speak to her or not or, if I spoke to her, how I could tell her of my confused adoration. But my body was like a harp and her words and gestures were like fingers running upon the wires.

One evening I went into the back drawing-room in which the priest had died. It was a dark rainy evening and there was no sound in the house. Through one of the broken panes I heard the rain impinge upon the earth, the fine incessant needles of water playing in the sodden beds. Some distant lamp or lighted window gleamed below me. I was thankful that I could see so little. All my senses seemed to desire to veil themselves and, feeling that I was about to slip from them, I pressed the palms of my hands together until they trembled, murmuring: *"O love! O love!"* many times.

At last she spoke to me. When she addressed the first words to me I was so confused that I did not know what to answer. She asked me was I

O'Donovan Rossa: Jeremiah O'Donovan (1831–1915) was nicknamed "Dynamite Rossa" for his militant pursuit of Irish independence.

going to *Araby*. I forgot whether I answered yes or no. It would be a splendid bazaar, she said she would love to go.

"And why can't you?" I asked.

While she spoke she turned a silver bracelet round and round her wrist. She could not go, she said, because there would be a retreat that week in her convent. Her brother and two other boys were fighting for their caps and I was alone at the railings. She held one of the spikes, bowing her head towards me. The light from the lamp opposite our door caught the white curve of her neck, lit up her hair that rested there and, falling, lit up the hand upon the railing. It fell over one side of her dress and caught the white border of a petticoat, just visible as she stood at ease.

"It's well for you," she said.

"If I go," I said, "I will bring you something."

What innumerable follies laid waste my waking and sleeping thoughts after that evening! I wished to annihilate the tedious intervening days. I chafed against the work of school. At night in my bedroom and by day in the classroom her image came between me and the page I strove to read. The syllables of the word *Araby* were called to me through the silence in which my soul luxuriated and cast an Eastern enchantment over me. I asked for leave to go to the bazaar on Saturday night. My aunt was surprised and hoped it was not some Freemason affair. I answered few questions in class. I watched my master's face pass from amiability to sternness; he hoped I was not beginning to idle. I could not call my wandering thoughts together. I had hardly any patience with the serious work of life which, now that it stood between me and my desire, seemed to me child's play, ugly monotonous child's play.

On Saturday morning I reminded my uncle that I wished to go to the bazaar in the evening. He was fussing at the hallstand, looking for the hat-brush, and answered me curtly:

"Yes, boy, I know."

As he was in the hall I could not go into the front parlour and lie at the window. I left the house in bad humour and walked slowly towards the school. The air was pitilessly raw and already my heart misgave me.

When I came home to dinner my uncle had not yet been home. Still it was early. I sat staring at the clock for some time and, when its ticking began to irritate me, I left the room. I mounted the staircase and gained the upper part of the house. The high cold empty gloomy rooms liberated me and I went from room to room singing. From the front window I saw my companions playing below in the street. Their cries reached me weakened and indistinct and, leaning my forehead against the cool glass, I looked over at the dark house where she lived. I may have stood there for an hour, seeing nothing but the brown-clad figure cast by my imagination, touched discreetly by the lamplight at the curved neck, at the hand upon the railings and at the border below the dress.

When I came downstairs again I found Mrs. Mercer sitting at the fire. She was an old garrulous woman, a pawnbroker's widow, who collected used stamps for some pious purpose. I had to endure the gossip of the tea-table. The meal was prolonged beyond an hour and still my uncle did not come. Mrs. Mercer stood up to go: she was sorry she couldn't wait any longer, but it was after eight o'clock and she did not like to be out late, as the night air was bad for her. When she had gone I began to walk up and down the room, clenching my fists. My aunt said:

"I'm afraid you may put off your bazaar for this night of Our Lord."

At nine o'clock I heard my uncle's latchkey in the halldoor. I heard him talking to himself and heard the hallstand rocking when it had received the weight of his overcoat. I could interpret these signs. When he was midway through his dinner I asked him to give me the money to go to the bazaar. He had forgotten.

"The people are in bed and after their first sleep now," he said.

I did not smile. My aunt said to him energetically:

"Can't you give him the money and let him go? You've kept him late enough as it is."

My uncle said he was very sorry he had forgotten. He said he believed in the old saying: "All work and no play makes Jack a dull boy." He asked me where I was going and, when I had told him a second time he asked me did I know *The Arab's Farewell to his Steed*.° When I left the kitchen he was about to recite the opening lines of the piece to my aunt.

I held a florin° tightly in my hand as I strode down Buckingham Street towards the station. The sight of the streets thronged with buyers and glaring with gas recalled to me the purpose of my journey. I took my seat in a third-class carriage of a deserted train. After an intolerable delay the train moved out of the station slowly. It crept onward among ruinous houses and over the twinkling river. At Westland Row Station a crowd of people pressed to the carriage doors; but the porters moved them back, saying that it was a special train for the bazaar. I remained alone in the bare carriage. In a few minutes the train drew up beside an improvised wooden platform. I passed out on to the road and saw by the lighted dial of a clock that it was ten minutes to ten. In front of me was a large building which displayed the magical name.

I could not find any sixpenny entrance and, fearing that the bazaar would be closed, I passed in quickly through a turnstile, handing a shil-

The Arab's Farewell to his Steed: A nostalgic poem by Caroline Norton (1808–1877).
Florin: A silver coin worth two shillings.

ling to a weary-looking man. I found myself in a big hall girdled at half its height by a gallery. Nearly all the stalls were closed and the greater part of the hall was in darkness. I recognised a silence like that which pervades a church after a service. I walked into the centre of the bazaar timidly. A few people were gathered about the stalls which were still open. Before a curtain, over which the words *Café Chantant* were written in coloured lamps, two men were counting money on a salver. I listened to the fall of the coins.

Remembering with difficulty why I had come I went over to one of the stalls and examined porcelain vases and flowered tea-sets. At the door of the stall a young lady was talking and laughing with two young gentlemen. I remarked their English accents and listened vaguely to their conversation.

"O, I never said such a thing!"

"O, but you did!"

"O, but I didn't!"

"Didn't she say that?"

"Yes. I heard her."

"O, there's a . . . fib!"

Observing me the young lady came over and asked me did I wish to buy anything. The tone of her voice was not encouraging; she seemed to have spoken to me out of a sense of duty. I looked humbly at the great jars that stood like eastern guards at either side of the dark entrance to the stall and murmured:

"No, thank you."

The young lady changed the position of one of the vases and went back to the two young men. They began to talk of the same subject. Once or twice the young lady glanced at me over her shoulder.

I lingered before her stall, though I knew my stay was useless, to make my interest in her wares seem the more real. Then I turned away slowly and walked down the middle of the bazaar. I allowed the two pennies to fall against the sixpence in my pocket. I heard a voice call from one end of the gallery that the light was out. The upper part of the hall was now completely dark.

Gazing up into the darkness I saw myself as a creature driven and derided by vanity; and my eyes burned with anguish and anger.

[1914]

FRANZ KAFKA [1883–1924]

The Metamorphosis

TRANSLATED BY ALEXIS WALKER, 2000

I

When Gregor Samsa awoke in his bed one morning from unquiet dreams, he found himself transformed into an enormous insect.° He lay on a back as hard as armor and saw, when he raised his head slightly, a jutting brown underbelly divided into arching segments. The bedcovers could barely cover it; they threatened to slide off altogether. His many legs, pitifully thin in comparison with the rest of his bulk, fluttered helplessly before his eyes.

"What has happened to me?" he thought. It wasn't a dream. His room—a decent enough room for a person, if slightly too small—lay quietly between the four familiar walls. Over the table on which was spread his unpacked collections of fabric samples—Samsa was a traveling salesman—hung the picture that he had recently cut out of an illustrated magazine and fit into an attractive gilt frame. The picture was of a woman clad in a fur hat and a fur stole; she sat upright and held out to the viewer a thick fur muff into which her entire forearm disappeared.

Gregor's gaze then directed itself to the window. The dreary weather—one could hear raindrops hit the metal awning over the window—made him quite melancholy. "What if I slept a bit longer and forgot all this foolishness," he thought. But that was altogether impossible, because he was used to sleeping on his right side, and his current condition made working himself into this position impossible. No matter how vigorously he swung himself over to the right, he immediately rolled again onto his back. He tried what seemed hundreds of times, closing his eyes

Translator's note: The closest English equivalents to the German word Kafka uses here (*Ungeziefer*) are "vermin" and "pest"—the German word denotes parasitic and otherwise objectionable creatures (including fleas, lice, rats, mice, etc.) and connotes uncleanness. "Insect" is a compromise: though at once more specific and less evocative than the original, it sidesteps problems of agreement ("vermin" being almost always plural in English) and of tone ("pest" being more colloquial than the German *Ungeziefer*).

in order to avoid having to see his wriggling legs. He finally gave up only when he began to feel in his side a small dull ache that he had never felt before.

"Oh, God," he thought, "what a strenuous profession I've chosen—traveling day in, day out! The demands of business are far greater on the road than they are at the home office, and I'm burdened with the annoyances of travel besides: the worry about train connections; the irregular, bad meals; a social life limited to passing acquaintances who never become real friends. To hell with it!" He felt an itch on his belly, and he shoved himself back against the bedpost so he could lift his head more easily. He found the spot that itched: it was covered with small white dots that he couldn't identify. He went to touch the spot with one of his legs but drew it back immediately, because the touch made him shudder.

He slid back into his former position. "This early rising," he thought, "can make you into a complete idiot. A man needs his sleep. Other travelers live like women in a harem. When, for example, I go back to my hotel during the course of the morning to write up orders, these gentlemen are just sitting down to breakfast. I should try that with the Director: I'd be fired on the spot. Who knows, though—that might be good for me. If it weren't for my parents, I would have given notice long ago: I would have confronted the Director and given him a piece of my mind. He would have fallen off his chair! It's incredible the way he has of sitting perched at his reading desk and speaking from on high to employees who, on top of everything, have to draw very near owing to his slight deafness. Oh well, I shouldn't give up hope altogether: once I have the money to pay off my parents' debt—it should only be another five or six years—I'll definitely do it. Then I'll make my big break. In the meantime, I have to get up—my train leaves at five."

And he looked over at the alarm clock that ticked on the bureau. "God in heaven!" he thought. It was six-thirty, and the hands of the clock went quietly on; it was even later than six-thirty—it was closer to six-forty-five. Shouldn't the alarm have gone off? He could see from the bed that it was correctly set for four o'clock; it must have gone off. But was it possible to sleep peacefully through that furniture-rattling noise? Of course, he hadn't actually slept peacefully, but he had no doubt for that reason slept more deeply. But what should he do now? The next train left at seven o'clock. In order to catch that one, he'd have to rush like a madman, and his samples weren't packed up yet. He hardly felt alert or energetic enough. And even if he caught the train, he wouldn't avoid the Director's wrath, because the office porter had been waiting at the five-o'clock train and would long since have reported his failure to appear. The porter was completely under the Director's thumb—he had neither a backbone nor brains. What if Gregor were to report himself sick? But that would be highly awkward and suspicious, because he had not been sick once in five years of service. The Director would certainly come with the insurance doctor. He would reproach his parents for their lazy son and dismiss all rejoinders by referring them to the doctor, who considered all people completely healthy, but work-averse. And would he be so wrong in this case? Gregor actually felt completely fine, despite a fatigue completely unwarranted after such a long sleep. He even had a powerful appetite.

As he thought all this over hurriedly, without being able to decide whether to leave his bed—the clock had just struck six-forty-five—there was a knock on the door near the head of his bed. "Gregor," he heard—it was his mother—"it's a quarter to seven. Weren't you going on a trip?" What a gentle voice! Gregor was terrified when he heard his answer. It was unmistakably in his old voice, but had mixed in, as if from down deep, an irrepressible, painful, squeaking noise, which allowed words to be heard clearly when first uttered, but as they resonated, distorted them to such an extent that they were difficult to understand. Gregor had wanted to answer in detail and explain everything, but in light of the circumstances he limited himself to saying: "Yes, yes, thanks, Mother, I'm getting up." The wooden door seemed to make the change in Gregor's voice imperceptible outside the room, because his mother was satisfied with his explanation and shuffled away. But through this brief exchange the other family members had become aware that Gregor was unexpectedly still at home, and his father was already knocking on one side door—lightly, but with his fist. "Gregor, Gregor," he called, "What's going on?" And after a short pause he urged again, with a deeper voice: "Gregor! Gregor!" At the other side door, his sister fretted softly: "Gregor? Are you ill? Do you need something?" To both sides, Gregor answered, "I'm just about ready to go," and he made an effort to ban anything conspicuous from his voice by the most painstaking enunciation and by inserting long pauses between individual words. His father returned to his breakfast, but his sister whispered: "Gregor, open up, I beg you." Gregor had no intention of opening the door, however—instead he gave thanks for his habitual precaution, born of much travel, of locking all doors during the night, even at home.

First he wanted to get up, quietly and undisturbed, get dressed, and above all eat breakfast—only then did he want to think over what came next, because he could see that he would come to no reasonable conclusions as long as he lay in bed. In the past he had often felt one mild pain or another while lying in bed, possibly from lying in an awkward position that proved to be sheer imagination once he got up. He was eager to see how today's fantasies would gradually resolve themselves. He didn't doubt in the least that the change in his voice was nothing more than the harbinger of a hearty cold, one of the occupational hazards of traveling salesmen.

Throwing off the covers was perfectly simple: he only needed to puff himself up a bit and they fell off on their own. But doing more than that was difficult, especially because he was so strangely broad. He would normally have used his arms and hands to get up; now, he had only the many little legs which were continuously moving in every direction and which he could not seem to control. If he meant to bend one, it would be the first one to stretch itself out, if he finally succeeded in enforcing his will with one leg, all the rest of them worked furiously, as if liberated, in extreme, painful agitation. "You can't just lie here in bed doing nothing," Gregor said to himself.

At first he intended to get out of the bed with the lower part of his body foremost, but this lower part, which he had moreover not yet seen and of which he could not form a proper mental image, proved too difficult to move. It went extremely slowly. When, nearly frantic, he finally gathered his strength and recklessly shoved himself forward, he misjudged the direction and violently struck the lower bed post. The burning pain he felt convinced him that the lower part of his body was at least at the moment the most sensitive part.

He afterwards attempted to get his upper body out of bed and carefully turned his head towards the edge of the bed. This he could do easily, and in spite of its bulk and weight, the mass of his body finally slowly followed the direction of his head. But when he held his head at last free of the bed, he became afraid to shift further in this direction, because if he ultimately let himself fall like that, it would be a miracle if his head were not injured. And now, of all times, he could not afford to lose consciousness; he would rather remain in bed.

After continued effort, however, he found himself lying exactly as before, and heaved a sigh. He saw his little legs struggling against one another even more furiously, if that were possible, and he saw no way of introducing calm and order to this anarchy. At this point he repeated to himself that he could not possibly lie in bed any longer and that it would be most sensible to risk everything, even if there were only the smallest hope of thereby freeing himself from bed. At the same time, however, he kept reminding himself that calm deliberation was always better than rash decision-making. All the while he tried hard to focus on the view from the window, but unfortunately there was little encouragement or cheer to gain from the sight of the morning fog, which shrouded even the opposite side of the narrow street. "Already seven o'clock," he said to himself with the latest striking of the alarm clock, "already seven o'clock and still such fog." And he lay quiet a short while, breathing shallowly, as if he thought complete stillness might restore things to their true and natural state.

After a bit, however, he said to himself, "Before it strikes seven-fifteen, I must without fail be completely out of bed. For one thing, someone from the company will have come by then to inquire after me, because the office opens before seven." And he concentrated his efforts toward swinging his entire body out of the bed all at the same time. If he let himself fall out of bed in this manner, his head, which he would raise sharply during the fall, would presumably remain uninjured. His back seemed to be hard; nothing would happen to it in the fall onto the carpet. His greatest source of misgiving was anticipation of the loud crash that would follow, which would probably arouse anxiety, if not terror, beyond the doors. That would have to be risked, however.

When, by rocking back and forth, Gregor moved halfway off of the bed—the new method was more a game than an exertion—it occurred to him how simple everything would be if someone would come help him. Two strong people—he thought of his father and the servant girl—would be more than adequate. They would only have to shove their arms under his domed back, pry him up out of bed, prop up his bulk by crouching low, and then help him complete the turn over onto the floor, where hopefully his little legs would gain some sense of purpose. Quite apart from the fact that the doors were locked, though, should he really call for help? In spite of his predicament he couldn't suppress a smile at the thought.

He was already so far along that he could hardly maintain his balance when he rocked forcefully. Very soon he would have to make a final decision, because in five minutes it would be seven-fifteen. Just then the front doorbell rang. "That's someone from the company," he said to himself and virtually froze, though his little legs only danced more hurriedly. Everything remained quiet for a moment. "They're not opening the door," Gregor said to himself, momentarily carried away by some absurd hope. But then, naturally, as always, the servant girl directed her firm step to the door and opened it. Gregor needed to hear only the first word of greeting from the visitor and he already knew who it was—the Deputy Director himself. Why was Gregor condemned to work at a company where the least infraction immediately attracted the greatest suspicion? Were all employees then without exception scoundrels; were there among them no loyal, devoted individuals who, when they had merely missed a few morning hours of service, would become so tormented by pangs of conscience that they would be frankly unable to leave their beds? Wouldn't it really have been enough to send an apprentice to inquire—if indeed this inquiry were necessary at all? Did the Deputy Director himself have to come, thereby showing the entire innocent family that the investigation of this suspicious situation could only be entrusted to the Deputy Director himself? And more as a result of the agitation into which this line of thought transported Gregor, than as a result of a proper decision, he swung himself with all his might out of the bed. There was a loud thump, but no actual crash. The fall was muffled a bit by the carpet, and his back was more elastic than Gregor had thought—these things accounted for the fairly inconspicuous dull thump. He had failed only to raise his head carefully enough and had struck it. He twisted it back and forth and rubbed it into the carpet out of anger and pain.

"Something happened inside there," said the Deputy Director in the room to the left. Gregor tried to imagine something similar to what had happened to him today happening to the Deputy Director; it really was possible, after all. But as if in cruel response to this question the Deputy Director took a few decisive steps in the next room, making his patent leather boots creak. From the room to the right Gregor's sister whispered to inform him: "Gregor, the Deputy Director is here." "I know," said Gregor to himself; but he did not dare to raise his voice loud enough for his sister to hear.

"Gregor," his father now said from the room to the left, "the Deputy Director has come and inquires as to why you did not leave with the early morning train. We don't know what we should say to him. Furthermore, he wants to speak to you directly. So please open the door. He will surely have the goodness to excuse the disorder of your room." "Good morning, Mr. Samsa," the Deputy Director called out at the same time in a friendly manner. "He is not well," his mother said to the Deputy Director, while his father still spoke at the door, "he is not well, believe me, sir. Why would Gregor otherwise miss a train? The boy has nothing in his head but the company. I almost worry that he never goes out at night; he has been in the city eight days now, but he was at home every night. He sits with us at the table and quietly reads the newspaper or studies train schedules. Busying himself with woodworking is as far as he goes in the way of amusement. In the course of two, three evenings, for example, he cut himself a small frame; you would be astounded at how pretty it is. It's hanging in his room; you will see it right away, when Gregor opens up. I am happy, in any case, that you're here, Deputy Director. We could not have persuaded Gregor to open the door alone; he is so stubborn; and there's certainly something wrong with him, although he denied it this morning." "I'm coming right away," said Gregor slowly and carefully, while not moving at all, in order not to miss a word of the conversation. "Otherwise, dear woman, I can't explain it myself, either," said the Deputy Director. "Hopefully it's nothing serious. Though I must say, that we businessmen—either fortunately or unfortunately, as you will—must often ignore a trivial indisposition in the interest of business." "So can the Deputy Director come in to see you?" asked his impatient father, knocking again at the door. "No," said Gregor. In the room to the left there arose an awkward silence; in the room to the right, his sister began sobbing.

Why didn't his sister join the others? She had most likely just now arisen from bed and had not yet begun to get dressed. And why was she crying? Because he did not stand up and let the Deputy Director in; because he was in danger of losing his position and because the Director would then persecute his parents with the old demands? Those were unnecessary worries, for the time being. Gregor was still here and did not in the least contemplate leaving his family. At the moment he was lying on the carpet, and no one who was aware of his condition would seriously request that he let the Deputy Director in. Gregor could not possibly be dismissed just for this minor breach of politeness; he could easily find a suitable excuse later. And it seemed to Gregor far more reasonable to leave him in peace now, instead of disturbing him with tears and entreaties. But it was the uncertainty of it all that distressed the others and so excused their behavior.

"Mr. Samsa," the Deputy Director now called in a raised voice, "what's the matter? You barricade yourself there in your room, answer merely with yes and no, burden your parents with profound, unnecessary worries and—this only mentioned incidentally—neglect your business responsibilities in an unheard-of way. I speak here in the name of your parents and your Director and earnestly request of you an immediate, clear explanation. I am amazed; I am amazed. I thought I knew you as a quiet, reasonable person, and now you suddenly begin to exhibit extraordinary capriciousness. The Director told me early this morning of a possible explanation for your dereliction—it related to the cash account recently entrusted to you—but I actually almost gave him my word of honor that this explanation could not be accurate. Now, however, I see your incomprehensible stubbornness here, and I lose any desire to vouch for you in the least. And your position is not the most secure. I originally had the intention of saying all of this just between the two of us, but since you force me to waste my time here needlessly, I don't know why your parents should not also hear it. Your performance recently has been very unsatisfying. It is not the time of the year, of course, to do extraordinary business, we recognize that; but there is no time of year in which to do *no* business, Mr. Samsa—there cannot be."

"But, sir," called out Gregor, beside himself, forgetting everything else in his agitation, "I'll open up immediately, this instant. A mild indisposition—an attack of dizziness—has kept me from getting up. I'm still lying in bed. I'm completely recovered now, though. I'm climbing out of bed right now. Just one moment of patience! I thought things were not quite back to normal yet. But I'm already well again. How it can sud-denly come over a person! I was fine yesterday evening, my parents know that, or perhaps I should say that yesterday evening I had a slight premo-nition of it. It must have been easy to see in me. Why didn't I report it to the office yesterday! But one always thinks that one can ride out illness without having to stay home. Sir! Spare my parents! There is no basis for all the reproaches you've made against me; no one said anything about them to me before now. Perhaps you haven't seen the latest orders that I sent in. In any case, I will be starting my trip on the eight o'clock train. These few hours of rest have strengthened me. Don't let me hold you up, though, sir; I'll soon be in the office myself, and please have the goodness to say so, and to send my greetings to the Director."

And while Gregor hurriedly blurted all this out, hardly knowing what he said, he moved effortlessly closer to the chest, thanks to the practice he had had in bed, and attempted to raise himself against it to an upright position. He actually wanted to open the door, actually wanted to let them see him and to speak with the Deputy Director. He was eager to know what they all would say to him when they finally saw him, after so much urging. Would they be afraid? If so, Gregor would be absolved of responsibility and could relax. If they took it all in stride, however, then, too, he would have no cause for worry, and he really could be at the train station at eight, if he hurried. At first he simply slid a few times down the side of the slippery chest; finally, however, he gave himself one last swing and stood upright. He ignored the pain in his lower body, despite the fact that it burned. Now he let himself fall against the back of a nearby chair and held tight to its sides with his legs. This helped him regain his self-control, and he stayed quiet, so that he could hear the Deputy Director speak.

"Did you understand one word?" the Deputy Director asked his par-ents. "Surely he's making fun of us?" "For God's sake," cried his mother in the midst of tears, "he might be seriously ill, and we're all plaguing him. Grete! Grete!" she then screamed. "Mother?" called his sister from the other side. They were communicating through Gregor's room. "You must go fetch the doctor this minute. Gregor is ill. Quickly, to the doctor. Did you hear Gregor speak just now?" "That was the voice of an animal," said the Deputy Director, noticeably quiet, by contrast with the scream-ing of his mother. "Anna! Anna!" called his father towards the kitchen, clapping his hands, "Get a locksmith immediately!" And the two girls ran, their skirts rustling, through the foyer—how had his sister gotten dressed so quickly?—and flung the apartment door open. There was no noise of the door slamming; they had probably left it open, as was usual in apartments where some great misfortune had occurred.

Gregor had become much calmer, however. It was true that they didn't understand his speech, but it sounded clear enough to him, clearer than previously, perhaps because his ear had adjusted to it. But they did still believe that something was wrong with him, and they were prepared to help him. He was pleased by the confidence and certainty with which the first arrangements had been made. He felt drawn once again into the circle of humanity and expected great things from both the doctor and the locksmith, without really making a distinction between them. In order to develop the clearest possible voice for the decisive discussions to come, he coughed a bit, although he tried to do this in a muted fashion, because this, too, might sound very different from a human cough—he no longer trusted himself to judge. It had now fallen completely silent in the next room. His parents might have been sitting at the table, whispering with the Deputy Director, or perhaps they were all pressed against the door, listening.

Using the chair, Gregor slowly shoved himself forward, and then let go, throwing himself against the door, and holding himself upright against it. The balls of his feet had some sticky substance on them. He took a moment to recover from the exertion. Then he applied himself to turning the key in the lock. Unfortunately, it seemed as if he had no real teeth—what then could he grip the key with?—but his jaws, on the other hand, were powerful. With their help he started to turn the key. He paid no attention to the fact that he obviously did some harm to himself in the process—a brown discharge came out from his mouth, flowing over the key and dripping on the floor. "Listen now," said the Deputy Director in the next room, "he's turning the key." That encouraged Gregor greatly, but all of them should have cheered him on, his father and mother, too: "Come on, Gregor," they should have called, "keep at it, keep working the lock!" And imagining that all his efforts were being watched with rapt attention, he recklessly bit down on the key with all his might. He danced around the lock, following the key as it turned; holding himself upright entirely with his mouth, he either pulled up on the key or forced it down with the full weight of his body, as necessary. The crisp click of the lock finally snapping back elated him. Breathing a sigh of relief he said to himself, "I didn't even need the locksmith," and he laid his head on the door handle, in order to open the door.

Because he had to open the door in this way, he was not yet visible even when it was opened wide. If he didn't want to fall flat on his back just before his entrance into the next room, he would first have to slowly make his way around the open panel of the double door. He was still busy with this difficult maneuver and had not yet had a moment to think of the others, when he heard the Deputy Director force out a loud "Oh!" It sounded like a gust of wind. Now he could also see the Deputy, who was nearest the door—he pressed his hand to his open mouth and slowly shrank back, as if an invisible, irresistible force drove him. His mother—who stood, despite the presence of the Deputy Director, with her hair still loose, and sticking up in parts from her night's sleep—first looked at his father with her hands clasped; then she walked two steps toward Gregor and sank to the ground in the midst of her billowing skirts, her face completely hidden, sunk upon her breast. His father balled his fist with a fierce expression, as if he wanted to knock Gregor back into his room; then he looked uncertainly around the living room, covered his eyes with his hands, and sobbed so that his powerful chest shook.

Gregor had not yet entered the outer room; instead, he leaned from within against the door panel that was still fastened, so that only half of his body and his head, craned to one side in order to see them, were visible. It had become much brighter outside in the meantime: one could clearly see a section of the endless, gray-black building—it was a hospital—that stood across the street, its severe, uniform windows breaking up its facade. The rain still fell, but only in large, singly visible and singly plummeting drops. The table teemed with breakfast dishes; his father considered breakfast the most important meal of the day, and he protracted it for hours reading various periodicals. On the wall just opposite hung a photograph of Gregor from his military days, which showed him dressed as a lieutenant, with a carefree smile, his hand on his dagger, his bearing and his uniform commanding respect. The door to the foyer was open, and because the door to the apartment was open as well, one could see the outer wall and the top of the staircase leading downwards.

"Now," said Gregor—and he was well aware that he was the only one remaining calm—"I will just get dressed, pack my samples up, and be off. Will you all allow me to go? Deputy Director, you see that I'm not obstinate and that I want to work. Traveling is demanding, but I couldn't live without it. Where do you intend to go now, Deputy Director? To the office? Yes? Will you report everything accurately? A person might be unable to work for a time, but it is precisely then that one must consider his past accomplishments and keep in mind that once the hindrance is past, he will certainly work even harder and more efficiently. I owe a great deal to the Director—you know that only too well. On the other hand, I have the care of my parents and sister. I'm in a fix, but I'll work my way out again. But please don't make it more difficult for me than it already is. Take my part in the office! I know the traveling salesmen aren't popular. People think we earn a huge amount of money and lead grand lives. People just don't have any particular reason to think this prejudice through carefully. You, however, Deputy Director, you have a better perspective on how things work than most of the staff—I might say, confidentially, a better perspective than even the Director himself, who, in his capacity as owner, can easily be misled in his judgment about an employee. You know very well that the traveling salesman, because he is away from the office the better part of the year, easily falls victim to gossip, to chance misfortune, and groundless complaints. It's impossible for him to defend himself against these complaints, as he ordinarily learns nothing of them; it's only when he comes home at the end of a trip completely exhausted that he feels the terrible consequences, whose origins he can't divine, in his very body. Deputy Director, don't leave without saying one word that shows me that you agree with me at least in part!"

But the Deputy Director had turned away at Gregor's first words, and was staring back at Gregor over one twitching shoulder, his mouth agape. During Gregor's speech he had not stood still for a moment, but, never taking his eyes off of Gregor, moved steadily but surreptitiously towards the door, as if there were some secret prohibition against leaving the room. He had already reached the foyer, and judging by the sudden movement with which he pulled his foot out of the room at his last step, one would have thought his sole was on fire. Once in the foyer, he stretched his hand out towards the staircase as if divine deliverance awaited him there.

Gregor realized that the Deputy Director could under no circumstances be allowed to leave this way, if his position at the company were not to be endangered. His parents didn't understand this as well as he did. They had over the years persuaded themselves that he was guaranteed permanent employment in the company, and besides, they had so much to do in dealing with their own distress at the moment, that their foresight had vanished. But Gregor had this foresight. The Deputy Director must be detained, calmed, persuaded, and finally won over—the future of Gregor and his family depended on it. If only his sister were here! She was clever: she was already crying when Gregor was still calmly lying on his back. And the Deputy Director, that ladies' man, would surely have let her sway him: she would have closed the apartment door and talked him out of his fear in the foyer. But his sister was not there, so Gregor would have to handle it himself. And without thinking about the fact that he had no idea yet how well he could move, without thinking that his speech was possibly—well, very probably—incomprehensible, he let go of the door panel, forcing himself through the opening, and headed for the Deputy Director, who was already at the landing in the hall and hugging himself in a comical manner. With a small cry, scrambling in vain for something to hold on to, Gregor immediately fell down onto his many little legs. This had hardly happened, when for the first time that morning he felt a sense of physical well-being. His little legs had solid ground beneath them; they obeyed him completely, as he noted to his delight. They even strove to carry him where he wanted to go.

Suddenly, he believed that the ultimate relief of all his suffering was at hand. But at that moment, as he lay on the floor trembling with suppressed energy, close to his mother and directly opposite her, she sprang up—she who had seemed so lost in thought—with her arms outstretched, her fingers splayed, and cried out: "Help, for God's sake, help!" She kept her head turned towards him, as if she wanted to be able to see him better, but, following a contradictory impulse, she ran heedlessly backwards, forgetting that the table full of dishes lay behind her. She quickly sat down when she reached it, as if absent-mindedly, seeming not to notice that next to her the coffeepot had been knocked over and coffee was streaming freely out onto the carpet.

"Mother, Mother," Gregor said softly, and looked up at her. The Deputy Director vanished from his mind momentarily, and he couldn't stop himself from snapping his jaws at the empty air several times at the sight of the flowing coffee. His mother began screaming again over this, fled from the table, and fell into the arms of his father, who was hurrying towards her. But Gregor had no time then for his parents. The Deputy Director was already on the stairs. His chin on the railing, he looked back one last time. Gregor took a running start, in order to have the best chance of catching up to him. The Deputy Director must have sensed something, as he sprang down several steps and then disappeared. "Ahh!" he screamed; it echoed throughout the entire stairwell.

Unfortunately, the flight of the Deputy Director seemed to have completely unhinged his father, who up until then had been relatively self-controlled. Instead of running after the Deputy Director or at least not restraining Gregor from pursuing him, with his right hand he grabbed the walking stick that the Deputy Director had left behind on an armchair together with his hat and coat; with his left hand he picked up a large newspaper from the table; then, stamping his feet, he began to drive Gregor back into his room by swatting at him with the stick and the newspaper. None of Gregor's pleas helped—none of his pleas were understood. The more submissively he bowed his head, the more vigorously his father stamped his feet. Across the room, despite the cool weather, his mother had thrown open a window and, leaning far out of the window, pressed her face into her hands. Between the street and the stairwell there arose a strong cross-draft: the window curtains flew up; the newspapers on the table rustled, and a few pages fluttered to the floor. His father drove him back mercilessly, spitting out hissing noises like a wild beast. Gregor, however, still was unpracticed in moving backwards, so he went very slowly. If he had only been allowed time to turn around, he would have gone immediately back into his room, but he was afraid of making his father impatient. At every moment the stick in his father's hand threatened to deal him a fatal blow to his back or head.

Finally, however, Gregor found he had no choice, as he noted with terror that he seemed unable to keep going in the right direction when he moved backwards. He therefore began, with frequent side-glances at his father, to turn around as quickly as he could, which was actually very slowly. His father might have understood his good intentions, because he did not disturb him while he was doing this; in fact, he actually directed him here and there from a distance with the point of his stick. If only there weren't this unbearable hissing from his father! It unnerved Gregor completely. He was already almost completely turned around when, listening to his hissing, he made a mistake and turned a bit in the wrong direction. When he was finally, fortunately, headfirst at the opening of the door, it appeared that his body was too wide to go through without further ado. In his present state of mind it was naturally far from occurring to his father to open the other door panel in order to make a wide enough passageway for Gregor. He was obsessed merely with getting Gregor into his room as quickly as possible. He would never have allowed the preparations necessary for Gregor to raise himself up and possibly go through the door that way. Instead, making a great deal of noise, he drove Gregor forward as if there were no obstacle before him. The noise coming from behind Gregor didn't sound any longer like the voice of his father. It was clearly no laughing matter, so Gregor forced himself—happen what would—through the door. One side of his body was hoisted upwards. He lay crookedly in the doorway. One of his flanks was rubbed raw, and on the white door ugly smears remained behind. He was soon stuck fast, and couldn't move at all anymore. His little legs hung twitching on one side, and those on the other side were pressed painfully against the floor. Then his father liberated him with a powerful shove from behind, and he flew, bleeding heavily, a long way into his room. The door was slammed shut with the stick, and then it was finally quiet.

II

It was already twilight when Gregor awoke from a deep, dreamless sleep. He would not have arisen much later even without having been disturbed, for he felt well rested and no longer sleepy, but it seemed to him that he had been awakened by the sounds of a fleeting footstep and of the door to the foyer carefully being shut. The glare from the electric street lamp outside lay palely here and there on the ceiling of his room and on the upper surfaces of the furniture, but down by Gregor it was dark. He shoved himself slowly towards the door, awkwardly groping with the feelers he had just then come to appreciate, in order to see what had happened there. His left side seemed to be a single, long, unpleasantly taut scar, and he had to positively limp on his row of legs. One leg had been seriously injured during the events of the morning: it dragged limply behind him.

It was only when he was at the door that he realized what had actually lured him there: it was the smell of something edible. Standing there was a basin filled with fresh milk, swimming with small pieces of white bread. He could almost have laughed for joy, for he was even hungrier than he had been that morning. He immediately dunked his head in the milk nearly up to his eyes. But he soon pulled back, disappointed. It wasn't only that his tender left side made it hard for him to eat—for it seemed he was able to eat only if his entire panting body cooperated—it was rather that the milk, which had always been his favorite drink, and which his sister certainly placed here for that reason, didn't taste good to him at all. He turned away from the basin with something like revulsion and crept back into the middle of the room.

The gas lamps had been turned on in the living room, as Gregor saw through the crack in the door. Whereas ordinarily at this hour his father would read the afternoon paper out loud to his mother and sometimes to his sister, now there wasn't a sound. Perhaps the reading, which his sister had frequently told him and wrote him about, had lately dropped out of their routine. It was completely quiet, though the apartment was certainly not empty. "What a quiet life the family leads," Gregor said to himself and felt great pride, as he stared into the darkness before him, that he had been able to provide his parents and his sister with such a life, in such a nice apartment. But what if terror now drove away all quiet, all prosperity, all contentment? Rather than surrender to such thoughts, Gregor preferred to move about, so he crawled back and forth in the room.

Once during the long evening one of the side doors and later the other was opened a crack and then hastily shut again. Someone had probably needed to come in, but had then thought better of it. Gregor now stopped directly in front of the door to the living room, determined somehow to get the hesitant visitor to come in, or at least to find out who it was, but the doors were not opened again and Gregor waited in vain. Early on, when the doors were locked, everyone had wanted to come in; now, when he had unlocked one door and the others had clearly been unlocked during the day, no one came, and the keys had been moved to the outside.

It was late at night before the light in the living room was turned out, and it was now clear that his parents and sister had been awake until then, for all three could clearly be heard departing on tiptoes. Now surely no one would come to see Gregor until morning; he therefore had quite a while in which to consider undisturbed how he should newly arrange his life. But he was uneasy lying flat on the ground in the high-ceilinged open room. He did not know why this should be, for he had lived in the room for five years already. Half unconsciously, and not without some shame, he scurried under the sofa where, despite the fact that his back was a bit crushed and he could no longer lift his head, he immediately felt more comfortable, regretting only that his body was too broad to fit completely underneath.

He remained there the entire night. He spent part of it in a light sleep, out of which hunger kept jolting him awake, and part of it awake, consumed by worries and by vague hopes that all led to the same conclusion: that for the time being he should keep calm and, by exercising patience and the greatest consideration for his family, try to make bearable the unpleasantness that he would in his present condition inevitably cause them.

Early the next morning—it was nearly still night—Gregor had a chance to test the firmness of his resolve, for his sister, already half-dressed, opened the door leading from the foyer and looked tensely inside. She couldn't find him right away, but when she noticed him under the sofa—God, he had to be someplace, he couldn't have just flown away—she was so shocked that without being able to stop herself, she slammed the door shut again. But as if she regretted her behavior, she opened the door again immediately, and came inside on tiptoe, as if she were in the presence of someone severely ill, or even a complete stranger. Gregor shoved his head forward just to the edge of the sofa and watched her. He wondered whether she would notice that he had left the milk standing, though not from lack of hunger, and whether she would bring him some other food that suited him better. If she didn't do it on her own, he would rather starve than make her aware of it, although he felt a strong urge to shoot out from beneath the sofa, throw himself at her feet, and beg her for something good to eat. But his sister, with some amazement, right away noticed the still full basin: only a bit of milk had been spilled around its edges. She picked it up immediately, though with a rag, not with her bare hands, and took it away. Gregor was extremely curious to see what she would bring as a replacement and thought a great deal about it. He could never have guessed, however, what his sister in her goodness actually did. In order to test his preferences, she brought him an entire assortment of foods spread out on an old newspaper. There were old, half-rotten vegetables; bones from last night's meal, covered with congealed white sauce; a few raisins and almonds; a cheese that Gregor had declared inedible two days before; a piece of dry bread, a piece of bread smeared with butter, and a piece with butter and salt. Beside this she placed the basin that seemed now to be designated permanently for Gregor, which she had filled with water. And out of tact, because she knew Gregor would not eat in front of her, she departed hastily, even going so far as to turn the key in the lock, just so that Gregor would know that he could make himself as comfortable as he wanted. Gregor's legs quivered, now that the meal lay waiting. His wounds must moreover have completely healed. He felt no impairment now, and was astonished at this, thinking of how he had cut himself very slightly with a knife more than a month ago, and how the wound had still hurt him considerably the day before yesterday. "Am I less sensitive than before?" he wondered, and sucked greedily at the cheese, to which he had found himself urgently drawn, before everything else. In rapid succession, amidst tears of joy, he devoured the cheese, the vegetables, and the sauce. He didn't like the taste of the fresh foods, however—he couldn't even bear their smell, and dragged the foods that he wanted to eat a bit farther away. He had long since finished everything and lay lazily in the same spot when his sister slowly turned the key in the lock, as a sign that he should withdraw. That jolted him awake immediately, though he was almost dozing, and he hurried back under the sofa. But it took great self-control for him to remain under the sofa even for the brief time that his sister was in the room, for his body had swelled a bit with the ample meal, and he could hardly breathe in the narrow space. Half-suffocating, he looked out with slightly bulging eyes as his sister, who noticed nothing, swept up with a broom not just the remainder of the food Gregor had eaten, but also the food that he had not even touched, as if this were no longer useable. She put it all in a container that she closed with a wooden lid, and then carried everything out. She had hardly turned around when Gregor pulled himself out from under the sofa and exhaled.

In this way Gregor now received his daily meals: the first in the morning, while his parents and the servant girl still slept, and the second after the common midday meal, for his parents slept a bit afterwards, and his sister sent the serving girl away on one errand or another. It was not that the others wanted him to starve, but experiencing his meals at secondhand might have been all they could bear; or perhaps his sister simply wanted to spare them even his minor source of sorrow, since they were already suffering enough.

With what kinds of excuses they had managed to get the doctor and the locksmith out of the apartment the first morning, Gregor didn't manage to find out. Because no one could understand him, it didn't occur to anyone—not even to his sister—that he could understand them, so he had to content himself, when his sister was in his room, with listening to her occasional sighs and appeals to the saints. It was only later, when she had gotten used to things a bit—getting used to them completely was out of the question, of course—that Gregor sometimes seized on a remark that was meant in a friendly way or that could be taken that way.

"Today he liked it," she said, if he had made a real dent in the meal, while in the contrary case, which occurred ever more frequently of late, she used to say almost sadly: "Everything untouched again."

Though Gregor could not learn any news directly, he overheard some from the rooms next door. The moment he heard voices, he immediately ran to the door and pressed his entire body up against it. Especially in the early days, there was no conversation that did not somehow, if only indirectly, relate to him. For two days there were consultations at every meal about what they should do; between meals, too, they discussed the same thing. There were always at least two family members at home, because no one wanted to remain home alone, and they couldn't under any circumstances all leave the apartment at the same time. On the very first day the girl who cooked for them had begged his mother on bended knee—it wasn't exactly clear what and how much she knew of what had happened—to dismiss her. As she departed fifteen minutes later, she tearfully thanked them for her dismissal, as if for the greatest favor that had ever been done her, and swore a terrible oath, without anyone having asked her to do so, not to betray the least of what she knew to anyone.

Now his sister had to do the cooking, together with his mother. This didn't take much effort, however, because they ate practically nothing. Gregor heard them again and again urge each other to eat and receive no other answer than "Thanks, I've had enough," or something similar. It seemed they didn't drink anything, either. His sister often asked his father if he would like a beer, cheerfully offering to get it herself. When his father said nothing, she offered to send the porter for it, in case he didn't want to trouble her. When his father finally uttered a firm "No," the subject was dropped.

In the course of the first few days his father explained their entire financial situation and their prospects to his mother and to his sister. Now and then he stood up from the table and took various documents and notebooks out of the small safe that he had rescued from the bankruptcy of his business five years before. He could be heard opening the complicated lock and closing it again after removing what he sought. His father's explanations contained the first heartening news that Gregor had heard since his imprisonment. He had been under the impression that his father had absolutely nothing left over from his business. At least, he had said nothing to the contrary, and Gregor had certainly never asked him about it. Gregor's concern at the time of the bankruptcy had been to arrange everything so that the family could forget as soon as possible the financial misfortune that had brought them to a state of complete despair. And so he had begun to work with pronounced fervor. Practically overnight he was elevated from a minor clerk into a traveling salesman, which naturally gave him completely different financial prospects. His successes at work translated directly into cash that he could lay on the table at home before his astonished and pleased family. Those had been fine times, but they had never recurred, at least not with the same warm feelings, although Gregor later earned so much money that he was in a position to support the entire family, and he did so. They simply got used to it—the family, as well as Gregor. They gratefully accepted his money, and he gladly offered it, but that special warmth did not reappear. Only his sister remained close to Gregor. Because she loved music very much, unlike Gregor, and could play the violin movingly, he secretly planned to send her to the conservatory next year, despite the great cost, which would have to be made up somehow. The conservatory came up often in conversations with his sister during Gregor's brief stays in the city, but only as a beautiful dream whose realization was unthinkable. His parents didn't even like to hear them utter those innocent musings. But Gregor had given it a good deal of thought and intended to announce his decision with due ceremony on Christmas Eve.

These thoughts, completely futile in his present situation, went through his head while he clung to the door and listened. Sometimes, from sheer exhaustion, he could listen no more and would let his head fall against the door, but then immediately catch himself, for even the faint noise that he made in doing so was heard next door and caused them all to fall silent. "What's he doing now?" said his father after a pause, obviously turned towards the door. Only then was the interrupted conversation gradually taken up again.

Gregor now learned—for his father tended to repeat himself often in his explanations, partly because he had not concerned himself with these matters for a long while, and partly, too, because his mother didn't immediately understand everything the first time—that despite all their misfortunes, a certain sum, though a very small one, was left over from the old days. The untouched interest on the sum had moreover in the meantime allowed it to grow a bit. Besides this, the money that Gregor had brought home every month—he had only kept a few florins for himself—had not been completely exhausted and had accumulated into a small amount of capital. Gregor, behind the door, nodded eagerly, overjoyed at this unexpected foresight and thriftiness. It occurred to him that he might have used that extra money to further pay down the debt his father owed the Director, bringing closer the day that he could quit his job, but the way his father had arranged things was no doubt better.

The sum that had been saved was not, however, large enough to allow his family to live off of the interest. It would have been enough to support them for a year, or at most two years, but no longer. The sum really shouldn't be touched: it should be set aside for emergencies. To live, money would have to be earned. His father was a healthy but old man, who had not worked now for five years and couldn't in any case take on too much. During these five years, which had been the first free time of his hardworking but unsuccessful life, he had put on a great deal of weight and had become downright sluggish. But was his elderly mother supposed to earn money now—his mother, who suffered from asthma, for whom even a stroll through the apartment was considerable exertion, and who spent every other day on the sofa by the open window, gasping for breath? Or his sister, who at seventeen was still a child, and whose lifestyle up to that point had consisted of dressing herself neatly, sleeping late, helping out in the household, taking part in a few modest pleasures, and above all playing the violin? Whenever the conversation turned towards the necessity of earning money, Gregor left the door and threw himself on the leather sofa that stood nearby, for he burned with shame and sorrow.

Often he lay there the long night through, though he was unable to sleep for a moment and just scratched for hours at the leather. Or he would go to great pains to shove an armchair to the window, then crawl up to the windowsill and, bolstered by the armchair, lean against the window. He did so only in some kind of nostalgia for the feeling of freedom he had previously found in looking out the window, for the fact was that every day he saw things that were even a short distance away less and less clearly. He could no longer see the hospital that lay across the way, whose all too massive prospect he had earlier cursed. If he had not known very well that he lived in the quiet, but distinctly urban Charlotte Street, he could have believed that he looked out of his window into a desert in which the gray sky and the gray earth merged indistinguishably. His alert sister only had to see the armchair standing by the window twice before she began to shove the chair precisely back to the spot by the window after she straightened up the room. She even left the inner casement open from then on.

If Gregor had been able to speak to his sister and thank her for everything she had to do for him, he would have been able to bear her assistance more easily; as it was, however, it caused him some pain. His sister tried to hide the awkwardness of the whole thing as much as possible, and the longer it went on, the better she succeeded, but Gregor felt everything more acutely as time went on. Even her entrance was terrible for him. She had hardly entered, when, without even taking the time to shut the doors, though she otherwise took such pains to spare everyone the sight of Gregor's room, she ran to the window and hastily flung it open, as if she were suffocating. Then she remained for a time by the window, cold as it still was, and breathed deeply. With this running and commotion she alarmed Gregor twice daily. He trembled under the sofa the entire time and yet he knew very well that she would gladly have spared him, if only it had been possible to stay in a room where Gregor was with the windows closed.

Once—one month had already passed since Gregor's transformation, and there was no longer any reason for his sister to be astonished by his appearance—she came a bit earlier than usual and encountered Gregor as he was staring out the window, motionless and perfectly positioned to frighten someone. Gregor would not have been surprised if she had not come in, since his position hindered her from immediately opening the window, but she not only refrained from coming in, she actually turned around and locked the door. A stranger would have thought that Gregor had lain in wait for her and tried to bite her. Gregor naturally hid himself immediately under the sofa, but he had to wait until midday for her return, and she seemed then more agitated than usual. He realized from this that his appearance was still unbearable to her and that it would remain so—that she had to steel herself to keep from running at the sight of even the small portion of his body that jutted out from beneath the sofa. In order to spare her the sight, one day he dragged a sheet onto the sofa—it took him four hours to do so—and arranged it in such a way that he was completely covered. His sister could not have seen him even if she bent down. If the sheet had not been necessary, in her opinion, she could have removed it, for it obviously couldn't be pleasant for Gregor to block himself off so completely. But she left the sheet where it was, and Gregor thought he even noticed a grateful glance when he once carefully lifted the sheet with his head in order to see how his sister liked the new arrangement.

In the first two weeks his parents could not bring themselves to come in to see him, and he often heard them praise his sister's current industry, whereas they had previously complained a great deal about her, as she had then seemed to them a rather idle girl. In those early days, both his father and his mother often waited in front of Gregor's room while his sister straightened up, and as soon as she came out, she had to tell them precisely what it looked like in the room, what Gregor had eaten, how he had behaved, and whether there were perhaps any slight improvement in his condition. His mother also wanted to visit Gregor early on, but his father and sister dissuaded her with sound reasons to which Gregor listened very attentively, and which he completely supported. Later, however, she had to be restrained with force. When she cried out, "Let me in to see Gregor; he's my poor son! Don't you understand that I must go to him?" Gregor thought that it might be good if his mother did come in—not every day, of course, but perhaps once a week. After all, she knew how to do things much better than his sister, who, despite her courage, was still only a child, and who likely took on such a heavy burden only out of childish thoughtlessness.

Gregor's wish to see his mother was soon fulfilled. During the day, for his parents' sake, Gregor did not want to show himself at the window, but he did not have much room to crawl in the few square meters of floor space. It was hard enough for him to bear lying quietly during the night, and eating soon gave him not the least bit of pleasure, so in order to distract himself, he had adopted the habit of crawling across the walls and ceiling. He especially liked hanging upside down from the ceiling. It was completely different from lying on the floor: he could breathe more freely; his entire body swayed gently; and in the nearly happy distraction in which he found himself above, it sometimes happened that he unexpectedly let himself fall and crashed to the ground. But these days he had better control of his body, so he did not hurt himself even in a great fall. His sister immediately noticed the new amusement that Gregor had found for himself—he left a trace of stickiness behind him here and there while crawling—and so she got it in her head to allow him to crawl to his utmost by removing the furniture that hindered it, especially the chest of drawers and desk. She was not capable of doing this herself, however. She didn't dare ask her father for help. The servant girl would certainly not help her: this roughly sixteen-year-old girl had stuck it out quite bravely since the dismissal of the former cook, but she had asked for the privilege of keeping the kitchen door always locked and only having to open it when specifically asked. So his sister had no choice but to enlist her mother one time when her father was absent. With cries of great joy his mother approached, but fell silent at the door of Gregor's room. His sister checked first, of course, to see that the room was in order; only then did she let her mother enter. In great haste, Gregor pulled the sheet lower and gathered more material around him. It looked like a sheet had merely been carelessly thrown over the sofa. Gregor also refrained from spying out from under the sheet. He deprived himself of the sight of his mother and took his pleasure entirely from the fact that she had come. "Come on, you can't see him," said his sister, and she apparently led her mother in by the hand. Gregor then heard the two frail women shove the heavy old chest of drawers from its place. His sister reserved the greatest part of the labor for herself, ignoring the warnings of her mother, who feared that she would overexert herself. It took a very long time. After fifteen minutes of work, his mother said that they should just leave the chest where it was, first, because it was too heavy—they wouldn't be finished before his father returned, and so would end up leaving the chest in the middle of the room, where it would block Gregor at every turn—and second, because it was not at all certain that they were doing Gregor a favor by removing the furniture. It seemed to her rather the opposite: the sight of the empty wall oppressed her heart. Why should Gregor not feel the same way? He had been used to the room's furniture for so long, that he would surely feel lost in an empty room. "And isn't it so," concluded his mother very softly—almost whispering, as if she wanted to keep Gregor, of whose precise whereabouts she wasn't certain, from hearing even the sound of her voice, for she was convinced that he could not understand the words—"isn't it so, that by removing the furniture we seem to be saying that we give up all hope of his recovery, and abandon him absolutely? I think it would be best if we left the room in exactly the same condition it was in before, so that when Gregor returns to us, he'll find everything unchanged, and so more easily forget what's happened in the meantime."

In listening to his mother's words, Gregor realized that the lack of any direct human communication over the course of the past two months, together with the monotonous life he led in the midst of the family, must have deranged his mind; otherwise he couldn't explain why he had earnestly desired that his room be emptied. Did he really want to let them transform the warm room, comfortably outfitted with inherited furnishings, into a cave? Granted, he would be able to crawl undisturbed in all directions, but he would at the same time forget, quickly and completely, his human past. He was already close to forgetting it, but his mother's voice, so long unheard, had roused him. Nothing should be removed; everything had to stay. He could not afford to lose the good influence the furniture had on his condition. If the furniture hindered him from carrying on his mindless crawling about, that was no drawback, it was rather a great advantage.

But his sister was unfortunately of a different opinion. She had become accustomed, not completely without justification, to playing the expert when it came to discussing anything that concerned Gregor with her parents. And so her mother's advice now led her to insist on the removal not only of the chest and the desk, which was all she had first intended, but of all of the furniture, with the exception of the indispensable sofa. Of course, it was not just childish stubbornness and the hard-won self-confidence she had recently and unexpectedly acquired that determined her on this course: she had actually observed that Gregor needed a great deal of room to crawl around in, and that he did not use the furniture at all, as far as she could see. It might also have been the romantic nature of girls of her age, which sought some outlet at every opportunity, and made her want Gregor's situation to be even more terrifying, so that she could do even more than before to help him. For in a space in which Gregor, completely alone, ruled the empty walls, no person but Grete would dare to enter.

And so she did not allow herself to be swayed by her mother, who faltered from sheer uneasiness at being in the room, soon fell silent, and finally helped his sister as much as she was able in shoving the chest out of the room. Gregor could spare the chest if he must, but the desk had to stay. The women had hardly left the room with the chest, pushing at it and gasping for air, when Gregor stuck his head out from under the sofa, in order to see where he could intervene, as carefully and as considerately as possible. But unfortunately it was his mother who returned first, while Grete in the next room gripped the chest and rocked it back and forth alone, without, naturally, being able to move it from its spot. His mother was not, however, used to the sight of Gregor—he might have made her sick—so Gregor, alarmed, rushed back to the opposite end of the sofa. He could not, however, prevent the sheet from moving a bit at the front. That was enough to put his mother on the alert. She froze, stood still a moment, and then returned to Grete.

Though Gregor kept telling himself that nothing extraordinary was happening—a few pieces of furniture were merely being moved around—he soon realized that this continual back and forth on the part of the women, their soft calls to one another, and the scraping of the furniture on the floor affected him like the greatest of commotions closing in on him from all sides. However closely he drew in his head and legs and however firmly he pressed his body to the floor, he realized he couldn't stand it much longer. They were emptying out his room; they were taking from him everything that he held dear. They had carried out the chest which held his fret saw and other tools; they were already working free the desk from the grooves it had worn into the floor—the desk at which he had written his exercises as a student at trade school, at secondary school, and even at primary school. At this point he did not have the patience to contemplate the women's good intentions, the existence of which he had at any rate almost forgotten. Exhausted, they worked now in complete silence, and only the heavy tread of their feet could be heard.

And so he burst forth from under the sofa—the women were just leaning against the desk in the next room, in order to catch their breath—though he changed the direction of his charge four times, for he really did not know what to save first. On one otherwise empty wall he distinctly saw the picture of the woman dressed entirely in furs. He crept hurriedly up to it and pressed himself against the glass, which held him fast and soothed his hot belly. At least no one could take away this picture, which Gregor now completely covered with his body. He turned his head towards the door of the living room in order to observe the women on their return.

They weren't allowing themselves much rest and so came back directly. Grete had put her arm around her mother and seemed practically to carry her. "Well, what should we take now?" said Grete and looked around. Then her glance met Gregor's as he clung to the wall. She maintained her composure—surely only due to her mother's presence—bent her face to her mother, in order to keep her from looking around, and said hastily, a tremor in her voice, "Come, let's go back in the living room for a moment." Grete's intention was clear to Gregor: she wanted to bring her mother to safety and then chase him down off of the wall. Well, she could try! He would sit on the picture and not give it up. He would rather spring in Grete's face.

But Grete's words had for the first time really unsettled his mother. She moved to the side, spotted the giant brown fleck on the flowered wallpaper, and cried out in a screeching, raw voice, before she was really fully conscious that it was Gregor that she saw, "Oh my God; oh my God!" She then fell onto the sofa with widespread arms, as if she were altogether giving up, and didn't move. "Gregor, you—!" cried his sister with a raised fist and piercing gaze. They were the first words she had directly addressed to Gregor since his transformation. She ran into the next room in order to get some scent with which she could wake her mother out of her faint. Gregor wanted to help, too—there was still time to save the picture—but he was stuck to the glass and had to tear himself free. He, too, ran into the next room, as if he could give his sister some advice, as in earlier days, but then he had to stand helplessly behind her while she rummaged through various bottles. She was startled when she turned around; a bottle fell to the floor and broke. A sliver of glass cut Gregor's face, and some burning medicine spilled over him. Grete took as many bottles as she could carry and ran with them in to her mother. She then slammed the door shut with her foot. Gregor was now shut off from his mother, who was through his fault possibly near death. He couldn't open the door, if he did not want to chase away his sister, who had to remain with his mother. He had nothing left to do but wait. Oppressed by self-reproaches and worry, he began to crawl. He crawled over everything—walls, furniture, and ceiling—and finally, in his despair, he fell, the entire room spinning around him, onto the center of the large table.

A short time passed, and Gregor lay limply there. All around was quiet. Perhaps that was a good sign. Then the bell rang. The servant girl was naturally locked into her kitchen, and so Grete had to go open the door. His father had returned. "What happened?" were his first words. The look on Grete's face betrayed everything to him. Grete answered with a muffled voice—she was obviously pressing her face against her father's chest. "Mother fainted, but she's already better. Gregor broke out." "I was waiting for this," said his father, "I always said it would happen, but you women didn't want to hear it." It was clear to Gregor that his father had interpreted Grete's all-too-brief announcement in the worst possible way, and assumed that Gregor had been guilty of some act of violence. Therefore Gregor had to try to mollify his father, for he had neither the time nor the ability to enlighten him. And so he fled to the door of his room and pressed against it, so that his father could see immediately on leaving the hallway that Gregor had every intention of returning right away to his room. It would not be necessary to drive him back, just to open the door, and he would disappear instantly.

But his father was not in the mood to notice such subtleties: "Ah!" he cried out on entering, in a tone that made him seem at once furious and glad. Gregor drew his head back from the door and turned it toward his father. His father's appearance was different from the way he remembered it. Lately, due to his new habit of crawling about, Gregor had concerned himself less with the goings-on in the rest of the apartment; he should therefore really have been prepared to encounter new developments. But still, still, was this really his father? The same man who lay, tired out, buried deep in his bed, when Gregor was all set to go on a business trip? The man who, dressed in a nightshirt, had greeted him when he returned in the evenings from an easy chair, and, unable to stand up, only raised his arms to show his joy at his return? The man who, on the rare walks he took together with Gregor and his mother on a few Sundays and the most important holidays of the year, walked packed into his old coat even more slowly than they did, though they walked slowly enough, laboring forward with a deliberately placed cane, and who nearly always stopped when he wanted to say something, gathering his companions around him? Now, he was quite well put together. He was dressed in the kind of close-fitting blue uniform with gold buttons that doormen at the banking houses wore; over the high stiff collar of the coat his pronounced double chin protruded; under his busy eyebrows the glance of his dark eyes sprang forth fresh and alert; the formerly disheveled white hair was combed flat into a painfully exact, shining part. He threw his hat, which bore a gold monogram—probably that of a bank— in an arc across the room and onto the sofa. He moved towards Gregor, the ends of his long coat pushed back, his hands in his pants pockets, his face grim. He probably did not know himself what he planned to do. In any case he lifted his feet unusually high, and Gregor was astonished at the gigantic size of the soles of his boots. But he didn't let his astonishment distract him. He had known from the first day of his new life that his father considered the greatest severity appropriate in dealing with him. And so he ran away from his father. He froze when his father stood still and hurried forward again when his father moved a muscle. In this way they circled the room several times, without anything decisive happening; the whole thing moved at such a slow tempo that it didn't even look like a pursuit. For the time being, Gregor stayed on the floor. He was afraid that his father might consider flight toward the walls or the ceiling as particular wickedness. But Gregor realized that he couldn't keep up even this pace for long, for when his father took a single step, he had to carry out myriad movements. He soon felt short of breath; his lungs had not been reliable even in the old days. As he staggered forward, he could barely keep his eyes open, so hard did he try to concentrate his energy for running. In his dullness he was simply unable to think of any other means of deliverance. He had almost forgotten already that the walls were open to him, though they were obstructed here by painstakingly carved furniture full of points and sharp edges. Suddenly something lightly thrown flew just past him and rolled ahead. It was an apple. Another immediately followed. Gregor froze in fear. Running further was pointless, for his father had decided to bombard him. He had filled his pockets from the fruit bowl on the credenza and now threw apple after apple, without for the time being aiming very carefully. These small red apples rolled around on the ground, knocking into each other as if charged with electricity. A weakly thrown apple strafed Gregor's back, but glanced off without doing any harm. One that flew immediately in its wake actually embedded itself in his back, however. Gregor tried to drag himself forward, as if he could outrun the unbelievable pain by changing position, but he felt as if he were nailed to the spot and lay sprawled upon the ground, in complete distraction of all of his senses. With his last conscious glance he watched as the door to his room was ripped open and, ahead of his screaming sister, his mother ran out of the room in her slip—for his sister had undressed her to let her breathe freely while in her faint—and raced towards his father, her untied skirts slipping down to the floor one after another; he watched as, stumbling on the skirts, she embraced his father, fully at one with him—but Gregor's vision now failed him utterly—and, with her hands clasped around the back of his head, begged him to spare Gregor's life.

III

The deep injury from which Gregor had suffered for over a month—the apple remained embedded in his flesh as a visible memento, as no one dared to remove it—seemed to have reminded even his father that despite his present sad and repulsive state, Gregor was a member of the family who should not be treated as an enemy. The law of familial obligation dictated, rather, that one had to swallow one's revulsion and be tolerant, simply be tolerant.

And though Gregor had probably permanently lost some mobility through his injury, and now, like an invalid, took many, many minutes to cross his room—crawling on high was out of the question—this degeneration in his condition brought with it a compensation that was to his mind completely satisfactory. Toward evening they now opened the living room door so that, lying in the darkness of his room and invisible from the living room, he could watch the entire family at the lighted table and listen to their conversation by general consent, as it were—a complete change from the early days when he used to watch the door like a hawk an hour or two before they gathered.

Of course, the conversations were not as lively as in earlier days. Gregor used to recall them longingly in the small hotel rooms where he had had to throw himself, exhausted, into the damp bedclothes. These days everything was mostly very quiet. His father fell asleep in his armchair soon after the evening meal; his mother and sister urged one another to silence. His mother now sewed fine lingerie for a boutique, bending close to her work under the light. His sister, who had taken a job as a salesclerk, studied stenography and French at night, in order to find a better position one day. Sometimes his father awoke and, as if he didn't realize that he had been sleeping, would say to his mother: "How long you're sewing again today!" Then he would fall asleep again immediately, while his mother and sister exchanged tired smiles.

With a kind of stubbornness his father refused to take off his work uniform when he returned home, and while his nightshirt hung, useless, on a clothes hook, he dozed at his place fully clothed, as if he were always on duty and awaited the call of his superiors. As a result, the uniform, which hadn't been new in the first place, became less than pristine, despite the care his mother and sister took with it. Gregor often spent whole evenings looking at the badly stained coat, its oft-polished gold buttons shining, in which the old man slept highly uncomfortably, but quietly.

As soon as the clock struck ten, his mother tried to wake his father by speaking softly to him, and tried to persuade him to go to bed, for he couldn't sleep well there, and a good sleep was absolutely essential, since he had to be at work by six. But in the stubbornness that had come over him since he became a bank employee, he always insisted on remaining longer where he was, although he regularly fell asleep again, and required much effort to persuade in exchanging the armchair for his bed. His mother and sister could press him with gentle remonstrances as much as they liked—for a quarter of an hour at a time he slowly shook his head, his eyes closed, and refused to stand up. His mother plucked at his sleeve, and whispered endearments in his ear; his sister left her work in order to help her mother, but got nowhere with him. He only sank deeper into his armchair. Only when the women grasped him under the arms would he open his eyes, look in turn at Gregor's mother and sister, and say, "What a life. This is the peace and quiet of my old age." And bracing himself against the women, he hoisted himself up laboriously, as if he were his own greatest burden, and allowed himself to be led to the door. He waved them off then and went on under his own power, but Gregor's mother would hastily throw down her sewing and his sister her quill in order to run after him and be of further help to him.

Who in this overworked and overtired family had time to worry about Gregor more than was absolutely necessary? The household was ever more reduced in circumstances. The servant girl had been dismissed, and a gigantic, bony servant with white hair that fluttered about her head came in the mornings and the evenings to do the hardest labor. Everything else his mother took care of, in addition to her abundant sewing work. It even came to pass that various pieces of family jewelry, which his mother and sister had previously worn with pleasure at parties and celebrations, were sold, as Gregor learned one evening from a general conversation about the prices obtained. Their greatest source of complaint, however, was that the apartment, far too large for them under the circumstances, could not be left, because it was unthinkable that Gregor be relocated. But Gregor realized that it was not consideration for him that hindered a relocation, for they could have transported him easily in a suitable carton with a few air holes. What really kept the family from changing apartments was despair, and the thought that they had been afflicted by misfortune such as had struck no one in their circle of relatives and acquaintances. They did everything that the world demanded of poor people—his father fetched breakfast for the junior bank clerks; his mother dedicated herself to making underwear for strangers; his sister ran back and forth behind the counter at the beck and call of customers—but they could do no more than that. And the wound in his back began to hurt Gregor anew when his mother and sister would return from putting his father to bed, let their work lie, and huddle close together, cheek to cheek. His mother, gesturing towards Gregor's room, said, "Close the door, Grete," and Gregor was in the dark again, while next door the women mingled tears or stared, dry-eyed and numb, down at the table.

Gregor passed the days and nights nearly without sleep. Sometimes he considered taking the affairs of the family in hand again, the next time the door was opened. After some time, he thought again about the Director and the Deputy Director, the clerks and the apprentices, the slow-witted porter, two or three friends from other companies, a chambermaid from a hotel in the provinces—a dear, fleeting memory—and a cashier from a hat store whom he had courted seriously, though too slowly. They reappeared in his thoughts together with strangers or people he had already forgotten, but instead of helping him and his family, they all remained detached, and he was glad when they disappeared. At other times, however, he was not in the mood to worry about his family. He was filled with rage at the poor care they took of him, and though he could think of nothing for which he had an appetite, he made plans to reach the pantry and take what was due him, even if he were not hungry. Without considering any longer what might especially please Gregor, mornings and afternoons before returning to the store his sister hurriedly shoved any old kind of food into his room with her foot, only in order to sweep it out with a whisk of the broom in the evenings, indifferent as to whether it might have been merely tasted or—as was usually the case—it remained completely untouched. Her cleaning of the room, which she now always did in the evening, could not have been done any more hastily. Smears of dirt ran along the walls, and here and there lay balls of dust and filth. In the early days Gregor used to position himself upon the arrival of his sister in a particularly grubby corner, in order to reproach her. But he could have remained there for weeks, and his sister would still not have changed her ways. She saw the dirt as well as he did, but she had simply decided to leave it there. At the same time, with a touchiness entirely new to her that had now possessed the entire family, she was vigilant in making sure that the straightening of Gregor's room was left to her. His mother once undertook a thorough cleaning of Gregor's room, which had required several buckets of water—the moisture bothered Gregor, and he lay broad, embittered, and unmoving on top of the sofa—but his mother did not go unpunished. That evening his sister had hardly registered the change in Gregor's room when, highly insulted, she ran into the living room, and despite her mother's beseechingly raised hands, broke into a spasm of tears that his parents—his father had naturally been frightened out of his seat—at first simply watched, helpless with astonishment. Then they, too, were affected: on one side, his father reproached his mother for not leaving the cleaning of Gregor's room to his sister; on the other side, he shouted at his sister that she would never be allowed to clean Gregor's room again. In the meantime, his mother tried to drag his father, who was beside himself with agitation, into the bedroom; his sister, racked by sobs, hammered the table with her small fists; and Gregor hissed loudly with fury that no one thought to close the door and so spare him the scene and the noise.

But even if his sister, exhausted from her work, could no longer manage to care for Gregor as she had earlier, his mother would still not have had to intervene in order to keep Gregor from being neglected. For there was still the servant. This old widow, who had weathered the worst in her long life with the help of a powerful frame, felt no especial revulsion towards Gregor. Without exactly being curious, she had once by chance opened the door to Gregor's room and stood staring at the sight of him, her hands folded across her chest. Gregor was completely taken by surprise, and despite the fact that no one was chasing him, he began to run back and forth. Since that time, she hadn't missed a chance to open the door quickly in the morning and the evening to look in at Gregor. At first she called him over to her with words that she probably considered friendly, like "Come on over here, you old dung beetle!" or "Look at the old dung beetle!" Gregor did not respond to such overtures, but remained motionless in his place, as if the door had not even been opened. If only they would order this servant to clean his room daily, instead of letting her needlessly disturb him at will! Once in the early morning—a hard rain, perhaps already a sign of the coming spring, beat on the window-panes—Gregor became so embittered when the servant began to speak that he turned towards her, as if to attack, though slowly and feebly. Instead of being afraid, however, the servant simply lifted high into the air a chair that stood in reach of the door. As she stood there with her mouth opened wide, it was clear that she intended to shut her mouth only after the chair in her hands had come down on Gregor's back. "That's it, then?" she asked, as Gregor turned around again, and she put the chair quietly back in its corner.

Gregor now ate almost nothing. When he happened to pass by the food prepared for him, he sometimes idly took a bite and held it in his mouth for an hour or so, only to spit most of it out again. At first he thought that his sorrow over the state of his room kept him from eating, but he had actually reconciled himself very soon to the changes. The family had gotten into the habit of putting into his room things that wouldn't fit anywhere else: there were now many such things, as they had rented one room in the apartment out to three lodgers. These three serious gentlemen—all three had full beards, as Gregor discovered once by looking through the crack in the door—were painfully focused on order, not only in their room, but, simply because they had taken lodgings there, in the entire household, especially in the kitchen. They would not put up with useless or dirty things. And in any case, they had brought with them most of their own furnishings. For this reason, many things that were not saleable, but that the family did not want to throw away, had become superfluous. All of this made its way into Gregor's room—even, eventually, the ash bin and the rubbish bin from the kitchen. The servant, who was always in a rush, simply slung anything that was at the moment unuseable into Gregor's room. Fortunately Gregor usually saw only the relevant object and the hand that held it. The servant might once have intended to take the things out again when time and opportunity permitted, or perhaps to throw them all out together once and for all, but in practice they lay wherever they were tossed, unless Gregor wound his way through the clutter and stirred it up—first because he had no other place to crawl, and later with growing pleasure, although after such forays, tired to death and full of sorrow, he could not stir for hours.

Because the lodgers sometimes took their evening meal in the common

142   FRANZ KAFKA

living room, the living room door remained closed on some evenings. Gregor managed without it very well. On some evenings when it was open he did not even take advantage of it, but without the family's knowing it, lay in the darkest corner of his room. Once, however, the servant left the door to his room open a bit, and it remained open, even as the lodgers came in that evening and the light was turned on. They sat at the head of the table, where in former days his father, mother, and Gregor had eaten, unfolded their napkins, and took their knives and forks in hand. His mother immediately appeared in the doorway with a dish of meat and his sister directly behind her with a dish piled high with potatoes. The steaming food gave off a rich smell. The lodgers bent over the dishes placed before them as if they wanted to check them before eating, and the one in the middle, whom the other two appeared to consider an authority, actually cut off a piece of meat still in the serving dish, obviously to test whether it were tender enough, or whether it might perhaps need to be sent back to the kitchen. He was satisfied, and mother and sister, who had watched the proceedings tensely, breathed again and smiled.

The family themselves ate in the kitchen. Nevertheless, his father, before he went into the kitchen, came into the room and made a single long bow while circling the table, cap in hand. The lodgers all rose together and murmured something into their beards. When they were alone again, they ate in near total silence. It seemed strange to Gregor that, among all the various sounds of eating, he could pick out the sound of their chewing teeth—it was as if Gregor were thereby reminded that one needed teeth in order to eat, and that one could do nothing with even the most beautiful toothless jaws. "I do have an appetite," said Gregor sorrowfully to himself, "but not for these things. How these lodgers feed themselves, while I'm dying of hunger!"

On this very evening, though Gregor did not remember having heard it once before during that whole time, the violin sounded from the kitchen. The lodgers had already finished their meal. The middle one had pulled out a newspaper and given each of the others one page. They now read, leaning back, and smoked. As the violin began to play, they became alert, arose and went on tiptoes to the hall door, where they stood pressed up against one another. They must have heard them in the kitchen, for his father called out: "Do you gentlemen perhaps dislike the playing? It can be stopped immediately." "On the contrary," said the lodger in the middle, "wouldn't the young lady like to come out and play here in this room, where it's much more comfortable and convenient?" "Oh, please!" called his father, as if he were the violin player. The lodgers moved back into the room and waited. His father soon came in with the music stand, his mother with the music, and his sister with the violin. His sister quietly prepared to play. His parents, who had never rented a room out before and so exaggerated the courtesy due the lodgers, did not dare to sit on their own chairs. His father leaned against the door, his right hand stuck between two buttons of his fastened livery coat. His mother, however, accepted a chair offered by one of the lodgers, and sat off in the corner where he had happened to place the chair.

His sister began to play. His father and mother, on either side of her, followed every note, attentive to the movements of her hands. Gregor, drawn by the music, had ventured a bit further forward. His head was already in the living room. He hardly wondered at himself for being so inconsiderate towards the others of late; earlier, this consideration had been a great source of pride. And just now he had more reason than before to hide himself. Because of the dust everywhere in his room that flew up at the least movement, he was himself covered in dust. Threads, hairs, and bits of leftover food stuck to his back and sides. His general apathy was much too great for him now to lie on his back and scrub himself on the carpet, as he used to do several times a day. Despite his condition, however, he had no qualms about advancing a bit onto the immaculate living room floor.

But no one paid any attention to him. His family was entirely absorbed in the playing of the violin. The lodgers, on the other hand, who had at first, their hands in their pants pockets, taken up positions inconveniently close to his sister's music stand, in order to see all the notes, soon withdrew to the window, their heads bowed amidst whispered conversation, and remained there with Gregor's father worriedly observing them. It was now painfully obvious that they were disappointed in what they had assumed would be a beautiful or entertaining performance, and that they were sick of the entire production and now allowed their quiet to be disturbed only out of politeness. The way they all blew their cigar smoke out of their mouths and noses indicated great irritation. But his sister played so beautifully! Her face was turned to the side; her gaze followed the lines of notes, searching and sorrowful. Gregor crept further forward and held his head close to the floor, in order to meet her gaze if possible. The music gripped him—was he then an animal? He felt as if he were being guided to the sustenance he had unknowingly desired. He was determined to press on all the way to his sister, to pull on her skirt and let her know that she could come into his room with her violin. No one here knew how to appreciate her playing the way he did. He wanted never to let her out of his room again, at least not as long as he lived. His terrifying shape would finally be of some use to him: he would be at all doors of his room at once, hissing at all intruders. His sister, though, would not be forced, but would rather stay with him willingly. She would sit next to him on the sofa, her ear inclined towards him, and he would confide in her that he had intended to send her to the conservatory, and that, were it not for the misfortune that had occurred, he had intended to announce it to everyone last Christmas—Christmas had surely passed already?—ignoring any possible objections. After this declaration, his sister would surely burst into tears of emotion, and Gregor would lift himself up to her shoulder and kiss her neck, which she now left uncovered, without ribbon or collar, since she had begun working at the store.

"Mr. Samsa!" called the middle lodger and without waiting another word, pointed at Gregor, who was slowly inching his way forward. The violin fell silent. The middle lodger smiled at first, shaking his head at his friends, and then looked down again at Gregor. His father seemed to consider it more urgent to reassure the lodgers than to drive Gregor back, despite the fact that they seemed calm and more entertained by Gregor than by the violin. He hurried over to them and tried with outspread arms to urge them into their room; at the same time, he wanted to block their view of Gregor with his body. They actually became a bit angry now, though it was unclear whether this was over his father's behavior or over the dawning recognition that, unbeknownst to them, they had all the while had a neighbor like Gregor. They asked his father for an explanation, raised their arms, pulled agitatedly at their beards, and only reluctantly retreated into their room. In the meantime his sister had come out of the trance into which she had fallen after her playing had been so suddenly broken off. For a time she had held her violin and bow in her limply hanging hands and continued to stare at the music, as if she were still playing. Now, all at once, she pulled herself together, laid the instrument in the lap of her mother, who, short of breath and gasping for air, was still seated, and ran into the next room, which the lodgers were now approaching more quickly at the urging of her father. Under her practiced hands, the covers and pillows flew high in the air and arranged themselves. Before the lodgers had reached the room, she was finished readying the beds and had slipped out. His father's stubbornness seemed to have returned to the extent that he forgot all respect that he owed his lodgers. He kept urging them and urging them, until finally at the threshold the gentleman in the middle resoundingly stamped his foot and so brought his father to a standstill. "I hereby declare," he said, and, raising his hand, sought the gaze of Gregor's mother and sister, as well, "that, in consideration of the revolting conditions existing in this apartment and this family"—and here, without a moment's hesitation, he spat on the ground—"I give notice this instant. I will naturally pay absolutely nothing for the days I have lived here; on the contrary, I will consider bringing charges against you, which will—believe me—be very easy to prove." He fell silent and stared straight ahead, as if he were waiting for something. His two friends then obliged him by chiming in with the words:

"We, too, give notice this instant." At that, he seized the door handle and shut the door with a crash.

His father staggered to his chair, his hands stretched out before him, and fell into it. It looked as if he were stretching himself out for his usual evening nap, but his head, sharply, ceaselessly nodding, showed that he was not sleeping at all. Gregor had lain all this time in the same spot where the lodgers had discovered him. His disappointment at the failure of his plans—perhaps, though, too, the weakness caused by his long hunger—made it impossible for him to move. He was distinctly afraid that in the next moment everything was going to come crashing down on top of him. He waited. Not even the violin roused him, which slipped from his mother's trembling fingers and fell from her lap, emitting a ringing tone.

"My dear parents," said his sister and struck her hand on the table by way of preamble, "we can't go on like this. If you can't see it, I can. I don't want to use the name of my brother in front of this monster, so let me just say this: we have to try to get rid of it. We have tried as much as humanly possible to care for it and to put up with it. I don't think it could reproach us in the least."

"She is absolutely right," said his father under his breath. His mother, who seemed not to have caught her breath yet, began to emit a muffled cough into the hand she held before her, a crazed expression in her eyes.

His sister hurried to his mother and put her hand to her forehead. His sister's words seemed to have put his father's thoughts in a surer course. He sat up straight, fiddling with his uniform cap amongst the plates that still sat on the table from the lodgers' evening meal, and looked for a time down at the quiet Gregor.

"We must try to get rid of it," his sister finally said to his father, for his mother heard nothing in the midst of her coughing. "It's going to kill you both; I can see it coming. When people have to work as hard as we do, they can't bear this kind of constant torture at home. I can't bear it any more." And she began crying so hard that her tears flowed down her mother's face, where she began mechanically wiping them away with her hand.

"But my child," said his father, sympathetically and with striking compassion, "what should we do?"

His sister only shrugged her shoulders as a sign of the helplessness that had during her crying spell taken the place of her former certainty. "But if he understood us—" his father said, half questioningly. His sister, in the midst of her tears, waved her hand violently as a sign that that was out of the question.

"If he understood us," his father repeated, and by closing his eyes, tried to absorb her certainty that it was impossible, "then we might be able to arrive at some arrangement with him. But as things stand—"

"It has to go," cried his sister. "That is the only way, father. You must simply try to rid yourself of the thought that it's Gregor. Our real misfortune is that we believed it for so long. But how can it be Gregor? If it were Gregor, he would have seen long ago that such an animal cannot live with people and he would have left voluntarily. We would then have had no brother, but we could have lived on and honored his memory. But this beast persecutes us, drives off the lodgers, and obviously wants to take over the apartment and force us to sleep out in the alley. Just look, Father," she suddenly screamed, "he's starting again!" And in a state of terror totally incomprehensible to Gregor, his sister abandoned his mother and practically vaulted off her chair, as if she would rather sacrifice her than remain in Gregor's vicinity. She hurried behind her father who, agitated entirely through her behavior, stood up as well and half raised his arms as if to protect her.

But it wasn't at all Gregor's intent to upset anyone, especially not his sister. He had just begun to turn himself around in order to make his way back into his room. Of course, that procedure looked peculiar enough, because his ailing condition meant that in order to turn even with difficulty he had to help with his head, which he lifted repeatedly and braced against the ground. He paused and looked around. His good intentions seemed to be recognized: it had only been a momentary fright. They all looked at him, silent and sorrowful. His mother lay in her chair, her legs stretched before her and pressed together; her eyes were nearly falling shut from exhaustion. His father and sister sat next to one another, his sister with her hand laid around her father's neck.

"Maybe they'll allow me to turn around now," thought Gregor, and started to work on it again. He could not suppress the wheezing caused by his exertion, and he had to stop and rest now and then. No one rushed him: he was left to his own devices. When he had completed the turn, he immediately headed straight back. He was astonished by the vast distance that divided him from his room, and he could not grasp how in his weakened condition he had put the entire distance behind him, almost without noticing it. Focused solely on crawling as quickly as possible, he hardly noticed that no word and no outcry from his family disturbed him. He turned his head only when he was already at the door—not all the way, for he felt his neck getting stiff, but enough to see that nothing had changed behind him, except for the fact that his sister had stood up. His last glance fell on his mother, who was now fast asleep.

He was hardly in his room when the door was hastily pushed to, bolted fast and locked. The sudden noise behind him frightened Gregor so much that his legs buckled beneath him. It was his sister who had rushed to do it. She had stood, waiting, and had suddenly sprung forward, light-footed — Gregor had not even heard her coming — crying out to her parents "Finally!" as she turned the key in the lock.

"And now?" Gregor asked himself, and looked around in the dark. He soon discovered that he could no longer move at all. He didn't wonder at this; on the contrary, it had seemed unnatural to him that he had actually been able to move before on such thin legs. Besides that, however, he felt relatively comfortable. He did have pains all over his body, but it seemed to him that they were becoming weaker and weaker and would finally die away altogether. He could hardly feel the rotten apple in his back or the inflamed surrounding area, which was now completely covered in moist dust. He thought of his family with compassion and love. His conviction that he had to disappear was even more definite than his sister's. He remained in this state of empty and peaceful contemplation until the clock tower struck three. He experienced once more the approach of daylight outside the window. Then, unwilled, his head sank fully down, and from his nostrils his last breath weakly streamed forth.

When the servant came in the early morning — though she had often been asked to refrain from doing so, she slammed all the doors out of sheer vigor and haste, to such an extent that it was not possible to sleep quietly anywhere in the apartment once she had arrived — she noticed nothing unusual at first in her morning visit to Gregor. She thought that he intentionally lay there motionless because he found her behavior insulting; she credited him with all manner of intelligence. As she happened to be holding her long broom in her hand, she tried to tickle Gregor with it from the door. When she met with no response, she became irritated and poked him a bit. Only when she had shoved him from his spot without meeting any resistance did she became alert. She soon understood the situation. Her eyes widened, and she whistled out loud. It wasn't long before she had flung the door of the master bedroom open and called loudly into the darkness: "Look, everyone, it's kicked the bucket; it's lying there, dead as a doornail!"

The Samsas sat bolt upright in bed and had first to overcome their alarm at the servant's behavior before they could understand her report. Then, however, they climbed hurriedly out of bed, one on each side. Mr. Samsa threw the blanket over his shoulders; Mrs. Samsa emerged in her nightgown. In this manner they entered Gregor's room. In the meantime Grete had opened the door to the living room, where she had been sleeping since the arrival of the lodgers. She was completely dressed, as if she had not slept; her pale face confirmed the impression. "Dead?" said Mrs. Samsa, and looked questioningly up at the servant, although she could have made her own investigation or even have recognized the fact without making any investigation. "I'd say so," said the servant, and as proof, she pushed Gregor's corpse further to one side with the broom. Mrs. Samsa moved as if she wanted to hold her back, but she didn't. "Well," said Mr. Samsa, "now we can thank God." He crossed himself, and the three women followed his example. Grete, who did not take her eyes from the corpse, said: "Just look at how thin he was. He hadn't eaten anything for so long. The food came out just the way it went in." Gregor's body was indeed completely flat and dry; it was really only possible to see it now that he was off his legs and nothing else distracted the eye.

"Come, Grete, come sit with us for a bit," said Mrs. Samsa with a wistful smile, and Grete followed her parents into their bedroom, though not without looking back at the corpse. The servant shut the door and opened the window wide. Despite the early morning the fresh air already had something mild mixed in it. It was, after all, already the end of March.

The three lodgers emerged from their room and looked in amazement for their breakfast. It had been forgotten. "Where is breakfast?" the middlemost of the men asked the servant sullenly. She laid a finger to her lips and then silently and hastily signaled to the men that they might come into Gregor's room. They came and stood around Gregor's corpse in the now completely bright room, their hands in the pockets of their somewhat shabby coats.

The door to the bedroom opened then, and Mr. Samsa appeared in his livery with his wife on one arm and his daughter on the other. They had all been crying; Grete pressed her face from time to time to her father's arm.

"Leave my apartment immediately!" said Mr. Samsa and pointed to the door, without letting the women leave his side. "What do you mean?" said the middle lodger, somewhat dismayed, and smiled mawkishly. The two others held their hands behind their backs and rubbed them together continuously, as if in joyful expectation of a great fight, which would, they were sure, end favorably for them. "I mean exactly what I say," answered Mr. Samsa, and advanced in a line with his companions toward the lodger. He stood quietly, at first, and looked at the ground, as if the things in his head were arranging themselves in a new order. "Then we'll go," he said and looked up at Mr. Samsa, as if a sudden access of humility required him to seek renewed approval even for this decision. Mr. Samsa merely nodded shortly several times, his eyes wide and staring. At this, the man immediately walked with long strides into the foyer. His two friends had listened at first, their hands completely still, and they now skipped after him directly, as if in fear that Mr. Samsa could step in front of them in the foyer and disrupt their connection to their leader. In the hall all three of them took their hats from the rack, drew their walking sticks from the stand, bowed mutely, and left the apartment. In what proved to be a completely unnecessary precaution, Mr. Samsa walked out with the two women onto the landing. Leaning on the railing, they watched as the three men slowly but steadily descended the stairs, disappearing on every floor at the turning of the stairwell, and emerging again after a few moments. The lower they went, the more the Samsa family lost interest in them, and as a butcher's boy carrying his burden on his head with dignity passed them and then climbed high above them, Mr. Samsa left the landing with the women and they all returned, as if freed from a burden, to their apartment.

They decided to spend the day resting and taking a stroll. They had not only earned this rest from work, they absolutely needed it. And so they sat at the table and wrote three letters of excuse, Mr. Samsa to the bank directors, Mrs. Samsa to her employer, and Grete to her supervisor. While they were writing the servant entered in order to say that she was leaving, as her morning work was finished. Writing, the three of them merely nodded at first, without looking up; only when the servant failed to depart did they look up angrily. "Well?" asked Mr. Samsa. The servant stood in the door, smiling, as if she had some great piece of good news to report to the family, but would only do so if she were thoroughly interrogated. The nearly upright little ostrich feather on her hat, which had annoyed Mr. Samsa the entire time she had been employed there, waved freely in all directions. "Well, what do you want?" asked Mrs. Samsa, for whom the servant had the most respect. "Well," the servant answered, and could say more right away, fairly bursting with friendly laughter, "well, you needn't worry about getting rid of that thing next door. It's all been taken care of." Mrs. Samsa and Grete bent to their letters again, as if they wanted to continue writing. Mr. Samsa, who saw that the servant was about to begin describing everything in great detail, decisively headed this off with an outstretched hand. Since she was not going to be allowed to tell her story, she suddenly remembered her great haste, and, obviously deeply insulted, called out, "'Bye, everyone," then spun around wildly and left the apartment amidst a terrific slamming of doors.

"Tonight we're firing her," said Mr. Samsa, but received no answer either from his wife or from his daughter, for the servant seemed to have disturbed their but newly restored calm. They rose, went to the window, and remained there, their arms around each other. Mr. Samsa turned in his chair as they went and quietly observed them for a while. Then he called out, "Well, come over here. Let what's past be past. And take some care of me, for once." The women obeyed immediately, hurrying over to him and caressing him, and then quickly finished their letters.

Then all three of them left the apartment together, which they had not done for months, and took a trolley to the open air beyond the city. The car they sat in was drenched with warm sunlight. Leaning back comfortably in their seats, they discussed their future prospects, and it emerged that these were not at all bad on closer inspection, for all three of their positions were altogether favorable at present and, most importantly, had great potential for the future. The great improvement of their present situation would have to come, naturally, from a change of apartments. They would want a smaller and cheaper apartment, but one that was better located and generally more convenient than their current apartment, which Gregor had originally found for them. While they conversed in this way, it occurred to both Mr. and Mrs. Samsa in the same moment in looking at their ever more lively daughter that despite the recent ordeals that had made her cheeks so pale, she had blossomed into a pretty and well-developed young woman. Becoming quieter and almost unconsciously communicating through glances, they realized that it would soon be time to look for a good husband for her. And it seemed to them a confirmation of their new dreams and good intentions, when, at the end of their journey, their daughter rose first and stretched her young body.

[1915]

D. H. LAWRENCE   [1885–1930]

The Rocking-Horse Winner

There was a woman who was beautiful, who started with all the advantages, yet she had no luck. She married for love, and the love turned to dust. She had bonny children, yet she felt they had been thrust upon her, and she could not love them. They looked at her coldly, as if they were finding fault with her. And hurriedly she felt she must cover up some fault in herself. Yet what it was that she must cover up she never knew. Nevertheless, when her children were present, she always felt the center of her heart go hard. This troubled her, and in her manner she was all the more gentle and anxious for her children, as if she loved them very much. Only she herself knew that at the center of her heart was a hard little place that could not feel love, no, not for anybody. Everybody else said of her: "She is such a good mother. She adores her children." Only she herself, and her children themselves, knew it was not so. They read it in each other's eyes.

There were a boy and two little girls. They lived in a pleasant house, with a garden, and they had discreet servants, and felt themselves superior to anyone in the neighborhood.

Although they lived in style, they felt always an anxiety in the house. There was never enough money. The mother had a small income, and the father had a small income, but not nearly enough for the social position which they had to keep up. The father went into town to some office. But though he had good prospects, these prospects never materialized. There was always the grinding sense of the shortage of money, though the style was always kept up.

At last the mother said: "I will see if *I* can't make something." But she did not know where to begin. She racked her brains, and tried this thing and the other, but could not find anything successful. The failure made deep lines come into her face. Her children were growing up, they would have to go to school. There must be more money, there must be more money. The father, who was always very handsome and expensive in his tastes, seemed as if he never *would* be able to do anything worth doing. And the mother, who had a great belief in herself, did not succeed any better, and her tastes were just as expensive.

And so the house came to be haunted by the unspoken phrase: *There must be more money! There must be more money!* The children could hear it all the time though nobody said it aloud. They heard it at Christmas, when the expensive and splendid toys filled the nursery. Behind the shining modern rocking horse, behind the smart doll's house, a voice would start whispering: "There *must* be more money! There *must* be more money!" And the children would stop playing, to listen for a moment. They would look into each other's eyes, to see if they had all heard. And each one saw in the eyes of the other two that they too had heard. "There *must* be more money! There *must* be more money!"

It came whispering from the springs of the still-swaying rocking horse, and even the horse, bending his wooden, champing head, heard it. The big doll, sitting so pink and smirking in her new pram, could hear it quite plainly, and seemed to be smirking all the more self-consciously because of it. The foolish puppy, too, that took the place of the teddy bear, he was looking so extraordinarily foolish for no other reason but that he heard the secret whisper all over the house: "There *must* be more money!"

Yet nobody ever said it aloud. The whisper was everywhere, and therefore no one spoke it. Just as no one ever says: "We are breathing!" in spite of the fact that breath is coming and going all the time.

"Mother," said the boy Paul one day, "why don't we keep a car of our own? Why do we always use Uncle's, or else a taxi?"

"Because we're the poor members of the family," said the mother.

"But why *are* we, Mother?"

"Well—I suppose," she said slowly and bitterly, "it's because your father has no luck."

The boy was silent for some time.

"Is luck money, Mother?" he asked rather timidly.

"No, Paul. Not quite. It's what causes you to have money."

"Oh!" said Paul vaguely. "I thought when Uncle Oscar said *filthy lucker*, it meant money."

"*Filthy lucre* does mean money," said the mother. "But it's lucre, not luck."

"Oh!" said the boy. "Then what *is* luck, Mother?"

"It's what causes you to have money. If you're lucky you have money. That's why it's better to be born lucky than rich. If you're rich, you may lose your money. But if you're lucky, you will always get more money."

"Oh! Will you? And is Father not lucky?"

"Very unlucky, I should say," she said bitterly.

The boy watched her with unsure eyes.

"Why?" he asked.

"I don't know. Nobody ever knows why one person is lucky and another unlucky."

"Don't they? Nobody at all? Does *nobody* know?"

"Perhaps God. But He never tells."

"He ought to, then. And aren't you lucky either, Mother?"

"I can't be, if I married an unlucky husband."

"But by yourself, aren't you?"

"I used to think I was, before I married. Now I think I am very unlucky indeed."

"Why?"

"Well—never mind! Perhaps I'm not really," she said.

The child looked at her, to see if she meant it. But he saw, by the lines of her mouth, that she was only trying to hide something from him.

"Well, anyhow," he said stoutly, "I'm a lucky person."

"Why?" said his mother, with a sudden laugh.

He stared at her. He didn't even know why he had said it.

"God told me," he asserted, brazening it out.

"I hope He did, dear!" she said, again with a laugh, but rather bitter.

"He did, Mother!"

"Excellent!" said the mother.

The boy saw she did not believe him; or, rather, that she paid no attention to his assertion. This angered him somewhat, and made him want to compel her attention.

He went off by himself, vaguely, in a childish way, seeking for the clue to "luck." Absorbed, taking no heed of other people, he went about with a sort of stealth, seeking inwardly for luck. He wanted luck, he wanted it, he wanted it. When the two girls were playing dolls in the nursery, he would sit on his big rocking horse, charging madly into space, with a frenzy that made the little girls peer at him uneasily. Wildly the horse careered, the waving dark hair of the boy tossed, his eyes had a strange glare in them. The little girls dared not speak to him.

When he had ridden to the end of his mad little journey, he climbed down and stood in front of his rocking horse, staring fixedly into its lowered face. Its red mouth was slightly open, its big eye was wide and glassy-bright.

Now! he could silently command the snorting steed. Now, take me to where there is luck! Now take me!

And he would slash the horse on the neck with the little whip he had asked Uncle Oscar for. He *knew* the horse could take him to where there was luck, if only he forced it. So he would mount again, and start on his furious ride, hoping at last to get there. He knew he could get there.

"You'll break your horse, Paul!" said the nurse.

"He's always riding like that! I wish he'd leave off!" said his elder sister Joan.

But he only glared down on them in silence. Nurse gave him up. She could make nothing of him. Anyhow he was growing beyond her.

One day his mother and his uncle Oscar came in when he was on one of his furious rides. He did not speak to them.

"Hallo, you young jockey! Riding a winner?" said his uncle.

"Aren't you growing too big for a rocking horse? You're not a very little boy any longer, you know," said his mother.

But Paul only gave a blue glare from his big, rather close-set eyes. He would speak to nobody when he was in full tilt. His mother watched him with an anxious expression on her face.

At last he suddenly stopped forcing his horse into the mechanical gallop, and slid down.

"Well, I got there!" he announced fiercely, his blue eyes still flaring, and his sturdy long legs straddling apart.

"Where did you get to?" asked his mother.

"Where I wanted to go," he flared back at her.

"That's right, son!" said Uncle Oscar. "Don't you stop till you get there. What's the horse's name?"

"He doesn't have a name," said the boy.

"Gets on without all right?" asked the uncle.

"Well, he has different names. He was called Sansovino last week."

"Sansovino, eh? Won the Ascot. How did you know his name?"

"He always talks about horse races with Bassett," said Joan.

The uncle was delighted to find that his small nephew was posted with all the racing news. Bassett, the young gardener, who had been wounded in the left foot in the war and had got his present job through Oscar Cresswell, whose batman he had been, was a perfect blade of the "turf." He lived in the racing events, and the small boy lived with him.

Oscar Cresswell got it all from Bassett.

"Master Paul comes and asks me, so I can't do more than tell him, sir," said Bassett, his face terribly serious, as if he were speaking of religious matters.

"And does he ever put anything on a horse he fancies?"

"Well—I don't want to give him away—he's a young sport, a fine sport, sir. Would you mind asking him himself? He sort of takes a pleasure in it, and perhaps he'd feel I was giving him away, sir, if you don't mind."

Bassett was serious as a church.

The uncle went back to his nephew and took him off for a ride in the car.

"Say, Paul, old man, do you ever put anything on a horse?" the uncle asked.

The boy watched the handsome man closely.

"Why, do you think I oughtn't to?" he parried.

"Not a bit of it! I thought perhaps you might give me a tip for the Lincoln."

The car sped on into the country, going down to Uncle Oscar's place in Hampshire.

"Honor bright?" said the nephew.

"Honor bright, son!" said the uncle.

"Well, then, Daffodil."

"Daffodil! I doubt it, sonny. What about Mirza?"

"I only know the winner," said the boy. "That's Daffodil."

"Daffodil, eh?"

There was a pause. Daffodil was an obscure horse comparatively.

"Uncle!"

"Yes, son?"

"You won't let it go any further, will you? I promised Bassett."

"Bassett be damned, old man! What's he got to do with it?"

"We're partners. We've been partners from the first. Uncle, he lent me my first five shillings, which I lost. I promised him, honor bright, it was only between me and him; only you gave me that ten-shilling note I started winning with, so I thought you were lucky. You won't let it go any further, will you?"

The boy gazed at his uncle from those big, hot, blue eyes, set rather close together. The uncle stirred and laughed uneasily.

"Right you are, son! I'll keep your tip private. Daffodil, eh? How much are you putting on him?"

"All except twenty pounds," said the boy. "I keep that in reserve."

The uncle thought it a good joke.

"You keep twenty pounds in reserve, do you, you young romancer? What are you betting, then?"

"I'm betting three hundred," said the boy gravely. "But it's between you and me, Uncle Oscar! Honor bright?"

The uncle burst into a roar of laughter.

"It's between you and me all right, you young Nat Gould,"° he said, laughing. "But where's your three hundred?"

"Bassett keeps it for me. We're partners."

"You are, are you! And what is Bassett putting on Daffodil?"

"He won't go quite as high as I do, I expect. Perhaps he'll go a hundred and fifty."

"What, pennies?" laughed the uncle.

"Pounds," said the child, with a surprised look at his uncle. "Bassett keeps a bigger reserve than I do."

Between wonder and amusement Uncle Oscar was silent. He pursued the matter no further, but he determined to take his nephew with him to the Lincoln races.

"Now, son," he said, "I'm putting twenty on Mirza, and I'll put five for you on any horse you fancy. What's your pick?"

"Daffodil, Uncle."

"No, not the fiver on Daffodil!"

"I should if it was my own fiver," said the child.

"Good! Good! Right you are! A fiver for me and a fiver for you on Daffodil."

The child had never been to a race meeting before, and his eyes were blue fire. He pursed his mouth tight, and watched. A Frenchman just in front had put his money on Lancelot. Wild with excitement, he flailed his arms up and down, yelling *Lancelot! Lancelot!* in his French accent.

Daffodil came in first, Lancelot second, Mirza third. The child, flushed and with eyes blazing, was curiously serene. His uncle brought him four five-pound notes, four to one.

"What am I to do with these?" he cried, waving them before the boy's eyes.

"I suppose we'll talk to Bassett," said the boy. "I expect I have fifteen hundred now; and twenty in reserve; and this twenty."

His uncle studied him for some moments.

"Look here, son!" he said. "You're not serious about Bassett and that fifteen hundred, are you?"

"Yes, I am. But it's between you and me, Uncle. Honor bright!"

"Honor bright all right, son! But I must talk to Bassett."

"If you'd like to be a partner, Uncle, with Bassett and me, we could all be partners. Only, you'd have to promise, honor bright, Uncle, not to let it go beyond us three. Bassett and I are lucky, and you must be lucky, because it was your ten shillings I started winning with. . . ."

Nat Gould: Nathaniel Gould (1857–1919), British novelist and sports columnist who wrote novels about horse racing.

Uncle Oscar took both Bassett and Paul into Richmond Park for an afternoon, and there they talked.

"It's like this, you see, sir," Bassett said. "Master Paul would get me talking about racing events, spinning yarns, you know, sir. And he was always keen on knowing if I'd made or if I'd lost. It's about a year since, now, that I put five shillings on Blush of Dawn for him—and we lost. Then the luck turned, with that ten shillings he had from you, that we put on Singhalese. And since then, it's been pretty steady, all things considering. What do you say, Master Paul?"

"We're all right when we're sure," said Paul. "It's when we're not quite sure that we go down."

"Oh, but we're careful then," said Bassett.

"But when are you *sure*?" Uncle Oscar smiled.

"It's Master Paul, sir," said Bassett, in a secret, religious voice. "It's as if he had it from heaven. Like Daffodil, now, for the Lincoln. That was as sure as eggs."

"Did you put anything on Daffodil?" asked Oscar Cresswell.

"Yes, sir. I made my bit."

"And my nephew?"

Bassett was obstinately silent, looking at Paul.

"I made twelve hundred, didn't I, Bassett? I told Uncle I was putting three hundred on Daffodil."

"That's right," said Bassett, nodding.

"But where's the money?" asked the uncle.

"I keep it safe locked up, sir. Master Paul he can have it any minute he likes to ask for it."

"What, fifteen hundred pounds?"

"And twenty! And *forty*, that is, with the twenty he made on the course."

"It's amazing!" said the uncle.

"If Master Paul offers you to be partners, sir, I would, if I were you; if you'll excuse me," said Bassett.

Oscar Cresswell thought about it.

"I'll see the money," he said.

They drove home again, and sure enough, Bassett came round to the garden house with fifteen hundred pounds in notes. The twenty pounds reserve was left with Joe Glee, in the Turf Commission deposit.

"You see, it's all right, Uncle, when I'm *sure*! Then we go strong, for all we're worth. Don't we, Bassett?"

"We do that, Master Paul."

"And when are you sure?" said the uncle, laughing.

"Oh, well, sometimes I'm *absolutely* sure, like about Daffodil," said the boy; "and sometimes I have an idea; and sometimes I haven't even an idea, have I, Bassett? Then we're careful, because we mostly go down."

"You do, do you! And when you're sure, like about Daffodil, what makes you sure, sonny?"

"Oh, well, I don't know," said the boy uneasily. "I'm sure, you know, Uncle; that's all."

"It's as if he had it from heaven, sir," Bassett reiterated.

"I should say so!" said the uncle.

But he became a partner. And when the Leger was coming on, Paul was "sure" about Lively Spark, which was a quite inconsiderable horse. The boy insisted on putting a thousand on the horse, Bassett went for five hundred, and Oscar Cresswell two hundred. Lively Spark came in first, and the betting had been ten to one against him. Paul had made ten thousand.

"You see," he said, "I was absolutely sure of him."

Even Oscar Cresswell had cleared two thousand.

"Look here, son," he said, "this sort of thing makes me nervous."

"It needn't, Uncle! Perhaps I shan't be sure again for a long time."

"But what are you going to do with your money?" asked the uncle.

"Of course," said the boy. "I started it for Mother. She said she had no luck, because Father is unlucky, so I thought if *I* was lucky, it might stop whispering."

"What might stop whispering?"

"Our house. I *hate* our house for whispering."

"What does it whisper?"

"Why—why"—the boy fidgeted—"why, I don't know. But it's always short of money, you know, Uncle."

"I know it, son, I know it."

"You know people send Mother writs, don't you, Uncle?"

"I'm afraid I do," said the uncle.

"And then the house whispers, like people laughing at you behind your back. It's awful, that is! I thought if I was lucky. . . ."

"You might stop it," added the uncle.

The boy watched him with big blue eyes, that had an uncanny cold fire in them, and he said never a word.

"Well, then!" said the uncle. "What are we doing?"

"I shouldn't like Mother to know I was lucky," said the boy.

"Why not, son?"

"She'd stop me."

"I don't think she would."

"Oh!"—and the boy writhed in an odd way—"I *don't* want her to know, Uncle."

"All right, son! We'll manage it without her knowing."

They managed it very easily. Paul, at the other's suggestion, handed over five thousand pounds to his uncle, who deposited it with the family lawyer, who was then to inform Paul's mother that a relative had put five thousand pounds into his hands, which sum was to be paid out a thousand pounds at a time, on the mother's birthday, for the next five years.

"So she'll have a birthday present of a thousand pounds for five successive years," said Uncle Oscar. "I hope it won't make it all the harder for her later."

Paul's mother had her birthday in November. The house had been "whispering" worse than ever lately, and, even in spite of his luck, Paul could not bear up against it. He was very anxious to see the effect of the birthday letter, telling his mother about the thousand pounds.

When there were no visitors, Paul now took his meals with his parents, as he was beyond the nursery control. His mother went into town nearly every day. She had discovered that she had an odd knack of sketching furs and dress materials, so she worked secretly in the studio of a friend who was the chief artist for the leading drapers. She drew the figures of ladies in furs and ladies in silk and sequins for the newspaper advertisements. This young woman artist earned several thousand pounds a year, but Paul's mother only made several hundreds, and she was again dissatisfied. She so wanted to be first in something, and she did not succeed, even in making sketches for drapery advertisements.

She was down to breakfast on the morning of her birthday. Paul watched her face as she read her letters. He knew the lawyer's letter. As his mother read it, her face hardened and became more expressionless. Then a cold, determined look came on her mouth. She hid the letter under the pile of others, and said not a word about it.

"Didn't you have anything nice in the post for your birthday, Mother?" said Paul.

"Quite moderately nice," she said, her voice cold and absent.

She went away to town without saying more.

But in the afternoon Uncle Oscar appeared. He said Paul's mother had had a long interview with the lawyer, asking if the whole five thousand could not be advanced at once, as she was in debt.

"What do you think, Uncle?" said the boy.

"I leave it to you, son."

"Oh, let her have it, then! We can get some more with the other," said the boy.

"A bird in the hand is worth two in the bush, laddie!" said Uncle Oscar.

"But I'm sure to *know* for the Grand National; or the Lincolnshire; or else the Derby. I'm sure to know for *one* of them," said Paul.

So Uncle Oscar signed the agreement, and Paul's mother touched the whole five thousand. Then something very curious happened. The voices in the house suddenly went mad, like a chorus of frogs on a spring evening. There were certain new furnishings, and Paul had a tutor. He was *really* going to Eton, his father's school, in the following autumn. There were flowers in the winter, and a blossoming of the luxury Paul's mother had been used to. And yet the voices in the house, behind the sprays of mimosa and almond blossom, and from under the piles of iridescent cushions, simply trilled and screamed in a sort of ecstasy: "There *must* be more money! Oh-h-h; there *must* be more money. Oh, now, now-w! Now-w-w—there *must* be more money!—more than ever! More than ever!"

It frightened Paul terribly. He studied away at his Latin and Greek. But his intense hours were spent with Bassett. The Grand National had gone by; he had not "known," and had lost a hundred pounds. Summer was at hand. He was in agony for the Lincoln. But even for the Lincoln he didn't "know," and he lost fifty pounds. He became wild-eyed and strange, as if something were going to explode in him.

"Let it alone, son! Don't you bother about it!" urged Uncle Oscar. But it was as if the boy couldn't really hear what his uncle was saying.

"I've got to know for the Derby! I've got to know for the Derby!" the child reiterated, his big blue eyes blazing with a sort of madness.

His mother noticed how overwrought he was.

"You'd better go to the seaside. Wouldn't you like to go now to the seaside, instead of waiting? I think you'd better," she said, looking down at him anxiously, her heart curiously heavy because of him.

But the child lifted his uncanny blue eyes. "I couldn't possibly go before the Derby, Mother!" he said. "I couldn't possibly!"

"Why not?" she said, her voice becoming heavy when she was opposed. "Why not? You can still go from the seaside to see the Derby with your uncle Oscar, if that's what you wish. No need for you to wait here. Besides, I think you care too much about these races. It's a bad sign. My family has been a gambling family, and you won't know till you grow up how much damage it has done. But it has done damage. I shall have to send Bassett away, and ask Uncle Oscar not to talk racing to you, unless you promise to be reasonable about it; go away to the seaside and forget it. You're all nerves!"

"I'll do what you like, Mother, so long as you don't send me away till after the Derby," the boy said.

"Send you away from where? Just from this house?"

"Yes," he said, gazing at her.

"Why, you curious child, what makes you care about this house so much, suddenly? I never knew you loved it."

He gazed at her without speaking. He had a secret within a secret, something he had not divulged, even to Bassett or to his uncle Oscar.

But his mother, after standing undecided and a little bit sullen for some moments, said:

"Very well, then! Don't go to the seaside till after the Derby, if you don't wish it. But promise me you won't let your nerves go to pieces. Promise you won't think so much about horse racing and *events*, as you call them!"

"Oh, no," said the boy casually. "I won't think much about them, Mother. You needn't worry. I wouldn't worry, Mother, if I were you."

"If you were me and I were you," said his mother, "I wonder what we *should* do!"

"But you know you needn't worry, Mother, don't you?" the boy repeated.

"I should be awfully glad to know it," she said wearily.

"Oh, well you *can*, you know. I mean, you *ought* to know you needn't worry," he insisted.

"Ought I? Then I'll see about it," she said.

Paul's secret of secrets was his wooden horse, that which had no name. Since he was emancipated from a nurse and a nursery governess, he had had his rocking horse removed to his own bedroom at the top of the house.

"Surely, you're too big for a rocking horse!" his mother had remonstrated.

"Well, you see, Mother, till I can have a *real* horse, I like to have *some* sort of animal about," had been his quaint answer.

"Do you feel he keeps you company?" She laughed.

"Oh, yes! He's very good, he always keeps me company, when I'm there," said Paul.

So the horse, rather shabby, stood in an arrested prance in the boy's bedroom.

The Derby was drawing near, and the boy grew more and more tense. He hardly heard what was spoken to him, he was very frail, and his eyes were really uncanny. His mother had sudden strange seizures of uneasiness about him. Sometimes, for half an hour, she would feel a sudden anxiety about him that was almost anguish. She wanted to rush to him at once, and know he was safe.

Two nights before the Derby, she was at a big party in town, when one of her rushes of anxiety about her boy, her firstborn, gripped her heart till she could hardly speak. She fought with the feeling, might and main, for she believed in common sense. But it was too strong. She had to leave the dance and go downstairs to telephone to the country. The children's nursery governess was terribly surprised and startled at being rung up in the night.

"Are the children all right, Miss Wilmot?"

"Oh, yes, they are quite all right."

"Master Paul? Is he all right?"

"He went to bed as right as a trivet. Shall I run up and look at him?"

"No," said Paul's mother reluctantly. "No! Don't trouble. It's all right.

Don't sit up. We shall be home fairly soon." She did not want her son's privacy intruded upon.

"Very good," said the governess.

It was about one o'clock when Paul's mother and father drove up to their house. All was still. Paul's mother went to her room and slipped off her white fur cloak. She had told her maid not to wait up for her. She heard her husband downstairs, mixing a whisky and soda.

And then, because of the strange anxiety at her heart, she stole upstairs to her son's room. Noiselessly she went along the upper corridor. Was there a faint noise? What was it?

She stood, with arrested muscles, outside his door, listening. There was a strange, heavy, and yet not loud noise. Her heart stood still. It was a soundless noise, yet rushing and powerful. Something huge, in violent, hushed motion. What was it? What in God's name was it? She ought to know. She felt that she knew the noise. She knew what it was.

Yet she could not place it. She couldn't say what it was. And on and on it went, like a madness.

Softly, frozen with anxiety and fear, she turned the door handle.

The room was dark. Yet in the space near the window, she heard and saw something plunging to and fro. She gazed in fear and amazement.

Then suddenly she switched on the light, and saw her son, in his green pajamas, madly surging on the rocking horse. The blaze of light suddenly lit him up, as he urged the wooden horse, and lit her up, as she stood, blonde, in her dress of pale green and crystal, in the doorway.

"Paul!" she cried. "Whatever are you doing?"

"It's Malabar!" he screamed, in a powerful, strange voice. "It's Malabar!"

His eyes blazed at her for one strange and senseless second, as he ceased urging his wooden horse. Then he fell with a crash to the ground, and she, all her tormented motherhood flooding upon her, rushed to gather him up.

But he was unconscious, and unconscious he remained, with some brain fever. He talked and tossed, and his mother sat stonily by his side.

"Malabar! It's Malabar! Bassett, Bassett, I *know*! It's Malabar!"

So the child cried, trying to get up and urge the rocking horse that gave him his inspiration.

"What does he mean by Malabar?" asked the heart-frozen mother.

"I don't know," said the father stonily.

"What does he mean by Malabar?" she asked her brother Oscar.

"It's one of the horses running for the Derby," was the answer.

And, in spite of himself, Oscar Cresswell spoke to Bassett, and himself put a thousand on Malabar: at fourteen to one.

The third day of the illness was critical: they were waiting for a change. The boy, with his rather long, curly hair, was tossing ceaselessly on the pillow. He never slept nor regained consciousness, and his eyes were like blue stones. His mother sat, feeling her heart had gone, turned actually into a stone.

In the evening, Oscar Cresswell did not come, but Bassett sent a message, saying could he come up for one moment, just one moment? Paul's mother was very angry at the intrusion, but on second thought she agreed. The boy was the same. Perhaps Bassett might bring him to consciousness.

The gardener, a shortish fellow with a little brown mustache, and sharp little brown eyes, tiptoed into the room, touched his imaginary cap to Paul's mother, and stole to the bedside, staring with glittering, smallish eyes at the tossing, dying child.

"Master Paul!" he whispered. "Master Paul! Malabar came in first all right, a clean win. I did as you told me. You've made over seventy thousand pounds, you have; you've got over eighty thousand. Malabar came in all right, Master Paul."

"Malabar! Malabar! Did I say Malabar, Mother? Did I say Malabar? Do you think I'm lucky, Mother? I knew Malabar, didn't I? Over eighty thousand pounds! I call that lucky, don't you, Mother? Over eighty thousand pounds! I knew, didn't I know I knew? Malabar came in all right. If I ride my horse till I'm sure, then I tell you, Bassett, you can go as high as you like. Did you go for all you were worth, Bassett?"

"I went a thousand on it, Master Paul."

"I never told you, Mother, that if I can ride my horse, and *get there*, then I'm absolutely sure—oh, absolutely! Mother, did I ever tell you? I *am* lucky!"

"No, you never did," said the mother.

But the boy died in the night.

And even as he lay dead, his mother heard her brother's voice saying to her: "My God, Hester, you're eighty-odd thousand to the good, and a poor devil of a son to the bad. But, poor devil, poor devil, he's best gone out of a life where he rides his rocking horse to find a winner."

[1926]

KATHERINE MANSFIELD   [1888–1923]

The Garden-Party

And after all the weather was ideal. They could not have had a more perfect day for a garden-party if they had ordered it. Windless, warm, the sky without a cloud. Only the blue was veiled with a haze of light gold, as it is sometimes in early summer. The gardener had been up since dawn, mowing the lawns and sweeping them, until the grass and the dark flat rosettes where the daisy plants had been seemed to shine. As for the roses, you could not help feeling they understood that roses are the only flowers that impress people at garden-parties; the only flowers that everybody is certain of knowing. Hundreds, yes, literally hundreds, had come out in a single night; the green bushes bowed down as though they had been visited by archangels.

Breakfast was not yet over before the men came to put up the marquee.

"Where do you want the marquee put, mother?"

"My dear child, it's no use asking me. I'm determined to leave everything to you children this year. Forget I am your mother. Treat me as an honoured guest."

But Meg could not possibly go and supervise the men. She had washed her hair before breakfast, and she sat drinking her coffee in a green turban, with a dark wet curl stamped on each cheek. Jose, the butterfly, always came down in a silk petticoat and a kimono jacket.

"You'll have to go, Laura; you're the artistic one."

Away Laura flew, still holding her piece of bread-and-butter. It's so delicious to have an excuse for eating out of doors, and besides, she loved having to arrange things; she always felt she could do it so much better than anybody else.

Four men in their shirt-sleeves stood grouped together on the garden path. They carried staves covered with rolls of canvas, and they had big tool-bags slung on their backs. They looked impressive. Laura wished now that she had not got the bread-and-butter, but there was nowhere to put it, and she couldn't possibly throw it away. She blushed and tried to look severe and even a little bit short-sighted as she came up to them.

"Good morning," she said, copying her mother's voice. But that sounded so fearfully affected that she was ashamed, and stammered like a little girl, "Oh—er—have you come—is it about the marquee?"

"That's right, miss," said the tallest of the men, a lanky, freckled fellow, and he shifted his tool-bag, knocked back his straw hat, and smiled down at her. "That's about it."

His smile was so easy, so friendly that Laura recovered. What nice eyes he had, small, but such a dark blue! And now she looked at the others, they were smiling too. "Cheer up, we won't bite," their smiles seemed to say. How very nice workmen were! And what a beautiful morning! She mustn't mention the morning; she must be businesslike. The marquee.

"Well, what about the lily-lawn? Would that do?"

And she pointed to the lily-lawn with the hand that didn't hold the bread-and-butter. They turned, they stared in the direction. A little fat chap thrust out his under-lip, and the tall fellow frowned.

"I don't fancy it," said he. "Not conspicuous enough. You see with a thing like a marquee," and he turned to Laura in his easy way, "you want to put it somewhere where it'll give you a bang slap in the eye, if you follow me."

Laura's upbringing made her wonder for a moment whether it was quite respectful of a workman to talk to her of bangs slap in the eye. But she did quite follow him.

"A corner of the tennis-court," she suggested. "But the band's going to be in one corner."

"H'm, going to have a band, are you?" said another of the workmen. He was pale. He had a haggard look as his dark eyes scanned the tennis-court. What was he thinking?

"Only a very small band," said Laura gently. Perhaps he wouldn't mind so much if the band was quite small. But the tall fellow interrupted.

"Look here, miss, that's the place. Against those trees. Over there. That'll do fine."

Against the karakas.° Then the karaka-trees would be hidden. And they were so lovely, with their broad, gleaming leaves, and their clusters of yellow fruit. They were like trees you imagined growing on a desert island, proud, solitary, lifting their leaves and fruits to the sun in a kind of silent splendour. Must they be hidden by a marquee?

They must. Already the men had shouldered their staves and were making for the place. Only the tall fellow was left. He bent down, pinched a sprig of lavender, put his thumb and forefinger to his nose, and snuffed up the smell. When Laura saw that gesture she forgot all about the karakas in her wonder at him caring for things like that—caring for the smell of lavender. How many men that she knew would have done such a

Karakas: Evergreen trees with large glossy leaves.

thing? Oh, how extraordinarily nice workmen were, she thought. Why couldn't she have workmen for friends rather than the silly boys she danced with and who came to Sunday night supper? She would get on much better with men like these.

It's all the fault, she decided, as the tall fellow drew something on the back of an envelope, something that was to be looped up or left to hang, of these absurd class distinctions. Well, for her part, she didn't feel them. Not a bit, not an atom. . . . And now there came the chock-chock of wooden hammers. Some one whistled, some one sang out, "Are you right there, matey?" "Matey!" The friendliness of it, the—the—Just to prove how happy she was, just to show the tall fellow how at home she felt, and how she despised stupid conventions, Laura took a big bite of her bread-and-butter as she stared at the little drawing. She felt just like a work-girl.

"Laura, Laura, where are you? Telephone, Laura!" a voice cried from the house.

"Coming!" Away she skimmed, over the lawn, up the path, up the steps, across the veranda, and into the porch. In the hall her father and Laurie were brushing their hats ready to go to the office.

"I say, Laura," said Laurie very fast, "you might just give a squiz° at my coat before this afternoon. See if it wants pressing."

"I will," said she. Suddenly she couldn't stop herself. She ran at Laurie and gave him a small, quick squeeze. "Oh, I do love parties, don't you?" gasped Laura.

"Ra-ther," said Laurie's warm, boyish voice, and he squeezed his sister too, and gave her a gentle push. "Dash off to the telephone, old girl."

The telephone. "Yes, yes; oh yes. Kitty? Good morning, dear. Come to lunch? Do, dear. Delighted of course. It will only be a very scratch meal—just the sandwich crusts and broken meringue-shells and what's left over. Yes, isn't it a perfect morning? Your white? Oh, I certainly should. One moment—hold the line. Mother's calling." And Laura sat back. "What, mother? Can't hear."

Mrs. Sheridan's voice floated down the stairs. "Tell her to wear that sweet hat she had on last Sunday."

"Mother says you're to wear that *sweet* hat you had on last Sunday. Good. One o'clock. Bye-bye."

Laura put back the receiver, flung her arms over her head, took a deep breath, stretched, and let them fall. "Huh," she sighed, and the moment after the sigh she sat up quickly. She was still, listening. All the doors in the house seemed to be open. The house was alive with soft, quick steps and running voices. The green baize door that led to the kitchen regions

Squiz: Australian slang, meaning a quick, close look.

swung open and shut with a muffled thud. And now there came a long, chuckling absurd sound. It was the heavy piano being moved on its stiff castors. But the air! If you stopped to notice, was the air always like this? Little faint winds were playing the chase, in at the tops of the windows, out at the doors. And there were two tiny spots of sun, one on the inkpot, one on a silver photograph frame, playing too. Darling little spots. Especially the one on the inkpot lid. It was quite warm. A warm little silver star. She could have kissed it.

The front door bell pealed, and there sounded the rustle of Sadie's print skirt on the stairs. A man's voice murmured; Sadie answered, careless, "I'm sure I don't know. Wait. I'll ask Mrs. Sheridan."

"What is it, Sadie?" Laura came into the hall.

"It's the florist, Miss Laura."

It was, indeed. There, just inside the door, stood a wide shallow tray full of pots of pink lilies. No other kind. Nothing but lilies—canna lilies, big pink flowers, wide open, radiant, almost frighteningly alive on bright crimson stems.

"O-oh, Sadie!" said Laura, and the sound was like a little moan. She crouched down as if to warm herself at that blaze of lilies; she felt they were in her fingers, on her lips, growing in her breast.

"It's some mistake," she said faintly. "Nobody ever ordered so many. Sadie, go and find mother."

But at that moment Mrs. Sheridan joined them.

"It's quite right," she said calmly. "Yes, I ordered them. Aren't they lovely?" She pressed Laura's arm. "I was passing the shop yesterday, and I saw them in the window. And I suddenly thought for once in my life I shall have enough canna lilies. The garden-party will be a good excuse."

"But I thought you said you didn't mean to interfere," said Laura. Sadie had gone. The florist's man was still outside at his van. She put her arm round her mother's neck and gently, very gently, she bit her mother's ear.

"My darling child, you wouldn't like a logical mother, would you? Don't do that. Here's the man."

He carried more lilies still, another whole tray.

"Bank them up, just inside the door, on both sides of the porch, please," said Mrs. Sheridan. "Don't you agree, Laura?"

"Oh, I *do* mother."

In the drawing-room Meg, Jose, and good little Hans had at last succeeded in moving the piano.

"Now, if we put this chesterfield against the wall and move everything out of the room except the chairs, don't you think?"

"Quite."

"Hans, move these tables into the smoking-room, and bring a sweeper to take these marks off the carpet and—one moment, Hans—" Jose loved giving orders to the servants, and they loved obeying her. She always made them feel they were taking part in some drama. "Tell mother and Miss Laura to come here at once."

"Very good, Miss Jose."

She turned to Meg. "I want to hear what the piano sounds like, just in case I'm asked to sing this afternoon. Let's try over 'This life is Weary.'"

Pom! Ta-ta-ta *Tee*-ta! The piano burst out so passionately that Jose's face changed. She clasped her hands. She looked mournfully and enigmatically at her mother and Laura as they came in.

This Life is *Wee*-ary,
A Tear—a Sigh.
A Love that *Chan*-ges,
   This Life is *Wee*-ary,
A Tear—a Sigh.
A Love that *Chan*-ges,
And then . . . Good-bye!

But at the word "Good-bye," and although the piano sounded more desperate than ever, her face broke into a brilliant, dreadfully unsympathetic smile.

"Aren't I in good voice, mummy?" she beamed.

This Life is *Wee*-ary,
Hope comes to Die.
A Dream—a *Wa*-kening.

But now Sadie interrupted them. "What is it, Sadie?"

"If you please, m'm, cook says have you got the flags for the sandwiches?"

"The flags for the sandwiches, Sadie?" echoed Mrs. Sheridan dreamily. And the children knew by her face that she hadn't got them. "Let me see." And she said to Sadie firmly, "Tell cook I'll let her have them in ten minutes."

Sadie went.

"Now, Laura," said her mother quickly. "Come with me into the smoking-room. I've got the names somewhere on the back of an envelope. You'll have to write them out for me. Meg, go upstairs this minute and take that wet thing off your head. Jose, run and finish dressing this instant. Do you hear me, children, or shall I have to tell your father when he comes home to-night? And—and, Jose, pacify cook if you do go into the kitchen, will you? I'm terrified of her this morning."

The envelope was found at last behind the dining-room clock, though how it had got there Mrs. Sheridan could not imagine.

"One of you children must have stolen it out of my bag, because I re-member vividly—cream cheese and lemon-curd. Have you done that?"

"Yes."

"Egg and—" Mrs. Sheridan held the envelope away from her. "It looks like mice. It can't be mice, can it?"

"Olive, pet," said Laura, looking over her shoulder.

"Yes, of course, olive. What a horrible combination it sounds. Egg and olive."

They were finished at last, and Laura took them off to the kitchen. She found Jose there pacifying the cook, who did not look at all terrifying.

"I have never seen such exquisite sandwiches," said Jose's rapturous voice. "How many kinds did you say there were, cook? Fifteen?"

"Fifteen, Miss Jose."

"Well, cook, I congratulate you."

Cook swept up crusts with the long sandwich knife, and smiled broadly.

"Godber's has come," announced Sadie, issuing out of the pantry. She had seen the man pass the window.

That meant the cream puffs had come. Godber's were famous for their cream puffs. Nobody ever thought of making them at home.

"Bring them in and put them on the table, my girl," ordered cook.

Sadie brought them in and went back to the door. Of course Laura and Jose were far too grown-up to really care about such things. All the same, they couldn't help agreeing that the puffs looked very attractive. Very. Cook began arranging them, shaking off the extra icing sugar.

"Don't they carry one back to all one's parties?" said Laura.

"I suppose they do," said practical Jose, who never liked to be carried back. "They look beautifully light and feathery, I must say."

"Have one each, my dears," said cook in her comfortable voice. "Yer ma won't know."

Oh, impossible. Fancy cream puffs so soon after breakfast. The very idea made one shudder. All the same, two minutes later Jose and Laura were licking their fingers with that absorbed inward look that only comes from whipped cream.

"Let's go into the garden, out by the back way," suggested Laura. "I want to see how the men are getting on with the marquee. They're such awfully nice men."

But the back door was blocked by cook, Sadie, Godber's man, and Hans.

Something had happened.

"Tuk-tuk-tuk," clucked cook like an agitated hen. Sadie had her hand clapped to her cheek as though she had toothache. Hans's face was screwed up in the effort to understand. Only Godber's man seemed to be enjoying himself; it was his story.

"What's the matter? What's happened?"

"There's been a horrible accident," said Cook. "A man killed."

"A man killed! Where? How? When?"

But Godber's man wasn't going to have his story snatched from under his very nose.

"Know those little cottages just below here, miss?" Know them? Of course, she knew them. "Well, there's a young chap living there, name of Scott, a carter. His horse shied at a traction-engine, corner of Hawke Street this morning, and he was thrown out on the back of his head. Killed."

"Dead!" Laura stared at Godber's man.

"Dead when they picked him up," said Godber's man with relish. "They were taking the body home as I come up here." And he said to the cook, "He's left a wife and five little ones."

"Jose, come here." Laura caught hold of her sister's sleeve and dragged her through the kitchen to the other side of the green baize door. There she paused and leaned against it. "Jose!" she said, horrified, "however are we going to stop everything?"

"Stop everything, Laura!" cried Jose in astonishment. "What do you mean?"

"Stop the garden-party, of course." Why did Jose pretend?

But Jose was still more amazed. "Stop the garden-party? My dear Laura, don't be so absurd. Of course we can't do anything of the kind. Nobody expects us to. Don't be so extravagant."

"But we can't possibly have a garden-party with a man dead just outside the front gate."

That really was extravagant, for the little cottages were in a lane to themselves at the very bottom of a steep rise that led up to the house. A broad road ran between. True, they were far too near. They were the greatest possible eyesore, and they had no right to be in that neighbourhood at all. They were little mean dwellings painted a chocolate brown. In the garden patches there was nothing but cabbage stalks, sick hens and tomato cans. The very smoke coming out of their chimneys was poverty-stricken. Little rags and shreds of smoke, so unlike the great silvery plumes that uncurled from the Sheridans' chimneys. Washerwomen lived in the lane and sweeps and a cobbler, and a man whose house-front was studded all over with minute bird-cages. Children swarmed. When the Sheridans were little they were forbidden to set foot there because of the revolting language and of what they might catch. But since they were grown up, Laura and Laurie on their prowls sometimes walked through. It was disgusting and sordid. They came out with a shudder. But still one must go everywhere; one must see everything. So through they went.

"And just think of what the band would sound like to that poor woman," said Laura.

"Oh, Laura!" Jose began to be seriously annoyed. "If you're going to stop a band playing every time some one has an accident, you'll lead a very strenuous life. I'm every bit as sorry about it as you. I feel just as sympathetic." Her eyes hardened. She looked at her sister just as she used to when they were little and fighting together. "You won't bring a drunken workman back to life by being sentimental," she said softly.

"Drunk! Who said he was drunk?" Laura turned furiously on Jose. She said, just as they had used to say on those occasions, "I'm going straight up to tell mother."

"Do, dear," cooed Jose.

"Mother, can I come into your room?" Laura turned the big glass door-knob.

"Of course, child. Why, what's the matter? What's given you such a colour?" And Mrs. Sheridan turned round from her dressing-table. She was trying on a new hat.

"Mother, a man's been killed," began Laura.

"*Not* in the garden?" interrupted her mother.

"No, no!"

"Oh, what a fright you gave me!" Mrs. Sheridan sighed with relief, and took off the big hat and held it on her knees.

"But listen, mother," said Laura. Breathless, half-choking, she told the dreadful story. "Of course, we can't have our party, can we?" she pleaded. "The band and everybody arriving. They'd hear us, mother; they're nearly neighbours!"

To Laura's astonishment her mother behaved just like Jose, it was harder to bear because she seemed amused. She refused to take Laura seriously.

"But, my dear child, use your common sense. It's only by accident we've heard of it. If some one had died there normally—and I can't understand how they keep alive in those poky little holes—we should still be having our party, shouldn't we?"

Laura had to say "yes" to that, but she felt it was all wrong. She sat down on her mother's sofa and pinched the cushion frill.

"Mother, isn't it really terribly heartless of us?" she asked.

"Darling!" Mrs. Sheridan got up and came over to her, carrying the hat. Before Laura could stop her she had popped it on. "My child!" said her mother, "the hat is yours. It's made for you. It's much too young for me.

I have never seen you look such a picture. Look at yourself!" And she held up her hand-mirror.

"But, mother," Laura began again. She couldn't look at herself; she turned aside.

This time Mrs. Sheridan lost patience just as Jose had done.

"You are being very absurd, Laura," she said coldly. "People like that don't expect sacrifices from us. And it's not very sympathetic to spoil everybody's enjoyment as you're doing now."

"I don't understand," said Laura, and she walked quickly out of the room into her own bedroom. There, quite by chance, the first thing she saw was this charming girl in the mirror, in her black hat trimmed with gold daisies, and a long black velvet ribbon. Never had she imagined she could look like that. Is mother right? she thought. And now she hoped her mother was right. Am I being extravagant? Perhaps it was extravagant. Just for a moment she had another glimpse of that poor woman and those little children, and the body being carried into the house. But it all seemed blurred, unreal, like a picture in the newspaper. I'll remember it again after the party's over, she decided. And somehow that seemed quite the best plan. . . .

Lunch was over by half-past one. By half-past two they were all ready for the fray. The green-coated band had arrived and was established in a corner of the tennis-court.

"My dear!" trilled Kitty Maitland, "aren't they too like frogs for words? You ought to have arranged them round the pond with the conductor in the middle on a leaf."

Laurie arrived and hailed them on his way to dress. At the sight of him Laura remembered the accident again. She wanted to tell him. If Laurie agreed with the others, then it was bound to be all right. And she followed him into the hall.

"Laurie!"

"Hallo!" He was half-way upstairs, but when he turned round and saw Laura he suddenly puffed out his cheeks and goggled his eyes at her. "My word, Laura; You do look stunning," said Laurie. "What an absolutely topping hat!"

Laura said faintly "Is it?" and smiled up at Laurie, and didn't tell him after all.

Soon after that people began coming in streams. The band struck up; the hired waiters ran from the house to the marquee. Wherever you looked there were couples strolling, bending to the flowers, greeting, moving on over the lawn. They were like bright birds that had alighted in the Sheridans' garden for this one afternoon, on their way to—where? Ah, what happiness it is to be with people who all are happy, to press hands, press cheeks, smile into eyes.

"Darling Laura, how well you look!"

"What a becoming hat, child!"

"Laura, you look quite Spanish. I've never seen you look so striking."

And Laura, glowing, answered softly, "Have you had tea? Won't you have an ice? The passion-fruit ices really are rather special." She ran to her father and begged him. "Daddy darling, can't the band have something to drink?"

And the perfect afternoon slowly ripened, slowly faded, slowly its petals closed.

"Never a more delightful garden-party . . ." "The greatest success . . ." "Quite the most . . ."

Laura helped her mother with the good-byes. They stood side by side in the porch till it was all over.

"All over, all over, thank heaven," said Mrs. Sheridan. "Round up the others, Laura. Let's go and have some fresh coffee. I'm exhausted. Yes, it's been very successful. But oh, these parties, these parties! Why will you children insist on giving parties!" And they all of them sat down in the deserted marquee.

"Have a sandwich, daddy dear. I wrote the flag."

"Thanks." Mr. Sheridan took a bite and the sandwich was gone. He took another. "I suppose you didn't hear of a beastly accident that happened to-day?" he said.

"My dear," said Mrs. Sheridan, holding up her hand, "we did. It nearly ruined the party. Laura insisted we should put it off."

"Oh, mother!" Laura didn't want to be teased about it.

"It was a horrible affair all the same," said Mr. Sheridan. "The chap was married too. Lived just below in the lane, and leaves a wife and half a dozen kiddies, so they say."

An awkward little silence fell. Mrs. Sheridan fidgeted with her cup. Really, it was very tactless of father . . .

Suddenly she looked up. There on the table were all those sandwiches, cakes, puffs, all uneaten, all going to be wasted. She had one of her brilliant ideas.

"I know," she said. "Let's make up a basket. Let's send that poor creature some of this perfectly good food. At any rate, it will be the greatest treat for the children. Don't you agree? And she's sure to have neighbours calling in and so on. What a point to have it all ready prepared. Laura!" She jumped up. "Get me the big basket out of the stairs cupboard."

"But, mother, do you really think it's a good idea?" said Laura.

Again, how curious, she seemed to be different from them all. To take scraps from their party. Would the poor woman really like that?

"Of course! What's the matter with you to-day? An hour or two ago you were insisting on us being sympathetic, and now—"

Oh, well! Laura ran for the basket. It was filled, it was heaped by her mother.

"Take it yourself, darling," said she. "Run down just as you are. No, wait, take the arum lilies too. People of that class are so impressed by arum lilies."

"The stems will ruin her lace frock," said practical Jose.

So they would. Just in time. "Only the basket, then. And, Laura!"—her mother followed her out of the marquee—"don't on any account—"

"What, mother?"

No, better not put such ideas into the child's head! "Nothing! Run along."

It was just growing dusky as Laura shut their garden gates. A big dog ran by like a shadow. The road gleamed white, and down below in the hollow the little cottages were in deep shade. How quiet it seemed after the afternoon. Here she was going down the hill to somewhere where a man lay dead, and she couldn't realize it. Why couldn't she? She stopped a minute. And it seemed to her that kisses, voices, tinkling spoons, laughter, the smell of crushed grass were somehow inside her. She had no room for anything else. How strange! She looked up at the pale sky, and all she thought was, "Yes, it was the most successful party."

Now the broad road was crossed. The lane began, smoky and dark. Women in shawls and men's tweed caps hurried by. Men hung over the palings; the children played in the doorways. A low hum came from the mean little cottages. In some of them there was a flicker of light, and a shadow, crab-like, moved across the window. Laura bent her head and hurried on. She wished now she had put on a coat. How her frock shone! And the big hat with the velvet streamer—if only it was another hat! Were the people looking at her? They must be. It was a mistake to have come; she knew all along it was a mistake. Should she go back even now?

No, too late. This was the house. It must be. A dark knot of people stood outside. Beside the gate an old, old woman with a crutch sat in a chair, watching. She had her feet on a newspaper. The voices stopped as Laura drew near. The group parted. It was as though she was expected, as though they had known she was coming here.

Laura was terribly nervous. Tossing the velvet ribbon over her shoulder, she said to a woman standing by, "Is this Mrs. Scott's house?" and the woman, smiling queerly, said, "It is, my lass."

Oh, to be away from this! She actually said, "Help me, God," as she walked up the tiny path and knocked. To be away from those staring eyes, or to be covered up in anything, one of those women's shawls even. I'll just leave the basket and go, she decided. I shan't even wait for it to be emptied.

Then the door opened. A little woman in black showed in the gloom.

Laura said, "Are you Mrs. Scott?" But to her horror the woman answered, "Walk in please, miss," and she was shut in the passage.

"No," said Laura, "I don't want to come in. I only want to leave this basket. Mother sent—"

The little woman in the gloomy passage seemed not to have heard her. "Step this way, please, miss," she said in an oily voice, and Laura followed her.

She found herself in a wretched little low kitchen, lighted by a smoky lamp. There was a woman sitting before the fire.

"Em," said the little creature who had let her in. "Em! It's a young lady." She turned to Laura. She said meaningly, "I'm 'er sister, Miss. You'll excuse 'er, won't you?"

"Oh, but of course!" said Laura. "Please, please don't disturb her. I—I only want to leave—"

But at that moment the woman at the fire turned round. Her face, puffed up, red, with swollen eyes and swollen lips, looked terrible. She seemed as though she couldn't understand why Laura was there. What did it mean? Why was this stranger standing in the kitchen with a basket? What was it all about? And the poor face puckered up again.

"All right, my dear," said the other. "I'll thenk the young lady."

And again she began, "You'll excuse her, miss, I'm sure," and her face, swollen too, tried an oily smile.

Laura only wanted to get out, to get away. She was back in the passage. The door opened. She walked straight through into the bedroom, where the dead man was lying.

"You'd like a look at 'im, wouldn't you?" said Em's sister, and she brushed past Laura over to the bed. "Don't be afraid, my lass, —" and now her voice sounded fond and sly, and fondly she drew down the sheet—"'e looks a picture. There's nothing to show. Come along, my dear."

Laura came.

There lay a young man, fast asleep—sleeping so soundly, so deeply, that he was far, far away from them both. Oh, so remote, so peaceful. He was dreaming. Never wake him up again. His head was sunk in the pillow, his eyes were closed; they were blind under the closed eyelids. He was given up to his dream. What did garden-parties and baskets and lace frocks matter to him? He was far from all those things. He was wonderful, beautiful. While they were laughing and while the band was playing, this marvel had come to the lane. Happy . . . happy. . . . All is well, said that sleeping face. This is just as it should be. I am content.

But all the same you had to cry, and she couldn't go out of the room without saying something to him. Laura gave a loud childish sob.

"Forgive my hat," she said.

And this time she didn't wait for Em's sister. She found her way out of the door, down the path, past all those dark people. At the corner of the lane she met Laurie.

He stepped out of the shadow. "Is that you, Laura?"

"Yes."

"Mother was getting anxious. Was it all right?"

"Yes, quite. Oh, Laurie!" She took his arm, she pressed up against him.

"I say, you're not crying, are you?" asked her brother.

Laura shook her head. She was.

Laurie put his arm round her shoulder. "Don't cry," he said in his warm, loving voice. "Was it awful?"

"No," sobbed Laura. "It was simply marvellous. But, Laurie—" She stopped, she looked at her brother. "Isn't life," she stammered, "isn't life—" But what life was she couldn't explain. No matter. He quite understood.

"*Isn't* it, darling?" said Laurie.

[1922]

ZORA NEALE HURSTON   [1891–1960]

Sweat

It was eleven o'clock of a Spring night in Florida. It was Sunday. Any other night, Delia Jones would have been in bed for two hours by this time. But she was a washwoman, and Monday morning meant a great deal to her. So she collected the soiled clothes on Saturday when she returned the clean things. Sunday night after church, she sorted them and put the white things to soak. It saved her almost a half day's start. A great hamper in the bedroom held the clothes that she brought home. It was so much neater than a number of bundles lying around.

She squatted in the kitchen floor beside the great pile of clothes, sorting them into small heaps according to color, and humming a song in a mournful key, but wondering through it all where Sykes, her husband, had gone with her horse and buckboard.

Just then something long, round, limp, and black fell upon her shoulders and slithered to the floor beside her. A great terror took hold of her. It softened her knees and dried her mouth so that it was a full minute before she could cry out or move. Then she saw that it was the big bull whip her husband liked to carry when he drove.

She lifted her eyes to the door and saw him standing there bent over with laughter at her fright. She screamed at him.

"Sykes, what you throw dat whip on me like dat? You know it would skeer me—looks just like a snake, an' you knows how skeered Ah is of snakes."

"Course Ah knowed it! That's how come Ah done it." He slapped his leg with his hand and almost rolled on the ground in his mirth. "If you such a big fool dat you got to have a fit over a earth worm or a string, Ah don't keer how bad Ah skeer you."

"You aint got no business doing it. Gawd knows it's a sin. Some day Ah'm gointuh drop dead from some of yo' foolishness. 'Nother thing, where you been wid mah rig? Ah feeds dat pony. He aint fuh you to be drivin' wid no bull whip."

"You sho is one aggravatin' nigger woman!" he declared and stepped into the room. She resumed her work and did not answer him at once. "Ah done tole you time and again to keep them white folks' clothes outa dis house."

He picked up the whip and glared down at her. Delia went on with her work. She went out into the yard and returned with a galvanized tub and sat it on the washbench. She saw that Sykes had kicked all of the clothes together again, and now stood in her way truculently, his whole manner hoping, *praying*, for an argument. But she walked calmly around him and commenced to re-sort the things.

"Next time, Ah'm gointer kick 'em outdoors," he threatened as he struck a match along the leg of his corduroy breeches.

Delia never looked up from her work, and her thin, stooped shoulders sagged further.

"Ah aint for no fuss t'night, Sykes. Ah just come from taking sacrament at the church house."

He snorted scornfully. "Yeah, you just come from de church house on a Sunday night, but heah you is gone to work on them clothes. You ain't nothing but a hypocrite. One of them amen-corner Christians—sing, whoop, and shout, then come home and wash white folks clothes on the Sabbath."

He stepped roughly upon the whitest pile of things, kicking them helter-skelter as he crossed the room. His wife gave a little scream of dismay, and quickly gathered them together again.

"Sykes, you quit grindin' dirt into these clothes! How can Ah git through by Sat'day if Ah don't start on Sunday?"

"Ah don't keer if you never git through. Anyhow, Ah done promised Gawd and a couple of other men, Ah aint gointer have it in mah house.

Don't gimme no lip neither, else Ah'll throw 'em out and put mah fist up side yo' head to boot."

Delia's habitual meekness seemed to slip from her shoulders like a blown scarf. She was on her feet; her poor little body, her bare knuckly hands bravely defying the strapping hulk before her.

"Looka heah, Sykes, you done gone too fur. Ah been married to you fur fifteen years, and Ah been takin' in washin' fur fifteen years. Sweat, sweat, sweat! Work and sweat, cry and sweat, pray and sweat!"

"What's that got to do with me?" he asked brutally.

"What's it got to do with you, Sykes? Mah tub of suds is filled yo' belly with vittles more times than yo' hands is filled it. Mah sweat is done paid for this house and Ah reckon Ah kin keep on sweatin' in it."

She seized the iron skillet from the stove and struck a defensive pose, which act surprised him greatly, coming from her. It cowed him and he did not strike her as he usually did.

"Naw you won't," she panted, "that ole snaggle-toothed black woman you runnin' with aint comin' heah to pile up on *mah* sweat and blood. You aint paid for nothin' on this place, and Ah'm gointer stay right heah till Ah'm toted out foot foremost."

"Well, you better quit gittin' me riled up, else they'll be totin' you out sooner than you expect. Ah'm so tired of you Ah don't know whut to do. Gawd! how Ah hates skinny wimmen!"

A little awed by this new Delia, he sidled out of the door and slammed the back gate after him. He did not say where he had gone, but she knew too well. She knew very well that he would not return until nearly daybreak also. Her work over, she went on to bed but not to sleep at once. Things had come to a pretty pass!

She lay awake, gazing upon the debris that cluttered their matrimonial trail. Not an image left standing along the way. Anything like flowers had long ago been drowned in the salty stream that had been pressed from her heart. Her tears, her sweat, her blood. She had brought love to the union and he had brought a longing after the flesh. Two months after the wedding, he had given her the first brutal beating. She had the memory of his numerous trips to Orlando with all of his wages when he had returned to her penniless, even before the first year had passed. She was young and soft then, but now she thought of her knotty, muscled limbs, her harsh knuckly hands, and drew herself up into an unhappy little ball in the middle of the big feather bed. Too late now to hope for love, even if it were not Bertha it would be someone else. This case differed from the others only in that she was bolder than the others. Too late for everything except her little home. She had built it for her old days, and planted one by one the trees and flowers there. It was lovely to her, lovely.

Somehow, before sleep came, she found herself saying aloud: "Oh well, whatever goes over the Devil's back, is got to come under his belly. Sometime or ruther, Sykes, like everybody else, is gointer reap his sowing." After that she was able to build a spiritual earthworks against her husband. His shells could no longer reach her. *Amen.* She went to sleep and slept until he announced his presence in bed by kicking her feet and rudely snatching the cover away.

"Gimme some kivah heah, an' git yo' damn foots over on yo' own side! Ah oughter mash you in yo' mouf fuh drawing dat skillet on me."

Delia went clear to the rail without answering him. A triumphant indifference to all that he was or did.

The week was as full of work for Delia as all other weeks, and Saturday found her behind her little pony, collecting and delivering clothes.

It was a hot, hot day near the end of July. The village men on Joe Clarke's porch even chewed cane listlessly. They did not hurl the caneknots as usual. They let them dribble over the edge of the porch. Even conversation had collapsed under the heat.

"Heah come Delia Jones," Jim Merchant said, as the shaggy pony came 'round the bend of the road toward them. The rusty buckboard was heaped with baskets of crisp, clean laundry.

"Yep," Joe Lindsay agreed. "Hot or col', rain or shine, jes ez reg'lar ez de weeks roll roun' Delia carries 'em an' fetches 'em on Sat'day."

"She better if she wanter eat," said Moss. "Sykes Jones aint wuth de shot an' powder hit would tek tuh kill 'em. Not to *huh* he aint."

"He sho' aint," Walter Thomas chimed in. "It's too bad, too, cause she wuz a right pritty li'l trick when he got huh. Ah'd uh mah'ied huh mahseff if he hadnter beat me to it."

Delia nodded briefly at the men as she drove past.

"Too much knockin' will ruin *any* 'oman. He done beat huh 'nough tuh kill three women, let 'lone change they looks," said Elijah Moseley. "How Sykes kin stommuck dat big black greasy Mogul he's layin' roun' wid, gits me. Ah swear dat eight-rock couldn't kiss a sardine can Ah done thowed out de back do' 'way las' yeah."

"Aw, she's fat, thass how come. He's allus been crazy 'bout fat women," put in Merchant. "He'd a' been tied up wid one long time ago if he could a' found one tuh have him. Did Ah tell yuh 'bout im come sidlin' roun' *mah* wife—bringin' her a basket uh pee-cans outa his yard fuh a present? Yessir, mah wife! She tol' him tuh take 'em right straight back home, cause Delia works so hard ovah dat washtub she reckon eveything on de place taste lak sweat an' soapsuds. Ah jus' wisht Ah'd a' caught 'im 'roun' dere! Ah'd a' made his hips ketch on fiah down dat shell road."

"Ah know he done it, too. Ah sees 'im grinnin' at every 'oman dat passes," Walter Thomas said. "But even so, he useter eat some mighty big hunks uh humble pie tuh git dat lil' 'oman he got. She wuz ez pritty ez a speckled pup! Dat wuz fifteen yeahs ago. He useter be so skeered uh losin' huh, she could make him do some parts of a husband's duty. Dey never wuz de same in de mind."

"There oughter be a law about him," said Lindsay. "He aint fit tuh carry guts tuh a bear."

Clarke spoke for the first time. "Taint no law on earth dat kin make a man be decent if it aint in 'im. There's plenty men dat takes a wife lak dey do a joint uh sugar-cane. It's round, juicy an' sweet when dey gits it. But dey squeeze an' grind, squeeze an' grind an' wring tell dey wring every drop uh pleasure dat's in 'em out. When dey's satisfied dat dey is wrung dry, dey treats 'em jes lak dey do a cane-chew. Dey throws 'em away. Dey knows whut dey is doin' while dey is at it, an' hates theirselves fuh it but they keeps on hangin' after huh tell she's empty. Den dey hates huh fuh bein' a cane-chew an' in de way."

"We oughter take Sykes an' dat stray 'oman uh his'n down in Lake Howell swamp an' lay on de rawhide till they cain't say 'Lawd a' mussy.' He allus wuz uh ovahbearin' niggah, but since dat white 'oman from up north done teached 'im how to run a automobile, he done got too biggety to live—an' we oughter kill 'im," Old Man Anderson advised.

A grunt of approval went around the porch. But the heat was melting their civic virtue and Elijah Moseley began to bait Joe Clarke.

"Come on, Joe, git a melon outa dere an' slice it up for yo' customers. We'se all sufferin' wid de heat. De bear's done got *me*!"

"Thass right, Joe, a watermelon is jes' whut Ah needs tuh cure de eppizudicks." Walter Thomas joined forces with Moseley. "Come on dere, Joe. We all is steady customers an' you aint set us up in a long time. Ah chooses dat long, bowlegged Floridy favorite."

"A god, an' be dough. You all gimme twenty cents and slice away," Clarke retorted. "Ah needs a col' slice m'self. Heah, everybody chip in. Ah'll lend y'all mah meat knife."

The money was quickly subscribed and the huge melon brought forth. At that moment, Sykes and Bertha arrived. A determined silence fell on the porch and the melon was put away again.

Merchant snapped down the blade of his jack-knife and moved toward the store door.

"Come on in, Joe, an' gimme a slab uh sow belly an' uh pound uh coffee—almost fuhgot 'twas Sat'day. Got to git on home." Most of the men left also.

Just then Delia drove past on her way home, as Sykes was ordering magnificently for Bertha. It pleased him for Delia to see.

"Git whutsoever yo' heart desires, Honey. Wait a minute, Joe. Give huh two botles uh strawberry soda-water, uh quart uh parched ground-peas, an a block uh chewin' gum."

With all this they left the store, with Sykes reminding Bertha that this was his town and she could have it if she wanted it.

The men returned soon after they left, and held their watermelon feast. "Where did Sykes Jones git dat 'oman from nohow?" Lindsay asked.

"Ovah Apopka. Guess dey musta been cleanin' out de town when she lef'. She don't look lak a thing but a hunk uh liver wid hair on it."

"Well, she sho' kin squall," Dave Carter contributed. "When she gits ready tuh laff, she jes' opens huh mouf an' latches it back tuh de las' notch. No ole grandpa alligator down in Lake Bell aint got nothin' on huh."

Bertha had been in town three months now. Sykes was still paying her room rent at Della Lewis'—the only house in town that would have taken her in. Sykes took her frequently to Winter Park to "stomps." He still assured her that he was the swellest man in the state.

"Sho' you kin have dat lil' ole house soon's Ah kin git dat 'oman outa dere. Everything b'longs tuh me an' you sho' kin have it. Ah sho' 'bominates uh skinny 'oman. Lawdy, you sho' is got one portly shape on you! You kin git *anything* you wants. Dis is *mah* town an' you sho' kin have it."

Delia's work-worn knees crawled over the earth in Gethsemane and up the rocks of Calvary many, many times during these months. She avoided the villagers and meeting places in her efforts to be blind and deaf. But Bertha nullified this to a degree, by coming to Delia's house to call Sykes out to her at the gate.

Delia and Sykes fought all the time now with no peaceful interludes. They slept and ate in silence. Two or three times Delia had attempted a timid friendliness, but she was repulsed each time. It was plain that the breaches must remain agape.

The sun had burned July to August. The heat streamed down like a million hot arrows, smiting all things living upon the earth. Grass withered, leaves browned, snakes went blind in shedding, and men and dogs went mad. Dog days!

Delia came home one day and found Sykes there before her. She wondered, but started to go on into the house without speaking, even though he was standing in the kitchen door and she must either stoop under his arm or ask him to move. He made no room for her. She noticed a soap box beside the steps, but paid no particular attention to it, knowing that he must have brought it there. As she was stooping to pass under his outstretched arm, he suddenly pushed her backward, laughingly.

"Look in de box dere Delia, Ah done brung yuh somethin'!"

She nearly fell upon the box in her stumbling, and when she saw what it held, she all but fainted outright.

"Sykes! Sykes, mah Gawd! You take dat rattlesnake 'way from heah! You *gottuh*. Oh, Jesus, have mussy!"

"Ah aint gut tuh do nothin' uh de kin'—fact is Ah aint got tuh do nothin' but die. Taint no use uh you puttin' on airs makin' out lak you skeered uh dat snake—he's gointer stay right heah tell he die. He wouldn't bite me cause Ah knows how tuh handle 'im. Nohow he wouldn't risk breakin' out his fangs 'gin *yo'* skinny laigs."

"Naw, now Sykes, don't keep dat thing 'roun' heah tuh skeer me tuh death. You knows Ah'm even feared uh earth worms. Thass de biggest snake Ah evah did see. Kill 'im Sykes, please."

"Doan ast me tuh do nothin' fuh yuh. Goin' 'roun' tryin' tuh be so damn astorperious. Naw, Ah aint gonna kill it. Ah think uh damn sight mo' uh him dan you! Dat's a nice snake an' anybody doan lak 'im kin jes' hit de grit."

The village soon heard that Sykes had the snake, and came to see and ask questions.

"How de hen-fire did you ketch dat six-foot rattler, Sykes?" Thomas asked.

"He's full uh frogs so he caint hardly move, thass how Ah eased up on 'm. But Ah'm a snake charmer an' knows how tuh handle 'em. Shux, dat aint nothin'. Ah could ketch one eve'y day if Ah so wanted tuh."

"Whut he needs is a heavy hick'ry club leaned real heavy on his head. Dat's de bes 'way tuh charm a rattlesnake."

"Naw, Walt, y'all jes' don't understand dese diamon' backs lak Ah do," said Sykes in a superior tone of voice.

The village agreed with Walter, but the snake stayed on. His box remained by the kitchen door with its screen wire covering. Two or three days later it had digested its meal of frogs and literally came to life. It rattled at every movement in the kitchen or the yard. One day as Delia came down the kitchen steps she saw his chalky-white fangs curved like scimitars hung in the wire meshes. This time she did not run away with averted eyes as usual. She stood for a long time in the doorway in a red fury that grew bloodier for every second that she regarded the creature that was her torment.

That night she broached the subject as soon as Sykes sat down to the table.

"Sykes, Ah wants you tuh take dat snake 'way fum heah. You done starved me an' Ah put up widcher, you done beat me an' Ah took dat, but you done kilt all mah insides bringin' dat varmint heah."

Sykes poured out a saucer full of coffee and drank it deliberately before he answered her.

"A whole lot Ah keer 'bout how you feels inside uh out. Dat snake aint goin' no damn wheah till Ah gits ready fuh 'im tuh go. So fur as beatin' is concerned, yuh aint took near all dat you gointer take ef yuh stay 'roun' *me*."

Delia pushed back her plate and got up from the table. "Ah hates you, Sykes," she said calmly. "Ah hates you tuh de same degree dat Ah useter love yuh. Ah done took an' took till mah belly is full up tuh mah neck. Dat's de reason Ah got mah letter fum de church an' moved mah membership tuh Woodbridge—so Ah don't haftuh take no sacrament wid yuh. Ah don't wantuh see yuh 'roun' me a-tall. Lay 'roun' wid dat 'oman all yuh wants tuh, but gwan 'way fum me an' mah house. Ah hates yuh lak uh suck-egg dog."

Sykes almost let the huge wad of corn bread and collard greens he was chewing fall out of his mouth in amazement. He had a hard time whipping himself up to the proper fury to try to answer Delia.

"Well, Ah'm glad you does hate me. Ah'm sho' tiahed uh you hangin' ontuh me. Ah don't want yuh. Look at yuh stringey ole neck! Yo' rawbony laigs an' arms is enough tuh cut uh man tuh death. You looks jes' lak de devvul's doll-baby tuh *me*. You cain't hate me no worse dan Ah hates you. Ah been hatin' *you* fuh years."

"Yo' ole black hide don't look lak nothin' tuh me, but uh passed uh wrinkled up rubber, wid yo' big ole yeahs flappin' on each side lak uh paih uh buzzard wings. Don't think Ah'm gointuh be run 'way fum mah house neither. Ah'm goin' tuh de white folks bout *you*, mah young man, de very nex' time you lay yo' han's on me. Mah cup is done run ovah." Delia said this with no signs of fear and Sykes departed from the house, threatening her, but made not the slightest move to carry out any of them.

That night he did not return at all, and the next day being Sunday, Delia was glad that she did not have to quarrel before she hitched up her pony and drove the four miles to Woodbridge.

She stayed to the night service—"love feast"—which was very warm and full of spirit. In the emotional winds her domestic trials were borne far and wide so that she sang as she drove homeward,

Jurden water, black an' col'
Chills de body, not de soul
An' Ah wantah cross Jurden in uh calm time.

She came from the barn to the kitchen door and stopped.

"Whut's de mattah, ol' satan, you aint kickin' up yo' racket?" She addressed the snake's box. Complete silence. She went on into the house with a new hope in its birth struggles. Perhaps her threat to go to the white folks had frightened Sykes! Perhaps he was sorry! Fifteen years of misery and suppression had brought Delia to the place where she would hope *anything* that looked towards a way over or through her wall of inhibitions.

She felt in the match safe behind the stove at once for a match. There was only one there.

"Dat niggah wouldn't fetch nothin' heah tuh save his rotten neck, but he kin run thew whut Ah brings quick enough. Now he done toted off nigh on tuh haff uh box uh matches. He done had dat 'oman heah in mah house, too."

Nobody but a woman could tell how she knew this even before she struck the match. But she did and it put her into a new fury.

Presently she brought in the tubs to put the white things to soak. This time she decided she need not bring the hamper out of the bedroom; she would go in there and do the sorting. She picked up the pot-bellied lamp and went in. The room was small and the hamper stood hard by the foot of the white iron bed. She could sit and reach through the bedposts — resting as she worked.

"Ah wantah cross Jurden in uh calm time." She was singing again. The mood of the "love feast" had returned. She threw back the lid of the basket almost gaily. Then, moved by both horror and terror, she sprung back toward the door. *There lay the snake in the basket!* He moved sluggishly at first, but even as she turned round and round, jumped up and down in an insanity of fear, he began to stir vigorously. She saw him pouring his awful beauty from the basket upon the bed, then she seized the lamp and ran as fast as she could to the kitchen. The wind from the open door blew out the light and the darkness added to her terror. She sped to the darkness of the yard, slamming the door after her before she thought to set down the lamp. She did not feel safe even on the ground, so she climbed up in the hay barn.

There for an hour or more she lay sprawled upon the hay a gibbering wreck.

Finally she grew quiet, and after that, coherent thought. With this, stalked through her a cold, bloody rage. Hours of this. A period of introspection, a space of retrospection, then a mixture of both. Out of this an awful calm.

"Well, Ah done de bes' Ah could. If things aint right, Gawd knows taint mah fault."

She went to sleep — a twitchy sleep — and woke up to a faint gray sky. There was a loud hollow sound below. She peered out. Sykes was at the wood-pile, demolishing a wire-covered box.

He hurried to the kitchen door, but hung outside there some minutes before he entered, and stood some minutes more inside before he closed it after him.

The gray in the sky was spreading. Delia descended without fear now, and crouched beneath the low bedroom window. The drawn shade shut out the dawn, shut in the night. But the thin walls held back no sound.

"Dat ol' scratch is woke up now!" She mused at the tremendous whirr inside, which every woodsman knows, is one of the sound illusions. The rattler is a ventriloquist. His whirr sounds to the right, to the left, straight ahead, behind, close under foot—everywhere but where it is. Woe to him who guesses wrong unless he is prepared to hold up his end of the argument! Sometimes he strikes without rattling at all.

Inside, Sykes heard nothing until he knocked a pot lid off the stove while trying to reach the match safe in the dark. He had emptied his pockets at Bertha's.

The snake seemed to wake up under the stove and Sykes made a quick leap into the bedroom. In spite of the gin he had had, his head was clearing now.

"Mah Gawd!" he chattered, "ef Ah could on'y strack uh light!"

The rattling ceased for a moment as he stood paralyzed. He waited. It seemed that the snake waited also.

"Oh fuh de light! Ah thought he'd be too sick"—Sykes was muttering to himself when the whirr began again, closer, right underfoot this time. Long before this, Sykes' ability to think had been flattened down to primitive instinct and he leaped—onto the bed.

Outside Delia hears a cry that might have come from a maddened chimpanzee, a stricken gorilla. All the terror, all the horror, all the rage that man possibly could express, without a recognizable human sound.

A tremendous stir inside there, another series of animal screams, the intermittent whirr of the reptile. The shade torn violently down from the window, letting in the red dawn, a huge brown hand seizing the window stick, great dull blows upon the wooden floor punctuating the gibberish of sound long after the rattle of the snake had abruptly subsided. All this Delia could see and hear from her place beneath the window, and it made her ill. She crept over to the four-o'clocks and stretched herself on the cool earth to recover.

She lay there. "Delia, Delia!" She could hear Sykes calling in a most despairing tone as one who expected no answer. The sun crept on up, and he called. Delia could not move—her legs were gone flabby. She never moved, he called, and the sun kept rising.

"Mah Gawd!" she heard him moan. "Mah Gawd fum Heben!" She heard him stumbling about and got up from her flower-bed. The sun was growing warm. As she approached the door she heard him call out hopefully, "Delia, is dat you Ah heah?"

She saw him on his hands and knees as soon as she reached the door. He crept an inch or two toward her—all that he was able, and she saw his horribly swollen neck and his one open eye shining with hope. A surge of pity too strong to support bore her away from that eye that must, could not, fail to see the tubs. He would see the lamp. Orlando with its doctors was too far. She could scarcely reach the Chinaberry tree, where she waited in the growing heat while inside she knew the cold river was creeping up and up to extinguish that eye which must know by now that she knew.

[1926]

F. SCOTT FITZGERALD   [1896–1940]

Winter Dreams

I

Some of the caddies were poor as sin and lived in one-room houses with a neurasthenic cow in the front yard, but Dexter Green's father owned the second best grocery-store in Black Bear—the best one was "The Hub," patronized by the wealthy people from Sherry Island—and Dexter caddied only for pocket-money.

In the fall when the days became crisp and gray, and the long Minnesota winter shut down like the white lid of a box, Dexter's skis moved over the snow that hid the fairways of the golf course. At these times the country gave him a feeling of profound melancholy—it offended him that the links should lie in enforced fallowness, haunted by ragged sparrows for the long season. It was dreary, too, that on the tees where the gay colors fluttered in summer there were now only the desolate sandboxes knee-deep in crusted ice. When he crossed the hills the wind blew cold as misery, and if the sun was out he tramped with his eyes squinted up against the hard dimensionless glare.

In April the winter ceased abruptly. The snow ran down into Black Bear Lake scarcely tarrying for the early golfers to brave the season with red and black balls. Without elation, without an interval of moist glory, the cold was gone.

Dexter knew that there was something dismal about this Northern spring, just as he knew there was something gorgeous about the fall. Fall made him clinch his hands and tremble and repeat idiotic sentences to himself, and make brisk abrupt gestures of command to imaginary audiences and armies. October filled him with hope which November raised to a sort of ecstatic triumph, and in this mood the fleeting brilliant impressions of the summer at Sherry Island were ready grist to his mill. He became a golf champion and defeated Mr. T. A. Hedrick in a marvellous match played a hundred times over the fairways of his imagination, a match each detail of which he changed about untiringly—sometimes he won with almost laughable ease, sometimes he came up magnificently from behind. Again, stepping from a Pierce-Arrow automobile, like Mr. Mortimer Jones, he strolled frigidly into the lounge of the Sherry Island Golf Club—or perhaps, surrounded by an admiring crowd, he gave an exhibition of fancy diving from the spring-board of the club raft. . . . Among those who watched him in open-mouthed wonder was Mr. Mortimer Jones.

And one day it came to pass that Mr. Jones—himself and not his ghost—came up to Dexter with tears in his eyes and said that Dexter was the—— best caddy in the club, and wouldn't he decide not to quit if Mr. Jones made it worth his while, because every other—— caddy in the club lost one ball a hole for him—regularly——

"No, sir," said Dexter decisively, "I don't want to caddy any more." Then, after a pause: "I'm too old."

"You're not more than fourteen. Why the devil did you decide just this morning that you wanted to quit? You promised that next week you'd go over to the State tournament with me."

"I decided I was too old."

Dexter handed in his "A Class" badge, collected what money was due him from the caddy master, and walked home to Black Bear Village.

"The best—— caddy I ever saw," shouted Mr. Mortimer Jones over a drink that afternoon. "Never lost a ball! Willing! Intelligent! Quiet! Honest! Grateful!"

The little girl who had done this was eleven—beautifully ugly as little girls are apt to be who are destined after a few years to be inexpressibly lovely and bring no end of misery to a great number of men. The spark, however, was perceptible. There was a general ungodliness in the way her lips twisted down at the corners when she smiled, and in the—Heaven help us!—in the almost passionate quality of her eyes. Vitality is born early in such women. It was utterly in evidence now, shining through her thin frame in a sort of glow.

She had come eagerly out on to the course at nine o'clock with a white linen nurse and five small new golf-clubs in a white canvas bag which the nurse was carrying. When Dexter first saw her she was standing by the caddy house, rather ill at ease and trying to conceal the fact by engaging her nurse in an obviously unnatural conversation graced by startling and irrelevant grimaces from herself.

"Well, it's certainly a nice day, Hilda," Dexter heard her say. She drew down the corners of her mouth, smiled, and glanced furtively around, her eyes in transit falling for an instant on Dexter.

Then to the nurse:

"Well, I guess there aren't very many people out here this morning, are there?"

The smile again—radiant, blatantly artificial—convincing.

"I don't know what we're supposed to do now," said the nurse, looking nowhere in particular.

"Oh, that's all right. I'll fix it up."

Dexter stood perfectly still, his mouth slightly ajar. He knew that if he moved forward a step his stare would be in her line of vision—if he moved backward he would lose his full view of her face. For a moment he had not realized how young she was. Now he remembered having seen her several times the year before—in bloomers.

Suddenly, involuntarily, he laughed, a short abrupt laugh—then, startled by himself, he turned and began to walk quickly away.

"Boy!"

Dexter stopped.

"Boy——"

Beyond question he was addressed. Not only that, but he was treated to that absurd smile, that preposterous smile—the memory of which at least a dozen men were to carry into middle age.

"Boy, do you know where the golf teacher is?"

"He's giving a lesson."

"Well, do you know where the caddy-master is?"

"He isn't here yet this morning."

"Oh." For a moment this baffled her. She stood alternately on her right and left foot.

"We'd like to get a caddy," said the nurse. "Mrs. Mortimer Jones sent us out to play golf, and we don't know how without we get a caddy."

Here she was stopped by an ominous glance from Miss Jones, followed immediately by the smile.

"There aren't any caddies here except me," said Dexter to the nurse, "and I got to stay here in charge until the caddy-master gets here."

"Oh."

Miss Jones and her retinue now withdrew, and at a proper distance from Dexter became involved in a heated conversation, which was concluded by Miss Jones taking one of the clubs and hitting it on the ground with violence. For further emphasis she raised it again and was about to bring it down smartly upon the nurse's bosom, when the nurse seized the club and twisted it from her hands.

"You damn little mean old *thing*!" cried Miss Jones wildly.

Another argument ensued. Realizing that the elements of the comedy were implied in the scene, Dexter several times began to laugh, but each time restrained the laugh before it reached audibility. He could not resist the monstrous conviction that the little girl was justified in beating the nurse.

The situation was resolved by the fortuitous appearance of the caddy-master, who was appealed to immediately by the nurse.

"Miss Jones is to have a little caddy, and this one says he can't go."

"Mr. McKenna said I was to wait here till you came," said Dexter quickly.

"Well, he's here now." Miss Jones smiled cheerfully at the caddy-master. Then she dropped her bag and set off at a haughty mince toward the first tee.

"Well?" The caddy-master turned to Dexter. "What you standing there like a dummy for? Go pick up the young lady's clubs."

"I don't think I'll go out to-day," said Dexter.

"You don't ——"

"I think I'll quit."

The enormity of his decision frightened him. He was a favorite caddy, and the thirty dollars a month he earned through the summer were not to be made elsewhere around the lake. But he had received a strong emotional shock, and his perturbation required a violent and immediate outlet.

It is not so simple as that, either. As so frequently would be the case in the future, Dexter was unconsciously dictated to by his winter dreams.

II

Now, of course, the quality and the seasonability of these winter dreams varied, but the stuff of them remained. They persuaded Dexter several years later to pass up a business course at the State university—his father, prospering now, would have paid his way—for the precarious advantage of attending an older and more famous university in the East, where he was bothered by his scanty funds. But do not get the impression, because his winter dreams happened to be concerned at first with musings on the rich, that there was anything merely snobbish in the boy. He wanted not association with glittering things and glittering people— he wanted the glittering things themselves. Often he reached out for the best without knowing why he wanted it—and sometimes he ran up against the mysterious denials and prohibitions in which life indulges. It is with one of those denials and not with his career as a whole that this story deals.

He made money. It was rather amazing. After college he went to the city from which Black Bear Lake draws its wealthy patrons. When he was only twenty-three and had been there not quite two years, there were already people who liked to say: "Now *there's* a boy—" All about him rich men's sons were peddling bonds precariously, or investing patrimonies precariously, or plodding through the two dozen volumes of the "George Washington Commercial Course," but Dexter borrowed a thousand dollars on his college degree and his confident mouth, and bought a partnership in a laundry.

It was a small laundry when he went into it but Dexter made a specialty of learning how the English washed fine woollen golf-stockings without shrinking them, and within a year he was catering to the trade that wore knickerbockers. Men were insisting that their Shetland hose and sweaters go to his laundry just as they had insisted on a caddy who could find golf-balls. A little later he was doing their wives' lingerie as well—and running five branches in different parts of the city. Before he was twenty-seven he owned the largest string of laundries in his section of the country. It was then that he sold out and went to New York. But the part of his story that concerns us goes back to the days when he was making his first big success.

When he was twenty-three Mr. Hart—one of the gray-haired men who like to say "Now there's a boy"—gave him a guest card to the Sherry Island Golf Club for a week-end. So he signed his name one day on the register, and that afternoon played golf in a foursome with Mr. Hart and Mr. Sandwood and Mr. T. A. Hedrick. He did not consider it necessary to remark that he had once carried Mr. Hart's bag over this same links, and that he knew every trap and gully with his eyes shut—but he found himself glancing at the four caddies who trailed them, trying to catch a gleam or gesture that would remind him of himself, that would lessen the gap which lay between his present and his past.

It was a curious day, slashed abruptly with fleeting, familiar impressions. One minute he had the sense of being a trespasser—in the next he was impressed by the tremendous superiority he felt toward Mr. T. A. Hedrick, who was a bore and not even a good golfer any more.

Then, because of a ball Mr. Hart lost near the fifteenth green, an enormous thing happened. While they were searching the stiff grasses of the rough there was a clear call of "Fore!" from behind a hill in their rear. And as they all turned abruptly from their search a bright new ball sliced abruptly over the hill and caught Mr. T. A. Hedrick in the abdomen.

"By Gad!" cried Mr. T. A. Hedrick, "they ought to put some of these crazy women off the course. It's getting to be outrageous."

A head and a voice came up together over the hill:

"Do you mind if we go through?"

"You hit me in the stomach!" declared Mr. Hedrick wildly.

"Did I?" The girl approached the group of men. "I'm sorry. I yelled 'Fore!'"

Her glance fell casually on each of the men—then scanned the fairway for her ball.

"Did I bounce into the rough?"

It was impossible to determine whether this question was ingenuous or malicious. In a moment, however, she left no doubt, for as her partner came up over the hill she called cheerfully:

"Here I am! I'd have gone on the green except that I hit something."

As she took her stance for a short mashie shot, Dexter looked at her closely. She wore a blue gingham dress, rimmed at throat and shoulders with a white edging that accentuated her tan. The quality of exaggeration, of thinness, which had made her passionate eyes and down-turning mouth absurd at eleven, was gone now. She was arrestingly beautiful. The color in her cheeks was centered like the color in a picture—it was not a "high" color, but a sort of fluctuating and feverish warmth, so shaded that it seemed at any moment it would recede and disappear. This color and the mobility of her mouth gave a continual impression of flux, of intense life, of passionate vitality—balanced only partially by the sad luxury of her eyes.

She swung her mashie impatiently and without interest, pitching the ball into a sand-pit on the other side of the green. With a quick, insincere smile and a careless "Thank you!" she went on after it.

"That Judy Jones!" remarked Mr. Hedrick on the next tee, as they waited—some moments—for her to play on ahead. "All she needs is to be turned up and spanked for six months and then to be married off to an old-fashioned cavalry captain."

"My God, she's good-looking!" said Mr. Sandwood, who was just over thirty.

"Good-looking!" cried Mr. Hedrick contemptuously, "she always looks as if she wanted to be kissed! Turning those big cow-eyes on every calf in town!"

It was doubtful if Mr. Hedrick intended a reference to the maternal instinct.

"She'd play pretty good golf if she'd try," said Mr. Sandwood.

"She has no form," said Mr. Hedrick solemnly.

"She has a nice figure," said Mr. Sandwood.

"Better thank the Lord she doesn't drive a swifter ball," said Mr. Hart, winking at Dexter.

Later in the afternoon the sun went down with a riotous swirl of gold and varying blues and scarlets, and left the dry, rustling night of Western summer. Dexter watched from the veranda of the Golf Club, watched the even overlap of the waters in the little wind, silver molasses under the harvest-moon. Then the moon held a finger to her lips and the lake be-came a clear pool, pale and quiet. Dexter put on his bathing-suit and swam out to the farthest raft, where he stretched dripping on the wet canvas of the spring-board.

There was a fish jumping and a star shining and the lights around the lake were gleaming. Over on a dark peninsula a piano was playing the songs of last summer and of summers before that—songs from "Chin-Chin" and "The Count of Luxemburg" and "The Chocolate Soldier"—and because the sound of a piano over a stretch of water had always seemed beautiful to Dexter he lay perfectly quiet and listened.

The tune the piano was playing at that moment had been gay and new five years before when Dexter was a sophomore at college. They had played it at a prom once when he could not afford the luxury of proms, and he had stood outside the gymnasium and listened. The sound of the tune precipitated in him a sort of ecstasy and it was with that ecstasy he viewed what happened to him now. It was a mood of intense apprecia-tion, a sense that, for once, he was magnificently attuned to life and that everything about him was radiating a brightness and a glamour he might never know again.

A low, pale oblong detached itself suddenly from the darkness of the Island, spitting forth the reverberate sound of a racing motor-boat. Two white streamers of cleft water rolled themselves out behind it and almost immediately the boat was beside him, drowning out the hot tinkle of the piano in the drone of its spray. Dexter raising himself on his arms was aware of a figure standing at the wheel, of two dark eyes regarding him over the lengthening space of water—then the boat had gone by and was sweeping in an immense and purposeless circle of spray round and round in the middle of the lake. With equal eccentricity one of the circles flattened out and headed back toward the raft.

"Who's that?" she called, shutting off her motor. She was so near now that Dexter could see her bathing-suit, which consisted apparently of pink rompers.

The nose of the boat bumped the raft, and as the latter tilted rakishly he was precipitated toward her. With different degrees of interest they recognized each other.

"Aren't you one of those men we played through this afternoon?" she demanded.

He was.

"Well, do you know how to drive a motor-boat? Because if you do I wish you'd drive this one so I can ride on the surf-board behind. My name is Judy Jones"—she favored him with an absurd smirk—rather, what tried to be a smirk, for, twist her mouth as she might, it was not grotesque, it was merely beautiful—"and I live in a house over there on the Island, and in that house there is a man waiting for me. When he drove up at the door I drove out of the dock because he says I'm his ideal."

There was a fish jumping and a star shining and the lights around the lake were gleaming. Dexter sat beside Judy Jones and she explained how her boat was driven. Then she was in the water, swimming to the floating surf-board with a sinuous crawl. Watching her was without effort to the eye, watching a branch waving or a sea-gull flying. Her arms, burned to butternut, moved sinuously among the dull platinum ripples, elbow appearing first, casting the forearm back with a cadence of falling water, then reaching out and down, stabbing a path ahead.

They moved out into the lake; turning, Dexter saw that she was kneeling on the low rear of the now uptilted surf-board.

"Go faster," she called, "fast as it'll go."

Obediently he jammed the lever forward and the white spray mounted at the bow. When he looked around again the girl was standing up on the rushing board, her arms spread wide, her eyes lifted toward the moon.

"It's awful cold," she shouted. "What's your name?"

He told her.

"Well, why don't you come to dinner to-morrow night?"

His heart turned over like the fly-wheel of the boat, and, for the second time, her casual whim gave a new direction to his life.

III

Next evening while he waited for her to come down-stairs, Dexter peopled the soft deep summer room and the sun-porch that opened from it with the men who had already loved Judy Jones. He knew the sort of men they were—the men who when he first went to college had entered from the great prep schools with graceful clothes and the deep tan of healthy summers. He had seen that, in one sense, he was better than these men. He was newer and stronger. Yet in acknowledging to himself that he wished his children to be like them he was admitting that he was but the rough, strong stuff from which they eternally sprang.

When the time had come for him to wear good clothes, he had known who were the best tailors in America, and the best tailors in America had made him the suit he wore this evening. He had acquired that particular reserve peculiar to his university, that set it off from other universities. He recognized the value to him of such a mannerism and he had adopted it; he knew that to be careless in dress and manner required more confidence than to be careful. But carelessness was for his children. His mother's name had been Krimslich. She was a Bohemian of the peasant class and she had talked broken English to the end of her days. Her son must keep to the set patterns.

At a little after seven Judy Jones came down-stairs. She wore a blue silk afternoon dress, and he was disappointed at first that she had not put on something more elaborate. This feeling was accentuated when, after a brief greeting, she went to the door of a butler's pantry and pushing it open called: "You can serve dinner, Martha." He had rather expected that a butler would announce dinner, that there would be a cocktail. Then he put these thoughts behind him as they sat down side by side on a lounge and looked at each other.

"Father and mother won't be here," she said thoughtfully.

He remembered the last time he had seen her father, and he was glad the parents were not to be here to-night—they might wonder who he was. He had been born in Keeble, a Minnesota village fifty miles farther north, and he always gave Keeble as his home instead of Black Bear Village. Country towns were well enough to come from if they weren't inconveniently in sight and used as footstools by fashionable lakes.

They talked of his university, which she had visited frequently during the past two years, and of the near-by city which supplied Sherry Island with its patrons, and whither Dexter would return next day to his prospering laundries.

During dinner she slipped into a moody depression which gave Dexter a feeling of uneasiness. Whatever petulance she uttered in her throaty voice worried him. Whatever she smiled at—at him, at a chicken liver, at nothing—it disturbed him that her smile could have no root in mirth, or even in amusement. When the scarlet corners of her lips curved down, it was less a smile than an invitation to a kiss.

Then, after dinner, she led him out on the dark sun-porch and deliberately changed the atmosphere.

"Do you mind if I weep a little?" she said.

"I'm afraid I'm boring you," he responded quickly.

"You're not. I like you. But I've just had a terrible afternoon. There was a man I cared about, and this afternoon he told me out of a clear sky that he was poor as a church-mouse. He'd never even hinted it before. Does this sound horribly mundane?"

"Perhaps he was afraid to tell you."

"Suppose he was," she answered. "He didn't start right. You see, if I'd thought of him as poor—well, I've been mad about loads of poor men, and fully intended to marry them all. But in this case, I hadn't thought of him that way, and my interest in him wasn't strong enough to survive the shock. As if a girl calmly informed her fiancé that she was a widow. He might not object to widows, but——

"Let's start right," she interrupted herself suddenly. "Who are you, any-how?"

For a moment Dexter hesitated. Then:

"I'm nobody," he announced. "My career is largely a matter of futures."

"Are you poor?"

"No," he said frankly, "I'm probably making more money than any man my age in the Northwest. I know that's an obnoxious remark, but you advised me to start right."

There was a pause. Then she smiled and the corners of her mouth drooped and an almost imperceptible sway brought her closer to him, looking up into his eyes. A lump rose in Dexter's throat, and he waited breathless for the experiment, facing the unpredictable compound that would form mysteriously from the elements of their lips. Then he saw—she communicated her excitement to him, lavishly, deeply, with kisses that were not a promise but a fulfillment. They aroused in him not hunger demanding renewal but surfeit that would demand more surfeit . . . kisses that were like charity, creating want by holding back nothing at all.

It did not take him many hours to decide that he had wanted Judy Jones ever since he was a proud, desirous little boy.

IV

It began like that—and continued, with varying shades of intensity, on such a note right up to the dénouement. Dexter surrendered a part of himself to the most direct and unprincipled personality with which he had ever come in contact. Whatever Judy wanted, she went after with the full pressure of her charm. There was no divergence of method, no jockeying for position or premeditation of effects—there was a very little mental side to any of her affairs. She simply made men conscious to the highest degree of her physical loveliness. Dexter had no desire to change her. Her deficiencies were knit up with a passionate energy that transcended and justified them.

When, as Judy's head lay against his shoulder that first night, she whispered, "I don't know what's the matter with me. Last night I thought I was in love with a man and to-night I think I'm in love with you——"—it seemed to him a beautiful and romantic thing to say. It was the exquisite excitability that for the moment he controlled and owned. But a week later he was compelled to view this same quality in a different light. She took him in her roadster to a picnic supper, and after supper she disappeared, likewise in her roadster, with another man. Dexter became enormously upset and was scarcely able to be decently civil to the other people present. When she assured him that she had not kissed the other man, he knew she was lying—yet he was glad that she had taken the trouble to lie to him.

He was, as he found before the summer ended, one of a varying dozen who circulated about her. Each of them had at one time been favored above all others—about half of them still basked in the solace of occasional sentimental revivals. Whenever one showed signs of dropping out through long neglect, she granted him a brief honeyed hour, which encouraged him to tag along for a year or so longer. Judy made these forays upon the helpless and defeated without malice, indeed half unconscious that there was anything mischievous in what she did.

When a new man came to town every one dropped out—dates were automatically cancelled.

The helpless part of trying to do anything about it was that she did it all herself. She was not a girl who could be "won" in the kinetic sense—she was proof against cleverness, she was proof against charm; if any of these assailed her too strongly she would immediately resolve the affair to a physical basis, and under the magic of her physical splendor the strong as well as the brilliant played her game and not their own. She was entertained only by the gratification of her desires and by the direct exercise of her own charm. Perhaps from so much youthful love, so many youthful lovers, she had come, in self-defense, to nourish herself wholly from within.

Succeeding Dexter's first exhilaration came restlessness and dissatisfaction. The helpless ecstasy of losing himself in her was opiate rather than tonic. It was fortunate for his work during the winter that those moments of ecstasy came infrequently. Early in their acquaintance it had seemed for a while that there was a deep and spontaneous mutual attraction—that first August, for example—three days of long evenings on her dusky veranda, of strange wan kisses through the late afternoon, in shadowy alcoves or behind the protecting trellises of the garden arbors, of mornings when she was fresh as a dream and almost shy at meeting him in the clarity of the rising day. There was all the ecstasy of an engagement about it, sharpened by his realization that there was no engagement. It was during those three days that, for the first time, he had asked her to marry him. She said "maybe some day," she said "kiss me," she said "I'd like to marry you," she said "I love you"—she said—nothing.

The three days were interrupted by the arrival of a New York man who visited at her house for half September. To Dexter's agony, rumor engaged them. The man was the son of the president of a great trust company. But at the end of a month it was reported that Judy was yawning. At a dance one night she sat all evening in a motor-boat with a local beau, while the New Yorker searched the club for her frantically. She told the local beau that she was bored with her visitor, and two days later he left. She was seen with him at the station, and it was reported that he looked very mournful indeed.

On this note the summer ended. Dexter was twenty-four, and he found himself increasingly in a position to do as he wished. He joined two clubs in the city and lived at one of them. Though he was by no means an integral part of the stag-lines at these clubs, he managed to be on hand at dances where Judy Jones was likely to appear. He could have gone out socially as much as he liked—he was an eligible young man, now, and popular with down-town fathers. His confessed devotion to Judy Jones had rather solidified his position. But he had no social aspirations and rather despised the dancing men who were always on tap for the Thursday or Saturday parties and who filled in at dinners with the younger married set. Already he was playing with the idea of going East to New York. He wanted to take Judy Jones with him. No disillusion as to the world in which she had grown up could cure his illusion as to her desirability.

Remember that—for only in the light of it can what he did for her be understood.

Eighteen months after he first met Judy Jones he became engaged to another girl. Her name was Irene Scheerer, and her father was one of the men who had always believed in Dexter. Irene was light-haired and sweet and honorable, and a little stout, and she had two suitors whom she pleasantly relinquished when Dexter formally asked her to marry him.

Summer, fall, winter, spring, another summer, another fall—so much he had given of his active life to the incorrigible lips of Judy Jones. She had treated him with interest, with encouragement, with malice, with indifference, with contempt. She had inflicted on him the innumerable little slights and indignities possible in such a case—as if in revenge for having ever cared for him at all. She had beckoned him and yawned at him and beckoned him again and he had responded often with bitterness and narrowed eyes. She had brought him ecstatic happiness and intolerable agony of spirit. She had caused him untold inconvenience and not a little trouble. She had insulted him, and she had ridden over him, and she had played his interest in her against his interest in his work—for fun. She had done everything to him except to criticise him—this she had not done—it seemed to him only because it might have sullied the utter indifference she manifested and sincerely felt toward him.

When autumn had come and gone again it occurred to him that he could not have Judy Jones. He had to beat this into his mind but he convinced himself at last. He lay awake at night for a while and argued it over. He told himself the trouble and the pain she had caused him, he enumerated her glaring deficiencies as a wife. Then he said to himself that he loved her, and after a while he fell asleep. For a week, lest he imagined her husky voice over the telephone or her eyes opposite him at lunch, he worked hard and late, and at night he went to his office and plotted out his years.

At the end of a week he went to a dance and cut in on her once. For almost the first time since they had met he did not ask her to sit out with him or tell her that she was lovely. It hurt him that she did not miss these things—that was all. He was not jealous when he saw that there was a new man to-night. He had been hardened against jealousy long before.

He stayed late at the dance. He sat for an hour with Irene Scheerer and talked about books and about music. He knew very little about either. But he was beginning to be master of his own time now, and he had a rather priggish notion that he—the young and already fabulously successful Dexter Green—should know more about such things.

That was in October, when he was twenty-five. In January, Dexter and Irene became engaged. It was to be announced in June, and they were to be married three months later.

The Minnesota winter prolonged itself interminably, and it was almost May when the winds came soft and the snow ran down into Black Bear Lake at last. For the first time in over a year Dexter was enjoying a certain tranquility of spirit. Judy Jones had been in Florida, and afterward in Hot Springs, and somewhere she had been engaged, and somewhere she had broken it off. At first, when Dexter had definitely given her up, it had made him sad that people still linked them together and asked for news of her, but when he began to be placed at dinner next to Irene Scheerer people didn't ask him about her any more—they told him about her. He ceased to be an authority on her.

May at last. Dexter walked the streets at night when the darkness was damp as rain, wondering that so soon, with so little done, so much of ecstasy had gone from him. May one year back had been marked by Judy's poignant, unforgivable, yet forgiven turbulence—it had been one of those rare times when he fancied she had grown to care for him. That old penny's worth of happiness he had spent for this bushel of content. He knew that Irene would be no more than a curtain spread behind him, a hand moving among gleaming teacups, a voice calling to children . . . fire and loveliness were gone, the magic of nights and the wonder of the varying hours and seasons . . . slender lips, down-turning, dropping to his lips and bearing him up into a heaven of eyes. . . . The thing was deep in him. He was too strong and alive for it to die lightly.

In the middle of May when the weather balanced for a few days on the thin bridge that led to deep summer he turned in one night at Irene's house. Their engagement was to be announced in a week now—no one would be surprised at it. And to-night they would sit together on the lounge at the University Club and look on for an hour at the dancers. It gave him a sense of solidity to go with her—she was so sturdily popular, so intensely "great."

He mounted the steps of the brownstone house and stepped inside.

"Irene," he called.

Mrs. Scheerer came out of the living-room to meet him.

"Dexter," she said, "Irene's gone up-stairs with a splitting headache. She wanted to go with you but I made her go to bed."

"Nothing serious, I——"

"Oh, no. She's going to play golf with you in the morning. You can spare her for just one night, can't you, Dexter?"

Her smile was kind. She and Dexter liked each other. In the living-room he talked for a moment before he said good-night.

Returning to the University Club, where he had rooms, he stood in the doorway for a moment and watched the dancers. He leaned against the door-post, nodded at a man or two—yawned.

"Hello, darling."

The familiar voice at his elbow startled him. Judy Jones had left a man and crossed the room to him—Judy Jones, a slender enamelled doll in cloth of gold: gold in a band at her head, gold in two slipper points at her dress's hem. The fragile glow of her face seemed to blossom as she smiled at him. A breeze of warmth and light blew through the room. His hands in the pockets of his dinner-jacket tightened spasmodically. He was filled with a sudden excitement.

"When did you get back?" he asked casually.

"Come here and I'll tell you about it."

She turned and he followed her. She had been away—he could have wept at the wonder of her return. She had passed through enchanted streets, doing things that were like provocative music. All mysterious happenings, all fresh and quickening hopes, had gone away with her, come back with her now.

She turned in the doorway.

"Have you a car here? If you haven't, I have."

"I have a coupé."

In then, with a rustle of golden cloth. He slammed the door. Into so many cars she had stepped—like this—like that—her back against the leather, so—her elbow resting on the door—waiting. She would have been soiled long since had there been anything to soil her—except herself—but this was her own self outpouring.

With an effort he forced himself to start the car and back into the street. This was nothing, he must remember. She had done this before, and he had put her behind him, as he would have crossed a bad account from his books.

He drove slowly down-town and, affecting abstraction, traversed the deserted streets of the business section, peopled here and there where a movie was giving out its crowd or where consumptive or pugilistic youth lounged in front of pool halls. The clink of glasses and the slap of hands on the bars issued from saloons, cloisters of glazed glass and dirty yellow light.

She was watching him closely and the silence was embarrassing, yet in this crisis he could find no casual word with which to profane the hour. At a convenient turning he began to zigzag back toward the University Club.

"Have you missed me?" she asked suddenly.

"Everybody missed you."

He wondered if she knew of Irene Scheerer. She had been back only a day—her absence had been almost contemporaneous with his engagement.

"What a remark!" Judy laughed sadly—without sadness. She looked at him searchingly. He became absorbed in the dashboard.

"You're handsomer than you used to be," she said thoughtfully. "Dexter, you have the most rememberable eyes."

He could have laughed at this, but he did not laugh. It was the sort of thing that was said to sophomores. Yet it stabbed at him.

"I'm awfully tired of everything, darling." She called every one darling, endowing the endearment with careless, individual comraderie. "I wish you'd marry me."

The directness of this confused him. He should have told her now that he was going to marry another girl, but he could not tell her. He could as easily have sworn that he had never loved her.

"I think we'd get along," she continued, on the same note, "unless probably you've forgotten me and fallen in love with another girl."

Her confidence was obviously enormous. She had said, in effect, that she found such a thing impossible to believe, that if it were true he had merely committed a childish indiscretion—and probably to show off. She would forgive him, because it was not a matter of any moment but rather something to be brushed aside lightly.

"Of course you could never love anybody but me," she continued. "I like the way you love me. Oh, Dexter, have you forgotten last year?"

"No, I haven't forgotten."

"Neither have I!"

Was she sincerely moved—or was she carried along by the wave of her own acting?

"I wish we could be like that again," she said, and he forced himself to answer:

"I don't think we can."

"I suppose not. . . . I hear you're giving Irene Scheerer a violent rush."

There was not the faintest emphasis on the name, yet Dexter was suddenly ashamed.

"Oh, take me home," cried Judy suddenly; "I don't want to go back to that idiotic dance—with those children."

Then, as he turned up the street that led to the residence district, Judy began to cry quietly to herself. He had never seen her cry before.

The dark street lightened, the dwellings of the rich loomed up around them, he stopped his coupé in front of the great white bulk of the Mortimer Joneses house, somnolent, gorgeous, drenched with the splendor of the damp moonlight. Its solidity startled him. The strong walls, the steel of the girders, the breadth and beam and pomp of it were there only to bring out the contrast with the young beauty beside him. It was sturdy to accentuate her slightness—as if to show what a breeze could be generated by a butterfly's wing.

He sat perfectly quiet, his nerves in wild clamor, afraid that if he moved he would find her irresistibly in his arms. Two tears had rolled down her wet face and trembled on her upper lip.

"I'm more beautiful than anybody else," she said brokenly, "why can't I be happy?" Her moist eyes tore at his stability—her mouth turned slowly downward with an exquisite sadness: "I'd like to marry you if you'll have me, Dexter. I suppose you think I'm not worth having, but I'll be so beautiful for you, Dexter."

A million phrases of anger, pride, passion, hatred, tenderness fought on his lips. Then a perfect wave of emotion washed over him, carrying off with it a sediment of wisdom, of convention, of doubt, of honor. This was his girl who was speaking, his own, his beautiful, his pride.

"Won't you come in?" He heard her draw in her breath sharply.

Waiting.

"All right," his voice was trembling, "I'll come in."

V

It was strange that neither when it was over nor a long time afterward did he regret that night. Looking at it from the perspective of ten years, the fact that Judy's flare for him endured just one month seemed of little importance. Nor did it matter that by his yielding he subjected himself to a deeper agony in the end and gave serious hurt to Irene Scheerer and to

Irene's parents, who had befriended him. There was nothing sufficiently pictorial about Irene's grief to stamp itself on his mind.

Dexter was at bottom hard-minded. The attitude of the city on his action was of no importance to him, not because he was going to leave the city, but because any outside attitude on the situation seemed superficial. He was completely indifferent to popular opinion. Nor, when he had seen that it was no use, that he did not possess in himself the power to move fundamentally or to hold Judy Jones, did he bear any malice toward her. He loved her, and he would love her until the day he was too old for loving—but he could not have her. So he tasted the deep pain that is reserved only for the strong, just as he had tasted for a little while the deep happiness.

Even the ultimate falsity of the grounds upon which Judy terminated the engagement that she did not want to "take him away" from Irene—Judy, who had wanted nothing else—did not revolt him. He was beyond any revulsion or any amusement.

He went East in February with the intention of selling out his laundries and settling in New York—but the war came to America in March and changed his plans. He returned to the West, handed over the management of the business to his partner, and went into the first officers' training-camp in late April. He was one of those young thousands who greeted the war with a certain amount of relief, welcoming the liberation from webs of tangled emotion.

VI

This story is not his biography, remember, although things creep into it which have nothing to do with those dreams he had when he was young. We are almost done with them and with him now. There is only one more incident to be related here, and it happens seven years farther on.

It took place in New York, where he had done well—so well that there were no barriers too high for him. He was thirty-two years old, and, except for one flying trip immediately after the war, he had not been West in seven years. A man named Devlin from Detroit came into his office to see him in a business way, and then and there this incident occurred, and closed out, so to speak, this particular side of his life.

"So you're from the Middle West," said the man Devlin with careless curiosity. "That's funny—I thought men like you were probably born and raised on Wall Street. You know—wife of one of my best friends in Detroit came from your city. I was usher at the wedding."

Dexter waited with no apprehension of what was coming.

"Judy Simms," said Devlin with no particular interest; "Judy Jones she was once."

"Yes, I knew her." A dull impatience spread over him. He had heard, of course, that she was married—perhaps deliberately he had heard no more.

"Awfully nice girl," brooded Devlin meaninglessly, "I'm sort of sorry for her."

"Why?" Something in Dexter was alert, receptive, at once.

"Oh, Lud Simms has gone to pieces in a way. I don't mean he ill-uses her, but he drinks and runs around——"

"Doesn't she run around?"

"No. Stays at home with her kids."

"Oh."

"She's a little too old for him," said Devlin.

"Too old!" cried Dexter. "Why, man, she's only twenty-seven."

He was possessed with a wild notion of rushing out into the streets and taking a train to Detroit. He rose to his feet spasmodically.

"I guess you're busy," Devlin apologized quickly. "I didn't realize——"

"No, I'm not busy," said Dexter, steadying his voice. "I'm not busy at all. Not busy at all. Did you say she was—twenty-seven? No, I said she was twenty-seven."

"Yes, you did," agreed Devlin dryly.

"Go on, then. Go on."

"What do you mean?"

"About Judy Jones."

Devlin looked at him helplessly.

"Well, that's—I told you all there is to it. He treats her like the devil. Oh, they're not going to get divorced or anything. When he's particularly outrageous she forgives him. In fact, I'm inclined to think she loves him. She was a pretty girl when she first came to Detroit."

A pretty girl! The phrase struck Dexter as ludicrous.

"Isn't she—a pretty girl, any more?"

"Oh, she's all right."

"Look here," said Dexter, sitting down suddenly, "I don't understand. You say she was a 'pretty girl' and now you say she's 'all right.' I don't understand what you mean—Judy Jones wasn't a pretty girl, at all. She was a great beauty. Why, I knew her, I knew her. She was——"

Devlin laughed pleasantly.

"I'm not trying to start a row," he said. "I think Judy's a nice girl and I like her. I can't understand how a man like Lud Simms could fall madly in love with her, but he did." Then he added: "Most of the women like her."

Dexter looked closely at Devlin, thinking wildly that there must be a reason for this, some insensitivity in the man or some private malice.

"Lots of women fade just like *that*," Devlin snapped his fingers. "You must have seen it happen. Perhaps I've forgotten how pretty she was at her wedding. I've seen her so much since then, you see. She has nice eyes."

A sort of dullness settled down upon Dexter. For the first time in his life he felt like getting very drunk. He knew that he was laughing loudly at something Devlin had said, but he did not know what it was or why it was funny. When, in a few minutes, Devlin went he lay down on his lounge and looked out the window at the New York sky-line into which the sun was sinking in dull lovely shades of pink and gold.

He had thought that having nothing else to lose he was invulnerable at last—but he knew that he had just lost something more, as surely as if he had married Judy Jones and seen her fade away before his eyes.

The dream was gone. Something had been taken from him. In a sort of panic he pushed the palms of his hands into his eyes and tried to bring up a picture of the waters lapping on Sherry Island and the moonlit veranda, and gingham on the golf-links and the dry sun and the gold color of her neck's soft down. And her mouth damp to his kisses and her eyes plaintive with melancholy and her freshness like new fine linen in the morning. Why, these things were no longer in the world! They had existed and they existed no longer.

For the first time in years the tears were streaming down his face. But they were for himself now. He did not care about mouth and eyes and moving hands. He wanted to care, and he could not care. For he had gone away and he could never go back any more. The gates were closed, the sun was gone down, and there was no beauty but the gray beauty of steel that withstands all time. Even the grief he could have borne was left behind in the country of illusion, of youth, of the richness of life, where his winter dreams had flourished.

"Long ago," he said, "long ago, there was something in me, but now that thing is gone. Now that thing is gone, that thing is gone. I cannot cry. I cannot care. That thing will come back no more."

[1922]

WILLIAM FAULKNER [1897–1962]

A Rose for Emily

1

When Miss Emily Grierson died, our whole town went to her funeral: the men through a sort of respectful affection for a fallen monument, the women mostly out of curiosity to see the inside of her house, which no one save an old manservant—a combined gardener and cook—had seen in at least ten years.

It was a big, squarish frame house that had once been white, decorated with cupolas and spires and scrolled balconies in the heavily lightsome style of the seventies, set on what had once been our most select street. But garages and cotton gins had encroached and obliterated even the august names of that neighborhood; only Miss Emily's house was left, lifting its stubborn and coquettish decay above the cotton wagons and the gasoline pumps—an eyesore among eyesores. And now Miss Emily had gone to join the representatives of those august names where they lay in the cedar-bemused cemetery among the ranked and anonymous graves of Union and Confederate soldiers who fell at the battle of Jefferson.

Alive, Miss Emily had been a tradition, a duty, and a care; a sort of hereditary obligation upon the town, dating from that day in 1894 when Colonel Sartoris, the mayor—he who fathered the edict that no Negro woman should appear on the streets without an apron—remitted her taxes, the dispensation dating from the death of her father on into perpetuity. Not that Miss Emily would have accepted charity. Colonel Sartoris invented an involved tale to the effect that Miss Emily's father had loaned money to the town, which the town, as a matter of business, preferred this way of repaying. Only a man of Colonel Sartoris's generation and thought could have invented it, and only a woman could have believed it.

When the next generation, with its more modern ideas, became mayors and aldermen, this arrangement created some little dissatisfaction. On the first of the year they mailed her a tax notice. February came, and there was no reply. They wrote her a formal letter, asked her to call at the sheriff's office at her convenience. A week later the mayor wrote her himself, offering to call or to send his car for her, and received in reply a note on paper of an archaic shape, in a thin, flowing calligraphy in faded ink, to the effect that she no longer went out at all. The tax notice was also enclosed, without comment.

They called a special meeting of the Board of Aldermen. A deputation waited upon her, knocked at the door through which no visitor had passed since she ceased giving china-painting lessons eight or ten years earlier. They were admitted by the old Negro into a dim hall from which a stairway mounted into still more shadow. It smelled of dust and disuse—a close, dank smell. The Negro led them into the parlor. It was furnished in heavy, leather-covered furniture. When the Negro opened the blinds of one window, they could see that the leather was cracked; and when they sat down, a faint dust rose sluggishly about their thighs, spinning with slow motes in the single sun-ray. On a tarnished gilt easel before the fireplace stood a crayon portrait of Miss Emily's father.

They rose when she entered—a small, fat woman in black, with a thin gold chain descending to her waist and vanishing into her belt, leaning on an ebony cane with a tarnished gold head. Her skeleton was small and spare; perhaps that was why what would have been merely plumpness in another was obesity in her. She looked bloated, like a body long submerged in motionless water, and of that pallid hue. Her eyes, lost in the fatty ridges of her face, looked like two small pieces of coal pressed into a lump of dough as they moved from one face to another while the visitors stated their errand.

She did not ask them to sit. She just stood in the door and listened quietly until the spokesman came to a stumbling halt. Then they could hear the invisible watch ticking at the end of the gold chain.

Her voice was dry and cold. "I have no taxes in Jefferson. Colonel Sartoris explained it to me. Perhaps one of you can gain access to the city records and satisfy yourselves."

"But we have. We are the city authorities, Miss Emily. Didn't you get a notice from the sheriff, signed by him?"

"I received a paper, yes," Miss Emily said. "Perhaps he considers himself the sheriff. . . . I have no taxes in Jefferson."

"But there is nothing on the books to show that, you see. We must go by the—"

"See Colonel Sartoris. I have no taxes in Jefferson."

"But, Miss Emily—"

"See Colonel Sartoris." (Colonel Sartoris had been dead almost ten years.) "I have no taxes in Jefferson. Tobe!" The Negro appeared. "Show these gentlemen out."

2

So she vanquished them, horse and foot, just as she had vanquished their fathers thirty years before about the smell. That was two years after her father's death and a short time after her sweetheart—the one we believed would marry her—had deserted her. After her father's death she went out very little; after her sweetheart went away, people hardly saw her at all. A few of the ladies had the temerity to call, but were not received, and the only sign of life about the place was the Negro man—a young man then—going in and out with a market basket.

"Just as if a man—any man—could keep a kitchen properly," the ladies said; so they were not surprised when the smell developed. It was another link between the gross, teeming world and the high and mighty Griersons.

A neighbor, a woman, complained to the mayor, Judge Stevens, eighty years old.

"But what will you have me do about it, madam?" he said.

"Why, send her word to stop it," the woman said. "Isn't there a law?"

"I'm sure that won't be necessary," Judge Stevens said. "It's probably just a snake or a rat that nigger of hers killed in the yard. I'll speak to him about it."

The next day he received two more complaints, one from a man who came in diffident deprecation. "We really must do something about it, Judge. I'd be the last one in the world to bother Miss Emily, but we've got to do something." That night the Board of Aldermen met—three gray-beards and one younger man, a member of the rising generation.

"It's simple enough," he said. "Send her word to have her place cleaned up. Give her a certain time to do it in, and if she don't. . . ."

"Dammit, sir," Judge Stevens said, "will you accuse a lady to her face of smelling bad?"

So the next night, after midnight, four men crossed Miss Emily's lawn and slunk about the house like burglars, sniffing along the base of the brickwork and at the cellar openings while one of them performed a regular sowing motion with his hand out of a sack slung from his shoulder. They broke open the cellar door and sprinkled lime there, and in all the outbuildings. As they recrossed the lawn, a window that had been dark was lighted and Miss Emily sat in it, the light behind her, and her upright torso motionless as that of an idol. They crept quietly across the lawn and into the shadow of the locusts that lined the street. After a week or two the smell went away.

That was when people had begun to feel really sorry for her. People in our town, remembering how old lady Wyatt, her great-aunt, had gone completely crazy at last, believed that the Griersons held themselves a little too high for what they really were. None of the young men were quite good enough for Miss Emily and such. We had long thought of them as a tableau. Miss Emily a slender figure in white in the background, her father a spraddled silhouette in the foreground, his back to her and clutching a horsewhip, the two of them framed by the backflung front door. So when she got to be thirty and was still single, we were not pleased exactly, but vindicated; even with insanity in the family she wouldn't have turned down all of her chances if they had really materialized.

When her father died, it got about that the house was all that was left to her; and in a way, people were glad. At last they could pity Miss Emily. Being left alone, and a pauper, she had become humanized. Now she too would know the old thrill and the old despair of a penny more or less.

The day after his death all the ladies prepared to call at the house and offer condolence and aid, as is our custom. Miss Emily met them at the door, dressed as usual and with no trace of grief on her face. She told them that her father was not dead. She did that for three days, with the ministers calling on her, and the doctors, trying to persuade her to let them dispose of the body. Just as they were about to resort to law and force, she broke down, and they buried her father quickly.

We did not say she was crazy then. We believed she had to do that. We remembered all the young men her father had driven away, and we knew that with nothing left, she would have to cling to that which had robbed her, as people will.

3

She was sick for a long time. When we saw her again, her hair was cut short, making her look like a girl, with a vague resemblance to those angels in colored church windows—sort of tragic and serene.

The town had just let the contracts for paving the sidewalks, and in the summer after her father's death they began the work. The construction company came with niggers and mules and machinery, and a foreman named Homer Barron, a Yankee—a big, dark, ready man, with a big voice and eyes lighter than his face. The little boys would follow in groups to hear him cuss the niggers, and the niggers singing in time to the rise and fall of picks. Pretty soon he knew everybody in town. Whenever you heard a lot of laughing anywhere about the square, Homer Barron would be in the center of the group. Presently, we began to see him and Miss Emily on Sunday afternoons driving in the yellow-wheeled buggy and the matched team of bays from the livery stable.

At first we were glad that Miss Emily would have an interest, because the ladies all said, "Of course a Grierson would not think seriously of a Northerner, a day laborer." But there were still others, older people, who said that even grief could not cause a real lady to forget *noblesse oblige*—without calling it *noblesse oblige*. They just said, "Poor Emily. Her kinsfolk should come to her." She had some kin in Alabama; but years ago her father had fallen out with them over the estate of old lady Wyatt, the crazy woman, and there was no communication between the two families. They had not even been represented at the funeral.

And as soon as the old people said, "Poor Emily," the whispering began. "Do you suppose it's really so?" they said to one another. "Of course it is. What else could. . . ." This behind their hands; rustling of craned silk and satin behind jalousies closed upon the sun of Sunday afternoon as the thin, swift clop-clop-clop of the matched team passed: "Poor Emily."

She carried her head high enough—even when we believed that she was fallen. It was as if she demanded more than ever the recognition of her dignity as the last Grierson; as if it had wanted that touch of earthiness to reaffirm her imperviousness. Like when she bought the rat poison, the arsenic. That was over a year after they had begun to say "Poor Emily," and while the two female cousins were visiting her.

"I want some poison," she said to the druggist. She was over thirty then, still a slight woman, though thinner than usual, with cold, haughty black eyes in a face the flesh of which was strained across the temples and about the eye-sockets as you imagine a lighthouse-keeper's face ought to look. "I want some poison," she said.

"Yes, Miss Emily. What kind? For rats and such? I'd recom——"

"I want the best you have. I don't care what kind."

The druggist named several. "They'll kill anything up to an elephant. But what you want is——"

"Arsenic," Miss Emily said. "Is that a good one?"

"Is . . . arsenic? Yes, ma'am. But what you want——"

"I want arsenic."

The druggist looked down at her. She looked back at him, erect, her face like a strained flag. "Why, of course," the druggist said. "If that's what you want. But the law requires you to tell what you are going to use it for."

Miss Emily just stared at him, her head tilted back in order to look him eye for eye, until he looked away and went and got the arsenic and wrapped it up. The Negro delivery boy brought her the package: the druggist didn't come back. When she opened the package at home there was written on the box, under the skull and bones: "For rats."

4

So the next day we all said, "She will kill herself"; and we said it would be the best thing. When she had first begun to be seen with Homer Barron, we had said, "She will marry him." Then we said, "She will persuade him yet," because Homer himself had remarked—he liked men, and it was known that he drank with the younger men in the Elks' Club—that he was not a marrying man. Later we said, "Poor Emily" behind the jalousies as they passed on Sunday afternoon in the glittering buggy, Miss Emily with her head high and Homer Barron with his hat cocked and a cigar in his teeth, reins and whip in a yellow glove.

Then some of the ladies began to say it was a disgrace to the town and a bad example to the young people. The men did not want to interfere; but at last the ladies forced the Baptist minister—Miss Emily's people were Episcopal—to call upon her. He would never divulge what happened during that interview, but he refused to go back again. The next Sunday they again drove about the streets, and the following day the minister's wife wrote to Miss Emily's relations in Alabama.

So she had blood-kin under her roof again and we sat back to watch developments. At first nothing happened. Then we were sure that they were to be married. We learned that Miss Emily had been to the jeweler's and ordered a man's toilet set in silver, with the letters H.B. on each piece. Two days later we learned that she had bought a complete outfit of men's clothing, including a nightshirt, and we said, "They are married." We were really glad. We were glad because the two female cousins were even more Grierson than Miss Emily had ever been.

So we were not surprised when Homer Barron—the streets had been finished some time since—was gone. We were a little disappointed that there was not a public blowing-off, but we believed that he had gone on to prepare for Miss Emily's coming, or to give her a chance to get rid of the cousins. (By that time it was a cabal, and we were all Miss Emily's allies to help circumvent the cousins.) Sure enough, after another week they departed. And, as we had expected all along, within three days Homer Barron was back in town. A neighbor saw the Negro man admit him at the kitchen door at dusk one evening.

And that was the last we saw of Homer Barron. And of Miss Emily for some time. The Negro man went in and out with the market basket, but the front door remained closed. Now and then we would see her at the window for a moment, as the men did that night when they sprinkled the lime, but for almost six months she did not appear on the streets. Then we knew that this was to be expected too; as if that quality of her father which had thwarted her woman's life so many times had been too virulent and too furious to die.

When we next saw Miss Emily, she had grown fat and her hair was turning gray. During the next few years it grew grayer and grayer until it attained an even pepper-and-salt iron-gray, when it ceased turning. Up to the day of her death at seventy-four it was still that vigorous iron-gray, like the hair of an active man.

From that time on her front door remained closed, save during a period of six or seven years, when she was about forty, during which she gave lessons in china-painting. She fitted up a studio in one of the downstairs rooms, where the daughters and granddaughters of Colonel Sartoris's contemporaries were sent to her with the same regularity and in the same spirit that they were sent to church on Sundays with a twenty-five-cent piece for the collection plate. Meanwhile her taxes had been remitted.

Then the newer generation became the backbone and the spirit of the town, and the painting pupils grew up and fell away and did not send their children to her with boxes of color and tedious brushes and pictures cut from the ladies' magazines. The front door closed upon the last one and remained closed for good. When the town got free postal delivery, Miss Emily alone refused to let them fasten the metal numbers above her door and attach a mailbox to it. She would not listen to them.

Daily, monthly, yearly we watched the Negro grow grayer and more stooped, going in and out with the market basket. Each December we sent her a tax notice, which would be returned by the post office a week later, unclaimed. Now and then we would see her in one of the downstairs windows—she had evidently shut up the top floor of the house—like the carven torso of an idol in a niche, looking or not looking at us, we could never tell which. Thus she passed from generation to generation—dear, inescapable, impervious, tranquil, and perverse.

And so she died. Fell ill in the house filled with dust and shadows, with only a doddering Negro man to wait on her. We did not even know she was sick; we had long since given up trying to get any information from the Negro. He talked to no one, probably not even to her, for his voice had grown harsh and rusty, as if from disuse.

She died in one of the downstairs rooms, in a heavy walnut bed with a curtain, her gray head propped on a pillow yellow and moldy with age and lack of sunlight.

5

The Negro met the first of the ladies at the front door and let them in, with their hushed, sibilant voices and their quick, curious glances, and then he disappeared. He walked right through the house and out the back and was not seen again.

The two female cousins came at once. They held the funeral on the second day, with the town coming to look at Miss Emily beneath a mass of bought flowers, with the crayon face of her father musing profoundly above the bier and the ladies sibilant and macabre; and the very old men—some in their brushed Confederate uniforms—on the porch and the lawn, talking of Miss Emily as if she had been a contemporary of theirs, believing that they had danced with her and courted her perhaps, confusing time with its mathematical progression, as the old do, to whom all the past is not a diminishing road but, instead, a huge meadow which no winter ever quite touches, divided from them now by the narrow bottleneck of the most recent decade of years.

Already we knew that there was one room in that region above stairs which no one had seen in forty years, and which would have to be forced. They waited until Miss Emily was decently in the ground before they opened it.

The violence of breaking down the door seemed to fill this room with pervading dust. A thin, acrid pall as of the tomb seemed to lie everywhere upon this room decked and furnished as for a bridal: upon the valance curtains of faded rose color, upon the rose-shaded lights, upon the dressing table, upon the delicate array of crystal and the man's toilet things backed with tarnished silver, silver so tarnished that the monogram was obscured. Among them lay a collar and tie, as if they had just been removed, which, lifted, left upon the surface a pale crescent in the dust. Upon a chair hung the suit, carefully folded; beneath it the two mute shoes and the discarded socks.

The man himself lay in the bed.

For a long while we just stood there, looking down at the profound and fleshless grin. The body had apparently once lain in the attitude of an embrace, but now the long sleep that outlasts love, that conquers even the grimace of love, had cuckolded him. What was left of him, rotted beneath what was left of the nightshirt, had become inextricable from the bed in which he lay; and upon him and upon the pillow beside him lay that even coating of the patient and biding dust.

Then we noticed that in the second pillow was the indentation of a head. One of us lifted something from it, and leaning forward, that faint and invisible dust dry and acrid in the nostrils, we saw a long strand of iron-gray hair.

[1931]

ERNEST HEMINGWAY [1899–1961]

Hills Like White Elephants

[handwritten: "fly on the Wall story"]

The hills across the valley of the Ebro were long and white. On this side there was no shade and no trees and the station was between two lines of rails in the sun. Close against the side of the station there was the warm shadow of the building and a curtain, made of strings of bamboo beads, hung across the open door into the bar, to keep out flies. The American and the girl with him sat at a table in the shade, outside the building. It was very hot and the express from Barcelona would come in forty minutes. It stopped at this junction for two minutes and went on to Madrid.

[handwritten: "Stations - tracks - symbolizes them"]

"What should we drink?" the girl asked. She had taken off her hat and put it on the table.

"It's pretty hot," the man said.

"Let's drink beer."

"*Dos cervezas,*" the man said into the curtain.

[handwritten: "Dialogue to help plot"]

"Big ones?" a woman asked from the doorway.

"Yes. Two big ones."

[handwritten: "Well off - Relaxed"]

The woman brought two glasses of beer and two felt pads. She put the felt pads and the beer glasses on the table and looked at the man and the girl. The girl was looking off at the line of hills. They were white in the sun and the country was brown and dry.

"They look like white elephants," she said.

"I've never seen one," the man drank his beer.

"No, you wouldn't have."

"I might have," the man said. "Just because you say I wouldn't have doesn't prove anything."

The girl looked at the bead curtain. "They've painted something on it," she said. "What does it say?"

"Anis del Toro. It's a drink."

"Could we try it?"

The man called "Listen" through the curtain. The woman came out from the bar.

"Four reales."°

"We want two Anis del Toro."

Reales: Spanish silver coins.

212

"With water?"

"Do you want it with water?"

"I don't know," the girl said. "Is it good with water?"

"It's all right."

"You want them with water?" asked the woman.

"Yes, with water."

"It tastes like licorice," the girl said and put the glass down.

"That's the way with everything."

"Yes," said the girl. "Everything tastes of licorice. Especially all the things you've waited so long for, like absinthe."

"Oh, cut it out."

"You started it," the girl said. "I was being amused. I was having a fine time."

"Well, let's try and have a fine time."

"All right. I was trying. I said the mountains looked like white elephants. Wasn't that bright?"

"That was bright."

"I wanted to try this new drink. That's all we do, isn't it—look at things and try new drinks?"

"I guess so."

The girl looked across at the hills.

"They're lovely hills," she said. "They don't really look like white elephants. I just meant the coloring of their skin through the trees."

"Should we have another drink?"

"All right."

The warm wind blew the bead curtain against the table.

"The beer's nice and cool," the man said.

"It's lovely," the girl said.

"It's really an awfully simple operation, Jig," the man said. "It's not really an operation at all."

The girl looked at the ground the table legs rested on.

"I know you wouldn't mind it, Jig. It's really not anything. It's just to let the air in."

The girl did not say anything.

"I'll go with you and I'll stay with you all the time. They just let the air in and then it's all perfectly natural."

"Then what will we do afterward?"

"We'll be fine afterward. Just like we were before."

"What makes you think so?"

"That's the only thing that bothers us. It's the only thing that's made us unhappy."

The girl looked at the bead curtain, put her hand out, and took hold of two of the strings of beads.

"And you think then we'll be all right and be happy."

"I know we will. You don't have to be afraid. I've known lots of people that have done it."

"So have I," said the girl. "And afterward they were all so happy."

"Well," the man said, "if you don't want to you don't have to. I wouldn't have you do it if you didn't want to. But I know it's perfectly simple."

"And you really want to?"

"I think it's the best thing to do. But I don't want you to do it if you don't really want to."

"And if I do it you'll be happy and things will be like they were and you'll love me?"

"I love you now. You know I love you."

"I know. But if I do it, then it will be nice again if I say things are like white elephants, and you'll like it?"

"I'll love it. I love it now but I just can't think about it. You know how I get when I worry."

"If I do it you won't ever worry?"

"I won't worry about that because it's perfectly simple."

"Then I'll do it. Because I don't care about me."

"What do you mean?"

"I don't care about me."

"Well, I care about you."

"Oh, yes. But I don't care about me. And I'll do it and then everything will be fine."

"I don't want you to do it if you feel that way."

The girl stood up and walked to the end of the station. Across, on the other side, were fields of grain and trees along the banks of the Ebro. Far away, beyond the river, were mountains. The shadow of a cloud moved across the field of grain and she saw the river through the trees.

"And we could have all this," she said. "And we could have everything and every day we make it more impossible."

"What did you say?"

"I said we could have everything."

"We can have everything."

"No, we can't."

"We can have the whole world."

"No, we can't."

"We can go everywhere."

"No, we can't. It isn't ours any more."

"It's ours."

"No, it isn't. And once they take it away, you never get it back."

"But they haven't taken it away."

"We'll wait and see."

"Come on back in the shade," he said. "You mustn't feel that way."

"I don't feel any way," the girl said. "I just know things."

"I don't want you to do anything that you don't want to do——"

"Nor that isn't good for me," she said. "I know. Could we have another beer?"

"All right. But you've got to realize——"

"I realize," the girl said. "Can't we maybe stop talking?"

They sat down at the table and the girl looked across at the hills on the dry side of the valley and the man looked at her and at the table.

"You've got to realize," he said, "that I don't want you to do it if you don't want to. I'm perfectly willing to go through with it if it means anything to you."

"Doesn't it mean anything to you? We could get along."

"Of course it does. But I don't want anybody but you. I don't want any one else. And I know it's perfectly simple."

"Yes, you know it's perfectly simple."

"It's all right for you to say that, but I do know it."

"Would you do something for me now?"

"I'd do anything for you."

"Would you please please please please please please please stop talking?"

He did not say anything but looked at the bags against the wall of the station. There were labels on them from all the hotels where they had spent nights.

"But I don't want you to," he said, "I don't care anything about it."

"I'll scream," the girl said.

The woman came out through the curtains with two glasses of beer and put them down on the damp felt pads. "The train comes in five minutes," she said.

"What did she say?" asked the girl.

"That the train is coming in five minutes."

The girl smiled brightly at the woman, to thank her.

"I'd better take the bags over to the other side of the station," the man said. She smiled at him.

"All right. Then come back and we'll finish the beer."

He picked up the two heavy bags and carried them around the station to the other tracks. He looked up the tracks but could not see the train. Coming back, he walked through the barroom, where people waiting for the train were drinking. He drank an Anis at the bar and looked at the people. They were all waiting reasonably for the train. He went out through the bead curtain. She was sitting at the table and smiled at him.

She isn't being reecsonable

"Do you feel better?" he asked.

epiphany "I feel fine," she said. "There's nothing wrong with me. I feel fine."

Ironic *⌐your the Asshole⌐*

[1927]

EUDORA WELTY   [1909–2001]

A Worn Path

It was December—a bright frozen day in the early morning. Far out in the country there was an old Negro woman with her head tied in a red rag, coming along a path through the pinewoods. Her name was Phoenix Jackson. She was very old and small and she walked slowly in the dark pine shadows, moving a little from side to side in her steps, with the balanced heaviness and lightness of a pendulum in a grandfather clock. She carried a thin, small cane made from an umbrella, and with this she kept tapping the frozen earth in front of her. This made a grave and persistent noise in the still air, that seemed meditative like the chirping of a solitary little bird.

She wore a dark striped dress reaching down to her shoe tops, and an equally long apron of bleached sugar sacks, with a full pocket: all neat and tidy, but every time she took a step she might have fallen over her shoelaces, which dragged from her unlaced shoes. She looked straight ahead. Her eyes were blue with age. Her skin had a pattern all its own of numberless branching wrinkles and as though a whole little tree stood in the middle of her forehead, but a golden color ran underneath, and the two knobs of her cheeks were illumined by a yellow burning under the dark. Under the red rag her hair came down on her neck in the frailest of ringlets, still black, and with an odor like copper.

Now and then there was a quivering in the thicket. Old Phoenix said, "Out of my way, all you foxes, owls, beetles, jack rabbits, coons and wild animals! . . . Keep out from under these feet, little bobwhites. . . . Keep the big wild hogs out of my path. Don't let none of those come running my direction. I got a long way." Under her small black-freckled hand her cane, limber as a buggy whip, would switch at the brush as if to rouse up any hiding things.

On she went. The woods were deep and still. The sun made the pine needles almost too bright to look at, up where the wind rocked. The cones dropped as light as feathers. Down in the hollow was the mourning dove—it was not too late for him.

The path ran up a hill. "Seem like there is chains about my feet, time I get this far," she said, in the voice of argument old people keep to use with themselves. "Something always take a hold of me on this hill—pleads I should stay."

After she got to the top she turned and gave a full, severe look behind her where she had come. "Up through pines," she said at length. "Now down through oaks."

Her eyes opened their widest, and she started down gently. But before she got to the bottom of the hill a bush caught her dress.

Her fingers were busy and intent, but her skirts were full and long, so that before she could pull them free in one place they were caught in another. It was not possible to allow the dress to tear. "I in the thorny bush," she said. "Thorns, you doing your appointed work. Never want to let folks pass, no sir. Old eyes thought you was a pretty little *green* bush."

Finally, trembling all over, she stood free, and after a moment dared to stoop for her cane.

"Sun so high!" she cried, leaning back and looking, while the thick tears went over her eyes. "The time getting all gone here."

At the foot of this hill was a place where a log was laid across the creek.

"Now comes the trial," said Phoenix.

Putting her right foot out, she mounted the log and shut her eyes. Lifting her skirt, leveling her cane fiercely before her, like a festival figure in some parade, she began to march across. Then she opened her eyes and she was safe on the other side.

"I wasn't as old as I thought," she said.

But she sat down to rest. She spread her skirts on the bank around her and folded her hands over her knees. Up above her was a tree in a pearly cloud of mistletoe. She did not dare to close her eyes, and when a little boy brought her a plate with a slice of marble-cake on it she spoke to him. "That would be acceptable," she said. But when she went to take it there was just her own hand in the air.

So she left that tree, and had to go through a barbed-wire fence. There she had to creep and crawl, spreading her knees and stretching her fingers like a baby trying to climb the steps. But she talked loudly to herself: she could not let her dress be torn now, so late in the day, and she could not pay for having her arm or her leg sawed off if she got caught fast where she was.

At last she was safe through the fence and risen up out in the clearing. Big dead trees, like black men with one arm, were standing in the purple stalks of the withered cotton field. There sat a buzzard.

"Who you watching?"

In the furrow she made her way along.

"Glad this not the season for bulls," she said, looking sideways, "and the good Lord made his snakes to curl up and sleep in the winter. A pleasure I don't see no two-headed snake coming around that tree, where it come once. It took a while to get by him, back in the summer."

She passed through the old cotton and went into a field of dead corn. It whispered and shook and was taller than her head. "Through the maze now," she said, for there was no path.

Then there was something tall, black, and skinny there, moving before her.

At first she took it for a man. It could have been a man dancing in the field. But she stood still and listened, and it did not make a sound. It was as silent as a ghost.

"Ghost," she said sharply, "who be you the ghost of? For I have heard of nary death close by."

But there was no answer—only the ragged dancing in the wind.

She shut her eyes, reached out her hand, and touched a sleeve. She found a coat and inside that an emptiness, cold as ice.

"You scarecrow," she said. Her face lighted. "I ought to be shut up for good," she said with laughter. "My senses is gone. I too old. I the oldest people I ever know. Dance, old scarecrow," she said, "while I dancing with you."

She kicked her foot over the furrow, and with mouth drawn down, shook her head once or twice in a little strutting way. Some husks blew down and whirled in streamers about her skirts.

Then she went on, parting her way from side to side with the cane, through the whispering field. At last she came to the end, to a wagon track where the silver grass blew between the red ruts. The quail were walking around like pullets, seeming all dainty and unseen.

"Walk pretty," she said. "This the easy place. This the easy going."

She followed the track, swaying through the quiet bare fields, through the little strings of trees silver in their dead leaves, past cabins silver from weather, with the doors and windows boarded shut, all like old women under a spell sitting there. "I walking in their sleep," she said, nodding her head vigorously.

In a ravine she went where a spring was silently flowing through a hollow log. Old Phoenix bent and drank. "Sweet-gum makes the water sweet," she said, and drank more. "Nobody know who made this well, for it was here when I was born."

The track crossed a swampy part where the moss hung as white as lace from every limb. "Sleep on, alligators, and blow your bubbles." Then the track went into the road.

Deep, deep the road went down between the high green-colored banks. Overhead the live-oaks met, and it was as dark as a cave.

A black dog with a lolling tongue came up out of the weeds by the ditch. She was meditating, and not ready, and when he came at her she only hit him a little with her cane. Over she went in the ditch, like a little puff of milkweed.

Down there, her senses drifted away. A dream visited her, and she reached her hand up, but nothing reached down and gave her a pull. So she lay there and presently went to talking. "Old woman," she said to herself, "that black dog come up out of the weeds to stall you off, and now there he sitting on his fine tail, smiling at you."

A white man finally came along and found her—a hunter, a young man, with his dog on a chain.

"Well, Granny!" he laughed. "What are you doing there?"

"Lying on my back like a June-bug waiting to be turned over, mister," she said, reaching up her hand.

He lifted her up, gave her a swing in the air, and set her down. "Anything broken, Granny?"

"No sir, them old dead weeds is springy enough," said Phoenix, when she had got her breath. "I thank you for your trouble."

"Where do you live, Granny?" he asked, while the two dogs were growling at each other.

"Away back yonder, sir, behind the ridge. You can't even see it from here."

"On your way home?"

"No sir, I going to town."

"Why, that's too far! That's as far as I walk when I come out myself, and I get something for my trouble." He patted the stuffed bag he carried, and there hung down a little closed claw. It was one of the bobwhites, with its beak hooked bitterly to show it was dead. "Now you go on home, Granny!"

"I bound to go to town, mister," said Phoenix. "The time come around."

He gave another laugh, filling the whole landscape. "I know you old colored people! Wouldn't miss going to town to see Santa Claus!"

But something held old Phoenix very still. The deep lines in her face went into a fierce and different radiation. Without warning, she had seen with her own eyes a flashing nickel fall out of the man's pocket onto the ground.

"How old are you, Granny?" he was saying.

"There is no telling, mister," she said, "no telling."

Then she gave a little cry and clapped her hands and said, "Git on away from here, dog! Look! Look at that dog!" She laughed as if in admiration. "He ain't scared of nobody. He a big black dog." She whispered, "Sic him!"

"Watch me get rid of that cur," said the man. "Sic him, Pete! Sic him!"

Phoenix heard the dogs fighting, and heard the man running and throwing sticks. She even heard a gunshot. But she was slowly bending forward by that time, further and further forward, the lid stretched down over her eyes, as if she were doing this in her sleep. Her chin was lowered almost to her knees. The yellow palm of her hand came out from the fold of her apron. Her fingers slid down and along the ground under the piece of money with the grace and care they would have in lifting an egg from under a setting hen. Then she slowly straightened up, she stood erect, and the nickel was in her apron pocket. A bird flew by. Her lips moved. "God watching me the whole time. I come to stealing."

The man came back, and his own dog panted about them. "Well, I scared him off that time," he said, and then he laughed and lifted his gun and pointed it at Phoenix.

She stood straight and faced him.

"Doesn't the gun scare you?" he said, still pointing it.

"No, sir, I seen plenty go off closer by, in my day, and for less than what I done," she said, holding utterly still.

He smiled, and shouldered the gun. "Well, Granny," he said, "you must be a hundred years old, and scared of nothing. I'd give you a dime if I had any money with me. But you take my advice and stay home, and nothing will happen to you."

"I bound to go on my way, mister," said Phoenix. She inclined her head in the red rag. Then they went in different directions, but she could hear the gun shooting again and again over the hill.

She walked on. The shadows hung from the oak trees to the road like curtains. Then she smelled wood-smoke, and smelled the river, and she saw a steeple and the cabins on their steep steps. Dozens of little black children whirled around her. There ahead was Natchez shining. Bells were ringing. She walked on.

In the paved city it was Christmas time. There were red and green electric lights strung and crisscrossed everywhere, and all turned on in the daytime. Old Phoenix would have been lost if she had not distrusted her eyesight and depended on her feet to know where to take her.

She paused quietly on the sidewalk where people were passing by. A lady came along in the crowd, carrying an armful of red-, green-, and silver-wrapped presents; she gave off perfume like the red roses in hot summer, and Phoenix stopped her.

"Please, missy, will you lace up my shoe?" She held up her foot.

"What do you want, Grandma?"

"See my shoe," said Phoenix. "Do all right for out in the country, but wouldn't look right to go in a big building."

"Stand still then, Grandma," said the lady. She put her packages down on the sidewalk beside her and laced and tied both shoes tightly.

"Can't lace 'em with a cane," said Phoenix. "Thank you, missy. I doesn't mind asking a nice lady to tie up my shoe, when I gets out on the street."

Moving slowly and from side to side, she went into the big building, and into a tower of steps, where she walked up and around and around until her feet knew to stop.

She entered a door, and there she saw nailed up on the wall the document that had been stamped with the gold seal and framed in the gold frame, which matched the dream that was hung up in her head.

"Here I be," she said. There was a fixed and ceremonial stiffness over her body.

"A charity case, I suppose," said an attendant who sat at the desk before her.

But Phoenix only looked above her head. There was sweat on her face, the wrinkles in her skin shone like a bright net.

"Speak up, Grandma," the woman said. "What's your name? We must have your history, you know. Have you been here before? What seems to be the trouble with you?"

Old Phoenix only gave a twitch to her face as if a fly were bothering her.

"Are you deaf?" cried the attendant.

But then the nurse came in.

"Oh, that's just old Aunt Phoenix," she said. "She doesn't come for herself—she has a little grandson. She makes these trips just as regular as clockwork. She lives away back off the Old Natchez Trace." She bent down. "Well, Aunt Phoenix, why don't you just take a seat? We won't keep you standing after your long trip." She pointed.

The old woman sat down, bolt upright in the chair.

"Now, how is the boy?" asked the nurse.

Old Phoenix did not speak.

"I said, how is the boy?"

But Phoenix only waited and stared straight ahead, her face very solemn and withdrawn into rigidity.

"Is his throat any better?" asked the nurse. "Aunt Phoenix, don't you hear me? Is your grandson's throat any better since the last time you came for the medicine?"

With her hands on her knees, the old woman waited, silent, erect and motionless, just as if she were in armor.

"You mustn't take up our time this way, Aunt Phoenix," the nurse said. "Tell us quickly about your grandson, and get it over. He isn't dead, is he?"

At last there came a flicker and then a flame of comprehension across her face, and she spoke.

"My grandson. It was my memory had left me. There I sat and forgot why I made my long trip."

"Forgot?" The nurse frowned. "After you came so far?"

Then Phoenix was like an old woman begging a dignified forgiveness for waking up frightened in the night. "I never did go to school, I was too old at the Surrender,"° she said in a soft voice. "I'm an old woman without an education. It was my memory fail me. My little grandson, he is just the same, and I forgot it in the coming."

"Throat never heals, does it?" said the nurse, speaking in a loud, sure voice to old Phoenix. By now she had a card with something written on it, a little list. "Yes. Swallowed lye. When was it?—January—two, three years ago—"

Phoenix spoke unasked now. "No, missy, he not dead, he just the same. Every little while his throat began to close up again, and he not able to swallow. He not get his breath. He not able to help himself. So the time come around, and I go on another trip for the soothing medicine."

"All right. The doctor said as long as you came to get it, you could have it," said the nurse. "But it's an obstinate case."

"My little grandson, he sit up there in the house all wrapped up, waiting by himself," Phoenix went on. "We is the only two left in the world. He suffer and it don't seem to put him back at all. He got a sweet look. He going to last. He wear a little patch quilt and peep out holding his mouth open like a little bird. I remembers so plain now. I not going to forget him again, no, the whole enduring time. I could tell him from all the others in creation."

"All right." The nurse was trying to hush her now. She brought her a bottle of medicine. "Charity," she said, making a check mark in a book.

Old Phoenix held the bottle close to her eyes, and then carefully put it into her pocket.

"I thank you," she said.

"It's Christmas time, Grandma," said the attendant. "Could I give you a few pennies out of my purse?"

"Five pennies is a nickel," said Phoenix stiffly.

"Here's a nickel," said the attendant.

Phoenix rose carefully and held out her hand. She received the nickel and then fished the other nickel out of her pocket and laid it beside the new one. She stared at her palm closely, with her head on one side.

Then she gave a tap with her cane on the floor.

The Surrender: General Robert E. Lee's surrender of the Confederacy to Union general Ulysses S. Grant, ending the Civil War.

"This is what come to me to do," she said. "I going to the store and buy my child a little windmill they sells, made out of paper. He going to find it hard to believe there such a thing in the world. I'll march myself back where he waiting, holding it straight up in this hand."

She lifted her free hand, gave a little nod, turned around, and walked out of the doctor's office. Then her slow step began on the stairs, going down.

[1941]

TILLIE OLSEN [1912–2007]

I Stand Here Ironing

I stand here ironing, and what you asked me moves tormented back and forth with the iron.

"I wish you would manage the time to come in and talk with me about your daughter. I'm sure you can help me understand her. She's a young-ster who needs help and whom I'm deeply interested in helping."

"Who needs help." . . . Even if I came, what good would it do? You think because I am her mother I have a key, or that in some way you could use me as a key? She has lived for nineteen years. There is all that life that has happened outside of me, beyond me.

And when is there time to remember, to sift, to weigh, to estimate, to total? I will start and there will be an interruption and I will have to gather it all together again. Or I will become engulfed with all I did or did not do, with what should have been and what cannot be helped.

She was a beautiful baby. The first and only one of our five that was beautiful at birth. You do not guess how new and uneasy her tenancy in her now-loveliness. You did not know her all those years she was thought homely, or see her poring over her baby pictures, making me tell her over and over how beautiful she had been—and would be, I would tell her—and was now, to the seeing eye. But the seeing eyes were few or nonexistent. Including mine.

I nursed her. They feel that's important nowadays. I nursed all the chil-dren, but with her, with all the fierce rigidity of first motherhood, I did like the books then said. Though her cries battered me to trembling and my breasts ached with swollenness, I waited till the clock decreed.

Why do I put that first? I do not even know if it matters, or if it explains anything.

She was a beautiful baby. She blew shining bubbles of sound. She loved motion, loved light, loved color and music and textures. She would lie on the floor in her blue overalls patting the surface so hard in ecstasy her hands and feet would blur. She was a miracle to me, but when she was eight months old I had to leave her daytimes with the woman downstairs to whom she was no miracle at all, for I worked or looked for work and for Emily's father, who "could no longer endure" (he wrote in his good-bye note) "sharing want with us."

I was nineteen. It was the pre-relief, pre-WPA world of the depression. I would start running as soon as I got off the streetcar, running up the stairs, the place smelling sour, and awake or asleep to startle awake, when she saw me she would break into a clogged weeping that could not be comforted, a weeping I can hear yet.

After a while I found a job hashing at night so I could be with her days, and it was better. But it came to where I had to bring her to his family and leave her.

It took a long time to raise the money for her fare back. Then she got chicken pox and I had to wait longer. When she finally came, I hardly knew her, walking quick and nervous like her father, looking like her father, thin, and dressed in a shoddy red that yellowed her skin and glared at the pockmarks. All the baby loveliness gone.

She was two. Old enough for nursery school they said, and I did not know then what I know now—the fatigue of the long day, and the lacerations of group life in the kinds of nurseries that are only parking places for children.

Except that it would have made no difference if I had known. It was the only place there was. It was the only way we could be together, the only way I could hold a job.

And even without knowing, I knew. I knew the teacher that was evil because all these years it has curdled into my memory, the little boy hunched in the corner, her rasp, "why aren't you outside, because Alvin hits you? that's no reason, go out, scaredy." I knew Emily hated it even if she did not clutch and implore "don't go Mommy" like the other children, mornings.

She always had a reason why we should stay home. Momma, you look sick, Momma, I feel sick. Momma, the teachers aren't there today, they're sick. Momma, we can't go, there was a fire there last night. Momma, it's a holiday today, no school, they told me.

But never a direct protest, never rebellion. I think of our others in their three-, four-year-oldness—the explosions, the tempers, the denunciations, the demands—and I feel suddenly ill. I put the iron down. What in me demanded that goodness in her? And what was the cost to her of such goodness?

The old man living in the back once said in his gentle way: "You should smile at Emily more when you look at her." What *was* in my face when I looked at her? I loved her. There were all the acts of love.

It was only with the others I remembered what he said, and it was the face of joy, and not of care or tightness or worry I turned to them—too late for Emily. She does not smile easily, let alone almost always as her brothers and sisters do. Her face is closed and somber, but when she wants, how fluid. You must have seen it in her pantomimes, you spoke of her rare gift for comedy on the stage that rouses a laughter out of the audience so dear they applaud and applaud and do not want to let her go.

Where does it come from, that comedy? There was none of it in her when she came back to me that second time, after I had had to send her away again. She had a new daddy now to learn to love, and I think perhaps it was a better time.

Except when we left her alone nights, telling ourselves she was old enough.

"Can't you go some other time, Mommy, like tomorrow?" she would ask. "Will it be just a little while you'll be gone? Do you promise?"

The time we came back, the front door open, the clock on the floor in the hall. She rigid awake. "It wasn't just a little while. I didn't cry. Three times I called you, just three times, and then I ran downstairs to open the door so you could come faster. The clock talked loud. I threw it away, it scared me what it talked."

She said the clock talked loud again that night I went to the hospital to have Susan. She was delirious with the fever that comes before red measles, but she was fully conscious all the week I was gone and the week after we were home when she could not come near the new baby or me.

She did not get well. She stayed skeleton thin, not wanting to eat, and night after night she had nightmares. She would call for me, and I would rouse from exhaustion to sleepily call back: "You're all right, darling, go to sleep, it's just a dream," and if she still called, in a sterner voice, "now go to sleep, Emily, there's nothing to hurt you." Twice, only twice, when I had to get up for Susan anyhow, I went in to sit with her.

Now when it is too late (as if she would let me hold and comfort her like I do the others) I get up and go to her at once at her moan or restless stirring. "Are you awake, Emily? Can I get you something?" And the answer is always the same: "No, I'm all right, go back to sleep, Mother."

They persuaded me at the clinic to send her away to a convalescent home in the country where "she can have the kind of food and care you can't manage for her, and you'll be free to concentrate on the new baby." They still send children to that place. I see pictures on the society page of sleek young women planning affairs to raise money for it, or dancing at the affairs, or decorating Easter eggs or filling Christmas stockings for the children.

They never have a picture of the children so I do not know if the girls still wear those gigantic red bows and the ravaged looks on the every other Sunday when parents can come to visit "unless otherwise notified"—as we were notified the first six weeks.

Oh it is a handsome place, green lawns and tall trees and fluted flower beds. High up on the balconies of each cottage the children stand, the girls in their red bows and white dresses, the boys in white suits and giant red ties. The parents stand below shrieking up to be heard and the children shriek down to be heard, and between them the invisible wall "Not To Be Contaminated by Parental Germs or Physical Affection."

There was a tiny girl who always stood hand in hand with Emily. Her parents never came. One visit she was gone. "They moved her to Rose Cottage" Emily shouted in explanation. "They don't like you to love anybody here."

She wrote once a week, the labored writing of a seven-year-old. "I am fine. How is the baby. If I write my leter nicly I will have a star. Love." There never was a star. We wrote every other day, letters she could never hold or keep but only hear read—once. "We simply do not have room for children to keep any personal possessions," they patiently explained when we pieced one Sunday's shrieking together to plead how much it would mean to Emily, who loved so to keep things, to be allowed to keep her letters and cards.

Each visit she looked frailer. "She isn't eating," they told us.

(They had runny eggs for breakfast or mush with lumps, Emily said later, I'd hold it in my mouth and not swallow. Nothing ever tasted good, just when they had chicken.)

It took us eight months to get her released home, and only the fact that she gained back so little of her seven lost pounds convinced the social worker.

I used to try to hold and love her after she came back, but her body would stay stiff, and after a while she'd push away. She ate little. Food sickened her, and I think much of life too. Oh she had physical lightness and brightness, twinkling by on skates, bouncing like a ball up and down up and down over the jump rope, skimming over the hill; but these were momentary.

She fretted about her appearance, thin and dark and foreign-looking at a time when every little girl was supposed to look or thought she should look a chubby blonde replica of Shirley Temple. The doorbell sometimes rang for her, but no one seemed to come and play in the house or be a best friend. Maybe because we moved so much.

There was a boy she loved painfully through two school semesters.

Months later she told me how she had taken pennies from my purse to buy him candy. "Licorice was his favorite and I brought him some every day, but he still liked Jennifer better'n me. Why, Mommy?" The kind of question for which there is no answer.

School was a worry to her. She was not glib or quick in a world where glibness and quickness were easily confused with ability to learn. To her overworked and exasperated teachers she was an overconscientious "slow learner" who kept trying to catch up and was absent entirely too often.

I let her be absent, though sometimes the illness was imaginary. How different from my now-strictness about attendance with the others. I wasn't working. We had a new baby, I was home anyhow. Sometimes, after Susan grew old enough, I would keep her home from school, too, to have them all together.

Mostly Emily had asthma, and her breathing, harsh and labored, would fill the house with a curiously tranquil sound. I would bring the two old dresser mirrors and her boxes of collections to her bed. She would select beads and single earrings, bottle tops and shells, dried flowers and pebbles, old postcards and scraps, all sorts of oddments; then she and Susan would play Kingdom, setting up landscapes and furniture, peopling them with action.

Those were the only times of peaceful companionship between her and Susan. I have edged away from it, that poisonous feeling between them, that terrible balancing of hurts and needs I had to do between the two, and did so badly, those earlier years.

Oh there are conflicts between the others too, each one human, needing, demanding, hurting, taking—but only between Emily and Susan, no, Emily toward Susan that corroding resentment. It seems so obvious on the surface, yet it is not obvious. Susan, the second child, Susan, golden- and curly-haired and chubby, quick and articulate and assured, everything in appearance and manner Emily was not; Susan, not able to resist Emily's precious things, losing or sometimes clumsily breaking them; Susan telling jokes and riddles to company for applause while Emily sat silent (to say to me later: that was *my* riddle, Mother, I told it to Susan); Susan, who for all the five years' difference in age was just a year behind Emily in developing physically.

I am glad for that slow physical development that widened the difference between her and her contemporaries, though she suffered over it. She was too vulnerable for that terrible world of youthful competition, of preening and parading, of constant measuring of yourself against every other, of envy, "If I had that copper hair," "If I had that skin. . . ." She tormented herself enough about not looking like the others, there was enough of the unsureness, the having to be conscious of words before you speak, the constant caring—what are they thinking of me? without having it all magnified by the merciless physical drives.

Ronnie is calling. He is wet and I change him. It is rare there is such a cry now. That time of motherhood is almost behind me when the ear is not one's own but must always be racked and listening for the child cry, the child call. We sit for a while and I hold him, looking out over the city spread in charcoal with its soft aisles of light. "*Shoogily*," he breathes and curls closer. I carry him back to bed, asleep. *Shoogily*. A funny word, a family word, inherited from Emily, invented by her to say: *comfort*.

In this and other ways she leaves her seal, I say aloud. And startle at my saying it. What do I mean? What did I start to gather together, to try and make coherent? I was at the terrible, growing years. War years. I do not remember them well. I was working, there were four smaller ones now, there was not time for her. She had to help be a mother, and house-keeper, and shopper. She had to set her seal. Mornings of crisis and near hysteria trying to get lunches packed, hair combed, coats and shoes found, everyone to school or Child Care on time, the baby ready for transportation. And always the paper scribbled on by a smaller one, the book looked at by Susan then mislaid, the homework not done. Running out to that huge school where she was one, she was lost, she was a drop; suffering over the unpreparedness, stammering and unsure in her classes.

There was so little time left at night after the kids were bedded down. She would struggle over books, always eating (it was in those years she developed her enormous appetite that is legendary in our family) and I would be ironing, or preparing food for the next day, or writing V-mail to Bill, or tending the baby. Sometimes, to make me laugh, or out of her despair, she would imitate happenings or types at school.

I think I said once: "Why don't you do something like this in the school amateur show?" One morning she phoned me at work, hardly under-standable through the weeping: "Mother, I did it. I won, I won; they gave me first prize; they clapped and clapped and wouldn't let me go."

Now suddenly she was Somebody, and as imprisoned in her difference as she had been in anonymity.

She began to be asked to perform at other high schools, even in col-leges, then at city and statewide affairs. The first one we went to, I only recognized her that first moment when thin, shy, she almost drowned herself into the curtains. Then: Was this Emily? The control, the com-mand, the convulsing and deadly clowning, the spell, then the roaring, stamping audience, unwilling to let this rare and precious laughter out of their lives.

Afterwards: You ought to do something about her with a gift like that—but without money or knowing how, what does one do? We have left it all to her, and the gift has as often eddied inside, clogged and clotted, as been used and growing.

She is coming. She runs up the stairs two at a time with her light graceful step, and I know she is happy tonight. Whatever it was that occasioned your call did not happen today.

"Aren't you ever going to finish the ironing, Mother? Whistler painted his mother in a rocker. I'd have to paint mine standing over an ironing board." This is one of her communicative nights and she tells me everything and nothing as she fixes herself a plate of food out of the icebox.

She is so lovely. Why did you want me to come in at all? Why were you concerned? She will find her way.

She starts up the stairs to bed. "Don't get me up with the rest in the morning." "But I thought you were having midterms." "Oh, those," she comes back in, kisses me, and says quite lightly, "in a couple of years when we'll all be atom-dead they won't matter a bit."

She has said it before. She *believes* it. But because I have been dredging the past, and all that compounds a human being is so heavy and meaningful in me, I cannot endure it tonight.

I will never total it all. I will never come in to say: She was a child seldom smiled at. Her father left me before she was a year old. I had to work her first six years when there was work, or I sent her home and to his relatives. There were years she had care she hated. She was dark and thin and foreign-looking in a world where the prestige went to blondeness and curly hair and dimples, she was slow where glibness was prized. She was a child of anxious, not proud, love. We were poor and could not afford for her the soil of easy growth. I was a young mother, I was a distracted mother. There were the other children pushing up, demanding. Her younger sister seemed all that she was not. There were years she did not want me to touch her. She kept too much in herself, her life was such she had to keep too much in herself. My wisdom came too late. She has much to her and probably little will come of it. She is a child of her age, of depression, of war, of fear.

Let her be. So all that is in her will not bloom—but in how many does it? There is still enough left to live by. Only help her to know—help make it so there is cause for her to know—that she is more than this dress on the ironing board, helpless before the iron.

[1961]

RALPH ELLISON   [1914–1994]

Battle Royal

It goes a long way back, some twenty years. All my life I had been looking for something, and everywhere I turned someone tried to tell me what it was. I accepted their answers too, though they were often in contradiction and even self-contradictory. I was naïve. I was looking for myself and asking everyone except myself questions which I, and only I, could answer. It took me a long time and much painful boomeranging of my expectations to achieve a realization everyone else appears to have been born with: That I am nobody but myself. But first I had to discover that I am an invisible man!

And yet I am no freak of nature, nor of history. I was in the cards, other things having been equal (or unequal) eighty-five years ago. I am not ashamed of my grandparents for having been slaves. I am only ashamed of myself for having at one time been ashamed. About eighty-five years ago they were told that they were free, united with others of our country in everything pertaining to the common good, and, in everything social, separate like the fingers of the hand. And they believed it. They exulted in it. They stayed in their place, worked hard, and brought up my father to do the same. But my grandfather is the one. He was an odd old guy, my grandfather, and I am told I take after him. It was he who caused the trouble. On his deathbed he called my father to him and said, "Son, after I'm gone I want you to keep up the good fight. I never told you, but our life is a war and I have been a traitor all my born days, a spy in the enemy's country ever since I give up my gun back in the Reconstruction. Live with your head in the lion's mouth. I want you to overcome 'em with yeses, undermine 'em with grins, agree 'em to death and destruction, let 'em swoller you till they vomit or bust wide open." They thought the old man had gone out of his mind. He had been the meekest of men. The younger children were rushed from the room, the shades drawn, and the flame of the lamp turned so low that it sputtered on the wick like the old man's breathing. "Learn it to the younguns," he whispered fiercely; then he died.

But my folks were more alarmed over his last words than over his dying. It was as though he had not died at all, his words caused so much anxiety. I was warned emphatically to forget what he had said and, indeed, this is the first time it has been mentioned outside the family circle. It had a tremendous effect upon me, however. I could never be sure of what he meant. Grandfather had been a quiet old man who never made any trouble, yet on his deathbed he had called himself a traitor and a spy, and he had spoken of his meekness as a dangerous activity. It became a constant puzzle which lay unanswered in the back of my mind. And whenever things went well for me I remembered my grandfather and felt guilty and uncomfortable. It was as though I was carrying out his advice in spite of myself. And to make it worse, everyone loved me for it. I was praised by the most lily-white men of the town. I was considered an example of desirable conduct—just as my grandfather had been. And what puzzled me was that the old man had defined it as *treachery*. When I was praised for my conduct I felt a guilt that in some way I was doing something that was really against the wishes of the white folks, that if they had understood they would have desired me to act just the opposite, that I should have been sulky and mean, and that that really would have been what they wanted, even though they were fooled and thought they wanted me to act as I did. It made me afraid that some day they would look upon me as a traitor and I would be lost. Still I was more afraid to act any other way because they didn't like that at all. The old man's words were like a curse. On my graduation day I delivered an oration in which I showed that humility was the secret, indeed, the very essence of progress. (Not that I believed this—how could I, remembering my grandfather?—I only believed that it worked.) It was a great success. Everyone praised me and I was invited to give the speech at a gathering of the town's leading white citizens. It was a triumph for our whole community.

It was in the main ballroom of the leading hotel. When I got there I discovered that it was on the occasion of a smoker, and I was told that since I was to be there anyway I might as well take part in the battle royal to be fought by some of my schoolmates as part of the entertainment. The battle royal came first.

All of the town's big shots were there in their tuxedoes, wolfing down the buffet foods, drinking beer and whiskey and smoking black cigars. It was a large room with a high ceiling. Chairs were arranged in neat rows around three sides of a portable boxing ring. The fourth side was clear, revealing a gleaming space of polished floor. I had some misgivings over the battle royal, by the way. Not from a distaste for fighting, but because I didn't care too much for the other fellows who were to take part. They were tough guys who seemed to have no grandfather's curse worrying their minds. No one could mistake their toughness. And besides, I suspected that fighting a battle royal might detract from the dignity of my speech. In those pre-invisible days I visualized myself as a potential

Booker T. Washington.° But the other fellows didn't care too much for me either, and there were nine of them. I felt superior to them in my way, and I didn't like the manner in which we were all crowded together into the servants' elevator. Nor did they like my being there. In fact, as the warmly lighted floors flashed past the elevator we had words over the fact that I, by taking part in the fight, had knocked one of their friends out of a night's work.

We were led out of the elevator through a rococo hall into an anteroom and told to get into our fighting togs. Each of us was issued a pair of boxing gloves and ushered out into the big mirrored hall, which we entered looking cautiously about us and whispering, lest we might accidentally be heard above the noise of the room. It was foggy with cigar smoke. And already the whiskey was taking effect. I was shocked to see some of the most important men of the town quite tipsy. They were all there — bankers, lawyers, judges, doctors, fire chiefs, teachers, merchants. Even one of the more fashionable pastors. Something we could not see was going on up front. A clarinet was vibrating sensuously and the men were standing up and moving eagerly forward. We were a small tight group, clustered together, our bare upper bodies touching and shining with anticipatory sweat; while up front the big shots were becoming increasingly excited over something we still could not see. Suddenly I heard the school superintendent, who had told me to come, yell, "Bring up the shines, gentlemen! Bring up the little shines!"

We were rushed up to the front of the ballroom, where it smelled even more strongly of tobacco and whiskey. Then we were pushed into place. I almost wet my pants. A sea of faces, some hostile, some amused, ringed around us, and in the center, facing us, stood a magnificent blonde — stark naked. There was dead silence. I felt a blast of cold air chill me. I tried to back away, but they were behind me and around me. Some of the boys stood with lowered heads, trembling. I felt a wave of irrational guilt and fear. My teeth chattered, my skin turned to goose flesh, my knees knocked. Yet I was strongly attracted and looked in spite of myself. Had the price of looking been blindness, I would have looked. The hair was yellow like that of a circus kewpie doll, the face heavily powdered and rouged, as though to form an abstract mask, the eyes hollow and smeared a cool blue, the color of a baboon's butt. I felt a desire to spit upon her as my eyes brushed slowly over her body. Her breasts were firm and round as the domes of East Indian temples, and I stood so close as to see the fine skin texture and beads of pearly perspiration glistening like dew around

Booker T. Washington (1856–1915): African American educator, reformer, and political leader. He advocated education in industry and economic security for post-Reconstruction African Americans.

the pink and erected buds of her nipples. I wanted at one and the same time to run from the room, to sink through the floor, or go to her and cover her from my eyes and the eyes of the others with my body; to feel the soft thighs, to caress her and destroy her, to love her and murder her, to hide from her, and yet to stroke where below the small American flag tattooed upon her belly her thighs formed a capital V. I had a notion that of all in the room she saw only me with her impersonal eyes.

And then she began to dance, a slow sensuous movement; the smoke of a hundred cigars clinging to her like the thinnest of veils. She seemed like a fair bird-girl girdled in veils calling to me from the angry surface of some gray and threatening sea. I was transported. Then I became aware of the clarinet playing and the big shots yelling at us. Some threatened us if we looked and others if we did not. On my right I saw one boy faint. And now a man grabbed a silver pitcher from a table and stepped close as he dashed ice water upon him and stood him up and forced two of us to support him as his head hung and moans issued from his thick bluish lips. Another boy began to plead to go home. He was the largest of the group, wearing dark red fighting trunks much too small to conceal the erection which projected from him as though in answer to the insinuating low-registered moaning of the clarinet. He tried to hide himself with his boxing gloves.

And all the while the blonde continued dancing, smiling faintly at the big shots who watched her with fascination, and faintly smiling at our fear. I noticed a certain merchant who followed her hungrily, his lips loose and drooling. He was a large man who wore diamond studs in a shirtfront which swelled with the ample paunch underneath, and each time the blonde swayed her undulating hips he ran his hand through the thin hair of his bald head and, with his arms upheld, his posture clumsy like that of an intoxicated panda, wound his belly in a slow and obscene grind. This creature was completely hypnotized. The music had quickened. As the dancer flung herself about with a detached expression on her face, the men began reaching out to touch her. I could see their beefy fingers sink into her soft flesh. Some of the others tried to stop them and she began to move around the floor in graceful circles, as they gave chase, slipping and sliding over the polished floor. It was mad. Chairs went crashing, drinks were spilt, as they ran laughing and howling after her. They caught her just as she reached a door, raised her from the floor, and tossed her as college boys are tossed at a hazing, and above her red fixed-smiling lips I saw the terror and disgust in her eyes, almost like my own terror and that which I saw in some of the other boys. As I watched, they tossed her twice and her soft breasts seemed to flatten against the air and her legs flung wildly as she spun. Some of the more sober ones helped her to escape. And I started off the floor, heading for the anteroom with the rest of the boys.

Some were still crying and in hysteria. But as we tried to leave we were stopped and ordered to get into the ring. There was nothing to do but what we were told. All ten of us climbed under the ropes and allowed ourselves to be blindfolded with broad bands of white cloth. One of the men seemed to feel a bit sympathetic and tried to cheer us up as we stood with our backs against the ropes. Some of us tried to grin. "See that boy over there?" one of the men said. "I want you to run across at the bell and give it to him right in the belly. If you don't get him, I'm going to get you. I don't like his looks." Each of us was told the same. The blindfolds were put on. Yet even then I had been going over my speech. In my mind each word was as bright as flame. I felt the cloth pressed into place, and frowned so that it would be loosened when I relaxed.

But now I felt a sudden fit of blind terror. I was unused to darkness. It was as though I had suddenly found myself in a dark room filled with poisonous cottonmouths. I could hear the bleary voices yelling insistently for the battle royal to begin.

"Get going in there!"

"Let me at that big nigger!"

I strained to pick up the school superintendent's voice, as though to squeeze some security out of that slightly more familiar sound.

"Let me at those black sonsabitches!" someone yelled.

"No, Jackson, no!" another voice yelled. "Here, somebody, help me hold Jack."

"I want to get at that ginger-colored nigger. Tear him limb from limb," the first voice yelled.

I stood against the ropes trembling. For in those days I was what they called ginger-colored, and he sounded as though he might crunch me between his teeth like a crisp ginger cookie.

Quite a struggle was going on. Chairs were being kicked about and I could hear voices grunting as with a terrific effort. I wanted to see, to see more desperately than ever before. But the blindfold was as tight as a thick skin-puckering scab and when I raised my gloved hands to push the layers of white aside a voice yelled, "Oh, no you don't, black bastard! Leave that alone!"

"Ring the bell before Jackson kills him a coon!" someone boomed in the sudden silence. And I heard the bell clang and the sound of the feet scuffling forward.

A glove smacked against my head. I pivoted, striking out stiffly as someone went past, and felt the jar ripple along the length of my arm to my shoulder. Then it seemed as though all nine of the boys had turned upon me at once. Blows pounded me from all sides while I struck out as best I could. So many blows landed upon me that I wondered if I were not the only blindfolded fighter in the ring, or if the man called Jackson hadn't succeeded in getting me after all.

Blindfolded, I could no longer control my motions. I had no dignity. I stumbled about like a baby or a drunken man. The smoke had become thicker and with each new blow it seemed to sear and further restrict my lungs. My saliva became like hot bitter glue. A glove connected with my head, filling my mouth with warm blood. It was everywhere. I could not tell if the moisture I felt upon my body was sweat or blood. A blow landed hard against the nape of my neck. I felt myself going over, my head hitting the floor. Streaks of blue light filled the black world behind the blindfold. I lay prone, pretending that I was knocked out, but felt myself seized by hands and yanked to my feet. "Get going, black boy! Mix it up!" My arms were like lead, my head smarting from blows. I managed to feel my way to the ropes and held on, trying to catch my breath. A glove landed in my midsection and I went over again, feeling as though the smoke had become a knife jabbed into my guts. Pushed this way and that by the legs milling around me, I finally pulled erect and discovered that I could see the black, sweat-washed forms weaving in the smoky-blue atmosphere like drunken dancers weaving to the rapid drum-like thuds of blows.

Everyone fought hysterically. It was complete anarchy. Everybody fought everybody else. No group fought together for long. Two, three, four, fought one, then turned to fight each other, were themselves attacked. Blows landed below the belt and in the kidney, with the gloves open as well as closed, and with my eye partly opened now there was not so much terror. I moved carefully, avoiding blows, although not too many to attract attention, fighting from group to group. The boys groped about like blind, cautious crabs crouching to protect their mid-sections, their heads pulled in short against their shoulders, their arms stretched nervously before them, with their fists testing the smoke-filled air like the knobbed feelers of hypersensitive snails. In one corner I glimpsed a boy violently punching the air and heard him scream in pain as he smashed his hand against a ring post. For a second I saw him bent over holding his hand, then going down as a blow caught his unprotected head. I played one group against the other, slipping in and throwing a punch then stepping out of range while pushing the others into the melee to take the blows blindly aimed at me. The smoke was agonizing and there were no rounds, no bells at three minute intervals to relieve our exhaustion. The room spun round me, a swirl of lights, smoke, sweating bodies surrounded by tense white faces. I bled from both nose and mouth, the blood spattering upon my chest.

The men kept yelling, "Slug him, black boy! Knock his guts out!"

"Uppercut him! Kill him! Kill that big boy!"

Taking a fake fall, I saw a boy going down heavily beside me as though we were felled by a single blow, saw a sneaker-clad foot shoot into his groin as the two who had knocked him down stumbled upon him. I rolled out of range, feeling a twinge of nausea.

The harder we fought the more threatening the men became. And yet, I had begun to worry about my speech again. How would it go? Would they recognize my ability? What would they give me?

I was fighting automatically and suddenly I noticed that one after another of the boys was leaving the ring. I was surprised, filled with panic, as though I had been left alone with an unknown danger. Then I understood. The boys had arranged it among themselves. It was the custom for the two men left in the ring to slug it out for the winner's prize. I discovered this too late. When the bell sounded two men in tuxedoes leaped into the ring and removed the blindfold. I found myself facing Tatlock, the biggest of the gang. I felt sick at my stomach. Hardly had the bell stopped ringing in my ears than it clanged again and I saw him moving swiftly toward me. Thinking of nothing else to do I hit him smash on the nose. He kept coming, bringing the rank sharp violence of stale sweat. His face was a black blank of a face, only his eyes alive—with hate of me and aglow with a feverish terror from what had happened to us all. I became anxious. I wanted to deliver my speech and he came at me as though he meant to beat it out of me. I smashed him again and again, taking his blows as they came. Then on a sudden impulse I struck him lightly and as we clinched, I whispered, "Fake like I knocked you out, you can have the prize."

"I'll break your behind," he whispered hoarsely.

"For *them*?"

"For *me*, sonofabitch!"

They were yelling for us to break it up and Tatlock spun me half around with a blow, and as a joggled camera sweeps in a reeling scene, I saw the howling red faces crouching tense beneath the cloud of blue-gray smoke. For a moment the world wavered, unraveled, flowed, then my head cleared and Tatlock bounced before me. That fluttering shadow before my eyes was his jabbing left hand. Then falling forward, my head against his damp shoulder, I whispered,

"I'll make it five dollars more."

"Go to hell!"

But his muscles relaxed a trifle beneath my pressure and I breathed, "Seven!"

"Give it to your ma," he said, ripping me beneath the heart.

And while I still held him I butted him and moved away. I felt myself bombarded with punches. I fought back with hopeless desperation. I wanted to deliver my speech more than anything else in the world, because I felt that only these men could judge truly my ability, and now this stupid clown was ruining my chances. I began fighting carefully now, moving in to punch him and out again with my greater speed. A lucky blow to his chin and I had him going too—until I heard a loud voice yell, "I got my money on the big boy."

Hearing this, I almost dropped my guard. I was confused: Should I try to win against the voice out there? Would not this go against my speech, and was not this a moment for humility, for nonresistance? A blow to my head as I danced about sent my right eye popping like a jack-in-the-box and settled my dilemma. The room went red as I fell. It was a dream fall, my body languid and fastidious as to where to land, until the floor became impatient and smashed up to meet me. A moment later I came to. An hypnotic voice said FIVE emphatically. And I lay there, hazily watching a dark red spot of my own blood shaping itself into a butterfly, glistening and soaking into the soiled gray world of the canvas.

When the voice drawled TEN I was lifted up and dragged to a chair. I sat dazed. My eye pained and swelled with each throb of my pounding heart and I wondered if now I would be allowed to speak. I was wringing wet, my mouth still bleeding. We were grouped along the wall now. The other boys ignored me as they congratulated Tatlock and speculated as to how much they would be paid. One boy whimpered over his smashed hand. Looking up front, I saw attendants in white jackets rolling the portable ring away and placing a small square rug in the vacant space surrounded by chairs. Perhaps, I thought, I will stand on the rug to deliver my speech.

Then the M.C. called to us, "Come on up here boys and get your money."

We ran forward to where the men laughed and talked in their chairs, waiting. Everyone seemed friendly now.

"There it is on the rug," the man said. I saw the rug covered with coins of all dimensions and a few crumpled bills. But what excited me, scattered here and there, were the gold pieces.

"Boys, it's all yours," the man said. "You get all you grab."

"That's right, Sambo," a blond man said, winking at me confidentially.

I trembled with excitement, forgetting my pain. I would get the gold and the bills, I thought. I would use both hands. I would throw my body against the boys nearest me to block them from the gold.

"Get down around the rug now," the man commanded, "and don't anyone touch it until I give the signal."

"This ought to be good," I heard.

As told, we got around the square rug on our knees. Slowly the man raised his freckled hand as we followed it upward with our eyes.

I heard, "These niggers look like they're about to pray!"

Then, "Ready," the man said. "Go!"

I lunged for a yellow coin lying on the blue design of the carpet, touching it and sending a surprised shriek to join those rising around me. I tried frantically to remove my hand but could not let go. A hot, violent force tore through my body, shaking me like a wet rat. The rug was electrified. The hair bristled up on my head as I shook myself free. My muscles jumped, my nerves jangled, writhed. But I saw that this was not stopping the other boys. Laughing in fear and embarrassment, some were holding back and scooping up the coins knocked off by the painful contortions of the others. The men roared above us as we struggled.

"Pick it up, goddamnit, pick it up!" someone called like a bass-voiced parrot. "Go on, get it!"

I crawled rapidly around the floor, picking up the coins, trying to avoid the coppers and to get greenbacks and the gold. Ignoring the shock by laughing, as I brushed the coins off quickly, I discovered that I could contain the electricity—a contradiction, but it works. Then the men began to push us onto the rug. Laughing embarrassedly, we struggled out of their hands and kept after the coins. We were all wet and slippery and hard to hold. Suddenly I saw a boy lifted into the air, glistening with sweat like a circus seal, and dropped, his wet back landing flush upon the charged rug, heard him yell and saw him literally dance upon his back, his elbows beating a frenzied tattoo upon the floor, his muscles twitching like the flesh of a horse stung by many flies. When he finally rolled off, his face was gray and no one stopped him when he ran from the floor amid booming laughter.

"Get the money," the M.C. called. "That's good hard American cash!"

And we snatched and grabbed, snatched and grabbed. I was careful not to come too close to the rug now, and when I felt the hot whiskey breath descend upon me like a cloud of foul air I reached out and grabbed the leg of a chair. It was occupied and I held on desperately.

"Leggo, nigger! Leggo!"

The huge face wavered down to mine as he tried to push me free. But my body was slippery and he was too drunk. It was Mr. Colcord, who owned a chain of movie houses and "entertainment palaces." Each time he grabbed me I slipped out of his hands. It became a real struggle. I feared the rug more than I did the drunk, so I held on, surprising myself for a moment by trying to topple *him* upon the rug. It was such an enormous idea that I found myself actually carrying it out. I tried not to be obvious, yet when I grabbed his leg, trying to tumble him out of the chair, he raised up roaring with laughter, and, looking at me with soberness dead in the eye, kicked me viciously in the chest. The chair leg flew out of my hand. I felt myself going and rolled. It was as though I had rolled through a bed of hot coals. It seemed a whole century would pass before I would roll free, a century in which I was seared through the deepest levels of my body to the fearful breath within me and the breath seared and heated to the point of explosion. It'll all be over in a flash, I thought as I rolled clear. It'll all be over in a flash.

But not yet, the men on the other side were waiting, red faces swollen as though from apoplexy as they bent forward in their chairs. Seeing their fingers coming toward me I rolled away as a fumbled football rolls off the receiver's fingertips, back into the coals. That time I luckily sent the rug sliding out of place and heard the coins ringing against the floor and the boys scuffling to pick them up and the M.C. calling, "All right, boys, that's all. Go get dressed and get your money."

I was limp as a dish rag. My back felt as though it had been beaten with wires.

When we had dressed the M.C. came in and gave us each five dollars, except Tatlock, who got ten for being last in the ring. Then he told us to leave. I was not to get a chance to deliver my speech, I thought. I was going out into the dim alley in despair when I was stopped and told to go back. I returned to the ballroom, where the men were pushing back their chairs and gathering in groups to talk.

The M.C. knocked on a table for quiet. "Gentlemen," he said, "we almost forgot an important part of the program. A most serious part, gentlemen. This boy was brought here to deliver a speech which he made at his graduation yesterday. . . ."

"Bravo!"

"I'm told that he is the smartest boy we've got out there in Greenwood. I'm told that he knows more big words than a pocket-sized dictionary."

Much applause and laughter.

"So now, gentlemen, I want you to give him your attention."

There was still laughter as I faced them, my mouth dry, my eye throbbing. I began slowly, but evidently my throat was tense, because they began shouting, "Louder! Louder!"

"We of the younger generation extol the wisdom of that great leader and educator," I shouted, "who first spoke these flaming words of wisdom: 'A ship lost at sea for many days suddenly sighted a friendly vessel. From the mast of the unfortunate vessel was seen a signal: "Water, water; we die of thirst!" The answer from the friendly vessel came back: "Cast down your bucket where you are." The captain of the distressed vessel, at last heeding the injunction, cast down his bucket, and it came up full of fresh sparkling water from the mouth of the Amazon River.' And like him I say, and in his words, 'To those of my race who depend upon bettering their condition in a foreign land, or who underestimate the importance of cultivating friendly relations with the Southern white man, who is his next-door neighbor, I would say: "Cast down your bucket where you are"—cast it down in making friends in every manly way of the people of all races by whom we are surrounded. . . .'"

I spoke automatically and with such fervor that I did not realize that the men were still talking and laughing until my dry mouth, filling up with blood from the cut, almost strangled me. I coughed, wanting to stop and go to one of the tall brass, sand-filled spittoons to relieve myself, but a few of the men, especially the superintendent, were listening and I was afraid. So I gulped it down, blood, saliva, and all, and continued. (What powers of endurance I had during those days! What enthusiasm! What a belief in the rightness of things!) I spoke even louder in spite of the pain. But still they talked and still they laughed, as though deaf with cotton in dirty ears. So I spoke with greater emotional emphasis. I closed my ears and swallowed blood until I was nauseated. The speech seemed a hundred times as long as before, but I could not leave out a single word. All had to be said, each memorized nuance considered, rendered. Nor was that all. Whenever I uttered a word of three or more syllables a group of voices would yell for me to repeat it. I used the phrase "social responsibility" and they yelled:

"What's the word you say, boy?"

"Social responsibility," I said.

"What?"

"Social . . ."

"Louder."

". . . responsibility."

"More!"

"Respon—"

"Repeat!"

"—sibility."

The room filled with the uproar of laughter until, no doubt, distracted by having to gulp down my blood, I made a mistake and yelled a phrase I had often seen denounced in newspaper editorials, heard debated in private.

"Social . . ."

"What?" they yelled.

". . . equality—"

The laughter hung smokelike in the sudden stillness. I opened my eyes, puzzled. Sounds of displeasure filled the room. The M.C. rushed forward. They shouted hostile phrases at me. But I did not understand.

A small dry mustached man in the front row blared out, "Say that slowly, son!"

"What sir?"

"What you just said!"

"Social responsibility, sir," I said.

"You weren't being smart, were you, boy?" he said, not unkindly.

"No, sir!"

"You sure that about 'equality' was a mistake?"

"Oh, yes, sir," I said. "I was swallowing blood."

"Well, you had better speak more slowly so we can understand. We mean to do right by you, but you've got to know your place at all times. All right, now, go on with your speech."

I was afraid. I wanted to leave but I wanted also to speak and I was afraid they'd snatch me down.

"Thank you, sir," I said, beginning where I had left off, and having them ignore me as before.

Yet when I finished there was a thunderous applause. I was surprised to see the superintendent come forth with a package wrapped in white tissue paper, and, gesturing for quiet, address the men.

"Gentlemen, you see that I did not overpraise this boy. He makes a good speech and some day he'll lead his people in the proper paths. And I don't have to tell you that that is important in these days and times. This is a good, smart boy, and so to encourage him in the right direction, in the name of the Board of Education I wish to present him a prize in the form of this . . ."

He paused, removing the tissue paper and revealing a gleaming calf-skin brief case.

". . . in the form of this first-class article from Shad Whitmore's shop."

"Boy," he said, addressing me, "take this prize and keep it well. Consider it a badge of office. Prize it. Keep developing as you are and some day it will be filled with important papers that will help shape the destiny of your people."

I was so moved that I could hardly express my thanks. A rope of bloody saliva forming a shape like an undiscovered continent drooled upon the leather and I wiped it quickly away. I felt an importance that I had never dreamed.

"Open it and see what's inside," I was told.

My fingers a-tremble, I complied, smelling the fresh leather and finding an official-looking document inside. It was a scholarship to the state college for Negroes. My eyes filled with tears and I ran awkwardly off the floor.

I was overjoyed; I did not even mind when I discovered that the gold pieces I had scrambled for were brass pocket tokens advertising a certain make of automobile.

When I reached home everyone was excited. Next day the neighbors came to congratulate me. I even felt safe from grandfather, whose death-bed curse usually spoiled my triumphs. I stood beneath his photograph with my brief case in hand and smiled triumphantly into his stolid black peasant's face. It was a face that fascinated me. The eyes seemed to follow everywhere I went.

That night I dreamed I was at a circus with him and that he refused to laugh at the clowns no matter what they did. Then later he told me to open my brief case and read what was inside and I did, finding an official envelope stamped with the state seal; and inside the envelope I found another and another, endlessly, and I thought I would fall of weariness. "Them's years," he said. "Now open that one." And I did and in it I found an engraved document containing a short message in letters of gold. "Read it," my grandfather said. "Out loud."

"To Whom It May Concern," I intoned. "Keep This Nigger-Boy Running."

I awoke with the old man's laughter ringing in my ears.

(It was a dream I was to remember and dream again for many years after. But at the time I had no insight into its meaning. First I had to attend college.)

[1952]

SHIRLEY JACKSON   [1919–1965]

The Lottery

The morning of June 27th was clear and sunny, with the fresh warmth of a full-summer day; the flowers were blossoming profusely and the grass was richly green. The people of the village began to gather in the square, between the post office and the bank, around ten o'clock; in some towns there were so many people that the lottery took two days and had to be started on June 26th, but in this village, where there were only about three hundred people, the whole lottery took less than two hours, so it could begin at ten o'clock in the morning and still be through in time to allow the villagers to get home for noon dinner.

The children assembled first, of course. School was recently over for the summer, and the feeling of liberty sat uneasily on most of them; they tended to gather together quietly for a while before they broke into boisterous play, and their talk was still of the classroom and teacher, of books and reprimands. Bobby Martin had already stuffed his pockets full of stones, and the other boys soon followed his example, selecting the smoothest and roundest stones; Bobby and Harry Jones and Dickie Delacroix—the villagers pronounced this name "Dellacroy"—eventually made a great pile of stones in one corner of the square and guarded it against the raids of the other boys. The girls stood aside, talking among themselves, looking over their shoulders at the boys, and the very small children rolled in the dust or clung to the hands of their older brothers or sisters.

Soon the men began to gather, surveying their own children, speaking of planting and rain, tractors and taxes. They stood together, away from the pile of stones in the corner, and their jokes were quiet and they smiled rather than laughed. The women, wearing faded house dresses and sweaters, came shortly after their menfolk. They greeted one another and exchanged bits of gossip as they went to join their husbands. Soon the women, standing by their husbands, began to call to their children, and the children came reluctantly, having to be called four or five times. Bobby Martin ducked under his mother's grasping hand and ran, laughing, back to the pile of stones. His father spoke up sharply, and Bobby came quickly and took his place between his father and his oldest brother.

The lottery was conducted—as were the square dances, the teen-age club, the Halloween program—by Mr. Summers, who had time and energy to devote to civic activities. He was a round-faced, jovial man and he ran the coal business, and people were sorry for him, because he had no children and his wife was a scold. When he arrived in the square, carrying the black wooden box, there was a murmur of conversation among the villagers, and he waved and called, "Little late today, folks." The postmaster, Mr. Graves, followed him, carrying a three-legged stool, and the stool was put in the center of the square and Mr. Summers set the black box down on it. The villagers kept their distance, leaving a space between themselves and the stool, and when Mr. Summers said, "Some of you fellows want to give me a hand?" there was a hesitation before two men, Mr. Martin and his oldest son, Baxter, came forward to hold the box steady on the stool while Mr. Summers stirred up the papers inside it.

The original paraphernalia for the lottery had been lost long ago, and the black box now resting on the stool had been put into use even before Old Man Warner, the oldest man in town, was born. Mr. Summers spoke frequently to the villagers about making a new box, but no one liked to upset even as much tradition as was represented by the black box. There was a story that the present box had been made with some pieces of the box that had preceded it, the one that had been constructed when the first people settled down to make a village here. Every year, after the lottery, Mr. Summers began talking again about a new box, but every year the subject was allowed to fade off without anything's being done. The black box grew shabbier each year; by now it was no longer completely black but splintered badly along one side to show the original wood color, and in some places faded or stained.

Mr. Martin and his oldest son, Baxter, held the black box securely on the stool until Mr. Summers had stirred the papers thoroughly with his hand. Because so much of the ritual had been forgotten or discarded, Mr. Summers had been successful in having slips of paper substituted for the chips of wood that had been used for generations. Chips of wood, Mr. Summers had argued, had been all very well when the village was tiny, but now that the population was more than three hundred and likely to keep on growing, it was necessary to use something that would fit more easily into the black box. The night before the lottery, Mr. Summers and Mr. Graves made up the slips of paper and put them in the box, and it was then taken to the safe of Mr. Summers's coal company and locked up until Mr. Summers was ready to take it to the square next morning. The rest of the year, the box was put away, sometimes one place, sometimes another; it had spent one year in Mr. Graves's barn and another year underfoot in the post office, and sometimes it was set on a shelf in the Martin grocery and left there.

There was a great deal of fussing to be done before Mr. Summers declared the lottery open. There were the lists to make up—of heads of families, heads of households in each family, members of each household in each family. There was the proper swearing-in of Mr. Summers by the postmaster, as the official of the lottery; at one time, some people remembered, there had been a recital of some sort, performed by the official of the lottery, a perfunctory, tuneless chant that had been rattled off duly each year; some people believed that the official of the lottery used to stand just so when he said or sang it, others believed that he was supposed to walk among the people, but years and years ago this part of the ritual had been allowed to lapse. There had been, also, a ritual salute, which the official of the lottery had had to use in addressing each person who came up to draw from the box, but this also had changed with time, until now it was felt necessary only for the official to speak to each person approaching. Mr. Summers was very good at all this; in his clean white shirt and blue jeans, with one hand resting carelessly on the black box, he seemed very proper and important as he talked interminably to Mr. Graves and the Martins.

Just as Mr. Summers finally left off talking and turned to the assembled villagers, Mrs. Hutchinson came hurriedly along the path to the square, her sweater thrown over her shoulders, and slid into place in the back of the crowd. "Clean forgot what day it was," she said to Mrs. Delacroix, who stood next to her, and they both laughed softly. "Thought my old man was out back stacking wood," Mrs. Hutchinson went on, "and then I looked out the window and the kids was gone, and then I remembered it was the twenty-seventh and came a-running." She dried her hands on her apron, and Mrs. Delacroix said, "You're in time, though. They're still talking away up there."

Mrs. Hutchinson craned her neck to see through the crowd and found her husband and children standing near the front. She tapped Mrs. Delacroix on the arm as a farewell and began to make her way through the crowd. The people separated good-humoredly to let her through; two or three people said, in voices just loud enough to be heard across the crowd, "Here comes your Missus, Hutchinson," and "Bill, she made it after all." Mrs. Hutchinson reached her husband, and Mr. Summers, who had been waiting, said cheerfully, "Thought we were going to have to get on without you, Tessie." Mrs. Hutchinson said, grinning, "Wouldn't have me leave m'dishes in the sink, now, would you, Joe?" and soft laughter ran through the crowd as the people stirred back into position after Mrs. Hutchinson's arrival.

"Well, now," Mr. Summers said soberly, "guess we better get started, get this over with, so's we can go back to work. Anybody ain't here?"

"Dunbar," several people said. "Dunbar, Dunbar."

Mr. Summers consulted his list. "Clyde Dunbar," he said. "That's right. He's broke his leg, hasn't he? Who's drawing for him?"

"Me, I guess," a woman said, and Mr. Summers turned to look at her. "Wife draws for her husband," Mr. Summers said. "Don't you have a grown boy to do it for you, Janey?" Although Mr. Summers and everyone else in the village knew the answer perfectly well, it was the business of the official of the lottery to ask such questions formally. Mr. Summers waited with an expression of polite interest while Mrs. Dunbar answered.

"Horace's not but sixteen yet," Mrs. Dunbar said regretfully. "Guess I gotta fill in for the old man this year."

"Right," Mr. Summers said. He made a note on the list he was holding. Then he asked, "Watson boy drawing this year?"

A tall boy in the crowd raised his hand. "Here," he said. "I'm drawing for m'mother and me." He blinked his eyes nervously and ducked his head as several voices in the crowd said things like "Good fellow, Jack," and "Glad to see your mother's got a man to do it."

"Well," Mr. Summers said, "guess that's everyone. Old Man Warner make it?"

"Here," a voice said, and Mr. Summers nodded.

A sudden hush fell on the crowd as Mr. Summers cleared his throat and looked at the list. "All ready?" he called. "Now, I'll read the names—heads of families first—and the men come up and take a paper out of the box. Keep the paper folded in your hand without looking at it until everyone has had a turn. Everything clear?"

The people had done it so many times that they only half listened to the directions; most of them were quiet, wetting their lips, not looking around. Then Mr. Summers raised one hand high and said, "Adams." A man disengaged himself from the crowd and came forward. "Hi, Steve," Mr. Summers said, and Mr. Adams said, "Hi, Joe." They grinned at one another humorlessly and nervously. Then Mr. Adams reached into the black box and took out a folded paper. He held it firmly by one corner as he turned and went hastily back to his place in the crowd, where he stood a little apart from his family, not looking down at his hand.

"Allen," Mr. Summers said, "Anderson. . . . Bentham."

"Seems like there's no time at all between lotteries any more," Mrs. Delacroix said to Mrs. Graves in the back row. "Seems like we got through with the last one only last week."

"Time sure goes fast," Mrs. Graves said.

"Clark. . . . Delacroix."

"There goes my old man," Mrs. Delacroix said. She held her breath while her husband went forward.

"Dunbar," Mr. Summers said, and Mrs. Dunbar went steadily to the box while one of the women said, "Go on, Janey," and another said, "There she goes."

"We're next," Mrs. Graves said. She watched while Mr. Graves came around from the side of the box, greeted Mr. Summers gravely, and selected a slip of paper from the box. By now, all through the crowd there were men holding the small folded papers in their large hands, turning them over and over nervously. Mrs. Dunbar and her two sons stood together, Mrs. Dunbar holding the slip of paper.

"Harburt. . . . Hutchinson."

"Get up there, Bill," Mrs. Hutchinson said, and the people near her laughed.

"Jones."

"They do say," Mr. Adams said to Old Man Warner, who stood next to him, "that over in the north village they're talking of giving up the lottery."

Old Man Warner snorted. "Pack of crazy fools," he said. "Listening to the young folks, nothing's good enough for *them*. Next thing you know, they'll be wanting to go back to living in caves, nobody work any more, live *that* way for a while. Used to be a saying about 'Lottery in June, corn be heavy soon.' First thing you know, we'd all be eating stewed chickweed and acorns. There's *always* been a lottery," he added petulantly. "Bad enough to see young Joe Summers up there joking with everybody."

"Some places have already quit lotteries," Mrs. Adams said.

"Nothing but trouble in *that*," Old Man Warner said stoutly. "Pack of young fools."

"Martin." And Bobby Martin watched his father go forward. "Overdyke. . . . Percy."

"I wish they'd hurry," Mrs. Dunbar said to her older son. "I wish they'd hurry."

"They're almost through," her son said.

"You get ready to run tell Dad," Mrs. Dunbar said.

Mr. Summers called his own name and then stepped forward precisely and selected a slip from the box. Then he called, "Warner."

"Seventy-seventh year I been in the lottery," Old Man Warner said as he went through the crowd. "Seventy-seventh time."

"Watson." The tall boy came awkwardly through the crowd. Someone said, "Don't be nervous, Jack," and Mr. Summers said, "Take your time, son."

"Zanini."

After that, there was a long pause, a breathless pause, until Mr. Summers, holding his slip of paper in the air, said, "All right, fellows." For a minute, no one moved, and then all the slips of paper were opened. Suddenly, all the women began to speak at once, saying, "Who is it?" "Who's got it?" "Is it the Dunbars?" "Is it the Watsons?" Then the voices began to say, "It's Hutchinson. It's Bill," "Bill Hutchinson's got it."

"Go tell your father," Mrs. Dunbar said to her older son.

People began to look around to see the Hutchinsons. Bill Hutchinson was standing quiet, staring down at the paper in his hand. Suddenly, Tessie Hutchinson shouted to Mr. Summers, "You didn't give him time enough to take any paper he wanted. I saw you. It wasn't fair!"

"Be a good sport, Tessie," Mrs. Delacroix called, and Mrs. Graves said, "All of us took the same chance."

"Shut up, Tessie," Bill Hutchinson said.

"Well, everyone," Mr. Summers said, "that was done pretty fast, and now we've got to be hurrying a little more to get done in time." He consulted his next list. "Bill," he said, "you draw for the Hutchinson family. You got any other households in the Hutchinsons?"

"There's Don and Eva," Mrs. Hutchinson yelled. "Make *them* take their chance!"

"Daughters drew with their husbands' families, Tessie," Mr. Summers said gently. "You know that as well as anyone else."

"It wasn't *fair*," Tessie said.

"I guess not, Joe," Bill Hutchinson said regretfully. "My daughter draws with her husband's family, that's only fair. And I've got no other family except the kids."

"Then, as far as drawing for families is concerned, it's you," Mr. Summers said in explanation, "and as far as drawing for households is concerned, that's you, too. Right?"

"Right," Bill Hutchinson said.

"How many kids, Bill?" Mr. Summers asked formally.

"Three," Bill Hutchinson said. "There's Bill, Jr., and Nancy, and little Dave. And Tessie and me."

"All right, then," Mr. Summers said. "Harry, you got their tickets back?"

Mr. Graves nodded and held up the slips of paper. "Put them in the box, then," Mr. Summers directed. "Take Bill's and put it in."

"I think we ought to start over," Mrs. Hutchinson said, as quietly as she could. "I tell you it wasn't *fair*. You didn't give him time enough to choose. *Every*body saw that."

Mr. Graves had selected the five slips and put them in the box, and he dropped all the papers but those onto the ground, where the breeze caught them and lifted them off.

"Listen, everybody," Mrs. Hutchinson was saying to the people around her.

"Ready, Bill?" Mr. Summers asked, and Bill Hutchinson, with one quick glance around at his wife and children, nodded.

"Remember," Mr. Summers said, "take the slips and keep them folded until each person has taken one. Harry, you help little Dave." Mr. Graves took the hand of the little boy, who came willingly with him up to the box. "Take a paper out of the box, Davy," Mr. Summers said. Davy put his hand into the box and laughed. "Take just *one* paper," Mr. Summers said. "Harry, you hold it for him." Mr. Graves took the child's hand and removed the folded paper from the tight fist and held it while little Dave stood next to him and looked up at him wonderingly.

"Nancy next," Mr. Summers said. Nancy was twelve, and her school friends breathed heavily as she went forward, switching her skirt, and took a slip daintily from the box. "Bill, Jr.," Mr. Summers said, and Billy, his face red and his feet overlarge, nearly knocked the box over as he got a paper out. "Tessie," Mr. Summers said. She hesitated for a minute, looking around defiantly, and then set her lips and went up to the box. She snatched a paper out and held it behind her.

"Bill," Mr. Summers said, and Bill Hutchinson reached into the box and felt around, bringing his hand out at last with the slip of paper in it.

The crowd was quiet. A girl whispered, "I hope it's not Nancy," and the sound of the whisper reached the edges of the crowd.

"It's not the way it used to be," Old Man Warner said clearly. "People ain't the way they used to be."

"All right," Mr. Summers said. "Open the papers. Harry, you open little Dave's."

Mr. Graves opened the slip of paper and there was a general sigh through the crowd as he held it up and everyone could see that it was blank. Nancy and Bill, Jr., opened theirs at the same time, and both beamed and laughed, turning around to the crowd and holding their slips of paper above their heads.

"Tessie," Mr. Summers said. There was a pause, and then Mr. Summers looked at Bill Hutchinson, and Bill unfolded his paper and showed it. It was blank.

"It's Tessie," Mr. Summers said, and his voice was hushed. "Show us her paper, Bill."

Bill Hutchinson went over to his wife and forced the slip of paper out of her hand. It had a black spot on it, the black spot Mr. Summers had made the night before with the heavy pencil in the coal-company office. Bill Hutchinson held it up and there was a stir in the crowd.

"All right, folks," Mr. Summers said. "Let's finish quickly."

Although the villagers had forgotten the ritual and lost the original black box, they still remembered to use stones. The pile of stones the boys had made earlier was ready; there were stones on the ground with the blowing scraps of paper that had come out of the box. Mrs. Delacroix selected a stone so large she had to pick it up with both hands and turned to Mrs. Dunbar. "Come on," she said. "Hurry up."

Mrs. Dunbar had small stones in both hands, and she said, gasping for breath, "I can't run at all. You'll have to go ahead and I'll catch up with you."

The children had stones already, and someone gave little Davy Hutchinson a few pebbles.

Tessie Hutchinson was in the center of a cleared space by now, and she held her hands out desperately as the villagers moved in on her. "It isn't fair," she said. A stone hit her on the side of the head.

Old Man Warner was saying, "Come on, come on, everyone." Steve Adams was in the front of the crowd of villagers, with Mrs. Graves beside him.

"It isn't fair, it isn't right," Mrs. Hutchinson screamed and then they were upon her.

[1948]

- blind Tradition
- lottery to Vietnam - who goes to
  War
- Natural this is the way we do it
- The Evil seems ordinary

JAMES BALDWIN   [1924–1987]

Sonny's Blues

I read about it in the paper, in the subway, on my way to work. I read it, and I couldn't believe it, and I read it again. Then perhaps I just stared at it, at the newsprint spelling out his name, spelling out the story. I stared at it in the swinging lights of the subway car, and in the faces and bodies of the people, and in my own face, trapped in the darkness which roared outside.

It was not to be believed and I kept telling myself that, as I walked from the subway station to the high school. And at the same time I couldn't doubt it. I was scared, scared for Sonny. He became real to me again. A great block of ice got settled in my belly and kept melting there slowly all day long, while I taught my classes algebra. It was a special kind of ice. It kept melting, sending trickles of ice water all up and down my veins, but it never got less. Sometimes it hardened and seemed to expand until I felt my guts were going to come spilling out or that I was going to choke or scream. This would always be at a moment when I was remembering some specific thing Sonny had once said or done.

When he was about as old as the boys in my classes his face had been bright and open, there was a lot of copper in it; and he'd had wonderfully direct brown eyes, and great gentleness and privacy. I wondered what he looked like now. He had been picked up, the evening before, in a raid on an apartment downtown, for peddling and using heroin.

I couldn't believe it: but what I mean by that is that I couldn't find any room for it anywhere inside me. I had kept it outside me for a long time. I hadn't wanted to know. I had had suspicions, but I didn't name them, I kept putting them away. I told myself that Sonny was wild, but he wasn't crazy. And he'd always been a good boy, he hadn't ever turned hard or evil or disrespectful, the way kids can, so quick, so quick, especially in Harlem. I didn't want to believe that I'd ever see my brother going down, coming to nothing, all that light in his face gone out, in the condition I'd already seen so many others. Yet it had happened and here I was, talking about algebra to a lot of boys who might, every one of them for all I knew, be popping off needles every time they went to the head. Maybe it did more for them than algebra could.

I was sure that the first time Sonny had ever had horse, he couldn't

250

have been much older than these boys were now. These boys, now, were living as we'd been living then, they were growing up with a rush and their heads bumped abruptly against the low ceiling of their actual possibilities. They were filled with rage. All they really knew were two darknesses, the darkness of their lives, which was now closing in on them, and the darkness of the movies, which had blinded them to that other darkness, and in which they now, vindictively, dreamed, at once more together than they were at any other time, and more alone.

When the last bell rang, the last class ended, I let out my breath. It seemed I'd been holding it for all that time. My clothes were wet — I may have looked as though I'd been sitting in a steam bath, all dressed up, all afternoon. I sat alone in the classroom a long time. I listened to the boys outside, downstairs, shouting and cursing and laughing. Their laughter struck me for perhaps the first time. It was not the joyous laughter which — God knows why — one associates with children. It was mocking and insular, its intent to denigrate. It was disenchanted, and in this, also, lay the authority of their curses. Perhaps I was listening to them because I was thinking about my brother and in them I heard my brother. And myself.

One boy was whistling a tune, at once very complicated and very simple, it seemed to be pouring out of him as though he were a bird, and it sounded very cool and moving through all that harsh, bright air, only just holding its own through all those other sounds.

I stood up and walked over to the window and looked down into the courtyard. It was the beginning of the spring and the sap was rising in the boys. A teacher passed through them every now and again, quickly, as though he or she couldn't wait to get out of that courtyard, to get those boys out of their sight and off their minds. I started collecting my stuff. I thought I'd better get home and talk to Isabel.

The courtyard was almost deserted by the time I got downstairs. I saw this boy standing in the shadow of a doorway, looking just like Sonny. I almost called his name. Then I saw that it wasn't Sonny, but somebody we used to know, a boy from around our block. He'd been Sonny's friend. He'd never been mine, having been too young for me, and, anyway, I'd never liked him. And now, even though he was a grown-up man, he still hung around that block, still spent hours on the street corners, was always high and raggy. I used to run into him from time to time and he'd often work around to asking me for a quarter or fifty cents. He always had some real good excuse, too, and I always gave it to him, I don't know why.

But now, abruptly, I hated him. I couldn't stand the way he looked at me, partly like a dog, partly like a cunning child. I wanted to ask him what the hell he was doing in the school courtyard.

He sort of shuffled over to me, and he said, "I see you got the papers. So you already know about it."

"You mean about Sonny? Yes, I already know about it. How come they didn't get you?"

He grinned. It made him repulsive and it also brought to mind what he'd looked like as a kid. "I wasn't there. I stay away from them people."

"Good for you." I offered him a cigarette and I watched him through the smoke. "You come all the way down here just to tell me about Sonny?"

"That's right." He was sort of shaking his head and his eyes looked strange, as though they were about to cross. The bright sun deadened his damp dark brown skin and it made his eyes look yellow and showed up the dirt in his kinked hair. He smelled funky. I moved a little away from him and I said, "Well, thanks. But I already know about it and I got to get home."

"I'll walk you a little ways," he said. We started walking. There were a couple of kids still loitering in the courtyard and one of them said good-night to me and looked strangely at the boy beside me.

"What're you going to do?" he asked me. "I mean, about Sonny?"

"Look. I haven't seen Sonny for over a year. I'm not sure I'm going to do anything. Anyway, what the hell *can* I do?"

"That's right," he said quickly, "ain't nothing you can do. Can't much help old Sonny no more, I guess."

It was what I was thinking and so it seemed to me he had no right to say it.

"I'm surprised at Sonny, though," he went on—he had a funny way of talking, he looked straight ahead as though he were talking to himself—"I thought Sonny was a smart boy, I thought he was too smart to get hung."

"I guess he thought so too," I said sharply, "and that's how he got hung. And how about you? You're pretty goddamn smart, I bet."

Then he looked directly at me, just for a minute. "I ain't smart," he said. "If I was smart, I'd have reached for a pistol a long time ago."

"Look. Don't tell *me* your sad story, if it was up to me, I'd give you one." Then I felt guilty—guilty, probably, for never having supposed that the poor bastard *had* a story of his own, much less a sad one, and I asked, quickly, "What's going to happen to him now?"

He didn't answer this. He was off by himself some place. "Funny thing," he said, and from his tone we might have been discussing the quickest way to get to Brooklyn, "when I saw the papers this morning, the first thing I asked myself was if I had anything to do with it. I felt sort of responsible."

I began to listen more carefully. The subway station was on the corner, just before us, and I stopped. He stopped, too. We were in front of a bar and he ducked slightly, peering in, but whoever he was looking for didn't seem to be there. The juke box was blasting away with something black and bouncy and I half watched the barmaid as she danced her way from the juke box to her place behind the bar. And I watched her face as she laughingly responded to something someone said to her, still keeping time to the music. When she smiled one saw the little girl, one sensed the doomed, still-struggling woman beneath the battered face of the semi-whore.

"I never *give* Sonny nothing," the boy said finally, "but a long time ago I come to school high and Sonny asked me how it felt." He paused, I couldn't bear to watch him, I watched the barmaid, and I listened to the music which seemed to be causing the pavement to shake. "I told him it felt great." The music stopped, the barmaid paused and watched the juke box until the music began again. "It did."

All this was carrying me some place I didn't want to go. I certainly didn't want to know how it felt. It filled everything, the people, the houses, the music, the dark, quicksilver barmaid, with menace; and this menace was their reality.

"What's going to happen to him now?" I asked again.

"They'll send him away some place and they'll try to cure him." He shook his head. "Maybe he'll even think he's kicked the habit. Then they'll let him loose"—he gestured, throwing his cigarette into the gutter. "That's all."

"What do you mean, that's *all*?"

But I knew what he meant.

"I *mean*, that's *all*." He turned his head and looked at me, pulling down the corners of his mouth. "Don't you know what I mean?" he asked, softly.

"How the hell *would* I know what you mean?" I almost whispered it, I don't know why.

"That's right," he said to the air, "how would *he* know what I mean?" He turned toward me again, patient and calm, and yet I somehow felt him shaking, shaking as though he were going to fall apart. I felt that ice in my guts again, the dread I'd felt all afternoon; and again I watched the barmaid, moving about the bar, washing glasses, and singing. "Listen. They'll let him out and then it'll just start all over again. That's what I mean."

"You mean—they'll let him out. And then he'll just start working his way back in again. You mean he'll never kick the habit. Is that what you mean?"

"That's right," he said, cheerfully. "*You* see what I mean."

"Tell me," I said at last, "why does he want to die? He must want to die, he's killing himself, why does he want to die?"

He looked at me in surprise. He licked his lips. "He don't want to die. He wants to live. Don't nobody want to die, ever."

Then I wanted to ask him—too many things. He could not have answered, or if he had, I could not have borne the answers. I started walking. "Well, I guess it's none of my business."

"It's going to be rough on old Sonny," he said. We reached the subway station. "This is your station?" he asked. I nodded. I took one step down. "Damn!" he said, suddenly. I looked up at him. He grinned again. "Damn it if I didn't leave all my money home. You ain't got a dollar on you, have you? Just for a couple of days, is all."

All at once something inside gave and threatened to come pouring out of me. I didn't hate him any more. I felt that in another moment I'd start crying like a child.

"Sure," I said. "Don't sweat." I looked in my wallet and didn't have a dollar, I only had a five. "Here," I said. "That hold you?"

He didn't look at it—he didn't want to look at it. A terrible closed look came over his face, as though he were keeping the number on the bill a secret from him and me. "Thanks," he said, and now he was dying to see me go. "Don't worry about Sonny. Maybe I'll write him or something."

"Sure," I said. "You do that. So long."

"Be seeing you," he said. I went on down the steps.

And I didn't write Sonny or send him anything for a long time. When I finally did, it was just after my little girl died, he wrote me back a letter which made me feel like a bastard.

Here's what he said:

Dear brother,

You don't know how much I needed to hear from you. I wanted to write you many a time but I dug how much I must have hurt you and so I didn't write. But now I feel like a man who's been trying to climb up out of some deep, real deep and funky hole and just saw the sun up there, outside. I got to get outside.

I can't tell you much about how I got here. I mean I don't know how to tell you. I guess I was afraid of something or I was trying to escape from something and you know I have never been very strong in the head (smile). I'm glad Mama and Daddy are dead and can't see what's happened to their son and I swear if I'd known what I was doing I would never have hurt you so, you and a lot of other fine people who were nice to me and who believed in me.

I don't want you to think it had anything to do with me being a musician. It's more than that. Or maybe less than that. I can't get anything straight in my head down here and I try not to think about what's going to happen to me when I get outside again. Sometime I think I'm going to flip and never get outside and sometime I think I'll come straight back. I tell you one thing, though, I'd rather blow my brains out than go through this again. But that's what they all say, so they tell me. If I tell you when I'm coming to New York and if you could meet me, I sure would appreciate it. Give my love to Isabel and the kids and I was sure sorry to hear about little Gracie. I wish I could be like Mama and say the Lord's will be done, but I don't know it seems to me that trouble is the one thing that never does get stopped and I don't know what good it does to blame it on the Lord. But maybe it does some good if you believe it.

Your brother,
Sonny

Then I kept in constant touch with him and I sent him whatever I could and I went to meet him when he came back to New York. When I saw him many things I thought I had forgotten came flooding back to me. This was because I had begun, finally, to wonder about Sonny, about the life that Sonny lived inside. This life, whatever it was, had made him older and thinner and it had deepened the distant stillness in which he had always moved. He looked very unlike my baby brother. Yet, when he smiled, when we shook hands, the baby brother I'd never known looked out from the depths of his private life, like an animal waiting to be coaxed into the light.

"How you been keeping?" he asked me.

"All right. And you?"

"Just fine." He was smiling all over his face. "It's good to see you again."

"It's good to see you."

The seven years' difference in our ages lay between us like a chasm: I wondered if these years would ever operate between us as a bridge. I was remembering, and it made it hard to catch my breath, that I had been there when he was born; and I had heard the first words he had ever spoken. When he started to walk, he walked from our mother straight to me. I caught him just before he fell when he took the first steps he ever took in this world.

"How's Isabel?"

"Just fine. She's dying to see you."

"And the boys?"

"They're fine, too. They're anxious to see their uncle."

"Oh, come on. You know they don't remember me."

"Are you kidding? Of course they remember you."

He grinned again. We got into a taxi. We had a lot to say to each other, far too much to know how to begin.

As the taxi began to move, I asked, "You still want to go to India?"

He laughed. "You still remember that. Hell, no. This place is Indian enough for me."

"It used to belong to them," I said.

And he laughed again. "They damn sure knew what they were doing when they got rid of it."

Years ago, when he was around fourteen, he'd been all hipped on the idea of going to India. He read books about people sitting on rocks, naked, in all kinds of weather, but mostly bad, naturally, and walking barefoot through hot coals and arriving at wisdom. I used to say that it sounded to me as though they were getting away from wisdom as fast as they could. I think he sort of looked down on me for that.

"Do you mind," he asked, "if we have the driver drive alongside the park? On the west side—I haven't seen the city in so long."

"Of course not," I said. I was afraid that I might sound as though I were humoring him, but I hoped he wouldn't take it that way.

So we drove along, between the green of the park and the stony, lifeless elegance of hotels and apartment buildings, toward the vivid, killing streets of our childhood. These streets hadn't changed, though housing projects jutted up out of them now like rocks in the middle of a boiling sea. Most of the houses in which we had grown up had vanished, as had the stores from which we had stolen, the basements in which we had first tried sex, the rooftops from which we had hurled tin cans and bricks. But houses exactly like the houses of our past yet dominated the landscape, boys exactly like the boys we once had been found themselves smothering in these houses, came down into the streets for light and air and found themselves encircled by disaster. Some escaped the trap, most didn't. Those who got out always left something of themselves behind, as some animals amputate a leg and leave it in the trap. It might be said, perhaps, that I had escaped, after all, I was a school teacher; or that Sonny had, he hadn't lived in Harlem for years. Yet, as the cab moved uptown through streets which seemed, with a rush, to darken with dark people, and as I covertly studied Sonny's face, it came to me that what we both were seeking through our separate cab windows was that part of ourselves which had been left behind. It's always at the hour of trouble and confrontation that the missing member aches.

We hit 110th Street and started rolling up Lenox Avenue. And I'd known this avenue all my life, but it seemed to me again, as it had seemed on the day I'd first heard about Sonny's trouble, filled with a hidden menace which was its very breath of life.

"We almost there," said Sonny.

"Almost." We were both too nervous to say anything more.

We live in a housing project. It hasn't been up long. A few days after it was up it seemed uninhabitably new, now, of course, it's already run-down.

It looks like a parody of the good, clean, faceless life—God knows the people who live in it do their best to make it a parody. The beat-looking grass lying around isn't enough to make their lives green, the hedges will never hold out the streets, and they know it. The big windows fool no one, they aren't big enough to make space out of no space. They don't bother with the windows, they watch the TV screen instead. The playground is most popular with the children who don't play at jacks, or skip rope, or roller skate, or swing, and they can be found in it after dark. We moved in partly because it's not too far from where I teach, and partly for the kids; but it's really just like the houses in which Sonny and I grew up. The same things happen, they'll have the same things to remember. The moment Sonny and I started into the house I had the feeling that I was simply bringing him back into the danger he had almost died trying to escape.

Sonny has never been talkative. So I don't know why I was sure he'd be dying to talk to me when supper was over the first night. Everything went fine, the oldest boy remembered him, and the youngest boy liked him, and Sonny had remembered to bring something for each of them; and Isabel, who is really much nicer than I am, more open and giving, had gone to a lot of trouble about dinner and was genuinely glad to see him. And she's always been able to tease Sonny in a way that I haven't. It was nice to see her face so vivid again and to hear her laugh and watch her make Sonny laugh. She wasn't, or, anyway, she didn't seem to be, at all uneasy or embarrassed. She chatted as though there were no subject which had to be avoided and she got Sonny past his first, faint stiffness. And thank God she was there, for I was filled with that icy dread again. Everything I did seemed awkward to me, and everything I said sounded freighted with hidden meaning. I was trying to remember everything I'd heard about dope addiction and I couldn't help watching Sonny for signs. I wasn't doing it out of malice. I was trying to find out something about my brother. I was dying to hear him tell me he was safe.

"Safe!" my father grunted, whenever Mama suggested trying to move to a neighborhood which might be safer for children. "Safe, hell! Ain't no place safe for kids, nor nobody."

He always went on like this, but he wasn't, ever, really as bad as he sounded, not even on weekends, when he got drunk. As a matter of fact, he was always on the lookout for "something a little better," but he died before he found it. He died suddenly, during a drunken weekend in the middle of the war, when Sonny was fifteen. He and Sonny hadn't ever got on too well. And this was partly because Sonny was the apple of his father's eye. It was because he loved Sonny so much and was frightened for him, that he was always fighting with him. It doesn't do any good to fight with Sonny. Sonny just moves back, inside himself, where he can't be reached. But the principal reason that they never hit it off is that they were so much alike. Daddy was big and rough and loud-talking, just the opposite of Sonny, but they both had—that same privacy.

Mama tried to tell me something about this, just after Daddy died. I was home on leave from the army.

This was the last time I ever saw my mother alive. Just the same, this picture gets all mixed up in my mind with pictures I had of her when she was younger. The way I always see her is the way she used to be on a Sunday afternoon, say, when the old folks were talking after the big Sunday dinner. I always see her wearing pale blue. She'd be sitting on the sofa. And my father would be sitting in the easy chair, not far from her. And the living room would be full of church folks and relatives. There they sit, in chairs all around the living room, and the night is creeping up outside, but nobody knows it yet. You can see the darkness growing against the windowpanes and you hear the street noises every now and again, or maybe the jangling beat of a tambourine from one of the churches close by, but it's real quiet in the room. For a moment nobody's talking, but every face looks darkening, like the sky outside. And my mother rocks a little from the waist, and my father's eyes are closed. Everyone is looking at something a child can't see. For a minute they've forgotten the children. Maybe a kid is lying on the rug, half asleep. Maybe somebody's got a kid in his lap and is absent-mindedly stroking the kid's head. Maybe there's a kid, quiet and big-eyed, curled up in a big chair in the corner. The silence, the darkness coming, and the darkness in the faces frightens the child obscurely. He hopes that the hand which strokes his forehead will never stop—will never die. He hopes that there will never come a time when the old folks won't be sitting around the living room, talking about where they've come from, and what they've seen, and what's happened to them and their kinfolk.

But something deep and watchful in the child knows that this is bound to end, is already ending. In a moment someone will get up and turn on the light. Then the old folks will remember the children and they won't talk any more that day. And when light fills the room, the child is filled with darkness. He knows that every time this happens he's moved just a little closer to that darkness outside. The darkness outside is what the old folks have been talking about. It's what they've come from. It's what they endure. The child knows that they won't talk any more because if he knows too much about what's happened to *them*, he'll know too much too soon, about what's going to happen to *him*.

The last time I talked to my mother, I remember I was restless. I wanted to get out and see Isabel. We weren't married then and we had a lot to straighten out between us.

There Mama sat, in black, by the window. She was humming an old church song, *Lord, you brought me from a long ways off.* Sonny was out somewhere. Mama kept watching the streets.

"I don't know," she said, "if I'll ever see you again, after you go off from here. But I hope you'll remember the things I tried to teach you."

"Don't talk like that," I said, and smiled. "You'll be here a long time yet."

She smiled, too, but she said nothing. She was quiet for a long time. And I said, "Mama, don't you worry about nothing. I'll be writing all the time, and you be getting the checks. . . ."

"I want to talk to you about your brother," she said, suddenly. "If anything happens to me he ain't going to have nobody to look out for him."

"Mama," I said, "ain't nothing going to happen to you or Sonny. Sonny's all right. He's a good boy and he's got good sense."

"It ain't a question of his being a good boy," Mama said, "nor of his having good sense. It ain't only the bad ones, nor yet the dumb ones that gets sucked under." She stopped, looking at me. "Your Daddy once had a brother," she said, and she smiled in a way that made me feel she was in pain. "You didn't never know that, did you?"

"No," I said, "I never knew that," and I watched her face.

"Oh, yes," she said, "your Daddy had a brother." She looked out of the window again. "I know you never saw your Daddy cry. But *I* did—many a time, through all these years."

I asked her, "What happened to his brother? How come nobody's ever talked about him?"

This was the first time I ever saw my mother look old.

"His brother got killed," she said, "when he was just a little younger than you are now. I knew him. He was a fine boy. He was maybe a little full of the devil, but he didn't mean nobody no harm."

Then she stopped and the room was silent, exactly as it had sometimes been on those Sunday afternoons. Mama kept looking out into the streets.

"He used to have a job in the mill," she said, "and, like all young folks, he just liked to perform on Saturday nights. Saturday nights, him and your father would drift around to different places, go to dances and things like that, or just sit around with people they knew, and your father's brother would sing, he had a fine voice, and play along with himself on his guitar. Well, this particular Saturday night, him and your father was coming home from some place, and they were both a little drunk and there was a moon that night, it was bright like day. Your father's brother was feeling kind of good, and he was whistling to himself, and he had his guitar slung over his shoulder. They was coming down a hill and beneath them was a road that turned off from the highway. Well, your father's brother, being always kind of frisky, decided to run down this hill, and he did, with that guitar banging and clanging behind him, and he ran across the road, and he was making water behind a tree. And your father was sort of amused at him and he was still coming down the hill, kind of slow. Then he heard a car motor and that same minute his brother stepped from behind the tree, into the road, in the moonlight.

And he started to cross the road. And your father started to run down the hill, he says he don't know why. This car was full of white men. They was all drunk, and when they seen your father's brother they let out a great whoop and holler and they aimed the car straight at him. They was having fun, they just wanted to scare him, the way they do sometimes, you know. But they was drunk. And I guess the boy, being drunk, too, and scared, kind of lost his head. By the time he jumped it was too late. Your father says he heard his brother scream when the car rolled over him, and he heard the wood of that guitar when it give, and he heard them strings go flying, and he heard them white men shouting, and the car kept on a-going and it ain't stopped till this day. And, time your father got down the hill, his brother weren't nothing but blood and pulp."

Tears were gleaming on my mother's face. There wasn't anything I could say.

"He never mentioned it," she said, "because I never let him mention it before you children. Your Daddy was like a crazy man that night and for many a night thereafter. He says he never in his life seen anything as dark as that road after the lights of that car had gone away. Weren't nothing, weren't nobody on that road, just your Daddy and his brother and that busted guitar. Oh, yes. Your Daddy never did really get right again. Till the day he died he weren't sure but that every white man he saw was the man that killed his brother."

She stopped and took out her handkerchief and dried her eyes and looked at me.

"I ain't telling you all this," she said, "to make you scared or bitter or to make you hate nobody. I'm telling you this because you got a brother. And the world ain't changed."

I guess I didn't want to believe this. I guess she saw this in my face. She turned away from me, toward the window again, searching those streets.

"But I praise my Redeemer," she said at last, "that He called your Daddy home before me. I ain't saying it to throw no flowers at myself, but, I declare, it keeps me from feeling too cast down to know I helped your father get safely through this world. Your father always acted like he was the roughest, strongest man on earth. And everybody took him to be like that. But if he hadn't had *me* there—to see his tears!"

She was crying again. Still, I couldn't move. I said, "Lord, Lord, Mama, I didn't know it was like that."

"Oh, honey," she said, "there's a lot that you don't know. But you are going to find it out." She stood up from the window and came over to me. "You got to hold on to your brother," she said, "and don't let him fall, no matter what it looks like is happening to him and no matter how evil you gets with him. You going to be evil with him many a time. But don't you forget what I told you, you hear?"

"I won't forget," I said. "Don't you worry, I won't forget. I won't let nothing happen to Sonny."

My mother smiled as though she were amused at something she saw in my face. Then, "You may not be able to stop nothing from happening. But you got to let him know you's *there*."

Two days later I was married, and then I was gone. And I had a lot of things on my mind and I pretty well forgot my promise to Mama until I got shipped home on a special furlough for her funeral.

And, after the funeral, with just Sonny and me alone in the empty kitchen, I tried to find out something about him.

"What do you want to do?" I asked him.

"I'm going to be a musician," he said.

For he had graduated, in the time I had been away, from dancing to the juke box to finding out who was playing what, and what they were doing with it, and he had bought himself a set of drums.

"You mean, you want to be a drummer?" I somehow had the feeling that being a drummer might be all right for other people but not for my brother Sonny.

"I don't think," he said, looking at me very gravely, "that I'll ever be a good drummer. But I think I can play a piano."

I frowned. I'd never played the role of the older brother quite so seriously before, had scarcely ever, in fact, *asked* Sonny a damn thing. I sensed myself in the presence of something I didn't really know how to handle, didn't understand. So I made my frown a little deeper as I asked: "What kind of musician do you want to be?"

He grinned. "How many kinds do you think there are?"

"Be *serious*," I said.

He laughed, throwing his head back, and then looked at me. "I *am* serious."

"Well, then, for Christ's sake, stop kidding around and answer a serious question. I mean, do you want to be a concert pianist, you want to play classical music and all that, or—or what?" Long before I finished he was laughing again. "For Christ's *sake*, Sonny!"

He sobered, but with difficulty. "I'm sorry. But you sound so—*scared*!" and he was off again.

"Well, you may think it's funny now, baby, but it's not going to be so funny when you have to make your living at it, let me tell you *that*." I was furious because I knew he was laughing at me and I didn't know why.

"No," he said, very sober now, and afraid, perhaps, that he'd hurt me, "I don't want to be a classical pianist. That isn't what interests me. I mean"—he paused, looking hard at me, as though his eyes would help me to understand, and then gestured helplessly, as though perhaps his hand would help—"I mean, I'll have a lot of studying to do, and I'll have to study *everything*, but, I mean, I want to play *with*—jazz musicians." He stopped. "I want to play jazz," he said.

Well, the word had never before sounded as heavy, as real, as it sounded that afternoon in Sonny's mouth. I just looked at him and I was probably frowning a real frown by this time. I simply couldn't see why on earth he'd want to spend his time hanging around nightclubs, clowning around on bandstands, while people pushed each other around a dance floor. It seemed—beneath him, somehow. I had never thought about it before, had never been forced to, but I suppose I had always put jazz musicians in a class with what Daddy called "good-time people."

"Are you *serious*?"

"Hell, *yes*, I'm serious."

He looked more helpless than ever, and annoyed, and deeply hurt.

I suggested, helpfully: "You mean—like Louis Armstrong?"

His face closed as though I'd struck him. "No. I'm not talking about none of that old-time, down home crap."

"Well, look, Sonny, I'm sorry, don't get mad. I just don't altogether get it, that's all. Name somebody—you know, a jazz musician you admire."

"Bird."

"Who?"

"Bird! Charlie Parker! Don't they teach you nothing in the goddamn army?"

I lit a cigarette. I was surprised and then a little amused to discover that I was trembling. "I've been out of touch," I said. "You'll have to be patient with me. Now. Who's this Parker character?"

"He's just one of the greatest jazz musicians alive," said Sonny, sullenly, his hands in his pockets, his back to me. "Maybe *the* greatest," he added, bitterly, "that's probably why *you* never heard of him."

"All right," I said, "I'm ignorant. I'm sorry. I'll go out and buy all the cat's records right away, all right?"

"It don't," said Sonny, with dignity, "make any difference to me. I don't care what you listen to. Don't do me no favors."

I was beginning to realize that I'd never seen him so upset before. With another part of my mind I was thinking that this would probably turn out to be one of those things kids go through and that I shouldn't make it seem important by pushing it too hard. Still, I didn't think it would do any harm to ask: "Doesn't all this take a lot of time? Can you make a living at it?"

He turned back to me and half leaned, half sat, on the kitchen table. "Everything takes time," he said, "and—well, yes, sure, I can make a living at it. But what I don't seem to be able to make you understand is that it's the only thing I want to do."

"Well, Sonny," I said, gently, "you know people can't always do exactly what they *want* to do—"

"*No*, I don't know that," said Sonny, surprising me. "I think people *ought* to do what they want to do, what else are they alive for?"

"You getting to be a big boy," I said desperately, "it's time you started thinking about your future."

"I'm thinking about my future," said Sonny, grimly. "I think about it all the time."

I gave up. I decided, if he didn't change his mind, that we could always talk about it later. "In the meantime," I said, "you got to finish school." We had already decided that he'd have to move in with Isabel and her folks. I knew this wasn't the ideal arrangement because Isabel's folks are inclined to be dicty° and they hadn't especially wanted Isabel to marry me. But I didn't know what else to do. "And we have to get you fixed up at Isabel's."

There was a long silence. He moved from the kitchen table to the window. "That's a terrible idea. You know it yourself."

"Do you have a *better* idea?"

He just walked up and down the kitchen for a minute. He was as tall as I was. He had started to shave. I suddenly had the feeling that I didn't know him at all.

He stopped at the kitchen table and picked up my cigarettes. Looking at me with a kind of mocking, amused defiance, he put one between his lips. "You mind?"

"You smoking already?"

He lit the cigarette and nodded, watching me through the smoke. "I just wanted to see if I'd have the courage to smoke in front of you." He grinned and blew a great cloud of smoke to the ceiling. "It was easy." He looked at my face. "Come on, now. I bet you was smoking at my age, tell the truth."

I didn't say anything but the truth was on my face, and he laughed. But now there was something very strained in his laugh. "Sure. And I bet that ain't all you was doing."

He was frightening me a little. "Cut the crap," I said. "We already decided that you was going to go and live at Isabel's. Now what's got into you all of a sudden?"

"*You* decided it," he pointed out. "*I* didn't decide nothing." He stopped in front of me, leaning against the stove, arms loosely folded. "Look, brother. I don't want to stay in Harlem no more, I really don't." He was very earnest. He looked at me, then over toward the kitchen window. There was something in his eyes I'd never seen before, some thoughtfulness, some

Dicty: High-class, snobbish.

worry all his own. He rubbed the muscle of one arm. "It's time I was getting out of here."

"Where do you want to *go*, Sonny?"

"I want to join the army. Or the navy, I don't care. If I say I'm old enough, they'll believe me."

Then I got mad. It was because I was so scared. "You must be crazy. You goddamn fool, what the hell do you want to go and join the *army* for?"

"I just told you. To get out of Harlem."

"Sonny, you haven't even finished *school*. And if you really want to be a musician, how do you expect to study if you're in the *army*?"

He looked at me, trapped, and in anguish. "There's ways. I might be able to work out some kind of deal. Anyway, I'll have the G.I. Bill when I come out."

"*If* you come out." We stared at each other. "Sonny, please. Be reasonable. I know the setup is far from perfect. But we got to do the best we can."

"I ain't learning nothing in school," he said. "Even when I go." He turned away from me and opened the window and threw his cigarette out into the narrow alley. I watched his back. "At least, I ain't learning nothing you'd want me to learn." He slammed the window so hard I thought the glass would fly out, and turned back to me. "And I'm sick of the stink of these garbage cans!"

"Sonny," I said, "I know how you feel. But if you don't finish school now, you're going to be sorry later that you didn't." I grabbed him by the shoulders. "And you only got another year. It ain't so bad. And I'll come back and I swear I'll help you do *whatever* you want to do. Just try to put up with it till I come back. Will you please do that? For me?"

He didn't answer and he wouldn't look at me.

"Sonny. You hear me?"

He pulled away. "I hear you. But you never hear anything *I* say."

I didn't know what to say to that. He looked out of the window and then back at me. "OK," he said, and sighed. "I'll try."

Then I said, trying to cheer him up a little, "They got a piano at Isabel's. You can practice on it."

And as a matter of fact, it did cheer him up for a minute. "That's right," he said to himself. "I forgot that." His face relaxed a little. But the worry, the thoughtfulness, played on it still, the way shadows play on a face which is staring into the fire.

But I thought I'd never hear the end of that piano. At first, Isabel would write me, saying how nice it was that Sonny was so serious about his music and how, as soon as he came in from school, or wherever he had been when he was supposed to be at school, he went straight to that piano and stayed there until suppertime. And, after supper, he went back to that piano and stayed there until everybody went to bed. He was at the piano all day Saturday and all day Sunday. Then he bought a record player and started playing records. He'd play one record over and over again, all day long sometimes, and he'd improvise along with it on the piano. Or he'd play one section of the record, one chord, one change, one progression, then he'd do it on the piano. Then back to the record. Then back to the piano.

Well, I really don't know how they stood it. Isabel finally confessed that it wasn't like living with a person at all, it was like living with sound. And the sound didn't make any sense to her, didn't make any sense to any of them—naturally. They began, in a way, to be afflicted by this presence that was living in their home. It was as though Sonny were some sort of god, or monster. He moved in an atmosphere which wasn't like theirs at all. They fed him and he ate, he washed himself, he walked in and out of their door; he certainly wasn't nasty or unpleasant or rude, Sonny isn't any of those things; but it was as though he were all wrapped up in some cloud, some fire, some vision all his own; and there wasn't any way to reach him.

At the same time, he wasn't really a man yet, he was still a child, and they had to watch out for him in all kinds of ways. They certainly couldn't throw him out. Neither did they dare to make a great scene about that piano because even they dimly sensed, as I sensed, from so many thousands of miles away, that Sonny was at that piano playing for his life.

But he hadn't been going to school. One day a letter came from the school board and Isabel's mother got it—there had, apparently, been other letters but Sonny had torn them up. This day, when Sonny came in, Isabel's mother showed him the letter and asked where he'd been spending his time. And she finally got it out of him that he'd been down in Greenwich Village, with musicians and other characters, in a white girl's apartment. And this scared her and she started to scream at him and what came up, once she began—though she denies it to this day—was what sacrifices they were making to give Sonny a decent home and how little he appreciated it.

Sonny didn't play the piano that day. By evening, Isabel's mother had calmed down but then there was the old man to deal with, and Isabel herself. Isabel says she did her best to be calm but she broke down and started crying. She says she just watched Sonny's face. She could tell, by watching him, what was happening with him. And what was happening was that they penetrated his cloud, they had reached him. Even if their fingers had been a thousand times more gentle than human fingers ever are, he could hardly help feeling that they had stripped him naked and were spitting on that nakedness. For he also had to see that his presence, that music, which was life or death to him, had been torture for them and that they had endured it, not at all for his sake, but only for mine. And Sonny couldn't take that. He can take it a little better today than he could then but he's still not very good at it and, frankly, I don't know anybody who is.

The silence of the next few days must have been louder than the sound of all the music ever played since time began. One morning, before she went to work, Isabel was in his room for something and she suddenly realized that all of his records were gone. And she knew for certain that he was gone. And he was. He went as far as the navy would carry him. He finally sent me a postcard from some place in Greece and that was the first I knew that Sonny was still alive. I didn't see him any more until we were both back in New York and the war had long been over.

He was a man by then, of course, but I wasn't willing to see it. He came by the house from time to time, but we fought almost every time we met. I didn't like the way he carried himself, loose and dreamlike all the time, and I didn't like his friends, and his music seemed to be merely an excuse for the life he led. It sounded just that weird and disordered.

Then we had a fight, a pretty awful fight, and I didn't see him for months. By and by I looked him up, where he was living, in a furnished room in the Village, and I tried to make it up. But there were lots of people in the room and Sonny just lay on his bed, and he wouldn't come downstairs with me, and he treated these other people as though they were his family and I weren't. So I got mad and then he got mad, and then I told him that he might just as well be dead as live the way he was living. Then he stood up and he told me not to worry about him any more in life, that he was dead as far as I was concerned. Then he pushed me to the door and the other people looked on as though nothing were happening, and he slammed the door behind me. I stood in the hallway, staring at the door. I heard somebody laugh in the room and then the tears came to my eyes. I started down the steps, whistling to keep from crying, I kept whistling to myself, *You going to need me, baby, one of these cold, rainy days.*

I read about Sonny's trouble in the spring. Little Grace died in the fall. She was a beautiful little girl. But she only lived a little over two years. She died of polio and she suffered. She had a slight fever for a couple of days, but it didn't seem like anything and we just kept her in bed. And we would certainly have called the doctor, but the fever dropped, she seemed to be all right. So we thought it had just been a cold. Then, one day, she was up, playing, Isabel was in the kitchen fixing lunch for the two boys when they'd come in from school, and she heard Grace fall down in the living room. When you have a lot of children you don't always start running when one of them falls, unless they start screaming or something.

And, this time, Grace was quiet. Yet, Isabel says that when she heard that *thump* and then that silence, something happened in her to make her afraid. And she ran to the living room and there was little Grace on the floor, all twisted up, and the reason she hadn't screamed was that she couldn't get her breath. And when she did scream, it was the worst sound, Isabel says, that she'd ever heard in all her life, and she still hears it sometimes in her dreams. Isabel will sometimes wake me up with a low, moaning, strangled sound and I have to be quick to awaken her and hold her to me and where Isabel is weeping against me seems a mortal wound.

I think I may have written Sonny the very day that little Grace was buried. I was sitting in the living room in the dark, by myself, and I suddenly thought of Sonny. My trouble made his real.

One Saturday afternoon, when Sonny had been living with us, or, anyway, been in our house, for nearly two weeks, I found myself wandering aimlessly about the living room, drinking from a can of beer, and trying to work up the courage to search Sonny's room. He was out, he was usually out whenever I was home, and Isabel had taken the children to see their grandparents. Suddenly I was standing still in front of the living room window, watching Seventh Avenue. The idea of searching Sonny's room made me still. I scarcely dared to admit to myself what I'd be searching for. I didn't know what I'd do if I found it. Or if I didn't.

On the sidewalk across from me, near the entrance to a barbecue joint, some people were holding an old-fashioned revival meeting. The barbecue cook, wearing a dirty white apron, his conked hair reddish and metallic in the pale sun, and a cigarette between his lips, stood in the doorway, watching them. Kids and older people paused in their errands and stood there, along with some older men and a couple of very tough-looking women who watched everything that happened on the avenue, as though they owned it, or were maybe owned by it. Well, they were watching this, too. The revival was being carried on by three sisters in black, and a brother. All they had were their voices and their Bibles and a tambourine. The brother was testifying and while he testified two of the sisters stood together, seeming to say, amen, and the third sister walked around with the tambourine outstretched and a couple of people dropped coins into it. Then the brother's testimony ended and the sister who had been taking up the collection dumped the coins into her palm and transferred them to the pocket of her long black robe. Then she raised both hands, striking the tambourine against the air, and then against one hand, and she started to sing. And the two other sisters and the brother joined in.

It was strange, suddenly, to watch, though I had been seeing these street meetings all my life. So, of course, had everybody else down there. Yet, they paused and watched and listened and I stood still at the window.

"Tis the old ship of Zion," they sang, and the sister with the tambourine kept a steady, jangling beat, *"it has rescued many a thousand!"* Not a soul under the sound of their voices was hearing this song for the first time, not one of them had been rescued. Nor had they seen much in the way of rescue work being done around them. Neither did they especially believe in the holiness of the three sisters and the brother, they knew too much about them, knew where they lived, and how. The woman with the tambourine, whose voice dominated the air, whose face was bright with joy, was divided by very little from the woman who stood watching her, a cigarette between her heavy, chapped lips, her hair a cuckoo's nest, her face scarred and swollen from many beatings, and her black eyes glittering like coal. Perhaps they both knew this, which was why, when, as rarely, they addressed each other, they addressed each other as Sister. As the singing filled the air the watching, listening faces underwent a change, the eyes focusing on something within; the music seemed to soothe a poison out of them; and time seemed, nearly, to fall away from the sullen, belligerent, battered faces, as though they were fleeing back to their first condition, while dreaming of their last. The barbecue cook half shook his head and smiled, and dropped his cigarette and disappeared into his joint. A man fumbled in his pockets for change and stood holding it in his hand impatiently, as though he had just remembered a pressing appointment further up the avenue. He looked furious. Then I saw Sonny, standing on the edge of the crowd. He was carrying a wide, flat notebook with a green cover, and it made him look, from where I was standing, almost like a schoolboy. The coppery sun brought out the copper in his skin, he was very faintly smiling, standing very still. Then the singing stopped, the tambourine turned into a collection plate again. The furious man dropped in his coins and vanished, so did a couple of the women, and Sonny dropped some change in the plate, looking directly at the woman with a little smile. He started across the avenue, toward the house. He has a slow, loping walk, something like the way Harlem hipsters walk, only he's imposed on this his own half-beat. I had never really noticed it before.

I stayed at the window, both relieved and apprehensive. As Sonny disappeared from my sight, they began singing again. And they were still singing when his key turned in the lock.

"Hey," he said.

"Hey, yourself. You want some beer?"

"No. Well, maybe." But he came up to the window and stood beside me, looking out. "What a warm voice," he said.

They were singing *If I could only hear my mother pray again!*

"Yes," I said, "and she can sure beat that tambourine."

"But what a terrible song," he said, and laughed. He dropped his notebook on the sofa and disappeared into the kitchen. "Where's Isabel and the kids?"

"I think they went to see their grandparents. You hungry?"

"No." He came back into the living room with his can of beer. "You want to come some place with me tonight?"

I sensed, I don't know how, that I couldn't possibly say no. "Sure. Where?"

He sat down on the sofa and picked up his notebook and started leafing through it. "I'm going to sit in with some fellows in a joint in the Village."

"You mean, you're going to play, tonight?"

"That's right." He took a swallow of his beer and moved back to the window. He gave me a sidelong look. "If you can stand it."

"I'll try," I said.

He smiled to himself and we both watched as the meeting across the way broke up. The three sisters and the brother, heads bowed, were singing *God be with you till we meet again*. The faces around them were very quiet. Then the song ended. The small crowd dispersed. We watched the three women and the lone man walk slowly up the avenue.

"When she was singing before," said Sonny, abruptly, "her voice reminded me for a minute of what heroin feels like sometimes—when it's in your veins. It makes you feel sort of warm and cool at the same time. And distant. And—and sure." He sipped his beer, very deliberately not looking at me. I watched his face. "It makes you feel—in control. Sometimes you've got to have that feeling."

"Do you?" I sat down slowly in the easy chair.

"Sometimes." He went to the sofa and picked up his notebook again. "Some people do."

"In order," I asked, "to play?" And my voice was very ugly, full of contempt and anger.

"Well"—he looked at me with great, troubled eyes, as though, in fact, he hoped his eyes would tell me things he could never otherwise say—"they *think* so. And *if* they think so—!"

"And what do *you* think?" I asked.

He sat on the sofa and put his can of beer on the floor. "I don't know," he said, and I couldn't be sure if he were answering my question or pursuing his thoughts. His face didn't tell me. "It's not so much to *play*. It's to *stand* it, to be able to make it at all. On any level." He frowned and smiled: "In order to keep from shaking to pieces."

"But these friends of yours," I said, "they seem to shake themselves to pieces pretty goddamn fast."

"Maybe." He played with the notebook. And something told me that I should curb my tongue, that Sonny was doing his best to talk, that I should listen. "But of course you only know the ones that've gone to pieces. Some don't—or at least they haven't *yet* and that's just about all *any* of us can say." He paused. "And then there are some who just live, really, in hell, and they know it and they see what's happening and they go right on. I don't know." He sighed, dropped the notebook, folded his arms. "Some guys, you can tell from the way they play, they on something *all* the time. And you can see that, well, it makes something real for them. But of course," he picked up his beer from the floor and sipped it and put the can down again, "they *want* to, too, you've got to see that. Even some of them that say they don't—*some*, not all."

"And what about you?" I asked—I couldn't help it. "What about you? Do *you* want to?"

He stood up and walked to the window and remained silent for a long time. Then he sighed. "Me," he said. Then: "While I was downstairs before, on my way here, listening to that woman sing, it struck me all of a sudden how much suffering she must have had to go through—to sing like that. It's *repulsive* to think you have to suffer that much."

I said: "But there's no way not to suffer—is there, Sonny?"

"I believe not," he said and smiled, "but that's never stopped anyone from trying." He looked at me. "Has it?" I realized, with this mocking look, that there stood between us, forever, beyond the power of time or forgiveness, the fact that I had held silence—so long!—when he had needed human speech to help him. He turned back to the window. "No, there's no way not to suffer. But you try all kinds of ways to keep from drowning in it, to keep on top of it, and to make it seem—well, like *you*. Like you did something, all right, and now you're suffering for it. You know?" I said nothing. "Well you know," he said, impatiently, "why *do* people suffer? Maybe it's better to do something to give it a reason, *any* reason."

"But we just agreed," I said, "that there's no way not to suffer. Isn't it better, then, just to—take it?"

"But nobody just takes it," Sonny cried, "that's what I'm telling you! *Everybody* tries not to. You're just hung up on the *way* some people try—it's not *your* way!"

The hair on my face began to itch, my face felt wet. "That's not true," I said, "that's not true. I don't give a damn what other people do, I don't even care how they suffer. I just care how *you* suffer." And he looked at me. "Please believe me," I said, "I don't want to see you—die—trying not to suffer."

"I won't," he said, flatly, "die trying not to suffer. At least, not any faster than anybody else."

"But there's no need," I said, trying to laugh, "is there? in killing yourself."

I wanted to say more, but I couldn't. I wanted to talk about will power and how life could be—well, beautiful. I wanted to say that it was all within; but was it? or, rather, wasn't that exactly the trouble? And I wanted to promise that I would never fail him again. But it would all have sounded—empty words and lies.

So I made the promise to myself and prayed that I would keep it.

"It's terrible sometimes, inside," he said, "that's what's the trouble. You walk these streets, black and funky and cold, and there's not really a living ass to talk to, and there's nothing shaking, and there's no way of getting it out—that storm inside. You can't talk it and you can't make love with it, and when you finally try to get with it and play it, you realize *nobody's* listening. So *you've* got to listen. You got to find a way to listen."

And then he walked away from the window and sat on the sofa again, as though all the wind had suddenly been knocked out of him. "Sometimes you'll do *anything* to play, even cut your mother's throat." He laughed and looked at me. "Or your brother's." Then he sobered. "Or your own." Then: "Don't worry. I'm all right now and I think I'll *be* all right. But I can't forget—where I've been. I don't mean just the physical place I've been, I mean where I've *been*. And *what* I've been."

"What have you been, Sonny?" I asked.

He smiled—but sat sideways on the sofa, his elbow resting on the back, his fingers playing with his mouth and chin, not looking at me. "I've been something I didn't recognize, didn't know I could be. Didn't know anybody could be." He stopped, looking inward, looking helplessly young, looking old. "I'm not talking about it now because I feel *guilty* or anything like that—maybe it would be better if I did, I don't know. Anyway, I can't really talk about it. Not to you, not to anybody," and now he turned and faced me. "Sometimes, you know, and it was actually when I was most *out* of the world, I felt that I was in it, that I was *with* it, really, and I could play or I didn't really have to *play*, it just came out of me, it was there. And I don't know how I played, thinking about it now, but I know I did awful things, those times, sometimes, to people. Or it wasn't that I *did* anything to them—it was that they weren't real." He picked up the beer can; it was empty; he rolled it between his palms: "And other times—well, I needed a fix, I needed to find a place to lean, I needed to clear a space to *listen*—and I couldn't find it, and I—went crazy, I did terrible things to *me*, I was terrible *for* me." He began pressing the beer can between his hands, I watched the metal begin to give. It glittered, as he played with it, like a knife, and I was afraid he would cut himself, but I said nothing. "Oh well. I can never tell you. I was all by myself at the bottom of something, stinking and sweating and crying and shaking, and I smelled it, you know? *my* stink, and I thought I'd die if I couldn't get away from it and yet, all the same, I knew that everything I was doing was just locking me in with it. And I didn't know," he paused, still flattening the beer can, "I didn't know, I still *don't* know, something kept telling me that maybe it was good to smell your own stink, but I didn't think that *that* was what I'd been trying to do—and—who can stand it?" and he abruptly dropped the ruined beer can, looking at me with a small, still smile, and then rose, walking to the window as though it were the lodestone rock. I watched his face, he watched the avenue. "I couldn't tell you when Mama died—but the reason I wanted to leave Harlem so bad was to get away from drugs. And then, when I ran away, that's what I was running from—really. When I came back, nothing had changed, *I* hadn't changed, I was just—older." And he stopped, drumming with his fingers on the windowpane. The sun had vanished, soon darkness would fall. I watched his face. "It can come again," he said, almost as though speaking to himself. Then he turned to me. "It can come again," he repeated. "I just want you to know that."

"All right," I said, at last. "So it can come again. All right."

He smiled, but the smile was sorrowful. "I had to try to tell you," he said.

"Yes," I said. "I understand that."

"You're my brother," he said, looking straight at me, and not smiling at all.

"Yes," I repeated, "yes. I understand that."

He turned back to the window, looking out. "All that hatred down there," he said, "all that hatred and misery and love. It's a wonder it doesn't blow the avenue apart."

We went to the only nightclub on a short, dark street, downtown. We squeezed through the narrow, chattering, jam-packed bar to the entrance of the big room, where the bandstand was. And we stood there for a moment, for the lights were very dim in this room and we couldn't see. Then, "Hello, boy," said a voice and an enormous black man, much older than Sonny or myself, erupted out of all that atmospheric lighting and put an arm around Sonny's shoulder. "I been sitting right here," he said, "waiting for you."

He had a big voice, too, and heads in the darkness turned toward us.

Sonny grinned and pulled a little away, and said, "Creole, this is my brother. I told you about him."

Creole shook my hand. "I'm glad to meet you, son," he said, and it was clear that he was glad to meet me *there*, for Sonny's sake. And he smiled, "You got a real musician in *your* family," and he took his arm from Sonny's shoulder and slapped him, lightly, affectionately, with the back of his hand.

"Well. Now I've heard it all," said a voice behind us. This was another musician, and a friend of Sonny's, a coal-black, cheerful-looking man, built close to the ground. He immediately began confiding to me, at the top of his lungs, the most terrible things about Sonny, his teeth gleaming like a lighthouse and his laugh coming up out of him like the beginning of an earthquake. And it turned out that everyone at the bar knew Sonny, or almost everyone; some were musicians, working there, or nearby, or not working, some were simply hangers-on, and some were there to hear Sonny play. I was introduced to all of them and they were all very polite to me. Yet, it was clear that, for them, I was only Sonny's brother. Here, I was in Sonny's world. Or, rather: his kingdom. Here, it was not even a question that his veins bore royal blood.

They were going to play soon and Creole installed me, by myself, at a table in a dark corner. Then I watched them, Creole, and the little black man, and Sonny, and the others, while they horsed around, standing just below the bandstand. The light from the bandstand spilled just a little short of them and, watching them laughing and gesturing and moving about, I had the feeling that they, nevertheless, were being most careful not to step into that circle of light too suddenly: that if they moved into the light too suddenly, without thinking, they would perish in flame. Then, while I watched, one of them, the small, black man, moved into the light and crossed the bandstand and started fooling around with his drums. Then—being funny and being, also, extremely ceremonious—Creole took Sonny by the arm and led him to the piano. A woman's voice called Sonny's name and a few hands started clapping. And Sonny, also being funny and being ceremonious, and so touched, I think, that he could have cried, but neither hiding it nor showing it, riding it like a man, grinned, and put both hands to his heart and bowed from the waist.

Creole then went to the bass fiddle and a lean, very bright-skinned brown man jumped up on the bandstand and picked up his horn. So there they were, and the atmosphere on the bandstand and in the room began to change and tighten. Someone stepped up to the microphone and announced them. Then there were all kinds of murmurs. Some people at the bar shushed others. The waitress ran around, frantically getting in the last orders, guys and chicks got closer to each other, and the lights on the bandstand, on the quartet, turned to a kind of indigo. Then they all looked different there. Creole looked about him for the last time, as though he were making certain that all his chickens were in the coop, and then he—jumped and struck the fiddle. And there they were.

All I know about music is that not many people ever really hear it. And even then, on the rare occasions when something opens within, and the music enters, what we mainly hear, or hear corroborated, are personal, private, vanishing evocations. But the man who creates the music is hearing something else, is dealing with the roar rising from the void and imposing order on it as it hits the air. What is evoked in him, then, is of another order, more terrible because it has no words, and triumphant, too, for that same reason. And his triumph, when he triumphs, is ours. I just watched Sonny's face. His face was troubled, he was working hard, but he wasn't with it. And I had the feeling that, in a way, everyone on the bandstand was waiting for him, both waiting for him and pushing him along. But as I began to watch Creole, I realized that it was Creole who held them all back. He had them on a short rein. Up there, keeping the beat with his whole body, wailing on the fiddle, with his eyes half closed, he was listening to everything, but he was listening to Sonny. He was having a dialogue with Sonny. He wanted Sonny to leave the shoreline and strike out for the deep water. He was Sonny's witness that deep water and drowning were not the same thing—he had been there, and he knew. And he wanted Sonny to know. He was waiting for Sonny to do the things on the keys which would let Creole know that Sonny was in the water.

And, while Creole listened, Sonny moved, deep within, exactly like someone in torment. I had never before thought of how awful the relationship must be between the musician and his instrument. He has to fill it, this instrument, with the breath of life, his own. He has to make it do what he wants it to do. And a piano is just a piano. It's made out of so much wood and wires and little hammers and big ones, and ivory. While there's only so much you can do with it, the only way to find this out is to try; to try and make it do everything.

And Sonny hadn't been near a piano for over a year. And he wasn't on much better terms with his life, not the life that stretched before him now. He and the piano stammered, started one way, got scared, stopped; started another way, panicked, marked time, started again; then seemed to have found a direction, panicked again, got stuck. And the face I saw on Sonny I'd never seen before. Everything had been burned out of it, and, at the same time, things usually hidden were being burned in, by the fire and fury of the battle which was occurring in him up there.

Yet, watching Creole's face as they neared the end of the first set, I had the feeling that something had happened, something I hadn't heard. Then they finished, there was scattered applause, and then, without an instant's warning, Creole started into something else, it was almost sardonic, it was *Am I Blue*. And, as though he commanded, Sonny began to play. Something began to happen. And Creole let out the reins. The dry, low, black man said something awful on the drums, Creole answered, and the drums talked back. Then the horn insisted, sweet and high, slightly detached perhaps, and Creole listened, commenting now and then, dry, and driving, beautiful and calm and old. Then they all came together again, and Sonny was part of the family again. I could tell this from his face. He seemed to have found, right there beneath his fingers, a damn brand-new piano. It seemed that he couldn't get over it. Then, for awhile, just being happy with Sonny, they seemed to be agreeing with him that brand-new pianos certainly were a gas.

Then Creole stepped forward to remind them that what they were playing was the blues. He hit something in all of them, he hit something in me, myself, and the music tightened and deepened, apprehension began to beat the air. Creole began to tell us what the blues were all about. They were not about anything very new. He and his boys up there were keeping it new, at the risk of ruin, destruction, madness, and death, in order to find new ways to make us listen. For, while the tale of how we suffer, and how we are delighted, and how we may triumph is never new, it always must be heard. There isn't any other tale to tell, it's the only light we've got in all this darkness.

And this tale, according to that face, that body, those strong hands on those strings, has another aspect in every country, and a new depth in every generation. Listen, Creole seemed to be saying, listen. Now these are Sonny's blues. He made the little black man on the drums know it, and the bright, brown man on the horn. Creole wasn't trying any longer to get Sonny in the water. He was wishing him Godspeed. Then he stepped back, very slowly, filling the air with the immense suggestion that Sonny speak for himself.

Then they all gathered around Sonny and Sonny played. Every now and again one of them seemed to say, amen. Sonny's fingers filled the air with life, his life. But that life contained so many others. And Sonny went all the way back, he really began with the spare, flat statement of the opening phrase of the song. Then he began to make it his. It was very beautiful because it wasn't hurried and it was no longer a lament. I seemed to hear with what burning he had made it his, with what burning we had yet to make it ours, how we could cease lamenting. Freedom lurked around us and I understood, at last, that he could help us to be free if we would listen, that he would never be free until we did. Yet, there was no battle in his face now. I heard what he had gone through, and would continue to go through until he came to rest in earth. He had made it his: that long line, of which we knew only Mama and Daddy. And he was giving it back, as everything must be given back, so that, passing through death, it can live forever. I saw my mother's face again, and felt, for the first time, how the stones of the road she had walked on must have bruised her feet. I saw the moonlit road where my father's brother died. And it brought something else back to me, and carried me past it. I saw my little girl again and felt Isabel's tears again, and I felt my own tears begin to rise. And I was yet aware that this was only a moment, that the world waited outside, as hungry as a tiger, and that trouble stretched above us, longer than the sky.

Then it was over. Creole and Sonny let out their breath, both soaking wet, and grinning. There was a lot of applause and some of it was real. In the dark, the girl came by and I asked her to take drinks to the bandstand. There was a long pause, while they talked up there in the indigo light and after awhile I saw the girl put a Scotch and milk on top of the piano for Sonny. He didn't seem to notice it, but just before they started playing again, he sipped from it and looked toward me, and nodded. Then he put it back on top of the piano. For me, then, as they began to play again, it glowed and shook above my brother's head like the very cup of trembling.

[1957]

FLANNERY O'CONNOR   [1925–1964]

A Good Man Is Hard to Find

*The dragon is by the side of the road, watching those who pass.
Beware lest he devour you. We go to the Father of Souls, but it is
necessary to pass by the dragon.* — ST. CYRIL OF JERUSALEM

The grandmother didn't want to go to Florida. She wanted to visit some of her connections in east Tennessee and she was seizing at every chance to change Bailey's mind. Bailey was the son she lived with, her only boy. He was sitting on the edge of his chair at the table, bent over the orange sports section of the *Journal*. "Now look here, Bailey," she said, "see here, read this," and she stood with one hand on her thin hip and the other rattling the newspaper at his bald head. "Here this fellow that calls himself The Misfit is aloose from the Federal Pen and headed toward Florida and you read here what it says he did to these people. Just you read it. I wouldn't take my children in any direction with a criminal like that aloose in it. I couldn't answer to my conscience if I did."

Bailey didn't look up from his reading so she wheeled around then and faced the children's mother, a young woman in slacks, whose face was as broad and innocent as a cabbage and was tied around with a green headkerchief that had two points on the top like rabbit's ears. She was sitting on the sofa, feeding the baby his apricots out of a jar. "The children have been to Florida before," the old lady said. "You all ought to take them somewhere else for a change so they would see different parts of the world and be broad. They never have been to east Tennessee."

The children's mother didn't seem to hear her but the eight-year-old boy, John Wesley, a stocky child with glasses, said, "If you don't want to go to Florida, why dontcha stay at home?" He and the little girl, June Star, were reading the funny papers on the floor.

"She wouldn't stay at home to be queen for a day," June Star said without raising her yellow head.

"Yes and what would you do if this fellow, The Misfit, caught you?" the grandmother asked.

"I'd smack his face," John Wesley said.

"She wouldn't stay at home for a million bucks," June Star said. "Afraid she'd miss something. She has to go everywhere we go."

"All right, Miss," the grandmother said. "Just remember that the next time you want me to curl your hair."

June Star said her hair was naturally curly.

The next morning the grandmother was the first one in the car, ready to go. She had her big black valise that looked like the head of a hippopotamus in one corner, and underneath it she was hiding a basket with Pitty Sing, the cat, in it. She didn't intend for the cat to be left alone in the house for three days because he would miss her too much and she was afraid he might brush against one of the gas burners and accidentally asphyxiate himself. Her son, Bailey, didn't like to arrive at a motel with a cat.

She sat in the middle of the back seat with John Wesley and June Star on either side of her. Bailey and the children's mother and the baby sat in front and they left Atlanta at eight forty-five with the mileage on the car at 55890. The grandmother wrote this down because she thought it would be interesting to say how many miles they had been when they got back. It took them twenty minutes to reach the outskirts of the city.

The old lady settled herself comfortably, removing her white cotton gloves and putting them up with her purse on the shelf in front of the back window. The children's mother still had on slacks and still had her head tied up in a green kerchief, but the grandmother had on a navy blue straw sailor hat with a bunch of white violets on the brim and a navy blue dress with a small white dot in the print. Her collars and cuffs were white organdy trimmed with lace and at her neckline she had pinned a purple spray of cloth violets containing a sachet. In case of an accident, anyone seeing her dead on the highway would know at once that she was a lady.

She said she thought it was going to be a good day for driving, neither too hot nor too cold, and she cautioned Bailey that the speed limit was fifty-five miles an hour and that the patrolmen hid themselves behind billboards and small clumps of trees and sped out after you before you had a chance to slow down. She pointed out interesting details of the scenery: Stone Mountain; the blue granite that in some places came up to both sides of the highway; the brilliant red clay banks slightly streaked with purple; and the various crops that made rows of green lace-work on the ground. The trees were full of silver-white sunlight and the meanest of them sparkled. The children were reading comic magazines and their mother had gone back to sleep.

"Let's go through Georgia fast so we won't have to look at it much," John Wesley said.

"If I were a little boy," said the grandmother, "I wouldn't talk about my native state that way. Tennessee has the mountains and Georgia has the hills."

"Tennessee is just a hillbilly dumping ground," John Wesley said, "and Georgia is a lousy state too."

"You said it," June Star said.

"In my time," said the grandmother, folding her thin veined fingers, "children were more respectful of their native states and their parents and everything else. People did right then. Oh look at the cute little pickaninny!" she said and pointed to a Negro child standing in the door of a shack. "Wouldn't that make a picture, now?" she asked and they all turned and looked at the little Negro out of the back window. He waved.

"He didn't have any britches on," June Star said.

"He probably didn't have any," the grandmother explained. "Little niggers in the country don't have things like we do. If I could paint, I'd paint that picture," she said.

The children exchanged comic books.

The grandmother offered to hold the baby and the children's mother passed him over the front seat to her. She set him on her knee and bounced him and told him about the things they were passing. She rolled her eyes and screwed up her mouth and stuck her leathery thin face into his smooth bland one. Occasionally he gave her a faraway smile. They passed a large cotton field with five or six graves fenced in the middle of it, like a small island. "Look at the graveyard!" the grandmother said, pointing it out. "That was the old family burying ground. That belonged to the plantation."

"Where's the plantation?" John Wesley asked.

"Gone with the Wind," said the grandmother. "Ha. Ha."

When the children finished all the comic books they had brought, they opened the lunch and ate it. The grandmother ate a peanut butter sandwich and an olive and would not let the children throw the box and the paper napkins out the window. When there was nothing else to do they played a game by choosing a cloud and making the other two guess what shape it suggested. John Wesley took one the shape of a cow and June Star guessed a cow and John Wesley said, no, an automobile, and June Star said he didn't play fair, and they began to slap each other over the grandmother.

The grandmother said she would tell them a story if they would keep quiet. When she told a story, she rolled her eyes and waved her head and was very dramatic. She said once when she was a maiden lady she had been courted by a Mr. Edgar Atkins Teagarden from Jasper, Georgia. She said he was a very good-looking man and a gentleman and that he brought her a watermelon every Saturday afternoon with his initials cut in it, E. A. T. Well, one Saturday, she said, Mr. Teagarden brought the watermelon and there was nobody at home and he left it on the front porch and returned in his buggy to Jasper, but she never got the watermelon, she said, because a nigger boy ate it when he saw the initials, E. A. T.! This story tickled John Wesley's funny bone and he giggled and giggled but June Star didn't think it was any good. She said she wouldn't marry a man that just brought her a watermelon on Saturday. The grandmother said she would have done well to marry Mr. Teagarden because he was a gentleman and had bought Coca-Cola stock when it first came out and that he had died only a few years ago, a very wealthy man.

They stopped at The Tower for barbecued sandwiches. The Tower was a part stucco and part wood filling station and dance hall set in a clearing outside of Timothy. A fat man named Red Sammy Butts ran it and there were signs stuck here and there on the building and for miles up and down the highway saying, TRY RED SAMMY'S FAMOUS BARBECUE. NONE LIKE FAMOUS RED SAMMY'S! RED SAM! THE FAT BOY WITH THE HAPPY LAUGH. A VETERAN! RED SAMMY'S YOUR MAN!

Red Sammy was lying on the bare ground outside The Tower with his head under a truck while a gray monkey about a foot high, chained to a small chinaberry tree, chattered nearby. The monkey sprang back into the tree and got on the highest limb as soon as he saw the children jump out of the car and run toward him.

Inside, The Tower was a long dark room with a counter at one end and tables at the other and dancing space in the middle. They all sat down at a board table next to the nickelodeon and Red Sam's wife, a tall burnt-brown woman with hair and eyes lighter than her skin, came and took their order. The children's mother put a dime in the machine and played "The Tennessee Waltz," and the grandmother said that tune always made her want to dance. She asked Bailey if he would like to dance but he only glared at her. He didn't have a naturally sunny disposition like she did and trips made him nervous. The grandmother's brown eyes were very bright. She swayed her head from side to side and pretended she was dancing in her chair. June Star said play something she could tap to so the children's mother put in another dime and played a fast number and June Star stepped out onto the dance floor and did her tap routine.

"Ain't she cute?" Red Sam's wife said, leaning over the counter. "Would you like to come be my little girl?"

"No I certainly wouldn't," June Star said. "I wouldn't live in a broken-down place like this for a million bucks!" and she ran back to the table.

"Ain't she cute?" the woman repeated, stretching her mouth politely.

"Aren't you ashamed?" hissed the grandmother.

Red Sam came in and told his wife to quit lounging on the counter and hurry up with these people's order. His khaki trousers reached just to his hip bones and his stomach hung over them like a sack of meal swaying under his shirt. He came over and sat down at a table nearby and let out a combination sigh and yodel. "You can't win," he said. "You can't win," and he wiped his sweating red face off with a gray handkerchief. "These days you don't know who to trust," he said. "Ain't that the truth?"

"People are certainly not nice like they used to be," said the grandmother.

"Two fellers come in here last week," Red Sammy said, "driving a Chrysler. It was a old beat-up car but it was a good one and these boys looked all right to me. Said they worked at the mill and you know I let them fellers charge the gas they bought? Now why did I do that?"

"Because you're a good man!" the grandmother said at once.

"Yes'm, I suppose so," Red Sam said as if he were struck with this answer.

His wife brought the orders, carrying the five plates all at once without a tray, two in each hand and one balanced on her arm. "It isn't a soul in this green world of God's that you can trust," she said. "And I don't count nobody out of that, not nobody," she repeated, looking at Red Sammy.

"Did you read about that criminal, The Misfit, that's escaped?" asked the grandmother.

"I wouldn't be a bit surprised if he didn't attack this place right here," said the woman. "If he hears about it being here, I wouldn't be none surprised to see him. If he hears it's two cent in the cash register, I wouldn't be a tall surprised if he . . ."

"That'll do," Red Sam said. "Go bring these people their Co'-Colas," and the woman went off to get the rest of the order.

"A good man is hard to find," Red Sammy said. "Everything is getting terrible. I remember the day you could go off and leave your screen door unlatched. Not no more."

He and the grandmother discussed better times. The old lady said that in her opinion Europe was entirely to blame for the way things were now. She said the way Europe acted you would think we were made of money and Red Sam said it was no use talking about it, she was exactly right. The children ran outside into the white sunlight and looked at the monkey in the lacy chinaberry tree. He was busy catching fleas on himself and biting each one carefully between his teeth as if it were a delicacy.

They drove off again into the hot afternoon. The grandmother took cat naps and woke up every few minutes with her own snoring. Outside of Toombsboro she woke up and recalled an old plantation that she had visited in this neighborhood once when she was a young lady. She said the house had six white columns across the front and that there was an avenue of oaks leading up to it and two little wooden trellis arbors on either side in front where you sat down with your suitor after a stroll in the garden. She recalled exactly which road to turn off to get to it. She knew that Bailey would not be willing to lose any time looking at an old house, but the more she talked about it, the more she wanted to see it once again and find out if the little twin arbors were still standing. "There was a secret panel in this house," she said craftily, not telling the truth but wishing that she were, "and the story went that all the family silver was hidden in it when Sherman came through but it was never found . . ."

"Hey!" John Wesley said. "Let's go see it! We'll find it! We'll poke all the woodwork and find it! Who lives there? Where do you turn off at? Hey Pop, can't we turn off there?"

"We never have seen a house with a secret panel!" June Star shrieked. "Let's go to the house with the secret panel! Hey Pop, can't we go see the house with the secret panel!"

"It's not far from here, I know," the grandmother said. "It wouldn't take over twenty minutes."

Bailey was looking straight ahead. His jaw was as rigid as a horseshoe. "No," he said.

The children began to yell and scream that they wanted to see the house with the secret panel. John Wesley kicked the back of the front seat and June Star hung over her mother's shoulder and whined desperately into her ear that they never had any fun even on their vacation, that they could never do what THEY wanted to do. The baby began to scream and John Wesley kicked the back of the seat so hard that his father could feel the blows in his kidney.

"All right!" he shouted and drew the car to a stop at the side of the road. "Will you all shut up? Will you all just shut up for one second? If you don't shut up, we won't go anywhere."

"It would be very educational for them," the grandmother murmured.

"All right," Bailey said, "but get this: this is the only time we're going to stop for anything like this. This is the one and only time."

"The dirt road that you have to turn down is about a mile back," the grandmother directed. "I marked it when we passed."

"A dirt road," Bailey groaned.

After they had turned around and were headed toward the dirt road, the grandmother recalled other points about the house, the beautiful glass over the front doorway and the candle-lamp in the hall. John Wesley said that the secret panel was probably in the fireplace.

"You can't go inside this house," Bailey said. "You don't know who lives there."

"While you all talk to the people in front, I'll run around behind and get in a window," John Wesley suggested.

"We'll all stay in the car," his mother said.

They turned onto the dirt road and the car raced roughly along in a swirl of pink dust. The grandmother recalled the times when there were no paved roads and thirty miles was a day's journey. The dirt road was hilly and there were sudden washes in it and sharp curves on dangerous embankments. All at once they would be on a hill, looking down over the blue tops of trees for miles around, then the next minute, they would be in a red depression with the dust-coated trees looking down on them.

"This place had better turn up in a minute," Bailey said, "or I'm going to turn around."

The road looked as if no one had traveled on it in months.

"It's not much farther," the grandmother said and just as she said it, a horrible thought came to her. The thought was so embarrassing that she turned red in the face and her eyes dilated and her feet jumped up, upsetting her valise in the corner. The instant the valise moved, the newspaper top she had over the basket under it rose with a snarl and Pitty Sing, the cat, sprang onto Bailey's shoulder.

The children were thrown to the floor and their mother, clutching the baby, was thrown out the door onto the ground; the old lady was thrown into the front seat. The car turned over once and landed right-side-up in a gulch off the side of the road. Bailey remained in the driver's seat with the cat—gray-striped with a broad white face and an orange nose—clinging to his neck like a caterpillar.

As soon as the children saw they could move their arms and legs, they scrambled out of the car, shouting, "We've had an ACCIDENT!" The grandmother was curled up under the dashboard, hoping she was injured so that Bailey's wrath would not come down on her all at once. The horrible thought she had had before the accident was that the house she had remembered so vividly was not in Georgia but in Tennessee.

Bailey removed the cat from his neck with both hands and flung it out the window against the side of a pine tree. Then he got out of the car and started looking for the children's mother. She was sitting against the side of the red gutted ditch, holding the screaming baby, but she only had a cut down her face and a broken shoulder. "We've had an ACCIDENT!" the children screamed in a frenzy of delight.

"But nobody's killed," June Star said with disappointment as the grandmother limped out of the car, her hat still pinned to her head but the broken front brim standing up at a jaunty angle and the violet spray hanging off the side. They all sat down in the ditch, except the children, to recover from the shock. They were all shaking.

"Maybe a car will come along," said the children's mother hoarsely.

"I believe I have injured an organ," said the grandmother, pressing her side, but no one answered her. Bailey's teeth were clattering. He had on a yellow sport shirt with bright blue parrots designed in it and his face was as yellow as the shirt. The grandmother decided that she would not mention that the house was in Tennessee.

The road was about ten feet above and they could only see the tops of the trees on the other side of it. Behind the ditch they were sitting in there were more woods, tall and dark and deep. In a few minutes they saw a car some distance away on top of a hill, coming slowly as if the occupants were watching them. The grandmother stood up and waved both arms dramatically to attract their attention. The car continued to come on slowly, disappeared around a bend and appeared again, moving even slower, on top of the hill they had gone over. It was a big black battered hearse-like automobile. There were three men in it.

It came to a stop just over them and for some minutes, the driver looked down with a steady expressionless gaze to where they were sitting, and didn't speak. Then he turned his head and muttered something to the other two and they got out. One was a fat boy in black trousers and a red sweat shirt with a silver stallion embossed on the front of it. He moved around on the right side of them and stood staring, his mouth partly open in a kind of loose grin. The other had on khaki pants and a blue striped coat and a gray hat pulled very low, hiding most of his face. He came around slowly on the left side. Neither spoke.

The driver got out of the car and stood by the side of it, looking down at them. He was an older man than the other two. His hair was just beginning to gray and he wore silver-rimmed spectacles that gave him a scholarly look. He had a long creased face and didn't have on any shirt or undershirt. He had on blue jeans that were too tight for him and was holding a black hat and a gun. The two boys also had guns.

"We've had an ACCIDENT!" the children screamed.

The grandmother had the peculiar feeling that the bespectacled man was someone she knew. His face was as familiar to her as if she had known him all her life but she could not recall who he was. He moved away from the car and began to come down the embankment, placing his feet carefully so that he wouldn't slip. He had on tan and white shoes and no socks, and his ankles were red and thin. "Good afternoon," he said. "I see you all had you a little spill."

"We turned over twice!" said the grandmother.

"Oncet," he corrected. "We seen it happen. Try their car and see will it run, Hiram," he said quietly to the boy with the gray hat.

"What you got that gun for?" John Wesley asked. "Whatcha gonna do with that gun?"

"Lady," the man said to the children's mother, "would you mind calling them children to sit down by you? Children make me nervous. I want all you all to sit down right together there where you're at."

"What are you telling US what to do for?" June Star asked.

Behind them the line of woods gaped like a dark open mouth. "Come here," said the mother.

"Look here now," Bailey began suddenly, "we're in a predicament! We're in . . ."

The grandmother shrieked. She scrambled to her feet and stood staring. "You're The Misfit!" she said. "I recognized you at once!"

"Yes'm," the man said, smiling slightly as if he were pleased in spite of himself to be known, "but it would have been better for all of you, lady, if you hadn't of reckernized me."

Bailey turned his head sharply and said something to his mother that shocked even the children. The old lady began to cry and The Misfit reddened.

"Lady," he said, "don't you get upset. Sometimes a man says things he don't mean. I don't reckon he meant to talk to you thataway."

"You wouldn't shoot a lady, would you?" the grandmother said and removed a clean handkerchief from her cuff and began to slap at her eyes with it.

The Misfit pointed the toe of his shoe into the ground and made a little hole and then covered it up again. "I would hate to have to," he said.

"Listen," the grandmother almost screamed, "I know you're a good man. You don't look a bit like you have common blood. I know you must come from nice people!"

"Yes mam," he said, "finest people in the world." When he smiled he showed a row of strong white teeth. "God never made a finer woman than my mother and my daddy's heart was pure gold," he said. The boy with the red sweat shirt had come around behind them and was standing with his gun at his hip. The Misfit squatted down on the ground. "Watch them children, Bobby Lee," he said. "You know they make me nervous." He looked at the six of them huddled together in front of him and he seemed to be embarrassed as if he couldn't think of anything to say. "Ain't a cloud in the sky," he remarked, looking up at it. "Don't see no sun but don't see no cloud neither."

"Yes, it's a beautiful day," said the grandmother. "Listen," she said, "you shouldn't call yourself The Misfit because I know you're a good man at heart. I can just look at you and tell."

"Hush!" Bailey yelled. "Hush! Everybody shut up and let me handle this!" He was squatting in the position of a runner about to sprint forward but he didn't move.

"I pre-chate that, lady," The Misfit said and drew a little circle in the ground with the butt of his gun.

"It'll take a half a hour to fix this here car," Hiram called, looking over the raised hood of it.

"Well, first you and Bobby Lee get him and that little boy to step over yonder with you," The Misfit said, pointing to Bailey and John Wesley. "The boys want to ast you something," he said to Bailey. "Would you mind stepping back in them woods there with them?"

"Listen," Bailey began, "we're in a terrible predicament! Nobody realizes what this is," and his voice cracked. His eyes were as blue and intense as the parrots in his shirt and he remained perfectly still.

The grandmother reached up to adjust her hat brim as if she were going to the woods with him but it came off in her hand. She stood staring at it and after a second she let it fall on the ground. Hiram pulled Bailey up by the arm as if he were assisting an old man. John Wesley caught hold of his father's hand and Bobby Lee followed. They went off toward the woods and just as they reached the dark edge, Bailey turned and supporting himself against a gray naked pine trunk, he shouted, "I'll be back in a minute, Mamma, wait on me!"

"Come back this instant!" his mother shrilled but they all disappeared into the woods.

"Bailey Boy!" the grandmother called in a tragic voice but she found she was looking at The Misfit squatting on the ground in front of her. "I just know you're a good man," she said desperately. "You're not a bit common!"

"Nome, I ain't a good man," The Misfit said after a second as if he had considered her statement carefully, "but I ain't the worst in the world neither. My daddy said I was a different breed of dog from my brothers and sisters. 'You know,' Daddy said, 'it's some that can live their whole life out without asking about it and it's others has to know why it is, and this boy is one of the latters. He's going to be into everything!'" He put on his black hat and looked up suddenly and then away deep into the woods as if he were embarrassed again. "I'm sorry I don't have on a shirt before you ladies," he said, hunching his shoulders slightly. "We buried our clothes that we had on when we escaped and we're just making do until we can get better. We borrowed these from some folks we met," he explained.

"That's perfectly all right," the grandmother said. "Maybe Bailey has an extra shirt in his suitcase."

"I'll look and see terrectly," The Misfit said.

"Where are they taking him?" the children's mother screamed.

"Daddy was a card himself," The Misfit said. "You couldn't put anything over on him. He never got in trouble with the Authorities though. Just had the knack of handling them."

"You could be honest too if you'd only try," said the grandmother. "Think how wonderful it would be to settle down and live a comfortable life and not have to think about somebody chasing you all the time."

The Misfit kept scratching in the ground with the butt of his gun as if he were thinking about it. "Yes'm, somebody is always after you," he murmured.

The grandmother noticed how thin his shoulder blades were just behind his hat because she was standing up looking down at him. "Do you ever pray?" she asked.

He shook his head. All she saw was the black hat wiggle between his shoulder blades. "Nome," he said.

There was a pistol shot from the woods, followed closely by another. Then silence. The old lady's head jerked around. She could hear the wind move through the tree tops like a long satisfied insuck of breath. "Bailey Boy!" she called.

"I was a gospel singer for a while," The Misfit said. "I been most everything. Been in the arm service, both land and sea, at home and abroad, been twict married, been an undertaker, been with the railroads, plowed Mother Earth, been in a tornado, seen a man burnt alive oncet," and he looked up at the children's mother and the little girl who were sitting close together, their faces white and their eyes glassy; "I even seen a woman flogged," he said.

"Pray, pray," the grandmother began, "pray, pray . . ."

"I never was a bad boy that I remember of," The Misfit said in an almost dreamy voice, "but somewheres along the line I done something wrong and got sent to the penitentiary. I was buried alive," and he looked up and held her attention to him by a steady stare.

"That's when you should have started to pray," she said. "What did you do to get sent to the penitentiary that first time?"

"Turn to the right, it was a wall," The Misfit said, looking up again at the cloudless sky. "Turn to the left, it was a wall. Look up it was a ceiling, look down it was a floor. I forgot what I done, lady. I set there and set there, trying to remember what it was I done and I ain't recalled it to this day. Oncet in a while, I would think it was coming to me, but it never come."

"Maybe they put you in by mistake," the old lady said vaguely.

"Nome," he said. "It wasn't no mistake. They had the papers on me."

"You must have stolen something," she said.

The Misfit sneered slightly. "Nobody had nothing I wanted," he said. "It was a head-doctor at the penitentiary said what I had done was kill my daddy but I known that for a lie. My daddy died in nineteen ought nineteen of the epidemic flu and I never had a thing to do with it. He was buried in the Mount Hopewell Baptist churchyard and you can go there and see for yourself."

"If you would pray," the old lady said, "Jesus would help you."

"That's right," The Misfit said.

"Well then, why don't you pray?" she asked trembling with delight suddenly.

"I don't want no hep," he said. "I'm doing all right by myself."

Bobby Lee and Hiram came ambling back from the woods. Bobby Lee was dragging a yellow shirt with bright blue parrots in it.

"Thow me that shirt, Bobby Lee," The Misfit said. The shirt came flying at him and landed on his shoulder and he put it on. The grandmother couldn't name what the shirt reminded her of. "No, lady," The Misfit said while he was buttoning it up, "I found out the crime don't matter. You can do one thing or you can do another, kill a man or take a tire off his car, because sooner or later you're going to forget what it was you done and just be punished for it."

The children's mother had begun to make heaving noises as if she couldn't get her breath. "Lady," he asked, "would you and that little girl like to step off yonder with Bobby Lee and Hiram and join your husband?"

"Yes, thank you," the mother said faintly. Her left arm dangled helplessly and she was holding the baby, who had gone to sleep, in the other. "Hep that lady up, Hiram," The Misfit said as she struggled to climb out of the ditch, "and Bobby Lee, you hold onto that little girl's hand."

"I don't want to hold hands with him," June Star said. "He reminds me of a pig."

The fat boy blushed and laughed and caught her by the arm and pulled her off into the woods after Hiram and her mother.

Alone with The Misfit, the grandmother found that she had lost her voice. There was not a cloud in the sky nor any sun. There was nothing around her but woods. She wanted to tell him that he must pray. She opened and closed her mouth several times before anything came out. Finally she found herself saying, "Jesus. Jesus," meaning, Jesus will help you, but the way she was saying it, it sounded as if she might be cursing.

"Yes'm," The Misfit said as if he agreed. "Jesus thown everything off balance. It was the same case with Him as with me except He hadn't committed any crime and they could prove I had committed one because they had the papers on me. Of course," he said, "they never shown me my papers. That's why I sign myself now. I said long ago, you get you a signature and sign everything you do and keep a copy of it. Then you'll know what you done and you can hold up the crime to the punishment and see do they match and in the end you'll have something to prove you ain't been treated right. I call myself The Misfit," he said, "because I can't make what all I done wrong fit what all I gone through in punishment."

There was a piercing scream from the woods, followed closely by a pistol report. "Does it seem right to you, lady, that one is punished a heap and another ain't punished at all?"

"Jesus!" the old lady cried. "You've got good blood! I know you wouldn't shoot a lady! I know you come from nice people! Pray! Jesus, you ought not to shoot a lady. I'll give you all the money I've got!"

"Lady," The Misfit said, looking beyond her far into the woods, "there never was a body that give the undertaker a tip."

There were two more pistol reports and the grandmother raised her head like a parched old turkey hen crying for water and called, "Bailey Boy, Bailey Boy!" as if her heart would break.

"Jesus was the only One that ever raised the dead," The Misfit continued, "and He shouldn't have done it. He thown everything off balance. If He did what He said, then it's nothing for you to do but thow away everything and follow Him, and if He didn't, then it's nothing for you to do but enjoy the few minutes you got left the best you can—by killing somebody or burning down his house or doing some other meanness to him. No pleasure but meanness," he said and his voice had become almost a snarl.

"Maybe He didn't raise the dead," the old lady mumbled, not knowing what she was saying and feeling so dizzy that she sank down in the ditch with her legs twisted under her.

"I wasn't there so I can't say He didn't," The Misfit said. "I wisht I had of been there," he said, hitting the ground with his fist. "It ain't right I wasn't there because if I had of been there I would of known. Listen lady," he said in a high voice, "if I had of been there I would of known and I wouldn't be like I am now." His voice seemed about to crack and the grandmother's head cleared for an instant. She saw the man's face twisted close to her own as if he were going to cry and she murmured, "Why you're one of my babies. You're one of my own children!" She reached out and touched him on the shoulder. The Misfit sprang back as if a snake had bitten him and shot her three times through the chest. Then he put his gun down on the ground and took off his glasses and began to clean them.

Hiram and Bobby Lee returned from the woods and stood over the ditch, looking down at the grandmother who half sat and half lay in a puddle of blood with her legs crossed under her like a child's and her face smiling up at the cloudless sky.

Without his glasses, The Misfit's eyes were red-rimmed and pale and defenseless-looking. "Take her off and thow her where you thown the others," he said, picking up the cat that was rubbing itself against his leg.

"She was a talker, wasn't she?" Bobby Lee said, sliding down the ditch with a yodel.

"She would of been a good woman," The Misfit said, "if it had been somebody there to shoot her every minute of her life."

"Some fun!" Bobby Lee said.

"Shut up, Bobby Lee," The Misfit said. "It's no real pleasure in life."

[1955]

GABRIEL GARCÍA MÁRQUEZ   [b. 1928]

The Handsomest Drowned Man in the World

TRANSLATED BY GREGORY RABASSA, 1972

The first children who saw the dark and slinky bulge approaching through the sea let themselves think it was an enemy ship. Then they saw it had no flags or masts and they thought it was a whale. But when it washed up on the beach, they removed the clumps of seaweed, the jelly-fish tentacles, and the remains of fish and flotsam, and only then did they see that it was a drowned man.

They had been playing with him all afternoon, burying him in the sand and digging him up again, when someone chanced to see them and spread the alarm in the village. The men who carried him to the nearest house noticed that he weighed more than any dead man they had ever known, almost as much as a horse, and they said to each other that maybe he'd been floating too long and the water had got into his bones. When they laid him on the floor they said he'd been taller than all other men because there was barely enough room for him in the house, but they thought that maybe the ability to keep on growing after death was part of the nature of certain drowned men. He had the smell of the sea about him and only his shape gave one to suppose that it was the corpse of a human being, because the skin was covered with a crust of mud and scales.

They did not even have to clean off his face to know that the dead man was a stranger. The village was made up of only twenty-odd wooden houses that had stone courtyards with no flowers and which were spread about on the end of a desertlike cape. There was so little land that moth-ers always went about with the fear that the wind would carry off their children and the few dead that the years had caused among them had to be thrown off the cliffs. But the sea was calm and bountiful and all the men fit into seven boats. So when they found the drowned man they simply had to look at one another to see that they were all there.

That night they did not go out to work at sea. While the men went to find out if anyone was missing in neighboring villages, the women stayed behind to care for the drowned man. They took the mud off with grass swabs, they removed the underwater stones entangled in his hair, and they scraped the crust off with tools used for scaling fish. As they were doing that they noticed that the vegetation on him came from faraway oceans and deep water and that his clothes were in tatters, as if he had sailed through labyrinths of coral. They noticed too that he bore his death with pride, for he did not have the lonely look of other drowned men who came out of the sea or that haggard, needy look of men who drowned in rivers. But only when they finished cleaning him off did they become aware of the kind of man he was and it left them breathless. Not only was he the tallest, strongest, most virile, and best built man they had ever seen, but even though they were looking at him there was no room for him in their imagination.

They could not find a bed in the village large enough to lay him on nor was there a table solid enough to use for his wake. The tallest men's holiday pants would not fit him, nor the fattest ones' Sunday shirts, nor the shoes of the one with the biggest feet. Fascinated by his huge size and his beauty, the women then decided to make him some pants from a large piece of sail and a shirt from some bridal brabant linen so that he could continue through his death with dignity. As they sewed, sitting in a circle and gazing at the corpse between stitches, it seemed to them that the wind had never been so steady nor the sea so restless as on that night and they supposed that the change had something to do with the dead man. They thought that if that magnificent man had lived in the village, his house would have had the widest doors, the highest ceiling, and the strongest floor, his bedstead would have been made from a midship frame held together by iron bolts, and his wife would have been the happiest woman. They thought that he would have had so much authority that he could have drawn fish out of the sea simply by calling their names and that he would have put so much work into his land that springs would have burst forth from among the rocks so that he would have been able to plant flowers on the cliffs. They secretly compared him to their own men, thinking that for all their lives theirs were incapable of doing what he could do in one night, and they ended up dismissing them deep in their hearts as the weakest, meanest, and most useless creatures on earth. They were wandering through that maze of fantasy when the oldest woman, who as the oldest had looked upon the drowned man with more compassion than passion, sighed:

"He has the face of someone called Esteban."

It was true. Most of them had only to take another look at him to see that he could not have any other name. The more stubborn among them, who were the youngest, still lived for a few hours with the illusion that when they put his clothes on and he lay among the flowers in patent leather shoes his name might be Lautaro. But it was a vain illusion.

There had not been enough canvas, the poorly cut and worse sewn pants were too tight, and the hidden strength of his heart popped the buttons on his shirt. After midnight the whistling of the wind died down and the sea fell into its Wednesday drowsiness. The silence put an end to any last doubts: he was Esteban. The women who had dressed him, who had combed his hair, had cut his nails and shaved him were unable to hold back a shudder of pity when they had to resign themselves to his being dragged along the ground. It was then that they understood how unhappy he must have been with that huge body since it bothered him even after death. They could see him in life, condemned to going through doors sideways, cracking his head on crossbeams, remaining on his feet during visits, not knowing what to do with his soft, pink, sea lion hands while the lady of the house looked for her most resistant chair and begged him, frightened to death, sit here, Esteban, please, and he, leaning against the wall, smiling, don't bother, ma'am, I'm fine where I am, his heels raw and his back roasted from having done the same thing so many times whenever he paid a visit, don't bother, ma'am, I'm fine where I am, just to avoid the embarrassment of breaking up the chair, and never knowing perhaps that the ones who said don't go, Esteban, at least wait till the coffee's ready, were the ones who later on would whisper the big boob finally left, how nice, the handsome fool has gone. That was what the women were thinking beside the body a little before dawn. Later, when they covered his face with a handkerchief so that the light would not bother him, he looked so forever dead, so defenseless, so much like their men that the first furrows of tears opened in their hearts. It was one of the younger ones who began the weeping. The others, coming to, went from sighs to wails, and the more they sobbed the more they felt like weeping, because the drowned man was becoming all the more Esteban for them, and so they wept so much, for he was the most destitute, most peaceful, and most obliging man on earth, poor Esteban. So when the men returned with the news that the drowned man was not from the neighboring villages either, the woman felt an opening of jubilation in the midst of their tears.

"Praise the Lord," they sighed, "he's ours!"

The men thought the fuss was only womanish frivolity. Fatigued because of the difficult nighttime inquiries, all they wanted was to get rid of the bother of the newcomer once and for all before the sun grew strong on that arid, windless day. They improvised a litter with the remains of foremasts and gaffs, tying it together with rigging so that it would bear the weight of the body until they reached the cliffs. They wanted to tie the anchor from a cargo ship to him so that he would sink easily into the deepest waves, where fish are blind and divers die of nostalgia, and bad currents would not bring him back to shore, as had happened with other bodies. But the more they hurried, the more the women thought of ways to waste time. They walked about like startled hens, pecking with the sea charms on their breasts, some interfering on one side to put a scapular of the good wind on the drowned man, some on the other side to put a wrist compass on him, and after a great deal of *get away from there, woman, stay out of the way, look, you almost made me fall on top of the dead man*, the men began to feel mistrust in their livers and started grumbling about why so many main-altar decorations for a stranger, because no matter how many nails and holy-water jars he had on him, the sharks would chew him all the same, but the women kept piling on their junk relics, running back and forth, stumbling, while they released in sighs what they did not in tears, so that the men finally exploded with *since when has there ever been such a fuss over a drifting corpse, a drowned nobody, a piece of cold Wednesday meat*. One of the women, mortified by so much lack of care, then removed the handkerchief from the dead man's face and the men were left breathless too.

He was Esteban. It was not necessary to repeat it for them to recognize him. If they had been told Sir Walter Raleigh, even they might have been impressed with his gringo accent, the macaw on his shoulder, his cannibal-killing blunderbuss, but there could be only one Esteban in the world and there he was, stretched out like a sperm whale, shoeless, wearing the pants of an undersized child, and with those stony nails that had to be cut with a knife. They only had to take the handkerchief off his face to see that he was ashamed, that it was not his fault that he was so big or so heavy or so handsome, and if he had known that this was going to happen, he would have looked for a more discreet place to drown in, seriously, I even would have tied the anchor off a galleon around my neck and staggered off a cliff like someone who doesn't like things in order not to be upsetting people now with this Wednesday dead body, as you people say, in order not to be bothering anyone with this filthy piece of cold meat that doesn't have anything to do with me. There was so much truth in his manner that even the most mistrustful men, the ones who felt the bitterness of endless nights at sea fearing that their women would tire of dreaming about them and begin to dream of drowned men, even they and others who were harder still shuddered in the marrow of their bones at Esteban's sincerity.

That was how they came to hold the most splendid funeral they could conceive of for an abandoned drowned man. Some women who had gone to get flowers in the neighboring villages returned with other women who could not believe what they had been told, and those women went back for more flowers when they saw the dead man, and they brought more and more until there were so many flowers and so many people that it was hard to walk about. At the final moment it pained them to return him to the waters as an orphan and they chose a father and mother from among the best people, and aunts and uncles and cousins, so that through him all the inhabitants of the village became kinsmen. Some sailors who heard the weeping from a distance went off course and people heard of one who had himself tied to the mainmast, remembering ancient fables about sirens. While they fought for the privilege of carrying him on their shoulders along the steep escarpment by the cliffs, men and women became aware for the first time of the desolation of their streets, the dryness of their courtyards, the narrowness of their dreams as they faced the splendor and beauty of their drowned man. They let him go without an anchor so that he could come back if he wished and whenever he wished, and they all held their breath for the fraction of centuries the body took to fall into the abyss. They did not need to look at one another to realize that they were no longer all present, that they would never be. But they also knew that everything would be different from then on, that their houses would have wider doors, higher ceilings, and stronger floors so that Esteban's memory could go everywhere without bumping into beams and so that no one in the future would dare whisper the big boob finally died, too bad, the handsome fool has finally died, because they were going to paint their house fronts gay colors to make Esteban's memory eternal and they were going to break their backs digging for springs among the stones and planting flowers on the cliffs so that in future years at dawn the passengers on great liners would awaken, suffocated by the smell of gardens on the high seas, and the captain would have to come down from the bridge in his dress uniform, with his astrolabe,° his pole star, and his row of war medals and, pointing to the promontory of roses on the horizon, he would say in fourteen languages, look there, where the wind is so peaceful now that it's gone to sleep beneath the beds, over there, where the sun's so bright that the sunflowers don't know which way to turn, yes, over there, that's Esteban's village.

[1968]

Astrolabe: A device used in classical antiquity to locate and predict the positions of stars, the sun, moon, and planets.

JOHN UPDIKE [1932–2009]

A & P

In walks these three girls in nothing but bathing suits. I'm in the third checkout slot, with my back to the door, so I don't see them until they're over by the bread. The one that caught my eye first was the one in the plaid green two-piece. She was a chunky kid, with a good tan and a sweet broad soft-looking can with those two crescents of white just under it, where the sun never seems to hit, at the top of the backs of her legs. I stood there with my hand on a box of HiHo crackers trying to remember if I rang it up or not. I ring it up again and the customer starts giving me hell. She's one of these cash-register-watchers, a witch about fifty with rouge on her cheekbones and no eyebrows, and I know it made her day to trip me up. She'd been watching cash registers for fifty years and probably never seen a mistake before.

By the time I got her feathers smoothed and her goodies into a bag—she gives me a little snort in passing, if she'd been born at the right time they would have burned her over in Salem—by the time I get her on her way the girls had circled around the bread and were coming back, without a pushcart, back my way along the counters, in the aisle between the checkouts and the Special bins. They didn't even have shoes on. There was this chunky one, with the two-piece—it was bright green and the seams on the bra were still sharp and her belly was still pretty pale so I guessed she just got it (the suit)—there was this one, with one of those chubby berry-faces, the lips all bunched together under her nose, this one, and a tall one, with black hair that hadn't quite frizzed right, and one of these sunburns right across under the eyes, and a chin that was too long—you know, the kind of girl other girls think is very "striking" and "attractive" but never quite makes it, as they very well know, which is why they like her so much—and then the third one, that wasn't quite so tall. She was the queen. She kind of led them, the other two peeking around and making their shoulders round. She didn't look around, not this queen, she just walked straight on slowly, on these long white prima-donna legs. She came down a little hard on her heels, as if she didn't walk in her bare feet that much, putting down her heels and then letting the weight move along to her toes as if she was testing the floor with every step, putting a little deliberate extra action into it. You never know for

294

sure how girls' minds work (do you really think it's a mind in there or just a little buzz like a bee in a glass jar?) but you got the idea she had talked the other two into coming in here with her, and now she was showing them how to do it, walk slow and hold yourself straight.

She had on a kind of dirty-pink — beige maybe, I don't know — bathing suit with a little nubble all over it, and what got me, the straps were down. They were off her shoulders looped loose around the cool tops of her arms, and I guess as a result the suit had slipped a little on her, so all around the top of the cloth there was this shining rim. If it hadn't been there you wouldn't have known there could have been anything whiter than those shoulders. With the straps pushed off, there was nothing between the top of the suit and the top of her head except just *her*, this clean bare plane of the top of her chest down from the shoulder bones like a dented sheet of metal tilted in the light. I mean, it was more than pretty.

She had sort of oaky hair that the sun and salt had bleached, done up in a bun that was unravelling, and a kind of prim face. Walking into the A & P with your straps down, I suppose it's the only kind of face you *can* have. She held her head so high her neck, coming up out of those white shoulders, looked kind of stretched, but I didn't mind. The longer her neck was, the more of her there was.

She must have felt in the corner of her eye me and over my shoulder Stokesie in the second slot watching, but she didn't tip. Not this queen. She kept her eyes moving across the racks, and stopped, and turned so slow it made my stomach rub the inside of my apron, and buzzed to the other two, who kind of huddled against her for relief, and then they all three of them went up the cat-and-dog-food-breakfast-cereal-macaroni-rice-raisins-seasonings-spreads-spaghetti-soft-drinks-crackers-and-cookies aisle. From the third slot I look straight up this aisle to the meat counter, and I watched them all the way. The fat one with the tan sort of fumbled with the cookies, but on second thought she put the package back. The sheep pushing their carts down the aisle — the girls were walking against the usual traffic (not that we have one-way signs or anything) — were pretty hilarious. You could see them, when Queenie's white shoulders dawned on them, kind of jerk, or hop, or hiccup, but their eyes snapped back to their own baskets and on they pushed. I bet you could set off dynamite in an A & P and the people would by and large keep reaching and checking oatmeal off their lists and muttering "Let me see, there was a third thing, began with A, asparagus, no, ah, yes, applesauce!" or whatever it is they do mutter. But there was no doubt, this jiggled them. A few houseslaves in pin curlers even looked around after pushing their carts past to make sure what they had seen was correct.

You know, it's one thing to have a girl in a bathing suit down on the beach, where what with the glare nobody can look at each other much anyway, and another thing in the cool of the A & P, under the fluorescent lights, against all those stacked packages, with her feet paddling along naked over our checkboard green-and-cream rubber-tile floor.

"Oh Daddy," Stokesie said beside me. "I feel so faint."

"Darling," I said. "Hold me tight." Stokesie's married, with two babies chalked up on his fuselage already, but as far as I can tell that's the only difference. He's twenty-two, and I was nineteen this April.

"Is it done?" he asks, the responsible married man finding his voice. I forgot to say he thinks he's going to be manager some sunny day, maybe in 1990 when it's called the Great Alexandrov and Petrooshki Tea Company or something.

What he meant was, our town is five miles from a beach, with a big summer colony out on the Point, but we're right in the middle of town, and the women generally put on a shirt or shorts or something before they get out of the car into the street. And anyway these are usually women with six children and varicose veins mapping their legs and nobody, including them, could care less. As I say, we're right in the middle of town, and if you stand at our front doors you can see two banks and the Congregational church and the newspaper store and three real-estate offices and about twenty-seven old freeloaders tearing up Central Street because the sewer broke again. It's not as if we're on the Cape; we're north of Boston and there's people in this town haven't seen the ocean for twenty years.

The girls had reached the meat counter and were asking McMahon something. He pointed, they pointed, and they shuffled out of sight behind a pyramid of Diet Delight peaches. All that was left for us to see was old McMahon patting his mouth and looking after them sizing up their joints. Poor kids, I began to feel sorry for them, they couldn't help it.

Now here comes the sad part of the story, at least my family says it's sad, but I don't think it's so sad myself. The store's pretty empty, it being Thursday afternoon, so there was nothing much to do except lean on the register and wait for the girls to show up again. The whole store was like a pinball machine and I didn't know which tunnel they'd come out of. After a while they come around out of the far aisle, around the light bulbs, records at discount of the Caribbean Six or Tony Martin Sings or some such gunk you wonder they waste the wax on, sixpacks of candy bars, and plastic toys done up in cellophane that fall apart when a kid looks at them anyway. Around they come, Queenie still leading the way, and holding a little gray jar in her hand. Slots Three through Seven are unmanned and I could see her wondering between Stokes and me, but Stokesie with his usual luck draws an old party in baggy gray pants who stumbles up with four giant cans of pineapple juice (what do these bums *do* with all that pineapple juice? I've often asked myself) so the girls come to me. Queenie puts down the jar and I take it into my fingers icy cold. Kingfish Fancy Herring Snacks in Pure Sour Cream: 49¢. Now her hands are empty, not a ring or a bracelet, bare as God made them, and I wonder where the money's coming from. Still with that prim look she lifts a folded dollar bill out of the hollow at the center of her nubbled pink top. The jar went heavy in my hand. Really, I thought that was so cute.

Then everybody's luck begins to run out. Lengel comes in from haggling with a truck full of cabbages on the lot and is about to scuttle into that door marked MANAGER behind which he hides all day when the girls touch his eye. Lengel's pretty dreary, teaches Sunday school and the rest, but he doesn't miss that much. He comes over and says, "Girls, this isn't the beach."

Queenie blushes, though maybe it's just a brush of sunburn I was noticing for the first time, now that she was so close. "My mother asked me to pick up a jar of herring snacks." Her voice kind of startled me, the way voices do when you see the people first, coming out so flat and dumb yet kind of tony, too, the way it ticked over "pick up" and "snacks." All of a sudden I slid right down her voice into her living room. Her father and the other men were standing around in ice-cream coats and bow ties and the women were in sandals picking up herring snacks on toothpicks off a big glass plate and they were all holding drinks the color of water with olives and sprigs of mint in them. When my parents have somebody over they get lemonade and if it's a real racy affair Schlitz in tall glasses with "They'll Do It Every Time" cartoons stencilled on.

"That's all right," Lengel said. "But this isn't the beach." His repeating this struck me as funny, as if it had just occurred to him, and he had been thinking all these years the A & P was a great big sand dune and he was the head lifeguard. He didn't like my smiling—as I say he doesn't miss much—but he concentrates on giving the girls that sad Sunday-school–superintendent stare.

Queenie's blush is no sunburn now, and the plump one in plaid, that I liked better from the back—a really sweet can—pipes up, "We weren't doing any shopping. We just came in for the one thing."

"That makes no difference," Lengel tells her, and I could see from the way his eyes went that he hadn't noticed she was wearing a two-piece before. "We want you decently dressed when you come in here."

"We *are* decent," Queenie says suddenly, her lower lip pushing, getting sore now that she remembers her place, a place from which the crowd that runs the A & P must look pretty crummy. Fancy Herring Snacks flashed in her very blue eyes.

"Girls, I don't want to argue with you. After this come in here with your shoulders covered. It's our policy." He turns his back. That's policy for you. Policy is what the kingpins want. What the others want is juvenile delinquency.

All this while, the customers had been showing up with their carts but, you know, sheep, seeing a scene, they had all bunched up on Stokesie, who shook open a paper bag as gently as peeling a peach, not wanting to miss a word. I could feel in the silence everybody getting nervous, most of all Lengel, who asks me, "Sammy, have you rung up their purchase?"

I thought and said "No" but it wasn't about that I was thinking. I go through the punches, 4, 9, GROC, TOT—it's more complicated than you think, and after you do it often enough, it begins to make a little song, that you hear words to, in my case "Hello (*bing*) there, you (*gung*) hap-py pee-pul (*splat*)!"—the *splat* being the drawer flying out. I uncrease the bill, tenderly as you may imagine, it just having come from between the two smoothest scoops of vanilla I had ever known were there, and pass a half and a penny into her narrow pink palm, and nestle the herrings in a bag and twist its neck and hand it over, all the time thinking.

The girls, and who'd blame them, are in a hurry to get out, so I say "I quit" to Lengel quick enough for them to hear, hoping they'll stop and watch me, their unsuspected hero. They keep right on going, into the electric eye; the door flies open and they flicker across the lot to their car, Queenie and Plaid and Big Tall Goony-Goony (not that as raw material she was so bad), leaving me with Lengel and a kink in his eyebrow.

"Did you say something, Sammy?"

"I said I quit."

"I thought you did."

"You didn't have to embarrass them."

"It was they who were embarrassing us."

I started to say something that came out "Fiddle-de-doo." It's a saying of my grandmother's, and I know she would have been pleased.

"I don't think you know what you're saying," Lengel said.

"I know you don't," I said. "But I do." I pull the bow at the back of my apron and start shrugging it off my shoulders. A couple customers that had been heading for my slot begin to knock against each other, like scared pigs in a chute.

Lengel sighs and begins to look very patient and old and gray. He's been a friend of my parents for years. "Sammy, you don't want to do this to your Mom and Dad," he tells me. It's true, I don't. But it seems to me that once you begin a gesture it's fatal not to go through with it. I fold the apron, "Sammy" stitched in red on the pocket, and put it on the counter, and drop the bow tie on top of it. The bow tie is theirs, if you've ever wondered. "You'll feel this for the rest of your life," Lengel says, and I know that's true, too, but remembering how he made that pretty girl blush makes me so scrunchy inside I punch the No Sale tab and the machine whirs "pee-pul" and the drawer splats out. One advantage to this scene taking place in summer, I can follow this up with a clean exit, there's no fumbling around getting your coat and galoshes, I just saunter into the electric eye in my white shirt that my mother ironed the night before, and the door heaves itself open, and outside the sunshine is skating around on the asphalt.

I look around for my girls, but they're gone, of course. There wasn't anybody but some young married screaming with her children about some candy they didn't get by the door of a powder-blue Falcon station wagon. Looking back in the big windows, over the bags of peat moss and aluminum lawn furniture stacked on the pavement, I could see Lengel in my place in the slot, checking the sheep through. His face was dark gray and his back stiff, as if he'd just had an injection of iron, and my stomach kind of fell as I felt how hard the world was going to be to me hereafter.

[1961]

RAYMOND CARVER   [1938–1988]

Cathedral

This blind man, an old friend of my wife's, he was on his way to spend the night. His wife had died. So he was visiting the dead wife's relatives in Connecticut. He called my wife from his in-laws'. Arrangements were made. He would come by train, a five-hour trip, and my wife would meet him at the station. She hadn't seen him since she worked for him one summer in Seattle ten years ago. But she and the blind man had kept in touch. They made tapes and mailed them back and forth. I wasn't enthusiastic about his visit. He was no one I knew. And his being blind bothered me. My idea of blindness came from the movies. In the movies, the blind moved slowly and never laughed. Sometimes they were led by seeing-eye dogs. A blind man in my house was not something I looked forward to.

That summer in Seattle she had needed a job. She didn't have any money. The man she was going to marry at the end of the summer was in officers' training school. He didn't have any money, either. But she was in love with the guy, and he was in love with her, etc. She'd seen something in the paper: HELP WANTED—*Reading to Blind Man*, and a telephone number. She phoned and went over, was hired on the spot. She'd worked with this blind man all summer. She read stuff to him, case studies, reports, that sort of thing. She helped him organize his little office in the county social-service department. They'd become good friends, my wife and the blind man. How do I know these things? She told me. And she told me something else. On her last day in the office, the blind man asked if he could touch her face. She agreed to this. She told me he touched his fingers to every part of her face, her nose—even her neck! She never forgot it. She even tried to write a poem about it. She was always trying to write a poem. She wrote a poem or two every year, usually after something really important had happened to her.

When we first started going out together, she showed me the poem. In the poem, she recalled his fingers and the way they had moved around over her face. In the poem, she talked about what she had felt at the time, about what went through her mind when the blind man touched her nose and lips. I can remember I didn't think much of the poem. Of course, I didn't tell her that. Maybe I just don't understand poetry. I admit it's not the first thing I reach for when I pick up something to read.

Anyway, this man who'd first enjoyed her favors, the officer-to-be, he'd been her childhood sweetheart. So okay. I'm saying that at the end of the summer she let the blind man run his hands over her face, said good-bye to him, married her childhood etc., who was now a commissioned officer, and she moved away from Seattle. But they'd kept in touch, she and the blind man. She made the first contact after a year or so. She called him up one night from an Air Force base in Alabama. She wanted to talk. They talked. He asked her to send him a tape and tell him about her life. She did this. She sent the tape. On the tape, she told the blind man about her husband and about their life together in the military. She told the blind man she loved her husband but she didn't like it where they lived and she didn't like it that he was part of the military-industrial thing. She told the blind man she'd written a poem and he was in it. She told him that she was writing a poem about what it was like to be an Air Force officer's wife. The poem wasn't finished yet. She was still writing it. The blind man made a tape. He sent her the tape. She made a tape. This went on for years. My wife's officer was posted to one base and then another. She sent tapes from Moody AFB, McGuire, McConnell, and finally Travis, near Sacramento, where one night she got to feeling lonely and cut off from the people she kept losing in that moving-around life. She got to feeling she couldn't go it another step. She went in and swallowed all the pills and capsules in the medicine chest and washed them down with a bottle of gin. Then she got into a hot bath and passed out.

But instead of dying, she got sick. She threw up. Her officer—why should he have a name? he was the childhood sweetheart, and what more does he want?—came home from somewhere, found her, and called the ambulance. In time, she put it all on a tape and sent the tape to the blind man. Over the years, she put all kinds of stuff on tapes and sent the tapes off lickety-split. Next to writing a poem every year, I think it was her chief means of recreation. On one tape, she told the blind man she'd decided to live away from her officer for a time. On another tape, she told him about her divorce. She and I began going out, and of course she told her blind man about it. She told him everything, or so it seemed to me. Once she asked me if I'd like to hear the latest tape from the blind man. This was a year ago. I was on the tape, she said. So I said okay, I'd listen to it. I got us drinks and we settled down in the living room. We made ready to listen. First she inserted the tape into the player and adjusted a couple of dials. Then she pushed a lever. The tape squeaked and someone began to talk in this loud voice. She lowered the volume. After a few minutes of harmless chitchat, I heard my own name in the mouth of this stranger, this blind man I didn't even know! And then this: "From all you've said about him, I can only conclude—" But we were interrupted, a knock at the door, something, and we didn't ever get back to the tape. Maybe it was just as well. I'd heard all I wanted to.

Now this same blind man was coming to sleep in my house.

"Maybe I could take him bowling," I said to my wife. She was at the draining board doing scalloped potatoes. She put down the knife she was using and turned around.

"If you love me," she said, "you can do this for me. If you don't love me, okay. But if you had a friend, any friend, and the friend came to visit, I'd make him feel comfortable." She wiped her hands with the dish towel.

"I don't have any blind friends," I said.

"You don't have *any* friends," she said. "Period. Besides," she said, "goddamn it, his wife's just died! Don't you understand that? The man's lost his wife!"

I didn't answer. She'd told me a little about the blind man's wife. Her name was Beulah. Beulah! That's a name for a colored woman.

"Was his wife a Negro?" I asked.

"Are you crazy?" my wife said. "Have you just flipped or something?" She picked up a potato. I saw it hit the floor, then roll under the stove. "What's wrong with you?" she said. "Are you drunk?"

"I'm just asking," I said.

Right then my wife filled me in with more detail than I cared to know. I made a drink and sat at the kitchen table to listen. Pieces of the story began to fall into place.

Beulah had gone to work for the blind man the summer after my wife had stopped working for him. Pretty soon Beulah and the blind man had themselves a church wedding. It was a little wedding—who'd want to go to such a wedding in the first place?—just the two of them, plus the minister and the minister's wife. But it was a church wedding just the same. It was what Beulah had wanted, he'd said. But even then Beulah must have been carrying the cancer in her glands. After they had been inseparable for eight years—my wife's word, *inseparable*—Beulah's health went into a rapid decline. She died in a Seattle hospital room, the blind man sitting beside the bed and holding on to her hand. They'd married, lived and worked together, slept together—had sex, sure—and then the blind man had to bury her. All this without his having ever seen what the goddamned woman looked like. It was beyond my understanding. Hearing this, I felt sorry for the blind man for a little bit. And then I found myself thinking what a pitiful life this woman must have led. Imagine a woman who could never see herself as she was seen in the eyes of her loved one. A woman who could go on day after day and never receive the smallest compliment from her beloved. A woman whose husband could never read the expression on her face, be it misery or something better. Someone who could wear makeup or not—what difference to him? She could, if she wanted, wear green eye-shadow around one eye, a straight pin in her nostril, yellow slacks and purple shoes, no matter. And then to slip off into death, the blind man's hand on her hand, his blind eyes streaming tears—I'm imagining now—her last thought maybe this: that he never even knew what she looked like, and she on an express to the grave. Robert was left with a small insurance policy and half of a twenty-peso Mexican coin. The other half of the coin went into the box with her. Pathetic.

So when the time rolled around, my wife went to the depot to pick him up. With nothing to do but wait—sure, I blamed him for that—I was having a drink and watching the TV when I heard the car pull into the drive. I got up from the sofa with my drink and went to the window to have a look.

I saw my wife laughing as she parked the car. I saw her get out of the car and shut the door. She was still wearing a smile. Just amazing. She went around to the other side of the car to where the blind man was already starting to get out. This blind man, feature this, he was wearing a full beard! A beard on a blind man! Too much, I say. The blind man reached into the back seat and dragged out a suitcase. My wife took his arm, shut the car door, and, talking all the way, moved him down the drive and then up the steps to the front porch. I turned off the TV. I finished my drink, rinsed the glass, dried my hands. Then I went to the door.

My wife said, "I want you to meet Robert. Robert, this is my husband. I've told you all about him." She was beaming. She had this blind man by his coat sleeve.

The blind man let go of his suitcase and up came his hand.

I took it. He squeezed hard, held my hand, and then he let it go.

"I feel like we've already met," he boomed.

"Likewise," I said. I didn't know what else to say. Then I said, "Welcome. I've heard a lot about you." We began to move then, a little group, from the porch into the living room, my wife guiding him by the arm. The blind man was carrying his suitcase in his other hand. My wife said things like, "To your left here, Robert. That's right. Now watch it, there's a chair. That's it. Sit down right here. This is the sofa. We just bought this sofa two weeks ago."

I started to say something about the old sofa. I'd liked that old sofa. But I didn't say anything. Then I wanted to say something else, small-talk, about the scenic ride along the Hudson. How going *to* New York, you should sit on the right-hand side of the train, and coming *from* New York, the left-hand side.

"Did you have a good train ride?" I said. "Which side of the train did you sit on, by the way?"

"What a question, which side!" my wife said. "What's it matter which side?" she said.

"I just asked," I said.

"Right side," the blind man said. "I hadn't been on a train in nearly forty years. Not since I was a kid. With my folks. That's been a long time. I'd nearly forgotten the sensation. I have winter in my beard now," he said. "So I've been told, anyway. Do I look distinguished, my dear?" the blind man said to my wife.

"You look distinguished, Robert," she said. "Robert," she said. "Robert, it's just so good to see you."

My wife finally took her eyes off the blind man and looked at me. I had the feeling she didn't like what she saw. I shrugged.

I've never met, or personally known, anyone who was blind. This blind man was late forties, a heavy-set, balding man with stooped shoulders, as if he carried a great weight there. He wore brown slacks, brown shoes, a light-brown shirt, a tie, a sports coat. Spiffy. He also had this full beard. But he didn't use a cane and he didn't wear dark glasses. I'd always thought dark glasses were a must for the blind. Fact was, I wished he had a pair. At first glance, his eyes looked like anyone else's eyes. But if you looked close, there was something different about them. Too much white in the iris, for one thing, and the pupils seemed to move around in the sockets without his knowing it or being able to stop it. Creepy. As I stared at his face, I saw the left pupil turn in toward his nose while the other made an effort to keep in one place. But it was only an effort, for that eye was on the roam without his knowing it or wanting it to be.

I said, "Let me get you a drink. What's your pleasure? We have a little of everything. It's one of our pastimes."

"Bub, I'm a Scotch man myself," he said fast enough in this big voice.

"Right," I said. Bub! "Sure you are. I knew it."

He let his fingers touch his suitcase, which was sitting alongside the sofa. He was taking his bearings. I didn't blame him for that.

"I'll move that up to your room," my wife said.

"No, that's fine," the blind man said loudly. "It can go up when I go up."

"A little water with the Scotch?" I said.

"Very little," he said.

"I knew it," I said.

He said, "Just a tad. The Irish actor, Barry Fitzgerald? I'm like that fellow. When I drink water, Fitzgerald said, I drink water. When I drink whiskey, I drink whiskey." My wife laughed. The blind man brought his hand up under his beard. He lifted his beard slowly and let it drop.

I did the drinks, three big glasses of Scotch with a splash of water in each. Then we made ourselves comfortable and talked about Robert's travels. First the long flight from the West Coast to Connecticut, we covered that. Then from Connecticut up here by train. We had another drink concerning that leg of the trip.

I remembered having read somewhere that the blind didn't smoke because, as speculation had it, they couldn't see the smoke they exhaled. I thought I knew that much and that much only about blind people. But this blind man smoked his cigarette down to the nubbin and then lit another one. This blind man filled his ashtray and my wife emptied it.

When we sat down at the table for dinner, we had another drink. My wife heaped Robert's plate with cube steak, scalloped potatoes, green beans. I buttered him up two slices of bread. I said, "Here's bread and butter for you." I swallowed some of my drink. "Now let us pray," I said, and the blind man lowered his head. My wife looked at me, her mouth agape. "Pray the phone won't ring and the food doesn't get cold," I said.

We dug in. We ate everything there was to eat on the table. We ate like there was no tomorrow. We didn't talk. We ate. We scarfed. We grazed that table. We were into serious eating. The blind man had right away located his foods, he knew just where everything was on his plate. I watched with admiration as he used his knife and fork on the meat. He'd cut two pieces of meat, fork the meat into his mouth, and then go all out for the scalloped potatoes, the beans next, and then he'd tear off a hunk of buttered bread and eat that. He'd follow this up with a big drink of milk. It didn't seem to bother him to use his fingers once in a while, either.

We finished everything, including half a strawberry pie. For a few moments, we sat as if stunned. Sweat beaded on our faces. Finally, we got up from the table and left the dirty plates. We didn't look back. We took ourselves into the living room and sank into our places again. Robert and my wife sat on the sofa. I took the big chair. We had us two or three more drinks while they talked about the major things that had come to pass for them in the past ten years. For the most part, I just listened. Now and then I joined in. I didn't want him to think I'd left the room, and I didn't want her to think I was feeling left out. They talked of things that had happened to them—to them!—these past ten years. I waited in vain to hear my name on my wife's sweet lips: "And then my dear husband came into my life"—something like that. But I heard nothing of the sort. More talk of Robert. Robert had done a little of everything, it seemed, a regular blind jack-of-all-trades. But most recently he and his wife had had an Amway distributorship, from which, I gathered, they'd earned their living, such as it was. The blind man was also a ham radio operator. He talked in his loud voice about conversations he'd had with fellow operators in Guam, in the Philippines, in Alaska, and even in Tahiti. He said he'd have a lot of friends there if he ever wanted to go visit those places. From time to time, he'd turn his blind face toward me, put his hand under his beard, ask me something. How long had I been in my present position? (Three years.) Did I like my work? (I didn't.) Was I going to stay with it? (What were the options?) Finally, when I thought he was beginning to run down, I got up and turned on the TV.

My wife looked at me with irritation. She was heading toward a boil. Then she looked at the blind man and said, "Robert, do you have a TV?"

The blind man said, "My dear, I have two TVs. I have a color set and a black-and-white thing, an old relic. It's funny, but if I turn the TV on, and I'm always turning it on, I turn on the color set. It's funny, don't you think?"

I didn't know what to say to that. I had absolutely nothing to say to that. No opinion. So I watched the news program and tried to listen to what the announcer was saying.

"This is a color TV," the blind man said. "Don't ask me how, but I can tell."

"We traded up a while ago," I said.

The blind man had another taste of his drink. He lifted his beard, sniffed it, and let it fall. He leaned forward on the sofa. He positioned his ashtray on the coffee table, then put the lighter to his cigarette. He leaned back on the sofa and crossed his legs at the ankles.

My wife covered her mouth, and then she yawned. She stretched. She said, "I think I'll go upstairs and put on my robe. I think I'll change into something else. Robert, you make yourself comfortable," she said.

"I'm comfortable," the blind man said.

"I want you to feel comfortable in this house," she said.

"I am comfortable," the blind man said.

After she'd left the room, he and I listened to the weather report and then to the sports roundup. By that time, she'd been gone so long I didn't know if she was going to come back. I thought she might have gone to bed. I wished she'd come back downstairs. I didn't want to be left alone with a blind man. I asked him if he wanted another drink, and he said sure. Then I asked if he wanted to smoke some dope with me. I said I'd just rolled a number. I hadn't, but I planned to do so in about two shakes.

"I'll try some with you," he said.

"Damn right," I said. "That's the stuff."

I got our drinks and sat down on the sofa with him. Then I rolled us two fat numbers. I lit one and passed it. I brought it to his fingers. He took it and inhaled.

"Hold it as long as you can," I said. I could tell he didn't know the first thing.

My wife came back downstairs wearing her pink robe and her pink slippers.

"What do I smell?" she said.

"We thought we'd have us some cannabis," I said.

My wife gave me a savage look. Then she looked at the blind man and said, "Robert, I didn't know you smoked."

He said, "I do now, my dear. There's a first time for everything. But I don't feel anything yet."

"This stuff is pretty mellow," I said. "This stuff is mild. It's dope you can reason with," I said. "It doesn't mess you up."

"Not much it doesn't, bub," he said, and laughed.

My wife sat on the sofa between the blind man and me. I passed her the number. She took it and toked and then passed it back to me. "Which way is this going?" she said. Then she said, "I shouldn't be smoking this. I can hardly keep my eyes open as it is. That dinner did me in. I shouldn't have eaten so much."

"It was the strawberry pie," the blind man said. "That's what did it," he said, and he laughed his big laugh. Then he shook his head.

"There's more strawberry pie," I said.

"Do you want some more, Robert?" my wife said.

"Maybe in a little while," he said.

We gave our attention to the TV. My wife yawned again. She said, "Your bed is made up when you feel like going to bed, Robert. I know you must have had a long day. When you're ready to go to bed, say so." She pulled his arm. "Robert?"

He came to and said, "I've had a real nice time. This beats tapes, doesn't it?"

I said, "Coming at you," and I put the number between his fingers. He inhaled, held the smoke, and then let it go. It was like he'd been doing it since he was nine years old.

"Thanks, bub," he said. "But I think this is all for me. I think I'm beginning to feel it," he said. He held the burning roach out for my wife.

"Same here," she said. "Ditto. Me, too." She took the roach and passed it to me. "I may just sit here for a while between you two guys with my eyes closed. But don't let me bother you, okay? Either one of you. If it bothers you, say so. Otherwise, I may just sit here with my eyes closed until you're ready to go to bed," she said. "Your bed's made up, Robert, when you're ready. It's right next to our room at the top of the stairs. We'll show you up when you're ready. You wake me up now, you guys, if I fall asleep." She said that and then she closed her eyes and went to sleep.

The news program ended. I got up and changed the channel. I sat back down on the sofa. I wished my wife hadn't pooped out. Her head lay across the back of the sofa, her mouth open. She'd turned so that her robe slipped away from her legs, exposing a juicy thigh. I reached to draw her robe back over her, and it was then that I glanced at the blind man. What the hell! I flipped the robe open again.

"You say when you want some strawberry pie," I said.

"I will," he said.

I said, "Are you tired? Do you want me to take you up to your bed? Are you ready to hit the hay?"

"Not yet," he said. "No, I'll stay up with you, bub. If that's all right. I'll stay up until you're ready to turn in. We haven't had a chance to talk. Know what I mean? I feel like me and her monopolized the evening." He lifted his beard and he let it fall. He picked up his cigarettes and his lighter.

"That's all right," I said. Then I said, "I'm glad for the company."

And I guess I was. Every night I smoked dope and stayed up as long as I could before I fell asleep. My wife and I hardly ever went to bed at the same time. When I did go to sleep, I had these dreams. Sometimes I'd wake up from one of them, my heart going crazy.

Something about the church and the Middle Ages was on the TV. Not your run-of-the-mill TV fare. I wanted to watch something else. I turned to the other channels. But there was nothing on them, either. So I turned back to the first channel and apologized.

"Bub, it's all right," the blind man said. "It's fine with me. Whatever you want to watch is okay. I'm always learning something. Learning never ends. It won't hurt me to learn something tonight. I got ears," he said.

We didn't say anything for a time. He was leaning forward with his head turned at me, his right ear aimed in the direction of the set. Very disconcerting. Now and then his eyelids drooped and then they snapped open again. Now and then he put his fingers into his beard and tugged, like he was thinking about something he was hearing on the television.

On the screen, a group of men wearing cowls was being set upon and tormented by men dressed in skeleton costumes and men dressed as devils. The men dressed as devils wore devil masks, horns, and long tails. This pageant was part of a procession. The Englishman who was narrating the thing said it took place in Spain once a year. I tried to explain to the blind man what was happening.

"Skeletons," he said. "I know about skeletons," he said, and he nodded.

The TV showed this one cathedral. Then there was a long, slow look at another one. Finally, the picture switched to the famous one in Paris, with its flying buttresses and its spires reaching up to the clouds. The camera pulled away to show the whole of the cathedral rising above the skyline.

There were times when the Englishman who was telling the thing would shut up, would simply let the camera move around over the cathedrals. Or else the camera would tour the countryside, men in fields walking behind oxen. I waited as long as I could. Then I felt I had to say something. I said, "They're showing the outside of this cathedral now. Gargoyles. Little statues carved to look like monsters. Now I guess they're in Italy. Yeah, they're in Italy. There's paintings on the walls of this one church."

"Are those fresco paintings, bub?" he asked, and he sipped from his drink.

I reached for my glass. But it was empty. I tried to remember what I could remember. "You're asking me are those frescoes?" I said. "That's a good question. I don't know."

The camera moved to a cathedral outside Lisbon. The differences in the Portuguese cathedral compared with the French and Italian were not that great. But they were there. Mostly the interior stuff. Then something occurred to me, and I said, "Something has occurred to me. Do you have any idea what a cathedral is? What they look like, that is? Do you follow me? If somebody says cathedral to you, do you have any notion what they're talking about? Do you know the difference between that and a Baptist church, say?"

He let the smoke dribble from his mouth. "I know they took hundreds of workers fifty or a hundred years to build," he said. "I just heard the man say that, of course. I know generations of the same families worked on a cathedral. I heard him say that, too. The men who began their life's work on them, they never lived to see the completion of their work. In that wise, bub, they're no different from the rest of us, right?" He laughed. Then his eyelids drooped again. His head nodded. He seemed to be snoozing. Maybe he was imagining himself in Portugal. The TV was showing another cathedral now. This one was in Germany. The Englishman's voice droned on. "Cathedrals," the blind man said. He sat up and rolled his head back and forth. "If you want the truth, bub, that's about all I know. What I just said. What I heard him say. But maybe you could describe one to me? I wish you'd do it. I'd like that. If you want to know, I really don't have a good idea."

I stared hard at the shot of the cathedral on the TV. How could I even begin to describe it? But say my life depended on it. Say my life was being threatened by an insane guy who said I had to do it or else.

I stared some more at the cathedral before the picture flipped off into the countryside. There was no use. I turned to the blind man and said, "To begin with, they're very tall." I was looking around the room for clues. "They reach way up. Up and up. Toward the sky. They're so big, some of them, they have to have these supports. To help hold them up, so to speak. These supports are called buttresses. They remind me of viaducts, for some reason. But maybe you don't know viaducts, either? Sometimes the cathedrals have devils and such carved into the front. Sometimes lords and ladies. Don't ask me why this is," I said.

He was nodding. The whole upper part of his body seemed to be moving back and forth.

"I'm not doing so good, am I?" I said.

He stopped nodding and leaned forward on the edge of the sofa. As he listened to me, he was running his fingers through his beard. I wasn't getting through to him, I could see that. But he waited for me to go on just the same. He nodded, like he was trying to encourage me. I tried to think what else to say. "They're really big," I said. "They're massive. They're built of stone. Marble, too, sometimes. In those olden days, when they built cathedrals, men wanted to be close to God. In those olden days, God was an important part of everyone's life. You could tell this from their cathedral-building. I'm sorry," I said, "but it looks like that's the best I can do for you. I'm just no good at it."

"That's all right, bub," the blind man said. "Hey, listen. I hope you don't mind my asking you. Can I ask you something? Let me ask you a simple question, yes or no. I'm just curious and there's no offense. You're my host. But let me ask if you are in any way religious? You don't mind my asking?"

I shook my head. He couldn't see that, though. A wink is the same as a nod to a blind man. "I guess I don't believe in it. In anything. Sometimes it's hard. You know what I'm saying?"

"Sure, I do," he said.

"Right," I said.

The Englishman was still holding forth. My wife sighed in her sleep. She drew a long breath and went on with her sleeping.

"You'll have to forgive me," I said. "But I can't tell you what a cathedral looks like. It just isn't in me to do it. I can't do any more than I've done."

The blind man sat very still, his head down, as he listened to me.

I said, "The truth is, cathedrals don't mean anything special to me. Nothing. Cathedrals. They're something to look at on late-night TV. That's all they are."

It was then that the blind man cleared his throat. He brought something up. He took a handkerchief from his back pocket. Then he said, "I get it, bub. It's okay. It happens. Don't worry about it," he said. "Hey, listen to me. Will you do me a favor? I got an idea. Why don't you find us some heavy paper? And a pen. We'll do something. We'll draw one together. Get us a pen and some heavy paper. Go on, bub, get the stuff," he said.

So I went upstairs. My legs felt like they didn't have any strength in them. They felt like they did after I'd done some running. In my wife's room, I looked around. I found some ballpoints in a little basket on her table. And then I tried to think where to look for the kind of paper he was talking about.

Downstairs, in the kitchen, I found a shopping bag with onion skins in the bottom of the bag. I emptied the bag and shook it. I brought it into the living room and sat down with it near his legs. I moved some things, smoothed the wrinkles from the bag, spread it out on the coffee table.

The blind man got down from the sofa and sat next to me on the carpet.

He ran his fingers over the paper. He went up and down the sides of the paper. The edges, even the edges. He fingered the corners.

"All right," he said. "All right, let's do her."

He found my hand, the hand with the pen. He closed his hand over my hand. "Go ahead, bub, draw," he said. "Draw. You'll see. I'll follow along with you. It'll be okay. Just begin now like I'm telling you. You'll see. Draw," the blind man said.

So I began. First I drew a box that looked like a house. It could have been the house I lived in. Then I put a roof on it. At either end of the roof, I drew spires. Crazy.

"Swell," he said. "Terrific. You're doing fine," he said. "Never thought anything like this could happen in your lifetime, did you, bub? Well, it's a strange life, we all know that. Go on now. Keep it up."

I put in windows with arches. I drew flying buttresses. I hung great doors. I couldn't stop. The TV station went off the air. I put down the pen and closed and opened my fingers. The blind man felt around over the paper. He moved the tips of his fingers over the paper, all over what I had drawn, and he nodded.

"Doing fine," the blind man said.

I took up the pen again, and he found my hand. I kept at it. I'm no artist. But I kept drawing just the same.

My wife opened up her eyes and gazed at us. She sat up on the sofa, her robe hanging open. She said, "What are you doing? Tell me, I want to know."

I didn't answer her.

The blind man said, "We're drawing a cathedral. Me and him are working on it. Press hard," he said to me. "That's right. That's good," he said. "Sure. You got it, bub. I can tell. You didn't think you could. But you can, can't you? You're cooking with gas now. You know what I'm saying? We're going to really have us something here in a minute. How's the old arm?" he said. "Put some people in there now. What's a cathedral without people?"

My wife said, "What's going on? Robert, what are you doing? What's going on?"

"It's all right," he said to her. "Close your eyes now," the blind man said to me.

I did it. I closed them just like he said.

"Are they closed?" he said. "Don't fudge."

"They're closed," I said.

"Keep them that way," he said. He said, "Don't stop now. Draw."

So we kept on with it. His fingers rode my fingers as my hand went over the paper. It was like nothing else in my life up to now.

Then he said, "I think that's it. I think you got it," he said. "Take a look. What do you think?"

But I had my eyes closed. I thought I'd keep them that way for a little longer. I thought it was something I ought to do.

"Well?" he said. "Are you looking?"

My eyes were still closed. I was in my house. I knew that. But I didn't feel like I was inside anything.

"It's really something," I said.

[1981]

JOYCE CAROL OATES [b. 1938]

Where Are You Going, Where Have You Been?

For Bob Dylan

Her name was Connie. She was fifteen and she had a quick nervous giggling habit of craning her neck to glance into mirrors, or checking other people's faces to make sure her own was all right. Her mother, who noticed everything and knew everything and who hadn't much reason any longer to look at her own face, always scolded Connie about it. "Stop gawking at yourself, who are you? You think you're so pretty?" she would say. Connie would raise her eyebrows at these familiar complaints and look right through her mother, into a shadowy vision of herself as she was right at that moment: she knew she was pretty and that was everything. Her mother had been pretty once too, if you could believe those old snapshots in the album, but now her looks were gone and that was why she was always after Connie.

"Why don't you keep your room clean like your sister? How've you got your hair fixed—what the hell stinks? Hair spray? You don't see your sister using that junk."

Her sister June was twenty-four and still lived at home. She was a secretary in the high school Connie attended, and if that wasn't bad enough—with her in the same building—she was so plain and chunky and steady that Connie had to hear her praised all the time by her mother and her mother's sisters. June did this, June did that, she saved money and helped clean the house and cooked and Connie couldn't do a thing, her mind was all filled with trashy daydreams. Their father was away at work most of the time and when he came home he wanted supper and he read the newspaper at supper and after supper he went to bed. He didn't bother talking much to them, but around his bent head Connie's mother kept picking at her until Connie wished her mother was dead and she herself was dead and it was all over. "She makes me want to throw up sometimes," she complained to her friends. She had a high, breathless, amused voice which made everything she said a little forced, whether it was sincere or not.

There was one good thing: June went places with girl friends of hers,

312

girls who were just as plain and steady as she, and so when Connie wanted to do that her mother had no objections. The father of Connie's best girl friend drove the girls the three miles to town and left them off at a shopping plaza, so that they could walk through the stores or go to a movie, and when he came to pick them up again at eleven he never bothered to ask what they had done.

They must have been familiar sights, walking around that shopping plaza in their shorts and flat ballerina slippers that always scuffed the sidewalk, with charm bracelets jingling on their thin wrists; they would lean together to whisper and laugh secretly if someone passed by who amused or interested them. Connie had long dark blond hair that drew anyone's eye to it, and she wore part of it pulled up on her head and puffed out and the rest of it she let fall down her back. She wore a pullover jersey blouse that looked one way when she was at home and another way when she was away from home. Everything about her had two sides to it, one for home and one for anywhere that was not home: her walk that could be childlike and bobbing, or languid enough to make anyone think she was hearing music in her head, her mouth which was pale and smirking most of the time, but bright and pink on these evenings out, her laugh which was cynical and drawling at home—"Ha, ha, very funny"—but high-pitched and nervous anywhere else, like the jingling of the charms on her bracelet.

Sometimes they did go shopping or to a movie, but sometimes they went across the highway, ducking fast across the busy road, to a drive-in restaurant where older kids hung out. The restaurant was shaped like a big bottle, though squatter than a real bottle, and on its cap was a revolving figure of a grinning boy who held a hamburger aloft. One night in midsummer they ran across, breathless with daring, and right away someone leaned out a car window and invited them over, but it was just a boy from high school they didn't like. It made them feel good to be able to ignore him. They went up through the maze of parked and cruising cars to the bright-lit, fly-infested restaurant, their faces pleased and expectant as if they were entering a sacred building that loomed out of the night to give them what haven and what blessing they yearned for. They sat at the counter and crossed their legs at the ankles, their thin shoulders rigid with excitement and listened to the music that made everything so good: the music was always in the background like music at a church service, it was something to depend upon.

A boy named Eddie came in to talk with them. He sat backwards on his stool, turning himself jerkily around in semi-circles and then stopping and turning again, and after a while he asked Connie if she would like something to eat. She said she did and so she tapped her friend's arm on her way out—her friend pulled her face up into a brave droll look—and Connie said she would meet her at eleven, across the way. "I just hate to leave her like that," Connie said earnestly, but the boy said that she wouldn't be alone for long. So they went out to his car and on the way Connie couldn't help but let her eyes wander over the windshields and faces all around her, her face gleaming with the joy that had nothing to do with Eddie or even this place; it might have been the music. She drew her shoulders up and sucked in her breath with the pure pleasure of being alive, and just at that moment she happened to glance at a face just a few feet from hers. It was a boy with shaggy black hair, in a convertible jalopy painted gold. He stared at her and then his lips widened into a grin. Connie slit her eyes at him and turned away, but she couldn't help glancing back and there he was still watching her. He wagged a finger and laughed and said, "Gonna get you, baby," and Connie turned away again without Eddie noticing anything.

She spent three hours with him, at the restaurant where they ate hamburgers and drank Cokes in wax cups that were always sweating, and then down an alley a mile or so away, and when he left her off at five to eleven only the movie house was still open at the plaza. Her girl friend was there, talking with a boy. When Connie came up the two girls smiled at each other and Connie said, "How was the movie?" and the girl said, "*You* should know." They rode off with the girl's father, sleepy and pleased, and Connie couldn't help but look at the darkened shopping plaza with its big empty parking lot and its signs that were faded and ghostly now, and over at the drive-in restaurant where cars were still circling tirelessly. She couldn't hear the music at this distance.

Next morning June asked her how the movie was and Connie said, "So-so."

She and that girl and occasionally another girl went out several times a week that way, and the rest of the time Connie spent around the house—it was summer vacation—getting in her mother's way and thinking, dreaming, about the boys she met. But all the boys fell back and dissolved into a single face that was not even a face, but an idea, a feeling, mixed up with the urgent insistent pounding of the music and the humid night air of July. Connie's mother kept dragging her back to the daylight by finding things for her to do or saying suddenly, "What's this about the Pettinger girl?"

And Connie would say nervously, "Oh, her. That dope." She always drew thick clear lines between herself and such girls, and her mother was simple and kindly enough to believe her. Her mother was so simple, Connie thought, that it was maybe cruel to fool her so much. Her mother went scuffling around the house in old bedroom slippers and complained over the telephone to one sister about the other, then the other called up and the two of them complained about the third one. If June's name was mentioned her mother's tone was approving, and if Connie's name was mentioned it was disapproving. This did not really mean she disliked Connie and actually Connie thought that her mother preferred her to June because she was prettier, but the two of them kept up a pretense of exasperation, a sense that they were tugging and struggling over something of little value to either of them. Sometimes, over coffee, they were almost friends, but something would come up—some vexation that was like a fly buzzing suddenly around their heads—and their faces went hard with contempt.

One Sunday Connie got up at eleven—none of them bothered with church—and washed her hair so that it could dry all day long, in the sun. Her parents and sister were going to a barbecue at an aunt's house and Connie said no, she wasn't interested, rolling her eyes, to let mother know just what she thought of it. "Stay home alone then," her mother said sharply. Connie sat out back in a lawn chair and watched them drive away, her father quiet and bald, hunched around so that he could back the car out, her mother with a look that was still angry and not at all softened through the windshield, and in the back seat poor old June all dressed up as if she didn't know what a barbecue was, with all the running yelling kids and the flies. Connie sat with her eyes closed in the sun, dreaming and dazed with the warmth about her as if this were a kind of love, the caresses of love, and her mind slipped over onto thoughts of the boy she had been with the night before and how nice he had been, how sweet it always was, not the way someone like June would suppose but sweet, gentle, the way it was in movies and promised in songs; and when she opened her eyes she hardly knew where she was, the back yard ran off into weeds and a fenceline of trees and behind it the sky was perfectly blue and still. The asbestos "ranch house" that was now three years old startled her—it looked small. She shook her head as if to get awake.

It was too hot. She went inside the house and turned on the radio to drown out the quiet. She sat on the edge of her bed, barefoot, and listened for an hour and a half to a program called XYZ Sunday Jamboree, record after record of hard, fast, shrieking songs she sang along with, interspersed by exclamations from "Bobby King": "An' look here you girls at Napoleon's—Son and Charley want you to pay real close attention to this song coming up!"

And Connie paid close attention herself, bathed in a glow of slow-pulsed joy that seemed to rise mysteriously out of the music itself and lay languidly about the airless little room, breathed in and breathed out with each gentle rise and fall of her chest.

After a while she heard a car coming up the drive. She sat up at once, startled, because it couldn't be her father so soon. The gravel kept crunching all the way in from the road—the driveway was long—and Connie ran to the window. It was a car she didn't know. It was an open jalopy, painted a bright gold that caught the sun opaquely. Her heart began to pound and her fingers snatched at her hair, checking it, and she whispered "Christ. Christ," wondering how bad she looked. The car came to a stop at the side door and the horn sounded four short taps as if this were a signal Connie knew.

She went into the kitchen and approached the door slowly, then hung out the screen door, her bare toes curling down off the step. There were two boys in the car and now she recognized the driver: he had shaggy, shabby black hair that looked crazy as a wig and he was grinning at her.

"I ain't late, am I?" he said.

"Who the hell do you think you are?" Connie said.

"Toldja I'd be out, didn't I?"

"I don't even know who you are."

She spoke sullenly, careful to show no interest or pleasure, and he spoke in a fast bright monotone. Connie looked past him to the other boy, taking her time. He had fair brown hair, with a lock that fell onto his forehead. His sideburns gave him a fierce, embarrassed look, but so far he hadn't even bothered to glance at her. Both boys wore sunglasses. The driver's glasses were metallic and mirrored everything in miniature.

"You wanta come for a ride?" he said.

Connie smirked and let her hair fall loose over one shoulder.

"Don'tcha like my car? New paint job," he said. "Hey."

"What?"

"You're cute."

She pretended to fidget, chasing flies away from the door.

"Don'tcha believe me, or what?" he said.

"Look, I don't even know who you are," Connie said in disgust.

"Hey, Ellie's got a radio, see. Mine's broke down." He lifted his friend's arm and showed her the little transistor the boy was holding, and now Connie began to hear the music. It was the same program that was playing inside the house.

"Bobby King?" she said.

"I listen to him all the time. I think he's great."

"He's kind of great," Connie said reluctantly.

"Listen, that guy's *great*. He knows where the action is."

Connie blushed a little, because the glasses made it impossible for her to see just what this boy was looking at. She couldn't decide if she liked him or if he was just a jerk, and so she dawdled in the doorway and wouldn't come down or go back inside. She said, "What's all that stuff painted on your car?"

"Can'tcha read it?" He opened the door very carefully, as if he was afraid it might fall off. He slid out just as carefully, planting his feet firmly

*Arnold=
Antagonist*

on the ground, the tiny metallic world in his glasses slowing down like gelatine hardening and in the midst of it Connie's bright green blouse. "This here is my name, to begin with," he said. ARNOLD FRIEND was written in tar-like black letters on the side, with a drawing of a round grinning face that reminded Connie of a pumpkin, except it wore sunglasses. "I wanta introduce myself, I'm Arnold Friend and that's my real name and I'm gonna be your friend, honey, and inside the car's Ellie Oscar, he's kinda shy." Ellie brought his transistor up to his shoulder and balanced it there. "Now these numbers are a secret code, honey," Arnold Friend explained. He read off the numbers 33, 19, 17 and raised his eyebrows at her to see what she thought of that, but she didn't think much of it. The left rear fender had been smashed and around it was written, on the gleaming gold background: DONE BY CRAZY WOMAN DRIVER. Connie had to laugh at that. Arnold Friend was pleased at her laughter and looked up at her. "Around the other side's a lot more—you wanta come and see them?"

"No."

"Why not?"

"Why should I?"

"Don'tcha wanta see what's on the car? Don'tcha wanta go for a ride?"

"I don't know."

"Why not?"

"I got things to do."

"Like what?"

"Things."

He laughed as if she had said something funny. He slapped his thighs. He was standing in a strange way, leaning back against the car as if he were balancing himself. He wasn't tall, only an inch or so taller than she would be if she came down to him. Connie liked the way he was dressed, which was the way all of them dressed: tight faded jeans stuffed into black, scuffed boots, a belt that pulled his waist in and showed how lean he was, and a white pull-over shirt that was a little soiled and showed the hard small muscles of his arms and shoulders. He looked as if he probably did hard work, lifting and carrying things. Even his neck looked muscular. And his face was a familiar face, somehow: the jaw and chin and cheeks slightly darkened, because he hadn't shaved for a day or two, and the nose long and hawk-like, sniffing as if she were a treat he was going to gobble up and it was all a joke.

"Connie, you ain't telling the truth. This is your day set aside for a ride with me and you know it," he said, still laughing. The way he straightened and recovered from his fit of laughing showed that it had been all fake.

"How do you know what my name is?" she said suspiciously.

"It's Connie."

"Maybe and maybe not."

"I know my Connie," he said, wagging his finger. Now she remembered him even better, back at the restaurant, and her cheeks warmed at the thought of how she sucked in her breath just at the moment she passed him—how she must have looked to him. And he had remembered her. "Ellie and I come out here especially for you," he said. "Ellie can sit in back. How about it?"

"Where?"

"Where what?"

"Where're we going?"

He looked at her. He took off the sunglasses and she saw how pale the skin around his eyes was, like holes that were not in shadow but instead in light. His eyes were like chips of broken glass that catch the light in an amiable way. He smiled. It was as if the idea of going for a ride somewhere, to some place, was a new idea to him.

"Just for a ride, Connie sweetheart."

"I never said my name was Connie," she said.

"But I know what it is. I know your name and all about you, lots of things," Arnold Friend said. He had not moved yet but stood still leaning back against the side of his jalopy. "I took a special interest in you, such a pretty girl, and found out all about you like I know your parents and sister are gone somewheres and I know where and how long they're going to be gone, and I know who you were with last night, and your best friend's name is Betty. Right?"

He spoke in a simple lilting voice, exactly as if he were reciting the words to a song. His smile assured her that everything was fine. In the car Ellie turned up the volume on his radio and did not bother to look around at them.

"Ellie can sit in the back seat," Arnold Friend said. He indicated his friend with a casual jerk of his chin, as if Ellie did not count and she could not bother with him.

"How'd you find out all that stuff?" Connie said.

"Listen: Betty Schultz and Tony Fitch and Jimmy Pettinger and Nancy Pettinger," he said, in a chant. "Raymond Stanley and Bob Hutter—"

"Do you know all those kids?"

"I know everybody."

"Look, you're kidding. You're not from around here."

"Sure."

"But—how come we never saw you before?"

"Sure you saw me before," he said. He looked down at his boots, as if he were a little offended. "You just don't remember."

"I guess I'd remember you," Connie said.

"Yeah?" He looked up at this, beaming. He was pleased. He began to mark time with the music from Ellie's radio, tapping his fists lightly together. Connie looked away from his smile to the car, which was painted so bright it almost hurt her eyes to look at it. She looked at that name, ARNOLD FRIEND. And up at the front fender was an expression that was familiar—MAN THE FLYING SAUCERS. It was an expression kids had used the year before, but didn't use this year. She looked at it for a while as if the words meant something to her that she did not yet know.

"What're you thinking about? Huh?" Arnold Friend demanded. "Not worried about your hair blowing around in the car, are you?"

"No."

"Think I maybe can't drive good?"

"How do I know?"

"You're a hard girl to handle. How come?" he said. "Don't you know I'm your friend? Didn't you see me put my sign in the air when you walked by?"

"What sign?"

"My sign." And he drew an X in the air, leaning out toward her. They were maybe ten feet apart. After his hand fell back to his side the X was still in the air, almost visible. Connie let the screen door close and stood perfectly still inside it, listening to the music from her radio and the boy's blend together. She stared at Arnold Friend. He stood there so stiffly relaxed, pretending to be relaxed, with one hand idly on the door handle as if he were keeping himself up that way and had no intention of ever moving again. She recognized most things about him, the tight jeans that showed his thighs and buttocks and the greasy leather boots and the tight shirt, and even that slippery friendly smile of his, that sleepy dreamy smile that all the boys used to get across ideas they didn't want to put into words. She recognized all this and also the singsong way he talked, slightly mocking, kidding, but serious and a little melancholy, and she recognized the way he tapped one fist against the other in homage to the perpetual music behind him. But all these things did not come together.

She said suddenly, "Hey, how old are you?"

His smile faded. She could see then that he wasn't a kid, he was much older—thirty, maybe more. At this knowledge her heart began to pound faster.

"That's a crazy thing to ask. Can'tcha see I'm your own age?"

"Like hell you are."

"Or maybe a coupla years older, I'm eighteen."

"Eighteen?" she said doubtfully.

He grinned to reassure her and lines appeared at the corners of his mouth. His teeth were big and white. He grinned so broadly his eyes became slits and she saw how thick the lashes were, thick and black as if painted with a black tar-like material. Then he seemed to become embarrassed, abruptly, and looked over his shoulder at Ellie. "*Him*, he's crazy," he said. "Ain't he a riot, he's a nut, a real character." Ellie was still listening to the music. His sunglasses told nothing about what he was thinking. He wore a bright orange shirt unbuttoned halfway to show his chest, which was a pale, bluish chest and not muscular like Arnold Friend's. His shirt collar was turned up all around and the very tips of the collar pointed out past his chin as if they were protecting him. He was pressing the transistor radio up against his ear and sat there in a kind of daze, right in the sun.

"He's kinda strange," Connie said.

"Hey, she says you're kinda strange! Kinda strange!" Arnold Friend cried. He pounded on the car to get Ellie's attention. Ellie turned for the first time and Connie saw with shock that he wasn't a kid either—he had a fair, hairless face, cheeks reddened slightly as if the veins grew too close to the surface of his skin, the face of a forty-year-old baby. Connie felt a wave of dizziness rise in her at this sight and she stared at him as if waiting for something to change the shock of the moment, make it all right again. Ellie's lips kept shaping words, mumbling along with the words blasting his ear.

"Maybe you two better go away," Connie said faintly.

"What? How come?" Arnold Friend cried. "We come out here to take you for a ride. It's Sunday." He had the voice of the man on the radio now. It was the same voice, Connie thought. "Don'tcha know it's Sunday all day and honey, no matter who you were with last night today you're with Arnold Friend and don't you forget it!—Maybe you better step out here," he said, and this last was in a different voice. It was a little flatter, as if the heat was finally getting to him.

"No. I got things to do."

"Hey."

"You two better leave."

"We ain't leaving until you come with us."

"Like hell I am—"

"Connie, don't fool around with me. I mean—I mean, don't fool *around*," he said, shaking his head. He laughed incredulously. He placed his sunglasses on top of his head, carefully, as if he were indeed wearing a wig, and brought the stems down behind his ears. Connie stared at him, another wave of dizziness and fear rising in her so that for a moment he wasn't even in focus but was just a blur, standing there against his gold car, and she had the idea that he had driven up the driveway all right but had come from nowhere before that and belonged nowhere and that everything about him and even the music that was so familiar to her was only half real.

"If my father comes and sees you—"

"He ain't coming. He's at a barbecue."

"How do you know that?"

"Aunt Tillie's. Right now they're—uh—they're drinking. Sitting around," he said vaguely, squinting as if he were staring all the way to town and over to Aunt Tillie's back yard. Then the vision seemed to clear and he nodded energetically. "Yeah. Sitting around. There's your sister in a blue dress, huh? And high heels, the poor sad bitch—nothing like you, sweetheart! And your mother's helping some fat woman with the corn, they're cleaning the corn—husking the corn—"

"What fat woman?" Connie cried.

"How do I know what fat woman. I don't know every goddamn fat woman in the world!" Arnold Friend laughed.

"Oh, that's Mrs. Hornby. . . . Who invited her?" Connie said. She felt a little light-headed. Her breath was coming quickly.

"She's too fat. I don't like them fat. I like them the way you are, honey," he said, smiling sleepily at her. They stared at each other for a while, through the screen door. He said softly, "Now what you're going to do is this: you're going to come out that door. You're going to sit up front with me and Ellie's going to sit in the back, the hell with Ellie, right? This isn't Ellie's date. You're my date. I'm your lover, honey."

"What? You're crazy—"

"Yes, I'm your lover. You don't know what that is but you will," he said. "I know that too. I know all about you. But look: it's real nice and you couldn't ask for nobody better than me, or more polite. I always keep my word. I'll tell you how it is, I'm always nice at first, the first time. I'll hold you so tight you won't think you have to try to get away or pretend anything because you'll know you can't. And I'll come inside you where it's all secret and you'll give in to me and you'll love me—"

"Shut up! You're crazy!" Connie said. She backed away from the door. She put her hands against her ears as if she'd heard something terrible, something not meant for her. "People don't talk like that, you're crazy," she muttered. Her heart was almost too big now for her chest and its pumping made sweat break out all over her. She looked out to see Arnold Friend pause and then take a step toward the porch lurching. He almost fell. But, like a clever drunken man, he managed to catch his balance. He wobbled in his high boots and grabbed hold of one of the porch posts.

"Honey?" he said. "You still listening?"

"Get the hell out of here!"

"Be nice, honey. Listen."

"I'm going to call the police—"

He wobbled again and out of the side of his mouth came a fast spat curse, an aside not meant for her to hear. But even this "Christ!" sounded forced. Then he began to smile again. She watched this smile come, awkward as if he were smiling from inside a mask. His whole face was a mask, she thought wildly, tanned down onto his throat but then running out as if he had plastered make-up on his face but had forgotten about his throat.

"Honey—? Listen, here's how it is. I always tell the truth and I promise you this: I ain't coming in that house after you."

"You better not! I'm going to call the police if you—if you don't—"

"Honey," he said, talking right through her voice, "honey, I'm not coming in there but you are coming out here. You know why?"

She was panting. The kitchen looked like a place she had never seen before, some room she had run inside but which wasn't good enough, wasn't going to help her. The kitchen window had never had a curtain, after three years, and there were dishes in the sink for her to do—probably—and if you ran your hand across the table you'd probably feel something sticky there.

"You listening, honey? Hey?"

"—going to call the police—"

"Soon as you touch the phone I don't need to keep my promise and can come inside. You won't want that."

She rushed forward and tried to lock the door. Her fingers were shaking. "But why lock it," Arnold Friend said gently, talking right into her face. "It's just a screen door. It's just nothing." One of his boots was at a strange angle, as if his foot wasn't in it. It pointed out to the left, bent at the ankle. "I mean, anybody can break through a screen door and glass and wood and iron or anything else if he needs to, anybody at all and specially Arnold Friend. If the place got lit up with a fire, honey, you'd come runnin' out into my arms, right into my arms an' safe at home—like you knew I was your lover and'd stopped fooling around, I don't mind a nice shy girl but I don't like no fooling around." Part of those words were spoken with a slight rhythmic lilt, and Connie somehow recognized them—the echo of a song from last year, about a girl rushing into her boy friend's arms and coming home again—

Connie stood barefoot on the linoleum floor, staring at him. "What do you want?" she whispered.

"I want you," he said.

"What?"

"Seen you that night and thought, that's the one, yes sir. I never needed to look any more."

"But my father's coming back. He's coming to get me. I had to wash my hair first—" She spoke in a dry, rapid voice, hardly raising it for him to hear.

"No, your daddy is not coming and yes, you had to wash your hair and you washed it for me. It's nice and shining and all for me. I thank you, sweetheart," he said, with a mock bow, but again he almost lost his balance. He had to bend and adjust his boots. Evidently his feet did not go all the way down; the boots must have been stuffed with something so that he would seem taller. Connie stared out at him and behind him at Ellie in the car, who seemed to be looking off toward Connie's right, into nothing. Then Ellie said, pulling the words out of the air one after another as if he were just discovering them, "You want me to pull out the phone?"

"Shut your mouth and keep it shut," Arnold Friend said, his face red from bending over or maybe from embarrassment because Connie had seen his boots. "This ain't none of your business."

"What—what are you doing? What do you want?" Connie said. "If I call the police they'll get you, they'll arrest you—"

"Promise was not to come in unless you touch that phone, and I'll keep that promise," he said. He resumed his erect position and tried to force his shoulders back. He sounded like a hero in a movie, declaring something important. He spoke too loudly and it was as if he were speaking to someone behind Connie. "I ain't made plans for coming in that house where I don't belong but just for you to come out to me, the way you should. Don't you know who I am?"

"You're crazy," she whispered. She backed away from the door but did not want to go into another part of the house, as if this would give him permission to come through the door. "What do you . . . You're crazy, you. . . ."

"Huh? What're you saying, honey?"

Her eyes darted everywhere in the kitchen. She could not remember what it was, this room.

"This is how it is, honey: you come out and we'll drive away, have a nice ride. But if you don't come out we're gonna wait till your people come home and then they're all going to get it."

"You want that telephone pulled out?" Ellie said. He held the radio away from his ear and grimaced, as if without the radio the air was too much for him.

"I toldja shut up, Ellie," Arnold Friend said, "you're deaf, get a hearing aid, right? Fix yourself up. This little girl's no trouble and's gonna be nice to me, so Ellie keep to yourself, this ain't your date—right? Don't hem in on me, don't hog, don't crush, don't bird dog, don't trail me," he said in a rapid, meaningless voice, as if he were running through all the expressions he'd learned but was no longer sure which one of them was in style, then rushing on to new ones, making them up with his eyes closed. "Don't crawl under my fence, don't squeeze in my chipmunk hole, don't sniff my glue, suck my popsicle, keep your own greasy fingers on yourself!" He shaded his eyes and peered in at Connie, who was backed against the kitchen table. "Don't mind him, honey, he's just a creep. He's a dope. Right? I'm the boy for you and like I said, you come out here nice like a lady and give me your hand, and nobody else gets hurt, I mean, your nice old bald-headed daddy and your mummy and your sister in her high heels. Because listen: why bring them in this?"

"Leave me alone," Connie whispered.

"Hey, you know that old woman down the road, the one with the chickens and stuff—you know her?"

"She's dead!"

"Dead? What? You know her?" Arnold Friend said.

"She's dead—"

"Don't you like her?"

"She's dead—she's—she isn't here any more—"

"But don't you like her, I mean, you got something against her? Some grudge or something?" Then his voice dipped as if he were conscious of rudeness. He touched the sunglasses on top of his head as if to make sure they were still there. "Now you be a good girl."

"What are you going to do?"

"Just two things, or maybe three," Arnold Friend said. "But I promise it won't last long and you'll like me that way you get to like people you're close to. You will. It's all over for you here, so come on out. You don't want your people in any trouble, do you?"

She turned and bumped against a chair or something, hurting her leg, but she ran into the back room and picked up the telephone. Something roared in her ear, a tiny roaring, and she was so sick with fear that she could do nothing but listen to it—the telephone was clammy and very heavy and her fingers groped down to the dial but were too weak to touch it. She began to scream into the phone, into the roaring. She cried out, she cried for her mother, she felt her breath start jerking back and forth in her lungs as if it were something Arnold Friend was stabbing her with again and again with no tenderness. A noisy sorrowful wailing rose all about her and she was locked inside it the way she was locked inside this house.

After a while she could hear again. She was sitting on the floor, with her wet back against the wall.

Arnold Friend was saying from the door, "That's a good girl. Put the phone back."

She kicked the phone away from her.

"No, honey. Pick it up. Put it back right."

She picked it up and put it back. The dial tone stopped.

"That's a good girl. Now you come outside."

She was hollow with what had been fear but what was now just an emptiness. All that screaming had blasted it out of her. She sat, one leg cramped under her, and deep inside her brain was something like a pinpoint of light that kept going and would not let her relax. She thought, I'm not going to see my mother again. She thought, I'm not going to sleep in my bed again. Her bright green blouse was all wet.

Arnold Friend said, in a gentle-loud voice that was like a stage voice, "The place where you came from ain't there any more, and where you had in mind to go is cancelled out. This place you are now—inside your daddy's house—is nothing but a cardboard box I can knock down any time. You know that and always did know it. You hear me?"

She thought, I have got to think. I have got to know what to do.

"We'll go out to a nice field, out in the country here where it smells so nice and it's sunny," Arnold Friend said. "I'll have my arms tight around you so you won't need to try to get away and I'll show you what love is like, what it does. The hell with this house! It looks solid all right," he said. He ran a fingernail down the screen and the noise did not make Connie shiver, as it would have the day before. "Now put your hand on your heart, honey. Feel that? That feels solid too but we know better. Be nice to me, be sweet like you can because what else is there for a girl like you but to be sweet and pretty and give in?—and get away before her people get back?"

She felt her pounding heart. Her hand seemed to enclose it. She thought for the first time in her life that it was nothing that was hers, that belonged to her, but just a pounding, living thing inside this body that wasn't really hers either.

"You don't want them to get hurt," Arnold Friend went on. "Now get up, honey. Get up all by yourself."

She stood.

"Now turn this way. That's right. Come over to me—Ellie, put that away, didn't I tell you? You dope. You miserable creepy dope," Arnold Friend said. His words were not angry but only part of an incantation. The incantation was kindly. "Now come out through the kitchen to me honey and let's see a smile, try it, you're a brave sweet little girl and now they're eating corn and hotdogs cooked to bursting over an outdoor fire, and they don't know one thing about you and never did and honey you're better than them because not a one of them would have done this for you."

Connie felt the linoleum under her feet; it was cool. She brushed her hair back out of her eyes. Arnold Friend let go of the post tentatively and opened his arms for her, his elbows pointing in toward each other and his wrists limp, to show that this was an embarrassed embrace and a little mocking, he didn't want to make her self-conscious.

She put out her hand against the screen. She watched herself push the door slowly open as if she were back safe somewhere in the other door-way, watching this body and this head of long hair moving out into the sunlight where Arnold Friend waited.

"My sweet little blue-eyed girl," he said in a half-sung sigh that had nothing to do with her brown eyes but was taken up just the same by the vast sunlit reaches of the land behind him and on all sides of him—so much land that Connie had never seen before and did not recognize ex-cept to know that she was going to it.

[1966]

MARGARET ATWOOD   [b. 1939]

Happy Endings

John and Mary meet.
>   What happens next?
>   If you want a happy ending, try A.

A.

John and Mary fall in love and get married. They both have worthwhile and remunerative jobs which they find stimulating and challenging. They buy a charming house. Real estate values go up. Eventually, when they can afford live-in help, they have two children, to whom they are devoted. The children turn out well. John and Mary have a stimulating and challenging sex life and worthwhile friends. They go on fun vaca-tions together. They retire. They both have hobbies which they find stim-ulating and challenging. Eventually they die. This is the end of the story.

B.

Mary falls in love with John but John doesn't fall in love with Mary. He merely uses her body for selfish pleasure and ego gratification of a tepid kind. He comes to her apartment twice a week and she cooks him dinner, you'll notice that he doesn't even consider her worth the price of a dinner out, and after he's eaten the dinner he fucks her and after that he falls asleep, while she does the dishes so he won't think she's untidy, having all those dirty dishes lying around, and puts on fresh lipstick so she'll look good when he wakes up, but when he wakes up he doesn't even notice, he puts on his socks and his shorts and his pants and his shirt and his tie and his shoes, the reverse order from the one in which he took them off. He doesn't take off Mary's clothes, she takes them off herself, she acts as if she's dying for it every time, not because she likes sex exactly, she doesn't, but she wants John to think she does because if they do it often enough surely he'll get used to her, he'll come to depend on her and they will get married, but John goes out the door with hardly so much as a goodnight and three days later he turns up at six o'clock and they do the whole thing over again.

Mary gets run down. Crying is bad for your face, everyone knows that and so does Mary but she can't stop. People at work notice. Her friends tell her John is a rat, a pig, a dog, he isn't good enough for her, but she can't believe it. Inside John, she thinks, is another John, who is much nicer. This other John will emerge like a butterfly from a cocoon, a Jack from a box, a pit from a prune, if the first John is only squeezed enough.

One evening John complains about the food. He has never complained about the food before. Mary is hurt.

Her friends tell her they've seen him in a restaurant with another woman, whose name is Madge. It's not even Madge that finally gets to Mary: it's the restaurant. John has never taken Mary to a restaurant. Mary collects all the sleeping pills and aspirins she can find, and takes them and half a bottle of sherry. You can see what kind of a woman she is by the fact that it's not even whiskey. She leaves a note for John. She hopes he'll discover her and get her to the hospital in time and repent and then they can get married, but this fails to happen and she dies.

John marries Madge and everything continues as in A.

C.

John, who is an older man, falls in love with Mary, and Mary, who is only twenty-two, feels sorry for him because he's worried about his hair falling out. She sleeps with him even though she's not in love with him. She met him at work. She's in love with someone called James, who is twenty-two also and not yet ready to settle down.

John on the contrary settled down long ago: this is what is bothering him. John has a steady respectable job and is getting ahead in his field, but Mary isn't impressed by him, she's impressed by James, who has a motorcycle and a fabulous record collection. But James is often away on his motorcycle, being free. Freedom isn't the same for girls, so in the meantime Mary spends Thursday evenings with John. Thursdays are the only days John can get away.

John is married to a woman called Madge and they have two children, a charming house which they bought just before the real estate values went up, and hobbies which they find stimulating and challenging, when they have the time. John tells Mary how important she is to him, but of course he can't leave his wife because a commitment is a commitment. He goes on about this more than is necessary and Mary finds it boring, but older men can keep it up longer so on the whole she has a fairly good time.

One day James breezes in on his motorcycle with some top-grade California hybrid and James and Mary get higher than you'd believe possible and they climb into bed. Everything becomes very underwater, but along comes John, who has a key to Mary's apartment. He finds them stoned and entwined. He's hardly in any position to be jealous, considering Madge, but nevertheless he's overcome with despair. Finally he's middle-aged, in two years he'll be bald as an egg, and he can't stand it. He purchases a handgun, saying he needs it for target practice—this is the thin part of the plot, but it can be dealt with later—and shoots the two of them and himself.

Madge, after a suitable period of mourning, marries an understanding man called Fred and everything continues as in A, but under different names.

D.

Fred and Madge have no problems. They get along exceptionally well and are good at working out any little difficulties that may arise. But their charming house is by the seashore and one day a giant tidal wave approaches. Real estate values go down. The rest of the story is about what caused the tidal wave and how they escape from it. They do, though thousands drown. Some of the story is about how the thousands drown, but Fred and Madge are virtuous and lucky. Finally on high ground they clasp each other, wet and dripping and grateful, and continue as in A.

E.

Yes, but Fred has a bad heart. The rest of the story is about how kind and understanding they both are until Fred dies. Then Madge devotes herself to charity work until the end of A. If you like, it can be "Madge," "cancer," "guilty and confused," and "bird watching."

F.

If you think this is all too bourgeois, make John a revolutionary and Mary a counterespionage agent and see how far that gets you. Remember, this is Canada. You'll still end up with A, though in between you may get a lustful brawling saga of passionate involvement, a chronicle of our times, sort of.

You'll have to face it, the endings are the same however you slice it. Don't be deluded by any other endings, they're all fake, either deliberately fake, with malicious intent to deceive, or just motivated by excessive optimism if not by downright sentimentality.

The only authentic ending is the one provided here:

John and Mary die. John and Mary die. John and Mary die.

So much for endings. Beginnings are always more fun. True connoisseurs, however, are known to favor the stretch in between, since it's the hardest to do anything with.

That's about all that can be said for plots, which anyway are just one thing after another, a what and a what and a what.

Now try How and Why.

[1994]

TONI CADE BAMBARA   [1939–1995]

The Lesson

Back in the days when everyone was old and stupid or young and foolish and me and Sugar were the only ones just right, this lady moved on our block with nappy hair and proper speech and no makeup. And quite naturally we laughed at her, laughed the way we did at the junk man who went about his business like he was some big-time president and his sorry-ass horse his secretary. And we kinda hated her too, hated the way we did the winos who cluttered up our parks and pissed on our handball walls and stank up our hallways and stairs so you couldn't halfway play hide-and-seek without a goddamn gas mask. Miss Moore was her name. The only woman on the block with no first name. And she was black as hell, cept for her feet, which were fish-white and spooky. And she was always planning these boring-ass things for us to do, us being my cousin, mostly, who lived on the block cause we all moved North the same time and to the same apartment then spread out gradual to breathe. And our parents would yank our heads into some kinda shape and crisp up our clothes so we'd be presentable for travel with Miss Moore, who always looked like she was going to church, though she never did. Which is just one of the things the grownups talked about when they talked behind her back like a dog. But when she came calling with some sachet she'd sewed up or some gingerbread she'd made or some book, why then they'd all be too embarrassed to turn her down and we'd get handed over all spruced up. She'd been to college and said it was only right that she should take responsibility for the young ones' education, and she not even related by marriage or blood. So they'd go for it. Specially Aunt Gretchen. She was the main gofer in the family. You got some ole dumb shit foolishness you want somebody to go for, you send for Aunt Gretchen. She been screwed into the go-along for so long, it's a blood-deep natural thing with her. Which is how she got saddled with me and Sugar and Junior in the first place while our mothers were in a la-de-da apartment up the block having a good ole time.

So this one day, Miss Moore rounds us all up at the mailbox and it's puredee hot and she's knockin herself out about arithmetic. And school suppose to let up in summer I heard, but she don't never let up. And the starch in my pinafore scratching the shit outta me and I'm really hating this nappy-head bitch and her goddamn college degree. I'd much rather go to the pool or to the show where it's cool. So me and Sugar leaning on the mailbox being surly, which is a Miss Moore word. And Flyboy checking out what everybody brought for lunch. And Fat Butt already wasting his peanut-butter-and-jelly sandwich like the pig he is. And Junebug punchin on Q.T.'s arm for potato chips. And Rosie Giraffe shifting from one hip to the other waiting for somebody to step on her foot or ask her if she from Georgia so she can kick ass, preferably Mercedes'. And Miss Moore asking us do we know what money is, like we a bunch of retards. I mean real money, she say, like it's only poker chips or monopoly papers we lay on the grocer. So right away I'm tired of this and say so. And would much rather snatch Sugar and go to the Sunset and terrorize the West Indian kids and take their hair ribbons and their money too. And Miss Moore files that remark away for next week's lesson on brotherhood, I can tell. And finally I say we oughta get to the subway cause it's cooler and besides we might meet some cute boys. Sugar done swiped her mama's lipstick, so we ready.

So we heading down the street and she's boring us silly about what things cost and what our parents make and how much goes for rent and how money ain't divided up right in this country. And then she gets to the part about we all poor and live in the slums, which I don't feature. And I'm ready to speak on that, but she steps out in the street and hails two cabs just like that. Then she hustles half the crew in with her and hands me a five-dollar bill and tells me to calculate 10 percent tip for the driver. And we're off. Me and Sugar and Junebug and Flyboy hangin out the window and hollering to everybody, putting lipstick on each other cause Flyboy a faggot anyway, and making farts with our sweaty armpits. But I'm mostly trying to figure how to spend this money. But they all fascinated with the meter ticking and Junebug starts laying bets as to how much it'll read when Flyboy can't hold his breath no more. Then Sugar lays bets as to how much it'll be when we get there. So I'm stuck. Don't nobody want to go for my plan, which is to jump out at the next light and run off to the first bar-b-que we can find. Then the driver tells us to get the hell out cause we there already. And the meter reads eighty-five cents. And I'm stalling to figure out the tip and Sugar say give him a dime. And I decide he don't need it bad as I do, so later for him. But then he tries to take off with Junebug foot still in the door so we talk about his mama something ferocious. Then we check out that we on Fifth Avenue and everybody dressed up in stockings. One lady in a fur coat, hot as it is. White folks crazy.

"This is the place," Miss Moore say, presenting it to us in the voice she uses at the museum. "Let's look in the windows before we go in."

"Can we steal?" Sugar asks very serious like she's getting the ground rules squared away before she plays. "I beg your pardon," say Miss Moore, and we fall out. So she leads us around the windows of the toy store and me and Sugar screamin, "This is mine, that's mine, I gotta have that, that was made for me, I was born for that," till Big Butt drowns us out.

"Hey, I'm going to buy that there."

"That there? You don't even know what it is, stupid."

"I do so," he say punchin on Rosie Giraffe. "It's a microscope."

"Whatcha gonna do with a microscope, fool?"

"Look at things."

"Like what, Ronald?" ask Miss Moore. And Big Butt ain't got the first notion. So here go Miss Moore gabbing about the thousands of bacteria in a drop of water and the somethinorother in a speck of blood and the million and one living things in the air around us is invisible to the naked eye. And what she say that for? Junebug go to town on that "naked" and we rolling. Then Miss Moore ask what it cost. So we all jam into the window smudgin it up and the price tag say $300. So then she ask how long'd take for Big Butt and Junebug to save up their allowances. "Too long," I say. "Yeh," adds Sugar, "outgrown it by that time." And Miss Moore say no, you never outgrow learning instruments. "Why, even medical students and interns and," blah, blah, blah. And we ready to choke Big Butt for bringing it up in the first damn place.

"This here costs four hundred eighty dollars," say Rosie Giraffe. So we pile up all over her to see what she pointin out. My eyes tell me it's a chunk of glass cracked with something heavy, and different-color inks dripped into the splits, then the whole thing put into a oven or something. But for $480 it don't make sense.

"That's a paperweight made of semi-precious stones fused together under tremendous pressure," she explains slowly, with her hands doing the mining and all the factory work.

"So what's a paperweight?" ask Rosie Giraffe.

"To weigh paper with, dumbbell," say Flyboy, the wise man from the East.

"Not exactly," say Miss Moore, which is what she say when you warm or way off too. "It's to weigh paper down so it won't scatter and make your desk untidy." So right away me and Sugar curtsy to each other and then to Mercedes who is more the tidy type.

"We don't keep paper on top of the desk in my class," say Junebug, figuring Miss Moore crazy or lyin one.

"At home, then," she say. "Don't you have a calendar and a pencil case and a blotter and a letter-opener on your desk at home where you do your homework?" And she know damn well what our homes look like cause she nosys around in them every chance she gets.

"I don't even have a desk," say Junebug. "Do we?"

"No. And I don't get no homework neither," say Big Butt.

"And I don't even have a home," say Flyboy like he do at school to keep the white folks off his back and sorry for him. Send this poor kid to camp posters, is his specialty.

"I do," says Mercedes. "I have a box of stationery on my desk and a picture of my cat. My godmother bought the stationery and the desk. There's a big rose on each sheet and the envelopes smell like roses."

"Who wants to know about your smelly-ass stationery," say Rosie Giraffe fore I can get my two cents in.

"It's important to have a work area all your own so that . . ."

"Will you look at this sailboat, please," say Flyboy, cutting her off and pointin to the thing like it was his. So once again we tumble all over each other to gaze at this magnificent thing in the toy store which is just big enough to maybe sail two kittens across the pond if you strap them to the posts tight. We all start reciting the price tag like we in assembly. "Hand-crafted sailboat of fiberglass at one thousand one hundred ninety-five dollars."

"Unbelievable," I hear myself say and am really stunned. I read it again for myself just in case the group recitation put me in a trance. Same thing. For some reason this pisses me off. We look at Miss Moore and she lookin at us, waiting for I dunno what.

"Who'd pay all that when you can buy a sailboat set for a quarter at Pop's, a tube of glue for a dime, and a ball of string for eight cents? It must have a motor and a whole lot else besides," I say. "My sailboat cost me about fifty cents."

"But will it take water?" say Mercedes with her smart ass.

"Took mine to Alley Pond Park once," say Flyboy. "String broke. Lost it. Pity."

"Sailed mine in Central Park and it keeled over and sank. Had to ask my father for another dollar."

"And you got the strap," laugh Big Butt. "The jerk didn't even have a string on it. My old man wailed on his behind."

Little Q.T. was staring hard at the sailboat and you could see he wanted it bad. But he too little and somebody'd just take it from him. So what the hell. "This boat for kids, Miss Moore?"

"Parents silly to buy something like that just to get all broke up," say Rosie Giraffe.

"That much money it should last forever," I figure.

"My father'd buy it for me if I wanted it."

"Your father, my ass," say Rosie Giraffe getting a chance to finally push Mercedes.

"Must be rich people shop here," say Q.T.

"You are a very bright boy," say Flyboy. "What was your first clue?" And he rap him on the head with the back of his knuckles, since Q.T. the only one he could get away with. Though Q.T. liable to come up behind you years later and get his licks in when you half expect it.

"What I want to know is," I says to Miss Moore though I never talk to her, I wouldn't give the bitch that satisfaction, "is how much a real boat costs? I figure a thousand'd get you a yacht any day."

"Why don't you check that out," she says, "and report back to the group?" Which really pains my ass. If you gonna mess up a perfectly good swim day least you could do is have some answers. "Let's go in," she say like she got something up her sleeve. Only she don't lead the way. So me and Sugar turn the corner to where the entrance is, but when we get there I kinda hang back. Not that I'm scared, what's there to be afraid of, just a toy store. But I feel funny, shame. But what I got to be shamed about? Got as much right to go in as anybody. But somehow I can't seem to get hold of the door, so I step away from Sugar to lead. But she hangs back too. And I look at her and she looks at me and this is ridiculous. I mean, damn, I have never been shy about doing nothing or going nowhere. But then Mercedes steps up and then Rosie Giraffe and Big Butt crowd in behind and shove, and next thing we all stuffed into the doorway with only Mercedes squeezing past us, smoothing out her jumper and walking right down the aisle. Then the rest of us tumble in like a glued-together jigsaw done all wrong. And people lookin at us. And it's like the time me and Sugar crashed into the Catholic church on a dare. But once we got in there and everything so hushed and holy and the candles and the bowin and the handkerchiefs on all the drooping heads, I just couldn't go through with the plan. Which was for me to run up to the altar and do a tap dance while Sugar played the nose flute and messed around in the holy water. And Sugar kept given me the elbow. Then later teased me so bad I tied her up in the shower and turned it on and locked her in. And she'd be there till this day if Aunt Gretchen hadn't finally figured I was lying about the boarder takin a shower.

Same thing in the store. We all walkin on tiptoe and hardly touchin the games and puzzles and things. And I watched Miss Moore who is steady watchin us like she waitin for a sign. Like Mama Drewery watches the sky and sniffs the air and takes note of just how much slant is in the bird formation. Then me and Sugar bump smack into each other, so busy gazing at the toys, 'specially the sailboat. But we don't laugh and go into our fat-lady bump-stomach routine. We just stare at that price tag. Then Sugar run a finger over the whole boat. And I'm jealous and want to hit her. Maybe not her, but I sure want to punch somebody in the mouth.

"Watcha bring us here for, Miss Moore?"

"You sound angry, Sylvia. Are you mad about something?" Givin me one of them grins like she tellin a grown-up joke that never turns out to be funny. And she's lookin very closely at me like maybe she plannin to do my portrait from memory. I'm mad, but I won't give her that satisfaction. So I slouch around the store being very bored and say, "Let's go."

Me and Sugar at the back of the train watchin the tracks whizzin by large then small then getting gobbled up in the dark. I'm thinkin about this tricky toy I saw in the store. A clown that somersaults on a bar then does chin-ups just cause you yank lightly at his leg. Cost $35. I could see me askin my mother for a $35 birthday clown. "You wanna who that costs what?" she'd say, cocking her head to the side to get a better view of the hole in my head. Thirty-five dollars could buy new bunk beds for Junior and Gretchen's boy. Thirty-five dollars and the whole household could go visit Grand-daddy Nelson in the country. Thirty-five dollars would pay for the rent and the piano bill too. Who are these people that spend that much for performing clowns and $1000 for toy sailboats? What kinda work they do and how they live and how come we ain't in on it? Where we are is who we are, Miss Moore always pointin out. But it don't necessarily have to be that way, she always adds then waits for somebody to say that poor people have to wake up and demand their share of the pie and don't none of us know what kind of pie she talking about in the first damn place. But she ain't so smart cause I still got her four dollars from the taxi and she sure ain't gettin it. Messin up my day with this shit. Sugar nudges me in my pocket and winks.

Miss Moore lines us up in front of the mailbox where we started from, seem like years ago, and I got a headache for thinkin so hard. And we lean all over each other so we can hold up under the draggy-ass lecture she always finishes us off with at the end before we thank her for borin us to tears. But she just looks at us like she readin tea leaves. Finally she say, "Well, what did you think of F.A.O. Schwarz?"

Rosie Giraffe mumbles, "White folks crazy."

"I'd like to go there again when I get my birthday money," says Mercedes, and we shove her out the pack so she has to lean on the mailbox by herself.

"I'd like a shower. Tiring day," say Flyboy.

Then Sugar surprises me by sayin, "You know, Miss Moore, I don't think all of us here put together eat in a year what that sailboat costs." And Miss Moore lights up like somebody goosed her. "And?" she say, urging Sugar on. Only I'm standin on her foot so she don't continue.

"Imagine for a minute what kind of society it is in which some people can spend on a toy what it would cost to feed a family of six or seven. What do you think?"

"I think," say Sugar pushing me off her feet like she never done before, cause I whip her ass in a minute, "that this is not much of a democracy if you ask me. Equal chance to pursue happiness means an equal crack at the dough, don't it?" Miss Moore is besides herself and I am disgusted with Sugar's treachery. So I stand on her foot one more time to see if she'll shove me. She shuts up, and Miss Moore looks at me, sorrowfully I'm thinkin. And somethin weird is goin on, I can feel it in my chest.

"Anybody else learn anything today?" lookin dead at me. I walk away and Sugar has to run to catch up and don't even seem to notice when I shrug her arm off my shoulder.

"Well, we got four dollars anyway," she says.

"Uh, hunh."

"We could go to Hascombs and get half a chocolate layer and then go to the Sunset and still have plenty money for potato chips and ice cream sodas."

"Uh, hunh."

"Race you to Hascombs," she say.

We start down the block and she gets ahead which is O.K. by me cause I'm going to the West End and then over to the Drive to think this day through. She can run if she want to and even run faster. But ain't nobody gonna beat me at nuthin.

[1972]

[handwritten: - Acceptance of who she is and not being Ms. Moore]
[handwritten: - Change in confidence]

ALICE WALKER   [b. 1944]

Everyday Use

For Your Grandmama

I will wait for her in the yard that Maggie and I made so clean and wavy yesterday afternoon. A yard like this is more comfortable than most people know. It is not just a yard. It is like an extended living room. When the hard clay is swept clean as a floor and the fine sand around the edges lined with tiny, irregular grooves, anyone can come and sit and look up into the elm tree and wait for the breezes that never come inside the house.

Maggie will be nervous until after her sister goes: she will stand hopelessly in corners, homely and ashamed of the burn scars down her arms and legs, eying her sister with a mixture of envy and awe. She thinks her sister has held life always in the palm of one hand, that "no" is a word the world never learned to say to her.

You've no doubt seen those TV shows where the child who has "made it" is confronted, as a surprise, by her own mother and father, tottering in weakly from backstage. (A pleasant surprise, of course: What would they do if parent and child came on the show only to curse out and insult each other?) On TV mother and child embrace and smile into each other's faces. Sometimes the mother and father weep, the child wraps them in her arms and leans across the table to tell how she would not have made it without their help. I have seen these programs.

Sometimes I dream a dream in which Dee and I are suddenly brought together on a TV program of this sort. Out of a dark and soft-seated limousine I am ushered into a bright room filled with many people. There I meet a smiling, gray, sporty man like Johnny Carson° who shakes my hand and tells me what a fine girl I have. Then we are on the stage and Dee is embracing me with tears in her eyes. She pins on my dress a large orchid, even though she has told me once that she thinks orchids are tacky flowers.

In real life I am a large, big-boned woman with rough, man-working hands. In the winter I wear flannel nightgowns to bed and overalls during the day. I can kill and clean a hog as mercilessly as a man. My fat keeps me hot in zero weather. I can work outside all day, breaking ice to get water for washing; I can eat pork liver cooked over the open fire minutes after it comes steaming from the hog. One winter I knocked a bull calf straight in the brain between the eyes with a sledge hammer and had the meat hung up to chill before nightfall. But of course all this does not show on television. I am the way my daughter would want me to be: a hundred pounds lighter, my skin like an uncooked barley pancake. My hair glistens in the hot bright lights. Johnny Carson has much to do to keep up with my quick and witty tongue.

But that is a mistake. I know even before I wake up. Who ever knew a Johnson with a quick tongue? Who can even imagine me looking a strange white man in the eye? It seems to me I have talked to them always with one foot raised in flight, with my head turned in whichever way is farthest from them. Dee, though. She would always look anyone in the eye. Hesitation was no part of her nature.

"How do I look, Mama?" Maggie says, showing just enough of her thin body enveloped in pink skirt and red blouse for me to know she's there, almost hidden by the door.

"Come out into the yard," I say.

Have you ever seen a lame animal, perhaps a dog run over by some careless person rich enough to own a car, sidle up to someone who is ignorant enough to be kind to him? That is the way my Maggie walks. She has been like this, chin on chest, eyes on ground, feet in shuffle, ever since the fire that burned the other house to the ground.

Johnny Carson (1925–2005): Late-night talk-show host and comedian. *The Tonight Show* starring Johnny Carson was on the air from 1962 to 1992.

Dee is lighter than Maggie, with nicer hair and a fuller figure. She's a woman now, though sometimes I forget. How long ago was it that the other house burned? Ten, twelve years? Sometimes I can still hear the flames and feel Maggie's arms sticking to me, her hair smoking and her dress falling off her in little black papery flakes. Her eyes seemed stretched open, blazed open by the flames reflected in them. And Dee. I see her standing off under the sweet gum tree she used to dig gum out of; a look of concentration on her face as she watched the last dingy gray board of the house fall in toward the red-hot brick chimney. Why don't you do a dance around the ashes? I'd want to ask her. She had hated the house that much.

I used to think she hated Maggie, too. But that was before we raised the money, the church and me, to send her to Augusta to school. She used to read to us without pity; forcing words, lies, other folks' habits, whole lives upon us two, sitting trapped and ignorant underneath her voice. She washed us in a river of make-believe, burned us with a lot of knowledge we didn't necessarily need to know. Pressed us to her with the serious way she read, to shove us away at just the moment, like dimwits, we seemed about to understand.

Dee wanted nice things. A yellow organdy dress to wear to her graduation from high school; black pumps to match a green suit she'd made from an old suit somebody gave me. She was determined to stare down any disaster in her efforts. Her eyelids would not flicker for minutes at a time. Often I fought off the temptation to shake her. At sixteen she had a style of her own: and knew what style was.

I never had an education myself. After second grade the school was closed down. Don't ask me why: in 1927 colored asked fewer questions than they do now. Sometimes Maggie reads to me. She stumbles along good-naturedly but can't see well. She knows she is not bright. Like good looks and money, quickness passed her by. She will marry John Thomas (who has mossy teeth in an earnest face) and then I'll be free to sit here and I guess just sing church songs to myself. Although I never was a good singer. Never could carry a tune. I was always better at a man's job. I used to love to milk till I was hooked in the side in '49. Cows are soothing and slow and don't bother you, unless you try to milk them the wrong way.

I have deliberately turned my back on the house. It is three rooms, just like the one that burned, except the roof is tin; they don't make shingle roofs any more. There are no real windows, just some holes cut in the sides, like the portholes in a ship, but not round and not square, with rawhide holding the shutters up on the outside. This house is in a pasture, too, like the other one. No doubt when Dee sees it she will want to tear it down. She wrote me once that no matter where we "choose" to live, she will manage to come see us. But she will never bring her friends. Maggie and I thought about this and Maggie asked me, "Mama, when did Dee ever *have* any friends?"

She had a few. Furtive boys in pink shirts hanging about on wash-day after school. Nervous girls who never laughed. Impressed with her they worshipped the well-turned phrase, the cute shape, the scalding humor that erupted like bubbles in lye. She read to them.

When she was courting Jimmy T she didn't have much time to pay to us, but turned all her faultfinding power on him. He *flew* to marry a cheap city girl from a family of ignorant flashy people. She hardly had time to recompose herself.

When she comes I will meet—but there they are!

Maggie attempts to make a dash for the house, in her shuffling way, but I stay her with my hand. "Come back here," I say. And she stops and tries to dig a well in the sand with her toe.

It is hard to see them clearly through the strong sun. But even the first glimpse of leg out of the car tells me it is Dee. Her feet were always neat-looking, as if God himself had shaped them with a certain style. From the other side of the car comes a short, stocky man. Hair is all over his head a foot long and hanging from his chin like a kinky mule tail. I hear Maggie suck in her breath. "Uhnnnh," is what it sounds like. Like when you see the wriggling end of a snake just in front of your foot on the road. "Uhnnnh."

Dee next. A dress down to the ground, in this hot weather. A dress so loud it hurts my eyes. There are yellows and oranges enough to throw back the light of the sun. I feel my whole face warming from the heat waves it throws out. Earrings gold, too, and hanging down to her shoulders. Bracelets dangling and making noises when she moves her arm up to shake the folds of the dress out of her armpits. The dress is loose and flows, and as she walks closer, I like it. I hear Maggie go "Uhnnnh" again. It is her sister's hair. It stands straight up like the wool on a sheep. It is black as night and around the edges are two long pigtails that rope about like small lizards disappearing behind her ears.

"Wa-su-zo-Tean-o!" she says, coming on in that gliding way the dress makes her move. The short stocky fellow with the hair to his navel is all grinning and he follows up with "Asalamalakim, my mother and sister!" He moves to hug Maggie but she falls back, right up against the back of my chair. I feel her trembling there and when I look up I see the perspiration falling off her chin.

"Don't get up," says Dee. Since I am stout it takes something of a push. You can see me trying to move a second or two before I make it. She turns, showing white heels through her sandals, and goes back to the car.

Out she peeks next with a Polaroid. She stoops down quickly and lines up picture after picture of me sitting there in front of the house with Maggie cowering behind me. She never takes a shot without making sure the house is included. When a cow comes nibbling around the edge of the yard she snaps it and me and Maggie *and* the house. Then she puts the Polaroid in the back seat of the car, and comes up and kisses me on the forehead.

Meanwhile Asalamalakim is going through motions with Maggie's hand. Maggie's hand is as limp as a fish, and probably as cold, despite the sweat, and she keeps trying to pull it back. It looks like Asalamalakim wants to shake hands but wants to do it fancy. Or maybe he don't know how people shake hands. Anyhow, he soon gives up on Maggie.

"Well," I say. "Dee."

"No, Mama," she says. "Not 'Dee,' Wangero Leewanika Kemanjo!"

"What happened to 'Dee'?" I wanted to know.

"She's dead," Wangero said. "I couldn't bear it any longer, being named after the people who oppress me."

"You know as well as me you was named after your aunt Dicie," I said. Dicie is my sister. She named Dee. We called her "Big Dee" after Dee was born.

"But who was *she* named after?" asked Wangero.

"I guess after Grandma Dee," I said.

"And who was she named after?" asked Wangero.

"Her mother," I said, and saw Wangero was getting tired. "That's about as far back as I can trace it," I said. Though, in fact, I probably could have carried it back beyond the Civil War through the branches.

"Well," said Asalamalakim, "there you are."

"Uhnnnh," I heard Maggie say.

"There I was not," I said, "before 'Dicie' cropped up in our family, so why should I try to trace it that far back?"

He just stood there grinning, looking down on me like somebody inspecting a Model A car. Every once in a while he and Wangero sent eye signals over my head.

"How do you pronounce this name?" I asked.

"You don't have to call me by it if you don't want to," said Wangero.

"Why shouldn't I?" I asked. "If that's what you want us to call you, we'll call you."

"I know it might sound awkward at first," said Wangero.

"I'll get used to it," I said. "Ream it out again."

Well, soon we got the name out of the way. Asalamalakim had a name twice as long and three times as hard. After I tripped over it two or three times he told me to just call him Hakim-a-barber. I wanted to ask him was he a barber, but I didn't really think he was, so I didn't ask.

"You must belong to those beef-cattle peoples down the road," I said. They said "Asalamalakim" when they met you, too, but they didn't shake hands. Always too busy: feeding the cattle, fixing the fences, putting up salt-lick shelters, throwing down hay. When the white folks poisoned some of the herd the men stayed up all night with rifles in their hands. I walked a mile and a half just to see the sight.

Hakim-a-barber said, "I accept some of their doctrines, but farming and raising cattle is not my style." (They didn't tell me, and I didn't ask, whether Wangero (Dee) had really gone and married him.)

We sat down to eat and right away he said he didn't eat collards and pork was unclean. Wangero, though, went on through the chitlins and corn bread, the greens and everything else. She talked a blue streak over the sweet potatoes. Everything delighted her. Even the fact that we still used the benches her daddy made for the table when we couldn't afford to buy chairs.

"Oh, Mama!" she cried. Then turned to Hakim-a-barber. "I never knew how lovely these benches are. You can feel the rump prints," she said, running her hands underneath her and long the bench. Then she gave a sigh and her hand closed over Grandma Dee's butter dish. "That's it!" she said. "I knew there was something I wanted to ask you if I could have." She jumped up from the table and went over in the corner where the churn stood, the milk in it clabber by now. She looked at the churn and looked at it.

"This churn top is what I need," she said. "Didn't Uncle Buddy whittle it out of a tree you all used to have?"

"Yes," I said.

"Uh huh," she said happily. "And I want the dasher, too."

"Uncle Buddy whittle that, too?" asked the barber.

Dee (Wangero) looked up at me.

"Aunt Dee's first husband whittled the dash," said Maggie so low you almost couldn't hear her. "His name was Henry, but they called him Stash."

"Maggie's brain is like an elephant's," Wangero said, laughing. "I can use the churn top as a centerpiece for the alcove table," she said, sliding a plate over the churn, "and I'll think of something artistic to do with the dasher."

When she finished wrapping the dasher the handle stuck out. I took it for a moment in my hands. You didn't even have to look close to see where hands pushing the dasher up and down to make butter had left a kind of sink in the wood. In fact, there were a lot of small sinks; you could see where thumbs and fingers had sunk into the wood. It was beautiful light yellow wood, from a tree that grew in the yard where Big Dee and Stash had lived.

After dinner Dee (Wangero) went to the trunk at the foot of my bed and started rifling through it. Maggie hung back in the kitchen over the dish-pan. Out came Wangero with two quilts. They had been pieced by Grandma Dee and then Big Dee and me had hung them on the quilt frames on the front porch and quilted them. One was in the Lone Star pattern. The other was Walk Around the Mountain. In both of them were scraps of dresses Grandma Dee had worn fifty and more years ago. Bits and pieces of Grandpa Jarrell's Paisley shirts. And one teeny faded blue piece, about the size of a penny matchbox, that was from Great Grandpa Ezra's uniform that he wore in the Civil War.

"Mama," Wangero said sweet as a bird. "Can I have these old quilts?"

I heard something fall in the kitchen, and a minute later the kitchen door slammed.

"Why don't you take one or two of the others?" I asked. "These old things was just done by me and Big Dee from some tops your grandma pieced before she died."

"No," said Wangero. "I don't want those. They are stitched around the borders by machine."

"That'll make them last better," I said.

"That's not the point," said Wangero. "These are all pieces of dresses Grandma used to wear. She did all this stitching by hand. Imagine!" She held the quilts securely in her arms, stroking them.

"Some of the pieces, like those lavender ones, come from old clothes her mother handed down to her," I said, moving up to touch the quilts. Dee (Wangero) moved back just enough so that I couldn't reach the quilts. They already belonged to her.

"Imagine!" she breathed again, clutching them closely to her bosom.

"The truth is," I said, "I promised to give them quilts to Maggie, for when she marries John Thomas."

She gasped like a bee had stung her.

"Maggie can't appreciate these quilts!" she said. "She'd probably be backward enough to put them to everyday use."

"I reckon she would," I said. "God knows I been saving 'em for long enough with nobody using 'em. I hope she will!" I didn't want to bring up how I had offered Dee (Wangero) a quilt when she went away to college. Then she had told me they were old-fashioned, out of style.

"But they're *priceless*!" she was saying now, furiously; for she has a temper. "Maggie would put them on the bed and in five years they'd be in rags. Less than that!"

"She can always make some more," I said. "Maggie knows how to quilt."

Dee (Wangero) looked at me with hatred. "You just will not understand. The point is these quilts, *these* quilts!"

"Well," I said, stumped. "What would *you* do with them?"

"Hang them," she said. As if that was the only thing you *could* do with quilts.

Maggie by now was standing in the door. I could almost hear the sound her feet made as they scraped over each other.

"She can have them, Mama," she said, like somebody used to never winning anything, or having anything reserved for her. "I can 'member Grandma Dee without the quilts."

I looked at her hard. She had filled her bottom lip with checkerberry snuff and it gave her face a kind of dopey, hangdog look. It was Grandma Dee and Big Dee who taught her how to quilt herself. She stood there with her scarred hands hidden in the folds of her skirt. She looked at her sister with something like fear but she wasn't mad at her. This was Maggie's portion. This was the way she knew God to work.

When I looked at her like that something hit me in the top of my head and ran down to the soles of my feet. Just like when I'm in church and the spirit of God touches me and I get happy and shout. I did something I never had done before: hugged Maggie to me, then dragged her on into the room, snatched the quilts out of Miss Wangero's hands and dumped them into Maggie's lap. Maggie just sat there on my bed with her mouth open.

"Take one or two of the others," I said to Dee.

But she turned without a word and went out to Hakim-a-barber.

"You just don't understand," she said, as Maggie and I came out to the car.

"What don't I understand?" I wanted to know.

"Your heritage," she said. And then she turned to Maggie, kissed her, and said, "You ought to try to make something of yourself, too, Maggie. It's really a new day for us. But from the way you and Mama still live you'd never know it."

She put on some sunglasses that hid everything above the tip of her nose and her chin.

Maggie smiled; maybe at the sunglasses. But a real smile, not scared. After we watched the car dust settle I asked Maggie to bring me a dip of snuff. And then the two of us sat there just enjoying, until it was time to go in the house and go to bed.

[1973]

TIM O'BRIEN [b. 1946]

The Things They Carried

First Lieutenant Jimmy Cross carried letters from a girl named Martha, a junior at Mount Sebastian College in New Jersey. They were not love letters, but Lieutenant Cross was hoping, so he kept them folded in plastic at the bottom of his rucksack. In the late afternoon, after a day's march, he would dig his foxhole, wash his hands under a canteen, unwrap the letters, hold them with the tips of his fingers, and spend the last hour of light pretending. He would imagine romantic camping trips into the White Mountains in New Hampshire. He would sometimes taste the envelope flaps, knowing her tongue had been there. More than anything, he wanted Martha to love him as he loved her, but the letters were mostly chatty, elusive on the matter of love. She was a virgin, he was almost sure. She was an English major at Mount Sebastian, and she wrote beautifully about her professors and roommates and midterm exams, about her respect for Chaucer and her great affection for Virginia Woolf. She often quoted lines of poetry; she never mentioned the war, except to say, Jimmy, take care of yourself. The letters weighed ten ounces. They were signed "Love, Martha," but Lieutenant Cross understood that "Love" was only a way of signing and did not mean what he sometimes pretended it meant. At dusk, he would carefully return the letters to his rucksack. Slowly, a bit distracted, he would get up and move among his men, checking the perimeter, then at full dark he would return to his hole and watch the night and wonder if Martha was a virgin.

The things they carried were largely determined by necessity. Among the necessities or near necessities were P-38 can openers, pocket knives, heat tabs, wrist watches, dog tags, mosquito repellant, chewing gum, candy, cigarettes, salt tablets, packets of Kool-Aid, lighters, matches, sewing kits, Military Payment Certificates, C rations,° and two or three canteens of water. Together, these items weighed between fifteen and twenty pounds, depending upon a man's habits or rate of metabolism. Henry Dobbins, who was a big man, carried extra rations; he was especially fond of canned peaches in heavy syrup over pound cake. Dave Jensen, who practiced field hygiene, carried a toothbrush, dental floss, and several hotel-size bars of

C rations: Combat rations.

soap he'd stolen on R&R in Sydney, Australia. Ted Lavender, who was scared, carried tranquilizers until he was shot in the head outside the village of Than Khe in mid-April. By necessity, and because it was SOP,° they all carried steel helmets that weighed five pounds including the liner and camouflage cover. They carried the standard fatigue jackets and trousers. Very few carried underwear. On their feet they carried jungle boots—2.1 pounds—and Dave Jensen carried three pairs of socks and a can of Dr. Scholl's foot powder as a precaution against trench foot. Until he was shot, Ted Lavender carried six or seven ounces of premium dope, which for him was a necessity. Mitchell Sanders, the RTO,° carried condoms. Norman Bowker carried a diary. Rat Kiley carried comic books. Kiowa, a devout Baptist, carried an illustrated New Testament that had been presented to him by his father, who taught Sunday school in Oklahoma City, Oklahoma. As a hedge against bad times, however, Kiowa also carried his grandmother's distrust of the white man, his grandfather's old hunting hatchet. Necessity dictated. Because the land was mined and booby-trapped, it was SOP for each man to carry a steel-centered, nylon-covered flak jacket, which weighed 6.7 pounds, but which on hot days seemed much heavier. Because you could die so quickly, each man carried at least one large compress bandage, usually in the helmet band for easy access. Because the nights were cold, and because the monsoons were wet, each carried a green plastic poncho that could be used as a raincoat or ground sheet or makeshift tent. With its quilted liner, the poncho weighed almost two pounds, but it was worth every ounce. In April, for instance, when Ted Lavender was shot, they used his poncho to wrap him up, then to carry him across the paddy, then to lift him into the chopper that took him away.

They were called legs or grunts.

To carry something was to "hump" it, as when Lieutenant Jimmy Cross humped his love for Martha up the hills and through the swamps. In its intransitive form, "to hump" meant "to walk," or "to march," but it implied burdens far beyond the intransitive.

Almost everyone humped photographs. In his wallet, Lieutenant Cross carried two photographs of Martha. The first was a Kodachrome snapshot signed "Love," though he knew better. She stood against a brick wall. Her eyes were gray and neutral, her lips slightly open as she stared straight-on at the camera. At night, sometimes, Lieutenant Cross wondered who had taken the picture, because he knew she had boyfriends, because he loved her so much, and because he could see the shadow of the picture taker spreading out against the brick wall. The second photograph

SOP: Standard operating procedure.
RTO: Radiotelephone operator.

had been clipped from the 1968 Mount Sebastian yearbook. It was an action shot—women's volleyball—and Martha was bent horizontal to the floor, reaching, the palms of her hands in sharp focus, the tongue taut, the expression frank and competitive. There was no visible sweat. She wore white gym shorts. Her legs, he thought, were almost certainly the legs of a virgin, dry and without hair, the left knee cocked and carrying her entire weight, which was just over one hundred pounds. Lieutenant Cross remembered touching that left knee. A dark theater, he remembered, and the movie was *Bonnie and Clyde*, and Martha wore a tweed skirt, and during the final scene, when he touched her knee, she turned and looked at him in a sad, sober way that made him pull his hand back, but he would always remember the feel of the tweed skirt and the knee beneath it and the sound of the gunfire that killed Bonnie and Clyde, how embarrassing it was, how slow and oppressive. He remembered kissing her good night at the dorm door. Right then, he thought, he should've done something brave. He should've carried her up the stairs to her room and tied her to the bed and touched that left knee all night long. He should've risked it. Whenever he looked at the photographs, he thought of new things he should've done.

What they carried was partly a function of rank, partly of field specialty.

As a first lieutenant and platoon leader, Jimmy Cross carried a compass, maps, code books, binoculars, and a .45-caliber pistol that weighed 2.9 pounds fully loaded. He carried a strobe light and the responsibility for the lives of his men.

As an RTO, Mitchell Sanders carried the PRC-25 radio, a killer, twenty-six pounds with its battery.

As a medic, Rat Kiley carried a canvas satchel filled with morphine and plasma and malaria tablets and surgical tape and comic books and all the things a medic must carry, including M&M's for especially bad wounds, for a total weight of nearly twenty pounds.

As a big man, therefore a machine gunner, Henry Dobbins carried the M-60, which weighed twenty-three pounds unloaded, but which was almost always loaded. In addition, Dobbins carried between ten and fifteen pounds of ammunition draped in belts across his chest and shoulders.

As PFCs° or Spec 4s,° most of them were common grunts and carried the standard M-16 gas-operated assault rifle. The weapon weighed 7.5 pounds unloaded, 8.2 pounds with its full twenty-round magazine. Depending on numerous factors, such as topography and psychology, the riflemen carried anywhere from twelve to twenty magazines, usually in

PFCs: Privates first class.
Spec 4s: Specialists fourth class, rank equivalent to that of corporal.

cloth bandoliers, adding on another 8.4 pounds at minimum, fourteen pounds at maximum. When it was available, they also carried M-16 maintenance gear—rods and steel brushes and swabs and tubes of LSA oil°—all of which weighed about a pound. Among the grunts, some carried the M-79 grenade launcher, 5.9 pounds unloaded, a reasonably light weapon except for the ammunition, which was heavy. A single round weighed ten ounces. The typical load was twenty-five rounds. But Ted Lavender, who was scared, carried thirty-four rounds when he was shot and killed outside Than Khe, and he went down under an exceptional burden, more than twenty pounds of ammunition, plus the flak jacket and helmet and rations and water and toilet paper and tranquilizers and all the rest, plus the unweighed fear. He was dead weight. There was no twitching or flopping. Kiowa, who saw it happen, said it was like watching a rock fall, or a big sandbag or something—just boom, then down—not like the movies where the dead guy rolls around and does fancy spins and goes ass over teakettle—not like that, Kiowa said, the poor bastard just flat-fuck fell. Boom. Down. Nothing else. It was a bright morning in mid-April. Lieutenant Cross felt the pain. He blamed himself. They stripped off Lavender's canteens and ammo, all the heavy things, and Rat Kiley said the obvious, the guy's dead, and Mitchell Sanders used his radio to report one U.S. KIA° and to request a chopper. Then they wrapped Lavender in his poncho. They carried him out to a dry paddy, established security, and sat smoking the dead man's dope until the chopper came. Lieutenant Cross kept to himself. He pictured Martha's smooth young face, thinking he loved her more than anything, more than his men, and now Ted Lavender was dead because he loved her so much and could not stop thinking about her. When the dust-off arrived, they carried Lavender aboard. Afterward they burned Than Khe. They marched until dusk, then dug their holes, and that night Kiowa kept explaining how you had to be there, how fast it was, how the poor guy just dropped like so much concrete. Boom-down, he said. Like cement.

In addition to the three standard weapons—the M-60, M-16, and M-79—they carried whatever presented itself, or whatever seemed appropriate as a means of killing or staying alive. They carried catch-as-catch-can. At various times, in various situations, they carried M-14s and CAR-15s and Swedish Ks and grease guns and captured AK-47s and Chi-Coms and RPGs and Simonov carbines and black-market Uzis and .38-caliber Smith & Wesson handguns and 66 mm LAWs and shotguns and silencers and blackjacks and bayonets and C-4 plastic explosives. Lee Strunk

LSA oil: Lube-small-arms oil.
KIA: Killed in action.

Plot-Lavender's early Death provides more empathy

carried a slingshot; a weapon of last resort, he called it. Mitchell Sanders carried brass knuckles. Kiowa carried his grandfather's feathered hatchet. Every third or fourth man carried a Claymore antipersonnel mine — 3.5 pounds with its firing device. They all carried fragmentation grenades — fourteen ounces each. They all carried at least one M-18 colored smoke grenade — twenty-four ounces. Some carried CS or tear-gas grenades. Some carried white-phosphorus grenades. They carried all they could bear, and then some, including a silent awe for the terrible power of the things they carried.

In the first week of April, before Lavender died, Lieutenant Jimmy Cross received a good-luck charm from Martha. It was a simple pebble, an ounce at most. Smooth to the touch, it was a milky-white color with flecks of orange and violet, oval-shaped, like a miniature egg. In the accompanying letter, Martha wrote that she had found the pebble on the Jersey shoreline, precisely where the land touched water at high tide, where things came together but also separated. It was this separate-but-together quality, she wrote, that had inspired her to pick up the pebble and to carry it in her breast pocket for several days, where it seemed weightless, and then to send it through the mail, by air, as a token of her truest feelings for him. Lieutenant Cross found this romantic. But he wondered what her truest feelings were, exactly, and what she meant by separate-but-together. He wondered how the tides and waves had come into play on that afternoon along the Jersey shoreline when Martha saw the pebble and bent down to rescue it from geology. He imagined bare feet. Martha was a poet, with the poet's sensibilities, and her feet would be brown and bare, the toenails unpainted, the eyes chilly and somber like the ocean in March, and though it was painful, he wondered who had been with her that afternoon. He imagined a pair of shadows moving along the strip of sand where things came together but also separated. It was phantom jealousy, he knew, but he couldn't help himself. He loved her so much. On the march, through the hot days of early April, he carried the pebble in his mouth, turning it with his tongue, tasting sea salts and moisture. His mind wandered. He had difficulty keeping his attention on the war. On occasion he would yell at his men to spread out the column, to keep their eyes open, but then he would slip away into daydreams, just pretending, walking barefoot along the Jersey shore, with Martha, carrying nothing. He would feel himself rising. Sun and waves and gentle winds, all love and lightness.

What they carried varied by mission.

When a mission took them to the mountains, they carried mosquito netting, machetes, canvas tarps, and extra bug juice.

If a mission seemed especially hazardous, or if it involved a place they knew to be bad, they carried everything they could. In certain heavily mined AOs,° where the land was dense with Toe Poppers° and Bouncing Betties,° they took turns humping a twenty-eight-pound mine detector. With its headphones and big sensing plate, the equipment was a stress on the lower back and shoulders, awkward to handle, often useless because of the shrapnel in the earth, but they carried it anyway, partly for safety, partly for the illusion of safety.

On ambush, or other night missions, they carried peculiar little odds and ends. Kiowa always took along his New Testament and a pair of moccasins for silence. Dave Jensen carried night-sight vitamins high in carotin. Lee Strunk carried his slingshot; ammo, he claimed, would never be a problem. Rat Kiley carried brandy and M&M's. Until he was shot, Ted Lavender carried the starlight scope, which weighed 6.3 pounds with its aluminum carrying case. Henry Dobbins carried his girlfriend's pantyhose wrapped around his neck as a comforter. They all carried ghosts. When dark came, they would move out single file across the meadows and paddies to their ambush coordinates, where they would quietly set up the Claymores and lie down and spend the night waiting.

Other missions were more complicated and required special equipment. In mid-April, it was their mission to search out and destroy the elaborate tunnel complexes in the Than Khe area south of Chu Lai. To blow the tunnels, they carried one-pound blocks of pentrite high explosives, four blocks to a man, sixty-eight pounds in all. They carried wiring, detonators, and battery-powered clackers. Dave Jensen carried earplugs. Most often, before blowing the tunnels, they were ordered by higher command to search them, which was considered bad news, but by and large they just shrugged and carried out orders. Because he was a big man, Henry Dobbins was excused from tunnel duty. The others would draw numbers. Before Lavender died there were seventeen men in the platoon, and whoever drew the number seventeen would strip off his gear and crawl in head first with a flashlight and Lieutenant Cross's .45-caliber pistol. The rest of them would fan out as security. They would sit down or kneel, not facing the hole, listening to the ground beneath them, imagining cobwebs and ghosts, whatever was down there—the tunnel walls squeezing in—how the flashlight seemed impossibly heavy in the hand and how it was tunnel vision in the very strictest sense, compression in all ways, even time, and how you had to wiggle in—ass and elbows—a swallowed-up feeling—and how you found yourself worrying

AOs: Areas of operations.
Toe Poppers: Viet Cong antipersonnel land mines with small firing pins.
Bouncing Betties: Bounding fragmentation land mines, the deadliest of all land mines.

about odd things—will your flashlight go dead? Do rats carry rabies? If you screamed, how far would the sound carry? Would your buddies hear it? Would they have the courage to drag you out? In some respects, though not many, the waiting was worse than the tunnel itself. Imagination was a killer.

On April 16, when Lee Strunk drew the number seventeen, he laughed and muttered something and went down quickly. The morning was hot and very still. Not good, Kiowa said. He looked at the tunnel opening, then out across a dry paddy toward the village of Than Khe. Nothing moved. No clouds or birds or people. As they waited, the men smoked and drank Kool-Aid, not talking much, feeling sympathy for Lee Strunk but also feeling the luck of the draw. You win some, you lose some, said Mitchell Sanders, and sometimes you settle for a rain check. It was a tired line and no one laughed.

Henry Dobbins ate a tropical chocolate bar. Ted Lavender popped a tranquilizer and went off to pee.

After five minutes, Lieutenant Jimmy Cross moved to the tunnel, leaned down, and examined the darkness. Trouble, he thought—a cave-in maybe. And then suddenly, without willing it, he was thinking about Martha. The stresses and fractures, the quick collapse, the two of them buried alive under all that weight. Dense, crushing love. Kneeling, watching the hole, he tried to concentrate on Lee Strunk and the war, all the dangers, but his love was too much for him, he felt paralyzed, he wanted to sleep inside her lungs and breathe her blood and be smothered. He wanted her to be a virgin and not a virgin, all at once. He wanted to know her. Intimate secrets—why poetry? Why so sad? Why the grayness in her eyes? Why so alone? Not lonely, just alone—riding her bike across campus or sitting off by herself in the cafeteria. Even dancing, she danced alone—and it was the aloneness that filled him with love. He remembered telling her that one evening. How she nodded and looked away. And how, later, when he kissed her, she received the kiss without returning it, her eyes wide open, not afraid, not a virgin's eyes, just flat and uninvolved.

Lieutenant Cross gazed at the tunnel. But he was not there. He was buried with Martha under the white sand at the Jersey shore. They were pressed together, and the pebble in his mouth was her tongue. He was smiling. Vaguely, he was aware of how quiet the day was, the sullen paddies, yet he could not bring himself to worry about matters of security. He was beyond that. He was just a kid at war, in love. He was twenty-two years old. He couldn't help it.

A few moments later Lee Strunk crawled out of the tunnel. He came up grinning, filthy but alive. Lieutenant Cross nodded and closed his eyes while the others clapped Strunk on the back and made jokes about rising from the dead.

Worms, Rat Kiley said. Right out of the grave. Fuckin' zombie.

The men laughed. They all felt great relief.

Spook City, said Mitchell Sanders.

Lee Strunk made a funny ghost sound, a kind of moaning, yet very happy, and right then, when Strunk made that high happy moaning sound, when he went *Ahhooooo*, right then Ted Lavender was shot in the head on his way back from peeing. He lay with his mouth open. The teeth were broken. There was a swollen black bruise under his left eye. The cheekbone was gone. Oh shit, Rat Kiley said, the guy's dead. The guy's dead, he kept saying, which seemed profound—the guy's dead. I mean really.

The things they carried were determined to some extent by superstition. Lieutenant Cross carried his good-luck pebble. Dave Jensen carried a rabbit's foot. Norman Bowker, otherwise a very gentle person, carried a thumb that had been presented to him as a gift by Mitchell Sanders. The thumb was dark brown, rubbery to the touch, and weighed four ounces at most. It had been cut from a VC° corpse, a boy of fifteen or sixteen. They'd found him at the bottom of an irrigation ditch, badly burned, flies in his mouth and eyes. The boy wore black shorts and sandals. At the time of his death he had been carrying a pouch of rice, a rifle, and three magazines of ammunition.

You want my opinion, Mitchell Sanders said, there's a definite moral here.

He put his hand on the dead boy's wrist. He was quiet for a time, as if counting a pulse, then he patted the stomach, almost affectionately, and used Kiowa's hunting hatchet to remove the thumb.

Henry Dobbins asked what the moral was.

Moral?

You know. *Moral.*

Sanders wrapped the thumb in toilet paper and handed it across to Norman Bowker. There was no blood. Smiling, he kicked the boy's head, watched the flies scatter, and said, It's like with that old TV show—Paladin. Have gun, will travel.

Henry Dobbins thought about it.

Yeah, well, he finally said. I don't see no moral.

There it *is*, man.

Fuck off.

They carried USO stationery and pencils and pens. They carried Sterno, safety pins, trip flares, signal flares, spools of wire, razor blades, chewing tobacco, liberated joss sticks° and statuettes of the smiling Buddha,

---

VC: Vietcong, a guerrilla fighter of the Vietnamese Communist movement.
Joss sticks: Slender sticks of incense.

candles, grease pencils, *The Stars and Stripes*, fingernail clippers, Psy Ops° leaflets, bush hats, bolos, and much more. Twice a week, when the resupply choppers came in, they carried hot chow in green Mermite cans and large canvas bags filled with iced beer and soda pop. They carried plastic water containers, each with a two-gallon capacity. Mitchell Sanders carried a set of starched tiger fatigues for special occasions. Henry Dobbins carried Black Flag insecticide. Dave Jensen carried empty sandbags that could be filled at night for added protection. Lee Strunk carried tanning lotion. Some things they carried in common. Taking turns, they carried the big PRC-77 scrambler radio, which weighed thirty pounds with its battery. They shared the weight of memory. They took up what others could no longer bear. Often, they carried each other, the wounded or weak. They carried infections. They carried chess sets, basketballs, Vietnamese-English dictionaries, insignia of rank, Bronze Stars and Purple Hearts, plastic cards imprinted with the Code of Conduct. They carried diseases, among them malaria and dysentery. They carried lice and ringworm and leeches and paddy algae and various rots and molds. They carried the land itself—Vietnam, the place, the soil—a powdery orange-red dust that covered their boots and fatigues and faces. They carried the sky. The whole atmosphere, they carried it, the humidity, the monsoons, the stink of fungus and decay, all of it, they carried gravity. They moved like mules. By daylight they took sniper fire, at night they were mortared, but it was not battle, it was just the endless march, village to village, without purpose, nothing won or lost. They marched for the sake of the march. They plodded along slowly, dumbly, leaning forward against the heat, unthinking, all blood and bone, simple grunts, soldiering with their legs, toiling up the hills and down into the paddies and across the rivers and up again and down, just humping, one step and then the next and then another, but no volition, no will, because it was automatic, it was anatomy, and the war was entirely a matter of posture and carriage, the hump was everything, a kind of inertia, a kind of emptiness, a dullness of desire and intellect and conscience and hope and human sensibility. Their principles were in their feet. Their calculations were biological. They had no sense of strategy or mission. They searched the villages without knowing what to look for, not caring, kicking over jars of rice, frisking children and old men, blowing tunnels, sometimes setting fires and sometimes not, then forming up and moving on to the next village, then other villages, where it would always be the same. They carried their own lives. The pressures were enormous. In the heat of early afternoon, they would remove their helmets and flak jackets, walking bare, which was dangerous but which

Psy Ops: Psychological operations.

helped ease the strain. They would often discard things along the route of march. Purely for comfort, they would throw away rations, blow their Claymores and grenades, no matter, because by nightfall the resupply choppers would arrive with more of the same, then a day or two later still more, fresh watermelons and crates of ammunition and sunglasses and woolen sweaters—the resources were stunning—sparklers for the Fourth of July, colored eggs for Easter. It was the great American war chest—the fruits of science, the smokestacks, the canneries, the arsenals at Hartford, the Minnesota forests, the machine shops, the vast fields of corn and wheat—they carried like freight trains; they carried it on their backs and shoulders—and for all the ambiguities of Vietnam, all the mysteries and unknowns, there was at least the single abiding certainty that they would never be at a loss for things to carry.

After the chopper took Lavender away, Lieutenant Jimmy Cross led his men into the village of Than Khe. They burned everything. They shot chickens and dogs, they trashed the village well, they called in artillery and watched the wreckage, then they marched for several hours through the hot afternoon, and then at dusk, while Kiowa explained how Lavender died, Lieutenant Cross found himself trembling.

He tried not to cry. With his entrenching tool, which weighed five pounds, he began digging a hole in the earth.

He felt shame. He hated himself. He had loved Martha more than his men, and as a consequence Lavender was now dead, and this was something he would have to carry like a stone in his stomach for the rest of the war.

All he could do was dig. He used his entrenching tool like an ax, slashing, feeling both love and hate, and then later, when it was full dark, he sat at the bottom of his foxhole and wept. It went on for a long while. In part, he was grieving for Ted Lavender, but mostly it was for Martha, and for himself, because she belonged to another world, which was not quite real, and because she was a junior at Mount Sebastian College in New Jersey, a poet and a virgin and uninvolved, and because he realized she did not love him and never would.

Like cement, Kiowa whispered in the dark. I swear to God—boom-down. Not a word.

I've heard this, said Norman Bowker.

A pisser, you know? Still zipping himself up. Zapped while zipping.

All right, fine. That's enough.

Yeah, but you had to see it, the guy just—

I *heard*, man. Cement. So why not shut the fuck *up*?

Kiowa shook his head sadly and glanced over at the hole where

Lieutenant Jimmy Cross sat watching the night. The air was thick and wet. A warm, dense fog had settled over the paddies and there was the stillness that precedes rain.

After a time Kiowa sighed.

One thing for sure, he said. The Lieutenant's in some deep hurt. I mean that crying jag—the way he was carrying on—it wasn't fake or anything, it was real heavy-duty hurt. The man cares.

Sure, Norman Bowker said.

Say what you want, the man does care.

We all got problems.

Not Lavender.

No, I guess not, Bowker said. Do me a favor, though.

Shut up?

That's a smart Indian. Shut up.

Shrugging, Kiowa pulled off his boots. He wanted to say more, just to lighten up his sleep, but instead he opened his New Testament and arranged it beneath his head as a pillow. The fog made things seem hollow and unattached. He tried not to think about Ted Lavender, but then he was thinking how fast it was, no drama, down and dead, and how it was hard to feel anything except surprise. It seemed un-Christian. He wished he could find some great sadness, or even anger, but the emotion wasn't there and he couldn't make it happen. Mostly he felt pleased to be alive. He liked the smell of the New Testament under his cheek, the leather and ink and paper and glue, whatever the chemicals were. He liked hearing the sounds of night. Even his fatigue, it felt fine, the stiff muscles and the prickly awareness of his own body, a floating feeling. He enjoyed not being dead. Lying there, Kiowa admired Lieutenant Jimmy Cross's capacity for grief. He wanted to share the man's pain, he wanted to care as Jimmy Cross cared. And yet when he closed his eyes, all he could think was Boom-down, and all he could feel was the pleasure of having his boots off and the fog curling in around him and the damp soil and the Bible smells and the plush comfort of night.

After a moment Norman Bowker sat up in the dark.

What the hell, he said. You want to talk, *talk*. Tell it to me.

Forget it.

No, man, go on. One thing I hate, it's a silent Indian.

For the most part they carried themselves with poise, a kind of dignity. Now and then, however, there were times of panic, when they squealed or wanted to squeal but couldn't, when they twitched and made moaning sounds and covered their heads and said Dear Jesus and flopped around on the earth and fired their weapons blindly and cringed and sobbed and begged for the noise to stop and went wild and made stupid promises to themselves and to God and to their mothers and fathers, hoping not to die. In different ways, it happened to all of them. Afterward, when the firing ended, they would blink and peek up. They would touch their bodies, feeling shame, then quickly hiding it. They would force themselves to stand. As if in slow motion, frame by frame, the world would take on the old logic—absolute silence, then the wind, then sunlight, then voices. It was the burden of being alive. Awkwardly, the men would reassemble themselves, first in private, then in groups, becoming soldiers again. They would repair the leaks in their eyes. They would check for casualties, call in dust-offs, light cigarettes, try to smile, clear their throats and spit and begin cleaning their weapons. After a time someone would shake his head and say, No lie, I almost shit my pants, and someone else would laugh, which meant it was bad, yes, but the guy had obviously not shit his pants, it wasn't that bad, and in any case nobody would ever do such a thing and then go ahead and talk about it. They would squint into the dense, oppressive sunlight. For a few moments, perhaps, they would fall silent, lighting a joint and tracking its passage from man to man, inhaling, holding in the humiliation. Scary stuff, one of them might say. But then someone else would grin or flick his eyebrows and say, Roger-dodger, almost cut me a new asshole, *almost*.

There were numerous such poses. Some carried themselves with a sort of wistful resignation, others with pride or stiff soldierly discipline or good humor or macho zeal. They were afraid of dying but they were even more afraid to show it.

They found jokes to tell.

They used a hard vocabulary to contain the terrible softness. *Greased*, they'd say. *Offed, lit up, zapped while zipping.* It wasn't cruelty, just stage presence. They were actors and the war came at them in 3-D. When someone died, it wasn't quite dying, because in a curious way it seemed scripted, and because they had their lines mostly memorized, irony mixed with tragedy, and because they called it by other names, as if to encyst and destroy the reality of death itself. They kicked corpses. They cut off thumbs. They talked grunt lingo. They told stories about Ted Lavender's supply of tranquilizers, how the poor guy didn't feel a thing, how incredibly tranquil he was.

There's a moral here, said Mitchell Sanders.

They were waiting for Lavender's chopper, smoking the dead man's dope.

The moral's pretty obvious, Sanders said, and winked. Stay away from drugs. No joke, they'll ruin your day every time.

Cute, said Henry Dobbins.

Mind-blower, get it? Talk about wiggy—nothing left, just blood and brains.

They made themselves laugh.

There it is, they'd say, over and over, as if the repetition itself were an act of poise, a balance between crazy and almost crazy, knowing without going. There it is, which meant be cool, let it ride, because oh yeah, man, you can't change what can't be changed, there it is, there it absolutely and positively and fucking well *is*.

They were tough.

They carried all the emotional baggage of men who might die. Grief, terror, love, longing—these were intangibles, but the intangibles had their own mass and specific gravity, they had tangible weight. They carried shameful memories. They carried the common secret of cowardice barely restrained, the instinct to run or freeze or hide, and in many respects this was the heaviest burden of all, for it could never be put down, it required perfect balance and perfect posture. They carried their reputations. They carried the soldier's greatest fear, which was the fear of blushing. Men killed, and died, because they were embarrassed not to. It was what had brought them to the war in the first place, nothing positive, no dreams of glory or honor, just to avoid the blush of dishonor. * They died so as not to die of embarrassment. They crawled into tunnels and walked point and advanced under fire. Each morning, despite the unknowns, they made their legs move. They endured. They kept humping. They did not submit to the obvious alternative, which was simply to close the eyes and fall. So easy, really. Go limp and tumble to the ground and let the muscles unwind and not speak and not budge until your buddies picked you up and lifted you into the chopper that would roar and dip its nose and carry you off to the world. A mere matter of falling, yet no one ever fell. It was not courage, exactly; the object was not valor. Rather, they were too frightened to be cowards.

By and large they carried these things inside, maintaining the masks of composure. They sneered at sick call. They spoke bitterly about guys who had found release by shooting off their own toes or fingers. Pussies, they'd say. Candyasses. It was fierce, mocking talk, with only a trace of envy or awe, but even so, the image played itself out behind their eyes.

They imagined the muzzle against flesh. They imagined the quick, sweet pain, then the evacuation to Japan, then a hospital with warm beds and cute geisha nurses.

They dreamed of freedom birds.

At night, on guard, staring into the dark, they were carried away by jumbo jets. They felt the rush of takeoff. *Gone!* they yelled. And then velocity, wings and engines, a smiling stewardess—but it was more than a plane, it was a real bird, a big sleek silver bird with feathers and talons and high screeching. They were flying. The weights fell off, there was nothing to bear. They laughed and held on tight, feeling the cold slap of wind and altitude, soaring, thinking *It's over, I'm gone!* — they were na-ked, they were light and free — it was all lightness, bright and fast and buoyant, light as light, a helium buzz in the brain, a giddy bubbling in the lungs as they were taken up over the clouds and the war, beyond duty, beyond gravity and mortification and global entanglements — *Sin loi!°* they yelled, *I'm sorry, motherfuckers, but I'm out of it, I'm goofed, I'm on a space cruise, I'm gone!* — and it was a restful, disencumbered sensation, just riding the light waves, sailing that big silver freedom bird over the mountains and oceans, over America, over the farms and great sleeping cities and cemeteries and highways and the golden arches of McDon-ald's. It was flight, a kind of fleeing, a kind of falling, falling higher and higher, spinning off the edge of the earth and beyond the sun and through the vast, silent vacuum where there were no burdens and where every-thing weighed exactly nothing. *Gone!* they screamed, *I'm sorry but I'm gone!* And so at night, not quite dreaming, they gave themselves over to lightness, they were carried, they were purely borne.

On the morning after Ted Lavender died, First Lieutenant Jimmy Cross crouched at the bottom of his foxhole and burned Martha's letters. Then he burned the two photographs. There was a steady rain falling, which made it difficult, but he used heat tabs and Sterno to build a small fire, screening it with his body, holding the photographs over the tight blue flame with the tips of his fingers.

He realized it was only a gesture. Stupid, he thought. Sentimental, too, but mostly just stupid.

Lavender was dead. You couldn't burn the blame.

Besides, the letters were in his head. And even now, without photo-graphs, Lieutenant Cross could see Martha playing volleyball in her white gym shorts and yellow T-shirt. He could see her moving in the rain.

When the fire died out, Lieutenant Cross pulled his poncho over his shoulders and ate breakfast from a can.

There was no great mystery, he decided.

In those burned letters Martha had never mentioned the war, except to say, Jimmy, take care of yourself. She wasn't involved. She signed the let-ters "Love," but it wasn't love, and all the fine lines and technicalities did not matter.

The morning came up wet and blurry. Everything seemed part of ev-erything else, the fog and Martha and the deepening rain.

It was a war, after all.

Half smiling, Lieutenant Jimmy Cross took out his maps. He shook his head hard, as if to clear it, then bent forward and began planning the

Sin loi!: "Sorry about that!"

day's march. In ten minutes, or maybe twenty, he would rouse the men and they would pack up and head west, where the maps showed the country to be green and inviting. They would do what they had always done. The rain might add some weight, but otherwise it would be one more day layered upon all the other days.

He was realistic about it. There was that new hardness in his stomach. No more fantasies, he told himself.

Henceforth, when he thought about Martha, it would be only to think that she belonged elsewhere. He would shut down the daydreams. This was not Mount Sebastian, it was another world, where there were no pretty poems or midterm exams, a place where men died because of carelessness and gross stupidity. Kiowa was right. Boom-down, and you were dead, never partly dead.

Briefly, in the rain, Lieutenant Cross saw Martha's gray eyes gazing back at him.

He understood.

It was very sad, he thought. The things men carried inside. The things men did or felt they had to do.

He almost nodded at her, but didn't.

Instead he went back to his maps. He was now determined to perform his duties firmly and without negligence. It wouldn't help Lavender, he knew that, but from this point on he would comport himself as a soldier. He would dispose of his good-luck pebble. Swallow it, maybe, or use Lee Strunk's slingshot, or just drop it along the trail. On the march he would impose strict field discipline. He would be careful to send out flank security, to prevent straggling or bunching up, to keep his troops moving at the proper pace and at the proper interval. He would insist on clean weapons. He would confiscate the remainder of Lavender's dope. Later in the day, perhaps, he would call the men together and speak to them plainly. He would accept the blame for what had happened to Ted Lavender. He would be a man about it. He would look them in the eyes, keeping his chin level, and he would issue the new SOPs in a calm, impersonal tone of voice, an officer's voice, leaving no room for argument or discussion. Commencing immediately, he'd tell them, they would no longer abandon equipment along the route of march. They would police up their acts. They would get their shit together, and keep it together, and maintain it neatly and in good working order.

He would not tolerate laxity. He would show strength, distancing himself.

Among the men there would be grumbling, of course, and maybe worse, because their days would seem longer and their loads heavier, but Lieutenant Cross reminded himself that his obligation was not to be loved but to lead. He would dispense with love; it was not now a factor.

And if anyone quarreled or complained, he would simply tighten his lips and arrange his shoulders in the correct command posture. He might give a curt little nod. Or he might not. He might just shrug and say Carry on, then they would saddle up and form into a column and move out toward the villages west of Than Khe.

[1986]

T. CORAGHESSAN BOYLE   [b. 1948]

Balto

There are two kinds of truths, good truths and hurtful ones. That was what her father's attorney was telling her, and she was listening, doing her best, her face a small glazed crescent of light where the sun glanced off the yellow kitchen wall to illuminate her, but it was hard. Hard because it was a weekday, after school, and this was her free time, her chance to breeze into the 7-Eleven or instant message her friends before dinner and homework closed the day down. Hard too because her father was there, sitting on a stool at the kitchen counter, sipping something out of a mug, not coffee, definitely not coffee. His face was soft, the lines at the corners of his eyes nearly erased in the gentle spill of light—his *crow's-feet*, and how she loved that word, as if the bird's scaly claws had taken hold there like something out of a horror story, Edgar Allan Poe, the raven, nevermore, but wasn't a raven different from a crow and why not call them raven's-feet? Or hawk's-feet? People could have a hawk's nose—they always did in stories—but they had crow's-feet, and that didn't make any sense at all.

"Angelle," the attorney said—*Mr. Apodaca*—and the sound of her own name startled her, "are you listening to me?"

She nodded her head. And because that didn't seem enough, she spoke up too. "Yes," she said, but her voice sounded strange in her ears, as if somebody else were speaking for her.

"Good," he said, "good," leaning into the table so that his big moist dog's eyes settled on her with a baleful look. "Because this is very important, I don't have to stress that—"

He waited for her to nod again before going on.

"There are two kinds of truths," he repeated, "just like lies. There are bad lies, we all know that, lies meant to cheat and deceive, and then there are white lies, little fibs that don't really hurt anybody"—he blew out a soft puff of air, as if he were just stepping into a hot tub—"and might actually do good. Do you understand what I'm saying?"

She held herself perfectly still. Of course she understood—he was treating her like a nine-year-old, like her sister, and she was twelve, almost thirteen, and this was an act of rebellion, to hold herself there, not answering, not nodding, not even blinking her eyes.

"Like in this case," he went on, "your father's case, I mean. You've seen TV, the movies. The judge asks you for the truth, the whole truth, and nothing but the truth, and you'll swear to it, everybody does—your father, me, anybody before the court." He had a mug too, one she recognized from her mother's college days—BU, it said in thick red letters, *Boston University*—but there was coffee in his, or there had been. Now he just pushed it around the table as if it were a chess piece and he couldn't decide where to play it. "All I want you to remember—and your father wants this too, or no, he needs it, and needs you to pay attention—is that there are good truths and bad truths, that's all. And your memory only serves to a point; I mean, who's to say what really happened, because everybody has their own version, that woman jogger, the boy on the bike—and the DA, the district attorney, he's the one who might ask you what happened that day, just him and me, that's all. Don't you worry about anything."

But she was worried, because Mr. Apodaca was there in the first place, with his perfect suit and perfect tie and his doggy eyes, and because her father had been handcuffed along the side of the road and taken to jail and the car had been impounded, which meant nobody could use it, not her father or her mother when she came back from France or Dolores the maid or Allie the au pair. There was all that, but there was something else too, something in her father's look and the attorney's sugary tones that hardened her: they were talking down to her. Talking down to her as if she had no more sense than her little sister. And she did. She did.

That day, the day of the incident—or accident, he'd have to call it an accident now—he'd met Marcy for lunch at a restaurant down by the marina where you could sit outside and watch the way the sun struck the masts of the ships as they rocked on the tide and the light shattered and regrouped and shattered again. It was one of his favorite spots in town—one of his favorite spots, period. No matter how overburdened he felt, no matter how life beat him down and every task and deadline seemed to swell up out of all proportion so that twenty people couldn't have dealt with it all—a team, an army—this place, this table in the far corner of the deck overlooking the jungle of masts, the bleached wooden catwalks, the glowing arc of the harbor and the mountains that framed it, always had a calming effect on him. That and the just-this-side-of-too-cold local sauvignon blanc they served by the glass. He was working on his second when Marcy came up the stairs, swaying over her heels like a model on the runway, and glided down the length of the deck to join him. She gave him an uncomplicated smile that lit her eyes and acknowledged everything—the day, the locale, the sun and the breeze and the clean pounded smell of the ocean and him perched there in the middle of it all—and bent to kiss him before easing herself into the chair beside him. "That looks nice," she said, referring to the wine dense as struck gold in the glass before him, and held up a finger for the waiter.

And what did they talk about? Little things. Her work, the pair of shoes she'd bought and returned and then bought all over again, the movie they'd seen two nights ago—the last time they'd been together—and how she still couldn't believe he liked that ending. "It's not that it was cheesy," she said, and here was her wine and should they get a bottle, yeah, sure, a bottle, why not, "and it was, but just that I didn't believe it."

"Didn't believe what—that the husband would take her back?"

"No," she said. "Or yes. It's idiotic. But what do you expect from a French movie? They always have these slinky-looking heroines in their thirties—"

"Or forties."

"—with great legs and mascara out of, I don't know, a Kiss revival, and then even though they're married to the greatest guy in the world they feel unfulfilled and they go out and fuck the whole village, starting with the butcher."

"Juliette Binoche," he said. He was feeling the wine. Feeling good.

"Yeah, right. Even though it wasn't her, it could have been. Should have been. Has been in every French movie but this one for the past what, twenty years?" She put down her glass and let out a short two-note laugh that was like birdsong, and laugh that entranced him, and he wasn't worried about work now, not work or anything else, and here was the bottle in the bucket, the wine cold as the cellar it came from. "And then the whole village comes out and applauds her at the end for staying true to her romantic ideals—and the *husband*, Jesus."

Nothing could irritate him. Nothing could touch him. He was in love, the pelicans were gliding over the belly of the bay and her eyes were lewd and beautiful and pleased with themselves, but he had to pull the stopper here for just a minute. "Martine's not like that," he said. "I'm not like that."

She looked over her shoulder before digging out a cigarette—this was California, after all—and when she bent to light it her hair fell across her face. She came up smiling, the smoke snatched away from her lips and neutralized on the breeze the moment she exhaled. Discussion over.

Marcy was twenty-eight, educated at Berkeley, and she and her sister had opened an artists' supply shop on a side street downtown. She'd been a double major in art and film. She rode a bike to work. She was Asian. Or Chinese, she corrected him. Of Chinese descent anyway. Her family, as she'd informed him on the first date with enough irony in her voice to foreground and bury the topic at the same time, went back four generations to the honorable great-grandfather who'd smuggled himself across the Pacific inside a clichéd flour barrel hidden in the clichéd hold of a clichéd merchant ship. She'd grown up in Syracuse, in a suburban development, and her accent—the a's flattened so that his name came out *Eelan* rather than Alan—just killed him, so incongruous coming from someone, as, well—the words out of his mouth before he knew what he was saying—as *exotic*-looking as her. And then, because he couldn't read her expression—had he gone too far? —he told her he was impressed because he only went back three generations, his grandfather having come over from Cork, but if it was in a barrel it would have been full of whiskey. "And Martine's from Paris," he'd added. "But you knew that already, didn't you?"

The bottle was half gone by the time they ordered—and there was no hurry, no hurry at all, because they were both taking the afternoon off, and no argument—and when the food came they looked at each other for just the briefest fleeting particle of a moment before he ordered a second bottle. And then they were eating and everything slowed down until all of creation seemed to come into focus in a new way. He sipped the wine, chewed, looked into her unparalleled eyes, and felt the sun lay a hand across his shoulders, and in a sudden blaze of apprehension he glanced up at the gull that appeared on the railing behind her and saw the way the breeze touched its feathers and the sun whitened its breast till there was nothing brighter and more perfect in the world—this creature, his fellow creature, and he was here to see it. He wanted to tell Marcy about it, about the miracle of the moment, the layers peeled back, revelatory, joyous, but instead he reached over to top off her glass and said, "So tell me about the shoes."

Later, after Mr. Apodaca had backed out of the driveway in his little white convertible with the Mercedes sign emblazoned on the front of it and the afternoon melted away in a slurry of phone calls and messages—*OMG! Chilty likes Alex Turtie!, can you believe it?*—Dolores made them chile rellenos with carrot and jicama sticks and ice cream for dessert. Then Allie quizzed her and Lisette over their homework until the house fell quiet and all she could hear was the faint pulse of her father's music from the family room. She'd done her math and was working on a report about Aaron Burr for her history teacher, Mr. Compson, when she got up and went to the kitchen for a glass of juice or maybe hot chocolate in the microwave—and she wouldn't know which till she was standing there in the kitchen with the recessed lights glowing over the stone counter-tops and the refrigerator door open wide. She wasn't thinking about anything in particular—Aaron Burr was behind her now, upstairs, on her desk—and when she passed the archway to the family room the flash of the TV screen caught her eye and she paused a moment. Her father was there still, stretched out on the couch with a book, the TV muted and some game on, football, baseball, and the low snarl of his music in the background. His face had that blank absorbed look he got while reading and sometimes when he was just sitting there staring across the room or out the window at nothing, and he had the mug cradled in one hand, balanced on his chest beside the book.

He'd sat with them over dinner, but he hadn't eaten—he was going out later, he told her. For dinner. A late dinner. He didn't say who with, but she knew it was the Asian woman. Marcy. She'd seen her exactly twice, from behind the window of her car, and Marcy had waved at her both times, a little curl of the fingers and a flash of the palm. There was an Asian girl in her class—she was Chinese—and her name was Xuan. That seemed right for an Asian girl, Xuan. Different. A name that said who she was and where she was from, far away, a whole ocean away. But Marcy? She didn't think so.

"Hey," her father said, lifting his head to peer over the butt of the couch, and she realized she'd been standing there watching him, "what's up? Homework done? Need any help? How about that essay—want me to proof that essay for you? What's it on, Madison? Or Burr. Burr, right?"

"That's okay."

"You sure?" His voice was slow and compacted, as if it wasn't composed of vibrations of the vocal cords, the air passing through the larynx like in her science book, but made of something heavier, denser. He would be taking a taxi tonight, she could see that, and then maybe she—*Marcy*—would drive him back home. "Because I could do it, no problem. I've got"—and she watched him lift his watch to his face and rotate his wrist—"half an hour or so, forty-five minutes."

"That's okay," she said.

She was sipping her hot chocolate and reading a story for English by William Faulkner, the author's picture in her textbook a freeze-frame of furious eyes and conquered hair, when she heard her father's voice riding a current down the hall, now murmurous, now pinched and electric, then dense and sluggish all over again. It took her a minute: he was reading Lisette her bedtime story. The house was utterly still and she held her breath, listening till all of a sudden she could make out the words. He was reading *Balto*, a story she'd loved when she was Lisette's age, and as his voice came to her down the hall she could picture the illustrations: Balto, the lead dog of the sled team, radiating light from a sunburst on his chest and the snowstorm like a monstrous hand closing over him, the team fighting through the Alaskan wind and ice and temperatures of forty below zero to deliver serum to the sick children in Nome—and those children would die if Balto didn't get through. Diphtheria. It was a diphtheria epidemic and the only plane available was broken down—or no, it couldn't fly in winter. *What's diphtheria?* she'd asked her father, and he'd gone to the shelf and pulled down the encyclopedia to give her the answer, and that was heroic in itself, because as he settled back onto her bed, Lisette snuggled up beside her and rain at the windows and the bedside lamp the only thing between them and darkness absolute, he'd said, *You see, there's everything in books, everything you could ever want.*

Balto's paws were bleeding. The ice froze between his toes. The other dogs kept holding back, but he was the lead dog and he turned on them and snarled, fought them just to keep them in their traces, to keep them going. *Balto.* With his harnessed shoulders and shaggy head and the furious unconquerable will that drove him all through that day and into the night that was so black there was no way of telling if they were on the trail or not.

Now, as she sat poised at the edge of her bed, listening to Lisette's silence and her father's limping voice, she waited for her sister to pipe up in her breathy little baby squeak and frame the inevitable questions: *Dad, Dad, how cold is forty below?* And: *Dad, what's diphtheria?*

The sun had crept imperceptibly across the deck, fingering the cracks in the varnished floorboards and easing up the low brass rail Marcy was using as a backrest. She was leaning into it, the rail, her chair tipped back, her elbows splayed behind her and her legs stretched out to catch the sun, shapely legs, stunning legs, legs long and burnished and firm, legs that made him think of the rest of her and the way she was in bed. There was a scar just under the swell of her left kneecap, the flesh annealed in an irregular oval as if it had been burned or scarified, and he'd never noticed that before. Well, he was in a new place, half a glass each left of the second bottle and the world sprung to life in the fullness of its detail, everything sharpened, in focus, as if he'd needed glasses all these years and just clapped them on. The gull was gone but it had been special, a very special gull, and there were sparrows now, or wrens, hopping along the floor in little streaks of color, snatching up a crumb of this or that and then hurtling away over the rail as if they'd been launched. He was thinking he didn't want any more wine—two bottles was plenty—but maybe something to cap off the afternoon, a cognac maybe, just one.

She'd been talking about one of the girls who worked for her, a girl he'd seen a couple of times, nineteen, soft-faced and pretty, and how she—her name was Bettina—was living the party life, every night at the clubs, and how thin she was.

"Cocaine?" he wondered, and she shrugged. "Has it affected her work?"

"No," she said, "not yet, anyway." And then she went on to qualify that with the litany of lateness in the morning, hyper behavior after lunch, and too many doctor's appointments. He waited a moment, watching her mouth and tongue, the beautiful unspooling way the words dropped from her lips, before he reached down and ran a finger over the blemish below her kneecap. "You have a scar," he said.

She looked at her knee as if she wasn't aware it was attached to her, then withdrew her leg momentarily to scrutinize it before giving it back to the sun and the deck and the waiting touch of his hand. "Oh, that?" she said. "That's from when I was a kid."

"A burn or what?"

"Bicycle." She teased the syllables out, slow and sure.

His hand was on her knee, the warmth of the contact, and he rubbed the spot a moment before straightening up in the chair and draining his glass. "Looks like a burn," he said.

"Nope. Just fell in the street." She let out that laugh again and he drank it in. "You should've seen my training wheels—or the one of them. It was as flat"—*flaat*—"as if a truck had run me over."

Her eyes flickered with the lingering seep of the memory and they both took a moment to picture it, the little girl with the wheel collapsed under her and the scraped knee—or it had to have been worse than that, punctured, shredded—and he didn't think of Lisette or Angelle, not yet, because he was deep into the drift of the day, so deep there was nothing else but this deck and this slow sweet sun and the gull that was gone now. "You want something else?" he heard himself say. "Maybe a Rémy, just to cap it off? I mean, I'm wined out, but just, I don't know, a taste of cognac?"

"Sure," she said, "why not?" and she didn't look at her watch and he didn't look at his either.

And then the waiter was there with two snifters and a little square of dark chocolate for each of them, compliments of the house. *Snifter*, he was thinking as he revolved the glass in his hand, what a perfect designation for the thing, a name that spoke to function, and he said it aloud, "Isn't it great that they have things like snifters, so you can stick your nose in it and sniff? And plus, it's named for what it is, unlike, say, a napkin or a fork. You don't nap napkins or fork forks, right?"

"Yeah," she said, and the sun had leveled on her hair now, picking out the highlights and illuminating the lobe of one ear, "I guess. But I was telling you about Bettina? Did you know that guy she picked up I told you about—not the boyfriend, but the one-night stand? He got her pregnant."

The waiter drifted by then, college kid, hair in his eyes, and asked if there'd be anything else. It was then that he thought to check his watch and the first little pulse of alarm began to make itself felt somewhere deep in the quiet lagoon of his brain: *Angelle*, the alarm said. *Lisette*. They had to be picked up at school after soccer practice every Wednesday because Wednesday was Allie's day off and Martine wasn't there to do it. Martine was in Paris, doing whatever she pleased. That much was clear. And today—today was Wednesday.

Angelle remembered waiting for him longer than usual that day. He'd been late before—he was almost always late, because of work, because he had such a hectic schedule—but this time she'd already got through half her homework, the blue backpack canted away from her and her notebook spread open across her knees as she sat at the curb, and still he wasn't there. The sun had sunk into the trees across the street and she felt a chill where she'd sweated through her shorts and T-shirt at soccer. Lisette's team had finished before hers and for a while her sister had sat beside her, drawing big X's and O's in two different colors on a sheet of loose-leaf paper, but she'd got bored and run off to play on the swings with two other kids whose parents were late.

Every few minutes a car would round the turn at the top of the street, and her eyes would jump to it, but it wasn't theirs. She watched a black SUV pull up in front of the school and saw Dani Mead and Sarah Schuster burst through the doors, laughing, their backpacks riding up off their shoulders and their hair swaying back and forth as they slid into the cavernous back seat and the door slammed shut. The car's brake lights flashed and then it rolled slowly out of the parking lot and into the street, and she watched it till it disappeared round the corner. He was always working, she knew that, trying to dig himself out from under all the work he had piled up—that was his phrase, *dig himself out*, and she pictured him in his office surrounded by towering stacks of papers, papers like the Leaning Tower of Pisa, and a shovel in his hands as if he were one of those men in the orange jackets bent over a hole in the road—but still, she felt impatient. Felt cold. Hungry. And where was he?

Finally, after the last two kids had been picked by their mothers and the sun reduced to a streak that ran across the tile roof of the school and up into the crowns of the palms behind it, after Lisette had come back to sit on the curb and whine and pout and complain like the baby she was *(He's just drunk, I bet that's it, just drunk like Mom said)* and she had to tell her she didn't know what she was talking about, there he was. Lisette saw the car first. It appeared at the top of the street like a mirage, coming so slowly round the turn it might have been rolling under its own power, with nobody in it, and Angelle remembered what her father had told her about always setting the handbrake, always, no matter what. She hadn't really wanted a lesson—she'd have to be sixteen for that—but they were up in the mountains, at the summer cabin, just after her mother had left for France, and there was nobody around. "You're a big girl," he'd told her, and she was, tall for her age—people always mistook her for an eighth-grader or even a freshman. "Go ahead, it's easy," he told her. "Like bumper cars. Only you don't bump anything." And she'd laughed and he laughed and she got behind the wheel with him guiding her and her heart was pounding till she thought she was going to lift right out of the seat. Everything looked different through the windshield, yellow spots and dirt, the world wrapped in a bubble. The sun was in her eyes. The road was a black river oozing through the dried-out weeds, the trees looming and receding as if a wave had passed through them. And the car crept down the road the way it was creeping now. Too slow. Much too slow.

When her father pulled up to the curb, she saw right away that something was wrong. He was smiling at them, or trying to smile, but his face was too heavy, his face weighed a thousand tons, carved of rock like the faces of the presidents on Mount Rushmore, and it distorted the smile till it was more like a grimace. A flare of anger rose in her—Lisette was right—and then it died away and she was scared. Just scared.

"Sorry," he murmured, "sorry I'm late, I—" and he didn't finish the thought or excuse or whatever it was because he was pushing open the door now, the driver's door, and pulling himself out onto the pavement. He took a minute to remove his sunglasses and polish them on the tail of his shirt before leaning heavily against the side of the car. He gave her a weak smile—half a smile, not even half—and carefully fitted them back over his ears, though it was too dark for sunglasses, anybody could see that. Plus, these were his old sunglasses—two shining blue disks in wire frames that made his eyes disappear—which meant that he must have lost his good ones, the ones that had cost him two hundred and fifty dollars on sale at the Sunglass Hut. "Listen," he said, as Lisette pulled open the rear door and flung her backpack across the seat. "I just—I forgot the time, is all. I'm sorry. I am. I really am."

She gave him a look that was meant to burn into him, to make him feel what she was feeling, but she couldn't tell if he was looking at her or not. "We've been sitting here since four," she said, and she heard the hurt and accusation in her own voice. She pulled open the other door, the one right beside him, because she was going to sit in back as a demonstration of her disapproval—they'd both sit in back, she and Lisette, and nobody up front—when he stopped her with a gesture, reaching out suddenly to brush the hair away from her face.

"You've got to help me out here," he said, and a pleading tone had come into his voice. "Because"—the words were stalling, congealing, sticking in his throat—"because, hey, why lie, huh? I wouldn't lie to you."

The sun faded. A car went up the street. There was a boy on a bicycle, a boy she knew, and he gave her a look as he cruised past, the wheels a blur.

"I was, I had lunch with Marcy, because, well, you know how hard I've been—and I just needed to kick back, you know? Everybody does. It's no sin." A pause, his hand going to his pocket and then back to her hair again. "And we had some wine. Some wine with lunch." He gazed off down the street then, as if he were looking for the tapering long-necked green bottles the wine had come in, as if he were going to produce them for evidence.

She just stood there staring at him, her jaw set, but she let his hand fall to her shoulder and give her a squeeze, the sort of squeeze he gave her when he was proud of her, when she got an A on a test or cleaned up the dishes all by herself without anybody asking.

"I know this is terrible," he was saying, "I mean I hate to do this, I hate to . . . but Angelle, I'm asking you just this once, because the thing is?"—and here he tugged down the little blue disks so that she could see the dull sheen of his eyes focused on her—"I don't think I can drive."

When the valet brought the car round, the strangest thing happened, a little lapse, and it was because he wasn't paying attention. He was distracted by Marcy in her low-slung Miata with the top down, the redness of it, a sleek thing, pin your ears back and fly, Marcy wheeling out of the lot with a wave and two fingers kissed to her lips, her hair lifting on the breeze. And there was the attendant, another college kid, shorter and darker than the one upstairs frowning over the tip but with the same haircut, as if they'd both been to the same barber or stylist or whatever, and the attendant had said something to him—*Your car, sir; here's your car, sir*—and the strange thing was that for a second there he didn't recognize it. Thought the kid was trying to put something over on him. Was this his car? Was this the sort of thing he'd own? This mud-splattered charcoal-gray SUV with the seriously depleted tires? And that dent in the front fender, the knee-high scrape that ran the length of the body as if some metallic claw had caught hold of it? Was this some kind of trick?

"Sir?"

"Yeah," he'd said, staring up into the sky now, and where were his shades? "Yeah, what? What do you want?"

The smallest beat. "Your car. Sir."

And then it all came clear to him the way these things do, and he flipped open his wallet to extract two singles—finger-softened money, as soft and pliable as felt—and the valet accepted them and he was in the car, looking to connect the male end of the seat belt to the female, and where was the damned thing? There was still a sliver of sun cutting in low over the ocean and he dug into the glove compartment for his old sunglasses, the emergency pair, because the new ones were someplace else altogether, apparently, and not in his pocket and not on the cord round his neck, and then he had them fitted over his ears and the radio was playing something with some real thump to it and he was rolling on out of the lot, looking to merge with the traffic on the boulevard.

That was when everything turned hard-edged and he knew he was drunk. He waited too long to merge—too cautious, too tentative—and the driver behind him laid on the horn and he had no choice but to give him the finger and he might have leaned his head out the window and barked something too, but the car came to life beneath him and somebody swerved wide and he was out in traffic. If he was thinking anything at all it probably had to do with his last DUI, which had come out of nowhere when he wasn't even that drunk, or maybe not drunk at all. He'd been coming back from Johnny's Rib Shack after working late, gnawing at a rib, a beer open between his legs, and he came down the slope beneath the underpass where you make a left to turn onto the freeway ramp and he was watching the light and didn't see the mustard-colored Volvo stopped there in front of him until it was too late. And he was so upset with himself—and not just himself, but the world at large and the way it presented these problems to him, these impediments, the unforeseen and the unexpected just laid out there in front of him as if it were some kind of conspiracy—that he got out of the car, the radiator crushed and hissing and beer pissed all over his lap, and shouted, "All right, so sue me!" at the dazed woman behind the wheel of the other car. But that wasn't going to happen now. Nothing was going to happen now.

The trees rolled by, people crossed at the crosswalk, lights turned yellow and then red and then green, and he was doing fine, just sailing, thinking he'd take the girls out for burritos or In-N-Out burgers on the way home, when a cop passed him going in the other direction and his heart froze like a block of ice and then thawed instantaneously, hammering so hard he thought it would punch right through his chest. *Signal, signal*, he told himself, keeping his eyes on the rearview, and he did, he signaled and made the first turn, a road he'd never been on before, and then he made the next turn after that, and the next, and when he looked up again he had no idea where he was.

Which was another reason why he was late, and there was Angelle giving him that hard cold judgmental look—her mother's look exactly—

because she was perfect, she was dutiful and put-upon and the single best kid in the world, in the history of the world, and he was a fuckup, pure and simple. It was wrong, what he asked her to do, but it happened nonetheless, and he guided her through each step, a straight shot on the way home, two and a half miles, that was all, and forget stopping at In-N-Out, they'd just go home and have a pizza delivered. He remembered going on in that vein, "Don't you girls want pizza tonight? Huh, Lisette? Peppers and onions? And those little roasted artichokes? Or maybe you'd prefer worm heads, mashed worm heads?"—leaning over the seat to cajole her, make it all right and take the tightness out of her face, and he didn't see the boy on the bicycle, didn't know anything about him until Angelle let out a choked little cry and there was the heart-stopping thump of something glancing off the fender.

The courtroom smelled of wax, the same kind of wax they used on the floors at school, sweet and acrid at the same time, a smell that was almost comforting in its familiarity. But she wasn't at school—she'd been excused for the morning—and she wasn't here to be comforted or to feel comfortable either. She was here to listen to Mr. Apodaca and the judge and the DA and the members of the jury decide her father's case and to testify on his behalf, tell what she knew, tell a kind of truth that wasn't maybe whole and pure but necessary, a necessary truth. That was what Mr. Apodaca was calling it now, *necessary*, and she'd sat with him and her father in one of the unused rooms off the main corridor—another courtroom—while he went over the whole business one more time for her, just to be sure she understood.

Her father had held her hand on the way in and he sat beside her on one of the wooden benches as his attorney went over the details of that day after school, because he wanted to make sure they were all on the same page. Those were his words exactly—"I want to make sure we're all on the same page on this"—as he loomed over her and her father, bracing himself on the gleaming wooden rail, his shoes competing with the floor for the brilliance of their shine, and she couldn't help picturing some Mexican boy, some dropout from the high school, laboring over those shoes while Mr. Apodaca sat high in a leather-backed chair, his feet in the stainless-steel stirrups. She pictured him behind his newspaper, looking stern, or going over his brief, the details, *these* details. When he'd gone through everything, minute by minute, gesture by gesture, coaching her, quizzing her—"And what did he say? What did you say?"—he asked her father if he could have a minute alone with her.

That was when her father gave her hand a final squeeze and then dropped it and got up from the bench. He was wearing a new suit, a navy so dark and severe it made his skin look like raw dough, and he'd had his hair cut so tight round the ears it was as if a machine had been at work there, an edger or a riding mower like the one they used on the soccer field at school, only in miniature, and for an instant she imagined tiny people like in *Gulliver's Travels* buzzing round her father's ears with their mowers and clippers and edgers. The tie he was wearing was the most boring one he owned, a blue fading to black, with no design, not even a stripe. His face was heavy, his crow's-feet right there for all the world to see—gouges, tears, slits, a butcher's shop of carved and abused skin—and for the first time she noticed the small gray dollop of loose flesh under his chin. It made him look old, worn-out, past his prime, as if he weren't the hero anymore but playing the hero's best friend, the one who never gets the girl and never gets the job. And what role was she playing? The star. She was the star here, and the more the attorney talked on and the heavier her father's face got, the more it came home to her.

Mr. Apodaca said nothing, just let the silence hang in the room till the memory of her father's footsteps had faded. Then he leaned over the back of the bench directly in front of her, the Great Seal of the State of California framed over the dais behind him, and he squeezed his eyes shut a moment so that when he opened them and fixed her with his gaze, there were tears there. Or the appearance of tears. His eyelashes were moist, and the moistness picked each of them out individually until all she could think of was the stalks of cane against the fence in the back corner of the yard. "I want you to listen very carefully to what I'm about to say, Angelle," he breathed, his voice so soft and constricted it was like the sound of the air being let out of a tire. "Because this concerns you and your sister. It could affect your whole life."

Another pause. Her stomach was crawling. She didn't want to say anything but he held the pause so long she had to bow her head and say, "Yeah. Yeah, I know."

And then suddenly, without warning, his voice was lashing out at her: "But you don't know it. Do you know what's at stake here? Do you really?"

"No," she said, and it was a whisper.

"Your father is going to plead no contest to the charge of driving under the influence. He was wrong, he admits it. And they'll take away his driving privileges and he'll have to go to counseling and find someone to drive you and your sister to school, and I don't mean to minimize that, that's very serious, but here's the thing you may not know." He held her eyes, though she wanted to look away. "The second charge is child endangerment, not for the boy on the bike, who barely even scraped a knee, luckily, luckily, and whose parents have already agreed to a settlement, but for you, for allowing you to do what you did. And do you know what will happen if the jury finds him guilty?"

She didn't know what was coming, not exactly, but the tone of what he was conveying—dark, ominous, fulminating with anger and the threat about to be revealed in the very next breath—made her feel small. And scared. Definitely scared. She shook her head.

"They'll take you and Lisette away from him." He clenched both hands, pushed himself up from the rail, and turned as if to pace off down the aisle in front of her, as if he was disgusted with the whole thing and had no more to say. But then, suddenly, he swung round on her with a furious twist of his shoulders and a hard accusatory stab of his balled-up right hand and a single rigid forefinger. "And no," he said, barely contained, barely able to keep his voice level, "in answer to your unasked question or objection or whatever you want to call it, your mother's not coming back for you, not now, maybe not ever."

Was he ashamed? Was he humiliated? Did he have to stop drinking and get his life in order? Yes, yes, and yes. But as he sat there in the court-room beside Jerry Apodaca at eleven-thirty in the morning, the high arched windows pregnant with light and his daughter, Marcy, Dolores, and the solemn-faced au pair sitting shoulder to shoulder on the gleaming wooden bench behind him, there was a flask in his inside pocket, and the faint burning pulse of single-malt scotch rode his veins. He'd taken a pull from it in the men's room not ten minutes ago, just to steady himself, and then he'd rinsed out his mouth and ground half a dozen Tic Tacs between his teeth to knock down any trace of alcohol on his breath. Jerry would have been furious with him if he so much as suspected . . . and it was a weak and cowardly thing to do, no excuse, no excuse at all, but he felt adrift, felt scared, and he needed an anchor to hold on to. Just for now. Just for today. And then he'd throw the thing away, because what was a flask for anyway except to provide a twenty-four hour teat for the kind of drunk who wore a suit and brushed his teeth.

He began to jiggle one foot and tap his knees together beneath the table, a nervous twitch no amount of scotch would cure. The judge was taking his time, the assistant DA smirking over a sheaf of papers at her own table off to the right. She wore a permanent self-congratulatory look, this woman, as if she were queen of the court and the county too, and she'd really laid into him before the recess, and that was nasty, purely nasty. She was the prosecution's attack dog, that was what Jerry called her, her voice tuned to a perpetual note of sarcasm, disbelief, and petulance, but he held to his story and never wavered. He was just glad Angelle hadn't had to see it.

She was here now, though, sitting right behind him, missing school—missing school because of him. And that was one more strike against him, he supposed, *because what kind of father would . . . ?* but the thought was too depressing and he let it die. He resisted the urge to turn round and give her a look, a smile, a wink, the least gesture, anything. It was too painful to see her there, under constraint, his daughter dragged out of school for this, and then he didn't want anybody to think he was coaching her or coercing her in any way. Jerry had no such scruples, though. He'd drilled her over and over and he'd even gone to the extreme of asking her—or no, *instructing* her—to wear something that might conform to the court's idea of what a good, honest, straightforward child was like, too young to bend the truth and far too young even to think about getting behind the wheel of a car.

Three times Jerry had sent her back to change outfits until finally, with a little persuasion from the au pair (*Allie*, and he'd have to remember to slip her a twenty, a twenty at least, because she was gold, pure gold), she put on a lacy white high-collared dress she'd worn for some kind of pageant at school, with matching white tights and patent-leather shoes. There was something wrong there in the living room, he could see that, something in the way she held her shoulders and stamped up the stairs to her room, her face clenched and her eyes burning into him, and he should have recognized it, should have given her just a hair more of his attention, but Marcy was there and she had her opinion and Jerry was being an autocrat and he himself had his hands full—he couldn't eat or think or do anything other than maybe slip into the pantry and tip the bottle of Macallan over the flask. By the time he thought of it, they were in the car, and he tried, he did, leaning across the seat to ply her with little jokes about getting a free day off and what her teachers were going to think and what Aaron Burr might have done—he would've just shot somebody, right?—but Jerry was drilling her one last time and she was sunk into the seat beside Marcy, already clamped up.

The courtroom, this courtroom, the one she was in now, was a duplicate of the one in which her father's attorney had quizzed her an hour and a half ago, except that it was filled with people. They were all old, or older, anyway, except for one woman in a form-fitting plaid jacket Angelle had seen in the window at Nordstrom's who must have been in her twenties. She was in the jury box, looking bored. The other jurors were mostly men, businessmen, she supposed, with balding heads and recessed eyes and big meaty hands clasped in their laps or grasping the rail in front of them. One of them looked like the principal of her school, Dr. Damon, but he wasn't.

The judge sat up at his desk in the front of the room, which they called a bench but wasn't a bench at all, the flag of the State of California on one side of him and the American flag on the other. She was seated in the front row, between Dolores and Allie, and her father and Mr. Apodaca sat at a desk in front of her, the shoulders of their suits puffed up as if they were wearing football pads. Her father's suit was so dark she could see the dandruff there, a little spray of it like dust on the collar of his jacket, and she felt embarrassed for him. And sorry for him too—and for herself. And Lisette. She looked up at the judge and then at the district attorney with his grim gray tight-shaven face and the scowling woman beside him, and couldn't help thinking about what Mr. Apodaca had told her, and it made her shrink into herself when Mr. Apodaca called her name and the judge, reading the look on her face, tried to give her a smile of encouragement.

She wasn't aware of walking across the floor or of the hush that fell over the courtroom or even of the bailiff who asked her to hold up her right hand and swear to tell the truth—all this, as if she were recalling a fragmented dream, would come to her later. But then she was seated in the witness chair and everything was bright and loud suddenly, as if she'd just switched channels on the TV. Mr. Apodaca was right there before her, his voice rising sweetly, almost as if he were singing, and he was leading her through the questions they'd rehearsed over and over again. Yes, she told him, her father was late, and yes, it was getting dark, and no, she didn't notice anything strange about him. He was her father and he always picked her sister and her up on Wednesdays, she volunteered, because Wednesdays were when Allie and Dolores both had their day off and there was no one else to do it because her mother was in France.

They were all watching her now, the court gone absolutely silent, so silent you would have thought everyone had tiptoed out the door, but there they all were, hanging on her every word. She wanted to say more about her mother, about how her mother was coming home soon—had promised as much the last time she'd called long distance from her apartment in Saint Germain des Prés—but Mr. Apodaca wouldn't let her. He kept leading her along, using his sugary voice now, talking down to her, and she wanted to speak up and tell him he didn't have to treat her like that, tell him about her mother, Lisette, the school and the lawn and the trees and the way the interior of the car smelled and the heat of the liquor on her father's breath—anything that would forestall the inevitable, the question that was tucked in just behind this last one, the question on the point of which everything turned, because now she heard it, murmurous and soft and sweet, on her father's attorney's lips: "Who was driving?"

"I just wanted to say one thing," she said, lifting her eyes now to look at Mr. Apodaca and only Mr. Apodaca, his dog's eyes, his pleading soft baby-talking face, "just because, well, I wanted to say you're wrong about my mother, because she *is* coming home—she told me so herself, on, on the phone—" She couldn't help herself. Her voice was cracking.

"Yes," he said, too quickly, a hiss of breath, "yes, I understand that, Angelle, but we need to establish . . . you need to answer the question."

Oh, and now the silence went even deeper, the silence of the deep sea, of outer space, of the Arctic night when you couldn't hear the runners of the sled or the feet of the dogs bleeding into the snow, and her eyes jumped to her father's then, the look on his face of hopefulness and fear and confusion, and she loved him in that moment more than she ever had.

"Angelle," Mr. Apodaca was saying, murmuring. "Angelle?"

She turned her face back to him, blotting out the judge, the DA, the woman in the plaid jacket who was probably a college student, probably cool, and waited for the question to drop.

"Who," Mr. Apodaca repeated, slowing it down now, "was"—slower, slower still—"driving?"

She lifted her chin then to look at the judge and heard the words coming out of her mouth as if they'd been planted there, telling the truth, the hurtful truth, the truth no one would have guessed because she was almost thirteen now, almost a teenager, and she let them know it. "*I* was," she said, and the courtroom roared to life with so many people buzzing at once she thought at first they hadn't heard her. So she said it again, said it louder, much louder, so loud she might have been shouting it to the man with the camera at the back of the long churchy room with its sweat-burnished pews and the flags and emblems and all the rest. And then she looked away from the judge, away from the spectators and the man with the camera and the court recorder and the bank of windows so brilliant with light you would have thought a bomb had gone off there, and looked directly at her father.

[2007]

LESLIE MARMON SILKO [b. 1948]

The Man to Send Rain Clouds

ONE

They found him under a big cottonwood tree. His Levi jacket and pants were faded light-blue so that he had been easy to find. The big cottonwood tree stood apart from a small grove of winterbare cottonwoods which grew in the wide, sandy arroyo. He had been dead for a day or more, and the sheep had wandered and scattered up and down the arroyo. Leon and his brother-in-law, Ken, gathered the sheep and left them in the pen at the sheep camp before they returned to the cottonwood tree. Leon waited under the tree while Ken drove the truck through the deep sand to the edge of the arroyo. He squinted up at the sun and unzipped his jacket—it sure was hot for this time of year. But high and northwest the blue mountains were still deep in snow. Ken came sliding down the low, crumbling bank about fifty yards down, and he was bringing the red blanket.

Before they wrapped the old man, Leon took a piece of string out of his pocket and tied a small gray feather in the old man's long white hair. Ken gave him the paint. Across the brown wrinkled forehead he drew a streak of white and along the high cheekbones he drew a strip of blue paint. He paused and watched Ken throw pinches of corn meal and pollen into the wind that fluttered the small gray feather. Then Leon painted with yellow under the old man's broad nose, and finally, when he had painted green across the chin, he smiled.

"Send us rain clouds, Grandfather." They laid the bundle in the back of the pickup and covered it with a heavy tarp before they started back to the pueblo.

They turned off the highway onto the sandy pueblo road. Not long after they passed the store and post office they saw Father Paul's car coming toward them. When he recognized their faces he slowed his car and waved for them to stop. The young priest rolled down the car window.

"Did you find old Teofilo?" he asked loudly.

Leon stopped the truck. "Good morning, Father. We were just out to the sheep camp. Everything is O.K. now."

376

"Thank God for that. Teofilo is a very old man. You really shouldn't allow him to stay at the sheep camp alone.

"No, he won't do that any more now."

"Well, I'm glad you understand. I hope I'll be seeing you at Mass this week—we missed you last Sunday. See if you can get old Teofilo to come with you." The priest smiled and waved at them as they drove away.

TWO

Louise and Teresa were waiting. The table was set for lunch, and the coffee was boiling on the black iron stove. Leon looked at Louise and then at Teresa.

"We found him under a cottonwood tree in the big arroyo near the sheep camp. I guess he sat down to rest in the shade and never got up again." Leon walked toward the old man's bed. The red plaid shawl had been shaken and spread carefully over the bed, and a new brown flannel shirt and pair of stiff new Levis were arranged neatly beside the pillow. Louise held the screen door open while Leon and Ken carried in the red blanket. He looked small and shriveled, and after they dressed him in the new shirt and pants he seemed more shrunken.

It was noontime now because the church bells rang the Angelus.° They ate the beans with hot bread, and nobody said anything until after Teresa poured the coffee.

Ken stood up and put on his jacket. "I'll see about the gravediggers. Only the top layer of soil is frozen. I think it can be ready before dark."

Leon nodded his head and finished his coffee. After Ken had been gone for a while, the neighbors and clanspeople came quietly to embrace Teofilo's family and to leave food on the table because the gravediggers would come to eat when they were finished.

THREE

The sky in the west was full of pale-yellow light. Louise stood outside with her hands in the pockets of Leon's green army jacket that was too big for her. The funeral was over, and the old men had taken their candles and medicine bags and were gone. She waited until the body was laid into the pickup before she said anything to Leon. She touched his arm, and he noticed that her hands were still dusty from the corn

Angelus: A devotional prayer commemorating the Annunciation (the angel Gabriel's announcement of the Incarnation of God in the human form of Jesus).

meal that she had sprinkled around the old man. When she spoke, Leon could not hear her.

"What did you say? I didn't hear you."

"I said that I had been thinking about something."

"About what?"

"About the priest sprinkling holy water for Grandpa. So he won't be thirsty."

Leon stared at the new moccasins that Teofilo had made for the ceremonial dances in the summer. They were nearly hidden by the red blanket. It was getting colder, and the wind pushed gray dust down the narrow pueblo road. The sun was approaching the long mesa where it disappeared during the winter. Louise stood there shivering and watching his face. Then he zipped up his jacket and opened the truck door. "I'll see if he's there."

FOUR

Ken stopped the pickup at the church, and Leon got out; and then Ken drove down the hill to the graveyard where people were waiting. Leon knocked at the old carved door with its symbols of the Lamb. While he waited he looked up at the twin bells from the king of Spain with the last sunlight pouring around them in their tower.

The priest opened the door and smiled when he saw who it was. "Come in! What brings you here this evening?"

The priest walked toward the kitchen, and Leon stood with his cap in his hand, playing with the earflaps and examining the living room—the brown sofa, the green armchair, and the brass lamp that hung down from the ceiling by links of chain. The priest dragged a chair out of the kitchen and offered it to Leon.

"No thank you, Father. I only came to ask you if you would bring your holy water to the graveyard."

The priest turned away from Leon and looked out the window at the patio full of shadows and the dining-room windows of the nuns' cloister across the patio. The curtains were heavy, and the light from within faintly penetrated; it was impossible to see the nuns inside eating supper. "Why didn't you tell me he was dead? I could have brought the Last Rites anyway."

Leon smiled. "It wasn't necessary, Father."

The priest stared down at his scuffed brown loafers and the worn hem of his cassock. "For a Christian burial it was necessary."

His voice was distant, and Leon thought that his blue eyes looked tired.

"It's O.K., Father, we just want him to have plenty of water."

The priest sank down in the green chair and picked up a glossy missionary magazine. He turned the colored pages full of lepers and pagans without looking at them.

"You know I can't do that, Leon. There should have been the Last Rites and a funeral Mass at the very least."

Leon put on his green cap and pulled the flaps down over his ears. "It's getting late, Father. I've got to go."

When Leon opened the door Father Paul stood up and said, "Wait." He left the room and came back wearing a long brown overcoat. He followed Leon out the door and across the dim churchyard to the adobe steps in front of the church. They both stooped to fit through the low adobe entrance. And when they started down the hill to the graveyard only half of the sun was visible above the mesa.

The priest approached the grave slowly, wondering how they had managed to dig into the frozen ground; and then he remembered that this was New Mexico, and saw the pile of cold loose sand beside the hole. The people stood close to each other with little clouds of steam puffing from their faces. The priest looked at them and saw a pile of jackets, gloves, and scarves in the yellow, dry tumbleweeds that grew in the graveyard. He looked at the red blanket, not sure that Teofilo was so small, wondering if it wasn't some perverse Indian trick—something they did in March to ensure a good harvest—wondering if maybe old Teofilo was actually at sheep camp corraling the sheep for the night. But there he was, facing into a cold dry wind and squinting at the last sunlight, ready to bury a red wool blanket while the faces of the parishioners were in shadow with the last warmth of the sun on their backs.

His fingers were stiff, and it took them a long time to twist the lid off the holy water. Drops of water fell on the red blanket and soaked into dark icy spots. He sprinkled the grave and the water disappeared almost before it touched the dim, cold sand; it reminded him of something—he tried to remember what it was, because he thought if he could remember he might understand this. He sprinkled more water; he shook the container until it was empty, and the water fell through the light from sundown like August rain that fell while the sun was still shining, almost evaporating before it touched the wilted squash flowers.

The wind pulled at the priest's brown Franciscan robe and swirled away the corn meal and pollen that had been sprinkled on the blanket. They lowered the bundle into the ground, and they didn't bother to untie the stiff pieces of new rope that were tied around the ends of the blanket. The sun was gone, and over on the highway the eastbound lane was full of headlights. The priest walked away slowly. Leon watched him climb the hill, and when he had disappeared within the tall, thick walls, Leon

turned to look up at the high blue mountains in the deep snow that reflected a faint red light from the west. He felt good because it was finished, and he was happy about the sprinkling of the holy water, now the
old man could send them big thunderclouds for sure.

[1969]

JAMAICA KINCAID [b. 1949]

Girl

Wash the white clothes on Monday and put them on the stone heap;
wash the color clothes on Tuesday and put them on the clothesline to
dry; don't walk barehead in the hot sun; cook pumpkin fritters in very
hot sweet oil; soak your little cloths right after you take them off; when
buying cotton to make yourself a nice blouse, be sure that it doesn't have
gum on it, because that way it won't hold up well after a wash; soak salt
fish overnight before you cook it; is it true that you sing benna° in Sunday school?; always eat your food in such a way that it won't turn someone else's stomach; on Sundays try to walk like a lady and not like the
slut you are so bent on becoming; don't sing benna in Sunday school; you
mustn't speak to wharf-rat boys, not even to give directions; don't eat
fruits on the street—flies will follow you; *but I don't sing benna on Sundays at all and never in Sunday school*; this is how to sew on a button; this
is how to make a button-hole for the button you have just sewed on; this
is how to hem a dress when you see the hem coming down and so to
prevent yourself from looking like the slut I know you are so bent on
becoming; this is how you iron your father's khaki shirt so that it doesn't
have a crease; this is how you iron your father's khaki pants so that they
don't have a crease; this is how you grow okra—far from the house, because okra tree harbors red ants; when you are growing dasheen,° make
sure it gets plenty of water or else it makes your throat itch when you are
eating it; this is how you sweep a corner; this is how you sweep a whole
house; this is how you sweep a yard; this is how you smile to someone
you don't like too much; this is how you smile to someone you don't like
at all; this is how you smile to someone you like completely; this is how

Benna: Calypso music.
Dasheen: Taro, an edible starchy plant.

you set a table for tea; this is how you set a table for dinner; this is how you set a table for dinner with an important guest; this is how you set a table for lunch; this is how you set a table for breakfast; this is how to behave in the presence of men who don't know you very well, and this way they won't recognize immediately the slut I have warned you against becoming; be sure to wash every day, even if it is with your own spit; don't squat down to play marbles—you are not a boy, you know; don't pick people's flowers—you might catch something; don't throw stones at blackbirds, because it might not be a blackbird at all; this is how to make a bread pudding; this is how to make doukona;° this is how to make pepper pot; this is how to make a good medicine for a cold; this is how to make a good medicine to throw away a child before it even becomes a child; this is how to catch a fish; this is how to throw back a fish you don't like, and that way something bad won't fall on you; this is how to bully a man; this is how a man bullies you; this is how to love a man, and if this doesn't work there are other ways, and if they don't work don't feel too bad about giving up; this is how to spit up in the air if you feel like it, and this is how to move quick so that it doesn't fall on you; this is how to make ends meet; always squeeze bread to make sure it's fresh; *but what if the baker won't let me feel the bread?*; you mean to say that after all you are really going to be the kind of woman who the baker won't let near the bread?

[1978]

Doukona: A spicy plantain pudding.

AMY TAN [b. 1952]

Two Kinds

My mother believed you could be anything you wanted to be in America. You could open a restaurant. You could work for the government and get good retirement. You could buy a house with almost no money down. You could become rich. You could become instantly famous.

"Of course you can be prodigy, too," my mother told me when I was nine. "You can be best anything. What does Auntie Lindo know? Her daughter, she is only best tricky."

America was where all my mother's hopes lay. She had come here in 1949 after losing everything in China: her mother and father, her family home, her first husband, and two daughters, twin baby girls. But she never looked back with regret. There were so many ways for things to get better.

We didn't immediately pick the right kind of prodigy. At first my mother thought I could be a Chinese Shirley Temple.° We'd watch Shirley's old movies on TV as though they were training films. My mother would poke my arm and say, "*Ni kan*"—You watch. And I would see Shirley tapping her feet, or singing a sailor song, or pursing her lips into a very round O while saying, "Oh my goodness."

"*Ni kan*," said my mother as Shirley's eyes flooded with tears. "You already know how. Don't need talent for crying!"

Soon after my mother got this idea about Shirley Temple, she took me to a beauty training school in the Mission district and put me in the hands of a student who could barely hold the scissors without shaking. Instead of getting big fat curls, I emerged with an uneven mass of crinkly black fuzz. My mother dragged me off to the bathroom and tried to wet down my hair.

"You look like Negro Chinese," she lamented, as if I had done this on purpose.

The instructor of the beauty training school had to lop off these soggy clumps to make my hair even again. "Peter Pan is very popular these days," the instructor assured my mother. I now had hair the length of a

Shirley Temple: Child movie star of the 1930s and 1940s, known for her blond ringlets.

boy's, with straight-across bangs that hung at a slant two inches above my eyebrows. I liked the haircut and it made me actually look forward to my future fame.

In fact, in the beginning, I was just as excited as my mother, maybe even more so. I pictured this prodigy part of me as many different images, trying each one on for size. I was a dainty ballerina girl standing by the curtains, waiting to hear the right music that would send me floating on my tiptoes. I was like the Christ child lifted out of the straw manger, crying with holy indignity. I was Cinderella stepping from her pumpkin carriage with sparkly cartoon music filling the air.

In all of my imaginings, I was filled with a sense that I would soon become *perfect*. My mother and father would adore me. I would be beyond reproach. I would never feel the need to sulk for anything.

But sometimes the prodigy in me became impatient. "If you don't hurry up and get me out of here, I'm disappearing for good," it warned. "And then you'll always be nothing."

Every night after dinner, my mother and I would sit at the Formica kitchen table. She would present new tests, taking her examples from stories of amazing children she had read in *Ripley's Believe It or Not*, or *Good Housekeeping*, *Reader's Digest*, and a dozen other magazines she kept in a pile in our bathroom. My mother got these magazines from people whose houses she cleaned. And since she cleaned many houses each week, we had a great assortment. She would look through them all, searching for stories about remarkable children.

The first night she brought out a story about a three-year-old boy who knew the capitals of all the states and even most of the European countries. A teacher was quoted as saying the little boy could also pronounce the names of the foreign cities correctly.

"What's the capital of Finland?" my mother asked me, looking at the magazine story.

All I knew was the capital of California, because Sacramento was the name of the street we lived on in Chinatown. "Nairobi!" I guessed, saying the most foreign word I could think of. She checked to see if that was possibly one way to pronounce "Helsinki" before showing me the answer.

The tests got harder—multiplying numbers in my head, finding the queen of hearts in a deck of cards, trying to stand on my head without using my hands, predicting the daily temperatures in Los Angeles, New York, and London.

One night I had to look at a page from the Bible for three minutes and then report everything I could remember. "Now Jehoshaphat had riches and honor in abundance and . . . that's all I remember, Ma," I said.

And after seeing my mother's disappointed face once again, something inside of me began to die. I hated the tests, the raised hopes and failed expectations. Before going to bed that night, I looked in the mirror above the bathroom sink and when I saw only my face staring back—and that it would always be this ordinary face—I began to cry. Such a sad, ugly girl! I made high-pitched noises like a crazed animal, trying to scratch out the face in the mirror.

And then I saw what seemed to be the prodigy side of me—because I had never seen that face before. I looked at my reflection, blinking so I could see more clearly. The girl staring back at me was angry, powerful. This girl and I were the same. I had new thoughts, willful thoughts, or rather thoughts filled with lots of won'ts. I won't let her change me, I promised myself. I won't be what I'm not.

So now on nights when my mother presented her tests, I performed listlessly, my head propped on one arm. I pretended to be bored. And I was. I got so bored I started counting the bellows of the foghorns out on the bay while my mother drilled me in other areas. The sound was comforting and reminded me of the cow jumping over the moon. And the next day, I played a game with myself, seeing if my mother would give up on me before eight bellows. After a while I usually counted only one, maybe two bellows at most. At last she was beginning to give up hope.

Two or three months had gone by without any mention of my being a prodigy again. And then one day my mother was watching *The Ed Sullivan Show*° on TV. The TV was old and the sound kept shorting out. Every time my mother got halfway up from the sofa to adjust the set, the sound would go back on and Ed would be talking. As soon as she sat down, Ed would go silent again. She got up, the TV broke into loud piano music. She sat down. Silence. Up and down, back and forth, quiet and loud. It was like a stiff embraceless dance between her and the TV set. Finally she stood by the set with her hand on the sound dial.

She seemed entranced by the music, a little frenzied piano piece with this mesmerizing quality, sort of quick passages and then teasing lilting ones before it returned to the quick playful parts.

"*Ni kan*," my mother said, calling me over with hurried hand gestures. "Look here."

I could see why my mother was fascinated by the music. It was being pounded out by a little Chinese girl, about nine years old, with a Peter Pan haircut. The girl had the sauciness of a Shirley Temple. She was proudly modest like a proper Chinese child. And she also did this fancy sweep of a curtsy, so that the fluffy skirt of her white dress cascaded slowly to the floor like the petals of a large carnation.

The Ed Sullivan Show: A variety show that ran from 1948 to 1971.

In spite of these warning signs, I wasn't worried. Our family had no piano and we couldn't afford to buy one, let alone reams of sheet music and piano lessons. So I could be generous in my comments when my mother bad-mouthed the little girl on TV.

"Play note right, but doesn't sound good! No singing sound," complained my mother.

"What are you picking on her for?" I said carelessly. "She's pretty good. Maybe she's not the best, but she's trying hard." I knew almost immediately I would be sorry I said that.

"Just like you," she said. "Not the best. Because you not trying." She gave a little huff as she let go of the sound dial and sat down on the sofa.

The little Chinese girl sat down also to play an encore of "Anitra's Dance" by Grieg. I remember the song, because later on I had to learn how to play it.

Three days after watching *The Ed Sullivan Show*, my mother told me what my schedule would be for piano lessons and piano practice. She had talked to Mr. Chong, who lived on the first floor of our apartment building. Mr. Chong was a retired piano teacher and my mother had traded housecleaning services for weekly lessons and a piano for me to practice on every day, two hours a day, from four until six.

When my mother told me this, I felt as though I had been sent to hell. I whined and then kicked my foot a little when I couldn't stand it anymore.

"Why don't you like me the way I am? I'm *not* a genius! I can't play the piano. And even if I could, I wouldn't go on TV if you paid me a million dollars!" I cried.

My mother slapped me. "Who ask you be genius?" she shouted. "Only ask you be your best. For you sake. You think I want you be genius? Hnnh! What for! Who ask you!"

"So ungrateful," I heard her mutter in Chinese. "If she had as much talent as she has temper, she would be famous now."

Mr. Chong, whom I secretly nicknamed Old Chong, was very strange, always tapping his fingers to the silent music of an invisible orchestra. He looked ancient in my eyes. He had lost most of the hair on top of his head and he wore thick glasses and had eyes that always looked tired and sleepy. But he must have been younger than I thought, since he lived with his mother and was not yet married.

I met Old Lady Chong once and that was enough. She had this peculiar smell like a baby that had done something in its pants. And her fingers felt like a dead person's, like an old peach I once found in the back of the refrigerator; the skin just slid off the meat when I picked it up.

I soon found out why Old Chong had retired from teaching piano. He was deaf. "Like Beethoven!" he shouted to me. "We're both listening only in our head!" And he would start to conduct his frantic silent sonatas.

Our lessons went like this. He would open the book and point to different things, explaining their purpose: "Key! Treble! Bass! No sharps or flats! So this is C major! Listen now and play after me!"

And then he would play the C scale a few times, a simple chord, and then, as if inspired by an old, unreachable itch, he gradually added more notes and running trills and a pounding bass until the music was really something quite grand.

I would play after him, the simple scale, the simple chord, and then I just played some nonsense that sounded like a cat running up and down on top of garbage cans. Old Chong smiled and applauded and then said, "Very good! But now you must learn to keep time!"

So that's how I discovered that Old Chong's eyes were too slow to keep up with the wrong notes I was playing. He went through the motions in half-time. To help me keep rhythm, he stood behind me, pushing down on my right shoulder for every beat. He balanced pennies on top of my wrists so I would keep them still as I slowly played scales and arpeggios. He had me curve my hand around an apple and keep that shape when playing chords. He marched stiffly to show me how to make each finger dance up and down, staccato like an obedient little soldier.

He taught me all these things, and that was how I also learned I could be lazy and get away with mistakes, lots of mistakes. If I hit the wrong notes because I hadn't practiced enough, I never corrected myself. I just kept playing in rhythm. And Old Chong kept conducting his own private reverie.

So maybe I never really gave myself a fair chance. I did pick up the basics pretty quickly, and I might have become a good pianist at that young age. But I was so determined not to try, not to be anybody different that I learned to play only the most ear-splitting preludes, the most discordant hymns.

Over the next year, I practiced like this, dutifully in my own way. And then one day I heard my mother and her friend Lindo Jong both talking in a loud bragging tone of voice so others could hear. It was after church, and I was leaning against the brick wall wearing a dress with stiff white petticoats. Auntie Lindo's daughter, Waverly, who was about my age, was standing farther down the wall about five feet away. We had grown up together and shared all the closeness of two sisters squabbling over crayons and dolls. In other words, for the most part, we hated each other. I thought she was snotty. Waverly Jong had gained a certain amount of fame as "Chinatown's Littlest Chinese Chess Champion."

"She bring home too many trophy," lamented Auntie Lindo that Sunday. "All day she play chess. All day I have no time do nothing but dust off her winnings." She threw a scolding look at Waverly, who pretended not to see her.

"You lucky you don't have this problem," said Auntie Lindo with a sigh to my mother.

And my mother squared her shoulders and bragged: "Our problem worser than yours. If we ask Jing-mei wash dish, she hear nothing but music. It's like you can't stop this natural talent."

And right then, I was determined to put a stop to her foolish pride.

A few weeks later, Old Chong and my mother conspired to have me play in a talent show which would be held in the church hall. By then, my parents had saved up enough to buy me a secondhand piano, a black Wurlitzer spinet with a scarred bench. It was the showpiece of our living room.

For the talent show, I was to play a piece called "Pleading Child" from Schumann's *Scenes from Childhood*. It was a simple, moody piece that sounded more difficult than it was. I was supposed to memorize the whole thing, playing the repeat parts twice to make the piece sound longer. But I dawdled over it, playing a few bars and then cheating, looking up to see what notes followed. I never really listened to what I was playing. I day-dreamed about being somewhere else, about being someone else.

The part I liked to practice best was the fancy curtsy: right foot out, touch the rose on the carpet with a pointed foot, sweep to the side, left leg bends, look up and smile.

My parents invited all the couples from the Joy Luck Club to witness my debut. Auntie Lindo and Uncle Tin were there. Waverly and her two older brothers had also come. The first two rows were filled with children both younger and older than I was. The littlest ones got to go first. They recited simple nursery rhymes, squawked out tunes on miniature violins, twirled Hula Hoops, pranced in pink ballet tutus, and when they bowed or curtsied, the audience would sigh in unison, "Awww," and then clap enthusiastically.

When my turn came, I was very confident. I remember my childish excitement. It was as if I knew, without a doubt, that the prodigy side of me really did exist. I had no fear whatsoever, no nervousness. I remember thinking to myself, This is it! This is it! I looked out over the audience, at my mother's blank face, my father's yawn, Auntie Lindo's stiff-lipped smile, Waverly's sulky expression. I had on a white dress layered with sheets of lace, and a pink bow in my Peter Pan haircut. As I sat down I envisioned people jumping to their feet and Ed Sullivan rushing up to introduce me to everyone on TV.

And I started to play. It was so beautiful. I was so caught up in how lovely I looked that at first I didn't worry how I would sound. So it was a surprise to me when I hit the first wrong note and I realized something didn't sound quite right. And then I hit another and another followed that. A chill started at the top of my head and began to trickle down. Yet I couldn't stop playing, as though my hands were bewitched. I kept thinking my fingers would adjust themselves back, like a train switching to the right track. I played this strange jumble through two repeats, the sour notes staying with me all the way to the end.

When I stood up, I discovered my legs were shaking. Maybe I had just been nervous and the audience, like Old Chong, had seen me go through the right motions and had not heard anything wrong at all. I swept my right foot out, went down on my knee, looked up and smiled. The room was quiet, except for Old Chong, who was beaming and shouting, "Bravo! Bravo! Well done!" But then I saw my mother's face, her stricken face. The audience clapped weakly, and as I walked back to my chair, with my whole face quivering as I tried not to cry, I heard a little boy whisper loudly to his mother, "That was awful," and the mother whispered back, "Well, she certainly tried."

And now I realized how many people were in the audience, the whole world it seemed. I was aware of eyes burning into my back. I felt the shame of my mother and father as they sat stiffly throughout the rest of the show.

We could have escaped during intermission. Pride and some strange sense of honor must have anchored my parents to their chairs. And so we watched it all: the eighteen-year-old boy with a fake mustache who did a magic show and juggled flaming hoops while riding a unicycle. The breasted girl with white makeup who sang from *Madama Butterfly* and got honorable mention. And the eleven-year-old boy who won first prize playing a tricky violin song that sounded like a busy bee.

After the show, the Hsus, the Jongs, and the St. Clairs from the Joy Luck Club came up to my mother and father.

"Lots of talented kids," Auntie Lindo said vaguely, smiling broadly.

"That was somethin' else," said my father, and I wondered if he was referring to me in a humorous way, or whether he even remembered what I had done.

Waverly looked at me and shrugged her shoulders. "You aren't a genius like me," she said matter-of-factly. And if I hadn't felt so bad, I would have pulled her braids and punched her stomach.

But my mother's expression was what devastated me: a quiet, blank look that said she had lost everything. I felt the same way, and it seemed as if everybody were now coming up, like gawkers at the scene of an accident, to see what parts were actually missing. When we got on the bus to go home, my father was humming the busy-bee tune and my mother was silent. I kept thinking she wanted to wait until we got home before shouting at me. But when my father unlocked the door to our apartment, my mother walked in and then went to the back, into the bedroom. No accusations. No blame. And in a way, I felt disappointed. I had been waiting for her to start shouting, so I could shout back and cry and blame her for all my misery.

I assumed my talent-show fiasco meant I never had to play the piano again. But two days later, after school, my mother came out of the kitchen and saw me watching TV.

"Four clock," she reminded me as if it were any other day. I was stunned, as though she were asking me to go through the talent-show torture again. I wedged myself more tightly in front of the TV.

"Turn off TV," she called from the kitchen five minutes later.

I didn't budge. And then I decided. I didn't have to do what my mother said anymore. I wasn't her slave. This wasn't China. I had listened to her before and look what happened. She was the stupid one.

She came out from the kitchen and stood in the arched entryway of the living room. "Four clock," she said once again, louder.

"I'm not going to play anymore," I said nonchalantly. "Why should I? I'm not a genius."

She walked over and stood in front of the TV. I saw her chest was heaving up and down in an angry way.

"No!" I said, and I now felt stronger, as if my true self had finally emerged. So this was what had been inside me all along.

"No! I won't!" I screamed.

She yanked me by the arm, pulled me off the floor, snapped off the TV. She was frighteningly strong, half pulling, half carrying me toward the piano as I kicked the throw rugs under my feet. She lifted me up and onto the hard bench. I was sobbing by now, looking at her bitterly. Her chest was heaving even more and her mouth was open, smiling crazily as if she were pleased I was crying.

"You want me to be someone that I'm not!" I sobbed. "I'll never be the kind of daughter you want me to be!"

"Only two kinds of daughters," she shouted in Chinese. "Those who are obedient and those who follow their own mind! Only one kind of daughter can live in this house. Obedient daughter!"

"Then I wish I wasn't your daughter. I wish you weren't my mother," I shouted. As I said these things I got scared. I felt like worms and toads and slimy things were crawling out of my chest, but it also felt good, as if this awful side of me had surfaced, at last.

"Too late change this," said my mother shrilly.

And I could sense her anger rising to its breaking point. I wanted to see it spill over. And that's when I remembered the babies she had lost in China, the ones we never talked about. "Then I wish I'd never been born!" I shouted. "I wish I were dead! Like them."

It was as if I had said the magic words, Alakazam!—and her face went blank, her mouth closed, her arms went slack, and she backed out of the room, stunned, as if she were blowing away like a small brown leaf, thin, brittle, lifeless.

It was not the only disappointment my mother felt in me. In the years that followed, I failed her so many times, each time asserting my own will, my right to fall short of expectations. I didn't get straight As. I didn't become class president. I didn't get into Stanford. I dropped out of college.

For unlike my mother, I did not believe I could be anything I wanted to be. I could only be me.

And for all those years, we never talked about the disaster at the recital or my terrible accusations afterward at the piano bench. All that remained unchecked, like a betrayal that was now unspeakable. So I never found a way to ask her why she had hoped for something so large that failure was inevitable.

And even worse, I never asked her what frightened me the most: Why had she given up hope?

For after our struggle at the piano, she never mentioned my playing again. The lessons stopped, the lid to the piano was closed, shutting out the dust, my misery, and her dreams.

So she surprised me. A few years ago, she offered to give me the piano, for my thirtieth birthday. I had not played in all those years. I saw the offer as a sign of forgiveness, a tremendous burden removed.

"Are you sure?" I asked shyly. "I mean, won't you and Dad miss it?"

"No, this your piano," she said firmly. "Always your piano. You only one can play."

"Well, I probably can't play anymore," I said. "It's been years."

"You pick up fast," said my mother, as if she knew this was certain. "You have natural talent. You could been genius if you want to."

"No I couldn't."

"You just not trying," said my mother. And she was neither angry nor sad. She said it as if to announce a fact that could never be disproved. "Take it," she said.

But I didn't at first. It was enough that she had offered it to me. And after that, every time I saw it in my parents' living room, standing in front of the bay windows, it made me feel proud, as if it were a shiny trophy I had won back.

Last week I sent a tuner over to my parents' apartment and had the piano reconditioned, for purely sentimental reasons. My mother had died a few months before and I had been getting things in order for my father, a little bit at a time. I put the jewelry in special silk pouches. The sweaters she had knitted in yellow, pink, bright orange—all the colors I hated—I put those in moth-proof boxes. I found some old Chinese silk dresses, the kind with little slits up the sides. I rubbed the old silk against my skin, then wrapped them in tissue and decided to take them home with me.

After I had the piano tuned, I opened the lid and touched the keys. It sounded even richer than I remembered. Really, it was a very good piano. Inside the bench were the same exercise notes with handwritten scales, the same secondhand music books with their covers held together with yellow tape.

I opened up the Schumann book to the dark little piece I had played at the recital. It was on the left-hand side of the page, "Pleading Child." It looked more difficult than I remembered. I played a few bars, surprised at how easily the notes came back to me.

And for the first time, or so it seemed, I noticed the piece on the right-hand side. It was called "Perfectly Contented." I tried to play this one as well. It had a lighter melody but the same flowing rhythm and turned out to be quite easy. "Pleading Child" was shorter but slower; "Perfectly Contented" was longer but faster. And after I played them both a few times, I realized they were two halves of the same song.

[1989]

SANDRA CISNEROS   [b. 1954]

The House on Mango Street

We didn't always live on Mango Street. Before that we lived on Loomis on the third floor, and before that we lived on Keeler. Before Keeler it was Paulina, and before that I can't remember. But what I remember most is moving a lot. Each time it seemed there'd be one more of us. By the time we got to Mango Street we were six—Mama, Papa, Carlos, Kiki, my sister Nenny, and me.

The house on Mango Street is ours, and we don't have to pay rent to anybody, or share the yard with the people downstairs, or be careful not to make too much noise, and there isn't a landlord banging on the ceiling with a broom. But even so, it's not the house we'd thought we'd get.

We had to leave the flat on Loomis quick. The water pipes broke and the landlord wouldn't fix them because the house was too old. We had to leave fast. We were using the washroom next door and carrying water over in empty milk gallons. That's why Mama and Papa looked for a house, and that's why we moved into the house on Mango Street, far away, on the other side of town.

They always told us that one day we would move into a house, a real house that would be ours for always so we wouldn't have to move each year. And our house would have running water and pipes that worked. And inside it would have real stairs, not hallway stairs, but stairs inside like the houses on T.V. And we'd have a basement and at least three washrooms so when we took a bath we wouldn't have to tell everybody. Our house would be white with trees around it, a great big yard and grass growing without a fence. This was the house Papa talked about when he held a lottery ticket and this was the house Mama dreamed up in the stories she told us before we went to bed.

But the house on Mango Street is not the way they told it at all. It's small and red with tight steps in front and windows so small you'd think they were holding their breath. Bricks are crumbling in places, and the front door is so swollen you have to push hard to get in. There is no front yard, only four little elms the city planted by the curb. Out back is a small garage for the car we don't own yet and a small yard that looks smaller between the two buildings on either side. There are stairs in our house, but they're ordinary hallway stairs, and the house has only one washroom. Everybody has to share a bedroom—Mama and Papa, Carlos and Kiki, me and Nenny.

Once when we were living on Loomis, a nun from my school passed by and saw me playing out front. The laundromat downstairs had been boarded up because it had been robbed two days before and the owner had painted on the wood YES WE'RE OPEN so as not to lose business.

Where do you live? she asked.

There, I said pointing up to the third floor.

You live *there*?

There. I had to look to where she pointed—the third floor, the paint peeling, wooden bars Papa had nailed on the windows so we wouldn't fall out. You live *there*? The way she said it made me feel like nothing. *There.* I lived *there.* I nodded.

I knew then I had to have a house. A real house. One I could point to. But this isn't it. The house on Mango Street isn't it. For the time being, Mama says. Temporary, says Papa. But I know how those things go.

[1983]

HA JIN   [b. 1956]

Saboteur

Mr. Chiu and his bride were having lunch in the square before Muji Train Station. On the table between them were two bottles of soda spewing out brown foam, and two paper boxes of rice and sautéed cucumber and pork. "Let's eat," he said to her, and broke the connected ends of the chopsticks. He picked up a slice of streaky pork and put it into his mouth. As he was chewing, a few crinkles appeared on his thin jaw.

To his right, at another table, two railroad policemen were drinking tea and laughing; it seemed that the stout, middle-aged man was telling a joke to his young comrade, who was tall and of athletic build. Now and again they would steal a glance at Mr. Chiu's table.

The air smelled of rotten melon. A few flies kept buzzing above the couple's lunch. Hundreds of people were rushing around to get on the platform or to catch buses to downtown. Food and fruit vendors were crying for customers in lazy voices. About a dozen young women, representing the local hotels, held up placards that displayed the daily prices and words as large as a palm, like *Free Meals*, *Air Conditioning*, and *On the River*. In the center of the square stood a concrete statue of Chairman Mao, at whose feet peasants were napping with their backs on the warm granite and with their faces toward the sunny sky. A flock of pigeons perched on the chairman's raised hand and forearm.

The rice and cucumber tasted good and Mr. Chiu was eating unhurriedly. His sallow face showed exhaustion. He was glad that the honeymoon was finally over and that he and his bride were heading for Harbin. During the two weeks' vacation, he had been worried about his liver because three months ago he had suffered from acute hepatitis; he was afraid he might have a relapse. But there had been no severe symptom, despite his liver being still big and tender. On the whole he was pleased with his health, which could even endure the strain of a honeymoon; indeed, he was on the course of recovery. He looked at his bride, who took off her wire glasses, kneading the root of her nose with her fingertips. Beads of sweat coated her pale cheeks.

"Are you all right, sweetheart?" he asked.

"I have a headache. I didn't sleep well last night."

"Take an aspirin, will you?"

393

"It's not that serious. Tomorrow is Sunday and I can sleep longer. Don't worry."

As they were talking, the stout policeman at the next table stood up and threw a bowl of tea in their direction. Both Mr. Chiu's and his bride's sandals were wet instantly.

"Hooligan!" she said in a low voice.

Mr. Chiu got to his feet and said out loud, "Comrade policeman, why did you do this?" He stretched out his right foot to show the wet sandal.

"Do what?" the stout man asked huskily, glaring at Mr. Chiu while the young fellow was whistling.

"See, you dumped water on our feet."

"You're lying. You wet your shoes yourself."

"Comrade policeman, your duty is to keep order, but you purposely tortured us common citizens. Why violate the law you are supposed to enforce?" As Mr. Chiu was speaking, dozens of people began gathering around.

With a wave of his hand, the man said to the young fellow, "Let's get hold of him!"

They grabbed Mr. Chiu and clamped handcuffs around his wrists. He cried, "You can't do this to me. This is utterly unreasonable."

"Shut up!" The man pulled out his pistol. "You can use your tongue at our headquarters."

The young fellow added, "You're a saboteur, you know? You're disrupting public order."

The bride was too terrified to say anything coherent. She was a recent college graduate, had majored in fine arts, and had never seen the police make an arrest. All she could say now was "Oh please, please!"

The policemen were pulling Mr. Chiu, but he refused to go with them, holding the corner of the table and shouting, "We have a train to catch. We already bought the tickets."

The stout man punched him in the chest. "Shut up. Let your ticket expire." With the pistol butt he chopped Mr. Chiu's hands, which at once released the table. Together the two men dragged him away to the police station.

Realizing he had to go with them, Mr. Chiu turned his head and shouted to his bride, "Don't wait for me here. Take the train. If I'm not back by tomorrow morning, send someone over to get me out."

She nodded, covering her sobbing mouth with her palm.

After removing his shoelaces, they locked Mr. Chiu into a cell in the back of the Railroad Police Station. The single window in the room was blocked by six steel bars; it faced a spacious yard in which stood a few pines. Beyond the trees two swings hung from an iron frame, swaying gently in the breeze. Somewhere in the building a cleaver was chopping rhythmically. There must be a kitchen upstairs, Mr. Chiu thought.

He was too exhausted to worry about what they would do to him, so he lay down on the narrow bed with his eyes shut. He wasn't afraid. The Cultural Revolution° was over already, and recently the Party had been propagating the idea that all citizens were equal before the law. The police ought to be a law-abiding model for common people. As long as he remained cool-headed and reasoned with them, they might not harm him.

Late in the afternoon he was taken to the Interrogation Bureau on the second floor. On his way there, in the stairwell, he ran into the middle-aged policeman who had manhandled him. The man grinned, rolling his bulgy eyes and pointing his fingers at him like firing a pistol. Egg of a tortoise!, Mr. Chiu cursed mentally.

The moment he sat down in the office, he burped, his palm shielding his mouth. In front of him, across the long desk, sat the chief of the bureau and a donkey-faced man. On the glass desktop was a folder containing information on his case. He felt it bizarre that in just a matter of hours they had accumulated a small pile of writing about him. On second thought, he began to wonder whether they had kept a file on him all the time. How could this have happened? He lived and worked in Harbin, more than three hundred miles away, and this was his first time in Muji City.

The chief of the bureau was a thin, bald man who looked serene and intelligent. His slim hands handled the written pages in the folder like those of a lecturing scholar. To Mr. Chiu's left sat a young scribe, with a clipboard on his knee and a black fountain pen in his hand.

"Your name?" the chief asked, apparently reading out the question from a form.

"Chiu Maguang."

"Age?"

"Thirty-four."

"Profession?"

"Lecturer."

"Work unit?"

"Harbin University."

"Political status?"

"Communist Party member."

The chief put down the paper and began to speak. "Your crime is sabotage, although it hasn't induced serious consequences yet. Because you

---

Cultural Revolution (1966–1976): A government action to eliminate Western ideas and enforce socialism in Chinese society.

are a Party member, you should be punished more. You have failed to be a model for the masses and you—"

"Excuse me, sir," Mr. Chiu cut him off.

"What?"

"I didn't do anything. Your men are the saboteurs of our social order. They threw hot tea on my feet and my wife's feet. Logically speaking, you should criticize them, if not punish them."

"That statement is groundless. You have no witness. How could I believe you?" the chief said matter-of-factly.

"This is my evidence." He raised his right hand. "Your man hit my fingers with a pistol."

"That can't prove how your feet got wet. Besides, you could hurt your fingers by yourself."

"But I told the truth!" Anger flared up in Mr. Chiu. "Your police station owes me an apology. My train ticket has expired, my new leather sandals are ruined, and I am late for a conference in the provincial capital. You must compensate me for the damage and losses. Don't mistake me for a common citizen who would tremble when you sneeze. I'm a scholar, a philosopher, and an expert in dialectical materialism. If necessary, we will argue about this in the *Northeastern Daily*, or we will go to the highest People's Court in Beijing. Tell me, what's your name?" He got carried away by his harangue, which was by no means trivial and had worked to his advantage on numerous occasions.

"Stop bluffing us," the donkey-faced man broke in. "We have seen a lot of your kind. We can easily prove you are guilty. Here are some of the statements given by the eyewitnesses." He pushed a few sheets of paper toward Mr. Chiu.

Mr. Chiu was dazed to see the different handwritings, which all stated that he had shouted in the square to attract attention and refused to obey the police. One of the witnesses had identified herself as a purchasing agent from a shipyard in Shanghai. Something stirred in Mr. Chiu's stomach, a pain rising to his ribs. He gave out a faint moan.

"Now, you have to admit you are guilty," the chief said. "Although it's a serious crime, we won't punish you severely, provided you write out a self-criticism and promise that you won't disrupt public order again. In other words, whether you will be released will depend on your attitude toward this crime."

"You're daydreaming," Mr. Chiu cried. "I won't write a word, because I'm innocent. I demand that you provide me with a letter of apology so I can explain to my university why I'm late."

Both the interrogators smiled with contempt. "Well, we've never done that," said the chief, taking a puff of his cigarette.

"Then make this a precedent."

"It's unnecessary. We are pretty certain that you will comply with our wishes." The chief blew a column of smoke at Mr. Chiu's face.

At the tilt of the chief's head, two guards stepped forward and grabbed the criminal by the arms. Mr. Chiu meanwhile went on saying, "I shall report you to the provincial administration. You'll have to pay for this! You are worse than the Japanese military police."

They dragged him out of the room.

After dinner, which consisted of a bowl of millet porridge, a corn bun, and a piece of pickled turnip, Mr. Chiu began to have a fever, shaking with a chill and sweating profusely. He knew that the fire of anger had got into his liver and that he was probably having a relapse. No medicine was available, because his briefcase had been left with his bride. At home it would have been time for him to sit in front of their color TV, drinking jasmine tea and watching the evening news. It was so lonesome in here. The orange bulb above the single bed was the only source of light, which enabled the guards to keep him under surveillance at night. A moment ago he had asked them for a newspaper or a magazine to read, but they had turned him down.

Through the small opening on the door, noises came in. It seemed that the police on duty were playing poker or chess in a nearby office; shouts and laughter could be heard now and then. Meanwhile, an accordion kept coughing from a remote corner of the building. Looking at the ballpoint and the letter paper left for him by the guards when they took him back from the Interrogation Bureau, Mr. Chiu remembered the old saying, "When a scholar runs into soldiers, the more he argues, the muddier his point becomes." How ridiculous this whole thing was. He ruffled his thick hair with his fingers.

He felt miserable, massaging his stomach continually. To tell the truth, he was more upset than frightened, because he would have to catch up with his work once he was back home—a paper that was to meet the publishing deadline next week, and two dozen books he ought to read for the course he was going to teach in the fall.

A human shadow flitted across the opening. Mr. Chiu rushed to the door and shouted through the hole, "Comrade guard, comrade guard!"

"What do you want?" a voice rasped.

"I want you to inform your leaders that I'm very sick. I have heart disease and hepatitis. I may die here if you keep me like this without medication."

"No leader is on duty on the weekend. You have to wait till Monday."

"What? You mean I'll stay in here tomorrow?"

"Yes."

"Your station will be held responsible if anything happens to me."

"We know that. Take it easy, you won't die."

It seemed illogical that Mr. Chiu slept quite well that night, though the light above his head had been on all the time and the straw mattress was hard and infested with fleas. He was afraid of ticks, mosquitoes, cockroaches—any kind of insect but fleas and bedbugs. Once in the countryside, where his school's faculty and staff had helped the peasants harvest crops for a week, his colleagues had joked about his flesh, which they said must have tasted nonhuman to fleas. Except for him, they were all afflicted with hundreds of bites.

More amazing now, he felt he didn't miss his bride a lot. He even enjoyed sleeping alone, perhaps because the honeymoon had tired him out and he needed more rest.

The back yard was quiet on Sunday morning. Pale sunlight streamed through the pine branches. A few sparrows were jumping on the ground, catching caterpillars and ladybugs. Holding the steel bars, Mr. Chiu inhaled the morning air, which smelled meaty. There must be a restaurant or a delicatessen nearby. He reminded himself that he should take this detention with ease. A sentence that Chairman Mao had written to a hospitalized friend rose in his mind: "Since you are already in here, you may as well stay and make the best of it."

His desire for peace of mind originated from his fear that his hepatitis might get worse. He tried to remain unperturbed. However, he was sure that his liver was swelling up, since the fever still persisted. For a whole day he lay in bed, thinking about his paper on the nature of contradictions. Time and again he was overwhelmed by anger, cursing aloud, "A bunch of thugs!" He swore that once he was out, he would write an article about this experience. He had better find out some of the policemen's names.

It turned out to be a restful day for the most part; he was certain that his university would send somebody to his rescue. All he should do now was remain clam and wait patiently. Sooner or later the police would have to release him, although they had no idea that he might refuse to leave unless they wrote him an apology. Damn those hoodlums, they had ordered more than they could eat!

When he woke up on Monday morning, it was already light. Somewhere a man was moaning; the sound came from the back yard. After a long yawn, and kicking off the tattered blanket, Mr. Chiu climbed out of bed and went to the window. In the middle of the yard, a young man was fastened to a pine, his wrists handcuffed from behind around the trunk. He was wriggling and swearing loudly, but there was no sign of anyone else in the yard. He looked familiar to Mr. Chiu.

Mr. Chiu squinted his eyes to see who it was. To his astonishment, he recognized the man, who was Fenjin, a recent graduate from the Law Department at Harbin University. Two years ago Mr. Chiu had taught a course in Marxist materialism in which Fenjin had been enrolled. Now, how on earth had this young devil landed here?

Then it dawned on him that Fenjin must have been sent over by his bride. What a stupid woman! What a bookworm, who knew only how to read foreign novels. He had expected that she would talk to the school's security section, which would for sure send a cadre here. Fenjin held no official position; he merely worked in a private law firm that had just two lawyers; in fact, they had little business except for some detective work for men and women who suspected their spouses of having extramarital affairs. Mr. Chiu was overcome with a wave of nausea.

Should he call out to let his student know he was nearby? He decided not to, because he didn't know what had happened. Fenjin must have quarreled with the police to incur such a punishment. Yet this would not have occurred if Fenjin hadn't come to his rescue. So no matter what, Mr. Chiu had to do something. But what could he do?

It was going to be a scorcher. He could see purple steam shimmering and rising from the ground among the pines. Poor devil, he thought, as he raised a bowl of corn glue to his mouth, sipped, and took a bite of a piece of salted celery.

When a guard came to collect the bowl and the chopsticks, Mr. Chiu asked what had happened to the man in the back yard. "He called our boss 'bandit,'" the guard said. "He claimed he was a lawyer or something. An arrogant son of a rabbit."

Now it was obvious that Mr. Chiu had to do something to help his rescuer. Before he could figure out a way, a scream broke out in the back yard. He rushed to the window and saw a tall policeman standing before Fenjin, an iron bucket on the ground. It was the same young fellow who had arrested Mr. Chiu in the square two days before. The man pinched Fenjin's nose, then raised his hand, which stayed in the air for a few seconds, then slapped the lawyer across the face. As Fenjin was groaning, the man lifted up the bucket and poured water on his head.

"This will keep you from getting sunstroke, boy. I'll give you some more every hour," the man said loudly.

Fenjin kept his eyes shut, yet his wry face showed that he was struggling to hold back from cursing the policeman or that he was probably sobbing in silence. He sneezed, then raised his face and shouted, "Let me go take a piss."

"Oh yeah?" the man bawled. "Pee in your pants."

Still Mr. Chiu didn't make any noise, holding the steel bars with both hands, his fingers white. The policeman turned and glanced at the cell's window; his pistol, partly holstered, glittered in the sun. With a snort he spat his cigarette butt to the ground and stamped it into the dust.

Then the cell door opened and the guards motioned Mr. Chiu to come out. Again they took him upstairs to the Interrogation Bureau.

The same men were in the office, though this time the scribe was sitting there empty-handed. At the sight of Mr. Chiu the chief said, "Ah, here you are. Please be seated."

After Mr. Chiu sat down, the chief waved a white silk fan and said to him, "You may have seen your lawyer. He's a young man without manners, so our director had him taught a crash lesson in the back yard."

"It's illegal to do that. Aren't you afraid to appear in a newspaper?"

"No, we are not, not even on TV. What else can you do? We are not afraid of any story you make up. We call it fiction. What we do care is that you cooperate with us; that's to say, you must admit your crime."

"What if I refuse to cooperate?"

"Then your lawyer will continue his education in the sunshine."

A swoon swayed Mr. Chiu, and he held the arms of the chair to steady himself. A numb pain stung him in the upper stomach and nauseated him, and his head was throbbing. He was sure that the hepatitis was finally attacking him. Anger was flaming up in his chest. His throat was tight and clogged.

The chief resumed, "As a matter of fact, you don't have to write out your self-criticism. We had your crime described clearly here. What we need is just your signature."

Holding back his rage, Mr. Chiu said, "Let me look at that."

With a smirk the donkey-faced man handed him a sheet, which carried these words: "I hereby admit that on July 13 I disrupted public order at Muji Train Station, and that I refused to listen to reason when the railroad police issued their warning. Thus I myself am responsible for my arrest. After two days' detention, I have realized the reactionary nature of my crime. From now on, I shall continue to educate myself with all my effort and shall never commit this kind of crime again."

A voice started screaming in Mr. Chiu's head, "Lie, lie!" But he shook his head and forced the voice away. He asked the chief, "If I sign this, will you release both my lawyer and me?"

"Of course, we'll do that." The chief was drumming his fingers on the blue folder—their file on him.

Mr. Chiu signed his name and put his thumbprint under his signature.

"Now you are free to go," the chief said with a smile, and handed him a piece of paper to wipe his thumb with.

Mr. Chiu was so sick that he didn't stand up from the chair at the first try. Then he doubled his effort and rose to his feet. He staggered out of the building to meet his lawyer in the back yard. In his chest he felt as though there were a bomb. If he were able to, he would have razed the entire police station and eliminated all their families. Though he knew he could do nothing like that, he made up his mind to do something.

"Sorry about this torture, Fenjin," Mr. Chiu said when they met.

"It doesn't matter. They are savages." The lawyer brushed a patch of dirt off his jacket with his trembling fingers. Water was still dribbling from the bottoms of his trouser legs.

"Let's go now," the teacher said.

The moment they came out of the police station, Mr. Chiu caught sight of a tea stand. He grabbed Fenjin's arm and walked over to the old woman at the table. "Two bowls of black tea," he said, and handed her a one-yuan note.

After the first bowl, they each had another one. Then they set out for the train station. But before they walked fifty yards, Mr. Chiu insisted on eating a bowl of tree-ear soup at a food stand. Fenjin agreed. He told his teacher, "Don't treat me like a guest."

"No, I want to eat something myself."

As if dying of hunger, Mr. Chiu dragged his lawyer from restaurant to restaurant near the police station, but at each place he ordered no more than two bowls of food. Fenjin wondered why his teacher wouldn't stay at one place and eat his fill.

Mr. Chiu bought noodles, wonton, eight-grain porridge, and chicken soup, respectively, at four restaurants. While eating, he kept saying through his teeth, "If only I could kill all the bastards!" At the last place he merely took a few sips of the soup without tasting the chicken cubes and mushrooms.

Fenjin was baffled by his teacher, who looked ferocious and muttered to himself mysteriously, and whose jaundiced face was covered with dark puckers. For the first time Fenjin thought of Mr. Chiu as an ugly man.

Within a month, over eight hundred people contracted acute hepatitis in Muji. Six died of the disease, including two children. Nobody knew how the epidemic had started.

[2000]

SHERMAN ALEXIE   [b. 1966]

The Lone Ranger and Tonto Fistfight in Heaven

[handwritten margin notes: Racial bias → Attitude About Life? Relationships we try to form]

Too hot to sleep so I walked down to the Third Avenue 7-11 for a Cream-sicle and the company of a graveyard-shift cashier. I know that game. I worked graveyard for a Seattle 7-11 and got robbed once too often. The last time the bastard locked me in the cooler. He even took my money and basketball shoes.

The graveyard-shift worker in the Third Avenue 7-11 looked like they all do. Acne scars and a bad haircut, work pants that showed off his white socks, and those cheap black shoes that have no support. My arches still ache from my year at the Seattle 7-11.

"Hello," he asked when I walked into his store. "How you doing?"

I gave him a half-wave as I headed back to the freezer. He looked me over so he could describe me to the police later. I knew the look. One of my old girlfriends said I started to look at her that way, too. She left me not long after that. No, I left her and don't blame her for anything. That's how it happened. When one person starts to look at another like a criminal, then the love is over. It's logical.

"I don't trust you," she said to me. "You get too angry."

She was white and I lived with her in Seattle. Some nights we fought so bad that I would just get in my car and drive all night, only stop to fill up on gas. In fact, I worked the graveyard shift to spend as much time away from her as possible. But I learned all about Seattle that way, driving its back ways and dirty alleys.

Sometimes, though, I would forget where I was and get lost. I'd drive for hours, searching for something familiar. Seems like I'd spent my whole life that way, looking for anything I recognized. Once, I ended up in a nice residential neighborhood and somebody must have been worried because the police showed up and pulled me over.

"What are you doing out here?" the police officer asked me as he looked over my license and registration.

"I'm lost."

"Well, where are you supposed to be?" he asked me, and I knew there

402

were plenty of places I wanted to be, but none where I was supposed
to be.

"I got in a fight with my girlfriend," I said. "I was just driving around,
blowing off steam, you know?"

"Well, you should be more careful where you drive," the officer said.
"You're making people nervous. You don't fit the profile of the neighborhood." Racial profiling

I wanted to tell him that I didn't really fit the profile of the country but
I knew it would just get me into trouble.

"Can I help you?" the 7-11 clerk asked me loudly, searching for some
response that would reassure him that I wasn't an armed robber. He
knew this dark skin and long, black hair of mine was dangerous. I had
potential.

"Just getting a Creamsicle," I said after a long interval. It was a sick
twist to pull on the guy, but it was late and I was bored. I grabbed my
Creamsicle and walked back to the counter slowly, scanned the aisles for
effect. I wanted to whistle low and menacingly but I never learned to
whistle.

"Pretty hot out tonight?" he asked, that old rhetorical weather bullshit
question designed to put us both at ease.

"Hot enough to make you go crazy," I said and smiled. He swallowed
hard like a white man does in those situations. I looked him over. Same
old green, red, and white 7-11 jacket and thick glasses. But he wasn't
ugly, just misplaced and marked by loneliness. If he wasn't working there
that night, he'd be at home alone, flipping through channels and wishing
he could afford HBO or Showtime.

"Will this be all?" he asked me, in that company effort to make me do
some impulse shopping. Like adding a clause onto a treaty. *We'll take
Washington and Oregon, and you get six pine trees and a brand-new Chrysler Cordoba.* I knew how to make and break promises.

"No," I said and paused. "Give me a Cherry Slushie, too."

"What size?" he asked, relieved.

"Large," I said, and he turned his back to me to make the drink. He
realized his mistake but it was too late. He stiffened, ready for the gunshot or the blow behind the ear. When it didn't come, he turned back
to me.

"I'm sorry," he said. "What size did you say?"

"Small," I said and changed the story.

"But I thought you said large."

"If you knew I wanted a large, then why did you ask me again?" I asked
him and laughed. He looked at me, couldn't decide if I was giving him
serious shit or just goofing. There was something about him I liked, even
if it was three in the morning and he was white.

"Hey," I said. "Forget the Slushie. What I want to know is if you know all the words to the theme from *The Brady Bunch*?"

He looked at me, confused at first, then laughed.

"Shit," he said. "I was hoping you weren't crazy. You were scaring me."

"Well, I'm going to get crazy if you don't know the words."

He laughed loudly then, told me to take the Creamsicle for free. He was the graveyard-shift manager and those little demonstrations of power tickled him. All seventy-five cents of it. I knew how much everything cost.

"Thanks," I said to him and walked out the door. I took my time walking home, let the heat of the night melt the Creamsicle all over my hand. At three in the morning I could act just as young as I wanted to act. There was no one around to ask me to grow up.

In Seattle, I broke lamps. She and I would argue and I'd break a lamp, just pick it up and throw it down. At first she'd buy replacement lamps, expensive and beautiful. But after a while she'd buy lamps from Goodwill or garage sales. Then she just gave up the idea entirely and we'd argue in the dark.

"You're just like your brother," she'd yell. "Drunk all the time and stupid."

"My brother don't drink that much."

She and I never tried to hurt each other physically. I did love her, after all, and she loved me. But those arguments were just as damaging as a fist. Words can be like that, you know? Whenever I get into arguments now, I remember her and I also remember Muhammad Ali. He knew the power of his fists but, more importantly, he knew the power of his words, too. Even though he only had an IQ of 80 or so, Ali was a genius. And she was a genius, too. She knew exactly what to say to cause me the most pain.

But don't get me wrong. I walked through that relationship with an executioner's hood. Or more appropriately, with war paint and sharp arrows. She was a kindergarten teacher and I continually insulted her for that.

"Hey, schoolmarm," I asked. "Did your kids teach you anything new today?"

And I always had crazy dreams. I always have had them, but it seemed they became nightmares more often in Seattle.

In one dream, she was a missionary's wife and I was a minor war chief. We fell in love and tried to keep it secret. But the missionary caught us fucking in the barn and shot me. As I lay dying, my tribe learned of the shooting and attacked the whites all across the reservation. I died and my soul drifted above the reservation.

Disembodied, I could see everything that was happening. Whites killing Indians and Indians killing whites. At first it was small, just my tribe and the few whites who lived there. But my dream grew, intensified. Other tribes arrived on horseback to continue the slaughter of whites, and the United States Cavalry rode into battle.

The most vivid image of that dream stays with me. Three mounted soldiers played polo with a dead Indian woman's head. When I first dreamed it, I thought it was just a product of my anger and imagination. But since then, I've read similar accounts of that kind of evil in the old West. Even more terrifying, though, is the fact that those kinds of brutal things are happening today in places like El Salvador.

All I know for sure, though, is that I woke from that dream in terror, packed up all my possessions, and left Seattle in the middle of the night.

"I love you," she said as I left her. "And don't ever come back."

I drove through the night, over the Cascades, down into the plains of central Washington, and back home to the Spokane Indian Reservation.

When I finished the Creamsicle that the 7-11 clerk gave me, I held the wooden stick up into the air and shouted out very loudly. A couple lights flashed on in windows and a police car cruised by me a few minutes later. I waved to the men in blue and they waved back accidentally. When I got home it was still too hot to sleep so I picked up a week-old newspaper from the floor and read.

There was another civil war, another terrorist bomb exploded, and one more plane crashed and all aboard were presumed dead. The crime rate was rising in every city with populations larger than 100,000, and a farmer in Iowa shot his banker after foreclosure on his 1,000 acres.

A kid from Spokane won the local spelling bee by spelling the word *rhinoceros*.

When I got back to the reservation, my family wasn't surprised to see me. They'd been expecting me back since the day I left for Seattle. There's an old Indian poet who said that Indians can reside in the city, but they can never live there. That's as close to truth as any of us can get.

Mostly I watched television. For weeks I flipped through channels, searched for answers in the game shows and soap operas. My mother would circle the want ads in red and hand the paper to me.

"What are you going to do with the rest of your life?" she asked.

"Don't know," I said, and normally, for almost any other Indian in the country, that would have been a perfectly fine answer. But I was special, a former college student, a smart kid. I was one of those Indians who was supposed to make it, to rise above the rest of the reservation like a fucking eagle or something. I was the new kind of warrior.

For a few months I didn't even look at the want ads my mother circled, just left the newspaper where she had set it down. After a while, though,

I got tired of television and started to play basketball again. I'd been a good player in high school, nearly great, and almost played at the college I attended for a couple years. But I'd been too out of shape from drinking and sadness to ever be good again. Still, I liked the way the ball felt in my hands and the way my feet felt inside my shoes.

Just About him

made a contribution

At first I just shot baskets by myself. It was selfish, and I also wanted to learn the game again before I played against anybody else. Since I had been good before and embarrassed fellow tribal members, I knew they would want to take revenge on me. Forget about the cowboys versus Indians business. The most intense competition on any reservation is Indians versus Indians.

But on the night I was ready to play for real, there was this white guy at the gym, playing with all the Indians.

"Who is that?" I asked Jimmy Seyler.

"He's the new BIA° chief's kid."

"Can he play?"

"Oh, yeah."

And he could play. He played Indian ball, fast and loose, better than all the Indians there.

"How long's he been playing here?" I asked.

"Long enough."

I stretched my muscles, and everybody watched me. All these Indians watched one of their old and dusty heroes. Even though I had played most of my ball at the white high school I went to, I was still all Indian, you know? I was Indian when it counted, and this BIA kid needed to be beaten by an Indian, any Indian.

I jumped into the game and played well for a little while. It felt good. I hit a few shots, grabbed a rebound or two, played enough defense to keep the other team honest. Then that white kid took over the game. He was too good. Later, he'd play college ball back East and would nearly make the Knicks team a couple years on. But we didn't know any of that would happen. We just knew he was better that day and every other day.

The next morning I woke up tired and hungry, so I grabbed the want ads, found a job I wanted, and drove to Spokane to get it. I've been working at the high school exchange program ever since, typing and answering phones. Sometimes I wonder if the people on the other end of the line know that I'm Indian and if their voices would change if they did know.

One day I picked up the phone and it was her, calling from Seattle.

"I got your number from your mom," she said. "I'm glad you're working."

BIA: Bureau of Indian Affairs.

"Yeah, nothing like a regular paycheck."

"Are you drinking?"

"No, I've been on the wagon for almost a year."

"Good. "

The connection was good. I could hear her breathing in the spaces between our words. How do you talk to the real person whose ghost has haunted you? How do you tell the difference between the two?

"Listen," I said. "I'm sorry for everything."

"Me, too."

"What's going to happen to us?" I asked her and wished I had the answer for myself.

"I don't know," she said. "I want to change the world."

These days, living alone in Spokane, I wish I lived closer to the river, to the falls where ghosts of salmon jump. I wish I could sleep. I put down my paper or book and turn off all the lights, lie quietly in the dark. It may take hours, even years, for me to sleep again. There's nothing surprising or disappointing in that.

I know how all my dreams end anyway. *The fact that he is Indian. uncomfortable in own skin.*

[1993]

JHUMPA LAHIRI   [b. 1967]

Interpreter of Maladies

At the tea stall Mr. and Mrs. Das bickered about who should take Tina to the toilet. Eventually Mrs. Das relented when Mr. Das pointed out that he had given the girl her bath the night before. In the rearview mirror Mr. Kapasi watched as Mrs. Das emerged slowly from his bulky white Ambassador, dragging her shaved, largely bare legs across the back seat. She did not hold the little girl's hand as they walked to the rest room.

They were on their way to see the Sun Temple at Konarak. It was a dry, bright Saturday, the mid-July heat tempered by a steady ocean breeze, ideal weather for sightseeing. Ordinarily Mr. Kapasi would not have stopped so soon along the way, but less than five minutes after he'd picked up the family that morning in front of Hotel Sandy Villa, the little girl had complained. The first thing Mr. Kapasi had noticed when he saw Mr. and Mrs. Das, standing with their children under the portico of the hotel, was that they were very young, perhaps not even thirty. In addition to Tina they had two boys, Ronny and Bobby, who appeared very close in age and had teeth covered in a network of flashing silver wires. The family looked Indian but dressed as foreigners did, the children in stiff, brightly colored clothing and caps with translucent visors. Mr. Kapasi was accustomed to foreign tourists; he was assigned to them regularly because he could speak English. Yesterday he had driven an elderly couple from Scotland, both with spotted faces and fluffy white hair so thin it exposed their sunburnt scalps. In comparison, the tanned, youthful faces of Mr. and Mrs. Das were all the more striking. When he'd introduced himself, Mr. Kapasi had pressed his palms together in greeting, but Mr. Das squeezed hands like an American so that Mr. Kapasi felt it in his elbow. Mrs. Das, for her part, had flexed one side of her mouth, smiling dutifully at Mr. Kapasi, without displaying any interest in him.

As they waited at the tea stall, Ronny, who looked like the older of the two boys, clambered suddenly out of the back seat, intrigued by a goat tied to a stake in the ground.

"Don't touch it," Mr. Das said. He glanced up from his paperback tour book, which said "INDIA" in yellow letters and looked as if it had been published abroad. His voice, somehow tentative and a little shrill, sounded as though it had not yet settled into maturity.

"I want to give it a piece of gum," the boy called back as he trotted ahead.

Mr. Das stepped out of the car and stretched his legs by squatting briefly to the ground. A clean-shaven man, he looked exactly like a magnified version of Ronny. He had a sapphire blue visor, and was dressed in shorts, sneakers, and a T-shirt. The camera slung around his neck, with an impressive telephoto lens and numerous buttons and markings, was the only complicated thing he wore. He frowned, watching as Ronny rushed toward the goat, but appeared to have no intention of intervening. "Bobby, make sure that your brother doesn't do anything stupid."

"I don't feel like it," Bobby said, not moving. He was sitting in the front seat beside Mr. Kapasi, studying a picture of the elephant god taped to the glove compartment.

"No need to worry," Mr. Kapasi said. "They are quite tame." Mr. Kapasi was forty-six years old, with receding hair that had gone completely silver, but his butterscotch complexion and his unlined brow, which he treated in spare moments to dabs of lotus-oil balm, made it easy to imagine what he must have looked like at an earlier age. He wore gray trousers and a matching jacket-style shirt, tapered at the waist, with short sleeves and a large pointed collar, made of a thin but durable synthetic material. He had specified both the cut and the fabric to his tailor—it was his preferred uniform for giving tours because it did not get crushed during his long hours behind the wheel. Through the windshield he watched as Ronny circled around the goat, touched it quickly on its side, then trotted back to the car.

"You left India as a child?" Mr. Kapasi asked when Mr. Das had settled once again into the passenger seat.

"Oh, Mina and I were both born in America," Mr. Das announced with an air of sudden confidence. "Born and raised. Our parents live here now, in Assansol. They retired. We visit them every couple years." He turned to watch as the little girl ran toward the car, the wide purple bows of her sundress flopping on her narrow brown shoulders. She was holding to her chest a doll with yellow hair that looked as if it had been chopped, as a punitive measure, with a pair of dull scissors. "This is Tina's first trip to India, isn't it, Tina?"

"I don't have to go to the bathroom anymore," Tina announced.

"Where's Mina?" Mr. Das asked.

Mr. Kapasi found it strange that Mr. Das should refer to his wife by her first name when speaking to the little girl. Tina pointed to where Mrs. Das was purchasing something from one of the shirtless men who worked at the tea stall. Mr. Kapasi heard one of the shirtless men sing a phrase from a popular Hindi love song as Mrs. Das walked back to the car, but she did not appear to understand the words of the song, for she did not express irritation, or embarrassment, or react in any other way to the man's declarations.

He observed her. She wore a red-and-white-checkered skirt that stopped above her knees, slip-on shoes with a square wooden heel, and a close-fitting blouse styled like a man's undershirt. The blouse was decorated at chest-level with a calico appliqué in the shape of a strawberry. She was a short woman, with small hands like paws, her frosty pink fingernails painted to match her lips, and was slightly plump in her figure. Her hair, shorn only a little longer than her husband's, was parted far to one side. She was wearing large dark brown sunglasses with a pinkish tint to them, and carried a big straw bag, almost as big as her torso, shaped like a bowl, with a water bottle poking out of it. She walked slowly, carrying some puffed rice tossed with peanuts and chili peppers in a large packet made from newspapers. Mr. Kapasi turned to Mr. Das.

"Where in America do you live?"

"New Brunswick, New Jersey."

"Next to New York."

"Exactly. I teach middle school there."

"What subject?"

"Science. In fact, every year I take my students on a trip to the Museum of Natural History in New York City. In a way we have a lot in common, you could say, you and I. How long have you been a tour guide, Mr. Kapasi?"

"Five years."

Mrs. Das reached the car. "How long's the trip?" she asked, shutting the door.

"About two and a half hours," Mr. Kapasi replied.

At this Mrs. Das gave an impatient sigh, as if she had been traveling her whole life without pause. She fanned herself with a folded Bombay film magazine written in English.

"I thought that the Sun Temple is only eighteen miles north of Puri," Mr. Das said, tapping on the tour book.

"The roads to Konarak are poor. Actually it is a distance of fifty-two miles," Mr. Kapasi explained.

Mr. Das nodded, readjusting the camera strap where it had begun to chafe the back of his neck.

Before starting the ignition, Mr. Kapasi reached back to make sure the cranklike locks on the inside of each of the back doors were secured. As soon as the car began to move the little girl began to play with the lock on her side, clicking it with some effort forward and backward, but Mrs. Das said nothing to stop her. She sat a bit slouched at one end of the back seat, not offering her puffed rice to anyone. Ronny and Tina sat on either side of her, both snapping bright green gum.

"Look," Bobby said as the car began to gather speed. He pointed with his finger to the tall trees that lined the road. "Look."

"Monkeys!" Ronny shrieked. "Wow!"

They were seated in groups along the branches, with shining black faces, silver bodies, horizontal eyebrows, and crested heads. Their long gray tails dangled like a series of ropes among the leaves. A few scratched themselves with black leathery hands, or swung their feet, staring as the car passed.

"We call them the hanuman," Mr. Kapasi said. "They are quite common in the area."

As soon as he spoke, one of the monkeys leaped into the middle of the road, causing Mr. Kapasi to brake suddenly. Another bounced onto the hood of the car, then sprang away. Mr. Kapasi beeped his horn. The children began to get excited, sucking in their breath and covering their faces partly with their hands. They had never seen monkeys outside of a zoo, Mr. Das explained. He asked Mr. Kapasi to stop the car so that he could take a picture.

While Mr. Das adjusted his telephoto lens, Mrs. Das reached into her straw bag and pulled out a bottle of colorless nail polish, which she proceeded to stroke on the tip of her index finger.

The little girl stuck out a hand. "Mine too. Mommy, do mine too."

"Leave me alone," Mrs. Das said, blowing on her nail and turning her body slightly. "You're making me mess up."

The little girl occupied herself by buttoning and unbuttoning a pinafore on the doll's plastic body.

"All set," Mr. Das said, replacing the lens cap.

The car rattled considerably as it raced along the dusty road, causing them all to pop up from their seats every now and then, but Mrs. Das continued to polish her nails. Mr. Kapasi eased up on the accelerator, hoping to produce a smoother ride. When he reached for the gearshift the boy in front accommodated him by swinging his hairless knees out of the way. Mr. Kapasi noted that this boy was slightly paler than the other children. "Daddy, why is the driver sitting on the wrong side in this car, too?" the boy asked.

"They all do that here, dummy," Ronny said.

"Don't call your brother a dummy," Mr. Das said. He turned to Mr. Kapasi. "In America, you know . . . it confuses them."

"Oh yes, I am well aware," Mr. Kapasi said. As delicately as he could, he shifted gears again, accelerating as they approached a hill in the road. "I see it on *Dallas*, the steering wheels are on the left-hand side."

"What's *Dallas*?" Tina asked, banging her now naked doll on the seat behind Mr. Kapasi.

"It went off the air," Mr. Das explained. "It's a television show."

They were all like siblings, Mr. Kapasi thought as they passed a row of date trees. Mr. and Mrs. Das behaved like an older brother and sister, not parents. It seemed that they were in charge of the children only for the day; it was hard to believe they were regularly responsible for anything other than themselves. Mr. Das tapped on his lens cap, and his tour book, dragging his thumbnail occasionally across the pages so that they made a scraping sound. Mrs. Das continued to polish her nails. She had still not removed her sunglasses. Every now and then Tina renewed her plea that she wanted her nails done, too, and so at one point Mrs. Das flicked a drop of polish on the little girl's finger before depositing the bottle back inside her straw bag.

"Isn't this an air-conditioned car?" she asked, still blowing on her hand. The window on Tina's side was broken and could not be rolled down.

"Quit complaining," Mr. Das said. "It isn't so hot."

"I told you to get a car with air-conditioning," Mrs. Das continued. "Why do you do this, Raj, just to save a few stupid rupees. What are you saving us, fifty cents?"

Their accents sounded just like the ones Mr. Kapasi heard on American television programs, though not like the ones on *Dallas*.

"Doesn't it get tiresome, Mr. Kapasi, showing people the same thing every day?" Mr. Das asked, rolling down his own window all the way. "Hey, do you mind stopping the car. I just want to get a shot of this guy."

Mr. Kapasi pulled over to the side of the road as Mr. Das took a picture of a barefoot man, his head wrapped in a dirty turban, seated on top of a cart of grain sacks pulled by a pair of bullocks. Both the man and the bullocks were emaciated. In the back seat Mrs. Das gazed out another window, at the sky, where nearly transparent clouds passed quickly in front of one another.

"I look forward to it, actually," Mr. Kapasi said as they continued on their way. "The Sun Temple is one of my favorite places. In that way it is a reward for me. I give tours on Fridays and Saturdays only. I have another job during the week."

"Oh? Where?" Mr. Das asked.

"I work in a doctor's office."

"You're a doctor?"

"I am not a doctor. I work with one. As an interpreter."

"What does the doctor need an interpreter for?"

"He has a number of Gujarati patients. My father was Gujarati, but many people do not speak Gujarati in this area, including the doctor. And so the doctor asked me to work in his office, interpreting what the patients say."

"Interesting. I've never heard of anything like that," Mr. Das said.

Mr. Kapasi shrugged. "It is a job like any other."

"But so romantic," Mrs. Das said dreamily, breaking her extended silence. She lifted her pinkish brown sunglasses and arranged them on top of her head like a tiara. For the first time, her eyes met Mr. Kapasi's in the rearview mirror: pale, a bit small, their gaze fixed but drowsy.

Mr. Das craned to look at her. "What's so romantic about it?"

"I don't know. Something." She shrugged, knitting her brows together for an instant. "Would you like a piece of gum, Mr. Kapasi?" she asked brightly. She reached into her straw bag and handed him a small square wrapped in green-and-white-striped paper. As soon as Mr. Kapasi put the gum in his mouth a thick sweet liquid burst onto his tongue.

"Tell us more about your job, Mr. Kapasi," Mrs. Das said.

"What would you like to know, madame?"

"I don't know," she shrugged, munching on some puffed rice and licking the mustard oil from the corners of her mouth. "Tell us a typical situation." She settled back in her seat, her head tilted in a patch of sun, and closed her eyes. "I want to picture what happens."

"Very well. The other day a man came in with a pain in his throat."

"Did he smoke cigarettes?"

"No. It was very curious. He complained that he felt as if there were long pieces of straw stuck in his throat. When I told the doctor he was able to prescribe the proper medicine."

"That's so neat."

"Yes," Mr. Kapasi agreed after some hesitation.

"So these patients are totally dependent on you," Mrs. Das said. She spoke slowly, as if she were thinking aloud. "In a way, more dependent on you than the doctor."

"How do you mean? How could it be?"

"Well, for example, you could tell the doctor that the pain felt like a burning, not straw. The patient would never know what you had told the doctor, and the doctor wouldn't know that you had told the wrong thing. It's a big responsibility."

"Yes, a big responsibility you have there, Mr. Kapasi," Mr. Das agreed.

Mr. Kapasi had never thought of his job in such complimentary terms. To him it was a thankless occupation. He found nothing noble in interpreting people's maladies, assiduously translating the symptoms of so many swollen bones, countless cramps of bellies and bowels, spots on people's palms that changed color, shape, or size. The doctor, nearly half his age, had an affinity for bell-bottom trousers and made humorless jokes about the Congress party. Together they worked in a stale little infirmary where Mr. Kapasi's smartly tailored clothes clung to him in the heat, in spite of the blackened blades of a ceiling fan churning over their heads.

The job was a sign of his failings. In his youth he'd been a devoted scholar of foreign languages, the owner of an impressive collection of dictionaries. He had dreamed of being an interpreter for diplomats and dignitaries, resolving conflicts between people and nations, settling disputes of which he alone could understand both sides. He was a self-educated man. In a series of notebooks, in the evenings before his parents settled his marriage, he had listed the common etymologies of words, and at one point in his life he was confident that he could converse, if given the opportunity, in English, French, Russian, Portuguese, and Italian, not to mention Hindi, Bengali, Orissi, and Gujarati. Now only a handful of European phrases remained in his memory, scattered words for things like saucers and chairs. English was the only non-Indian language he spoke fluently anymore. Mr. Kapasi knew it was not a remarkable talent. Sometimes he feared that his children knew better English than he did, just from watching television. Still, it came in handy for the tours.

He had taken the job as an interpreter after his first son, at the age of seven, contracted typhoid—that was how he had first made the acquaintance of the doctor. At the time Mr. Kapasi had been teaching English in a grammar school, and he bartered his skills as an interpreter to pay the increasingly exorbitant medical bills. In the end the boy had died one evening in his mother's arms, his limbs burning with fever, but then there was the funeral to pay for, and the other children who were born soon enough, and the newer, bigger house, and the good schools and tutors, and the fine shoes and the television, and the countless other ways he tried to console his wife and to keep her from crying in her sleep, and so when the doctor offered to pay him twice as much as he earned at the grammar school, he accepted. Mr. Kapasi knew that his wife had little regard for his career as an interpreter. He knew it reminded her of the son she'd lost, and that she resented the other lives he helped, in his own small way, to save. If ever she referred to his position, she used the phrase "doctor's assistant," as if the process of interpretation were equal to taking someone's temperature, or changing a bedpan. She never asked him about the patients who came to the doctor's office, or said that his job was a big responsibility.

For this reason it flattered Mr. Kapasi that Mrs. Das was so intrigued by his job. Unlike his wife, she had reminded him of its intellectual challenges. She had also used the word "romantic." She did not behave in a romantic way toward her husband, and yet she had used the word to describe him. He wondered if Mr. and Mrs. Das were a bad match, just as he and his wife were. Perhaps they, too, had little in common apart from three children and a decade of their lives. The signs he recognized from his own marriage were there—the bickering, the indifference, the protracted silences. Her sudden interest in him, an interest she did not express in either her husband or her children, was mildly intoxicating. When Mr. Kapasi thought once again about how she had said "romantic," the feeling of intoxication grew.

He began to check his reflection in the rearview mirror as he drove, feeling grateful that he had chosen the gray suit that morning and not the brown one, which tended to sag a little in the knees. From time to time he glanced through the mirror at Mrs. Das. In addition to glancing at her face he glanced at the strawberry between her breasts, and the golden brown hollow in her throat. He decided to tell Mrs. Das about another patient, and another: the young woman who had complained of a sensation of raindrops in her spine, the gentleman whose birthmark had begun to sprout hairs. Mrs. Das listened attentively, stroking her hair with a small plastic brush that resembled an oval bed of nails, asking more questions, for yet another example. The children were quiet, intent on spotting more monkeys in the trees, and Mr. Das was absorbed by his tour book, so it seemed like a private conversation between Mr. Kapasi and Mrs. Das. In this manner the next half hour passed, and when they stopped for lunch at a roadside restaurant that sold fritters and omelette sandwiches, usually something Mr. Kapasi looked forward to on his tours so that he could sit in peace and enjoy some hot tea, he was disappointed. As the Das family settled together under a magenta umbrella fringed with white and orange tassels, and placed their orders with one of the waiters who marched about in tricornered caps, Mr. Kapasi reluctantly headed toward a neighboring table.

"Mr. Kapasi, wait. There's room here," Mrs. Das called out. She gathered Tina onto her lap, insisting that he accompany them. And so, together, they had bottled mango juice and sandwiches and plates of onions and potatoes deep-fried in graham-flour batter. After finishing two omelette sandwiches Mr. Das took more pictures of the group as they ate.

"How much longer?" he asked Mr. Kapasi as he paused to load a new roll of film in the camera.

"About half an hour more."

By now the children had gotten up from the table to look at more monkeys perched in a nearby tree, so there was a considerable space between Mrs. Das and Mr. Kapasi. Mr. Das placed the camera to his face and squeezed one eye shut, his tongue exposed at one corner of his mouth. "This looks funny. Mina, you need to lean in closer to Mr. Kapasi."

She did. He could smell a scent on her skin, like a mixture of whiskey and rosewater. He worried suddenly that she could smell his perspiration, which he knew had collected beneath the synthetic material of his shirt. He polished off his mango juice in one gulp and smoothed his silver hair with his hands. A bit of juice dripped onto his chin. He wondered if Mrs. Das had noticed.

She had not. "What's your address, Mr. Kapasi?" she inquired, fishing for something inside her straw bag.

"You would like my address?"

"So we can send you copies," she said. "Of the pictures." She handed him a scrap of paper which she had hastily ripped from a page of her film magazine. The blank portion was limited, for the narrow strip was crowded by lines of text and a tiny picture of a hero and heroine embracing under a eucalyptus tree.

The paper curled as Mr. Kapasi wrote his address in clear, careful letters. She would write to him, asking about his days interpreting at the doctor's office, and he would respond eloquently, choosing only the most entertaining anecdotes, ones that would make her laugh out loud as she read them in her house in New Jersey. In time she would reveal the disappointment of her marriage, and he his. In this way their friendship would grow, and flourish. He would possess a picture of the two of them, eating fried onions under a magenta umbrella, which he would keep, he decided, safely tucked between the pages of his Russian grammar. As his mind raced, Mr. Kapasi experienced a mild and pleasant shock. It was similar to a feeling he used to experience long ago when, after months of translating with the aid of a dictionary, he would finally read a passage from a French novel, or an Italian sonnet, and understand the words, one after another, unencumbered by his own efforts. In those moments Mr. Kapasi used to believe that all was right with the world, that all struggles were rewarded, that all of life's mistakes made sense in the end. The promise that he would hear from Mrs. Das now filled him with the same belief.

When he finished writing his address Mr. Kapasi handed her the paper, but as soon as he did so he worried that he had either misspelled his name, or accidentally reversed the numbers of his postal code. He dreaded the possibility of a lost letter, the photograph never reaching him, hovering somewhere in Orissa, close but ultimately unattainable. He thought of asking for the slip of paper again, just to make sure he had written his address accurately, but Mrs. Das had already dropped it into the jumble of her bag.

They reached Konarak at two-thirty. The temple, made of sandstone, was a massive pyramid-like structure in the shape of a chariot. It was dedicated to the great master of life, the sun, which struck three sides of the edifice as it made its journey each day across the sky. Twenty-four giant wheels were carved on the north and south sides of the plinth. The whole thing was drawn by a team of seven horses, speeding as if through the heavens. As they approached, Mr. Kapasi explained that the temple had been built between A.D. 1243 and 1255, with the efforts of twelve hundred artisans, by the great ruler of the Ganga dynasty, King Narasimhadeva the First, to commemorate his victory against the Muslim army.

"It says the temple occupies about a hundred and seventy acres of land," Mr. Das said, reading from his book.

"It's like a desert," Ronny said, his eyes wandering across the sand that stretched on all sides beyond the temple.

"The Chandrabhaga River once flowed one mile north of here. It is dry now," Mr. Kapasi said, turning off the engine.

They got out and walked toward the temple, posing first for pictures by the pair of lions that flanked the steps. Mr. Kapasi led them next to one of the wheels of the chariot, higher than any human being, nine feet in diameter.

"'The wheels are supposed to symbolize the wheel of life,'" Mr. Das read. "'They depict the cycle of creation, preservation, and achievement of realization.' Cool." He turned the page of his book. "'Each wheel is divided into eight thick and thin spokes, dividing the day into eight equal parts. The rims are carved with designs of birds and animals, whereas the medallions in the spokes are carved with women in luxurious poses, largely erotic in nature.'"

What he referred to were the countless friezes of entwined naked bodies, making love in various positions, women clinging to the necks of men, their knees wrapped eternally around their lovers' thighs. In addition to these were assorted scenes from daily life, of hunting and trading, of deer being killed with bows and arrows and marching warriors holding swords in their hands.

It was no longer possible to enter the temple, for it had filled with rubble years ago, but they admired the exterior, as did all the tourists Mr. Kapasi brought there, slowly strolling along each of its sides. Mr. Das trailed behind, taking pictures. The children ran ahead, pointing to figures of naked people, intrigued in particular by the Nagamithunas, the half-human, half-serpentine couples who were said, Mr. Kapasi told them, to live in the deepest waters of the sea. Mr. Kapasi was pleased that they liked the temple, pleased especially that it appealed to Mrs. Das. She stopped every three or four paces, staring silently at the carved lovers, and the processions of elephants, and the topless female musicians beating on two-sided drums.

Though Mr. Kapasi had been to the temple countless times, it occurred to him, as he, too, gazed at the topless women, that he had never seen his own wife fully naked. Even when they had made love she kept the panels of her blouse hooked together, the string of her petticoat knotted around her waist. He had never admired the backs of his wife's legs the way he now admired those of Mrs. Das, walking as if for his benefit alone. He had, of course, seen plenty of bare limbs before, belonging to the American and European ladies who took his tours. But Mrs. Das was different. Unlike the other women, who had an interest only in the temple, and kept their noses buried in a guidebook, or their eyes behind the lens of a camera, Mrs. Das had taken an interest in him.

Mr. Kapasi was anxious to be alone with her, to continue their private conversation, yet he felt nervous to walk at her side. She was lost behind her sunglasses, ignoring her husband's requests that she pose for another picture, walking past her children as if they were strangers. Worried that he might disturb her, Mr. Kapasi walked ahead, to admire, as he always did, the three life-sized bronze avatars of Surya, the sun god, each emerging from its own niche on the temple facade to greet the sun at dawn, noon, and evening. They wore elaborate headdresses, their languid, elongated eyes closed, their bare chests draped with carved chains and amulets. Hibiscus petals, offerings from previous visitors, were strewn at their gray-green feet. The last statue, on the northern wall of the temple, was Mr. Kapasi's favorite. This Surya had a tired expression, weary after a hard day of work, sitting astride a horse with folded legs. Even his horse's eyes were drowsy. Around his body were smaller sculptures of women in pairs, their hips thrust to one side.

"Who's that?" Mrs. Das asked. He was startled to see that she was standing beside him.

"He is the Astachala-Surya," Mr. Kapasi said. "The setting sun."

"So in a couple of hours the sun will set right here?" She slipped a foot out of one of her square-heeled shoes, rubbed her toes on the back of her other leg.

"That is correct."

She raised her sunglasses for a moment, then put them back on again. "Neat."

Mr. Kapasi was not certain exactly what the word suggested, but he had a feeling it was a favorable response. He hoped that Mrs. Das had understood Surya's beauty, his power. Perhaps they would discuss it further in their letters. He would explain things to her, things about India, and she would explain things to him about America. In its own way this correspondence would fulfill his dream, of serving as an interpreter between nations. He looked at her straw bag, delighted that his address lay nestled among its contents. When he pictured her so many thousands of miles away he plummeted, so much so that he had an overwhelming urge to wrap his arms around her, to freeze with her, even for an instant, in an embrace witnessed by his favorite Surya. But Mrs. Das had already started walking.

"When do you return to America?" he asked, trying to sound placid.

"In ten days."

He calculated: A week to settle in, a week to develop the pictures, a few days to compose her letter, two weeks to get to India by air. According to his schedule, allowing room for delays, he would hear from Mrs. Das in approximately six weeks' time.

The family was silent as Mr. Kapasi drove them back, a little past four-thirty, to Hotel Sandy Villa. The children had bought miniature granite versions of the chariot's wheels at a souvenir stand, and they turned them round in their hands. Mr. Das continued to read his book. Mrs. Das untangled Tina's hair with her brush and divided it into two little ponytails.

Mr. Kapasi was beginning to dread the thought of dropping them off. He was not prepared to begin his six-week wait to hear from Mrs. Das. As he stole glances at her in the rearview mirror, wrapping elastic bands around Tina's hair, he wondered how he might make the tour last a little longer. Ordinarily he sped back to Puri using a shortcut, eager to return home, scrub his feet and hands with sandalwood soap, and enjoy the evening newspaper and a cup of tea that his wife would serve him in silence. The thought of that silence, something to which he'd long been resigned, now oppressed him. It was then that he suggested visiting the hills at Udayagiri and Khandagiri, where a number of monastic dwellings were hewn out of the ground, facing one another across a defile. It was some miles away, but well worth seeing, Mr. Kapasi told them.

"Oh yeah, there's something mentioned about it in this book," Mr. Das said. "Built by a Jain king or something."

"Shall we go then?" Mr. Kapasi asked. He paused at a turn in the road. "It's to the left."

Mr. Das turned to look at Mrs. Das. Both of them shrugged.

"Left, left," the children chanted.

Mr. Kapasi turned the wheel, almost delirious with relief. He did not know what he would do or say to Mrs. Das once they arrived at the hills. Perhaps he would tell her what a pleasing smile she had. Perhaps he would compliment her strawberry shirt, which he found irresistibly becoming. Perhaps, when Mr. Das was busy taking a picture, he would take her hand.

He did not have to worry. When they got to the hills, divided by a steep path thick with trees, Mrs. Das refused to get out of the car. All along the path, dozens of monkeys were seated on stones, as well as on the branches of the trees. Their hind legs were stretched out in front and raised to shoulder level, their arms resting on their knees.

"My legs are tired," she said, sinking low in her seat. "I'll stay here."

"Why did you have to wear those stupid shoes?" Mr. Das said. "You won't be in the pictures."

"Pretend I'm there."

"But we could use one of these pictures for our Christmas card this year. We didn't get one of all five of us at the Sun Temple. Mr. Kapasi could take it."

"I'm not coming. Anyway, those monkeys give me the creeps."

"But they're harmless," Mr. Das said. He turned to Mr. Kapasi. "Aren't they?"

"They are more hungry than dangerous," Mr. Kapasi said. "Do not provoke them with food, and they will not bother you."

Mr. Das headed up the defile with the children, the boys at his side, the little girl on his shoulders. Mr. Kapasi watched as they crossed paths with a Japanese man and woman, the only other tourists there, who paused for a final photograph, then stepped into a nearby car and drove away. As the car disappeared out of view some of the monkeys called out, emitting soft whooping sounds, and then walked on their flat black hands and feet up the path. At one point a group of them formed a little ring around Mr. Das and the children. Tina screamed in delight. Ronny ran in circles around his father. Bobby bent down and picked up a fat stick on the ground. When he extended it, one of the monkeys approached him and snatched it, then briefly beat the ground.

"I'll join them," Mr. Kapasi said, unlocking the door on his side. "There is much to explain about the caves."

"No. Stay a minute," Mrs. Das said. She got out of the back seat and slipped in beside Mr. Kapasi. "Raj has his dumb book anyway." Together, through the windshield, Mrs. Das and Mr. Kapasi watched as Bobby and the monkey passed the stick back and forth between them.

"A brave little boy," Mr. Kapasi commented.

"It's not so surprising," Mrs. Das said.

"No?"

"He's not his."

"I beg your pardon?"

"Raj's. He's not Raj's son."

Mr. Kapasi felt a prickle on his skin. He reached into his shirt pocket for the small tin of lotus-oil balm he carried with him at all times, and applied it to three spots on his forehead. He knew that Mrs. Das was watching him, but he did not turn to face her. Instead he watched as the figures of Mr. Das and the children grew smaller, climbing up the steep path, pausing every now and then for a picture, surrounded by a growing number of monkeys.

"Are you surprised?" The way she put it made him choose his words with care.

"It's not the type of thing one assumes," Mr. Kapasi replied slowly. He put the tin of lotus-oil balm back in his pocket.

"No, of course not. And no one knows, of course. No one at all. I've kept it a secret for eight whole years." She looked at Mr. Kapasi, tilting her chin as if to gain a fresh perspective. "But now I've told you."

Mr. Kapasi nodded. He felt suddenly parched, and his forehead was warm and slightly numb from the balm. He considered asking Mrs. Das for a sip of water, then decided against it.

"We met when we were very young," she said. She reached into her straw bag in search of something, then pulled out a packet of puffed rice. "Want some?"

"No, thank you."

She put a fistful in her mouth, sank into the seat a little, and looked away from Mr. Kapasi, out the window on her side of the car. "We married when we were still in college. We were in high school when he proposed. We went to the same college, of course. Back then we couldn't stand the thought of being separated, not for a day, not for a minute. Our parents were best friends who lived in the same town. My entire life I saw him every weekend, either at our house or theirs. We were sent upstairs to play together while our parents joked about our marriage. Imagine! They never caught us at anything, though in a way I think it was all more or less a setup. The things we did those Friday and Saturday nights, while our parents sat downstairs drinking tea . . . I could tell you stories, Mr. Kapasi."

As a result of spending all her time in college with Raj, she continued, she did not make many close friends. There was no one to confide in about him at the end of a difficult day, or to share a passing thought or a worry. Her parents now lived on the other side of the world, but she had never been very close to them, anyway. After marrying so young she was overwhelmed by it all, having a child so quickly, and nursing, and warming up bottles of milk and testing their temperature against her wrist while Raj was at work, dressed in sweaters and corduroy pants, teaching his students about rocks and dinosaurs. Raj never looked cross or harried, or plump as she had become after the first baby.

Always tired, she declined invitations from her one or two college girl-friends, to have lunch or shop in Manhattan. Eventually the friends stopped calling her, so that she was left at home all day with the baby, surrounded by toys that made her trip when she walked or wince when she sat, always cross and tired. Only occasionally did they go out after Ronny was born, and even more rarely did they entertain. Raj didn't mind; he looked forward to coming home from teaching and watching television and bouncing Ronny on his knee. She had been outraged when Raj told her that a Punjabi friend, someone whom she had once met but did not remember, would be staying with them for a week for some job interviews in the New Brunswick area.

Bobby was conceived in the afternoon, on a sofa littered with rubber teething toys, after the friend learned that a London pharmaceutical company had hired him, while Ronny cried to be freed from his playpen. She made no protest when the friend touched the small of her back as she was about to make a pot of coffee, then pulled her against his crisp navy suit. He made love to her swiftly, in silence, with an expertise she had never known, without the meaningful expressions and smiles Raj always insisted on afterward. The next day Raj drove the friend to JFK. He was married now, to a Punjabi girl, and they lived in London still, and every year they exchanged Christmas cards with Raj and Mina, each couple tucking photos of their families into the envelopes. He did not know that he was Bobby's father. He never would.

"I beg your pardon, Mrs. Das, but why have you told me this information?" Mr. Kapasi asked when she had finally finished speaking, and had turned to face him once again.

"For God's sake, stop calling me Mrs. Das. I'm twenty-eight. You probably have children my age."

"Not quite." It disturbed Mr. Kapasi to learn that she thought of him as a parent. The feeling he had had toward her, that had made him check his reflection in the rearview mirror as they drove, evaporated a little.

"I told you because of your talents." She put the packet of puffed rice back into her bag without folding over the top.

"I don't understand," Mr. Kapasi said.

"Don't you see? For eight years I haven't been able to express this to anybody, not to friends, certainly not to Raj. He doesn't even suspect it. He thinks I'm still in love with him. Well, don't you have anything to say?"

"About what?"

"About what I've just told you. About my secret, and about how terrible it makes me feel. I feel terrible looking at my children, and at Raj, always terrible. I have terrible urges, Mr. Kapasi, to throw things away. One day I had the urge to throw everything I own out the window, the television, the children, everything. Don't you think it's unhealthy?"

He was silent.

"Mr. Kapasi, don't you have anything to say? I thought that was your job."

"My job is to give tours, Mrs. Das."

"Not that. Your other job. As an interpreter."

"But we do not face a language barrier. What need is there for an interpreter?"

"That's not what I mean. I would never have told you otherwise. Don't you realize what it means for me to tell you?"

"What does it mean?"

"It means that I'm tired of feeling so terrible all the time. Eight years, Mr. Kapasi, I've been in pain eight years. I was hoping you could help me feel better, say the right thing. Suggest some kind of remedy."

He looked at her, in her red plaid skirt and strawberry T-shirt, a woman not yet thirty, who loved neither her husband nor her children, who had already fallen out of love with life. Her confession depressed him, depressed him all the more when he thought of Mr. Das at the top of the path, Tina clinging to his shoulders, taking pictures of ancient monastic cells cut into the hills to show his students in America, unsuspecting and unaware that one of his sons was not his own. Mr. Kapasi felt insulted that Mrs. Das should ask him to interpret her common, trivial little secret. She did not resemble the patients in the doctor's office, those who came glassy-eyed and desperate, unable to sleep or breathe or urinate with ease, unable, above all, to give words to their pains. Still, Mr. Kapasi believed it was his duty to assist Mrs. Das. Perhaps he ought to tell her to confess the truth to Mr. Das. He would explain that honesty was the best policy. Honesty, surely, would help her feel better, as she'd put it. Perhaps he would offer to preside over the discussion, as a mediator. He decided to begin with the most obvious question, to get to the heart of the matter, and so he asked, "Is it really pain you feel, Mrs. Das, or is it guilt?"

She turned to him and glared, mustard oil thick on her frosty pink lips.

She opened her mouth to say something, but as she glared at Mr. Kapasi some certain knowledge seemed to pass before her eyes, and she stopped. It crushed him; he knew at that moment that he was not even important enough to be properly insulted. She opened the car door and began walking up the path, wobbling a little on her square wooden heels, reaching into her straw bag to eat handfuls of puffed rice. It fell through her fingers, leaving a zigzagging trail, causing a monkey to leap down from a tree and devour the little white grains. In search of more, the monkey began to follow Mrs. Das. Others joined him, so that she was soon being followed by about half a dozen of them, their velvety tails dragging behind.

Mr. Kapasi stepped out of the car. He wanted to holler, to alert her in some way, but he worried that if she knew they were behind her, she would grow nervous. Perhaps she would lose her balance. Perhaps they would pull at her bag or her hair. He began to jog up the path, taking a fallen branch in his hand to scare away the monkeys. Mrs. Das continued walking, oblivious, trailing grains of puffed rice. Near the top of the incline, before a group of cells fronted by a row of squat stone pillars, Mr. Das was kneeling on the ground, focusing the lens of his camera. The children stood under the arcade, now hiding, now emerging from view.

"Wait for me," Mrs. Das called out. "I'm coming."

Tina jumped up and down. "Here comes Mommy!"

"Great," Mr. Das said without looking up. "Just in time. We'll get Mr. Kapasi to take a picture of the five of us."

Mr. Kapasi quickened his pace, waving his branch so that the monkeys scampered away, distracted, in another direction.

"Where's Bobby?" Mrs. Das asked when she stopped.

Mr. Das looked up from the camera. "I don't know. Ronny, where's Bobby?"

Ronny shrugged. "I thought he was right here."

"Where is he?" Mrs. Das repeated sharply. "What's wrong with all of you?"

They began calling his name, wandering up and down the path a bit. Because they were calling, they did not initially hear the boy's screams. When they found him, a little farther down the path under a tree, he was surrounded by a group of monkeys, over a dozen of them, pulling at his T-shirt with their long black fingers. The puffed rice Mrs. Das had spilled was scattered at his feet, raked over by the monkeys' hands. The boy was silent, his body frozen, swift tears running down his startled face. His bare legs were dusty and red with welts from where one of the monkeys struck him repeatedly with the stick he had given to it earlier.

"Daddy, the monkey's hurting Bobby," Tina said.

Mr. Das wiped his palms on the front of his shorts. In his nervousness he accidentally pressed the shutter on his camera; the whirring noise of the advancing film excited the monkeys, and the one with the stick began to beat Bobby more intently. "What are we supposed to do? What if they start attacking?"

"Mr. Kapasi," Mrs. Das shrieked, noticing him standing to one side. "Do something, for God's sake, do something!"

Mr. Kapasi took his branch and shooed them away, hissing at the ones that remained, stomping his feet to scare them. The animals retreated slowly, with a measured gait, obedient but unintimidated. Mr. Kapasi gathered Bobby in his arms and brought him back to where his parents and siblings were standing. As he carried him he was tempted to whisper a secret into the boy's ear. But Bobby was stunned, and shivering with fright, his legs bleeding slightly where the stick had broken the skin. When Mr. Kapasi delivered him to his parents, Mr. Das brushed some dirt off the boy's T-shirt and put the visor on him the right way. Mrs. Das reached into her straw bag to find a bandage which she taped over the cut on his knee. Ronny offered his brother a fresh piece of gum. "He's fine. Just a little scared, right, Bobby?" Mr. Das said, patting the top of his head.

"God, let's get out of here," Mrs. Das said. She folded her arms across the strawberry on her chest. "This place gives me the creeps."

"Yeah. Back to the hotel, definitely," Mr. Das agreed.

"Poor Bobby," Mrs. Das said. "Come here a second. Let Mommy fix your hair." Again she reached into her straw bag, this time for her hairbrush, and began to run it around the edges of the translucent visor. When she whipped out the hairbrush, the slip of paper with Mr. Kapasi's address on it fluttered away in the wind. No one but Mr. Kapasi noticed. He watched as it rose, carried higher and higher by the breeze, into the trees where the monkeys now sat, solemnly observing the scene below. Mr. Kapasi observed it too, knowing that this was the picture of the Das family he would preserve forever in his mind.

[1999]

JUNOT DÍAZ   [b. 1968]

Drown

My mother tells me Beto's home, waits for me to say something, but I keep watching the TV. Only when she's in bed do I put on my jacket and swing through the neighborhood to see. He's a <u>pato</u> now but two years ago we were friends and he would walk into the apartment without knocking, his heavy voice rousing my mother from the Spanish of her room and drawing me up from the basement, a voice that crackled and made you think of uncles or grandfathers.

We were raging then, crazy the way we stole, broke windows, the way we pissed on people's steps and then challenged them to come out and stop us. Beto was leaving for college at the end of the summer and was delirious from the thought of it—he hated everything about the neighborhood, the break-apart buildings, the little strips of grass, the piles of garbage around the cans, and the dump, especially the dump.

I don't know how you can do it, he said to me. I would just find me a job anywhere and go.

Yeah, I said. I wasn't like him. I had another year to go in high school, no promises elsewhere.

Days we spent in the mall or out in the parking lot playing stickball, but nights were what we waited for. The heat in the apartments was like something heavy that had come inside to die. Families arranged on their porches, the glow from their TVs washing blue against the brick. From my family apartment you could smell the pear trees that had been planted years ago, four to a court, probably to save us all from asphyxiation. Nothing moved fast, even the daylight was slow to fade, but as soon as night settled Beto and I headed down to the community center and sprang the fence into the pool. We were never alone, every kid with legs was there. We lunged from the boards and swam out of the deep end, wrestling and farting around. At around midnight abuelas, with their night hair swirled around spiky rollers, shouted at us from their apartment windows. ¡Sinvergüenzas! Go home!

I pass his apartment but the windows are dark; I put my ear to the busted-up door and hear only the familiar hum of the air conditioner. I haven't decided yet if I'll talk to him. I can go back to my dinner and two years will become three.

Even from four blocks off I can hear the racket from the pool—radios too—and wonder if we were ever that loud. Little has changed, not the stink of chlorine, not the bottles exploding against the lifeguard station. I hook my fingers through the plastic-coated hurricane fence. Something tells me that he will be here; I hop the fence, feeling stupid when I sprawl on the dandelions and the grass.

Nice one, somebody calls out.

Fuck me, I say. I'm not the oldest motherfucker in the place, but it's close. I take off my shirt and my shoes and then knife in. Many of the kids here are younger brothers of the people I used to go to school with. Two of them swim past, black and Latino, and they pause when they see me, recognizing the guy who sells them their shitty dope. The crackheads have their own man, Lucero, and some other guy who drives in from Paterson, the only full-time commuter in the area.

The water feels good. Starting at the deep end I glide over the slick-tiled bottom without kicking up a spume or making a splash. Sometimes another swimmer churns past me, more a disturbance of water than a body. I can still go far without coming up. While everything above is loud and bright, everything below is whispers. And always the risk of coming up to find the cops stabbing their searchlights out across the water. And then everyone running, wet feet slapping against the concrete, yelling, Fuck you, officers, you puto sucios, fuck you.

When I'm tired I wade through to the shallow end, past some kid who's kissing his girlfriend, watching me as though I'm going to try to cut in, and I sit near the sign that runs the pool during the day. *No Horseplay, No Running, No Defecating, No Urinating, No Expectorating*. At the bottom someone has scrawled in *No Whites, No Fat Chiks* and someone else has provided the missing *c*. I laugh. Beto hadn't known what expectorating meant though he was the one leaving for college. I told him, spitting a greener by the side of the pool.

Shit, he said. Where did you learn that?

I shrugged.

Tell me. He hated when I knew something he didn't. He put his hands on my shoulders and pushed me under. He was wearing a cross and cut-off jeans. He was stronger than me and held me down until water flooded my nose and throat. Even then I didn't tell him; he thought I didn't read, not even dictionaries.

We live alone. My mother has enough for the rent and groceries and I cover the phone bill, sometimes the cable. She's so quiet that most of the time I'm startled to find her in the apartment. I'll enter a room and she'll stir, detaching herself from the cracking plaster walls, from the stained cabinets, and fright will pass through me like a wire. She has discovered the secret to silence: pouring café without a splash, walking between rooms as if gliding on a cushion of felt, crying without a sound. You have traveled to the East and learned many secret things, I've told her. You're like a shadow warrior.

And you're like a crazy, she says. Like a big crazy.

When I come in she's still awake, her hands picking clots of lint from her skirt. I put a towel down on the sofa and we watch television together. We settle on the Spanish-language news: drama for her, violence for me. Today a child has survived a seven-story fall, busting nothing but his diaper. The hysterical baby-sitter, about three hundred pounds of her, is head-butting the microphone.

It's a goddamn miraclevilla, she cries.

My mother asks if I found Beto. I tell her that I didn't look.

That's too bad. He was telling me that he might be starting at a school for business.

So what?

She's never understood why we don't speak anymore. I've tried to explain, all wise-like, that everything changes, but she thinks that sort of saying is only around so you can prove it wrong.

He asked me what you were doing.

What did you say?

I told him you were fine.

You should have told him I moved.

And what if he ran into you?

I'm not allowed to visit my mother?

She notices the tightening of my arms. You should be more like me and your father.

Can't you see I'm watching television?

I was angry at him, wasn't I? But now we can talk to each other.

Am I watching television here or what?

Saturdays she asks me to take her to the mall. As a son I feel I owe her that much, even though neither of us has a car and we have to walk two miles through redneck territory to catch the M15.

Before we head out she drags us through the apartment to make sure the windows are locked. She can't reach the latches so she has me test them. With the air conditioner on we never open windows but I go through the routine anyway. Putting my hand on the latch is not enough—she wants to hear it rattle. This place just isn't safe, she tells me. Lorena got lazy and look what they did to her. They punched her and kept her locked up in her place. Those morenos ate all her food and even made phone calls. Phone calls!

That's why we don't have long-distance, I tell her but she shakes her head. That's not funny, she says.

She doesn't go out much, so when she does it's a big deal. She dresses up, even puts on makeup. Which is why I don't give her lip about taking her to the mall even though I usually make a fortune on Saturdays, selling to those kids going down to Belmar or out to Spruce Run.

I recognize like half the kids on the bus. I keep my head buried in my cap, praying that nobody tries to score. She watches the traffic, her hands somewhere inside her purse, doesn't say a word.

When we arrive at the mall I give her fifty dollars. Buy something, I say, hating the image I have of her, picking through the sale bins, wrinkling everything. Back in the day, my father would give her a hundred dollars at the end of each summer for my new clothes and she would take nearly a week to spend it, even though it never amounted to more than a couple of t-shirts and two pairs of jeans. She folds the bills into a square. I'll see you at three, she says.

I wander through the stores, staying in sight of the cashiers so they won't have reason to follow me. The circuit I make has not changed since my looting days. Bookstore, record store, comic-book shop, Macy's. Me and Beto used to steal like mad from these places, two, three hundred dollars of shit in an outing. Our system was simple—we walked into a store with a shopping bag and came out loaded. Back then security wasn't tight. The only trick was in the exit. We stopped right at the entrance of the store and checked out some worthless piece of junk to stop people from getting suspicious. What do you think? we asked each other. Would she like it? Both of us had seen bad shoplifters at work. All grab and run, nothing smooth about them. Not us. We idled out of the stores slow, like a fat seventies car. At this, Beto was the best. He even talked to mall security, asked them for directions, his bag all loaded up, and me, standing ten feet away, shitting my pants. When he finished he smiled, swinging his shopping bag up to hit me.

You got to stop that messing around, I told him. I'm not going to jail for bullshit like that.

You don't go to jail for shoplifting. They just turn you over to your old man.

I don't know about you, but my pops hits like a motherfucker.

He laughed. You know my dad. He flexed his hands. The nigger's got arthritis.

My mother never suspected, even when my clothes couldn't all fit in the closet, but my father wasn't that easy. He knew what things cost and knew that I didn't have a regular job.

You're going to get caught, he told me one day. Just you wait. When you do I'll show them everything you've taken and then they'll throw your stupid ass away like a bad piece of meat.

He was a charmer, my pop, a real asshole, but he was right. Nobody can stay smooth forever, especially kids like us. One day at the bookstore, we didn't even hide the drops. Four issues of the same *Playboy* for kicks, enough audio books to start our own library. No last minute juke either. The lady who stepped in front of us didn't look old, even with her white hair. Her silk shirt was half unbuttoned and a silver horn necklace sat on the freckled top of her chest. I'm sorry fellows, but I have to check your bag, she said. I kept moving, and looked back all annoyed, like she was asking us for a quarter or something. Beto got polite and stopped. No problem, he said, slamming the heavy bag into her face. She hit the cold tile with a squawk, her palms slapping the ground. There you go, Beto said.

Security found us across from the bus stop, under a Jeep Cherokee. A bus had come and gone, both of us too scared to take it, imagining a plainclothes waiting to clap the cuffs on. I remember that when the rent-a-cop tapped his nightstick against the fender and said, You little shits better come out here real slow, I started to cry. Beto didn't say a word, his face stretched out and gray, his hand squeezing mine, the bones in our fingers pressing together.

Nights I drink with Alex and Danny. The Malibou Bar is no good, just washouts and the sucias we can con into joining us. We drink too much, roar at each other, and make the skinny bartender move closer to the phone. On the wall hangs a cork dartboard and a Brunswick Gold Crown blocks the bathroom, its bumpers squashed, the felt pulled like old skin.

When the bar begins to shake back and forth like a rumba, I call it a night and go home, through the fields that surround the apartments. In the distance you can see the Raritan, as shiny as an earthworm, the same river my homeboy goes to school on. The dump has long since shut down, and grass has spread over it like a sickly fuzz, and from where I stand, my right hand directing a colorless stream of piss downward, the landfill might be the top of a blond head, square and old.

In the mornings I run. My mother is already up, dressing for her housecleaning job. She says nothing to me, would rather point to the mangú she has prepared than speak.

I run three miles easily, could have pushed a fourth if I were in the mood. I keep an eye out for the recruiter who prowls around our neighborhood in his dark K-car. We've spoken before. He was out of uniform and called me over, jovial, and I thought I was helping some white dude with directions. Would you mind if I asked you a question?

No.

Do you have a job?

Not right now.

Would you like one? A real career, more than you'll get around here?

I remember stepping back. Depends on what it is, I said.

Son, I know somebody who's hiring. It's the United States government.

Well. Sorry, but I ain't Army material.

That's exactly what I used to think, he said, his ten piggy fingers buried in his carpeted steering wheel. But now I have a house, a car, a gun, and a wife. Discipline. Loyalty. Can you say that you have those things? Even one?

He's a southerner, red-haired, his drawl so out of place that the people around here laugh just hearing him. I take to the bushes when I see his car on the road. These days my guts feel loose and cold and I want to be away from here. He won't have to show me his Desert Eagle or flash the photos of the skinny Filipino girls sucking dick. He'll only have to smile and name the places and I'll listen.

When I reach the apartment, I lean against my door, waiting for my heart to slow, for the pain to lose its edge. I hear my mother's voice, a whisper from the kitchen. She sounds hurt or nervous, maybe both. At first I'm terrified that Beto's inside with her but then I look and see the phone cord, swinging lazily. She's talking to my father, something she knows I disapprove of. He's in Florida now, a sad guy who calls her and begs for money. He swears that if she moves down there he'll leave the woman he's living with. These are lies, I've told her, but she still calls him. His words coil inside of her, wrecking her sleep for days. She opens the refrigerator door slightly so that the whir of the compressor masks their conversation. I walk in on her and hang up the phone. That's enough, I say.

She's startled, her hand squeezing the loose folds of her neck. That was him, she says quietly.

On school days Beto and I chilled at the stop together but as soon as the bus came over the Parkwood hill I got to thinking about how I was failing gym and screwing up math and how I hated every single living teacher on the planet.

I'll see *you* in the p.m., I said.

He was already standing on line. I just stood back and grinned, my hands in my pockets. With our bus drivers you didn't have to hide. Two of them didn't give a rat fuck and the third one, the Brazilian preacher, was too busy talking Bible to notice anything but the traffic in front of him.

Being truant without a car was no easy job but I managed. I watched a lot of TV and when it got boring I trooped down to the mall or the Sayreville library, where you could watch old documentaries for free. I always came back to the neighborhood late, so the bus wouldn't pass me on Ernston and nobody could yell Asshole! out the windows. Beto would usually be home or down by the swings, but other times he wouldn't be around at all. Out visiting other neighborhoods. He knew a lot of folks I didn't—a messed-up black kid from Madison Park, two brothers who were into that N.Y. club scene, who spent money on platform shoes and leather backpacks. I'd leave a message with his parents and then watch some more TV. The next day he'd be out at the bus stop, too busy smoking a cigarette to say much about the day before.

You need to learn how to walk the world, he told me. There's a lot out there.

Some nights me and the boys drive to New Brunswick. A nice city, the Raritan so low and silty that you don't have to be Jesus to walk over it. We hit the Melody and the Roxy, stare at the college girls. We drink a lot and then spin out onto the dance floor. None of the chicas ever dance with us, but a glance or a touch can keep us talking shit for hours.

Once the clubs close we go to the Franklin Diner, gorge ourselves on pancakes, and then, after we've smoked our pack, head home. Danny passes out in the back seat and Alex cranks the window down to keep the wind in his eyes. He's fallen asleep in the past, wrecked two cars before this one. The streets have been picked clean of students and townies and we blow through every light, red or green. At the Old Bridge Turnpike we pass the fag bar, which never seems to close. Patos are all over the parking lot, drinking and talking.

Sometimes Alex will stop by the side of the road and say, Excuse me. When somebody comes over from the bar he'll point his plastic pistol at them, just to see if they'll run or shit their pants. Tonight he just puts his head out the window. Fuck you! he shouts and then settles back in his seat, laughing.

That's original, I say.

He puts his head out the window again. Eat me, then!

Yeah, Danny mumbles from the back. Eat me.

Twice. That's it.

The first time was at the end of the summer. We had just come back from the pool and were watching a porn video at his parents' apartment. His father was a nut for these tapes, ordering them from wholesalers in California and Grand Rapids. Beto used to tell me how his pop would watch them in the middle of the day, not caring a lick about his moms, who spent the time in the kitchen, taking hours to cook a pot of rice and gandules. Beto would sit down with his pop and neither of them would say a word, except to laugh when somebody caught it in the eye or the face.

We were an hour into the new movie, some vaina that looked like it had been filmed in the apartment next door, when he reached into my shorts. What the fuck are you doing? I asked, but he didn't stop. His hand was dry. I kept my eyes on the television, too scared to watch. I came right away, smearing the plastic sofa covers. My legs started shaking and suddenly I wanted out. He didn't say anything to me as I left, just sat there watching the screen.

The next day he called and when I heard his voice I was cool but I wouldn't go to the mall or anywhere else. My mother sensed that something was wrong and pestered me about it, but I told her to leave me the fuck alone, and my pops, who was home on a visit, stirred himself from the couch to slap me down. Mostly I stayed in the basement, terrified that I would end up abnormal, a fucking pato, but he was my best friend and back then that mattered to me more than anything. This alone got me out of the apartment and over to the pool that night. He was already there, his body pale and flabby under the water. Hey, he said. I was beginning to worry about you.

Nothing to worry about, I said.

We swam and didn't talk much and later we watched a Skytop crew pull a bikini top from a girl stupid enough to hang out alone. Give it, she said, covering herself, but these kids howled, holding it up over her head, the shiny laces flopping just out of reach. When they began to pluck at her arms, she walked away, leaving them to try the top on over their flat pecs.

He put his hand on my shoulder, my pulse a code under his palm. Let's go, he said. Unless of course you're not feeling good.

I'm feeling fine, I said.

Since his parents worked nights we pretty much owned the place until six the next morning. We sat in front of his television, in our towels, his hands bracing against my abdomen and thighs. I'll stop if you want, he said and I didn't respond. After I was done, he laid his head in my lap. I wasn't asleep or awake, but caught somewhere in between, rocked slowly back and forth the way surf holds junk against the shore, rolling it over and over. In three weeks he was leaving. Nobody can touch me, he kept saying. We'd visited the school and I'd seen how beautiful the campus was, with all the students drifting from dorm to class. I thought of how in high school our teachers loved to crowd us into their lounge every time a space shuttle took off from Florida. One teacher, whose family had two grammar schools named after it, compared us to the shuttles. A few of you are going to make it. Those are the orbiters. But the majority of you are just going to burn out. Going nowhere. He dropped his hand onto his desk. I could already see myself losing altitude, fading, the earth spread out beneath me, hard and bright.

I had my eyes closed and the television was on and when the hallway door crashed open, he jumped up and I nearly cut my dick off struggling with my shorts. It's just the neighbor, he said, laughing. He was laughing, but I was saying, Fuck this, and getting my clothes on.

I believe I see him in his father's bottomed-out Cadillac, heading towards the turnpike, but I can't be sure. He's probably back in school already. I deal close to home, trooping up and down the same dead-end street where the kids drink and smoke. These punks joke with me, pat me down for taps, sometimes too hard. Now that strip malls line Route 9, a lot of folks have part-time jobs; the kids stand around smoking in their aprons, name tags dangling heavily from pockets.

When I get home, my sneakers are filthy so I take an old toothbrush to their soles, scraping the crap into the tub. My mother has thrown open the windows and propped open the door. It's cool enough, she explains. She has prepared dinner—rice and beans, fried cheese, tostones. Look what I bought, she says, showing me two blue t-shirts. They were two for one so I bought you one. Try it on.

It fits tight but I don't mind. She cranks up the television. A movie dubbed into Spanish, a classic, one that everyone knows. The actors throw themselves around, passionate, but their words are plain and deliberate. It's hard to imagine anybody going through life this way. I pull out the plug of bills from my pockets. She takes it from me, her fingers soothing the creases. A man who treats his plata like this doesn't deserve to spend it, she says.

We watch the movie and the two hours together makes us friendly. She puts her hand on mine. Near the end of the film, just as our heroes are about to fall apart under a hail of bullets, she takes off her glasses and kneads her temples, the light of the television flickering across her face. She watches another minute and then her chin lists to her chest. Almost immediately her eyelashes begin to tremble, a quiet semaphore. She is dreaming, dreaming of Boca Raton, of strolling under the jacarandas with my father. You can't be anywhere forever, was what Beto used to say, what he said to me the day I went to see him off. He handed me a gift, a book, and after he was gone I threw it away, didn't even bother to open it and read what he'd written.

I let her sleep until the end of the movie and when I wake her she shakes her head, grimacing. You better check those windows, she says. I promise her I will.

[1996]

CHIMAMANDA NGOZI ADICHIE   [b. 1977]

Birdsong

The woman, a stranger, was looking at me. In the glare of the hot afternoon, in the swirl of motorcycles and hawkers, she was looking down at me from the back seat of her jeep. Her stare was too direct, not sufficiently vacant. She was not merely resting her eyes on the car next to hers, as people often do in Lagos traffic; she was *looking* at me. At first, I glanced away, but then I stared back, at the haughty silkiness of the weave that fell to her shoulders in loose curls, the kind of extension called Brazilian Hair and paid for in dollars at Victoria Island hair salons; at her fair skin, which had the plastic sheen that comes from expensive creams; and at her hand, forefinger bejeweled, which she raised to wave a magazine hawker away, with the ease of a person used to waving people away. She was beautiful, or perhaps she was just so unusual-looking, with wide-set eyes sunk deep in her face, that "beautiful" was the easiest way of describing her. She was the kind of woman I imagined my lover's wife was, a woman for whom things were done.

My lover. It sounds a little melodramatic, but I never knew how to refer to him. "Boyfriend" seemed wrong for an urbane man of forty-five who carefully slipped off his wedding ring before he touched me. Chikwado called him "your man," with a faintly sneering smile, as though we were both in on the joke: he was not, of course, mine. "Ah, you are always rushing to leave because of this your man," she would say, leaning back in her chair and smacking her head with her hand, over and over. Her scalp was itchy beneath her weave, and this was the only way she could come close to scratching it. "Have fun oh, as long as your spirit accepts it, but as for me, I cannot spread my legs for a married man." She said this often, with a clear-eyed moral superiority, as I packed my files and shut down my computer for the day.

We were friends out of necessity, because we had both graduated from Enugu Campus and ended up working for Celnet Telecom, in Lagos, as the only females in the community-relations unit. Otherwise, we would not have been friends. I was irritated by how full of simplified certainties she was, and I knew that she thought I behaved like an irresponsible, vaguely foreign teen-ager: wearing my hair in a natural low-cut, smoking cigarettes right in front of the building, where everyone could see, and refusing to join in the prayer sessions our boss led after Monday meetings. I would not have told her about my lover—I did not tell her about my personal life—but she was there when he first walked into our office, a lean, dark man with a purple tie and a moneyed manner. He was full of the glossy self-regard of men who shrugged off their importance in a way that only emphasized it. Our boss shook his hand with both hands and said, "Welcome, sir, it is good to see you, sir, how are you doing, sir, please come and sit down, sir." Chikwado was there when he looked at me and I looked at him and then he smiled, of all things, a warm, open smile. She heard when he said to our boss, "My family lives in America," a little too loudly, for my benefit, with that generic foreign accent of the worldly Nigerian, which, I would discover later, disappeared when he became truly animated about something. She saw him walk over and give me his business card. She was there, a few days later, when his driver came to deliver a gift bag. Because she had seen, and because I was swamped with emotions that I could not name for a man I knew was wrong for me, I showed her the perfume and the card that said, "I am thinking of you."

"*Na wa!* Look at how your eyes are shining because of a married man. You need deliverance prayers," Chikwado said, half joking. She went to night-vigil services often, at different churches, but all with the theme Finding Your God-Given Mate; she would come to work the next morning sleepy, the whites of her eyes flecked with red, but already planning to attend another service. She was thirty-two and tottering under the weight of her desire: to settle down. It was all she talked about. It was all our female co-workers talked about when we had lunch at the cafeteria. *Yewande is wasting her time with that man—he is not ready to settle down. Please ask him oh, if he does not see marriage in the future then you better look elsewhere; nobody is getting any younger. Ekaete is lucky, just six months and she is already engaged.* While they talked, I would look out the window, high up above Lagos, at the acres of rusted roofs, at the rise and fall of hope in this city full of tarnished angels.

Even my lover spoke of this desire. "You'll want to settle down soon," he said. "I just want you to know I'm not going to stand in your way." We were naked in bed; it was our first time. A feather from the pillow was stuck in his hair, and I had just picked it out and showed it to him. I could not believe, in the aftermath of what had just happened, both of us still flush from each other's warmth, how easily the words rolled out of his mouth. "I'm not like other men, who think they can dominate your life and not let you move forward," he continued, propping himself up on his elbow to look at me. He was telling me that he played the game better than others, while I had not yet conceived of the game itself. From the moment I met him, I had had the sensation of possibility, but for him the path was already closed, had indeed never been open; there was no room for things to sweep in and disrupt.

"You're very thoughtful," I said, with the kind of overdone mockery that masks damage. He nodded, as though he agreed with me. I pulled the covers up to my chin. I should have got dressed, gone back to my flat in Surulere, and deleted his number from my phone. But I stayed. I stayed for thirteen months and eight days, mostly in his house in Victoria Island—a faded-white house, with its quiet grandeur and airy spaces, which was built during British colonial rule and sat in a compound full of fruit trees, the enclosing wall wreathed in creeping bougainvillea. He had told me he was taking me to a Lebanese friend's guesthouse, where he was staying while his home in Ikoyi was being refurbished. When I stepped out of the car, I felt as though I had stumbled into a secret garden. A dense mass of periwinkles, white and pink, bordered the walkway to the house. The air was clean here, even fragrant, and there was something about it all that made me think of renewal. He was watching me; I could sense how much he wanted me to like it.

"This is your house, isn't it?" I said. "It doesn't belong to your Lebanese friend."

He moved closer to me, surprised. "Please don't misunderstand. I was going to tell you. I just didn't want you to think it was some kind of . . ." He paused and took my hand. "I know what other men do, and I am not like that. I don't bring women here. I bought it last year to knock it down and build an apartment block, but it was so beautiful. My friends think I'm mad for keeping it. You know nobody respects old things in this country. I work from here most days now, instead of going to my office."

We were standing by sliding glass doors that led to a veranda, over which a large flame tree spread its branches. Wilted red flowers had fallen on the cane chairs. "I like to sit there and watch birds," he said, pointing.

He liked birds. Birds had always been just birds to me, but with him I became someone else: I became a person who liked birds. The following Sunday morning, on our first weekend together, as we passed sections of *Next* to each other in the quiet of that veranda, he looked up at the sky and said, "There's a magpie. They like shiny things." I imagined putting his wedding ring on the cane table so that the bird would swoop down and carry it away forever.

"I knew you were different!" he said, thrilled, when he noticed that I read the business and sports sections, as though my being different reflected his good taste. And so we talked eagerly about newspapers, and about the newscasts on AIT and CNN, marvelling at how similar our opinions were. We never discussed my staying. It was not safe to drive back to Surulere late, and he kept saying, "Why don't you bring your things tomorrow so you can go to work from here?" until most of my clothes were in the wardrobe and my moisturizers were on the bathroom ledge. He left me money on the table, in brown envelopes on which he wrote "For your fuel," as if I could possibly spend fifty thousand naira on petrol. Sometimes, he asked if I needed privacy to change, as if he had not seen me naked many times.

We did not talk about his wife or his children or my personal life or when I would want to settle down so that he could avoid standing in my way. Perhaps it was all the things we left unsaid that made me watch him. His skin was so dark that I teased him about being from Gambia; if he were a woman, I told him, he would never find a face powder that matched his tone. I watched as he carefully unwrapped scented moist tissues to clean his glasses, or cut the chicken on his plate, or tied his towel round his waist in a knot that seemed too elaborate for a mere towel, just below the embossed scar by his navel. I memorized him, because I did not know him. He was courtly, his life lived in well-oiled sequences, his cufflinks always tasteful.

His three cell phones rang often; I knew when it was his wife, because he would go to the toilet or out to the veranda, and I knew when it was a government official, because he would say afterward, "Why won't these governors leave somebody alone?" But it was clear that he liked the governors' calls, and the restaurant manager who came to our table to say, "We are so happy to see you, sah." He searched the Sunday-magazine pullouts for pictures of himself, and when he found one he said in a mildly complaining tone, "Look at this, why should they turn businessmen into celebrities?" Yet he would not wear the same suit to two events because of the newspaper photographers. He had a glowing ego, like a globe, round and large and in constant need of polishing. He did things for people. He gave them money, introduced them to contacts, helped their relatives get jobs, and when the gratitude and praise came—he showed me text messages thanking him; I remember one that read "History will immortalize you as a great man"—his eyes would glaze over, and I could almost hear him purr.

One day he told me, while we were watching two kingfishers do a mating dance on a guava tree, that most birds did not have penises. I had never thought about the penises of birds.

"My mother had chickens in the yard when I was growing up, and I used to watch them mating," I said.

"Of course they mate, but not with penises," he said. "Did you ever see a cock with a dick?"

I laughed, and he, only just realizing the joke, laughed, too. It became our endearment. "Cock with a dick," I would whisper, hugging him in greeting, and we would burst out laughing. He sent me texts signed "CwithaD." And each time I turned off the potholed road in Victoria Island and into that compound full of birdsong I felt as though I were home.

The woman was still looking at me. Traffic was at a standstill, unusual this early in the afternoon. A tanker must have fallen across the road—tankers were always falling across the road—or a bus had broken down, or cars had formed a line outside a petrol station, blocking the road. My fuel gauge was close to empty. I switched off the ignition and rolled down the window, wondering if the woman would roll down hers as well and say something to me. I stared back at her, and yet she did not waver, her eyes remaining firm, until I looked away. There were many more hawkers now, holding out magazines, phone cards, plantain chips, newspapers, cans of Coke and Amstel Malta dipped in water to make them look cold. The driver in front of me was buying a phone card. The hawker, a boy in a red Arsenal shirt, scratched the card with his finger-nail, and then waited for the driver to enter the numbers in his phone to make sure the card was not fake.

I turned again to look at the woman. I was reminded of what Chik-wado had said about my lover the first day that he came to our office: "His face is full of overseas." The woman, too, had a face full of overseas, the face of a person whose life was a blur of comforts. There was some-thing in the set of her lips, which were lined with cocoa pencil, that sug-gested an unsatisfying triumph, as though she had won a battle but hated having had to fight in the first place. Perhaps she was indeed my lover's wife and she had come back to Lagos and just found out about me, and then, as though in a bad farce, ended up next to me in traffic. But his wife could not possibly know; he had been so careful.

"I wish I could," he always said, when I asked him to spend Saturday afternoon with me at Jazz Hole, or when I suggested we go to a play at Terra Kulture on Sunday, or when I asked if we could try dinner at a dif-ferent restaurant. We only ever went to one on a dark street off Awolowo Road, a place with expensive wines and no sign on the gate. He said "I wish I could" as though some great and ineluctable act of nature made it impossible for him to be seen publicly with me. And impossible for him to keep my text messages. I wanted to ask how he could so efficiently delete my texts as soon as he read them, why he felt no urge to keep them on his phone, even if only for a few hours, even if only for a day. There were reams of questions unasked, gathering like rough pebbles in my throat. It was a strange thing to feel so close to a man—to tell him about my resentment of my parents, to lie supine for him with an abandon that was unfamiliar to me—and yet be unable to ask him questions, bound as I was by insecurity and unnamed longings.

The first time we quarreled, he said to me accusingly, "You don't cry." I realized that his wife cried, that he could handle tears but not my cold defiance.

The fight was about his driver, Emmanuel, an elderly man who might have looked wise if his features were not so snarled with dissatisfaction. It was a Saturday afternoon. I had been at work that morning. My boss had called an emergency meeting that I thought was unnecessary: we all knew that His Royal Highness, the Oba of the town near the lagoon, was causing trouble, saying that Celnet Telecom had made him look bad in front of his people. He had sent many messages asking how we could build a big base station on his ancestral land and yet donate only a small borehole to his people. That morning, his guards had blocked off our building site, shoved some of our engineers around, and punctured the tires of their van. My boss was furious, and he slammed his hand on the table as he spoke at the meeting. I, too, slammed my hand on the cane table as I imitated him later, while my lover laughed. "That is the problem with these godless, demon-worshipping traditional rulers," my boss said. "The man is a crook. A common crook! What happened to the one million naira we gave him? Should we also bring bags of rice and beans for all his people before we put up our base station? Does he want a supply of meat pies every day? Nonsense!"

"Meat pies" had made Chikwado and me laugh, even though our boss was not being funny. "Why not something more ordinary, like bread?" Chikwado whispered to me, and then promptly raised her hand when our boss asked for volunteers to go see the Oba right away. I never volunteered. I disliked those visits—villagers watching us with awed eyes, young men asking for free phone cards, even free phones—because it all made me feel helplessly powerful.

"Why meat pies?" my lover asked, still laughing.

"I have no idea."

"Actually, I would like to have a meat pie right now."

"Me, too."

We were laughing, and with the sun shining, the sound of birds above, the slight flutter of the curtains against the sliding door, I was already thinking of future Saturdays that we would spend together, laughing at funny stories about my boss. My lover summoned Emmanuel and asked him to take me to the supermarket to buy the meat pies. When I got into the car, Emmanuel did not greet me. He simply stared straight ahead. It was the first time that he had driven me without my lover. The silence was tense. Perhaps he was thinking that all his children were older than me.

"Well done, Emmanuel!" I said finally, greeting him with forced brightness. "Do you know the supermarket on Kofo Abayomi Street?"

He said nothing and started the car. When we arrived, he stopped at the gate. "Come out here, let me go and park," he said.

"Please drop me at the entrance," I said. Every other driver did that, before looking for a parking space.

"Come out here." He still did not look at me. Rage rose under my skin, making me feel detached and bloodless, suspended in air; I could not sense the ground under my feet as I climbed out. After I had selected some meat pies from the display case, I called my lover and told him that Emmanuel had been rude and that I would be taking a taxi back.

"Emmanuel said the road was bad," my lover said when I got back, his tone conciliatory.

"The man insulted me," I said.

"No, he's not like that. Maybe he didn't understand you."

Emmanuel had shown me the power of my lover's wife; he would not have been so rude if he feared he might be reprimanded. I wanted to fling the bag of meat pies through the window.

"Is this what you do, have your driver remind your girlfriends of their place?" I was shrill and I disliked myself for it. Worse, I was horrified to notice that my eyes were watering. My lover gently wrapped his arms around me, as though I were an irrational child, and asked whether I would give him a meat pie.

"You've brought other women here, haven't you?" I asked, not entirely sure how this had become about other women.

He shook his head. "No, I have not. No more of this talk. Let's eat the meat pies and watch a film."

I let myself be mollified, be held, be caressed. Later, he said, "You know, I have had only two affairs since I got married. I'm not like other men."

"You sound as if you think you deserve a prize," I said.

He was smiling. "Both of them were like you." He paused to search for a word, and when he found it he said it with enjoyment. "Feisty. They were feisty like you."

I looked at him. How could he not see that there were things he should not say to me, and that there were things I longed to have with him? It was a willed blindness; it had to be. He chose not to see. "You are such a bastard," I said.

"What?"

I repeated myself.

He looked as though he had just been stung by an insect. "Get out. Leave this house right now," he said, and then muttered, "This is unacceptable."

I had never before been thrown out of a house. Emmanuel sat in a chair in the shade of the garage and watched stone-faced as I hurried to my car. My lover did not call me for five days, and I did not call him. When he finally called, his first words were "There are two pigeons on the flame tree. I'd like you to see them."

"You are acting as if nothing happened."

"I called *you*," he said, as though the call itself were an apology. Later, he told me that if I had cried instead of calling him a bastard he would have behaved better. I should not have gone back—I knew that even then.

The woman, still staring at me, was talking on her cell phone. Her jeep was black and silver and miraculously free of scratches. How was that possible in this city where okada° after okada sped through the narrow slices of space between cars in traffic as though motorcycles could shrink to fit any gap? Perhaps whenever her car was hit a mechanic descended from the sky and made the dent disappear. The car in front of me had a gash on its tail-light; it looked like one of the many cars that dripped oil, turning the roads into a slick sheet when the rains came. My own car was full of wounds. The biggest, a mangled bumper, was from a taxi that rammed into me at a red light on Kingsway Road a month before. The driver had jumped out with his shirt unbuttoned, all sweaty bravado, and screamed at me.

"Stupid girl! You are a common nuisance. Why did you stop like that? Nonsense!"

I stared at him, stunned, until he drove away, and then I began to think of what I could have said, what I could have shouted back.

"If you were wearing a wedding ring, he would not have shouted at you like that," Chikwado said when I told her, as she punched the redial button on her desk phone. At the cafeteria, she told our co-workers about it. *Ah, ah, stupid man! Of course he was shouting because he knew he was wrong—that is the Lagos way. So he thinks he can speak big English. Where did he even learn the word "nuisance"?* They sucked their teeth, telling their own stories about taxi-drivers, and then their outrage fizzled and they began to talk, voices lowered and excited, about a fertility biscuit that the new pastor at Redemption Church was giving women.

"It worked for my sister oh. First she did a dry fast for two days, then the pastor did a special deliverance prayer for her before she ate the biscuit. She had to eat it at exactly midnight. The next month, the very next month, she missed her period, I'm telling you," one of them, a contract staffer who was doing a master's degree part time at Ibadan, said.

Okada: Motorcycles used as vehicles for hire in Nigeria.

"Is it an actual biscuit?" another asked.

"Yes now. But they bless the ingredients before they make the biscuits. God can work through anything, *sha*. I heard about a pastor that uses handkerchiefs."

I looked away and wondered what my lover would make of this story. He was visiting his family in America for two weeks. That evening, he sent me a text. "At a concert with my wife. Beautiful music. Will call you in ten minutes and leave phone on so you can listen in. CwithaD." I read it twice and then, even though I had saved all his other texts, I deleted it, as though my doing so would mean that it had never been sent. When he called, I let my phone ring and ring. I imagined them at the concert, his wife reaching out to hold his hand, because I could not bear the thought that it might be he who would reach out. I knew then that he could not possibly see me, the inconvenient reality of me; instead, all he saw was himself in an exciting game.

He came back from his trip wearing shoes I did not recognize, made of rich brown leather and much more tapered than his other shoes, almost comically pointy. He was in high spirits, twirling me around when we hugged, caressing the tightly coiled hair at the nape of my neck and saying, "So soft." He wanted to go out to dinner, he said, because he had a surprise for me, and when he went into the bathroom one of his phones rang. I took it and looked at his text messages. It was something I had never thought of doing before, and yet I suddenly felt compelled to do it. Text after text in his "sent" box were to Baby. The most recent said he had arrived safely. What struck me was not how often he texted his wife, or how short the texts were—"stuck in traffic," "missing you," "almost there"—but that all of them were signed "CwithaD." Inside me, something snagged. Had he choreographed a conversation with her, nimbly made the joke about a "cock with a dick" and then found a way to turn it into a shared endearment for the two of them? I thought of the effort it would take to do that. I put the phone down and glanced at the mirror, half expecting to see myself morphing into a slack, stringless marionette.

In the car, he asked, "Is something wrong? Are you feeling well?"

"I can't believe you called me so that I could listen to the music you and your wife were listening to."

"I did that because I missed you so much," he said. "I really wanted to be there with you."

"But you *weren't* there with me."

"You're in a bad mood."

"Don't you see? You weren't there with *me*."

He reached over and took my hand, rubbing his thumb on my palm. I looked out at the dimly lit street. We were on our way to our usual hidden restaurant, where I had eaten everything on the menu a hundred times. A mosquito, now sluggish with my blood, had got in the car. I slapped myself as I tried to hit it.

"Good evening, sah," the waiter said when we were seated. "You are welcome, sah."

"Have you noticed that they never greet me?" I asked my lover.

"Well . . ." he said, and adjusted his glasses.

The waiter came back, a sober-faced man with a gentle demeanor, and I waited until he had opened the bottle of red wine before I asked, "Why don't you greet me?"

The waiter glanced at my lover, as though seeking guidance, and this infuriated me even more. "Am I invisible? I am the one who asked you a question. Why do all of you waiters and gatemen and drivers in this Lagos refuse to greet me? Do you not see me?"

"Come back in ten minutes," my lover said to the waiter in his courteous, deep-voiced way. "You need to calm down," he told me. "Do you want us to go?"

"Why don't they greet me?" I asked, and gulped down half my glass of wine.

"I have a surprise for you. I've bought you a new car."

I looked at him blankly.

"Did you hear me?" he asked.

"I heard you." I was supposed to get up and hug him and tell him that history would remember him as a great man. A new car. I drank more wine.

"Did I tell you about my first bus ride when I arrived in Lagos, six years ago?" I asked. "When I got on the bus, a boy was screaming in shock because a stranger had found his lost wallet and given it back to him. The boy looked like me, a green, eager job seeker, and he, too, must have come from his home town armed with warnings. You know all the things they tell you: don't give to street beggars because they are only pretending to be lame; look through tomato pyramids for the rotten ones the hawkers hide underneath; don't help people whose cars have broken down, because they are really armed robbers. And then somebody found his wallet and gave it back to him."

My lover looked puzzled.

"Rituals of distrust," I said. "That is how we relate to one another here, through rituals of distrust. Do you know how carefully I watch the fuel gauge when I buy petrol just to make sure the attendant hasn't tampered with it? We know the rules and we follow them, and we never make room for things we might not have imagined. We close the door too soon." I felt a little silly, saying things I knew he did not understand and did not want to understand, and also a little cowardly, saying them the way I did. He was resting his elbows on the table, watching me, and I knew that all he wanted was my excitement, my gratitude, my questions about when I could see the new car. I began to cry, and he came around and cradled me against his waist. My nose was running and my eyes itched as I dabbed them with my napkin. I never cried elegantly, and I imagined that his wife did; she was probably one of those women who could just have the tears trail down her cheeks, leaving her makeup intact, her nose dry.

The traffic had started to move a little. I saw an okada in my side mirror, coming too fast, swerving and honking, and I waited to hear the crunch as it hit my car. But it didn't. The driver was wearing a helmet, while his passenger merely held hers over her head—the smelly foam inside would have ruined her hair—close enough so that she could slip it on as soon as she saw a LASTMA official ahead. My lover once called it fatalism. He had given free helmets to all his staff, but most of them still got on an okada without one. The day before, an okada, the driver bareheaded and blindly speeding, had hit me as I turned onto Ogunlana Drive; the driver stuck his finger into his mouth and ran it over the scratch on the side of my car. "Auntie, sorry oh! Nothing happen to the car," he said, and continued his journey.

I laughed. I had not laughed in the three weeks since I had left work at lunchtime and driven to my lover's house. I had packed all my clothes, my books, and my toiletries and gone back to my flat, consumed as I went by how relentlessly unpretty Lagos was, with houses sprouting up unplanned like weeds.

During those three weeks, I had said little at work. Our office was suddenly very uncomfortable, the air-conditioning always too cold. His Royal Highness, the Oba of the town near the lagoon, was asking for more money; his town council had written a letter saying that the borehole was spewing blackish water. My boss was calling too many meetings.

"Let us give thanks," he said after one of the meetings.

"Why should we be praying in the workplace?" I asked. "Why must you assume that we are all Christians?"

He looked startled. He knew that I never joined in, never said "Amen," but I had never been vocal about it.

"It is not by force to participate in thanking the Lord," he said, and then in the same breath continued, "In Jesus' name!"

"Amen!" the others chorused.

I turned to leave the meeting room.

"Don't go," my co-worker Gerald whispered to me. "Akin brought his birthday cake."

I stood outside the meeting room until the prayer ended, and then we sang "Happy Birthday" to Akin. His cake looked like the unpretentious kind I liked, probably from Sweet Sensation, the kind that sometimes had bits of forgotten eggshells in it. Our boss asked him to give me or Chikwado the cake to serve.

"Why do we always have to serve the cake?" I asked. "Every time somebody brings in a cake, it is either Chikwado serves it or I serve it. You, Gerald, serve the cake. Or you, Emeka, since you are the most junior."

They stared at me. Chikwado got up hurriedly and began to slice the cake. "Please, don't mind her," she said to everyone, but her eyes were on our boss. "She is behaving like this because she did not take her madness medicine today."

Later, she said to me, "Why have you been behaving somehow? What's the problem? Did something happen with your man?"

For a moment, I wanted to tell her how I felt: as though bits of my skin had warped and cracked and peeled off, leaving patches of raw flesh so agonizingly painful I did not know what to do. I wanted to tell her how often I stared at my phone, even though he had sent two feeble texts saying he did not understand why I'd left and then nothing else; and how I remembered clearly, too clearly, the scent of the moist tissues he used to clean his glasses. I didn't tell her, because I was sure she would deliver one of her petty wisdoms, like "If you see fire and you put your hand in fire, then fire will burn you." Still, there was a softness in her expression, something like sympathy, when I looked up from my computer screen and saw her watching me while her hand went slap, slap, slap on her head. Her weave was a new style, too long and too wiggy, with reddish highlights that brought to mind the hair of cheap plastic dolls. Yet there was an honesty about it; Chikwado owned it in a way that the woman in the jeep did not own her Brazilian hair.

A young boy approached my car, armed with a spray bottle of soapy water and a rag. I turned on my wipers to discourage him, but he still squirted my windscreen. I increased the wiper speed. The boy glared at me and moved on to the car behind me. I was seized with a sudden urge to step out and slap him. For a moment, my vision blurred. It was really the woman I wanted to slap. I turned to her jeep and, because she had looked away, I pressed my horn. I leaned out of my window.

"What is your problem? Why have you been staring at me? Do I owe you?" I shouted.

The traffic began to move. I thought she would roll down her window, too. She made as if to lean toward it, then turned away, the slightest of smiles on her face, her head held high, and I watched the jeep pick up speed and head to the bridge.

[2010]

PART TWO

200 Poems

ANONYMOUS

Lord Randal

1

"O where ha' you been, Lord Randal, my son?
And where ha' you been, my handsome young man?"
"I ha' been at the greenwood; mother, mak my bed soon,
For I'm wearied wi' huntin', and fain wad° lie down."   *gladly would*

2

"And wha° met ye there, Lord Randal, my son?   *who*   5
And wha met you there, my handsome young man?"
"O I met wi' my true-love; mother, mak my bed soon,
For I'm wearied wi' huntin', and fain wad lie down."

3

"And what did she give you, Lord Randal, my son?
And what did she give you, my handsome young man?"   10
"Eels fried in a pan; mother, mak my bed soon,
For I'm wearied wi' huntin', and fain wad lie down."

4

"And wha gat your leavin's, Lord Randal, my son?
And wha gat your leavin's, my handsome young man?"
"My hawks and my hounds; mother, mak my bed soon,   15
For I'm wearied wi' huntin', and fain wad lie down."

5

"And what becam of them, Lord Randal, my son?
And what becam of them, my handsome young man?"
"They stretched their legs out and died; mother, mak my bed soon,
For I'm wearied wi' huntin', and fain wad lie down."   20

6

"O I fear you are poisoned, Lord Randal, my son!
I fear you are poisoned, my handsome young man!"
"O yes, I am poisoned; mother, mak my bed soon,
For I'm sick at the heart, and I fain wad lie down."

7

"What d' ye leave to your mother, Lord Randal, my son?
What d' ye leave to your mother, my handsome young man?"
"Four and twenty milk kye;° mother, mak my bed soon,   cows
For I'm sick at the heart, and I fain wad lie down."

8

"What d' ye leave to your sister, Lord Randal, my son?
What d' ye leave to your sister, my handsome young man?"
"My gold and my silver; mother, mak my bed soon,
For I'm sick at the heart, and I fain wad lie down."

9

"What d' ye leave to your brother, Lord Randal, my son?
What d' ye leave to your brother, my handsome young man?"
"My houses and my lands; mother, mak my bed soon,
For I'm sick at the heart, and I fain wad lie down."

10

"What d' ye leave to your true-love, Lord Randal, my son?
What d' ye leave to your true-love, my handsome young man?"
"I leave her hell and fire; mother, mak my bed soon,
For I'm sick at the heart, and I fain wad lie down."

[1803]

SIR THOMAS WYATT [1503–1542]

They flee from me

They flee from me, that sometime did me seek,
With naked foot stalking in my chamber.
I have seen them, gentle, tame, and meek,
That now are wild, and do not remember
That sometime they put themselves in danger   5
To take bread at my hand; and now they range,
Busily seeking with a continual change.

Thankèd be fortune it hath been otherwise,
Twenty times better; but once in special,
In thin array, after a pleasant guise,°   *manner of dress* 10
When her loose gown from her shoulders did fall,
And she me caught in her arms long and small,°   *slender*
Therewithall sweetly did me kiss
And softly said, "Dear heart,° how like you this?"

It was no dream, I lay broad waking.   15
But all is turned, thorough° my gentleness,   *through*
Into a strange fashion of forsaking;
And I have leave to go, of° her goodness,   *out of (motivated by)*
And she also to use newfangleness.
But since that I so kindly° am served,   20
I fain would know what she hath deserved.

[from an undated manuscript]

14. **Dear heart** (pun): Heart, and hart (deer).
20. **kindly** (pun): Graciously (ironic), and "in kind"; i.e., in a way typical of
female nature.

EDMUND SPENSER   [1552–1599]

what guile is this,
that those her golden tresses

What guile is this, that those her golden tresses
She doth attire under a net of gold;
And with sly skill so cunningly them dresses,
That which is gold or hair may scarce be told?
Is it that men's frail eyes, which gaze too bold,
She may entangle in that golden snare;
And, being caught, may craftily enfold
Their weaker hearts, which are not well aware?
Take heed, therefore, mine eyes, how ye do stare
Henceforth too rashly on that guileful net,
In which, if ever ye entrappèd are,
Out of her bands ye by no means shall get.
   Fondness it were for any, being free,
    To cover fetters, though they golden be.

[c. 1593–1595]

CHRISTOPHER MARLOWE   [1564–1593]

The Passionate Shepherd
to His Love

Come live with me and be my love,
And we will all the pleasures prove
That valleys, groves, hills, and fields,
Woods, or steepy mountain yields.

452

And we will sit upon the rocks,   5
Seeing the shepherds feed their flocks,
By shallow rivers, to whose falls
Melodious birds sing madrigals.

And I will make thee beds of roses
And a thousand fragrant posies,   10
A cap of flowers, and a kirtle°   *a long gown*
Embroidered all with leaves of myrtle.

A gown made of the finest wool
Which from our pretty lambs we pull,
Fair lined slippers for the cold,   15
With buckles of the purest gold.

A belt of straw and ivy buds,
With coral clasps and amber studs,
And if these pleasures may thee move,
Come live with me, and be my love.   20

The shepherd swains shall dance and sing
For thy delight each May morning.
If these delights thy mind may move,
Then live with me and be my love.

                                                                           [1599]

WILLIAM SHAKESPEARE   [1564–1616]

Sonnet 18

Shall I compare thee to a summer's day?
Thou art more lovely and more temperate:
Rough winds do shake the darling buds of May,
And summer's lease° hath all too short a date;°   *allotted time/duration*
Sometimes too hot the eye of heaven shines,   5
And often is his gold complexion dimmed;
And every fair° from fair° sometimes declines,   *beautiful thing/beauty*
By chance or nature's changing course untrimmed;°   *stripped of its beauty*
But thy eternal summer shall not fade,

Nor lose possession of that fair thou ow'st;°   *beauty you own*
Nor shall death brag thou wand'rest in his shade,
When in eternal lines° to time thou grow'st:°
  So long as men can breathe, or eyes can see,
  So long lives this,° and this gives life to thee.   *this sonnet*

[1609]

12. **lines:** (Of poetry); **to . . . grow'st:** You are grafted to time.

WILLIAM SHAKESPEARE [1564–1616]

Sonnet 73

That time of year thou mayst in me behold
When yellow leaves, or none, or few, do hang
Upon those boughs which shake against the cold,
Bare ruined choirs,° where late° the sweet birds sang.   *choir stalls/lately*
In me thou seest the twilight of such day
As after sunset fadeth in the west,
Which by and by black night doth take away,
Death's second self, that seals up all in rest.
In me thou seest the glowing of such fire
That on the ashes of his youth doth lie,
As the deathbed whereon it must expire,
Consumed with that which it was nourished by.
  This thou perceiv'st, which makes thy love more strong,
  To love that well which thou must leave ere long.

[1609]

WILLIAM SHAKESPEARE   [1564–1616]

Sonnet 116

Let me not to the marriage of true minds
Admit impediments. Love is not love
Which alters when it alteration finds,
Or bends with the remover to remove:
Oh, no! it is an ever-fixed mark,   5
That looks on tempests and is never shaken;
It is the star to every wandering bark,°   *a small sailing ship*
Whose worth's unknown, although his height be taken.
Love's not Time's fool, though rosy lips and cheeks
Within his bending sickle's compass come;   10
Love alters not with his brief hours and weeks,
But bears it out even to the edge of doom.
     If this be error, and upon me prov'd,
     I never writ, nor no man ever lov'd.

[1609]

JOHN DONNE   [1572–1631]

A Valediction:
Forbidding Mourning

As virtuous men pass mildly away,
     And whisper to their souls to go,
Whilst some of their sad friends do say
     The breath goes now, and some say, No;

So let us melt, and make no noise,
  No tear-floods, nor sigh-tempests move;
'Twere profanation of our joys
  To tell the laity our love.

Moving of th' earth brings harms and fears,
  Men reckon what it did and meant;
But trepidation of the spheres,
  Though greater far, is innocent.°

Dull sublunary° lovers' love   *under the moon; hence, inconstant*
  (Whose soul is sense) cannot admit
Absence, because it doth remove
  Those things which elemented° it.   *composed*

But we, by a love so much refined
  That our selves know not what it is,
Inter-assurèd of the mind,
  Care less, eyes, lips, and hands to miss.

Our two souls therefore, which are one,
  Though I must go, endure not yet
A breach, but an expansion,
  Like gold to airy thinness beat.

If they be two, they are two so
  As stiff twin compasses° are two;   *drawing compasses*
Thy soul, the fixed foot, makes no show
  To move, but doth, if th' other do.

And though it in the center sit,
  Yet when the other far doth roam,
It leans and hearkens after it,
  And grows erect, as that comes home.

Such wilt thou be to me, who must,
  Like th' other foot, obliquely run;
Thy firmness makes my circle just,
  And makes me end where I begun.

[1633]

9–12. Moving . . . innocent: Earthquakes cause damage and were taken as portending further changes or dangers. Trepidation (an oscillating motion of the eighth or ninth sphere, in the Ptolemaic cosmological system) is greater than an earthquake, but not harmful or ominous.

JOHN DONNE   [1572–1631]

Death, be not proud

Death, be not proud, though some have callèd thee
Mighty and dreadful, for thou art not so;
For those whom thou think'st thou dost overthrow
Die not, poor Death, nor yet canst thou kill me.
From rest and sleep, which but thy pictures be,   5
Much pleasure; then from thee much more must flow,
And soonest our best men with thee do go,
Rest of their bones, and soul's delivery.
Thou art slave to fate, chance, kings, and desperate men,
And dost with poison, war, and sickness dwell,   10
And poppy° or charms can make us sleep as well   *opium*
And better than thy stroke; why swell'st° thou then?   *(with pride)*
One short sleep past, we wake eternally
And death shall be no more; Death, thou shalt die.

[1633]

BEN JONSON   [1572–1637]

On My First Son

Farewell, thou child of my right hand,° and joy;
My sin was too much hope of thee, loved boy:
Seven years thou'wert lent to me, and I thee pay,
Exacted by thy fate, on the just day.
O could I lose all father now! for why   5

1. child . . . hand: A literal translation of the Hebrew name "Benjamin." The boy,
named for his father, was born in 1596 and died on his birthday ("the [exact]
day"—that on which the loan came due) in 1603.

Will man lament the state he should envy,
To have so soon 'scaped world's and flesh's rage,
And, if no other misery, yet age?
Rest in soft peace, and asked, say, "Here doth lie
Ben Jonson his best piece of poetry."
For whose sake henceforth all his° vows be such   *(the father's)*
As what he loves may never like° too much.

[1616]

12. **like:** Archaic meaning "please."

LADY MARY WROTH   [1587–1653]

Am I Thus Conquer'd?

Am I thus conquer'd? have I lost the powers,
    That to withstand which joyes to ruine me?
    Must I bee still, while it my strength devoures,
    And captive leads me prisoner bound, unfree?

Love first shall leane mens fant'sies to them free,
    Desire shall quench loves flames, Spring, hate sweet showers,
    Love shall loose all his Darts, have sight, and see
    His shame and wishings, hinder happy houres.

Why should we not Loves purblinde charmes resist?
    Must we be servile, doing what he list?
    No, seeke some host to harbour thee: I flye

Thy Babish° tricks, and freedome doe professe:
    But O, my hurt makes my lost heart confesse:
    I love, and must; so farewell liberty.

[1621]

12. **Babish:** Like a babe, childish, babyish.

ROBERT HERRICK   [1591–1674]

To the Virgins, to Make Much of Time

Gather ye rosebuds while ye may,
  Old time is still a-flying;
And this same flower that smiles today
  Tomorrow will be dying.

The glorious lamp of heaven, the sun,   5
  The higher he's a-getting,
The sooner will his race be run,
  And nearer he's to setting.

That age is best which is the first,
  When youth and blood are warmer;   10
But being spent, the worse, and worst
  Times still succeed the former.

Then be not coy, but use your time,
  And while ye may, go marry;
For having lost but once your prime,   15
  You may forever tarry.

                                                        [1648]

GEORGE HERBERT [1593–1633]

Easter-wings°

Lord, who createdst man in wealth and store,°
  Though foolishly he lost the same,°
    Decaying more and more
       Till   he   became
        Most   poor:
        With   thee
      O let me rise
    As   larks,   harmoniously,
  And sing this day thy victories:
Then shall the fall further the flight in me.

My tender age in sorrow did begin:
  And still with sicknesses and shame
    Thou didst so punish sin,
       That   I   became
        Most   thin.
        With   thee
      Let me combine,
    And   feel thy victory;
For, if I imp° my wing on thine,
Affliction shall advance the flight in me.

[1633]

Easter-wings: Originally the stanzas were printed on facing pages, lines 1–10 on the right page, to be read first, then lines 11–20 on the left page.
1. Store: Abundance.
2. lost the same: Through the Fall in the Garden of Eden. Early editions include the words "this day" in line 18 (perhaps repeated by mistake from line 9); they do not appear in the only surviving manuscript and are not required for the meter.
19. imp: A term from falconry—to graft additional feathers onto the wings of a hawk to improve its flight.

GEORGE HERBERT   [1593–1633]

The Collar

I struck the board° and cried,"No more;	*table*
I will abroad!	
What? shall I ever sigh and pine?	
My lines and life are free, free as the road,	
Loose as the wind, as large as store.°	*abundance* 5
Shall I be still in suit?	
Have I no harvest but a thorn	
To let me blood, and not restore	
What I have lost with cordial° fruit?	*life-giving*
Sure there was wine	10
Before my sighs did dry it; there was corn	
Before my tears did drown it.	
Is the year only lost to me?	
Have I no bays° to crown it,	
No flowers, no garlands gay? All blasted?	15
All wasted?	
Not so, my heart; but there is fruit,	
And thou hast hands.	
Recover all thy sigh-blown age	
On double pleasures: leave thy cold dispute	20
Of what is fit and not. Forsake thy cage,	
Thy rope of sands,°	
Which petty thoughts have made, and made to thee	
Good cable, to enforce and draw,	
And be thy law,	25
While thou didst wink° and wouldst not see.	*shut your eyes*
Away! take heed;	
I will abroad.	
Call in thy death's-head there; tie up thy fears.	
He that forbears	30

14. bays: A laurel garland, signifying poetic fame.
22. rope of sands: Restrictions on behavior, which thoughts have made into
"strong cable."

To suit and serve his need,
    Deserves his load."
But as I raved and grew more fierce and wild
    At every word,
Methought I heard one calling, *Child!*
    And I replied, *My Lord*.

[1633]

JOHN MILTON   [1608–1674]

When I consider
how my light is spent

When I consider how my light is spent°
   Ere half my days, in this dark world and wide,
   And that one talent which is death to hide
   Lodged with me useless, though my soul more bent
To serve therewith my Maker, and present
   My true account, lest he returning chide.
   "Doth God exact day-labor, light denied?"
   I fondly ask; but patience to prevent
That murmur, soon replies, "God doth not need
   Either man's work or his own gifts; who best
   Bear his mild yoke, they serve him best. His state
Is kingly. Thousands at his bidding speed
   And post o'er land and ocean without rest:
   They also serve who only stand and wait."

[*c. 1652*; 1673]°

1. When . . . spent: Milton went blind in 1652. Lines 1–2 allude to Matthew
25:1–13; line 3, to Matthew 25:14–30; and line 11, to Matthew 11:30.
[*c. 1652*; 1673]: When two dates appear, the first date (in italics) is an approximate time of composition and the second date is the year of earliest publication.
Both dates are included when two dates are so far apart that publication doesn't
reflect the time the poem was written.

ANNE BRADSTREET [c. 1612–1672]

To My Dear and Loving Husband

If ever two were one, then surely we.
If ever man were loved by wife, then thee;
If ever wife was happy in a man,
Compare with me ye women if you can.
I prize thy love more than whole mines of gold,   5
Or all the riches that the East doth hold.
My love is such that rivers cannot quench,
Nor ought but love from thee give recompense.
Thy love is such I can no way repay;
The heavens reward thee manifold, I pray.   10
Then while we live, in love let's so persever,
That when we live no more we may live ever.

[1678]

RICHARD LOVELACE [1618–1657]

To Lucasta, Going to the Wars

Tell me not, Sweet, I am unkind,
   That from the nunnery
Of thy chaste breast and quiet mind
   To war and arms I fly.

True, a new mistress now I chase,
  The first foe in the field;
And with a stronger faith embrace
  A sword, a horse, a shield.

Yet this inconstancy is such
  As you too shall adore;
I could not love thee, dear, so much,
  Loved I not honor more.

[1649]

ANDREW MARVELL   [1621–1678]

To His Coy Mistress°

Had we but world enough, and time,
This coyness, lady, were no crime.
We would sit down, and think which way
To walk, and pass our long love's day.
Thou by the Indian Ganges' side
Shouldst rubies find; I by the tide
Of Humber would complain.° I would
Love you ten years before the Flood,
And you should, if you please, refuse
Till the conversion of the Jews.°
My vegetable° love should grow   *living and growing*
Vaster than empires, and more slow;
An hundred years should go to praise
Thine eyes, and on thy forehead gaze;
Two hundred to adore each breast,

Coy: In the seventeenth century, "coy" could carry its older meaning, "shy," or the modern sense of "coquettish." "Mistress" then could mean "a woman loved and courted by a man; a female sweetheart."
5–7. Indian Ganges', Humber: The Ganges River in India, with its distant, romantic associations, contrasts with the Humber River, running through Hull in northeast England, Marvell's hometown.
10. conversion . . . Jews: An occurrence foretold, in some traditions, as one of the concluding events of human history.

But thirty thousand to the rest;
An age at least to every part,
And the last age should show your heart.
For, lady, you deserve this state,°   *dignity*
Nor would I love at lower rate.   20
   But at my back I always hear
Time's wingèd chariot hurrying near;
And yonder all before us lie
Deserts of vast eternity.
Thy beauty shall no more be found,   25
Nor, in thy marble vault, shall sound
My echoing song; then worms shall try
That long-preserved virginity,
And your quaint honor turn to dust,
And into ashes all my lust: 30
The grave's a fine and private place,
But none, I think, do there embrace.
   Now therefore, while the youthful hue
Sits on thy skin like morning dew,
And while thy willing soul transpires°   *breathes forth*   35
At every pore with instant fires,°   *urgent passion*
Now let us sport us while we may,
And now, like amorous birds of prey,
Rather at once our time devour
Than languish in his slow-chapped° power.   40
Let us roll all our strength and all
Our sweetness up into one ball,
And tear our pleasures with rough strife
Thorough° the iron gates of life;   *through*
Thus, though we cannot make our sun   45
Stand still,° yet we will make him run.

[*c. 1650;* 1681]

40. slow-chapped: Slow-jawed, devouring slowly.
45–46. make our sun stand still: An allusion to Joshua 10:12. In answer to
Joshua's prayer, God made the sun stand still, to prolong the day and give the
Israelites more time to defeat the Amorites.

JONATHAN SWIFT   [1667–1745]

A Description
of the Morning

Now hardly here and there a hackney-coach
Appearing, showed the ruddy morn's approach.
Now Betty from her master's bed had flown,
And softly stole to discompose her own;
The slip-shod 'prentice from his master's door
Had pared the dirt and sprinkled round the floor.
Now Moll had whirled her mop with dext'rous airs,
Prepared to scrub the entry and the stairs.
The youth with broomy stumps° began to trace   *worn broom*
The kennel-edge,° where wheels had worn the place.   *gutter*
The small-coal man° was heard with cadence deep,   *coal vendor*
Till drowned in shriller notes of chimney-sweep:
Duns° at his lordship's gate began to meet;   *debt collectors*
And brickdust Moll° had screamed through half the street.
The turnkey° now his flock° returning sees,   *jailer/inmates*
Duly let out a-nights to steal for fees:°
The watchful bailiffs take their silent stands,
And schoolboys lag with satchels in their hands.

[1709]

14. **brickdust Moll:** Woman selling powdered brick.
16. **fees:** Payments for food and better treatment.

ALEXANDER POPE   [1688–1744]

From An Essay on Criticism, Part 2°

But most by numbers° judge a poet's song,   *versification*
And smooth or rough, with them, is right or wrong.
In the bright Muse though thousand charms conspire,
Her voice is all these tuneful fools admire,   340
Who haunt Parnassus but to please their ear,
Not mend their minds; as some to church repair,
Not for the doctrine, but the music there.
These equal syllables alone require,°
Though oft the ear the open vowels tire,   345
While expletives° their feeble aid do join,
And ten low words oft creep in one dull line:
While they ring round the same unvaried chimes,
With sure returns of still expected rhymes;
Where'er you find "the cooling western breeze,"   350
In the next line, it "whispers through the trees";
If crystal streams "with pleasing murmurs creep,"
The reader's threatened (not in vain) with "sleep";
Then, at the last and only couplet fraught
With some unmeaning thing they call a thought,   355

An Essay on Criticism: An Essay on Criticism is a verse epistle addressed to
literary critics. In it Pope satirizes the pedantic judgments of inferior literary
critics (as he does in lines 337–61, on critics who care only about the way a
poem sounds and thus praise poets who produce rhyme and meter mechanically); he points out the characteristics of excellent poetry (ll. 362–83); and he
offers advice to critics on how to critique literature sensibly and helpfully
(ll. 384–93).
344–57. These . . . along: In alternating lines, Pope describes, then illustrates
satirically, the kinds of metrics or diction these critics advocate ("these . . .
require"). **equal syllables:** Mechanically regular accents.
346. expletives: Unnecessary words added to give a line the number of syllables
its meter requires, like *do* in this line.

A needless Alexandrine° ends the song,
That, like a wounded snake, drags its slow length along.
Leave such to tune their own dull rhymes, and know
What's roundly smooth or languishingly slow;
And praise the easy vigor of a line
Where Denham's strength and Waller's sweetness join.°
True ease in writing comes from art, not chance,
As those move easiest who have learned to dance.
'Tis not enough no harshness gives offense,
The sound must seem an echo to the sense.°
Soft is the strain when Zephyr° gently blows,   *the West Wind*
And the smooth stream in smoother numbers flows;
But when loud surges lash the sounding shore,
The hoarse, rough verse should like the torrent roar.
When Ajax° strives some rock's vast weight to throw,
The line too labors, and the words move slow;
Not so, when swift Camilla° scours the plain,
Flies o'er the unbending corn, and skims along the main.
Hear how Timotheus'° varied lays surprise,
And bid alternate passions fall and rise!
While at each change the son of Libyan Jove°
Now burns with glory, and then melts with love;
Now his fierce eyes with sparkling fury glow,
Now sighs steal out, and tears begin to flow:
Persians and Greeks like turns of nature° found
And the world's victor stood subdued by sound!
The power of music all our hearts allow,

356. Alexandrine: A metrical line with six iambic feet, illustrated in the following line.
361. Denham's . . . join: Combining the qualities attributed to two important shapers of the late-seventeenth-century heroic couplet: the "strength" (conciseness and emphasis on content) of Sir John Denham (1615–1669) and the "sweetness" (smoothness and musical qualities) of Edmund Waller (1606–1687).
365. sound . . . sense: Lines 366–83 provide examples of the precept that sound should echo sense in poetry.
370. Ajax: The rough hero in Homer's *Iliad* 12.378–86.
372. Camilla: The female warrior in Virgil's *Aeneid* (see especially 7.808ff).
374. Timotheus': A Theban musician in the court of Alexander the Great, whose music had powerful emotional effects. Lines 374–83 sum up the story told in John Dryden's ode "Alexander's Feast" (1697).
376. Libyan Jove: Alexander the Great.
380. like turns of nature: Similar alternations of feelings.

And what Timotheus was, is Dryden° now.
   Avoid extremes; and shun the fault of such
Who still° are pleased too little or too much.   *always* 385
At every trifle scorn to take offense:
That always shows great pride, or little sense.
Those heads, as stomachs, are not sure the best,
Which nauseate all, and nothing can digest.
Yet let not each gay turn° thy rapture move;   390
For fools admire,° but men of sense approve:°
As things seem large which we through mists descry,
Dullness is ever apt to magnify.

                                                [1711]

383. Dryden: John Dryden (1631–1700) was the dominant poet in England from
1660 until his death.
390. gay turn: Apt and pleasing turn of phrase.
391. admire: Marvel; **approve:** Commend thoughtfully as good.

THOMAS GRAY   [1716–1771]

Elegy Written in a Country Churchyard

The curfew° tolls the knell of parting day,   *evening bell*
   The lowing herd wind slowly o'er the lea,
The plowman homeward plods his weary way,
   And leaves the world to darkness and to me.

Now fades the glimmering landscape on the sight,   5
   And all the air a solemn stillness holds,
Save where the beetle wheels his droning flight,
   And drowsy tinklings lull the distant folds;

Save that from yonder ivy-mantled tower
   The moping owl does to the moon complain   10
Of such, as wandering near her secret bower,
   Molest her ancient solitary reign.

Beneath those rugged elms, that yew tree's shade,
  Where heaves the turf in many a moldering heap,
Each in his narrow cell forever laid,
  The rude forefathers° of the hamlet sleep.   *humble ancestors*

The breezy call of incense-breathing morn,
  The swallow twittering from the straw-built shed,
The cock's shrill clarion, or the echoing horn,°   *(of a hunter)*
  No more shall rouse them from their lowly bed.

For them no more the blazing hearth shall burn,
  Or busy housewife ply her evening care;
No children run to lisp their sire's return,
  Or climb his knees the envied kiss to share.

Oft did the harvest to their sickle yield,
  Their furrow oft the stubborn glebe° has broke;   *soil*
How jocund did they drive their team afield!
  How bowed the woods beneath their sturdy stroke!

Let not Ambition mock their useful toil,
  Their homely joys, and destiny obscure;
Nor Grandeur hear with a disdainful smile
  The short and simple annals of the poor.

The boast of heraldry,° the pomp of power,   *noble ancestry*
  And all that beauty, all that wealth e'er gave,
Awaits alike the inevitable hour.
  The paths of glory lead but to the grave.

Nor you, ye proud, impute to these the fault,
  If memory o'er their tomb no trophies° raise,   *memorials*
Where through the long-drawn aisle and fretted° vault   *ornamented*
  The pealing anthem swells the note of praise.

Can storied° urn or animated° bust   *decorated/lifelike*
  Back to its mansion call the fleeting breath?
Can Honor's voice provoke° the silent dust,   *call forth*
  Or Flattery soothe the dull cold ear of Death?

Perhaps in this neglected spot is laid
  Some heart once pregnant with celestial fire;
Hands that the rod of empire might have swayed,
  Or waked to ecstasy the living lyre.

But Knowledge to their eyes her ample page
    Rich with the spoils of time did ne'er unroll;   50
Chill Penury repressed their noble rage,
    And froze the genial current of the soul.

Full many a gem of purest ray serene,
    The dark unfathomed caves of ocean bear:
Full many a flower is born to blush unseen,   55
    And waste its sweetness on the desert air.

Some village Hampden,° that with dauntless breast
    The little tyrant of his fields withstood;
Some mute inglorious Milton here may rest,
    Some Cromwell guiltless of his country's blood.   60

The applause of listening senates to command,
    The threats of pain and ruin to despise,
To scatter plenty o'er a smiling land,
    And read their history in a nation's eyes,

Their lot forbade: nor° circumscribed alone   *not* 65
    Their growing virtues, but their crimes confined;
Forbade to wade through slaughter to a throne,
    And shut the gates of mercy on mankind,

The struggling pangs of conscious truth to hide,
    To quench the blushes of ingenuous shame,   70
Or heap the shrine of Luxury and Pride
    With incense kindled at the Muse's flame.

Far from the madding crowd's ignoble strife,
    Their sober wishes never learned to stray;
Along the cool sequestered vale of life   75
    They kept the noiseless tenor of their way.

Yet even these bones from insult to protect
    Some frail memorial° still erected nigh,   *(simple tombstone)*
With uncouth rhymes and shapeless sculpture decked,
    Implores the passing tribute of a sigh.   80

57–60. Hampden, Cromwell: John Hampden (1594–1643) refused to pay a
special tax imposed in 1636 and led a defense of the people's rights in Parliament. Oliver Cromwell (1599–1658) was a rebel leader in the English Civil War.

Their name, their years, spelt by the unlettered Muse,
    The place of fame and elegy supply:
And many a holy text around she strews,
    That teach the rustic moralist to die.

For who to dumb Forgetfulness a prey,
    This pleasing anxious being e'er resigned,
Left the warm precincts of the cheerful day,
    Nor cast one longing lingering look behind?

On some fond breast the parting soul relies,
    Some pious drops° the closing eye requires;   *tears*
Even from the tomb the voice of Nature cries,
    Even in our ashes live their wonted fires.

For thee,° who mindful of the unhonored dead   *(the poet himself)*
    Dost in these lines their artless tale relate;
If chance, by lonely contemplation led,
    Some kindred spirit shall inquire thy fate,

Haply° some hoary-headed swain° may say,   *perhaps/elderly shepherd*
    "Oft have we seen him° at the peep of dawn   *the poet*
Brushing with hasty steps the dews away
    To meet the sun upon the upland lawn.

"There at the foot of yonder nodding beech
    That wreathes its old fantastic roots so high,
His listless length at noontide would he stretch,
    And pore upon the brook that babbles by.

"Hard by yon wood, now smiling as in scorn,
    Muttering his wayward fancies he would rove,
Now drooping, woeful wan, like one forlorn,
    Or crazed with care, or crossed in hopeless love.

"One morn I missed him on the customed hill,
    Along the heath and near his favorite tree;
Another° came; nor yet beside the rill,°   *(another day)/small brook*
    Nor up the lawn, nor at the wood was he;

"The next with dirges due in sad array
    Slow through the churchway path we saw him borne.
Approach and read (for thou canst read) the lay,
    Graved on the stone beneath yon aged thorn."

THE EPITAPH

Here rests his head upon the lap of Earth
  A youth to fortune and to Fame unknown.
Fair Science° frowned not on his humble birth,   learning
  And Melancholy marked him for her own.   120

Large was his bounty, and his soul sincere,
  Heaven did a recompense as largely send:
He gave to Misery all he had, a tear,
  He gained from Heaven ('twas all he wished) a friend.

No farther seek his merits to disclose,   125
  Or draw his frailties from their dread abode
(There they alike in trembling hope repose),
  The bosom of his Father and his God.

[1751]

WILLIAM BLAKE [1757–1827]

The Lamb

  Little Lamb, who made thee?
  Dost thou know who made thee?
Gave thee life & bid thee feed,
By the stream & o'er the mead;
Gave thee clothing of delight,   5
Softest clothing wooly bright;
Gave thee such a tender voice,
Making all the vales rejoice!
  Little Lamb who made thee?
  Dost thou know who made thee?   10

  Little Lamb I'll tell thee,
  Little Lamb I'll tell thee!
He is callèd by thy name,
For he calls himself a Lamb:
He is meek & he is mild,   15

He became a little child:
I a child & thou a lamb,
We are callèd by his name.
   Little Lamb God bless thee.
   Little Lamb God bless thee.

[1789]

WILLIAM BLAKE   [1757–1827]

The Tyger

Tyger, Tyger, burning bright
In the forests of the night,
What immortal hand or eye
Could frame thy fearful symmetry?

In what distant deeps or skies
Burnt the fire of thine eyes?
On what wings dare he aspire?
What the hand, dare seize the fire?

And what shoulder, & what art,
Could twist the sinews of thy heart?
And when thy heart began to beat,
What dread hand? & what dread feet?

What the hammer? what the chain?
In what furnace was thy brain?
What the anvil? what dread grasp
Dare its deadly terrors clasp?

When the stars threw down their spears
And water'd heaven with their tears,
Did he smile his work to see?
Did he who made the Lamb make thee?

Tyger, Tyger, burning bright
In the forests of the night,
What immortal hand or eye
Dare frame thy fearful symmetry?

[1794]

WILLIAM BLAKE   [1757–1827]

A Poison Tree

I was angry with my friend;
I told my wrath, my wrath did end.
I was angry with my foe:
I told it not, my wrath did grow.

And I watered it in fears,   5
Night & morning with my tears:
And I sunned it with smiles,
And with soft deceitful wiles.

And it grew both day and night.
Till it bore an apple bright.   10
And my foe beheld it shine,
And he knew that it was mine.

And into my garden stole,
When the night had veiled the pole;
In the morning glad I see;   15
My foe outstretched beneath the tree.

[1794]

ROBERT BURNS   [1759–1796]

A Red, Red Rose

O my luve's like a red, red rose,
   That's newly sprung in June;
O my luve's like the melodie
   That's sweetly played in tune.

As fair art thou, my bonnie lass,
    So deep in luve am I;
And I will luve thee still, my dear,
    Till a' the seas gang dry.

Till a' the seas gang dry, my dear,
    And the rocks melt wi' the sun:
O I will love thee still, my dear,
    While the sands o' life shall run.

And fare thee weel, my only luve,
    And fare thee weel awhile!
And I will come again, my luve,
    Though it were ten thousand mile.

[1796]

WILLIAM WORDSWORTH   [1770–1850]

I wandered lonely as a cloud

I wandered lonely as a cloud
That floats on high o'er vales and hills,
When all at once I saw a crowd,
A host, of golden daffodils;
Beside the lake, beneath the trees,
Fluttering and dancing in the breeze.

Continuous as the stars that shine
And twinkle on the milky way,
They stretched in never-ending line
Along the margin of a bay:
Ten thousand saw I at a glance,
Tossing their heads in sprightly dance.

The waves beside them danced; but they
Outdid the sparkling waves in glee:
A poet could not but be gay,
In such a jocund company:
I gazed—and gazed—but little thought
What wealth the show to me had brought:

For oft, when on my couch I lie
In vacant or in pensive mood,   20
They flash upon that inward eye
Which is the bliss of solitude;
And then my heart with pleasure fills,
And dances with the daffodils.

[1807]

WILLIAM WORDSWORTH [1770–1850]

Ode

*Intimations of Immortality from Recollections
of Early Childhood*

*The Child is father of the Man;
And I could wish my days to be
Bound each to each by natural piety.*°

1

There was a time when meadow, grove, and stream,
The earth, and every common sight,
        To me did seem
        Appareled in celestial light,
The glory and the freshness of a dream.   5
It is not now as it hath been of yore—
        Turn whereso'er I may,
        By night or day,
The things which I have seen I now can see no more.

2

        The Rainbow comes and goes,   10
        And lovely is the Rose,
        The Moon doth with delight
Look round her when the heavens are bare,
        Waters on a starry night

Epigraph: The final lines of Wordsworth's "My Heart Leaps Up."

Are beautiful and fair;
  The sunshine is a glorious birth;
  But yet I know, where'er I go,
That there hath passed away a glory from the earth.

3

Now, while the birds thus sing a joyous song,
  And while the young lambs bound
    As to the tabor's° sound,
To me alone there came a thought of grief:
A timely utterance gave that thought relief,
    And I again am strong:
The cataracts blow their trumpets from the steep;
No more shall grief of mine the season wrong;
I hear the Echoes through the mountains throng,
The Winds come to me from the fields of sleep,
    And all the earth is gay;
      Land and sea
    Give themselves up to jollity,
      And with the heart of May
    Doth every Beast keep holiday—
      Thou Child of Joy,
Shout round me, let me hear thy shouts, thou happy Shepherd-boy!

4

Ye blessèd Creatures, I have heard the call
  Ye to each other make; I see
The heavens laugh with you in your jubilee;
  My heart is at your festival,
    My head hath its coronal,°
The fullness of your bliss, I feel—I feel it all.
    Oh, evil day! if I were sullen
    While Earth herself is adorning,
      This sweet May morning,
    And the Children are culling
      On every side,
    In a thousand valleys far and wide,
    Fresh flowers; while the sun shines warm,
And the Babe leaps up on his Mother's arm—
    I hear, I hear, with joy I hear!

---

21. tabor: A small drum, used chiefly as an accompaniment to the pipe or trumpet.
40. coronal: A wreath of flowers or leaves for the head; a garland.

—But there's a Tree, of many, one,
A single Field which I have looked upon,
Both of them speak of something that is gone:
  The Pansy at my feet
  Doth the same tale repeat: 55
Whither is fled the visionary gleam?
Where is it now, the glory and the dream?

5

Our birth is but a sleep and a forgetting:
The Soul that rises with us, our life's Star,
  Hath had elsewhere its setting,   60
   And cometh from afar:
  Not in entire forgetfulness,
  And not in utter nakedness,
But trailing clouds of glory do we come
  From God, who is our home: 65
Heaven lies about us in our infancy!
Shades of the prison-house begin to close
  Upon the growing Boy
   But he
Beholds the light, and whence it flows,   70
  He sees it in his joy;
The Youth, who daily farther from the east
  Must travel, still is Nature's Priest,
  And by the vision splendid
  Is on his way attended;   75
At length the Man perceives it die away,
And fade into the light of common day.°

6

Earth fills her lap with pleasures of her own;
Yearnings she hath in her own natural kind,
And, even with something of a Mother's mind, 80
  And no unworthy aim,

---

77. Lines 58–77 reflect Plato's belief that human souls inhabit "a pre-existent state" (in Wordsworth's terms) before being born into this world. Though imprisoned in a physical body and the material world, the soul of the infant has recollections of and longs to return to the perfect world of ideas. As the child grows older, those memories begin to fade, though reminders of that primal glory recur (usually from experiences with things in nature). By adulthood, such glimpses become rare and the adult becomes reconciled to the material world and its values.

The homely° Nurse doth all she can   *simple, kindly*
To make her foster child, her Inmate Man,
    Forget the glories he hath known,
And that imperial palace whence he came.

7

Behold the Child among his newborn blisses,
A six-years' Darling of a pygmy size!
See, where 'mid work of his own hand he lies,
Fretted° by sallies of his mother's kisses,   *annoyed*
With light upon him from his father's eyes!
See, at his feet, some little plan or chart,
Some fragment from his dream of human life,
Shaped by himself with newly-learnèd art;
    A wedding or a festival,
    A mourning or a funeral;
      And this hath now his heart,
    And unto this he frames his song;
      Then will he fit his tongue
To dialogues of business, love, or strife;
    But it will not be long
    Ere this be thrown aside,
    And with new joy and pride
The little Actor cons° another part;   *learns*
Filling from time to time his "humorous stage"°
With all the Persons,° down to palsied Age,   *dramatis personae*
That Life brings with her in her equipage;°
    As if his whole vocation
    Were endless imitation.

8

Thou, whose exterior semblance doth belie
    Thy Soul's immensity;
Thou best Philosopher, who yet dost keep
Thy heritage, thou Eye among the blind,

---

104. "humorous stage": Quoted from a sonnet by the Elizabethan poet Samuel
Daniel: the varied temperaments (humors) of characters represented on the stage.
Lines 103–05 echo Jaques's "All the world's a stage" speech in Shakespeare's *As
You Like It* (2.7.138–65), with its description of the "seven ages" in the life of a
person.
105–06. all . . . equipage: All that is needed for a military operation, a journey,
or a domestic establishment.

That, deaf and silent, read'st the eternal deep,
Haunted forever by the eternal mind—
     Mighty Prophet! Seer blest!   115
     On whom those truths do rest,
Which we are toiling all our lives to find,
In darkness lost, the darkness of the grave;
Thou, over whom thy Immortality
Broods like the Day, a Master o'er a Slave,   120
A Presence which is not to be put by;
Thou little Child, yet glorious in the might
Of heaven-born freedom on thy being's height,
Why with such earnest pains dost thou provoke
The years to bring the inevitable yoke,   125
Thus blindly with thy blessedness at strife?
Full soon thy Soul shall have her earthly freight,
And custom lie upon thee with a weight,
Heavy as frost, and deep almost as life!

9

     O joy! that in our embers   130
     Is something that doth live,
     That nature yet remembers
     What was so fugitive!
The thought of our past years in me doth breed
Perpetual benediction: not indeed   135
For that which is most worthy to be blest;
Delight and liberty, the simple creed
Of Childhood, whether busy or at rest,
With new-fledged hope still fluttering in his breast—
     Not for these I raise   140
     The song of thanks and praise;
    But for those obstinate questionings
    Of sense and outward things,
    Fallings from us, vanishings;
    Blank misgivings of a Creature   145
Moving about in worlds not realized,°   *not seeming real*
High instincts before which our mortal Nature
Did tremble like a guilty Thing surprised;
     But for those first affections,
     Those shadowy recollections,   150
    Which, be they what they may,
Are yet the fountain light of all our day,
Are yet a master light of all our seeing;

Uphold us, cherish, and have power to make
Our noisy years seem moments in the being
Of the eternal Silence: truths that wake,
     To perish never;
Which neither listlessness, nor mad endeavor,
     Nor Man nor Boy,
Nor all that is at enmity with joy,
Can utterly abolish or destroy!
     Hence in a season of calm weather
     Though inland far we be,
Our Souls have sight of that immortal sea
     Which brought us hither,
     Can in a moment travel thither,
And see the Children sport upon the shore,
And hear the mighty waters rolling evermore.

10

Then sing, ye Birds, sing, sing a joyous song!
     And let the young Lambs bound
     As to the tabor's sound!
We in thought will join your throng,
     Ye that pipe and ye that play,
     Ye that through your hearts today
     Feel the gladness of the May!
What though the radiance which was once so bright
Be now forever taken from my sight,
     Though nothing can bring back the hour
Of splendor in the grass, of glory in the flower;
     We will grieve not, rather find
     Strength in what remains behind;
     In the primal sympathy
     Which having been must ever be;
     In the soothing thoughts that spring
     Out of human suffering;
     In the faith that looks through death,
In years that bring the philosophic mind.

11

And O, ye Fountains, Meadows, Hills, and Groves,
Forebode not any severing of our loves!
Yet in my heart of hearts I feel your might;
I only have relinquished one delight

To live beneath your more habitual sway.
I love the Brooks which down their channels fret,°   *move in agitated waves*
Even more than when I tripped lightly as they;
The innocent brightness of a newborn Day   195
          Is lovely yet;
The clouds that gather round the setting sun
Do take a sober coloring from an eye
That hath kept watch o'er man's mortality;
Another race hath been, and other palms° are won.   *symbols of victory* 200
Thanks to the human heart by which we live,
Thanks to its tenderness, its joys, and fears,
To me the meanest° flower that blows° can give   *most ordinary/blooms*
Thoughts that do often lie too deep for tears.

[1807]

WILLIAM WORDSWORTH   [1770–1850]

It is a beauteous evening

It is a beauteous evening, calm and free,
The holy time is quiet as a Nun
Breathless with adoration; the broad sun
Is sinking down in its tranquility;
The gentleness of heaven broods o'er the Sea;   5
Listen! the mighty Being is awake,
And doth with his eternal motion make
A sound like thunder—everlastingly.
Dear Child! dear Girl! that walkest with me here,
If thou appear untouched by solemn thought,   10
Thy nature is not therefore less divine:
Thou liest in Abraham's bosom all the year;
And worshipp'st at the Temple's inner shrine,°
God being with thee when we know it not.

[1807]

13. Temple's inner shrine: Referring to the ancient temple in Jerusalem—the
holy of holies, where it is said God dwells.

SAMUEL TAYLOR COLERIDGE   [1772–1834]

Kubla Khan

Or, a Vision in a Dream. A Fragment°

In Xanadu did Kubla Khan
A stately pleasure dome decree:°
Where Alph,° the sacred river, ran
Through caverns measureless to man
  Down to a sunless sea.
So twice five miles of fertile ground
With walls and towers were girdled round:
And there were gardens bright with sinuous rills,°   *small brooks*
Where blossomed many an incense-bearing tree;
And here were forests ancient as the hills,
Enfolding sunny spots of greenery.

But oh! that deep romantic chasm which slanted
Down the green hill athwart a cedarn cover!
A savage place! as holy and enchanted
As e'er beneath a waning moon was haunted
By woman wailing for her demon lover!
And from this chasm, with ceaseless turmoil seething,
As if this earth in fast thick pants were breathing,
A mighty fountain momently was forced:
Amid whose swift half-intermitted burst

Or, a Vision . . . A Fragment: Coleridge stated in a preface that this poem composed itself in his mind during "a profound sleep" (actually an opium-induced
reverie); that he began writing it down immediately upon waking but was interrupted by a caller; and that when he returned to his room an hour later he could
not complete it.
1–2. In . . . decree: "In Xamdu did Cublai Can build a stately Palace, encom-
passing sixteene miles of plaine ground with a wall" (Samuel Purchas, *Purchas
his Pilgrimage* [1613]). The historical Kublai Khan (1215–1294) was the founder
of the Yüan dynasty of China and overlord of the Mongol Empire.
3. Alph: Probably derived from the name of the River Alpheus in southern
Greece, which according to mythology ran under the sea and emerged at Syracuse (Italy) in the fountain of Arethusa.

Huge fragments vaulted like rebounding hail,
Or chaffy grain beneath the thresher's flail:
And 'mid these dancing rocks at once and ever
It flung up momently the sacred river.
Five miles meandering with a mazy motion   25
Through wood and dale the sacred river ran,
Then reached the caverns measureless to man,
And sank in tumult to a lifeless ocean:
And 'mid this tumult Kubla heard from far
Ancestral voices prophesying war!   30
   The shadow of the dome of pleasure
   Floated midway on the waves;
   Where was heard the mingled measure
   From the fountain and the caves.
It was a miracle of rare device,   35
A sunny pleasure dome with caves of ice!

   A damsel with a dulcimer
   In a vision once I saw:
   It was an Abyssinian maid,
   And on her dulcimer she played,   40
   Singing of Mount Abora.°
   Could I revive within me
   Her symphony and song,
   To such a deep delight 'twould win me,
That with music loud and long,   45
I would build that dome in air,
That sunny dome! those caves of ice!
And all who heard should see them there,
And all should cry, Beware! Beware!
His flashing eyes, his floating hair!   50
Weave a circle round him thrice,
And close your eyes with holy dread,
For he on honey-dew hath fed,
And drunk the milk of Paradise.

[*c. 1797–1798;* 1813]

39–41. **Abyssinian . . . Abora:** See *Paradise Lost* 4.280–82: "where Abassin Kings
their issue Guard, / Mount Amara, though this by some supposed / True Paradise
under the Ethiop Line."

GEORGE GORDON, LORD BYRON   [1788–1824]

She walks in beauty

1

She walks in beauty, like the night
   Of cloudless climes and starry skies;
And all that's best of dark and bright
   Meet in her aspect and her eyes:
Thus mellowed to that tender light
   Which heaven to gaudy day denies.

2

One shade the more, one ray the less,
   Had half impaired the nameless grace
Which waves in every raven tress,
   Or softly lightens o'er her face;
Where thoughts serenely sweet express
   How pure, how dear their dwelling place.

3

And on that cheek, and o'er that brow,
   So soft, so calm, yet eloquent,
The smiles that win, the tints that glow,
   But tell of days in goodness spent,
A mind at peace with all below,
   A heart whose love is innocent!

[1815]

PERCY BYSSHE SHELLEY [1792–1822]

Ozymandias°

I met a traveler from an antique land
Who said: Two vast and trunkless legs of stone
Stand in the desert. Near them, on the sand,
Half sunk, a shattered visage lies, whose frown,
And wrinkled lip, and sneer of cold command,   5
Tell that its sculptor well those passions read
Which yet survive, stamped on these lifeless things,
The hand that mocked them, and the heart that fed:
And on the pedestal these words appear:
"My name is Ozymandias, king of kings: 10
Look on my works, ye Mighty, and despair!"
Nothing beside remains. Round the decay
Of that colossal wreck, boundless and bare
The lone and level sands stretch far away.

[1818]

Ozymandias: The Greek name for Ramses II of Egypt (thirteenth century B.C.E.), who erected the largest statue in Egypt as a memorial to himself.

PERCY BYSSHE SHELLEY [1792–1822]

To a Skylark

Hail to thee, blithe spirit!
    Bird thou never wert—
That from Heaven or near it
    Pourest thy full heart
In profuse strains of unpremeditated art.   5

Higher still and higher
   From the earth thou springest,
Like a cloud of fire;
   The blue deep thou wingest,
And singing still dost soar, and soaring ever singest.

In the golden lightning
   Of the sunken sun,
O'er which clouds are bright'ning,
   Thou dost float and run;
Like an unbodied joy whose race is just begun.

The pale purple even
   Melts around thy flight;
Like a star of Heaven,
   In the broad daylight
Thou art unseen, but yet I hear thy shrill delight,

Keen as are the arrows
   Of that silver sphere
Whose intense lamp narrows
   In the white dawn clear
Until we hardly see, we feel that it is there.

All the earth and air
   With thy voice is loud,
As when night is bare
   From one lonely cloud
The moon rains out her beams, and Heaven is overflow'd.

What thou art we know not;
   What is most like thee?
From rainbow clouds there flow not
   Drops so bright to see,
As from thy presence showers a rain of melody.

Like a Poet hidden
   In the light of thought,
Singing hymns unbidden,
   Till the world is wrought
To sympathy with hopes and fears it heeded not:

Like a high-born maiden
   In a palace tower,
Soothing her love-laden
   Soul in secret hour
With music sweet as love, which overflows her bower:

Like a glow-worm golden
   In a dell of dew,
Scattering unbeholden
   Its aërial hue
Among the flowers and grass which screen it from the view: 50

Like a rose embower'd
   In its own green leaves,
By warm winds deflower'd,
   Till the scent it gives
Makes faint with too much sweet those heavy-wingèd thieves: 55

Sound of vernal showers
   On the twinkling grass,
Rain-awaken'd flowers,
   All that ever was
Joyous, and clear, and fresh thy music doth surpass.   60

Teach us, Sprite or Bird,
   What sweet thoughts are thine:
I have never heard
   Praise of love or wine
That panted forth a flood of rapture so divine.   65

Chorus Hymeneal,°   *nuptial*
   Or triumphal chant,
Match'd with thine would be all
   But an empty vaunt,
A thing wherein we feel there is some hidden want.   70

What objects are the fountains
   Of thy happy strain?
What fields, or waves, or mountains?
   What shapes of sky or plain?
What love of thine own kind? what ignorance of pain?   75

With thy clear keen joyance
   Languor cannot be:
Shadow of annoyance
   Never came near thee:
Thou lovest, but ne'er knew love's sad satiety.   80

Waking or asleep,
   Thou of death must deem
Things more true and deep
   Than we mortals dream,
Or how could thy notes flow in such a crystal stream?   85

We look before and after,
    And pine for what is not:
Our sincerest laughter
    With some pain is fraught;
Our sweetest songs are those that tell of saddest thought.

    Yet if we could scorn
        Hate and pride and fear,
If we were things born
        Not to shed a tear,
I know not how thy joy we ever should come near.

    Better than all measures
        Of delightful sound,
Better than all treasures
        That in books are found,
Thy skill to poet were, thou scorner of the ground!

    Teach me half the gladness
        That thy brain must know,
Such harmonious madness
        From my lips would flow,
The world should listen then, as I am listening now.

[1820]

JOHN KEATS   [1795–1821]

When I have fears
that I may cease to be

When I have fears that I may cease to be
    Before my pen has gleaned my teeming brain,
Before high piled books, in charactry,°   *writing*
    Hold like rich garners° the full ripened grain;   *granaries*
When I behold, upon the night's starred face,
    Huge cloudy symbols of a high romance,
And think that I may never live to trace
    Their shadows, with the magic hand of chance;

And when I feel, fair creature of an hour,
  That I shall never look upon thee more,
Never have relish in the fairy power
  Of unreflecting love;—then on the shore 10
Of the wide world I stand alone, and think
Till love and fame to nothingness do sink.

[*1818;* 1848]

JOHN KEATS [1795–1821]

La Belle Dame sans Merci°

O what can ail thee, Knight at arms,
  Alone and palely loitering?
The sedge° has withered from the Lake   *rushes*
  And no birds sing!

O what can ail thee, Knight at arms, 5
  So haggard, and so woebegone?
The squirrel's granary is full
  And the harvest's done.

I see a lily on thy brow
  With anguish moist and fever dew,
And on thy cheeks a fading rose 10
  Fast withereth too.

"I met a Lady in the Meads,°   *meadows*
  Full beautiful, a faery's child,
Her hair was long, her foot was light
  And her eyes were wild. 15

"I made a Garland for her head,
  And bracelets too, and fragrant Zone;°   *girdle*
She looked at me as she did love
  And made sweet moan. 20

La Belle Dame sans Merci: "The beautiful lady without pity" (French). This text is an earlier, and generally preferred, version of a poem first published in 1820.

"I set her on my pacing steed
  And nothing else saw all day long,
For sidelong would she bend and sing
  A faery's song.

"She found me roots of relish sweet,
  And honey wild, and manna dew,
And sure in language strange she said
  'I love thee true.'

"She took me to her elfin grot°   *grotto, cave*
  And there she wept and sighed full sore,
And there I shut her wild wild eyes
  With kisses four.

"And there she lullèd me asleep,
  And there I dreamed, Ah Woe betide!
The latest° dream I ever dreamt   *last*
  On the cold hill side.

"I saw pale Kings, and Princes too,
  Pale warriors, death-pale were they all;
They cried, 'La belle dame sans merci
  Hath thee in thrall!'

"I saw their starved lips in the gloam°   *twilight*
  With horrid warning gapèd wide,
And I awoke, and found me here
  On the cold hill's side.

"And this is why I sojourn here,
  Alone and palely loitering;
Though the sedge is withered from the Lake
  And no birds sing."

                                     [*1819; 1888*]

JOHN KEATS [1795–1821]

To Autumn

Season of mists and mellow fruitfulness
  Close bosom-friend of the maturing sun;
Conspiring with him how to load and bless
  With fruit the vines that round the thatch-eves run;
To bend with apples the moss'd cottage-trees,   5
  And fill all fruit with ripeness to the core;
    To swell the gourd, and plump the hazel shells
  With a sweet kernel; to set budding more,
And still more, later flowers for the bees,
Until they think warm days will never cease,   10
  For Summer has o'er-brimm'd their clammy cells.

Who hath not seen thee oft amid thy store?
  Sometimes whoever seeks abroad may find
Thee sitting careless on a granary floor,
  Thy hair soft-lifted by the winnowing wind;   15
Or on a half-reap'd furrow sound asleep,
  Drowsed with the fume of poppies, while thy hook
    Spares the next swath and all its twinèd flowers:
And sometimes like a gleaner thou dost keep
  Steady thy laden head across a brook;   20
  Or by a cider-press, with patient look,
    Thou watchest the last oozings hours by hours.

Where are the songs of Spring? Ay, where are they?
  Think not of them, thou hast thy music too,—
While barrèd clouds bloom the soft-dying day,   25
  And touch the stubble-plains with rosy hue;
Then in a wailful choir the small gnats mourn
  Among the river sallows, borne aloft
    Or sinking as the light wind lives or dies;
And full-grown lambs loud bleat from hilly bourn;°   *stream* 30
  Hedge-crickets sing; and now with treble soft

The redbreast whistles from a garden-croft;
And gathering swallows twitter in the skies.

[1820]

ELIZABETH BARRETT BROWNING [1806–1861]

How do I love thee? Let me count the ways

How do I love thee? Let me count the ways.
I love thee to the depth and breadth and height
My soul can reach, when feeling out of sight
For the ends of Being and ideal Grace.
I love thee to the level of everyday's
Most quiet need, by sun and candlelight.
I love thee freely, as men strive for Right;
I love thee purely, as they turn from Praise.
I love thee with the passion put to use
In my old griefs, and with my childhood's faith.
I love thee with a love I seemed to lose
With my lost saints—I love thee with the breath,
Smiles, tears, of all my life!—and, if God choose,
I shall but love thee better after death.

[1850]

EDGAR ALLAN POE [1809–1849]

Annabel Lee

It was many and many a year ago,
    In a kingdom by the sea,
That a maiden there lived whom you may know

By the name of Annabel Lee;
And this maiden she lived with no other thought   5
   Than to love and be loved by me.

She was a child and *I* was a child,
   In this kingdom by the sea,
But we loved with a love that was more than love—
   I and my Annabel Lee—   10
With a love that the wingèd seraphs° of Heaven   *angels of the highest order*
   Coveted her and me.

And this was the reason that, long ago,
   In this kingdom by the sea,
A wind blew out of a cloud by night   15
   Chilling my Annabel Lee;
So that her highborn kinsmen came
   And bore her away from me,
To shut her up in a sepulchre
   In this kingdom by the sea.   20

The angels, not half so happy in Heaven,
   Went envying her and me:
Yes! that was the reason (as all men know,
   In this kingdom by the sea)
That the wind came out of the cloud, chilling   25
   And killing my Annabel Lee.

But our love it was stronger by far than the love
   Of those who were older than we—
   Of many far wiser than we—
And neither the angels in Heaven above   30
   Nor the demons down under the sea,
Can ever dissever my soul from the soul
   Of the beautiful Annabel Lee:

For the moon never beams without bringing me dreams
   Of the beautiful Annabel Lee;   35
And the stars never rise but I see the bright eyes
   Of the beautiful Annabel Lee;
And so, all the night-tide, I lie down by the side
Of my darling, my darling, my life and my bride,
   In her sepulchre there by the sea—   40
   In her tomb by the side of the sea.

[1849]

ALFRED, LORD TENNYSON   [1809–1892]

Ulysses°

It little profits that an idle king,
By this still hearth, among these barren crags,
Matched with an agèd wife, I mete and dole
Unequal laws unto a savage race,°
That hoard, and sleep, and feed, and know not me.

   I cannot rest from travel; I will drink
Life to the lees.° All times I have enjoyed
Greatly, have suffered greatly, both with those
That loved me, and alone; on shore, and when
Through scudding drifts° the rainy Hyades°
Vexed the dim sea. I am become a name;
For always roaming with a hungry heart
Much have I seen and known—cities of men
And manners, climates, councils, governments,
Myself not least, but honored of them all—
And drunk delight of battle with my peers,

Ulysses (the Roman form of Odysseus): The hero of Homer's epic *The Odyssey*,
which tells the story of Odysseus's adventures on his voyage back to Ithaca, the
small island of which he was king, after he and the other Greek heroes defeated
Troy. It took Odysseus ten years to reach Ithaca, where his wife (Penelope) and
son (Telemachus) were waiting for him. Upon his return, he defeated the suitors
who had been trying to marry the faithful Penelope, and he resumed the kingship and his old ways of life. Here Homer's story ends, but in Canto 26 of the
Inferno, Dante extended the story: Odysseus eventually became restless and
dissatisfied with his settled life and decided to return to the sea and sail west,
into the unknown sea, and seek whatever adventures he might find there. Tennyson's poem amplifies the speech delivered in Dante's poem as Ulysses challenges
his men to accompany him on this new voyage.
3–4. mete . . . race: Administer inadequate (unequal to what is needed) laws to a
still somewhat lawless race.
6–7. drink . . . lees: Lees refers to the dregs or sediment at the bottom of beer or
wine, so Ulysses is vowing to live his life to the fullest, to drink to the last drop.
10. scudding drifts: Wind-driven spray; **Hyades:** Five stars in the constellation
Taurus whose rising was assumed to be followed by rain.

Far on the ringing plains of windy Troy.
I am a part of all that I have met;
Yet all experience is an arch wherethrough
Gleams that untraveled world whose margin fades   20
Forever and forever when I move.
How dull it is to pause, to make an end,
To rust unburnished, not to shine in use!
As though to breathe were life! Life piled on life
Were all too little, and of one to me   25
Little remains; but every hour is saved
From that eternal silence, something more,
A bringer of new things; and vile it were
For some three suns° to store and hoard myself,   *years*
And this gray spirit yearning in desire   30
To follow knowledge like a sinking star,
Beyond the utmost bound of human thought.

　　This is my son, mine own Telemachus,
To whom I leave the scepter and the isle—
Well-loved of me, discerning to fulfill   35
This labor, by slow prudence to make mild
A rugged people, and through soft degrees
Subdue them to the useful and the good.
Most blameless is he, centered in the sphere
Of common duties, decent not to fail   40
In offices of tenderness, and pay
Meet° adoration to my household gods,   *proper*
When I am gone. He works his work, I mine.

　　There lies the port; the vessel puffs her sail;
There gloom the dark, broad seas. My mariners,   45
Souls that have toiled, and wrought, and thought with me—
That ever with a frolic welcome took
The thunder and the sunshine, and opposed
Free hearts, free foreheads—you and I are old;
Old age hath yet his honor and his toil.   50
Death closes all; but something ere the end,
Some work of noble note, may yet be done,
Not unbecoming men that strove with Gods.
The lights begin to twinkle from the rocks;
The long day wanes; the slow moon climbs; the deep   55
Moans round with many voices. Come, my friends,
'Tis not too late to seek a newer world.
Push off, and sitting well in order smite

The sounding furrows; for my purpose holds
To sail beyond the sunset, and the baths°
Of all the western stars, until I die.
It may be that the gulfs will wash us down;
It may be we shall touch the Happy Isles,°
And see the great Achilles,° whom we knew.
Though much is taken, much abides; and though
We are not now that strength which in old days
Moved earth and heaven, that which we are, we are—
One equal temper of heroic hearts,
Made weak by time and fate, but strong in will
To strive, to seek, to find, and not to yield.

[1833]

60. **baths:** The outer river or ocean surrounding the flat earth, in Greek cosmology, into which the stars descended upon setting.
63. **Happy Isles:** The Islands of the Blessed, or Elysian Fields, in Greek myth, which lay in the western seas beyond the Strait of Gibraltar and were the abode of heroes after death.
64. **Achilles:** The hero of the Greeks, and Odysseus's comrade, in Homer's *Iliad*.

ALFRED, LORD TENNYSON   [1809–1892]

The Lady of Shalott

PART I

On either side the river lie
Long fields of barley and of rye,
That clothe the wold° and meet the sky;   *plain*
And through the field the road runs by
        To many towered Camelot;°
And up and down the people go,
Gazing where the lilies blow°   *bloom*
Round an island there below,
        The island of Shalott.

Willows whiten, aspens quiver,
Little breezes dusk and shiver

5. **Camelot:** King Arthur's castle.

Through the wave that runs for ever
By the island in the river
    Flowing down to Camelot.
Four gray walls, and four gray towers,   15
Overlook a space of flowers,
And the silent isle imbowers
    The Lady of Shalott.

By the margin, willow-veiled,
Slide the heavy barges trailed   20
By slow horses; and unhailed
The shallop° flitteth silken-sailed   *small boat*
    Skimming down to Camelot:
But who hath seen her wave her hand?
Or at the casement seen her stand?   25
Or is she known in all the land,
    The Lady of Shalott?

Only reapers, reaping early
In among the bearded barley,
Hear a song that echoes cheerly   30
From the river winding clearly,
    Down to towered Camelot:
And by the moon the reaper weary,
Piling sheaves in uplands airy,
Listening, whispers " 'Tis the fairy   35
    Lady of Shalott."

PART II

There she weaves by night and day
A magic web with colors gay.
She has heard a whisper say,
A curse is on her if she stay°   *pause* 40
    To look down to Camelot.
She knows not what the curse may be,
And so she weaveth steadily,
And little other care hath she,
    The Lady of Shalott.   45

And moving through a mirror clear°
That hangs before her all the year,
Shadows of the world appear.

46. mirror clear: Weavers placed mirrors facing their looms to watch the progress of their work.

There she sees the highway near
    Winding down to Camelot:
There the river eddy whirls,
And there the surly village-churls,°   *peasants*
And the red cloaks of market girls,
    Pass onward from Shalott.

Sometimes a troop of damsels glad,
An abbot on an ambling pad,°   *easy-paced horse*
Sometimes a curly shepherd-lad,
Or long-haired page in crimson clad,
    Goes by to towered Camelot;
And sometimes through the mirror blue
The knights come riding two and two:
She hath no loyal knight and true,
    The Lady of Shalott.

But in her web she still delights
To weave the mirror's magic sights,
For often through the silent nights
A funeral, with plumes and lights
    And music, went to Camelot;
Or when the moon was overhead,
Came two young lovers lately wed;
"I am half sick of shadows," said
    The Lady of Shalott.

PART III

A bow-shot from her bower-eaves,
He rode between the barley-sheaves,
The sun came dazzling through the leaves,
And flamed upon the brazen greaves°
    Of bold Sir Lancelot.
A red-cross knight for ever kneeled
To a lady in his shield,
That sparkled on the yellow field,
    Beside remote Shalott.

The gemmy bridle glittered free,
Like to some branch of stars we see
Hung in the golden Galaxy.
The bridle bells rang merrily
    As he rode down to Camelot:

76. brazen greaves: Brass armor for the leg below the knee.

And from his blazoned° baldric° slung
A mighty silver bugle hung,
And as he rode his armor rung,
    Beside remote Shalott.   90

All in the blue unclouded weather
Thick-jewelled shone the saddle-leather,
The helmet and the helmet-feather
Burned like one burning flame together,
    As he rode down to Camelot.   95
As often through the purple night,
Below the starry clusters bright,
Some bearded meteor, trailing light,
    Moves over still Shalott.

His broad clear brow in sunlight glowed;   100
On burnished hooves his war-horse trode;
From underneath his helmet flowed
His coal-black curls as on he rode,
    As he rode down to Camelot.
From the bank and from the river   105
He flashed into the crystal mirror,
"Tirra lirra," by the river
    Sang Sir Lancelot.

She left the web, she left the loom,
She made three paces through the room,   110
She saw the water-lily bloom,
She saw the helmet and the plume,
    She looked down to Camelot.
Out flew the web and floated wide;
The mirror cracked from side to side;   115
"The curse is come upon me," cried
    The Lady of Shalott.

PART IV

In the stormy east-wind straining,
The pale yellow woods were waning,
The broad stream in his banks complaining.   120
Heavily the low sky raining
    Over towered Camelot;
Down she came and found a boat

---

87. blazoned: Painted with a heraldic device; **baldric:** Belt worn diagonally
from the shoulder to the opposite hip to support a sword or bugle.

Beneath a willow left afloat,
And round about the prow she wrote
    The Lady of Shalott.

And down the river's dim expanse
Like some bold seër in a trance,
Seeing all his own mischance—
With a glassy countenance
    Did she look to Camelot.
And at the closing of the day
She loosed the chain, and down she lay;
The broad stream bore her far away,
    The Lady of Shalott.

Lying, robed in snowy white
That loosely flew to left and right—
The leaves upon her falling light—
Through the noises of the night
    She floated down to Camelot:
And as the boat-head wound along
The willowy hills and fields among,
They heard her singing her last song,
    The Lady of Shalott.

Heard a carol, mournful, holy,
Chanted loudly, chanted lowly,
Till her blood was frozen slowly,
And her eyes were darkened wholly,
    Turned to towered Camelot.
For ere she reached upon the tide
The first house by the water-side,
Singing in her song she died,
    The Lady of Shalott.

Under tower and balcony,
By garden-wall and gallery,
A gleaming shape she floated by,
Dead-pale between the houses high,
    Silent into Camelot.
Out upon the wharfs they came,
Knight and burgher, lord and dame,
And round the prow they read her name,
    The Lady of Shalott.

Who is this? and what is here?
And in the lighted palace near

Died the sound of royal cheer;   165
And they crossed themselves for fear,
　　All the knights at Camelot:
But Lancelot mused a little space;
He said, "She has a lovely face;
God in his mercy lend her grace,   170
　　The Lady of Shalott."

[1832]

ROBERT BROWNING   [1812–1889]

My Last Duchess

Ferrara°

That's my last Duchess° painted on the wall,
Looking as if she were alive. I call
That piece a wonder, now: Frà Pandolf's° hands
Worked busily a day, and there she stands.
Will't please you sit and look at her? I said   5
"Frà Pandolf" by design, for never read
Strangers like you that pictured countenance,
The depth and passion of its earnest glance,
But to myself they turned (since none puts by
The curtain I have drawn for you, but I)   10
And seemed as they would ask me, if they durst,
How such a glance came there; so, not the first
Are you to turn and ask thus. Sir, 'twas not
Her husband's presence only, called that spot
Of joy into the Duchess' cheek: perhaps   15
Frà Pandolf chanced to say "Her mantle laps
Over my lady's wrist too much," or "Paint

Ferrara: The poem is based on events that occurred in the life of Alfonso II,
duke of Ferrara in Italy, in the sixteenth century.
1. last Duchess: Ferrara's first wife, Lucrezia, died in 1561 at age seventeen after
three years of marriage.
3. Frà Pandolf: Brother Pandolf, a fictional painter.

Must never hope to reproduce the faint
Half-flush that dies along her throat": such stuff
Was courtesy, she thought, and cause enough
For calling up that spot of joy. She had
A heart—how shall I say?—too soon made glad,
Too easily impressed; she liked whate'er
She looked on, and her looks went everywhere.
Sir, 'twas all one! My favor at her breast,
The dropping of the daylight in the West,
The bough of cherries some officious fool
Broke in the orchard for her, the white mule
She rode with round the terrace—all and each
Would draw from her alike the approving speech,
Or blush, at least. She thanked men,—good! but thanked
Somehow—I know not how—as if she ranked
My gift of a nine-hundred-years-old name
With anybody's gift. Who'd stoop to blame
This sort of trifling? Even had you skill
In speech—(which I have not)—to make your will
Quite clear to such an one, and say, "Just this
Or that in you disgusts me; here you miss,
Or there exceed the mark"—and if she let
Herself be lessoned so, nor plainly set
Her wits to yours, forsooth, and made excuse,
—E'en then would be some stooping; and I choose
Never to stoop. Oh sir, she smiled, no doubt,
Whene'er I passed her; but who passed without
Much the same smile? This grew; I gave commands;
Then all smiles stopped together. There she stands
As if alive. Will't please you rise? We'll meet
The company below, then. I repeat,
The Count your master's known munificence
Is ample warrant that no just pretense
Of mine for dowry will be disallowed;
Though his fair daughter's self, as I avowed
At starting, is my object. Nay, we'll go
Together down, sir. Notice Neptune, though,
Taming a sea-horse, thought a rarity,
Which Claus of Innsbruck° cast in bronze for me!

[1842]

56. **Claus of Innsbruck:** A fictional sculptor.

WALT WHITMAN   [1819–1892]

From Song of Myself°

1

I celebrate myself, and sing myself,
And what I assume you shall assume,
For every atom belonging to me as good belongs to you.

I loafe and invite my soul,
I lean and loafe at my ease observing a spear of summer grass.   5

My tongue, every atom of my blood, form'd from this soil, this air,
Born here of parents born here from parents the same, and their
    parents the same,
I, now thirty-seven years old in perfect health begin,
Hoping to cease not till death.

Creeds and schools in abeyance,   10
Retiring back a while sufficed at what they are, but never forgotten,
I harbor for good or bad, I permit to speak at every hazard,
Nature without check with original energy.

2

Houses and rooms are full of perfumes, the shelves are crowded with
    perfumes,
I breathe the fragrance myself and know it and like it,   15

Song of Myself: The poem was first published in 1855 as an untitled section of
Leaves of Grass. It was a rough, rude, and vigorous example of antebellum American cultural politics and free verse experimentation. The version used here,
from the sixth edition (1891–1892), is much longer, more carefully crafted, and
more conventionally punctuated. Sections 1–3 introduce the persona and the
scope and method of the poem; section 6 explains grass as a symbol; sections
7–10, examples of Whitman's dynamic panoramic miniatures, are also of historical significance regarding Native and African Americans; section 14 extends the
outward sweep of 7–10; section 21 develops Whitman's theme of sex and nature;
section 24 extends the handling of the poem's persona; sections 46 and 48 reca-
pitulate the major themes of the poem; sections 51 and 52 deal with the absorp-
tion of the poet's persona into the converted reader.

The distillation would intoxicate me also, but I shall not let it.
The atmosphere is not a perfume, it has no taste of the distillation,
    it is odorless,
It is for my mouth forever, I am in love with it,
I will go to the bank by the wood and become undisguised and naked,
I am mad for it to be in contact with me.

The smoke of my own breath,
Echoes, ripples, buzz'd whispers, love-root, silk-thread, crotch and
    vine,
My respiration and inspiration, the beating of my heart, the passing of
    blood and air through my lungs,
The sniff of green leaves and dry leaves, and of the shore and
    dark-color'd sea-rocks, and of hay in the barn,
The sound of the belch'd words of my voice loos'd to the eddies of the
    wind,
A few light kisses, a few embraces, a reaching around of arms,
The play of shine and shade on the trees as the supple boughs wag,
The delight alone or in the rush of the streets, or along the fields and
    hill-sides,
The feeling of health, the full-noon trill, the song of me rising from bed
    and meeting the sun.

Have you reckon'd a thousand acres much? have you reckon'd the earth
    much?
Have you practis'd so long to learn to read?
Have you felt so proud to get at the meaning of poems?

Stop this day and night with me and you shall possess the origin of all
    poems,
You shall possess the good of the earth and sun, (there are millions of
    suns left,)
You shall no longer take things at second or third hand, nor look
    through the eyes of the dead, nor feed on the spectres in books,
You shall not look through my eyes either, nor take things from me,
You shall listen to all sides and filter them from your self.

3

I have heard what the talkers were talking, the talk of the beginning
    and the end,
But I do not talk of the beginning or the end.

There was never any more inception than there is now,
Nor any more youth or age than there is now,

And will never be any more perfection than there is now,
Nor any more heaven or hell than there is now.
Urge and urge and urge,
Always the procreant urge of the world.   45

Out of the dimness opposite equals advance, always substance and
     increase, always sex,
Always a knit of identity, always distinction, always a breed of life.

To elaborate is no avail, learn'd and unlearn'd feel that it is so.

Sure as the most certain sure, plumb in the uprights, well entretied,°
     braced in the beams,
Stout as a horse, affectionate, haughty, electrical,   50
I and this mystery here we stand.

Clear and sweet is my soul, and clear and sweet is all that is not my
     soul.

Lack one lacks both, and the unseen is proved by the seen,
Till that becomes unseen and receives proof in its turn.

Showing the best and dividing it from the worst age vexes age,   55
Knowing the perfect fitness and equanimity of things, while they
     discuss I am silent, and go bathe and admire myself.

Welcome is every organ and attribute of me, and of any man hearty
     and clean,
Not an inch nor a particle of an inch is vile, and none shall be less
     familiar than the rest.

I am satisfied—I see, dance, laugh, sing;
As the hugging and loving bed-fellow sleeps at my side through the
     night, and withdraws at the peep of the day with stealthy tread,   60
Leaving me baskets cover'd with white towels swelling the house with
     their plenty,
Shall I postpone my acceptation and realization and scream at
     my eyes,
That they turn from gazing after and down the road,
And forthwith cipher and show me to a cent,
Exactly the value of one and exactly the value of two, and which is
     ahead?   65

·   ·   ·

---

49. entretied: Cross-braced, as between two joists in carpentry.

6

A child said *What is the grass?* fetching it to me with full hands;
How could I answer the child? I do not know what it is any more
than he.

I guess it must be the flag of my disposition, out of hopeful green stuff
woven.

Or I guess it is the handkerchief of the Lord,
A scented gift and remembrancer designedly dropt,
Bearing the owner's name someway in the corners, that we may see and
remark, and say *Whose?*

Or I guess the grass is itself a child, the produced babe of the vegetation.

Or I guess it is a uniform hieroglyphic,
And it means, Sprouting alike in broad zones and narrow zones,
Growing among black folks as among white,
Kanuck,° Tuckahoe,° Congressman, Cuff,° I give them the same, I receive
them the same.

And now it seems to me the beautiful uncut hair of graves.

Tenderly will I use you curling grass,
It may be you transpire from the breasts of young men,
It may be if I had known them I would have loved them,
It may be you are from old people, or from offspring taken soon out of
their mothers' laps,
And here you are the mothers' laps.

This grass is very dark to be from the white heads of old mothers,
Darker than the colorless beards of old men,
Dark to come from under the faint red roofs of mouths.

O I perceive after all so many uttering tongues,
And I perceive they do not come from the roofs of mouths for nothing.

I wish I could translate the hints about the dead young men and women,
And the hints about old men and mothers, and the offspring taken soon
out of their laps.
What do you think has become of the young and old men?
And what do you think has become of the women and children?
They are alive and well somewhere,
The smallest sprout shows there is really no death,

---

109. Kanuck: A French Canadian; **Tuckahoe:** A Virginian living in the tide-
water region and eating tuckahoe, a fungus; **Cuff:** A black person.

And if ever there was it led forward life, and does not wait at the end to
    arrest it,
And ceas'd the moment life appear'd.

All goes onward and outward, nothing collapses,
And to die is different from what any one supposed, and luckier.   130

7

Has any one supposed it lucky to be born?
I hasten to inform him or her it is just as lucky to die, and I know it.

I pass death with the dying and birth with the new-wash'd babe, and am
    not contain'd between my hat and boots,
And peruse manifold objects, no two alike and every one good,
The earth good and the stars good, and their adjuncts all good.   135

I am not an earth nor an adjunct of an earth,
I am the mate and companion of people, all just as immortal and
    fathomless as myself,
(They do not know how immortal, but I know.)

Every kind for itself and its own, for me mine male and female,
For me those that have been boys and that love women,   140
For me the man that is proud and feels how it stings to be slighted,
For me the sweet-heart and the old maid, for me mothers and the
    mothers of mothers,
For me lips that have smiled, eyes that have shed tears,
For me children and the begetters of children.

Undrape! you are not guilty to me, nor stale nor discarded,   145
I see through the broadcloth and gingham whether or no,
And am around, tenacious, acquisitive, tireless, and cannot be shaken
    away.

8

The little one sleeps in its cradle,
I lift the gauze and look a long time, and silently brush away flies with
    my hand.

The youngster and the red-faced girl turn aside up the bushy hill,   150
I peeringly view them from the top.
The suicide sprawls on the bloody floor of the bedroom,
I witness the corpse with its dabbled hair, I note where the pistol has
    fallen.

The blab of the pave, tires of carts, sluff of boot-soles, talk of the
    promenaders,
The heavy omnibus, the driver with his interrogating thumb, the clank
    of the shod horses on the granite floor,
The snow-sleighs, clinking, shouted jokes, pelts of snow-balls,
The hurrahs for popular favorites, the fury of rous'd mobs,
The flap of the curtain'd litter, a sick man inside borne to the hospital,
The meeting of enemies, the sudden oath, the blows and fall,
The excited crowd, the policeman with his star quickly working his
    passage to the centre of the crowd,
The impassive stones that receive and return so many echoes,
What groans of over-fed or half-starv'd who fall sunstruck or in fits,
What exclamations of women taken suddenly who hurry home and give
    birth to babes,
What living and buried speech is always vibrating here, what howls
    restrain'd by decorum,
Arrests of criminals, slights, adulterous offers made, acceptances,
    rejections with convex lips,
I mind them or the show or resonance of them—I come and I depart.

9

The big doors of the country barn stand open and ready,
The dried grass of the harvest-time loads the slow-drawn wagon,
The clear light plays on the brown gray and green intertinged,
The armfuls are pack'd to the sagging mow.

I am there, I help, I came stretch'd atop of the load,
I felt its soft jolts, one leg reclined on the other,
I jump from the cross-beams and seize the clover and timothy,
And roll head over heels and tangle my hair full of wisps.

10

Alone far in the wilds and mountains I hunt,
Wandering amazed at my own lightness and glee,
In the late afternoon choosing a safe spot to pass the night,
Kindling a fire and broiling the fresh-kill'd game,
Falling asleep on the gather'd leaves with my dog and gun by my side.

The Yankee clipper is under her sky-sails, she cuts the sparkle and
    scud,
My eyes settle the land, I bend at her prow or shout joyously from
    the deck.

The boatmen and clam-diggers arose early and stopt for me,
I tuck'd my trowser-ends in my boots and went and had a good time;
You should have been with us that day round the chowder-kettle.

I saw the marriage of the trapper in the open air in the far west, the
    bride was a red girl,   185
Her father and his friends sat near cross-legged and dumbly smoking,
    they had moccasins to their feet and large thick blankets hanging
    from their shoulders,
On a bank lounged the trapper, he was drest mostly in skins, his
    luxuriant beard and curls protected his neck, he held his bride by
    the hand,
She had long eyelashes, her head was bare, her coarse straight locks
    descended upon her voluptuous limbs and reach'd to her feet.

The runaway slave came to my house and stopt outside,
I heard his motions crackling the twigs of the woodpile,   190
Through the swung half-door of the kitchen I saw him limpsy and
    weak,
And went where he sat on a log and led him in and assured him,
And brought water and fill'd a tub for his sweated body and bruis'd feet,
And gave him a room that enter'd from my own, and gave him some
    coarse clean clothes,
And remember perfectly well his revolving eyes and his awkwardness,   195
And remember putting plasters on the galls of his neck and ankles;
He staid with me a week before he was recuperated and pass'd north,
I had him sit next me at table, my fire-lock lean'd in the corner.

14

The wild gander leads his flock through the cool night,   245
Ya-honk he says, and sounds it down to me like an invitation,
The pert may suppose it meaningless, but I listening close,
Find its purpose and place up there toward the wintry sky.

The sharp-hoof'd moose of the north, the cat on the house-sill, the
    chickadee, the prairie-dog,
The litter of the grunting sow as they tug at her teats,   250
The brood of the turkey-hen and she with her half-spread wings,
I see in them and myself the same old law.

The press of my foot to the earth springs a hundred affections,
They scorn the best I can do to relate them.
I am enamour'd of growing out-doors,   255
Of men that live among cattle or taste of the ocean or woods,

Of the builders and steerers of ships and the wielders of axes and mauls,
and the drivers of horses,
I can eat and sleep with them week in and week out.

What is commonest, cheapest, nearest, easiest, is Me,
Me going in for my chances, spending for vast returns,
Adorning myself to bestow myself on the first that will take me,
Not asking the sky to come down to my good will,
Scattering it freely forever.

21

I am the poet of the Body and I am the poet of the Soul,
The pleasures of heaven are with me and the pains of hell are with me,
The first I graft and increase upon myself, the latter I translate into a
new tongue.

I am the poet of the woman the same as the man,
And I say it is as great to be a woman as to be a man,
And I say there is nothing greater than the mother of men.

I chant the chant of dilation or pride,
We have had ducking and deprecating about enough,
I show that size is only development.

Have you outstript the rest? are you the President?
It is a trifle, they will more than arrive there every one, and still
pass on.

I am he that walks with the tender and growing night,
I call to the earth and sea half-held by the night.

Press close bare-bosom'd night—press close magnetic nourishing night!
Night of south winds—night of the large few stars!
Still nodding night—mad naked summer night.

Smile O voluptuous cool-breath'd earth!
Earth of the slumbering and liquid trees!
Earth of departed sunset—earth of the mountains misty-topt!
Earth of the vitreous pour of the full moon just tinged with blue!
Earth of shine and dark mottling the tide of the river!
Earth of the limpid gray of clouds brighter and clearer for my sake!
Far-swooping elbow'd earth—rich apple-blossom'd earth!
Smile, for your lover comes.
Prodigal, you have given me love—therefore I to you give love!
O unspeakable passionate love.

24

Walt Whitman, a kosmos, of Manhattan the son,
Turbulent, fleshy, sensual, eating, drinking and breeding,
No sentimentalist, no stander above men and women or apart from them,
No more modest than immodest.   500

Unscrew the locks from the doors!
Unscrew the doors themselves from their jambs!

Whoever degrades another degrades me,
And whatever is done or said returns at last to me.

Through me the afflatus° surging and surging, through me the current
    and index.   505

I speak the pass-word primeval, I give the sign of democracy,
By God! I will accept nothing which all cannot have their counterpart
    of on the same terms.

Through me many long dumb voices,
Voices of the interminable generations of prisoners and slaves,
Voices of the diseas'd and despairing and of thieves and dwarfs,   510
Voices of cycles of preparation and accretion,
And of the threads that connect the stars, and of wombs and of the
    father-stuff,
And of the rights of them the others are down upon,
Of the deform'd, trivial, flat, foolish, despised,
Fog in the air, beetles rolling balls of dung.   515

Through me forbidden voices,
Voices of sexes and lusts, voices veil'd and I remove the veil,
Voices indecent by me clarified and transfigur'd.

I do not press my fingers across my mouth,
I keep as delicate around the bowels as around the head and heart,   520
Copulation is no more rank to me than death is.

I believe in the flesh and the appetites,
Seeing, hearing, feeling, are miracles, and each part and tag of me is a
    miracle.
Divine am I inside and out, and I make holy whatever I touch or am
    touch'd from,
The scent of these arm-pits aroma finer than prayer,   525
This head more than churches, bibles, and all the creeds.

---

505. afflatus: Inspiration (from the Latin for "to blow on").

If I worship one thing more than another it shall be the spread of my
    own body, or any part of it,
Translucent mould of me it shall be you!
Shaded ledges and rests it shall be you!
Firm masculine colter° it shall be you!   5
Whatever goes to the tilth° of me it shall be you!
You my rich blood! your milky stream pale strippings of my life!
Breast that presses against other breasts it shall be you!
My brain it shall be your occult convolutions!
Root of wash'd sweet-flag! timorous pond-snipe! nest of guarded
    duplicate eggs! it shall be you!   5
Mix'd tussled hay of head, beard, brawn, it shall be you!
Trickling sap of maple, fibre of manly wheat, it shall be you!
Sun so generous it shall be you!
Vapors lighting and shading my face it shall be you!
You sweaty brooks and dews it shall be you!   5
Winds whose soft-tickling genitals rub against me it shall be you!
Broad muscular fields, branches of live oak, loving lounger in my
    winding paths, it shall be you!
Hands I have taken, face I have kiss'd, mortal I have ever touch'd, it
    shall be you.

46

I know I have the best of time and space, and was never measured and
    never will be measured.

I tramp a perpetual journey, (come listen all!)
My signs are a rain-proof coat, good shoes, and a staff cut from the woods,
No friend of mine takes his ease in my chair,
I have no chair, no church, no philosophy,   120
I lead no man to a dinner-table, library, exchange,
But each man and each woman of you I lead upon a knoll,
My left hand hooking you round the waist,
My right hand pointing to landscapes of continents and the public road.
Not I, not any one else can travel that road for you,   121
You must travel it for yourself.

It is not far, it is within reach,
Perhaps you have been on it since you were born and did not know,
Perhaps it is everywhere on water and on land.

---

530. colter: Blade or disk on a plow for cutting the earth.
531. tilth: Cultivation of land.

Shoulder your duds dear son, and I will mine, and let us hasten forth,   1215
Wonderful cities and free nations we shall fetch as we go.

If you tire, give me both burdens, and rest the chuff° of your hand
    on my hip,
And in due time you shall repay the same service to me,
For after we start we never lie by again.

This day before dawn I ascended a hill and look'd at the crowded
    heaven,   1220
And I said to my spirit *When we become the enfolders of those orbs, and*
    the pleasure and knowledge of every thing in them, shall we be fill'd and
    satisfied then?
And my spirit said *No, we but level that lift to pass and continue beyond.*

You are also asking me questions and I hear you,
I answer that I cannot answer, you must find out for yourself.

Sit a while dear son,   1225
Here are biscuits to eat and here is milk to drink,
But as soon as you sleep and renew yourself in sweet clothes, I kiss you
    with a good-by kiss and open the gate for your egress hence.

Long enough have you dream'd contemptible dreams,
Now I wash the gum from your eyes,
You must habit yourself to the dazzle of the light and of every moment
    of your life.   1230

Long have you timidly waded holding a plank by the shore,
Now I will you to be a bold swimmer,
To jump off in the midst of the sea, rise again, nod to me, shout, and
    laughingly dash with your hair.

48

I have said that the soul is not more than the body,
And I have said that the body is not more than the soul,   1270
And nothing, not God, is greater to one than one's self is,
And whoever walks a furlong without sympathy walks to his own
    funeral drest in his shroud,
And I or you pocketless of a dime may purchase the pick of the earth,
And to glance with an eye or show a bean in its pod confounds the
    learning of all times,
And there is no trade or employment but the young man following it
    may become a hero,   1275

1217. chuff: Weight.

And there is no object so soft but it makes a hub for the wheel'd
   universe,
And I say to any man or woman, Let your soul stand cool and composed
   before a million universes.

And I say to mankind, Be not curious about God,
For I who am curious about each am not curious about God,
(No array of terms can say how much I am at peace about God and
   about death.)

I hear and behold God in every object, yet understand God not in the
   least,
Nor do I understand who there can be more wonderful than myself.

Why should I wish to see God better than this day?
I see something of God each hour of the twenty-four, and each
   moment then,
In the faces of men and women I see God, and in my own face in the
   glass,
I find letters from God dropt in the street, and every one is sign'd by
   God's name,
And I leave them where they are, for I know that wheresoe'er I go,
Others will punctually come for ever and ever.

51

The past and present wilt—I have fill'd them, emptied them,
And proceed to fill my next fold of the future.

Listener up there! what have you to confide to me?
Look in my face while I snuff° the sidle° of evening,
(Talk honestly, no one else hears you, and I stay only a minute longer.)

Do I contradict myself?
Very well then I contradict myself,
(I am large, I contain multitudes.)
I concentrate toward them that are nigh, I wait on the door-slab.

Who has done his day's work? who will soonest be through with his
   supper?
Who wishes to walk with me?

Will you speak before I am gone? will you prove already too late?

1322. snuff: Snuff out; **sidle:** Sidewise or stealthy movement.

52

The spotted hawk swoops by and accuses me, he complains of my gab
   and my loitering.

I too am not a bit tamed, I too am untranslatable,
I sound my barbaric yawp over the roofs of the world.

The last scud of day holds back for me,
It flings my likeness after the rest and true as any on the shadow'd
   wilds,   1335
It coaxes me to the vapor and the dusk.

I depart as air, I shake my white locks at the runaway sun,
I effuse my flesh in eddies, and drift it in lacy jags.

I bequeath myself to the dirt to grow from the grass I love,
If you want me again look for me under your boot-soles.   1340

You will hardly know who I am or what I mean,
But I shall be good health to you nevertheless,
And filter and fibre your blood.

Failing to fetch me at first keep encouraged,
Missing me one place search another,   1345
I stop somewhere waiting for you.

                                           [*1855;* 1891–1892]

WALT WHITMAN   [1819–1892]

A Noiseless Patient Spider

A noiseless patient spider,
I mark'd where on a little promontory it stood isolated,
Mark'd how to explore the vacant vast surrounding,
It launch'd forth filament, filament, filament, out of itself,
Ever unreeling them, ever tirelessly speeding them.   5

And you O my soul where you stand,
Surrounded, detached, in measureless oceans of space,
Ceaselessly musing, venturing, throwing, seeking the spheres to connect
   them,

Till the bridge you will need be form'd, till the ductile anchor hold,
Till the gossamer thread you fling catch somewhere, O my soul.

[1868–1881]

MATTHEW ARNOLD   [1822–1888]

Dover Beach

The sea is calm tonight.
The tide is full, the moon lies fair
Upon the straits; on the French coast the light
Gleams and is gone; the cliffs of England stand,
Glimmering and vast, out in the tranquil bay.
Come to the window, sweet is the night-air!
Only, from the long line of spray
Where the sea meets the moon-blanched land,
Listen! you hear the grating roar
Of pebbles which the waves draw back, and fling,
At their return, up the high strand,
Begin, and cease, and then again begin,
With tremulous cadence slow, and bring
The eternal note of sadness in.

Sophocles long ago   1
Heard it on the Aegean, and it brought
Into his mind the turbid ebb and flow
Of human misery; we
Find also in the sound a thought,
Hearing it by this distant northern sea.   2

The Sea of Faith
Was once, too, at the full, and round earth's shore
Lay like the folds of a bright girdle furled.
But now I only hear
Its melancholy, long, withdrawing roar,   2
Retreating, to the breath
Of the night-wind, down the vast edges drear
And naked shingles° of the world.   *pebble-covered beaches*

Ah, love, let us be true
To one another! for the world, which seems   30
To lie before us like a land of dreams,
So various, so beautiful, so new,
Hath really neither joy, nor love, nor light,
Nor certitude, nor peace, nor help for pain;
And we are here as on a darkling plain   35
Swept with confused alarms of struggle and flight,
Where ignorant armies clash by night.

[*c. 1851;* 1867]

EMILY DICKINSON   [1830–1886]

Wild Nights — Wild Nights!

Wild Nights — Wild Nights!
Were I with thee
Wild Nights should be
Our luxury!

Futile — the Winds —   5
To a Heart in port —
Done with the Compass —
Done with the Chart!

Rowing in Eden —
Ah, the Sea!   10
Might I but moor — Tonight —
In Thee!

[*c. 1861;* 1891]

EMILY DICKINSON   [1830–1886]

It sifts from Leaden Sieves

It sifts from Leaden Sieves—
It powders all the Wood.
It fills with Alabaster Wool
The Wrinkles of the Road—

It makes an Even Face
Of Mountain, and of Plain—
Unbroken Forehead from the East
Unto the East again—

It reaches to the Fence—
It wraps it Rail by Rail
Till it is lost in Fleeces—
It deals Celestial Vail

To Stump, and Stack— and Stem—
A Summer's empty Room—
Acres of Joints, where Harvests were,
Recordless, but for them—

It Ruffles Wrists of Posts
As Ankles of a Queen—
Then stills its Artisans— like Ghosts—
Denying they have been—

[c. 1867; 1891]

EMILY DICKINSON   [1830–1886]

I like to see it lap the Miles

I like to see it lap the Miles—
And lick the Valleys up—
And stop to feed itself at Tanks—
And then—prodigious step

Around a Pile of Mountains—   5
And supercilious peer
In Shanties—by the sides of Roads—
And then a Quarry pare

To fit its Ribs
And crawl between   10
Complaining all the while
In horrid—hooting stanza—
Then chase itself down Hill—

And neigh like Boanerges°—
Then—punctual as a Star   15
Stop—docile and omnipotent
At its own stable door—

[*c. 1862;* 1891]

14. like Boanerges: As loud as thunder. *Boanerges* is the surname given by Jesus
to James and John in Mark 3:17, translated there as "the sons of thunder."

EMILY DICKINSON   [1830–1886]

Much Madness is divinest Sense

Much Madness is divinest Sense—
To a discerning Eye—
Much Sense—the starkest Madness—
'Tis the Majority
In this, as All, prevail—
Assent—and you are sane—
Demur—you're straightway dangerous—
And handled with a Chain—

[*c. 1862;* 1890]

EMILY DICKINSON   [1830–1886]

I heard a Fly buzz— when I died

I heard a Fly buzz—when I died—
The Stillness in the Room
Was like the Stillness in the Air—
Between the Heaves of Storm—

The Eyes around—had wrung them dry—
And Breaths were gathering firm
For that last Onset—when the King
Be witnessed—in the Room—

I willed my Keepsakes—Signed away
What portion of me be   10
Assignable—and then it was
There interposed a Fly—

With Blue—uncertain stumbling Buzz—
Between the light—and me—
And then the Windows failed—and then   15
I could not see to see—

[*c. 1862;* 1890]

EMILY DICKINSON   [1830–1886]

Because I could not stop for Death

Because I could not stop for Death—
He kindly stopped for me—
The Carriage held but just Ourselves—
And Immortality.

We slowly drove—He knew no haste   5
And I had put away
My labor and my leisure too,
For His Civility—

We passed the School, where Children strove
At Recess—in the Ring—   10
We passed the Fields of Gazing Grain—
We passed the Setting Sun—

Or rather—He passed Us—
The Dews drew quivering and chill—
For only Gossamer, my Gown—   15
My Tippet°—only Tulle°—   *scarf/silk net*

We paused before a House that seemed
A Swelling of the Ground—
The Roof was scarcely visible—
The Cornice—in the Ground—   20

Since then—'tis Centuries—and yet
Feels shorter than the Day
I first surmised the Horses' Heads
Were toward Eternity—

[c. 1863; 1890]

THOMAS HARDY   [1840–1928]

The Convergence of the Twain

Lines on the Loss of the Titanic°

1

    In a solitude of the sea
    Deep from human vanity,
And the Pride of Life that planned her, stilly couches she.

2

    Steel chambers, late the pyres
    Of her salamandrine° fires,
Cold currents thrid,° and turn to rhythmic tidal lyres.   *thread*

3

    Over the mirrors meant
    To glass the opulent
The sea-worm crawls—grotesque, slimed, dumb, indifferent.

Titanic: A famous luxury ocean liner, largest of its time and considered unsink-
able. It collided with an iceberg on its maiden voyage and sank on 15 April 1912.
Of some 2,200 people aboard, more than 1,500 were lost.
5. salamandrine: Fierce, inextinguishable (the lizardlike salamander supposedly
is able to resist or live in fire).

4

Jewels in joy designed   10
To ravish the sensuous mind
Lie lightless, all their sparkles bleared and black and blind.

5

Dim moon-eyed fishes near
Gaze at the gilded gear
And query: "What does this vaingloriousness down here?"   15

6

Well: while was fashioning
This creature of cleaving wing,
The Immanent Will that stirs and urges everything

7

Prepared a sinister mate
For her—so gaily great—   20
A Shape of Ice, for the time far and dissociate.

8

And as the smart ship grew
In stature, grace, and hue,
In shadowy silent distance grew the Iceberg too.

9

Alien they seemed to be: 25
No mortal eye could see
The intimate welding of their later history,

10

Or sign that they were bent
By paths coincident
On being anon twin halves of one august event,   30

11

Till the Spinner of the Years
Said "Now!" And each one hears,
And consummation comes, and jars two hemispheres.

[1912]

GERARD MANLEY HOPKINS [1844–1889]

God's Grandeur

The world is charged wíth the grándeur of God.
  It will flame out, like shining from shook foil;°   *shaken gold foil*
  It gathers to a greatness, like the ooze of oil°   *(from olives)*
Crushed. Why do men then now not reck° his rod°?   *recognize/discipline*
Génerátions have trod, have trod, have trod;
  And all is seared with trade; bleared, smeared, with toil;
  And wears man's smudge and shares man's smell: the soil
Is bare now, nor can foot feel, being shod.

Ánd, for° all this, náture is never spent;   *despite*
  There lives the dearest freshness deep down things;
And though the last lights off the black West went
  Oh, morning, at the brown brink eastward, springs—
Because the Holy Ghost óver the bent
  World broods with warm breast and with ah! bright wings.

[*1877;* 1918]

GERARD MANLEY HOPKINS [1844–1889]

Pied° Beauty   *multicolored, variegated*

Glóry be to God for dappled things—
  For skies of couple-colour as a brinded° cow;   *streaked*
    For rose-moles all in stipple upon trout that swim;
Fresh-firecoal chestnut-fálls; fínches' wings;
  Lándscape plotted and pieced—fold, fallow, and plough;
    And áll trádes, their gear and tackle and trim.

All things counter, original, spáre, stránge;
  Whatever is fickle, freckled (who knows how?)

With swift, slow; sweet, sour; adazzle, dim;
He fathers-forth whose beauty is pást chánge: 10
   Práise hím.

[*1877;* 1918]

GERARD MANLEY HOPKINS   [1844–1889]

Spring and Fall

to a young child

Márgarét, áre you gríeving
Over Goldengrove unleaving?
Leáves, líke the things of mán, you
With your fresh thoughts care for, can you?
Áh! ás the héart grows ólder   5
It will come to such sights colder
By and by, nor spare a sigh
Though worlds of wanwood leafmeal° lie;
And yet you *will* weep and know why.
Now no matter, child, the name: 10
Sórrow's spríngs áre the sáme.
Nor mouth had, no nor mind, expressed
What héart héard of, ghóst° guéssed: *spirit*
It ís the blíght man was bórn for,
It is Margaret you mourn for.   15

[*1880;* 1918]

8. **wanwood leafmeal:** Colorless forest with scattered leaves.

A. E. HOUSMAN [1859–1936]

Loveliest of trees,
the cherry now

Loveliest of trees, the cherry now
Is hung with bloom along the bough,
And stands about the woodland ride
Wearing white for Eastertide.

Now, of my threescore years and ten,
Twenty will not come again,
And take from seventy springs a score,
It only leaves me fifty more.

And since to look at things in bloom
Fifty springs are little room,
About the woodlands I will go
To see the cherry hung with snow.

[1896]

A. E. HOUSMAN [1859–1936]

To an Athlete Dying Young

The time you won your town the race
We chaired you through the market-place;
Man and boy stood cheering by,
And home we brought you shoulder-high.

To-day, the road all runners come,
Shoulder-high we bring you home,
And set you at your threshold down,
Townsman of a stiller town.

Smart lad, to slip betimes away
From fields where glory does not stay
And early though the laurel grows   10
It withers quicker than the rose.

Eyes the shady night has shut
Cannot see the record cut,°   *broken*
And silence sounds no worse than cheers   15
After earth has stopped the ears:

Now you will not swell the rout
Of lads that wore their honours out,
Runners whom renown outran
And the name died before the man.   20

So set, before its echoes fade,
The fleet foot on the sill of shade,
And hold to the low lintel up
The still-defended challenge-cup.

And round that early-laurelled head   25
Will flock to gaze the strengthless dead,
And find unwithered on its curls
The garland briefer than a girl's.

[1896]

WILLIAM BUTLER YEATS   [1865–1939]

The Lake Isle of Innisfree

I will arise and go now, and go to Innisfree,
And a small cabin build there, of clay and wattles made:
Nine bean-rows will I have there, a hive for the honey-bee,
And live alone in the bee-loud glade.

And I shall have some peace there, for peace comes dropping slow,   5
Dropping from the veils of the morning to where the cricket sings;
There midnight's all a glimmer, and noon a purple glow,
And evening full of the linnet's wings.

I will arise and go now, for always night and day
I hear lake water lapping with low sounds by the shore;
While I stand on the roadway, or on the pavements grey,
I hear it in the deep heart's core.

[1892]

WILLIAM BUTLER YEATS   [1865–1939]

The Second Coming°

Turning and turning in the widening gyre
The falcon cannot hear the falconer;
Things fall apart; the centre cannot hold;
Mere anarchy is loosed upon the world,
The blood-dimmed tide is loosed, and everywhere
The ceremony of innocence is drowned;
The best lack all conviction, while the worst
Are full of passionate intensity.

Surely some revelation is at hand;
Surely the Second Coming is at hand.
The Second Coming! Hardly are those words out
When a vast image out of *Spiritus Mundi*°
Troubles my sight: somewhere in sands of the desert
A shape with lion body and the head of a man,
A gaze blank and pitiless as the sun,
Is moving its slow thighs, while all about it

The Second Coming: Alludes to Matthew 24:3–44, on the return of Christ at
the end of the present age. Yeats viewed history as a series of 2,000-year cycles
(imaged as gyres, cone-shaped motions). The birth of Christ in Bethlehem
brought to an end the cycle that ran from the Babylonians through the Greeks
and Romans. The approach of the year 2000, then, anticipated for Yeats the end
of another era (the Christian age). Yeats wrote this poem shortly after the Russian Revolution of 1917 (lines 4–8), which may have confirmed his sense of
imminent change and of a new beginning of an unpredictable nature (Yeats
expected the new era to be violent and despotic).
12. *Spiritus Mundi:* Latin, "the spirit of the universe." Yeats believed in a Great
Memory, a universal storehouse of symbolic images from the past. Individuals,
drawing on it for images, are put in touch with the soul of the universe.

Reel shadows of the indignant desert birds.
The darkness drops again; but now I know
That twenty centuries of stony sleep
Were vexed to nightmare by a rocking cradle,   20
And what rough beast, its hour come round at last,
Slouches towards Bethlehem to be born?

[1921]

WILLIAM BUTLER YEATS   [1865–1939]

Leda and the Swan°

A sudden blow: the great wings beating still
Above the staggering girl, her thighs caressed
By the dark webs, her nape caught in his bill,
He holds her helpless breast upon his breast.

How can those terrified vague fingers push   5
The feathered glory from her loosening thighs?
And how can body, laid in that white rush,
But feel the strange heart beating where it lies?

A shudder in the loins engenders there
The broken wall, the burning roof and tower   10
And Agamemnon dead.
                    Being so caught up,
So mastered by the brute blood of the air,
Did she put on his knowledge with his power
Before the indifferent beak could let her drop?   15

[1928]

Leda and the Swan: In Greek mythology, Leda was seduced (or raped) by Zeus,
who approached her in the form of a swan. She gave birth to Helen, whose
abduction by Paris gave rise to the Trojan War (referred to in line 10). The Greek
forces were headed by Agamemnon, who was killed (line 11) upon his return to
Greece by his wife, Clytemnestra, daughter of Leda by her husband, Tyndareus.
Yeats regarded Zeus's visit as a "violent annunciation" of the founding of Greek
civilization, with parallels to the annunciation to Mary (Luke 1:26–38), 2,000
years later, of the coming of the Christian age. See the note to "The Second
Coming" for Yeats's view of historical eras (p. 530).

WILLIAM BUTLER YEATS   [1865–1939]

Sailing to Byzantium°

1

That is no country for old men. The young
In one another's arms, birds in the trees
—Those dying generations—at their song,
The salmon-falls, the mackerel-crowded seas,
Fish, flesh, or fowl, commend all summer long
Whatever is begotten, born, and dies.
Caught in that sensual music all neglect
Monuments of unaging intellect.

2

An aged man is but a paltry thing,
A tattered coat upon a stick, unless
Soul clap its hands and sing, and louder sing
For every tatter in its mortal dress,
Nor is there singing school but studying
Monuments of its own magnificence;
And therefore I have sailed the seas and come
To the holy city of Byzantium.

Sailing to Byzantium: Yeats wrote in *A Vision* (1925): "I think if I could be given
a month of Antiquity and leave to spend it where I chose, I would spend it in
Byzantium [modern Istanbul] a little before Justinian [ruled 527 to 565] opened
St. Sophia and closed the Academy of Plato. . . . I think that in early Byzantium,
and maybe never before or since in recorded history, religious, aesthetic and
practical life were one, and that architect and artificers . . . spoke to the multitude and the few alike. The painter and the mosaic worker, the worker in gold
and silver, the illuminator of Sacred Books were almost impersonal, almost
perhaps without the consciousness of individual design, absorbed in their subject matter and that the vision of a whole people" (3.3). Byzantium becomes for
Yeats a symbol of eternity, a place of perfection where the growth and change
that characterize nature and physical life do not occur.

532

3

O sages standing in God's holy fire
As in the gold mosaic of a wall,
Come from the holy fire, perne in a gyre,°
And be the singing-masters of my soul.   20
Consume my heart away; sick with desire
And fastened to a dying animal
It knows not what it is; and gather me
Into the artifice of eternity.

4

Once out of nature I shall never take   25
My bodily form from any natural thing,
But such a form as Grecian goldsmiths make
Of hammered gold and gold enamelling
To keep a drowsy Emperor awake;°
Or set upon a golden bough to sing   30
To lords and ladies of Byzantium
Of what is past, or passing, or to come.

[1928]

19. gyre: Whirl in a spiral motion (a *perne* is a spool or bobbin on which something is wound; a *gyre* is a spiral).
25–29. Once . . . awake: Yeats wrote in a note, "I have read somewhere that in the Emperor's palace at Byzantium was a tree made of gold and silver, and artificial birds that sang." He may have been thinking of Hans Christian Andersen's *The Emperor's Nightingale.*

EDWIN ARLINGTON ROBINSON   [1869–1935]

Richard Cory

Whenever Richard Cory went down town,
We people on the pavement looked at him:
He was a gentleman from sole to crown,
Clean favored, and imperially slim.

And he was always quietly arrayed,
And he was always human when he talked;
But still he fluttered pulses when he said,
"Good-morning," and he glittered when he walked.

And he was rich—yes, richer than a king—
And admirably schooled in every grace:
In fine, we thought that he was everything
To make us wish that we were in his place.

So on we worked, and waited for the light,
And went without the meat, and cursed the bread;
And Richard Cory, one calm summer night,
Went home and put a bullet through his head.

[1897]

PAUL LAURENCE DUNBAR   [1872–1906]

We Wear the Mask

We wear the mask that grins and lies,
It hides our cheeks and shades our eyes,—
This debt we pay to human guile;
With torn and bleeding hearts we smile,
And mouth with myriad subtleties.
Why should the world be over-wise,
In counting all our tears and sighs?
Nay, let them only see us, while
    We wear the mask.

We smile, but, O great Christ, our cries
To thee from tortured souls arise.
We sing, but oh the clay is vile
Beneath our feet, and long the mile;
But let the world dream otherwise,
    We wear the mask!

[1896]

ROBERT FROST   [1874–1963]

After Apple-Picking

My long two-pointed ladder's sticking through a tree
Toward heaven still,
And there's a barrel that I didn't fill
Beside it, and there may be two or three
Apples I didn't pick upon some bough.   5
But I am done with apple-picking now.
Essence of winter sleep is on the night,
The scent of apples: I am drowsing off.
I cannot rub the strangeness from my sight
I got from looking through a pane of glass   10
I skimmed this morning from the drinking trough
And held against the world of hoary grass.
It melted, and I let it fall and break.
But I was well
Upon my way to sleep before it fell,   15
And I could tell
What form my dreaming was about to take.
Magnified apples appear and disappear,
Stem end and blossom end,
And every fleck of russet showing clear.   20
My instep arch not only keeps the ache,
It keeps the pressure of a ladder-round.
I feel the ladder sway as the boughs bend.
And I keep hearing from the cellar bin
The rumbling sound   25
Of load on load of apples coming in.
For I have had too much
Of apple-picking: I am overtired
Of the great harvest I myself desired.
There were ten thousand thousand fruit to touch,   30
Cherish in hand, lift down, and not let fall.
For all
That struck the earth,
No matter if not bruised or spiked with stubble,

Went surely to the cider-apple heap
As of no worth.
One can see what will trouble
This sleep of mine, whatever sleep it is.
Were he not gone,
The woodchuck could say whether it's like his
Long sleep, as I describe its coming on,
Or just some human sleep.

[1914]

ROBERT FROST   [1874–1963]

The Road Not Taken

Two roads diverged in a yellow wood,
And sorry I could not travel both
And be one traveler, long I stood
And looked down one as far as I could
To where it bent in the undergrowth;

Then took the other, as just as fair,
And having perhaps the better claim,
Because it was grassy and wanted wear;
Though as for that, the passing there
Had worn them really about the same,

And both that morning equally lay
In leaves no step had trodden black.
Oh, I kept the first for another day!
Yet knowing how way leads on to way,
I doubted if I should ever come back.

I shall be telling this with a sigh
Somewhere ages and ages hence:
Two roads diverged in a wood, and I—
I took the one less traveled by,
And that has made all the difference.

[1916]

ROBERT FROST   [1874–1963]

Birches

When I see birches bend to left and right
Across the lines of straighter darker trees,
I like to think some boy's been swinging them.
But swinging doesn't bend them down to stay
As ice storms do. Often you must have seen them   5
Loaded with ice a sunny winter morning
After a rain. They click upon themselves
As the breeze rises, and turn many-colored
As the stir cracks and crazes their enamel.
Soon the sun's warmth makes them shed crystal shells   10
Shattering and avalanching on the snow crust—
Such heaps of broken glass to sweep away
You'd think the inner dome of heaven had fallen.
They are dragged to the withered bracken by the load,
And they seem not to break; though once they are bowed   15
So low for long, they never right themselves:
You may see their trunks arching in the woods
Years afterwards, trailing their leaves on the ground
Like girls on hands and knees that throw their hair
Before them over their heads to dry in the sun.   20
But I was going to say when Truth broke in
With all her matter of fact about the ice storm,
I should prefer to have some boy bend them
As he went out and in to fetch the cows—
Some boy too far from town to learn baseball,   25
Whose only play was what he found himself,
Summer or winter, and could play alone.
One by one he subdued his father's trees
By riding them down over and over again
Until he took the stiffness out of them,   30
And not one but hung limp, not one was left
For him to conquer. He learned all there was
To learn about not launching out too soon
And so not carrying the tree away

Clear to the ground. He always kept his poise
To the top branches, climbing carefully
With the same pains you use to fill a cup
Up to the brim, and even above the brim.
Then he flung outward, feet first, with a swish,
Kicking his way down through the air to the ground.
So was I once myself a swinger of birches.
And so I dream of going back to be.
It's when I'm weary of considerations,
And life is too much like a pathless wood
Where your face burns and tickles with the cobwebs
Broken across it, and one eye is weeping
From a twig's having lashed across it open.
I'd like to get away from earth awhile
And then come back to it and begin over.
May no fate willfully misunderstand me
And half grant what I wish and snatch me away
Not to return. Earth's the right place for love:
I don't know where it's likely to go better.
I'd like to go by climbing a birch tree,
And climb black branches up a snow-white trunk
Toward heaven, till the tree could bear no more,
But dipped its top and set me down again.
That would be good both going and coming back.
One could do worse than be a swinger of birches.

[1916]

ROBERT FROST   [1874–1963]

"Out, Out—"

The buzz saw snarled and rattled in the yard
And made dust and dropped stove-length sticks of wood,
Sweet-scented stuff when the breeze drew across it.
And from there those that lifted eyes could count
Five mountain ranges one behind the other
Under the sunset far into Vermont.

And the saw snarled and rattled, snarled and rattled,
As it ran light, or had to bear a load.
And nothing happened: day was all but done.
Call it a day, I wish they might have said   10
To please the boy by giving him the half hour
That a boy counts so much when saved from work.
His sister stood beside them in her apron
To tell them "Supper." At the word, the saw,
As if to prove saws knew what supper meant,   15
Leaped out at the boy's hand, or seemed to leap—
He must have given the hand. However it was,
Neither refused the meeting. But the hand!
The boy's first outcry was a rueful laugh,
As he swung toward them holding up the hand,   20
Half in appeal, but half as if to keep
The life from spilling. Then the boy saw all—
Since he was old enough to know, big boy
Doing a man's work, though a child at heart—
He saw all spoiled. "Don't let him cut my hand off—   25
The doctor, when he comes. Don't let him, sister!"
So. But the hand was gone already.
The doctor put him in the dark of ether.
He lay and puffed his lips out with his breath.
And then—the watcher at his pulse took fright.   30
No one believed. They listened at his heart.
Little—less—nothing!—and that ended it.
No more to build on there. And they, since they
Were not the one dead, turned to their affairs.

[1916]

ROBERT FROST [1874–1963]

Stopping by Woods on a Snowy Evening

Whose woods these are I think I know.
His house is in the village, though;
He will not see me stopping here
To watch his woods fill up with snow.

My little horse must think it queer
To stop without a farmhouse near
Between the woods and frozen lake
The darkest evening of the year.

He gives his harness bells a shake
To ask if there is some mistake.
The only other sound's the sweep
Of easy wind and downy flake.

The woods are lovely, dark, and deep,
But I have promises to keep,
And miles to go before I sleep,
And miles to go before I sleep.

[1923]

ROBERT FROST [1874–1963]

Acquainted with the Night

I have been one acquainted with the night.
I have walked out in rain—and back in rain.
I have outwalked the furthest city light.

I have looked down the saddest city lane.
I have passed by the watchman on his beat   5
And dropped my eyes, unwilling to explain.

I have stood still and stopped the sound of feet
When far away an interrupted cry
Came over houses from another street,

But not to call me back or say good-bye;   10
And further still at an unearthly height,
One luminary clock against the sky

Proclaimed the time was neither wrong nor right.
I have been one acquainted with the night.

[1928]

WALLACE STEVENS   [1879–1955]

Anecdote of the Jar

I placed a jar in Tennessee,
And round it was, upon a hill.
It made the slovenly wilderness
Surround that hill.

The wilderness rose up to it,   5
And sprawled around, no longer wild.
The jar was round upon the ground
And tall and of a port in air.

It took dominion everywhere.
The jar was gray and bare.   10
It did not give of bird or bush,
Like nothing else in Tennessee.

[1923]

WALLACE STEVENS   [1879–1955]

The Emperor of Ice-Cream

Call the roller of big cigars,
The muscular one, and bid him whip
In kitchen cups concupiscent curds.
Let the wenches dawdle in such dress
As they are used to wear, and let the boys
Bring flowers in last month's newspapers.
Let be be finale of seem.
The only emperor is the emperor of ice-cream.

Take from the dresser of deal,°
Lacking the three glass knobs, that sheet
On which she embroidered fantails once
And spread it so as to cover her face.
If her horny feet protrude, they come
To show how cold she is, and dumb.
Let the lamp affix its beam.
The only emperor is the emperor of ice-cream.

[1923]

9. **deal:** Fir or pine wood.

WILLIAM CARLOS WILLIAMS   [1883–1963]

The Red Wheelbarrow

concrete
poem

so much depends
upon

a red wheel
barrow

glazed with rain   5
water

beside the white
chickens.

[1923]

WILLIAM CARLOS WILLIAMS   [1883–1963]

Spring and All

By the road to the contagious hospital
under the surge of the blue
mottled clouds driven from the
northeast—a cold wind. Beyond, the
waste of broad, muddy fields   5
brown with dried weeds, standing and fallen

patches of standing water
the scattering of tall trees

All along the road the reddish
purplish, forked, upstanding, twiggy   10
stuff of bushes and small trees
with dead, brown leaves under them
leafless vines—

Lifeless in appearance, sluggish
dazed spring approaches—   15

They enter the new world naked,
cold, uncertain of all
save that they enter. All about them
the cold, familiar wind—

Now the grass, tomorrow   20
the stiff curl of wildcarrot leaf

One by one objects are defined—
It quickens: clarity, outline of leaf

But now the stark dignity of
entrance—Still, the profound change
has come upon them: rooted, they
grip down and begin to awaken

[1923]

WILLIAM CARLOS WILLIAMS [1883–1963]

This Is Just to Say

I have eaten
the plums
that were in
the icebox

and which
you were probably
saving
for breakfast

Forgive me
they were delicious
so sweet
and so cold

[1934]

EZRA POUND [1885–1972]

The River-Merchant's Wife:
A Letter

While my hair was still cut straight across my forehead
I played about the front gate, pulling flowers.
You came by on bamboo stilts, playing horse,
You walked about my seat, playing with blue plums.
And we went on living in the village of Chokan: 5
Two small people, without dislike or suspicion.

At fourteen I married My Lord you.
I never laughed, being bashful.
Lowering my head, I looked at the wall.
Called to, a thousand times, I never looked back.   10

At fifteen I stopped scowling,
I desired my dust to be mingled with yours
Forever and forever and forever.
Why should I climb the look out?

At sixteen you departed,   15
You went into far Ku-to-yen, by the river of swirling eddies,
And you have been gone five months.
The monkeys make sorrowful noise overhead.

You dragged your feet when you went out.
By the gate now, the moss is grown, the different mosses,   20
Too deep to clear them away!
The leaves fall early this autumn, in wind.
The paired butterflies are already yellow with August
Over the grass in the West garden;
They hurt me. I grow older.   25
If you are coming down through the narrows of the river Kiang,
Please let me know beforehand,

And I will come out to meet you
        As far as Cho-fu-Sa.

                                                    By Rihaku°

                                                    [1915]

By Rihaku: An adaptation of a Chinese poem by the famous poet Li Po
(701–762 C.E.), whose Japanese name is Rihaku.

MARIANNE MOORE   [1887–1972]

Poetry

I, too, dislike it: there are things that are important beyond all this fiddle.
    Reading it, however, with a perfect contempt for it, one discovers in
    it after all, a place for the genuine.
        Hands that can grasp, eyes
        that can dilate, hair that can rise
            if it must, these things are important not because a

high-sounding interpretation can be put upon them but because they are
    useful. When they become so derivative as to become unintelligible,
    the same thing may be said for all of us, that we
        do not admire what
        we cannot understand: the bat
            holding on upside down or in quest of something to

eat, elephants pushing, a wild horse taking a roll, a tireless wolf under
    a tree, the immovable critic twitching his skin like a horse that feels a
                                                    flea, the base-
    ball fan, the statistician—
        nor is it valid
            to discriminate against "business documents and

school-books"; all these phenomena are important. One must make a
                                                    distinction
    however: when dragged into prominence by half poets, the result is
                                                    not poetry,

nor till the poets among us can be   20
   "literalists of
the imagination"—above
    insolence and triviality and can present

for inspection, "imaginary gardens with real toads in them," shall we
                              have
  it. In the meantime, if you demand on the one hand,   25
the raw material of poetry in
   all its rawness and
    that which is on the other hand
      genuine, you are interested in poetry.

[1921]

T. S. ELIOT [1888–1965]

The Love Song of J. Alfred Prufrock

S'io credesse che mia risposta fosse
A persona che mai tornasse al mondo,
Questa fiamma staria senza piu scosse.
Ma perciocche giammai di questo fondo
Non torno vivo alcun, s'i'odo il vero,
Senza tema d'infamia ti rispondo.°

Let us go then, you and I,
When the evening is spread out against the sky
Like a patient etherised upon a table;

Epigraph: "If I thought that my answer were being made to someone who
would ever return to earth, this flame would remain without further movement;
but since no one has ever returned alive from this depth, if what I hear is true, I
answer you without fear of infamy" (Dante, *Inferno* 27.61–66). Dante encounters
Guido de Montefeltro in the eighth circle of hell, where souls are trapped within
flames (tongues of fire) as punishment for giving evil counsel. Guido tells Dante
details about his evil life only because he assumes that Dante is on his way to an
even deeper circle in hell and will never return to earth and be able to repeat
what he has heard.

Let us go, through certain half-deserted streets,
The muttering retreats
Of restless nights in one-night cheap hotels
And sawdust restaurants with oyster-shells:
Streets that follow like a tedious argument
Of insidious intent
To lead you to an overwhelming question . . .
Oh, do not ask, "What is it?"
Let us go and make our visit.

In the room the women come and go
Talking of Michelangelo.

The yellow fog that rubs its back upon the window-panes,
The yellow smoke that rubs its muzzle on the window-panes
Licked its tongue into the corners of the evening,
Lingered upon the pools that stand in drains,
Let fall upon its back the soot that falls from chimneys,
Slipped by the terrace, made a sudden leap,
And seeing that it was a soft October night,
Curled once about the house, and fell asleep.

And indeed there will be time
For the yellow smoke that slides along the street,
Rubbing its back upon the window-panes;
There will be time, there will be time
To prepare a face to meet the faces that you meet;
There will be time to murder and create,
And time for all the works and days° of hands
That lift and drop a question on your plate;
Time for you and time for me,
And time yet for a hundred indecisions,
And for a hundred visions and revisions,
Before the taking of a toast and tea.

In the room the women come and go
Talking of Michelangelo.

And indeed there will be time
To wonder, "Do I dare?" and, "Do I dare?"
Time to turn back and descend the stair,
With a bald spot in the middle of my hair—

29. **works and days:** *Works and Days* is the title of a didactic poem about farming by the Greek poet Hesiod (eighth century B.C.E.) that includes instruction about doing each task at the proper time.

(They will say: "How his hair is growing thin!")
My morning coat, my collar mounting firmly to the chin,
My necktie rich and modest, but asserted by a simple pin—
(They will say: "But how his arms and legs are thin!")
Do I dare   45
Disturb the universe?
In a minute there is time
For decisions and revisions which a minute will reverse.

    For I have known them all already, known them all:—
Have known the evenings, mornings, afternoons,   50
I have measured out my life with coffee spoons;
I know the voices dying with a dying fall°
Beneath the music from a farther room.
    So how should I presume?

    And I have known the eyes already, known them all—   55
The eyes that fix you in a formulated phrase,
And when I am formulated, sprawling on a pin,
When I am pinned and wriggling on the wall,
Then how should I begin
To spit out all the butt-ends of my days and ways?   60
    And how should I presume?

    And I have known the arms already, known them all—
Arms that are braceleted and white and bare
(But in the lamplight, downed with light brown hair!)
Is it perfume from a dress   65
That makes me so digress?
Arms that lie along a table, or wrap about a shawl.
    And should I then presume?
    And how should I begin?

            •   •   •

Shall I say, I have gone at dusk through narrow streets   70
And watched the smoke that rises from the pipes
Of lonely men in shirt-sleeves, leaning out of windows? . . .

    I should have been a pair of ragged claws
Scuttling across the floors of silent seas.

            •   •   •

52. a dying fall: An allusion to Shakespeare's *Twelfth Night* (1.1.4): "That strain
[of music] again! It had a dying fall" (a cadence that falls away).

And the afternoon, the evening, sleeps so peacefully!
Smoothed by long fingers,
Asleep . . . tired . . . or it malingers,
Stretched on the floor, here beside you and me.
Should I, after tea and cakes and ices,
Have the strength to force the moment to its crisis?
But though I have wept and fasted, wept and prayed,
Though I have seen my head (grown slightly bald) brought in upon a
               platter,°
I am no prophet—and here's no great matter;
I have seen the moment of my greatness flicker,
And I have seen the eternal Footman hold my coat, and snicker,
And in short, I was afraid.

    And would it have been worth it, after all,
After the cups, the marmalade, the tea,
Among the porcelain, among some talk of you and me,
Would it have been worth while,
To have bitten off the matter with a smile,
To have squeezed the universe into a ball
To roll it toward some overwhelming question,
To say: "I am Lazarus,° come from the dead,
Come back to tell you all, I shall tell you all"—
If one, settling a pillow by her head,
    Should say: "That is not what I meant at all.
    That is not it, at all."

    And would it have been worth it, after all,
Would it have been worth while,
After the sunsets and the dooryards and the sprinkled streets,
After the novels, after the teacups, after the skirts that trail along the
               floor—
And this, and so much more?—
It is impossible to say just what I mean!
But as if a magic lantern threw the nerves in patterns on a screen:
Would it have been worth while
If one, settling a pillow or throwing off a shawl,
And turning toward the window, should say:

82. **head . . . platter:** As a reward for dancing before King Herod, Salome, his
stepdaughter, asked for the head of John the Baptist to be presented to her on a
platter (Matthew 14:1–12; Mark 6:17–28).
94. **Lazarus:** Either the beggar Lazarus, who in Luke 16:19–31 did not return
from the dead, or Jesus's friend Lazarus, who did (John 11:1–44).

"That is not it at all,
That is not what I meant, at all."   110

    •   •   •

No! I am not Prince Hamlet, nor was meant to be;
Am an attendant lord, one that will do
To swell a progress,° start a scene or two,
Advise the prince; no doubt, an easy tool,
Deferential, glad to be of use,   115
Politic, cautious, and meticulous;
Full of high sentence,° but a bit obtuse;   *sententiousness*
At times, indeed, almost ridiculous—
Almost, at times, the Fool.

    I grow old . . . I grow old . . .   120
I shall wear the bottoms of my trousers rolled.°   *turned up, with cuffs*

    Shall I part my hair behind? Do I dare to eat a peach?
I shall wear white flannel trousers, and walk upon the beach.
I have heard the mermaids singing, each to each.

    I do not think that they will sing to me.   125

    I have seen them riding seaward on the waves
Combing the white hair of the waves blown back
When the wind blows the water white and black.

    We have lingered in the chambers of the sea
By sea-girls wreathed with seaweed red and brown   130
Till human voices wake us, and we drown.

                         [1915]

113. progress: Ceremonial journey made by a royal court.

T. S. ELIOT   [1888–1965]

Preludes

I

The winter evening settles down
With smell of steaks in passageways.
Six o'clock.
The burnt-out ends of smoky days.
And now a gusty shower wraps
The grimy scraps
Of withered leaves about your feet
And newspapers from vacant lots;
The showers beat
On broken blinds and chimney-pots,
And at the corner of the street
A lonely cab-horse steams and stamps.
And then the lighting of the lamps.

II

The morning comes to consciousness
Of faint stale smells of beer
From the sawdust-trampled street
With all its muddy feet that press
To early coffee-stands.
With the other masquerades
That time resumes,
One thinks of all the hands
That are raising dingy shades
In a thousand furnished rooms.

III

You tossed a blanket from the bed,
You lay upon your back, and waited;
You dozed, and watched the night revealing
The thousand sordid images
Of which your soul was constituted;

They flickered against the ceiling.
And when all the world came back   30
And the light crept up between the shutters
And you heard the sparrows in the gutters,
You had such a vision of the street
As the street hardly understands;
Sitting along the bed's edge, where   35
You curled the papers from your hair,
Or clasped the yellow soles of feet
In the palms of both soiled hands.

IV

His soul stretched tight across the skies
That fade behind a city block,   40
Or trampled by insistent feet
At four and five and six o'clock;
And short square fingers stuffing pipes,
And evening newspapers, and eyes
Assured of certain certainties,   45
The conscience of a blackened street
Impatient to assume the world.

   I am moved by fancies that are curled
Around these images, and cling:
The notion of some infinitely gentle   50
Infinitely suffering thing.

   Wipe your hand across your mouth, and laugh;
The worlds revolve like ancient women
Gathering fuel in vacant lots.

[1917]

JOHN CROWE RANSOM   [1888–1974]

Bells for John Whiteside's Daughter

There was such speed in her little body,
And such lightness in her footfall,
It is no wonder her brown study°
Astonishes us all.

Her wars were bruited in our high window.
We looked among orchard trees and beyond
Where she took arms against her shadow,
Or harried unto the pond

The lazy geese, like a snow cloud
Dripping their snow on the green grass,
Tricking and stopping, sleepy and proud,
Who cried in goose, Alas,

For the tireless heart within the little
Lady with rod that made them rise
From their noon apple-dreams and scuttle
Goose-fashion under the skies!

But now go the bells, and we are ready,
In one house we are sternly stopped
To say we are vexed at her brown study,
Lying so primly propped.

[1924]

3. **brown study:** Being deeply absorbed in one's thoughts; reverie.

CLAUDE McKAY   [1890–1948]

America

Although she feeds me bread of bitterness,
And sinks into my throat her tiger's tooth,
Stealing my breath of life, I will confess
I love this cultured hell that tests my youth!
Her vigor flows like tides into my blood,   5
Giving me strength erect against her hate.
Her bigness sweeps my being like a flood.
Yet as a rebel fronts a king in state,
I stand within her walls with not a shred
Of terror, malice, not a word of jeer.   10
Darkly I gaze into the days ahead,
And see her might and granite wonders there,
Beneath the touch of Time's unerring hand,
Like priceless treasures sinking in the sand.

[1922]

WILFRED OWEN   [1893–1918]

Dulce et Decorum Est

Bent double, like old beggars under sacks,
Knock-kneed, coughing like hags, we cursed through sludge,
Till on the haunting flares we turned our backs
And towards our distant rest began to trudge.
Men marched asleep. Many had lost their boots   5
But limped on, blood-shod. All went lame; all blind;
Drunk with fatigue; deaf even to the hoots
Of tired, outstripped Five-Nines° that dropped behind.

8. **Five-Nines:** 5.9-inch caliber shells.

Gas! GAS! Quick, boys!—An ecstasy of fumbling,
Fitting the clumsy helmets just in time;
But someone still was yelling out and stumbling
And flound'ring like a man in fire or lime . . .
Dim, through the misty panes° and thick green light,   *of a gas mask*
As under a green sea, I saw him drowning.

In all my dreams, before my helpless sight,
He plunges at me, guttering, choking, drowning.

If in some smothering dreams you too could pace
Behind the wagon that we flung him in,
And watch the white eyes writhing in his face,
His hanging face, like a devil's sick of sin;
If you could hear, at every jolt, the blood
Come gargling from the froth-corrupted lungs,
Obscene as cancer, bitter as the cud
Of vile, incurable sores on innocent tongues,—
My friend, you would not tell with such high zest
To children ardent for some desperate glory,
The old Lie: Dulce et decorum est
Pro patria mori.°

[1920]

27–28. Dulce . . . mori: It is sweet and fitting / to die for one's country (Horace, *Odes* 3.12.13).

E. E. CUMMINGS   [1894–1962]

in Just-

in Just-
spring   when the world is mud-
luscious the little
lame balloonman

whistles   far   and wee

and eddieandbill come
running from marbles and
piracies and it's
spring

when the world is puddle-wonderful   10

the queer
old balloonman whistles
far   and   wee
and bettyandisbel come dancing

from hop-scotch and jump-rope and   15

it's
spring
and
   the

      goat-footed   20

balloonMan   whistles
far
and
wee

[1923]

E. E. CUMMINGS   [1894–1962]

"next to of course god america i

"next to of course god america i
love you land of the pilgrims' and so forth oh
say can you see by the dawn's early my
country 'tis of centuries come and go
and are no more what of it we should worry   5
in every language even deafanddumb
thy sons acclaim your glorious name by gorry
by jingo by gee by gosh by gum
why talk of beauty what could be more beautiful than these heroic happy dead   10

who rushed like lions to the roaring slaughter
they did not stop to think they died instead
then shall the voice of liberty be mute?"

He spoke.   And drank rapidly a glass of water

[1926]

JEAN TOOMER   [1894–1967]

Face

Hair—
silver-gray,
like streams of stars,
Brows—
recurved canoes
quivered by the ripples blown by pain,
Her eyes—
mist of tears
condensing on the flesh below
And her channeled muscles
are cluster grapes of sorrow
purple in the evening sun
nearly ripe for worms.

[1923]

ROBERT FRANCIS   [1901-1987]

The Base Stealer

Poised between going on and back, pulled
Both ways taut like a tightrope-walker,
Fingertips pointing the opposites,

Now bouncing tiptoe like a dropped ball
Or a kid skipping rope, come on, come on,   5
Running a scattering of steps sidewise,
How he teeters, skitters, tingles, teases,
Taunts them, hovers like an ecstatic bird,
He's only flirting, crowd him, crowd him,
Delicate, delicate, delicate, delicate—now!   10

[1953]

LANGSTON HUGHES   [1902–1967]

Mother to Son

Well, son, I'll tell you:
Life for me ain't been no crystal stair.
It's had tacks in it,
And splinters,
And boards torn up,   5
And places with no carpet on the floor—
Bare.
But all the time
I'se been a-climbin' on,
And reachin' landin's,   10
And turnin' corners,
And sometimes goin' in the dark
Where there ain't been no light.
So boy, don't you turn back.
Don't you set down on the steps   15
'Cause you finds it's kinder hard.
Don't you fall now—
For I'se still goin', honey,
I'se still climbin',
And life for me ain't been no crystal stair.   20

[1922]

LANGSTON HUGHES   [1902–1967]

Harlem

What happens to a dream deferred?

Does it dry up
like a raisin in the sun?
Or fester like a sore—
And then run?
Does it stink like rotten meat?
Or crust and sugar over—
like a syrupy sweet?

Maybe it just sags
like a heavy load.

Or does it explode?

[1951]

COUNTEE CULLEN   [1903–1946]

Incident

for Eric Walrond

Once riding in old Baltimore,
  Heart-filled, head-filled with glee,
I saw a Baltimorean
  Keep looking straight at me.

Now I was eight and very small,
  And he was no whit bigger,
And so I smiled, but he poked out
  His tongue, and called me, "Nigger."

I saw the whole of Baltimore
  From May until December;   10
Of all the things that happened there
  That's all that I remember.

[1925]

LORINE NIEDECKER   [1903–1970]

My Life by Water

My life
  by water—
    Hear

spring's
  first frog   5
    or board

out on the cold
  ground
    giving

Muskrats   10
  gnawing
    doors

to wild green
  arts and letters
    Rabbits   15

raided
  my lettuce
    One boat

two—
  pointed toward
    my shore   20

thru birdstart
  wingdrip
    weed-drift

of the soft
  and serious—
    Water

[1985]

STANLEY KUNITZ   [1905–2006]

The War Against the Trees

The man who sold his lawn to standard oil
Joked with his neighbors come to watch the show
While the bulldozers, drunk with gasoline,
Tested the virtue of the soil
Under the branchy sky
By overthowing first the privet-row.

Forsythia-forays and hydrangea-raids
Were but preliminaries to a war
Against the great-grandfathers of the town,
So freshly lopped and maimed.
They struck and struck again,
And with each elm a century went down.

All day the hireling engines charged the trees,
Subverting them by hacking underground
In grub-dominions, where dark summer's mole
Rampages through his halls,
Till a northern seizure shook
Those crowns, forcing the giants to their knees.

I saw the ghosts of children at their games
Racing beyond their childhood in the shade,
And while the green world turned its death-foxed page
And a red wagon wheeled,
I watched them disappear
Into the suburbs of their grievous age.

Ripped from the craters much too big for hearts
The club-roots bared their amputated coils,

Raw gorgons° matted blind, whose pocks and scars
Cried Moon! On a corner lot
One witness-moment, caught
In the rear-view mirrors of the passing cars.   30

[1958]

27. gorgons: Found in Greek mythology, the Gorgon was a female creature with snakes for hair.

W. H. AUDEN [1907–1973]

Stop All the Clocks

Stop all the clocks, cut off the telephone,
Prevent the dog from barking with a juicy bone,
Silence the pianos and with muffled drum
Bring out the coffin, let the mourners come.

Let aeroplanes circle moaning overhead   5
Scribbling on the sky the message He Is Dead,
Put crêpe bows round the white necks of the public doves,
Let the traffic policemen wear black cotton gloves.

He was my North, my South, my East and West,
My working week and my Sunday rest,   10
My noon, my midnight, my talk, my song;
I thought that love would last for ever: I was wrong.

The stars are not wanted now; put out every one:
Pack up the moon and dismantle the sun;
Pour away the ocean and sweep up the woods: 15
For nothing now can ever come to any good.

[1936]

W. H. AUDEN   [1907–1973]

Musée des Beaux Arts°

About suffering they were never wrong,
The Old Masters: how well they understood
Its human position; how it takes place
While someone else is eating or opening a window or just walking dully
    along;
How, when the aged are reverently, passionately waiting
For the miraculous birth, there always must be
Children who did not specially want it to happen, skating
On a pond at the edge of the wood:
They never forgot
That even the dreadful martyrdom must run its course
Anyhow in a corner, some untidy spot
Where the dogs go on with their doggy life and the torturer's horse
Scratches its innocent behind on a tree.
In Brueghel's *Icarus*, for instance: how everything turns away
Quite leisurely from the disaster; the ploughman may
Have heard the splash, the forsaken cry,
But for him it was not an important failure; the sun shone
As it had to on the white legs disappearing into the green
Water; and the expensive delicate ship that must have seen
Something amazing, a boy falling out of the sky,
Had somewhere to get to and sailed calmly on.

[1940]

Musée des Beaux Arts: The painting *Landscape with the Fall of Icarus* by Pieter Brueghel the Elder, on which the poem is based, is in the Musées Royaux des Beaux-Arts in Brussels.

Brueghel, *Landscape with the Fall of Icarus*

THEODORE ROETHKE [1908–1963]

My Papa's Waltz

The whiskey on your breath
Could make a small boy dizzy;
But I hung on like death:
Such waltzing was not easy.

We romped until the pans   5
Slid from the kitchen shelf;
My mother's countenance
Could not unfrown itself.

The hand that held my wrist
Was battered on one knuckle;   10
At every step you missed
My right ear scraped a buckle.

You beat time on my head
With a palm caked hard by dirt,
Then waltzed me off to bed
Still clinging to your shirt.

[1948]

ELIZABETH BISHOP   [1911–1979]

The Fish

I caught a tremendous fish
and held him beside the boat
half out of water, with my hook
fast in a corner of his mouth.
He didn't fight.
He hadn't fought at all.
He hung a grunting weight,
battered and venerable
and homely. Here and there
his brown skin hung in strips
like ancient wallpaper,
and its pattern of darker brown
was like wallpaper:
shapes like full-blown roses
stained and lost through age.
He was speckled with barnacles,
fine rosettes of lime,
and infested
with tiny white sea-lice,
and underneath two or three
rags of green weed hung down.
While his gills were breathing in
the terrible oxygen
—the frightening gills,
fresh and crisp with blood,
that can cut so badly—
I thought of the coarse white flesh
packed in like feathers,
the big bones and the little bones,

the dramatic reds and blacks   30
of his shiny entrails,
and the pink swim-bladder
like a big peony.
I looked into his eyes
which were far larger than mine   35
but shallower, and yellowed,
the irises backed and packed
with tarnished tinfoil
seen through the lenses
of old scratched isinglass.°   *transparent sheet of mica*   40
They shifted a little, but not
to return my stare.
—It was more like the tipping
of an object toward the light.
I admired his sullen face,   45
the mechanism of his jaw,
and then I saw
that from his lower lip
—if you could call it a lip—
grim, wet, and weaponlike,   50
hung five old pieces of fish-line,
or four and a wire leader
with the swivel still attached,
with all their five big hooks
grown firmly in his mouth.   55
A green line, frayed at the end
where he broke it, two heavier lines,
and a fine black thread
still crimped from the strain and snap
when it broke and he got away.   60
Like medals with their ribbons
frayed and wavering,
a five-haired beard of wisdom   *respect*
trailing from his aching jaw.
I stared and stared   65
and victory filled up
the little rented boat,
from the pool of bilge
where oil had spread a rainbow
around the rusted engine   70
to the bailer rusted orange,
the sun-cracked thwarts,
the oarlocks on their strings,

the gunnels—until everything
was rainbow, rainbow, rainbow!
And I let the fish go.

[1946]

ELIZABETH BISHOP   [1911–1979]

In the Waiting Room

In Worcester, Massachusetts,
I went with Aunt Consuelo
to keep her dentist's appointment
and sat and waited for her
in the dentist's waiting room.
It was winter. It got dark
early. The waiting room
was full of grown-up people,
arctics and overcoats,
lamps and magazines.
My aunt was inside
what seemed like a long time
and while I waited I read
the *National Geographic*
(I could read) and carefully
studied the photographs:
the inside of a volcano,
black, and full of ashes;
then it was spilling over
in rivulets of fire.
Osa and Martin Johnson°
dressed in riding breeches,
laced boots, and pith helmets.
A dead man slung on a pole
—"Long Pig,"° the caption said.
Babies with pointed heads
wound round and round with string;
black, naked women with necks

21. **Osa and Martin Johnson:** Husband-and-wife explorers and naturalists.
25. **Long Pig:** Polynesian cannibals' name for a human carcass.

wound round and round with wire
like the necks of light bulbs.   30
Their breasts were horrifying.
I read it right straight through.
I was too shy to stop.
And then I looked at the cover:
the yellow margins, the date.   35
Suddenly, from inside,
came an *oh!* of pain
—Aunt Consuelo's voice—
not very loud or long.
I wasn't at all surprised;   40
even then I knew she was
a foolish, timid woman.
I might have been embarrassed,
but wasn't. What took me
completely by surprise   45
was that it was *me*:
my voice, in my mouth.
Without thinking at all
I was my foolish aunt,
I—we—were falling, falling,   50
our eyes glued to the cover
of the *National Geographic*,
February, 1918.

I said to myself: three days
and you'll be seven years old.   55
I was saying it to stop
the sensation of falling off
the round, turning world
into cold, blue-black space.
But I felt: you are an *I*,   60
you are an *Elizabeth*,
you are one of *them*.
Why should you be one, too?
I scarcely dared to look
to see what it was I was.   65
I gave a sidelong glance
—I couldn't look any higher—
at shadowy gray knees,
trousers and skirts and boots
and different pairs of hands   70
lying under the lamps.

I knew that nothing stranger
had ever happened, that nothing
stranger could ever happen.
Why should I be my aunt,
or me, or anyone?
What similarities—
boots, hands, the family voice
I felt in my throat, or even
the *National Geographic*
and those awful hanging breasts—
held us all together
or made us all just one?
How—I didn't know any
word for it—how "unlikely" . . .
How had I come to be here,
like them, and overhear
a cry of pain that could have
got loud and worse but hadn't?

The waiting room was bright
and too hot. It was sliding
beneath a big black wave,
another, and another.

Then I was back in it.
The War was on. Outside,
in Worcester, Massachusetts,
were night and slush and cold,
and it was still the fifth
of February, 1918.

[1976]

ELIZABETH BISHOP   [1911–1979]

One Art

The art of losing isn't hard to master;
so many things seem filled with the intent
to be lost that their loss is no disaster.

Lose something every day. Accept the fluster
of lost door keys, the hour badly spent.   5
The art of losing isn't hard to master.

Then practice losing farther, losing faster:
places, and names, and where it was you meant
to travel. None of these will bring disaster.

I lost my mother's watch. And look! my last, or   10
next-to-last, of three loved houses went.
The art of losing isn't hard to master.

I lost two cities, lovely ones. And, vaster,
some realms I owned, two rivers, a continent.
I miss them, but it wasn't a disaster.   15

—Even losing you (the joking voice, a gesture
I love) I shan't have lied. It's evident
the art of losing's not too hard to master
though it may look like (*Write it!*) like disaster.

[1976]

JOHN FREDERICK NIMS   [1913–1999]

Love Poem

My clumsiest dear, whose hands shipwreck vases,
At whose quick touch all glasses chip and ring,
Whose palms are bulls in china, burs in linen,
And have no cunning with any soft thing

Except all ill-at-ease fidgeting people: 5
The refugee uncertain at the door
You make at home; deftly you steady
The drunk clambering on his undulant floor.

Unpredictable dear, the taxi drivers' terror,
Shrinking from far headlights pale as a dime   10
Yet leaping before red apoplectic streetcars—
Misfit in any space. And never on time.

A wrench in clocks and the solar system. Only
With words and people and love you move at ease;
In traffic of wit expertly maneuver
And keep us, all devotion, at your knees.

Forgetting your coffee spreading on our flannel,
Your lipstick grinning on our coat,
So gaily in love's unbreakable heaven
Our souls on glory of spilt bourbon float.

Be with me, darling, early and late. Smash glasses—
I will study wry music for your sake.
For should your hands drop white and empty
All the toys of the world would break.

[1947]

ROBERT HAYDEN   [1913–1980]

Those Winter Sundays

Sundays too my father got up early
and put his clothes on in the blueblack cold,
then with cracked hands that ached
from labor in the weekday weather made
banked fires blaze. No one ever thanked him.

I'd wake and hear the cold splintering, breaking.
When the rooms were warm, he'd call,
and slowly I would rise and dress,
fearing the chronic angers of that house,

Speaking indifferently to him,
who had driven out the cold
and polished my good shoes as well.
What did I know, what did I know
of love's austere and lonely offices?

[1962]

DUDLEY RANDALL [1914–2000]

Ballad of Birmingham

On the bombing of a church in Birmingham, Alabama, 1963

"Mother dear, may I go downtown
Instead of out to play,
And march the streets of Birmingham
In a Freedom March today?"

"No, baby, no, you may not go,   5
For the dogs are fierce and wild,
And clubs and hoses, guns and jails
Aren't good for a little child."

"But, mother, I won't be alone.
Other children will go with me,   10
And march the streets of Birmingham
To make our country free."

"No, baby, no, you may not go,
For I fear those guns will fire.
But you may go to church instead   15
And sing in the children's choir."

She has combed and brushed her night-dark hair,
And bathed rose petal sweet,
And drawn white gloves on her small brown hands,
And white shoes on her feet.   20

The mother smiled to know her child
Was in the sacred place,
But that smile was the last smile
To come upon her face.

For when she heard the explosion,   25
Her eyes grew wet and wild.
She raced through the streets of Birmingham
Calling for her child.

She clawed through bits of glass and brick,
Then lifted out a shoe.
"Oh, here's the shoe my baby wore,
But, baby, where are you?"

[1969]

WILLIAM STAFFORD   [1914–1995]

Traveling through the Dark

Traveling through the dark I found a deer
dead on the edge of the Wilson River road.
It is usually best to roll them into the canyon:
that road is narrow; to swerve might make more dead.

By glow of the tail-light I stumbled back of the car
and stood by the heap, a doe, a recent killing;
she had stiffened already, almost cold.
I dragged her off; she was large in the belly.

My fingers touching her side brought me the reason—
her side was warm; her fawn lay there waiting,
alive, still, never to be born.
Beside that mountain road I hesitated.

The car aimed ahead its lowered parking lights;
under the hood purred the steady engine.
I stood in the glare of the warm exhaust turning red;
around our group I could hear the wilderness listen.

I thought hard for us all—my only swerving—,
then pushed her over the edge into the river.

[1962]

DYLAN THOMAS   [1914–1953]

Fern Hill

Now as I was young and easy under the apple boughs
About the lilting house and happy as the grass was green,
   The night above the dingle° starry,   *small wooded valley*
     Time let me hail and climb
     Golden in the heydays of his eyes,   5
And honoured among wagons I was prince of the apple towns
And once below a time I lordly had the trees and leaves
     Trail with daisies and barley
     Down the rivers of the windfall light.

And as I was green and carefree, famous among the barns   10
About the happy yard and singing as the farm was home,
     In the sun that is young once only,
       Time let me play and be
     Golden in the mercy of his means,
And green and golden I was huntsman and herdsman, the calves   15
Sang to my horn, the foxes on the hills barked clear and cold,
     And the sabbath rang slowly
     In the pebbles of the holy streams.

All the sun long it was running, it was lovely, the hay
Fields high as the house, the tunes from the chimneys, it was air   20
     And playing, lovely and watery
       And fire green as grass.
     And nightly under the simple stars
As I rode to sleep the owls were bearing the farm away,
All the moon long I heard, blessed among stables, the nightjars   25
     Flying with the ricks, and the horses
       Flashing into the dark.

And then to awake, and the farm, like a wanderer white
With the dew, come back, the cock on his shoulder: it was all
     Shining, it was Adam and maiden,   30
       The sky gathered again
     And the sun grew round that very day.

So it must have been after the birth of the simple light
In the first, spinning place, the spellbound horses walking warm
　　Out of the whinnying green stable
　　　On to the fields of praise.

And honoured among foxes and pheasants by the gay house
Under the new made clouds and happy as the heart was long,
　　In the sun born over and over,
　　　I ran my heedless ways,
　　My wishes raced through the house high hay
And nothing I cared, at my sky blue trades, that time allows
In all his tuneful turning so few and such morning songs
　　Before the children green and golden
　　　Follow him out of grace,

Nothing I cared, in the lamb white days, that time would take me
Up to the swallow thronged loft by the shadow of my hand,
　　In the moon that is always rising,
　　　Nor that riding to sleep
　　I should hear him fly with the high fields
And wake to the farm forever fled from the childless land.
Oh as I was young and easy in the mercy of his means,
　　　Time held me green and dying
　　Though I sang in my chains like the sea.

[1946]

DYLAN THOMAS   [1914–1953]

Do not go gentle into that good night

Do not go gentle into that good night,
Old age should burn and rave at close of day;
Rage, rage against the dying of the light.

Though wise men at their end know dark is right,
Because their words had forked no lightning they
Do not go gentle into that good night.

Good men, the last wave by, crying how bright
Their frail deeds might have danced in a green bay,
Rage, rage against the dying of the light.

Wild men who caught and sang the sun in flight,   10
And learn, too late, they grieved it on its way,
Do not go gentle into that good night.

Grave men, near death, who see with blinding sight
Blind eyes could blaze like meteors and be gay,
Rage, rage against the dying of the light.   15

And you, my father, there on the sad height,
Curse, bless, me now with your fierce tears, I pray.
Do not go gentle into that good night.
Rage, rage against the dying of the light.

[1952]

RANDALL JARRELL   [1914–1965]

The Death of the
Ball Turret Gunner°

From my mother's sleep I fell into the State,
And I hunched in its belly till my wet fur froze.
Six miles from earth, loosed from its dream of life,
I woke to black flak and the nightmare fighters.
When I died they washed me out of the turret with a hose.   5

[1945]

Ball Turret Gunner: "A ball turret was a plexiglass sphere set into the belly of a
B-17 or B-24, and inhabited by two .50 caliber machine-guns and one man, a
short small man. When this gunner tracked with his machine guns a fighter
attacking his bomber from below, he revolved with the turret; hunched upside-
down in his little sphere, he looked like the foetus in the womb. The fighters that
attacked him were armed with cannon-firing explosive shells. The hose was a
steam hose" [Jarrell's note].

GWENDOLYN BROOKS [1917–2000]

We Real Cool

The Pool Players.
Seven at the Golden Shovel.

We real cool. We
Left school. We

Lurk late. We
Strike straight. We

Sing sin. We
Thin gin. We

Jazz° June. We   *have sexual intercourse (with)*
Die soon.

[1960]

GWENDOLYN BROOKS [1917–2000]

The Bean Eaters

They eat beans mostly, this old yellow pair.
Dinner is a casual affair.
Plain chipware on a plain and creaking wood,
Tin flatware.

Two who are Mostly Good.
Two who have lived their day,
But keep on putting on their clothes
and putting things away.

And remembering . . .
Remembering, with twinklings and twinges,   10
As they lean over the beans in their rented back room that
   is full of beads and receipts and dolls and cloths,
    tobacco crumbs, vases and fringes.

                                 [1960]

ROBERT LOWELL   [1917–1978]

Skunk Hour

for Elizabeth Bishop

Nautilus Island's hermit
heiress still lives through winter in her Spartan cottage;
her sheep still graze above the sea.
Her son's a bishop. Her farmer
is first selectman in our village;   5
she's in her dotage.

Thirsting for
the hierarchic privacy
of Queen Victoria's century,
she buys up all   10
the eyesores facing her shore,
and lets them fall.

The season's ill—
we've lost our summer millionaire,
who seemed to leap from an L. L. Bean   15
catalogue. His nine-knot yawl
was auctioned off to lobstermen.
A red fox stain covers Blue Hill.

And now our fairy
decorator brightens his shop for fall;   20
his fishnet's filled with orange cork,
orange, his cobbler's bench and awl;
there is no money in his work,
he'd rather marry.

One dark night,
my Tudor Ford climbed the hill's skull;
I watched for love-cars. Lights turned down,
they lay together, hull to hull,
where the graveyard shelves on the town. . . .
My mind's not right.

A car radio bleats,
"Love, O careless Love. . . ." I hear
my ill-spirit sob in each blood cell,
as if my hand were at its throat. . . .
I myself am hell;
nobody's here—

only skunks, that search
in the moonlight for a bite to eat.
They march on their soles up Main Street:
white stripes, moonstruck eyes' red fire
under the chalk-dry and spar spire
of the Trinitarian Church.

I stand on top
of our back steps and breathe the rich air—
a mother skunk with her column of kittens swills the garbage pail.
She jabs her wedge-head in a cup
of sour cream, drops her ostrich tail,
and will not scare.

[1963]

ROBERT DUNCAN   [1919–1988]

The Torso

Passages 18

Most beautiful!   the red-flowering eucalyptus,
        the madrone,° the yew

    Is he . . .

2. madrone: A type of evergreen tree.

So thou wouldst smile, and take me in thine arms
The sight of London to my exiled eyes   5
Is as Elysium° to a new-come soul   paradise

    If he be Truth
    I would dwell in the illusion of him

His hands unlocking from chambers of my male body

      such an idea in man's image   10

  rising tides that sweep me towards him

      . . . *homosexual?*

      and at the treasure of his mouth

     pour forth my soul

        his soul   commingling   15

I thought a Being more than vast, His body leading
    into Paradise,   his eyes
      quickening a fire in me,   a trembling

   hieroglyph:°   At the root of the neck

the clavicle, for the neck is the stem of the great artery   20
   upward into his head that is beautiful

      At the rise of the pectoral muscle,

the nipples, for the breasts are like sleeping fountains
   of feeling in man, waiting above the beat of his heart,
   shielding the rise and fall of his breath, to be   25
   awakend

      At the axis of his mid hriff

the navel, for in the pit of his stomach the chord from
   which first he was fed has its temple

      At the root of the groin   30

the pubic hair, for the torso is the stem in which the man
   flowers forth and leads to the stamen of flesh in which
   his seed rises

a wave of need and desire over   taking me

      cried out my name   35

---

19. hieroglyph: A picture or symbol representing a word or sound.

(This was long ago.   It was another life)

and said,

What do you want of me?

I do not know, I said.   I have fallen in love.   He
has brought me into heights and depths my heart
would fear   without him.   His look

pierces my side   •   fire eyes   •

I have been waiting for you, he said:
I know what you desire

you do not yet know   but through me   •

And I am with you everywhere.   In your falling

I have fallen from a high place.   I have raised myself

from darkness in your   rising

wherever you are

my hand in your hand   seeking   the locks, the keys

I am there.   Gathering me, you gather

your Self   •

For my Other is not a woman but a man

the King upon whose bosom let me lie.

[1968]

RICHARD WILBUR   [b. 1921]

Love Calls Us to the Things of This World

The eyes open to a cry of pulleys,
And spirited from sleep, the astounded soul
Hangs for a moment bodiless and simple

As false dawn.
                    Outside the open window   5
The morning air is all awash with angels.

    Some are in bed-sheets, some are in blouses,
Some are in smocks: but truly there they are.
Now they are rising together in calm swells
Of halcyon feeling, filling whatever they wear   10
With the deep joy of their impersonal breathing;

    Now they are flying in place, conveying
The terrible speed of their omnipresence, moving
And staying like white water; and now of a sudden
They swoon down into so rapt a quiet   15
That nobody seems to be there.
                              The soul shrinks

From all that it is about to remember,
From the punctual rape of every blessèd day,
And cries,   20
            "Oh, let there be nothing on earth but laundry,
Nothing but rosy hands in the rising steam
And clear dances done in the sight of heaven."

    Yet, as the sun acknowledges
With a warm look the world's hunks and colors,   25
The soul descends once more in bitter love
To accept the waking body, saying now
In a changed voice as the man yawns and rises,

    "Bring them down from their ruddy gallows;
Let there be clean linen for the backs of thieves;   30
Let lovers go fresh and sweet to be undone,
And the heaviest nuns walk in a pure floating
Of dark habits,
                    keeping their difficult balance."

                                                                     [1956]

DENISE LEVERTOV   [1923–1997]

Talking to Grief

Ah, grief, I should not treat you
like a homeless dog
who comes to the back door
for a crust, for a meatless bone.
I should trust you.

I should coax you
into the house and give you
your own corner,
a worn mat to lie on,
your own water dish.

You think I don't know you've been living
under my porch.
You long for your real place to be readied
before winter comes. You need
your name,
your collar and tag. You need
the right to warn off intruders,
to consider
my house your own
and me your person
and yourself
my own dog.

[1978]

MAXINE KUMIN   [b. 1925]

The Sound of Night

And now the dark comes on, all full of chitter noise.
Birds huggermugger crowd the trees,
the air thick with their vesper cries,
and bats, snub seven-pointed kites,
skitter across the lake, swing out,   5
squeak, chirp, dip, and skim on skates
of air, and the fat frogs wake and prink°   *primp*
wide-lipped, noisy as ducks, drunk
on the boozy black, gloating chink-chunk.

And now on the narrow beach we defend ourselves from dark.   10
The cooking done, we build our firework
bright and hot and less for outlook
than for magic, and lie in our blankets
while night nickers around us. Crickets
chorus hallelujahs; paws, quiet   15
and quick as raindrops, play on the stones
expertly soft, run past and are gone;
fish pulse in the lake; the frogs hoarsen.

Now every voice of the hour—the known, the supposed, the strange,
the mindless, the witted, the never seen—   20
sing, thrum, impinge, and rearrange
endlessly; and debarred from sleep we wait
for the birds, importantly silent,
for the crease of first eye-licking light,
for the sun, lost long ago and sweet.   25
By the lake, locked black away and tight,
we lie, day creatures, overhearing night.

[1961]

585

GERALD STERN   [b. 1925]

The Dog

What I was doing with my white teeth exposed
like that on the side of the road I don't know,
and I don't know why I lay beside the sewer
so that lover of dead things could come back
with his pencil sharpened and his piece of white paper.
I was there for a good two hours whistling
dirges, shrieking a little, terrifying
hearts with my whimpering cries before I died
by pulling the one leg up and stiffening.
There is a look we have with the hair of the chin
curled in mid-air, there is a look with the belly
stopped in the midst of its greed. The lover of dead things
stoops to feel me, his hand is shaking. I know
his mouth is open and his glasses are slipping.
I think his pencil must be jerking and the terror
of smell—and sight—is overtaking him;
I know he has that terrified faraway look
that death brings—he is contemplating. I want him
to touch my forehead once and rub my muzzle
before he lifts me up and throws me into
that little valley. I hope he doesn't use
his shoe for fear of touching me; I know,
or used to know, the grasses down there; I think
I knew a hundred smells. I hope the dog's way
doesn't overtake him, one quick push,
barely that, and the mind freed, something else,
some other thing, to take its place. Great heart,
great human heart, keep loving me as you lift me,
give me your tears, great loving stranger, remember
the death of dogs, forgive the yapping, forgive
the shitting, let there be pity, give me your pity.
How could there be enough? I have given
my life for this, emotion has ruined me, oh lover,
I have exchanged my wildness—little tricks

with the mouth and feet, with the tail, my tongue is a parrot's,   35
I am a rampant horse, I am a lion,
I wait for the cookie, I snap my teeth—
as you have taught me, oh distant and brilliant and lonely.

[1987]

FRANK O'HARA   [1926–1966]

The Day Lady° Died

It is 12:20 in New York a Friday
three days after Bastille day,° yes   *(July 14)*
it is 1959 and I go get a shoeshine
because I will get off the 4:19 in Easthampton
at 7:15 and then go straight to dinner   5
and I don't know the people who will feed me

I walk up the muggy street beginning to sun
and have a hamburger and a malted and buy
an ugly NEW WORLD WRITING to see what the poets
in Ghana are doing these days   10
                    I go on to the bank
and Miss Stillwagon (first name Linda I once heard)
doesn't even look up my balance for once in her life
and in the GOLDEN GRIFFIN I get a little Verlaine°   *French poet*
for Patsy with drawings by Bonnard° although I do   15
think of Hesiod,° trans. Richmond Lattimore or   *Greek poet*
Brendan Behan's° new play or *Le Balcon or Les Nègres*   *Irish playwright*
of Genet,° but I don't, I stick with Verlaine
after practically going to sleep with quandariness

and for Mike I just stroll into the PARK LANE   20
Liquor Store and ask for a bottle of Strega and
then I go back where I came from to 6th Avenue
and the tobacconist in the Ziegfeld Theatre and

Lady: Jazz singer Billie Holiday (1915–1959).
15. Bonnard: French modernist painter.
18. Genet: French playwright and novelist.

casually ask for a carton of Gauloises° and a carton   *French cigarettes*
of Picayunes,° and a NEW YORK POST with her face on it   *southern cigarettes*

and I am sweating a lot by now and thinking of
leaning on the john door in the 5 SPOT
while she whispered a song along the keyboard
to Mal Waldron and everyone and I stopped breathing

[1964]

ALLEN GINSBERG   [1926–1997]

A Supermarket in California

What thoughts I have of you tonight, Walt Whitman, for I walked down the sidestreets under the trees with a headache self-conscious looking at the full moon.

In my hungry fatigue, and shopping for images, I went into the neon fruit supermarket, dreaming of your enumerations!

What peaches and what penumbras! Whole families shopping at night! Aisles full of husbands! Wives in the avocados, babies in the tomatoes!—and you, García Lorca,° what were you doing down by the watermelons?

I saw you, Walt Whitman, childless, lonely old grubber, poking among the meats in the refrigerator and eyeing the grocery boys.

I heard you asking questions of each: Who killed the pork chops? What price bananas? Are you my Angel?

I wandered in and out of the brilliant stacks of cans following you, and followed in my imagination by the store detective.

We strode down the open corridors together in our solitary fancy tasting artichokes, possessing every frozen delicacy, and never passing the cashier.

Where are we going, Walt Whitman? The doors close in an hour. Which way does your beard point tonight?

(I touch your book and dream of our odyssey in the supermarket and feel absurd.)

3. **García Lorca:** Spanish surrealist poet and playwright (1899–1936).

Will we walk all night through solitary streets? The trees add shade to shade, lights out in the houses, we'll both be lonely.   10

Will we stroll dreaming of the lost America of love past blue automobiles in driveways, home to our silent cottage?

Ah, dear father, graybeard, lonely old courage-teacher, what America did you have when Charon° quit poling his ferry and you got out on a smoking bank and stood watching the boat disappear on the black waters of Lethe?°

Berkeley, 1955

[1956]

12. **Charon:** The boatman in Greek mythology who carried the dead across the river Styx to Hades. **Lethe:** River of Forgetfulness in Hades.

GALWAY KINNELL [b. 1927]

The Bear

1

In late winter
I sometimes glimpse bits of steam
coming up from
some fault in the old snow
and bend close and see it is lung-colored   5
and put down my nose
and know
the chilly, enduring odor of bear.

2

I take a wolf's rib and whittle
it sharp at both ends   10
and coil it up
and freeze it in blubber and place it out
on the fairway of the bears.

And when it has vanished
I move out on the bear tracks,   15

roaming in circles
until I come to the first, tentative, dark
splash on the earth.

And I set out
running, following the splashes
of blood wandering over the world.
At the cut, gashed resting places
I stop and rest,
at the crawl-marks
where he lay out on his belly
to overpass some stretch of bauchy° ice   *weak, thin*
I lie out
dragging myself forward with bear-knives in my fists.

3

On the third day I begin to starve,
at nightfall I bend down as I knew I would
at a turd sopped in blood,
and hesitate, and pick it up,
and thrust it in my mouth, and gnash it down,
and rise
and go on running.

4

On the seventh day,
living by now on bear blood alone,
I can see his upturned carcass far out ahead, a scraggled,
steamy hulk,
the heavy fur riffling in the wind.

I come up to him
and stare at the narrow-spaced, petty eyes,
the dismayed
face laid back on the shoulder, the nostrils
flared, catching
perhaps the first taint of me as he
died.

I hack
a ravine in his thigh, and eat and drink,
and tear him down his whole length
and open him and climb in
and close him up after me, against the wind,
and sleep.

5

And dream
of lumbering flatfooted   55
over the tundra,
stabbed twice from within,
splattering a trail behind me,
splattering it out no matter which way I lurch,
no matter which parabola of bear-transcendence,   60
which dance of solitude I attempt,
which gravity-clutched leap,
which trudge, which groan.

6

Until one day I totter and fall—
fall on this   65
stomach that has tried so hard to keep up,
to digest the blood as it leaked in,
to break up
and digest the bone itself: and now the breeze
blows over me, blows off   70
the hideous belches of ill-digested bear blood
and rotted stomach
and the ordinary, wretched odor of bear,

blows across
my sore, lolled tongue a song   75
or screech, until I think I must rise up
and dance. And I lie still.

7

I awaken I think. Marshlights
reappear, geese
come trailing again up the flyway.   80
In her ravine under old snow the dam-bear
lies, licking
lumps of smeared fur
and drizzly eyes into shapes
with her tongue. And one   85
hairy-soled trudge stuck out before me,
the next groaned out,
the next,
the next,
the rest of my days I spend   90

wandering: wondering
what, anyway,
was that sticky infusion, that rank flavor of blood, that poetry, by which
   I lived?

[1967]

JAMES WRIGHT   [1927–1980]

A Blessing

Just off the highway to Rochester, Minnesota,
Twilight bounds softly forth on the grass.
And the eyes of those two Indian ponies
Darken with kindness.
They have come gladly out of the willows
To welcome my friend and me.
We step over the barbed wire into the pasture
Where they have been grazing all day, alone.

They ripple tensely, they can hardly contain their happiness
That we have come.
They bow shyly as wet swans. They love each other.
There is no loneliness like theirs.
At home once more,
They begin munching the young tufts of spring in the darkness.
I would like to hold the slenderer one in my arms,
For she has walked over to me
And nuzzled my left hand.
She is black and white,
Her mane falls wild on her forehead,
And the light breeze moves me to caress her long ear
That is delicate as the skin over a girl's wrist.
Suddenly I realize
That if I stepped out of my body I would break
Into blossom.

[1963]

PHILIP LEVINE   [b. 1928]

What Work Is

We stand in the rain in a long line
waiting at Ford Highland Park. For work.
You know what work is — if you're
old enough to read this you know what
work is, although you may not do it.   5
Forget you. This is about waiting,
shifting from one foot to another.
Feeling the light rain falling like mist
into your hair, blurring your vision
until you think you see your own brother   10
ahead of you, maybe ten places.
You rub your glasses with your fingers,
and of course it's someone else's brother,
narrower across the shoulders than
yours but with the same sad slouch, the grin   15
that does not hide the stubbornness,
the sad refusal to give in to
rain, to the hours wasted waiting,
to the knowledge that somewhere ahead
a man is waiting who will say, "No,   20
we're not hiring today," for any
reason he wants. You love your brother,
now suddenly you can hardly stand
the love flooding you for your brother,
who's not beside you or behind or   25
ahead because he's home trying to
sleep off a miserable night shift
at Cadillac so he can get up
before noon to study his German.
Works eight hours a night so he can sing   30
Wagner, the opera you hate most,
the worst music ever invented.
How long has it been since you told him
you loved him, held his wide shoulders,

opened your eyes wide and said those words,
and maybe kissed his cheek? You've never
done something so simple, so obvious,
not because you're too young or too dumb,
not because you're jealous or even mean
or incapable of crying in
the presence of another man, no,
just because you don't know what work is.

[1991]

CONRAD HILBERRY   [b. 1928]

Player Piano

She was right: basement was the place for it.
Who wants a Pianola in the dining room?
It's not an instrument, not a household
object even, more a curiosity.

So with a rented dolly and four big friends
from work, he eased it down the cellar stairs,
across the concrete to its place against
the wall. Now he leans back on the bench

and pumps the Basement Rag. His youngest daughter
sits beside him on the bench within
the light of the gooseneck lamp, the dog curls
on the rug, and always the ghostly fingers move,

the left hand striding and the right hand climbing
down out of the high notes. Four of them,
father, daughter, dog, and piano player,
all in a circle of light, the roll unwinding

its dots and dashes, music clattering out,
and no one saying anything. "Hey,
Cosby's on,"° his wife calls down the stairs.
"Why not come on up?" And so they sit

19. Cosby's on: *The Cosby Show* was a popular television situation comedy
(1984–1992) starring Bill Cosby and Phylicia Rashad.

in the kitchen, laughing at Rudy and the Cos.
Afterwards, homework and bed—and he drifts
back to the basement, back to the wooden music.
Gradually, his wife becomes sarcastic,

as if he were counterfeiting bills down there,   25
or dissecting cats. His daughter says she isn't
coming down. But he believes the piano
brings him closer to them all. It's something

he can count on, almost like a law
of nature, not needing praise or inspiration,   30
sticking to its version of the story.
The roll scrolling in front of him is

Morse code talking to people in other basements
or in huts or lean-to's—Sarasota, Caracas,
up-country Liberia. The key taps out   35
news of high winds, the river rising, families

sheltered in the local school, news
of people he's never met, clicking in a voice
without inflection, neither speech
nor silence. The longs and shorts, the steady   40

white keys and the black must carry
through the studs of the house, he thinks,
easing the children into sleep.
He hears a pipe muttering

and knows his wife is drawing water for   45
a bath. It stops. She must be in the tub.
He taps a message on the pipe, binary,
the way nerves talk, signaling across

the gaps, need and love condensed to dots
and dashes. She must hear it as she steams   50
and lathers in the bath, metallic music
played by no one's fingers on the pipes.

[1999]

SAMUEL HAZO [b. 1928]

For Fawzi in Jerusalem

Leaving a world too old to name
and too undying to forsake,
I flew the cold, expensive sea
toward Columbus' mistake
where life could never be the same

for me. In Jerash° on the sand
I saw the colonnades of Rome
bleach in the sun like skeletons.
Behind a convalescent home,
armed soldiers guarded no man's land

between Jordanians and Jews.
Opposing sentries frowned and spat.
Fawzi, you mocked in Arabic
this justice from Jehoshophat°
before you shined my Pittsburgh shoes

for nothing. Why you never kept
the coins I offered you is still
your secret and your victory.
Saying you saw marauders kill
your father while Beershebans° wept

for mercy in their holy war,
you told me how you stole to stay
alive. You must have thought I thought

---

6. Jerash: The ancient city of Gerasa, twenty-two miles north of Amman in present-day Jordan. Called Jerash by the Romans who rebuilt it in 65 C.E., it is the best-preserved Palestinian city of Roman times.
14. Jehoshophat: Hebrew king of Judah (c. 873–849 B.C.E.), the first to make a treaty with the neighboring kingdom of Israel.
20. Beershebans: Inhabitants of Beersheba, a city in southern Israel. Given to the Arabs in the partition of Palestine (1948), it was retaken by Israel in the Arab-Israeli war of 1948.

your history would make me pay
a couple of piastres more   25

than any shine was worth—and I
was ready to—when you said, "No,
I never take. I never want
America to think I throw
myself on you. I never lie."   30

I watched your young but old man's stare
demand the sword to flash again
in blood and flame from Jericho°
and leave the bones of these new men
of Judah bleaching in the air   35

like Roman stones upon the plain
of Jerash. Then you faced away.
Jerusalem, Jerusalem,
I asked myself if I could pray
for peace and not recall the pain   40

you spoke. But what could praying do?
Today I live your loss in no
man's land but mine, and every time
I talk of fates not just but so,
Fawzi, my friend, I think of you.   45

                                                          [1968]

33. **Jericho:** Ancient city in biblical Palestine, in the Jordan valley north of the
Dead Sea, captured from the Canaanites by Joshua and destroyed (Joshua 6:1–21).

ANNE SEXTON   [1928–1974]

Cinderella

You always read about it:
the plumber with twelve children
who wins the Irish Sweepstakes.
From toilets to riches.
That story.   5

Or the nursemaid,
some luscious sweet from Denmark
who captures the oldest son's heart.
From diapers to Dior.°
That story.

Or a milkman who serves the wealthy,
eggs, cream, butter, yogurt, milk,
the white truck like an ambulance
who goes into real estate
and makes a pile.
From homogenized to martinis at lunch.

Or the charwoman
who is on the bus when it cracks up
and collects enough from the insurance.
    From mops to Bonwit Teller.°
    That story.

Once
the wife of a rich man was on her deathbed
and she said to her daughter Cinderella:
Be devout. Be good. Then I will smile
down from heaven in the seam of a cloud.
The man took another wife who had
two daughters, pretty enough
but with hearts like blackjacks.
Cinderella was their maid.
She slept on the sooty hearth each night
and walked around looking like Al Jolson.°
Her father brought presents home from town,
jewels and gowns for the other women
but the twig of a tree for Cinderella.
She planted that twig on her mother's grave
and it grew to a tree where a white dove sat.
Whenever she wished for anything the dove
would drop it like an egg upon the ground.
The bird is important, my dears, so heed him.

---

9. Dior: Fashions designed by the French house of Dior, established by Christian Dior (1905–1957).
20. Bonwit Teller: A fashionable and expensive department store.
32. Al Jolson: American entertainer (1888–1950), known particularly for singing in blackface.

Next came the ball, as you all know.
It was a marriage market.
The prince was looking for a wife.
All but Cinderella were preparing
and gussying up for the big event.   45
Cinderella begged to go too.
Her stepmother threw a dish of lentils
into the cinders and said: Pick them
up in an hour and you shall go.
The white dove brought all his friends;   50
all the warm wings of the fatherland came,
and picked up the lentils in a jiffy.
No, Cinderella, said the stepmother,
you have no clothes and cannot dance.
That's the way with stepmothers.   55

Cinderella went to the tree at the grave
and cried forth like a gospel singer:
Mama! Mama! My turtledove,
send me to the prince's ball!
The bird dropped down a golden dress   60
and delicate little gold slippers.
Rather a large package for a simple bird.
So she went. Which is no surprise.
Her stepmother and sisters didn't
recognize her without her cinder face   65
and the prince took her hand on the spot
and danced with no other the whole day.

As nightfall came she thought she'd better
get home. The prince walked her home
and she disappeared into the pigeon house   70
and although the prince took an axe and broke
it open she was gone. Back to her cinders.
These events repeated themselves for three days.
However on the third day the prince
covered the palace steps with cobbler's wax   75
and Cinderella's gold shoe stuck upon it.

Now he would find whom the shoe fit
and find his strange dancing girl for keeps.
He went to their house and the two sisters
were delighted because they had lovely feet.   80
The eldest went into a room to try the slipper on

but her big toe got in the way so she simply
sliced it off and put on the slipper.
The prince rode away with her until the white dove
told him to look at the blood pouring forth.
That is the way with amputations.
They don't just heal up like a wish.
The other sister cut off her heel
but the blood told as blood will.
The prince was getting tired.
He began to feel like a shoe salesman.
But he gave it one last try.
This time Cinderella fit into the shoe
like a love letter into its envelope.

At the wedding ceremony
the two sisters came to curry favor
and the white dove pecked their eyes out.
Two hollow spots were left
like soup spoons.

Cinderella and the prince
lived, they say, happily ever after,
like two dolls in a museum case
never bothered by diapers or dust,
never arguing over the timing of an egg,
never telling the same story twice,
never getting a middle-aged spread,
their darling smiles pasted on for eternity.
Regular Bobbsey Twins.°
That story.

[1971]

108. Bobbsey Twins: Principal characters in a popular series of children's
books, published between 1904 and 1979. In illustrations they are depicted as
carefully dressed, always smiling, and in idyllic circumstances.

ADRIENNE RICH   [b. 1929–2012]

Aunt Jennifer's Tigers

Aunt Jennifer's tigers prance across a screen,
Bright topaz denizens of a world of green.
They do not fear the men beneath the tree;
They pace in sleek chivalric certainty.

Aunt Jennifer's fingers fluttering through her wool   5
Find even the ivory needle hard to pull.
The massive weight of Uncle's wedding band
Sits heavily upon Aunt Jennifer's hand.

When Aunt is dead, her terrified hands will lie
Still ringed with ordeals she was mastered by.   10
The tigers in the panel that she made
Will go on prancing, proud and unafraid.

                                              [1951]

ADRIENNE RICH   [b. 1929–2012]

Diving into the Wreck

First having read the book of myths,
and loaded the camera,
and checked the edge of the knife-blade,
I put on
the body-armor of black rubber   5
the absurd flippers
the grave and awkward mask.
I am having to do this

601

not like Cousteau° with his
assiduous team
aboard the sun-flooded schooner
but here alone.

There is a ladder.
The ladder is always there
hanging innocently
close to the side of the schooner.
We know what it is for,
we who have used it.
Otherwise
it's a piece of maritime floss
some sundry equipment.

I go down.
Rung after rung and still
the oxygen immerses me
the blue light
the clear atoms
of our human air.
I go down.
My flippers cripple me,
I crawl like an insect down the ladder
and there is no one
to tell me when the ocean
will begin.

First the air is blue and then
it is bluer and then green and then
black I am blacking out and yet
my mask is powerful
it pumps my blood with power
the sea is another story
the sea is not a question of power
I have to learn alone
to turn my body without force
in the deep element.

And now: it is easy to forget
what I came for
among so many who have always

9. **Cousteau:** Jacques-Yves Cousteau (1910–1997), French underwater explorer, photographer, and author.

lived here
swaying their crenellated° fans
between the reefs
and besides   50
you breathe differently down here.

I came to explore the wreck.
The words are purposes.
The words are maps.
I came to see the damage that was done   55
and the treasures that prevail.
I stroke the beam of my lamp
slowly along the flank
of something more permanent
than fish or weed   60

the thing I came for:
the wreck and not the story of the wreck
the thing itself and not the myth
the drowned face° always staring
toward the sun   65
the evidence of damage
worn by salt and sway into this threadbare beauty
the ribs of the disaster
curving their assertion
among the tentative haunters.   70

This is the place.
And I am here, the mermaid whose dark hair
streams black, the merman in his armored body
We circle silently
about the wreck   75
we dive into the hold.
I am she: I am he

whose drowned face sleeps with open eyes
whose breasts still bear the stress
whose silver, copper, vermeil° cargo lies   80
obscurely inside barrels

---

48. crenellated: Notched; *crenels* are the open spaces between the solid portions
of a battlement.
64. drowned face: The ornamental female figurehead on the prow of an old
sailing ship.
80. vermeil: Gilded silver, bronze, or copper.

half-wedged and left to rot
we are the half-destroyed instruments
that once held to a course
the water-eaten log
the fouled compass

We are, I am, you are
by cowardice or courage
the one who find our way
back to this scene
carrying a knife, a camera
a book of myths
in which
our names do not appear.

[1973]

GARY SNYDER   [b. 1930]

Hitch Haiku

They didn't hire him
            so he ate his lunch alone:
the noon whistle

                        • • •

Cats shut down
            deer thread through
men all eating lunch

                        • • •

Frying hotcakes in a dripping shelter
            Fu Manchu°
Queets Indian Reservation in the rain

                        • • •

A truck went by
            three hours ago:
Smoke Creek desert

---

8. Fu Manchu: Master criminal in a series of "Yellow Peril Thrillers" by Sax
Rohmer (pen name of Arthur Henry Sarsfield Ward, 1883–1959) that were immensely popular in the first half of the twentieth century.

● ● ●

Jackrabbit eyes all night
   breakfast in Elko.

             ● ● ●

Old kanji° hid by dirt   15
on skidroad Jap town walls
         down the hill
to the Wobbly hall

                        Seattle

             ● ● ●

Spray drips from the cargo-booms   20
a fresh-chipped winch
         spotted with red lead
young fir—
       soaking in summer rain

             ● ● ●

Over the Mindanao Deep   25

Scrap bass
       dumpt off the fantail
falling six miles

             ● ● ●

[*The following two were written on classical
themes while traveling through Sappho, Washington.
The first is by Thomas L. Hoodlatch.*]

Moonlight on the burned-out temple—
       wooden horse shit.   30
Sunday dinner in Ithaca—
      the twang of a bowstring

            ● ● ●

After weeks of watching the roof leak
     I fixed it tonight
by moving a single board   35

           ● ● ●

*A freezing morning in October in the high
Sierra crossing Five Lakes Basin to the
Kaweahs with Bob Greensfelder and Claude Dalenburg*

Stray white mare
       neck rope dangling   40
forty miles from farms.

---

15. kanji: Japanese written characters, or ideographs, borrowed and adapted
from Chinese ideographs.

• • •

Back from the Kaweahs

Sundown, Timber Gap
　　　—sat down—
　　　　　dark firs.
　dirty;　cold;
too tired to talk

• • •

Cherry blossoms at Hood river
　　　　　rusty sand near Tucson
mudflats of Willapa Bay

• • •

Pronghorn country

Steering into the sun
　　　　　glittering jewel-road
shattered obsidian

• • •

The mountain walks over the water!
Rain down from the mountain!
　　　　high bleat of a
cow elk
　　　over blackberries

• • •

A great freight truck
　　　　lit like a town
through the dark stony desert

• • •

Drinking hot saké
　　　　　toasting fish on coals
　the motorcycle
out　　parked in the rain.

• • •

Switchback

turn, turn,
and again,　　hard-
scrabble
steep travel a-
head.

[1968]

LINDA PASTAN   [b. 1932]

love poem

I want to write you
a love poem as headlong
as our creek
after thaw
when we stand   5
on its dangerous
banks and watch it carry
with it every twig
every dry leaf and branch
in its path   10
every scruple
when we see it
so swollen
with runoff
that even as we watch   15
we must grab
each other
and step back
we must grab each
other or   20
get our shoes
soaked we must
grab each other

[1988]

SYLVIA PLATH   [1932–1963]

Metaphors

I'm a riddle in nine syllables,
An elephant, a ponderous house,
A melon strolling on two tendrils.
O red fruit, ivory, fine timbers!
This loaf's big with its yeasty rising.
Money's new-minted in this fat purse.
I'm a means, a stage, a cow in calf.
I've eaten a bag of green apples,
Boarded the train there's no getting off.

[1960]

SYLVIA PLATH   [1932–1963]

Morning Song

Love set you going like a fat gold watch.
The midwife slapped your footsoles, and your bald cry
Took its place among the elements.

Our voices echo, magnifying your arrival. New statue
In a drafty museum, your nakedness
Shadows our safety. We stand round blankly as walls.

I'm no more your mother
Than the cloud that distils a mirror to reflect its own slow
Effacement at the wind's hand.

All night your moth-breath
Flickers among the flat pink roses. I wake to listen:
A far sea moves in my ear.

One cry, and I stumble from bed, cow-heavy and floral
In my Victorian nightgown.
Your mouth opens clean as a cat's. The window square   15

Whitens and swallows its dull stars. And now you try
Your handful of notes;
The clear vowels rise like balloons.

[*1961*; 1965]

SYLVIA PLATH   [1932–1963]

Daddy

You do not do, you do not do
Any more, black shoe
In which I have lived like a foot
For thirty years, poor and white,
Barely daring to breathe or Achoo.   5

Daddy, I have had to kill you.
You died before I had time—
Marble-heavy, a bag full of God,
Ghastly statue with one grey toe
Big as a Frisco seal   10

And a head in the freakish Atlantic
Where it pours bean green over blue
In the waters off beautiful Nauset.
I used to pray to recover you.
Ach, du.°   *Oh, you (German)*   15

In the German tongue, in the Polish town
Scraped flat by the roller
Of wars, wars, wars.
But the name of the town is common.
My Polack friend   20

Says there are a dozen or two.
So I never could tell where you
Put your foot, your root,

I never could talk to you.
The tongue stuck in my jaw.

It stuck in a barb wire snare.
Ich, ich, ich, ich,°   *I (German)*
I could hardly speak.
I thought every German was you.
And the language obscene

An engine, an engine
Chuffing me off like a Jew.
A Jew to Dachau, Auschwitz, Belsen.°
I began to talk like a Jew.
I think I may well be a Jew.

The snows of the Tyrol,° the clear beer of Vienna
Are not very pure or true.
With my gypsy ancestress and my weird luck
And my Taroc pack and my Taroc pack
I may be a bit of a Jew.

I have always been scared of *you*,
With your Luftwaffe,° your gobbledygoo.
And your neat moustache
And your Aryan eye, bright blue.
Panzer°-man, panzer-man, O You—

Not God but a swastika
So black no sky could squeak through.
Every woman adores a Fascist,
The boot in the face, the brute
Brute heart of a brute like you.

You stand at the blackboard, daddy,
In the picture I have of you,
A cleft in your chin instead of your foot
But no less a devil for that, no not
Any less the black man who

Bit my pretty red heart in two.
I was ten when they buried you.

33. **Dachau, Auschwitz, Belsen:** Nazi concentration camps.
36. **the Tyrol:** An alpine region in western Austria and northern Italy.
42. **Luftwaffe:** The Nazi air force in World War II.
45. **Panzer:** An armored unit in the German army in World War II.

At twenty I tried to die
And get back, back, back to you.
I thought even the bones would do.   60

But they pulled me out of the sack,
And they stuck me together with glue.
And then I knew what to do.
I made a model of you,
A man in black with a Meinkampf° look   65

And a love of the rack and the screw.
And I said I do, I do.
So daddy, I'm finally through.
The black telephone's off at the root,
The voices just can't worm through.   70

If I've killed one man, I've killed two—
The vampire who said he was you
And drank my blood for a year,
Seven years, if you want to know.
Daddy, you can lie back now.   75

There's a stake in your fat black heart
And the villagers never liked you.
They are dancing and stamping on you.
They always *knew* it was you.
Daddy, daddy, you bastard, I'm through.   80

[1962]

65. MeinKampf: *Mein Kampf* (or *My Struggle*), the title of Adolf Hitler's autobiography.

ETHERIDGE KNIGHT   [1933–1991]

Hard Rock Returns to Prison from the Hospital for the Criminal Insane

Hard Rock / was / "known not to take no shit
From nobody," and he had the scars to prove it:
Split purple lips, lumbed ears, welts above
His yellow eyes, and one long scar that cut
Across his temple and plowed through a thick
Canopy of kinky hair.

The WORD / was / that Hard Rock wasn't a mean nigger
Anymore, that the doctors had bored a hole in his head,
Cut out part of his brain, and shot electricity
Through the rest. When they brought Hard Rock back,
Handcuffed and chained, he was turned loose,
Like a freshly gelded stallion, to try his new status.
And we all waited and watched, like a herd of sheep,
To see if the WORD was true.

As we waited we wrapped ourselves in the cloak
Of his exploits: "Man, the last time, it took eight
Screws° to put him in the Hole."° "Yeah, remember when he
Smacked the captain with his dinner tray?" "He set
The record for time in the Hole—67 straight days!"
"Ol Hard Rock! man, that's one crazy nigger."
And then the jewel of a myth that Hard Rock had once bit
A screw on the thumb and poisoned him with syphilitic spit.

The testing came, to see if Hard Rock was really tame.
A hillbilly called him a black son of a bitch
And didn't lose his teeth, a screw who knew Hard Rock
From before shook him down and barked in his face.

17. Screws: Guards; **Hole:** Solitary confinement.

612

And Hard Rock did *nothing*. Just grinned and looked silly,
His eyes empty like knot holes in a fence.

And even after we discovered that it took Hard Rock
Exactly 3 minutes to tell you his first name,   30
We told ourselves that he had just wised up,
Was being cool; but we could not fool ourselves for long,
And we turned away, our eyes on the ground. Crushed.
He had been our Destroyer, the doer of things
We dreamed of doing but could not bring ourselves to do,   35
The fears of years, like a biting whip,
Had cut deep bloody grooves
Across our backs.

[1968]

JIM BARNES   [b. 1933]

Return to La Plata, Missouri

The warping bandstand reminds you of the hard rage
you felt in the heart of the town the day you said goodbye
to the park, silver jet, and cicadas dead in the sage.

The town is basic red, although it browns. A cry
of murder, rape, or wrong will always bend the night   5
hard into the broken grass. You listen close for sighs

of lovers on the ground. The darkness gathers light
and throws it down: something glows that you cannot name,
something fierce, abstract, given time and space you might

on a journey leave behind, a stone to carve your fame   10
on, or a simple word like *love*. The sun is down
or always going down in La Plata, the same

sun. Same too the child's cry that turns the mother's frown
brittle as chalk or the town's face against the moon.
Same too the moan of dog and diesel circling the town   15

in an air so heavy with cloud that there is little room
for breath or moon. Strange: in a town so country, so
foreign, you never hear a song nor see a loom

pattern dark threads into a history you would know
and would not know. You think you see one silver star.
But the town offers only itself, and you must go.

[1982]

WENDELL BERRY   [b. 1934]

The Peace of Wild Things

When despair for the world grows in me
and I wake in the night at the least sound
in fear of what my life and my children's lives may be,
I go and lie down where the wood drake
rests in his beauty on the water, and the great heron feeds.
I come into the peace of wild things
who do not tax their lives with forethought
of grief. I come into the presence of still water.
And I feel above me the day-blind stars
waiting with their light. For a time
I rest in the grace of the world, and am free.

[1968]

AUDRE LORDE   [1934–1992]

Coal

I   is the total black
being spoken
from the earth's inside.

There are many kinds of open
how a diamond comes   5
into a knot of flame
how sound comes into a word
colored
by who pays what for speaking.

Some words are open   10
diamonds on a glass window
singing out within the crash
of passing sun
other words are stapled wagers
in a perforated book   15
buy and sign and tear apart
and come whatever wills all chances
the stub remains
an ill-pulled tooth
with a ragged edge.   20

Some words live in my throat
breeding like adders
others
know sun
seeking like gypsies   25
over my tongue
to explode through my lips
like young sparrows
bursting from shell.

Some words   30
bedevil me.

Love is a word, another kind of open.
As the diamond comes
into a knot of flame
I am Black   35
because I come from the earth's inside
take my word for jewel
in the open light.

[*1962;* rev. 1992]

MARK STRAND   [b. 1934]

Eating Poetry

Ink runs from the corners of my mouth.
There is no happiness like mine.
I have been eating poetry.

The librarian does not believe what she sees.
Her eyes are sad
and she walks with her hands in her dress.

The poems are gone.
The light is dim.
The dogs are on the basement stairs and coming up.

Their eyeballs roll,
their blond legs burn like brush.
The poor librarian begins to stamp her feet and weep.

She does not understand.
When I get on my knees and lick her hand,
she screams.

I am a new man.
I snarl at her and bark.
I romp with joy in the bookish dark.

[1968]

PAUL ZIMMER   [b. 1934]

The Poets' Strike

On the stroke of this midnight
Let us cover our typewriters,
Throw down all pens and papers,
Build kindling fires in oil drums.
Let there be no more poems,   5
Not one more metaphor nor image,
No loose nor strict iambics,
No passion, anger, laughter.
Let no one cheat nor scab,
No furtive peeks in notebooks,   10
No secret scribbling in closets,
Let us dwell together in a void
Removed from beauty and truth.

Then let us see what happens,
How many trees will blight,   15
How earth wobbles and fractures,
Words loosen and fall from dictionaries.
People will move through life
Like worms swallowing
And excreting their tedious passage.   20
They'll beg us for one crippled line,
One near rhyme, One feeble dream,
And they will be so sorry
They will pay and pay and pay.

                                                        [1989]

617

CHARLES WRIGHT   [b. 1935]

March Journal

—After the Rapture° comes, and everyone goes away
Quicker than cream in a cat's mouth,
                                    all of them gone
In an endless slipknot down the sky
                                    and its pink tongue
Into the black hole of Somewhere Else,

What will we do, left with the empty spaces of our lives
Intact,
          the radio frequencies still unchanged,
The same houses up for sale,
Same books unread,
                    all comfort gone and its comforting . . .

For us, the earth is a turbulent rest,
                                    a different bed
Altogether, and kinder than that—
After the first death is the second,
A little fire in the afterglow,
                              somewhere to warm your hands.

—The clean, clear line, incised, unbleeding,
Sharp and declarative as a cut
                              the instant before the blood wells out . . .

—*March Blues*
The insides were blue, the color of Power Putty,
When Luke dissected the dogfish,
                                    a plastic blue
In the whey
          sharkskin infenestrated:
Its severed tailfin bobbed like a wing nut in another pan

1. the Rapture: Refers to the Christian idea of Jesus Christ's second coming,
during which the righteous will be caught up into heaven.

As he explained the dye job
                              and what connected with what,   30
Its pursed lips skewed and pointed straight-lined at the ceiling,
The insides so blue, so blue . . .

March gets its second wind,
                              starlings high shine in the trees
As dread puts its left foot down and then the other.   35
Buds hold their breaths and sit tight.
The weeping cherries
                    lower their languorous necks and nibble the grass
Sprout ends that jump headfirst from the ground,
Magnolia drums blue weight   40
                              next door when the sun is right.

—Rhythm comes from the roots of the world,
                                    rehearsed and expandable.

—After the ice storm a shower of crystal down from the trees
Shattering over the ground   45
                         like cut glass twirling its rainbows,
Sunlight in flushed layers under the clouds,
Twirling and disappearing into the clenched March grass.

—Structure is binary, intent on a resolution,
Its parts tight but the whole loose   50
                         and endlessly repetitious.

—And here we stand, caught
In the crucifixal noon
                    with its bled, attendant bells,
And nothing to answer back with.   55
Forsythia purrs in its burning shell,
Jonquils, like Dante's angels, appear from their blue shoots.

How can we think to know of another's desire for darkness,
That low coo like a dove's
                         insistent outside the heart's window?   60
How can we think to think this?
How can we sit here, crossing out line after line,
Such five-finger exercises
                    up and down, learning our scales,

And say that all quartets are eschatological°   *pertaining to the end times*   65

Heuristically
            when the willows swim like medusas through the trees,
Their skins beginning to blister into a thousand green welts?
How can we think to know these things,
Clouds like full suds in the sky
                          keeping away, keeping away?

—Form is finite, an undestroyable hush over all things.

[1988]

MARY OLIVER   [b. 1935]

First Snow

The snow
began here
this morning and all day
continued, its white
rhetoric everywhere
calling us back to *why*, *how*,
whence such beauty and *what*
the meaning; such
an oracular fever! flowing
past windows, an energy it seemed
would never ebb, never settle
less than lovely! and only now,
deep into night,
it has finally ended.
The silence
is immense,
and the heavens still hold
a million candles; nowhere
the familiar things:
stars, the moon,
the darkness we expect
and nightly turn from. Trees
glitter like castles
of ribbons, the broad fields

smolder with light, a passing   25
creekbed lies
heaped with shining hills;
and though the questions
that have assailed us all day
remain—not a single   30
answer has been found—
walking out now
into the silence and the light
under the trees,
and through the fields,   35
feels like one.

[1983]

LUCILLE CLIFTON   [b. 1936]

at the cemetery,
walnut grove plantation,
south carolina, 1989

among the rocks
at walnut grove
your silence drumming
in my bones,
tell me your names.   5

nobody mentioned slaves
and yet the curious tools
shine with your fingerprints.
nobody mentioned slaves
but somebody did this work   10
who had no guide, no stone,
who moulders under rock.

tell me your names,
tell me your bashful names
and i will testify.   15

the inventory lists ten slaves
but only men were recognized.

among the rocks
at walnut grove
some of these honored dead
were dark
some of these dark
were slaves
some of these slaves
were women
some of them did this
honored work.
tell me your names
foremothers, brothers,
tell me your dishonored names.
here lies
here lies
here lies
here lies
hear

[1991]

NANCY WILLARD   [b. 1936]

Questions My Son Asked Me, Answers I Never Gave Him

1. Do gorillas have birthdays?
    Yes. Like the rainbow, they happen.
    Like the air, they are not observed.

2. Do butterflies make a noise?
    The wire in the butterfly's tongue
    hums gold. Some men hear butterflies
    even in winter.

3. Are they part of our family?
   They forgot us, who forgot how to fly.

4. Who tied my navel? Did God tie it?   10
   God made the thread: O man, live forever!
   Man made the knot: enough is enough.

5. If I drop my tooth in the telephone
   will it go through the wires and bite someone's ear?
   I have seen earlobes pierced by a tooth of steel.   15
   It loves what lasts.
   It does not love flesh.
   It leaves a ring of gold in the wound.

6. If I stand on my head
   will the sleep in my eye roll up into my head?
   Does the dream know its own father?   20
   Can bread go back to the field of its birth?

7. Can I eat a star?
   Yes, with the mouth of time
   that enjoys everything.   25

8. Could we Xerox the moon?
   This is the first commandment:
   I am the moon, thy moon.
   Thou shalt have no other moons before thee.

9. Who invented water?   30
   The hands of the air, that wanted to wash each other.

10. What happens at the end of numbers?
    I see three men running toward a field.
    At the edge of the tall grass, they turn into light.

11. Do the years ever run out?   35
    God said, I will break time's heart.
    Time ran down like an old phonograph.
    It lay flat as a carpet.
    At rest on its threads, I am learning to fly.

[1982]

MARGE PIERCY [b. 1936]

Barbie Doll

This girlchild was born as usual
and presented dolls that did pee-pee
and miniature GE stoves and irons
and wee lipsticks the color of cherry candy.
Then in the magic of puberty, a classmate said:
You have a great big nose and fat legs.

She was healthy, tested intelligent,
possessed strong arms and back,
abundant sexual drive and manual dexterity.
She went to and fro apologizing.
Everyone saw a fat nose on thick legs.

She was advised to play coy,
exhorted to come on hearty,
exercise, diet, smile and wheedle.
Her good nature wore out
like a fan belt.
So she cut off her nose and her legs
and offered them up.

In the casket displayed on satin she lay
with the undertaker's cosmetics painted on,
a turned-up putty nose,
dressed in a pink and white nightie.
Doesn't she look pretty? everyone said.
Consummation at last.
To every woman a happy ending.

[1973]

624

CHARLES SIMIC [b. 1938]

Begotten of the Spleen°

The Virgin Mother° walked barefoot
Among the land mines.
She carried an old man in her arms
Like a howling babe.

The earth was an old people's home.   5
Judas was the night nurse,
Emptying bedpans into the river Jordan,
Tying people on a dog chain.

The old man had two stumps for legs.
St. Peter came pushing a cart   10
Loaded with flying carpets.
They were not flying carpets.

They were piles of bloody diapers.
The Magi° stood around
Cleaning their nails with bayonets.   15
The old man gave little Mary Magdalene°

A broken piece of a mirror.
She hid in the church outhouse.
When she got thirsty she licked
the steam off the glass.   20

That leaves Joseph.° Poor Joseph,
Standing naked in the snow.
He only had a rat
To load his suitcases on.

Spleen: Once believed to be the source in a person either of high spirit, courage,
and resolute mind or of ill-nature, ill-humor, and irritable or peevish temper.
1. The Virgin Mother: Mary, the mother of Jesus.
14. Magi: The wise men from the East who visited the baby Jesus.
16. Mary Magdalene: A follower of Jesus who was present at his crucifixion and
burial and who went to the tomb on Easter Sunday to anoint his body.
21. Joseph: The husband of Mary, the mother of Jesus.

The rat wouldn't run into its hole.
Even when the lights came on—
And the lights came on:
The floodlights in the guard towers.

[*1980;* 1999]

MICHAEL S. HARPER   [b. 1938]

Nightmare Begins Responsibility

I place these numbed wrists to the pane
watching white uniforms whisk over
him in the tube-kept
prison
fear what they will do in experiment
watch my gloved stickshifting gasolined hands
breathe *boxcar-information-please* infirmary tubes
distrusting white-pink mending paperthin
silkened end hairs, distrusting tubes
shrunk in his *trunk-skincapped*
shaven head, in thighs
distrusting-white-hands-picking-baboon-light
on this son who will not make his second night
of this wardstrewn intensive airpocket
where his father's asthmatic
hymns of *night-train*, train done gone
his mother can only know that he has flown
up into essential calm unseen corridor
going boxscarred home, *mamaborn, sweetsonchild*
gonedowntown into *researchtestingwarehousebatteryacid*
mama-son-done-gone/me telling her 'nother
train tonight, no music, no breathstroked
heartbeat in my infinite distrust of them:

and of my distrusting self
white-doctor-who-breathed-for-him-all-night

say it for two sons gone,
say nightmare, say it loud
panebreaking heartmadness:
nightmare begins responsibility.

[1975]

SEAMUS HEANEY   [b. 1939]

Mid-Term Break

I sat all morning in the college sick bay
Counting bells knelling classes to a close.
At two o'clock our neighbours drove me home.

In the porch I met my father crying—
He had always taken funerals in his stride—   5
And Big Jim Evans saying it was a hard blow.

The baby cooed and laughed and rocked the pram°   *baby carriage*
When I came in, and I was embarrassed
By old men standing up to shake my hand

And tell me they were "sorry for my trouble,"   10
Whispers informed strangers I was the eldest,
Away at school, as my mother held my hand

In hers and coughed out angry tearless sighs.
At ten o'clock the ambulance arrived
With the corpse, stanched and bandaged by the nurses.   15

Next morning I went up into the room. Snowdrops
And candles soothed the bedside; I saw him
For the first time in six weeks. Paler now,

Wearing a poppy bruise on his left temple,
He lay in the four foot box as in his cot.   20
No gaudy scars, the bumper knocked him clear.

A four foot box, a foot for every year.

[1966]

MARGARET ATWOOD   [b. 1939]

True Stories

I

Don't ask for the true story;
why do you need it?

It's not what I set out with
or what I carry.

What I'm sailing with,
a knife, blue fire,

luck, a few good words
that still work, and the tide.

II

The true story was lost
on the way down to the beach, it's something

I never had, that black tangle
of branches in a shifting light,

my blurred footprints
filling with salt

water, this handful
of tiny bones, this owl's kill;

a moon, crumpled papers, a coin,
the glint of an old picnic,

the hollows made by lovers
in sand a hundred

years ago: no clue.

III

The true story lies
among the other stories,

a mess of colours, like jumbled clothing
thrown off or away,   25

like hearts on marble, like syllables, like
butchers' discards.

The true story is vicious
and multiple and untrue

after all. Why do you   30
need it? Don't ever

ask for the true story.

[1981]

TED KOOSER [b. 1939]

Student

The green shell of his backpack makes him lean
into wave after wave of responsibility,
and he swings his stiff arms and cupped hands,

paddling ahead. He has extended his neck
to its full length, and his chin, hard as a beak,   5
breaks the cold surf. He's got his baseball cap on

backward as up he crawls, out of the froth
of a hangover and onto the sand of the future,
and lumbers, heavy with hope, into the library.

[2004]

AL YOUNG   [b. 1939]

A Dance for Ma Rainey°

I'm going to be just like you, Ma
Rainey this monday morning
clouds puffing up out of my head
like those balloons
that float above the faces of white people
in the funnypapers

I'm going to hover in the corners
of the world, Ma
& sing from the bottom of hell
up to the tops of high heaven
& send out scratchless waves of yellow
& brown & that basic black honey
misery

I'm going to cry so sweet
& so low
& so dangerous,
Ma,
that the message is going to reach you
back in 1922
where you shimmer
snaggle-toothed
perfumed &
powdered
in your bauble beads

hair pressed & tied back
throbbing with that sick pain
I know
& hide so well

Ma Rainey: Gertrude Pridgett (1886–1939), known after her marriage as Ma
Rainey, was a noted vaudeville entertainer and blues singer, credited as being the
"Mother of the Blues."

that pain that blues
jives the world with   30
aching to be heard
that downness
that bottomlessness
first felt by some stolen delta nigger
swamped under with redblooded american agony;   35
reduced to the sheer shit
of existence
that bred
& battered us all,
Ma,   40
the beautiful people
our beautiful brave black people
who no longer need to jazz
or sing to themselves in murderous vibrations
or play the veins of their strong tender arms   45
with needles
to prove we're still here

[1969]

JAMES WELCH   [b. 1940]

Christmas Comes to Moccasin Flat

Christmas comes like this: Wise men
unhurried, candles bought on credit (poor price
for calves), warriors face down in wine sleep.
Winds cheat to pull heat from smoke.

Friends sit in chinked cabins, stare out   5
plastic windows and wait for commodities.
Charlie Blackbird, twenty miles from church
and bar, stabs his fire with flint.

When drunks drain radiators for love
or need, chiefs eat snow and talk of change,   10

an urge to laugh pounding their ribs.
Elk play games in high country.

Medicine Woman, clay pipe and twist tobacco,
calls each blizzard by name and predicts
five o'clock by spitting at her television.
Children lean into her breath to beg a story:

Something about honor and passion,
warriors back with meat and song,
a peculiar evening star, quick vision of birth.
Blackbird feeds his fire. Outside, a quick 30 below.

[1976]

ROBERT PINSKY   [b. 1940]

Shirt

The back, the yoke, the yardage. Lapped seams,
The nearly invisible stitches along the collar
Turned in a sweatshop by Koreans or Malaysians

Gossiping over tea and noodles on their break
Or talking money or politics while one fitted
This armpiece with its overseam to the band

Of cuff I button at my wrist. The presser, the cutter,
The wringer, the mangle. The needle, the union,
The treadle, the bobbin. The code. The infamous blaze

At the Triangle Factory° in nineteen-eleven.   *(in New York City)*
One hundred and forty-six died in the flames
On the ninth floor, no hydrants, no fire escapes—

The witness in a building across the street
Who watched how a young man helped a girl to step
Up to the windowsill, then held her out

Away from the masonry wall and let her drop.
And then another. As if he were helping them up
To enter a streetcar, and not eternity.

A third before he dropped her put her arms
Around his neck and kissed him. Then he held   20
Her into space, and dropped her. Almost at once

He stepped to the sill himself, his jacket flared
And fluttered up from his shirt as he came down,
Air filling up the legs of his gray trousers—

Like Hart Crane's Bedlamite,° "shrill shirt ballooning."   25
Wonderful how the pattern matches perfectly
Across the placket and over the twin bar-tacked

Corners of both pockets, like a strict rhyme
Or a major chord. Prints, plaids, checks,
Houndstooth, Tattersall, Madras. The clan tartans   30

Invented by mill-owners inspired by the hoax of Ossian,°
To control their savage Scottish workers, tamed
By a fabricated heraldry: MacGregor,

Bailey, MacMartin. The kilt, devised for workers
To wear among the dusty clattering looms.   35
Weavers, carders, spinners. The loader,

The docker, the navvy.° The planter, the picker, the sorter
Sweating at her machine in a litter of cotton
As slaves in calico headrags sweated in fields:

George Herbert,° your descendant is a Black   40
Lady in South Carolina, her name is Irma
And she inspected my shirt. Its color and fit

And feel and its clean smell have satisfied
Both her and me. We have culled its cost and quality
Down to the buttons of simulated bone,   45

25. Bedlamite: Reference to image in Hart Crane's famous book-length poem
The Bridge (lines 17–20 of the section titled, "The Brooklyn Bridge.")
31. Ossian: Legendary Gaelic poet, hero of a cycle of traditional tales and poems
that place him in the third century CE. The hoax involved Scottish author James
Macpherson (1736–1796), who published two epic poems that he said were
translations of works written by Ossian but were in fact mostly composed by
Macpherson himself.
37. navvy: An unskilled laborer.
40. George Herbert: English metaphysical poet (1593–1633). See Biographical
Notes (p. 1304).

The buttonholes, the sizing, the facing, the characters
Printed in black on neckband and tail. The shape,
The label, the labor, the color, the shade. The shirt.

[1990]

BILLY COLLINS   [b. 1941]

I Chop Some Parsley While Listening to Art Blakey's Version of "Three Blind Mice"

And I start wondering how they came to be blind.
If it was congenital, they could be brothers and sisters,
and I think of the poor mother
brooding over her sightless young triplets.

Or was it a common accident, all three caught
in a searing explosion, a firework perhaps?
If not,
if each came to his or her blindness separately,

how did they ever manage to find one another?
Would it not be difficult for a blind mouse
to locate even one fellow mouse with vision
let alone two other blind ones?

And how, in their tiny darkness,
could they possibly have run after a farmer's wife
or anyone else's wife for that matter?
Not to mention why.

Just so she could cut off their tails
with a carving knife, is the cynic's answer,
but the thought of them without eyes
and now without tails to trail through the moist grass

or slip around the corner of a baseboard
has the cynic who always lounges within me

up off his couch and at the window
trying to hide the rising softness that he feels.

By now I am on to dicing an onion   25
which might account for the wet stinging
in my own eyes, though Freddie Hubbard's
mournful trumpet on "Blue Moon,"

which happens to be the next cut,
cannot be said to be making matters any better.   30

[2001]

RICHARD GARCIA   [b. 1941]

Why I Left the Church

Maybe it was
because the only time
I hit a baseball
it smashed the neon cross
on the church across   5
the street. Even
twenty-five years later
when I saw Father Harris
I would wonder
if he knew it was me.   10
Maybe it was the demon-stoked
rotisseries of purgatory
where we would roast
hundreds of years
for the smallest of sins.   15
Or was it the day
I wore my space helmet
to catechism? Clear plastic
with a red-and-white
inflatable rim.   20
Sister Mary Bernadette
pointed toward the door
and said, "Out! Come back

when you're ready."
I rose from my chair
and kept rising
toward the ceiling
while the children
screamed and Sister
kept crossing herself.
The last she saw of me
was my shoes disappearing
through cracked plaster.
I rose into the sky and beyond.
It is a good thing
I am wearing my helmet,
I thought as I floated
and turned in the blackness
and brightness of outer space,
my body cold on one side and hot
on the other. It would
have been very quiet
if my blood had not been
rumbling in my ears so loud.
I remember thinking,
Maybe I will come back
when I'm ready.
But I won't tell
the other children
what it was like.
I'll have to make something up.

[1993]

ROBERT HASS   [b. 1941]

A Story about the Body

The young composer, working that summer at an artists' colony, had watched her for a week. She was Japanese, a painter, almost sixty, and he thought he was in love with her. He loved her work, and her work was like the way she moved her body, used her hands, looked at him directly when she made amused and considered answers to his questions. One night, walking back from a concert, they came to her door and she turned to him and said, "I think you would like to have me. I would like that too, but I must tell you that I have had a double mastectomy," and when he didn't understand, "I've lost both my breasts." The radiance that he had carried around in his belly and chest cavity—like music—withered very quickly, and he made himself look at her when he said, "I'm sorry. I don't think I could." He walked back to his own cabin through the pines, and in the morning he found a small blue bowl on the porch outside his door. It looked to be full of rose petals, but he found when he picked it up that the rose petals were on top; the rest of the bowl—she must have swept them from the corners of her studio—was full of dead bees.

[1989]

SIMON J. ORTIZ   [b. 1941]

Speaking

I take him outside
under the trees,
have him stand on the ground.
We listen to the crickets,
cicadas, million years old sound.   5
Ants come by us.
I tell them,
"This is he, my son.
This boy is looking at you.
I am speaking for him."   10

The crickets, cicadas,
the ants, the millions of years
are watching us,
hearing us.
My son murmurs infant words,   15
speaking, small laughter
bubbles from him.
Tree leaves tremble.

They listen to this boy
speaking for me.

[1977]

TOI DERRICOTTE   [b. 1941]

A Note on My Son's Face

I

Tonight, I look, thunderstruck
at the gold head of my grandchild.
Almost asleep, he buries his feet
between my thighs;
his little straw eyes
close in the near dark.
I smell the warmth of his raw
slightly foul breath, the new death
waiting to rot inside him.
Our breaths equalize our heartbeats;
every muscle of the chest uncoils,
the arm bones loosen in the nest
of nerves. I think of the peace
of walking through the house,
pointing to the name of this, the name of that,
an educator of a new man.

Mother. Grandmother. Wise
Snake-woman who will show the way;
Spider-woman whose black tentacles
hold him precious. Or will tear off his head,
her teeth over the little husband,
the small fist clotted in trust at her breast.

This morning, looking at the face of his father,
I remembered how, an infant, his face was too dark,
nose too broad, mouth too wide.
I did not look in that mirror
and see the face that could save me

from my own darkness.
Did he, looking in my eye, see
what I turned from: 30
my own dark grandmother
bending over gladioli in the field,
her shaking black hand defenseless
at the shining cock of flower?

I wanted that face to die, 35
to be reborn in the face of a white child.
I wanted the soul to stay the same,
for I loved to death,
to damnation and God-death,
the soul that broke out of me. 40
I crowed: My Son! My Beautiful!
But when I peeked in the basket,
I saw the face of a black man.

Did I bend over his nose
and straighten it with my fingers 45
like a vine growing the wrong way?
Did he feel my hand in malice?

Generations we prayed and fucked
for this light child,
the shining god of the second coming; 50
we bow down in shame
and carry the children of the past
in our wallets, begging forgiveness.

II

A picture in a book,
a lynching. 55
The bland faces of men who watch
a Christ go up in flames, smiling,
as if he were a hooked
fish, a felled antelope, some
wild thing tied to boards and burned. 60
His charring body
gives off light—a halo
burns out of him.
His face scorched featureless;
the hair matted to the scalp 65
like feathers.

One man stands with his hand on his hip,
another with his arm
slung over the shoulder of a friend,
as if this moment were large enough
to hold affection.

III

How can we wake
from a dream
we are born into,
that shines around us,
the terrible bright air?

Having awakened,
having seen our own bloody hands,
how can we ask forgiveness,
bring before our children the real
monster of their nightmares?

The worst is true.
Everything you did not want to know.

[1989]

SHARON OLDS   [b. 1942]

I Go Back to May 1937

I see them standing at the formal gates of their colleges,
I see my father strolling out
under the ochre sandstone arch, the
red tiles glinting like bent
plates of blood behind his head, I
see my mother with a few light books at her hip
standing at the pillar made of tiny bricks with the
wrought-iron gate still open behind her, its
sword-tips black in the May air,
they are about to graduate, they are about to get married,
they are kids, they are dumb, all they know is they are

innocent, they would never hurt anybody.
I want to go up to them and say Stop,
don't do it—she's the wrong woman,
he's the wrong man, you are going to do things   15
you cannot imagine you would ever do,
you are going to do bad things to children,
you are going to suffer in ways you never heard of,
you are going to want to die. I want to go
up to them there in the late May sunlight and say it,   20
her hungry pretty blank face turning to me,
her pitiful beautiful untouched body,
his arrogant handsome blind face turning to me,
his pitiful beautiful untouched body,
but I don't do it. I want to live. I   25
take them up like the male and female
paper dolls and bang them together
at the hips like chips of flint as if to
strike sparks from them, I say
Do what you are going to do, and I will tell about it.   30

[1987]

MARILYN HACKER   [b. 1942]

Villanelle

Every day our bodies separate,
explode torn and dazed.
Not understanding what we celebrate

we grope through languages and hesitate
and touch each other, speechless and amazed;   5
and every day our bodies separate

us further from our planned, deliberate
ironic lives. I am afraid, disphased,
not understanding what we celebrate

when our fused limbs and lips communicate   10
the unlettered power we have raised.
Every day our bodies' separate

routines are harder to perpetuate.
In wordless darkness we learn wordless praise,
not understanding what we celebrate;

wake to ourselves, exhausted, in the late
morning as the wind tears off the haze,
not understanding how we celebrate
our bodies. Every day we separate.

[1974]

JAMES TATE   [b. 1943]

The Wheelchair Butterfly

O sleepy city of reeling wheelchairs
where a mouse can commit suicide if he can

concentrate long enough
on the history book of rodents
in this underground town

of electrical wheelchairs!
The girl who is always pregnant and bruised
like a pear

rides her many-stickered bicycle
backward up the staircase
of the abandoned trolleybarn.

Yesterday was warm. Today a butterfly froze
in midair; and was plucked like a grape
by a child who swore he could take care

of it. O confident city where
the seeds of poppies pass for carfare,

where the ordinary hornets in a human's heart
may slumber and snore, where bifocals bulge

in an orange garage of daydreams,
we wait in our loose attics for a new season

as if for an ice-cream truck.
An Indian pony crosses the plains

whispering Sanskrit prayers to a crater of fleas.
Honeysuckle says: I thought I could swim.

The Mayor is urinating on the wrong side   25
of the street! A dandelion sends off sparks:
beware your hair is locked!

Beware the trumpet wants a glass of water!
Beware a velvet tabernacle!

Beware the Warden of Light has married   30
an old piece of string!

[1969]

QUINCY TROUPE [b. 1943]

A Poem For "Magic"°

*for Earvin "Magic" Johnson,
Donnell Reid & Richard Franklin*

take it to the hoop, "magic" johnson,
take the ball dazzling down the open lane
herk & jerk & raise your six-feet, nine-inch frame
into air sweating screams of your neon name
"magic" johnson, nicknamed "windex" way back   5
in high school
            cause you wiped glass backboards
so clean, where you first juked & shook
wiled your way to glory
            a new-style fusion of shake-&-bake   10
energy, using everything possible, you created your own

"**Magic**": Earvin "Magic" Johnson Jr. (b. 1959), star basketball player at Lansing
(Michigan) Everett High School (1973–77) and Michigan State University (1977–
79) and for the Los Angeles Lakers (1979–91 and 1996). He was honored in 1996
as one of the Fifty Greatest Players in National Basketball Association History.

space to fly through—any moment now
we expect your wings to spread feathers for that spooky takeoff
of yours—then, shake & glide & ride up in space
till you hammer home a clothes-lining deuce off glass
now, come back down with a reverse hoodoo gem
off the spin & stick in sweet, popping nets clean
from twenty feet, right side
put the ball on the floor again, "magic"
slide the dribble behind your back, ease it deftly
between your bony stork legs, head bobbing everwhichaway
up & down, you see everything on the court
off the high yoyo patter
                              stop & go dribble
you thread a needle-rope pass sweet home
to kareem cutting through the lane
                                                  his skyhook pops the cords
now, lead the fastbreak, hit worthy on the fly
now, blindside a pinpoint behind-the-back pass for two more
off the fake, looking the other way, you raise off-balance
into electric space
sweating chants of your name
turn, 180 degrees off the move, your legs scissoring space
like a swimmer's yoyoing motion in deep water
stretching out now toward free flight
you double-pump through human trees
                                        hang in place
slip the ball into your left hand
then deal it like a las vegas card dealer off squared glass
into nets, living up to your singular nickname
so "bad" you cartwheel the crowd toward frenzy
wearing now your electric smile, neon as your name

in victory, we suddenly sense your glorious uplift
your urgent need to be champion
& so we cheer with you, rejoice with you
                                        for this quicksilver, quicksilver,
quicksilver moment of fame
so put the ball on the floor again, "magic"
juke & dazzle, shake & bake down the lane
take the sucker to the hoop, "magic" johnson,
recreate reverse hoodoo gems off the spin
deal alley-oop dunkathon magician passes
now, double-pump, scissor, vamp through space

hang in place
                        & put it all up in the sucker's face, "magic" johnson,   55
& deal the roundball like the juju man that you am
like the sho-nuff shaman that you am, "magic,"
like the sho-nuff spaceman you am

                                         [*1991*; rev. 1996]

EAVAN BOLAND   [b. 1944]

The Pomegranate

The only legend I have ever loved is
the story of a daughter lost in hell.
And found and rescued there.
Love and blackmail are the gist of it.
Ceres° and Persephone the names.   5
And the best thing about the legend is
I can enter it anywhere. And have.
As a child in exile in
a city of fogs and strange consonants,
I read it first and at first I was   10
an exiled child in the crackling dusk of
the underworld, the stars blighted. Later
I walked out in a summer twilight
searching for my daughter at bed-time.
When she came running I was ready   15
to make any bargain to keep her.
I carried her back past whitebeams

5. **Ceres:** Roman name of Demeter, the goddess of crops and harvest. Her daughter Persephone was kidnapped by Pluto (or Hades) and taken to the underworld. Demeter, grieving and angry, refused to let seeds germinate or crops grow. To save the human race from extinction, Zeus finally ordered Pluto to release Persephone. Pluto told her she was free to leave but tricked her by offering a pomegranate seed; anyone who eats food in the underworld must return there. Zeus therefore arranged a compromise: Persephone would spend a third of each year in the land of the dead with Pluto (winter, when Demeter went into mourning), but she would be with her mother for the other two-thirds of each year (spring and summer).

and wasps and honey-scented buddleias.
But I was Ceres then and I knew
winter was in store for every leaf
on every tree on that road.
Was inescapable for each one we passed.
And for me.
                                    It is winter
and the stars are hidden.
I climb the stairs and stand where I can see
my child asleep beside her teen magazines,
her can of Coke, her plate of uncut fruit.
The pomegranate! How did I forget it?
She could have come home and been safe
and ended the story and all
our heart-broken searching but she reached
out a hand and plucked a pomegranate.
She put out her hand and pulled down
the French sound for apple° and   *pomme*
the noise of stone° and the proof   *granite*
that even in the place of death,
at the heart of legend, in the midst
of rocks full of unshed tears
ready to be diamonds by the time
the story was told, a child can be
hungry. I could warn her. There is still a chance.
The rain is cold. The road is flint-coloured.
The suburb has cars and cable television.
The veiled stars are above ground.
It is another world. But what else
can a mother give her daughter but such
beautiful rifts in time?
If I defer the grief I will diminish the gift.
The legend will be hers as well as mine.
She will enter it. As I have.
She will wake up. She will hold
the papery flushed skin in her hand.
And to her lips. I will say nothing.

[*1994;* 1995]

LARRY LEVIS   [1946–1996]

The Poem You Asked For

My poem would eat nothing.
I tried giving it water
but it said no,

worrying me.
Day after day,   5
I held it up to the light,

turning it over,
but it only pressed its lips
more tightly together.

It grew sullen, like a toad   10
through with being teased.
I offered it all my money,

my clothes, my car with a full tank.
But the poem stared at the floor.
Finally I cupped it in   15

my hands, and carried it gently
out into the soft air, into the
evening traffic, wondering how

to end things between us.
For now it had begun breathing,   20
putting on more and

more hard rings of flesh.
And the poem demanded the food,
it drank up all the water,

beat me and took my money,   25
tore the faded clothes
off my back,

said Shit,
and walked slowly away,
slicking its hair down.   30

Said it was going
over to your place.

[1972]

MARILYN NELSON   [b. 1946]

Minor Miracle

Which reminds me of another knock-on-wood
memory. I was cycling with a male friend,
through a small midwestern town. We came to a 4-way
stop and stopped, chatting. As we started again,
a rusty old pick-up truck, ignoring the stop sign,
hurricaned past scant inches from our front wheels.
My partner called, "Hey, that was a 4-way stop!"
The truck driver, stringy blond hair a long fringe
under his brand-name beer cap, looked back and yelled,
          "You fucking niggers!"
And sped off.
My friend and I looked at each other and shook our heads.
We remounted our bikes and headed out of town.
We were pedaling through a clear blue afternoon
between two fields of almost-ripened wheat
bordered by cornflowers and Queen Anne's lace
when we heard an unmuffled motor, a honk-honking.
We stopped, closed ranks, made fists.
It was the same truck. It pulled over.
A tall, very much in shape young white guy slid out:
greasy jeans, homemade finger tattoos, probably
a Marine Corps boot-camp footlockerful
of martial arts techniques.

"What did you say back there!" he shouted.
My friend said, "I said it was a 4-way stop.
You went through it."
"And what did I say?" the white guy asked.
"You said: "'You fucking niggers.'"
The afternoon froze.

"Well," said the white guy,   30
shoving his hands into his pockets
and pushing dirt around with the pointed toe of his boot,
"I just want to say I'm sorry."
He climbed back into his truck
and drove away.   35

[1997]

AI [b. 1947]

Why Can't I Leave You?

You stand behind the old black mare,
dressed as always in that red shirt,
stained from sweat, the crying of the armpits,
that will not stop for anything,
stroking her rump, while the barley goes unplanted.   5
I pick up my suitcase and set it down,
as I try to leave you again.
I smooth the hair back from your forehead.
I think with your laziness and the drought too,
you'll be needing my help more than ever.   10
You take my hands, I nod
and go to the house to unpack,
having found another reason to stay.

I undress, then put on my white lace slip
for you to take off, because you like that   15
and when you come in, you pull down the straps
and I unbutton your shirt.
I know we can't give each other any more
or any less than what we have.
There is safety in that, so much   20
that I can never get past the packing,
the begging you to please, if I can't make you happy,
come close between my thighs
and let me laugh for you from my second mouth.

[1972]

LINDA HOGAN   [b. 1947]

Crow Law

The temple where crow worships
walks forward in tall, black grass.
Betrayal is crow's way of saying grace
to the wolf
so it can eat
what is left
when blood is on the ground,
until what remains of moose
is crow
walking out
the sacred temple of ribs
in a dance of leaving
the red tracks of scarce and private gods.
It is the oldest war
where moose becomes wolf and crow,
where the road ceases
to become the old forest
where crow is calling,
where we are still afraid.

[1993]

YUSEF KOMUNYAKAA   [b. 1947]

Facing It

My black face fades,
hiding inside the black granite.
I said I wouldn't,
dammit: No tears.

650

I'm stone. I'm flesh.   5
My clouded reflection eyes me
like a bird of prey, the profile of night
slanted against morning. I turn
this way—the stone lets me go.
I turn that way—I'm inside   10
the Vietnam Veterans Memorial
again, depending on the light
to make a difference.
I go down the 58,022 names,
half-expecting to find   15
my own in letters like smoke.
I touch the name Andrew Johnson;
I see the booby trap's white flash.
Names shimmer on a woman's blouse
but when she walks away   20
the names stay on the wall.
Brushstrokes flash, a red bird's
wings cutting across my stare.
The sky. A plane in the sky.
A white vet's image floats   25
closer to me, then his pale eyes
look through mine. I'm a window.
He's lost his right arm
inside the stone. In the black mirror
a woman's trying to erase names: 30
No, she's brushing a boy's hair.

[1988]

JANE KENYON   [1947–1995]

A Boy Goes into the World

My brother rode off on his bike
into the summer afternoon, but
Mother called me back
from the end of the sandy drive:
"It's different for girls."   5

He'd be gone for hours, come back
with things: a cocoon, gray-brown
and papery around a stick;
a puff ball, ripe, wrinkled,
and exuding spores; owl pellets—
bits of undigested bone and fur;
and pieces of moss that might
have made toupees for preposterous
green men, but went instead
into a wide-necked jar for a terrarium.

He mounted his plunder on poster
board, gluing and naming
each piece. He has long since
forgotten those days and things, but
I at last can claim them as my own.

[1990]

HEATHER McHUGH   [b. 1948]

What He Thought

for Fabbio Doplicher

We were supposed to do a job in Italy
and, full of our feeling for
ourselves (our sense of being
Poets from America) we went
from Rome to Fano, met
the mayor, mulled
a couple matters over (what's
cheap date, they asked us; what's
flat drink). Among Italian literati

we could recognize our counterparts:
the academic, the apologist,
the arrogant, the amorous,
the brazen and the glib—and there was one

administrator (the conservative), in suit
of regulation gray, who like a good tour guide   15
with measured pace and uninflected tone narrated
sights and histories the hired van hauled us past.
Of all, he was most politic and least poetic,
so it seemed. Our last few days in Rome
(when all but three of the New World Bards had flown)   20
I found a book of poems this
unprepossessing one had written: it was there
in the *pensione* room (a room he'd recommended)
where it must have been abandoned by
the German visitor (was there a bus of *them*?)   25
to whom he had inscribed and dated it a month before.
I couldn't read Italian, either, so I put the book
back into the wardrobe's dark. We last Americans

were due to leave tomorrow. For our parting evening then
our host chose something in a family restaurant, and there   30
we sat and chatted, sat and chewed,
till, sensible it was our last
big chance to be poetic, make
our mark, one of us asked

                        "What's poetry?   35
Is it the fruits and vegetables and
marketplace of Campo dei Fiori, or
the statue there?" Because I was

the glib one, I identified the answer
instantly, I didn't have to think—"The truth   40
is both, it's both," I blurted out. But that
was easy. That was easiest to say. What followed
taught me something about difficulty,
for our underestimated host spoke out,
all of a sudden, with a rising passion, and he said: 45

The statue represents Giordano Bruno,
brought to be burned in the public square
because of his offense against
authority, which is to say
the Church. His crime was his belief   50
the universe does not revolve around
the human being: God is no
fixed point or central government, but rather is
poured in waves through all things. All things

move. "If God is not the soul itself, He is
the soul of the soul of the world." Such was
his heresy. The day they brought him
forth to die, they feared he might
incite the crowd (the man was famous
for his eloquence). And so his captors
placed upon his face
an iron mask, in which

he could not speak. That's
how they burned him. That is how
he died: without a word, in front
of everyone.
                    And poetry—
                              (we'd all
put down our forks by now, to listen to
the man in gray; he went on
softly)—
                    poetry is what

he thought, but did not say.

                                                [1994]

LESLIE MARMON SILKO   [b. 1948]

Prayer to the Pacific

I traveled to the ocean
                    distant
                              from my southwest land of sandrock
                              to the moving blue water
                    Big as the myth of origin.

Pale
pale water in the yellow-white light of
                              sun   floating west
                                        to China
                              where ocean herself was born.
Clouds that blow across the sand are wet.

Squat in the wet sand and speak to the Ocean:
      I return to you   turquoise   the red coral you sent us,
               sister spirit of Earth.
Four round stones in my pocket   I carry back the ocean   15
               to suck and to taste.

Thirty thousand years ago
          Indians came riding across the ocean
          carried by giant sea turtles.

Waves were high that day   20
         great sea turtles waded   slowly out
                   from the gray sundown sea.

Grandfather Turtle rolled in the sand   four times
          and disappeared
                   swimming into the sun.   25

And so   from that time
         immemorial,
               as the old people say,
rain clouds drift from the west
               gift from the ocean.   30

Green leaves in the wind
Wet earth on my feet
         swallowing raindrops
              clear from China.

                                   [1981]

SEKOU SUNDIATA   [1948–2007]

Blink Your Eyes

Remembering Sterling A. Brown

I was on my way to see my woman
but the Law said I was on my way
thru a red light red light red light
and if you saw my woman

you could understand,
I was just being a man
It wasn't about no light
it was about my ride
and if you saw my ride
you could dig that too, you dig?
Sunroof stereo radio black leather
bucket seats sit low you know,
the body's cool, but the tires are worn.
Ride when the hard time come, ride
when they're gone, in other words
the light was green.

I could wake up in the morning
without a warning
and my world could change:
blink your eyes.
All depends, all depends on the skin,
all depends on the skin you're living in.

Up to the window comes the Law
with his hand on his gun
what's up? what's happening?
I said I guess
that's when I really broke the law.
He said *a routine, step out the car*
a routine, assume the position.
Put your hands up in the air
you know the routine, like you just don't care.
License and registration.
Deep was the night and the light
from the North Star on the car door, deja vu
we've been through this before,
why did you stop me?
Somebody had to stop you.
I watch the news, you always lose.
You're unreliable, that's undeniable.
This is serious, you could be dangerous.

I could wake up in the morning
without a warning
and my world could change:
blink your eyes.
All depends, all depends on the skin,
all depends on the skin you're living in.

New York City, they got laws
can't no bruthas drive outdoors,
in certain neighborhoods, on particular streets
near and around certain types of people.   50
They got laws.
All depends, all depends on the skin,
all depends on the skin you're living in.

[1995]

VICTOR HERNÁNDEZ CRUZ   [b. 1949]

Problems with Hurricanes

A campesino° looked at the air
And told me:
With hurricanes it's not the wind
or the noise or the water.
I'll tell you he said: 5
it's the mangoes, avocados
Green plantains and bananas
flying into town like projectiles.

How would your family
feel if they had to tell   10
The generations that you
got killed by a flying
Banana.

Death by drowning has honor
If the wind picked you up   15
and slammed you
Against a mountain boulder
This would not carry shame
But
to suffer a mango smashing   20
Your skull

1. campesino: Someone (particularly a farmer or farm laborer) who lives in a
rural area in Latin America.

or a plantain hitting your
Temple at 70 miles per hour
is the ultimate disgrace.

The campesino takes off his hat—
As a sign of respect
towards the fury of the wind
And says:
Don't worry about the noise
Don't worry about the water
Don't worry about the wind—
If you are going out
beware of mangoes
And all such beautiful
sweet things.

[1991]

AGHA SHAHID ALI   [1949–2001]

I Dream It Is Afternoon
When I Return to Delhi

At Purana Qila I am alone, waiting
for the bus to Daryaganj. I see it coming,
but my hands are empty.
"Jump on, jump on," someone shouts,
"I've saved this change for you
for years. Look!"
A hand opens, full of silver rupees.
"Jump on, jump on." The voice doesn't stop.
There's no one I know. A policeman,
handcuffs silver in his hands,
asks for my ticket.

I jump off the running bus,
sweat pouring from my hair.
I run past the Doll Museum, past
headlines on the Times of India

building, PRISONERS BLINDED IN A BIHAR
JAIL, HARIJAN VILLAGES BURNED BY LANDLORDS.
Panting, I stop in Daryaganj,
outside Golcha Cinema.

Sunil is there, lighting   20
a cigarette, smiling. I say,
"It must be ten years, you haven't changed,
it was your voice on the bus!"
He says, "The film is about to begin,
I've bought an extra ticket for you,"   25
and we rush inside:

Anarkali is being led away,
her earrings lying on the marble floor.
Any moment she'll be buried alive.
"But this is the end," I turn   30
toward Sunil. He is nowhere.
The usher taps my shoulder, says
my ticket is ten years old.

Once again my hands are empty.
I am waiting, alone, at Purana Qila.   35
Bus after empty bus is not stopping.
Suddenly, beggar women with children
are everywhere, offering
me money, weeping for me.

                                                          [1987]

OLGA BROUMAS   [b. 1949]

Cinderella

> . . . the joy that isn't shared
> I heard, dies young.
> —ANNE SEXTON, 1928–1974

Apart from my sisters, estranged
from my mother, I am a woman alone
in a house of men

who secretly
call themselves princes, alone
with me usually, under cover of dark. I am the one allowed in

to the royal chambers, whose small foot conveniently
fills the slipper of glass. The woman writer, the lady
umpire, the madam chairman, anyone's wife.
I know what I know.
And I once was glad

of the chance to use it, even alone
in a strange castle, doing overtime on my own, cracking
the royal code. The princes spoke
in their fathers' language, were eager to praise me
my nimble tongue. I am a woman in a state of siege, alone

as one piece of laundry, strung on a windy clothesline a
mile long. A woman co-opted by promises: the lure
of a job, the ruse of a choice, a woman forced
to bear witness, falsely
against my kind, as each
other sister was judged inadequate, bitchy, incompetent,
jealous, too thin, too fat. I know what I know.
What sweet bread I make

for myself in this prosperous house
is dirty, what good soup I boil turns
in my mouth to mud. Give
me my ashes. A cold stove, a cinder-block pillow, wet
canvas shoes in my sisters', my sisters' hut. Or I swear

I'll die young
like those favored before me, hand-picked each one
for her joyful heart.

[1977]

RAY A. YOUNG BEAR   [b. 1950]

From the Spotted Night

In the blizzard
while chopping wood
the mystical whistler
beckons my attention.
Once there were longhouses   5
here. A village.
In the abrupt spring floods
swimmers retrieved our belief.
So their spirit remains.
From the spotted night   10
distant jets transform
into fireflies who float
towards me like incandescent
snowflakes.
The leather shirt   15
which is suspended
on a wire hanger
above the bed's headboard
is humanless; yet when one
stands outside the house,   20
the strenuous sounds
of dressers and boxes
being moved can be heard.
We believe someone wears
the shirt and rearranges   25
the heavy furniture,
although nothing
is actually changed.
Unlike the Plains Indian shirts
which repelled lead bullets,   30
ricocheting from them
in fiery sparks,

this shirt is the means;
this shirt *is* the bullet.

[1990]

CAROLYN FORCHÉ   [b. 1950]

The Colonel

What you have heard is true. I was in his house. His wife carried a tray
of coffee and sugar. His daughter filed her nails, his son went out for the
night. There were daily papers, pet dogs, a pistol on the cushion beside
him. The moon swung bare on its black cord over the house. On the television was a cop show. It was in English. Broken bottles were embedded
in the walls around the house to scoop the kneecaps from a man's legs or
cut his hands to lace. On the windows there were gratings like those in
liquor stores. We had dinner, rack of lamb, good wine, a gold bell was on
the table for calling the maid. The maid brought green mangoes, salt, a
type of bread. I was asked how I enjoyed the country. There was a brief
commercial in Spanish. His wife took everything away. There was some
talk then of how difficult it had become to govern. The parrot said hello
on the terrace. The colonel told it to shut up, and pushed himself from
the table. My friend said to me with his eyes: say nothing. The colonel
returned with a sack used to bring groceries home. He spilled many human ears on the table. They were like dried peach halves. There is no
other way to say this. He took one of them in his hands, shook it in our
faces, dropped it into a water glass. It came alive there. I am tired of fooling around he said. As for the rights of anyone, tell your people they can
go fuck themselves. He swept the ears to the floor with his arm and held
the last of his wine in the air. Something for your poetry, no? he said.
Some of the ears on the floor caught this scrap of his voice. Some of the
ears on the floor were pressed to the ground.

[1978]

JULIA ALVAREZ   [b. 1950]

How I Learned to Sweep

My mother never taught me sweeping.
One afternoon she found me watching
t.v. She eyed the dusty floor
boldly, and put a broom before
me, and said she'd like to be able   5
to eat her dinner off that table,
and nodded at my feet, then left.
I knew right off what she expected
and went at it. I stepped and swept;
the t.v. blared the news; I kept   10
my mind on what I had to do,
until in minutes, I was through.
Her floor was as immaculate
as a just-washed dinner plate.
I waited for her to return   15
and turned to watch the President,
live from the White House, talk of war:
in the Far East our soldiers were
landing in their helicopters
into jungles their propellers   20
swept like weeds seen underwater
while perplexing shots were fired
from those beautiful green gardens
into which these dragonflies
filled with little men descended.   25
I got up and swept again
as they fell out of the sky.
I swept all the harder when
I watched a dozen of them die—
as if their dust fell through the screen   30
upon the floor I had just cleaned.
She came back and turned the dial;
the screen went dark. *That's beautiful*,
she said, and ran her clean hand through

my hair, and on, over the window-sill,
coffee table, rocker, desk,
and held it up—I held my breath—
That's beautiful, she said, impressed,
she hadn't found a speck of death.

[1996]

JOY HARJO   [b. 1951]

She Had Some Horses

She had some horses.

She had horses who were bodies of sand.
She had horses who were maps drawn of blood.
She had horses who were skins of ocean water.
She had horses who were the blue air of sky.
She had horses who were fur and teeth.
She had horses who were clay and would break.
She had horses who were splintered red cliff.

She had some horses.

She had horses with long, pointed breasts.
She had horses with full, brown thighs.
She had horses who laughed too much.
She had horses who threw rocks at glass houses.
She had horses who licked razor blades.

She had some horses.

She had horses who danced in their mothers' arms.
She had horses who thought they were the sun and their
bodies shone and burned like stars.
She had horses who waltzed nightly on the moon.
She had horses who were much too shy, and kept quiet
in stalls of their own making.

She had some horses.

She had horses who liked Creek Stomp Dance songs.
She had horses who cried in their beer.
She had horses who spit at male queens who made   25
them afraid of themselves.
She had horses who said they weren't afraid.
She had horses who lied.
She had horses who told the truth, who were stripped
bare of their tongues.   30

She had some horses.

She had horses who called themselves, "horse."
She had horses who called themselves, "spirit," and kept
their voices secret and to themselves.
She had horses who had no names.   35
She had horses who had books of names.

She had some horses.

She had horses who whispered in the dark, who were afraid to speak.
She had horses who screamed out of fear of the silence, who
carried knives to protect themselves from ghosts.   40
She had horses who waited for destruction.
She had horses who waited for resurrection.

She had some horses.

She had horses who got down on their knees for any saviour.
She had horses who thought their high price had saved them.   45
She had horses who tried to save her, who climbed in her
bed at night and prayed as they raped her.

She had some horses.

She had some horses she loved.
She had some horses she hated.   50

These were the same horses.

[1983]

GARRETT KAORU HONGO   [b. 1951]

Yellow Light

One arm hooked around the frayed strap
of a tar-black, patent-leather purse,
the other cradling something for dinner:
fresh bunches of spinach from a J-Town *yaoya*,°   *vegetable stand or seller*
sides of split Spanish mackerel from Alviso's,
maybe a loaf of Langendorf;° she steps
off the hissing bus at Olympic and Fig,
begins the three-block climb up the hill,
passing gangs of schoolboys playing war,
Japs against Japs, Chicanas chalking sidewalks
with the holy double-yoked crosses of hopscotch,
and the Korean grocer's wife out for a stroll
around this neighborhood of Hawaiian apartments
just starting to steam with cooking
and the anger of young couples coming home
from work, yelling at kids, flicking on
TV sets for the Wednesday Night Fights.

If it were May, hydrangeas and jacaranda
flowers in the streetside trees would be
blooming through the smog of late spring.
Wisteria in Masuda's front yard would be
shaking out the long tresses of its purple hair.
Maybe mosquitoes, moths, a few orange butterflies
settling on the lattice of monkey flowers
tangled in chain-link fences by the trash.

But this is October, and Los Angeles
seethes like a billboard under twilight.
From used-car lots and the movie houses uptown,
long silver sticks of light probe the sky.
From the Miracle Mile, whole freeways away,
a brilliant fluorescence breaks out

6. **Langendorf:** A well-known bakery in California.

and makes war with the dim squares
of yellow kitchen light winking on
in all the side streets of the Barrio.

She climbs up the two flights of flagstone   35
stairs to 201-B, the spikes of her high heels
clicking like kitchen knives on a cutting board,
props the groceries against the door,
fishes through memo pads, a compact,
empty packs of chewing gum, and finds her keys.   40

The moon then, cruising from behind
a screen of eucalyptus across the street,
covers everything, everything in sight,
in a heavy light like yellow onions.

[1982]

RITA DOVE   [b. 1952]

Fifth Grade Autobiography

I was four in this photograph fishing
with my grandparents at a lake in Michigan.
My brother squats in poison ivy.
His Davy Crockett cap
sits squared on his head so the raccoon tail   5
flounces down the back of his sailor suit.

My grandfather sits to the far right
in a folding chair,
and I know his left hand is on
the tobacco in his pants pocket   10
because I used to wrap it for him
every Christmas. Grandmother's hips
bulge from the brush, she's leaning
into the ice chest, sun through the trees
printing her dress with soft   15
luminous paws.

I am staring jealously at my brother;
the day before he rode his first horse, alone.

I was strapped in a basket
behind my grandfather.
He smelled of lemons. He's died—

but I remember his hands.

[1989]

NAOMI SHIHAB NYE   [b. 1952]

The Small Vases from Hebron°

Tip their mouths open to the sky.
Turquoise, amber,
the deep green with fluted handle,
pitcher the size of two thumbs,
tiny lip and graceful waist.
Here we place the smallest flower
which could have lived invisibly
in loose soil beside the road,
sprig of succulent rosemary,
bowing mint.

They grow deeper in the center of the table.

Here we entrust the small life,
thread, fragment, breath.
And it bends. It waits all day.
As the bread cools and the children
open their gray copybooks
to shape the letter that looks like
a chimney rising out of a house.

And what do the headlines say?

Nothing of the smaller petal
perfectly arranged inside the larger petal
or the way tinted glass filters light.

Hebron: An ancient city in the West Bank area of Israel, a sacred place for both Muslims and Jews. It has been a focus of tension between Israelis and Palestinians since the 1967 Arab-Israeli war.

Men and boys, praying when they died,
fall out of their skins.
The whole alphabet of living,   25
heads and tails of words,
sentences, the way they said,
"Ya'Allah!" when astonished,
or "ya'ani" for "I mean"—
a crushed glass under the feet   30
still shines.
But the child of Hebron sleeps
with the thud of her brothers falling
and the long sorrow of the color red.

                                                              [1998]

ALBERTO RÍOS   [b. 1952]

Nani°

Sitting at her table, she serves
the sopa de arroz° to me   *rice soup*
instinctively, and I watch her,
the absolute *mamá*, and eat words
I might have had to say more   5
out of embarrassment. To speak,
now-foreign words I used to speak,
too, dribble down her mouth as she serves
me albondigas.° No more   *meatballs*
than a third are easy to me.   10
By the stove she does something with words
and looks at me only with her
back. I am full. I tell her
I taste the mint, and watch her speak
smiles at the stove. All my words   15
make her smile. Nani never serves
herself, she only watches me
with her skin, her hair. I ask for more.

Nani: Diminutive for "grandmother."

I watch the *mamá* warming more
tortillas for me. I watch her
fingers in the flame for me.
Near her mouth, I see a wrinkle speak
of a man whose body serves
the ants like she serves me, then more words
from more wrinkles about children, words
about this and that, flowing more
easily from these other mouths. Each serves
as a tremendous string around her,
holding her together. They speak
nani was this and that to me
and I wonder just how much of me
will die with her, what were the words
I could have been, was. Her insides speak
through a hundred wrinkles, now, more
than she can bear, steel around her,
shouting, then, What is this thing she serves?

She asks me if I want more.
I own no words to stop her.
Even before I speak, she serves.

[1982]

MARY RUEFLE   [b. 1952]

Barbarians

Here and there, between trees,
cows lie down in the forest
in the mid-afternoon
as though sleep were an idea
for which they were willing
to die.

[1987]

GARY SOTO [b. 1952]

Moving Away

Remember that we are moving away   brother
From those years
In the same house with a white stepfather
What troubled him has been forgotten

But what troubled us has settled   5
Like dirt
In the nests of our knuckles
And cannot be washed away

All those times you woke shivering
In the night   10
From a coldness I
Could not understand
And cupped a crucifix beneath the covers

All those summers we hoed our yard
In the afternoon sun   15
The heat waving across our faces
And we waved back wasps
While the one we hated
Watched us from under a tree and said nothing

We will remember those moments   brother   20

And now that we are far
From one another
What I want to speak of
Is the quiet of a room just before daybreak
And you next to me   sleeping   25

[1977]

JIMMY SANTIAGO BACA   [b. 1952]

Family Ties

Mountain barbecue.
They arrive, young cousins singly,
older aunts and uncles in twos and threes,
like trees. I play with a new generation
of children, my hands in streambed silt
of their lives, a scuba diver's hands, dusting
surface sand for buried treasure.
Freshly shaved and powdered faces
of uncles and aunts surround taco
and tamale tables. Mounted elk head on wall,
brass rearing horse cowboy clock
on fireplace mantle. Sons and daughters
converse round beer and whiskey table.
Tempers ignite on land grant issues.
Children scurry round my legs.
Old bow-legged men toss horseshoes on lawn,
other farmhands from Mexico sit on a bench,
broken lives repaired for this occasion.
I feel no love or family tie here. I rise
to go hiking, to find abandoned rock cabins
in the mountains. We come to a grass clearing,
my wife rolls her jeans up past ankles,
wades ice cold stream, and I barefooted,
carry a son in each arm and follow.
We cannot afford a place like this.
At the party again, I eat bean and chile
burrito, and after my third glass of rum,
we climb in the car and my wife drives
us home. My sons sleep in the back,
dream of the open clearing,
they are chasing each other with cattails
in the sunlit pasture, giggling,

as I stare out the window
at no trespassing signs white flashing past.

[1989]

JUDITH ORTIZ COFER   [b. 1952]

Cold as Heaven

Before there is a breeze again
before the cooling days of Lent, she may be gone.
My grandmother asks me to tell her
again about the snow.
We sit on her white bed   5
in this white room, while outside
the Caribbean sun winds up the world
like an old alarm clock. I tell her
about the enveloping blizzard I lived through
that made everything and everyone the same;   10
how we lost ourselves in drifts so tall
we fell through our own footprints;
how wrapped like mummies in layers of wool
that almost immobilized us, we could only
take hesitant steps like toddlers   15
toward food, warmth, shelter.
I talk winter real for her,
as she would once conjure for me to dream
at sweltering siesta time,
cool stone castles in lands far north.   20
Her eyes wander to the window,
to the teeming scene of children
pouring out of a yellow bus, then to the bottle
dripping minutes through a tube
into her veins. When her eyes return to me,   25
I can see she's waiting to hear more
about the purifying nature of ice,
how snow makes way for a body,
how you can make yourself an angel
by just lying down and waving your arms   30

as you do when you say
good-bye.

[1995]

ANITA ENDREZZE   [b. 1952]

The Girl Who Loved the Sky

Outside the second grade room,
the jacaranda tree blossomed
into purple lanterns, the papery petals
drifted, darkening the windows.
Inside, the room smelled like glue.
The desks were made of yellowed wood,
the tops littered with eraser rubbings,
rulers, and big fat pencils.
Colored chalk meant special days.
The walls were covered with precise
bright tulips and charts with shiny stars
by certain names. There, I learned
how to make butter by shaking a jar
until the pale cream clotted
into one sweet mass. There, I learned
that numbers were fractious beasts
with dens like dim zeros. And there,
I met a blind girl who thought the sky
tasted like cold metal when it rained
and whose eyes were always covered
with the bruised petals of her lids.

She loved the formless sky, defined
only by sounds, or the cool umbrellas
of clouds. On hot, still days
we listened to the sky falling
like chalk dust. We heard the noon
whistle of the pig-mash factory,
smelled the sourness of home-bound men.
I had no father; she had no eyes;

we were best friends. The other girls   30
drew shaky hop-scotch squares
on the dusty asphalt, talked about
pajama parties, weekend cook-outs,
and parents who bought sleek-finned cars.
Alone, we sat in the canvas swings,   35
our shoes digging into the sand, then pushing,
until we flew high over their heads,
our hands streaked with red rust
from the chains that kept us safe.

I was born blind, she said, an act of nature.   40
Sure, I thought, like birds born
without wings, trees without roots.
I didn't understand. The day she moved
I saw the world clearly; the sky
backed away from me like a departing father.   45
I sat under the jacaranda, catching
the petals in my palm, enclosing them
until my fist was another lantern
hiding a small and bitter flame.

[1988]

RAY GONZÁLEZ   [b. 1952]

Praise the Tortilla,
Praise Menudo,
Praise Chorizo

I praise the tortilla in honor of El Panzón,
who hit me in school every day and made me see
how the bruises on my arms looked like
the brown clouds on my mother's tortillas.
I praise the tortilla because I know   5
they can fly into our hands like
eager flesh of the one we love,

those soft yearnings we delight in biting
as we tear the tortilla and wipe the plate clean.

I praise the menudo° as visionary food that it is,
the tripas y posole° tight flashes of color
we see as the red caldo° smears across our notebooks
like a vision we have not had in years,
our lives going down like the empty bowl
of menudo exploding in our stomachs
with the chili piquin° of our poetic dreams.

I praise the chorizo° and smear it
across my face and hands,
the dayglow brown of it painting me
with the desire to find out
what happened to la familia,
why the chorizo sizzled in the pan
and covered the house with a smell
of childhood we will never have again,
the chorizo burrito hot in our hands,
as we ran out to play and show the vatos°
it's time to cut the chorizo,
tell it like it is before la manteca° runs down
our chins and drips away.

[1992]

10. menudo: Mexican soup made with hominy and tripe; said to have special powers.
11. tripas y posole: Tripe and hominy.
12. caldo: Soup.
16. chili piquin: Type of pepper, added to menudo or other soups.
17. chorizo: Mexican sausage.
26. vatos: Guys.
28. la manteca: Lard or grease.

MARK DOTY [b. 1953]

Tiara

Peter died in a paper tiara
cut from a book of princess paper dolls;
he loved royalty, sashes

and jewels. I don't know,
he said, when he woke in the hospice,   5
I was watching the Bette Davis film festival

on Channel 57 and then—
At the wake, the tension broke
when someone guessed

the casket closed because   10
he was *in there in a big wig*
and heels, and someone said,

You know he's always late,
he probably isn't here yet—
he's still fixing his makeup.   15

And someone said he asked for it.
Asked for it—
when all he did was go down

into the salt tide
of wanting as much as he wanted,   20
giving himself over so drunk

or stoned it almost didn't matter who,
though they were beautiful,
stampeding into him in the simple,

ravishing music of their hurry.   25
I think heaven is perfect stasis
poised over the realms of desire,

677

where dreaming and waking men lie
on the grass while wet horses
roam among them, huge fragments

of the music we die into
in the body's paradise.
Sometimes we wake not knowing

how we came to lie here,
or who has crowned us with these temporary,
precious stones. And given

the world's perfectly turned shoulders,
the deep hollows blued by longing,
given the irreplaceable silk

of horses rippling in orchards,
fruit thundering and chiming down,
given the ordinary marvels of form

and gravity, what could he do,
what could any of us ever do
but ask for it?

[1991]

TONY HOAGLAND   [b. 1953]

History of Desire

When you're seventeen, and drunk
on the husky, late-night flavor
of your first girlfriend's voice
along the wires of the telephone

what else to do but steal
your father's El Dorado from the drive,
and cruise out to the park on Driscoll Hill?
Then climb the county water tower

and aerosol her name in spraycan orange
a hundred feet above the town?

Because only the letters of that word,
DORIS, next door to yours,

in yard-high, iridescent script,
are amplified enough to tell the world
who's playing lead guitar   15
in the rock band of your blood.

You don't consider for a moment
the shock in store for you in 10 A.D.,
a decade after Doris, when,
out for a drive on your visit home,   20

you take the Smallville Road, look up
and see *RON LOVES DORIS*
still scorched upon the reservoir.
This is how history catches up—

by holding still until you   25
bump into yourself.
What makes you blush, and shove
the pedal of the Mustang

almost through the floor
as if you wanted to spray gravel   30
across the features of the past,
or accelerate into oblivion?

Are you so out of love that you
can't move fast enough away?
But if desire is acceleration,   35
experience is circular as any

Indianapolis. We keep coming back
to what we are—each time older,
more freaked out, or less afraid.
And you are older now.   40

You should stop today.
In the name of Doris, stop.

[1992]

RICHARD JONES [b. 1953]

Cathedral

Songbirds live
in the old cathedral,
caged birds bought at the street market
and freed as a kind of offering.
Now doves and finches and parakeets
nest in the crooks of the nave's highest arches,
roosting on the impossibly high
sills of stained glass windows,
looking down into the valley of the altar
as if from cliffs.

Twice a day, you'll hear them singing:
at dawn
when the blue light
of angels' wings
and the yellow light of halos
flood into their nests to wake them;
and during mass
when the organ fills
the valley below with thunder.
These birds love thunder,
never having seen a drop of rain.
They love it when the people below stand up
and sing. They fly
in mad little loops
from window to window,
from the tops of arches
down toward the candles and tombs,
making the sign of the cross.

If you look up during mass
to the world's light falling
through the arms of saints
you can see birds flying
through blue columns of incense

as if it were simple wood smoke
rising from a cabin's chimney
in a remote and hushed forest.   35

[1994]

JANE HIRSHFIELD [b. 1953]

To Drink

I want to gather your darkness
in my hands, to cup it like water
and drink.
I want this in the same way
as I want to touch your cheek—   5
it is the same—
the way a moth will come
to the bedroom window in late September,
beating and beating its wings against cold glass;
the way a horse will lower   10
his long head to water, and drink,
and pause to lift his head and look,
and drink again,
taking everything in with the water,
everything.   15

[1988]

LORNA DEE CERVANTES [b. 1954]

Freeway 280

Las casitas° near the gray cannery,   *little houses*
nestled amid wild abrazos° of climbing roses   *bear hugs*
and man-high red geraniums

are gone now. The freeway conceals it
all beneath a raised scar.

But under the fake windsounds of the open lanes,
in the abandoned lots below, new grasses sprout,
wild mustard remembers, old gardens
come back stronger than they were,
trees have been left standing in their yards.
Albaricoqueros, cerezos, nogales° . . .   *apple, cherry, walnut trees*
Viejitas° come here with paper bags to gather greens.   *old women*
Espinaca, verdolagas, yerbabuena° . . .   *spinach, purslane, mint*

I scramble over the wire fence
that would have kept me out.
Once, I wanted out, wanted the rigid lanes
to take me to a place without sun,
without the smell of tomatoes burning
on swing shift in the greasy summer air.

Maybe it's here
en los campos extraños de esta ciudad°
where I'll find it, that part of me
mown under
like a corpse
or a loose seed.

[1981]

21. en . . . ciudad: In the strange fields of this city.

THYLIAS MOSS   [b. 1954]

The Lynching

They should have slept, would have
but had to fight the darkness, had
to build a fire and bathe a man in
flames. No

other soap's as good when
the dirt is the skin. Black since

birth, burnt by birth. His father
is not in heaven. No parent

of atrocity is in heaven. My father chokes
in the next room. It is night, darkness   10
has replaced air. We are white like
incandescence

yet lack light. The God in my father
does not glow. The only lamp
is the burning black man. Holy   15
burning, holy longing, remnants of

a genie after greed. My father
baptizes by fire same as Jesus will.
Becomes a holy ghost when
he dons his sheet, a clerical collar   20

out of control, Dundee Mills percale,
fifty percent cotton, dixie, confederate
and fifty percent polyester, man-made, man-
ipulated, unnatural, mulatto fiber, warp

of miscegenation.   25
After the bath, the man is hung as if
just his washed shirt, the parts
of him most capable of sin removed.

Charred, his flesh is bark, his body
a trunk. No sign of roots. I can't leave   30
him. This is limbo. This is the life after
death coming if God is an invention as were

slaves. So I spend the night, his thin moon-begot
shadow as mattress; something smoldering
keeps me warm. Patches of skin fall onto me   35
in places I didn't know needed mending.

[1991]

CORNELIUS EADY [b. 1954]

My Mother, If She Had Won Free Dance Lessons

Would she have been a person
With a completely different outlook on life?
There are times when I visit
And find her settled on a chair
In our dilapidated house,
The neighborhood crazy lady
Doing what the neighborhood crazy lady is supposed to do,
Which is absolutely nothing

And I wonder as we talk our sympathetic talk,
Abandoned in easy dialogue,
I, the son of the crazy lady,
Who crosses easily into her point of view
As if yawning
Or taking off an overcoat.
Each time I visit
I walk back into our lives

And I wonder, like any child who wakes up one day to find themself
Abandoned in a world larger than their
    Bad dreams,
I wonder as I see my mother sitting there,
Landed to the right-hand window in the living room,
Pausing from time to time in the endless loop of our dialogue
To peek for rascals through the
Venetian blinds,
I wonder a small thought.
I walk back into our lives.
Given the opportunity,
How would she have danced?
Would it have been as easily

As we talk to each other now,
The crazy lady

And the crazy lady's son,
As if we were old friends from opposite coasts
Picking up the thread of a long conversation,

Or two ballroom dancers   35
Who only know
One step?

What would have changed
If the phone had rung like a suitor,
If the invitation had arrived in the mail   40
Like Jesus, extending a hand?

[1986]

MARILYN CHIN   [b. 1955]

How I Got That Name

an essay on assimilation

I am Marilyn Mei Ling Chin.
Oh, how I love the resoluteness
of that first person singular
followed by that stalwart indicative
of "be," without the uncertain i-n-g   5
of "becoming." Of course,
the name had been changed
somewhere between Angel Island° and the sea,
when my father the paperson°
in the late 1950s   10
obsessed with a bombshell blonde°   *(Marilyn Monroe)*
transliterated "Mei Ling" to "Marilyn."
And nobody dared question
his initial impulse—for we all know

8. Angel Island: An island in San Francisco Bay, site of the Angel Island Immigration Station that processed approximately one million Asian immigrants between 1910 and 1940.
9. paperson: A "paper son" is a term used for young Chinese males entering the United States who claimed to be sons of U.S. citizens but were, in fact, sons on paper only.

lust drove men to greatness,
not goodness, not decency.
And there I was, a wayward pink baby,
named after some tragic white woman
swollen with gin and Nembutal.°
My mother couldn't pronounce the "r."
She dubbed me "Numba one female offshoot"
for brevity: henceforth, she will live and die
in sublime ignorance, flanked
by loving children and the "kitchen deity."
While my father dithers,
a tomcat in Hong Kong trash—
a gambler, a petty thug,
who bought a chain of chopsuey joints
in Piss River, Oregon,
with bootlegged Gucci cash.
Nobody dared question his integrity given
his nice, devout daughters,
and his bright, industrious sons
as if filial piety were the standard
by which all earthly men were measured.

*

Oh, how trustworthy our daughters,
how thrifty our sons!
How we've managed to fool the experts
in education, statistics and demography—
We're not very creative but not adverse to rote-learning.
Indeed, they can *use* us.
But the "Model Minority" is a tease.
We know you are watching now,
so we refuse to give you any!
Oh, bamboo shoots, bamboo shoots!
The further west we go, we'll hit east;
the deeper down we dig, we'll find China.
History has turned its stomach
on a black polluted beach—
where life doesn't hinge
on that red, red wheelbarrow,°

19. **Nembutal:** A short-acting barbituate (Pentobarbital) prescribed as a sedative but also used as an intoxicant.
51. **red wheelbarrow:** See the poem by William Carlos Williams on page 542.

but whether or not our new lover
in the final episode of *Santa Barbara*°
will lean over a scented candle
and call us a "bitch."
Oh God, where have we gone wrong?   55
We have no inner resources!

*

Then, one redolent spring morning
the Great Patriarch Chin
peered down from his kiosk in heaven   60
and saw that his descendants were ugly.
One had a squarish head and a nose without a bridge.
Another's profile—long and knobbed as a gourd.
A third, the sad, brutish one
may never, never marry.   65
And I, his least favorite—
"not quite boiled, not quite cooked,"
a plump pomfret simmering in my juices—
too listless to fight for my people's destiny.
"To kill without resistance is not slaughter"   70
says the proverb. So, I wait for imminent death.
The fact that this death is also metaphorical
is testament to my lethargy.

*

So here lies Marilyn Mei Ling Chin,
married once, twice to so-and-so, a Lee and a Wong,   75
granddaughter of Jack "the patriarch"
and the brooding Suilin Fong,
daughter of the virtuous Yuet Kuen Wong
and G. G. Chin the infamous,
sister of a dozen, cousin of a million,   80
survived by everybody and forgotten by all.
She was neither black nor white,
neither cherished nor vanquished,
just another squatter in her own bamboo grove
minding her poetry—   85
when one day heaven was unmerciful,

53. **"Santa Barbara":** American television soap opera, 1984-1993, that focused
on the lives of the wealthy Capwell family of Santa Barbara, California.

and a chasm opened where she stood.
Like the jowls of a mighty white whale,°
or the jaws of a metaphysical Godzilla,°
it swallowed her whole.
She did not flinch nor writhe,
nor fret about the afterlife,
but stayed! Solid as wood, happily
a little gnawed, tattered, mesmerized
by all that was lavished upon her
and all that was taken away!

[1994]

88. **mighty white whale:** The whale in Herman Melville's 1851 novel *Moby Dick*.
89. **Godzilla:** A monster which appeared first in Ishirō Honda's 1954 film *Godzilla* and became a pop culture icon in twenty-eight additional films.

CATHY SONG   [b. 1955]

Heaven

He thinks when we die we'll go to China.
Think of it—a Chinese heaven
where, except for his blond hair,
the part that belongs to his father,
everyone will look like him.
China, that blue flower on the map,
bluer than the sea
his hand must span like a bridge
to reach it.
An octave away.

I've never seen it.
It's as if I can't sing that far.
But look—
on the map, this black dot.
Here is where we live,
on the pancake plains
just east of the Rockies,

on the other side of the clouds.
A mile above the sea,
the air is so thin, you can starve on it.   20
No bamboo trees
but the alpine equivalent,
reedy aspen with light, fluttering leaves.
Did a boy in Guangzhou° dream of this
as his last stop?   25

I've heard the trains at night
whistling past our yards,
what we've come to own,
the broken fences, the whiny dog, the rattletrap cars.
It's still the wild west,   30
mean and grubby,
the shootouts and fistfights in the back alley.
With my son the dreamer
and my daughter, who is too young to walk,
I've sat in this spot   35
and wondered why here?
Why in this short life,
this town, this creek they call a river?

He had never planned to stay,
the boy who helped to build   40
the railroads° for a dollar a day.
He had always meant to go back.
When did he finally know
that each mile of track led him further away,
that he would die in his sleep,   45
dispossessed,
having seen Gold Mountain,°
the icy wind tunneling through it,
these landlocked, makeshift ghost towns?

It must be in the blood,   50
this notion of returning.

24. Guangzhou: A large seaport city in southeastern China (also known as Canton).
40–41. build the railroads: The Central Pacific Railroad used mostly Chinese immigrant laborers to lay the western section of tracks for the first transcontinental railroad.
47. Gold Mountain: The name the Chinese gave to California and British Columbia during the gold rush of the nineteenth century.

It skipped two generations, lay fallow,
the garden an unmarked grave.
On a spring sweater day
it's as if we remember him.
I call to the children.
We can see the mountains
shimmering blue above the air.
If you look really hard
says my son the dreamer,
leaning out from the laundry's rigging,
the work shirts fluttering like sails,
you can see all the way to heaven.

[1988]

KIMIKO HAHN   [b. 1955]

Mother's Mother

. . . There is no mother tongue.
—ELAINE SHOWALTER

The mother draws the shade down halfway
so the sunlight does not blind the pages
and she reads the story, *mukashi mukashi aruhi,*°
which is the way every story begins
whether about a boy riding a tortoise beneath the sea
or a girl born from a bamboo stalk.
Her daughter does not speak Japanese
though she can write her name in the *kana*°
that resembles tv antennae

キ ミ コ°

---

3. *mukashi mukashi aruhi:* Once upon a time.
8. *kana:* A general term for the syllabic Japanese scripts *hiragana* and *katakana*,
which were adapted from the logographic characters of Chinese origin known in
Japan as *Kanji* and are easier to master.
9. キ ミ コ: Ki-mi-ko.

and she knows not everyone speaks the same language: 10
see you, ciao, adios, sayonara. She knows
her mother knows more than one way to say things
and Japanese, which is also how she *looks*,
is the language her mother was taught,
like the island of Japan,   15
almost as far from this little house on the island of Maui.

The chickens are so loud grandma.
Ursuai ne.°
So dusty.
Kitanai°   20
So—
She wants to learn every word her grandma knows.
She wants to be like her grandma
who she sees her mother loves and does not want to leave.
She wants to stay with her grandma also   25
and knows from her mother's shoulders they will not see her again.

If there is no mother tongue for women
there is for immigrant children
who play on the black volcanic beaches,
on the sharp coral reefs, in the salty rain, the plantation houses,   30
the fields of burning cane, the birds-of-paradise.
Who see the shark fins in the sunlight and linger on the blanket.

There is a mother's tongue and it is conveyed
by this mother to her daughters
who will carry the words at least in song   35
because when mother dies there will be no one else
unless there is an aunt or cousin
to correct the tense or word choice
with such affection and cause.

そうよね。°

The same cause found in domestic arts and survival.   40
When the mother dies the daughter
or the daughter-in-law, or even the son,
becomes that figure in part
and the words the older woman knew

18. *Ursuai ne:* Annoying, isn't it?
20. *Kitanai:* Dirty, filthy.
39. そうよね.: That's just the way it is, isn't it?

are the words this person will parent
despite lineage and its repressive roots.
Its often awful branches.
The root words and radicals the daughter memorizes.

水   シ°

So when I toss my hair from my eyes I feel
it's mother tossing her head and when I cough
it is her cough I hear.
And when I tell my child to say *mama*
it may be that I am speaking to myself
as much as I am speaking to the small mouth
a few inches from my face.

[1999]

48. 水 シ: It is endless (the process of learning Japanese characters).

LI-YOUNG LEE [b. 1957]

Eating Alone

I've pulled the last of the year's young onions.
The garden is bare now. The ground is cold,
brown and old. What is left of the day flames
in the maples at the corner of my
eye. I turn, a cardinal vanishes.
By the cellar door, I wash the onions,
then drink from the icy metal spigot.

Once, years back, I walked beside my father
among the windfall pears. I can't recall
our words. We may have strolled in silence. But
I still see him bend that way—left hand braced
on knee, creaky—to lift and hold to my
eye a rotten pear. In it, a hornet
spun crazily, glazed in slow, glistening juice.

It was my father I saw this morning
waving to me from the trees. I almost

called to him, until I came close enough
to see the shovel, leaning where I had
left it, in the flickering, deep green shade.

White rice steaming, almost done. Sweet green peas   20
fried in onions. Shrimp braised in sesame
oil and garlic. And my own loneliness.
What more could I, a young man, want.

[1986]

LI-YOUNG LEE   [b. 1957]

Visions and Interpretations

Because this graveyard is a hill,
I must climb up to see my dead,
stopping once midway to rest
beside this tree.

It was here, between the anticipation   5
of exhaustion, and exhaustion,
between vale and peak,
my father came down to me

and we climbed arm in arm to the top.
He cradled the bouquet I'd brought,   10
and I, a good son, never mentioned his grave,
erect like a door behind him.

And it was here, one summer day, I sat down
to read an old book. When I looked up
from the noon-lit page, I saw a vision   15
of a world about to come, and a world about to go.

Truth is, I've not seen my father
since he died, and, no, the dead
do not walk arm in arm with me.

If I carry flowers to them, I do so without their help,   20
the blossoms not always bright, torch-like,
but often heavy as sodden newspaper.

Truth is, I came here with my son one day,
and we rested against this tree,
and I fell asleep, and dreamed

a dream which, upon my boy waking me, I told.
Neither of us understood.
Then we went up.

Even this is not accurate.
Let me begin again:

Between two griefs, a tree.
Between my hands, white chrysanthemums, yellow chrysanthemums.

The old book I finished reading
I've since read again and again.

And what was far grows near,
and what is near grows more dear,

and all of my visions and interpretations
depend on what I see,

and between my eyes is always
the rain, the migrant rain.

[1986]

MARTÍN ESPADA   [b. 1957]

Latin Night at the Pawnshop

Chelsea, Massachusetts,
Christmas, 1987

The apparition of a salsa band
gleaming in the Liberty Loan
pawnshop window:

Golden trumpet,
silver trombone,
congas, maracas, tambourine,
all with price tags dangling

like the city morgue ticket
on a dead man's toe.

[1990]

BOB HICOK   [b. 1960]

In the Loop

I heard from people after the shootings. People
I knew well or barely or not at all. Largely
the same message: how horrible it was, how little
there was to say about how horrible it was.
People wrote, called, mostly e-mailed   5
to say, there's nothing to say. Eventually
I answered these messages: there's nothing
to say back of course there's nothing
to say, thank you for your willingness to say it.
Because this was about nothing. A boy who felt   10
that he was nothing, who erased and entered
that erasure, and guns that are good for nothing,
and talk of guns that is good for nothing,
and spring that is good for flowers, and Jesus
for some, and scotch for others, and "and"   15
for me in this poem, "and" that is good
for sewing the minutes together, which otherwise
go about going away, bereft of us and us
of them, like a scarf left on a train
and nothing like a scarf left on a train,   20
like the train, empty of everything but a scarf,
and still it opens its doors at every stop,
because this is what a train does,
this is what a man does with his hand on a lever,
because otherwise why the lever, why the hand,   25
and then it was over, and then it had just begun.

[2010]

VIRGIL SUÁREZ [b. 1962]

Tea Leaves, *Caracoles*, Coffee Beans

My mother, who in those Havana days believed in divination,
found her tea leaves at *El Volcán*, the Chinese market/apothecary,

brought the leaves in a precious silk paper bundle, unwrapped
them as if unwrapping her own skin, and then boiled water

to make my dying grandmother's tea; while my mother read
its leaves, I simply saw *leaves floating* in steaming water,

vapor kissed my skin, my nose became moist as a puppy's.
My mother did this because my grandmother, her mother-in-law,

believed in all things. Her appetite for knowledge was vast,
the one thing we all agreed she passed down to me, the skinny

kid sent to search for *caracoles*, these snail shells
that littered the underbrush of the empty lot next door.

My mother threw them on top of the table, cleaned them of dirt,
kept them in a mason jar and every morning before breakfast,

read them on top of the table, their way of falling, some up,
some down, their ridges, swirls of creamy lines, their broken

edges. . . . Everything she read looked bad, for my grandmother,
for us, for staying in our country, this island of suspended

disbelief. My mother read coffee beans too, with their wrinkled,
fleshy green and red skin. Orange-skinned beans she kept aside.

Orange meant death, and my mother didn't want to accept it.
I learned mostly of death from the way a sparrow fell

when I hit it in the chest with my slingshot and a lead pellet
I made by melting my toy soldiers. The sparrow's eyes

always hid behind droopy eyelids, which is how my grandmother
died, by closing her eyes to the world; truth became this fading

696

light, a tunnel, as everybody says, but instead of heaven
she went into the ground, to that one place that still nourishes

the tea leaves, *caracoles*, and the coffee beans, which, if I didn't
know better, I'd claim shone; those red-glowing beans   30

in starlight were the eyes of the dead looking out through
the darkness as those of us who believed in such things walked

through life with a lightness of feet, spirit, a vapor-aura
that could be read or sung.

[2005]

A. VAN JORDAN [b. 1965]

From

from (⟹) *prep.* 1. Starting at (a particular place or time): As in, John was
from Chicago, but he played guitar straight *from* the Delta; he wore a
blue suit *from* Robert Hall's; his hair smelled like coconut; his breath,
like mint and bourbon; his hands felt like they were *from* slave times
when he touched me—hungry, stealthy, trembling. 2. Out of: He pulled a
knot of bills *from* his pocket, paid the man and we went upstairs. 3. Not
near to or in contact with: He smoked the weed, but, surprisingly, he kept
it *from* me. He said it would make me too self-conscious, and he wanted
those feelings as far away *from* us as possible; he said a good part of my
beauty was that I wasn't conscious of my beauty. Isn't that funny? So we
drank Bloody Mothers (Hennessey and tomato juice), which was hard to
keep *from* him—he always did like to drink. 4. Out of the control or authority of: I was released *from* my mama's house, *from* dreams of hands
holding me down, *from* the threat of hands not pulling me up, *from* the
man that knew me, but of whom I did not know; released *from* the dim-
ming of twilight, *from* the brightness of morning; *from* the love I thought
had to look like love; *from* the love I thought had to taste like love, *from*
the love I thought I had to love like love. 5. Out of the totality of: I came
from a family full of women; I came *from* a family full of believers; I
came *from* a pack of witches—I'm just waiting to conjure my powers; I
came *from* a legacy of lovers—I'm just waiting to seduce my seducer;
I came *from* a pride of proud women, and we take good care of our

young. 6. As being other or another than: He couldn't tell me *from* his
mother; he couldn't tell me *from* his sister; he couldn't tell me *from* the
last woman he had before me, and why should he—we're all the same
woman. 7. With (some person, place, or thing) as the instrument, maker,
or source: Here's a note *from* my mother, and you can take it as advice
from me: A weak lover is more dangerous than a strong enemy; if you're
going to love someone, make sure you know where they're coming *from*.
8. Because of: Becoming an alcoholic, learning to walk away, being a
good speller, being good in bed, falling in love—they all come *from* practice. 9. Outside or beyond the possibility of: In the room, he kept me *from*
leaving by keeping me curious; he kept me *from* drowning by holding my
breath in his mouth; yes, he kept me *from* leaving till the next day when
he said *Leave*. Then, he couldn't keep me *from* coming back.

[2004]

SHERMAN ALEXIE   [b. 1966]

Postcards to Columbus

Beginning at the front door of the White House, travel west
for 500 years, pass through small towns and house fires, ignore
hitchhikers and stranded motorists, until you find yourself
back at the beginning of this journey, this history and country

folded over itself like a Mobius strip. Christopher Columbus
where have you been? Lost between Laramie and San Francisco
or in the reservation HUD house, building a better mousetrap?
Seymour saw you shooting free throws behind the Tribal School

in a thunderstorm. Didn't you know lightning strikes the earth
800 times a second? But, Columbus, how could you ever imagine
how often our lives change? *Electricity is lightning pretending
to be permanent* and when the Indian child pushes the paper clip

into the electrical outlet, it's applied science, insane economics
of supply and demand, the completion of a 20th century circuit.
Christopher Columbus, you are the most successful real estate agent
who ever lived, sold acres and acres of myth, a house built on stilts

above the river salmon travel by genetic memory. Beneath the burden
of 15,000 years my tribe celebrated this country's 200th birthday
by refusing to speak English and we'll honor the 500th anniversary
of your invasion, Columbus, by driving blindfolded cross-country   20

naming the first tree we destroy *America*. We'll make the first guardrail
we crash through our national symbol. Our flag will be a white sheet
stained with blood and piss. Columbus, can you hear me over white
noise of your television set? Can you hear ghosts of drums approaching?

[1993]

NATASHA TRETHEWEY   [b. 1966]

History Lesson

I am four in this photograph, standing
on a wide strip of Mississippi beach,
my hands on the flowered hips

of a bright bikini. My toes dig in,
curl around wet sand. The sun cuts   5
the rippling Gulf in flashes with each

tidal rush. Minnows dart at my feet
glinting like switchblades. I am alone
except for my grandmother, other side

of the camera, telling me how to pose.   10
It is 1970, two years after they opened
the rest of this beach to us,

forty years since the photograph
where she stood on a narrow plot
of sand marked *colored*, smiling,   15

her hands on the flowered hips
of a cotton meal-sack dress.

[2000]

HONORÉE FANONNE JEFFERS   [b. 1967]

Unidentified Female Student,
Former Slave
(Talladega College, circa 1885)

You might have heard a story like this one well
but I'm telling this one to you now.
I was five when the soldiers came.

Master worked me twenty years longer.
How could I know? One day he left me alone
and an unwatched pot started to boil. By the time

he came back home I was cleaned of him and singing,
There's a man going round taking names.
Ready, set, and I was gone, walking. Could I see

beyond his yard? Did I have a thought to read or write
or count past God's creation? A barefooted
girl!—and you remember, you woman who will take

your pen to write my life. This is what the truth was like:
Master's clouds followed me to the steps of this school.
Dear reader, when you think on this years after I have died

and I am dust, think on a great and awful morning
when I learned my freedom. Think that the skin on my
back was scared when I dared step out into the world,

when my Master stood trembling and weeping
on his front porch and he cursed me beyond knowing.

[2003]

700

ALLISON JOSEPH   [b. 1967]

On Being Told I Don't Speak
Like a Black Person

Emphasize the "h," you hignorant ass,
was what my mother was told
when colonial-minded teachers
slapped her open palm with a ruler
in that Jamaican schoolroom.   5
Trained in England, they tried
to force their pupils to speak
like Eliza Doolittle after
her transformation, fancying themselves
British as Henry Higgins,°   10
despite dark, sun-ripened skin.
Mother never lost her accent,
though, the music of her voice
charming everyone, an infectious lilt
I can imitate, not duplicate.   15
No one in the States told her
to eliminate the accent,
my high school friends adoring
the way her voice would lift
when she called me to the phone,   20
A-ll-i-son, it's friend Cathy.
Why don't you sound like her?,
they'd ask. I didn't sound
like anyone or anything,
no grating New Yorker nasality,   25
no fastidious British mannerisms
like the ones my father affected

8–10. Eliza Doolittle . . . Henry Higgins: Flower-girl with a strong Cockney
(working-class) accent in George Bernard Shaw's play *Pygmalion* and the musical
based on it, *My Fair Lady*. Henry Higgins, a linguistic professor, takes on the challenge of teaching her how to speak (and act and dress) like a proper British lady.

when he wanted to sell someone
something. And I didn't sound
like a Black American,
college acquaintances observed,
sure they knew what a black person
was supposed to sound like.
Was I supposed to sound lazy,
dropping syllables here, there,
not finishing words but
slurring the final letter so that
each sentence joined the next,
sliding past the listener?
Were certain words off limits,
too erudite, too scholarly
for someone with a natural tan?
I asked what they meant,
and they stuttered, blushed,
said you know, Black English,
applying what they'd learned
from that semester's text.
Does everyone in your family
speak alike?, I'd question,
and they'd say don't take this the
wrong way, nothing personal.

Now I realize there's nothing
more personal than speech,
that I don't have to defend
how I speak, how any person,
black, white, chooses to speak.
Let us speak. Let us talk
with the sounds of our mothers
and fathers still reverberating
in our minds, wherever our mothers
or fathers come from:
Arkansas, Belize, Alabama,
Brazil, Aruba, Arizona.
Let us simply speak
to one another,
listen and prize the inflections,
differences, never assuming
how any person will sound
until her mouth opens,

until his mouth opens,   70
greetings familiar
in any language.

[1999]

TERRANCE HAYES   [b. 1971]

Talk

like a nigger now, my white friend, M, said
after my M.L.K. and Ronald Reagan impersonations,
the two of us alone and shirtless in the locker room,

and if you're thinking my knuckles knocked
a few times against his jaw or my fingers knotted   5
at his throat, you're wrong because I pretended

I didn't hear him, and when he didn't ask it again,
we slipped into our middle school uniforms
since it was November, the beginning

of basketball season, and jogged out   10
onto the court to play together
in that vision all Americans wish for

their children, and the point is we slipped
into our uniform harmony, and spit out *Go Team!*,
our hands stacked on and beneath the hands   15

of our teammates and that was as close
as I have come to passing for one
of the members of The Dream, my white friend

thinking I was so far from that word
that he could say it to me, which I guess   20
he could since I didn't let him taste the salt

and iron in the blood, I didn't teach him
what it's like to squint through a black eye,
and if I had I wonder if he would have grown

up to be the kind of white man who believes
all blacks are thugs or if he would have learned
to bite his tongue or let his belly be filled

by shame, but more importantly, would I be
the kind of black man who believes silence
is worth more than talk or that it can be

a kind of grace, though I'm not sure
that's the kind of black man I've become,
and in any case, M, wherever you are,

I'd just like to say I heard it, but let it go
because I was afraid to lose our friendship
or afraid we'd lose the game—which we did anyway.

[2006]

PART THREE

9 Plays

SOPHOCLES   [c. 496–c. 406 B.C.E.]

Oedipus Rex

TRANSLATED BY DUDLEY FITTS AND ROBERT FITZGERALD

Characters

OEDIPUS, *King of Thebes, supposed son of Polybos and Merope, King and Queen of Corinth*
IOKASTE,° *wife of Oedipus and widow of the late King Laios*
KREON,° *brother of Iokaste, a prince of Thebes*
TEIRESIAS, *a blind seer who serves Apollo*
PRIEST
MESSENGER, *from Corinth*
SHEPHERD, *former servant of Laios*
SECOND MESSENGER, *from the palace*
CHORUS OF THEBAN ELDERS
CHORAGOS, *leader of the Chorus*
ANTIGONE AND ISMENE, *young daughters of Oedipus and Iokaste. They appear in the Exodos but do not speak.*
SUPPLIANTS, GUARDS, SERVANTS

Scene: *Before the palace of Oedipus, King of Thebes. A central door and two lateral doors open onto a platform which runs the length of the facade. On the platform, right and left, are altars; and three steps lead down into the orchestra, or chorus-ground. At the beginning of the action these steps are crowded by suppliants who have brought branches and chaplets of olive leaves and who sit in various attitudes of despair. Oedipus enters.*

PROLOGUE°

OEDIPUS: My children, generations of the living
 In the line of Kadmos,° nursed at his ancient hearth:

Iokaste: Traditional Western spelling is *Jocasta*.   **Kreon:** Traditional Western spelling is *Creon*.   **Prologue:** First part of the play explaining the background and introducing the scene.   **2. Kadmos:** Founder of Thebes.

707

Why have you strewn yourselves before these altars
In supplication, with your boughs and garlands?
The breath of incense rises from the city
With a sound of prayer and lamentation.
　　Children,
I would not have you speak through messengers,
And therefore I have come myself to hear you—
I, Oedipus, who bear the famous name.
(*To a Priest.*) You, there, since you are eldest in the company,
Speak for them all, tell me what preys upon you,
Whether you come in dread, or crave some blessing:
Tell me, and never doubt that I will help you
In every way I can; I should be heartless
Were I not moved to find you suppliant here.

PRIEST: Great Oedipus, O powerful king of Thebes!
You see how all the ages of our people
Cling to your altar steps: here are boys
Who can barely stand alone, and here are priests
By weight of age, as I am a priest of God,
And young men chosen from those yet unmarried;
As for the others, all that multitude,
They wait with olive chaplets in the squares,
At the two shrines of Pallas,° and where Apollo°
Speaks in the glowing embers.
　　　　　　　　　　　　Your own eyes
Must tell you: Thebes is tossed on a murdering sea
And can not lift her head from the death surge.
A rust consumes the buds and fruits of the earth;
The herds are sick; children die unborn,
And labor is vain. The god of plague and pyre
Raids like detestable lightning through the city,
And all the house of Kadmos is laid waste,
All emptied, and all darkened: Death alone
Battens upon the misery of Thebes.

You are not one of the immortal gods, we know;
Yet we have come to you to make our prayer
As to the man surest in mortal ways
And wisest in the ways of God. You saved us

---

24. Pallas: Daughter of Zeus, goddess of wisdom, and protectress of Athens.
Apollo: Son of Zeus and god of the sun, of light, and of healing.

From the Sphinx,° that flinty singer, and the tribute
We paid to her so long; yet you were never   40
Better informed than we, nor could we teach you:
A god's touch, it seems, enabled you to help us.

Therefore, O mighty power, we turn to you:
Find us our safety, find us a remedy,
Whether by counsel of the gods or of men.   45
A king of wisdom tested in the past
Can act in a time of troubles, and act well.
Noblest of men, restore
Life to your city! Think how all men call you
Liberator for your boldness long ago;   50
Ah, when your years of kingship are remembered,
Let them not say *We rose, but later fell*—
Keep the State from going down in the storm!
Once, years ago, with happy augury,
You brought us fortune; be the same again!   55
No man questions your power to rule the land:
But rule over men, not over a dead city!
Ships are only hulls, high walls are nothing,
When no life moves in the empty passageways.
OEDIPUS: Poor children! You may be sure I know   60
  All that you longed for in your coming here.
  I know that you are deathly sick; and yet,
  Sick as you are, not one is as sick as I.
  Each of you suffers in himself alone
  His anguish, not another's; but my spirit   65
  Groans for the city, for myself, for you.

  I was not sleeping, you are not waking me.
  No, I have been in tears for a long while
  And in my restless thought walked many ways.
  In all my search I found one remedy,   70
  And I have adopted it: I have sent Kreon,
  Son of Menoikeus, brother of the queen,

---

39. Sphinx: A winged monster with the body of a lion and the face of a woman.
The Sphinx tormented Thebes with a riddle—"What goes on four legs in the
morning, two at noon, and three in the evening?"—and killed those who could
not answer correctly. When Oedipus solved the riddle, the Sphinx killed herself.

To Delphi,° Apollo's place of revelation,
To learn there, if he can,
What act or pledge of mine may save the city.
I have counted the days, and now, this very day,
I am troubled, for he has overstayed his time.
What is he doing? He has been gone too long.
Yet whenever he comes back, I should do ill
Not to take any action the god orders.

PRIEST: It is a timely promise. At this instant
They tell me Kreon is here.

OEDIPUS: O Lord Apollo!
May his news be fair as his face is radiant!

PRIEST: Good news, I gather! he is crowned with bay,
The chaplet is thick with berries.

OEDIPUS: We shall soon know;
He is near enough to hear us now. (*Enter Kreon.*) O prince:
Brother: son of Menoikeus:
What answer do you bring us from the god?

KREON: A strong one. I can tell you, great afflictions
Will turn out well, if they are taken well.

OEDIPUS: What was the oracle? These vague words
Leave me still hanging between hope and fear.

KREON: Is it your pleasure to hear me with all these
Gathered around us? I am prepared to speak,
But should we not go in?

OEDIPUS: Speak to them all,
It is for them I suffer, more than for myself.

KREON: Then I will tell you what I heard at Delphi.
In plain words
The god commands us to expel from the land of Thebes
An old defilement we are sheltering.
It is a deathly thing, beyond cure;
We must not let it feed upon us longer.

OEDIPUS: What defilement? How shall we rid ourselves of it?

KREON: By exile or death, blood for blood. It was
Murder that brought the plague-wind on the city.

OEDIPUS: Murder of whom? Surely the god has named him?

KREON: My Lord: Laios once ruled this land,
Before you came to govern us.

OEDIPUS: I know;
I learned of him from others; I never saw him.

73. Delphi: Site of the oracle, the preeminent shrine of Apollo.

KREON: He was murdered; and Apollo commands us now   110
   To take revenge upon whoever killed him.
OEDIPUS: Upon whom? Where are they? Where shall we find a clue
   To solve that crime, after so many years?
KREON: Here in this land, he said. Search reveals
   Things that escape an inattentive man.   115
OEDIPUS: Tell me: Was Laios murdered in his house,
   Or in the fields, or in some foreign country?
KREON: He said he planned to make a pilgrimage.
   He did not come home again.
OEDIPUS: And was there no one,
   No witness, no companion, to tell what happened?   120
KREON: They were all killed but one, and he got away
   So frightened that he could remember one thing only.
OEDIPUS: What was that one thing? One may be the key
   To everything, if we resolve to use it.
KREON: He said that a band of highwaymen attacked them,   125
   Outnumbered them, and overwhelmed the king.
OEDIPUS: Strange, that a highwayman should be so daring—
   Unless some faction here bribed him to do it.
KREON: We thought of that. But after Laios' death
   New troubles arose and we had no avenger.   130
OEDIPUS: What troubles could prevent your hunting down the killers?
KREON: The riddling Sphinx's song
   Made us deaf to all mysteries but her own.
OEDIPUS: Then once more I must bring what is dark to light.
   It is most fitting that Apollo shows,   135
   As you do, this compunction for the dead.
   You shall see how I stand by you, as I should,
   Avenging this country and the god as well,
   And not as though it were for some distant friend,
   But for my own sake, to be rid of evil.   140
   Whoever killed King Laios might—who knows?—
   Lay violent hands even on me—and soon.
   I act for the murdered king in my own interest.

   Come, then, my children: leave the altar steps,
   Lift up your olive boughs!
                 One of you go   145
   And summon the people of Kadmos to gather here.
   I will do all that I can; you may tell them that.   (*Exit a Page.*)
   So, with the help of God,
   We shall be saved—or else indeed we are lost.

PRIEST: Let us rise, children. It was for this we came,   1
    And now the king has promised it.
    Phoibos° has sent us an oracle; may he descend
    Himself to save us and drive out the plague.

(*Exeunt° Oedipus and Kreon into the palace by the central door. The Priest and
the Suppliants disperse right and left. After a short pause the Chorus enters the
orchestra.*)

PARODOS°   *Strophe° 1*

CHORUS: What is God singing in his profound
    Delphi of gold and shadow?
    What oracle for Thebes, the Sunwhipped city?
    Fear unjoints me, the roots of my heart tremble.
    Now I remember, O Healer, your power, and wonder:
    Will you send doom like a sudden cloud, or weave it
    Like nightfall of the past?
    Speak to me, tell me, O
    Child of golden Hope, immortal Voice.

Antistrophe° 1

Let me pray to Athene, the immortal daughter of Zeus,
    And to Artemis° her sister
    Who keeps her famous throne in the market ring,
    And to Apollo, archer from distant heaven—
    O gods, descend! Like three streams leap against
    The fires of our grief, the fires of darkness;
    Be swift to bring us rest!
    As in the old time from the brilliant house
    Of air you stepped to save us, come again!

Strophe 2

Now our afflictions have no end,
    Now all our stricken host lies down

152. Phoibos: Apollo.   [S.D.] *Exeunt:* Latin for "they go out."   **Parodos:** The
song chanted by the Chorus on their entry.   **Strophe:** Song sung by the Chorus
as they danced from stage right to stage left.   **Antistrophe:** Song sung by the
Chorus as they danced from stage left back to stage right.   **11. Artemis:** Daughter
of Zeus, twin sister of Apollo, goddess of the hunt and female chastity.

And no man fights off death with his mind;
The noble plowland bears no grain,
And groaning mothers can not bear—
See, how our lives like birds take wing,
Like sparks that fly when a fire soars,   25
To the shore of the god of evening.

Antistrophe 2

The plague burns on, it is pitiless,
Though pallid children laden with death
Lie unwept in the stony ways,
And old gray women by every path   30
Flock to the strand about the altars
There to strike their breasts and cry
Worship of Phoibos in wailing prayers:
Be kind, God's golden child!

Strophe 3

There are no swords in this attack by fire,   35
No shields, but we are ringed with cries.
Send the besieger plunging from our homes
Into the vast sea-room of the Atlantic
Or into the waves that foam eastward of Thrace—
For the day ravages what the night spares—   40
Destroy our enemy, lord of the thunder!
Let him be riven by lightning from heaven!

Antistrophe 3

Phoibos Apollo, stretch the sun's bowstring,
That golden cord, until it sing for us,
Flashing arrows in heaven!
                            Artemis, Huntress,   45
Race with flaring lights upon our mountains!
O scarlet god,° O golden-banded brow,
O Theban Bacchos in a storm of Maenads,°

(*Enter Oedipus, center.*)

47. scarlet god: Bacchus, god of wine (also called Dionysus).   **48. Maenads:**
Bacchus's female devotees.

Whirl upon Death, that all the Undying hate!
Come with blinding torches, come in joy!

SCENE 1

OEDIPUS: Is this your prayer? It may be answered. Come,
Listen to me, act as the crisis demands,
And you shall have relief from all these evils.

Until now I was a stranger to this tale,
As I had been a stranger to the crime.
Could I track down the murderer without a clue?
But now, friends,
As one who became a citizen after the murder,
I make this proclamation to all Thebans:
If any man knows by whose hand Laios, son of Labdakos,
Met his death, I direct that man to tell me everything,
No matter what he fears for having so long withheld it.
Let it stand as promised that no further trouble
Will come to him, but he may leave the land in safety.
Moreover: If anyone knows the murderer to be foreign,
Let him not keep silent: he shall have his reward from me.
However, if he does conceal it; if any man
Fearing for his friend or for himself disobeys this edict,
Hear what I propose to do:

I solemnly forbid the people of this country,
Where power and throne are mine, ever to receive that man
Or speak to him, no matter who he is, or let him
Join in sacrifice, lustration,° or in prayer.
I decree that he be driven from every house,
Being, as he is, corruption itself to us: the Delphic
Voice of Apollo has pronounced this revelation.
Thus I associate myself with the oracle
And take the side of the murdered king.

As for the criminal, I pray to God—
Whether it be a lurking thief, or one of a number—
I pray that that man's life be consumed in evil and wretchedness.
And as for me, this curse applies no less

23. lustration: A ceremonial purification.

If it should turn out that the culprit is my guest here,
Sharing my hearth.
                    You have heard the penalty.
I lay it on you now to attend to this   35
For my sake, for Apollo's, for the sick
Sterile city that heaven has abandoned.
Suppose the oracle had given you no command:
Should this defilement go uncleansed for ever?
You should have found the murderer: your king,   40
A noble king, had been destroyed!
                              Now I,
Having the power that he held before me,
Having his bed, begetting children there
Upon his wife, as he would have, had he lived—
Their son would have been my children's brother,   45
If Laios had had luck in fatherhood!
(And now his bad fortune has struck him down)—
I say I take the son's part, just as though
I were his son, to press the fight for him
And see it won! I'll find the hand that brought   50
Death to Labdakos' and Polydoros' child,
Heir of Kadmos' and Agenor's line.°
And as for those who fail me,
May the gods deny them the fruit of the earth,
Fruit of the womb, and may they rot utterly!   55
Let them be wretched as we are wretched, and worse!

For you, for loyal Thebans, and for all
Who find my actions right, I pray the favor
Of justice, and of all the immortal gods.
CHORAGOS:° Since I am under oath, my lord, I swear   60
    I did not do the murder, I can not name
    The murderer. Phoibos ordained the search;
    Why did he not say who the culprit was?
OEDIPUS: An honest question. But no man in the world
    Can make the gods do more than the gods will.   65
CHORAGOS: There is an alternative, I think—
OEDIPUS: Tell me.
    Any or all, you must not fail to tell me.
CHORAGOS: A lord clairvoyant to the lord Apollo,

51–52. Labdakos, Polydoros, Kadmos, and Agenor: Father, grandfather, great-grandfather, and great-great-grandfather of Laios.   **60. Choragos:** Chorus leader.

As we all know, is the skilled Teiresias.
One might learn much about this from him, Oedipus.
OEDIPUS: I am not wasting time:
   Kreon spoke of this, and I have sent for him—
   Twice, in fact; it is strange that he is not here.
CHORAGOS: The other matter—that old report—seems useless.
OEDIPUS: What was that? I am interested in all reports.
CHORAGOS: The king was said to have been killed by highwaymen.
OEDIPUS: I know. But we have no witnesses to that.
CHORAGOS: If the killer can feel a particle of dread,
   Your curse will bring him out of hiding!
OEDIPUS: No.
   The man who dared that act will fear no curse.

(*Enter the blind seer Teiresias, led by a Page.*)

CHORAGOS: But there is one man who may detect the criminal.
   This is Teiresias, this is the holy prophet
   In whom, alone of all men, truth was born.
OEDIPUS: Teiresias: seer: student of mysteries,
   Of all that's taught and all that no man tells,
   Secrets of Heaven and secrets of the earth:
   Blind though you are, you know the city lies
   Sick with plague; and from this plague, my lord,
   We find that you alone can guard or save us.

   Possibly you did not hear the messengers?
   Apollo, when we sent to him,
   Sent us back word that this great pestilence
   Would lift, but only if we established clearly
   The identity of those who murdered Laios.
   They must be killed or exiled.
                                 Can you use
   Birdflight° or any art of divination
   To purify yourself, and Thebes, and me
   From this contagion? We are in your hands.
   There is no fairer duty
   Than that of helping others in distress.
TEIRESIAS: How dreadful knowledge of the truth can be
   When there's no help in truth! I knew this well,
   But did not act on it; else I should not have come.

96. Birdflight: Prophets believed they could predict the future based on the
flight of birds.

OEDIPUS: What is troubling you? Why are your eyes so cold?

TEIRESIAS: Let me go home. Bear your own fate, and I'll   105
    Bear mine. It is better so: trust what I say.

OEDIPUS: What you say is ungracious and unhelpful
    To your native country. Do not refuse to speak.

TEIRESIAS: When it comes to speech, your own is neither temperate
    Nor opportune. I wish to be more prudent.   110

OEDIPUS: In God's name, we all beg you—

TEIRESIAS: You are all ignorant.
    No; I will never tell you what I know.
    Now it is my misery; then, it would be yours.

OEDIPUS: What! You do know something, and will not tell us?
    You would betray us all and wreck the State?   115

TEIRESIAS: I do not intend to torture myself, or you.
    Why persist in asking? You will not persuade me.

OEDIPUS: What a wicked old man you are! You'd try a stone's
    Patience! Out with it! Have you no feeling at all?

TEIRESIAS: You call me unfeeling. If you could only see   120
    The nature of your own feelings . . .

OEDIPUS: Why,
    Who would not feel as I do? Who could endure
    Your arrogance toward the city?

TEIRESIAS: What does it matter?
    Whether I speak or not, it is bound to come.

OEDIPUS: Then, if "it" is bound to come, you are bound to tell me.   125

TEIRESIAS: No, I will not go on. Rage as you please.

OEDIPUS: Rage? Why not!
                And I'll tell you what I think:
    You planned it, you had it done, you all but
    Killed him with your own hands: if you had eyes,
    I'd say the crime was yours, and yours alone.   130

TEIRESIAS: So? I charge you, then,
    Abide by the proclamation you have made:
    From this day forth
    Never speak again to these men or to me;
    You yourself are the pollution of this country.   135

OEDIPUS: You dare say that! Can you possibly think you have
    Some way of going free, after such insolence?

TEIRESIAS: I have gone free. It is the truth sustains me.

OEDIPUS: Who taught you shamelessness? It was not your craft.

TEIRESIAS: You did. You made me speak. I did not want to.   140

OEDIPUS: Speak what? Let me hear it again more clearly.

TEIRESIAS: Was it not clear before? Are you tempting me?

OEDIPUS: I did not understand it. Say it again.
TEIRESIAS: I say that you are the murderer whom you seek.
OEDIPUS: Now twice you have spat out infamy. You'll pay for it!
TEIRESIAS: Would you care for more? Do you wish to be really angry?
OEDIPUS: Say what you will. Whatever you say is worthless.
TEIRESIAS: I say you live in hideous shame with those
    Most dear to you. You can not see the evil.
OEDIPUS: Can you go on babbling like this for ever?
TEIRESIAS: I can, if there is power in truth.
OEDIPUS: There is:
    But not for you, not for you,
    You sightless, witless, senseless, mad old man!
TEIRESIAS: You are the madman. There is no one here
    Who will not curse you soon, as you curse me.
OEDIPUS: You child of total night! I would not touch you;
    Neither would any man who sees the sun.
TEIRESIAS: True: it is not from you my fate will come.
    That lies within Apollo's competence,
    As it is his concern.
OEDIPUS: Tell me, who made
    These fine discoveries? Kreon? or someone else?
TEIRESIAS: Kreon is no threat. You weave your own doom.
OEDIPUS: Wealth, power, craft of statemanship!
    Kingly position, everywhere admired!
    What savage envy is stored up against these,
    If Kreon, whom I trusted, Kreon my friend,
    For this great office which the city once
    Put in my hands unsought—if for this power
    Kreon desires in secret to destroy me!

    He has bought this decrepit fortune-teller, this
    Collector of dirty pennies, this prophet fraud—
    Why, he is no more clairvoyant than I am!
                                            Tell us:
    Has your mystic mummery ever approached the truth?
    When that hellcat the Sphinx was performing here,
    What help were you to these people?
    Her magic was not for the first man who came along:
    It demanded a real exorcist. Your birds—
    What good were they? or the gods, for the matter of that?
    But I came by,
    Oedipus, the simple man, who knows nothing—
    I thought it out for myself, no birds helped me!
    And this is the man you think you can destroy,

That you may be close to Kreon when he's king!
Well, you and your friend Kreon, it seems to me,
Will suffer most. If you were not an old man,   185
You would have paid already for your plot.
CHORAGOS: We can not see that his words or yours
    Have been spoken except in anger, Oedipus,
    And of anger we have no need. How to accomplish
    The god's will best: that is what most concerns us.   190
TEIRESIAS: You are a king. But where argument's concerned
    I am your man, as much a king as you.
    I am not your servant, but Apollo's.
    I have no need of Kreon or Kreon's name.

Listen to me. You mock my blindness, do you?   195
But I say that you, with both your eyes, are blind:
You can not see the wretchedness of your life,
Nor in whose house you live, no, nor with whom.
Who are your father and mother? Can you tell me?
You do not even know the blind wrongs   200
That you have done them, on earth and in the world below.
But the double lash of your parents' curse will whip you
Out of this land some day, with only night
Upon your precious eyes.
Your cries then—where will they not be heard?   205
What fastness of Kithairon° will not echo them?
And that bridal-descant of yours—you'll know it then,
The song they sang when you came here to Thebes
And found your misguided berthing.
All this, and more, that you can not guess at now,   210
Will bring you to yourself among your children.

Be angry, then. Curse Kreon. Curse my words.
I tell you, no man that walks upon the earth
Shall be rooted out more horribly than you.
OEDIPUS: Am I to bear this from him?—Damnation   215
    Take you! Out of this place! Out of my sight!
TEIRESIAS: I would not have come at all if you had not asked me.
OEDIPUS: Could I have told that you'd talk nonsense, that
    You'd come here to make a fool of yourself, and of me?
TEIRESIAS: A fool? Your parents thought me sane enough.   220

206. Kithairon: The mountain near Thebes where Oedipus was abandoned as
an infant.

OEDIPUS: My parents again!—Wait: who were my parents?
TEIRESIAS: This day will give you a father, and break your heart.
OEDIPUS: Your infantile riddles! Your damned abracadabra!
TEIRESIAS: You were a great man once at solving riddles.
OEDIPUS: Mock me with that if you like; you will find it true.
TEIRESIAS: It was true enough. It brought about your ruin.
OEDIPUS: But if it saved this town?
TEIRESIAS (*to the Page*):   Boy, give me your hand.
OEDIPUS: Yes, boy; lead him away.
                                    —While you are here
   We can do nothing. Go; leave us in peace.
TEIRESIAS: I will go when I have said what I have to say.
   How can you hurt me? And I tell you again:
   The man you have been looking for all this time,
   The damned man, the murderer of Laios,
   That man is in Thebes. To your mind he is foreign-born,
   But it will soon be shown that he is a Theban,
   A revelation that will fail to please.
                                    A blind man,
   Who has his eyes now; a penniless man, who is rich now;
   And he will go tapping the strange earth with his staff.
   To the children with whom he lives now he will be
   Brother and father—the very same; to her
   Who bore him, son and husband—the very same
   Who came to his father's bed, wet with his father's blood.
   Enough. Go think that over.
   If later you find error in what I have said,
   You may say that I have no skill in prophecy.

(*Exit Teiresias, led by his Page. Oedipus goes into the palace.*)

ODE° 1   *Strophe 1*

CHORUS: The Delphic stone of prophecies
   Remembers ancient regicide
   And a still bloody hand.
   That killer's hour of flight has come.
   He must be stronger than riderless
   Coursers of untiring wind,
   For the son of Zeus° armed with his father's thunder

Ode: Song sung by the Chorus. **7. son of Zeus:** Apollo.

Leaps in lightning after him;
And the Furies° hold his track, the sad Furies.

Antistrophe 1

Holy Parnassos'° peak of snow   10
Flashes and blinds that secret man,
That all shall hunt him down:
Though he may roam the forest shade
Like a bull gone wild from pasture
To rage through glooms of stone.   15
Doom comes down on him; flight will not avail him;
For the world's heart calls him desolate,
And the immortal voices follow, for ever follow.

Strophe 2

But now a wilder thing is heard
From the old man skilled at hearing Fate in the wing-beat of a bird.   20
Bewildered as a blown bird, my soul hovers and can not find
Foothold in this debate, or any reason or rest of mind.
But no man ever brought—none can bring
Proof of strife between Thebes' royal house,
Labdakos' line,° and the son of Polybos;°   25
And never until now has any man brought word
Of Laios' dark death staining Oedipus the King.

Antistrophe 2

Divine Zeus and Apollo hold
Perfect intelligence alone of all tales ever told;
And well though this diviner works, he works in his own night;   30
No man can judge that rough unknown or trust in second sight,
For wisdom changes hands among the wise.
Shall I believe my great lord criminal
At a raging word that a blind old man let fall?
I saw him, when the carrion woman° faced him of old,   35
Prove his heroic mind. These evil words are lies.

9. **Furies:** Powerful avenging divinities.   10. **Parnassos:** Mountain sacred to
Apollo.   25. **Labdakos' line:** Laios's family.   **Polybos:** King of Corinth who
adopted Oedipus.   35. **woman:** The Sphinx.

SCENE 2

KREON: Men of Thebes:
   I am told that heavy accusations
   Have been brought against me by King Oedipus.

   I am not the kind of man to bear this tamely.

   If in these present difficulties
   He holds me accountable for any harm to him
   Through anything I have said or done—why, then,
   I do not value life in this dishonor.
   It is not as though this rumor touched upon
   Some private indiscretion. The matter is grave.
   The fact is that I am being called disloyal
   To the State, to my fellow citizens, to my friends.
CHORAGOS: He may have spoken in anger, not from his mind.
KREON: But did you not hear him say I was the one
   Who seduced the old prophet into lying?
CHORAGOS: The thing was said; I do not know how seriously.
KREON: But you were watching him! Were his eyes steady?
   Did he look like a man in his right mind?
CHORAGOS: I do not know.
   I can not judge the behavior of great men.
   But here is the king himself.

(*Enter Oedipus.*)

OEDIPUS: So you dared come back.
   Why? How brazen of you to come to my house,
   You murderer!
                       Do you think I do not know
   That you plotted to kill me, plotted to steal my throne?
   Tell me, in God's name: am I coward, a fool,
   That you should dream you could accomplish this?
   A fool who could not see your slippery game?
   A coward, not to fight back when I saw it?
   You are the fool, Kreon, are you not? hoping
   Without support or friends to get a throne?
   Thrones may be won or bought: you could do neither.
KREON: Now listen to me. You have talked; let me talk, too.
   You can not judge unless you know the facts.
OEDIPUS: You speak well: there is one fact; but I find it hard
   To learn from the deadliest enemy I have.

KREON: That above all I must dispute with you.   35
OEDIPUS: That above all I will not hear you deny.
KREON: If you think there is anything good in being stubborn
    Against all reason, then I say you are wrong.
OEDIPUS: If you think a man can sin against his own kind
    And not be punished for it, I say you are mad.   40
KREON: I agree. But tell me: what have I done to you?
OEDIPUS: You advised me to send for that wizard, did you not?
KREON: I did. I should do it again.
OEDIPUS: Very well. Now tell me:
    How long has it been since Laios—
KREON: What of Laios?
OEDIPUS: Since he vanished in that onset by the road?   45
KREON: It was long ago, a long time.
OEDIPUS: And this prophet,
    Was he practicing here then?
KREON: He was; and with honor, as now.
OEDIPUS: Did he speak of me at that time?
KREON: He never did,
    At least, not when I was present.
OEDIPUS: But . . . the enquiry?
    I suppose you held one?
KREON: We did, but we learned nothing.   50
OEDIPUS: Why did the prophet not speak against me then?
KREON: I do not know; and I am the kind of man
    Who holds his tongue when he has no facts to go on.
OEDIPUS: There's one fact that you know, and you could tell it.
KREON: What fact is that? If I know it, you shall have it.   55
OEDIPUS: If he were not involved with you, he could not say
    That it was I who murdered Laios.
KREON: If he says that, you are the one that knows it!—
    But now it is my turn to question you.
OEDIPUS: Put your questions. I am no murderer.   60
KREON: First, then: You married my sister?
OEDIPUS: I married your sister.
KREON: And you rule the kingdom equally with her?
OEDIPUS: Everything that she wants she has from me.
KREON: And I am the third, equal to both of you?
OEDIPUS: That is why I call you a bad friend.   65
KREON: No. Reason it out, as I have done.
    Think of this first: would any sane man prefer
    Power, with all a king's anxieties,
    To that same power and the grace of sleep?

Certainly not I.
I have never longed for the king's power—only his rights.
Would any wise man differ from me in this?
As matters stand, I have my way in everything
With your consent, and no responsibilities.
If I were king, I should be a slave to policy.
How could I desire a scepter more
Than what is now mine—untroubled influence?
No, I have not gone mad; I need no honors,
Except those with the perquisites I have now.
I am welcome everywhere; every man salutes me,
And those who want your favor seek my ear,
Since I know how to manage what they ask.
Should I exchange this ease for that anxiety?
Besides, no sober mind is treasonable.
I hate anarchy
And never would deal with any man who likes it.
Test what I have said. Go to the priestess
At Delphi, ask if I quoted her correctly.
And as for this other thing: if I am found
Guilty of treason with Teiresias,
Then sentence me to death. You have my word
It is a sentence I should cast my vote for—
But not without evidence!
                              You do wrong
When you take good men for bad, bad men for good.
A true friend thrown aside—why, life itself
Is not more precious!
                              In time you will know this well:
For time, and time alone, will show the just man,
Though scoundrels are discovered in a day.
CHORAGOS: This is well said, and a prudent man would ponder it.
   Judgments too quickly formed are dangerous.
OEDIPUS: But is he not quick in his duplicity?
   And shall I not be quick to parry him?
   Would you have me stand still, hold my peace, and let
   This man win everything, through my inaction?
KREON: And you want—what is it, then? To banish me?
OEDIPUS: No, not exile. It is your death I want,
   So that all the world may see what treason means.
KREON: You will persist, then? You will not believe me?
OEDIPUS: How can I believe you?
KREON: Then you are a fool.

OEDIPUS: To save myself?
KREON: In justice, think of me.   110
OEDIPUS: You are evil incarnate.
KREON: But suppose that you are wrong?
OEDIPUS: Still I must rule.
KREON: But not if you rule badly.
OEDIPUS: O city, city!
KREON: It is my city, too!
CHORAGOS: Now, my lords, be still. I see the queen,
  Iokaste, coming from her palace chambers;   115
  And it is time she came, for the sake of you both.
  This dreadful quarrel can be resolved through her.

(*Enter Iokaste.*)

IOKASTE: Poor foolish men, what wicked din is this?
  With Thebes sick to death, is it not shameful
  That you should take some private quarrel up?   120
  (*To Oedipus.*) Come into the house.
                              —And you, Kreon, go now:
  Let us have no more of this tumult over nothing.
KREON: Nothing? No, sister: what your husband plans for me
  Is one of two great evils: exile or death.
OEDIPUS: He is right.
                    Why, woman I have caught him squarely   125
  Plotting against my life.
KREON: No! Let me die
  Accurst if ever I have wished you harm!
IOKASTE: Ah, believe it, Oedipus!
  In the name of the gods, respect this oath of his
  For my sake, for the sake of these people here!   130

Strophe 1

CHORAGOS: Open your mind to her, my lord. Be ruled by her, I beg you!
OEDIPUS: What would you have me do?
CHORAGOS: Respect Kreon's word. He has never spoken like a fool,
  And now he has sworn an oath.
OEDIPUS: You know what you ask?
CHORAGOS: I do.
OEDIPUS: Speak on, then.
CHORAGOS: A friend so sworn should not be baited so,   135
  In blind malice, and without final proof.

OEDIPUS: You are aware, I hope, that what you say
   Means death for me, or exile at the least.

Strophe 2

CHORAGOS: No, I swear by Helios,° first in heaven!
      May I die friendless and accurst,
   The worst of deaths, if ever I meant that!
   It is the withering fields
      That hurt my sick heart:
   Must we bear all these ills,
   And now your bad blood as well?
OEDIPUS: Then let him go. And let me die, if I must,
   Or be driven by him in shame from the land of Thebes.
   It is your unhappiness, and not his talk,
   That touches me.
                  As for him—
   Wherever he goes, hatred will follow him.
KREON: Ugly in yielding, as you were ugly in rage!
   Natures like yours chiefly torment themselves.
OEDIPUS: Can you not go? Can you not leave me?
KREON: I can.
   You do not know me; but the city knows me,
   And in its eyes I am just, if not in yours.   (*Exit Kreon.*)

Antistrophe 1

CHORAGOS: Lady Iokaste, did you not ask the King to go to his
   chambers?
IOKASTE: First tell me what has happened.
CHORAGOS: There was suspicion without evidence; yet it rankled
   As even false charges will.
IOKASTE: On both sides?
CHORAGOS: On both.
IOKASTE: But what was said?
CHORAGOS: Oh let it rest, let it be done with!
   Have we not suffered enough?
OEDIPUS: You see to what your decency has brought you:
   You have made difficulties where my heart saw none.

139. Helios: The sun god.

Antistrophe 2

CHORAGOS: Oedipus, it is not once only I have told you—   165
  You must know I should count myself unwise
  To the point of madness, should I now forsake you—
        You, under whose hand,
          In the storm of another time,
          Our dear land sailed out free.   170
        But now stand fast at the helm!
IOKASTE: In God's name, Oedipus, inform your wife as well:
  Why are you so set in this hard anger?
OEDIPUS: I will tell you, for none of these men deserves
  My confidence as you do. It is Kreon's work,   175
  His treachery, his plotting against me.
IOKASTE: Go on, if you can make this clear to me.
OEDIPUS: He charges me with the murder of Laios.
IOKASTE: Has he some knowledge? Or does he speak from
    hearsay?
OEDIPUS: He would not commit himself to such a charge,   180
  But he has brought in that damnable soothsayer
  To tell his story.
IOKASTE: Set your mind at rest.
  If it is a question of soothsayers, I tell you
  That you will find no man whose craft gives knowledge
  Of the unknowable.
            Here is my proof: 185
  An oracle was reported to Laios once
  (I will not say from Phoibos himself, but from
  His appointed ministers, at any rate)
  That his doom would be death at the hands of his own son—
  His son, born of his flesh and of mine!   190

  Now, you remember the story: Laios was killed
  By marauding strangers where three highways meet;
  But his child had not been three days in this world
  Before the king had pierced the baby's ankles
  And left him to die on a lonely mountainside.   195

  Thus, Apollo never caused that child
  To kill his father, and it was not Laios' fate
  To die at the hands of his son, as he had feared.
  This is what prophets and prophecies are worth!

Have no dread of them.
                        It is God himself
Who can show us what he wills, in his own way.

OEDIPUS: How strange a shadowy memory crossed my mind,
   Just now while you were speaking; it chilled my heart.

IOKASTE: What do you mean? What memory do you speak of?

OEDIPUS: If I understand you, Laios was killed
   At a place where three roads meet.

IOKASTE: So it was said;
   We have no later story.

OEDIPUS: Where did it happen?

IOKASTE: Phokis, it is called: at a place where the Theban Way
   Divides into the roads toward Delphi and Daulia.

OEDIPUS: When?

IOKASTE: We had the news not long before you came
   And proved the right to your succession here.

OEDIPUS: Ah, what net has God been weaving for me?

IOKASTE: Oedipus! Why does this trouble you?

OEDIPUS: Do not ask me yet.
   First, tell me how Laios looked, and tell me
   How old he was.

IOKASTE: He was tall, his hair just touched
   With white; his form was not unlike your own.

OEDIPUS: I think that I myself may be accurst
   By my own ignorant edict.

IOKASTE: You speak strangely.
   It makes me tremble to look at you, my king.

OEDIPUS: I am not sure that the blind man can not see.
   But I should know better if you were to tell me—

IOKASTE: Anything—though I dread to hear you ask it.

OEDIPUS: Was the king lightly escorted, or did he ride
   With a large company, as a ruler should?

IOKASTE: There were five men with him in all: one was a herald;
   And a single chariot, which he was driving.

OEDIPUS: Alas, that makes it plain enough!
                              But who—
   Who told you how it happened?

IOKASTE: A household servant,
   The only one to escape.

OEDIPUS: And is he still
   A servant of ours?

IOKASTE: No; for when he came back at last
   And found you enthroned in the place of the dead king,

He came to me, touched my hand with his, and begged
That I would send him away to the frontier district
Where only the shepherds go—
As far away from the city as I could send him.   235
I granted his prayer; for although the man was a slave,
He had earned more than this favor at my hands.
OEDIPUS: Can he be called back quickly?
IOKASTE: Easily.
     But why?
OEDIPUS: I have taken too much upon myself   240
     Without enquiry; therefore I wish to consult him.
IOKASTE: Then he shall come.
                         But am I not one also
To whom you might confide these fears of yours?
OEDIPUS: That is your right; it will not be denied you,
     Now least of all; for I have reached a pitch   245
     Of wild foreboding. Is there anyone
     To whom I should sooner speak?

Polybos of Corinth is my father.
My mother is a Dorian: Merope.
I grew up chief among the men of Corinth   250
Until a strange thing happened—
Not worth my passion, it may be, but strange.
At a feast, a drunken man maundering in his cups
Cries out that I am not my father's son!
I contained myself that night, though I felt anger   255
And a sinking heart. The next day I visited
My father and mother, and questioned them. They stormed,
Calling it all the slanderous rant of a fool;
And this relieved me. Yet the suspicion
Remained always aching in my mind;   260
I knew there was talk; I could not rest;
And finally, saying nothing to my parents,
I went to the shrine at Delphi.

The god dismissed my question without reply;
He spoke of other things.
                         Some were clear,   265
Full of wretchedness, dreadful, unbearable:
As, that I should lie with my own mother, breed
Children from whom all men would turn their eyes;
And that I should be my father's murderer.

I heard all this, and fled. And from that day
Corinth to me was only in the stars
Descending in that quarter of the sky,
As I wandered farther and farther on my way
To a land where I should never see the evil
Sung by the oracle. And I came to this country
Where, so you say, King Laios was killed.

I will tell you all that happened there, my lady.
There were three highways
Coming together at a place I passed;
And there a herald came towards me, and a chariot
Drawn by horses, with a man such as you describe
Seated in it. The groom leading the horses
Forced me off the road at his lord's command;
But as this charioteer lurched over towards me
I struck him in my rage. The old man saw me
And brought his double goad° down upon my head
As I came abreast.

                          He was paid back, and more!
Swinging my club in this right hand I knocked him
Out of his car, and he rolled on the ground.

                                          I killed him.

I killed them all.
Now if that stranger and Laios were—kin,
Where is a man more miserable than I?
More hated by the gods? Citizen and alien alike
Must never shelter me or speak to me—
I must be shunned by all.

                          And I myself
Pronounced this malediction upon myself!

Think of it: I have touched you with these hands,
These hands that killed your husband. What defilement!

Am I all evil, then? It must be so,
Since I must flee from Thebes, yet never again
See my own countrymen, my own country,
For fear of joining my mother in marriage

---

286. **goad:** A pointed rod used to urge on an animal.

And killing Polybos, my father.
                              Ah,
If I was created so, born to this fate,
Who could deny the savagery of God?   305

O holy majesty of heavenly powers!
May I never see that day! Never!
Rather let me vanish from the race of men
Than know the abomination destined me!
CHORAGOS: We too, my lord, have felt dismay at this.   310
   But there is hope: you have yet to hear the shepherd.
OEDIPUS: Indeed, I fear no other hope is left me.
IOKASTE: What do you hope from him when he comes?
OEDIPUS: This much:
   If his account of the murder tallies with yours,
   Then I am cleared.
IOKASTE: What was it that I said   315
   Of such importance?
OEDIPUS: Why, "marauders," you said,
   Killed the king, according to this man's story.
   If he maintains that still, if there were several,
   Clearly the guilt is not mine: I was alone.
   But if he says one man, singlehanded, did it,   320
   Then the evidence all points to me.
IOKASTE: You may be sure that he said there were several;
   And can he call back that story now? He can not.
   The whole city heard it as plainly as I.
   But suppose he alters some detail of it: 325
   He can not ever show that Laios' death
   Fulfilled the oracle: for Apollo said
   My child was doomed to kill him; and my child—
   Poor baby!—it was my child that died first.

   No. From now on, where oracles are concerned,   330
   I would not waste a second thought on any.
OEDIPUS: You may be right.
                        But come: let someone go
   For the shepherd at once. This matter must be settled.
IOKASTE: I will send for him.
   I would not wish to cross you in anything,   335
   And surely not in this.—Let us go in.

                                        (*Exeunt into the palace.*)

ODE 2   *Strophe 1*

CHORUS: Let me be reverent in the ways of right,
　　　　Lowly the paths I journey on;
　　　　Let all my words and actions keep
　　　　The laws of the pure universe
　　　　From highest Heaven handed down.
　　　　For Heaven is their bright nurse,
　　　　Those generations of the realms of light;
　　　　Ah, never of mortal kind were they begot,
　　　　Nor are they slaves of memory, lost in sleep:
　　　　Their Father is greater than Time, and ages not.

Antistrophe 1

　　　　The tyrant is a child of Pride
　　　　Who drinks from his great sickening cup
　　　　Recklessness and vanity,
　　　　Until from his high crest headlong
　　　　He plummets to the dust of hope.
　　　　That strong man is not strong.
　　　　But let no fair ambition be denied;
　　　　May God protect the wrestler for the State
　　　　In government, in comely policy,
　　　　Who will fear God, and on his ordinance wait.

Strophe 2

　　　　Haughtiness and the high hand of disdain
　　　　Tempt and outrage God's holy law;
　　　　And any mortal who dares hold
　　　　No immortal Power in awe
　　　　Will be caught up in a net of pain:
　　　　The price for which his levity is sold.
　　　　Let each man take due earnings, then,
　　　　And keep his hands from holy things,
　　　　And from blasphemy stand apart—
　　　　Else the crackling blast of heaven
　　　　Blows on his head, and on his desperate heart.
　　　　Though fools will honor impious men,
　　　　In their cities no tragic poet sings.

Antistrophe 2

Shall we lose faith in Delphi's obscurities,
We who have heard the world's core   35
Discredited, and the sacred wood
Of Zeus at Elis praised no more?
The deeds and the strange prophecies
Must make a pattern yet to be understood.
Zeus, if indeed you are lord of all,   40
Throned in light over night and day,
Mirror this in your endless mind:
Our masters call the oracle
Words on the wind, and the Delphic vision blind!
Their hearts no longer know Apollo,   45
And reverence for the gods has died away.

SCENE 3

(*Enter Iokaste.*)

IOKASTE: Princes of Thebes, it has occurred to me
    To visit the altars of the gods, bearing
    These branches as a suppliant, and this incense.
    Our king is not himself: his noble soul
    Is overwrought with fantasies of dread,   5
    Else he would consider
    The new prophecies in the light of the old.
    He will listen to any voice that speaks disaster,
    And my advice goes for nothing. (*She approaches the
        altar, right.*)
                        To you, then, Apollo,
    Lycean lord, since you are nearest, I turn in prayer   10
    Receive these offerings, and grant us deliverance
    From defilement. Our hearts are heavy with fear
    When we see our leader distracted, as helpless sailors
    Are terrified by the confusion of their helmsman.

(*Enter Messenger.*)

MESSENGER: Friends, no doubt you can direct me: 15
    Where shall I find the house of Oedipus,
    Or, better still, where is the king himself?

CHORAGOS: It is this very place, stranger; he is inside.
   This is his wife and mother of his children.
MESSENGER: I wish her happiness in a happy house,
   Blest in all the fulfillment of her marriage.
IOKASTE: I wish as much for you: your courtesy
   Deserves a like good fortune. But now, tell me:
   Why have you come? What have you to say to us?
MESSENGER: Good news, my lady, for your house and your husband.
IOKASTE: What news? Who sent you here?
MESSENGER: I am from Corinth.
   The news I bring ought to mean joy for you,
   Though it may be you will find some grief in it.
IOKASTE: What is it? How can it touch us in both ways?
MESSENGER: The word is that the people of the Isthmus
   Intend to call Oedipus to be their king.
IOKASTE: But old King Polybos—is he not reigning still?
MESSENGER: No. Death holds him in his sepulchre.
IOKASTE: What are you saying? Polybos is dead?
MESSENGER: If I am not telling the truth, may I die myself.
IOKASTE (*to a Maidservant*): Go in, go quickly; tell this to your master.
   O riddlers of God's will, where are you now!
   This was the man whom Oedipus, long ago,
   Feared so, fled so, in dread of destroying him—
   But it was another fate by which he died.

(*Enter Oedipus, center.*)

OEDIPUS: Dearest Iokaste, why have you sent for me?
IOKASTE: Listen to what this man says, and then tell me
   What has become of the solemn prophecies.
OEDIPUS: Who is this man? What is his news for me?
IOKASTE: He has come from Corinth to announce your father's death!
OEDIPUS: Is it true, stranger? Tell me in your own words.
MESSENGER: I can not say it more clearly: the king is dead.
OEDIPUS: Was it by treason? Or by an attack of illness?
MESSENGER: A little thing brings old men to their rest.
OEDIPUS: It was sickness, then?
MESSENGER: Yes, and his many years.
OEDIPUS: Ah!
   Why should a man respect the Pythian hearth,° or
   Give heed to the birds that jangle above his head?
   They prophesied that I should kill Polybos,

52. **Pythian hearth:** A site in Delphi where ritualistic offerings were made.

Kill my own father; but he is dead and buried,   55
And I am here—I never touched him, never,
Unless he died of grief for my departure,
And thus, in a sense, through me. No. Polybos
Has packed the oracles off with him underground.
They are empty words.

IOKASTE: Had I not told you so?   60

OEDIPUS: You had; it was my faint heart that betrayed me.

IOKASTE: From now on never think of those things again.

OEDIPUS: And yet—must I not fear my mother's bed?

IOKASTE: Why should anyone in this world be afraid
          Since Fate rules us and nothing can be foreseen?   65
          A man should live only for the present day.

          Have no more fear of sleeping with your mother:
          How many men, in dreams, have lain with their mothers!
          No reasonable man is troubled by such things.

OEDIPUS: That is true, only—   70
          If only my mother were not still alive!
          But she is alive. I can not help my dread.

IOKASTE: Yet this news of your father's death is wonderful.

OEDIPUS: Wonderful. But I fear the living woman.

MESSENGER: Tell me, who is this woman that you fear?   75

OEDIPUS: It is Merope, man; the wife of King Polybos.

MESSENGER: Merope? Why should you be afraid of her?

OEDIPUS: An oracle of the gods, a dreadful saying.

MESSENGER: Can you tell me about it or are you sworn to silence?

OEDIPUS: I can tell you, and I will.   80
          Apollo said through his prophet that I was the man
          Who should marry his own mother, shed his father's blood
          With his own hands. And so, for all these years
          I have kept clear of Corinth, and no harm has come—
          Though it would have been sweet to see my parents again.   85

MESSENGER: And is this the fear that drove you out of Corinth?

OEDIPUS: Would you have me kill my father?

MESSENGER: As for that
          You must be reassured by the news I gave you.

OEDIPUS: If you could reassure me, I would reward you.

MESSENGER: I had that in mind, I will confess: I thought   90
          I could count on you when you returned to Corinth.

OEDIPUS: No: I will never go near my parents again.

MESSENGER: Ah, son, you still do not know what you are doing—

OEDIPUS: What do you mean? In the name of God tell me!

MESSENGER: —If these are your reasons for not going home.
OEDIPUS: I tell you, I fear the oracle may come true.
MESSENGER: And guilt may come upon you through your parents?
OEDIPUS: That is the dread that is always in my heart.
MESSENGER: Can you not see that all your fears are groundless?
OEDIPUS: Groundless? Am I not my parents' son?
MESSENGER: Polybos was not your father.
OEDIPUS: Not my father?
MESSENGER: No more your father than the man speaking to you.
OEDIPUS: But you are nothing to me!
MESSENGER: Neither was he.
OEDIPUS: Then why did he call me son?
MESSENGER: I will tell you:
    Long ago he had you from my hands, as a gift.
OEDIPUS: Then how could he love me so, if I was not his?
MESSENGER: He had no children, and his heart turned to you.
OEDIPUS: What of you? Did you buy me? Did you find me by chance?
MESSENGER: I came upon you in the woody vales of Kithairon.
OEDIPUS: And what were you doing there?
MESSENGER: Tending my flocks.
OEDIPUS: A wandering shepherd?
MESSENGER: But your savior, son, that day.
OEDIPUS: From what did you save me?
MESSENGER: Your ankles should tell you that.
OEDIPUS: Ah, stranger, why do you speak of that childhood pain?
MESSENGER: I pulled the skewer that pinned your feet together.
OEDIPUS: I have had the mark as long as I can remember.
MESSENGER: That was why you were given the name you bear.°
OEDIPUS: God! Was it my father or my mother who did it?
    Tell me!
MESSENGER: I do not know. The man who gave you to me
    Can tell you better than I.
OEDIPUS: It was not you that found me, but another?
MESSENGER: It was another shepherd gave you to me.
OEDIPUS: Who was he? Can you tell me who he was?
MESSENGER: I think he was said to be one of Laios' people.
OEDIPUS: You mean the Laios who was king here years ago?
MESSENGER: Yes; King Laios; and the man was one of his herdsmen.
OEDIPUS: Is he still alive? Can I see him?
MESSENGER: These men here
    Know best about such things.

116. **name you bear:** *Oedipus* literally means "swollen foot."

OEDIPUS: Does anyone here
  Know this shepherd that he is talking about?
  Have you seen him in the fields, or in the town?
  If you have, tell me. It is time things were made plain.   130
CHORAGOS: I think the man he means is that same shepherd
  You have already asked to see. Iokaste perhaps
  Could tell you something.
OEDIPUS: Do you know anything
  About him, Lady? Is he the man we have summoned?
  Is that the man this shepherd means?
IOKASTE: Why think of him?   135
  Forget this herdsman. Forget it all.
  This talk is a waste of time.
OEDIPUS: How can you say that,
  When the clues to my true birth are in my hands?
IOKASTE: For God's love, let us have no more questioning!
  Is your life nothing to you?   140
  My own is pain enough for me to bear.
OEDIPUS: You need not worry. Suppose my mother a slave,
  And born of slaves: no baseness can touch you.
IOKASTE: Listen to me, I beg you: do not do this thing!
OEDIPUS: I will not listen; the truth must be made known.   145
IOKASTE: Everything that I say is for your own good!
OEDIPUS: My own good
  Snaps my patience, then; I want none of it.
IOKASTE: You are fatally wrong! May you never learn who you are!
OEDIPUS: Go, one of you, and bring the shepherd here.
  Let us leave this woman to brag of her royal name.   150
IOKASTE: Ah, miserable!
  That is the only word I have for you now.
  That is the only word I can ever have.   (*Exit into the palace.*)
CHORAGOS: Why has she left us, Oedipus? Why has she gone
  In such a passion of sorrow? I fear this silence: 155
  Something dreadful may come of it.
OEDIPUS: Let it come!
  However base my birth, I must know about it.
  The Queen, like a woman, is perhaps ashamed
  To think of my low origin. But I
  Am a child of Luck, I can not be dishonored.   160
  Luck is my mother; the passing months, my brothers,
  Have seen me rich and poor.
                              If this is so,
  How could I wish that I were someone else?
  How could I not be glad to know my birth?

ODE 3 *Strophe*

CHORUS: If ever the coming time were known
  To my heart's pondering,
  Kithairon, now by Heaven I see the torches
  At the festival of the next full moon
  And see the dance, and hear the choir sing
  A grace to your gentle shade:
  Mountain where Oedipus was found,
  O mountain guard of a noble race!
  May the god° who heals us lend his aid,
  And let that glory come to pass
  For our king's cradling-ground.

Antistrophe

Of the nymphs that flower beyond the years,
  Who bore you, royal child,
  To Pan° of the hills or the timberline Apollo,
  Cold in delight where the upland clears,
  Or Hermes° for whom Kyllene's° heights are piled?
  Or flushed as evening cloud,
  Great Dionysos, roamer of mountains,
  He—was it he who found you there,
  And caught you up in his own proud
  Arms from the sweet god-ravisher
  Who laughed by the Muses'° fountains?

SCENE 4

OEDIPUS: Sirs: though I do not know the man,
  I think I see him coming, this shepherd we want:
  He is old, like our friend here, and the men
  Bringing him seem to be servants of my house.
  But you can tell, if you have ever seen him.

(*Enter Shepherd escorted by Servants.*)

CHORAGOS: I know him, he was Laios' man. You can trust him.

9. god: Apollo.　14. Pan: God of nature and fertility, depicted as an ugly man
with the horns and legs of a goat. Pan was considered playful and amorous.
16. Hermes: Son of Zeus, messenger of the gods.　Kyllene: Hermes' birthplace.
22. Muses: Nine sister goddesses of poetry, music, art, and sciences.

OEDIPUS: Tell me first, you from Corinth: is this the shepherd
  We were discussing?
MESSENGER: This is the very man.
OEDIPUS (*to Shepherd*): Come here. No, look at me. You must answer
  Everything I ask.—You belonged to Laios?   10
SHEPHERD: Yes: born his slave, brought up in his house.
OEDIPUS: Tell me: what kind of work did you do for him?
SHEPHERD: I was a shepherd of his, most of my life.
OEDIPUS: Where mainly did you go for pasturage?
SHEPHERD: Sometimes Kithairon, sometimes the hills near-by.   15
OEDIPUS: Do you remember ever seeing this man out there?
SHEPHERD: What would he be doing there? This man?
OEDIPUS: This man standing here. Have you ever seen him before?
SHEPHERD: No. At least, not to my recollection.
MESSENGER: And that is not strange, my lord. But I'll refresh   20
  His memory: he must remember when we two
  Spent three whole seasons together, March to September,
  On Kithairon or thereabouts. He had two flocks;
  I had one. Each autumn I'd drive mine home
  And he would go back with his to Laios' sheepfold.—   25
  Is this not true, just as I have described it?
SHEPHERD: True, yes; but it was all so long ago.
MESSENGER: Well, then: do you remember, back in those days,
  That you gave me a baby boy to bring up as my own?
SHEPHERD: What if I did? What are you trying to say?   30
MESSENGER: King Oedipus was once that little child.
SHEPHERD: Damn you, hold your tongue!
OEDIPUS: No more of that!
  It is your tongue needs watching, not this man's.
SHEPHERD: My king, my master, what is it I have done wrong?
OEDIPUS: You have not answered his question about the boy.   35
SHEPHERD: He does not know . . . He is only making trouble . . .
OEDIPUS: Come, speak plainly, or it will go hard with you.
SHEPHERD: In God's name, do not torture an old man!
OEDIPUS: Come here, one of you; bind his arms behind him.
SHEPHERD: Unhappy king! What more do you wish to learn?   40
OEDIPUS: Did you give this man the child he speaks of?
SHEPHERD: I did.
  And I would to God I had died that very day.
OEDIPUS: You will die now unless you speak the truth.
SHEPHERD: Yet if I speak the truth, I am worse than dead.
OEDIPUS (*to Attendant*): He intends to draw it out, apparently—   45
SHEPHERD: No! I have told you already that I gave him the boy.

OEDIPUS: Where did you get him? From your house? From somewhere
    else?
SHEPHERD: Not from mine, no. A man gave him to me.
OEDIPUS: Is that man here? Whose house did he belong to?
SHEPHERD: For God's love, my king, do not ask me any more!
OEDIPUS: You are a dead man if I have to ask you again.
SHEPHERD: Then . . . Then the child was from the palace of Laios.
OEDIPUS: A slave child? or a child of his own line?
SHEPHERD: Ah, I am on the brink of dreadful speech!
OEDIPUS: And I of dreadful hearing. Yet I must hear.
SHEPHERD: If you must be told, then . . .
                                  They said it was Laios' child;
  But it is your wife who can tell you about that.
OEDIPUS: My wife—Did she give it to you?
SHEPHERD: My lord, she did.
OEDIPUS: Do you know why?
SHEPHERD: I was told to get rid of it.
OEDIPUS: Oh heartless mother!
SHEPHERD: But in dread of prophecies . . .
OEDIPUS: Tell me.
SHEPHERD: It was said that the boy would kill his own father.
OEDIPUS: Then why did you give him over to this old man?
SHEPHERD: I pitied the baby, my king,
  And I thought that this man would take him far away
  To his own country.
                He saved him—but for what a fate!
  For if you are what this man says you are,
  No man living is more wretched than Oedipus.
OEDIPUS: Ah God!
  It was true!
      All the prophecies!
                —Now,
  O Light, may I look on you for the last time!
  I, Oedipus,
  Oedipus, damned in his birth, in his marriage damned,
  Damned in the blood he shed with his own hand!

(*He rushes into the palace.*)

ODE 4   *Strophe 1*

CHORUS: Alas for the seed of men.
  What measure shall I give these generations
  That breathe on the void and are void

And exist and do not exist?
Who bears more weight of joy   5
Than mass of sunlight shifting in images,
Or who shall make his thought stay on
That down time drifts away?
Your splendor is all fallen.
O naked brow of wrath and tears,   10
O change of Oedipus!
I who saw your days call no man blest—
Your great days like ghosts gone.

Antistrophe 1

That mind was a strong bow.
Deep, how deep you drew it then, hard archer,   15
At a dim fearful range,
And brought dear glory down!
You overcame the stranger°—
The virgin with her hooking lion claws—
And though death sang, stood like a tower   20
To make pale Thebes take heart.
Fortress against our sorrow!
True king, giver of laws,
Majestic Oedipus!
No prince in Thebes had ever such renown,   25
No prince won such grace of power.

Strophe 2

And now of all men ever known
Most pitiful is this man's story:
His fortunes are most changed; his state
Fallen to a low slave's   30
Ground under bitter fate.
O Oedipus, most royal one!
The great door° that expelled you to the light
Gave at night—ah, gave night to your glory:
As to the father, to the fathering son.   35
All understood too late.
How could that queen whom Laios won,
The garden that he harrowed at his height,
Be silent when that act was done?

18. **stranger:** The Sphinx.   33. **door:** Iokaste's womb.

Antistrophe 2

But all eyes fail before time's eye,
All actions come to justice there.
Though never willed, though far down the deep past,
Your bed, your dread sirings,
Are brought to book at last.
Child by Laios doomed to die,
Then doomed to lose that fortunate little death,
Would God you never took breath in this air
That with my wailing lips I take to cry:
For I weep the world's outcast.
I was blind, and now I can tell why:
Asleep, for you had given ease of breath
To Thebes, while the false years went by.

EXODOS°

(*Enter, from the palace, Second Messenger.*)

SECOND MESSENGER: Elders of Thebes, most honored in this land,
   What horrors are yours to see and hear, what weight
   Of sorrow to be endured, if, true to your birth,
   You venerate the line of Labdakos!
   I think neither Istros nor Phasis, those great rivers,
   Could purify this place of all the evil
   It shelters now, or soon must bring to light—
   Evil not done unconsciously, but willed.

   The greatest griefs are those we cause ourselves.
CHORAGOS: Surely, friend, we have grief enough already;
   What new sorrow do you mean?
SECOND MESSENGER: The queen is dead.
CHORAGOS: O miserable queen! But at whose hand?
SECOND MESSENGER: Her own.
   The full horror of what happened you can not know,
   For you did not see it; but I, who did, will tell you
   As clearly as I can how she met her death.

   When she had left us,
   In passionate silence, passing through the court,

Exodos: Final scene.

She ran to her apartment in the house,
Her hair clutched by the fingers of both hands.
She closed the doors behind her; then, by that bed   20
Where long ago the fatal son was conceived—
That son who should bring about his father's death—
We heard her call upon Laios, dead so many years,
And heard her wail for the double fruit of her marriage,
A husband by her husband, children by her child.   25

Exactly how she died I do not know:
For Oedipus burst in moaning and would not let us
Keep vigil to the end: it was by him
As he stormed about the room that our eyes were caught.
From one to another of us he went, begging a sword,   30
Hunting the wife who was not his wife, the mother
Whose womb had carried his own children and himself.
I do not know: it was none of us aided him,
But surely one of the gods was in control!
For with a dreadful cry   35
He hurled his weight, as though wrenched out of himself,
At the twin doors: the bolts gave, and he rushed in.
And there we saw her hanging, her body swaying
From the cruel cord she had noosed about her neck.
A great sob broke from him, heartbreaking to hear,   40
As he loosed the rope and lowered her to the ground.

I would blot out from my mind what happened next!
For the king ripped from her gown the golden brooches
That were her ornament, and raised them, and plunged them down
Straight into his own eyeballs, crying, "No more,   45
No more shall you look on the misery about me,
The horrors of my own doing! Too long you have known
The faces of those whom I should never have seen,
Too long been blind to those for whom I was searching!
From this hour, go in darkness!" And as he spoke,   50
He struck at his eyes—not once, but many times;
And the blood spattered his beard,
Bursting from his ruined sockets like red hail.

So from the unhappiness of two this evil has sprung,
A curse on the man and woman alike. The old   55
Happiness of the house of Labdakos
Was happiness enough: where is it today?
It is all wailing and ruin, disgrace, death—all

The misery of mankind that has a name—
And it is wholly and for ever theirs.

CHORAGOS: Is he in agony still? Is there no rest for him?

SECOND MESSENGER: He is calling for someone to open the
    doors wide
So that all the children of Kadmos may look upon
His father's murderer, his mother's—no,
I can not say it!
                              And then he will leave Thebes,
Self-exiled, in order that the curse
Which he himself pronounced may depart from the house.
He is weak, and there is none to lead him,
So terrible is his suffering.
                                           But you will see:
Look, the doors are opening; in a moment
You will see a thing that would crush a heart of stone.

(*The central door is opened; Oedipus, blinded, is led in.*)

CHORAGOS: Dreadful indeed for men to see.
    Never have my own eyes
    Looked on a sight so full of fear.

    Oedipus!
    What madness came upon you, what demon
    Leaped on your life with heavier
    Punishment than a mortal man can bear?
    No: I can not even
    Look at you, poor ruined one.
    And I would speak, question, ponder,
    If I were able. No.
    You make me shudder.

OEDIPUS: God. God.
    Is there a sorrow greater?
    Where shall I find harbor in this world?
    My voice is hurled far on a dark wind.
    What has God done to me?

CHORAGOS: Too terrible to think of, or to see.

Strophe 1

OEDIPUS: O cloud of night,
    Never to be turned away: night coming on,

I can not tell how: night like a shroud!
My fair winds brought me here.
                      O God. Again
The pain of the spikes where I had sight,
The flooding pain   95
Of memory, never to be gouged out.
CHORAGOS: This is not strange.
    You suffer it all twice over, remorse in pain,
    Pain in remorse.

Antistrophe 1

OEDIPUS: Ah dear friend   100
    Are you faithful even yet, you alone?
    Are you still standing near me, will you stay here,
    Patient, to care for the blind?
                    The blind man!
    Yet even blind I know who it is attends me,
    By the voice's tone—   105
    Though my new darkness hide the comforter.
CHORAGOS: Oh fearful act!
    What god was it drove you to rake black
    Night across your eyes?

Strophe 2

OEDIPUS: Apollo. Apollo. Dear   110
    Children, the god was Apollo.
    He brought my sick, sick fate upon me.
    But the blinding hand was my own!
    How could I bear to see
    When all my sight was horror everywhere?   115
CHORAGOS: Everywhere; that is true.
OEDIPUS: And now what is left?
    Images? Love? A greeting even,
    Sweet to the senses? Is there anything?
    Ah, no, friends: lead me away.
    Lead me away from Thebes.   120
                    Lead the great wreck
    And hell of Oedipus, whom the gods hate.
CHORAGOS: Your misery, you are not blind to that.
    Would God you had never found it out!

Antistrophe 2

OEDIPUS: Death take the man who unbound
  My feet on that hillside
  And delivered me from death to life! What life?
  If only I had died,
  This weight of monstrous doom
  Could not have dragged me and my darlings down.
CHORAGOS: I would have wished the same.
OEDIPUS: Oh never to have come here
  With my father's blood upon me! Never
  To have been the man they call his mother's husband!
  Oh accurst! Oh child of evil,
  To have entered that wretched bed—
                                    the selfsame one!
  More primal than sin itself, this fell to me.
CHORAGOS: I do not know what words to offer you.
  You were better dead than alive and blind.
OEDIPUS: Do not counsel me any more. This punishment
  That I have laid upon myself is just.
  If I had eyes,
  I do not know how I could bear the sight
  Of my father, when I came to the house of Death,
  Or my mother: for I have sinned against them both
  So vilely that I could not make my peace
  By strangling my own life.
                            Or do you think my children,
  Born as they were born, would be sweet to my eyes?
  Ah never, never! Nor this town with its high walls,
  Nor the holy images of the gods.
                        For I,
  Thrice miserable!—Oedipus, noblest of all the line
  Of Kadmos, have condemned myself to enjoy
  These things no more, by my own malediction
  Expelling that man whom the gods declared
  To be a defilement in the house of Laios.
  After exposing the rankness of my own guilt,
  How could I look men frankly in the eyes?
  No, I swear it,
  If I could have stifled my hearing at its source,
  I would have done it and made all this body
  A tight cell of misery, blank to light and sound:
  So I should have been safe in my dark mind
  Beyond external evil.

Ah Kithairon!
Why did you shelter me? When I was cast upon you,
Why did I not die? Then I should never   165
Have shown the world my execrable birth.

Ah Polybos! Corinth, city that I believed
The ancient seat of my ancestors: how fair
I seemed, your child! And all the while this evil
Was cancerous within me!
                                    For I am sick   170
In my own being, sick in my origin.
O three roads, dark ravine, woodland and way
Where three roads met; you, drinking my father's blood,
My own blood, spilled by my own hand: can you remember
The unspeakable things I did there, and the things   175
I went on from there to do?
                                    O marriage, marriage!
The act that engendered me, and again the act
Performed by the son in the same bed—
                                    Ah, the net
Of incest, mingling fathers, brothers, sons,
With brides, wives, mothers: the last evil   180
That can be known by men: no tongue can say
How evil!
          No. For the love of God, conceal me
Somewhere far from Thebes; or kill me; or hurl me
Into the sea, away from men's eyes for ever.

Come, lead me. You need not fear to touch me.   185
Of all men, I alone can bear this guilt.

(*Enter Kreon.*)

CHORAGOS: Kreon is here now. As to what you ask,
     He may decide the course to take. He only
     Is left to protect the city in your place.
OEDIPUS: Alas, how can I speak to him? What right have I   190
     To beg his courtesy whom I have deeply wronged?
KREON: I have not come to mock you, Oedipus,
     Or to reproach you, either.
     (*To Attendants.*)   —You, standing there:
     If you have lost all respect for man's dignity,
     At least respect the flame of Lord Helios: 195
     Do not allow this pollution to show itself
     Openly here, an affront to the earth

And Heaven's rain and the light of day. No, take him
Into the house as quickly as you can.
For it is proper
That only the close kindred see his grief.

OEDIPUS: I pray you in God's name, since your courtesy
Ignores my dark expectation, visiting
With mercy this man of all men most execrable:
Give me what I ask—for your good, not for mine.

KREON: And what is it that you turn to me begging for?

OEDIPUS: Drive me out of this country as quickly as may be
To a place where no human voice can ever greet me.

KREON: I should have done that before now—only,
God's will had not been wholly revealed to me.

OEDIPUS: But his command is plain: the parricide
Must be destroyed. I am that evil man.

KREON: That is the sense of it, yes; but as things are,
We had best discover clearly what is to be done.

OEDIPUS: You would learn more about a man like me?

KREON: You are ready now to listen to the god.

OEDIPUS: I will listen. But it is to you
That I must turn for help. I beg you, hear me.

The woman is there—
Give her whatever funeral you think proper:
She is your sister.
                    —But let me go, Kreon!
Let me purge my father's Thebes of the pollution
Of my living here, and go out to the wild hills,
To Kithairon, that has won such fame with me,
The tomb my mother and father appointed for me,
And let me die there, as they willed I should.
And yet I know
Death will not ever come to me through sickness
Or in any natural way: I have been preserved
For some unthinkable fate. But let that be.

As for my sons, you need not care for them.
They are men, they will find some way to live.
But my poor daughters, who have shared my table,
Who never before have been parted from their father—
Take care of them, Kreon; do this for me.

And will you let me touch them with my hands
A last time, and let us weep together?

Be kind, my lord,
Great prince, be kind!
                    Could I but touch them,
They would be mine again, as when I had my eyes.   240

(*Enter Antigone and Ismene, attended.*)

Ah, God!
Is it my dearest children I hear weeping?
Has Kreon pitied me and sent my daughters?
KREON: Yes, Oedipus: I knew that they were dear to you
In the old days, and know you must love them still.   245
OEDIPUS: May God bless you for this—and be a friendlier
Guardian to you than he has been to me!

Children, where are you?
Come quickly to my hands: they are your brother's—
Hands that have brought your father's once clear eyes   250
To this way of seeing—
                    Ah dearest ones,
I had neither sight nor knowledge then, your father
By the woman who was the source of his own life!
And I weep for you—having no strength to see you—,
I weep for you when I think of the bitterness   255
That men will visit upon you all your lives.
What homes, what festivals can you attend
Without being forced to depart again in tears?
And when you come to marriageable age,
Where is the man, my daughters, who would dare   260
Risk the bane that lies on all my children?
Is there any evil wanting? Your father killed
His father; sowed the womb of her who bore him;
Engendered you at the fount of his own existence!
That is what they will say of you.

                                   Then, whom   265
Can you ever marry? There are no bridegrooms for you,
And your lives must wither away in sterile dreaming.

O Kreon, son of Menoikeus!
You are the only father my daughters have,
Since we, their parents, are both of us gone for ever.   270
They are your own blood: you will not let them
Fall into beggary and loneliness;
You will keep them from the miseries that are mine!

Take pity on them; see, they are only children,
Friendless except for you. Promise me this,
Great prince, and give me your hand in token of it.

(*Kreon clasps his right hand.*)

Children:
I could say much, if you could understand me,
But as it is, I have only this prayer for you:
Live where you can, be as happy as you can—
Happier, please God, than God has made your father.
KREON: Enough. You have wept enough. Now go within.
OEDIPUS: I must, but it is hard.
KREON: Time eases all things.
OEDIPUS: You know my mind, then?
KREON: Say what you desire.
OEDIPUS: Send me from Thebes!
KREON: God grant that I may!
OEDIPUS: But since God hates me . . .
KREON: No, he will grant your wish.
OEDIPUS: You promise?
KREON: I can not speak beyond my knowledge.
OEDIPUS: Then lead me in.
KREON: Come now, and leave your children.
OEDIPUS: No! Do not take them from me!
KREON: Think no longer
    That you are in command here, but rather think
    How, when you were, you served your own destruction.

(*Exeunt into the house all but the Chorus; the Choragos chants directly to the
audience.*)

CHORAGOS: Men of Thebes: look upon Oedipus.

This is the king who solved the famous riddle
And towered up, most powerful of men.
No mortal eyes but looked on him with envy,
Yet in the end ruin swept over him.

Let every man in mankind's frailty
Consider his last day; and let none
Presume on his good fortune until he find
Life, at his death, a memory without pain.

[C. 430 B.C.E.]

WILLIAM SHAKESPEARE [1564–1616]

Othello the Moor of Venice

The Names of the Actors

OTHELLO, THE MOOR
BRABANTIO, [*a Venetian senator,*] *father to Desdemona*
CASSIO, *an honorable lieutenant* [*to Othello*]
IAGO, [*Othello's ancient,*] *a villain*
RODERIGO, *a gulled gentleman*
DUKE OF VENICE
SENATORS [*of Venice*]
MONTANO, *governor of Cyprus*
LODOVICO AND GRATIANO, [*kinsmen to Brabantio,*] *two noble Venetians*
SAILORS
CLOWNS
DESDEMONA, *wife to Othello*
EMILIA, *wife to Iago*
BIANCA, *a courtesan*
[MESSENGER, HERALD, OFFICERS, VENETIAN GENTLEMEN, MUSICIANS, ATTENDANTS]

Scene: *Venice and Cyprus*

ACT I   *Scene I*

(*A street in Venice.*)

(*Enter Roderigo and Iago.*)

RODERIGO: Tush, never tell me! I take it much unkindly

Note: *Othello* was first published in 1622, some six years after Shakespeare's death, in a slender book called a "quarto" (made up of printer's paper folded twice, creating four leaves—eight pages—approximately 9½ by 12 inches in size). The following year the play was printed a second time, in the 1623 collected edition of Shakespeare's plays called the First Folio (with paper folded once, creating pages twice as large as a quarto). The Folio text is around 160 lines longer, but the quarto text contains some things omitted from the Folio text. The play as printed here mainly follows the Folio text, but passages from the quarto text have been inserted and enclosed in square brackets.

That thou, Iago, who hast had my purse
As if the strings were thine, shouldst know of this.°
IAGO: 'Sblood,° but you'll not hear me!
If ever I did dream of such a matter,
Abhor me.
RODERIGO: Thou told'st me thou didst hold him in thy hate.
IAGO: Despise me if I do not. Three great ones of the city,
In personal suit to make me his lieutenant,
Off-capped to him;° and, by the faith of man,
I know my price; I am worth no worse a place.
But he, as loving his own pride and purposes,
Evades them with a bombast circumstance,°
Horribly stuffed with epithets of war;
[And, in conclusion,]
Nonsuits° my mediators; for, "Certes," says he,
"I have already chose my officer."
And what was he?
Forsooth, a great arithmetician,°
One Michael Cassio, a Florentine
(A fellow almost damned in a fair wife°)
That never set a squadron in the field,
Nor the division of a battle knows
More than a spinster; unless the bookish theoric,
Wherein the togèd consuls can propose°
As masterly as he. Mere prattle without practice
Is all his soldiership. But he, sir, had th' election;
And I (of whom his eyes had seen the proof
At Rhodes, at Cyprus, and on other grounds
Christian and heathen) must be belee'd and calmed°
By debitor and creditor; this counter-caster,°
He, in good time, must his lieutenant be,
And I—God bless the mark!—his Moorship's ancient.°
RODERIGO: By heaven, I rather would have been his hangman.
IAGO: Why, there's no remedy; 'tis the curse of service.
Preferment goes by letter and affection,°

3. this: I.e., Desdemona's elopement.   4. 'Sblood: By God's blood.   10. him:
I.e., Othello.   13. a bombast circumstance: Pompous circumlocutions.
16. Nonsuits: Rejects.   19. arithmetician: Theoretician.   21. almost . . . wife:
(An obscure allusion; Cassio is unmarried, but see 4.1.125–26).   25. Wherein . . .
propose: In which the toga-wearing senators can debate.   30. belee'd and
calmed: Left in the lurch.   31. counter-caster: Bookkeeper.   33. ancient:
Ensign.   36. affection: Favoritism.

And not by old gradation, where each second
Stood heir to th' first. Now, sir, be judge yourself,
Whether I in any just term am affined°
To love the Moor.
RODERIGO: I would not follow him then.   40
IAGO: O, sir, content you;
I follow him to serve my turn upon him.
We cannot all be masters, nor all masters
Cannot be truly followed. You shall mark
Many a duteous and knee-crooking knave   45
That, doting on his own obsequious bondage,
Wears out his time, much like his master's ass,
For naught but provender; and when he's old, cashiered.°
Whip me such honest knaves! Others there are
Who, trimmed° in forms and visages of duty,   50
Keep yet their hearts attending on themselves;
And, throwing but shows of service on their lords,
Do well thrive by them, and when they have lined their coats,°
Do themselves homage. These fellows have some soul;
And such a one do I profess myself. For, sir,   55
It is as sure as you are Roderigo,
Were I the Moor, I would not be Iago.
In following him, I follow but myself;
Heaven is my judge, not I for love and duty,
But seeming so, for my peculiar end;   60
For when my outward action doth demonstrate
The native act and figure of my heart°
In compliment extern,° 'tis not long after
But I will wear my heart upon my sleeve
For daws to peck at; I am not what I am.°   65
RODERIGO: What a full fortune does the thick-lips° owe°
If he can carry't thus!
IAGO: Call up her father,
Rouse him. Make after him, poison his delight,
Proclaim him in the streets. Incense her kinsmen,
And though he in a fertile climate dwell,   70
Plague him with flies; though that his joy be joy,

39. affined: Obliged.   48. cashiered: Dismissed.   50. trimmed: Dressed
up.   53. lined their coats: Filled their purses.   62. The . . . heart: What I really
believe and intend.   63. compliment extern: Outward appearance.   65. What I
am: What I seem.   66. thick-lips: An Elizabethan epithet for blacks, including
Moors; owe: Own.

Yet throw such changes of vexation on't
As it may lose some color.
RODERIGO: Here is her father's house. I'll call aloud.
IAGO: Do, with like timorous° accent and dire yell
As when, by night and negligence, the fire
Is spied in populous cities.
RODERIGO: What, ho, Brabantio! Signior Brabantio, ho!
IAGO: Awake! What, ho, Brabantio! Thieves! thieves! thieves!
Look to your house, your daughter, and your bags!
Thieves! thieves!

(*Brabantio at a window.*°)

BRABANTIO (*above*): What is the reason of this terrible summons?
What is the matter there?
RODERIGO: Signior, is all your family within?
IAGO: Are your doors locked?
BRABANTIO: Why, wherefore ask you this?
IAGO: Zounds, sir, y' are robbed! For shame, put on your gown!
Your heart is burst; you have lost half your soul.
Even now, now, very now, an old black ram
Is tupping° your white ewe. Arise, arise!
Awake the snorting° citizens with the bell.
Or else the devil will make a grandsire of you.
Arise, I say!
BRABANTIO: What, have you lost your wits?
RODERIGO: Most reverend signior, do you know my voice?
BRABANTIO: Not I. What are you?
RODERIGO: My name is Roderigo.
BRABANTIO: The worser welcome!
I have charged thee not to haunt about my doors.
In honest plainness thou hast heard me say
My daughter is not for thee; and now, in madness,
Being full of supper and distemp'ring° draughts,
Upon malicious knavery dost thou come
To start° my quiet.
RODERIGO: Sir, sir, sir—
BRABANTIO: But thou must needs be sure
My spirit and my place have in them power
To make this bitter to thee.

---

75. timorous: Terrifying.   [s.d.] **Brabantio at a window:** (added from quarto).
89. tupping: Copulating with.   **90. snorting:** Snoring.   **100. distemp'ring:**
Intoxicating.   **102. start:** Startle, disturb.

RODERIGO: Patience, good sir.
BRABANTIO: What tell'st thou me of robbing? This is Venice;
  My house is not a grange.°
RODERIGO: Most grave Brabantio,
  In simple° and pure soul I come to you.
IAGO: Zounds, sir, you are one of those that will not serve God if the devil   110
  bid you. Because we come to do you service, and you think we are ruf-
  fians, you'll have your daughter covered with a Barbary horse; you'll
  have your nephews° neigh to you; you'll have coursers for cousins, and
  gennets for germans.°
BRABANTIO: What profane wretch art thou?   115
IAGO: I am one, sir, that comes to tell you your daughter and the Moor
  are now making the beast with two backs.
BRABANTIO: Thou art a villain.
IAGO: You are—a senator.
BRABANTIO: This thou shalt answer. I know thee, Roderigo.
RODERIGO: Sir, I will answer anything. But I beseech you,   120
  If 't be your pleasure and most wise consent,
  As partly I find it is, that your fair daughter,
  At this odd-even° and dull watch o' th' night,
  Transported, with° no worse nor better guard
  But with a knave of common hire, a gondolier,   125
  To the gross clasps of a lascivious Moor—
  If this be known to you, and your allowance,°
  We then have done you bold and saucy wrongs;
  But if you know not this, my manners tell me
  We have your wrong rebuke. Do not believe   130
  That, from the sense° of all civility,
  I thus would play and trifle with your reverence.
  Your daughter, if you have not given her leave,
  I say again, hath made a gross revolt,
  Tying her duty, beauty, wit, and fortunes   135
  In an extravagant and wheeling° stranger
  Of here and everywhere. Straight satisfy yourself.
  If she be in her chamber, or your house,
  Let loose on me the justice of the state
  For thus deluding you.

108. **grange:** Isolated farmhouse.   109. **simple:** Sincere.   113. **nephews:** I.e.,
grandsons.   114. **gennets for germans:** Spanish horses for near kinsmen.
123. **odd-even:** Between night and morning.   124. **with:** By.   127. **allowance:**
Approval.   131. **from the sense:** Contrary to.   136. **extravagant and wheeling:**
Expatriate and roving.

BRABANTIO: Strike on the tinder, ho!
  Give me a taper!° Call up all my people!
  This accident° is not unlike my dream.
  Belief of it oppresses me already.
  Light, I say! light!   (*Exit [above]*.)
IAGO: Farewell, for I must leave you.
  It seems not meet,° nor wholesome to my place,°
  To be produced°—as, if I stay, I shall—
  Against the Moor. For I do know the state,
  However this may gall him with some check,°
  Cannot with safety cast° him; for he's embarked
  With such loud reason to the Cyprus wars,
  Which even now stand in act,° that for their souls
  Another of his fathom° they have none
  To lead their business; in which regard,
  Though I do hate him as I do hell-pains,
  Yet, for necessity of present life,°
  I must show out a flag and sign of love,
  Which is indeed but sign. That you shall surely find him,
  Lead to the Sagittary° the raisèd search;
  And there will I be with him. So farewell.   (*Exit.*)

(*Enter [below] Brabantio in his nightgown,° and Servants with torches.*)

BRABANTIO: It is too true an evil. Gone she is;
  And what's to come of my despisèd time
  Is naught but bitterness. Now, Roderigo,
  Where didst thou see her?—O unhappy girl!—
  With the Moor, say'st thou?—Who would be a father?—
  How didst thou know 'twas she!—O, she deceives me
  Past thought!—What said she to you?—Get moe° tapers!
  Raise all my kindred!—Are they married, think you?
RODERIGO: Truly I think they are.
BRABANTIO: O heaven! How got she out? O treason of the blood!
  Fathers, from hence trust not your daughters' minds
  By what you see them act. Is there not charms
  By which the property° of youth and maidhood
  May be abused? Have you not read, Roderigo,
  Of some such thing?

---

141. **taper:** Candle.   142. **accident:** Occurrence.   145. **meet:** Fitting.   **place:**
Position.   146. **produced:** Called as a witness.   148. **check:** Reprimand.
149. **cast:** Discharge.   151. **stand in act:** Are going on.   152. **fathom:** Capacity.   155. **life:** Livelihood.   158. **Sagittary:** An inn.   [s.d.] **nightgown:** Dressing gown.   166. **moe:** More.   172. **property:** Nature.

RODERIGO: Yes, sir, I have indeed.
BRABANTIO: Call up my brother.—O, would you had had her!—   175
   Some one way, some another.—Do you know
   Where we may apprehend her and the Moor?
RODERIGO: I think I can discover him, if you please
   To get good guard and go along with me.
BRABANTIO: I pray you lead on. At every house I'll call;   180
   I may command at most.—Get weapons, ho!
   And raise some special officers of night.—
   On, good Roderigo; I'll deserve° your pains.   (*Exeunt.*)

Scene II

(*Before the lodgings of Othello.*)

(*Enter Othello, Iago, and Attendants with torches.*)

IAGO: Though in the trade of war I have slain men,
   Yet do I hold it very stuff o' th' conscience
   To do no contrived° murther. I lack iniquity
   Sometimes to do me service. Nine or ten times
   I had thought t' have yerked° him here under the ribs.   5
OTHELLO: 'Tis better as it is.
IAGO: Nay, but he prated,
   And spoke such scurvy and provoking terms
   Against your honor
   That with the little godliness I have
   I did full hard forbear him.° But I pray you, sir,   10
   Are you fast° married? Be assured of this,
   That the magnifico° is much beloved,
   And hath in his effect° a voice potential°
   As double° as the Duke's. He will divorce you,
   Or put upon you what restraint and grievance   15
   The law, with all his might to enforce it on,
   Will give him cable.
OTHELLO: Let him do his spite.
   My services which I have done the signiory°
   Shall out-tongue his complaints. 'Tis yet to know°—

---

183. **deserve:** Show gratitude for.   SCENE II.   3. **contrived:** Premeditated
5. **yerked:** Stabbed.   10. **I . . . him:** I restrained myself with difficulty from
attacking him.   11. **fast:** Securely.   12. **magnifico:** Grandee (Brabantio).
13. **in his effect:** At his command.   **potential:** Powerful.   14. **double:** Doubly
influential.   18. **signiory:** Venetian government.   19. **yet to know:** Still not
generally known.

Which, when I know that boasting is an honor,
I shall promulgate—I fetch my life and being
From men of royal siege;° and my demerits°
May speak unbonneted to as proud a fortune
As this that I have reached.° For know, Iago,
But that I love the gentle Desdemona,
I would not my unhousèd° free condition
Put into circumscription and confine
For the sea's worth. But look what lights come yond?
IAGO: Those are the raisèd father and his friends.
  You were best go in.
OTHELLO: Not I; I must be found.
  My parts, my title, and my perfect soul°
  Shall manifest me rightly. Is it they?
IAGO: By Janus, I think no.

(*Enter Cassio, with torches, Officers.*)

OTHELLO: The servants of the Duke, and my lieutenant.
  The goodness of the night upon you, friends!
  What is the news?
CASSIO: The Duke does greet you, general;
  And he requires your haste-post-haste appearance
  Even on the instant.
OTHELLO: What's the matter, think you?
CASSIO: Something from Cyprus, as I may divine.
  It is a business of some heat.° The galleys
  Have sent a dozen sequent° messengers
  This very night at one another's heels,
  And many of the consuls,° raised and met,
  Are at the Duke's already. You have been hotly called for;
  When, being not at your lodging to be found,
  The Senate hath sent about three several° quests
  To search you out.
OTHELLO: 'Tis well I am found by you.
  I will but spend a word here in the house,
  And go with you.   [*Exit.*]
CASSIO: Ancient, what makes° he here?

22. **siege:** Rank; **demerits:** Deserts.   23–24. **May speak . . . reached:** Are equal,
I modestly assert, to those of Desdemona's family.   26. **unhousèd:** Unrestrained.
31. **my perfect . . . soul:** My natural gifts, my position, and my Stainless conscience.   40. **heat:** Urgency.   41. **sequent:** Consecutive.   43. **consuls:** Senators.
46. **several:** Separate.   49. **makes:** Does.

IAGO: Faith, he to-night hath boarded a land carack.°   50
  If it prove lawful prize,° he's made for ever.
CASSIO: I do not understand.
IAGO: He's married.
CASSIO: To who?

[Enter Othello.]

IAGO: Marry,° to—Come, captain, will you go?
OTHELLO: Have with you.
CASSIO: Here comes another troop to seek for you.

(Enter Brabantio, Roderigo, and others with lights and weapons.)

IAGO: It is Brabantio. General, be advised.°   55
  He comes to bad intent.
OTHELLO: Holla! stand there!
RODERIGO: Signior, it is the Moor.
BRABANTIO: Down with him, thief!

[They draw on both sides.]

IAGO: You, Roderigo! Come, sir, I am for you.
OTHELLO: Keep up° your bright swords, for the dew will rust them.
  Good signior, you shall more command with years   60
  Than with your weapons.
BRABANTIO: O thou foul thief, where hast thou stowed my daughter?
  Damned as thou art, thou hast enchanted her!
  For I'll refer me to all things of sense,°
  If she in chains of magic were not bound,   65
  Whether a maid so tender, fair, and happy,
  So opposite to marriage that she shunned
  The wealthy curlèd darlings of our nation,
  Would ever have, t' incur a general mock,
  Run from her guardage° to the sooty bosom   70
  Of such a thing as thou—to fear, not to delight.
  Judge me the world if 'tis not gross in sense°
  That thou hast practiced on her with foul charms,
  Abused her delicate youth with drugs or minerals
  That weaken motion.° I'll have't disputed on;   75
  'Tis probable, and palpable to thinking.

---

50. carack: Treasure ship. **51. prize:** Booty. **53. Marry:** By Mary (a mild oath).
55. be advised: Be on your guard. **59. Keep up:** I.e., sheath. **64. I'll . . . sense:**
I'll submit my case to everyone. **70. guardage:** Guardianship. **72. gross in
sense:** Obvious. **75. motion:** Perception.

I therefore apprehend and do attach° thee
For an abuser of the world, a practicer
Of arts inhibited° and out of warrant.°
Lay hold upon him. If he do resist,
Subdue him at his peril.

OTHELLO: Hold your hands,
Both you of my inclining and the rest.
Were it my cue to fight, I should have known it
Without a prompter. Where will you that I go
To answer this your charge?

BRABANTIO: To prison, till fit time
Of law and course of direct session°
Call thee to answer.

OTHELLO: What if I do obey?
How may the Duke be therewith satisfied,
Whose messengers are here about my side
Upon some present business of the state
To bring me to him?

OFFICER: 'Tis true, most worthy signior.
The Duke's in council, and your noble self
I am sure is sent for.

BRABANTIO: How? The Duke in council?
In this time of the night? Bring him away.
Mine's not an idle° cause. The Duke himself,
Or any of my brothers of the state,
Cannot but feel this wrong as 'twere their own;
For if such actions may have passage free,°
Bondslaves and pagans shall our statesmen be.   (*Exeunt.*)

Scene III

(*The Venetian Senate Chamber.*)

(*Enter Duke and Senators, set at a table, with lights and Attendants.*)

DUKE: There is no composition° in these news
That gives them credit.

FIRST SENATOR: Indeed they are disproportioned.°
My letters say a hundred and seven galleys.

---

77. attach: Arrest.   **79. arts inhibited:** Prohibited arts, black magic.   **out of warrant:** Illegal.   **86. direct session:** Regular trial.   **95. idle:** Trifling.   **98. may . . . free:** Are allowed to go unrestrained.   SCENE III.   **1. composition:** Consistency.   **2. disproportioned:** Inconsistent.

DUKE: And mine a hundred forty.
SECOND SENATOR: And mine two hundred.
  But though they jump° not on a just° account— 5
  As in these cases where the aim° reports
  'Tis oft with difference—yet do they all confirm
  A Turkish fleet, and bearing up to Cyprus.
DUKE: Nay, it is possible enough to judgment.
  I do not so secure me° in the error 10
  But the main article° I do approve°
  In fearful sense.
SAILOR (*within*):   What, ho! what, ho! what, ho!
OFFICER: A messenger from the galleys.

(*Enter Sailor.*)

DUKE: Now, what's the business?
SAILOR: The Turkish preparation makes for Rhodes.
  So was I bid report here to the state 15
  By Signior Angelo.
DUKE: How say you by° this change?
FIRST SENATOR: This cannot be
  By no assay° of reason. 'Tis a pageant
  To keep us in false gaze.° When we consider
  Th' importancy of Cyprus to the Turk, 20
  And let ourselves again but understand
  That, as it more concerns the Turk than Rhodes,
  So may he with more facile question bear° it,
  For that it stands not in such warlike brace,°
  But altogether lacks th' abilities 25
  That Rhodes is dressed in—if we make thought of this,
  We must not think the Turk is so unskillful
  To leave that latest which concerns him first,
  Neglecting an attempt of ease and gain
  To wake and wage° a danger profitless. 30
DUKE: Nay, in all confidence, he's not for Rhodes.
OFFICER: Here is more news.

(*Enter a Messenger.*)

MESSENGER: The Ottomites, reverend and gracious,

---

5. **jump:** Agree; **just:** Exact. 6. **aim:** Conjecture. 10. **so secure me:** Take such comfort. 11. **article:** Substance; **approve:** Accept. 17. **by:** About. 18. **assay:** Test. 19. **in false gaze:** Looking the wrong way. 23. **with . . . bear:** More easily capture. 24. **brace:** Posture of defense. 30. **wake and wage:** Rouse and risk.

Steering with due course toward the isle of Rhodes,
Have there injointed them° with an after fleet.
FIRST SENATOR: Ay, so I thought. How many, as you guess?
MESSENGER: Of thirty sail; and now they do restem°
  Their backward course, bearing with frank appearance°
  Their purposes toward Cyprus. Signior Montano,
  Your trusty and most valiant servitor,
  With his free duty recommends you thus,
  And prays you to believe him.
DUKE: 'Tis certain then for Cyprus.
  Marcus Luccicos,° is not he in town?
FIRST SENATOR: He's now in Florence.
DUKE: Write from us to him, post, post-haste. Dispatch.
FIRST SENATOR: Here comes Brabantio and the valiant Moor.

(*Enter Brabantio, Othello, Cassio, Iago, Roderigo, and Officers.*)

DUKE: Valiant Othello, we must straight employ you
  Against the general enemy Ottoman.   [*To Brabantio.*]
  I did not see you. Welcome, gentle signior.
  We lacked your counsel and your help to-night.
BRABANTIO: So did I yours. Good your grace, pardon me.
  Neither my place, nor aught I heard of business,
  Hath raised me from my bed; nor doth the general care
  Take hold on me; for my particular grief
  Is of so floodgate° and o'erbearing nature
  That it engluts° and swallows other sorrows,
  And it is still itself.
DUKE: Why, what's the matter?
BRABANTIO: My daughter! O, my daughter!
ALL: Dead?
BRABANTIO: Ay, to me.
  She is abused,° stol'n from me, and corrupted
  By spells and medicines bought of mountebanks;
  For nature so prepost'rously to err,
  Being not deficient,° blind, or lame of sense,
  Sans witchcraft could not.
DUKE: Whoe'er he be that in this foul proceeding
  Hath thus beguiled your daughter of herself,

---

35. injointed them: Joined themselves.   37. restem: Steer again.   38. frank
appearance: Undisguised intent.   44. Marcus Luccicos: (Presumably a Venetian envoy).   56. floodgate: Torrential.   57. engluts: Engulfs.   60. abused:
Deceived.   63. deficient: Feeble-minded.

And you of her, the bloody book of law
You shall yourself read in the bitter letter
After your own sense; yea, though our proper° son
Stood in your action.°

BRABANTIO: Humbly I thank your grace.   70
  Here is the man—this Moor, whom now, it seems,
  Your special mandate for the state affairs
  Hath hither brought.

ALL: We are very sorry for't.

DUKE [to Othello]: What, in your own part, can you say to this?

BRABANTIO: Nothing, but this is so.   75

OTHELLO: Most potent, grave, and reverend signiors,
  My very noble, and approved° good masters,
  That I have ta'en away this old man's daughter,
  It is most true; true I have married her.
  The very head and front of my offending   80
  Hath this extent, no more. Rude° am I in my speech,
  And little blessed with the soft phrase of peace;
  For since these arms of mine had seven years' pith°
  Till now some nine moons wasted,° they have used
  Their dearest action in the tented field;   85
  And little of this great world can I speak
  More than pertains to feats of broil and battle;
  And therefore little shall I grace my cause
  In speaking for myself. Yet, by your gracious patience,
  I will a round° unvarnished tale deliver   90
  Of my whole course of love—what drugs, what charms,
  What conjuration, and what mighty magic
  (For such proceeding am I charged withal°)
  I won his daughter.

BRABANTIO: A maiden never bold;
  Of spirit so still and quiet that her motion   95
  Blushed° at herself; and she—in spite of nature,
  Of years,° of country, credit, everything—
  To fall in love with what she feared to look on!
  It is a judgment maimed and most imperfect
  That will confess perfection so could err   100

---

69. **our proper:** My own.   70. **Stood in your action:** Were accused by you.
77. **approved:** Tested by experience.   81. **Rude:** Unpolished.   83. **pith:** Strength
(i.e., since I was seven years old).   84. **Till . . . wasted:** Until about nine months
ago.   90. **round:** Plain.   93. **withal:** With.   95–96. **her motion Blushed:** Her
own emotions caused her to blush.   97. **years:** (Difference in age).

Against all rules of nature, and must be driven
To find out practices° of cunning hell
Why this should be. I therefore vouch° again
That with some mixtures pow'rful o'er the blood,°
Or with some dram, conjured° to this effect,
He wrought upon her.

DUKE: To vouch this is no proof,
Without more certain and more overt test
Than these thin habits° and poor likelihoods
Of modern seeming° do prefer against him.

FIRST SENATOR: But, Othello, speak.
Did you by indirect and forcèd° courses
Subdue and poison this young maid's affections?
Or came it by request, and such fair question°
As soul to soul affordeth?

OTHELLO: I do beseech you,
Send for the lady to the Sagittary
And let her speak of me before her father.
If you do find me foul in her report,
The trust, the office, I do hold of you
Not only take away, but let your sentence
Even fall upon my life.

DUKE: Fetch Desdemona hither.

OTHELLO: Ancient, conduct them; you best know the place.

                    (*Exit [Iago, with] two or three [Attendants].*)

And till she come, as truly as to heaven
I do confess the vices of my blood,
So justly to your grave ears I'll present
How I did thrive in this fair lady's love,
And she in mine.

DUKE: Say it, Othello.

OTHELLO: Her father loved me, oft invited me;
Still° questioned me the story of my life
From year to year—the battles, sieges, fortunes
That I have passed.
I ran it through, even from my boyish days
To th' very moment that he bade me tell it.
Wherein I spoke of most disastrous chances,

---

102. **practices:** Plots.   103. **vouch:** Assert.   104. **blood:** Passions.   105. **dram, conjured:** Potion, prepared by magic.   108. **thin habits:** Slight appearances.
109. **modern seeming:** Everyday supposition.   111. **forcèd:** Violent.
113. **question:** Conversation.   129. **Still:** Continually.

Of moving accidents by flood and field;   135
Of hairbreadth scapes i' th' imminent deadly breach;
Of being taken by the insolent foe
And sold to slavery; of my redemption thence
And portance° in my travels' history;
Wherein of anters° vast and deserts idle,   140
Rough quarries, rocks, and hills whose heads touch heaven,
It was my hint° to speak—such was the process;
And of the Cannibals that each other eat,
The Anthropophagi,° and men whose heads
Do grow beneath their shoulders. This to hear   145
Would Desdemona seriously incline;
But still the house affairs would draw her thence;
Which ever as she could with haste dispatch,
She'ld come again, and with a greedy ear
Devour up my discourse. Which I observing,   150
Took once a pliant° hour, and found good means
To draw from her a prayer of earnest heart
That I would all my pilgrimage dilate,°
Whereof by parcels° she had something heard,
But not intentively.° I did consent,   155
And often did beguile her of her tears
When I did speak of some distressful stroke
That my youth suffered. My story being done,
She gave me for my pains a world of sighs.
She swore, i' faith, 'twas strange, 'twas passing° strange;   160
'Twas pitiful, 'twas wondrous pitiful.
She wished she had not heard it; yet she wished
That heaven had made her such a man. She thanked me;
And bade me, if I had a friend that loved her,
I should but teach him how to tell my story,   165
And that would woo her. Upon this hint° I spake.
She loved me for the dangers I had passed,
And I loved her that she did pity them.
This only is the witchcraft I have used.
Here comes the lady. Let her witness it.   170

(*Enter Desdemona, Iago, Attendants.*)

139. **portance:** Behavior.   140. **anters:** Propitous Caves.   142. **hint:** Occasion.
144. **Anthropophagi:** Man-eaters.   151. **pliant:** Suitable.   153. **dilate:** Recount
in full.   154. **parcels:** Portions.   155. **intentively:** With full attention.
160. **passing:** Exceedingly.   166. **hint:** Opportunity.

DUKE: I think this tale would win my daughter too.
  Good Brabantio,
  Take up this mangled matter at the best.°
  Men do their broken weapons rather use
  Than their bare hands.
BRABANTIO: I pray you hear her speak.
  If she confess that she was half the wooer,
  Destruction on my head if my bad blame
  Light on the man! Come hither, gentle mistress.
  Do you perceive in all this noble company
  Where most you owe obedience?
DESDEMONA: My noble father,
  I do perceive here a divided duty.
  To you I am bound for life and education;°
  My life and education both do learn me
  How to respect you: you are the lord of duty;°
  I am hitherto your daughter. But here's my husband;
  And so much duty as my mother showed
  To you, preferring you before her father,
  So much I challenge° that I may profess
  Due to the Moor my lord.
BRABANTIO: God be with you! I have done.
  Please it your grace, on to the state affairs.
  I had rather to adopt a child than get° it.
  Come hither, Moor.
  I here do give thee that with all my heart
  Which, but thou hast already, with all my heart
  I would keep from thee. For your sake,° jewel,
  I am glad at soul I have no other child;
  For thy escape° would teach me tyranny,
  To hang clogs on them. I have done, my lord.
DUKE: Let me speak like yourself° and lay a sentence°
  Which, as a grise° or step, may help these lovers
  [Into your favor.]
  When remedies are past, the griefs are ended
  By seeing the worst, which late on hopes depended.
  To mourn a mischief that is past and gone
  Is the next way to draw new mischief on.

---

173. Take . . . best: Make the best of this situation.   182. education: Upbringing.   184. of duty: To whom duty is due.   188. challenge: Claim the right.
191. get: Beget.   195. For your sake: Because of you.   197. escape: Esca-
pade.   199. like yourself: As you should; sentence: Maxim.   200. grise: Step.

What cannot be preserved when fortune takes,
Patience her injury a mock'ry makes.
The robbed that smiles steals something from the thief;
He robs himself that spends a bootless grief.
BRABANTIO: So let the Turk of Cyprus us beguile: 210
We lose it not so long as we can smile.
He bears the sentence well that nothing bears
But the free comfort which from thence he hears;
But he bears both the sentence and the sorrow
That to pay grief must of poor patience borrow.   215
These sentences, to sugar, or to gall,
Being strong on both sides, are equivocal.
But words are words. I never yet did hear
That the bruisèd heart was piercèd through the ear.
Beseech you, now to the affairs of state.   220
DUKE: The Turk with a most mighty preparation makes for Cyprus.
    Othello, the fortitude° of the place is best known to you; and though
    we have there a substitute of most allowed° sufficiency, yet opinion,° a
    more sovereign mistress of effects, throws a more safer voice on you.
    You must therefore be content to slubber° the gloss of your new for-   225
    tunes with this more stubborn and boist'rous expedition.
OTHELLO: The tyrant custom, most grave senators,
    Hath made the flinty and steel couch of war
    My thrice-driven bed of down. I do agnize
    A natural and prompt alacrity   230
    I find in hardness;° and do undertake
    These present wars against the Ottomites.
    Most humbly, therefore, bending to your state,
    I crave fit disposition for my wife,
    Due reference of place, and exhibition,°   235
    With such accommodation and besort°
    As levels° with her breeding.
DUKE: If you please,
    Be't at her father's.
BRABANTIO: I will not have it so.
OTHELLO: Nor I.
DESDEMONA: Nor I. I would not there reside,   240
    To put my father in impatient thoughts

---

222. **fortitude:** Fortification.   223. **allowed:** Acknowledged; **opinion:** Public
opinion.   225. **slubber:** Sully.   229–31. **agnize . . . hardness:** Recognize in
myself a natural and easy response to hardship.   235. **exhibition:** Allowance of
money.   236. **besort:** Suitable company.   237. **levels:** Corresponds.

By being in his eye. Most gracious Duke,
To my unfolding lend your prosperous° ear,
And let me find a charter in your voice,
T' assist my simpleness.°

DUKE: What would you, Desdemona?

DESDEMONA: That I did love the Moor to live with him,
My downright violence, and storm of fortunes,°
May trumpet to the world. My heart's subdued
Even to the very quality of my lord.
I saw Othello's visage in his mind,
And to his honors and his valiant parts
Did I my soul and fortunes consecrate.
So that, dear lords, if I be left behind,
A moth of peace, and he go to the war,
The rites for which I love him are bereft me,
And I a heavy interim shall support
By his dear° absence. Let me go with him.

OTHELLO: Let her have your voice.°
Vouch with me, heaven, I therefore beg it not
To please the palate of my appetite,
Not to comply with heat°—the young affects°
In me defunct—and proper satisfaction;
But to be free and bounteous to her mind;
And heaven defend your good souls that you think
I will your serious and great business scant
When she is with me. No, when light-winged toys
Of feathered Cupid seel° with wanton dullness
My speculative and officed instruments,°
That° my disports corrupt and taint my business,
Let housewives make a skillet of my helm,
And all indign° and base adversities
Make head against my estimation!°

DUKE: Be it as you shall privately determine,
Either for her stay or going. Th' affair cries haste,
And speed must answer it.

FIRST SENATOR: You must away to-night.

---

243. prosperous: Favorable. 245. simpleness: Lack of skill. 248. My ...
fortunes: My clear and complete breaking of social customs. 258. dear: Grievous. 259. voice: Consent. 262. heat: Passions. young affects: Tendencies of
youth. 268. seel: Blind. 269. My ... instruments: My perceptive and responsible faculties. 270. That: So that. 272. indign: Unworthy. 273. estimation:
Reputation.

OTHELLO: With all my heart.
DUKE: At nine i' th' morning here we'll meet again.
  Othello, leave some officer behind,
  And he shall our commission bring to you,   280
  With such things else of quality and respect
  As doth import° you.
OTHELLO: So please your grace, my ancient;
  A man he is of honesty and trust.
  To his conveyance I assign my wife,
  With what else needful your good grace shall think   285
  To be sent after me.
DUKE: Let it be so.
  Good night to every one.
    [*To Brabantio.*]   And, noble signior,
  If virtue no delighted° beauty lack,
  Your son-in-law is far more fair than black.
FIRST SENATOR: Adieu, brave Moor. Use Desdemona well.   290
BRABANTIO: Look to her, Moor, if thou hast eyes to see:
  She has deceived her father, and may thee.
               (*Exeunt* [*Duke, Senators, Officers, &c.*].)
OTHELLO: My life upon her faith!—Honest Iago,
  My Desdemona must I leave to thee.
  I prithee let thy wife attend on her,   295
  And bring them after in the best advantage.°
  Come, Desdemona. I have but an hour
  Of love, of worldly matters and direction,
  To spend with thee. We must obey the time.
               (*Exit Moor and Desdemona.*)
RODERIGO: Iago,—   300
IAGO: What say'st thou, noble heart?
RODERIGO: What will I do, think'st thou?
IAGO: Why, go to bed and sleep.
RODERIGO: I will incontinently° drown myself.
IAGO: If thou dost, I shall never love thee after. Why, thou silly gentle-   305
  man!
RODERIGO: It is silliness to live when to live is torment; and then have we
  a prescription to die when death is our physician.
IAGO: O villainous! I have looked upon the world for four times seven
  years; and since I could distinguish betwixt a benefit and an injury, I   310
  never found man that knew how to love himself. Ere I would say I

282. import: Concern.   **288. delighted:** Delightful.   **296. in the best advan-**
tage: At the best opportunity.   **304. incontinently:** Forthwith.

would drown myself for the love of a guinea hen,° I would change my
humanity with a baboon.

RODERIGO: What should I do? I confess it is my shame to be so fond,° but
it is not in my virtue° to amend it.

IAGO: Virtue? a fig! 'Tis in ourselves that we are thus or thus. Our bodies
are our gardens, to which our wills are gardeners; so that if we will
plant nettles or sow lettuce, set hyssop and weed up thyme, supply it
with one gender° of herbs or distract it with many—either to have it
sterile with idleness or manured with industry—why, the power and
corrigible authority° of this lies in our wills. If the balance of our lives
had not one scale of reason to poise° another of sensuality, the blood
and baseness° of our natures would conduct us to most preposterous
conclusions. But we have reason to cool our raging motions,° our carnal strings, our unbitted° lusts; whereof I take this that you call love to
be a sect or scion.°

RODERIGO: It cannot be.

IAGO: It is merely a lust of the blood and a permission of the will. Come,
be a man! Drown thyself? Drown cats and blind puppies! I have pro-
fessed me thy friend, and I confess me knit to thy deserving with cables
of perdurable toughness. I could never better stead thee than now.
Put money in thy purse. Follow thou the wars; defeat thy favor° with
an usurped beard. I say, put money in thy purse. It cannot be that
Desdemona should long continue her love to the Moor—put money in
thy purse—nor he his to her. It was a violent commencement in her,
and thou shalt see an answerable sequestration°—put but money in
thy purse. These Moors are changeable in their wills—fill thy purse
with money. The food that to him now is as luscious as locusts shall be
to him shortly as bitter as coloquintida.° She must change for youth:
when she is sated with his body, she will find the error of her choice.
[She must have change, she must.] Therefore put money in thy purse.
If thou wilt needs damn thyself, do it a more delicate way than drowning. Make° all the money thou canst. If sanctimony and a frail vow
betwixt an erring° barbarian and a supersubtle Venetian be not too
hard for my wits and all the tribe of hell, thou shalt enjoy her. Therefore make money. A pox of drowning thyself! 'Tis clean out of the way.

---

312. **guinea hen:** Prostitute (slang).   314. **fond:** Foolish.   315. **virtue:** Strength,
ability.   319. **gender:** Species.   321. **corrigible authority:** Corrective power.
322. **poise:** Counterbalance.   322–23. **blood and baseness:** Animal instincts.
324. **motions:** Appetites.   325. **unbitted:** Uncontrolled.   326. **sect or scion:**
Offshoot, cutting.   332. **defeat thy favor:** Disguise thy appearance.   336. **seques-
tration:** Estrangement.   339. **coloquintida:** A medicine.   343. **Make:** Raise.
344. **erring:** Wandering.

Seek thou rather to be hanged in compassing thy joy than to be
drowned and go without her.

RODERIGO: Wilt thou be fast to my hopes, if I depend on the issue?

IAGO: Thou art sure of me. Go, make money. I have told thee often, and I   350
retell thee again and again, I hate the Moor. My cause is hearted;° thine
hath no less reason. Let us be conjunctive° in our revenge against him.
If thou canst cuckold him, thou dost thyself a pleasure, me a sport.
There are many events in the womb of time, which will be delivered.
Traverse,° go, provide thy money! We will have more of this to-morrow.   355
Adieu.

RODERIGO: Where shall we meet i' th' morning?

IAGO: At my lodging.

RODERIGO: I'll be with thee betimes.°

IAGO: Go to, farewell—Do you hear, Roderigo?   360

[RODERIGO: What say you?

IAGO: No more of drowning, do you hear?

RODERIGO: I am changed.

IAGO: Go to, farewell. Put money enough in your purse.]

RODERIGO: I'll sell all my land.   (*Exit.*) 365

IAGO: Thus do I ever make my fool my purse;
   For I mine own gained knowledge should profane
   If I would time expend with such a snipe°
   But for my sport and profit. I hate the Moor;
   And it is thought abroad° that 'twixt my sheets   370
   H'as done my office. I know not if't be true;
   But I, for mere suspicion in that kind,
   Will do as if for surety.° He holds me well;°
   The better shall my purpose work on him.
   Cassio's a proper man. Let me see now: 375
   To get his place, and to plume up° my will
   In double knavery—How, how?—Let's see:—
   After some time, to abuse° Othello's ears
   That he° is too familiar with his° wife.
   He hath a person and a smooth dispose°   380
   To be suspected—framed to make women false.
   The Moor is of a free° and open nature
   That thinks men honest that but seem to be so;

---

351. **hearted:** Fixed in my heart.   352. **conjunctive:** United.   355. **Traverse:**
Forward march.   359. **betimes:** Early.   368. **snipe:** Fool.   370. **thought abroad:**
Rumored.   373. **do . . . surety:** Act on it as if certain; **well:** In high regard.
376. **plume up:** Gratify.   378. **abuse:** Deceive.   379. **he:** (Cassio); **his:**
(Othello's).   380. **dispose:** Manner.   382. **free:** Frank.

And will as tenderly be led by th' nose
As asses are.
I have't! It is engend'red! Hell and night
Must bring this monstrous birth to the world's light.   (*Exit.*)

ACT II   *Scene I*

(*An open place in Cyprus, near the harbor.*)

(*Enter Montano and two Gentlemen.*)

MONTANO: What from the cape can you discern at sea?
FIRST GENTLEMAN: Nothing at all: it is a high-wrought flood.°
   I cannot 'twixt the heaven and the main
   Descry a sail.
MONTANO: Methinks the wind hath spoke aloud at land;
   A fuller blast ne'er shook our battlements.
   If it hath ruffianed° so upon the sea,
   What ribs of oak, when mountains° melt on them,
   Can hold the mortise?° What shall we hear of this?
SECOND GENTLEMAN: A segregation° of the Turkish fleet.
   For do but stand upon the foaming shore,
   The chidden billow seems to pelt the clouds;
   The wind-shaked surge, with high and monstrous mane,
   Seems to cast water on the burning Bear
   And quench the Guards° of th' ever-fixèd pole.°
   I never did like molestation° view
   On the enchafèd° flood.
MONTANO: If that° the Turkish fleet
   Be not ensheltered and embayed, they are drowned;
   It is impossible to bear it out.

(*Enter a third Gentleman.*)

THIRD GENTLEMAN: News, lads! Our wars are done.
   The desperate tempest hath so banged the Turks
   That their designment halts.° A noble ship of Venice
   Hath seen a grievous wrack° and sufferance°
   On most part of their fleet.

ACT II, SCENE I.   **2. high-wrought flood:** Very agitated sea.   **7. ruffianed:** Raged.
8. mountains: I.e., of water.   **9. hold the mortise:** Hold their joints together.
10. segregation: Scattering.   **15. Guards:** Stars near the North Star; **pole:** Pole-
star.   **16. molestation:** Tumult.   **17. enchafèd:** Angry; **If that:** If.   **22. designment halts:** Plan is crippled.   **23. wrack:** Shipwreck; **sufferance:** Disaster.

MONTANO: How? Is this true?

THIRD GENTLEMAN: The ship is here put in,   25
  A Veronesa;° Michael Cassio,
  Lieutenant to the warlike Moor Othello,
  Is come on shore; the Moor himself at sea,
  And is in full commission here for Cyprus.

MONTANO: I am glad on't. 'Tis a worthy governor.   30

THIRD GENTLEMAN: But this same Cassio, though he speak of comfort
  Touching the Turkish loss, yet he looks sadly
  And prays the Moor be safe, for they were parted
  With foul and violent tempest.

MONTANO: Pray heaven he be;
  For I have served him, and the man commands   35
  Like a full° soldier. Let's to the seaside, ho!
  As well to see the vessel that's come in
  As to throw out our eyes for brave Othello,
  Even till we make the main and th' aerial blue
  An indistinct regard.°

THIRD GENTLEMAN: Come, let's do so;   40
  For every minute is expectancy
  Of more arrivance.

(*Enter Cassio.*)

CASSIO: Thanks, you the valiant of this warlike isle,
  That so approve° the Moor! O, let the heavens
  Give him defense against the elements,   45
  For I have lost him on a dangerous sea!

MONTANO: Is he well shipped?

CASSIO: His bark is stoutly timbered, and his pilot
  Of very expert and approved allowance;°
  Therefore my hopes, not surfeited to death,°   50
  Stand in bold cure.°
  (*Within.*)   A sail, a sail, a sail!   (*Enter a messenger.*)

CASSIO: What noise?

MESSENGER: The town is empty; on the brow o' th' sea
  Stand ranks of people, and they cry "A sail!"

CASSIO: My hopes do shape him for the governor.   55

(*A shot.*)

---

26. Veronesa: Ship furnished by Verona.   **36. full:** Perfect.   **40. An indistinct regard:** Indistinguishable.   **44. approve:** Commend, admire.   **49. approved allowance:** Tested reputation.   **50. surfeited to death:** Overindulged.   **51. in bold cure:** A good chance of fulfillment.

SECOND GENTLEMAN: They do discharge their shot of courtesy:
  Our friends at least.
CASSIO: I pray you, sir, go forth
  And give us truth who 'tis that is arrived.
SECOND GENTLEMAN: I shall.   (*Exit.*)
MONTANO: But, good lieutenant, is your general wived?
CASSIO: Most fortunately. He hath achieved a maid
  That paragons° description and wild fame;
  One that excels the quirks° of blazoning° pens,
  And in th' essential vesture of creation
  Does tire the ingener.°

(*Enter Second Gentleman.*)

                        How now? Who has put in?
SECOND GENTLEMAN: 'Tis one Iago, ancient to the general.
CASSIO: He's had most favorable and happy speed:
  Tempests themselves, high seas, and howling winds,
  The guttered° rocks and congregated sands,
  Traitors ensteeped° to clog the guiltless keel,
  As having sense of beauty, do omit
  Their mortal° natures, letting go safely by
  The divine Desdemona.
MONTANO: What is she?
CASSIO: She that I spake of, our great captain's captain,
  Left in the conduct of the bold Iago,
  Whose footing° here anticipates our thoughts
  A se'nnight's° speed. Great Jove, Othello guard,
  And swell his sail with thine own pow'rful breath,
  That he may bless this bay with his tall ship,
  Make love's quick pants in Desdemona's arms,
  Give renewed fire to our extinct spirits,
  [And bring all Cyprus comfort!]

(*Enter Desdemona, Iago, Roderigo, and Emilia* [*with Attendants*].)

                        O, behold!
  The riches of the ship is come on shore!
  You men of Cyprus, let her have your knees.°
  Hail to thee, lady! and the grace of heaven,

---

62. **paragons:** Surpasses.   63. **quirks:** Ingenuities; **blazoning:** Describing in
heraldic language.   64–65. **And . . . ingener:** Merely to describe her as God made
her exhaust her praiser.   69. **guttered:** Jagged.   70. **ensteeped:** Submerged.
72. **mortal:** Deadly.   76. **footing:** Landing.   77. **se'nnight's:** Week's.   84. **knees:**
I.e., kneeling.

Before, behind thee, and on every hand,
  Enwheel thee round!
DESDEMONA: I thank you, valiant Cassio.
  What tidings can you tell me of my lord?
CASSIO: He is not yet arrived; nor know I aught
  But that he's well and will be shortly here.   90
DESDEMONA: O but I fear! How lost you company?
CASSIO: The great contention of the sea and skies
  Parted our fellowship.
      (*Within.*)   A sail, a sail! [*A shot.*]
                                         But hark. A sail!
SECOND GENTLEMAN: They give their greeting to the citadel;
  This likewise is a friend.
CASSIO: See for the news.   95
                                    [*Exit Gentleman.*]
Good ancient, you are welcome.
      [*To Emilia.*]   Welcome, mistress.—
  Let it not gall your patience, good Iago,
  That I extend my manners. 'Tis my breeding
  That gives me this bold show of courtesy.
      [*Kisses Emilia.°*]
IAGO: Sir, would she give you so much of her lips   100
  As of her tongue she oft bestows on me,
  You would have enough.
DESDEMONA: Alas, she has no speech!
IAGO: In faith, too much.
  I find it still° when I have list° to sleep.
  Marry, before your ladyship, I grant,   105
  She puts her tongue a little in her heart
  And chides with thinking.
EMILIA: You have little cause to say so.
IAGO: Come on, come on! You are pictures out of doors,°
  Bells° in your parlors, wildcats in your kitchens,   110
  Saints° in your injuries, devils being offended,
  Players in your housewifery,° and housewives° in your beds.
DESDEMONA: O, fie upon thee, slanderer!
IAGO: Nay, it is true, or else I am a Turk:°
  You rise to play, and go to bed to work.   115

[S.D.] **Kisses Emilia:** (Kissing was a common Elizabethan form of social courtesy).   **104. still:** Always; **list:** Desire.   **109. pictures out of doors:** Well-
behaved in public.   **110. Bells:** Noisy, jangling.   **111. Saints:** Martyrs.
112. housewifery: Housekeeping; **housewives:** Hussies.   **114. Turk:** Infidel,
not to be believed.

EMILIA: You shall not write my praise.

IAGO: No, let me not.

DESDEMONA: What wouldst thou write of me, if thou shouldst praise me?

IAGO: O gentle lady, do not put me to't,
    For I am nothing if not critical.

DESDEMONA: Come on, assay.°—There's one gone to the harbor?

IAGO: Ay, madam.

DESDEMONA: I am not merry; but I do beguile
    The thing I am by seeming otherwise.—
    Come, how wouldst thou praise me?

IAGO: I am about it; but indeed my invention
    Comes from my pate as birdlime° does from frieze°—
    It plucks out brains and all. But my Muse labors,
    And thus she is delivered:
    If she be fair and wise, fairness and wit—
    The one's for use, the other useth it.

DESDEMONA: Well praised! How if she be black° and witty?

IAGO: If she be black, and thereto have a wit,
    She'll find a white° that shall her blackness fit.

DESDEMONA: Worse and worse!

EMILIA: How if fair and foolish?

IAGO: She never yet was foolish that was fair,
    For even her folly° helped her to an heir.

DESDEMONA: These are old fond° paradoxes to make fools laugh i' th'
    alehouse. What miserable praise hast thou for her that's foul° and
    foolish?

IAGO: There's none so foul, and foolish thereunto,
    But does foul pranks which fair and wise ones do.

DESDEMONA: O heavy ignorance! Thou praisest the worst best. But what
    praise couldst thou bestow on a deserving woman indeed—one that in
    the authority of her merit did justly put on the vouch° of very malice
    itself?

IAGO: She that was ever fair, and never proud;
    Had tongue at will, and yet was never loud;
    Never lacked gold, and yet went never gay;°
    Fled from her wish, and yet said "Now I may";°
    She that, being ang'red, her revenge being nigh,

120. assay: Try.   126. birdlime: A sticky paste; frieze: Rough cloth.   131. black:
Brunette.   133. white: Wight (a person), and a fair person (pun).   137. folly:
Wantonness.   138. fond: Foolish.   139. foul: Ugly.   145. put on the vouch:
Compel the approval.   149. gay: Lavishly clothed.   150. Fled ... may": Resisted
temptation even when she had a choice.

Bade her wrong stay,° and her displeasure fly;
She that in wisdom never was so frail
To change the cod's head for the salmon's tail;°
She that could think, and ne'er disclose her mind;   155
See suitors following, and not look behind:
She was a wight (if ever such wight° were)—

DESDEMONA: To do what?

IAGO: To suckle fools and chronicle small beer.°

DESDEMONA: O most lame and impotent conclusion! Do not learn of him, 160
    Emilia, though he be thy husband. How say you, Cassio? Is he not a
    most profane and liberal° counsellor?

CASSIO: He speaks home,° madam. You may relish him more in the sol-
    dier than in the scholar.

IAGO [aside]: He takes her by the palm. Ay, well said, whisper! With as 165
    little a web as this will I ensnare as great a fly as Cassio. Ay, smile upon
    her, do! I will give thee in thine own courtship.° — You say true; 'tis so,
    indeed! — If such tricks as these strip you out of your lieutenantry, it
    had been better you had not kissed your three fingers so oft—which
    now again you are most apt to play the sir° in. Very good! well kissed! 170
    an excellent courtesy! 'Tis so, indeed. Yet again your fingers to your
    lips? Would they were clyster pipes° for your sake! (Trumpet within.)
    The Moor! I know his trumpet.

CASSIO: 'Tis truly so.

DESDEMONA: Let's meet him and receive him.   175

CASSIO: Lo, where he comes.

(Enter Othello and Attendants.)

OTHELLO: O my fair warrior!

DESDEMONA: My dear Othello!

OTHELLO: It gives me wonder great as my content
    To see you here before me. O my soul's joy!
    If after every tempest come such calms,   180
    May the winds blow till they have wakened death!
    And let the laboring bark climb hills of seas
    Olympus-high, and duck again as low
    As hell's from heaven! If it were now to die,

152. **Bade . . . stay:** Decided to put up with her injury patiently.   154. **To . . . tail:**
I.e., to exchange the good for the poor but expensive.   157. **wight:** Person, human
being.   159. **chronicle small beer:** Keep petty household accounts.   162. **profane and liberal:** Worldly and licentious.   163. **home:** Bluntly.   167. **give . . .
courtship:** Manacle you by means of your courtly manners.   170. **sir:** Courtly
gentleman.   172. **clyster pipes:** Syringes.

'Twere now to be most happy;° for I fear   1
My soul hath her content so absolute
That not another comfort like to this
Succeeds in unknown fate.

DESDEMONA: The heavens forbid
But that our loves and comforts should increase
Even as our days do grow.

OTHELLO: Amen to that, sweet powers!
I cannot speak enough of this content;
It stops me here; it is too much of joy.
And this, and this, the greatest discords be

(*They kiss.*)

That e'er our hearts shall make!

IAGO [*aside*]:   O, you are well tuned now!
But I'll set down° the pegs that make this music,
As honest as I am.

OTHELLO: Come, let us to the castle.
News, friends! Our wars are done; the Turks are drowned.
How does my old acquaintance of this isle?—
Honey, you shall be well desired° in Cyprus;
I have found great love amongst them. O my sweet,
I prattle out of fashion, and I dote
In mine own comforts. I prithee, good Iago,
Go to the bay and disembark my coffers.
Bring thou the master° to the citadel;
He is a good one, and his worthiness
Does challenge° much respect.—Come, Desdemona,
Once more well met at Cyprus.

(*Exit Othello [with all but Iago and Roderigo].*)

IAGO [*to an Attendant, who goes out*]: Do thou meet me presently at the
harbor. [*To Roderigo.*] Come hither. If thou be'st valiant (as they say
base men being in love have then a nobility in their natures more than
is native to them), list me. The lieutenant to-night watches on the court
of guard.° First, I must tell thee this: Desdemona is directly in love
with him.

RODERIGO: With him? Why, 'tis not possible.

IAGO: Lay thy finger thus,° and let thy soul be instructed. Mark me with
what violence she first loved the Moor, but° for bragging and telling

---

185. **happy:** Fortunate.   195. **set down:** Loosen.   199. **well desired:** Warmly
welcomed.   204. **master:** Ship captain.   206. **challenge:** Deserve.   211–12. **court
of guard:** Headquarters.   215. **thus:** I.e., on your lips.   216. **but:** Only.

her fantastical lies; and will she love him still for prating? Let not thy
discreet heart think it. Her eye must be fed; and what delight shall she
have to look on the devil? When the blood is made dull with the act of
sport,° there should be, again to inflame it and to give satiety a fresh   220
appetite, loveliness in favor,° sympathy° in years, manners, and beauties; all which the Moor is defective in. Now for want of these required
conveniences,° her delicate tenderness will find itself abused,° begin to
heave the gorge,° disrelish and abhor the Moor. Very nature° will instruct her in it and compel her to some second choice. Now, sir, this   225
granted—as it is a most pregnant° and unforced position—who
stands so eminent in the degree of° this fortune as Cassio does? A
knave very voluble; no further conscionable° than in putting on the
mere form of civil and humane° seeming for the better compassing of
his salt° and most hidden loose affection? Why, none! why, none! A   230
slipper° and subtle knave; a finder-out of occasions; that has an eye can
stamp° and counterfeit advantages,° though true advantage never
present itself; a devilish knave! Besides, the knave is handsome, young,
and hath all those requisites in him that folly and green° minds look
after. A pestilent complete knave! and the woman hath found him   235
already.

RODERIGO: I cannot believe that in her; she's full of most blessed
condition.°

IAGO: Blessed fig's-end! The wine she drinks is made of grapes. If she had
been blessed, she would never have loved the Moor. Blessed pudding!   240
Didst thou not see her paddle with the palm of his hand? Didst not
mark that?

RODERIGO: Yes, that I did; but that was but courtesy.

IAGO: Lechery, by this hand! an index° and obscure° prologue to the history of lust and foul thoughts. They met so near with their lips that   245
their breaths embraced together. Villainous thoughts, Roderigo! When
these mutualities° so marshal the way, hard at hand comes the master
and main exercise, th' incorporate° conclusion. Pish! But, sir, be you
ruled by me: I have brought you from Venice. Watch you to-night;

220. **the act of sport:** Sex.   221. **favor:** Appearance; **sympathy:** Similarity.
223. **conveniences:** Compatibilities.   **abused:** Cheated.   224. **heave the gorge:**
Be nauseated.   224. **Very nature:** Her very instincts.   226. **pregnant:** Evident.   227. **in the degree of:** As next in line for.   228. **conscionable:** Conscientious.   229. **humane:** Polite.   230. **salt:** Lecherous.   231. **slipper:** Slippery.
232. **stamp:** Coin; **advantages:** Opportunities.   234. **folly and green:** Foolish
and inexperienced.   237–238. **condition:** Character.   244. **index:** Table of contents; **obscure:** Hidden.   247. **mutualities:** Exchanges.   248. **incorporate:**
Carnal.

for the command, I'll lay't upon you.° Cassio knows you not. I'll not be
far from you: do you find some occasion to anger Cassio, either by
speaking too loud, or tainting° his discipline, or from what other
course you please which the time shall more favorably minister.°

RODERIGO: Well.

IAGO: Sir, he's rash and very sudden in choler,° and haply with his trun-
cheon may strike at you. Provoke him that he may; for even out of that
will I cause these of Cyprus to mutiny; whose qualification° shall come
into no true taste° again but by the displanting of Cassio. So shall you
have a shorter journey to your desires by the means I shall then have
to prefer° them; and the impediment most profitably removed without the which there were no expectation of our prosperity.

RODERIGO: I will do this if you can bring it to any opportunity.

IAGO: I warrant thee. Meet me by and by at the citadel; I must fetch his
necessaries ashore. Farewell.

RODERIGO: Adieu.   (*Exit.*)

IAGO: That Cassio loves her, I do well believe't;
    That she loves him, 'tis apt° and of great credit.
    The Moor, howbeit that I endure him not,
    Is of a constant, loving, noble nature,
    And I dare think he'll prove to Desdemona
    A most dear husband. Now I do love her too;
    Not out of absolute lust, though peradventure
    I stand accountant° for as great a sin,
    But partly led to diet° my revenge,
    For that I do suspect the lusty Moor
    Hath leaped into my seat; the thought whereof
    Doth, like a poisonous mineral, gnaw my innards;
    And nothing can or shall content my soul
    Till I am evened with him, wife for wife;
    Or failing so, yet that I put the Moor
    At least into a jealousy so strong
    That judgment cannot cure. Which thing to do,
    If this poor trash of Venice, whom I trash°
    For° his quick hunting, stand the putting on,°

---

250. for . . . you: I'll put you in charge. **252. tainting:** Discrediting. **253. minister:** Provide. **255. sudden in choler:** Violent in anger. **257. qualification:**
Appeasement. **258. true taste:** Satisfactory state. **260. prefer:** Advance.
267. apt: Probable. **273. accountant:** Accountable. **274. diet:** Feed. **283. I
trash:** I weight down (in order to keep under control). **284. For:** In order to
develop; **stand the putting on:** Responds to my inciting.

I'll have our Michael Cassio on the hip,°   285
Abuse him to the Moor in the rank garb°
(For I fear Cassio with my nightcap too),
Make the Moor thank me, love me, and reward me
For making him egregiously an ass
And practicing upon° his peace and quiet   290
Even to madness. 'Tis here, but yet confused:
Knavery's plain face is never seen till used.   (*Exit.*)

Scene II

(*A street in Cyprus.*)

(*Enter Othello's Herald, with a proclamation.*)

HERALD: It is Othello's pleasure, our noble and valiant general, that,
upon certain tidings now arrived, importing the mere perdition° of the
Turkish fleet, every man put himself into triumph; some to dance,
some to make bonfires, each man to what sport and revels his addiction leads him. For, besides these beneficial news, it is the celebration   5
of his nuptial. So much was his pleasure should be proclaimed. All
offices° are open, and there is full liberty of feasting from the present hour of five till the bell have told eleven. Heaven bless the isle of
Cyprus and our noble general Othello!   (*Exit.*)

Scene III

(*The Cyprian Castle.*)

(*Enter Othello, Desdemona, Cassio, and Attendants.*)

OTHELLO: Good Michael, look you to the guard to-night.
  Let's teach ourselves that honorable stop,
  Not to outsport discretion.°
CASSIO: Iago hath direction what to do;
  But not withstanding, with my personal eye   5
  Will I look to't.
OTHELLO: Iago is most honest.
  Michael, good night. To-morrow with your earliest

---

285. on the hip: At my mercy.   **286. rank garb:** Gross manner.   **290. practicing
upon:** Plotting against.   SCENE II.   **2. mere perdition:** Complete destruction.
7. offices: Kitchens and storerooms.   SCENE III.   **3. outsport discretion:** Let
celebrating go too far.

Let me have speech with you.
    [*To Desdemona.*]   Come, my dear love.
The purchase made, the fruits are to ensue;
That profit 's yet to come 'tween me and you.—
Good night.

                      (*Exit [Othello with Desdemona and Attendants].*)

(*Enter Iago.*)

CASSIO: Welcome, Iago. We must to the watch.

IAGO: Not this hour, lieutenant; 'tis not yet ten o' th' clock. Our general cast° us thus early for the love of his Desdemona; who let us not therefore blame. He hath not yet made wanton the night with her, and she is sport for Jove.

CASSIO: She's a most exquisite lady.

IAGO: And, I'll warrant her, full of game.

CASSIO: Indeed, she's a most fresh and delicate creature.

IAGO: What an eye she has! Methinks it sounds a parley to provocation.

CASSIO: An inviting eye; and yet methinks right modest.

IAGO: And when she speaks, is it not an alarum to love?

CASSIO: She is indeed perfection.

IAGO: Well, happiness to their sheets! Come, lieutenant, I have a stoup° of wine, and here without are a brace of Cyprus gallants that would fain have a measure to the health of black Othello.

CASSIO: Not to-night, good Iago. I have very poor and unhappy brains for drinking; I could well wish courtesy would invent some other custom of entertainment.

IAGO: O, they are our friends. But one cup! I'll drink for you.

CASSIO: I have drunk but one cup to-night, and that was craftily qualified° too; and behold what innovation° it makes here. I am unfortunate in the infirmity and dare not task my weakness with any more.

IAGO: What, man! 'Tis a night of revels: the gallants desire it.

CASSIO: Where are they?

IAGO: Here at the door; I pray you call them in.

CASSIO: I'll do't, but it dislikes me.   (*Exit.*)

IAGO: If I can fasten but one cup upon him
    With that which he hath drunk to-night already,
    He'll be as full of quarrel and offense
    As my young mistress' dog. Now my sick fool Roderigo,
    Whom love hath turned almost the wrong side out,
    To Desdemona hath to-night caroused

---

14. **cast:** Dismissed.   24. **stoup:** Two-quart tankard.   31–32. **qualified:** Diluted.
32. **innovation:** Disturbance.

Potations pottle-deep;° and he's to watch.
Three lads of Cyprus—noble swelling spirits,   45
That hold their honors in a wary distance,°
The very elements° of this warlike isle—
Have I to-night flustered with flowing cups,
And they watch too. Now, 'mongst this flock of drunkards
Am I to put our Cassio in some action   50
That may offend the isle.

(*Enter Cassio, Montano, and Gentlemen[; Servants following with wine].*)

                    But here they come.
If consequence do but approve my dream,
  My boat sails freely, both with wind and stream.
CASSIO: 'Fore God, they have given me a rouse° already.
MONTANO: Good faith, a little one; not past a pint, as I am a soldier.   55
IAGO: Some wine, ho!
  [*Sings.*]   And let me the canakin° clink, clink;
                And let me the canakin clink
                    A soldier's a man;
                    A life's but a span,   60
                  Why then, let a soldier drink.
  Some wine, boys!
CASSIO: 'Fore God, an excellent song!
IAGO: I learned it in England, where indeed they are most potent in pot-
  ting. Your Dane, your German, and your swag-bellied Hollander—   65
  Drink, ho!—are nothing to your English.
CASSIO: Is your Englishman so expert in his drinking?
IAGO: Why, he drinks you with facility your Dane dead drunk; he sweats
  not to overthrow your Almain;° he gives your Hollander a vomit ere
  the next pottle can be filled.   70
CASSIO: To the health of our general!
MONTANO: I am for it, lieutenant, and I'll do you justice.
IAGO: O sweet England!
  [*Sings.*]   King Stephen was a worthy peer;
                His breeches cost him but a crown;   75
                He held 'em sixpence all too dear,
                    With that he called the tailor lown.°
                He was a wight of high renown,
                    And thou art but of low degree.

---

44. pottle-deep: Bottoms up.   **46. That ... distance:** Are very sensitive about
their honor.   **47. very elements:** True representatives.   **54. rouse:** Bumper.
57. canakin: Small drinking cup.   **69. Almain:** German.   **77. lown:** Rascal.

'Tis pride that pulls the country down;
   Then take thine auld cloak about thee.
Some wine, ho!

CASSIO: 'Fore God, this is a more exquisite song than the other.

IAGO: Will you hear't again?

CASSIO: No, for I hold him to be unworthy of his place that does those things.° Well, God's above all; and there be souls must be saved, and there be souls must not be saved.

IAGO: It's true, good lieutenant.

CASSIO: For mine own part—no offense to the general, nor any man of quality—I hope to be saved.

IAGO: And so do I too, lieutenant.

CASSIO: Ay, but, by your leave, not before me. The lieutenant is to be saved before the ancient. Let's have no more of this; let's to our affairs.—God forgive us our sins!—Gentlemen, let's look to our business. Do not think, gentlemen, I am drunk. This is my ancient; this is my right hand, and this is my left. I am not drunk now. I can stand well enough, and I speak well enough.

ALL: Excellent well!

CASSIO: Why, very well then. You must not think then that I am drunk.
                                                                    (*Exit.*)

MONTANO: To th' platform, masters. Come, let's set the watch.

IAGO: You see this fellow that is gone before.
   He's a soldier fit to stand by Caesar
   And give direction; and do but see his vice.
   'Tis to his virtue a just equinox,°
   The one as long as th' other. 'Tis pity of him.
   I fear the trust Othello puts him in,
   On some odd time of his infirmity,
   Will shake this island.

MONTANO: But is he often thus?

IAGO: 'Tis evermore his prologue to his sleep:
   He'll watch the horologe a double set°
   If drink rock not his cradle.

MONTANO: It were well
   The general were put in mind of it.
   Perhaps he sees it not, or his good nature
   Prizes the virtue that appears in Cassio
   And looks not on his evils. Is not this true?

(*Enter Roderigo.*)

85–86. does . . . things: I.e., behaves in this fashion.   **104. just equinox:** Exact
equivalent.   **110. watch . . . set:** Stay awake twice around the clock (horologe).

IAGO [*aside to him*]: How now, Roderigo?
  I pray you, after the lieutenant, go!   (*Exit Roderigo.*)
MONTANO: And 'tis great pity that the noble Moor
  Should hazard such a place as his own second
  With one of an ingraft° infirmity.   120
  It were an honest action to say
  So to the Moor.
IAGO: Not I, for this fair island!
  I do love Cassio well and would do much
  To cure him of this evil.
         (*Within.*) Help! help!
                    But hark! What noise?   125

(*Enter Cassio, driving in Roderigo.*)

CASSIO: Zounds, you rogue! you rascal!
MONTANO: What's the matter, lieutenant?
CASSIO: A knave to teach me my duty?
  I'll beat the knave into a twiggen° bottle.
RODERIGO: Beat me?
CASSIO: Dost thou prate, rogue? [*Strikes him.*]
MONTANO: Nay, good lieutenant!
                    [*Stays him.*]
  I pray you, sir, hold your hand.
CASSIO: Let me go, sir,   130
  Or I'll knock you o'er the mazzard.°
MONTANO: Come, come, you're drunk!
CASSIO: Drunk?

(*They fight.*)

IAGO [*aside to Roderigo*]: Away, I say! Go out and cry a mutiny!
                    (*Exit Roderigo.*)
  Nay, good lieutenant. God's will, gentlemen!
  Help, ho!—lieutenant—sir—Montano—sir—   135
  Help, masters!—Here's a goodly watch indeed!

(*A bell rung.*)

  Who's that which rings the bell? Diablo,° ho!
  The town will rise.° God's will, lieutenant, hold!
  You'll be shamed for ever.

(*Enter Othello and Gentlemen with weapons.*)

---

120. ingraft: I.e., ingrained. **128. twiggen:** Wicker-covered. **131. mazzard:** Head. **137. Diablo:** The devil. **138. rise:** Grow riotous.

OTHELLO: What is the matter here?
MONTANO: Zounds, I bleed still. I am hurt to th' death.
    He dies!
OTHELLO: Hold for your lives!
IAGO: Hold, hold! Lieutenant—sir—Montano—gentlemen!
    Have you forgot all sense of place and duty?
    Hold! The general speaks to you. Hold, for shame!
OTHELLO: Why, how now ho? From whence ariseth this?
    Are we turned Turks, and to ourselves do that
    Which heaven hath forbid the Ottomites?
    For Christian shame put by this barbarous brawl!
    He that stirs next to carve for° his own rage
    Holds his soul light;° he dies upon his motion.°
    Silence that dreadful bell! It frights the isle
    From her propriety.° What is the matter, masters?
    Honest Iago, that looks dead with grieving,
    Speak. Who began this? On thy love, I charge thee.
IAGO: I do not know. Friends all, but now, even now,
    In quarter,° and in terms like bride and groom
    Devesting them for bed; and then, but now—
    As if some planet had unwitted men—
    Swords out, and tilting one at other's breast
    In opposition bloody. I cannot speak
    Any beginning to this peevish odds,°
    And would in action glorious I had lost
    Those legs that brought me to a part of it!
OTHELLO: How comes it, Michael, you are thus forgot?°
CASSIO: I pray you pardon me; I cannot speak.
OTHELLO: Worthy Montano, you were wont to be civil;
    The gravity and stillness of your youth
    The world hath noted, and your name is great
    In mouths of wisest censure.° What's the matter
    That you unlace° your reputation thus
    And spend your rich opinion° for the name
    Of a night-brawler? Give me answer to it.
MONTANO: Worthy Othello, I am hurt to danger.
    Your officer, Iago, can inform you,

---

150. carve for: Indulge.   **151. Holds . . . light:** Values his life lightly; **upon his motion:** If he moves.   **153. propriety:** Proper self.   **157. quarter:** Friendliness.   **162. peevish odds:** Childish quarrel.   **165. are thus forgot:** Have forgotten yourself this way.   **170. censure:** Judgment.   **171. unlace:** Undo.   **172. rich opinion:** High reputation.

While I spare speech, which something now offends° me,
Of all that I do know; nor know I aught
By me that's said or done amiss this night,
Unless self-charity be sometimes a vice,
And to defend ourselves it be a sin   180
When violence assails us.

OTHELLO: Now, by heaven,
My blood° begins my safer guides° to rule,
And passion, having my best judgment collied,°
Assays° to lead the way. If I once stir
Or do but lift this arm, the best of you   185
Shall sink in my rebuke. Give me to know
How this foul rout began, who set it on;
And he that is approved in° this offense,
Though he had twinned with me, both at a birth,
Shall lose me. What! in a town of war,   190
Yet wild, the people's hearts brimful of fear,
To manage° private and domestic quarrel?
In night, and on the court and guard of safety?
'Tis monstrous. Iago, who began't?

MONTANO: If partially affined, or leagued in office,°   195
Thou dost deliver more or less than truth,
Thou art no soldier.

IAGO: Touch me not so near.
I had rather have this tongue cut from my mouth
Than it should do offense to Michael Cassio;
Yet I persuade myself, to speak the truth   200
Shall nothing wrong him. This it is, general.
Montano and myself being in speech,
There comes a fellow crying out for help,
And Cassio following him with determined sword
To execute° upon him. Sir, this gentleman   205
Steps in to Cassio and entreats his pause.°
Myself the crying fellow did pursue,
Lest by his clamor—as it so fell out—
The town might fall in fright. He, swift of foot,
Outran my purpose; and I returned then rather°   210

---

176. offends: Pains. **182. blood:** Passion. **safer guides:** Reason. **183. collied:**
Darkened. **184. Assays:** Tries. **188. approved in:** Proved guilty of. **192. manage:** Carry on. **195. partially . . . office:** Prejudiced by comradeship or official relations. **205. execute:** Work his will. **206. his pause:** Him to stop.
210. rather: Sooner.

For that I heard the clink and fall of swords,
And Cassio high in oath;° which till to-night
I ne'er might say before. When I came back—
For this was brief—I found them close together
At blow and thrust, even as again they were
When you yourself did part them.
More of this matter cannot I report;
But men are men; the best sometimes forget.°
Though Cassio did some little wrong to him,
As men in rage strike those that wish them best,
Yet surely Cassio I believe received
From him that fled some strange indignity,
Which patience could not pass.°

OTHELLO: I know, Iago,
Thy honesty and love doth mince this matter,
Making it light to Cassio. Cassio, I love thee;
But never more be officer of mine.

(*Enter Desdemona, attended.*)

Look if my gentle love be not raised up!
I'll make thee an example.

DESDEMONA: What's the matter?

OTHELLO: All's well now, sweeting; come away to bed.
[*To Montano.*]
Sir, for your hurts, myself will be your surgeon.
Lead him off.

[*Montano is led off.*]

Iago, look with care about the town
And silence those whom this vile brawl distracted.°
Come, Desdemona; 'tis the soldiers' life
To have their balmy slumbers waked with strife.
                                (*Exit* [*with all but Iago and Cassio*].)

IAGO: What, are you hurt, lieutenant?

CASSIO: Ay, past all surgery.

IAGO: Marry, God forbid!

CASSIO: Reputation, reputation, reputation! O, I have lost my reputation!
I have lost the immortal part of myself, and what remains is bestial.
My reputation, Iago, my reputation!

IAGO: As I am an honest man, I thought you had received some bodily
wound. There is more sense in that than in reputation. Reputation is

212. high in oath: Cursing.   **218. forget:** Forget themselves.   **223. pass:** Pass
over, ignore.   **233. distracted:** Excited.

an idle and most false imposition; oft got without merit and lost without deserving. You have lost no reputation at all unless you repute 245
yourself such a loser. What, man! there are ways to recover° the general again. You are but now cast in his mood°—a punishment more in
policy than in malice, even so as one would beat his offenseless dog to
affright an imperious lion. Sue to him again, and he's yours.

CASSIO: I will rather sue to be despised than to deceive so good a com- 250
mander with so slight, so drunken, and so indiscreet an officer. Drunk!
and speak parrot!° and squabble! swagger! swear! and discourse fus-
tian° with one's own shadow! O thou invisible spirit of wine, if thou
hast no name to be known by, let us call thee devil!

IAGO: What was he that you followed with your sword? What had he 255
done to you?

CASSIO: I know not.

IAGO: Is't possible?

CASSIO: I remember a mass of things, but nothing distinctly; a quarrel,
but nothing wherefore. O God, that men should put an enemy in their 260
mouths to steal away their brains! that we should with joy, pleasance,
revel, and applause° transform ourselves into beasts!

IAGO: Why, but you are now well enough. How came you thus recovered?

CASSIO: It hath pleased the devil drunkenness to give place to the devil
wrath. One unperfectness shows me another, to make me frankly de- 265
spise myself.

IAGO: Come, you are too severe a moraler.° As the time, the place, and the
condition of this country stands, I could heartily wish this had not so
befall'n; but since it is as it is, mend it for your own good.

CASSIO: I will ask him for my place again: he shall tell me I am a drunk- 270
ard! Had I as many mouths as Hydra,° such an answer would stop
them all. To be now a sensible man, by and by a fool, and presently a
beast! O strange! Every inordinate° cup is unblest, and the ingredient°
is a devil.

IAGO: Come, come, good wine is a good familiar creature if it be well 275
used. Exclaim no more against it. And, good lieutenant, I think you
think I love you.

CASSIO: I have well approved it,° sir. I drunk!

IAGO: You or any man living may be drunk at some time, man. I'll tell you
what you shall do. Our general's wife is now the general. I may say so 280
in this respect, for that he hath devoted and given up himself to the

246. recover: Regain favor with.   247. in his mood: Dismissed because of his
anger.   252. parrot: Meaningless phrases.   252–53. fustian: Bombastic nonsense.   262. applause: Desire to please.   267. moraler: Moralizer.   271. Hydra: Monster with many heads.   273. inordinate: Excessive; ingredient: Contents.   278. approved: Proved.

contemplation, mark, and denotement of her parts and graces. Confess yourself freely to her; importune her help to put you in your place again. She is of so free,° so kind, so apt, so blessed a disposition she holds it a vice in her goodness not to do more than she is requested. This broken joint between you and her husband entreat her to splinter;° and my fortunes against any lay° worth naming, this crack of your love shall grow stronger than it was before.

CASSIO: You advise me well.

IAGO: I protest, in the sincerity of love and honest kindness.

CASSIO: I think it freely; and betimes in the morning will I beseech the virtuous Desdemona to undertake for me. I am desperate of my fortunes if they check me here.°

IAGO: You are in the right. Good night, lieutenant; I must to the watch.

CASSIO: Good night, honest Iago.   (*Exit Cassio.*)

IAGO: And what's he then that says I play the villain,
    When this advice is free I give and honest,
    Probal° to thinking, and indeed the course
    To win the Moor again? For 'tis most easy
    Th' inclining Desdemona to subdue°
    In any honest suit; she's framed as fruitful
    As the free elements. And then for her
    To win the Moor—were't to renounce his baptism,
    All seals and symbols of redeemèd sin—
    His soul is so enfettered to her love
    That she may make, unmake, do what she list,
    Even as her appetite shall play the god
    With his weak function.° How am I then a villain
    To counsel Cassio to this parallel° course,
    Directly to his good? Divinity° of hell!
    When devils will the blackest sins put on,°
    They do suggest at first with heavenly shows,
    As I do now. For whiles this honest fool
    Plies Desdemona to repair his fortunes,
    And she for him pleads strongly to the Moor,
    I'll pour this pestilence into his ear,
    That she repeals him° for her body's lust;
    And by how much she strives to do him good,

---

284. **free:** Bounteous.   286–87. **splinter:** Bind up with splints; **lay:** Wager.
292–93. **I . . . here:** I despair of my future if my career is stopped short here.
298. **Probal:** Probable.   300. **subdue:** Persuade.   308. **function:** Intelligence (weakened by his fondness for her).   309. **parallel:** Corresponding.   310. **Divinity:** Theology.   311. **put on:** Incite.   317. **repeals him:** Seeks his recall.

She shall undo her credit with the Moor.
So will I turn her virtue into pitch,   320
And out of her own goodness make the net
That shall enmesh them all.

(*Enter Roderigo.*)

               How, now, Roderigo?

RODERIGO: I do follow here in the chase, not like a hound that hunts, but
one that fills up the cry.° My money is almost spent; I have been to-
night exceedingly well cudgelled; and I think the issue will be—I shall   325
have so much experience for my pains; and so, with no money at all,
and a little more wit, return again to Venice.

IAGO: How poor are they that have not patience!
What wound did ever heal but by degrees?
Thou know'st we work by wit, and not by witchcraft;   330
And wit depends on dilatory time.
Does't not go well? Cassio hath beaten thee,
And thou by that small hurt hast cashiered Cassio.°
Though other things grow fair against the sun,
Yet fruits that blossom first will first be ripe.°   335
Content thyself awhile. By the mass, 'tis morning!
Pleasure and action make the hours seem short.
Retire thee; go where thou art billeted.
Away, I say! Thou shalt know more hereafter.
Nay, get thee gone!   (*Exit Roderigo.*)
             Two things are to be done: 340
My wife must move for Cassio to her mistress;
I'll set her on;
Myself the while to draw the Moor apart
And bring him jump° when he may Cassio find
Soliciting his wife. Ay, that's the way!   345
Dull no device by coldness and delay.   (*Exit.*)

ACT III   *Scene I*

(*Before the chamber of Othello and Desdemona.*)

(*Enter Cassio, with Musicians and the Clown.*)

324. cry: Pack.   **333. cashiered Cassio:** Maneuvered Cassio's discharge.   **334–
35. Though . . . ripe:** Although fruit ripens in the sun, yet the first fruit to ripen
will come from the earliest blossoms.   **344. jump:** At the exact moment.

CASSIO: Masters, play here, I will content° your pains:
   Something that's brief; and bid "Good morrow, general."

[*They play.*]

CLOWN: Why, masters, ha' your instruments been in Naples,° that they
   speak i' th' nose thus?
MUSICIAN: How, sir, how?
CLOWN: Are these, I pray you, called wind instruments?
MUSICIAN: Ay, marry, are they, sir.
CLOWN: O, thereby hangs a tail.
MUSICIAN: Whereby hangs a tale, sir?
CLOWN: Marry, sir, by many a wind instrument that I know. But, masters,
   here's money for you; and the general so likes your music that he de-
   sires you, for love's sake, to make no more noise with it.
MUSICIAN: Well, sir, we will not.
CLOWN: If you have any music that may not be heard, to't again: but, as
   they say, to hear music the general does not greatly care.
MUSICIAN: We have none such, sir.
CLOWN: Then put up your pipes in your bag, for I'll away. Go, vanish into
   air, away!   (*Exit Musician [with his fellows].*)
CASSIO: Dost thou hear, my honest friend?
CLOWN: No, I hear not your honest friend. I hear you.
CASSIO: Prithee keep up thy quillets.° There's a poor piece of gold for
   thee. If the gentlewoman that attends the general's wife be stirring, tell
   her there's one Cassio entreats her a little favor of speech. Wilt thou do
   this?
CLOWN: She is stirring sir. If she will stir hither, I shall seem to notify
   unto her.
CASSIO: [Do, good my friend.]   (*Exit Clown.*)

(*Enter Iago.*)

                                   In happy time,° Iago.
IAGO: You have not been abed then?
CASSIO: Why, no; the day had broke
   Before we parted. I have made bold, Iago,
   To send in to your wife: my suit to her
   Is that she will to virtuous Desdemona
   Procure me some access.
IAGO: I'll send her to you presently;
   And I'll devise a mean to draw the Moor

ACT III, SCENE I.   **1. content:** Reward.   **3. Naples:** (Notorious for its association
with venereal disease).   **21. quillets:** Quips.   **27. In happy time:** Well met.

Out of the way, that your converse and business   35
  May be more free.
CASSIO: I humbly thank you for't.   (*Exit* [*Iago*].)
                   I never knew
  A Florentine° more kind and honest.

(*Enter Emilia.*)

EMILIA: Good morrow, good lieutenant. I am sorry
  For your displeasure:° but all will sure be well.   40
  The general and his wife are talking of it,
  And she speaks for you stoutly. The Moor replied
  That he you hurt is of great fame in Cyprus
  And great affinity,° and that in wholesome wisdom
  He might not but refuse you; but he protests he loves you,   45
  And needs no other suitor but his likings
  [To take the safest occasion° by the front°]
  To bring you in again.
CASSIO: Yet I beseech you,
  If you think fit, or that it may be done,
  Give me advantage of some brief discourse   50
  With Desdemona alone.
EMILIA: Pray you come in.
  I will bestow you where you shall have time
  To speak your bosom° freely.
CASSIO: I am much bound to you.   (*Exeunt.*)

Scene II

(*The castle.*)

(*Enter Othello, Iago, and Gentlemen.*)

OTHELLO: These letters give, Iago, to the pilot
  And by him do my duties° to the Senate.
  That done, I will be walking on the works;°
  Repair there to me.
IAGO: Well, my good lord, I'll do't.
OTHELLO: This fortification, gentlemen, shall we see't?   5
GENTLEMEN: We'll wait upon your lordship.   (*Exeunt.*)

38. Florentine: I.e., even a Florentine (like Cassio; Iago was a Venetian).
40. displeasure: Fall from favor.   **44. affinity:** Family connections.   **47. occasion:** Opportunity; **front:** Forelock.   **54. your bosom:** Your inmost thoughts.
SCENE II.   **2. do my duties:** Convey my respects.   **3. works:** Fortifications.

Scene III

(*The castle grounds.*)

(*Enter Desdemona, Cassio, and Emilia.*)

DESDEMONA: Be thou assured, good Cassio, I will do
    All my abilities in thy behalf.
EMILIA: Good madam, do. I warrant it grieves my husband
    As if the cause were his.
DESDEMONA: O, that's an honest fellow. Do not doubt, Cassio,
    But I will have my lord and you again
    As friendly as you were.
CASSIO: Bounteous madam,
    Whatever shall become of Michael Cassio,
    He's never anything but your true servant.
DESDEMONA: I know't; I thank you. You do love my lord;
    You have known him long; and be you well assured
    He shall in strangeness° stand no farther off
    Than in a politic distance.°
CASSIO: Ay, but, lady,
    That policy may either last so long,
    Or feed upon such nice and waterish diet,°
    Or breed itself so out of circumstance,
    That, I being absent, and my place supplied,
    My general will forget my love and service.
DESDEMONA: Do not doubt° that; before Emilia here
    I give thee warrant of thy place. Assure thee,
    If I do vow a friendship, I'll perform it
    To the last article. My lord shall never rest;
    I'll watch him tame° and talk him out of patience;
    His bed shall seem a school, his board a shrift;°
    I'll intermingle everything he does
    With Cassio's suit. Therefore be merry, Cassio,
    For thy solicitor shall rather die
    Than give thy cause away.

(*Enter Othello and Iago* [*at a distance*].)

EMILIA: Madam, here comes my lord.
CASSIO: Madam, I'll take my leave.

SCENE III.   **12. strangeness:** Aloofness.   **13. Than ... distance:** Than wise policy
requires.   **15. Or ... diet:** Or be continued for such slight reasons.   **19. doubt:**
Fear.   **23. watch him tame:** Keep him awake until he gives in.   **24. board a
shrift:** Confessional.

DESDEMONA: Why, stay, and hear me speak.
CASSIO: Madam, not now: I am very ill at ease,
    Unfit for mine own purposes.
DESDEMONA: Well, do your discretion.   (*Exit Cassio.*)
IAGO: Ha! I like not that.
OTHELLO: What dost thou say?   35
IAGO: Nothing, my lord; or if—I know not what.
OTHELLO: Was not that Cassio parted from my wife?
IAGO: Cassio, my lord? No, sure, I cannot think it,
    That he would steal away so guilty-like,
    Seeing your coming.
OTHELLO: I do believe 'twas he.   40
DESDEMONA: How now, my lord?
    I have been talking with a suitor here,
    A man that languishes in your displeasure.
OTHELLO: What is't you mean?
DESDEMONA: Why, your lieutenant, Cassio. Good my lord,   45
    If I have any grace or power to move you,
    His present° reconciliation take;
    For if he be not one that truly loves you,
    That errs in ignorance, and not in cunning,°
    I have no judgment in an honest face,   50
    I prithee call him back.
OTHELLO: Went he hence now?
DESDEMONA: Yes, faith; so humbled
    That he hath left part of his grief with me
    To suffer with him. Good love, call him back.
OTHELLO: Not now, sweet Desdemon; some other time.   55
DESDEMONA: But shall't be shortly?
OTHELLO: The sooner, sweet, for you.
DESDEMONA: Shall't be to-night at supper?
OTHELLO: No, not to-night.
DESDEMONA: To-morrow dinner then?
OTHELLO: I shall not dine at home;
    I meet the captains at the citadel.
DESDEMONA: Why then, to-morrow night, or Tuesday morn,   60
    On Tuesday noon or night, or Wednesday morn.
    I prithee name the time, but let it not
    Exceed three days. I' faith, he's penitent;
    And yet his trespass, in our common reason
    (Save that, they say, the wars must make examples   65

47. present: Immediate.   49. in cunning: Knowingly.

Out of their best), is not almost° a fault
T' incur a private check.° When shall he come?
Tell me, Othello. I wonder in my soul
What you could ask me that I should deny
Or stand so mamm'ring on.° What? Michael Cassio,
That came a-wooing with you, and so many a time,
When I have spoke of you dispraisingly,
Hath ta'en your part—to have so much to do
To bring him in?° By'r Lady, I could do much—

OTHELLO: Prithee no more. Let him come when he will!
I will deny thee nothing.

DESDEMONA: Why, this is not a boon;
'Tis as I should entreat you wear your gloves,
Or feed on nourishing dishes, or keep you warm,
Or sue to you to do a peculiar profit
To your own person. Nay, when I have a suit
Wherein I mean to touch your love indeed,
It shall be full of poise and difficult weight,
And fearful° to be granted.

OTHELLO: I will deny thee nothing!
Whereon I do beseech thee grant me this,
To leave me but a little to myself.

DESDEMONA: Shall I deny you? No. Farewell, my lord.

OTHELLO: Farewell, my Desdemon: I'll come to thee straight.°

DESDEMONA: Emilia, come.—Be as your fancies teach you;°
Whate'er you be, I am obedient.   (Exit [with Emilia].)

OTHELLO: Excellent wretch!° Perdition catch my soul
But I do love thee! and when I love thee not,
Chaos is come again.

IAGO: My noble lord—

OTHELLO: What dost thou say, Iago?

IAGO: Did Michael Cassio, when you wooed my lady,
Know of your love?

OTHELLO: He did, from first to last. Why dost thou ask?

IAGO: But for a satisfaction of my thought;
No further harm.

OTHELLO: Why of thy thought, Iago?

IAGO: I did not think he had been acquainted with her.

66. not almost: Hardly.   67. a private check: Even a private reprimand.
70. mamm'ring on: Hesitating about.   74. To bring him in: To restore him to
favor.   83. fearful: Dangerous.   87. straight: Straightway.   88. Be . . . you:
Please yourself.   90. wretch: (A term of endearment).

OTHELLO: O, yes, and went between us° very oft.   100

IAGO: Indeed?

OTHELLO: Indeed? Ay, indeed! Discern'st thou aught in that?
  Is he not honest?

IAGO: Honest, my lord?

OTHELLO: Honest. Ay, honest.

IAGO: My lord, for aught I know.

OTHELLO: What dost thou think?

IAGO: Think, my lord?

OTHELLO: Think, my lord?   105
  By heaven, he echoes me,
  As if there were some monster in his thought
  Too hideous to be shown. Thou dost mean something:
  I heard thee say even now, thou lik'st not that,
  When Cassio left my wife. What didst not like?   110
  And when I told thee he was of my counsel
  In my whole course of wooing, thou cried'st "Indeed?"
  And didst contract and purse thy brow together,
  As if thou then hadst shut up in thy brain
  Some horrible conceit.° If thou dost love me,   115
  Show me thy thought

IAGO: My lord, you know I love you.

OTHELLO: I think thou dost;
  And, for° I know thou'rt full of love and honesty
  And weigh'st thy words before thou giv'st them breath,
  Therefore these stops° of thine fright me the more;   120
  For such things in a false disloyal knave
  Are tricks of custom;° but in a man that's just
  They are close dilations, working from the heart
  That passion cannot rule.°

IAGO: For Michael Cassio,
  I dare be sworn I think that he is honest.   125

OTHELLO: I think so too.

IAGO: Men should be what they seem;
  Or those that be not, would they might seem none!°

OTHELLO: Certain, men should be what they seem.

IAGO: Why then, I think Cassio's an honest man.

---

100. **went . . . us:** (I.e., as messenger).   115. **conceit:** Fancy.   118. **for:** Because.   120. **stops:** Pauses.   122. **tricks of custom:** Customary, or usual, tricks.   123–24. **close dilations . . . rule:** Secret emotions which well up and cannot be restrained.   127. **seem none:** I.e., not pretend to be men when they are really monsters.

OTHELLO: Nay, yet there's more in this.
   I prithee speak to me as to thy thinkings,
   As thou dost ruminate, and give thy worst of thoughts
   The worst of words.
IAGO: Good my lord, pardon me:
   Though I am bound to every act of duty,
   I am not bound to that all slaves are free to.°
   Utter my thoughts? Why, say they are vile and false,
   As where's that palace whereinto foul things
   Sometimes intrude not? Who has a breast so pure
   But some uncleanly apprehensions
   Keep leets and law days,° and in Sessions sit
   With meditations lawful?
OTHELLO: Thou dost conspire against thy friend, Iago,
   If thou but think'st him wronged, and mak'st his ear
   A stranger to thy thoughts.
IAGO: I do beseech you—
   Though I perchance am vicious° in my guess
   (As I confess it is my nature's plague
   To spy into abuses, and oft my jealousy°
   Shapes faults that are not), that your wisdom yet
   From one that so imperfectly conjects°
   Would take no notice, nor build yourself a trouble
   Out of his scattering° and unsure observance.
   It were not for your quiet nor your good,
   Nor for my manhood, honesty, and wisdom,
   To let you know my thoughts.
OTHELLO: What dost thou mean?
IAGO: Good name in man and woman, dear my lord,
   Is the immediate° jewel of their souls.
   Who steals my purse steals trash; 'tis something, nothing;
   'Twas mine, 'tis his, and has been slave to thousands;
   But he that filches from me my good name
   Robs me of that which not enriches him
   And makes me poor indeed.
OTHELLO: By heaven, I'll know thy thoughts!
IAGO: You cannot, if° my heart were in your hand;
   Nor shall not whilst 'tis in my custody.

---

135. bound . . . free to: Bound to tell that which even slaves are allowed to keep
to themselves.   140. leets and law days: Sittings of the courts.   145. vicious:
Wrong.   147. jealousy: Suspicion.   149. conjects: Conjectures.   151. scattering: Random.   156. immediate: Nearest the heart.   163. if: Even if.

OTHELLO: Ha!

IAGO: O, beware, my lord, of jealousy!   165
  It is the green-eyed monster, which doth mock°
  The meat it feeds on. That cuckold lives in bliss
  Who, certain of his fate, loves not his wronger;
  But O, what damnèd minutes tells he o'er
  Who dotes, yet doubts—suspects, yet strongly loves!   170

OTHELLO: O misery!

IAGO: Poor and content is rich, and rich enough;
  But riches fineless° is as poor as winter
  To him that ever fears he shall be poor.
  Good God, the souls of all my tribe defend   175
  From jealousy!

OTHELLO: Why, why is this?
  Think'st thou I'ld make a life of jealousy,
  To follow still the changes of the moon
  With fresh suspicions? No! To be once in doubt
  Is once to be resolved. Exchange me for a goat   180
  When I shall turn the business of my soul
  To such exsufflicate and blown° surmises,
  Matching this inference. 'Tis not to make me jealous
  To say my wife is fair, feeds well, loves company,
  Is free of speech, sings, plays, and dances;   185
  Where virtue is, these are more virtuous.
  Nor from mine own weak merits will I draw
  The smallest fear or doubt of her revolt,°
  For she had eyes, and chose me. No, Iago;
  I'll see before I doubt; when I doubt, prove;   190
  And on the proof there is no more but this—
  Away at once with love or jealousy!

IAGO: I am glad of this; for now I shall have reason
  To show the love and duty that I bear you
  With franker spirit. Therefore, as I am bound,   195
  Receive it from me. I speak not yet of proof.
  Look to your wife; observe her well with Cassio;
  Wear your eyes thus, not jealous nor secure:°
  I would not have your free and noble nature,
  Out of self-bounty,° be abused. Look to't.   200
  I know our country disposition well:

---

166. mock: Play with, like a cat with a mouse.   **173. fineless:** Unlimited.
182. exsufflicate and blown: Spat out and flyblown.   **188. revolt:** Unfaithful-
ness.   **198. secure:** Overconfident.   **200. self-bounty:** Natural goodness.

In Venice they do let God see the pranks
They dare not show their husbands; their best conscience
Is not to leave't undone, but keep't unknown.

OTHELLO: Dost thou say so?

IAGO: She did deceive her father, marrying you;
    And when she seemed to shake and fear your looks,
    She loved them most.

OTHELLO: And so she did.

IAGO: Why, go to then!
    She that, so young, could give out such a seeming
    To seel° her father's eyes up close as oak°—
    He thought 'twas witchcraft—but I am much to blame.
    I humbly do beseech you of your pardon
    For too much loving you.

OTHELLO: I am bound to thee for ever.

IAGO: I see this hath a little dashed your spirits.

OTHELLO: Not a jot, not a jot.

IAGO: I' faith, I fear it has.
    I hope you will consider what is spoke
    Comes from my love. But I do see y' are moved.
    I am to pray you not to strain my speech
    To grosser issues° nor to larger reach
    Than to suspicion.

OTHELLO: I will not.

IAGO: Should you do so, my lord,
    My speech should fall into such vile success°
    As my thoughts aim not at. Cassio's my worthy friend—
    My lord, I see y' are moved.

OTHELLO: No, not much moved:
    I do not think but Desdemona's honest.°

IAGO: Long live she so! and long live you to think so!

OTHELLO: And yet, how nature erring from itself—

IAGO: Ay, there's the point! as (to be bold with you)
    Not to affect° many proposèd matches
    Of her own clime, complexion, and degree,°
    Whereto we see in all things nature tends—
    Foh! one may smell in such a will most rank,°

---

210. seel: Close (a term from falconry); close as oak: Tight as oak grain.
219. To grosser issues: To mean something more monstrous.   222. vile
success: Evil outcome.   225. honest: Chaste.   229. affect: Prefer.
230. clime . . . degree: Country, color, and rank.   232. will most rank: Desire
most lustful.

Foul disproportions,° thought unnatural—
But pardon me—I do not in position°
Distinctly speak of her; though I may fear   235
Her will, recoiling° to her better judgment,
May fall to match° you with her country forms,
And happily° repent.

OTHELLO: Farewell, farewell!
If more thou dost perceive, let me know more.
Set on thy wife to observe. Leave me, Iago.   240

IAGO: My lord, I take my leave.   [*Going.*]

OTHELLO: Why did I marry? This honest creature doubtless
Sees and knows more, much more, than he unfolds.

IAGO [*returns*]: My lord, I would I might entreat your honor
To scan this thing no further: leave it to time.   245
Although 'tis fit that Cassio have his place,
For sure he fills it up with great ability,
Yet, if you please to hold off a while,
You shall by that perceive him and his means.
Note if your lady strain his entertainment°   250
With any strong or vehement importunity;
Much will be seen in that. In the mean time
Let me be thought too busy° in my fears
(As worthy cause I have to fear I am)
And hold her free,° I do beseech your honor.   255

OTHELLO: Fear not my government.°

IAGO: I once more take my leave.   (*Exit.*)

OTHELLO: This fellow 's of exceeding honesty,
And knows all qualities,° with a learned spirit
Of° human dealings. If I do prove her haggard,°   260
Though that her jesses° were my dear heartstrings,
I'd whistle her off and let her down the wind
To prey at fortune.° Haply, for I am black
And have not those soft parts of conversation°
That chamberers° have, or for I am declined   265

---

233. disproportions: Abnormality.   **234. position:** Definite assertion.
236. recoiling: Reverting.   **237. fall to match:** Happen to compare.
238. happily: Haply, perhaps.   **250. strain his entertainment:** Urge his recall.
253. busy: Meddlesome.   **255. hold her free:** Consider her guiltless.
256. government: Self-control.   **259. qualities:** Natures.   **259–60. learnèd
spirit Of:** Mind informed about.   **260. haggard:** A wild hawk.   **261. jesses:**
Thongs for controlling a hawk.   **262–63. whistle . . . fortune:** Turn her out and
let her take care of herself.   **264. soft . . . conversation:** Ingratiating manners.
265. chamberers: Courtiers.

Into the vale of years—yet that's not much—
She's gone. I am abused, and my relief
Must be to loathe her. O curse of marriage,
That we can call these delicate creatures ours,
And not their appetites! I had rather be a toad
And live upon the vapor of a dungeon
Than keep a corner in the thing I love
For others' uses. Yet 'tis the plague of great ones;°
Prerogatived° are they less than the base.
'Tis destiny unshunnable, like death.
Even then this forkèd plague° is fated to us
When we do quicken.° Look where she comes.

(*Enter Desdemona and Emilia.*)

If she be false, O, then heaven mocks itself!
I'll not believe't.
DESDEMONA: How now, my dear Othello?
Your dinner, and the generous° islanders
By you invited, do attend your presence.
OTHELLO: I am to blame.
DESDEMONA: Why do you speak so faintly?
Are you not well?
OTHELLO: I have a pain upon my forehead, here.
DESDEMONA: Faith, that's with watching;° 'twill away again.
Let me but bind it hard, within this hour
It will be well.
OTHELLO: Your napkin° is too little;

[*He pushes the handkerchief from him, and it falls unnoticed.*]

Let it° alone. Come, I'll go in with you.
DESDEMONA: I am very sorry that you are not well.   (*Exit* [*with Othello*].)
EMILIA: I am glad I have found this napkin;
This was her first remembrance from the Moor,
My wayward husband hath a hundred times
Wooed me to steal it; but she so loves the token
(For he conjured her she should ever keep it)
That she reserves it evermore about her
To kiss and talk to. I'll have the work ta'en out°
And give't Iago.

___

273. great ones: Prominent men.   274. Prerogatived: Privileged.   276. forkèd
plague: I.e., horns of a cuckold.   277. do quicken: Are born.   280. generous:
Noble.   285. watching: Working late.   287. napkin: Handkerchief.   288. it:
I.e., his forehead.   296. work ta'en out: Pattern copied.

What he will do with it heaven knows, not I;
I nothing but to please his fantasy.°

(*Enter Iago.*)

IAGO: How now? What do you here alone?   300
EMILIA: Do not you chide; I have a thing for you.
IAGO: A thing for me? It is a common° thing° —
EMILIA: Ha?
IAGO: To have a foolish wife.
EMILIA: O, is that all? What will you give me now   305
    For that same handkerchief?
IAGO: What handkerchief?
EMILIA: What handkerchief!
    Why, that the Moor first gave to Desdemona;
    That which so often you did bid me steal.
IAGO: Hast stol'n it from her?   310
EMILIA: No, faith; she let it drop by negligence,
    And to th' advantage,° I, being here, took't up.
    Look, here it is.
IAGO: A good wench! Give it me.
EMILIA: What will you do with't, that you have been so earnest
    To have me filch it?
IAGO: Why, what is that to you?   315

[*Snatches it.*]

EMILIA: If it be not for some purpose of import,°
    Give't me again. Poor lady, she'll run mad
    When she shall lack it.
IAGO: Be not acknown on't;° I have use for it.
    Go, leave me.   (*Exit Emilia.*)   320
    I will in Cassio's lodgings lose this napkin
    And let him find it. Trifles light as air
    Are to the jealous confirmations strong
    As proofs of holy writ. This may do something.
    The Moor already changes with my poison: 325
    Dangerous conceits° are in their nature poisons,
    Which at the first are scarce found to distaste,°
    But with a little act° upon the blood
    Burn like the mines of sulphur.

299. fantasy: Whim.   302. common: Available to everyone; thing: Slang term
for vagina.   312. to th' advantage: Opportunely.   316. import: Importance.
319. Be . . . on't: Do not acknowledge it.   326. conceits: Ideas.   327. distaste:
Be distasteful.   328. act: Action.

(*Enter Othello.*)

                                I did say so.
Look where he comes! Not poppy nor mandragora,°
Nor all the drowsy syrups of the world,
Shall ever med'cine thee to that sweet sleep
Which thou owedst yesterday.
OTHELLO: Ha! ha! false to me?
IAGO: Why, how now, general? No more of that!
OTHELLO: Avaunt! be gone! Thou hast set me on the rack.
  I swear 'tis better to be much abused
  Than but to know't a little.
IAGO: How now, my lord?
OTHELLO: What sense had I of her stol'n hours of lust?
  I saw't not, thought it not, it harmed not me;
  I slept the next night well, fed well, was free° and merry;
  I found not Cassio's kisses on her lips
  He that is robbed, not wanting° what is stol'n,
  Let him not know't, and he's not robbed at all.
IAGO: I am sorry to hear this.
OTHELLO: I had been happy if the general camp,
  Pioneers° and all, had tasted her sweet body,
  So° I had nothing known. O, now for ever
  Farewell the tranquil mind! farewell content!
  Farewell the plumèd troop, and the big° wars
  That make ambition virtue! O, farewell!
  Farewell the neighing steed and the shrill trump,
  The spirit-stirring drum, th' ear-piercing fife,
  The royal banner, and all quality,
  Pride, pomp, and circumstance° of glorious war!
  And O you mortal engines° whose rude throats
  Th' immortal Jove's dread clamors counterfeit,°
  Farewell! Othello's occupation's gone!
IAGO: Is't possible, my lord?
OTHELLO: Villain, be sure thou prove my love a whore!
  Be sure of it; give me the ocular proof;
  Or, by the worth of mine eternal soul,
  Thou hadst been better have been born a dog
  Than answer my waked wrath!

---

330. mandragora: A sleep-inducing drug made from mandrake roots. 340. free:
Carefree. 342. wanting: Missing. 346. Pioneers: Sappers, laborers. 347. So:
So long as. 349. big: Mighty. 354. circumstance: Pageantry. 355. mortal
engines: Deadly artillery. 356. counterfeit: Imitate.

IAGO: Is't come to this?

OTHELLO: Make me to see't; or at the least so prove it
   That the probation° bear no hinge nor loop   365
   To hang a doubt on—or woe upon thy life!

IAGO: My noble lord—

OTHELLO: If thou dost slander her and torture me,
   Never pray more; abandon all remorse;°
   On horror's head horrors accumulate;   370
   Do deeds to make heaven weep, all earth amazed;
   For nothing canst thou to damnation add
   Greater than that.

IAGO: O grace! O heaven forgive me!
   Are you a man? Have you a soul or sense?—
   God b' wi' you! take mine office. O wretched fool,°   375
   That lov'st to make thine honesty a vice!°
   O monstrous world! Take note, take note, O world,
   To be direct and honest is not safe.
   I thank you for this profit;° and from hence°
   I'll love no friend, sith love breeds such offense.   380

OTHELLO: Nay, stay. Thou shouldst be honest.

IAGO: I should be wise; for honesty's a fool
   And loses that it works for.

OTHELLO: By the world,
   I think my wife be honest, and think she is not;
   I think that thou art just, and think thou art not.   385
   I'll have some proof. Her name, that was as fresh
   As Dian's° visage, is now begrimed and black
   As mine own face. If there be cords, or knives,
   Poison, or fire, or suffocating streams,
   I'll not endure it. Would I were satisfied!°   390

IAGO: I see, sir, you are eaten up with passion:
   I do repent me that I put it to you.
   You would be satisfied?

OTHELLO: Would? Nay, I will.

IAGO: And may; but how? how satisfied, my lord?
   Would you, the supervisor,° grossly gape on?   395
   Behold her topped?

---

365. probation: Proof.   **369. remorse:** Penitence, hope of salvation.   **375. O
wretched fool:** (Iago addressing himself).   **376. make . . . vice:** Take honesty
too far.   **379. profit:** Profitable lesson.   **hence:** Henceforth.   **387. Dian:** Diana,
goddess of the moon and of chastity.   **390. satisfied:** Completely informed.
395. supervisor: Spectator.

OTHELLO: Death and damnation! O!
IAGO: It were a tedious difficulty, I think,
    To bring them to that prospect. Damn them then,
    If ever mortal eyes do see them bolster°
    More than their own! What then? How then?
    What shall I say? Where's satisfaction?
    It is impossible you should see this,
    Were they as prime° as goats, as hot as monkeys,
    As salt° as wolves in pride,° and fools as gross
    As ignorance made drunk. But yet, I say,
    If imputation and strong circumstances
    Which lead directly to the door of truth
    Will give you satisfaction, you may have't.
OTHELLO: Give me a living reason she's disloyal.
IAGO: I do not like the office.
    But sith I am ent'red in this cause so far,
    Pricked° to't by foolish honesty and love,
    I will go on. I lay with Cassio lately,
    And being troubled with a raging tooth,
    I could not sleep.
    There are a kind of men so loose of soul
    That in their sleeps will mutter their affairs.
    One of this kind is Cassio.
    In sleep I heard him say, "Sweet Desdemona,
    Let us be wary, let us hide our loves!"
    And then, sir, would he grip and wring my hand,
    Cry "O sweet creature!" and then kiss me hard,
    As if he plucked up kisses by the roots
    That grew upon my lips; then laid his leg
    Over my thigh, and sighed, and kissed, and then
    Cried "Cursèd fate that gave thee to the Moor!"
OTHELLO: O monstrous! monstrous!
IAGO: Nay, this was but his dream.
OTHELLO: But this denoted a foregone conclusion;°
    'Tis a shrewd doubt,° though it be but a dream.
IAGO: And this may help to thicken other proofs
    That do demonstrate thinly.
OTHELLO: I'll tear her all to pieces!
IAGO: Nay, but be wise. Yet we see nothing done;

399. bolster: Lie together. **403. prime:** Lustful. **404. salt:** Lecherous; **pride:**
Heat. **412. Pricked:** Spurred. **428. foregone conclusion:** Previous experience.
429. a shrewd doubt: Cursedly suspicious.

She may be honest yet. Tell me but this—
Have you not sometimes seen a handkerchief
Spotted with strawberries in your wife's hand?   435
OTHELLO: I gave her such a one; 'twas my first gift.
IAGO: I know not that; but such a handkerchief—
  I am sure it was your wife's—did I to-day
  See Cassio wipe his beard with.
OTHELLO: If it be that—
IAGO: If it be that, or any that was hers,   440
  It speaks against her with the other proofs.
OTHELLO: O, that the slave had forty thousand lives!
  One is too poor, too weak for my revenge.
  Now do I see 'tis true. Look here, Iago:
  All my fond love thus do I blow to heaven.   445
  'Tis gone.
  Arise, black vengeance, from the hollow hell!
  Yield up, O love, thy crown and hearted throne
  To tyrannous hate! Swell, bosom, with thy fraught,°
  For 'tis of aspics'° tongues!
IAGO: Yet be content.   450
OTHELLO: O, blood, blood, blood!
IAGO: Patience, I say. Your mind perhaps may change.
OTHELLO: Never, Iago. Like to the Pontic sea,°
  Whose icy current and compulsive course
  Ne'er feels retiring ebb, but keeps due on   455
  To the Propontic and the Hellespont,
  Even so my bloody thoughts, with violent pace,
  Shall ne'er look back, ne'er ebb to humble love,
  Till that a capable° and wide revenge
  Swallow them up.
  (He kneels.)   Now, by yond marble heaven,   460
  In the due reverence of a sacred vow
  I here engage my words.
IAGO: Do not rise yet.
(Iago kneels.)
  Witness, you ever-burning lights above,
  You elements that clip° us round about,
  Witness that here Iago doth give up   465
  The execution° of his wit,° hands, heart

---

449. **fraught:** Burden.   450. **aspics:** Deadly poisonous snakes.   453. **Pontic sea:** Black Sea.   459. **capable:** All-embracing.   464. **clip:** Encompass.
466. **execution:** Activities; **wit:** Mind.

To wronged Othello's service! Let him command,
And to obey shall be in me remorse,°
What bloody business ever.°

[*They rise.*]

OTHELLO: I greet thy love,
   Not with vain thanks but with acceptance bounteous,
   And will upon the instant put thee to't.
   Within these three days let me hear thee say
   That Cassio's not alive.
IAGO: My friend is dead; 'tis done at your request.
   But let her live.
OTHELLO: Damn her, lewd minx!° O, damn her! damn her!
   Come, go with me apart. I will withdraw
   To furnish me with some swift means of death
   For the fair devil. Now art thou my lieutenant.
IAGO: I am your own forever.   (*Exeunt.*)

Scene IV

(*The environs of the castle.*)

(*Enter Desdemona, Emilia, and Clown.*)

DESDEMONA: Do you know, sirrah, where Lieutenant Cassio lies?°
CLOWN: I dare not say he lies anywhere.
DESDEMONA: Why, man?
CLOWN: He's a soldier, and for me to say a soldier lies is stabbing.
DESDEMONA: Go to. Where lodges he?
CLOWN: To tell you where he lodges is to tell you where I lie.
DESDEMONA: Can anything be made of this?
CLOWN: I know not where he lodges; and for me to devise a lodging, and
   say he lies here or he lies there, were to lie in mine own throat.
DESDEMONA: Can you enquire him out, and be edified by report?
CLOWN: I will catechize the world for him; that is, make questions, and
   by them answer.
DESDEMONA: Seek him, bid him come hither. Tell him I have moved° my
   lord on his behalf and hope all will be well.
CLOWN: To do this is within the compass of man's wit, and therefore I'll
   attempt the doing of it.   (*Exit.*)

---

468. remorse: Pity. **469. ever:** Soever. **476. minx:** Wanton. SCENE IV. **1. lies:**
Lives, lodges. **13. moved:** Made proposals to.

DESDEMONA: Where should I lose that handkerchief, Emilia?
EMILIA: I know not, madam.
DESDEMONA: Believe me, I had rather have lost my purse
    Full of crusadoes;° and but my noble Moor   20
    Is true of mind, and made of no such baseness
    As jealous creatures are, it were enough
    To put him to ill thinking.
EMILIA: Is he not jealous?
DESDEMONA: Who? he? I think the sun where he was born
    Drew all such humors° from him.

(*Enter Othello.*)

EMILIA: Look where he comes.   25
DESDEMONA: I will not leave him now till Cassio
    Be called to him—How is't with you, my lord?
OTHELLO: Well, my good lady. [*Aside.*] O, hardness to dissemble!—
    How do you, Desdemona?
DESDEMONA: Well, my good lord.
OTHELLO: Give me your hand. This hand is moist, my lady.   30
DESDEMONA: It yet hath felt no age nor known no sorrow.
OTHELLO: This argues fruitfulness and liberal heart.
    Hot, hot, and moist. This hand of yours requires
    A sequester° from liberty, fasting and prayer,
    Much castigation, exercise devout;   35
    For here's a young and sweating devil here
    That commonly rebels. 'Tis a good hand,
    A frank one.
DESDEMONA: You may, indeed, say so;
    For 'twas that hand that gave away my heart.   40
OTHELLO: A liberal hand! The hearts of old gave hands;
    But our new heraldry° is hands, not hearts.
DESDEMONA: I cannot speak of this. Come now, your promise!
OTHELLO: What promise, chuck?
DESDEMONA: I have sent to bid Cassio come speak with you.   45
OTHELLO: I have a salt and sorry rheum° offends me.
    Lend me thy handkerchief.
DESDEMONA: Here, my lord.
OTHELLO: That which I gave you.
DESDEMONA: I have it not about me.

---

20. **crusadoes:** Portuguese gold coins.   **24. humors:** Inclinations.   **34. seques-
ter:** Removal.   **42. heraldry:** Heraldic symbolism.   **46. salt . . . rheum:** Dis-
tressing head cold.

OTHELLO: Not?

DESDEMONA: No, faith, my lord.

OTHELLO: That's a fault.
   That handkerchief
   Did an Egyptian° to my mother give.
   She was a charmer,° and could almost read
   The thoughts of people. She told her, while she kept it,
   'Twould make her amiable° and subdue my father
   Entirely to her love; but if she lost it
   Or made a gift of it, my father's eye
   Should hold her loathèd, and his spirits should hunt
   After new fancies. She, dying, gave it me,
   And bid me, when my fate would have me wive,
   To give it her. I did so; and take heed on't;
   Make it a darling like your precious eye.
   To lose't or give't away were such perdition°
   As nothing else could match.

DESDEMONA: Is't possible?

OTHELLO: 'Tis true. There's magic in the web of it.
   A sibyl that had numb'red in the world
   The sun to course two hundred compasses,°
   In her prophetic fury sewed the work;
   The worms were hallowed that did breed the silk;
   And it was dyed in mummy° which the skillful
   Conserved of maidens' hearts.

DESDEMONA: I' faith? Is't true?

OTHELLO: Most veritable. Therefore look to't well.

DESDEMONA: Then would to God that I had never seen't!

OTHELLO: Ha! Wherefore?

DESDEMONA: Why do you speak so startingly and rash?

OTHELLO: Is't lost? Is't gone? Speak, is it out o' th' way?

DESDEMONA: Heaven bless us!

OTHELLO: Say you?

DESDEMONA: It is not lost. But what an if it were?

OTHELLO: How?

DESDEMONA: I say it is not lost.

OTHELLO: Fetch't, let me see't!

DESDEMONA: Why, so I can, sir; but I will not now.
   This is a trick to put° me from my suit:
   Pray you let Cassio be received again.

---

51. **Egyptian:** Gypsy.   52. **charmer:** Sorceress.   54. **amiable:** Lovable.
62. **perdition:** Disaster.   66. **compasses:** Annual rounds.   69. **mummy:** A drug
made from mummies.   82. **put:** Divert.

OTHELLO: Fetch me the handkerchief! My mind misgives.
DESDEMONA: Come, come!   85
  You'll never meet a more sufficient man.
OTHELLO: The handkerchief!
[DESDEMONA: I pray talk me of Cassio.
OTHELLO: The handkerchief!]
DESDEMONA: A man that all his time°
  Hath founded his good fortunes on your love,
  Shared dangers with you—   90
OTHELLO: The handkerchief!
DESDEMONA: I' faith, you are to blame.
OTHELLO: Zounds!   (*Exit Othello.*)
EMILIA: Is not this man jealous?
DESDEMONA: I ne'er saw this before.   95
  Sure there's some wonder in this handkerchief;
  I am most unhappy in the loss of it.
EMILIA: 'Tis not a year or two shows us a man.
  They are all but° stomachs, and we all but food;
  They eat us hungerly, and when they are full,   100
  They belch us.

(*Enter Iago and Cassio.*)

        Look you—Cassio and my husband!
IAGO: There is no other way; 'tis she must do't.
  And lo the happiness!° Go and importune her.
DESDEMONA: How now, good Cassio? What's the news with you?
CASSIO: Madam, my former suit. I do beseech you   105
  That by your virtuous means I may again
  Exist, and be a member of his love
  Whom I with all the office° of my heart
  Entirely honor. I would not be delayed.
  If my offense be of such mortal° kind   110
  That neither service past, nor present sorrows,
  Nor purposed merit in futurity,
  Can ransom me into his love again,
  But to know so must be my benefit.
  So shall I clothe me in a forced content,   115
  And shut myself up in° some other course,
  To fortune's alms.
DESDEMONA: Alas, thrice-gentle Cassio!

---

88. all . . . time: During his whole career.   99. but: Nothing but.   103. happiness: Good luck.   108. office: Loyal service.   110. mortal: Fatal.   116. shut
myself up in: Confine myself to.

My advocation° is not now in tune.
My lord is not my lord; nor should I know him,
Were he in favor° as in humor altered.
So help me every spirit sanctified
As I have spoken for you all my best
And stood within the blank° of his displeasure
For my free speech! You must a while be patient.
What I can do I will; and more I will
Than for myself I dare. Let that suffice you.

IAGO: Is my lord angry?

EMILIA: He went hence but now,
And certainly in strange unquietness.

IAGO: Can he be angry? I have seen the cannon
When it hath blown his ranks into the air
And, like the devil, from his very arm
Puffed his own brother—and is he angry?
Something of moment then. I will go meet him.
There's matter in't indeed if he be angry.

DESDEMONA: I prithee do so.   (*Exit [Iago]*.)
                  Something sure of state,°
Either from Venice or some unhatched practice°
Made demonstrable here in Cyprus to him,
Hath puddled° his clear spirit; and in such cases
Men's natures wrangle with inferior things,
Though great ones are their object. 'Tis even so;
For let our finger ache, and it endues°
Our other, healthful members even to a sense
Of pain. Nay, we must think men are not gods,
Nor of them look for such observancy°
As fits the bridal. Beshrew me much, Emilia,
I was, unhandsome warrior° as I am,
Arraigning his unkindness with my soul;°
But now I find I had suborned the witness,
And he's indicted falsely.

EMILIA: Pray heaven it be state matters, as you think,
And no conception nor no jealous toy°
Concerning you.

DESDEMONA: Alas the day! I never gave him cause.

---

118. **advocation:** Advocacy.   120. **favor:** Appearance.   123. **blank:** Bull's-eye of
the target.   135. **state:** Public affairs.   136. **unhatched practice:** Budding plot.
138. **puddled:** Muddied.   141. **endues:** Brings.   144. **observancy:** Attentive-
ness.   146. **unhandsome warrior:** Inadequate soldier.   147. **Arraigning . . . soul:**
Indicting his unkindness before the bar of my soul.   151. **toy:** Fancy.

EMILIA: But jealous souls will not be answered so;
    They are not ever jealous for the cause,
    But jealous for° they're jealous. 'Tis a monster   155
    Begot upon itself,° born on itself.
DESDEMONA: Heaven keep that monster from Othello's mind!
EMILIA: Lady, amen.
DESDEMONA: I will go seek him. Cassio, walk here about: 160
    If I do find him fit, I'll move your suit
    And seek to effect it to my uttermost.
CASSIO: I humbly thank your ladyship.

                     (Exeunt Desdemona and Emilia.)

(Enter Bianca.)

BIANCA: Save° you, friend Cassio!
CASSIO: What make you from home?
    How is't with you, my most fair Bianca?
    I' faith, sweet love, I was coming to your house.   165
BIANCA: And I was going to your lodging, Cassio.
    What, keep a week away? seven days and nights?
    Eightscore eight hours? and lovers' absent hours,
    More tedious than the dial° eightscore times?   170
    O weary reck'ning!
CASSIO: Pardon me, Bianca:
    I have this while with leaden thoughts been pressed;
    But I shall in a more continuate° time
    Strike off this score° of absence. Sweet Bianca,

[Gives her Desdemona's handkerchief.]

    Take me this work out.°
BIANCA: O Cassio, whence came this?   175
    This is some token from a newer friend.
    To the felt absence now I feel a cause.
    Is't come to this? Well, well.
CASSIO: Go to, woman!
    Throw your vile guesses in the devil's teeth,
    From whence you have them. You are jealous now   180
    That this is from some mistress, some remembrance.
    No, by my faith, Bianca.
BIANCA: Why, whose is it?

---

156. for: Because. **157. Begot . . . itself:** Self-engendered. **164. Save:** God
save. **170. dial:** Complete revolution of the clock (or sundial). **173. continuate:**
Uninterrupted. **174. Strike . . . score:** Settle this account. **175. Take . . . out:**
Copy this embroidery for me.

CASSIO: I know not, sweet; I found it in my chamber.
  I like the work° well; ere it be demanded,
  As like enough it will, I'd have it copied.
  Take it and do't, and leave me for this time.
BIANCA: Leave you? Wherefore?
CASSIO: I do attend here on the general
  And think it no addition,° nor my wish,
  To have him see me womaned.
BIANCA: Why, I pray you?
CASSIO: Not that I love you not.
BIANCA: But that you do not love me!
  I pray you bring me on the way a little,
  And say if I shall see you soon at night.
CASSIO: 'Tis but a little way that I can bring you,
  For I attend here; but I'll see you soon.
BIANCA: 'Tis very good. I must be circumstanced.°   (*Exeunt.*)

ACT IV   *Scene I*

(*The environs of the castle.*)

(*Enter Othello and Iago.*)

IAGO: Will you think so?
OTHELLO: Think so, Iago?
IAGO: What,
  To kiss in private?
OTHELLO: An unauthorized kiss.
IAGO: Or to be naked with her friend in bed
  An hour or more, not meaning any harm?
OTHELLO: Naked in bed, Iago, and not mean harm?
  It is hypocrisy against the devil.°
  They that mean virtuously, and yet do so,
  The devil their virtue tempts, and they tempt heaven.
IAGO: So° they do nothing, 'tis a venial slip.
  But if I give my wife a handkerchief—
OTHELLO: What then?
IAGO: Why, then 'tis hers, my lord; and being hers,
  She may, I think, bestow't on any man.

---

184. work: Needlework.   **189. addition:** (To my reputation).   **196. circum-stanced:** Governed by circumstances.   ACT IV, SCENE I.   **6. hypocrisy . . . devil:** I.e., feigned sin instead of feigned virtue.   **9. So:** So long as.

OTHELLO: She is protectress of her honor too;
  May she give that?   15
IAGO: Her honor is an essence that's not seen;
  They have it very oft that have it not.
  But for the handkerchief—
OTHELLO: By heaven, I would most gladly have forgot it!
  Thou said'st—O, it comes o'er my memory   20
  As doth the raven o'er the infected° house,
  Boding to all!—he had my handkerchief.
IAGO: Ay, what of that?
OTHELLO: That's not so good now.
IAGO: What
  If I had said I had seen him do you wrong?
  Or heard him say—as knaves be such abroad   25
  Who having, by their own importunate suit,
  Or voluntary dotage of some mistress,
  Convincèd or supplied° them, cannot choose
  But they must blab—
OTHELLO: Hath he said anything?
IAGO: He hath, my lord; but be you well assured,   30
  No more than he'll unswear.
OTHELLO: What hath he said?
IAGO: Faith, that he did—I know not what he did.
OTHELLO: What? what?
IAGO: Lie—
OTHELLO: With her?
IAGO: With her, on her; what you will.   35
OTHELLO: Lie with her? lie on her?—We say "lie on her" when they be-
  lie° her.—Lie with her! Zounds, that's fulsome.°—Handkerchief—
  confessions—handkerchief!—To confess, and be hanged for his
  labor—first to be hanged, and then to confess! I tremble at it. Nature
  would not invest herself in such shadowing passion without some in-   40
  struction.° It is not words that shakes me thus.—Pish! Noses, ears,
  and lips? Is't possible?—Confess?—Handkerchief?—O devil!

(*Falls in a trance.*)

IAGO: Work on,
  My med'cine, work! Thus credulous fools are caught,
  And many worthy and chaste dames even thus,   45

---

21. **infected:** Plague-stricken.   28. **Convincèd or supplied:** Overcome or grati-
fied.   36–37. **belie:** Slander.   37. **fulsome:** Foul.   39–41. **Nature . . . instruction:**
My natural faculties would not be so overcome by passion without reason.

All guiltless, meet reproach. —What, ho! my lord!
My lord, I say! Othello!
    (*Enter Cassio.*)   How now, Cassio?
CASSIO: What's the matter?
IAGO: My lord is fall'n into an epilepsy.
    This is his second fit; he had one yesterday.
CASSIO: Rub him about the temples.
IAGO: No, forbear.
    The lethargy° must have his quiet course.
    If not, he foams at mouth, and by and by
    Breaks out to savage madness. Look, he stirs.
    Do you withdraw yourself a little while.
    He will recover straight. When he is gone,
    I would on great occasion speak with you.   [*Exit Cassio.*]
    How is it, general? Have you not hurt your head?
OTHELLO: Dost thou mock me?
IAGO: I mock you? No, by heaven.
    Would you would bear your fortune like a man!
OTHELLO: A hornèd man's° a monster and a beast.
IAGO: There's many a beast then in a populous city,
    And many a civil° monster.
OTHELLO: Did he confess it?
IAGO: Good sir, be a man.
    Think every bearded fellow that's but yoked
    May draw with you. There's millions now alive
    That nightly lie in those unproper° beds
    Which they dare swear peculiar:° your case is better.
    O, 'tis the spite of hell, the fiend's arch-mock,
    To lip a wanton in a secure° couch,
    And to suppose her chaste! No, let me know;
    And knowing what I am, I know what she shall be.
OTHELLO: O, thou art wise! 'Tis certain.
IAGO: Stand you awhile apart;
    Confine yourself but in a patient list.°
    Whilst you were here, o'erwhelmèd with your grief—
    A passion most unsuiting such a man—
    Cassio came hither. I shifted him away
    And laid good 'scuse upon your ecstasy;°

52. **lethargy:** Coma.   61. **hornèd man:** Cuckold.   63. **civil:** City-dwelling.
67. **unproper:** Not exclusively their own.   68. **peculiar:** Exclusively their own.
70. **secure:** Free from fear of rivalry.   74. **in a patient list:** Within the limits of
self-control.   78. **ecstasy:** Trance.

Bade him anon return, and here speak with me;
The which he promised. Do but encave° yourself   80
And mark the fleers, the gibes, and notable scorns
That dwell in every region of his face;
For I will make him tell the tale anew—
Where, how, how oft, how long ago, and when
He hath, and is again to cope° your wife.   85
I say, but mark his gesture. Marry, patience!
Or I shall say y'are all in all in spleen,°
And nothing of a man.

OTHELLO: Dost thou hear, Iago?
  I will be found most cunning in my patience;
  But—dost thou hear?—most bloody.

IAGO: That's not amiss: 90
  But yet keep time in all. Will you withdraw?

                                        [*Othello retires.*]

  Now will I question Cassio of Bianca,
  A huswife° that by selling her desires
  Buys herself bread and clothes. It is a creature
  That dotes on Cassio, as 'tis the strumpet's plague   95
  To beguile many and be beguiled by one.
  He, when he hears of her, cannot refrain
  From the excess of laughter. Here he comes.

(*Enter Cassio.*)

  As he shall smile, Othello shall go mad;
  And his unbookish° jealousy must conster°   100
  Poor Cassio's smiles, gestures, and light behavior
  Quite in the wrong. How do you now, lieutenant?

CASSIO: The worser that you give me the addition°
  Whose want even kills me.

IAGO: Ply Desdemona well, and you are sure on't.   105
  Now, if this suit lay in Bianca's power,
  How quickly should you speed!

CASSIO: Alas, poor caitiff!°

OTHELLO: Look how he laughs already!

IAGO: I never knew a woman love man so.

CASSIO: Alas, poor rogue! I think, i' faith, she loves me.   110

---

80. encave: Conceal. 85. cope: Meet. 87. all in all in spleen: Wholly overcome
by your passion. 93. huswife: Hussy. 100. unbookish: Uninstructed; **conster:**
Construe, interpret. 103. addition: Title. 107. caitiff: Wretch.

OTHELLO: Now he denies it faintly, and laughs it out.

IAGO: Do you hear, Cassio?

OTHELLO: Now he importunes him
To tell it o'er. Go to! Well said, well said!

IAGO: She gives out that you shall marry her.
Do you intend it?

CASSIO: Ha, ha, ha!

OTHELLO: Do you triumph, Roman? Do you triumph?

CASSIO: I marry her? What, a customer?° Prithee bear some charity to
my wit;° do not think it so unwholesome.° Ha, ha, ha!

OTHELLO: So, so, so, so! They laugh that win!

IAGO: Faith, the cry goes that you shall marry her.

CASSIO: Prithee, say true.

IAGO: I am a very villain else.

OTHELLO: Have you scored me?° Well.

CASSIO: This is the monkey's own giving out. She is persuaded I will
marry her out of her own love and flattery, not out of my promise.

OTHELLO: Iago beckons° me; now he begins the story.

CASSIO: She was here even now; she haunts me in every place. I was t'
other day talking on the sea bank with certain Venetians, and thither
comes the bauble,° and, by this hand, she falls me thus about my
neck—

OTHELLO: Crying "O dear Cassio!" as it were. His gesture imports it.

CASSIO: So hangs, and lolls, and weeps upon me; so shakes and pulls me!
Ha, ha, ha!

OTHELLO: Now he tells how she plucked him to my chamber. O, I see that
nose of yours, but not that dog I shall throw it to.

CASSIO: Well, I must leave her company.

(*Enter Bianca.*)

IAGO: Before me!° Look where she comes.

CASSIO: 'Tis such another fitchew!° marry, a perfumed one. What do you
mean by this haunting of me?

BIANCA: Let the devil and his dam haunt you! What did you mean by that
same handkerchief you gave me even now? I was a fine fool to take it.
I must take out the whole work? A likely piece of work that you should
find it in your chamber and know not who left it there! This is some

---

118. customer: Prostitute. 118–19. bear . . . wit: Be more generous in assessing my intelligence. 119. unwholesome: Impaired, defective. 124. scored me: Settled my account (?). 127. beckons: Signals. 130. bauble: Plaything. 138. Before me: By my soul. 139. fitchew: Polecat (slang for whore).

minx's token, and I must take out the work? There! Give it your hobby- 145
horse.° Wheresoever you had it, I'll take out no work on't.

CASSIO: How now, my sweet Bianca? How now? how now?

OTHELLO: By heaven, that should be my handkerchief!

BIANCA: An° you'll come to supper to-night, you may; an you will not,
   come when you are next prepared for.   (*Exit.*) 150

IAGO: After her, after her!

CASSIO: Faith, I must; she'll rail in the street else.

IAGO: Will you sup there?

CASSIO: Yes, I intend so.

IAGO: Well, I may chance to see you; for I would very fain speak with 155
   you.

CASSIO: Prithee come. Will you?

IAGO: Go to! say no more.   (*Exit Cassio.*)

OTHELLO [*comes forward*]: How shall I murder him, Iago?

IAGO: Did you perceive how he laughed at his vice?°   160

OTHELLO: O Iago!

IAGO: And did you see the handkerchief?

OTHELLO: Was that mine?

IAGO: Yours, by this hand! And to see how he prizes° the foolish woman
   your wife! She gave it him, and he hath giv'n it his whore.   165

OTHELLO: I would have him nine years a-killing—A fine woman! a fair
   woman! a sweet woman!

IAGO: Nay, you must forget that.

OTHELLO: Ay, let her rot, and perish, and be damned to-night; for she
   shall not live. No, my heart is turned to stone; I strike it, and it hurts 170
   my hand. O, the world hath not a sweeter creature! She might lie by an
   emperor's side and command him tasks.

IAGO: Nay, that's not your way.

OTHELLO: Hang her! I do but say what she is. So delicate with her needle!
   an admirable musician! O, she will sing the savageness out of a bear! 175
   Of so high and plenteous wit and invention°—

IAGO: She's the worse for all this.

OTHELLO: O, a thousand thousand times! And then, of so gentle a condition!°

IAGO: Ay, too gentle.°   180

OTHELLO: Nay, that's certain. But yet the pity of it, Iago! O Iago, the pity
   of it, Iago!

145–46. **hobby-horse:** Harlot.   **149. An:** If.   **160. vice:** I.e., vicious conduct.
164. prizes: Values.   **176. invention:** Imagination.   **178–79. condition:** Disposition.   **180. gentle:** Generous.

IAGO: If you are so fond over her iniquity, give her patent° to offend; for if it touch not you, it comes near nobody.

OTHELLO: I will chop her into messes!° Cuckold me!

IAGO: O, 'tis foul in her.

OTHELLO: With mine officer!

IAGO: That's fouler.

OTHELLO: Get me some poison, Iago, this night. I'll not expostulate with her, lest her body and beauty unprovide° my mind again. This night, Iago!

IAGO: Do it not with poison. Strangle her in her bed, even the bed she hath contaminated.

OTHELLO: Good, good! The justice of it pleases. Very good!

IAGO: And for Cassio, let me be his undertaker;° you shall hear more by midnight.

OTHELLO: Excellent good!

(A trumpet.)

What trumpet is that same?

IAGO: I warrant something from Venice.

(Enter Lodovico, Desdemona, and Attendants.)

                                                        'Tis Lodovico.
This comes from the Duke; and see, your wife is with him.

LODOVICO: God save you, worthy general!

OTHELLO: With all my heart, sir.

LODOVICO: The Duke and senators of Venice greet you.

[Gives him a letter.]

OTHELLO: I kiss the instrument of their pleasures.

[Opens the letter and reads.]

DESDEMONA: And what's the news, good cousin Lodovico?

IAGO: I am very glad to see you, signior.
    Welcome to Cyprus.

LODOVICO: I thank you. How does Lieutenant Cassio?

IAGO: Lives, sir.

DESDEMONA: Cousin, there's fall'n between him and my lord
    An unkind° breach; but you shall make all well.

OTHELLO: Are you sure of that?

DESDEMONA: My lord?

---

183. patent: License.   **185. messes:** Small pieces.   **190. unprovide:** Disarm.
195. be his undertaker: Undertake to deal with him.   **209. unkind:** Unnatural.

OTHELLO [reads]: "This fail you not to do, as you will—"
LODOVICO: He did not call; he's busy in the paper.
   Is there division 'twixt thy lord and Cassio?
DESDEMONA: A most unhappy one. I would do much   215
   T' atone° them, for the love I bear to Cassio.
OTHELLO: Fire and brimstone!
DESDEMONA: My lord?
OTHELLO: Are you wise?
DESDEMONA: What, is he angry?
LODOVICO: May be the letter moved him;
   For, as I think, they do command him home,
   Deputing Cassio in his government.   220
DESDEMONA: By my troth, I am glad on't.
OTHELLO: Indeed?
DESDEMONA: My lord?
OTHELLO: I am glad to see you mad.°
DESDEMONA: Why, sweet Othello—
OTHELLO: Devil!

[Strikes her.]

DESDEMONA: I have not deserved this.
LODOVICO: My lord, this would not be believed in Venice,   225
   Though I should swear I saw't. 'Tis very much.
   Make her amends; she weeps.
OTHELLO: O devil, devil!
   If that the earth could teem° with woman's tears,
   Each drop she falls would prove a crocodile.°
   Out of my sight!
DESDEMONA: I will not stay to offend you.   [Going.] 230
LODOVICO: Truly, an obedient lady.
   I do beseech your lordship call her back.
OTHELLO: Mistress!
DESDEMONA: My lord?
OTHELLO: What would you with her, sir?
LODOVICO: Who? I, my lord?   235
OTHELLO: Ay! You did wish that I would make her turn.
  Sir, she can turn, and turn, and yet go on
  And turn again; and she can weep, sir, weep;
  And she's obedient; as you say, obedient,

---

216. atone: Reconcile.   222. mad: I.e., waggish.   228. teem: Breed.
229. crocodile: (Crocodiles were supposed to shed hypocritical tears to lure
men to destruction.)

Very obedient.—Proceed you in your tears.—
Concerning this, sir—O well-painted passion!°—
I am commanded home.—Get you away;
I'll send for you anon.—Sir, I obey the mandate
And will return to Venice.—Hence, avaunt!

[*Exit Desdemona.*]

Cassio shall have my place. And, sir, to-night
I do entreat that we may sup together.
You are welcome, sir, to Cyprus—Goats and monkeys!

[*Exit.*]

LODOVICO: Is this the noble Moor whom our full Senate
　Call all in all sufficient? Is this the nature
　Whom passion could not shake? whose solid virtue
　The shot of accident nor dart of chance
　Could neither graze nor pierce?
IAGO:　　　　　　　　　　He is much changed.
LODOVICO: Are his wits safe? Is he not light of brain?
IAGO: He's that he is; I may not breathe my censure.
　What he might be—if what he might he is not—
　I would to heaven he were!
LODOVICO:　　　　　　What, strike his wife?
IAGO: Faith, that was not so well; yet would I knew
　That stroke would prove the worst!
LODOVICO:　　　　　　　　　Is it his use?°
　Or did the letters work upon his blood°
　And new-create this fault?
IAGO:　　　　　　　　Alas, alas!
　It is not honesty in me to speak
　What I have seen and known. You shall observe him,
　And his own courses will denote° him so
　That I may save my speech. Do but go after
　And mark how he continues.
LODOVICO: I am sorry that I am deceived in him.　　　(*Exeunt.*)

Scene II

(*Within the castle.*)

(*Enter Othello and Emilia.*)

OTHELLO: You have seen nothing then?
EMILIA: Nor ever heard, nor ever did suspect.

241. passion: Grief.　258. use: Custom.　259. blood: Passions.　263. courses will denote: Actions will reveal.

OTHELLO: Yes, you have seen Cassio and she together.
EMILIA: But then I saw no harm, and then I heard
   Each syllable that breath made up between them.   5
OTHELLO: What, did they never whisper?
EMILIA: Never, my lord.
OTHELLO: Nor send you out o' th' way?
EMILIA: Never.
OTHELLO: To fetch her fan, her gloves, her mask, nor nothing?
EMILIA: Never, my lord.   10
OTHELLO: That's strange.
EMILIA: I durst, my lord, to wager she is honest,
   Lay down my soul at stake.° If you think other,
   Remove your thought; it doth abuse your bosom.°
   If any wretch have put this in your head,   15
   Let heaven requite it with the serpent's curse!°
   For if she be not honest, chaste, and true,
   There's no man happy; the purest of their wives
   Is foul as slander.
OTHELLO: Bid her come hither. Go.   (*Exit Emilia.*)
   She says enough; yet she's a simple bawd   20
   That cannot say as much.° This is a subtle whore,
   A closet lock and key of villainous secrets;
   And yet she'll kneel and pray; I have seen her do't.

(*Enter Desdemona and Emilia.*)

DESDEMONA: My lord, what is your will?
OTHELLO: Pray, chuck, come hither.
DESDEMONA: What is your pleasure?
OTHELLO: Let me see your eyes.   25
   Look in my face.
DESDEMONA: What horrible fancy's this?
OTHELLO [*to Emilia*]: Some of your function, mistress.
   Leave procreants° alone and shut the door;
   Cough or cry hem if anybody come.
   Your mystery, your mystery!° Nay, dispatch!   30
                         (*Exit Emilia.*)
DESDEMONA: Upon my knees, what doth your speech import?
   I understand a fury in your words,
   [But not the words.]

SCENE II.   **13. at stake:** As the wager.   **14. abuse your bosom:** Deceive your heart.
16. serpent's curse: (cf. Genesis 3:14).   **20–21. yet . . . much:** Yet any procuress
who couldn't make up as believable a story as this would have to be pretty stupid.   **28. procreants:** Mating couples.   **30. mystery:** Trade, occupation.

OTHELLO: Why, what art thou?
DESDEMONA: Your wife, my lord; your true
   And loyal wife.
OTHELLO: Come, swear it, damn thyself;
   Lest, being like one of heaven,° the devils themselves
   Should fear to seize thee. Therefore be double-damned—
   Swear thou art honest.°
DESDEMONA: Heaven doth truly know it.
OTHELLO: Heaven truly knows that thou art false as hell.
DESDEMONA: To whom, my lord? With whom? How am I false?
OTHELLO: Ah, Desdemona! away! away! away!
DESDEMONA: Alas the heavy day! Why do you weep?
   Am I the motive of these tears, my lord?
   If haply you my father do suspect
   An instrument° of this your calling back,
   Lay not your blame on me. If you have lost him,
   Why, I have lost him too.
OTHELLO: Had it pleased heaven
   To try me with affliction, had they rained
   All kinds of sores and shames on my bare head,
   Steeped me in poverty to the very lips,
   Given to captivity me and my utmost hopes,
   I should have found in some place of my soul
   A drop of patience. But, alas, to make me
   A fixèd figure for the time of scorn°
   To point his slow unmoving finger at!
   Yet could I bear that too; well, very well.
   But there where I have garnered up my heart,
   Where either I must live or bear no life,
   The fountain from the which my current runs
   Or else dries up—to be discarded thence,
   Or keep it as a cistern for foul toads
   To knot and gender in—turn thy complexion there,°
   Patience, thou young and rose-lipped cherubin!
   Ay, there look grim as hell!
DESDEMONA: I hope my noble lord esteems me honest.
OTHELLO: O, ay; as summer flies are in the shambles,°
   That quicken° even with blowing. O thou weed,

36. being . . . heaven: Looking like an angel.   38. honest: Chaste.   45. An
instrument: To be the cause.   54. time of scorn: Scornful world.   62. turn thy
complexion there: Change thy color at that point.   66. shambles: Slaughter-
house.   67. quicken: Come to life.

Who art so lovely fair, and smell'st so sweet,
That the sense aches at thee, would thou hadst ne'er been born!

DESDEMONA: Alas, what ignorant sin have I committed?   70

OTHELLO: Was this fair paper, this most goodly book,
Made to write "whore" upon? What committed?
Committed? O thou public commoner!°
I should make very forges of my cheeks
That would to cinders burn up modesty,   75
Did I but speak thy deeds. What committed?
Heaven stops the nose at it, and the moon winks;°
The bawdy wind, that kisses all it meets,
Is hushed within the hollow mine of earth
And will not hear it. What committed?   80
Impudent strumpet!

DESDEMONA: By heaven, you do me wrong!

OTHELLO: Are not you a strumpet?

DESDEMONA: No, as I am a Christian!
If to preserve this vessel for my lord
From any other foul unlawful touch
Be not to be a strumpet, I am none.   85

OTHELLO: What, not a whore?

DESDEMONA: No, as I shall be saved!

OTHELLO: Is't possible?

DESDEMONA: O, heaven forgive us!

OTHELLO: I cry you mercy° then.
I took you for that cunning whore of Venice
That married with Othello.—[Calling.] You, mistress,   90
That have the office opposite to Saint Peter
And keep the gate of hell!

(Enter Emilia.)

                              You, you, ay, you!
We have done our course; there's money for your pains:
I pray you turn the key, and keep our counsel.

EMILIA: Alas, what does this gentleman conceive?   95
How do you, madam? How do you, my good lady?

DESDEMONA: Faith, half asleep.°

EMILIA: Good madam, what's the matter with my lord?

DESDEMONA: With who?

73. commoner: Harlot.   77. winks: Closes her eyes.   88. cry you mercy: Beg
your pardon.   97. half asleep: I.e., stunned.

EMILIA: Why, with my lord, madam.
DESDEMONA: Who is thy lord?
EMILIA: He that is yours, sweet lady.
DESDEMONA: I have none. Do not talk to me, Emilia.
  I cannot weep; nor answer have I none
  But what should go by water. Prithee to-night
  Lay on my bed my wedding sheets, remember;
  And call thy husband hither.
EMILIA: Here's a change indeed!   (*Exit.*)
DESDEMONA: 'Tis meet° I should be used so, very meet.
  How have I been behaved, that he might stick
  The small'st opinion° on my least misuse?°

(*Enter Iago and Emilia.*)

IAGO: What is your pleasure, madam? How is't with you?
DESDEMONA: I cannot tell. Those that do teach young babes
  Do it with gentle means and easy tasks:
  He might have chid me so; for, in good faith,
  I am a child to chiding.
IAGO: What is the matter, lady?
EMILIA: Alas, Iago, my lord hath so bewhored her,
  Thrown such despite and heavy terms upon her
  As true hearts cannot bear.
DESDEMONA: Am I that name, Iago?
IAGO: What name, fair lady?
DESDEMONA: Such as she said my lord did say I was.
EMILIA: He called her whore. A beggar in his drink
  Could not have laid such terms upon his callet.°
IAGO: Why did he so?
DESDEMONA: I do not know; I am sure I am none such.
IAGO: Do not weep, do not weep. Alas the day!
EMILIA: Hath she forsook so many noble matches,
  Her father and her country, and her friends,
  To be called whore? Would it not make one weep?
DESDEMONA: It is my wretched fortune.
IAGO: Beshrew him for't!
  How comes this trick° upon him?
DESDEMONA: Nay, heaven doth know.
EMILIA: I will be hanged if some eternal villain,
  Some busy and insinuating° rogue,

---

107. meet: Fitting.   **109. small'st opinion:** Least suspicion; **least misuse:** Slightest misconduct.   **121. callet:** Whore.   **129. trick:** Freakish behavior.
131. insinuating: Ingratiating.

Some cogging, cozening° slave, to get some office,
  Have not devised this slander. I'll be hanged else.
IAGO: Fie, there is no such man! It is impossible.
DESDEMONA: If any such there be, heaven pardon him!
EMILIA: A halter° pardon him! and hell gnaw his bones!   135
  Why should he call her whore? Who keeps her company?
  What place? what time? what form? what likelihood?
  The Moor 's abused by some most villainous knave,
  Some base notorious knave, some scurvy fellow.   140
  O heaven, that such companions° thou 'dst unfold,°
  And put in every honest hand a whip
  To lash the rascals naked through the world
  Even from the east to th' west!
IAGO: Speak within door.°
EMILIA: O, fie upon them! Some such squire he was   145
  That turned your wit the seamy side without
  And made you to suspect me with the Moor.
IAGO: You are a fool. Go to.
DESDEMONA: Alas, Iago,
  What shall I do to win my lord again?
  Good friend, go to him; for, by this light of heaven,   150
  I know not how I lost him. Here I kneel:
  If e'er my will did trespass 'gainst his love
  Either in discourse° of thought or actual deed,
  Or that° mine eyes, mine ears, or any sense
  Delighted them in any other form,
  Or that I do not yet,° and ever did,   155
  And ever will (though he do shake me off
  To beggarly divorcement) love him dearly,
  Comfort forswear° me! Unkindness may do much;
  And his unkindness may defeat° my life,
  But never taint my love. I cannot say "whore."   160
  It does abhor me now I speak the word;
  To do the act that might the addition° earn
  Not the world's mass of vanity° could make me.
IAGO: I pray you be content. 'Tis but his humor.   165
  The business of the state does him offense,
  [And he does chide with you.]

---

132. **cogging, cozening:** Cheating, defrauding.   136. **halter:** Hangman's noose.
141. **companions:** Rogues; **unfold:** Expose.   144. **within door:** With restraint.
153. **discourse:** Course.   154. **that:** If.   156. **yet:** Still.   159. **Comfort forswear:**
May happiness forsake.   160. **defeat:** Destroy.   163. **addition:** Title.   164. **vanity:** Showy riches.

DESDEMONA: If 'twere no other—

IAGO: 'Tis but so, I warrant.

[*Trumpets within.*]

Hark how these instruments summon you to supper.
The messengers of Venice stay the meat:
Go in, and weep not. All things shall be well.

(*Exeunt Desdemona and Emilia.*)

(*Enter Roderigo.*)

How now, Roderigo?

RODERIGO: I do not find that thou deal'st justly with me.

IAGO: What in the contrary?

RODERIGO: Every day thou daff'st me with some device,° Iago, and rather,
as it seems to me now, keep'st from me all conveniency° than suppliest
me with the least advantage° of hope. I will indeed no longer endure it;
nor am I yet persuaded to put up° in peace what already I have foolishly suffered.

IAGO: Will you hear me, Roderigo?

RODERIGO: Faith, I have heard too much; for your words and performances are no kin together.

IAGO: You charge me most unjustly.

RODERIGO: With naught but truth. I have wasted myself out of my means.
The jewels you have had from me to deliver to Desdemona would half
have corrupted a votarist.° You have told me she hath received them,
and returned me expectations and comforts of sudden respect° and
acquaintance; but I find none.

IAGO: Well, go to; very well.

RODERIGO: Very well! go to! I cannot go to, man; nor 'tis not very well. By
this hand, I say 'tis very scurvy, and begin to find myself fopped° in it.

IAGO: Very well.

RODERIGO: I tell you 'tis not very well. I will make myself known to Desdemona. If she will return me my jewels, I will give over my suit and
repent my unlawful solicitation; if not, assure yourself I will seek satisfaction of you.

IAGO: You have said now.

RODERIGO: Ay, and said nothing but what I protest intendment° of doing.

IAGO: Why, now I see there's mettle in thee; and even from this instant do
build on thee a better opinion than ever before. Give me thy hand,

---

175. thou . . . device: You put me off with some trick.   **176. conveniency:** Favorable opportunities.   **177. advantage:** Increase.   **178. put up:** Tolerate.
186. votarist: Nun.   **187. sudden respect:** Immediate notice.   **191. fopped:**
Duped.   **198. protest intendment:** Declare my intention.

Roderigo. Thou has taken against me a most just exception; but yet I protest I have dealt most directly° in thy affair.

RODERIGO: It hath not appeared.

IAGO: I grant indeed it hath not appeared, and your suspicion is not without wit and judgment. But, Roderigo, if thou hast that in thee indeed   205
which I have greater reason to believe now than ever, I mean purpose,
courage, and valor, this night show it. If thou the next night following
enjoy not Desdemona, take me from this world with treachery and
devise engines for° my life.

RODERIGO: Well, what is it? Is it within reason and compass?   210

IAGO: Sir, there is especial commission come from Venice to depute
Cassio in Othello's place.

RODERIGO: Is that true? Why, then Othello and Desdemona return again
to Venice.

IAGO: O, no; he goes into Mauritania and takes away with him the fair   215
Desdemona, unless his abode be lingered here° by some accident;
wherein none can be so determinate° as the removing of Cassio.

RODERIGO: How do you mean removing of him?

IAGO: Why, by making him uncapable of Othello's place—knocking out
his brains.   220

RODERIGO: And that you would have me to do?

IAGO: Ay, if you dare do yourself a profit and a right. He sups to-night
with a harlotry, and thither will I go to him. He knows not yet of his
honorable fortune. If you will watch his going thence, which I will
fashion to fall out° between twelve and one, you may take him at your   225
pleasure. I will be near to second your attempt, and he shall fall between
us. Come, stand not amazed at it, but go along with me. I will
show you such a necessity in his death that you shall think yourself
bound to put it on him. It is now high supper time, and the night grows
to waste. About it!   230

RODERIGO: I will hear further reason for this.

IAGO: And you shall be satisfied.   (*Exeunt.*)

Scene III

(*Within the castle.*)

(*Enter Othello, Lodovico, Desdemona, Emilia, and Attendants.*)

LODOVICO: I do beseech you, sir, trouble yourself no further.

202. **directly:** Straightforwardly.   209. **engines for:** Plots against.
216. **abode . . . here:** Stay here be extended.   217. **determinate:** Effective.
225. **fall out:** Occur.

OTHELLO: O, pardon me; 'twill do me good to walk.
LODOVICO: Madam, good night. I humbly thank your ladyship.
DESDEMONA: Your honor is most welcome.
OTHELLO: Will you walk, sir?
    O, Desdemona—
DESDEMONA: My lord?
OTHELLO: Get you to bed on th' instant; I will be returned forthwith.
    Dismiss your attendant there. Look't be done.
DESDEMONA: I will, my lord.

                            (*Exit* [*Othello, with Lodovico and Attendants*].)

EMILIA: How goes it now? He looks gentler than he did.
DESDEMONA: He says he will return incontinent.°
    He hath commanded me to go to bed,
    And bade me to dismiss you.
EMILIA: Dismiss me?
DESDEMONA: It was his bidding; therefore, good Emilia,
    Give me my nightly wearing, and adieu.
    We must not now displease him.
EMILIA: I would you had never seen him!
DESDEMONA: So would not I. My love doth so approve him
    That even his stubbornness,° his checks,° his frowns—
    Prithee unpin me—have grace and favor in them.
EMILIA: I have laid those sheets you bade me on the bed.
DESDEMONA: All's one.° Good faith, how foolish are our minds!
    If I do die before thee, prithee shroud me
    In one of those same sheets.
EMILIA: Come, come! You talk.°
DESDEMONA: My mother had a maid called Barbary.
    She was in love; and he she loved proved mad°
    And did forsake her. She had a song of "Willow";
    An old thing 'twas; but it expressed her fortune,
    And she died singing it. That song to-night
    Will not go from my mind; I have much to do
    But to go hang° my head all at one side
    And sing it like poor Barbary. Prithee dispatch.
EMILIA: Shall I go fetch your nightgown?°
DESDEMONA: No, unpin me here.
    This Lodovico is a proper man.

SCENE III. **11. incontinent:** At once. **19. stubbornness:** Roughness; **checks:** Rebukes. **22. All's one:** It doesn't matter. **24. talk:** Prattle. **26. mad:** Wild, faithless. **30–31. I . . . hang:** I can hardly keep from hanging. **33. nightgown:** Dressing gown.

EMILIA: A very handsome man.   35
DESDEMONA: He speaks well.
EMILIA: I know a lady in Venice would have walked barefoot to Pales-
 tine for a touch of his nether lip.
DESDEMONA (*sings*): "The poor soul sat sighing by a sycamore tree
   Sing all a green willow;   40
  Her hand on her bosom, her head on her knee,
   Sing willow, willow, willow.
  The fresh streams ran by her and murmured her moans;
   Sing willow, willow, willow;
  Her salt tears fell from her, and soft'ned the stones"—   45
 Lay by these.
   "Sing willow, willow, willow"—
 Prithee hie thee;° he'll come anon.
   "Sing all a green willow must be my garland.
  Let nobody blame him; his scorn I approve"—   50
 Nay, that's not next. Hark! who is't that knocks?
EMILIA: It's the wind.
DESDEMONA (*sings*): "I called my love false love; but what said he then?
   Sing willow, willow, willow:
  If I court moe women, you'll couch with moe men."   55
 So get thee gone; good night. Mine eyes do itch.
 Doth that bode weeping?
EMILIA: 'Tis neither here nor there.
DESDEMONA: I have heard it said so. O, these men, these men!
 Dost thou in conscience think—tell me, Emilia—
 That there be women do abuse their husbands   60
 In such gross kind?
EMILIA: There be some such, no question.
DESDEMONA: Wouldst thou do such a deed for all the world?
EMILIA: Why, would not you?
DESDEMONA: No, by this heavenly light!
EMILIA: Nor I neither by this heavenly light.
 I might do't as well i' th' dark.   65
DESDEMONA: Wouldst thou do such a deed for all the world?
EMILIA: The world's a huge thing; it is a great price for a small vice.
DESDEMONA: In troth, I think thou wouldst not.
EMILIA: In troth, I think I should; and undo't when I had done it. Marry,
 I would not do such a thing for a joint-ring,° nor for measures of   70
 lawn, nor for gowns, petticoats, nor caps, nor any petty exhibition;°
 but, for all the whole world—'Ud's pity! who would not make her

---

48. hie thee: Hurry.   **70. joint-ring:** Ring made in separable halves.
71. exhibition: Gift.

husband a cuckold to make him a monarch? I should venture purgatory for't.

DESDEMONA: Beshrew me if I would do such a wrong
For the whole world.

EMILIA: Why, the wrong is but a wrong i' th' world; and having the world
for your labor, 'tis a wrong in your own world, and you might quickly
make it right.

DESDEMONA: I do not think there is any such woman.

EMILIA: Yes, a dozen; and as many to th' vantage° as
would store° the world they played for.
But I do think it is their husbands' faults
If wives do fall. Say that they slack their duties
And pour our treasures into foreign laps;°
Or else break out in peevish° jealousies,
Throwing restraint upon us; or say they strike us,
Or scant our former having° in despite—
Why, we have galls;° and though we have some grace,
Yet have we some revenge. Let husbands know
Their wives have sense like them. They see, and smell,
And have their palates both for sweet and sour,
As husbands have. What is it that they do
When they change us for others? Is it sport?
I think it is. And doth affection breed it?
I think it doth. Is't frailty that thus errs?
It is so too. And have not we affections,
Desires for sport, and frailty, as men have?
Then let them use us well; else let them know,
The ills we do, their ills instruct us so.

DESDEMONA: Good night, good night. God me such usage° send,
Not to pick bad from bad, but by bad mend!°   (*Exeunt.*)

ACT V   *Scene I*

(*A street in Cyprus.*)

(*Enter Iago and Roderigo.*)

---

81. **to th' vantage:** Besides.   82. **store:** Populate.   84–85. **slack . . . laps:** Are
unfaithful.   86. **peevish:** Senseless.   88. **having:** Allowance.   89. **galls:** Spirits
to resent.   101. **usage:** Habits.   102. **Not . . . mend:** As not to learn bad ways
from others' badness, but to mend my ways by learning what evil is.

IAGO: Here, stand behind this bulk;° straight will he come.
   Wear thy good rapier bare, and put it home.
   Quick, quick! Fear nothing; I'll be at thy elbow.
   It makes us, or it mars us—think on that,
   And fix most firm thy resolution.   5
RODERIGO: Be near at hand; I may miscarry in't.
IAGO: Here, at thy hand. Be bold, and take thy stand.

[*Stands aside.*]

RODERIGO: I have no great devotion to the deed,
   And yet he hath given me satisfying reasons.
   'Tis but a man gone. Forth my sword! He dies!   10
IAGO: I have rubbed this young quat° almost to the sense,°
   And he grows angry. Now whether he kill Cassio,
   Or Cassio him, or each do kill the other,
   Every way makes my gain. Live Roderigo,
   He calls me to a restitution large   15
   Of gold and jewels that I bobbed° from him
   As gifts to Desdemona.
   It must not be. If Cassio do remain,
   He hath a daily beauty in his life
   That makes me ugly; and besides, the Moor   20
   May unfold me to him; there stand I in much peril.
   No, he must die. Be't so! I hear him coming.

(*Enter Cassio.*)

RODERIGO: I know his gait. 'Tis he. Villain, thou diest!

[*Makes a pass at Cassio.*]

CASSIO: That thrust had been mine enemy indeed
   But that my coat° is better than thou know'st.
   I will make proof° of thine.   25

[*Draws, and wounds Roderigo.*]

RODERIGO: O, I am slain!

[*Iago darts from concealment behind Cassio, wounds him in the leg, and exits.*]

CASSIO: I am maimed for ever. Help, ho! Murder! murder!

[*Falls.*]

(*Enter Othello.*)

ACT V, SCENE I. **1. bulk:** Projecting shop-front. **11. quat:** Pimple; **sense:** Quick.
16. bobbed: Swindled. **25. coat:** Undershirt of mail. **26. proof:** A test.

OTHELLO: The voice of Cassio. Iago keeps his word.
RODERIGO: O, villain that I am!
OTHELLO: It is even so.
CASSIO: O, help, ho! light! a surgeon!
OTHELLO: 'Tis he. O brave Iago, honest and just,
   That hast such noble sense of thy friend's wrong!
   Thou teachest me. Minion,° your dear lies dead,
   And your unblest fate hies.° Strumpet, I come.
   Forth of my heart those charms, thine eyes, are blotted.
   Thy bed, lust-stained, shall with lust's blood be spotted.

                                                   (*Exit Othello.*)

(*Enter Lodovico and Gratiano.*)

CASSIO: What, ho? No watch? No passage?° Murder! murder!
GRATIANO: 'Tis some mischance. The cry is very direful.
CASSIO: O, help!
LODOVICO: Hark!
RODERIGO: O wretched villain!
LODOVICO: Two or three groan. It is a heavy° night.
   These may be counterfeits. Let's think't unsafe
   To come in to the cry without more help.
RODERIGO: Nobody come? Then shall I bleed to death.
LODOVICO: Hark!

(*Enter Iago, with a light.*)

GRATIANO: Here's one comes in his shirt, with light and weapons.
IAGO: Who's there? Whose noise is this that cries on° murder?
LODOVICO: We do not know.
IAGO: Did not you hear a cry?
CASSIO: Here, here! For heaven's sake, help me!
IAGO: What's the matter?
GRATIANO: This is Othello's ancient, as I take it.
LODOVICO: The same indeed, a very valiant fellow.
IAGO: What are you here that cry so grievously?
CASSIO: Iago? O, I am spoiled, undone by villains!
   Give me some help.
IAGO: O me, lieutenant! What villains have done this?
CASSIO: I think that one of them is hereabout
   And cannot make° away.
IAGO: O treacherous villains!

---

33. **Minion:** Mistress (Desdemona).   34. **hies:** Hurries on.   37. **passage:** Pass-
ersby.   42. **heavy:** Cloudy, dark.   48. **cries on:** Raises the cry of.   58. **make:** Get.

[*To Lodovico and Gratiano.*]

What are you there? Come in, and give some help.
RODERIGO: O, help me here!   60
CASSIO: That's one of them.
IAGO: O murd'rous slave! O villain!

[*Stabs Roderigo.*]

RODERIGO: O damned Iago! O inhuman dog!
IAGO: Kill men i' th' dark?—Where be these bloody thieves?—
    How silent is this town!—Ho! murder! murder!—
    What may you be? Are you of good or evil?   65
LODOVICO: As you shall prove us, praise us.
IAGO: Signior Lodovico?
LODOVICO: He, sir.
IAGO: I cry you mercy.° Here's Cassio hurt by villains.
GRATIANO: Cassio?   70
IAGO: How is't, brother?
CASSIO: My leg is cut in two.
IAGO: Marry,° heaven forbid!
    Light, gentlemen. I'll bind it with my shirt.

(*Enter Bianca.*)

BIANCA: What is the matter, ho? Who is't that cried?
IAGO: Who is't that cried?   75
BIANCA: O my dear Cassio! my sweet Cassio!
    O Cassio, Cassio, Cassio!
IAGO: O notable strumpet!—Cassio, may you suspect
    Who they should be that have thus mangled you?
CASSIO: No.   80
GRATIANO: I am sorry to find you thus. I have been to seek you.
IAGO: Lend me a garter. So. O for a chair°
    To bear him easily hence!
BIANCA: Alas, he faints! O Cassio, Cassio, Cassio!
IAGO: Gentlemen all, I do suspect this trash   85
    To be a party in this injury.—
    Patience a while, good Cassio.—Come, come!
    Lend me a light. Know we this face or no?
    Alas, my friend and my dear countryman
    Roderigo? No—Yes, sure.—O heaven, Roderigo!   90
GRATIANO: What, of Venice?

69. I . . . mercy: I beg your pardon. **72. Marry:** (From "By Mary"). **82. chair:**
Litter (an enclosed seat carried on poles by two bearers).

IAGO: Even he, sir. Did you know him?
GRATIANO:　　　　　　　　　　　　Know him? Ay.
IAGO: Signior Gratiano? I cry your gentle° pardon.
　These bloody accidents° must excuse my manners
　That so neglected you.
GRATIANO:　　　　　　　I am glad to see you.
IAGO: How do you, Cassio?—O, a chair, a chair!
GRATIANO: Roderigo?
IAGO: He, he, 'tis he!

[*A chair brought in.*]

　O, that's well said;° the chair.
　Some good man bear him carefully from hence.
　I'll fetch the general's surgeon. [*To Bianca.*] For you, mistress,
　Save you your labor.—He that lies slain here, Cassio,
　Was my dear friend. What malice was between you?
CASSIO: None in the world; nor do I know the man.
IAGO [*To Bianca*]: What, look you pale?—O, bear him out o' th' air.

　　　　　　　　　　　[*Cassio and Roderigo are borne off.*]

　Stay you, good gentlemen.—Look you pale, mistress?—
　Do you perceive the gastness° of her eye?—
　Nay, if you stare, we shall hear more anon.
　Behold her well; I pray you look upon her.
　Do you see, gentlemen? Nay, guiltiness will speak.
　Though tongues were out of use.

(*Enter Emilia.*)

EMILIA: 'Las, what's the matter? What's the matter, husband?
IAGO: Cassio hath here been set on in the dark
　By Roderigo, and fellows that are scaped.
　He's almost slain, and Roderigo dead.
EMILIA: Alas, good gentlemen! alas, good Cassio!
IAGO: This is the fruits of whoring. Prithee, Emilia,
　Go know of° Cassio where he supped to-night.

[*To Bianca.*]

　What, do you shake at that?
BIANCA: He supped at my house; but I therefore shake not.
IAGO: O, did he so? I charge you go with me.
EMILIA: Fie, fie upon thee, strumpet!

93. **gentle:** Noble.　94. **accidents:** Sudden events.　99. **well said:** Well done.
107. **gastness:** Terror.　118. **know of:** Learn from.

BIANCA: I am no strumpet, but of life as honest°
  As you that thus abuse me.
EMILIA: As I? Foh! fie upon thee!
IAGO: Kind gentlemen, let's go see poor Cassio dressed.°   125

[*To Bianca.*]

  Come, mistress, you must tell 's another tale.
  Emilia, run you to the citadel
  And tell my lord and lady what hath happed.
                                           [*Exit Emilia.*]
  Will you go on afore?   (*Exeunt [all but Iago].*)
                      This is the night
  That either makes me or fordoes° me quite.   [*Exit.*]   130

Scene II

(*A bedchamber in the castle.*)

(*Desdemona [asleep] in her bed. Enter Othello with a light.*)

OTHELLO: It is the cause, it is the cause,° my soul.
  Let me not name it to you, you chaste stars!
  It is the cause. Yet I'll not shed her blood,
  Nor scar that whiter skin of hers than snow,
  And smooth as monumental alabaster.°   5
  Yet she must die, else she'll betray more men.
  Put out the light, and then put out the light.
  If I quench thee, thou flaming minister,°
  I can again thy former light restore,
  Should I repent me;° but once put out thy light,   10
  Thou cunning'st pattern° of excelling nature,
  I know not where is that Promethean heat°
  That can thy light relume.° When I have plucked the rose,
  I cannot give it vital growth again;
  It needs must wither. I'll smell thee on the tree.   15

(*He kisses her.*)

  O balmy breath, that dost almost persuade
  Justice to break her sword! One more, one more!

---

123. honest: Chaste.   **125. Cassio dressed:** Cassio's wounds dressed.   **130. for-**
does: Destroys.   SCENE II.   **1. cause:** Cause of justice.   **5. monumental alabas-**
ter: Alabaster stone used for tombs and monuments.   **8. minister:** Servant.
10. repent me: Change my mind.   **11. cunning'st pattern:** Skillfully wrought
example.   **12. Promethean heat:** Divine fire.   **13. relume:** Relight.

Be thus when thou art dead, and I will kill thee,
And love thee after. One more, and that's the last!
So sweet was ne'er so fatal. I must weep,
But they are cruel tears. This sorrow's heavenly;
It strikes where it doth love. She wakes.

DESDEMONA: Who's there? Othello?

OTHELLO: Ay, Desdemona.

DESDEMONA: Will you come to bed, my lord?

OTHELLO: Have you prayed to-night, Desdemon?

DESDEMONA: Ay, my lord.

OTHELLO: If you bethink yourself of any crime°
Unreconciled as yet to heaven and grace,
Solicit° for it straight.

DESDEMONA: Alack, my lord, what may you mean by that?

OTHELLO: Well, do it, and be brief; I will walk by.
I would not kill thy unprepared spirit.
No, heaven forfend!° I would not kill thy soul.

DESDEMONA: Talk you of killing?

OTHELLO: Ay, I do.

DESDEMONA: Then heaven
Have mercy on me!

OTHELLO: Amen, with all my heart!

DESDEMONA: If you say so, I hope you will not kill me.

OTHELLO: Hum!

DESDEMONA: And yet I fear you; for you're fatal then
When your eyes roll so. Why I should fear I know not,
Since guiltiness I know not; but yet I feel I fear.

OTHELLO: Think on thy sins.

DESDEMONA: They are loves I bear to you.

OTHELLO: Ay, and for that thou diest.

DESDEMONA: That death 's unnatural that kills for loving.
Alas, why gnaw you so your nether lip?
Some bloody passion shakes your very frame.
These are portents,° but yet I hope, I hope,
They do not point on me.

OTHELLO: Peace and be still!

DESDEMONA: I will so. What's the matter?

OTHELLO: That handkerchief which I so loved and gave thee
Thou gav'st to Cassio.

DESDEMONA: No, by my life and soul!
Send for the man and ask him.

---

26. crime: Sin. **28. Solicit:** Pray. **32. forfend:** Forbid. **45. portents:** Signs
of impending violence.

OTHELLO: Sweet soul, take heed,   50
  Take heed of perjury; thou art on thy deathbed.
DESDEMONA: Ay, but not yet to die.
OTHELLO: Yes, presently.°
  Therefore confess thee freely of thy sin;
  For to deny each article with oath
  Cannot remove nor choke the strong conception°   55
  That I do groan withal. Thou art to die.
DESDEMONA: Then Lord have mercy on me!
OTHELLO: I say amen.
DESDEMONA: And have you mercy too! I never did
  Offend° you in my life; never loved Cassio
  But with such general warranty of heaven   60
  As I might love. I never gave him token.
OTHELLO: By heaven, I saw my handkerchief in's hand!
  O perjured woman! thou dost stone my heart,°
  And mak'st me call what I intend to do
  A murder, which I thought a sacrifice.   65
  I saw the handkerchief.
DESDEMONA: He found it then.
  I never gave it him. Send for him hither.
  Let him confess a truth.
OTHELLO: He hath confessed.
DESDEMONA: What, my lord?
OTHELLO: That he hath used thee.
DESDEMONA: How? Unlawfully?
OTHELLO: Ay.   70
DESDEMONA: He will not say so.
OTHELLO: No, his mouth is stopped.
  Honest Iago hath ta'en order° for't.
DESDEMONA: O, my fear interprets. What, is he dead?
OTHELLO: Had all his hairs been lives, my great revenge
  Had stomach for them all.   75
DESDEMONA: Alas, he is betrayed, and I undone!   [*She weeps.*]
OTHELLO: Out, strumpet! Weep'st thou for him to my face?
DESDEMONA: O, banish me, my lord, but kill me not!
OTHELLO: Down, strumpet!
DESDEMONA: Kill me to-morrow; let me live to-night!   80
OTHELLO: Nay, if you strive—
DESDEMONA: But half an hour!
OTHELLO: Being done, there is no pause.

---

52. **presently:** At once.   55. **conception:** Belief.   59. **Offend:** Wrong.   63. **stone my heart:** Turn my heart to stone.   72. **ta'en order:** Taken measures.

DESDEMONA: But while I say one prayer!
OTHELLO: It is too late.

(*Smothers her.*)

   [DESDEMONA: O Lord, Lord, Lord!]

(*Emilia at the door.*)

EMILIA (*calls within*): My lord, my lord! What, ho! my lord, my lord!
OTHELLO: What noise is this? Not dead? not yet quite dead?
   I that am cruel am yet merciful;
   I would not have thee linger in thy pain.
   So, so.
EMILIA (*within*): What, ho! my lord, my lord!
OTHELLO: Who's there?
EMILIA (*within*): O, good my lord, I would speak a word with you!
OTHELLO: Yes, 'tis Emilia.—By and by.°—She's dead.—
   'Tis like° she comes to speak of Cassio's death.
   The noise was here. Ha! no more moving?
   Still as the grave.—Shall she come in? Were't good!—
   I think she stirs again. No.—What's best to do?
   If she come in, she'll sure speak to my wife.
   My wife! my wife! what wife? I have no wife.
   O, insupportable! O heavy hour!
   Methinks it should be now a huge eclipse
   Of sun and moon, and that th' affrighted globe
   Should yawn° at alteration.
EMILIA (*within*):   I do beseech you
   That I may speak with you, O good my lord!
OTHELLO: I had forgot thee. O, come in, Emilia.
   Soft, by and by.—Let me the curtains draw.—

[*Closes the bed-curtains.*]

   Where art thou?

[*Opens the door.*]

(*Enter Emilia.*)

                       What's the matter with thee now?
EMILIA: O my good lord, yonder's foul murder done!
OTHELLO: What? Now?

---

92. By and by: Just a moment (addressed to Emilia).   **93. like:** Likely.
102. yawn: Open, as in an earthquake.

EMILIA: But now, my lord.

OTHELLO: It is the very error° of the moon.   110
  She comes more nearer earth than she was wont
  And makes men mad.

EMILIA: Cassio, my lord, hath killed a young Venetian
  Called Roderigo.

OTHELLO: Roderigo killed?
  And Cassio killed?

EMILIA: No, Cassio is not killed.   115

OTHELLO: Not Cassio killed? Then murder's out of tune,
  And sweet revenge grows harsh.

DESDEMONA: O, falsely, falsely murdered?

EMILIA: O, Lord! what cry is that?

OTHELLO: That? What?

EMILIA: Out and alas! that was my lady's voice.   120
  Help! help, ho! help! O lady, speak again!
  Sweet Desdemona! O sweet mistress, speak!

DESDEMONA: A guiltless death I die.

EMILIA: O, who hath done this deed?

DESDEMONA: Nobody—I myself. Farewell.   125
  Commend° me to my kind lord. O, farewell!

(*She dies.*)

OTHELLO: Why, how should she be murd'red?

EMILIA: Alas, who knows?

OTHELLO: You heard her say herself, it was not I.

EMILIA: She said so. I must needs report the truth.

OTHELLO: She's like a liar gone to burning hell!   130
  'Twas I that killed her.

EMILIA: O, the more angel she,
  And you the blacker devil!

OTHELLO: She turned to folly, and she was a whore.

EMILIA: Thou dost belie° her, and thou art a devil.

OTHELLO: She was false as water.°

EMILIA: Thou art rash as fire to say   135
  That she was false. O, she was heavenly true!

OTHELLO: Cassio did top her. Ask thy husband else.°
  O, I were damned beneath all depth in hell
  But that I did proceed upon just grounds
  To this extremity. Thy husband knew it all.   140

---

110. **error:** Straying off course. 126. **Commend:** Remember. 134. **belie:** Slander. 135. **water:** (Which is yielding). 137. **else:** If you don't believe me.

EMILIA: My husband?

OTHELLO: Thy husband.

EMILIA: That she was false to wedlock?

OTHELLO: Ay, with Cassio. Nay, had she been true,
  If heaven would make me such another world
  Of one entire and perfect chrysolite,°
  I'ld not have sold her for it.

EMILIA: My husband?

OTHELLO: Ay 'twas he that told me first.
  An honest man he is, and hates the slime
  That sticks on filthy deeds.

EMILIA: My husband?

OTHELLO: What needs this iterance,° woman? I say thy husband.

EMILIA: O mistress, villainy hath made mocks with° love!
  My husband say that she was false?

OTHELLO: He, woman.
  I say, thy husband. Dost understand the word?
  My friend, thy husband; honest, honest Iago.

EMILIA: If he say so, may his pernicious soul
  Rot half a grain a day! he lies to th' heart.
  She was too fond of her most filthy bargain.

OTHELLO: Ha! [He draws.]

EMILIA: Do thy worst.
  This deed of thine is no more worthy heaven
  Than thou wast worthy her.

OTHELLO: Peace, you were best.°

EMILIA: Thou hast not half the power to do me harm
  As I have to be hurt.° O gull! O dolt!
  As ignorant as dirt! thou hast done a deed—
  I care not for thy sword; I'll make thee known,
  Though I lost twenty lives. Help! help! Ho! help!
  The Moor hath killed my mistress! Murder! murder!

(*Enter Montano, Gratiano, Iago, and others.*)

MONTANO: What is the matter? How now, general?

EMILIA: O, are you come, Iago? You have done well,
  That men must lay their murders on your neck.°

GRATIANO: What is the matter?

EMILIA: Disprove this villain, if thou be'st a man.

---

146. chrysolite: (Precious topaz).   **151. iterance:** Repetition.   **152. mocks with:** A mockery of.   **162. Peace . . . best:** You had better keep quiet.   **164. to be hurt:** To endure hurt.   **171. on your neck:** To your charge.

He says thou told'st him that his wife was false.
I know thou didst not; thou'rt not such a villain.   175
Speak, for my heart is full.
IAGO: I told him what I thought, and told no more
  Than what he found himself was apt and true.
EMILIA: But did you ever tell him she was false?
IAGO: I did.   180
EMILIA: You told a lie, an odious damnèd lie!
  Upon my soul, a lie! a wicked lie!
  She false with Cassio? Did you say with Cassio?
IAGO: With Cassio, mistress. Go to, charm° your tongue.
EMILIA: I will not charm my tongue; I am bound to speak: 185
  My mistress here lies murdered in her bed—
ALL: O heavens forfend!
EMILIA: And your reports have set the murder on.
OTHELLO: Nay, stare not, masters. It is true indeed.
GRATIANO: 'Tis a strange truth.   190
MONTANO: O monstrous act!
EMILIA: Villainy, villainy, villainy!
  I think upon't—I think I smell't!—O villainy!
  I thought so then.—I'll kill myself for grief.—
  O villainy, villainy!
IAGO: What, are you mad? I charge you get you home.   195
EMILIA: Good gentlemen, let me have leave to speak.
  'Tis proper I obey him, but not now.
  Perchance, Iago, I will ne'er go home.
OTHELLO: O! O! O!   (*Falls on the bed.*)
EMILIA: Nay, lay thee down and roar!
  For thou hast killed the sweetest innocent   200
  That e'er did lift up eye.°
OTHELLO: O, she was foul!

[*Rises.*]

  I scarce did know you, uncle. There lies your niece,
  Whose breath, indeed, these hands have newly stopped.
  I know this act shows° horrible and grim.
GRATIANO: Poor Desdemon! I am glad thy father's dead.   205
  Thy match was mortal to him, and pure grief
  Shore his old thread in twain. Did he live now,
  This sight would make him do a desperate turn;°

184. charm: Cast a spell on, silence. **201. lift up eye:** Lift her eyes to heaven.
204. shows: Appears. **208. turn:** Act.

Yea, curse his better angel from his side,
And fall to reprobation.°
OTHELLO: 'Tis pitiful; but yet Iago knows
   That she with Cassio hath the act of shame
   A thousand times committed. Cassio confessed it;
   And she did gratify° his amorous works
   With that recognizance° and pledge of love
   Which I first gave her. I saw it in his hand.
   It was a handkerchief, an antique token
   My father gave my mother.
EMILIA: O God! O heavenly God!
IAGO: Zounds, hold your peace!
EMILIA: 'Twill out, 'twill out! I peace?
   No, I will speak as liberal as the north,°
   Let heaven and men and devils, let them all,
   All, all, cry shame against me, yet I'll speak.
IAGO: Be wise, and get you home.
EMILIA: I will not.

[*Iago draws and threatens Emilia.*]

GRATIANO: Fie!
   Your sword upon a woman?
EMILIA: O thou dull Moor, that handkerchief thou speak'st of
   I found by fortune, and did give my husband;
   For often with a solemn earnestness—
   More than indeed belonged to such a trifle—
   He begged of me to steal't.
IAGO: Villainous whore!
EMILIA: She give it Cassio? No, alas, I found it,
   And I did give't my husband.
IAGO: Filth, thou liest!
EMILIA: By heaven, I do not, I do not, gentlemen.
   O murd'rous coxcomb!° what should such a fool
   Do with so good a wife?
OTHELLO: Are there no stones° in heaven
   But what serves for the thunder? Precious° villain!

(*The Moor runs at Iago* [*but is disarmed by Montano*].)

210. reprobation: Rejection by God, damnation.   214. gratify: Reward.
215. recognizance: Token.   221. liberal as the north: Unchecked as the north
wind blows.   234. coxcomb: Fool.   235. stones: Bolts like those used for
thunderbolts.   236. Precious: Absolute.

(*Iago kills his wife.*)

GRATIANO: The woman falls. Sure he hath killed his wife.
EMILIA: Ay, ay. O, lay me by my mistress' side.   (*Exit Iago.*)
GRATIANO: He's gone, but his wife's killed.
MONTANO: 'Tis a notorious° villain. Take you this weapon,   240
  Which I have here recovered from the Moor.
  Come, guard the door without. Let him not pass,
  But kill him rather. I'll after that same villain,
  For 'tis a damnèd slave.

              (*Exit [Montano, with all but Othello and Emilia].*)

OTHELLO: I am not valiant neither;
  But every puny whipster° gets my sword.   245
  But why should honor outlive honesty?
  Let it go all.
EMILIA: What did thy song bode, lady?
  Hark, canst thou hear me? I will play the swan,
  And die in music. [*Sings.*] "Willow, willow, willow."
  Moor, she was chaste. She loved thee, cruel Moor: 250
  So come my soul to bliss as I speak true.
  So speaking as I think, alas, I die.

(*She dies.*)

OTHELLO: I have another weapon in this chamber;
  It is a sword of Spain, the ice brook's° temper.
  O, here it is.—Uncle, I must come forth.   255
GRATIANO (*within*): If thou attempt it, it will cost thee dear.
  Thou hast no weapon, and perforce must suffer.
OTHELLO: Look in upon me then and speak with me,
  Or, naked° as I am, I will assault thee.

[*Enter Gratiano.*]

GRATIANO: What is the matter?
OTHELLO: Behold, I have a weapon;   260
  A better never did itself sustain
  Upon a soldier's thigh. I have seen the day
  That with this little arm and this good sword
  I have made my way through more impediments
  Than twenty times your stop.° But O vain boast!   265

240. **notorious:** Reprehensible. 245. **puny whipster:** Whippersnapper.
254. **ice brook:** I.e., a Spanish blade, tempered in cold running water.
259. **naked:** Disarmed. 265. **stop:** Power to stop.

Who can control his fate? 'Tis not so now.
Be not afraid, though you do see me weaponed.
Here is my journey's end, here is my butt,°
And very seamark° of my utmost sail:
Do you go back dismayed? 'Tis a lost° fear.
Man but a rush° against Othello's breast,
And he retires. Where should Othello go?
Now, how dost thou look now? O ill-starred wench!
Pale as thy smock! When we shall meet at compt,°
This look of thine will hurl my soul from heaven,
And fiends will snatch at it. Cold, cold, my girl?
Even like thy chastity.
O cursèd, cursèd slave! Whip me, ye devils,
From the possession of this heavenly sight!
Blow me about in winds! roast me in sulphur!
Wash me in steep-down gulfs of liquid fire!
Oh Desdemon! dead Desdemon! dead! Oh! Oh!

(*Enter Lodovico, Montano, Iago* [*as prisoner*]*, and Officers; Cassio in a chair.*)

LODOVICO: Where is this rash and most unfortunate man?
OTHELLO: That's he that was Othello. Here I am.
LODOVICO: Where is that viper? Bring the villain forth.
OTHELLO: I look down towards his feet°—but that's a fable.
   If that thou be'st a devil, I cannot kill thee.

[*Wounds Iago.*]

LODOVICO: Wrench his sword from him.

[*Othello is disarmed.*]

IAGO: I bleed, sir, but not killed.
OTHELLO: I am not sorry neither. I'ld have thee live;
   For in my sense, 'tis happiness to die.
LODOVICO: O thou Othello that wert once so good,
   Fall'n in the practice° of a damnèd slave,
   What shall be said to thee?
OTHELLO: Why, anything;
   An honorable murderer, if you will;
   For naught did I in hate, but all in honor.

268. butt: Limit.   269. seamark: Beacon, destination.   270. lost: Wasted.
271. Man but a rush: Wield only a reed.   274. compt: Final accounting, Last
Judgment.   286. I . . . feet: I.e., to see if they are cloven, like the Devil's.
292. practice: Plot.

LODOVICO: This wretch hath part confessed his villainy.
  Did you and he consent in° Cassio's death?
OTHELLO: Ay.
CASSIO: Dear general, I never gave you cause.
OTHELLO: I do believe it, and I ask your pardon.   300
  Will you, I pray, demand that demi-devil
  Why he hath thus ensnared my soul and body?
IAGO: Demand me nothing. What you know, you know.
  From this time forth I never will speak word.
LODOVICO: What, not to pray?
GRATIANO: Torments° will ope your lips.   305
OTHELLO: Well, thou dost best.
LODOVICO: Sir, you shall understand what hath befall'n,
  Which, as I think, you know not. Here is a letter
  Found in the pocket of the slain Roderigo;
  And here another. The one of them imports   310
  The death of Cassio to be undertook
  By Roderigo.
OTHELLO: O villain!
CASSIO: Most heathenish and most gross!
LODOVICO: Now here's another discontented° paper
  Found in the pocket too; and this, it seems,   315
  Roderigo meant t' have sent this damnèd villain;
  But that, belike, Iago in the nick°
  Came in and satisfied him.
OTHELLO: O thou pernicious caitiff!—
  How came you, Cassio, by that handkerchief
  That was my wife's?
CASSIO: I found it in my chamber;   320
  And he himself confessed but even now
  That there he dropped it for a special purpose
  Which wrought to his desire.
OTHELLO: O fool! fool! fool!
CASSIO: There is besides in Roderigo's letter,
  How he upbraids Iago that he made him   325
  Brave° me upon the watch; whereon it came°
  That I was cast;° and even but now he spake,
  After long seeming dead—Iago hurt him,
  Iago set him on.

297. consent in: Agree upon.   305. Torments: Torture.   314. discontented:
Full of discontent.   317. nick: Nick of time.   326. Brave: Defy; Whereon it
came: whereof it came about.   327. cast: Dismissed.

LODOVICO [*to Othello*]: You must forsake this room and go with us.   3
   Your power and your command is taken off,°
   And Cassio rules in Cyprus. For this slave,
   If there be any cunning cruelty
   That can torment him much and hold him long,°
   It shall be his. You shall close prisoner rest°   3
   Till that the nature of your fault be known
   To the Venetian state. Come, bring away.
OTHELLO: Soft you!° a word or two before you go.
   I have done the state some service, and they know't.
   No more of that. I pray you, in your letters,
   When you shall these unlucky° deeds relate,
   Speak of me as I am. Nothing extenuate,
   Nor set down aught in malice. Then must you speak
   Of one that loved not wisely, but too well;
   Of one not easily jealous, but, being wrought,°   3
   Perplexed° in the extreme; of one whose hand,
   Like the base Judean,° threw a pearl away
   Richer than all his tribe; of one whose subdued° eyes,
   Albeit unusèd to the melting mood,
   Drop tears as fast as the Arabian trees
   Their med'cinable gum. Set you down this.
   And say besides that in Aleppo once,
   Where a malignant and a turbaned Turk
   Beat a Venetian and traduced the state,
   I took by th' throat the circumcisèd dog
   And smote him—thus.

(*He stabs himself.*)

LODOVICO: O bloody period!°
GRATIANO: All that's spoke is marred.
OTHELLO: I kissed thee ere I killed thee. No way but this,
   Killing myself, to die upon a kiss.

(*He [falls upon the bed and] dies.*)

CASSIO: This did I fear, but thought he had no weapon;
   For he was great of heart.

---

331. off: Away.   **334. hold him long:** Keep him alive a long time.   **335. rest:**
Remain.   **338. Soft you:** Wait a moment.   **341. unlucky:** Fatal.   **345. wrought:**
Worked into a frenzy.   **346. Perplexed:** Distraught.   **347. Judean:** Judas Iscariot
(?) (quarto reads "Indian").   **348. subdued:** I.e., conquered by grief.   **357. period:**
Ending.

LODOVICO [*to Iago*]:   O Spartan dog,
  More fell° than anguish, hunger, or the sea!
  Look on the tragic loading of this bed.
  This is thy work. The object poisons sight;
  Let it be hid.° Gratiano, keep° the house,   365
  And seize upon° the fortunes of the Moor,
  For they succeed on you. [*To Cassio*] To you, lord governor,
  Remains the censure° of this hellish villain,
  The time, the place, the torture. O, enforce it!
  Myself will straight aboard, and to the state   370
  This heavy act with heavy heart relate.

                                    (*Exeunt.*)

                                    [1604]

---

363. fell: Cruel.   **365. Let it be hid:** I.e., draw the bed curtains.   **366. seize upon:** Take legal possession of.   **368. censure:** Judicial sentence.

HENRIK IBSEN   [1828–1906]

A Doll House

TRANSLATED BY ROLF FJELDE

The Characters
TORVALD HELMER, *a lawyer*
NORA, *his wife*
DR. RANK
MRS. LINDE
NILS KROGSTAD, *a bank clerk*
THE HELMERS' THREE SMALL CHILDREN
ANNE-MARIE, *their nurse*
HELENE, *a maid*
A DELIVERY BOY

The action takes place in Helmer's residence.

ACT I

(*A comfortable room, tastefully but not expensively furnished. A door to the right in the back wall leads to the entryway; another to the left leads to Helmer's study. Between these doors, a piano. Midway in the left-hand wall a door, and further back a window. Near the window a round table with an armchair and a small sofa. In the right-hand wall, toward the rear, a door, and nearer the foreground a porcelain stove with two armchairs and a rocking chair beside it. Between the stove and the side door, a small table. Engravings on the walls. An étagère° with china figures and other small art objects; a small bookcase with richly bound books; the floor carpeted; a fire burning in the stove. It is a winter day.*)

Note: As Fjelde explains in his foreword to the translation, he does not use the possessive "A Doll's House" because "the house is not Nora's, as the possessive implies." Fjelde believes that Ibsen includes Torvald with Nora in the original title, "for the two of them at the play's opening are still posing like the little marzipan bride and groom atop the wedding cake."
[s.d.] *étagère:* Cabinet with shelves.

(*A bell rings in the entryway; shortly after we hear the door being unlocked. Nora comes into the room, humming happily to herself; she is wearing street clothes and carries an armload of packages, which she puts down on the table to the right. She has left the hall door open, and through it a Delivery Boy is seen holding a Christmas tree and a basket, which he gives to the Maid who lets them in.*)

NORA: Hide the tree well, Helene. The children mustn't get a glimpse of it till this evening, after it's trimmed. (*To the Delivery Boy, taking out her purse.*) How much?

DELIVERY BOY: Fifty, ma'am.

NORA: There's a crown. No, keep the change. (*The Boy thanks her and leaves. Nora shuts the door. She laughs softly to herself while taking off her street things. Drawing a bag of macaroons from her pocket, she eats a couple, then steals over and listens at her husband's study door.*) Yes, he's home. (*Hums again as she moves to the table right.*)

HELMER (*from the study*): Is that my little lark twittering out there?

NORA (*busy opening some packages*): Yes, it is.

HELMER: Is that my squirrel rummaging around?

NORA: Yes!

HELMER: When did my squirrel get in?

NORA: Just now. (*Putting the macaroon bag in her pocket and wiping her mouth.*) Do come in, Torvald, and see what I've bought.

HELMER: Can't be disturbed. (*After a moment he opens the door and peers in, pen in hand.*) Bought, you say? All that there? Has the little spendthrift been out throwing money around again?

NORA: Oh, but Torvald, this year we really should let ourselves go a bit. It's the first Christmas we haven't had to economize.

HELMER: But you know we can't go squandering.

NORA: Oh yes, Torvald, we can squander a little now. Can't we? Just a tiny, wee bit. Now that you've got a big salary and are going to make piles and piles of money.

HELMER: Yes—starting New Year's. But then it's a full three months till the raise comes through.

NORA: Pooh! We can borrow that long.

HELMER: Nora! (*Goes over and playfully takes her by the ear.*) Are your scatterbrains off again? What if today I borrowed a thousand crowns, and you squandered them over Christmas week, and then on New Year's Eve a roof tile fell on my head, and I lay there—

NORA (*putting her hand on his mouth*): Oh! Don't say such things!

HELMER: Yes, but what if it happened—then what?

NORA: If anything so awful happened, then it just wouldn't matter if I had debts or not.

HELMER: Well, but the people I'd borrowed from?

NORA: Them? Who cares about them! They're strangers.

HELMER: Nora, Nora, how like a woman! No, but seriously, Nora, you know what I think about that. No debts! Never borrow! Something of freedom's lost—and something of beauty, too—from a home that's founded on borrowing and debt. We've made a brave stand up to now, the two of us; and we'll go right on like that the little while we have to.

NORA (*going toward the stove*): Yes, whatever you say, Torvald.

HELMER (*following her*): Now, now, the little lark's wings mustn't droop. Come on, don't be a sulky squirrel. (*Taking out his wallet.*) Nora, guess what I have here.

NORA (*turning quickly*): Money!

HELMER: There, see. (*Hands her some notes.*) Good grief, I know how costs go up in a house at Christmastime.

NORA: Ten—twenty—thirty—forty. Oh, thank you, Torvald; I can manage no end on this.

HELMER: You really will have to.

NORA: Oh yes, I promise I will! But come here so I can show you everything I bought. And so cheap! Look, new clothes for Ivar here—and a sword. Here a horse and a trumpet for Bob. And a doll and a doll's bed here for Emmy; they're nothing much, but she'll tear them to bits in no time anyway. And here I have dress material and handkerchiefs for the maids. Old Anne-Marie really deserves something more.

HELMER: And what's in that package there?

NORA (*with a cry*): Torvald, no! You can't see that till tonight!

HELMER: I see. But tell me now, you little prodigal, what have you thought of for yourself?

NORA: For myself? Oh, I don't want anything at all.

HELMER: Of course you do. Tell me just what—within reason—you'd most like to have.

NORA: I honestly don't know. Oh, listen, Torvald—

HELMER: Well?

NORA (*fumbling at his coat buttons, without looking at him*): If you want to give me something, then maybe you could—you could—

HELMER: Come on, out with it.

NORA (*hurriedly*): You could give me money, Torvald. No more than you think you can spare; then one of these days I'll buy something with it.

HELMER: But Nora—

NORA: Oh, please, Torvald darling, do that! I beg you, please. Then I could hang the bills in pretty gilt paper on the Christmas tree. Wouldn't that be fun?

HELMER: What are those little birds called that always fly through their fortunes?

NORA: Oh yes, spendthrifts; I know all that. But let's do as I say, Torvald;

then I'll have time to decide what I really need most. That's very sensible, isn't it?

HELMER (*smiling*): Yes, very—that is, if you actually hung onto the money I give you, and you actually used it to buy yourself something. But it goes for the house and for all sorts of foolish things, and then I only have to lay out some more.

NORA: Oh, but Torvald—

HELMER: Don't deny it, my dear little Nora. (*Putting his arm around her waist.*) Spendthrifts are sweet, but they use up a frightful amount of money. It's incredible what it costs a man to feed such birds.

NORA: Oh, how can you say that! Really, I save everything I can.

HELMER (*laughing*): Yes, that's the truth. Everything you can. But that's nothing at all.

NORA (*humming, with a smile of quiet satisfaction*): Hm, if you only knew what expenses we larks and squirrels have, Torvald.

HELMER: You're an odd little one. Exactly the way your father was. You're never at a loss for scaring up money; but the moment you have it, it runs right out through your fingers; you never know what you've done with it. Well, one takes you as you are. It's deep in your blood. Yes, these things are hereditary, Nora.

NORA: Ah, I could wish I'd inherited many of Papa's qualities.

HELMER: And I couldn't wish you anything but just what you are, my sweet little lark. But wait; it seems to me you have a very—what should I call it?—a very suspicious look today—

NORA: I do?

HELMER: You certainly do. Look me straight in the eye.

NORA (*looking at him*): Well?

HELMER (*shaking an admonitory finger*): Surely my sweet tooth hasn't been running riot in town today, has she?

NORA: No. Why do you imagine that?

HELMER: My sweet tooth really didn't make a little detour through the confectioner's?

NORA: No, I assure you, Torvald—

HELMER: Hasn't nibbled some pastry?

NORA: No, not at all.

HELMER: Not even munched a macaroon or two?

NORA: No, Torvald, I assure you, really—

HELMER: There, there now. Of course I'm only joking.

NORA (*going to the table, right*): You know I could never think of going against you.

HELMER: No, I understand that; and you *have* given me your word. (*Going over to her.*) Well, you keep your little Christmas secrets to yourself, Nora darling. I expect they'll come to light this evening, when the tree is lit.

NORA: Did you remember to ask Dr. Rank?

HELMER: No. But there's no need for that, it's assumed he'll be dining with us. All the same, I'll ask him when he stops by here this morning. I've ordered some fine wine. Nora, you can't imagine how I'm looking forward to this evening.

NORA: So am I. And what fun for the children, Torvald!

HELMER: Ah, it's so gratifying to know that one's gotten a safe, secure job, and with a comfortable salary. It's a great satisfaction, isn't it?

NORA: Oh, it's wonderful!

HELMER: Remember last Christmas? Three whole weeks before, you shut yourself in every evening till long after midnight, making flowers for the Christmas tree, and all the other decorations to surprise us. Ugh, that was the dullest time I've ever lived through.

NORA: It wasn't at all dull for me.

HELMER (smiling): But the outcome *was* pretty sorry, Nora.

NORA: Oh, don't tease me with that again. How could I help it that the cat came in and tore everything to shreds.

HELMER: No, poor thing, you certainly couldn't. You wanted so much to please us all, and that's what counts. But it's just as well that the hard times are past.

NORA: Yes, it's really wonderful.

HELMER: Now I don't have to sit here alone, boring myself, and you don't have to tire your precious eyes and your fair little delicate hands—

NORA (clapping her hands): No, is it really true, Torvald, I don't have to? Oh, how wonderfully lovely to hear! (Taking his arm.) Now I'll tell you just how I've thought we should plan things. Right after Christmas—(The doorbell rings.) Oh, the bell. (Straightening the room up a bit.) Somebody would have to come. What a bore!

HELMER: I'm not at home to visitors, don't forget.

MAID (from the hall doorway): Ma'am, a lady to see you—

NORA: All right, let her come in.

MAID (to Helmer): And the doctor's just come too.

HELMER: Did he go right to my study?

MAID: Yes, he did.

(Helmer goes into his room. The Maid shows in Mrs. Linde, dressed in traveling clothes, and shuts the door after her.)

MRS. LINDE (in a dispirited and somewhat hesitant voice): Hello, Nora.

NORA (uncertain): Hello—

MRS. LINDE: You don't recognize me.

NORA: No, I don't know—but wait, I think—(Exclaiming.) What! Kristine! Is it really you?

MRS. LINDE: Yes, it's me.

NORA: Kristine! To think I didn't recognize you. But then, how could I? (*More quietly.*) How you've changed, Kristine!

MRS. LINDE: Yes, no doubt I have. In nine—ten long years.

NORA: Is it so long since we met! Yes, it's all of that. Oh, these last eight years have been a happy time, believe me. And so now you've come in to town, too. Made the long trip in the winter. That took courage.

MRS. LINDE: I just got here by ship this morning.

NORA: To enjoy yourself over Christmas, of course. Oh, how lovely! Yes, enjoy ourselves, we'll do that. But take your coat off. You're not still cold? (*Helping her.*) There now, let's get cozy here by the stove. No, the easy chair there! I'll take the rocker here. (*Seizing her hands.*) Yes, now you have your old look again; it was only in that first moment. You're a bit more pale, Kristine—and maybe a bit thinner.

MRS. LINDE: And much, much older, Nora.

NORA: Yes, perhaps a bit older; a tiny, tiny bit; not much at all. (*Stopping short; suddenly serious.*) Oh, but thoughtless me, to sit here, chattering away. Sweet, good Kristine, can you forgive me?

MRS. LINDE: What do you mean, Nora?

NORA (*softly*): Poor Kristine, you've become a widow.

MRS. LINDE: Yes, three years ago.

NORA: Oh, I knew it, of course; I read it in the papers. Oh, Kristine, you must believe me; I often thought of writing you then, but I kept postponing it, and something always interfered.

MRS. LINDE: Nora dear, I understand completely.

NORA: No, it was awful of me, Kristine. You poor thing, how much you must have gone through. And he left you nothing?

MRS. LINDE: No.

NORA: And no children?

MRS. LINDE: No.

NORA: Nothing at all, then?

MRS. LINDE: Not even a sense of loss to feed on.

NORA (*looking incredulously at her*): But Kristine, how could that be?

MRS. LINDE (*smiling wearily and smoothing her hair*): Oh, sometimes it happens, Nora.

NORA: So completely alone. How terribly hard that must be for you. I have three lovely children. You can't see them now; they're out with the maid. But now you must tell me everything—

MRS. LINDE: No, no, no, tell me about yourself.

NORA: No, you begin. Today I don't want to be selfish. I want to think only of you today. But there is something I must tell you. Did you hear of the wonderful luck we had recently?

MRS. LINDE: No, what's that?

NORA: My husband's been made manager in the bank, just think!

MRS. LINDE: Your husband? How marvelous!

NORA: Isn't it? Being a lawyer is such an uncertain living, you know, especially if one won't touch any cases that aren't clean and decent. And of course Torvald would never do that, and I'm with him completely there. Oh, we're simply delighted, believe me! He'll join the bank right after New Year's and start getting a huge salary and lots of commissions. From now on we can live quite differently—just as we want. Oh, Kristine, I feel so light and happy! Won't it be lovely to have stacks of money and not a care in the world?

MRS. LINDE: Well, anyway, it would be lovely to have enough for necessities.

NORA: No, not just for necessities, but stacks and stacks of money!

MRS. LINDE (smiling): Nora, Nora, aren't you sensible yet? Back in school you were such a free spender.

NORA (with a quiet laugh): Yes, that's what Torvald still says. (Shaking her finger.) But "Nora, Nora" isn't as silly as you all think. Really, we've been in no position for me to go squandering. We've had to work, both of us.

MRS. LINDE: You too?

NORA: Yes, at odd jobs—needlework, crocheting, embroidery, and such—(casually) and other things too. You remember that Torvald left the department when we were married? There was no chance of promotion in his office, and of course he needed to earn more money. But that first year he drove himself terribly. He took on all kinds of extra work that kept him going morning and night. It wore him down, and then he fell deathly ill. The doctors said it was essential for him to travel south.

MRS. LINDE: Yes, didn't you spend a whole year in Italy?

NORA: That's right. It wasn't easy to get away, you know. Ivar had just been born. But of course we had to go. Oh, that was a beautiful trip, and it saved Torvald's life. But it cost a frightful sum, Kristine.

MRS. LINDE: I can well imagine.

NORA: Four thousand, eight hundred crowns it cost. That's really a lot of money.

MRS. LINDE: But it's lucky you had it when you needed it.

NORA: Well, as it was, we got it from Papa.

MRS. LINDE: I see. It was just about the time your father died.

NORA: Yes, just about then. And, you know, I couldn't make that trip out to nurse him. I had to stay here, expecting Ivar any moment, and with my poor sick Torvald to care for. Dearest Papa, I never saw him again, Kristine. Oh, that was the worst time I've known in all my marriage.

MRS. LINDE: I know how you loved him. And then you went off to Italy?

NORA: Yes. We had the means now, and the doctors urged us. So we left a month after.

MRS. LINDE: And your husband came back completely cured?

NORA: Sound as a drum!

MRS. LINDE: But—the doctor?

NORA: Who?

MRS. LINDE: I thought the maid said he was a doctor, the man who came in with me.

NORA: Yes, that was Dr. Rank—but he's not making a sick call. He's our closest friend, and he stops by at least once a day. No, Torvald hasn't had a sick moment since, and the children are fit and strong, and I am, too. (*Jumping up and clapping her hands.*) Oh, dear God, Kristine, what a lovely thing to live and be happy! But how disgusting of me—I'm talking of nothing but my own affairs. (*Sits on a stool close by Kristine, arms resting across her knees.*) Oh, don't be angry with me! Tell me, is it really true that you weren't in love with your husband? Why did you marry him, then?

MRS. LINDE: My mother was still alive, but bedridden and helpless—and I had my two younger brothers to look after. In all conscience, I didn't think I could turn him down.

NORA: No, you were right there. But was he rich at the time?

MRS. LINDE: He was very well off, I'd say. But the business was shaky, Nora. When he died, it all fell apart, and nothing was left.

NORA: And then—?

MRS. LINDE: Yes, so I had to scrape up a living with a little shop and a little teaching and whatever else I could find. The last three years have been like one endless workday without a rest for me. Now, it's over, Nora. My poor mother doesn't need me, for she's passed on. Nor the boys, either; they're working now and can take care of themselves.

NORA: How free you must feel—

MRS. LINDE: No—only unspeakably empty. Nothing to live for now. (*Standing up anxiously.*) That's why I couldn't take it any longer out in that desolate hole. Maybe here it'll be easier to find something to do and keep my mind occupied. If I could only be lucky enough to get a steady job, some office work—

NORA: Oh, but Kristine, that's so dreadfully tiring, and you already look so tired. It would be much better for you if you could go off to a bathing resort.

MRS. LINDE (*going toward the window*): I have no father to give me travel money, Nora.

NORA (*rising*): Oh, don't be angry with me.

MRS. LINDE (*going to her*): Nora dear, don't you be angry with me. The worst of my kind of situation is all the bitterness that's stored away. No one to work for, and yet you're always having to snap up your opportunities. You have to live; and so you grow selfish. When you told me the happy change in your lot, do you know I was delighted less for your sakes than for mine?

NORA: How so? Oh, I see. You think maybe Torvald could do something for you.

MRS. LINDE: Yes, that's what I thought.

NORA: And he will, Kristine! Just leave it to me; I'll bring it up so delicately—find something attractive to humor him with. Oh, I'm so eager to help you.

MRS. LINDE: How very kind of you, Nora, to be so concerned over me—doubly kind, considering you really know so little of life's burdens yourself.

NORA: I—? I know so little—?

MRS. LINDE (*smiling*): Well, my heavens—a little needlework and such—Nora, you're just a child.

NORA (*tossing her head and pacing the floor*): You don't have to act so superior.

MRS. LINDE: Oh?

NORA: You're just like the others. You all think I'm incapable of anything serious—

MRS. LINDE: Come now—

NORA: That I've never had to face the raw world.

MRS. LINDE: Nora dear, you've just been telling me all your troubles.

NORA: Hm! Trivial! (*Quietly.*) I haven't told you the big thing.

MRS. LINDE: Big thing? What do you mean?

NORA: You look down on me so, Kristine, but you shouldn't. You're proud that you worked so long and hard for your mother.

MRS. LINDE: I don't look down on a soul. But it is true: I'm proud—and happy, too—to think it was given to me to make my mother's last days almost free of care.

NORA: And you're also proud thinking of what you've done for your brothers.

MRS. LINDE: I feel I've a right to be.

NORA: I agree. But listen to this, Kristine—I've also got something to be proud and happy for.

MRS. LINDE: I don't doubt it. But whatever do you mean?

NORA: Not so loud. What if Torvald heard! He mustn't, not for anything in the world. Nobody must know, Kristine. No one but you.

MRS. LINDE: But what is it, then?

NORA: Come here. (*Drawing her down beside her on the sofa.*) It's true—I've also got something to be proud and happy for. I'm the one who saved Torvald's life.

MRS. LINDE: Saved—? Saved how?

NORA: I told you about the trip to Italy. Torvald never would have lived if he hadn't gone south—

MRS. LINDE: Of course; your father gave you the means—

NORA (*smiling*): That's what Torvald and all the rest think, but—

MRS. LINDE: But—?

NORA: Papa didn't give us a pin. I was the one who raised the money.

MRS. LINDE: You? That whole amount?

NORA: Four thousand, eight hundred crowns. What do you say to that?

MRS. LINDE: But Nora, how was it possible? Did you win the lottery?

NORA (*disdainfully*): The lottery? Pooh! No art to that.

MRS. LINDE: But where did you get it from then?

NORA (*humming, with a mysterious smile*): Hmm, tra-la-la-la.

MRS. LINDE: Because you couldn't have borrowed it.

NORA: No? Why not?

MRS. LINDE: A wife can't borrow without her husband's consent.

NORA (*tossing her head*): Oh, but a wife with a little business sense, a wife who knows how to manage—

MRS. LINDE: Nora, I simply don't understand—

NORA: You don't have to. Whoever said I *borrowed* the money? I could have gotten it other ways. (*Throwing herself back on the sofa.*) I could have gotten it from some admirer or other. After all, a girl with my ravishing appeal—

MRS. LINDE: You lunatic.

NORA: I'll bet you're eaten up with curiosity, Kristine.

MRS. LINDE: Now listen here, Nora—you haven't done something indiscreet?

NORA (*sitting up again*): Is it indiscreet to save your husband's life?

MRS. LINDE: I think it's indiscreet that without his knowledge you—

NORA: But that's the point: He mustn't know! My Lord, can't you understand? He mustn't ever know the close call he had. It was to *me* the doctors came to say his life was in danger—that nothing could save him but a stay in the south. Didn't I try strategy then! I began talking about how lovely it would be for me to travel abroad like other young wives; I begged and I cried; I told him please to remember my condition, to be kind and indulge me; and then I dropped a hint that he could easily take out a loan. But at that, Kristine, he nearly exploded. He said I was frivolous, and it was his duty as man of the house not to indulge me in whims and fancies—as I think he called them. Aha, I thought, now you'll just have to be saved—and that's when I saw my chance.

MRS. LINDE: And your father never told Torvald the money wasn't from him?

NORA: No, never. Papa died right about then. I'd considered bringing him into my secret and begging him never to tell. But he was too sick at the time—and then, sadly, it didn't matter.

MRS. LINDE: And you've never confided in your husband since?

NORA: For heaven's sake, no! Are you serious? He's so strict on that subject. Besides—Torvald, with all his masculine pride—how painfully humiliating for him if he ever found out he was in debt to me. That would just ruin our relationship. Our beautiful, happy home would never be the same.

MRS. LINDE: Won't you ever tell him?

NORA (*thoughtfully, half smiling*): Yes—maybe sometime years from now, when I'm no longer so attractive. Don't laugh! I only mean when Torvald loves me less than now, when he stops enjoying my dancing and dressing up and reciting for him. Then it might be wise to have something in reserve—(*Breaking off.*) How ridiculous! That'll never happen—Well, Kristine, what do you think of my big secret? I'm capable of something too, hm? You can imagine, of course, how this thing hangs over me. It really hasn't been easy meeting the payments on time. In the business world there's what they call quarterly interest and what they call amortization, and these are always so terribly hard to manage. I've had to skimp a little here and there, wherever I could, you know. I could hardly spare anything from my house allowance, because Torvald has to live well. I couldn't let the children go poorly dressed; whatever I got for them, I felt I had to use up completely—the darlings!

MRS. LINDE: Poor Nora, so it had to come out of your own budget, then?

NORA: Yes, of course. But I was the one most responsible, too. Every time Torvald gave me money for new clothes and such, I never used more than half; always bought the simplest, cheapest outfits. It was a godsend that everything looks so well on me that Torvald never noticed. But it did weigh me down at times, Kristine. It *is* such a joy to wear fine things. You understand.

MRS. LINDE: Oh, of course.

NORA: And then I found other ways of making money. Last winter I was lucky enough to get a lot of copying to do. I locked myself in and sat writing every evening till late in the night. Ah, I was tired so often, dead tired. But still it was wonderful fun, sitting and working like that, earning money. It was almost like being a man.

MRS. LINDE: But how much have you paid off this way so far?

NORA: That's hard to say, exactly. These accounts, you know, aren't easy to figure. I only know that I've paid out all I could scrape together. Time and again I haven't known where to turn. (*Smiling.*) Then I'd sit here dreaming of a rich old gentleman who had fallen in love with me—

MRS. LINDE: What! Who is he?

NORA: Oh, really! And that he'd died, and when his will was opened, there in big letters it said, "All my fortune shall be paid over in cash, immediately, to that enchanting Mrs. Nora Helmer."

MRS. LINDE: But Nora dear—who *was* this gentleman?

NORA: Good grief, can't you understand? The old man never existed; that was only something I'd dream up time and again whenever I was at my wits' end for money. But it makes no difference now; the old fossil can go where he pleases for all I care; I don't need him or his will—because now I'm free. (*Jumping up.*) Oh, how lovely to think of that, Kristine! Carefree! To know you're carefree, utterly carefree; to be able to romp and play with the children, and to keep up a beautiful, charming home—everything just the way Torvald likes it! And think, spring is coming, with big blue skies. Maybe we can travel a little then. Maybe I'll see the ocean again. Oh yes, it *is* so marvelous to live and be happy!

(*The front doorbell rings.*)

MRS. LINDE (*rising*): There's the bell. It's probably best that I go.

NORA: No, stay. No one's expected. It must be for Torvald.

MAID (*from the hall doorway*): Excuse me, ma'am—there's a gentleman here to see Mr. Helmer, but I didn't know—since the doctor's with him—

NORA: Who is the gentleman?

KROGSTAD (*from the doorway*): It's me, Mrs. Helmer.

(*Mrs. Linde starts and turns away toward the window.*)

NORA (*stepping toward him, tense, her voice a whisper*): You? What is it? Why do you want to speak to my husband?

KROGSTAD: Bank business—after a fashion. I have a small job in the investment bank, and I hear now your husband is going to be our chief—

NORA: In other words, it's—

KROGSTAD: Just dry business, Mrs. Helmer. Nothing but that.

NORA: Yes, then please be good enough to step into the study. (*She nods indifferently as she sees him out by the hall door, then returns and begins stirring up the stove.*)

MRS. LINDE: Nora—who was that man?

NORA: That was a Mr. Krogstad—a lawyer.

MRS. LINDE: Then it really was him.

NORA: Do you know that person?

MRS. LINDE: I did once—many years ago. For a time he was a law clerk in our town.

NORA: Yes, he's been that.

MRS. LINDE: How he's changed.

NORA: I understand he had a very unhappy marriage.

MRS. LINDE: He's a widower now.

NORA: With a number of children. There now, it's burning. (*She closes the stove door and moves the rocker a bit to one side.*)

MRS. LINDE: They say he has a hand in all kinds of business.

NORA: Oh? That may be true; I wouldn't know. But let's not think about business. It's so dull.

(*Dr. Rank enters from Helmer's study.*)

RANK (*still in the doorway*): No, no, really—I don't want to intrude, I'd just as soon talk a little while with your wife. (*Shuts the door, then notices Mrs. Linde.*) Oh, beg pardon. I'm intruding here too.

NORA: No, not at all. (*Introducing him.*) Dr. Rank, Mrs. Linde.

RANK: Well now, that's a name much heard in this house. I believe I passed the lady on the stairs as I came.

MRS. LINDE: Yes, I take the stairs very slowly. They're rather hard on me.

RANK: Uh-hm, some touch of internal weakness?

MRS. LINDE: More overexertion, I'd say.

RANK: Nothing else? Then you're probably here in town to rest up in a round of parties?

MRS. LINDE: I'm here to look for work.

RANK: Is that the best cure for overexertion?

MRS. LINDE: One has to live, Doctor.

RANK: Yes, there's a common prejudice to that effect.

NORA: Oh, come on, Dr. Rank—you really do want to live yourself.

RANK: Yes, I really do. Wretched as I am, I'll gladly prolong my torment indefinitely. All my patients feel like that. And it's quite the same, too, with the morally sick. Right at this moment there's one of those moral invalids in there with Helmer—

MRS. LINDE (*softly*): Ah!

NORA: Who do you mean?

RANK: Oh, it's a lawyer, Krogstad, a type you wouldn't know. His character is rotten to the root—but even he began chattering all-importantly about how he had to *live*.

NORA: Oh? What did he want to talk to Torvald about?

RANK: I really don't know. I only heard something about the bank.

NORA: I didn't know that Krog—that this man Krogstad had anything to do with the bank.

RANK: Yes, he's gotten some kind of berth down there. (*To Mrs. Linde.*) I don't know if you also have, in your neck of the woods, a type of person who scuttles about breathlessly, sniffing out hints of moral corruption, and then maneuvers his victim into some sort of key position where he can keep an eye on him. It's the healthy these days that are out in the cold.

MRS. LINDE: All the same, it's the sick who most need to be taken in.
RANK (*with a shrug*): Yes, there we have it. That's the concept that's turning society into a sanatorium.

(*Nora, lost in her thoughts, breaks out into quiet laughter and claps her hands.*)

RANK: Why do you laugh at that? Do you have any real idea of what society is?
NORA: What do I care about dreary old society? I was laughing at something quite different—something terribly funny. Tell me, Doctor—is everyone who works in the bank dependent now on Torvald?
RANK: Is that what you find so terribly funny?
NORA (*smiling and humming*): Never mind, never mind! (*Pacing the floor.*) Yes, that's really immensely amusing: that we—that Torvald has so much power now over all those people. (*Taking the bag out of her pocket.*) Dr. Rank, a little macaroon on that?
RANK: See here, macaroons! I thought they were contraband here.
NORA: Yes, but these are some that Kristine gave me.
MRS. LINDE: What? I—?
NORA: Now, now, don't be afraid. You couldn't possibly know that Torvald had forbidden them. You see, he's worried they'll ruin my teeth. But hmp! Just this once! Isn't that so, Dr. Rank? Help yourself! (*Puts a macaroon in his mouth.*) And you too, Kristine. And I'll also have one, only a little one—or two, at the most. (*Walking about again.*) Now I'm really tremendously happy. Now's there's just one last thing in the world that I have an enormous desire to do.
RANK: Well! And what's that?
NORA: It's something I have such a consuming desire to say so Torvald could hear.
RANK: And why can't you say it?
NORA: I don't dare. It's quite shocking.
MRS. LINDE: Shocking?
RANK: Well, then it isn't advisable. But in front of us you certainly can. What do you have such a desire to say so Torvald could hear?
NORA: I have such a huge desire to say—to hell and be damned!
RANK: Are you crazy?
MRS. LINDE: My goodness, Nora!
RANK: Go on, say it. Here he is.
NORA (*hiding the macaroon bag*): Shh, shh, shh!

(*Helmer comes in from his study, hat in hand, overcoat over his arm.*)

NORA (*going toward him*): Well, Torvald dear, are you through with him?
HELMER: Yes, he just left.
NORA: Let me introduce you—this is Kristine, who's arrived here in town.
HELMER: Kristine—? I'm sorry, but I don't know—

NORA: Mrs. Linde, Torvald dear. Mrs. Kristine Linde.

HELMER: Of course. A childhood friend of my wife's, no doubt?

MRS. LINDE: Yes, we knew each other in those days.

NORA: And just think, she made the long trip down here in order to talk with you.

HELMER: What's this?

MRS. LINDE: Well, not exactly—

NORA: You see, Kristine is remarkably clever in office work, and so she's terribly eager to come under a capable man's supervision and add more to what she already knows—

HELMER: Very wise, Mrs. Linde.

NORA: And then when she heard that you'd become a bank manager—the story was wired out to the papers—then she came in as fast as she could and—Really, Torvald, for my sake you can do a little something for Kristine, can't you?

HELMER: Yes, it's not at all impossible. Mrs. Linde, I suppose you're a widow?

MRS. LINDE: Yes.

HELMER: Any experience in office work?

MRS. LINDE: Yes, a good deal.

HELMER: Well, it's quite likely that I can make an opening for you—

NORA (clapping her hands): You see, you see!

HELMER: You've come at a lucky moment, Mrs. Linde.

MRS. LINDE: Oh, how can I thank you?

HELMER: Not necessary. (Putting his overcoat on.) But today you'll have to excuse me—

RANK: Wait, I'll go with you. (He fetches his coat from the hall and warms it at the stove.)

NORA: Don't stay out long, dear.

HELMER: An hour; no more.

NORA: Are you going too, Kristine?

MRS. LINDE (putting on her winter garments): Yes, I have to see about a room now.

HELMER: Then perhaps we can all walk together.

NORA (helping her): What a shame we're so cramped here, but it's quite impossible for us to—

MRS. LINDE: Oh, don't even think of it! Good-bye, Nora dear, and thanks for everything.

NORA: Good-bye for now. Of course you'll be back this evening. And you too, Dr. Rank. What? If you're well enough? Oh, you've got to be! Wrap up tight now.

(In a ripple of small talk the company moves out into the hall; children's voices are heard outside on the steps.)

NORA: There they are! There they are! (*She runs to open the door. The children come in with their nurse, Anne-Marie.*) Come in, come in! (*Bends down and kisses them.*) Oh, you darlings—! Look at them, Kristine. Aren't they lovely!

RANK: No loitering in the draft here.

HELMER: Come, Mrs. Linde—this place is unbearable now for anyone but mothers.

Dr. Rank, Helmer, and Mrs. Linde go down the stairs. Anne-Marie goes into the living room with the children. Nora follows, after closing the hall door.)

NORA: How fresh and strong you look. Oh, such red cheeks you have! Like apples and roses. (*The children interrupt her throughout the following.*) And it was so much fun? That's wonderful. Really? You pulled both Emmy and Bob on the sled? Imagine, all together! Yes, you're a clever boy, Ivar. Oh, let me hold her a bit, Anne-Marie. My sweet little doll baby! (*Takes the smallest from the nurse and dances with her.*) Yes, yes, Mama will dance with Bob as well. What? Did you throw snowballs? Oh, if I'd only been there! No, don't bother, Anne-Marie—I'll undress them myself. Oh yes, let me. It's such fun. Go in and rest; you look half frozen. There's hot coffee waiting for you on the stove. (*The nurse goes into the room to the left. Nora takes the children's winter things off, throwing them about, while the children talk to her all at once.*) Is that so? A big dog chased you? But it didn't bite? No, dogs never bite little, lovely doll babies. Don't peek in the packages, Ivar! What is it? Yes, wouldn't you like to know. No, no, it's an ugly something. Well? Shall we play? What shall we play? Hide-and-seek? Yes, let's play hide-and-seek. Bob must hide first. I must? Yes, let me hide first. (*Laughing and shouting, she and the children play in and out of the living room and the adjoining room to the right. At last Nora hides under the table. The children come storming in, search, but cannot find her, then hear her muffled laughter, dash over to the table, lift the cloth up and find her. Wild shouting. She creeps forward as if to scare them. More shouts. Meanwhile, a knock at the hall door; no one has noticed it. Now the door half opens, and Krogstad appears. He waits a moment; the game goes on.*)

KROGSTAD: Beg pardon, Mrs. Helmer—

NORA (*with a strangled cry, turning and scrambling to her knees*): Oh! What do you want?

KROGSTAD: Excuse me. The outer door was ajar; it must be someone forgot to shut it—

NORA (*rising*): My husband isn't home, Mr. Krogstad.

KROGSTAD: I know that.

NORA: Yes—then what do you want here?

KROGSTAD: A word with you.

NORA: With—? (*To the children, quietly.*) Go in to Anne-Marie. What? No,

the strange man won't hurt Mama. When he's gone, we'll play some
more. (*She leads the children into the room to the left and shuts the door*
after them. Then, tense and nervous:) You want to speak to me?

KROGSTAD: Yes, I want to.

NORA: Today? But it's not yet the first of the month—

KROGSTAD: No, it's Christmas Eve. It's going to be up to you how merry a
Christmas you have.

NORA: What is it you want? Today I absolutely can't—

KROGSTAD: We won't talk about that till later. This is something else. You
do have a moment to spare, I suppose?

NORA: Oh yes, of course—I do, except—

KROGSTAD: Good. I was sitting over at Olsen's Restaurant when I saw
your husband go down the street—

NORA: Yes?

KROGSTAD: With a lady.

NORA: Yes. So?

KROGSTAD: If you'll pardon my asking: Wasn't that lady a Mrs. Linde?

NORA: Yes.

KROGSTAD: Just now come into town?

NORA: Yes, today.

KROGSTAD: She's a good friend of yours?

NORA: Yes, she is. But I don't see—

KROGSTAD: I also knew her once.

NORA: I'm aware of that.

KROGSTAD: Oh? You know all about it. I thought so. Well, then let me ask
you short and sweet: Is Mrs. Linde getting a job in the bank?

NORA: What makes you think you can cross-examine me, Mr. Krogstad—
you, one of my husband's employees? But since you ask, you might as
well know—yes, Mrs. Linde's going to be taken on at the bank. And I'm
the one who spoke for her, Mr. Krogstad. Now you know.

KROGSTAD: So I guessed right.

NORA (*pacing up and down*): Oh, one does have a tiny bit of influence, I
should hope. Just because I am a woman, don't think it means
that—When one has a subordinate position, Mr. Krogstad, one really
ought to be careful about pushing somebody who—hm—

KROGSTAD: Who has influence?

NORA: That's right.

KROGSTAD (*in a different tone*): Mrs. Helmer, would you be good enough to
use your influence on my behalf?

NORA: What? What do you mean?

KROGSTAD: Would you please make sure that I keep my subordinate position in the bank?

NORA: What does that mean? Who's thinking of taking away your
position?

KROGSTAD: Oh, don't play the innocent with me. I'm quite aware that your friend would hardly relish the chance of running into me again; and I'm also aware now whom I can thank for being turned out.

NORA: But I promise you—

KROGSTAD: Yes, yes, yes, to the point: There's still time, and I'm advising you to use your influence to prevent it.

NORA: But Mr. Krogstad, I have absolutely no influence.

KROGSTAD: You haven't? I thought you were just saying—

NORA: You shouldn't take me so literally. I! How can you believe that I have any such influence over my husband?

KROGSTAD: Oh, I've known your husband from our student days. I don't think the great bank manager's more steadfast than any other married man.

NORA: You speak insolently about my husband, and I'll show you the door.

KROGSTAD: The lady has spirit.

NORA: I'm not afraid of you any longer. After New Year's, I'll soon be done with the whole business.

KROGSTAD (*restraining himself*): Now listen to me, Mrs. Helmer. If necessary, I'll fight for my little job in the bank as if it were life itself.

NORA: Yes, so it seems.

KROGSTAD: It's not just a matter of income; that's the least of it. It's something else—All right, out with it! Look, this is the thing. You know, just like all the others, of course, that once, a good many years ago, I did something rather rash.

NORA: I've heard rumors to that effect.

KROGSTAD: The case never got into court; but all the same, every door was closed in my face from then on. So I took up those various activities you know about. I had to grab hold somewhere; and I dare say I haven't been among the worst. But now I want to drop all that. My boys are growing up. For their sakes, I'll have to win back as much respect as possible here in town. That job in the bank was like the first rung in my ladder. And now your husband wants to kick me right back down in the mud again.

NORA: But for heaven's sake, Mr. Krogstad, it's simply not in my power to help you.

KROGSTAD: That's because you haven't the will to—but I have the means to make you.

NORA: You certainly won't tell my husband that I owe you money?

KROGSTAD: Hm—what if I told him that?

NORA: That would be shameful of you. (*Nearly in tears.*) This secret—my joy and my pride—that he should learn it in such a crude and disgusting way—learn it from you. You'd expose me to the most horrible unpleasantness—

KROGSTAD: Only unpleasantness?

NORA (*vehemently*): But go on and try. It'll turn out the worse for you, because then my husband will really see what a crook you are, and then you'll never be able to hold your job.

KROGSTAD: I asked if it was just domestic unpleasantness you were afraid of?

NORA: If my husband finds out, then of course he'll pay what I owe at once, and then we'd be through with you for good.

KROGSTAD (*a step closer*): Listen, Mrs. Helmer—you've either got a very bad memory, or else no head at all for business. I'd better put you a little more in touch with the facts.

NORA: What do you mean?

KROGSTAD: When your husband was sick, you came to me for a loan of four thousand, eight hundred crowns.

NORA: Where else could I go?

KROGSTAD: I promised to get you that sum—

NORA: And you got it.

KROGSTAD: I promised to get you that sum, on certain conditions. You were so involved in your husband's illness, and so eager to finance your trip, that I guess you didn't think out all the details. It might just be a good idea to remind you. I promised you the money on the strength of a note I drew up.

NORA: Yes, and that I signed.

KROGSTAD: Right. But at the bottom I added some lines for your father to guarantee the loan. He was supposed to sign down there.

NORA: Supposed to? He did sign.

KROGSTAD: I left the date blank. In other words, your father would have dated his signature himself. Do you remember that?

NORA: Yes, I think—

KROGSTAD: Then I gave you the note for you to mail to your father. Isn't that so?

NORA: Yes.

KROGSTAD: And naturally you sent it at once—because only some five, six days later you brought me the note, properly signed. And with that, the money was yours.

NORA: Well, then; I've made my payments regularly, haven't I?

KROGSTAD: More or less. But—getting back to the point—those were hard times for you then, Mrs. Helmer.

NORA: Yes, they were.

KROGSTAD: Your father was very ill, I believe.

NORA: He was near the end.

KROGSTAD: He died soon after?

NORA: Yes.

KROGSTAD: Tell me, Mrs. Helmer, do you happen to recall the date of your father's death? The day of the month, I mean.

NORA: Papa died the twenty-ninth of September.

KROGSTAD: That's quite correct; I've already looked into that. And now we come to a curious thing — (*taking out a paper*) which I simply cannot comprehend.

NORA: Curious thing? I don't know —

KROGSTAD: This is the curious thing: that your father co-signed the note for your loan three days after his death.

NORA: How—? I don't understand.

KROGSTAD: Your father died the twenty-ninth of September. But look. Here your father dated his signature October second. Isn't that curious, Mrs. Helmer? (*Nora is silent.*) Can you explain it to me? (*Nora remains silent.*) It's also remarkable that the words "October second" and the year aren't written in your father's hand, but rather in one that I think I know. Well, it's easy to understand. Your father forgot perhaps to date his signature, and then someone or other added it, a bit sloppily, before anyone knew of his death. There's nothing wrong in that. It all comes down to the signature. And there's no question about *that*, Mrs. Helmer. It really *was* your father who signed his own name here, wasn't it?

NORA (*after a short silence, throwing her head back and looking squarely at him*): No, it wasn't. *I* signed Papa's name.

KROGSTAD: Wait, now—are you fully aware that this is a dangerous confession?

NORA: Why? You'll soon get your money.

KROGSTAD: Let me ask you a question—why didn't you send the paper to your father?

NORA: That was impossible. Papa was so sick. If I'd asked him for his signature, I also would have had to tell him what the money was for. But I couldn't tell him, sick as he was, that my husband's life was in danger. That was just impossible.

KROGSTAD: Then it would have been better if you'd given up the trip abroad.

NORA: I couldn't possibly. The trip was to save my husband's life. I couldn't give that up.

KROGSTAD: But didn't you ever consider that this was a fraud against me?

NORA: I couldn't let myself be bothered by that. You weren't any concern of mine. I couldn't stand you, with all those cold complications you made, even though you knew how badly off my husband was.

KROGSTAD: Mrs. Helmer, obviously you haven't the vaguest idea of what you've involved yourself in. But I can tell you this: It was nothing more and nothing worse that I once did—and it wrecked my whole reputation.

NORA: You? Do you expect me to believe that you ever acted bravely to save your wife's life?

KROGSTAD: Laws don't inquire into motives.

NORA: Then they must be very poor laws.

KROGSTAD: Poor or not—if I introduce this paper in court, you'll be judged according to law.

NORA: This I refuse to believe. A daughter hasn't a right to protect her dying father from anxiety and care? A wife hasn't a right to save her husband's life? I don't know much about laws, but I'm sure that somewhere in the books these things are allowed. And you don't know anything about it—you who practice the law? You must be an awful lawyer, Mr. Krogstad.

KROGSTAD: Could be. But business—the kind of business we two are mixed up in—don't you think I know about that? All right. Do what you want now. But I'm telling you *this*: If I get shoved down a second time, you're going to keep me company. (*He bows and goes out through the hall.*)

NORA (*pensive for a moment, then tossing her head*): Oh, really! Trying to frighten me! I'm not so silly as all that. (*Begins gathering up the children's clothes, but soon stops.*) But—? No, but that's impossible! I did it out of love.

THE CHILDREN (*in the doorway, left*): Mama, that strange man's gone out the door.

NORA: Yes, yes, I know it. But don't tell anyone about the strange man. Do you hear? Not even Papa!

THE CHILDREN: No, Mama. But now will you play again?

NORA: No, not now.

THE CHILDREN: Oh, but Mama, you promised.

NORA: Yes, but I can't now. Go inside; I have too much to do. Go in, go in, my sweet darlings. (*She herds them gently back in the room and shuts the door after them. Settling on the sofa, she takes up a piece of embroidery and makes some stitches, but soon stops abruptly.*) No! (*Throws the work aside, rises, goes to the hall door and calls out.*) Helene! Let me have the tree in here. (*Goes to the table, left, opens the table drawer, and stops again.*) No, but that's utterly impossible!

MAID (*with the Christmas tree*): Where should I put it, ma'am?

NORA: There. The middle of the floor.

MAID: Should I bring anything else?

NORA: No, thanks. I have what I need.

(*The Maid, who has set the tree down, goes out.*)

NORA (*absorbed in trimming the tree*): Candles here—and flowers here. That terrible creature! Talk, talk, talk! There's nothing to it at all. The tree's going to be lovely. I'll do anything to please you Torvald. I'll sing for you, dance for you—

(*Helmer comes in from the hall, with a sheaf of papers under his arm.*)

NORA: Oh! You're back so soon?

HELMER: Yes. Has anyone been here?

NORA: Here? No.

HELMER: That's odd. I saw Krogstad leaving the front door.

NORA: So? Oh yes, that's true. Krogstad was here a moment.

HELMER: Nora, I can see by your face that he's been here, begging you to put in a good word for him.

NORA: Yes.

HELMER: And it was supposed to seem like your own idea? You were to hide it from me that he'd been here. He asked you that, too, didn't he?

NORA: Yes, Torvald, but—

HELMER: Nora, Nora, and you could fall for that? Talk with that sort of person and promise him anything? And then in the bargain, tell me an untruth.

NORA: An untruth—?

HELMER: Didn't you say that no one had been here? (*Wagging his finger.*) My little songbird must never do that again. A songbird needs a clean beak to warble with. No false notes. (*Putting his arm about her waist.*) That's the way it should be, isn't it? Yes, I'm sure of it. (*Releasing her.*) And so, enough of that. (*Sitting by the stove.*) Ah, how snug and cozy it is here. (*Leafing among his papers.*)

NORA (*busy with the tree, after a short pause*): Torvald!

HELMER: Yes.

NORA: I'm so much looking forward to the Stenborgs' costume party, day after tomorrow.

HELMER: And I can't wait to see what you'll surprise me with.

NORA: Oh, that stupid business!

HELMER: What?

NORA: I can't find anything that's right. Everything seems so ridiculous, so inane.

HELMER: So my little Nora's come to *that* recognition?

NORA (*going behind his chair, her arms resting on its back*): Are you very busy, Torvald?

HELMER: Oh—

NORA: What papers are those?

HELMER: Bank matters.

NORA: Already?

HELMER: I've gotten full authority from the retiring management to make all necessary changes in personnel and procedure. I'll need

Christmas week for that. I want to have everything in order by New Year's.

NORA: So that was the reason this poor Krogstad—

HELMER: Hm.

NORA (*still leaning on the chair and slowly stroking the nape of his neck*): If you weren't so very busy, I would have asked you an enormous favor, Torvald.

HELMER: Let's hear. What is it?

NORA: You know, there isn't anyone who has your good taste—and I want so much to look well at the costume party. Torvald, couldn't you take over and decide what I should be and plan my costume?

HELMER: Ah, is my stubborn little creature calling for a lifeguard?

NORA: Yes, Torvald, I can't get anywhere without your help.

HELMER: All right—I'll think it over. We'll hit on something.

NORA: Oh, how sweet of you. (*Goes to the tree again. Pause.*) Aren't the red flowers pretty—? But tell me, was it really such a crime that this Krogstad committed?

HELMER: Forgery. Do you have any idea what that means?

NORA: Couldn't he have done it out of need?

HELMER: Yes, or thoughtlessness, like so many others. I'm not so heartless that I'd condemn a man categorically for just one mistake.

NORA: No, of course not, Torvald!

HELMER: Plenty of men have redeemed themselves by openly confessing their crimes and taking their punishment.

NORA: Punishment—?

HELMER: But now Krogstad didn't go that way. He got himself out by sharp practices, and that's the real cause of his moral breakdown.

NORA: Do you really think that would—?

HELMER: Just imagine how a man with that sort of guilt in him has to lie and cheat and deceive on all sides, has to wear a mask even with the nearest and dearest he has, even with his own wife and children. And with the children, Nora—that's where it's most horrible.

NORA: Why?

HELMER: Because that kind of atmosphere of lies infects the whole life of a home. Every breath the children take in is filled with the germs of something degenerate.

NORA (*coming closer behind him*): Are you sure of that?

HELMER: Oh, I've seen it often enough as a lawyer. Almost everyone who goes bad early in life has a mother who's a chronic liar.

NORA: Why just—the mother?

HELMER: It's usually the mother's influence that's dominant, but the father's works in the same way, of course. Every lawyer is quite familiar with it. And still this Krogstad's been going home year in, year out, poisoning his own children with lies and pretense; that's why I call him morally lost. (*Reaching his hands out toward her.*) So my sweet little Nora must promise me never to plead his cause. Your hand on it. Come, come, what's this? Give me your hand. There, now. All settled. I can tell you it'd be impossible for me to work alongside of him. I literally feel physically revolted when I'm anywhere near such a person.

NORA (*withdraws her hand and goes to the other side of the Christmas tree*): How hot it is here! And I've got so much to do.

HELMER (*getting up and gathering his papers*): Yes, and I have to think about getting some of these read through before dinner. I'll think about your costume, too. And something to hang on the tree in gilt paper, I may even see about that. (*Putting his hand on her head.*) Oh you, my darling little songbird. (*He goes into his study and closes the door after him.*)

NORA (*softly, after a silence*): Oh, really! It isn't so. It's impossible. It must be impossible.

ANNE-MARIE (*in the doorway left*): The children are begging so hard to come in to Mama.

NORA: No, no, no, don't let them in to me! You stay with them, Anne-Marie.

ANNE-MARIE: Of course, ma'am. (*Closes the door.*)

NORA (*pale with terror*): Hurt my children—! Poison my home? (*A moment's pause; then she tosses her head.*) That's not true. Never. Never in all the world.

ACT II

(*Same room. Beside the piano the Christmas tree now stands stripped of ornament, burned-down candle stubs on its ragged branches. Nora's street clothes lie on the sofa. Nora, alone in the room, moves restlessly about; at last she stops at the sofa and picks up her coat.*)

NORA (*dropping the coat again*): Someone's coming! (*Goes toward the door, listens.*) No—there's no one. Of course—nobody's coming today, Christmas Day—or tomorrow, either. But maybe—(*Opens the door and looks out.*) No, nothing in the mailbox. Quite empty. (*Coming forward.*) What nonsense! He won't do anything serious. Nothing terrible could happen. It's impossible. Why, I have three small children.

(*Anne-Marie, with a large carton, comes in from the room to the left.*)

ANNE-MARIE: Well, at last I found the box with the masquerade clothes.

NORA: Thanks. Put it on the table.

ANNE-MARIE (*does so*): But they're all pretty much of a mess.

NORA: Ahh! I'd love to rip them in a million pieces!

ANNE-MARIE: Oh, mercy, they can be fixed right up. Just a little patience.

NORA: Yes, I'll go get Mrs. Linde to help me.

ANNE-MARIE: Out again now? In this nasty weather? Miss Nora will catch cold—get sick.

NORA: Oh, worse things could happen—How are the children?

ANNE-MARIE: The poor mites are playing with their Christmas presents, but—

NORA: Do they ask for me much?

ANNE-MARIE: They're so used to having Mama around, you know.

NORA: Yes, but Anne-Marie, I *can't* be together with them as much as I was.

ANNE-MARIE: Well, small children get used to anything.

NORA: You think so? Do you think they'd forget their mother if she was gone for good?

ANNE-MARIE: Oh, mercy—gone for good!

NORA: Wait, tell me. Anne-Marie—I've wondered so often—how could you ever have the heart to give your child over to strangers?

ANNE-MARIE: But I had to, you know, to become little Nora's nurse.

NORA: Yes, but how could you *do* it?

ANNE-MARIE: When I could get such a good place? A girl who's poor and who's gotten in trouble is glad enough for that. Because that slippery fish, he didn't do a thing for me, you know.

NORA: But your daughter's surely forgotten you.

ANNE-MARIE: Oh, she certainly has not. She's written to me, both when she was confirmed and when she was married.

NORA (*clasping her about the neck*): You old Anne-Marie, you were a good mother for me when I was little.

ANNE-MARIE: Poor little Nora, with no other mother but me.

NORA: And if the babies didn't have one, then I know that you'd—What silly talk! (*Opening the carton.*) Go in to them. Now I'll have to—Tomorrow you can see how lovely I'll look.

ANNE-MARIE: Oh, there won't be anyone at the party as lovely as Miss Nora. (*She goes off into the room, left.*)

NORA (*begins unpacking the box, but soon throws it aside*): Oh, if I dared to go out. If only nobody would come. If only nothing would happen here while I'm out. What craziness—nobody's coming. Just don't think. This muff—needs a brushing. Beautiful gloves, beautiful gloves. Let it go. Let it go! One, two, three, four, five, six—(*With a cry.*) Oh, there they are! (*Poises to move toward the door, but remains irresolutely standing. Mrs. Linde enters from the hall, where she has removed her street clothes.*)

NORA: Oh, it's you, Kristine. There's no one else out there? How good that you've come.

MRS. LINDE: I hear you were up asking for me.

NORA: Yes, I just stopped by. There's something you really can help me with. Let's get settled on the sofa. Look, there's going to be a costume party tomorrow evening at the Stenborgs' right above us, and now Torvald wants me to go as a Neapolitan peasant girl and dance the tarantella that I learned in Capri.

MRS. LINDE: Really, are you giving a whole performance?

NORA: Torvald says yes, I should. See, here's the dress. Torvald had it made for me down there; but now it's all so tattered that I just don't know—

MRS. LINDE: Oh, we'll fix that up in no time. It's nothing more than the trimmings—they're a bit loose here and there. Needle and thread? Good, now we have what we need.

NORA: Oh, how sweet of you!

MRS. LINDE (*sewing*): So you'll be in disguise tomorrow, Nora. You know what? I'll stop by then for a moment and have a look at you all dressed up. But listen, I've absolutely forgotten to thank you for that pleasant evening yesterday.

NORA (*getting up and walking about*): I don't think it was as pleasant as usual yesterday. You should have come to town a bit sooner, Kristine—Yes, Torvald really knows how to give a home elegance and charm.

MRS. LINDE: And you do, too, if you ask me. You're not your father's daughter for nothing. But tell me, is Dr. Rank always so down in the mouth as yesterday?

NORA: No, that was quite an exception. But he goes around critically ill all the time—tuberculosis of the spine, poor man. You know, his father was a disgusting thing who kept mistresses and so on—and that's why the son's been sickly from birth.

MRS. LINDE (*lets her sewing fall to her lap*): But my dearest Nora, how do you know about such things?

NORA (*walking more jauntily*): Hmp! When you've had three children, then you've had a few visits from—from women who know something of medicine, and they tell you this and that.

MRS. LINDE (*resumes sewing; a short pause*): Does Dr. Rank come here every day?

NORA: Every blessed day. He's Torvald's best friend from childhood, and *my* good friend, too. Dr. Rank almost belongs to this house.

MRS. LINDE: But tell me—is he quite sincere? I mean, doesn't he rather enjoy flattering people?

NORA: Just the opposite. Why do you think that?

MRS. LINDE: When you introduced us yesterday, he was proclaiming that he'd often heard my name in this house; but later I noticed that your husband hadn't the slightest idea who I really was. So how could Dr. Rank—?

NORA: But it's all true, Kristine. You see, Torvald loves me beyond words, and, as he puts it, he'd like to keep me all to himself. For a long time he'd almost be jealous if I even mentioned any of my old friends back home. So of course I dropped that. But with Dr. Rank I talk a lot about such things because he likes hearing about them.

MRS. LINDE: Now listen, Nora; in many ways you're still like a child. I'm a good deal older than you, with a little more experience. I'll tell you something: You ought to put an end to all this with Dr. Rank.

NORA: What should I put an end to?

MRS. LINDE: Both parts of it, I think. Yesterday you said something about a rich admirer who'd provide you with money—

NORA: Yes, one who doesn't exist—worse luck. So?

MRS. LINDE: Is Dr. Rank well off?

NORA: Yes, he is.

MRS. LINDE: With no dependents?

NORA: No, no one. But—

MRS. LINDE: And he's over here every day?

NORA: Yes, I told you that.

MRS. LINDE: How can a man of such refinement be so grasping?

NORA: I don't follow you at all.

MRS. LINDE: Now don't try to hide it, Nora. You think I can't guess who loaned you the forty-eight hundred crowns?

NORA: Are you out of your mind? How could you think such a thing! A friend of ours, who comes here every single day. What an intolerable situation that would have been!

MRS. LINDE: Then it really wasn't him.

NORA: No, absolutely not. It never even crossed my mind for a moment—And he had nothing to lend in those days; his inheritance came later.

MRS. LINDE: Well, I think that was a stroke of luck for you, Nora dear.

NORA: No, it never would have occurred to me to ask Dr. Rank—Still, I'm quite sure that if I had asked him—

MRS. LINDE: Which you won't, of course.

NORA: No, of course not. I can't see that I'd ever need to. But I'm quite positive that if I talked to Dr. Rank—

MRS. LINDE: Behind your husband's back?

NORA: I've got to clear up this other thing; *that's* also behind his back. I've *got* to clear it all up.

MRS. LINDE: Yes, I was saying that yesterday, but—

NORA (*pacing up and down*): A man handles these problems so much better than a woman—

MRS. LINDE: One's husband does, yes.

NORA: Nonsense. (*Stopping.*) When you pay everything you owe, then you get your note back, right?

MRS. LINDE: Yes, naturally.

NORA: And can rip it into a million pieces and burn it up—that filthy scrap of paper!

MRS. LINDE (*looking hard at her, laying her sewing aside, and rising slowly*): Nora, you're hiding something from me.

NORA: You can see it in my face?

MRS. LINDE: Something's happened to you since yesterday morning. Nora, what is it?

NORA (*hurrying toward her*): Kristine! (*Listening.*) Shh! Torvald's home. Look, go in with the children a while. Torvald can't bear all this snipping and stitching. Let Anne-Marie help you.

MRS. LINDE (*gathering up some of the things*): All right, but I'm not leaving here until we've talked this out. (*She disappears into the room, left, as Torvald enters from the hall.*)

NORA: Oh, how I've been waiting for you, Torvald dear.

HELMER: Was that the dressmaker?

NORA: No, that was Kristine. She's helping me fix up my costume. You know, it's going to be quite attractive.

HELMER: Yes, wasn't that a bright idea I had?

NORA: Brilliant! But then wasn't I good as well to give in to you?

HELMER: Good—because you give in to your husband's judgment? All right, you little goose, I know you didn't mean it like that. But I won't disturb you. You'll want to have a fitting, I suppose.

NORA: And you'll be working?

HELMER: Yes. (*Indicating a bundle of papers.*) See. I've been down to the bank. (*Starts toward his study.*)

NORA: Torvald.

HELMER (*stops*): Yes.

NORA: If your little squirrel begged you, with all her heart and soul, for something—?

HELMER: What's that?

NORA: Then would you do it?

HELMER: First, naturally, I'd have to know what it was.

NORA: Your squirrel would scamper about and do tricks, if you'd only be sweet and give in.

HELMER: Out with it.

NORA: Your lark would be singing high and low in every room—

HELMER: Come on, she does that anyway.

NORA: I'd be a wood nymph and dance for you in the moonlight.

HELMER: Nora—don't tell me it's that same business from this morning?

NORA (*coming closer*): Yes, Torvald, I beg you, please!

HELMER: And you actually have the nerve to drag that up again?

NORA: Yes, yes, you've got to give in to me; you *have* to let Krogstad keep his job in the bank.

HELMER: My dear Nora, I've slated his job for Mrs. Linde.

NORA: That's awfully kind of you. But you could just fire another clerk instead of Krogstad.

HELMER: This is the most incredible stubbornness! Because you go and give an impulsive promise to speak up for him, I'm expected to—

NORA: That's not the reason, Torvald. It's for your own sake. That man does writing for the worst papers; you said it yourself. He could do you any amount of harm. I'm scared to death of him—

HELMER: Ah, I understand. It's the old memories haunting you.

NORA: What do you mean by that?

HELMER: Of course, you're thinking about your father.

NORA: Yes, all right. Just remember how those nasty gossips wrote in the papers about Papa and slandered him so cruelly. I think they'd have had him dismissed if the department hadn't sent you up to investigate, and if you hadn't been so kind and open-minded toward him.

HELMER: My dear Nora, there's a notable difference between your father and me. Your father's official career was hardly above reproach. But mine is; and I hope it'll stay that way as long as I hold my position.

NORA: Oh, who can ever tell what vicious minds can invent? We could be so snug and happy now in our quiet, carefree home—you and I and the children, Torvald! That's why I'm pleading with you so—

HELMER: And just by pleading for him you make it impossible for me to keep him on. It's already known at the bank that I'm firing Krogstad. What if it's rumored around now that the new bank manager was vetoed by his wife—

NORA: Yes, what then—?

HELMER: Oh yes—as long as our little bundle of stubbornness gets her way—! I should go and make myself ridiculous in front of the whole office—give people the idea I can be swayed by all kinds of outside pressure. Oh, you can bet I'd feel the effects of that soon enough! Besides—there's something that rules Krogstad right out at the bank as long as I'm the manager.

NORA: What's that?

HELMER: His moral failings I could maybe overlook if I had to—

NORA: Yes, Torvald, why not?

HELMER: And I hear he's quite efficient on the job. But he was a crony of mine back in my teens—one of those rash friendships that crop up again and again to embarrass you later in life. Well, I might as well say it straight out: We're on a first-name basis. And that tactless fool makes no effort at all to hide it in front of others. Quite the contrary—he thinks that entitles him to take a familiar air around me, and so every other second he comes booming out with his, "Yes, Torvald!" and "Sure thing, Torvald!" I tell you, it's been excruciating for me. He's out to make my place in the bank unbearable.

NORA: Torvald, you can't be serious about all this.

HELMER: Oh no? Why not?

NORA: Because these are such petty considerations.

HELMER: What are you saying? Petty? You think I'm petty!

NORA: No, just the opposite, Torvald dear. That's exactly why—

HELMER: Never mind. You call my motives petty; then I might as well be just that. Petty! All right! We'll put a stop to this for good. (*Goes to the hall door and calls.*) Helene!

NORA: What do you want?

HELMER (*searching among his papers*): A decision. (*The Maid comes in.*) Look here; take this letter; go out with it at once. Get hold of a messenger and have him deliver it. Quick now. It's already addressed. Wait, here's some money.

MAID: Yes, sir. (*She leaves with the letter.*)

HELMER (*straightening his papers*): There, now, little Miss Willful.

NORA (*breathlessly*): Torvald, what was that letter?

HELMER: Krogstad's notice.

NORA: Call it back, Torvald! There's still time. Oh, Torvald, call it back! Do it for my sake—for your sake, for the children's sake! Do you hear, Torvald; do it! You don't know how this can harm us.

HELMER: Too late.

NORA: Yes, too late.

HELMER: Nora, dear, I can forgive you this panic, even though basically you're insulting me. Yes, you are! Or isn't it an insult to think that *I* should be afraid of a courtroom hack's revenge? But I forgive you anyway, because this shows so beautifully how much you love me. (*Takes her in his arms.*) This is the way it should be, my darling Nora. Whatever comes, you'll see: When it really counts, I have strength and courage enough as a man to take on the whole weight myself.

NORA (*terrified*): What do you mean by that?

HELMER: The whole weight, I said.

NORA (*resolutely*): No, never in all the world.

HELMER: Good. So we'll share it, Nora, as man and wife. That's as it should be. (*Fondling her.*) Are you happy now? There, there, there—not these frightened dove's eyes. It's nothing at all but empty fantasies— Now you should run through your tarantella and practice your tambourine. I'll go to the inner office, and shut both doors, so I won't hear a thing; you can make all the noise you like. (*Turning in the doorway.*)

And when Rank comes, just tell him where he can find me. (*He nods to her and goes with his papers into the study, closing the door.*)

NORA (*standing as though rooted, dazed with fright, in a whisper*): He really could do it. He will do it. He'll do it in spite of everything. No, not that, never, never! Anything but that! Escape! A way out—(*The doorbell rings.*) Dr. Rank! Anything but that! *Anything*, whatever it is! (*Her hands pass over her face, smoothing it; she pulls herself together, goes over and opens the hall door. Dr. Rank stands outside, hanging his fur coat up. During the following scene, it begins getting dark.*)

NORA: Hello, Dr. Rank. I recognized your ring. But you mustn't go in to Torvald yet; I believe he's working.

RANK: And you?

NORA: For you, I always have an hour to spare—you know that. (*He has entered, and she shuts the door after him.*)

RANK: Many thanks. I'll make use of these hours while I can.

NORA: What do you mean by that? While you can?

RANK: Does that disturb you?

NORA: Well, it's such an odd phrase. Is anything going to happen?

RANK: What's going to happen is what I've been expecting so long—but I honestly didn't think it would come so soon.

NORA (*gripping his arm*): What is it you've found out? Dr. Rank, you have to tell me!

RANK (*sitting by the stove*): It's all over with me. There's nothing to be done about it.

NORA (*breathing easier*): Is it you—then—?

RANK: Who else? There's no point in lying to one's self. I'm the most miserable of all my patients, Mrs. Helmer. These past few days I've been auditing my internal accounts. Bankrupt! Within a month I'll probably be laid out and rotting in the churchyard.

NORA: Oh, what a horrible thing to say.

RANK: The thing itself is horrible. But the worst of it is all the other horror before it's over. There's only one final examination left; when I'm finished with that, I'll know about when my disintegration will begin. There's something I want to say. Helmer with his sensitivity has such a sharp distaste for anything ugly. I don't want him near my sickroom.

NORA: Oh, but Dr. Rank—

RANK: I won't have him in there. Under no condition. I'll lock my door to him—As soon as I'm completely sure of the worst, I'll send you my calling card marked with a black cross, and you'll know then the wreck has started to come apart.

NORA: No, today you're completely unreasonable. And I wanted you so much to be in a really good humor.

RANK: With death up my sleeve? And then to suffer this way for some-body else's sins. Is there any justice in that? And in every single family, in some way or another, this inevitable retribution of nature goes on—

NORA (*her hands pressed over her ears*): Oh, stuff! Cheer up! Please—be gay!

RANK: Yes, I'd just as soon laugh at it all. My poor, innocent spine, serving time for my father's gay army days.

NORA (*by the table, left*): He was so infatuated with asparagus tips and pâté de foie gras, wasn't that it?

RANK: Yes—and with truffles.

NORA: Truffles, yes. And then with oysters, I suppose?

RANK: Yes, tons of oysters, naturally.

NORA: And then the port and champagne to go with it. It's so sad that all these delectable things have to strike at our bones.

RANK: Especially when they strike at the unhappy bones that never shared in the fun.

NORA: Ah, that's the saddest of all.

RANK (*looks searchingly at her*): Hm.

NORA (*after a moment*): Why did you smile?

RANK: No, it was you who laughed.

NORA: No, it was you who smiled, Dr. Rank!

RANK (*getting up*): You're even a bigger tease than I'd thought.

NORA: I'm full of wild ideas today.

RANK: That's obvious.

NORA (*putting both hands on his shoulders*): Dear, dear Dr. Rank, you'll never die for Torvald and me.

RANK: Oh, that loss you'll easily get over. Those who go away are soon forgotten.

NORA (*looks fearfully at him*): You believe that?

RANK: One makes new connections, and then—

NORA: Who makes new connections?

RANK: Both you and Torvald will when I'm gone. I'd say you're well under way already. What was that Mrs. Linde doing here last evening?

NORA: Oh, come—you can't be jealous of poor Kristine?

RANK: Oh yes, I am. She'll be my successor here in the house. When I'm down under, that woman will probably—

NORA: Shh! Not so loud. She's right in there.

RANK: Today as well. So you see.

NORA: Only to sew on my dress. Good gracious, how unreasonable you are. (*Sitting on the sofa.*) Be nice now, Dr. Rank. Tomorrow you'll see how beautifully I'll dance; and you can imagine then that I'm dancing only for you—yes, and of course for Torvald, too—that's understood.

(*Takes various items out of the carton.*) Dr. Rank, sit over here and I'll show you something.

RANK (*sitting*): What's that?

NORA: Look here. Look.

RANK: Silk stockings.

NORA: Flesh-colored. Aren't they lovely? Now it's so dark here, but to-morrow—No, no, no, just look at the feet. Oh well, you might as well look at the rest.

RANK: Hm—

NORA: Why do you look so critical? Don't you believe they'll fit?

RANK: I've never had any chance to form an opinion on that.

NORA (*glancing at him a moment*): Shame on you. (*Hits him lightly on the ear with the stockings.*) That's for you. (*Puts them away again.*)

RANK: And what other splendors am I going to see now?

NORA: Not the least bit more, because you've been naughty. (*She hunts a little and rummages among her things.*)

RANK (*after a short silence*): When I sit here together with you like this, completely easy and open, then I don't know—I simply can't imagine—whatever would have become of me if I'd never come into this house.

NORA (*smiling*): Yes, I really think you feel completely at ease with us.

RANK (*more quietly, staring straight ahead*): And then to have to go away from it all—

NORA: Nonsense, you're not going away.

RANK (*his voice unchanged*): —and not even be able to leave some poor show of gratitude behind, scarcely a fleeting regret—no more than a vacant place that anyone can fill.

NORA: And if I asked you now for—No—

RANK: For what?

NORA: For a great proof of your friendship—

RANK: Yes, yes?

NORA: No, I mean—for an exceptionally big favor—

RANK: Would you really, for once, make me so happy?

NORA: Oh, you haven't the vaguest idea what it is.

RANK: All right, then tell me.

NORA: No, but I can't, Dr. Rank—it's all out of reason. It's advice and help, too—and a favor—

RANK: So much the better. I can't fathom what you're hinting at. Just speak out. Don't you trust me?

NORA: Of course. More than anyone else. You're my best and truest friend, I'm sure. That's why I want to talk to you. All right, then, Dr. Rank: There's something you can help me prevent. You know how deeply, how inexpressibly dearly Torvald loves me; he'd never hesitate a second to give up his life for me.

RANK (*leaning close to her*): Nora—do you think he's the only one—

NORA (*with a slight start*): Who—?

RANK: Who'd gladly give up his life for you.

NORA (*heavily*): I see.

RANK: I swore to myself you should know this before I'm gone. I'll never find a better chance. Yes, Nora, now you know. And also you know now that you can trust me beyond anyone else.

NORA (*rising, natural and calm*): Let me by.

RANK (*making room for her, but still sitting*): Nora—

NORA (*in the hall doorway*): Helene, bring the lamp in. (*Goes over to the stove.*) Ah, dear Dr. Rank, that was really mean of you.

RANK (*getting up*): That I've loved you just as deeply as somebody else? Was *that* mean?

NORA: No, but that you came out and told me. That was quite unnecessary—

RANK: What do you mean? Have you known—?

(*The Maid comes in with the lamp, sets it on the table, and goes out again.*)

RANK: Nora—Mrs. Helmer—I'm asking you: Have you known about it?

NORA: Oh, how can I tell what I know or don't know? Really, I don't know what to say—Why did you have to be so clumsy, Dr. Rank! Everything was so good.

RANK: Well, in any case, you now have the knowledge that my body and soul are at your command. So won't you speak out?

NORA (*looking at him*): After that?

RANK: Please, just let me know what it is.

NORA: You can't know anything now.

RANK: I have to. You mustn't punish me like this. Give me the chance to do whatever is humanly possible for you.

NORA: Now there's nothing you can do for me. Besides, actually, I don't need any help. You'll see—it's only my fantasies. That's what it is. Of course! (*Sits in the rocker, looks at him, and smiles.*) What a nice one you are, Dr. Rank. Aren't you a little bit ashamed, now that the lamp is here?

RANK: No, not exactly. But perhaps I'd better go—for good?

NORA: No, you certainly can't do that. You must come here just as you always have. You know Torvald can't do without you.

RANK: Yes, but *you*?

NORA: You know how much I enjoy it when you're here.

RANK: That's precisely what threw me off. You're a mystery to me. So many times I've felt you'd almost rather be with me than with Helmer.

NORA: Yes—you see, there are some people that one loves most and other people that one would almost prefer being with.

RANK: Yes, there's something to that.

NORA: When I was back home, of course I loved Papa most. But I always thought it was so much fun when I could sneak down to the maids' quarters, because they never tried to improve me, and it was always so amusing, the way they talked to each other.

RANK: Aha, so it's their place that I've filled.

NORA (*jumping up and going to him*): Oh, dear, sweet Dr. Rank, that's not what I meant at all. But you can understand that with Torvald it's just the same as with Papa—

(*The Maid enters from the hall.*)

MAID: Ma'am—please! (*She whispers to Nora and hands her a calling card.*)

NORA (*glancing at the card*): Ah! (*Slips it into her pocket.*)

RANK: Anything wrong?

NORA: No, no, not at all. It's only some—it's my new dress—

RANK: Really? But—there's your dress.

NORA: Oh, that. But this is another one—I ordered it—Torvald mustn't know—

RANK: Ah, now we have the big secret.

NORA: That's right. Just go in with him—he's back in the inner study. Keep him there as long as—

RANK: Don't worry. He won't get away. (*Goes into the study.*)

NORA (*to the Maid*): And he's standing waiting in the kitchen?

MAID: Yes, he came up by the back stairs.

NORA: But didn't you tell him somebody was here?

MAID: Yes, but that didn't do any good.

NORA: He won't leave?

MAID: No, he won't go till he's talked with you, ma'am.

NORA: Let him come in, then—but quietly. Helene, don't breathe a word about this. It's a surprise for my husband.

MAID: Yes, yes, I understand—(*Goes out.*)

NORA: This horror—it's going to happen. No, no, no, it can't happen, it mustn't. (*She goes and bolts Helmer's door. The Maid opens the hall door for Krogstad and shuts it behind him. He is dressed for travel in a fur coat, boots, and a fur cap.*)

NORA (*going toward him*): Talk softly. My husband's home.

KROGSTAD: Well, good for him.

NORA: What do you want?

KROGSTAD: Some information.

NORA: Hurry up, then. What is it?

KROGSTAD: You know, of course, that I got my notice.

NORA: I couldn't prevent it, Mr. Krogstad. I fought for you to the bitter end, but nothing worked.

KROGSTAD: Does your husband's love for you run so thin? He knows everything I can expose you to, and all the same he dares to—

NORA: How can you imagine he knows anything about this?

KROGSTAD: Ah, no—I can't imagine it either, now. It's not at all like my fine Torvald Helmer to have so much guts—

NORA: Mr. Krogstad, I demand respect for my husband!

KROGSTAD: Why, of course—all due respect. But since the lady's keeping it so carefully hidden, may I presume to ask if you're also a bit better informed than yesterday about what you've actually done?

NORA: More than you ever could teach me.

KROGSTAD: Yes, I *am* such an awful lawyer.

NORA: What is it you want from me?

KROGSTAD: Just a glimpse of how you are, Mrs. Helmer. I've been thinking about you all day long. A cashier, a night-court scribbler, a—well, a type like me also has a little of what they call a heart, you know.

NORA: Then show it. Think of my children.

KROGSTAD: Did you or your husband ever think of mine? But never mind. I simply wanted to tell you that you don't need to take this thing too seriously. For the present, I'm not proceeding with any action.

NORA: Oh no, really! Well—I knew that.

KROGSTAD: Everything can be settled in a friendly spirit. It doesn't have to get around town at all; it can stay just among us three.

NORA: My husband must never know anything of this.

KROGSTAD: How can you manage that? Perhaps you can pay me the balance?

NORA: No, not right now.

KROGSTAD: Or you know some way of raising the money in a day or two?

NORA: No way that I'm willing to use.

KROGSTAD: Well, it wouldn't have done you any good, anyway. If you stood in front of me with a fistful of bills, you still couldn't buy your signature back.

NORA: Then tell me what you're going to do with it.

KROGSTAD: I'll just hold onto it—keep it on file. There's no outsider who'll even get wind of it. So if you've been thinking of taking some desperate step—

NORA: I have.

KROGSTAD: Been thinking of running away from home—

NORA: I have!

KROGSTAD: Or even of something worse—

NORA: How could you guess that?

KROGSTAD: You can drop those thoughts.

NORA: How could you guess I was thinking of *that*?

KROGSTAD: Most of us think about *that* at first. I thought about it too, but I discovered I hadn't the courage—

NORA (*lifelessly*): I don't either.

KROGSTAD (*relieved*): That's true, you haven't the courage? You too?

NORA: I don't have it—I don't have it.

KROGSTAD: It would be terribly stupid, anyway. After that first storm at home blows out, why, then—I have here in my pocket a letter for your husband—

NORA: Telling everything?

KROGSTAD: As charitably as possible.

NORA (*quickly*): He mustn't ever get that letter. Tear it up. I'll find some way to get money.

KROGSTAD: Beg pardon, Mrs. Helmer, but I think I just told you—

NORA: Oh, I don't mean the money I owe you. Let me know how much you want from my husband, and I'll manage it.

KROGSTAD: I don't want any money from your husband.

NORA: What do you want, then?

KROGSTAD: I'll tell you what. I want to recoup, Mrs. Helmer; I want to get on in the world—and there's where your husband can help me. For a year and a half I've kept myself clean of anything disreputable—all that time struggling with the worst conditions; but I was satisfied, working my way up step by step. Now I've been written right off, and I'm just not in the mood to come crawling back. I tell you, I want to move on. I want to get back in the bank—in a better position. Your husband can set up a job for me—

NORA: He'll never do that!

KROGSTAD: He'll do it. I know him. He won't dare breathe a word of protest. And once I'm in there together with him, you just wait and see! Inside of a year, I'll be the manager's right-hand man. It'll be Nils Krogstad, not Torvald Helmer, who runs the bank.

NORA: You'll never see the day!

KROGSTAD: Maybe you think you can—

NORA: I have the courage now—for *that*.

KROGSTAD: Oh, you don't scare me. A smart, spoiled lady like you—

NORA: You'll see; you'll see!

KROGSTAD: Under the ice, maybe? Down in the freezing, coal-black water? There, till you float up in the spring, ugly, unrecognizable, with your hair falling out—

NORA: You don't frighten me.

KROGSTAD: Nor do you frighten me. One doesn't do these things, Mrs. Helmer. Besides what good would it be? I'd still have him safe in my pocket.

NORA: Afterwards? When I'm no longer—?

KROGSTAD: Are you forgetting that *I'll* be in control then over your final reputation? (*Nora stands speechless, staring at him.*) Good; now I've warned you. Don't do anything stupid. When Helmer's read my letter, I'll be waiting for his reply. And bear in mind that it's your husband himself who's forced me back to my old ways. I'll never forgive him for that. Good-bye, Mrs. Helmer. (*He goes out through the hall.*)

NORA (*goes to the hall door, opens it a crack, and listens*): He's gone. Didn't leave the letter. Oh no, no, that's impossible too! (*Opening the door more and more.*) What's that? He's standing outside—not going downstairs. He's thinking it over? Maybe he'll—? (*A letter falls in the mailbox; then Krogstad's footsteps are heard, dying away down a flight of stairs. Nora gives a muffled cry and runs over toward the sofa table. A short pause.*) In the mailbox. (*Slips warily over to the hall door.*) It's lying there. Torvald, Torvald—now we're lost!

MRS. LINDE (*entering with the costume from the room, left*): There now, I can't see anything else to mend. Perhaps you'd like to try—

NORA (*in a hoarse whisper*): Kristine, come here.

MRS. LINDE (*tossing the dress on the sofa*): What's wrong? You look upset.

NORA: Come here. See that letter? There! Look—through the glass in the mailbox.

MRS. LINDE: Yes, yes, I see it.

NORA: That letter's from Krogstad—

MRS. LINDE: Nora—it's Krogstad who loaned you the money!

NORA: Yes, and now Torvald will find out everything.

MRS. LINDE: Believe me, Nora, it's best for both of you.

NORA: There's more you don't know. I forged a name.

MRS. LINDE: But for heaven's sake—?

NORA: I only want to tell you that, Kristine, so that you can be my witness.

MRS. LINDE: Witness? Why should I—?

NORA: If I should go out of my mind—it could easily happen—

MRS. LINDE: Nora!

NORA: Or anything else occurred—so I couldn't be present here—

MRS. LINDE: Nora, Nora, you aren't yourself at all!

NORA: And someone should try to take on the whole weight, all of the guilt, you follow me—

MRS. LINDE: Yes, of course, but why do you think—?

NORA: Then you're the witness that it isn't true, Kristine. I'm very much myself; my mind right now is perfectly clear; and I'm telling you: Nobody else has known about this; I alone did everything. Remember that.

MRS. LINDE: I will. But I don't understand all this.

NORA: Oh, how could you ever understand it? It's the miracle now that's going to take place.

MRS. LINDE: The miracle?

NORA: Yes, the miracle. But it's so awful, Kristine. It mustn't take place, not for anything in the world.

MRS. LINDE: I'm going right over and talk with Krogstad.

NORA: Don't go near him; he'll do you some terrible harm!

MRS. LINDE: There was a time once when he'd gladly have done anything for me.

NORA: He?

MRS. LINDE: Where does he live?

NORA: Oh, how do I know? Yes. (*Searches in her pocket.*) Here's his card. But the letter, the letter—!

HELMER (*from the study, knocking on the door*): Nora!

NORA (*with a cry of fear*): Oh! What is it? What do you want?

HELMER: Now, now, don't be so frightened. We're not coming in. You locked the door—are you trying on the dress?

NORA: Yes, I'm trying it. I'll look just beautiful, Torvald.

MRS. LINDE (*who has read the card*): He's living right around the corner.

NORA: Yes, but what's the use? We're lost. The letter's in the box.

MRS. LINDE: And your husband has the key?

NORA: Yes, always.

MRS. LINDE: Krogstad can ask for his letter back unread; he can find some excuse—

NORA: But it's just this time that Torvald usually—

MRS. LINDE: Stall him. Keep him in there. I'll be back as quick as I can. (*She hurries out through the hall entrance.*)

NORA (*goes to Helmer's door, opens it, and peers in*): Torvald!

HELMER (*from the inner study*): Well—does one dare set foot in one's own living room at last? Come on, Rank, now we'll get a look—(*In the doorway.*) But what's this?

NORA: What, Torvald dear?

HELMER: Rank had me expecting some grand masquerade.

RANK (*in the doorway*): That was my impression, but I must have been wrong.

NORA: No one can admire me in my splendor—not till tomorrow.

HELMER: But Nora dear, you look so exhausted. Have you practiced too hard?

NORA: No, I haven't practiced at all yet.

HELMER: You know, it's necessary—

NORA: Oh, it's absolutely necessary, Torvald. But I can't get anywhere without your help. I've forgotten the whole thing completely.

HELMER: Ah, we'll soon take care of that.

NORA: Yes, take care of me, Torvald, please! Promise me that? Oh, I'm so nervous. That big party—You must give up everything this evening for me. No business—don't even touch your pen. Yes? Dear Torvald, promise?

HELMER: It's a promise. Tonight I'm totally at your service—you little helpless thing. Hm—but first there's one thing I want to—(*Goes toward the hall door.*)

NORA: What are you looking for?

HELMER: Just to see if there's any mail.

NORA: No, no, don't do that, Torvald!

HELMER: Now what?

NORA: Torvald, please. There isn't any.

HELMER: Let me look, though. (*Starts out. Nora, at the piano, strikes the first notes of the tarantella. Helmer, at the door, stops.*) Aha!

NORA: I can't dance tomorrow if I don't practice with you.

HELMER (*going over to her*): Nora dear, are you really so frightened?

NORA: Yes, so terribly frightened. Let me practice right now; there's still time before dinner. Oh, sit down and play for me, Torvald. Direct me. Teach me, the way you always have.

HELMER: Gladly, if it's what you want. (*Sits at the piano.*)

NORA (*snatches the tambourine up from the box, then a long, varicolored shawl, which she throws around herself, whereupon she springs forward and cries out*): Play for me now! Now I'll dance!

(*Helmer plays and Nora dances. Rank stands behind Helmer at the piano and looks on.*)

HELMER (*as he plays*): Slower. Slow down.

NORA: Can't change it.

HELMER: Not so violent, Nora!

NORA: Has to be just like this.

HELMER (*stopping*): No, no, that won't do at all.

NORA (*laughing and swinging her tambourine*): Isn't that what I told you?

RANK: Let me play for her.

HELMER (*getting up*): Yes, go on. I can teach her more easily then.

(*Rank sits at the piano and plays, Nora dances more and more wildly. Helmer has stationed himself by the stove and repeatedly gives her directions; she seems not to hear them; her hair loosens and falls over her shoulders; she does not notice, but goes on dancing. Mrs. Linde enters.*)

MRS. LINDE (*standing dumbfounded at the door*): Ah—!

NORA (*still dancing*): See what fun, Kristine!

HELMER: But Nora darling, you dance as if your life were at stake.

NORA: And it is.

HELMER: Rank, stop! This is pure madness. Stop it, I say!

(*Rank breaks off playing, and Nora halts abruptly.*)

HELMER (*going over to her*): I never would have believed it. You've forgotten everything I taught you.

NORA (*throwing away the tambourine*): You see for yourself.

HELMER: Well, there's certainly room for instruction here.

NORA: Yes, you see how important it is. You've got to teach me to the very last minute. Promise me that, Torvald?

HELMER: You can bet on it.

NORA: You mustn't, either today or tomorrow, think about anything else but me; you mustn't open any letters—or the mailbox—

HELMER: Ah, it's still the fear of that man—

NORA: Oh yes, yes, that too.

HELMER: Nora, it's written all over you—there's already a letter from him out there.

NORA: I don't know. I guess so. But you mustn't read such things now; there mustn't be anything ugly between us before it's all over.

RANK (*quietly to Helmer*): You shouldn't deny her.

HELMER (*putting his arm around her*): The child can have her way. But tomorrow night, after you've danced—

NORA: Then you'll be free.

MAID (*in the doorway, right*): Ma'am, dinner is served.

NORA: We'll be wanting champagne, Helene.

MAID: Very good, ma'am. (*Goes out.*)

HELMER: So—a regular banquet, hm?

NORA: Yes, a banquet—champagne till daybreak! (*Calling out.*) And some macaroons, Helene. Heaps of them—just this once.

HELMER (*taking her hands*): Now, now, now—no hysterics. Be my own little lark again.

NORA: Oh, I will soon enough. But go on in—and you, Dr. Rank. Kristine, help me put up my hair.

RANK (*whispering, as they go*): There's nothing wrong—really wrong, is there?

HELMER: Oh, of course not. It's nothing more than this childish anxiety I was telling you about. (*They go out, right.*)

NORA: Well?

MRS. LINDE: Left town.

NORA: I could see by your face.

MRS. LINDE: He'll be home tomorrow evening. I wrote him a note.

NORA: You shouldn't have. Don't try to stop anything now. After all, it's a wonderful joy, this waiting here for the miracle.

MRS. LINDE: What is it you're waiting for?

NORA: Oh, you can't understand that. Go in to them; I'll be along in a moment.

(*Mrs. Linde goes into the dining room. Nora stands a short while as if composing herself; then she looks at her watch.*)

NORA: Five. Seven hours to midnight. Twenty-four hours to the midnight after, and then the tarantella's done. Seven and twenty-four? Thirty-one hours to live.

HELMER (*in the doorway, right*): What's become of the little lark?

NORA (*going toward him with open arms*): Here's your lark!

ACT III

(*Same scene. The table, with chairs around it, has been moved to the center of the room. A lamp on the table is lit. The hall door stands open. Dance music drifts down from the floor above. Mrs. Linde sits at the table, absently paging through a book, trying to read, but apparently unable to focus her thoughts. Once or twice she pauses, tensely listening for a sound at the outer entrance.*)

MRS. LINDE (*glancing at her watch*): Not yet—and there's hardly any time left. If only he's not—(*Listening again.*) Ah, there it is. (*She goes out in the hall and cautiously opens the outer door. Quiet footsteps are heard on the stairs. She whispers.*) Come in. Nobody's here.

KROGSTAD (*in the doorway*): I found a note from you at home. What's back of all this?

MRS. LINDE: I just *had* to talk to you.

KROGSTAD: Oh? And it just *had* to be here in this house?

MRS. LINDE: At my place it was impossible; my room hasn't a private entrance. Come in, we're all alone. The maid's asleep, and the Helmers are at the dance upstairs.

KROGSTAD (*entering the room*): Well, well, the Helmers are dancing tonight? Really?

MRS. LINDE: Yes, why not?

KROGSTAD: How true—why not?

MRS. LINDE: All right, Krogstad, let's talk.

KROGSTAD: Do we two have anything more to talk about?

MRS. LINDE: We have a great deal to talk about.

KROGSTAD: I wouldn't have thought so.

MRS. LINDE: No, because you've never understood me, really.

KROGSTAD: Was there anything more to understand—except what's all too common in life? A calculating woman throws over a man the moment a better catch comes by.

MRS. LINDE: You think I'm so thoroughly calculating? You think I broke it off lightly?

KROGSTAD: Didn't you?

MRS. LINDE: Nils—is that what you really thought?

KROGSTAD: If you cared, then why did you write me the way you did?

MRS. LINDE: What else could I do? If I had to break off with you, then it was my job as well to root out everything you felt for me.

KROGSTAD (*wringing his hands*): So that was it. And this—all this, simply for money!

MRS. LINDE: Don't forget I had a helpless mother and two small brothers. We couldn't wait for you, Nils; you had such a long road ahead of you then.

KROGSTAD: That may be; but you still hadn't the right to abandon me for somebody else's sake.

MRS. LINDE: Yes—I don't know. So many, many times I've asked myself if I did have that right.

KROGSTAD (*more softly*): When I lost you, it was as if all the solid ground dissolved from under my feet. Look at me; I'm a half-drowned man now, hanging onto a wreck.

MRS. LINDE: Help may be near.

KROGSTAD: It was near—but then you came and blocked it off.

MRS. LINDE: Without my knowing it, Nils. Today for the first time I learned that it's you I'm replacing at the bank.

KROGSTAD: All right—I believe you. But now that you know, will you step aside?

MRS. LINDE: No, because that wouldn't benefit you in the slightest.

KROGSTAD: Not "benefit" me, hm! I'd step aside anyway.

MRS. LINDE: I've learned to be realistic. Life and hard, bitter necessity have taught me that.

KROGSTAD: And life's taught me never to trust fine phrases.

MRS. LINDE: Then life's taught you a very sound thing. But you do have to trust in actions, don't you?

KROGSTAD: What does that mean?

MRS. LINDE: You said you were hanging on like a half-drowned man to a wreck.

KROGSTAD: I've good reason to say that.

MRS. LINDE: I'm also like a half-drowned woman on a wreck. No one to suffer with; no one to care for.

KROGSTAD: You made your choice.

MRS. LINDE: There wasn't any choice then.

KROGSTAD: So—what of it?

MRS. LINDE: Nils, if only we two shipwrecked people could reach across to each other.

KROGSTAD: What are you saying?

MRS. LINDE: Two on one wreck are at least better off than each on his own.

KROGSTAD: Kristine!

MRS. LINDE: Why do you think I came into town?

KROGSTAD: Did you really have some thought of me?

MRS. LINDE: I have to work to go on living. All my born days, as long as I can remember, I've worked, and it's been my best and my only joy. But now I'm completely alone in the world; it frightens me to be so empty and lost. To work for yourself—there's no joy in that. Nils, give me something—someone to work for.

KROGSTAD: I don't believe all this. It's just some hysterical feminine urge to go out and make a noble sacrifice.

MRS. LINDE: Have you ever found me to be hysterical?

KROGSTAD: Can you honestly mean this? Tell me—do you know everything about my past?

MRS. LINDE: Yes.

KROGSTAD: And you know what they think I'm worth around here.

MRS. LINDE: From what you were saying before, it would seem that with me you could have been another person.

KROGSTAD: I'm positive of that.

MRS. LINDE: Couldn't it happen still?

KROGSTAD: Kristine—you're saying this in all seriousness? Yes, you are! I can see it in you. And do you really have the courage, then—?

MRS. LINDE: I need to have someone to care for, and your children need a mother. We both need each other. Nils, I have faith that you're good at heart—I'll risk everything together with you.

KROGSTAD (*gripping her hands*): Kristine, thank you, thank you—Now I know I can win back a place in their eyes. Yes—but I forgot—

MRS. LINDE (*listening*): Shh! The tarantella. Go now! Go on!

KROGSTAD: Why? What is it?

MRS. LINDE: Hear the dance up there? When that's over, they'll be coming down.

KROGSTAD: Oh, then I'll go. But—it's all pointless. Of course, you don't know the move I made against the Helmers.

MRS. LINDE: Yes, Nils, I know.

KROGSTAD: And all the same, you have the courage to—?

MRS. LINDE: I know how far despair can drive a man like you.

KROGSTAD: Oh, if I only could take it all back.

MRS. LINDE: You easily could—your letter's still lying in the mailbox.

KROGSTAD: Are you sure of that?

MRS. LINDE: Positive. But—

KROGSTAD (*looks at her searchingly*): Is that the meaning of it, then? You'll save your friend at any price. Tell me straight out. Is that it?

MRS. LINDE: Nils—anyone who's sold herself for somebody else once isn't going to do it again.

KROGSTAD: I'll demand my letter back.

MRS. LINDE: No, no.

KROGSTAD: Yes, of course. I'll stay here till Helmer comes down; I'll tell him to give me my letter again—that it only involves my dismissal— that he shouldn't read it—

MRS. LINDE: No, Nils, don't call the letter back.

KROGSTAD: But wasn't that exactly why you wrote me to come here?

MRS. LINDE: Yes, in that first panic. But it's been a whole day and night since then, and in that time I've seen such incredible things in this house. Helmer's got to learn everything; this dreadful secret has to be aired; those two have to come to a full understanding; all these lies and evasions can't go on.

KROGSTAD: Well, then, if you want to chance it. But at least there's one thing I can do, and do right away—

MRS. LINDE (*listening*): Go now, go, quick! The dance is over. We're not safe another second.

KROGSTAD: I'll wait for you downstairs.

MRS. LINDE: Yes, please do; take me home.

KROGSTAD: I can't believe it; I've never been so happy. (*He leaves by way of the outer door; the door between the room and the hall stays open.*)

MRS. LINDE (*straightening up a bit and getting together her street clothes*): How different now! How different! Someone to work for, to live for—a home to build. Well, it is worth the try! Oh, if they'd only come! (*Listening.*) Ah, there they are. Bundle up. (*She picks up her hat and coat. Nora's and Helmer's voices can be heard outside; a key turns in the lock, and Helmer brings Nora into the hall almost by force. She is wearing the Italian costume with a large black shawl about her; he has on evening dress, with a black domino open over it.*)

NORA (*struggling in the doorway*): No, no, no, not inside! I'm going up again. I don't want to leave so soon.

HELMER: But Nora dear—

NORA: Oh, I beg you, please, Torvald. From the bottom of my heart, *please*—only an hour more!

HELMER: Not a single minute, Nora darling. You know our agreement. Come on, in we go; you'll catch cold out here. (*In spite of her resistance, he gently draws her into the room.*)

MRS. LINDE: Good evening.

NORA: Kristine!

HELMER: Why, Mrs. Linde—are you here so late?

MRS. LINDE: Yes, I'm sorry, but I did want to see Nora in costume.

NORA: Have you been sitting here, waiting for me?

MRS. LINDE: Yes. I didn't come early enough; you were all upstairs; and then I thought I really couldn't leave without seeing you.

HELMER (*removing Nora's shawl*): Yes, take a good look. She's worth looking at, I can tell you that, Mrs. Linde. Isn't she lovely?

MRS. LINDE: Yes, I should say —

HELMER: A dream of loveliness, isn't she? That's what everyone thought at the party, too. But she's horribly stubborn—this sweet little thing. What's to be done with her? Can you imagine, I almost had to use force to pry her away.

NORA: Oh, Torvald, you're going to regret you didn't indulge me, even for just a half hour more.

HELMER: There, you see. She danced her tarantella and got a tumultuous hand—which was well earned, although the performance may have been a bit too naturalistic—I mean it rather overstepped the proprieties of art. But never mind—what's important is, she made a success, an overwhelming success. You think I could let her stay on after that and spoil the effect? Oh no; I took my lovely little Capri girl—my capricious little Capri girl, I should say—took her under my arm; one quick tour of the ballroom, a curtsy to every side, and then—as they say in novels—the beautiful vision disappeared. An exit should always be effective, Mrs. Linde, but that's what I can't get Nora to grasp. Phew, it's hot in here. (*Flings the domino on a chair and opens the door to his room.*) Why's it dark in here? Oh yes, of course. Excuse me. (*He goes in and lights a couple of candles.*)

NORA (*in a sharp, breathless whisper*): So?

MRS. LINDE (*quietly*): I talked with him.

NORA: And—?

MRS. LINDE: Nora—you must tell your husband everything.

NORA (*dully*): I knew it.

MRS. LINDE: You've got nothing to fear from Krogstad, but you have to speak out.

NORA: I won't tell.

MRS. LINDE: Then the letter will.

NORA: Thanks, Kristine. I know now what's to be done. Shh!

HELMER (*reentering*): Well, then, Mrs. Linde—have you admired her?

MRS. LINDE: Yes, and now I'll say good night.

HELMER: Oh, come, so soon? Is this yours, this knitting?

MRS. LINDE: Yes, thanks. I nearly forgot it.

HELMER: Do you knit, then?

MRS. LINDE: Oh yes.

HELMER: You know what? You should embroider instead.

MRS. LINDE: Really? Why?

HELMER: Yes, because it's a lot prettier. See here, one holds the embroidery so, in the left hand, and then one guides the needle with the right—so—in an easy, sweeping curve—right?

MRS. LINDE: Yes, I guess that's—

HELMER: But, on the other hand, knitting—it can never be anything but ugly. Look, see here, the arms tucked in, the knitting needles going up and down—there's something Chinese about it. Ah, that was really a glorious champagne they served.

MRS. LINDE: Yes, good night, Nora, and don't be stubborn anymore.

HELMER: Well put, Mrs. Linde!

MRS. LINDE: Good night, Mr. Helmer.

HELMER (*accompanying her to the door*): Good night, good night. I hope you get home all right. I'd be very happy to—but you don't have far to go. Good night, good night. (*She leaves. He shuts the door after her and returns.*) There, now, at last we got her out the door. She's a deadly bore, that creature.

NORA: Aren't you pretty tired, Torvald?

HELMER: No, not a bit.

NORA: You're not sleepy?

HELMER: Not at all. On the contrary, I'm feeling quite exhilarated. But you? Yes, you really look tired and sleepy.

NORA: Yes, I'm very tired. Soon now I'll sleep.

HELMER: See! You see! I was right all along that we shouldn't stay longer.

NORA: Whatever you do is always right.

HELMER (*kissing her brow*): Now my little lark talks sense. Say, did you notice what a time Rank was having tonight?

NORA: Oh, was he? I didn't get to speak with him.

HELMER: I scarcely did either, but it's a long time since I've seen him in such high spirits. (*Gazes at her a moment, then comes nearer her.*) Hm—it's marvelous, though, to be back home again—to be completely alone with you. Oh, you bewitchingly lovely young woman!

NORA: Torvald, don't look at me like that!

HELMER: Can't I look at my richest treasure? At all that beauty that's mine, mine alone—completely and utterly.

NORA (*moving around to the other side of the table*): You mustn't talk to me that way tonight.

HELMER (*following her*): The tarantella is still in your blood. I can see—and it makes you even more enticing. Listen. The guests are beginning to go. (*Dropping his voice.*) Nora—it'll soon be quiet through this whole house.

NORA: Yes, I hope so.

HELMER: You do, don't you, my love? Do you realize—when I'm out at a party like this with you—do you know why I talk to you so little, and keep such a distance away; just send you a stolen look now and then—you know why I do it? It's because I'm imagining then that you're my secret darling, my secret young bride-to-be, and that no one suspects there's anything between us.

NORA: Yes, yes; oh, yes, I know you're always thinking of me.

HELMER: And then when we leave and I place the shawl over those fine young rounded shoulders—over that wonderful curving neck—then I pretend that you're my young bride, that we're just coming from the wedding, that for the first time I'm bringing you into my house—that for the first time I'm alone with you—completely alone with you, your trembling young beauty! All this evening I've longed for nothing but you. When I saw you turn and sway in the tarantella—my blood was pounding till I couldn't stand it—that's why I brought you down here so early—

NORA: Go away, Torvald! Leave me alone. I don't want all this.

HELMER: What do you mean? Nora, you're teasing me. You will, won't you? Aren't I your husband—?

(*A knock at the outside door.*)

NORA (*startled*): What's that?

HELMER (*going toward the hall*): Who is it?

RANK (*outside*): It's me. May I come in a moment?

HELMER (*with quiet irritation*): Oh, what does he want now? (*Aloud.*) Hold on. (*Goes and opens the door.*) Oh, how nice that you didn't just pass us by!

RANK: I thought I heard your voice, and then I wanted so badly to have a look in. (*Lightly glancing about.*) Ah, me, these old familiar haunts. You have it snug and cozy in here, you two.

HELMER: You seemed to be having it pretty cozy upstairs, too.

RANK: Absolutely. Why shouldn't I? Why not take in everything in life? As much as you can, anyway, and as long as you can. The wine was superb—

HELMER: The champagne especially.

RANK: You noticed that too? It's amazing how much I could guzzle down.

NORA: Torvald also drank a lot of champagne this evening.

RANK: Oh?

NORA: Yes, and that always makes him so entertaining.

RANK: Well, why shouldn't one have a pleasant evening after a well-spent day?

HELMER: Well spent? I'm afraid I can't claim that.

RANK (*slapping him on the back*): But I can, you see!

NORA: Dr. Rank, you must have done some scientific research today.

RANK: Quite so.

HELMER: Come now—little Nora talking about scientific research!

NORA: And can I congratulate you on the results?

RANK: Indeed you may.

NORA: Then they were good?

RANK: The best possible for both doctor and patient—certainty.

NORA (*quickly and searchingly*): Certainty?

RANK: Complete certainty. So don't I owe myself a gay evening afterwards?

NORA: Yes, you're right, Dr. Rank.

HELMER: I'm with you—just so long as you don't have to suffer for it in the morning.

RANK: Well, one never gets something for nothing in life.

NORA: Dr. Rank—are you very fond of masquerade parties?

RANK: Yes, if there's a good array of odd disguises—

NORA: Tell me, what should we two go as at the next masquerade?

HELMER: You little featherhead—already thinking of the next!

RANK: We two? I'll tell you what: You must go as Charmed Life—

HELMER: Yes, but find a costume for that!

RANK: Your wife can appear just as she looks every day.

HELMER: That was nicely put. But don't you know what you're going to be?

RANK: Yes, Helmer, I've made up my mind.

HELMER: Well?

RANK: At the next masquerade I'm going to be invisible.

HELMER: That's a funny idea.

RANK: They say there's a hat—black, huge—have you never heard of the hat that makes you invisible? You put it on, and then no one on earth can see you.

HELMER (*suppressing a smile*): Ah, of course.

RANK: But I'm quite forgetting what I came for. Helmer, give me a cigar, one of the dark Havanas.

HELMER: With the greatest pleasure. (*Holds out his case.*)

RANK: Thanks. (*Takes one and cuts off the tip.*)

NORA (*striking a match*): Let me give you a light.

RANK: Thank you. (*She holds the match for him; he lights the cigar.*) And now good-bye.

HELMER: Good-bye, good-bye, old friend.

NORA: Sleep well, Doctor.

RANK: Thanks for that wish.

NORA: Wish me the same.

RANK: You? All right, if you like—Sleep well. And thanks for the light. (*He nods to them both and leaves.*)

HELMER (*his voice subdued*): He's been drinking heavily.

NORA (*absently*): Could be. (*Helmer takes his keys from his pocket and goes out in the hall.*) Torvald—what are you after?

HELMER: Got to empty the mailbox; it's nearly full. There won't be room for the morning papers.

NORA: Are you working tonight?

HELMER: You know I'm not. Why—what's this? Someone's been at the lock.

NORA: At the lock—?

HELMER: Yes, I'm positive. What do you suppose—? I can't imagine one of the maids—? Here's a broken hairpin. Nora, it's yours—

NORA (*quickly*): Then it must be the children—

HELMER: You'd better break them of that. Hm, hm—well, opened it after all. (*Takes the contents out and calls into the kitchen.*) Helene! Helene, would you put out the lamp in the hall. (*He returns to the room, shutting the hall door, then displays the handful of mail.*) Look how it's piled up. (*Sorting through them.*) Now what's this?

NORA (*at the window*): The letter! Oh, Torvald, no!

HELMER: Two calling cards—from Rank.

NORA: From Dr. Rank?

HELMER (*examining them*): "Dr. Rank, Consulting Physician." They were on top. He must have dropped them in as he left.

NORA: Is there anything on them?

HELMER: There's a black cross over the name. See? That's a gruesome notion. He could almost be announcing his own death.

NORA: That's just what he's doing.

HELMER: What! You've heard something? Something he's told you?

NORA: Yes. That when those cards came, he'd be taking his leave of us. He'll shut himself in now and die.

HELMER: Ah, my poor friend! Of course I knew he wouldn't be here much longer. But so soon—And then to hide himself away like a wounded animal.

NORA: If it has to happen, then it's best it happens in silence—don't you think so, Torvald?

HELMER (*pacing up and down*): He's grown right into our lives. I simply can't imagine him gone. He with his suffering and loneliness—like a dark cloud setting off our sunlit happiness. Well, maybe it's best this way. For him, at least. (*Standing still.*) And maybe for us too, Nora. Now we're thrown back on each other, completely. (*Embracing her.*) Oh you, my darling wife, how can I hold you close enough? You know what, Nora—time and again I've wished you were in some terrible danger, just so I could stake my life and soul and everything, for your sake.

NORA (*tearing herself away, her voice firm and decisive*): Now you must read your mail, Torvald.

HELMER: No, no, not tonight. I want to stay with you, dearest.

NORA: With a dying friend on your mind?

HELMER: You're right. We've both had a shock. There's ugliness between us—these thoughts of death and corruption. We'll have to get free of them first. Until then—we'll stay apart.

NORA (*clinging about his neck*): Torvald—good night! Good night!

HELMER (*kissing her on the cheek*): Good night, little songbird. Sleep well, Nora. I'll be reading my mail now. (*He takes the letters into his room and shuts the door after him.*)

NORA (*with bewildered glances, groping about, seizing Helmer's domino, throwing it around her, and speaking in short, hoarse, broken whispers*): Never see him again. Never, never. (*Putting her shawl over her head.*) Never see the children either—them, too. Never, never. Oh, the freezing black water! The depths—down—Oh, I wish it were over—He has it now; he's reading it—now. Oh no, no, not yet. Torvald, good-bye, you and the children—(*She starts for the hall; as she does, Helmer throws open his door and stands with an open letter in his hand.*)

HELMER: Nora!

NORA (*screams*): Oh—!

HELMER: What is this? You know what's in this letter?

NORA: Yes, I know. Let me go! Let me out!

HELMER (*holding her back*): Where are you going?

NORA (*struggling to break loose*): You can't save me, Torvald!

HELMER (*slumping back*): True! Then it's true what he writes? How horrible! No, no, it's impossible—it can't be true.

NORA: It *is* true. I've loved you more than all this world.

HELMER: Ah, none of your slippery tricks.

NORA (*taking one step toward him*): Torvald—!

HELMER: What *is* this you've blundered into!

NORA: Just let me loose. You're not going to suffer for my sake. You're not going to take on my guilt.

HELMER: No more playacting. (*Locks the hall door.*) You stay right here and give me a reckoning. You understand what you've done? Answer! You understand?

NORA (*looking squarely at him, her face hardening*): Yes. I'm beginning to understand everything now.

HELMER (*striding about*): Oh, what an awful awakening! In all these eight years—she who was my pride and joy—a hypocrite, a liar—worse, worse—a criminal! How infinitely disgusting it all is! The shame! (*Nora says nothing and goes on looking straight at him. He stops in front of her.*) I should have suspected something of the kind. I should have known. All your father's flimsy values—Be still! All your father's flimsy values have come out in you. No religion, no morals, no sense of duty—Oh, how I'm punished for letting him off! I did it for your sake, and you repay me like this.

NORA: Yes, like this.

HELMER: Now you've wrecked all my happiness—ruined my whole future. Oh, it's awful to think of. I'm in a cheap little grafter's hands; he can do anything he wants with me, ask for anything, play with me like a puppet—and I can't breathe a word. I'll be swept down miserably into the depths on account of a featherbrained woman.

NORA: When I'm gone from this world, you'll be free.

HELMER: Oh, quit posing. Your father had a mess of those speeches too. What good would that ever do me if you were gone from this world, as you say? Not the slightest. He can still make the whole thing known; and if he does, I could be falsely suspected as your accomplice. They might even think that I was behind it—that I put you up to it. And all that I can thank you for—you that I've coddled the whole of our marriage. Can you see now what you've done to me?

NORA (*icily calm*): Yes.

HELMER: It's so incredible, I just can't grasp it. But we'll have to patch up whatever we can. Take off the shawl. I said, take it off! I've got to appease him somehow or other. The thing has to be hushed up at any cost. And as for you and me, it's got to seem like everything between us is just as it was—to the outside world, that is. You'll go right on living in this house, of course. But you can't be allowed to bring up the children; I don't dare trust you with them—Oh, to have to say this to someone I've loved so much! Well, that's done with. From now on happiness doesn't matter; all that matters is saving the bits and pieces, the appearance—(*The doorbell rings. Helmer starts.*) What's that? And so late. Maybe the worst—? You think he'd—? Hide, Nora! Say you're sick. (*Nora remains standing motionless. Helmer goes and opens the door.*)

MAID (*half dressed, in the hall*): A letter for Mrs. Helmer.

HELMER: I'll take it. (*Snatches the letter and shuts the door.*) Yes, it's from him. You don't get it; I'm reading it myself.

NORA: Then read it.

HELMER (*by the lamp*): I hardly dare. We may be ruined, you and I. But—I've got to know. (*Rips open the letter, skims through a few lines, glances at an enclosure, then cries out joyfully.*) Nora! (*Nora looks inquiringly at him.*) Nora! Wait—better check it again—Yes, yes, it's true. I'm saved. Nora, I'm saved!

NORA: And I?

HELMER: You too, of course. We're both saved, both of us. Look. He's sent back your note. He says he's sorry and ashamed—that a happy development in his life—oh, who cares what he says! Nora, we're saved! No one can hurt you. Oh, Nora, Nora—but first, this ugliness all has to go. Let me see—(*Takes a look at the note.*) No, I don't want to see it; I want the whole thing to fade like a dream. (*Tears the note and both letters to pieces, throws them into the stove and watches them burn.*) There—now there's nothing left—He wrote that since Christmas Eve you—Oh, they must have been three terrible days for you, Nora.

NORA: I fought a hard fight.

HELMER: And suffered pain and saw no escape but—No, we're not going to dwell on anything unpleasant. We'll just be grateful and keep on repeating: It's over now, it's over! You hear me, Nora? You don't seem to realize—it's over. What's it mean—that frozen look? Oh, poor little Nora, I understand. You can't believe I've forgiven you. But I have, Nora; I swear I have. I know that what you did, you did out of love for me.

NORA: That's true.

HELMER: You loved me the way a wife ought to love her husband. It's simply the means that you couldn't judge. But you think I love you any the less for not knowing how to handle your affairs? No, no—just lean on me; I'll guide you and teach you. I wouldn't be a man if this feminine helplessness didn't make you twice as attractive to me. You mustn't mind those sharp words I said—that was all in the first confusion of thinking my world had collapsed. I've forgiven you, Nora; I swear I've forgiven you.

NORA: My thanks for your forgiveness. (*She goes out through the door, right.*)

HELMER: No, wait—(*Peers in.*) What are you doing in there?

NORA (*inside*): Getting out of my costume.

HELMER (*by the open door*): Yes, do that. Try to calm yourself and collect your thoughts again, my frightened little songbird. You can rest easy now; I've got wide wings to shelter you with. (*Walking about close by the door.*) How snug and nice our home is, Nora. You're safe here; I'll keep you like a hunted dove I've rescued out of a hawk's claws. I'll bring peace to your poor, shuddering heart. Gradually it'll happen, Nora; you'll see. Tomorrow all this will look different to you; then everything will be as it was. I won't have to go on repeating I forgive you; you'll feel it for yourself. How can you imagine I'd ever conceivably want to disown you—or even blame you in any way? Ah, you don't know a man's heart, Nora. For a man there's something indescribably sweet and satisfying in knowing he's forgiven his wife—and forgiven her out of a full and open heart. It's as if she belongs to him in two ways now: In a sense he's given her fresh into the world again, and she's become his wife and his child as well. From now on that's what you'll be to me—you little, bewildered, helpless thing. Don't be afraid of anything, Nora; just open your heart to me, and I'll be conscience and will to you both—(*Nora enters in her regular clothes.*) What's this? Not in bed? You've changed your dress?

NORA: Yes, Torvald, I've changed my dress.

HELMER: But why now, so late?

NORA: Tonight I'm not sleeping.

HELMER: But Nora dear—

NORA (*looking at her watch*): It's still not so very late. Sit down, Torvald; we have a lot to talk over. (*She sits at one side of the table.*)

HELMER: Nora—what is this? That hard expression—

NORA: Sit down. This'll take some time. I have a lot to say.

HELMER (*sitting at the table directly opposite her*): You worry me, Nora. And I don't understand you.

NORA: No, that's exactly it. You don't understand me. And I've never understood you either—until tonight. No, don't interrupt. You can just listen to what I say. We're closing out accounts, Torvald.

HELMER: How do you mean that?

NORA (*after a short pause*): Doesn't anything strike you about our sitting here like this?

HELMER: What's that?

NORA: We've been married now eight years. Doesn't it occur to you that this is the first time we two, you and I, man and wife, have ever talked seriously together?

HELMER: What do you mean—seriously?

NORA: In eight whole years—longer even—right from our first acquaintance, we've never exchanged a serious word on any serious thing.

HELMER: You mean I should constantly go and involve you in problems you couldn't possibly help me with?

NORA: I'm not talking of problems. I'm saying that we've never sat down seriously together and tried to get to the bottom of anything.

HELMER: But dearest, what good would that ever do you?

NORA: That's the point right there: You've never understood me. I've been wronged greatly, Torvald—first by Papa, and then by you.

HELMER: What! By us—the two people who've loved you more than anyone else?

NORA (*shaking her head*): You never loved me. You've thought it fun to be in love with me, that's all.

HELMER: Nora, what a thing to say!

NORA: Yes, it's true now, Torvald. When I lived at home with Papa, he told me all his opinions, so I had the same ones too; or if they were different I hid them, since he wouldn't have cared for that. He used to call me his doll-child, and he played with me the way I played with my dolls. Then I came into your house—

HELMER: How can you speak of our marriage like that?

NORA (*unperturbed*): I mean, then I went from Papa's hands into yours. You arranged everything to your own taste, and so I got the same taste as you—or I pretended to; I can't remember. I guess a little of both, first one, then the other. Now when I look back, it seems as if I'd lived here like a beggar—just from hand to mouth. I've lived by doing tricks for you, Torvald. But that's the way you wanted it. It's a great sin what you and Papa did to me. You're to blame that nothing's become of me.

HELMER: Nora, how unfair and ungrateful you are! Haven't you been happy here?

NORA: No, never. I thought so—but I never have.

HELMER: Not—not happy!

NORA: No, only lighthearted. And you've always been so kind to me. But our home's been nothing but a playpen. I've been your doll-wife here, just as at home I was Papa's doll-child. And in turn the children have been my dolls. I thought it was fun when you played with me, just as they thought it fun when I played with them. That's been our marriage, Torvald.

HELMER: There's some truth in what you're saying—under all the raving exaggeration. But it'll all be different after this. Playtime's over; now for the schooling.

NORA: Whose schooling—mine or the children's?

HELMER: Both yours and the children's, dearest.

NORA: Oh, Torvald, you're not the man to teach me to be a good wife to you.

HELMER: And you can say that?

NORA: And I—how am I equipped to bring up children?

HELMER: Nora!

NORA: Didn't you say a moment ago that that was no job to trust me with?

HELMER: In a flare of temper! Why fasten on that?

NORA: Yes, but you were so very right. I'm not up to the job. There's another job I have to do first. I have to try to educate myself. You can't help me with that. I've got to do it alone. And that's why I'm leaving you now.

HELMER (jumping up): What's that?

NORA: I have to stand completely alone, if I'm ever going to discover myself and the world out there. So I can't go on living with you.

HELMER: Nora, Nora!

NORA: I want to leave right away. Kristine should put me up for the night—

HELMER: You're insane! You've no right! I forbid you!

NORA: From here on, there's no use forbidding me anything. I'll take with me whatever is mine. I don't want a thing from you, either now or later.

HELMER: What kind of madness is this!

NORA: Tomorrow I'm going home—I mean, home where I came from. It'll be easier up there to find something to do.

HELMER: Oh, you blind, incompetent child!

NORA: I must learn to be competent, Torvald.

HELMER: Abandon your home, your husband, your children! And you're not even thinking what people will say.

NORA: I can't be concerned about that. I only know how essential this is.

HELMER: Oh, it's outrageous. So you'll run out like this on your most sacred vows.

NORA: What do you think are my most sacred vows?

HELMER: And I have to tell you that! Aren't they your duties to your husband and children?

NORA: I have other duties equally sacred.

HELMER: That isn't true. What duties are they?

NORA: Duties to myself.

HELMER: Before all else, you're a wife and a mother.

NORA: I don't believe in that anymore. I believe that before all else, I'm a human being, no less than you—or anyway, I ought to try to become one. I know the majority thinks you're right, Torvald, and plenty of books agree with you, too. But I can't go on believing what the majority says, or what's written in books. I have to think over these things myself and try to understand them.

HELMER: Why can't you understand your place in your own home? On a point like that, isn't there one everlasting guide you can turn to? Where's your religion?

NORA: Oh, Torvald, I'm really not sure what religion is.

HELMER: What—?

NORA: I only know what the minister said when I was confirmed. He told me religion was this thing and that. When I get clear and away by myself, I'll go into that problem too. I'll see if what the minister said was right, or, in any case, if it's right for me.

HELMER: A young woman your age shouldn't talk like that. If religion can't move you, I can try to rouse your conscience. You do have some moral feeling? Or, tell me—has that gone too?

NORA: It's not easy to answer that, Torvald. I simply don't know. I'm all confused about these things. I just know I see them so differently from you. I find out for one thing, that the law's not at all what I'd thought—but I can't get it through my head that the law is fair. A woman hasn't a right to protect her dying father or save her husband's life! I can't believe that.

HELMER: You talk like a child. You don't know anything of the world you live in.

NORA: No, I don't. But now I'll begin to learn for myself. I'll try to discover who's right, the world or I.

HELMER: Nora, you're sick; you've got a fever. I almost think you're out of your head.

NORA: I've never felt more clearheaded and sure in my life.

HELMER: And—clearheaded and sure—you're leaving your husband and children?

NORA: Yes.

HELMER: Then there's only one possible reason.

NORA: What?

HELMER: You no longer love me.

NORA: No. That's exactly it.

HELMER: Nora! You can't be serious!

NORA: Oh, this is so hard, Torvald—you've been so kind to me always. But I can't help it. I don't love you anymore.

HELMER (*struggling for composure*): Are you also clearheaded and sure about that?

NORA: Yes, completely. That's why I can't go on staying here.

HELMER: Can you tell me what I did to lose your love?

NORA: Yes, I can tell you. It was this evening when the miraculous thing didn't come—then I knew you weren't the man I'd imagined.

HELMER: Be more explicit; I don't follow you.

NORA: I've waited now so patiently eight long years—for, my Lord, I know miracles don't come every day. Then this crisis broke over me, and such a certainty filled me: *Now* the miraculous event would occur. While Krogstad's letter was lying out there, I never for an instant dreamed that you could give in to his terms. I was so utterly sure you'd say to him: Go on, tell your tale to the whole wide world. And when he'd done that—

HELMER: Yes, what then? When I'd delivered my own wife into shame and disgrace—!

NORA: When he'd done that, I was so utterly sure that you'd step forward, take the blame on yourself and say: I am the guilty one.

HELMER: Nora—!

NORA: You're thinking I'd never accept such a sacrifice from you? No, of course not. But what good would my protests be against you? That was the miracle I was waiting for, in terror and hope. And to stave that off, I would have taken my life.

HELMER: I'd gladly work for you day and night, Nora—and take on pain and deprivation. But there's no one who gives up honor for love.

NORA: Millions of women have done just that.

HELMER: Oh, you think and talk like a silly child.

NORA: Perhaps. But you neither think nor talk like the man I could join myself to. When your big fright was over—and it wasn't from any threat against me, only for what might damage you—when all the danger was past, for you it was just as if nothing had happened. I was exactly the same, your little lark, your doll, that you'd have to handle with double care now that I'd turned out so brittle and frail. (*Gets up.*)

Torvald—in that instant it dawned on me that for eight years I've been living here with a stranger, and that I'd even conceived three children—oh, I can't stand the thought of it! I could tear myself to bits.

HELMER (*heavily*): I see. There's a gulf that's opened between us—that's clear. Oh, but Nora, can't we bridge it somehow?

NORA: The way I am now, I'm no wife for you.

HELMER: I have the strength to make myself over.

NORA: Maybe—if your doll gets taken away.

HELMER: But to part! To part from you! No, Nora, no—I can't imagine it.

NORA (*going out, right*): All the more reason why it has to be. (*She reenters with her coat and a small overnight bag, which she puts on a chair by the table.*)

HELMER: Nora, Nora, not now! Wait till tomorrow.

NORA: I can't spend the night in a strange man's room.

HELMER: But couldn't we live here like brother and sister—

NORA: You know very well how long that would last. (*Throws her shawl about her.*) Good-bye, Torvald. I won't look in on the children. I know they're in better hands than mine. The way I am now, I'm no use to them.

HELMER: But someday, Nora—someday—?

NORA: How can I tell? I haven't the least idea what'll become of me.

HELMER: But you're my wife, now and wherever you go.

NORA: Listen, Torvald—I've heard that when a wife deserts her husband's house just as I'm doing, then the law frees him from all responsibility. In any case, I'm freeing you from being responsible. Don't feel yourself bound, any more than I will. There has to be absolute freedom for us both. Here, take your ring back. Give me mine.

HELMER: That too?

NORA: That too.

HELMER: There it is.

NORA: Good. Well, now it's all over. I'm putting the keys here. The maids know all about keeping up the house—better than I do. Tomorrow, after I've left town, Kristine will stop by to pack up everything that's mine from home. I'd like those things shipped up to me.

HELMER: Over! All over! Nora, won't you ever think about me?

NORA: I'm sure I'll think of you often, and about the children and the house here.

HELMER: May I write you?

NORA: No—never. You're not to do that.

HELMER: Oh, but let me send you—

NORA: Nothing. Nothing.

HELMER: Or help you if you need it.

NORA: No. I accept nothing from strangers.

HELMER: Nora—can I never be more than a stranger to you?

NORA (*picking up the overnight bag*): Ah, Torvald—it would take the greatest miracle of all—

HELMER: Tell me the greatest miracle!

NORA: You and I both would have to transform ourselves to the point that—Oh, Torvald, I've stopped believing in miracles.

HELMER: But I'll believe. Tell me! Transform ourselves to the point that—?

NORA: That our living together could be a true marriage. (*She goes out down the hall.*)

HELMER (*sinks down on a chair by the door, face buried in his hands*): Nora! Nora! (*Looking about and rising.*) Empty. She's gone. (*A sudden hope leaps in him.*) The greatest miracle—?

(*From below, the sound of a door slamming shut.*)

[1879]

SUSAN GLASPELL   [1882–1948]

Trifles

Characters

GEORGE HENDERSON, *county attorney*
HENRY PETERS, *sheriff*
LEWIS HALE, *a neighboring farmer*
MRS. PETERS
MRS. HALE

Scene: *The kitchen in the now abandoned farmhouse of John Wright, a gloomy kitchen, and left without having been put in order—the walls covered with a faded wall paper. Down right is a door leading to the parlor. On the right wall above this door is a built-in kitchen cupboard with shelves in the upper portion and drawers below. In the rear wall at right, up two steps is a door opening onto stairs leading to the second floor. In the rear wall at left is a door to the shed and from there to the outside. Between these two doors is an old-fashioned black iron stove. Running along the left wall from the shed door is an old iron sink and sink shelf, in which is set a hand pump. Downstage of the sink is an uncurtained window. Near the window is an old wooden rocker. Center stage is an unpainted wooden kitchen table with straight chairs on either side. There is a small chair down right. Unwashed pans under the sink, a loaf of bread outside the breadbox, a dish towel on the table—other signs of incompleted work. At the rear the shed door opens and the Sheriff comes in followed by the County Attorney and Hale. The Sheriff and Hale are men in middle life, the County Attorney is a young man; all are much bundled up and go at once to the stove. They are followed by the two women—the Sheriff's wife, Mrs. Peters, first: she is a slight wiry woman, a thin nervous face. Mrs. Hale is larger and would ordinarily be called more comfortable looking, but she is disturbed now and looks fearfully about as she enters. The women have come in slowly, and stand close together near the door.*

COUNTY ATTORNEY (*at stove rubbing his hands*): This feels good. Come up to the fire, ladies.

MRS. PETERS (*after taking a step forward*): I'm not—cold.

SHERIFF (*unbuttoning his overcoat and stepping away from the stove to right of table as if to mark the beginning of official business*): Now, Mr. Hale, before we move things about, you explain to Mr. Henderson just what you saw when you came here yesterday morning.

COUNTY ATTORNEY (*crossing down to left of the table*): By the way, has anything been moved? Are things just as you left them yesterday?

909

SHERIFF (*looking about*): It's just about the same. When it dropped below zero last night I thought I'd better send Frank out this morning to make a fire for us—(*sits right of center table*) no use getting pneumonia with a big case on, but I told him not to touch anything except the stove—and you know Frank.

COUNTY ATTORNEY: Somebody should have been left here yesterday.

SHERIFF: Oh—yesterday. When I had to send Frank to Morris Center for that man who went crazy—I want you to know I had my hands full yesterday. I knew you could get back from Omaha by today and as long as I went over everything here myself———

COUNTY ATTORNEY: Well, Mr. Hale, tell just what happened when you came here yesterday morning.

HALE (*crossing down to above table*): Harry and I had started to town with a load of potatoes. We came along the road from my place and as I got here I said, "I'm going to see if I can't get John Wright to go in with me on a party telephone." I spoke to Wright about it once before and he put me off, saying folks talked too much anyway, and all he asked was peace and quiet—I guess you know about how much he talked himself; but I thought maybe if I went to the house and talked about it before his wife, though I said to Harry that I didn't know as what his wife wanted made much difference to John———

COUNTY ATTORNEY: Let's talk about that later, Mr. Hale. I do want to talk about that, but tell now just what happened when you got to the house.

HALE: I didn't hear or see anything; I knocked at the door, and still it was all quiet inside. I knew they must be up, it was past eight o'clock. So I knocked again, and I thought I heard someone say, "Come in." I wasn't sure, I'm not sure yet, but I opened the door—this door (*indicating the door by which the two women are still standing*) and there in that rocker—(*pointing to it*) sat Mrs. Wright. (*They all look at the rocker down left.*)

COUNTY ATTORNEY: What—was she doing?

HALE: She was rockin' back and forth. She had her apron in her hand and was kind of—pleating it.

COUNTY ATTORNEY: And how did she—look?

HALE: Well, she looked queer.

COUNTY ATTORNEY: How do you mean—queer?

HALE: Well, as if she didn't know what she was going to do next. And kind of done up.

COUNTY ATTORNEY (*takes out notebook and pencil and sits left of center table*): How did she seem to feel about your coming?

HALE: Why, I don't think she minded—one way or other. She didn't pay much attention. I said, "How do, Mrs. Wright, it's cold, ain't it?" And she said, "Is it?"—and went on kind of pleating at her apron. Well, I was surprised: she didn't ask me to come up to the stove, or to set down, but just sat there, not even looking at me, so I said, "I want to see John." And then she—laughed. I guess you would call it a laugh. I thought of Harry and the team outside, so I said a little sharp: "Can't I see John?" "No," she says, kind o' dull like. "Ain't he home?" says I. "Yes," says she, "he's home." "Then why can't I see him?" I asked her, out of patience. "'Cause he's dead," says she. "*Dead?*" says I. She just nodded her head, not getting a bit excited, but rockin' back and forth. "Why—where is he?" says I, not knowing what to say. She just pointed upstairs—like that. (*Himself pointing to the room above.*) I started for the stairs, with the idea of going up there. I walked from there to here—then I says, "Why, what did he die of?" "He died of a rope round his neck," says she, and just went on pleatin' at her apron. Well, I went out and called Harry. I thought I might—need help. We went upstairs and there he was lyin'———

COUNTY ATTORNEY: I think I'd rather have you go into that upstairs, where you can point it all out. Just go on now with the rest of the story.

HALE: Well, my first thought was to get that rope off. It looked . . . (*stops: his face twitches*) . . . but Harry, he went up to him, and he said, "No, he's dead all right, and we'd better not touch anything." So we went right back downstairs. She was still sitting that same way. "Has anybody been notified?" I asked. "No," says she, unconcerned. "Who did this, Mrs. Wright?" said Harry. He said it businesslike—and she stopped pleatin' of her apron. "I don't know," she says. "You don't *know*?" says Harry. "No," says she. "Weren't you sleepin' in the bed with him?" says Harry. "Yes," says she, "but I was on the inside." "Somebody slipped a rope round his head and strangled him and you didn't wake up?" says Harry. "I didn't wake up," she said after him. We must 'a' looked as if we didn't see how that could be, for after a minute she said, "I sleep sound." Harry was going to ask her more questions but I said maybe we ought to let her tell her story first to the coroner, or the sheriff, so Harry went fast as he could to Rivers' place, where there's a telephone.

COUNTY ATTORNEY: And what did Mrs. Wright do when she knew that you had gone for the coroner?

HALE: She moved from the rocker to that chair over there (*pointing to a small chair in the down right corner*) and just sat there with her hands held together and looking down. I got a feeling that I ought to make some conversation, so I said I had come in to see if John wanted to put in a telephone, and at that she started to laugh, and then she stopped and looked at me—scared. (*The County Attorney, who has had his notebook out, makes a note.*) I dunno, maybe it wasn't scared. I wouldn't like to say it was. Soon Harry got back, and then Dr. Lloyd came and you, Mr. Peters, and so I guess that's all I know that you don't.

COUNTY ATTORNEY (*rising and looking around*): I guess we'll go upstairs first—and then out to the barn and around there. (*To the Sheriff.*) You're convinced that there was nothing important here—nothing that would point to any motive?

SHERIFF: Nothing here but kitchen things. (*The County Attorney, after again looking around the kitchen, opens the door of a cupboard closet in right wall. He brings a small chair from right—gets on it and looks on a shelf. Pulls his hand away, sticky.*)

COUNTY ATTORNEY: Here's a nice mess. (*The women draw nearer up to center.*)

MRS. PETERS (*to the other woman*): Oh, her fruit; it did freeze. (*To the Lawyer.*) She worried about that when it turned so cold. She said the fire'd go out and her jars would break.

SHERIFF (*rises*): Well, can you beat the woman! Held for murder and worryin' about her preserves.

COUNTY ATTORNEY (*getting down from chair*): I guess before we're through she may have something more serious than preserves to worry about. (*Crosses down right center.*)

HALE: Well, women are used to worrying over trifles. (*The two women move a little closer together.*)

COUNTY ATTORNEY (*with the gallantry of a young politician*): And yet, for all their worries, what would we do without the ladies? (*The women do not unbend. He goes below the center table to the sink, takes a dipperful of water from the pail, and pouring it into a basin, washes his hands. While he is doing this the Sheriff and Hale cross to cupboard, which they inspect. The County Attorney starts to wipe his hands on the roller towel, turns it for a cleaner place.*) Dirty towels! (*Kicks his foot against the pans under the sink.*) Not much of a housekeeper, would you say, ladies?

MRS. HALE (*stiffly*): There's a great deal of work to be done on a farm.

COUNTY ATTORNEY: To be sure. And yet (*with a little bow to her*) I know there are some Dickson County farmhouses which do not have such roller towels. (*He gives it a pull to expose its full-length again.*)

MRS. HALE: Those towels get dirty awful quick. Men's hands aren't always clean as they might be.

COUNTY ATTORNEY: Ah, loyal to your sex, I see. But you and Mrs. Wright were neighbors. I suppose you were friends, too.

MRS. HALE (*shaking her head*): I've not seen much of her of late years. I've not been in this house—it's more than a year.

COUNTY ATTORNEY (*crossing to women up center*): And why was that? You didn't like her?

MRS. HALE: I liked her all well enough. Farmer's wives have their hands full, Mr. Henderson. And then——

COUNTY ATTORNEY: Yes——?

MRS. HALE (*looking about*): It never seemed a very cheerful place.

COUNTY ATTORNEY: No—it's not cheerful. I shouldn't say she had the homemaking instinct.

MRS. HALE: Well, I don't know as Wright had, either.

COUNTY ATTORNEY: You mean that they didn't get on very well?

MRS. HALE: No, I don't mean anything. But I don't think a place'd be any cheerfuller for John Wright's being in it.

COUNTY ATTORNEY: I'd like to talk more of that a little later. I want to get the lay of things upstairs now. (*He goes past the women to up right where the steps lead to a stair door.*)

SHERIFF: I suppose anything Mrs. Peters does'll be all right. She was to take in some clothes for her, you know, and a few little things. We left in such a hurry yesterday.

COUNTY ATTORNEY: Yes, but I would like to see what you take, Mrs. Peters, and keep an eye out for anything that might be of use to us.

MRS. PETERS: Yes, Mr. Henderson. (*The men leave by up right door to stairs. The women listen to the men's steps on the stairs, then look about the kitchen.*)

MRS. HALE (*crossing left to sink*): I'd hate to have men coming into my kitchen, snooping around and criticizing. (*She arranges the pans under sink which the lawyer had shoved out of place.*)

MRS. PETERS: Of course it's no more than their duty. (*Crosses to cupboard up right.*)

MRS. HALE: Duty's all right, but I guess that deputy sheriff that came out to make the fire might have got a little of this on. (*Gives the roller towel a pull.*) Wish I'd thought of that sooner. Seems mean to talk about her for not having things slicked up when she had to come away in such a hurry. (*Crosses right to Mrs. Peters at cupboard.*)

MRS. PETERS (*who has been looking through cupboard, lifts one end of towel that covers a pan*): She had bread set. (*Stands still.*)

MRS. HALE (*eyes fixed on a loaf of bread beside the breadbox, which is on a low shelf of the cupboard*): She was going to put this in there. (*Picks up loaf, abruptly drops it. In a manner of returning to familiar things.*) It's a shame about her fruit. I wonder if it's all gone. (*Gets up on chair and looks.*) I think there's some here that's all right, Mrs. Peters. Yes—here; (*holding it toward the window*) this is cherries, too. (*Looking again.*) I declare I believe that's the only one. (*Gets down, jar in hand. Goes to the sink and wipes it off on the outside.*) She'll feel awful bad after all her hard work in the hot weather. I remember the afternoon I put up my cherries last summer. (*She puts the jar on the big kitchen table, center of the room. With a sigh, is about to sit down in the rocking chair. Before she is seated realizes what chair it is; with a slow look at it, steps back. The chair which she has touched rocks back and forth. Mrs. Peters moves to center table and they both watch the chair rock for a moment or two.*)

MRS. PETERS (*shaking off the mood which the empty rocking chair has evoked.*)

Now in a businesslike manner she speaks): Well I must get those things from the front room closet. (*She goes to the door at the right but, after looking into the other room, steps back.*) You coming with me, Mrs. Hale? You could help me carry them. (*They go in the other room; reappear, Mrs. Peters carrying a dress, petticoat, and skirt, Mrs. Hale following with a pair of shoes.*) My, it's cold in there. (*She puts the clothes on the big table and hurries to the stove.*)

MRS. HALE (*right of center table examining the skirt*): Wright was close. I think maybe that's why she kept so much to herself. She didn't even belong to the Ladies' Aid. I suppose she felt she couldn't do her part, and then you don't enjoy things when you feel shabby. I heard she used to wear pretty clothes and be lively, when she was Minnie Foster, one of the town girls singing in the choir. But that—oh, that was thirty years ago. This all you want to take in?

MRS. PETERS: She said she wanted an apron. Funny thing to want, for there isn't much to get you dirty in jail, goodness knows. But I suppose just to make her feel more natural. (*Crosses to cupboard.*) She said they was in the top drawer in this cupboard. Yes, here. And then her little shawl that always hung behind the door. (*Opens stair door and looks.*) Yes, here it is. (*Quickly shuts door leading upstairs.*)

MRS. HALE (*abruptly moving toward her*): Mrs. Peters?

MRS. PETERS: Yes, Mrs. Hale? (*At up right door.*)

MRS. HALE: Do you think she did it?

MRS. PETERS (*in a frightened voice*): Oh, I don't know.

MRS. HALE: Well, I don't think she did. Asking for an apron and her little shawl. Worrying about her fruit.

MRS. PETERS (*starts to speak, glances up, where footsteps are heard in the room above. In a low voice*): Mr. Peters says it looks bad for her. Mr. Henderson is awful sarcastic in a speech and he'll make fun of her sayin' she didn't wake up.

MRS. HALE: Well, I guess John Wright didn't wake when they was slipping that rope under his neck.

MRS. PETERS (*crossing slowly to table and placing shawl and apron on table with other clothing*): No, it's strange. It must have been done awful crafty and still. They say it was such a—funny way to kill a man, rigging it all up like that.

MRS. HALE (*crossing to left of Mrs. Peters at table*): That's just what Mr. Hale said. There was a gun in the house. He says that's what he can't understand.

MRS. PETERS: Mr. Henderson said coming out that what was needed for the case was a motive: something to show anger, or—sudden feeling.

MRS. HALE (*who is standing by the table*): Well, I don't see any signs of anger around here. (*She puts her hand on the dish towel, which lies on the table, stands looking down at table, one-half of which is clean, the other half messy.*) It's wiped to here. (*Makes a move as if to finish work, then turns and looks at loaf of bread outside the breadbox. Drops towel. In that voice of coming back to familiar things.*) Wonder how they are finding things upstairs. (*Crossing below table to down right.*) I hope she had it a little more red-up up there. You know, it seems kind of *sneaking*. Locking her up in town and then coming out here and trying to get her own house to turn against her!

MRS. PETERS: But, Mrs. Hale, the law is the law.

MRS. HALE: I s'pose 'tis. (*Unbuttoning her coat.*) Better loosen up your things, Mrs. Peters. You won't feel them when you go out. (*Mrs. Peters takes off her fur tippet, goes to hang it on chair back left of table, stands looking at the work basket on floor near down left window.*)

MRS. PETERS: She was piecing a quilt. (*She brings the large sewing basket to the center table and they look at the bright pieces, Mrs. Hale above the table and Mrs. Peters left of it.*)

MRS. HALE: It's a log cabin pattern. Pretty, isn't it? I wonder if she was goin' to quilt it or just knot it? (*Footsteps have been heard coming down the stairs. The Sheriff enters followed by Hale and the County Attorney.*)

SHERIFF: They wonder if she was going to quilt it or just knot it! (*The men laugh, the women look abashed.*)

COUNTY ATTORNEY (*rubbing his hands over the stove*): Frank's fire didn't do much up there, did it? Well, let's go out to the barn and get that cleared up. (*The men go outside by up left door.*)

MRS. HALE (*resentfully*): I don't know as there's anything so strange, our takin' up our time with little things while we're waiting for them to get the evidence. (*She sits in chair right of table smoothing out a block with decision.*) I don't see as it's anything to laugh about.

MRS. PETERS (*apologetically*): Of course they've got awful important things on their minds. (*Pulls up a chair and joins Mrs. Hale at the left of the table.*)

MRS. HALE (*examining another block*): Mrs. Peters, look at this one. Here, this is the one she was working on, and look at the sewing! All the rest of it has been so nice and even. And look at this! It's all over the place! Why, it looks as if she didn't know what she was about! (*After she has said this they look at each other, then start to glance back at the door. After an instant Mrs. Hale has pulled at a knot and ripped the sewing.*)

MRS. PETERS: Oh, what are you doing, Mrs. Hale?

MRS. HALE (*mildly*): Just pulling out a stitch or two that's not sewed very good. (*Threading a needle.*) Bad sewing always made me fidgety.

MRS. PETERS (*with a glance at the door, nervously*): I don't think we ought to touch things.

MRS. HALE: I'll just finish up this end. (*Suddenly stopping and leaning forward.*) Mrs. Peters?

MRS. PETERS: Yes, Mrs. Hale?

MRS. HALE: What do you suppose she was so nervous about?

MRS. PETERS: Oh—I don't know. I don't know as she was nervous. I sometimes sew awful queer when I'm just tired. (*Mrs. Hale starts to say something, looks at Mrs. Peters, then goes on sewing.*) Well, I must get these things wrapped up. They may be through sooner than we think. (*Putting apron and other things together.*) I wonder where I can find a piece of paper, and string. (*Rises.*)

MRS. HALE: In that cupboard, maybe.

MRS. PETERS (*crosses right looking in cupboard*): Why, here's a bird-cage. (*Holds it up.*) Did she have a bird, Mrs. Hale?

MRS. HALE: Why, I don't know whether she did or not—I've not been here for so long. There was a man around last year selling canaries cheap, but I don't know as she took one; maybe she did. She used to sing real pretty herself.

MRS. PETERS (*glancing around*): Seems funny to think of a bird here. But she must have had one, or why would she have a cage? I wonder what happened to it?

MRS. HALE: I s'pose maybe the cat got it.

MRS. PETERS: No, she didn't have a cat. She's got that feeling some people have about cats—being afraid of them. My cat got in her room and she was real upset and asked me to take it out.

MRS. HALE: My sister Bessie was like that. Queer, ain't it?

MRS. PETERS (*examining the cage*): Why, look at this door. It's broke. One hinge is pulled apart. (*Takes a step down to Mrs. Hale's right.*)

MRS. HALE (*looking too*): Looks as if someone must have been rough with it.

MRS. PETERS: Why, yes. (*She brings the cage forward and puts it on the table.*)

MRS. HALE (*glancing toward up left door*): I wish if they're going to find any evidence they'd be about it. I don't like this place.

MRS. PETERS: But I'm awful glad you came with me, Mrs. Hale. It would be lonesome for me sitting here alone.

MRS. HALE: It would, wouldn't it? (*Dropping her sewing.*) But I tell you what I do wish, Mrs. Peters. I wish I had come over sometimes when she was here. I—(*looking around the room*)—wish I had.

MRS. PETERS: But of course you were awful busy, Mrs. Hale—your house and your children.

MRS. HALE (*rises and crosses left*): I could've come. I stayed away because it weren't cheerful—and that's why I ought to have come. I—(*looking out left window*)—I've never liked this place. Maybe it's because it's down in a hollow and you don't see the road. I dunno what it is, but it's a lonesome place and always was. I wish I had come over to see Minnie Foster sometimes. I can see now—(*Shakes her head.*)

MRS. PETERS (*left of table and above it*): Well, you mustn't reproach your-self, Mrs. Hale. Somehow we just don't see how it is with other folks until—something turns up.

MRS. HALE: Not having children makes less work—but it makes a quiet house, and Wright out to work all day, and no company when he did come in. (*Turning from window.*) Did you know John Wright, Mrs. Peters?

MRS. PETERS: Not to know him; I've seen him in town. They say he was a good man.

MRS. HALE: Yes—good; he didn't drink, and kept his word as well as most, I guess, and paid his debts. But he was a hard man, Mrs. Peters. Just to pass the time of day with him—(*Shivers.*) Like a raw wind that gets to the bone. (*Pauses, her eye falling on the cage.*) I should think she would 'a' wanted a bird. But what do you suppose went with it?

MRS. PETERS: I don't know, unless it got sick and died. (*She reaches over and swings the broken door, swings it again, both women watch it.*)

MRS. HALE: You weren't raised round here, were you? (*Mrs. Peters shakes her head.*) You didn't know—her?

MRS. PETERS: Not till they brought her yesterday.

MRS. HALE: She—come to think of it, she was kind of like a bird her-self—real sweet and pretty, but kind of timid and—fluttery. How—she—did—change. (*Silence: then as if struck by a happy thought and relieved to get back to everyday things. Crosses right above Mrs. Peters to cupboard, replaces small chair used to stand on to its original place down right.*) Tell you what, Mrs. Peters, why don't you take the quilt in with you? It might take up her mind.

MRS. PETERS: Why, I think that's a real nice idea, Mrs. Hale. There couldn't possibly be any objection to it could there? Now, just what would I take? I wonder if her patches are in here—and her things. (*They look in the sewing basket.*)

MRS. HALE (*crosses to right of table*): Here's some red. I expect this has got sewing things in it. (*Brings out a fancy box.*) What a pretty box. Looks like something somebody would give you. Maybe her scissors are in here. (*Opens box. Suddenly puts her hand to her nose.*) Why———(*Mrs. Peters bends nearer, then turns her face away.*) There's something wrapped up in this piece of silk.

MRS. PETERS: Why, this isn't her scissors.

MRS. HALE (*lifting the silk*): Oh, Mrs. Peters—it's———(*Mrs. Peters bends closer.*)

MRS. PETERS: It's the bird.

MRS. HALE: But, Mrs. Peters—look at it! Its neck! Look at its neck! It's all—other side *to*.

MRS. PETERS: Somebody—wrung—its—neck. (*Their eyes meet. A look of growing comprehension, of horror. Steps are heard outside. Mrs. Hale slips*

box under quilt pieces, and sinks into her chair. Enter Sheriff and County
Attorney. Mrs. Peters steps down left and stands looking out of window.)

COUNTY ATTORNEY (*as one turning from serious things to little pleasant-
ries*): Well, ladies, have you decided whether she was going to quilt it
or knot it? (*Crosses to center above table.*)

MRS. PETERS: We think she was going to—knot it. (*Sheriff crosses to right
of stove, lifts stove lid, and glances at fire, then stands warming hands at
stove.*)

COUNTY ATTORNEY: Well, that's interesting, I'm sure. (*Seeing the bird-cage.*)
Has the bird flown?

MRS. HALE (*putting more quilt pieces over the box*): We think the—cat
got it.

COUNTY ATTORNEY (*preoccupied*): Is there a cat? (*Mrs. Hale glances in a
quick covert way at Mrs. Peters.*)

MRS. PETERS (*turning from window takes a step in*): Well, not *now*. They're
superstitious, you know. They leave.

COUNTY ATTORNEY (*to Sheriff Peters, continuing an interrupted conversation*): No sign at all of anyone having come from the outside. Their
own rope. Now let's go up again and go over it piece by piece. (*They
start upstairs.*) It would have to have been someone who knew just
the———(*Mrs. Peters sits down left of table. The two women sit there not
looking at one another, but as if peering into something and at the same time
holding back. When they talk now it is in the manner of feeling their way over
strange ground, as if afraid of what they are saying, but as if they cannot help
saying it.*)

MRS. HALE (*hesitatively and in hushed voice*): She liked the bird. She was
going to bury it in that pretty box.

MRS. PETERS (*in a whisper*): When I was a girl—my kitten—there was a
boy took a hatchet, and before my eyes—and before I could get
there———(*Covers her face an instant.*) If they hadn't held me back I
would have—(*catches herself, looks upstairs where steps are heard, falters
weakly*)—hurt him.

MRS. HALE (*with a slow look around her*): I wonder how it would seem
never to have had any children around. (*Pause.*) No, Wright wouldn't
like the bird—a thing that sang. She used to sing. He killed that, too.

MRS. PETERS (*moving uneasily*): We don't know who killed the bird.

MRS. HALE: I knew John Wright.

MRS. PETERS: It was an awful thing was done in this house that night,
Mrs. Hale. Killing a man while he slept, slipping a rope around his
neck that choked the life out of him.

MRS. HALE: His neck. Choked the life out of him. (*Her hand goes out and
rests on the bird-cage.*)

MRS. PETERS (*with rising voice*): We don't know who killed him. We don't know.

MRS. HALE (*her own feelings not interrupted*): If there'd been years and years of nothing, then a bird to sing to you, it would be awful—still, after the bird was still.

MRS. PETERS (*something within her speaking*): I know what stillness is. When we homesteaded in Dakota, and my first baby died—after he was two years old, and me with no other then——

MRS. HALE (*moving*): How soon do you suppose they'll be through looking for the evidence?

MRS. PETERS: I know what stillness is. (*Pulling herself back.*) The law has got to punish crimes, Mrs. Hale.

MRS. HALE (*not as if answering that*): I wish you'd seen Minnie Foster when she wore a white dress with blue ribbons and stood up there in the choir and sang. (*A look around the room.*) Oh, I *wish* I'd come over here once in a while! That was a crime! That was a crime! Who's going to punish that?

MRS. PETERS (*looking upstairs*): We mustn't—take on.

MRS. HALE: I might have known she needed help! I know how things can be—for women. I tell you, it's queer, Mrs. Peters. We live close together and we live far apart. We all go through the same things—it's all just a different kind of the same thing. (*Brushes her eyes, noticing the jar of fruit, reaches out for it.*) If I was you I wouldn't tell her her fruit was gone. Tell her it ain't. Tell her it's all right. Take this in to prove it to her. She—she may never know whether it was broke or not.   ☉

MRS. PETERS (*takes the jar, looks about for something to wrap it in; takes petticoat from the clothes brought from the other room, very nervously begins winding this around the jar. In a false voice*): My, it's a good thing the men couldn't hear us. Wouldn't they just laugh! Getting all stirred up over a little thing like a—dead canary. As if that could have anything to do with—with—wouldn't they *laugh*! (*The men are heard coming downstairs.*)

MRS. HALE (*under her breath*): Maybe they would—maybe they wouldn't.

COUNTY ATTORNEY: No, Peters, it's all perfectly clear except a reason for doing it. But you know juries when it comes to women. If there was some definite thing. (*Crosses slowly to above table. Sheriff crosses down right. Mrs. Hale and Mrs. Peters remain seated at either side of table.*) Something to show—something to make a story about—a thing that would connect up with this strange way of doing it——(*The women's eyes meet for an instant. Enter Hale from outer door.*)

HALE (*remaining by door*): Well, I've got the team around. Pretty cold out there.

COUNTY ATTORNEY: I'm going to stay awhile by myself. (*To the Sheriff.*) You can send Frank out for me, can't you? I want to go over everything. I'm not satisfied that we can't do better.

SHERIFF: Do you want to see what Mrs. Peters is going to take in? (*The Lawyer picks up the apron, laughs.*)

COUNTY ATTORNEY: Oh, I guess they're not very dangerous things the ladies have picked out. (*Moves a few things about, disturbing the quilt pieces which cover the box. Steps back.*) No, Mrs. Peters doesn't need supervising. For that matter a sheriff's wife is married to the law. Ever think of it that way, Mrs. Peters?

MRS. PETERS: Not—just that way. *—Obstruct Justice—don't tell them the mot*

SHERIFF (*chuckling*): Married to the law. (*Moves to down right door to the other room.*) I just want you to come in here a minute, George. We ought to take a look at these windows.

COUNTY ATTORNEY (*scoffingly*): Oh, windows!

SHERIFF: We'll be right out, Mr. Hale. (*Hale goes outside. The Sheriff follows the County Attorney into the room. Then Mrs. Hale rises, hands tight together, looking intensely at Mrs. Peters, whose eyes make a slow turn, finally meeting Mrs. Hale's. A moment Mrs. Hale holds her, then her own eyes point the way to where the box is concealed. Suddenly Mrs. Peters throws back quilt pieces and tries to put the box in the bag she is carrying. It is too big. She opens box, starts to take bird out, cannot touch it, goes to pieces, stands there helpless. Sound of a knob turning in the other room. Mrs. Hale snatches the box and puts it in the pocket of her big coat. Enter County Attorney and Sheriff, who remains down right.*)

COUNTY ATTORNEY (*crosses to up left door facetiously*): Well, Henry, at least we found out that she was not going to quilt it. She was going to—what is it you call it, ladies?

MRS. HALE (*standing center below table facing front, her hand against her pocket*): We call it—knot it, Mr. Henderson.

[1916]

Why not tell them?
- they feel bad for her & can relate
Play Raises questions About marriage, womens role in marriage in this time period (1916)

TENNESSEE WILLIAMS [1911–1983]

The Glass Menagerie

nobody, not even the rain, has such small hands
— E. E. CUMMINGS

Production Notes by Tennessee Williams

Being a "memory play," *The Glass Menagerie* can be presented with unusual freedom of convention. Because of its considerably delicate or tenuous material, atmospheric touches and subtleties of direction play a particularly important part. Expressionism and all other unconventional techniques in drama have only one valid aim, and this is a closer approach to truth. When a play employs unconventional techniques, it is not, or certainly shouldn't be, trying to escape its responsibility of dealing with reality, or interpreting experience, but is actually or should be attempting to find a closer approach, or more penetrating and vivid expression of things as they are. The straight realistic play with its genuine frigidaire and authentic ice cubes, its characters that speak exactly as its audience speaks, corresponds to the academic landscape and has the same virtue of a photographic likeness. Everyone should know nowadays the unimportance of the photographic in art: that truth, life, or reality is an organic thing which the poetic imagination can represent or suggest, in essence, only through transformation, through changing into other forms than those which were merely present in appearance.

These remarks are not meant as a preface only to this particular play. They have to do with a conception of a new, plastic theatre which must take the place of the exhausted theatre of realistic conventions if the theatre is to resume vitality as a part of our culture.

The Screen Device: There is *only one important difference between the original and acting version of the play* and that is the *omission* in the latter of the device which I tentatively included in my *original* script. This device was the use of a screen on which were projected magic-lantern slides bearing images or titles. I do not regret the omission of this device from the present Broadway production. The extraordinary power of Miss Taylor's° performance made it suitable to have the utmost simplicity in the physical production. But I

Miss Taylor: Referring to the performance of Laurette Taylor, who played Amanda Wingfield in the original Broadway production in 1945.

think it may be interesting to some readers to see how this device was conceived. So I am putting it into the published manuscript. These images and legends, projected from behind, were cast on a section of wall between the front-room and dining-room areas, which should be indistinguishable from the rest when not in use.

The purpose of this will probably be apparent. It is to give accent to certain values in each scene. Each scene contains a particular point (or several) which is structurally the most important. In an episodic play, such as this, the basic structure or narrative line may be obscured from the audience; the effect may seem fragmentary rather than architectural. This may not be the fault of the play so much as a lack of attention in the audience. The legend or image upon the screen will strengthen the effect of what is merely allusion in the writing and allow the primary point to be made more simply and lightly than if the entire responsibility were on the spoken lines. Aside from this structural value, I think the screen will have a definite emotional appeal, less definable but just as important. An imaginative producer or director may invent many other uses for this device than those indicated in the present script. In fact the possibilities of the device seem much larger to me than the instance of this play can possibly utilize.

The Music: Another extra-literary accent in this play is provided by the use of music. A single recurring tune, "The Glass Menagerie," is used to give emotional emphasis to suitable passages. This tune is like circus music, not when you are on the grounds or in the immediate vicinity of the parade, but when you are at some distance and very likely thinking of something else. It seems under those circumstances to continue almost interminably and it weaves in and out of your preoccupied consciousness; then it is the lightest, most delicate music in the world and perhaps the saddest. It expresses the surface vivacity of life with the underlying strain of immutable and inexpressible sorrow. When you look at a piece of delicately spun glass you think of two things: how beautiful it is and how easily it can be broken. Both of those ideas should be woven into the recurring tune, which dips in and out of the play as if it were carried on a wind that changes. It serves as a thread of connection and allusion between the narrator with his separate point in time and space and the subject of his story. Between each episode it returns as reference to the emotion, nostalgia, which is the first condition of the play. It is primarily Laura's music and therefore comes out most clearly when the play focuses upon her and the lovely fragility of glass which is her image.

The Lighting: The lighting in the play is not realistic. In keeping with the atmosphere of memory, the stage is dim. Shafts of light are focused on selected areas or actors, sometimes in contradistinction to what is the apparent center. For instance, in the quarrel scene between Tom and Amanda, in which Laura has no active part, the clearest pool of light is on her figure. This is also true of the supper scene, when her silent figure on the sofa should remain the visual center. The light upon Laura should be distinct from the others, having a peculiar pristine clarity such as light used in early religious portraits of female saints or madonnas. A certain correspondence to light in religious paintings, such as El Greco's, where the figures are radiant in atmosphere that is relatively dusky, could be effectively used throughout the play. (It will also permit a more effective use of the screen.) A free, imaginative use of light can be of enormous value in giving a mobile, plastic quality to plays of a more or less static nature.

Characters

AMANDA WINGFIELD, *the mother. A little woman of great but confused vitality clinging frantically to another time and place. Her characterization must be carefully created, not copied from type. She is not paranoiac, but her life is paranoia. There is much to admire in Amanda, and as much to love and pity as there is to laugh at. Certainly she has endurance and a kind of heroism, and though her foolishness makes her unwittingly cruel at times, there is tenderness in her slight person.*

LAURA WINGFIELD, *her daughter. Amanda, having failed to establish contact with reality, continues to live vitally in her illusions, but Laura's situation is even graver. A childhood illness has left her crippled, one leg slightly shorter than the other, and held in a brace. This defect need not be more than suggested on the stage. Stemming from this, Laura's separation increases till she is like a piece of her own glass collection, too exquisitely fragile to move from the shelf.*

TOM WINGFIELD, *her son. And the narrator of the play. A poet with a job in a warehouse. His nature is not remorseless, but to escape from a trap he has to act without pity.*

JIM O'CONNOR, *the gentleman caller. A nice, ordinary, young man.*

Scene: *An alley in St. Louis.*
Part I: *Preparation for a Gentleman Caller.*
Part II: *The Gentleman Calls.*
Time: *Now and the Past.*

SCENE 1

(The Wingfield apartment is in the rear of the building, one of those vast hive-like conglomerations of cellular living-units that flower as warty growths in over-crowded urban centers of lower middle-class population and are symptomatic of the impulse of this largest and fundamentally enslaved section of American society to avoid fluidity and differentiation and to exist and function as one interfused mass of automatism.)

(The apartment faces an alley and is entered by a fire escape, a structure whose name is a touch of accidental poetic truth, for all of these huge buildings are always

burning with the slow and implacable fires of human desperation. The fire escape is included in the set — that is, the landing of it and steps descending from it.)

(The scene is memory and is therefore nonrealistic. Memory takes a lot of poetic license. It omits some details; others are exaggerated, according to the emotional value of the articles it touches, for memory is seated predominantly in the heart. The interior is therefore rather dim and poetic.)

(At the rise of the curtain, the audience is faced with the dark, grim rear wall of the Wingfield tenement. This building, which runs parallel to the footlights, is flanked on both sides by dark, narrow alleys which run into murky canyons of tangled clothes-lines, garbage cans, and the sinister latticework of neighboring fire escapes. It is up and down these side alleys that exterior entrances and exits are made, during the play. At the end of Tom's opening commentary, the dark tenement wall slowly reveals [by means of a transparency] the interior of the ground floor Wingfield apartment.)

(Downstage is the living room, which also serves as a sleeping room for Laura, the sofa unfolding to make her bed. Upstage, center, and divided by a wide arch or second proscenium with transparent faded portieres [or second curtain], is the dining room. In an old-fashioned what-not in the living room are seen scores of transparent glass animals. A blown-up photograph of the father hangs on the wall of the living room, facing the audience, to the left of the archway. It is the face of a very handsome young man in a doughboy's First World War cap. He is gallantly smiling, ineluctably smiling, as if to say, "I will be smiling forever.")

(The audience hears and sees the opening scene in the dining room through both the transparent fourth wall of the building and the transparent gauze portieres of the dining-room arch. It is during this revealing scene that the fourth wall slowly ascends, out of sight. This transparent exterior wall is not brought down again until the very end of the play, during Tom's final speech.)

(The narrator is an undisguised convention of the play. He takes whatever license with dramatic convention as is convenient to his purposes.)

(Tom enters dressed as a merchant sailor from alley, stage left, and strolls across the front of the stage to the fire escape. There he stops and lights a cigarette. He addresses the audience.)

TOM: Yes, I have tricks in my pocket, I have things up my sleeve. But I am the opposite of a stage magician. He gives you illusion that has the appearance of truth. I give you truth in the pleasant disguise of illusion. To begin with, I turn back time. I reverse it to that quaint period, the thirties, when the huge middle class of America was matriculating in a school for the blind. Their eyes had failed them, or they had failed their eyes, and so they were having their fingers pressed forcibly down on the fiery Braille alphabet of a dissolving economy. In Spain there was revolution. Here there was only shouting and confusion. In Spain there was Guernica.° Here there were disturbances of labor, sometimes pretty violent, in otherwise peaceful cities such as Chicago, Cleveland, Saint Louis. . . . This is the social background of the play.

Guernica: A Spanish town bombed by Germany during the Spanish Civil War.

(*Music.*)

The play is memory. Being a memory play, it is dimly lighted, it is sentimental, it is not realistic. In memory everything seems to happen to music. That explains the fiddle in the wings. I am the narrator of the play, and also a character in it. The other characters are my mother, Amanda, my sister, Laura, and a gentleman caller who appears in the final scenes. He is the most realistic character in the play, being an emissary from a world of reality that we were somehow set apart from. But since I have a poet's weakness for symbols, I am using this character also as a symbol; he is the long delayed but always expected something that we live for. There is a fifth character in the play who doesn't appear except in this larger-than-life photograph over the mantel. This is our father who left us a long time ago. He was a telephone man who fell in love with long distances; he gave up his job with the telephone company and skipped the light fantastic out of town . . . The last we heard of him was a picture postcard from Mazatlan, on the Pacific coast of Mexico, containing a message of two words—"Hello—Good-bye!" and no address. I think the rest of the play will explain itself. . . .

(*Amanda's voice becomes audible through the portieres.*)
     (*Legend on Screen: "Où Sont les Neiges."*°)
     (*He divides the portieres and enters the upstage area.*)
     (*Amanda and Laura are seated at a drop-leaf table. Eating is indicated by gestures without food or utensils. Amanda faces the audience. Tom and Laura are seated in profile.*)
     (*The interior has lit up softly and through the scrim we see Amanda and Laura seated at the table in the upstage area.*)

AMANDA (*calling*): Tom?
TOM: Yes, Mother.
AMANDA: We can't say grace until you come to the table!
TOM: Coming, Mother. (*He bows slightly and withdraws, reappearing a few moments later in his place at the table.*)
AMANDA (*to her son*): Honey, don't *push* with your *fingers*. If you have to push with something, the thing to push with is a crust of bread. And chew—chew! Animals have sections in their stomachs which enable them to digest food without mastication, but human beings are supposed to chew their food before they swallow it down. Eat food leisurely, son, and really enjoy it. A well-cooked meal has lots of delicate flavors that have to be held in the mouth for appreciation. So chew your food and give your salivary glands a chance to function!

"Où Sont les Neiges": "Où sont les neiges d'antan?" ("Where are the snows of yesteryear?") is a line from a poem by fifteenth-century French poet François Villon.

(*Tom deliberately lays his imaginary fork down and pushes his chair back from the table.*)

Tom: I haven't enjoyed one bite of this dinner because of your constant directions on how to eat it. It's you that makes me rush through meals with your hawk-like attention to every bite I take. Sickening—spoils my appetite—all this discussion of animals' secretion—salivary glands—mastication!

Amanda (*lightly*): Temperament like a Metropolitan° star! (*He rises and crosses downstage.*) You're not excused from the table.

Tom: I'm getting a cigarette.

Amanda: You smoke too much.

(*Laura rises.*)

Laura: I'll bring in the blancmange.

(*He remains standing with his cigarette by the portieres during the following.*)

Amanda (*rising*): No, sister, no, sister—you be the lady this time and I'll be the darky.

Laura: I'm already up.

Amanda: Resume your seat, little sister—I want you to stay fresh and pretty—for gentlemen callers!

Laura: I'm not expecting any gentlemen callers.

Amanda (*crossing out to kitchenette. Airily*): Sometimes they come when they are least expected! Why, I remember one Sunday afternoon in Blue Mountain—(*Enters kitchenette.*)

Tom: I know what's coming!

Laura: Yes. But let her tell it.

Tom: Again?

Laura: She loves to tell it.

(*Amanda returns with bowl of dessert.*)

Amanda: One Sunday afternoon in Blue Mountain—your mother received—*seventeen!*—gentlemen callers! Why, sometimes there weren't chairs enough to accommodate them all. We had to send the nigger over to bring in folding chairs from the parish house.

Tom (*remaining at portieres*): How did you entertain those gentlemen callers?

Amanda: I understood the art of conversation!

Tom: I bet you could talk.

Amanda: Girls in those days *knew* how to talk, I can tell you.

Tom: Yes?

Metropolitan: Metropolitan Opera.

(*Image: Amanda as a girl on a porch greeting callers.*)

AMANDA: They knew how to entertain their gentlemen callers. It wasn't enough for a girl to be possessed of a pretty face and a graceful figure—although I wasn't slighted in either respect. She also needed to have a nimble wit and a tongue to meet all occasions.

TOM: What did you talk about?

AMANDA: Things of importance going on in the world! Never anything coarse or common or vulgar. (*She addresses Tom as though he were seated in the vacant chair at the table though he remains by portieres. He plays this scene as though he held the book.*) My callers were gentlemen—all! Among my callers were some of the most prominent young planters of the Mississippi Delta—planters and sons of planters!

(*Tom motions for music and a spot of light on Amanda.*)
    (*Her eyes lift, her face glows, her voice becomes rich and elegiac.*)
    (*Screen legend: "Où Sont les Neiges."*)

There was young Champ Laughlin who later became vice-president of the Delta Planters Bank. Hadley Stevenson who was drowned in Moon Lake and left his widow one hundred and fifty thousand in Government bonds. There were the Cutrere brothers, Wesley and Bates. Bates was one of my bright particular beaux! He got in a quarrel with that wild Wainright boy. They shot it out on the floor of Moon Lake Casino. Bates was shot through the stomach. Died in the ambulance on his way to Memphis. His widow was also well-provided for, came into eight or ten thousand acres, that's all. She married him on the rebound—never loved her—carried my picture on him the night he died! And there was that boy that every girl in the Delta had set her cap for! That beautiful, brilliant young Fitzhugh boy from Greene County!

TOM: What did he leave his widow?

AMANDA: He never married! Gracious, you talk as though all of my old admirers had turned up their toes to the daisies!

TOM: Isn't this the first you mentioned that still survives?

AMANDA: That Fitzhugh boy went North and made a fortune—came to be known as the Wolf of Wall Street! He had the Midas touch, whatever he touched turned to gold! And I could have been Mrs. Duncan J. Fitzhugh, mind you! But—I picked your *father*!

LAURA (*rising*): Mother, let me clear the table.

AMANDA: No, dear, you go in front and study your typewriter chart. Or practice your shorthand a little. Stay fresh and pretty!—It's almost time for our gentlemen callers to start arriving. (*She flounces girlishly toward the kitchenette.*) How many do you suppose we're going to entertain this afternoon?

(*Tom throws down the paper and jumps up with a groan.*)

LAURA (*alone in the dining room*): I don't believe we're going to receive any, Mother.

AMANDA (*reappearing, airily*): What? No one—not one? You must be joking! (*Laura nervously echoes her laugh. She slips in a fugitive manner through the half-open portieres and draws them gently behind her. A shaft of very clear light is thrown on her face against the faded tapestry of the curtains. Music: "The Glass Menagerie" under faintly. Lightly.*) Not one gentleman caller? It can't be true! There must be a flood, there must have been a tornado!

LAURA: It isn't a flood, it's not a tornado, Mother. I'm just not popular like you were in Blue Mountain. . . . (*Tom utters another groan. Laura glances at him with a faint, apologetic smile. Her voice catching a little.*) Mother's afraid I'm going to be an old maid.

(*The scene dims out with "Glass Menagerie" music.*)

SCENE 2

("*Laura, Haven't You Ever Liked Some Boy?*")
(*On the dark stage the screen is lighted with the image of blue roses.*)
(*Gradually Laura's figure becomes apparent and the screen goes out.*)
(*The music subsides.*)
(*Laura is seated in the delicate ivory chair at the small clawfoot table.*)
(*She wears a dress of soft violet material for a kimono—her hair tied back from her forehead with a ribbon.*)
(*She is washing and polishing her collection of glass.*)
(*Amanda appears on the fire escape steps. At the sound of her ascent, Laura catches her breath, thrusts the bowl of ornaments away and seats herself stiffly before the diagram of the typewriter keyboard as though it held her spellbound. Something has happened to Amanda. It is written in her face as she climbs to the landing: a look that is grim and hopeless and a little absurd.*)
(*She has on one of those cheap or imitation velvety-looking cloth coats with imitation fur collar. Her hat is five or six years old, one of those dreadful cloche hats that were worn in the late twenties, and she is clasping an enormous black patent-leather pocketbook with nickel clasp and initials. This is her full-dress outfit, the one she usually wears to the D.A.R.°*)
(*Before entering she looks through the door.*)

D.A.R.: Daughters of the American Revolution is a patriotic organization for women whose ancestors were part of the American War of Independence.

(*She purses her lips, opens her eyes wide, rolls them upward and shakes her head.*)

(*Then she slowly lets herself in the door. Seeing her mother's expression Laura touches her lips with a nervous gesture.*)

LAURA: Hello, Mother, I was—(*She makes a nervous gesture toward the chart on the wall. Amanda leans against the shut door and stares at Laura with a martyred look.*)

AMANDA: Deception? Deception? (*She slowly removes her hat and gloves, continuing the swift suffering stare. She lets the hat and gloves fall on the floor—a bit of acting.*)

LAURA (*shakily*): How was the D.A.R. meeting? (*Amanda slowly opens her purse and removes a dainty white handkerchief which she shakes out delicately and delicately touches to her lips and nostrils.*) Didn't you go to the D.A.R. meeting, Mother?

AMANDA (*faintly, almost inaudibly*): —No.—No. (*Then more forcibly*). I did not have the strength—to go to the D.A.R. In fact, I did not have the courage! I wanted to find a hole in the ground and hide myself in it forever! (*She crosses slowly to the wall and removes the diagram of the typewriter keyboard. She holds it in front of her for a second, staring at it sweetly and sorrowfully—then bites her lips and tears it in two pieces.*)

LAURA (*faintly*): Why did you do that, Mother? (*Amanda repeats the same procedure with the chart of the Gregg Alphabet.*) Why are you—

AMANDA: Why? Why? How old are you, Laura?

LAURA: Mother, you know my age.

AMANDA: I thought that you were an adult; it seems that I was mistaken. (*She crosses slowly to the sofa and sinks down and stares at Laura.*)

LAURA: Please don't stare at me, Mother.

(*Amanda closes her eyes and lowers her head. Count ten.*)

AMANDA: What are we going to do, what is going to become of us, what is the future?

(*Count ten.*)

LAURA: Has something happened, Mother? (*Amanda draws a long breath and takes out the handkerchief again. Dabbing process.*) Mother, has—something happened?

AMANDA: I'll be all right in a minute. I'm just bewildered—(*Count five.*)—by life. . . .

LAURA: Mother, I wish that you would tell me what's happened.

AMANDA: As you know, I was supposed to be inducted into my office at the D.A.R. this afternoon. (*Image: a swarm of typewriters.*) But I stopped off at Rubicam's Business College to speak to your teachers about your having a cold and ask them what progress they thought you were making down there.

LAURA: Oh. . . .

AMANDA: I went to the typing instructor and introduced myself as your mother. She didn't know who you were. Wingfield, she said. We don't have any such student enrolled at the school! I assured her she did, that you had been going to classes since early in January. "I wonder," she said, "if you could be talking about that terribly shy little girl who dropped out of school after only a few days' attendance?" "No," I said, "Laura, my daughter, has been going to school every day for the past six weeks!" "Excuse me," she said. She took the attendance book out and there was your name, unmistakably printed, and all the dates you were absent until they decided that you had dropped out of school. I still said, "No, there must have been some mistake! There must have been some mix-up in the records!" And she said, "No—I remember her perfectly now. Her hands shook so that she couldn't hit the right keys! The first time we gave a speed test, she broke down completely—was sick at the stomach and almost had to be carried into the wash-room! After that morning she never showed up any more. We phoned the house but never got any answer"—while I was working at Famous and Barr, I suppose, demonstrating those—Oh! I felt so weak I could barely keep on my feet. I had to sit down while they got me a glass of water! Fifty dollars' tuition, all of our plans—my hopes and ambitions for you—just gone up the spout, just gone up the spout like that. (*Laura draws a long breath and gets awkwardly to her feet. She crosses to the victrola and winds it up.*) What are you doing?

LAURA: Oh! (*She releases the handle and returns to her seat.*)

AMANDA: Laura, where have you been going when you've gone out pretending that you were going to business college?

LAURA: I've just been going out walking.

AMANDA: That's not true.

LAURA: It is. I just went walking.

AMANDA: Walking? Walking? In winter? Deliberately courting pneumonia in that light coat? Where did you walk to, Laura?

LAURA: All sorts of places—mostly in the park.

AMANDA: Even after you'd started catching that cold?

LAURA: It was the lesser of two evils, Mother. (*Image: winter scene in park.*) I couldn't go back up. I—threw up—on the floor!

AMANDA: From half past seven till after five every day you mean to tell me you walked around in the park, because you wanted to make me think that you were still going to Rubicam's Business College?

LAURA: It wasn't as bad as it sounds. I went inside places to get warmed up.

AMANDA: Inside where?

LAURA: I went in the art museum and the bird houses at the Zoo. I visited the penguins every day! Sometimes I did without lunch and went to the movies. Lately I've been spending most of my afternoons in the Jewel-box, that big glass house where they raise the tropical flowers.

AMANDA: You did all this to deceive me, just for the deception? (*Laura looks down.*) Why?

LAURA: Mother, when you're disappointed, you get that awful suffering look on your face, like the picture of Jesus' mother in the museum!

AMANDA: Hush!

LAURA: I couldn't face it.

(*Pause. A whisper of strings.*)
(*Legend: "The Crust of Humility."*)

AMANDA (*hopelessly fingering the huge pocketbook*): So what are we going to do the rest of our lives? Stay home and watch the parades go by? Amuse ourselves with the glass menagerie, darling? Eternally play those worn-out phonograph records your father left as a painful reminder of him? We won't have a business career—we've given that up because it gave us nervous indigestion! (*Laughs wearily.*) What is there left but dependency all our lives? I know so well what becomes of unmarried women who aren't prepared to occupy a position. I've seen such pitiful cases in the South—barely tolerated spinsters living upon the grudging patronage of sister's husband or brother's wife!—stuck away in some little mousetrap of a room—encouraged by one in-law to visit another—little birdlike women without any nest—eating the crust of humility all their life! Is that the future that we've mapped out for ourselves? I swear it's the only alternative I can think of! It isn't a very pleasant alternative, is it? Of course—some girls do *marry*. (*Laura twists her hands nervously.*) Haven't you ever liked some boy?

LAURA: Yes. I liked one once. (*Rises.*) I came across his picture a while ago.

AMANDA (*with some interest*): He gave you his picture?

LAURA: No, it's in the yearbook.

AMANDA (*disappointed*): Oh—a high-school boy.

(*Screen image: Jim as high school hero bearing a silver cup.*)

LAURA: Yes. His name was Jim. (*Laura lifts the heavy annual from the clawfoot table.*) Here he is in The Pirates of Penzance.

AMANDA (*absently*): The what?

LAURA: The operetta the senior class put on. He had a wonderful voice and we sat across the aisle from each other Mondays, Wednesdays, and Fridays in the Aud. Here he is with the silver cup for debating! See his grin?

AMANDA (*absently*): He must have had a jolly disposition.
LAURA: He used to call me—Blue Roses.

(*Image: blue roses.*)

AMANDA: Why did he call you such a name as that?
LAURA: When I had that attack of pleurosis—he asked me what was the matter when I came back. I said pleurosis—he thought that I said Blue Roses! So that's what he always called me after that. Whenever he saw me, he'd holler, "Hello, Blue Roses!" I didn't care for the girl that he went out with. Emily Meisenbach. Emily was the best-dressed girl at Soldan. She never struck me, though, as being sincere . . . It says in the Personal Section—they're engaged. That's—six years ago! They must be married by now.
AMANDA: Girls that aren't cut out for business careers usually wind up married to some nice man. (*Gets up with a spark of revival.*) Sister, that's what you'll do!

(*Laura utters a startled, doubtful laugh. She reaches quickly for a piece of glass.*)

LAURA: But, Mother—
AMANDA: Yes? (*Crossing to photograph.*)
LAURA (*in a tone of frightened apology*): I'm—crippled!

(*Image: screen.*)

AMANDA: Nonsense! Laura, I've told you never, never to use that word. Why, you're not crippled, you just have a little defect—hardly noticeable, even! When people have some slight disadvantage like that, they cultivate other things to make up for it—develop charm—and vivacity—and—*charm*! That's all you have to do! (*She turns again to the photograph.*) One thing your father had *plenty of*—was *charm*!

(*Tom motions to the fiddle in the wings.*)
(*The scene fades out with music.*)

SCENE 3

(*Legend on screen: "After the Fiasco—"*)
(*Tom speaks from the fire escape landing.*)

TOM: After the fiasco at Rubicam's Business College, the idea of getting a gentleman caller for Laura began to play a more important part in Mother's calculations. It became an obsession. Like some archetype of the universal unconscious, the image of the gentleman caller haunted our small apartment. . . . (*Image: young man at door with flowers.*) An evening at home rarely passed without some allusion to this image, this specter, this hope. . . . Even when he wasn't mentioned, his presence hung in Mother's preoccupied look and in my sister's frightened, apologetic manner—hung like a sentence passed upon the Wingfields! Mother was a woman of action as well as words. She began to take logical steps in the planned direction. Late that winter and in the early spring—realizing that extra money would be needed to properly feather the nest and plume the bird—she conducted a vigorous campaign on the telephone, roping in subscribers to one of those magazines for matrons called *The Home-maker's Companion*, the type of journal that features the serialized sublimations of ladies of letters who think in terms of delicate cuplike breasts, slim, tapering waists, rich, creamy thighs, eyes like wood smoke in autumn, fingers that soothe and caress like strains of music, bodies as powerful as Etruscan sculpture.

(*Screen image: glamor magazine cover.*)
(*Amanda enters with phone on long extension cord. She is spotted in the dim stage.*)

AMANDA: Ida Scott? This is Amanda Wingfield! We *missed* you at the D.A.R. last Monday! I said to myself: She's probably suffering with that sinus condition! How is that sinus condition? Horrors! Heaven have mercy!—You're a Christian martyr, yes, that's what you are, a Christian martyr! Well I just now happened to notice that your subscription to the *Companion's* about to expire! Yes, it expires with the next issue, honey!—just when that wonderful new serial by Bessie Mae Hopper is getting off to such an exciting start. Oh, honey, it's something that you can't miss! You remember how *Gone with the Wind* took everybody by storm? You simply couldn't go out if you hadn't read it. All everybody *talked* was Scarlett O'Hara. Well, this is a book that critics already compare to *Gone with the Wind*. It's the *Gone with the Wind* of the post–World War generation!—What?—Burning?—Oh, honey, don't let them burn, go take a look in the oven and I'll hold the wire! Heavens—I think she's hung up!

(*Dim out.*)
(*Legend on screen: "You Think I'm in Love with Continental Shoemakers?"*)
(*Before the stage is lighted, the violent voices of Tom and Amanda are heard.*)
(*They are quarreling behind the portieres. In front of them stands Laura with clenched hands and panicky expression.*)
(*A clear pool of light on her figure throughout this scene.*)

TOM: What in Christ's name am I—
AMANDA (*shrilly*): Don't you use that—

Tom: Supposed to do!

Amanda: Expression! Not in my—

Tom: Ohhh!

Amanda: Presence! Have you gone out of your senses?

Tom: I have, that's true, *driven* out!

Amanda: What is the matter with you, you—big—big—idiot!

Tom: Look—I've got no *thing*, no single thing—

Amanda: Lower your voice!

Tom: In my life here that I can call my OWN! Everything is—

Amanda: Stop that shouting!

Tom: Yesterday you confiscated my books! You had the nerve to—

Amanda: I took that horrible novel back to the library—yes! That hideous book by that insane Mr. Lawrence. (*Tom laughs wildly.*) I cannot control the output of diseased minds or people who cater to them— (*Tom laughs still more wildly.*) BUT I WON'T ALLOW SUCH FILTH BROUGHT INTO MY HOUSE! No, no, no, no, no!

Tom: House, house! Who pays rent on it, who makes a slave of himself to—

Amanda (*fairly screeching*): Don't you DARE to—

Tom: No, no, *I* mustn't say things! *I've* got to just—

Amanda: Let me tell you—

Tom: I don't want to hear any more! (*He tears the portieres open. The upstage area is lit with a turgid smoky red glow.*)

(*Amanda's hair is in metal curlers and she wears a very old bathrobe, much too large for her slight figure, a relic of the faithless Mr. Wingfield.*)

  (*An upright typewriter and a wild disarray of manuscripts are on the dropleaf table. The quarrel was probably precipitated by Amanda's interruption of his creative labor. A chair lying overthrown on the floor.*)

  (*Their gesticulating shadows are cast on the ceiling by the fiery glow.*)

Amanda: You *will* hear more, you—

Tom: No, I won't hear more, I'm going out!

Amanda: You come right back in—

Tom: Out, out out! Because I'm—

Amanda: Come back here, Tom Wingfield! I'm not through talking to you!

Tom: Oh, go—

Laura (*desperately*): Tom!

Amanda: You're going to listen, and no more insolence from you! I'm at the end of my patience! (*He comes back toward her.*)

Tom: What do you think I'm at? Aren't I supposed to have any patience to reach the end of, Mother? I know, I know. It seems unimportant to you, what I'm *doing*—what I *want* to do—having a little *difference* between them! You don't think that—

AMANDA: I think you've been doing things that you're ashamed of. That's why you act like this. I don't believe that you go every night to the movies. Nobody goes to the movies night after night. Nobody in their right minds goes to the movies as often as you pretend to. People don't go to the movies at nearly midnight, and movies don't let out at two a.m. Come in stumbling. Muttering to yourself like a maniac! You get three hours' sleep and then go to work. Oh, I can picture the way you're doing down there. Moping, doping, because you're in no condition.

TOM (*wildly*): No, I'm in no condition!

AMANDA: What right have you got to jeopardize your job? Jeopardize the security of us all? How do you think we'd manage if you were—

TOM: Listen! You think I'm *crazy* about the *warehouse*? (*He bends fiercely toward her slight figure.*) You think I'm in love with the Continental Shoemakers? You think I want to spend fifty-five *years* down there in that—*celotex interior!* with—*fluorescent—tubes!* Look! I'd rather somebody picked up a crowbar and battered out my brains—than go back mornings! I *go!* Every time you come in yelling that God damn "*Rise and Shine!*" "*Rise and Shine!*" I say to myself, "*How lucky dead people are!*" But I get up. I *go!* For sixty-five dollars a month I give up all that I dream of doing and being *ever!* And you say self—*self's* all I ever think of. Why, listen, if self is what I thought of, Mother, I'd be where he is—GONE! (*Pointing to father's picture.*) As far as the system of transportation reaches! (*He starts past her. She grabs his arm.*) Don't grab at me, Mother!

AMANDA: Where are you going?

TOM: I'm going to the *movies!*

AMANDA: I don't believe that lie!

TOM (*Crouching toward her, overtowering her tiny figure. She backs away, gasping.*): I'm going to opium dens! Yes, opium dens, dens of vice and criminals' hangouts, Mother. I've joined the Hogan gang, I'm a hired assassin, I carry a tommy-gun in a violin case! I run a string of cathouses in the Valley! They call me Killer, Killer Wingfield, I'm leading a double life, a simple, honest warehouse worker by day, by night, a dynamic *czar* of the *underworld, Mother*. I go to gambling casinos, I spin away fortunes on the roulette table! I wear a patch over one eye and a false mustache, sometimes I put on green whiskers. On those occasions they call me—*El Diablo!* Oh, I could tell you things to make you sleepless! My enemies plan to dynamite this place. They're going to blow us all skyhigh some night! I'll be glad, very happy, and so will you! You'll go up, up on a broomstick, over Blue Mountain with seventeen gentlemen callers! You ugly—babbling old—*witch. . . .* (*He goes through a series of violent, clumsy movements, seizing his overcoat, lunging to the door, pulling it fiercely open. The women watch him, aghast. His arm catches in the sleeve of the coat as he struggles to pull it on. For a moment he is pinioned by the bulky garment. With an outraged groan he tears the coat off again, splitting the shoulders of it, and hurls it across the room. It strikes against the shelf of Laura's glass collection, there is a tinkle of shattering glass. Laura cries out as if wounded.*)

(*Music legend: "The Glass Menagerie."*)

LAURA (*shrilly*): My glass! —menagerie. . . . (*She covers her face and turns away.*)

(*But Amanda is still stunned and stupefied by the "ugly witch" so that she barely notices this occurrence. Now she recovers her speech.*)

AMANDA (*in an awful voice*): I won't speak to you—until you apologize!
(*She crosses through portieres and draws them together behind her. Tom is left with Laura. Laura clings weakly to the mantel with her face averted. Tom stares at her stupidly for a moment. Then he crosses to shelf. Drops awkwardly to his knees to collect the fallen glass, glancing at Laura as if he would speak but couldn't.*)

(*"The Glass Menagerie" steals in as the scene dims out.*)

SCENE 4

(*The interior is dark. Faint light in the alley.*)

(*A deep-voiced bell in a church is tolling the hour of five as the scene commences.*)

(*Tom appears at the top of the alley. After each solemn boom of the bell in the tower, he shakes a little noisemaker or rattle as if to express the tiny spasm of man in contrast to the sustained power and dignity of the Almighty. This and the unsteadiness of his advance make it evident that he has been drinking.*)

(*As he climbs the few steps to the fire escape landing light steals up inside. Laura appears in nightdress, observing Tom's empty bed in the front room.*)

(*Tom fishes in his pockets for the door key, removing a motley assortment of articles in the search, including a perfect shower of movie ticket stubs and an empty bottle. At last he finds the key, but just as he is about to insert it, it slips from his fingers. He strikes a match and crouches below the door.*)

TOM (*bitterly*): One crack—and it falls through!

(*Laura opens the door.*)

LAURA: Tom! Tom, what are you doing?
TOM: Looking for a door key.

LAURA: Where have you been all this time?

TOM: I have been to the movies.

LAURA: All this time at the movies?

TOM: There was a very long program. There was a Garbo picture and a Mickey Mouse and a travelogue and a newsreel and a preview of coming attractions. And there was an organ solo and a collection for the milk fund—simultaneously—which ended up in a terrible fight between a fat lady and an usher!

LAURA (*innocently*): Did you have to stay through everything?

TOM: Of course! And, oh, I forgot! There was a big stage show! The headliner on this stage show was Malvolio the Magician. He performed wonderful tricks, many of them, such as pouring water back and forth between pitchers. First it turned to wine and then it turned to beer and then it turned to whiskey. I know it was whiskey it finally turned into because he needed somebody to come up out of the audience to help him, and I came up—both shows! It was Kentucky Straight Bourbon. A very generous fellow, he gave souvenirs. (*He pulls from his back pocket a shimmering rainbow-colored scarf.*) He gave me this. This is his magic scarf. You can have it, Laura. You wave it over a canary cage and you get a bowl of goldfish. You wave it over the goldfish bowl and they fly away canaries. . . . But the wonderfullest trick of all was the coffin trick. We nailed him into a coffin and he got out of the coffin without removing one nail. (*He has come inside.*) There is a trick that would come in handy for me—get me out of this 2 by 4 situation! (*Flops onto bed and starts removing shoes.*)

LAURA: Tom—Shhh!

TOM: What you shushing me for?

LAURA: You'll wake up Mother.

TOM: Goody, goody! Pay 'er back for all those "Rise an' Shines." (*Lies down, groaning.*) You know it don't take much intelligence to get yourself into a nailed-up coffin, Laura. But who in hell ever got himself out of one without removing one nail?

(*As if in answer, the father's grinning photograph lights up.*)

   (*Scene dims out.*)

   (*Immediately following: The church bell is heard striking six. At the sixth stroke the alarm clock goes off in Amanda's room, and after a few moments we hear her calling: "Rise and Shine! Rise and Shine! Laura, go tell your brother to rise and shine!"*)

TOM (*sitting up slowly*): I'll rise—but I won't shine.

(*The light increases.*)

AMANDA: Laura, tell your brother his coffee is ready.

(*Laura slips into front room.*)

LAURA: Tom! it's nearly seven. Don't make Mother nervous. (*He stares at her stupidly. Beseechingly.*) Tom, speak to Mother this morning. Make up with her, apologize, speak to her!

TOM: She won't to me. It's her that started not speaking.

LAURA: If you just say you're sorry she'll start speaking.

TOM: Her not speaking—is that such a tragedy?

LAURA: Please—please!

AMANDA (*calling from kitchenette*): Laura, are you going to do what I asked you to do, or do I have to get dressed and go out myself?

LAURA: Going, going—soon as I get on my coat! (*She pulls on a shapeless felt hat with nervous, jerky movement, pleadingly glancing at Tom. Rushes awkwardly for coat. The coat is one of Amanda's, inaccurately made over, the sleeves too short for Laura.*) Butter and what else?

AMANDA (*entering upstage*): Just butter. Tell them to charge it.

LAURA: Mother, they make such faces when I do that.

AMANDA: Sticks and stones may break my bones, but the expression on Mr. Garfinkel's face won't harm us! Tell your brother his coffee is getting cold.

LAURA (*at door*): Do what I asked you, will you, will you, Tom?

(*He looks sullenly away.*)

AMANDA: Laura, go now or just don't go at all!

LAURA (*rushing out*): Going—going! (*A second later she cries out. Tom springs up and crosses to the door. Amanda rushes anxiously in. Tom opens the door.*)

TOM: Laura?

LAURA: I'm all right. I slipped, but I'm all right.

AMANDA (*peering anxiously after her*): If anyone breaks a leg on those fire escape steps, the landlord ought to be sued for every cent he possesses! (*She shuts door. Remembers she isn't speaking and returns to other room.*)

(*As Tom enters listlessly for his coffee, she turns her back to him and stands rigidly facing the window on the gloomy gray vault of the areaway. Its light on her face with its aged but childish features is cruelly sharp, satirical as a Daumier print.*)

(*Music under: "Ave Maria."*)

(*Tom glances sheepishly but sullenly at her averted figure and slumps at the table. The coffee is scalding hot; he sips it and gasps and spits it back in the cup. At his gasp, Amanda catches her breath and half turns. Then catches herself and turns back to window.*)

(*Tom blows on his coffee, glancing sidewise at his mother. She clears her*) *throat. Tom clears his. He starts to rise. Sinks back down again, scratches his head, clears his throat again. Amanda coughs. Tom raises his cup in both hands to blow on it, his eyes staring over the rim of it at his mother for several moments. Then he slowly sets the cup down and awkwardly and hesitantly rises from the chair.)*

TOM (*hoarsely*): Mother. I—I apologize. Mother. (*Amanda draws a quick, shuddering breath. Her face works grotesquely. She breaks into childlike tears.*) I'm sorry for what I said, for everything that I said, I didn't mean it.

AMANDA (*sobbingly*): My devotion has made me a witch and so I make myself hateful to my children!

TOM: No, you don't.

AMANDA: I worry so much, don't sleep, it makes me nervous!

TOM (*gently*): I understand that.

AMANDA: I've had to put up a solitary battle all these years. But you're my right-hand bower! Don't fall down, don't fail!

TOM (*gently*): I try, Mother.

AMANDA (*with great enthusiasm*): Try and you will SUCCEED! (*The notion makes her breathless.*) Why, you—you're just *full* of natural endowments! Both of my children—they're *unusual* children! Don't you think I know it? I'm so—*proud*! Happy and—feel I've—so much to be thankful for but—Promise me one thing, son!

TOM: What, Mother?

AMANDA: Promise, son, you'll—never be a drunkard!

TOM (*turns to her grinning*): I will never be a drunkard, Mother.

AMANDA: That's what frightened me so, that you'd be drinking! Eat a bowl of Purina!

TOM: Just coffee, Mother.

AMANDA: Shredded wheat biscuit?

TOM: No, no, Mother, just coffee.

AMANDA: You can't put in a day's work on an empty stomach. You've got ten minutes—don't gulp! Drinking too-hot liquids makes cancer of the stomach. . . . Put cream in.

TOM: No, thank you.

AMANDA: To cool it.

TOM: No! No, thank you, I want it black.

AMANDA: I know, but it's not good for you. We have to do all that we can to build ourselves up. In these trying times we live in, all that we have to cling to is—each other. . . . That's why it's so important to—Tom, I—I sent out your sister so I could discuss something with you. If you hadn't spoken I would have spoken to you. (*Sits down.*)

TOM (*gently*): What is it, Mother, that you want to discuss?

AMANDA: *Laura!*

(*Tom puts his cup down slowly.*)
  (*Legend on screen: "Laura."*)
  (*Music: "The Glass Menagerie."*)

TOM: —Oh.—Laura . . .

AMANDA (*touching his sleeve*): You know how Laura is. So quiet but—still water runs deep! She notices things and I think she—broods about them. (*Tom looks up.*) A few days ago I came in and she was crying.

TOM: What about?

AMANDA: You.

TOM: Me?

AMANDA: She has an idea that you're not happy here.

TOM: What gave her that idea?

AMANDA: What gives her any idea? However, you do act strangely. I—I'm not criticizing, understand *that*! I know your ambitions do not lie in the warehouse, that like everybody in the whole wide world—you've had to—make sacrifices, but—Tom—Tom—life's not easy, it calls for—Spartan endurance! There's so many things in my heart that I cannot describe to you! I've never told you but I—*loved your father*. . . .

TOM (*gently*): I know that, Mother.

AMANDA: And you—when I see you taking after his ways! Staying out late—and—well, you *had* been drinking the night you were in that—terrifying condition! Laura says that you hate the apartment and that you go out nights to get away from it! Is that true, Tom?

TOM: No. You say there's so much in your heart that you can't describe to me. That's true of me, too. There's so much in my heart that I can't describe to *you*! So let's respect each other's—

AMANDA: But, why—*why*, Tom—are you always so *restless*? Where do you go to, nights?

TOM: I—go to the movies.

AMANDA: Why do you go to the movies so much, Tom?

TOM: I go to the movies because—I like adventure. Adventure is something I don't have much of at work, so I go to the movies.

AMANDA: But, Tom, you go to the movies *entirely* too *much*!

TOM: I like a lot of adventure.

(*Amanda looks baffled, then hurt. As the familiar inquisition resumes he becomes hard and impatient again. Amanda slips back into her querulous attitude toward him.*)
  (*Image on screen: sailing vessel with Jolly Roger.°*)

AMANDA: Most young men find adventure in their careers.

Jolly Roger: A black flag with a white skull and crossbones formerly used by pirates.

TOM: Then most young men are not employed in a warehouse.

AMANDA: The world is full of young men employed in warehouses and offices and factories.

TOM: Do all of them find adventure in their careers?

AMANDA: They do or they do without it! Not everybody has a craze for adventure.

TOM: Man is by instinct a lover, a hunter, a fighter, and none of those instincts are given much play at the warehouse!

AMANDA: Man is by instinct! Don't quote instinct to me! Instinct is something that people have got away from! It belongs to animals! Christian adults don't want it!

TOM: What do Christian adults want, then, Mother?

AMANDA: Superior things! Things of the mind and the spirit! Only animals have to satisfy instincts! Surely your aims are somewhat higher than theirs! Than monkeys—pigs—

TOM: I reckon they're not.

AMANDA: You're joking. However, that isn't what I wanted to discuss.

TOM (*rising*): I haven't much time.

AMANDA (*pushing his shoulders*): Sit down.

TOM: You want me to punch in red at the warehouse, Mother?

AMANDA: You have five minutes. I want to talk about Laura.

(*Legend: "Plans and Provisions."*)

TOM: All right! What about Laura?

AMANDA: We have to be making plans and provisions for her. She's older than you, two years, and nothing has happened. She just drifts along doing nothing. It frightens me terribly how she just drifts along.

TOM: I guess she's the type that people call home girls.

AMANDA: There's no such type, and if there is, it's a pity! That is unless the home is hers, with a husband!

TOM: What?

AMANDA: Oh, I can see the handwriting on the wall as plain as I see the nose in front of my face! It's terrifying! More and more you remind me of your father! He was out all hours without explanation—Then *left*! *Good-bye*! And me with a bag to hold. I saw that letter you got from the Merchant Marine. I know what you're dreaming of. I'm not standing here blindfolded. Very well, then. Then *do* it! But not till there's somebody to take your place.

TOM: What do you mean?

AMANDA: I mean that as soon as Laura has got somebody to take care of her, married, a home of her own, independent—why, then you'll be free to go wherever you please, on land, on sea, whichever way the wind blows you! But until that time you've got to look out for your sister. I don't say me because I'm old and don't matter! I say for your sister because she's young and dependent. I put her in business college—a dismal failure! Frightened her so it made her sick to her stomach. I took her over to the Young People's League at the church. Another fiasco. She spoke to nobody, nobody spoke to her. Now all she does is fool with those pieces of glass and play those worn-out records. What kind of a life is that for a girl to lead!

TOM: What can I do about it?

AMANDA: Overcome selfishness! Self, self, self is all that you ever think of! (*Tom springs up and crosses to get his coat. It is ugly and bulky. He pulls on a cap with earmuffs.*) Where is your muffler? Put your wool muffler on! (*He snatches it angrily from the closet and tosses it around his neck and pulls both ends tight.*) Tom! I haven't said what I had in mind to ask you.

TOM: I'm too late to—

AMANDA (*Catching his arms—very importunately. Then shyly*): Down at the warehouse, aren't there some—nice young men?

TOM: No!

AMANDA: There *must* be—*some* . . .

TOM: Mother—

(*Gesture.*)

AMANDA: Find out one that's clean-living—doesn't drink and—ask him out for sister!

TOM: What?

AMANDA: For *sister*! To *meet*! Get *acquainted*!

TOM (*stamping to door*): Oh, my *go-osh*!

AMANDA: Will you? (*He opens door. Imploringly.*) Will you? (*He starts down.*) Will you? *Will* you, dear?

TOM (*calling back*): YES!

(*Amanda closes the door hesitantly and with a troubled but faintly hopeful expression.*)
  (*Screen image: glamor magazine cover.*)
  (*Spot° Amanda at phone.*)

AMANDA: Ella Cartwright? This is Amanda Wingfield! How are you, honey? How is that kidney condition? (*Count five.*) *Horrors!* (*Count five.*) You're a Christian martyr, yes, honey, that's what you are, a Christian martyr! Well, I just happened to notice in my little red book that your subscription to the *Companion* has just run out! I knew that you wouldn't want to miss out on the wonderful serial starting in this new issue. It's by Bessie Mae Hopper, the first thing she's written since

Spot: Spotlight.

Honeymoon for Three. Wasn't that a strange and interesting story? Well, this one is even lovelier, I believe. It has a sophisticated society background. It's all about the horsey set on Long Island!

(*Fade out.*)

SCENE 5

(*Legend on screen "Annunciation." Fade with music.*)

(*It is early dusk of a spring evening. Supper has just been finished in the Wingfield apartment. Amanda and Laura in light colored dresses are removing dishes from the table, in the upstage area, which is shadowy, their movements formalized almost as a dance or ritual, their moving forms as pale and silent as moths.*)

(*Tom, in white shirt and trousers, rises from the table and crosses toward the fire escape.*)

AMANDA (*as he passes her*): Son, will you do me a favor?

TOM: What?

AMANDA: Comb your hair! You look so pretty when your hair is combed! (*Tom slouches on sofa with evening paper. Enormous caption "Franco Triumphs."*) There is only one respect in which I would like you to emulate your father.

TOM: What respect is that?

AMANDA: The care he always took of his appearance. He never allowed himself to look untidy. (*He throws down the paper and crosses to fire escape.*) Where are you going?

TOM: I'm going out to smoke.

AMANDA: You smoke too much. A pack a day at fifteen cents a pack. How much would that amount to in a month? Thirty times fifteen is how much, Tom? Figure it out and you will be astounded at what you could save. Enough to give you a night school course in accounting at Washington U! Just think what a wonderful thing that would be for you, son!

(*Tom is unmoved by the thought.*)

TOM: I'd rather smoke. (*He steps out on landing, letting the screen door slam.*)

AMANDA (*sharply*): I know! That's the tragedy of it. . . . (*Alone, she turns to look at her husband's picture.*)

(*Dance music: "All the World Is Waiting for the Sunrise!"*)

TOM (*to the audience*): Across the alley from us was the Paradise Dance Hall. On evenings in spring the windows and doors were open and the music came outdoors. Sometimes the lights were turned out except for a large glass sphere that hung from the ceiling. It would turn slowly about and filter the dusk with delicate rainbow colors. Then the orchestra played a waltz or a tango, something that had a slow and sensuous rhythm. Couples would come outside, to the relative privacy of the alley. You could see them kissing behind ash-pits and telephone poles. This was the compensation for lives that passed like mine, without any change or adventure. Adventure and change were imminent in this year. They were waiting around the corner for all these kids. Suspended in the mist over Berchtesgaden, caught in the folds of Chamberlain's° umbrella—In Spain there was Guernica! But here there was only hot swing music and liquor, dance halls, bars, and movies, and sex that hung in the gloom like a chandelier and flooded the world with brief, deceptive rainbows. . . . All the world was waiting for bombardments!

(*Amanda turns from the picture and comes outside.*)

AMANDA (*sighing*): A fire escape landing's a poor excuse for a porch. (*She spreads a newspaper on a step and sits down, gracefully and demurely as if she were settling into a swing on a Mississippi veranda.*) What are you looking at?

TOM: The moon.

AMANDA: Is there a moon this evening?

TOM: It's rising over Garfinkel's Delicatessen.

AMANDA: So it is! A little silver slipper of a moon. Have you made a wish on it yet?

TOM: Um-hum.

AMANDA: What did you wish for?

TOM: That's a secret.

AMANDA: A secret, huh? Well, I won't tell mine either. I will be just as mysterious as you.

TOM: I bet I can guess what yours is.

AMANDA: Is my head so transparent?

TOM: You're not a sphinx.

AMANDA: No, I don't have secrets. I'll tell you what I wished for on the moon. Success and happiness for my precious children! I wish for that whenever there's a moon, and when there isn't a moon, I wish for it, too.

TOM: I thought perhaps you wished for a gentleman caller.

AMANDA: Why do you say that?

Berchtesgaden . . . Chamberlain's: Berchtesgaden was Hitler's summer home. Neville Chamberlain was a British prime minister who tried to avoid war with Hitler through the Munich Pact.

TOM: Don't you remember asking me to fetch one?

AMANDA: I remember suggesting that it would be nice for your sister if you brought home some nice young man from the warehouse. I think I've made that suggestion more than once.

TOM: Yes, you have made it repeatedly.

AMANDA: Well?

TOM: We are going to have one.

AMANDA: *What?*

TOM: A gentleman caller!

(The annunciation is celebrated with music.)
  (Amanda rises.)
  (Image on screen: caller with bouquet.)

AMANDA: You mean you have asked some nice young man to come over?

TOM: Yep. I've asked him to dinner.

AMANDA: You really did?

TOM: I did!

AMANDA: You did, and did he—*accept?*

TOM: He did!

AMANDA: Well, well—well, well! That's—lovely!

TOM: I thought that you would be pleased.

AMANDA: It's definite, then?

TOM: Very definite.

AMANDA: Soon?

TOM: Very soon.

AMANDA: For heaven's sake, stop putting on and tell me some things, will you?

TOM: What things do you want me to tell you?

AMANDA: *Naturally* I would like to know when he's *coming!*

TOM: He's coming tomorrow.

AMANDA: *Tomorrow?*

TOM: Yep. Tomorrow.

AMANDA: But, Tom!

TOM: Yes, Mother?

AMANDA: Tomorrow gives me no time!

TOM: Time for what?

AMANDA: Preparations! Why didn't you phone me at once, as soon as you asked him, the minute that he accepted? Then, don't you see, I could have been getting ready!

TOM: You don't have to make any fuss.

AMANDA: Oh, Tom, Tom, Tom, of course I have to make a fuss! I want things nice, not sloppy! Not thrown together. I'll certainly have to do some fast thinking, won't I?

TOM: I don't see why you have to think at all.

AMANDA: You just don't know. We can't have a gentleman caller in a pig-sty! All my wedding silver has to be polished, the monogrammed table linen ought to be laundered! The windows have to be washed and fresh curtains put up. And how about clothes? We have to *wear* something, don't we?

TOM: Mother, this boy is no one to make a fuss over!

AMANDA: Do you realize he's the first young man we've introduced to your sister? It's terrible, dreadful, disgraceful that poor little sister has never received a single gentleman caller! Tom, come inside! (*She opens the screen door.*)

TOM: What for?

AMANDA: I want to ask you some things.

TOM: If you're going to make such a fuss, I'll call it off, I'll tell him not to come.

AMANDA: You certainly won't do anything of the kind. Nothing offends people worse than broken engagements. It simply means I'll have to work like a Turk! We won't be brilliant, but we'll pass inspection. Come on inside. (*Tom follows, groaning.*) Sit down.

TOM: Any particular place you would like me to sit?

AMANDA: Thank heavens I've got that new sofa! I'm also making pay-ments on a floor lamp I'll have sent out! And put the chintz covers on, they'll brighten things up! Of course I'd hoped to have these walls re-papered. . . . What is the young man's name?

TOM: His name is O'Connor.

AMANDA: That, of course, means fish—tomorrow is Friday!° I'll have that salmon loaf—with Durkee's dressing! What does he do? He works at the warehouse?

TOM: Of course! How else would I—

AMANDA: Tom, he—doesn't drink?

TOM: Why do you ask me that?

AMANDA: Your father *did*!

TOM: Don't get started on that!

AMANDA: He *does* drink, then?

TOM: Not that I know of!

AMANDA: Make sure, be certain! The last thing I want for my daughter's a boy who drinks!

TOM: Aren't you being a little premature? Mr. O'Connor has not yet ap-peared on the scene!

AMANDA: But will tomorrow. To meet your sister, and what do I know about his character? Nothing! Old maids are better off than wives of drunkards!

---

fish . . . Friday: Reference to the religious doctrine that prohibited Catholics from eating meat on Fridays.

Tom: Oh, my God!

Amanda: Be still!

Tom (*leaning forward to whisper*): Lots of fellows meet girls whom they don't marry!

Amanda: Oh, talk sensibly, Tom — and don't be sarcastic! (*She has gotten a hairbrush.*)

Tom: What are you doing?

Amanda: I'm brushing that cowlick down! What is this young man's position at the warehouse?

Tom (*submitting grimly to the brush and the interrogation*): This young man's position is that of a shipping clerk, Mother.

Amanda: Sounds to me like a fairly responsible job, the sort of a job *you* would be in if you just had more *get-up*. What is his salary? Have you got any idea?

Tom: I would judge it to be approximately eighty-five dollars a month.

Amanda: Well — not princely, but —

Tom: Twenty more than I make.

Amanda: Yes, how well I know! But for a family man, eighty-five dollars a month is not much more than you can just get by on. . . .

Tom: Yes, but Mr. O'Connor is not a family man.

Amanda: He might be, mightn't he? Some time in the future?

Tom: I see. Plans and provisions.

Amanda: You are the only young man that I know of who ignores the fact that the future becomes the present, the present the past, and the past turns into everlasting regret if you don't plan for it!

Tom: I will think that over and see what I can make of it.

Amanda: Don't be supercilious with your mother! Tell me some more about this — what do you call him?

Tom: James D. O'Connor. The D. is for Delaney.

Amanda: Irish on *both* sides! *Gracious!* And doesn't drink?

Tom: Shall I call him up and ask him right this minute?

Amanda: The only way to find out about those things is to make discreet inquiries at the proper moment. When I was a girl in Blue Mountain and it was suspected that a young man drank, the girl whose attentions he had been receiving, if any girl was, would sometimes speak to the minister of his church, or rather her father would if her father was living, and sort of feel him out on the young man's character. That is the way such things are discreetly handled to keep a young woman from making a tragic mistake!

Tom: Then how did you happen to make a tragic mistake?

Amanda: That innocent look of your father's had everyone fooled! He *smiled* — the world was *enchanted*! No girl can do worse than put herself at the mercy of a handsome appearance! I hope that Mr. O'Connor is not too good-looking.

Том: No, he's not too good-looking. He's covered with freckles and hasn't too much of a nose.

AMANDA: He's not right-down homely, though?

Том: Not right-down homely. Just medium homely, I'd say.

AMANDA: Character's what to look for in a man.

Том: That's what I've always said, Mother.

AMANDA: You've never said anything of the kind and I suspect you would never give it a thought.

Том: Don't be suspicious of me.

AMANDA: At least I hope he's the type that's up and coming.

Том: I think he really goes in for self-improvement.

AMANDA: What reason have you to think so?

Том: He goes to night school.

AMANDA (*beaming*): Splendid! What does he do, I mean study?

Том: Radio engineering and public speaking!

AMANDA: Then he has visions of being advanced in the world! Any young man who studies public speaking is aiming to have an executive job some day! And radio engineering? A thing for the future! Both of these facts are very illuminating. Those are the sort of things that a mother should know concerning any young man who comes to call on her daughter. Seriously or—not.

Том: One little warning. He doesn't know about Laura. I didn't let on that we had dark ulterior motives. I just said, why don't you come have dinner with us? He said okay and that was the whole conversation.

AMANDA: I bet it was! You're eloquent as an oyster. However, he'll know about Laura when he gets here. When he sees how lovely and sweet and pretty she is, he'll thank his lucky stars he was asked to dinner.

Том: Mother, you mustn't expect too much of Laura.

AMANDA: What do you mean?

Том: Laura seems all those things to you and me because she's ours and we love her. We don't even notice she's crippled anymore.

AMANDA: Don't say crippled! You know that I never allow that word to be used!

Том: But face facts, Mother. She is and—that's not all—

AMANDA: What do you mean not all?

Том: Laura is very different from other girls.

AMANDA: I think the difference is all to her advantage.

Том: Not quite all—in the eyes of others—strangers—she's terribly shy and lives in a world of her own and those things make her seem a little peculiar to people outside the house.

AMANDA: Don't say peculiar.

Том: Face the facts. She is.

(*The dance-hall music changes to a tango that has a minor and somewhat ominous tone.*)

AMANDA: In what way is she peculiar—may I ask?

TOM (*gently*): She lives in a world of her own—a world of—little glass ornaments, Mother. . . . (*Gets up. Amanda remains holding brush, looking at him, troubled.*) She plays old phonograph records and—that's about all—(*He glances at himself in the mirror and crosses to door.*)

AMANDA (*sharply*): Where are you going?

TOM: I'm going to the movies. (*Out screen door.*)

AMANDA: Not to the movies, every night to the movies! (*Follows quickly to screen door.*) I don't believe you always go to the movies! (*He is gone. Amanda looks worriedly after him for a moment. Then vitality and optimism return and she turns from the door. Crossing to portieres.*) Laura! Laura! (*Laura answers from kitchenette.*)

LAURA: Yes, Mother.

AMANDA: Let those dishes go and come in front! (*Laura appears with dish towel. Gaily.*) Laura, come here and make a wish on the moon!

LAURA (*entering*): Moon—moon?

AMANDA: A little silver slipper of a moon. Look over your left shoulder, Laura, and make a wish! (*Laura looks faintly puzzled as if called out of sleep. Amanda seizes her shoulders and turns her at an angle by the door.*) Now! Now, darling, *wish*!

LAURA: What shall I wish for, Mother?

AMANDA (*her voice trembling and her eyes suddenly filling with tears*): Happiness! Good Fortune!

(*The violin rises and the stage dims out.*)

SCENE 6

(*Image: high school hero.*)

TOM: And so the following evening I brought Jim home to dinner. I had known Jim slightly in high school. In high school Jim was a hero. He had tremendous Irish good nature and vitality with the scrubbed and polished look of white chinaware. He seemed to move in a continual spotlight. He was a star in basketball, captain of the debating club, president of the senior class and the glee club and he sang the male lead in the annual light operas. He was always running or bounding, never just walking. He seemed always at the point of defeating the law of gravity. He was shooting with such velocity through his adolescence that you would logically expect him to arrive at nothing short of the

White House by the time he was thirty. But Jim apparently ran into more interference after his graduation from Soldan. His speed had definitely slowed. Six years after he left high school he was holding a job that wasn't much better than mine.

(*Image: clerk.*)

He was the only one at the warehouse with whom I was on friendly terms. I was valuable to him as someone who could remember his former glory, who had seen him win basketball games and the silver cup in debating. He knew of my secret practice of retiring to a cabinet of the washroom to work on poems when business was slack in the warehouse. He called me Shakespeare. And while the other boys in the warehouse regarded me with suspicious hostility, Jim took a humorous attitude toward me. Gradually his attitude affected the others, their hostility wore off and they also began to smile at me as people smile at an oddly fashioned dog who trots across their path at some distance.

I knew that Jim and Laura had known each other at Soldan, and I had heard Laura speak admiringly of his voice. I didn't know if Jim remembered her or not. In high school Laura had been as unobtrusive as Jim had been astonishing. If he did remember Laura, it was not as my sister, for when I asked him to dinner, he grinned and said, "You know, Shakespeare, I never thought of you as having folks!"

He was about to discover that I did. . . .

(*Light up stage.*)
(*Legend on screen: "The Accent of a Coming Foot."*)
(*Friday evening. It is about five o'clock of a late spring evening which comes "scattering poems in the sky."*)
(*A delicate lemony light is in the Wingfield apartment.*)
(*Amanda has worked like a Turk in preparation for the gentleman caller. The results are astonishing. The new floor lamp with its rose-silk shade is in place, a colored paper lantern conceals the broken light fixture in the ceiling, new billowing white curtains are at the windows, chintz covers are on chairs and sofa, a pair of new sofa pillows make their initial appearance.*)
(*Open boxes and tissue paper are scattered on the floor.*)
(*Laura stands in the middle with lifted arms while Amanda crouches before her, adjusting the hem of the new dress, devout and ritualistic. The dress is colored and designed by memory. The arrangement of Laura's hair is changed; it is softer and more becoming. A fragile, unearthly prettiness has come out in Laura: she is like a piece of translucent glass touched by light, given a momentary radiance, not actual, not lasting.*)

AMANDA (*impatiently*): Why are you trembling?
LAURA: Mother, you've made me so nervous!

AMANDA: How have I made you nervous?

LAURA: By all this fuss! You make it seem so important!

AMANDA: I don't understand you, Laura. You couldn't be satisfied with just sitting home, and yet whenever I try to arrange something for you, you seem to resist it. (*She gets up.*) Now take a look at yourself. No, wait! Wait just a moment—I have an idea!

LAURA: What is it now?

(*Amanda produces two powder puffs which she wraps in handkerchiefs and stuffs in Laura's bosom.*)

LAURA: Mother, what are you doing?

AMANDA: They call them "Gay Deceivers"!

LAURA: I won't wear them!

AMANDA: You will!

LAURA: Why should I?

AMANDA: Because, to be painfully honest, your chest is flat.

LAURA: You make it seem like we were setting a trap.

AMANDA: All pretty girls are a trap, a pretty trap, and men expect them to be. (*Legend: "A Pretty Trap."*) Now look at yourself, young lady. This is the prettiest you will ever be! I've got to fix myself now! You're going to be surprised by your mother's appearance! (*She crosses through portieres, humming gaily.*)

(*Laura moves slowly to the long mirror and stares solemnly at herself.*)

(*A wind blows the white curtains inward in a slow, graceful motion and with a faint, sorrowful sighing.*)

AMANDA (*offstage*): It isn't dark enough yet. (*She turns slowly before the mirror with a troubled look.*)

(*Legend on screen: "This Is My Sister: Celebrate Her with Strings!" Music.*)

AMANDA (*laughing, off*): I'm going to show you something. I'm going to make a spectacular appearance!

LAURA: What is it, Mother?

AMANDA: Possess your soul in patience—you will see! Something I've resurrected from that old trunk! Styles haven't changed so terribly much after all. . . . (*She parts the portieres.*) Now just look at your mother! (*She wears a girlish frock of yellowed voile with a blue silk sash. She carries a bunch of jonquils—the legend of her youth is nearly revived. Feverishly.*) This is the dress in which I led the cotillion. Won the cakewalk twice at Sunset Hill, wore one spring to the Governor's ball in Jackson! See how I sashayed around the ballroom, Laura? (*She raises her skirt and does a mincing step around the room.*) I wore it on Sundays for my gentlemen callers! I had it on the day I met your father—I had malaria fever all that spring. The change of climate from East Tennessee to the Delta—weakened resistance—I had a little temperature all the time—not enough to be serious—just enough to make me restless and giddy! Invitations poured in—parties all over the Delta!—"Stay in bed," said Mother, "you have fever!"—but I just wouldn't.—I took quinine but kept on going, going!—Evenings, dances!—Afternoons, long, long rides! Picnics—lovely!—So lovely, that country in May.—All lacy with dogwood, literally flooded with jonquils!—That was the spring I had the craze for jonquils. Jonquils became an absolute obsession. Mother said, "Honey, there's no more room for jonquils." And still I kept on bringing in more jonquils. Whenever, wherever I saw them, I'd say, "Stop! Stop! I see jonquils!" I made the young men help me gather the jonquils! It was a joke, Amanda and her jonquils! Finally there were no more vases to hold them, every available space was filled with jonquils. No vases to hold them? All right, I'll hold them myself! And then I—(*She stops in front of the picture. Music.*) met your father! Malaria fever and jonquils and then—this—boy. . . . (*She switches on the rose-colored lamp.*) I hope they get here before it starts to rain. (*She crosses upstage and places the jonquils in bowl on table.*) I gave your brother a little extra change so he and Mr. O'Connor could take the service car home.

LAURA (*with altered look*): What did you say his name was?

AMANDA: O'Connor.

LAURA: What is his first name?

AMANDA: I don't remember. Oh, yes, I do. It was—Jim!

(*Laura sways slightly and catches hold of a chair.*)
  (*Legend on screen: "Not Jim!"*)

LAURA (*faintly*): Not—Jim!

AMANDA: Yes, that was it, it was Jim! I've never known a Jim that wasn't nice!

(*Music: ominous.*)

LAURA: Are you sure his name is Jim O'Connor?

AMANDA: Yes. Why?

LAURA: Is he the one that Tom used to know in high school?

AMANDA: He didn't say so. I think he just got to know him at the warehouse.

LAURA: There was a Jim O'Connor we both knew in high school—(*Then, with effort.*) If that is the one that Tom is bringing to dinner—you'll have to excuse me, I won't come to the table.

AMANDA: What sort of nonsense is this?

LAURA: You asked me once if I'd ever liked a boy. Don't you remember I showed you this boy's picture?

AMANDA: You mean the boy you showed me in the yearbook?

LAURA: Yes, that boy.

AMANDA: Laura, Laura, were you in love with that boy?

LAURA: I don't know, Mother. All I know is I couldn't sit at the table if it was him!

AMANDA: It won't be him! It isn't the least bit likely. But whether it is or not, you will come to the table. You will not be excused.

LAURA: I'll have to be, Mother.

AMANDA: I don't intend to humor your silliness, Laura. I've had too much from you and your brother, both! So just sit down and compose yourself till they come. Tom has forgotten his key so you'll have to let them in, when they arrive.

LAURA (*panicky*): Oh, Mother—you answer the door!

AMANDA (*lightly*): I'll be in the kitchen—busy!

LAURA: Oh, Mother, please answer the door, don't make me do it!

AMANDA (*crossing into kitchenette*): I've got to fix the dressing for the salmon. Fuss, fuss—silliness!—over a gentleman caller!

(*Door swings shut. Laura is left alone.*)
  (*Legend: "Terror!"*)
  (*She utters a low moan and turns off the lamp—sits stiffly on the edge of the sofa, knotting her fingers together.*)
  (*Legend on screen: "The Opening of a Door!"*)
  (*Tom and Jim appear on the fire escape steps and climb to landing. Hearing their approach, Laura rises with a panicky gesture. She retreats to the portieres.*)
  (*The doorbell. Laura catches her breath and touches her throat. Low drums.*)

AMANDA (*calling*): Laura, sweetheart! The door!

(*Laura stares at it without moving.*)

JIM: I think we just beat the rain.

TOM: Uh-huh. (*He rings again, nervously. Jim whistles and fishes for a cigarette.*)

AMANDA (*very, very gaily*): Laura, that is your brother and Mr. O'Connor! Will you let them in, darling?

(*Laura crosses toward kitchenette door.*)

LAURA (*breathlessly*): Mother—you go to the door!

(*Amanda steps out of kitchenette and stares furiously at Laura. She points imperiously at the door.*)

LAURA: Please, please!

AMANDA (*in a fierce whisper*): What is the matter with you, you silly thing?

LAURA (*desperately*): Please, you answer it, *please*!

AMANDA: I told you I wasn't going to humor you, Laura. Why have you chosen this moment to lose your mind?

LAURA: Please, please, please, you go!

AMANDA: You'll have to go to the door because I can't!

LAURA (*despairingly*): I can't either!

AMANDA: *Why?*

LAURA: I'm *sick*!

AMANDA: I'm sick, too—of your nonsense! Why can't you and your brother be normal people? Fantastic whims and behavior! (*Tom gives a long ring.*) Preposterous goings on! Can you give me one reason—(*Calls out lyrically.*) COMING! JUST ONE SECOND!—why should you be afraid to open a door? Now you answer it, Laura!

LAURA: Oh, oh, oh . . . (*She returns through the portieres. Darts to the victrola and winds it frantically and turns it on.*)

AMANDA: Laura Wingfield, you march right to that door!

LAURA: Yes—yes, Mother!

(*A faraway, scratchy rendition of "Dardanella" softens the air and gives her strength to move through it. She slips to the door and draws it cautiously open.*)
(*Tom enters with the caller, Jim O'Connor.*)

TOM: Laura, this is Jim. Jim, this is my sister, Laura.

JIM (*stepping inside*): I didn't know that Shakespeare had a sister!

LAURA (*retreating stiff and trembling from the door*): How—how do you do?

JIM (*heartily extending his hand*): Okay!

(*Laura touches it hesitantly with hers.*)

JIM: Your hand's *cold*, Laura!

LAURA: Yes, well—I've been playing the victrola. . . .

JIM: Must have been playing classical music on it! You ought to play a little hot swing music to warm you up!

LAURA: Excuse me—I haven't finished playing the victrola. . . .

(*She turns awkwardly and hurries into the front room. She pauses a second by the victrola. Then catches her breath and darts through the portieres like a frightened deer.*)

JIM (*grinning*): What was the matter?

TOM: Oh—with Laura? Laura is—terribly shy.

JIM: Shy, huh? It's unusual to meet a shy girl nowadays. I don't believe you ever mentioned you had a sister.

TOM: Well, now you know. I have one. Here is the *Post Dispatch*. You want a piece of it?

JIM: Uh-huh.

TOM: What piece? The comics?

JIM: Sports! (*Glances at it.*) Ole Dizzy Dean is on his bad behavior.

TOM (*disinterest*): Yeah? (*Lights cigarette and crosses back to fire escape door.*)

JIM: Where are *you* going?

TOM: I'm going out on the terrace.

JIM (*goes after him*): You know, Shakespeare—I'm going to sell you a bill of goods!

TOM: What goods?

JIM: A course I'm taking.

TOM: Huh?

JIM: In public speaking! You and me, we're not the warehouse type.

TOM: Thanks—that's good news. But what has public speaking got to do with it?

JIM: It fits you for—executive positions!

TOM: Awww.

JIM: I tell you it's done a helluva lot for me.

(*Image: executive at desk.*)

TOM: In what respect?

JIM: In every! Ask yourself what is the difference between you an' me and men in the office down front? Brains?—No!—Ability?—No! Then what? Just one little thing—

TOM: What is that one little thing?

JIM: Primarily it amounts to—social poise! Being able to square up to people and hold your own on any social level!

AMANDA (*offstage*): Tom?

TOM: Yes, Mother?

AMANDA: Is that you and Mr. O'Connor?

TOM: Yes, Mother.

AMANDA: Well, you just make yourselves comfortable in there.

TOM: Yes, Mother.

AMANDA: Ask Mr. O'Connor if he would like to wash his hands.

JIM: Aw,—no—no—thank you—I took care of that at the warehouse. Tom—

TOM: Yes?

JIM: Mr. Mendoza was speaking to me about you.

TOM: Favorably?

JIM: What do you think?

TOM: Well—

JIM: You're going to be out of a job if you don't wake up.

TOM: I am waking up—

JIM: You show no signs.

TOM: The signs are interior.

(*Image on screen: the sailing vessel with Jolly Roger again.*)

TOM: I'm planning to change. (*He leans over the rail speaking with quiet exhilaration. The incandescent marquees and signs of the first-run movie houses light his face from across the alley. He looks like a voyager.*) I'm right at the point of committing myself to a future that doesn't include the warehouse and Mr. Mendoza or even a night school course in public speaking.

JIM: What are you gassing about?

TOM: I'm tired of the movies.

JIM: Movies!

TOM: Yes, movies! Look at them—(*A wave toward the marvels of Grand Avenue.*) All of those glamorous people—having adventures—hogging it all, gobbling the whole thing up! You know what happens? People go to the *movies* instead of *moving*! Hollywood characters are supposed to have all the adventures for everybody in America, while everybody in America sits in a dark room and watches them have them! Yes, until there's a war. That's when adventure becomes available to the masses! *Everyone's* dish, not only Gable's! Then the people in the dark room come out of the dark room to have some adventures themselves—Goody, goody!—It's our turn now, to go to the South Sea Island—to make a safari—to be exotic, far-off!—But I'm not patient. I don't want to wait till then. I'm tired of the *movies* and I am *about* to *move*!

JIM (*incredulously*): Move?

TOM: Yes.

JIM: When?

TOM: Soon!

JIM: Where? Where?

(*Theme three music seems to answer the question, while Tom thinks it over. He searches among his pockets.*)

TOM: I'm starting to boil inside. I know I seem dreamy, but inside—well, I'm boiling! Whenever I pick up a shoe, I shudder a little thinking how short life is and what I am doing!—Whatever that means. I know it doesn't mean shoes—except as something to wear on a traveler's feet! (*Finds paper.*) Look—

JIM: What?

TOM: I'm a member.

JIM (*reading*): The Union of Merchant Seamen.

TOM: I paid my dues this month, instead of the light bill.

JIM: You will regret it when they turn the lights off.

Toм: I won't be here.

JIM: How about your mother?

Toм: I'm like my father. The bastard son of a bastard! See how he grins?
And he's been absent going on sixteen years!

JIM: You're just talking, you drip. How does your mother feel about it?

Toм: Shhh!—Here comes Mother! Mother is not acquainted with my
plans!

AMANDA (*enters portieres*): Where are you all?

Toм: On the terrace, Mother.

(*They start inside. She advances to them. Tom is distinctly shocked at her appearance. Even Jim blinks a little. He is making his first contact with girlish
Southern vivacity and in spite of the night school course in public speaking is
somewhat thrown off the beam by the unexpected outlay of social charm.*)

(*Certain responses are attempted by Jim but are swept aside by Amanda's gay
laughter and chatter. Tom is embarrassed but after the first shock Jim reacts
very warmly. Grins and chuckles, is altogether won over.*)

(*Image: Amanda as a girl.*)

AMANDA (*coyly smiling, shaking her girlish ringlets*): Well, well, well, so this
is Mr. O'Connor. Introductions entirely unnecessary. I've heard so
much about you from my boy. I finally said to him, Tom—good gracious!—why don't you bring this paragon to supper? I'd like to meet
this nice young man at the warehouse!—Instead of just hearing him
sing your praises so much! I don't know why my son is so standoff-
ish—that's not Southern behavior! Let's sit down and—I think we
could stand a little more air in here! Tom, leave the door open. I felt a
nice fresh breeze a moment ago. Where has it gone to? Mmm, so warm
already! And not quite summer, even. We're going to burn up when
summer really gets started. However, we're having—we're having a
very light supper. I think light things are better fo' this time of year. The
same as light clothes are. Light clothes an' light food are what warm
weather calls fo'. You know our blood gets so thick during th' winter—it takes a while fo' us to *adjust* ou'selves!—when the season
changes ... It's come so quick this year. I wasn't prepared. All of a sudden—heavens! Already summer!—I ran to the trunk an' pulled out
this light dress—Terribly old! Historical almost! But feels so good—so
good an' co-ol, y'know. . . .

Toм: Mother—

AMANDA: Yes, honey?

Toм: How about—supper?

AMANDA: Honey, you go ask Sister if supper is ready! You know that Sister is in full charge of supper! Tell her you hungry boys are waiting for
it. (*To Jim.*) Have you met Laura?

JIM: She—

AMANDA: Let you in? Oh, good, you've met already! It's rare for a girl as
sweet an' pretty as Laura to be domestic! But Laura is, thank heavens,
not only pretty but also very domestic. I'm not at all. I never was a bit.
I never could make a thing but angel food cake. Well, in the South we
had so many servants. Gone, gone, gone. All vestiges of gracious living!
Gone completely! I wasn't prepared for what the future brought me.
All of my gentlemen callers were sons of planters and so of course I
assumed that I would be married to one and raise my family on a large
piece of land with plenty of servants. But man proposes—and woman
accepts the proposal!—To vary that old, old saying a little bit—I married no planter! I married a man who worked for the telephone company!—That gallantly smiling gentleman over there! (*Points to the picture.*) A telephone man who—fell in love with long distance!—Now
he travels and I don't even know where!—But what am I going on
for about my—tribulations! Tell me yours—I hope you don't have
any! Tom?

TOM (*returning*): Yes, Mother?

AMANDA: Is supper nearly ready?

TOM: It looks to me like supper is on the table.

AMANDA: Let me look—(*She rises prettily and looks through portieres.*) Oh,
lovely!—But where is Sister?

TOM: Laura is not feeling well and she says that she thinks she'd better
not come to the table.

AMANDA: What?—Nonsense!—Laura? Oh, Laura!

LAURA (*offstage, faintly*): Yes, Mother.

AMANDA: You really must come to the table. We won't be seated until you
come to the table! Come in, Mr. O'Connor. You sit over there, and
I'll—Laura? Laura Wingfield! You're keeping us waiting, honey! We
can't say grace until you come to the table!

(*The back door is pushed weakly open and Laura comes in. She is obviously
quite faint, her lips trembling, her eyes wide and staring. She moves unsteadily
toward the table.*)
   (*Legend: "Terror!"*)
   (*Outside a summer storm is coming abruptly. The white curtains billow inward at the windows and there is a sorrowful murmur and deep blue dusk.*)
   (*Laura suddenly stumbles—she catches at a chair with a faint moan.*)

TOM: Laura!

AMANDA: Laura! (*There is a clap of thunder.*) (*Legend: "Ah!"*) (*Despairingly.*)
Why, Laura, you are sick, darling! Tom, help your sister into the living
room, dear! Sit in the living room, Laura—rest on the sofa. Well! (*To
the gentleman caller.*) Standing over the hot stove made her ill!—I told

her that it was just too warm this evening, but—(*Tom comes back in. Laura is on the sofa.*) Is Laura all right now?

TOM: Yes.

AMANDA: What is that? Rain? A nice cool rain has come up! (*She gives the gentleman caller a frightened look.*) I think we may—have grace—now . . . (*Tom looks at her stupidly.*) Tom, honey—you say grace!

TOM: Oh . . . "For these and all thy mercies—" (*They bow their heads, Amanda stealing a nervous glance at Jim. In the living room Laura, stretched on the sofa, clenches her hand to her lips, to hold back a shuddering sob.*) God's Holy Name be praised—

(*The scene dims out.*)

SCENE 7

(*A Souvenir*)

(*Half an hour later. Dinner is just being finished in the upstage area which is concealed by the drawn portieres.*)

(*As the curtain rises Laura is still huddled upon the sofa, her feet drawn under her, her head resting on a pale blue pillow, her eyes wide and mysteriously watchful. The new floor lamp with its shade of rose-colored silk gives a soft, becoming light to her face, bringing out the fragile, unearthly prettiness which usually escapes attention. There is a steady murmur of rain, but it is slackening and stops soon after the scene begins; the air outside becomes pale and luminous as the moon breaks out.*)

(*A moment after the curtain rises, the lights in both rooms flicker and go out.*)

JIM: Hey, there, Mr. Light Bulb!

(*Amanda laughs nervously.*)

(*Legend: "Suspension of a Public Service."*)

AMANDA: Where was Moses when the lights went out? Ha-ha. Do you know the answer to that one, Mr. O'Connor?

JIM: No, Ma'am, what's the answer?

AMANDA: In the dark! (*Jim laughs appreciably.*) Everybody sit still. I'll light the candles. Isn't it lucky we have them on the table? Where's a match? Which of you gentlemen can provide a match?

JIM: Here.

AMANDA: Thank you, sir.

JIM: Not at all, Ma'am!

AMANDA: I guess the fuse has burnt out. Mr. O'Connor, can you tell a burnt-out fuse? I know I can't and Tom is a total loss when it comes to mechanics. (*Sound: getting up: voices recede a little to kitchenette.*) Oh, be careful you don't bump into something. We don't want our gentleman caller to break his neck. Now wouldn't that be a fine howdy-do?

JIM: Ha-ha! Where is the fuse box?

AMANDA: Right here next to the stove. Can you see anything?

JIM: Just a minute.

AMANDA: Isn't electricity a mysterious thing? Wasn't it Benjamin Franklin who tied a key to a kite? We live in such a mysterious universe, don't we? Some people say that science clears up all the mysteries for us. In my opinion it only creates more! Have you found it yet?

JIM: No, Ma'am. All these fuses look okay to me.

AMANDA: Tom!

TOM: Yes, Mother?

AMANDA: That light bill I gave you several days ago. The one I told you we got the notices about?

TOM: Oh.—Yeah.

(Legend: "Ha!")

AMANDA: You didn't neglect to pay it by any chance?

TOM: Why, I—

AMANDA: Didn't! I might have known it!

JIM: Shakespeare probably wrote a poem on that light bill, Mrs. Wingfield.

AMANDA: I might have known better than to trust him with it! There's such a high price for negligence in this world!

JIM: Maybe the poem will win a ten-dollar prize.

AMANDA: We'll just have to spend the remainder of the evening in the nineteenth century, before Mr. Edison made the Mazda lamp!

JIM: Candlelight is my favorite kind of light.

AMANDA: That shows you're romantic! But that's no excuse for Tom. Well, we got through dinner. Very considerate of them to let us get through dinner before they plunged us into everlasting darkness, wasn't it, Mr. O'Connor?

JIM: Ha-ha!

AMANDA: Tom, as a penalty for your carelessness you can help me with the dishes.

JIM: Let me give you a hand.

AMANDA: Indeed you will not!

JIM: I ought to be good for something.

AMANDA: Good for something? *(Her tone is rhapsodic.) You?* Why, Mr. O'Connor, nobody, *nobody's* given me this much entertainment in years—as you have!

JIM: Aw, now, Mrs. Wingfield!

AMANDA: I'm not exaggerating, not one bit! But Sister is all by her lonesome. You go keep her company in the parlor! I'll give you this lovely old candelabrum that used to be on the altar at the church of the Heavenly Rest. It was melted a little out of shape when the church burnt down. Lightning struck it one spring. Gypsy Jones was holding a revival at the time and he intimated that the church was destroyed because the Episcopalians gave card parties.

JIM: Ha-ha.

AMANDA: And how about coaxing Sister to drink a little wine? I think it would be good for her! Can you carry both at once?

JIM: Sure. I'm Superman!

AMANDA: Now, Thomas, get into this apron!

(*The door of kitchenette swings closed on Amanda's gay laughter; the flickering light approaches the portieres.*)

(*Laura sits up nervously as he enters. Her speech at first is low and breathless from the almost intolerable strain of being alone with a stranger.*)

(*The legend: "I Don't Suppose You Remember Me at All!"*)

(*In her first speeches in this scene, before Jim's warmth overcomes her paralyzing shyness, Laura's voice is thin and breathless as though she has just run up a steep flight of stairs.*)

(*Jim's attitude is gently humorous. In playing this scene it should be stressed that while the incident is apparently unimportant, it is to Laura the climax of her secret life.*)

JIM: Hello, there, Laura.

LAURA (*faintly*): Hello. (*She clears her throat.*)

JIM: How are you feeling now? Better?

LAURA: Yes. Yes, thank you.

JIM: This is for you. A little dandelion wine. (*He extends it toward her with extravagant gallantry.*)

LAURA: Thank you.

JIM: Drink it—but don't get drunk! (*He laughs heartily. Laura takes the glass uncertainly; laughs shyly.*) Where shall I set the candles?

LAURA: Oh—oh, anywhere . . .

JIM: How about here on the floor? Any objections?

LAURA: No.

JIM: I'll spread a newspaper under to catch the drippings. I like to sit on the floor. Mind if I do?

LAURA: Oh, no.

JIM: Give me a pillow?

LAURA: What?

JIM: A pillow!

LAURA: Oh . . . (*Hands him one quickly.*)

JIM: How about you? Don't you like to sit on the floor?

LAURA: Oh—yes.

JIM: Why don't you, then?

LAURA: I—will.

JIM: Take a pillow! (*Laura does. Sits on the other side of the candelabrum. Jim crosses his legs and smiles engagingly at her.*) I can't hardly see you sitting way over there.

LAURA: I can—see you.

JIM: I know, but that's not fair, I'm in the limelight. (*Laura moves her pillow closer.*) Good! Now I can see you! Comfortable?

LAURA: Yes.

JIM: So am I. Comfortable as a cow. Will you have some gum?

LAURA: No, thank you.

JIM: I think that I will indulge, with your permission. (*Musingly unwraps it and holds it up.*) Think of the fortune made by the guy that invented the first piece of chewing gum. Amazing, huh? The Wrigley Building is one of the sights of Chicago.—I saw it summer before last when I went up to the Century of Progress. Did you take in the Century of Progress?

LAURA: No, I didn't.

JIM: Well, it was quite a wonderful exposition. What impressed me most was the Hall of Science. Gives you an idea of what the future will be in America, even more wonderful than the present time is! (*Pause. Smiling at her.*) Your brother tells me you're shy. Is that right, Laura?

LAURA: I—don't know.

JIM: I judge you to be an old-fashioned type of girl. Well, I think that's a pretty good type to be. Hope you don't think I'm being too personal—do you?

LAURA (*hastily, out of embarrassment*): I believe I *will* take a piece of gum, if you—don't mind. (*Clearing her throat.*) Mr. O'Connor, have you—kept up with your singing?

JIM: Singing? Me?

LAURA: Yes. I remember what a beautiful voice you had.

JIM: When did you hear me sing?

(*Voice offstage in the pause.*)

VOICE (*offstage*): O blow, ye winds, heigh-ho,
    A-roving I will go!
    I'm off to my love
    With a boxing glove—
    Ten thousand miles away!

JIM: You say you've heard me sing?

LAURA: Oh, yes! Yes, very often ... I—don't suppose you remember me—at all?

JIM (*smiling doubtfully*): You know I have an idea I've seen you before. I had that idea soon as you opened the door. It seemed almost like I was about to remember your name. But the name that I started to call you—wasn't a name! And so I stopped myself before I said it.

LAURA: Wasn't it—Blue Roses?

JIM (*Springs up. Grinning.*): Blue Roses! My gosh, yes—Blue Roses! That's what I had on my tongue when you opened the door! Isn't it funny what tricks your memory plays? I didn't connect you with the high school somehow or other. But that's where it was; it was high school. I didn't even know you were Shakespeare's sister! Gosh, I'm sorry.

LAURA: I didn't expect you to. You—barely knew me!

JIM: But we did have a speaking acquaintance, huh?

LAURA: Yes, we—spoke to each other.

JIM: When did you recognize me?

LAURA: Oh, right away!

JIM: Soon as I came in the door?

LAURA: When I heard your name I thought it was probably you. I knew that Tom used to know you a little in high school. So when you came in the door—Well, then I was—sure.

JIM: Why didn't you *say* something, then?

LAURA (*breathlessly*): I didn't know what to say, I was—too surprised!

JIM: For goodness' sakes! You know, this sure is funny!

LAURA: Yes! Yes, isn't it, though . . .

JIM: Didn't we have a class in something together?

LAURA: Yes, we did.

JIM: What class was that?

LAURA: It was—singing—Chorus!

JIM: Aw!

LAURA: I sat across the aisle from you in the Aud.

JIM: Aw.

LAURA: Mondays, Wednesdays, and Fridays.

JIM: Now I remember—you always came in late.

LAURA: Yes, it was so hard for me, getting upstairs. I had that brace on my leg—it clumped so loud!

JIM: I never heard any clumping.

LAURA (*wincing at the recollection*): To me it sounded like—thunder!

JIM: Well, well, well, I never even noticed.

LAURA: And everybody was seated before I came in. I had to walk in front of all those people. My seat was in the back row. I had to go clumping all the way up the aisle with everyone watching!

JIM: You shouldn't have been self-conscious.

LAURA: I know, but I was. It was always such a relief when the singing started.

JIM: Aw, yes, I've placed you now! I used to call you Blue Roses. How was it that I got started calling you that?

LAURA: I was out of school a little while with pleurosis. When I came back you asked me what was the matter. I said I had pleurosis—you thought I said Blue Roses. That's what you always called me after that!

JIM: I hope you didn't mind.

LAURA: Oh, no—I liked it. You see, I wasn't acquainted with many—people . . .

JIM: As I remember you sort of stuck by yourself.

LAURA: I—I—never had much luck at—making friends.

JIM: I don't see why you wouldn't.

LAURA: Well, I—started out badly.

JIM: You mean being—

LAURA: Yes, it sort of—stood between me—

JIM: You shouldn't have let it!

LAURA: I know, but it did, and—

JIM: You were shy with people!

LAURA: I tried not to be but never could—

JIM: Overcome it?

LAURA: No, I—I never could!

JIM: I guess being shy is something you have to work out of kind of gradually.

LAURA (*sorrowfully*): Yes—I guess it—

JIM: Takes time!

LAURA: Yes—

JIM: People are not so dreadful when you know them. That's what you have to remember! And everybody has problems, not just you, but practically everybody has got some problems. You think of yourself as having the only problems, as being the only one who is disappointed. But just look around you and you will see lots of people as disappointed as you are. For instance, I hoped when I was going to high school that I would be further along at this time, six years later, than I am now—You remember that wonderful write-up I had in *The Torch*?

LAURA: Yes! (*She rises and crosses to table.*)

JIM: It said I was bound to succeed in anything I went into! (*Laura returns with the annual.*) Holy Jeez! *The Torch!* (*He accepts it reverently. They smile across it with mutual wonder. Laura crouches beside him and they begin to turn through it. Laura's shyness is dissolving in his warmth.*)

LAURA: Here you are in *Pirates of Penzance*!

JIM (*wistfully*): I sang the baritone lead in that operetta.

LAURA (*rapidly*): So—*beautifully*!

JIM (*protesting*): Aw—

LAURA: Yes, yes—beautifully—beautifully!

JIM: You heard me?

LAURA: All three times!

JIM: No!

LAURA: Yes!

JIM: All three performances?

LAURA (*looking down*): Yes.

JIM: Why?

LAURA: I—wanted to ask you to—autograph my program.

JIM: Why didn't you ask me to?

LAURA: You were always surrounded by your own friends so much that I never had a chance to.

JIM: You should have just—

LAURA: Well, I—thought you might think I was—

JIM: Thought I might think you was—what?

LAURA: Oh—

JIM (*with reflective relish*): I was beleaguered by females in those days.

LAURA: You were terribly popular!

JIM: Yeah—

LAURA: You had such a—friendly way—

JIM: I was spoiled in high school.

LAURA: Everybody—liked you!

JIM: Including you?

LAURA: I—yes, I—I did, too—(*She gently closes the book in her lap.*)

JIM: Well, well, well!—Give me that program, Laura. (*She hands it to him. He signs it with a flourish.*) There you are—better late than never!

LAURA: Oh, I—what a—surprise!

JIM: My signature isn't worth very much right now. But some day—maybe—it will increase in value! Being disappointed is one thing and being discouraged is something else. I am disappointed but I am not discouraged. I'm twenty-three years old. How old are you?

LAURA: I'll be twenty-four in June.

JIM: That's not old age!

LAURA: No, but—

JIM: You finished high school?

LAURA (*with difficulty*): I didn't go back.

JIM: You mean you dropped out?

LAURA: I made bad grades in my final examinations. (*She rises and replaces the book and the program. Her voice strained.*) How is—Emily Meisenbach getting along?

JIM: Oh, that kraut-head!

LAURA: Why do you call her that?

JIM: That's what she was.

LAURA: You're not still—going with her?

JIM: I never see her.

LAURA: It said in the Personal Section that you were—engaged!

JIM: I know, but I wasn't impressed by that—propaganda!

LAURA: It wasn't—the truth?

JIM: Only in Emily's optimistic opinion!

LAURA: Oh—

(*Legend: "What Have You Done since High School?"*)

(*Jim lights a cigarette and leans indolently back on his elbows smiling at Laura with a warmth and charm which lights her inwardly with altar candles. She remains by the table and turns in her hands a piece of glass to cover her tumult.*)

JIM (*after several reflective puffs on a cigarette*): What have you done since high school? (*She seems not to hear him.*) Huh? (*Laura looks up.*) I said what have you done since high school, Laura?

LAURA: Nothing much.

JIM: You must have been doing something these six long years.

LAURA: Yes.

JIM: Well, then, such as what?

LAURA: I took a business course at business college—

JIM: How did that work out?

LAURA: Well, not very—well—I had to drop out, it gave me—indigestion—

(*Jim laughs gently.*)

JIM: What are you doing now?

LAURA: I don't do anything—much. Oh, please don't think I sit around doing nothing! My glass collection takes up a good deal of my time. Glass is something you have to take good care of.

JIM: What did you say—about glass?

LAURA: Collection I said—I have one—(*She clears her throat and turns away again, acutely shy.*)

JIM (*abruptly*): You know what I judge to be the trouble with you? Inferiority complex! Know what that is? That's what they call it when someone low-rates himself! I understand it because I had it, too. Although my case was not so aggravated as yours seems to be. I had it until I took up public speaking, developed my voice, and learned that I had an aptitude for science. Before that time I never thought of myself as being outstanding in any way whatsoever! Now I've never made a regular study of it, but I have a friend who says I can analyze people better than doctors that make a profession of it. I don't claim that to be necessarily true, but I can sure guess a person's psychology, Laura! (*Takes out his gum.*) Excuse me, Laura. I always take it out when the flavor is gone. I'll use this scrap of paper to wrap it in. I know how it is to get it stuck on a shoe. Yep—that's what I judge to be your principal trouble. A lack of confidence in yourself as a person. You don't have the proper amount of faith in yourself. I'm basing that fact on a number of your remarks and also on certain observations I've made. For instance that clumping you thought was so awful in high school. You say that you even dreaded to walk into class. You see what you did? You dropped out of school, you gave up an education because of a clump, which as far as I know was practically nonexistent! A little physical defect is what you have. Hardly noticeable even! Magnified thousands of times by imagination! You know what my strong advice to you is? Think of yourself as *superior* in some way!

LAURA: In what way would I think?

JIM: Why, man alive, Laura! Just look about you a little. What do you see? A world full of common people! All of 'em born and all of 'em going to die! Which of them has one-tenth of your good points! Or mine! Or anyone else's, as far as that goes—Gosh! Everybody excels in some one thing. Some in many! (*Unconsciously glances at himself in the mirror.*) All you've got to do is discover in what! Take me, for instance. (*He adjusts his tie at the mirror.*) My interest happens to lie in electrodynamics. I'm taking a course in radio engineering at night school, Laura, on top of a fairly responsible job at the warehouse. I'm taking that course and studying public speaking.

LAURA: Ohhhh.

JIM: Because I believe in the future of television! (*Turning back to her.*) I wish to be ready to go up right along with it. Therefore I'm planning to get in on the ground floor. In fact, I've already made the right connections and all that remains is for the industry itself to get under way! Full steam—(*His eyes are starry.*) *Knowledge*—Zzzzzp! *Money*—Zzzzzzp!—*Power*! That's the cycle democracy is built on! (*His attitude is convincingly dynamic. Laura stares at him, even her shyness eclipsed in her absolute wonder. He suddenly grins.*) I guess you think I think a lot of myself!

LAURA: No—o-o-o, I—

JIM: Now how about you? Isn't there something you take more interest in than anything else?

LAURA: Well, I do—as I said—have my—glass collection—

(*A peal of girlish laughter from the kitchen.*)

JIM: I'm not right sure I know what you're talking about. What kind of glass is it?

LAURA: Little articles of it, they're ornaments mostly! Most of them are little animals made out of glass, the tiniest little animals in the world.

Mother calls them a glass menagerie! Here's an example of one, if you'd like to see it! This one is one of the oldest. It's nearly thirteen. (*He stretches out his hand.*) (*Music: "The Glass Menagerie."*) Oh, be careful—if you breathe, it breaks!

JIM: I'd better not take it. I'm pretty clumsy with things.

LAURA: Go on, I trust you with him! (*Places it in his palm.*) There now—you're holding him gently! Hold him over the light, he loves the light! You see how the light shines through him?

JIM: It sure does shine!

LAURA: I shouldn't be partial, but he is my favorite one.

JIM: What kind of a thing is this one supposed to be?

LAURA: Haven't you noticed the single horn on his forehead?

JIM: A unicorn, huh?

LAURA: Mmm-hmmm!

JIM: Unicorns, aren't they extinct in the modern world?

LAURA: I know!

JIM: Poor little fellow, he must feel sort of lonesome.

LAURA (*smiling*): Well, if he does he doesn't complain about it. He stays on a shelf with some horses that don't have horns and all of them seem to get along nicely together.

JIM: How do you know?

LAURA (*lightly*): I haven't heard any arguments among them!

JIM (*grinning*): No arguments, huh? Well, that's a pretty good sign! Where shall I set him?

LAURA: Put him on the table. They all like a change of scenery once in a while!

JIM (*stretching*): Well, well, well, well—Look how big my shadow is when I stretch!

LAURA: Oh, oh, yes—it stretches across the ceiling!

JIM (*crossing to door*): I think it's stopped raining. (*Opens fire escape door.*) Where does the music come from?

LAURA: From the Paradise Dance Hall across the alley.

JIM: How about cutting the rug a little, Miss Wingfield?

LAURA: Oh, I—

JIM: Or is your program filled up? Let me have a look at it. (*Grasps imaginary card.*) Why, every dance is taken! I'll just have to scratch some out. (*Waltz music: "La Golondrina."*) Ahhh, a waltz! (*He executes some sweeping turns by himself then holds his arms toward Laura.*)

LAURA (*breathlessly*): I—can't dance!

JIM: There you go, that inferiority stuff!

LAURA: I've never danced in my life!

JIM: Come on, try!

LAURA: Oh, but I'd step on you!

JIM: I'm not made out of glass.

LAURA: How—how—how do we start?

JIM: Just leave it to me. You hold your arms out a little.

LAURA: Like this?

JIM: A little bit higher. Right. Now don't tighten up, that's the main thing about it—relax.

LAURA (*laughing breathlessly*): It's hard not to.

JIM: Okay.

LAURA: I'm afraid you can't budge me.

JIM: What do you bet I can't? (*He swings her into motion.*)

LAURA: Goodness, yes, you can!

JIM: Let yourself go, now, Laura, just let yourself go.

LAURA: I'm—

JIM: Come on!

LAURA: Trying!

JIM: Not so stiff—Easy does it!

LAURA: I know but I'm—

JIM: Loosen th' backbone! There now, that's a lot better.

LAURA: Am I?

JIM: Lots, lots better! (*He moves her about the room in a clumsy waltz.*)

LAURA: Oh, my!

JIM: Ha-ha!

LAURA: Oh, my goodness!

JIM: Ha-ha-ha! (*They suddenly bump into the table. Jim stops.*) What did we hit on?

LAURA: Table.

JIM: Did something fall off it? I think—

LAURA: Yes.

JIM: I hope that it wasn't the little glass horse with the horn!

LAURA: Yes.

JIM: Aw, aw, aw. Is it broken?

LAURA: Now it is just like all the other horses.

JIM: It's lost its—

LAURA: Horn! It doesn't matter. Maybe it's a blessing in disguise.

JIM: You'll never forgive me. I bet that that was your favorite piece of glass.

LAURA: I don't have favorites much. It's no tragedy, Freckles. Glass breaks so easily. No matter how careful you are. The traffic jars the shelves and things fall off them.

JIM: Still I'm awfully sorry that I was the cause.

LAURA (*smiling*): I'll just imagine he had an operation. The horn was removed to make him feel less—freakish! (*They both laugh.*) Now he will feel more at home with the other horses, the ones that don't have horns . . .

JIM: Ha-ha, that's very funny! (*Suddenly serious.*) I'm glad to see that you have a sense of humor. You know—you're—well—very different! Surprisingly different from anyone else I know! (*His voice becomes soft and hesitant with a genuine feeling.*) Do you mind me telling you that? (*Laura is abashed beyond speech.*) I mean it in a nice way . . . (*Laura nods shyly, looking away.*) You make me feel sort of—I don't know how to put it! I'm usually pretty good at expressing things, but—This is something that I don't know how to say! (*Laura touches her throat and clears it—turns the broken unicorn in her hands.*) (*Even softer.*) Has anyone ever told you that you were pretty? (*Pause: Music.*) (*Laura looks up slowly, with wonder, and shakes her head.*) Well, you are! In a very different way from anyone else. And all the nicer because of the difference, too. (*His voice becomes low and husky. Laura turns away, nearly faint with the novelty of her emotions.*) I wish that you were my sister. I'd teach you to have some confidence in yourself. The different people are not like other people, but being different is nothing to be ashamed of. Because other people are not such wonderful people. They're one hundred times one thousand. You're one times one! They walk all over the earth. You just stay here. They're common as—weeds, but—you—well, you're—*Blue Roses!*

(*Image on screen: blue roses.*)
   (*Music changes.*)

LAURA: But blue is wrong for—roses . . .
JIM: It's right for you—You're—pretty!
LAURA: In what respect am I pretty?
JIM: In all respects—believe me! Your eyes—your hair—are pretty! Your hands are pretty! (*He catches hold of her hand.*) You think I'm making this up because I'm invited to dinner and have to be nice. Oh, I could do that! I could put on an act for you, Laura, and say lots of things without being very sincere. But this time I am. I'm talking to you sincerely. I happened to notice you had this inferiority complex that keeps you from feeling comfortable with people. Somebody needs to build your confidence up and make you proud instead of shy and turning away and—blushing—Somebody ought to—Ought to—kiss you, Laura! (*His hand slips slowly up her arm to her shoulder.*) (*Music swells tumultuously.*) (*He suddenly turns her about and kisses her on the lips. When he releases her Laura sinks on the sofa with a bright, dazed look. Jim backs away and fishes in his pocket for a cigarette.*) (*Legend on screen: "Souvenir."*) Stumble-john! (*He lights the cigarette, avoiding her look. There is a peal of girlish laughter from Amanda in the kitchen. Laura slowly raises and opens her hand. It still contains the little broken glass animal. She looks at it with a tender, bewildered expression.*) Stumble-john! I shouldn't have done that—That was way off the beam. You don't smoke, do you? (*She*

looks up, smiling, not hearing the question. He sits beside her a little gingerly. She looks at him speechlessly—waiting. He coughs decorously and moves a little farther aside as he considers the situation and senses her feelings, dimly, with perturbation. Gently.) Would you—care for a—mint? (*She doesn't seem to hear him but her look grows brighter even.*) Peppermint—Life Saver? My pocket's a regular drugstore—wherever I go . . . (*He pops a mint in his mouth. Then gulps and decides to make a clean breast of it. He speaks slowly and gingerly.*) Laura, you know, if I had a sister like you, I'd do the same thing as Tom. I'd bring out fellows and—introduce her to them. The right type of boys of a type to—appreciate her. Only—well—he made a mistake about me. Maybe I've got no call to be saying this. That may not have been the idea in having me over. But what if it was? There's nothing wrong about that. The only trouble is that in my case—I'm not in a situation to—do the right thing. I can't take down your number and say I'll phone. I can't call up next week and—ask for a date. I thought I had better explain the situation in case you misunderstood it and—hurt your feelings. . . . (*Pause. Slowly, very slowly, Laura's look changes, her eyes returning slowly from his to the ornament in her palm.*)

(*Amanda utters another gay laugh in the kitchen.*)

LAURA (*faintly*): You—won't—call again?

JIM: No, Laura, I can't. (*He rises from the sofa.*) As I was just explaining, I've—got strings on me, Laura, I've—been going steady! I go out all the time with a girl named Betty. She's a home-girl like you, and Catholic, and Irish, and in a great many ways we—get along fine. I met her last summer on a moonlight boat trip up the river to Alton, on the *Majestic*. Well—right away from the start it was—love! (*Legend: Love!*) (*Laura sways slightly forward and grips the arm of the sofa. He fails to notice, now enrapt in his own comfortable being.*) Being in love has made a new man of me! (*Leaning stiffly forward, clutching the arm of the sofa, Laura struggles visibly with her storm. But Jim is oblivious, she is a long way off.*) The power of love is really pretty tremendous! Love is something that—changes the whole world, Laura! (*The storm abates a little and Laura leans back. He notices her again.*) It happened that Betty's aunt took sick, she got a wire and had to go to Centralia. So Tom—when he asked me to dinner—I naturally just accepted the invitation, not knowing that you—that he—that I—(*He stops awkwardly.*) Huh—I'm a stumble-john! (*He flops back on the sofa. The holy candles in the altar of Laura's face have been snuffed out! There is a look of almost infinite desolation. Jim glances at her uneasily.*) I wish that you would—say something. (*She bites her lip which was trembling and then bravely smiles. She opens her hand again on the broken glass ornament. Then she gently takes his hand and raises it level with her own. She carefully places the unicorn in the palm of his hand, then pushes his fingers closed upon it.*) What are you—doing that for? You want me to have him?—Laura? (*She nods.*) What for?

LAURA: A—souvenir . . .

(*She rises unsteadily and crouches beside the victrola to wind it up.*)
  (*Legend on screen: "Things Have a Way of Turning out so Badly."*)
  (*Or Image: "Gentleman Caller Waving Good-bye!—Gaily."*)
  (*At this moment Amanda rushes brightly back in the front room. She bears a pitcher of fruit punch in an old-fashioned cut-glass pitcher and a plate of macaroons. The plate has a gold border and poppies painted on it.*)

AMANDA: Well, well, well! Isn't the air delightful after the shower? I've made you children a little liquid refreshment. (*Turns gaily to the gentleman caller.*) Jim, do you know that song about lemonade?
  "Lemonade, lemonade
    Made in the shade and stirred with a spade—
    Good enough for any old maid!"

JIM (*uneasily*): Ha-ha! No—I never heard it.

AMANDA: Why, Laura! You look so serious!

JIM: We were having a serious conversation.

AMANDA: Good! Now you're better acquainted!

JIM (*uncertainly*): Ha-ha! Yes.

AMANDA: You modern young people are much more serious-minded than my generation. I was so gay as a girl!

JIM: You haven't changed, Mrs. Wingfield.

AMANDA: Tonight I'm rejuvenated! The gaiety of the occasion, Mr. O'Connor! (*She tosses her head with a peal of laughter. Spills lemonade.*) Oooo! I'm baptizing myself!

JIM: Here—let me—

AMANDA (*setting the pitcher down*): There now. I discovered we had some maraschino cherries. I dumped them in, juice and all!

JIM: You shouldn't have gone to that trouble, Mrs. Wingfield.

AMANDA: Trouble, trouble? Why it was loads of fun! Didn't you hear me cutting up in the kitchen? I bet your ears were burning! I told Tom how out-done with him I was for keeping you to himself so long a time! He should have brought you over much, much sooner! Well, now that you've found your way, I want you to be a very frequent caller! Not just occasional but all the time. Oh, we're going to have a lot of gay times together! I see them coming! Mmm, just breathe that air! So fresh, and the moon's so pretty! I'll skip back out—I know where my place is when young folks are having a—serious conversation!

JIM: Oh, don't go out, Mrs. Wingfield. The fact of the matter is I've got to be going.

AMANDA: Going, now? You're joking! Why, it's only the shank of the evening, Mr. O'Connor!

JIM: Well, you know how it is.

AMANDA: You mean you're a young workingman and have to keep workingmen's hours. We'll let you off early tonight. But only on the condition that next time you stay later. What's the best night for you? Isn't Saturday night the best night for you workingmen?

JIM: I have a couple of time clocks to punch, Mrs. Wingfield. One at morning, another one at night!

AMANDA: My, but you *are* ambitious! You work at night, too?

JIM: No, Ma'am, not work but—Betty! (*He crosses deliberately to pick up his hat. The band at the Paradise Dance Hall goes into a tender waltz.*)

AMANDA: Betty? Betty? Who's—Betty! (*There is an ominous cracking sound in the sky.*)

JIM: Oh, just a girl. The girl I go steady with! (*He smiles charmingly. The sky falls.*)

(*Legend: "The Sky Falls."*)

AMANDA (*a long-drawn exhalation*): Ohhhh . . . Is it a serious romance, Mr. O'Connor?

JIM: We're going to be married the second Sunday in June.

AMANDA: Ohhhh—how nice! Tom didn't mention that you were engaged to be married.

JIM: The cat's not out of the bag at the warehouse yet. You know how they are. They call you Romeo and stuff like that. (*He stops at the oval mirror to put on his hat. He carefully shapes the brim and the crown to give a discreetly dashing effect.*) It's been a wonderful evening, Mrs. Wingfield. I guess this is what they mean by Southern hospitality.

AMANDA: It really wasn't anything at all.

JIM: I hope it don't seem like I'm rushing off. But I promised Betty I'd pick her up at the Wabash depot, an' by the time I get my jalopy down there her train'll be in. Some women are pretty upset if you keep 'em waiting.

AMANDA: Yes, I know—The tyranny of women! (*Extends her hand.*) Goodbye, Mr. O'Connor. I wish you luck—and happiness—and success! All three of them, and so does Laura!—Don't you, Laura?

LAURA: Yes!

JIM (*taking her hand*): Good-bye, Laura. I'm certainly going to treasure that souvenir. And don't you forget the good advice I gave you. (*Raises his voice to a cheery shout.*) So long, Shakespeare! Thanks again, ladies—Good night!

(*He grins and ducks jauntily out.*)

(*Still bravely grimacing, Amanda closes the door on the gentleman caller. Then she turns back to the room with a puzzled expression. She and Laura don't dare to face each other. Laura crouches beside the victrola to wind it.*)

AMANDA (*faintly*): Things have a way of turning out so badly. I don't believe that I would play the victrola. Well, well—well—Our gentleman caller was engaged to be married! Tom!

TOM (*from back*): Yes, Mother?

AMANDA: Come in here a minute. I want to tell you something awfully funny.

TOM (*enters with macaroon and a glass of the lemonade*): Has the gentleman caller gotten away already?

AMANDA: The gentleman caller has made an early departure. What a wonderful joke you played on us!

TOM: How do you mean?

AMANDA: You didn't mention that he was engaged to be married.

TOM: Jim? Engaged?

AMANDA: That's what he just informed us.

TOM: I'll be jiggered! I didn't know about that.

AMANDA: That seems very peculiar.

TOM: What's peculiar about it?

AMANDA: Didn't you call him your best friend down at the warehouse?

TOM: He is, but how did I know?

AMANDA: It seems extremely peculiar that you wouldn't know your best friend was going to be married!

TOM: The warehouse is where I work, not where I know things about people!

AMANDA: You don't know things anywhere! You live in a dream; you manufacture illusions! (*He crosses to door.*) Where are you going?

TOM: I'm going to the movies.

AMANDA: That's right, now that you've had us make such fools of ourselves. The effort, the preparations, all the expense! The new floor lamp, the rug, the clothes for Laura! All for what? To entertain some other girl's fiancé! Go to the movies, go! Don't think about us, a mother deserted, an unmarried sister who's crippled and has no job! Don't let anything interfere with your selfish pleasure! Just go, go, go—to the movies!

TOM: All right, I will! The more you shout about my selfishness to me the quicker I'll go, and I won't go to the movies!

AMANDA: Go, then! Then go to the moon—you selfish dreamer!

(*Tom smashes his glass on the floor. He plunges out on the fire escape, slamming the door. Laura screams—cut by door.*)

(*Dance hall music up. Tom goes to the rail and grips it desperately, lifting his face in the chill white moonlight penetrating the narrow abyss of the alley.*)

(*Legend on screen: "And so Good-bye . . ."*)

(*Tom's closing speech is timed with the interior pantomime. The interior scene is played as though viewed through soundproof glass. Amanda appears to be making a comforting speech to Laura who is huddled upon the sofa. Now that we cannot hear the mother's speech, her silliness is gone and she has dignity and tragic beauty. Laura's dark hair hides her face until at the end of the speech she lifts it to smile at her mother. Amanda's gestures are slow and graceful, almost dancelike, as she comforts the daughter. At the end of her speech she glances a moment at the father's picture—then withdraws through the portieres. At close of Tom's speech, Laura blows out the candles, ending the play.*)

TOM: I didn't go to the moon, I went much further—for time is the longest distance between two places—Not long after that I was fired for writing a poem on the lid of a shoebox. I left Saint Louis. I descended the steps of this fire escape for a last time and followed, from then on, in my father's footsteps, attempting to find in motion what was lost in space—I traveled around a great deal. The cities swept about me like dead leaves, leaves that were brightly colored but torn away from the branches. I would have stopped, but I was pursued by something. It always came upon me unawares, taking me altogether by surprise. Perhaps it was a familiar bit of music. Perhaps it was only a piece of transparent glass—Perhaps I am walking along a street at night, in some strange city, before I have found companions. I pass the lighted window of a shop where perfume is sold. The window is filled with pieces of colored glass, tiny transparent bottles in delicate colors, like bits of a shattered rainbow. Then all at once my sister touches my shoulder. I turn around and look into her eyes . . . Oh, Laura, Laura, I tried to leave you behind me, but I am more faithful than I intended to be! I reach for a cigarette, I cross the street, I run into the movies or a bar, I buy a drink, I speak to the nearest stranger—anything that can blow your candles out! (*Laura bends over the candles.*)—for nowadays the world is lit by lightning! Blow out your candles, Laura—and so good-bye. . . .

(*She blows the candles out.*)
(*The scene dissolves.*)

[1944]

LORRAINE HANSBERRY [1930–1965]

A Raisin in the Sun°

HARLEM

What happens to a dream deferred?

Is the American Dream possible? [handwritten]

Does it dry up
like a raisin in the sun?
Or fester like a sore —
And then run?
Does it stink like rotten meat?
Or crust and sugar over —
like a syrupy sweet?

Maybe it just sags
like a heavy load.

Or does it explode?
— LANGSTON HUGHES

Characters

RUTH YOUNGER — *Walter's wife* [handwritten]
TRAVIS YOUNGER — *kid of Walter's, Ruth* [handwritten]
WALTER LEE YOUNGER, *Brother* — ~~Beau~~ *Drives White Rich Man Around* [handwritten] *WALTER: Personal Dream: own his own liquor Dept.* [handwritten]
BENEATHA YOUNGER — *Sister of Walter* [handwritten] *another* [handwritten, left margin]
LENA YOUNGER, *Mama* — *wants A house* [handwritten]
JOSEPH ASAGAI
GEORGE MURCHISON
KARL LINDNER
BOBO
MOVING MEN

Act I
Scene 1: *Friday morning.*
Scene 2: *The following morning.*

See Langston Hughes, "Harlem" (p. 560).

976

Act II

Scene 1: *Later, the same day.*
Scene 2: *Friday night, a few weeks later.*
Scene 3: *Moving day, one week later.*

Act III

An hour later.

Scene

The action of the play is set in Chicago's Southside, sometime between World War II and the present.

ACT I   *Scene 1*

(*The Younger living room would be a comfortable and well-ordered room if it were not for a number of indestructible contradictions to this state of being. Its furnishings are typical and undistinguished and their primary feature now is that they have clearly had to accommodate the living of* too many people for too many years—*and* they are tired. *Still, we can see that at some time, a time probably no longer remembered by the family* (*except perhaps for Mama*), *the furnishings of this room were actually selected with care and love and even hope—and brought to this apartment and arranged with taste and pride.*) ⟶metaphor

(*That was a long time ago. Now the* once loved *pattern of the couch upholstery has to fight to show itself from under acres of crocheted doilies and couch covers which have themselves finally come to be more important than the upholstery. And here a table or a chair has been moved to disguise the worn places in the carpet; but the carpet has fought back by showing its* weariness, *with depressing uniformity, elsewhere on its surface.*)

(*Weariness has, in fact, won in this room. Everything has been polished, washed, sat on, used, scrubbed too often. All pretenses but living itself have long since vanished from the very atmosphere of this room.*) ⟶have care best they can—Pride

(*Moreover, a section of this room, for it is not really a room unto itself, though the landlord's lease would make it seem so, slopes backward to provide a small kitchen area, where the family prepares the meals that are eaten in the living room proper, which must also serve as dining room. The single window that has been provided for these "two" rooms is located in this kitchen area. The sole natural light the family may enjoy in the course of a day is only that which fights its way through this little window.*)

(*At left, a door leads to a bedroom which is shared by Mama and her daughter, Beneatha. At right, opposite, is a second room* (*which in the beginning of the life of this apartment was probably a breakfast room*) *which serves as a bedroom for Walter and his wife, Ruth.*)

(*Time: Sometime between World War II and the present.*)

(*Place: Chicago's Southside.*)

(*At Rise: It is morning dark in the living room, Travis is asleep on the make-down bed at center. An alarm clock sounds from within the bedroom at right, and presently Ruth enters from that room and closes the door behind her. She crosses sleepily toward the window. As she passes her sleeping son she reaches down and shakes him a little. At the window she raises the shade and a dusky Southside morning light comes in feebly. She fills a pot with water and puts it on to boil. She calls to the boy, between yawns, in a slightly muffled voice.)*

(Ruth is about thirty. We can see that she was a pretty girl, even exceptionally so, but now it is apparent that life has been little that she expected, and disappointment has already begun to hang in her face. In a few years, before thirty-five even, she will be known among her people as a "settled woman.")

(She crosses to her son and gives him a good, final, rousing shake.)

RUTH: Come on now, boy, it's seven thirty! *(Her son sits up at last, in a stupor of sleepiness)* I say hurry up, Travis! You ain't the only person in the world got to use a bathroom! *(The child, a sturdy, handsome little boy of ten or eleven, drags himself out of the bed and almost blindly takes his towels and "today's clothes" from drawers and a closet and goes out to the bathroom, which is in an outside hall and which is shared by another family or families on the same floor. Ruth crosses to the bedroom door at right and opens it and calls in to her husband)* Walter Lee! . . . It's after seven thirty! Lemme see you do some waking up in there now! *(She waits)* You better get up from there, man! It's after seven thirty I tell you. *(She waits again)* All right, you just go ahead and lay there and next thing you know Travis be finished and Mr. Johnson'll be in there and you'll be fussing and cussing round here like a madman! And be late too! *(She waits, at the end of patience)* Walter Lee—it's time for you to GET UP!

(She waits another second and then starts to go into the bedroom, but is apparently satisfied that her husband has begun to get up. She stops, pulls the door to, and returns to the kitchen area. She wipes her face with a moist cloth and runs her fingers through her sleep-disheveled hair in a vain effort and ties an apron around her housecoat. The bedroom door at right opens and her husband stands in the doorway in his pajamas, which are rumpled and mismated. He is a lean, intense young man in his middle thirties, inclined to quick nervous movements and erratic speech habits—and always in his voice there is a quality of indictment)

WALTER: Is he out yet?

RUTH: What you mean *out*? He ain't hardly got in there good yet.

WALTER *(Wandering in, still more oriented to sleep than to a new day)*: Well, what was you doing all that yelling for if I can't even get in there yet? *(Stopping and thinking)* Check coming today?

RUTH: They *said* Saturday and this is just Friday and I hopes to God you ain't going to get up here first thing this morning and start talking to me 'bout no money—'cause I 'bout don't want to hear it.

WALTER: Something the matter with you this morning?

RUTH: No—I'm just sleepy as the devil. What kind of eggs you want?

WALTER: Not scrambled. (*Ruth starts to scramble eggs*) Paper come? (*Ruth points impatiently to the rolled up* Tribune *on the table, and he gets it and spreads it out and vaguely reads the front page*) Set off another bomb yesterday.

RUTH (*Maximum indifference*): Did they?

WALTER (*Looking up*): What's the matter with you?

RUTH: Ain't nothing the matter with me. And don't keep asking me that this morning.

WALTER: Ain't nobody bothering you. (*Reading the news of the day absently again*) Say Colonel McCormick is sick.

RUTH (*Affecting tea-party interest*): Is he now? Poor thing.

WALTER (*Sighing and looking at his watch*): Oh, me. (*He waits*) Now what is that boy doing in that bathroom all this time? He just going to have to start getting up earlier. I can't be being late to work on account of him fooling around in there.

RUTH (*Turning on him*): Oh, no he ain't going to be getting up no earlier no such thing! It ain't his fault that he can't get to bed no earlier nights 'cause he got a bunch of crazy good-for-nothing clowns sitting up running their mouths in what is supposed to be his bedroom after ten o'clock at night . . .

WALTER: That's what you mad about, ain't it? The things I want to talk about with my friends just couldn't be important in your mind, could they?

(*He rises and finds a cigarette in her handbag on the table and crosses to the little window and looks out, smoking and deeply enjoying this first one*)

RUTH (*Almost matter of factly, a complaint too automatic to deserve emphasis*): Why you always got to smoke before you eat in the morning?

WALTER (*At the window*): Just look at 'em down there . . . Running and racing to work . . . (*He turns and faces his wife and watches her a moment at the stove, and then, suddenly*) You look young this morning, baby.

RUTH (*Indifferently*): Yeah?

WALTER: Just for a second—stirring them eggs. Just for a second it was— you looked real young again. (*He reaches for her; she crosses away. Then, drily*) It's gone now—you look like yourself again!

RUTH: Man, if you don't shut up and leave me alone.

WALTER (*Looking out to the street again*): First thing a man ought to learn in life is not to make love to no colored woman first thing in the morning. You all some eeeevil people at eight o'clock in the morning.

(*Travis appears in the hall doorway, almost fully dressed and quite wide awake now, his towels and pajamas across his shoulders. He opens the door and signals for his father to make the bathroom in a hurry*)

TRAVIS (*Watching the bathroom*): Daddy, come on! (*Walter gets his bathroom utensils and flies out to the bathroom*)

RUTH: Sit down and have your breakfast, Travis.

TRAVIS: Mama, this is Friday. (*Gleefully*) Check coming tomorrow, huh?

RUTH: You get your mind off money and eat your breakfast.

TRAVIS (*Eating*): This is the morning we supposed to bring the fifty cents to school.

RUTH: Well, I ain't got no fifty cents this morning.

TRAVIS: Teacher say we have to.

RUTH: I don't care what teacher say. I ain't got it. Eat your breakfast, Travis.

TRAVIS: I *am* eating.

RUTH: Hush up now and just eat!

(*The boy gives her an exasperated look for her lack of understanding, and eats grudgingly*)

TRAVIS: You think Grandmama would have it?

RUTH: No! And I want you to stop asking your grandmother for money, you hear me?

TRAVIS (*Outraged*): Gaaaleee! I don't ask her, she just gimme it sometimes!

RUTH: Travis Willard Younger—I got too much on me this morning to be—

TRAVIS: Maybe Daddy—

RUTH: *Travis!*

(*The boy hushes abruptly. They are both quiet and tense for several seconds*)

TRAVIS (*Presently*): Could I maybe go carry some groceries in front of the supermarket for a little while after school then?

RUTH: Just hush, I said. (*Travis jabs his spoon into his cereal bowl viciously, and rests his head in anger upon his fists*) If you through eating, you can get over there and make up your bed.

(*The boy obeys stiffly and crosses the room, almost mechanically, to the bed and more or less folds the bedding into a heap, then angrily gets his books and cap*)

TRAVIS (*Sulking and standing apart from her unnaturally*): I'm gone.

RUTH (*Looking up from the stove to inspect him automatically*): Come here. (*He crosses to her and she studies his head*) If you don't take this comb and fix this here head, you better! (*Travis puts down his books with a great sigh of oppression, and crosses to the mirror. His mother mutters under her breath about his "slubbornness"*) 'Bout to march out of here with that head looking just like chickens slept in it! I just don't know where you get your slubborn ways . . . And get your jacket, too. Looks chilly out this morning.

TRAVIS (*With conspicuously brushed hair and jacket*): I'm gone.

RUTH: Get carfare and milk money—(*Waving one finger*)—and not a single penny for no caps°, you hear me?

TRAVIS (*With sullen politeness*): Yes'm.

(*He turns in outrage to leave. His mother watches after him as in his frustration he approaches the door almost comically. When she speaks to him, her voice has become a very gentle tease*)

RUTH (*Mocking; as she thinks he would say it*): Oh, Mama makes me so mad sometimes, I don't know what to do! (*She waits and continues to his back as he stands stock-still in front of the door*) I wouldn't kiss that woman good-bye for nothing in this world this morning! (*The boy finally turns around and rolls his eyes at her, knowing the mood has changed and he is vindicated; he does not, however, move toward her yet*) Not for nothing in this world! (*She finally laughs aloud at him and holds out her arms to him and we see that it is a way between them, very old and practiced. He crosses to her and allows her to embrace him warmly but keeps his face fixed with masculine rigidity. She holds him back from her presently and looks at him and runs her fingers over the features of his face. With utter gentleness—*) Now—whose little old angry man are you?

TRAVIS (*The masculinity and gruffness start to fade at last*): Aw gaalee—Mama . . .

RUTH (*Mimicking*): Aw gaaaaalleeeee, Mama! (*She pushes him, with rough playfulness and finality, toward the door*) Get on out of here or you going to be late.

TRAVIS (*In the face of love, new aggressiveness*): Mama, could I *please* go carry groceries?

RUTH: Honey, it's starting to get so cold evenings.

WALTER (*Coming in from the bathroom and drawing a make-believe gun from a make-believe holster and shooting at his son*): What is it he wants to do?

RUTH: Go carry groceries after school at the supermarket.

WALTER: Well, let him go . . .

TRAVIS (*Quickly, to the ally*): I *have* to—she won't gimme the fifty cents . . .

WALTER (*To his wife only*): Why not?

RUTH (*Simply, and with flavor*): 'Cause we don't have it.

WALTER (*To Ruth only*): What you tell the boy things like that for? (*Reaching down into his pants with a rather important gesture*) Here, son—

(*He hands the boy the coin, but his eyes are directed to his wife's. Travis takes the money happily*)

TRAVIS: Thanks, Daddy.

caps: For his cap gun, a very popular toy in the 1950s and 1960s.

(*He starts out. Ruth watches both of them with murder in her eyes. Walter stands and stares back at her with defiance, and suddenly reaches into his pocket again on an afterthought*)

WALTER (*Without even looking at his son, still staring hard at his wife*): In fact, here's another fifty cents . . . Buy yourself some fruit today— or take a taxicab to school or something!

TRAVIS: Whoopee—

(*He leaps up and clasps his father around the middle with his legs, and they face each other in mutual appreciation; slowly Walter Lee peeks around the boy to catch the violent rays from his wife's eyes and draws his head back as if shot*)

WALTER: You better get down now—and get to school, man.

TRAVIS (*At the door*): O.K. Good-bye.

(*He exits*)

WALTER (*After him, pointing with pride*): That's *my* boy. (*She looks at him in disgust and turns back to her work*) You know what I was thinking 'bout in the bathroom this morning?

RUTH: No.

WALTER: How come you always try to be so pleasant!

RUTH: What is there to be pleasant 'bout!

WALTER: You want to know what I was thinking 'bout in the bathroom or not!

RUTH: I know what you thinking 'bout.

WALTER (*Ignoring her*): 'Bout what me and Willy Harris was talking about last night.

RUTH (*Immediately—a refrain*): Willy Harris is a good-for-nothing loud-mouth.

WALTER: Anybody who talks to me has got to be a good-for-nothing loud-mouth, ain't he? And what you know about who is just a good-for-nothing loudmouth? Charlie Atkins was just a "good-for-nothing loud-mouth" too, wasn't he! When he wanted me to go in the dry-cleaning business with him. And now—he's grossing a hundred thousand a year. A hundred thousand dollars a year! You still call *him* a loudmouth!

RUTH (*Bitterly*): Oh, Walter Lee . . .

(*She folds her head on her arms over the table*)

WALTER (*Rising and coming to her and standing over her*): You tired, ain't you? Tired of everything. Me, the boy, the way we live—this beat-up hole— everything. Ain't you? (*She doesn't look up, doesn't answer*) So tired— moaning and groaning all the time, but you wouldn't do nothing to help, would you? You couldn't be on my side that long for nothing, could you?

RUTH: Walter, please leave me alone.

WALTER: A man needs for a woman to back him up . . .

RUTH: Walter—

WALTER: Mama would listen to you. You know she listen to you more than she do me and Bennie. She think more of you. All you have to do is just sit down with her when you drinking your coffee one morning and talking 'bout things like you do and—(*He sits down beside her and demonstrates graphically what he thinks her methods and tone should be*)— you just sip your coffee, see, and say easy like that you been thinking 'bout that deal Walter Lee is so interested in, 'bout the store and all, and sip some more coffee, like what you saying ain't really that important to you—And the next thing you know, she be listening good and asking you questions and when I come home—I can tell her the details. This ain't no fly-by-night proposition, baby. I mean we figured it out, me and Willy and Bobo.

RUTH (*With a frown*): Bobo?

WALTER: Yeah. You see, this little liquor store we got in mind cost seventy-five thousand and we figured the initial investment on the place be 'bout thirty thousand, see. That be ten thousand each. Course, there's a couple of hundred you got to pay so's you don't spend your life just waiting for them clowns to let your license get approved—

RUTH: You mean graft?

WALTER (*Frowning impatiently*): Don't call it that. See there, that just goes to show you what women understand about the world. Baby, don't *nothing* happen for you in this world 'less you pay *somebody* off!

RUTH: Walter, leave me alone! (*She raises her head and stares at him vigorously— then says, more quietly*) *Eat* your eggs, they gonna be cold.

WALTER (*Straightening up from her and looking off*): That's it. There you are. Man say to his woman: I got me a dream. His woman say: Eat your eggs. (*Sadly, but gaining in power*) Man say: I got to take hold of this here world, baby! And a woman will say: Eat your eggs and go to work. (*Passionately now*) Man say: I got to change my life, I'm choking to death, baby! And his woman say—(*In utter anguish as he brings his fists down on his thighs*)—Your eggs is getting cold!

RUTH (*Softly*): Walter, that ain't none of our money.

WALTER (*Not listening at all or even looking at her*): This morning, I was lookin' in the mirror and thinking about it . . . I'm thirty-five years old; I been married eleven years and I got a boy who sleeps in the living room—(*Very, very quietly*)—and all I got to give him is stories about how rich white people live . . .

RUTH: Eat your eggs, Walter.

WALTER (*Slams the table and jumps up*): —DAMN MY EGGS—DAMN ALL THE EGGS THAT EVER WAS!

RUTH: Then go to work.

WALTER (*Looking up at her*): See—I'm trying to talk to you 'bout myself—(*Shaking his head with the repetition*)—and all you can say is eat them eggs and go to work.

RUTH (*Wearily*): Honey, you never say nothing new. I listen to you every day, every night and every morning, and you never say nothing new. (*Shrugging*) So you would rather *be* Mr. Arnold than be his chauffeur. So—I would *rather* be living in Buckingham Palace.°

WALTER: That is just what is wrong with the colored woman in this world . . . Don't understand about building their men up and making 'em feel like they somebody. Like they can do something.

RUTH (*Drily, but to hurt*): There *are* colored men who do things.

WALTER: No thanks to the colored woman.

RUTH: Well, being a colored woman, I guess I can't help myself none.

(*She rises and gets the ironing board and sets it up and attacks a huge pile of rough-dried clothes, sprinkling them in preparation for the ironing and then rolling them into tight fat balls*)

WALTER (*Mumbling*): We one group of men tied to a race of women with small minds!

full of herself

(*His sister Beneatha enters. She is about twenty, as slim and intense as her brother. She is not as pretty as her sister-in-law, but her lean, almost intellectual face has a handsomeness of its own. She wears a bright-red flannel nightie, and her thick hair stands wildly about her head. Her speech is a mixture of many things; it is different from the rest of the family's insofar as education has permeated her sense of English—and perhaps the Midwest rather than the South has finally—at last—won out in her inflection; but not altogether, because over all of it is a soft slurring and transformed use of vowels which is the decided influence of the Southside. She passes through the room without looking at either Ruth or Walter and goes to the outside door and looks, a little blindly, out to the bathroom. She sees that it has been lost to the Johnsons. She closes the door with a sleepy vengeance and crosses to the table and sits down a little defeated*)

[handwritten left margin: originally from South→ Move to Chicago–was Chicago Accent vs South]

BENEATHA: I am going to start timing those people.

WALTER: You should get up earlier.

BENEATHA (*Her face in her hands. She is still fighting the urge to go back to bed*): Really—would you suggest dawn? Where's the paper?

WALTER (*Pushing the paper across the table to her as he studies her almost clinically, as though he has never seen her before*): You a horrible-looking chick at this hour.

BENEATHA (*Drily*): Good morning, everybody.

WALTER (*Senselessly*): How is school coming?

Buckingham Palace: The London residence of the British royal family.

BENEATHA (*In the same spirit*): Lovely. Lovely. And you know, biology is the greatest. (*Looking up at him*) I dissected something that looked just like you yesterday.

WALTER: I just wondered if you've made up your mind and everything.

BENEATHA (*Gaining in sharpness and impatience*): And what did I answer yesterday morning—and the day before that?

RUTH (*From the ironing board, like someone disinterested and old*): Don't be so nasty, Bennie.

BENEATHA (*Still to her brother*): And the day before that and the day before that!

WALTER (*Defensively*): I'm interested in you. Something wrong with that? Ain't many girls who decide—

WALTER AND BENEATHA (*In unison*): —"to be a doctor." (*Silence*)

WALTER: Have we figured out yet just exactly how much medical school is going to cost?

RUTH: Walter Lee, why don't you leave that girl alone and get out of here to work?

BENEATHA (*Exits to the bathroom and bangs on the door*): Come on out of there, please!

(*She comes back into the room*)

WALTER (*Looking at his sister intently*): You know the check is coming tomorrow.

BENEATHA (*Turning on him with a sharpness all her own*): That money belongs to Mama, Walter, and it's for her to decide how she wants to use it. I don't care if she wants to buy a house or a rocket ship or just nail it up somewhere and look at it. It's hers. Not ours—*hers*.

WALTER (*Bitterly*): Now ain't that fine! You just got your mother's interest at heart, ain't you, girl? You such a nice girl—but if Mama got that money she can always take a few thousand and help you through school too—can't she?

BENEATHA: I have never asked anyone around here to do anything for me!

WALTER: No! And the line between asking and just accepting when the time comes is big and wide—ain't it!

BENEATHA (*With fury*): What do you want from me, Brother—that I quit school or just drop dead, which!

WALTER: I don't want nothing but for you to stop acting holy 'round here. Me and Ruth done made some sacrifices for you—why can't you do something for the family?

RUTH: Walter, don't be dragging me in it.

WALTER: You are in it—Don't you get up and go work in somebody's kitchen for the last three years to help put clothes on her back?

RUTH: Oh, Walter—that's not fair . . .

WALTER: It ain't that nobody expects you to get on your knees and say thank you, Brother; thank you, Ruth; thank you, Mama—and thank you, Travis, for wearing the same pair of shoes for two semesters—

BENEATHA (*Dropping to her knees*): Well—I *do*—all right?—thank everybody! And forgive me for ever wanting to be anything at all! (*Pursuing him on her knees across the floor*) FORGIVE ME, FORGIVE ME, FORGIVE ME!

RUTH: Please stop it! Your mama'll hear you.

WALTER: Who the hell told you you had to be a doctor? If you so crazy 'bout messing 'round with sick people—then go be a nurse like other women—or just get married and be quiet . . .

BENEATHA: Well—you finally got it said . . . It took you three years but you finally got it said. Walter, give up; leave me alone—it's Mama's money.

WALTER: *He was my father, too!*

BENEATHA: So what? He was mine, too—and Travis's grandfather—but the insurance money belongs to Mama. Picking on me is not going to make her give it to you to invest in any liquor stores—(*Underbreath, dropping into a chair*)—and I for one say, God bless Mama for that!

WALTER (*To Ruth*): See—did you hear? Did you hear!

RUTH: Honey, please go to work.

WALTER: Nobody in this house is ever going to understand me.

BENEATHA: Because you're a nut.

WALTER: Who's a nut?

BENEATHA: You—you are a nut. Thee is mad, boy.

WALTER (*Looking at his wife and his sister from the door, very sadly*): The world's most backward race of people, and that's a fact.

BENEATHA (*Turning slowly in her chair*): And then there are all those prophets who would lead us out of the wilderness—(*Walter slams out of the house*)—into the swamps!

RUTH: Bennie, why you always gotta be pickin' on your brother? Can't you be a little sweeter sometimes? (*Door opens. Walter walks in. He fumbles with his cap, starts to speak, clears throat, looks everywhere but at Ruth. Finally:*)

WALTER (*To Ruth*): I need some money for carfare.

RUTH (*Looks at him, then warms; teasing, but tenderly*): Fifty cents? (She goes to her bag and gets money) Here—take a taxi!

(*Walter exits, Mama enters. She is a woman in her early sixties, full-bodied and strong. She is one of those women of a certain grace and beauty who wear it so unobtrusively that it takes a while to notice. Her dark-brown face is surrounded by the total whiteness of her hair, and, being a woman who has adjusted to many things in life and overcome many more, her face is full of strength. She has, we*

*can see, wit and faith of a kind that keep her eyes lit and full of interest and ex-
pectancy. She is, in a word, a beautiful woman. Her bearing is perhaps most
like the noble bearing of the women of the Hereros of Southwest Africa—rather
as if she imagines that as she walks she still bears a basket or a vessel upon her
head. Her speech, on the other hand, is as careless as her carriage is precise—she
is inclined to slur everything—but her voice is perhaps not so much quiet as
simply soft)*

MAMA: Who that 'round here slamming doors at this hour?

*(She crosses through the room, goes to the window, opens it, and brings in a
feeble little plant growing doggedly in a small pot on the windowsill. She feels
the dirt and puts it back out)*

RUTH: That was Walter Lee. He and Bennie was at it again.

MAMA: My children and they tempers. Lord, if this little old plant don't get
more sun than it's been getting it ain't never going to see spring again.
(She turns from the window) What's the matter with you this morning,
Ruth? You looks right peaked. You aiming to iron all them things? Leave
some for me. I'll get to 'em this afternoon. Bennie honey, it's too drafty
for you to be sitting 'round half dressed. Where's your robe?

BENEATHA: In the cleaners.

MAMA: Well, go get mine and put it on.

BENEATHA: I'm not cold, Mama, honest.

MAMA: I know—but you so thin . . .

BENEATHA *(Irritably)*: Mama, I'm not cold.

MAMA *(Seeing the make-down bed as Travis has left it)*: Lord have mercy, look
at that poor bed. Bless his heart—he tries, don't he?

(She moves to the bed Travis has sloppily made up)

RUTH: No—he don't half try at all 'cause he knows you going to come
along behind him and fix everything. That's just how come he don't
know how to do nothing right now—you done spoiled that boy so.

MAMA *(Folding bedding)*: Well—he's a little boy. Ain't supposed to know
'bout housekeeping. My baby, that's what he is. What you fix for his
breakfast this morning?

RUTH *(Angrily)*: I feed my son, Lena!

MAMA: I ain't meddling—*(Underbreath; busy-bodyish)* I just noticed all last
week he had cold cereal, and when it starts getting this chilly in the fall
a child ought to have some hot grits or something when he goes out in
the cold—

RUTH *(Furious)*: I gave him hot oats—is that all right!

MAMA: I ain't meddling. *(Pause)* Put a lot of nice butter on it? *(Ruth shoots
her an angry look and does not reply)* He likes lots of butter.

RUTH *(Exasperated)*: Lena—

MAMA (*To Beneatha. Mama is inclined to wander conversationally sometimes*):
What was you and your brother fussing 'bout this morning?

BENEATHA: It's not important, Mama.

(*She gets up and goes to look out at the bathroom, which is apparently free, and she picks up her towels and rushes out*)

MAMA: What was they fighting about?

RUTH: Now you know as well as I do.

MAMA (*Shaking her head*): Brother still worrying hisself sick about that money?

RUTH: You know he is.

MAMA: You had breakfast?

RUTH: Some coffee.

MAMA: Girl, you better start eating and looking after yourself better. You almost thin as Travis.

RUTH: Lena—

MAMA: Un-hunh?

RUTH: What are you going to do with it?

MAMA: Now don't you start, child. It's too early in the morning to be talking about money. It ain't Christian.

RUTH: It's just that he got his heart set on that store—

MAMA: You mean that liquor store that Willy Harris want him to invest in?

RUTH: Yes—

MAMA: We ain't no business people, Ruth. We just plain working folks.

RUTH: Ain't nobody business people till they go into business. Walter Lee say colored people ain't never going to start getting ahead till they start gambling on some different kinds of things in the world—investments and things.

MAMA: What done got into you, girl? Walter Lee done finally sold you on investing.

RUTH: No. Mama, something is happening between Walter and me. I don't know what it is—but he needs something—something I can't give him anymore. He needs this chance, Lena.

MAMA (*Frowning deeply*): But liquor, honey—

RUTH: Well—like Walter say—I spec people going to always be drinking themselves some liquor.

MAMA: Well—whether they drinks it or not ain't none of my business. But whether I go into business selling it to 'em *is*, and I don't want that on my ledger this late in life. (*Stopping suddenly and studying her daughter-in-law*) Ruth Younger, what's the matter with you today? You look like you could fall over right there.

RUTH: I'm tired.

MAMA: Then you better stay home from work today.

RUTH: I can't stay home. She'd be calling up the agency and screaming at them, "My girl didn't come in today—send me somebody! My girl didn't come in!" Oh, she just have a fit . . .

MAMA: Well, let her have it. I'll just call her up and say you got the flu—

RUTH (*Laughing*): Why the flu?

MAMA: 'Cause it sounds respectable to 'em. Something white people get, too. They know 'bout the flu. Otherwise they think you been cut up or something when you tell 'em you sick.

RUTH: I got to go in. We need the money.

MAMA: Somebody would of thought my children done all but starved to death the way they talk about money here late. Child, we got a great big old check coming tomorrow.

RUTH (*Sincerely, but also self-righteously*): Now that's your money. It ain't got nothing to do with me. We all feel like that—Walter and Bennie and me—even Travis.

MAMA (*Thoughtfully, and suddenly very far away*): Ten thousand dollars—

RUTH: Sure is wonderful.

MAMA: Ten thousand dollars.

RUTH: You know what you should do, Miss Lena? You should take yourself a trip somewhere. To Europe or South America or someplace—

MAMA (*Throwing up her hands at the thought*): Oh, child!

RUTH: I'm serious. Just pack up and leave! Go on away and enjoy yourself some. Forget about the family and have yourself a ball for once in your life—

MAMA (*Drily*): You sound like I'm just about ready to die. Who'd go with me? What I look like wandering 'round Europe by myself?

RUTH: Shoot—these here rich white women do it all the time. They don't think nothing of packing up they suitcases and piling on one of them big steamships and—swoosh!—they gone, child.

MAMA: Something always told me I wasn't no rich white woman.

RUTH: Well—what are you going to do with it then?

MAMA: I ain't rightly decided. (*Thinking. She speaks now with emphasis*) Some of it got to be put away for Beneatha and her schoolin'—and ain't nothing going to touch that part of it. Nothing. (*She waits several seconds, trying to make up her mind about something, and looks at Ruth a little tentatively before going on*) Been thinking that we maybe could meet the notes on a little old two-story somewhere, with a yard where Travis could play in the summertime, if we use part of the insurance for a down payment and everybody kind of pitch in. I could maybe take on a little day work again, few days a week— *[margin note: Mama's Dream]*

RUTH (*Studying her mother-in-law furtively and concentrating on her ironing, anxious to encourage without seeming to*): Well, Lord knows, we've put enough rent into this here rat trap to pay for four houses by now . . .

MAMA (*Looking up at the words "rat trap" and then looking around and leaning back and sighing—in a suddenly reflective mood—*): "Rat trap"—yes, that's all it is. (*Smiling*) I remember just as well the day me and Big Walter moved in here. Hadn't been married but two weeks and wasn't planning on living here no more than a year. (*She shakes her head at the dissolved dream*) We was going to set away, little by little, don't you know, and buy a little place out in Morgan Park. We had even picked out the house. (*Chuckling a little*) Looks right dumpy today. But Lord, child, you should know all the dreams I had 'bout buying that house and fixing it up and making me a little garden in the back—(*She waits and stops smiling*) And didn't none of it happen.

(*Dropping her hands in a futile gesture*)

RUTH (*Keeps her head down, ironing*): Yes, life can be a barrel of disappointments, sometimes.

MAMA: Honey, Big Walter would come in here some nights back then and slump down on that couch there and just look at the rug, and look at me and look at the rug and then back at me—and I'd know he was down then . . . really down. (*After a second very long and thoughtful pause; she is seeing back to times that only she can see*) And then, Lord, when I lost that baby—little Claude—I almost thought I was going to lose Big Walter too. Oh, that man grieved hisself! He was one man to love his children.

RUTH: Ain't nothin' can tear at you like losin' your baby.

MAMA: I guess that's how come that man finally worked hisself to death like he done. Like he was fighting his own war with this here world that took his baby from him.

RUTH: He sure was a fine man, all right. I always liked Mr. Younger.

MAMA: Crazy 'bout his children! God knows there was plenty wrong with Walter Younger—hard-headed, mean, kind of wild with women—plenty wrong with him. But he sure loved his children. Always wanted them to have something—be something. That's where Brother gets all these notions, I reckon. Big Walter used to say, he'd get right wet in the eyes sometimes, lean his head back with the water standing in his eyes and say, "Seem like God didn't see fit to give the black man nothing but dreams—but He did give us children to make them dreams seem worth while." (*She smiles*) He could talk like that, don't you know.

RUTH: Yes, he sure could. He was a good man, Mr. Younger.

MAMA: Yes, a fine man—just couldn't never catch up with his dreams, that's all.

(*Beneatha comes in, brushing her hair and looking up to the ceiling, where the sound of a vacuum cleaner has started up*)

BENEATHA: What could be so dirty on that woman's rugs that she has to vacuum them every single day?

RUTH: I wish certain young women 'round here who I could name would take inspiration about certain rugs in a certain apartment I could also mention.

BENEATHA (*Shrugging*): How much cleaning can a house need, for Christ's sakes.

MAMA (*Not liking the Lord's name used thus*): Bennie!

RUTH: Just listen to her—just listen!

BENEATHA: Oh, God!

MAMA: If you use the Lord's name just one more time—

BENEATHA (*A bit of a whine*): Oh, Mama—

RUTH: Fresh—just fresh as salt, this girl!

BENEATHA (*Drily*): Well—if the salt loses its savor—

MAMA: Now that will do. I just ain't going to have you 'round here reciting the scriptures in vain—you hear me?

BENEATHA: How did I manage to get on everybody's wrong side by just walking into a room?

RUTH: If you weren't so fresh—

BENEATHA: Ruth, I'm twenty years old.

MAMA: What time you be home from school today?

BENEATHA: Kind of late. (*With enthusiasm*) Madeline is going to start my guitar lessons today.

(*Mama and Ruth look up with the same expression*)

MAMA: Your *what* kind of lessons?

BENEATHA: Guitar.

RUTH: Oh, Father!

MAMA: How come you done taken it in your mind to learn to play the guitar?

BENEATHA: I just want to, that's all.

MAMA (*Smiling*): Lord, child, don't you know what to do with yourself? How long it going to be before you get tired of this now—like you got tired of that little playacting group you joined last year? (*Looking at Ruth*) And what was it the year before that?

RUTH: The horseback-riding club for which she bought that fifty-five-dollar riding habit that's been hanging in the closet ever since!

MAMA (*To Beneatha*): Why you got to flit so from one thing to another, baby?

BENEATHA (*Sharply*): I just want to learn to play the guitar. Is there anything wrong with that?

MAMA: Ain't nobody trying to stop you. I just wonders sometimes why you has to flit so from one thing to another all the time. You ain't never done nothing with all that camera equipment you brought home—

BENEATHA: I don't flit! I—I experiment with different forms of expression—
RUTH: Like riding a horse?
BENEATHA: —People have to express themselves one way or another.
MAMA: What is it you want to express?
BENEATHA (*Angrily*): Me! (*Mama and Ruth look at each other and burst into raucous laughter*) Don't worry—I don't expect you to understand.
MAMA (*To change the subject*): Who you going out with tomorrow night?
BENEATHA (*With displeasure*): George Murchison again.
MAMA (*Pleased*): Oh—you getting a little sweet on him?
RUTH: You ask me, this child ain't sweet on nobody but herself— (*Underbreath*) Express herself!

(*They laugh*)

BENEATHA: Oh—I like George all right, Mama. I mean I like him enough to go out with him and stuff, but—
RUTH (*For devilment*): What does *and stuff* mean?
BENEATHA: Mind your own business.
MAMA: Stop picking at her now, Ruth. (*She chuckles—then a suspicious sudden look at her daughter as she turns in her chair for emphasis*) What DOES it mean?
BENEATHA (*Wearily*): Oh, I just mean I couldn't ever really be serious about George. He's—he's so shallow.
RUTH: Shallow—what do you mean he's shallow? He's *rich*!
MAMA: Hush, Ruth.
BENEATHA: I know he's rich. He knows he's rich, too.
RUTH: Well—what other qualities a man got to have to satisfy you, little girl?
BENEATHA: You wouldn't even begin to understand. Anybody who married Walter could not possibly understand.
MAMA (*Outraged*): What kind of way is that to talk about your brother?
BENEATHA: Brother is a flip—let's face it.
MAMA (*To Ruth, helplessly*): What's a flip?
RUTH (*Glad to add kindling*): She's saying he's crazy.
BENEATHA: Not crazy. Brother isn't really crazy yet—he—he's an elaborate neurotic.
MAMA: Hush your mouth!
BENEATHA: As for George. Well. George looks good—he's got a beautiful car and he takes me to nice places and, as my sister-in-law says, he is probably the richest boy I will ever get to know and I even like him sometimes—but if the Youngers are sitting around waiting to see if their little Bennie is going to tie up the family with the Murchisons, they are wasting their time.

RUTH: You mean you wouldn't marry George Murchison if he asked you someday? That pretty, rich thing? Honey, I knew you was odd—

BENEATHA: No I would not marry him if all I felt for him was what I feel now. Besides, George's family wouldn't really like it.

MAMA: Why not?

BENEATHA: Oh, Mama—The Murchisons are honest-to-God-real-*live*-rich colored people, and the only people in the world who are more snobbish than rich white people are rich colored people. I thought everybody knew that. I've met Mrs. Murchison. She's a scene!

MAMA: You must not dislike people 'cause they well off, honey.

BENEATHA: Why not? It makes just as much sense as disliking people 'cause they are poor, and lots of people do that.

RUTH (*A wisdom-of-the-ages manner. To Mama*): Well, she'll get over some of this—

BENEATHA: Get over it? What are you talking about, Ruth? Listen, I'm going to be a doctor. I'm not worried about who I'm going to marry yet—if I ever get married.

MAMA AND RUTH: *If!*

MAMA: Now, Bennie—

BENEATHA: Oh, I probably will . . . but first I'm going to be a doctor, and George, for one, still thinks that's pretty funny. I couldn't be bothered with that. I am going to be a doctor and everybody around here better understand that!

MAMA (*Kindly*): 'Course you going to be a doctor, honey, God willing.

BENEATHA (*Drily*): God hasn't got a thing to do with it.

MAMA: Beneatha—that just wasn't necessary.

BENEATHA: Well—neither is God. I get sick of hearing about God.

MAMA: Beneatha!

BENEATHA: I mean it! I'm just tired of hearing about God all the time. What has He got to do with anything? Does he pay tuition?

MAMA: You 'bout to get your fresh little jaw slapped!

RUTH: That's just what she needs, all right!

BENEATHA: Why? Why can't I say what I want to around here, like everybody else?

MAMA: It don't sound nice for a young girl to say things like that—you wasn't brought up that way. Me and your father went to trouble to get you and Brother to church every Sunday.

BENEATHA: Mama, you don't understand. It's all a matter of ideas, and God is just one idea I don't accept. It's not important. I am not going out and be immoral or commit crimes because I don't believe in God. I don't even think about it. It's just that I get tired of Him getting credit for all the things the human race achieves through its own stubborn effort.

There simply is no blasted God—there is only man and it is *he* who makes miracles!

(*Mama absorbs this speech, studies her daughter and rises slowly and crosses to Beneatha and slaps her powerfully across the face. After, there is only silence and the daughter drops her eyes from her mother's face, and Mama is very tall before her*)

MAMA: Now—you say after me, in my mother's house there is still God. (*There is a long pause and Beneatha stares at the floor wordlessly. Mama repeats the phrase with precision and cool emotion*) In my mother's house there is still God.

BENEATHA: In my mother's house there is still God.

(*A long pause*)

MAMA (*Walking away from Beneatha, too disturbed for triumphant posture. Stopping and turning back to her daughter*): There are some ideas we ain't going to have in this house. Not long as I am at the head of this family.

BENEATHA: Yes, ma'am.

(*Mama walks out of the room*)

RUTH (*Almost gently, with profound understanding*): You think you a woman, Bennie—but you still a little girl. What you did was childish—so you got treated like a child.

BENEATHA: I see. (*Quietly*) I also see that everybody thinks it's all right for Mama to be a tyrant. But all the tyranny in the world will never put a God in the heavens!

(*She picks up her books and goes out. Pause*)

RUTH (*Goes to Mama's door*): She said she was sorry.

MAMA (*Coming out, going to her plant*): They frightens me, Ruth. My children.

RUTH: You got good children, Lena. They just a little off sometimes—but they're good.

MAMA: No—there's something come down between me and them that don't let us understand each other and I don't know what it is. One done almost lost his mind thinking 'bout money all the time and the other done commence to talk about things I can't seem to understand in no form or fashion. What is it that's changing, Ruth.

RUTH (*Soothingly, older than her years*): Now . . . you taking it all too seriously. You just got strong-willed children and it takes a strong woman like you to keep 'em in hand.

MAMA (*Looking at her plant and sprinkling a little water on it*): They spirited all right, my children. Got to admit they got spirit—Bennie and Walter. Like this little old plant that ain't never had enough sunshine or nothing— and look at it . . .

(*She has her back to Ruth, who has had to stop ironing and lean against something and put the back of her hand to her forehead*)

RUTH (*Trying to keep Mama from noticing*): You . . . sure . . . loves that little old thing, don't you? . . .

MAMA: Well, I always wanted me a garden like I used to see sometimes at the back of the houses down home. This plant is close as I ever got to having one. (*She looks out of the window as she replaces the plant*) Lord, ain't nothing as dreary as the view from this window on a dreary day, is there? Why ain't you singing this morning, Ruth? Sing that "No Ways Tired." That song always lifts me up so—(*She turns at last to see that Ruth has slipped quietly to the floor, in a state of semiconsciousness*) Ruth! Ruth honey—what's the matter with you . . . Ruth!

[handwritten margin note: Dream house]

Scene 2

(*It is the following morning; a Saturday morning, and house cleaning is in progress at the Youngers. Furniture has been shoved hither and yon and Mama is giving the kitchen-area walls a washing down. Beneatha, in dungarees, with a handkerchief tied around her face, is spraying insecticide into the cracks in the walls. As they work, the radio is on and a Southside disk-jockey program is inappropriately filling the house with a rather exotic saxophone blues. Travis, the sole idle one, is leaning on his arms, looking out of the window.*)

TRAVIS: Grandmama, that stuff Bennie is using smells awful. Can I go downstairs, please?

MAMA: Did you get all them chores done already? I ain't seen you doing much.

TRAVIS: Yes'm—finished early. Where did Mama go this morning?

MAMA (*Looking at Beneatha*): She had to go on a little errand.

(*The phone rings. Beneatha runs to answer it and reaches it before Walter, who has entered from bedroom*)

TRAVIS: Where?

MAMA: To tend to her business.

BENEATHA: Haylo . . . (*Disappointed*) Yes, he is. (*She tosses the phone to Walter, who barely catches it*) It's Willie Harris again.

WALTER (*As privately as possible under Mama's gaze*): Hello, Willie. Did you get the papers from the lawyer? . . . No, not yet. I told you the mailman doesn't get here till ten-thirty . . . No, I'll come there . . . Yeah! Right away. (*He hangs up and goes for his coat*)

BENEATHA: Brother, where did Ruth go?

WALTER (*As he exits*): How should I know!

TRAVIS: Aw come on, Grandma. Can I go outside?

MAMA: Oh, I guess so. You stay right in front of the house, though, and keep a good lookout for the postman.

TRAVIS: Yes'm. (*He darts into bedroom for stickball and bat, reenters, and sees Beneatha on her knees spraying under sofa with behind upraised. He edges closer to the target, takes aim, and lets her have it. She screams*) Leave them poor little cockroaches alone, they ain't bothering you none! (*He runs as she swings the spray gun at him viciously and playfully*) Grandma! Grandma!

MAMA: Look out there, girl, before you be spilling some of that stuff on that child!

TRAVIS (*Safely behind the bastion of Mama*): That's right—look out, now! (*He exits*)

BENEATHA (*Drily*): I can't imagine that it would hurt him—it has never hurt the roaches.

MAMA: Well, little boys' hides ain't as tough as Southside roaches. You better get over there behind the bureau. I seen one marching out of there like Napoleon yesterday.

BENEATHA: There's really only one way to get rid of them, Mama—

MAMA: How?

BENEATHA: Set fire to this building! Mama, where did Ruth go?

MAMA (*Looking at her with meaning*): To the doctor, I think.

BENEATHA: The doctor? What's the matter? (*They exchange glances*) You don't think—

MAMA (*With her sense of drama*): Now I ain't saying what I think. But I ain't never been wrong 'bout a woman neither.

(*The phone rings*)

BENEATHA (*At the phone*): Hay-lo . . . (*Pause, and a moment of recognition*) Well—when did you get back! . . . And how was it? . . . Of course I've missed you—in my way . . . This morning? No . . . house cleaning and all that and Mama hates it if I let people come over when the house is like this . . . You *have*? Well, that's different . . . What is it— Oh, what the hell, come on over . . . Right, see you then. *Arrivederci*.

(*She hangs up*)

MAMA (*Who has listened vigorously, as is her habit*): Who is that you inviting over here with this house looking like this? You ain't got the pride you was born with!

BENEATHA: Asagai doesn't care how houses look, Mama—he's an intellectual.

MAMA: *Who?*

BENEATHA: Asagai—Joseph Asagai. He's an African boy I met on campus. He's been studying in Canada all summer.

MAMA: What's his name?

BENEATHA: Asagai, Joseph. Ah-sah-guy . . . He's from Nigeria.

MAMA: Oh, that's the little country that was founded by slaves way back . . .

BENEATHA: No, Mama—that's Liberia.

MAMA: I don't think I never met no African before.

BENEATHA: Well, do me a favor and don't ask him a whole lot of ignorant questions about Africans. I mean, do they wear clothes and all that—

MAMA: Well, now, I guess if you think we so ignorant 'round here maybe you shouldn't bring your friends here—

BENEATHA: It's just that people ask such crazy things. All anyone seems to know about when it comes to Africa is Tarzan—

MAMA (*Indignantly*): Why should I know anything about Africa?

BENEATHA: Why do you give money at church for the missionary work?

MAMA: Well, that's to help save people.

BENEATHA: You mean save them from *heathenism*—

MAMA (*Innocently*): Yes.

BENEATHA: I'm afraid they need more salvation from the British and the French.

(*Ruth comes in forlornly and pulls off her coat with dejection. They both turn to look at her*)

RUTH (*Dispiritedly*): Well, I guess from all the happy faces—everybody knows.

BENEATHA: You pregnant?

MAMA: Lord have mercy, I sure hope it's a little old girl. Travis ought to have a sister.

(*Beneatha and Ruth give her a hopeless look for this grandmotherly enthusiasm*)

BENEATHA: How far along are you?

RUTH: Two months.

BENEATHA: Did you mean to? I mean did you plan it or was it an accident?

MAMA: What do you know about planning or not planning?

BENEATHA: Oh, Mama.

RUTH (*Wearily*): She's twenty years old, Lena.

BENEATHA: Did you plan it, Ruth?

RUTH: Mind your own business.

BENEATHA: It is my business—where is he going to live, on the *roof*? (*There is silence following the remark as the three women react to the sense of it*) Gee—I didn't mean that, Ruth, honest. Gee, I don't feel like that at all. I—I think it is wonderful.

RUTH (*Dully*): Wonderful.

BENEATHA: Yes—really. (*There is a sudden commotion from the street and she goes to the window to look out*) What on earth is going on out there? These kids. (*There are, as she throws open the window, the shouts of children rising up from the street. She sticks her head out to see better and calls out)* TRAVIS! TRAVIS . . . WHAT ARE YOU DOING DOWN THERE? (*She sees*) Oh Lord, they're chasing a rat!

(*Ruth covers her face with hands and turns away*)

MAMA (*Angrily*): Tell that youngun to get himself up here, at once!

BENEATHA: TRAVIS . . . YOU COME UPSTAIRS . . . AT ONCE!

RUTH (*Her face twisted*): Chasing a rat. . . . .

MAMA (*Looking at Ruth, worried*): Doctor say everything going to be all right?

RUTH (*Far away*): Yes—she says everything is going to be fine . . .

MAMA (*Immediately suspicious*): "She"—What doctor you went to?

(*Ruth just looks at Mama meaningfully and Mama opens her mouth to speak as Travis bursts in*)

TRAVIS (*Excited and full of narrative, coming directly to his mother*): Mama, you should of seen the rat . . . Big as a cat, honest! (*He shows an exaggerated size with his hands*) Gaaleee, that rat was really cuttin' and Bubber caught him with his heel and the janitor, Mr. Barnett, got him with a stick—and then they got him in a corner and—BAM! BAM! BAM!—and he was still jumping around and bleeding like everything too—there's rat blood all over the street—

(*Ruth reaches out suddenly and grabs her son without even looking at him and clamps her hand over his mouth and holds him to her. Mama crosses to them rapidly and takes the boy from her*)

MAMA: You hush up now . . . talking all that terrible stuff. . . . (*Travis is staring at his mother with a stunned expression, Beneatha comes quickly and takes him away from his grandmother and ushers him to the door*)

BENEATHA: You go back outside and play . . . but not with any rats. (*She pushes him gently out the door with the boy straining to see what is wrong with his mother*)

MAMA (*Worriedly hovering over Ruth*): Ruth honey—what's the matter with you—you sick?

(*Ruth has her fists clenched on her thighs and is fighting hard to suppress a scream that seems to be rising in her*)

BENEATHA: What's the matter with her, Mama?

MAMA (*Working her fingers in Ruth's shoulders to relax her*): She be all right. Women gets right depressed sometimes when they get her way. (*Speaking softly, expertly, rapidly*) Now you just relax. That's right . . . just lean back, don't think 'bout nothing at all . . . nothing at all—

RUTH: I'm all right . . .

(*The glassy-eyed look melts and then she collapses into a fit of heavy sobbing. The bell rings*)

BENEATHA: Oh, my God—that must be Asagai.

MAMA (*To Ruth*): Come on now, honey. You need to lie down and rest awhile . . . then have some nice hot food.

(*They exit, Ruth's weight on her mother-in-law. Beneatha, herself profoundly disturbed, opens the door to admit a rather dramatic-looking young man with a large package*)

ASAGAI: Hello, Alaiyo—

BENEATHA (*Holding the door open and regarding him with pleasure*): Hello . . . (*Long pause*) Well—come in. And please excuse everything. My mother was very upset about my letting anyone come here with the place like this.

ASAGAI (*Coming into the room*): You look disturbed too . . . Is something wrong?

BENEATHA (*Still at the door, absently*): Yes . . . we've all got acute ghetto-itis. (*She smiles and comes toward him, finding a cigarette and sitting*) So—sit down! No! Wait! (*She whips the spray gun off sofa where she had left it and puts the cushions back. At last perches on arm of sofa. He sits*) So, how was Canada?

ASAGAI (*A sophisticate*): Canadian.

BENEATHA (*Looking at him*): Asagai, I'm very glad you are back.

ASAGAI (*Looking back at her in turn*): Are you really?

BENEATHA: Yes—very.

ASAGAI: Why?—you were quite glad when I went away. What happened?

BENEATHA: You went away.

ASAGAI: Ahhhhhhhh.

BENEATHA: Before—you wanted to be so serious before there was time.

ASAGAI: How much time must there be before one knows what one feels?

BENEATHA (*Stalling this particular conversation. Her hands pressed together, in a deliberately childish gesture*): What did you bring me?

ASAGAI (*Handing her the package*): Open it and see.

BENEATHA (*Eagerly opening the package and drawing out some records and the colorful robes of a Nigerian woman*): Oh, Asagai! . . . You got them for me! . . . How beautiful . . . and the records too! (*She lifts out the robes and runs to the mirror with them and holds the drapery up in front of herself*)

ASAGAI (*Coming to her at the mirror*): I shall have to teach you how to drape it properly. (*He flings the material about her for the moment and stands back to look at her*) Ah—*Oh-pay-gay-day, oh-gbah-mu-shay*. (*A Yoruba° exclamation for admiration*) You wear it well . . . very well . . . mutilated hair and all.

BENEATHA (*Turning suddenly*): My hair—what's wrong with my hair?

___

Yoruba: One of the largest ethnic groups in West Africa, known for its political and military strength and rich culture from A.D. 1100 to 1700.

ASAGAI (*Shrugging*): Were you born with it like that?

BENEATHA (*Reaching up to touch it*): No . . . of course not.

(*She looks back to the mirror, disturbed*)

ASAGAI (*Smiling*): How then?

BENEATHA: You know perfectly well how . . . as crinkly as yours . . . that's how.

ASAGAI: And it is ugly to you that way?

BENEATHA (*Quickly*): Oh, no—not ugly . . . (*More slowly, apologetically*) But it's so hard to manage when it's, well—raw.

ASAGAI: And so to accommodate that—you mutilate it every week?

BENEATHA: It's not mutilation!

ASAGAI (*Laughing aloud at her seriousness*): Oh . . . please! I am only teasing you because you are so very serious about these things. (*He stands back from her and folds his arms across his chest as he watches her pulling at her hair and frowning in the mirror*) Do you remember the first time you met me at school? . . . (*He laughs*) You came up to me and you said—and I thought you were the most serious little thing I had ever seen—you said: (*He imitates her*) "Mr. Asagai—I want very much to talk with you. About Africa. You see, Mr. Asagai, I am looking for my *identity*!"

(*He laughs*)

BENEATHA (*Turning to him, not laughing*): Yes—

(*Her face is quizzical, profoundly disturbed*)

ASAGAI (*Still teasing and reaching out and taking her face in his hands and turning her profile to him*): Well . . . it is true that this is not so much a profile of a Hollywood queen as perhaps a queen of the Nile—(*A mock dismissal of the importance of the question*) But what does it matter? Assimilationism is so popular in your country.

BENEATHA (*Wheeling, passionately, sharply*): I am not an assimilationist!

ASAGAI (*The protest hangs in the room for a moment and Asagai studies her, his laughter fading*): Such a serious one. (*There is a pause*) So—you like the robes? You must take excellent care of them—they are from my sister's personal wardrobe.

BENEATHA (*With incredulity*): You—you sent all the way home—for me?

ASAGAI (*With charm*): For you—I would do much more . . . Well, that is what I came for. I must go.

BENEATHA: Will you call me Monday?

ASAGAI: Yes . . . We have a great deal to talk about. I mean about identity and time and all that.

BENEATHA: Time?

ASAGAI: Yes. About how much time one needs to know what one feels.

BENEATHA: You see! You never understood that there is more than one kind of feeling which can exist between a man and a woman—or, at least, there should be.

ASAGAI (*Shaking his head negatively but gently*): No. Between a man and a woman there need be only one kind of feeling. I have that for you . . . Now even . . . right this moment . . .

BENEATHA: I know—and by itself—it won't do. I can find that anywhere.

ASAGAI: For a woman it should be enough.

BENEATHA: I know—because that's what it says in all the novels that men write. But it isn't. Go ahead and laugh—but I'm not interested in being someone's little episode in America or—(*With feminine vengeance*)—one of them! (*Asagai has burst into laughter again*) That's funny as hell, huh!

ASAGAI: It's just that every American girl I have known has said that to me. White—black—in this you are all the same. And the same speech, too!

BENEATHA (*Angrily*): Yuk, yuk, yuk!

ASAGAI: It's how you can be sure that the world's most liberated women are not liberated at all. You all talk about it too much!

(*Mama enters and is immediately all social charm because of the presence of a guest*)

BENEATHA: Oh—Mama—this is Mr. Asagai.

MAMA: How do you do?

ASAGAI (*Total politeness to an elder*): How do you do, Mrs. Younger. Please forgive me for coming at such an outrageous hour on a Saturday.

MAMA: Well, you are quite welcome. I just hope you understand that our house don't always look like this. (*Chatterish*) You must come again. I would love to hear all about—(*Not sure of the name*)—your country. I think it's so sad the way our American Negroes don't know nothing about Africa 'cept Tarzan and all that. And all that money they pour into these churches when they ought to be helping you people over there drive out them French and Englishmen done taken away your land.

(*The mother flashes a slightly superior look at her daughter upon completion of the recitation*)

ASAGAI (*Taken aback by this sudden and acutely unrelated expression of sympathy*): Yes . . . yes . . .

MAMA (*Smiling at him suddenly and relaxing and looking him over*): How many miles is it from here to where you come from?

ASAGAI: Many thousands.

MAMA (*Looking at him as she would Walter*): I bet you don't half look after yourself, being away from your mama either. I spec you better come 'round here from time to time to get yourself some decent home-cooked meals . . .

ASAGAI (*Moved*): Thank you. Thank you very much. (*They are all quiet, then—*) Well . . . I must go. I will call you Monday, Alaiyo.

MAMA: What's that he call you?

ASAGAI: Oh—"Alaiyo." I hope you don't mind. It is what you would call a nickname, I think. It is a Yoruba word. I am a Yoruba.

MAMA (*Looking at Beneatha*): I—I thought he was from—(*Uncertain*)

ASAGAI (*Understanding*): Nigeria is my country. Yoruba is my tribal origin—

BENEATHA: You didn't tell us what Alaiyo means . . . for all I know, you might be calling me Little Idiot or something . . .

ASAGAI: Well . . . let me see . . . I do not know how just to explain it . . . The sense of a thing can be so different when it changes languages.

BENEATHA: You're evading.

ASAGAI: No—really it is difficult . . . (*Thinking*) It means . . . it means One for Whom Bread—Food—Is Not Enough. (*He looks at her*) Is that all right?

BENEATHA (*Understanding, softly*): Thank you.

MAMA (*Looking from one to the other and not understanding any of it*): Well . . . that's nice . . . You must come see us again—Mr.——

ASAGAI: Ah-sah-guy . . .

MAMA: Yes . . . Do come again.

ASAGAI: Good-bye.

(*He exits*)

MAMA (*After him*): Lord, that's a pretty thing just went out here! (*Insinuatingly, to her daughter*) Yes, I guess I see why we done commence to get so interested in Africa 'round here. Missionaries my aunt Jenny!

(*She exits*)

BENEATHA: Oh, Mama! . . .

(*She picks up the Nigerian dress and holds it up to her in front of the mirror again. She sets the headdress on haphazardly and then notices her hair again and clutches at it and then replaces the headdress and frowns at herself. Then she starts to wriggle in front of the mirror as she thinks a Nigerian woman might. Travis enters and stands regarding her*)

TRAVIS: What's the matter, girl, you cracking up?

BENEATHA: Shut up.

(*She pulls the headdress off and looks at herself in the mirror and clutches at her hair again and squinches her eyes as if trying to imagine something. Then, suddenly, she gets her raincoat and kerchief and hurriedly prepares for going out*)

MAMA (*Coming back into the room*): She's resting now. Travis, baby, run next door and ask Miss Johnson to please let me have a little kitchen cleanser. This here can is empty as Jacob's kettle.

TRAVIS: I just came in.

MAMA: Do as you told. (*He exits and she looks at her daughter*) Where you going?

BENEATHA (*Halting at the door*): To become a queen of the Nile!

(*She exits in a breathless blaze of glory. Ruth appears in the bedroom doorway*)

MAMA: Who told you to get up?

RUTH: Ain't nothing wrong with me to be lying in no bed for. Where did Bennie go?

MAMA (*Drumming her fingers*): Far as I could make out—to Egypt. (*Ruth just looks at her*) What time is it getting to?

RUTH: Ten twenty. And the mailman going to ring that bell this morning just like he done every morning for the last umpteen years.

(*Travis comes in with the cleanser can*)

TRAVIS: She say to tell you that she don't have much.

MAMA (*Angrily*): Lord, some people I could name sure is tight-fisted! (*Directing her grandson*) Mark two cans of cleanser down on the list there. If she that hard up for kitchen cleanser, I sure don't want to forget to get her none!

RUTH: Lena—maybe the woman is just short on cleanser—

MAMA (*Not listening*): —Much baking powder as she done borrowed from me all these years, she could of done gone into the baking business!

(*The bell sounds suddenly and sharply and all three are stunned—serious and silent—mid-speech. In spite of all the other conversations and distractions of the morning, this is what they have been waiting for, even Travis who looks helplessly from his mother to his grandmother. Ruth is the first to come to life again*)

RUTH (*To Travis*): Get down them steps, boy!

(*Travis snaps to life and flies out to get the mail*)

MAMA (*Her eyes wide, her hand to her breast*): You mean it done really come?

RUTH (*Excited*): Oh, Miss Lena!

MAMA (*Collecting herself*): Well . . . I don't know what we all so excited about 'round here for. We known it was coming for months.

RUTH: That's a whole lot different from having it come and being able to hold it in your hands . . . a piece of paper worth ten thousand dollars . . . (*Travis bursts back into the room. He holds the envelope high above his head, like a little dancer, his face is radiant and he is breathless. He moves to his grandmother with sudden slow ceremony and puts the envelope into her hands. She accepts it, and then merely holds it and looks at it*) Come on! Open it . . . Lord have mercy, I wish Walter Lee was here!

TRAVIS: Open it, Grandmama!

MAMA (*Staring at it*): Now you all be quiet. It's just a check.

RUTH: Open it . . .

MAMA (*Still staring at it*): Now don't act silly . . . We ain't never been no people to act silly 'bout no money—

RUTH (*Swiftly*): We ain't never had none before—OPEN IT!

(*Mama finally makes a good strong tear and pulls out the thin blue slice of paper and inspects it closely. The boy and his mother study it raptly over Mama's shoulders*)

MAMA: *Travis!* (*She is counting off with doubt*) Is that the right number of zeros?

TRAVIS: Yes'm . . . ten thousand dollars. Gaalee, Grandmama, you rich.

MAMA (*She holds the check away from her, still looking at it. Slowly her face sobers into a mask of unhappiness*): Ten thousand dollars. (*She hands it to Ruth*) Put it away somewhere, Ruth. (*She does not look at Ruth; her eyes seem to be seeing something somewhere very far off*) Ten thousand dollars they give you. Ten thousand dollars.

TRAVIS (*To his mother, sincerely*): What's the matter with Grandmama—don't she want to be rich?

RUTH (*Distractedly*): You go on out and play now, baby. (*Travis exits. Mama starts wiping dishes absently, humming intently to herself. Ruth turns to her, with kind exasperation*) You've gone and got yourself upset.

MAMA (*Not looking at her*): I spec if it wasn't for you all . . . I would just put that money away or give it to the church or something.

RUTH: Now what kind of talk is that. Mr. Younger would just be plain mad if he could hear you talking foolish like that.

MAMA (*Stopping and staring off*): Yes . . . he sure would. (*Sighing*) We got enough to do with that money, all right. (*She halts then, and turns and looks at her daughter-in-law hard; Ruth avoids her eyes and Mama wipes her hands with finality and starts to speak firmly to Ruth*) Where did you go today, girl?

RUTH: To the doctor.

MAMA (*Impatiently*): Now, Ruth . . . you know better than that. Old Doctor Jones is strange enough in his way but there ain't nothing 'bout him make somebody slip and call him "she"—like you done this morning.

RUTH: Well, that's what happened—my tongue slipped.

MAMA: You went to see that woman, didn't you?

RUTH (*Defensively, giving herself away*): What woman you talking about?

MAMA (*Angrily*): That woman who—

(*Walter enters in great excitement*)

WALTER: Did it come?

MAMA (*Quietly*): Can't you give people a Christian greeting before you start asking about money?

WALTER (*To Ruth*): Did it come? (*Ruth unfolds the check and lays it quietly before him, watching him intently with thoughts of her own. Walter sits down and grasps it close and counts off the zeros*) Ten thousand dollars—(*He turns suddenly, frantically to his mother and draws some papers out of his breast pocket*) Mama—look. Old Willy Harris put everything on paper—

MAMA: Son—I think you ought to talk to your wife . . . I'll go on out and leave you alone if you want—

WALTER: I can talk to her later—Mama, look—

MAMA: Son—

WALTER: WILL SOMEBODY PLEASE LISTEN TO ME TODAY!

MAMA (*Quietly*): I don't 'low no yellin' in this house, Walter Lee, and you know it—(*Walter stares at them in frustration and starts to speak several times*) And there ain't going to be no investing in no liquor stores.

WALTER: But, Mama, you ain't even looked at it.

MAMA: I don't aim to have to speak on that again.

(*A long pause*)

WALTER: You ain't looked at it and you don't aim to have to speak on that again? You ain't even looked at it and you have decided—(*Crumpling his papers*) Well, *you* tell that to my boy tonight when you put him to sleep on the living-room couch . . . (*Turning to Mama and speaking directly to her*) Yeah—and tell it to my wife, Mama, tomorrow when she has to go out of here to look after somebody else's kids. And tell it to *me*, Mama, every time we need a new pair of curtains and I have to watch *you* go out and work in somebody's kitchen. Yeah, you tell me then!

(*Walter starts out*)

RUTH: Where you going?

WALTER: I'm going out!

RUTH: Where?

WALTER: Just out of this house somewhere—

RUTH (*Getting her coat*): I'll come too.

WALTER: I don't want you to come!

RUTH: I got something to talk to you about, Walter.

WALTER: That's too bad.

MAMA (*Still quietly*): Walter Lee—(*She waits and he finally turns and looks at her*) Sit down.

WALTER: I'm a grown man, Mama.

MAMA: Ain't nobody said you wasn't grown. But you still in my house and my presence. And as long as you are—you'll talk to your wife civil. Now sit down.

RUTH (*Suddenly*): Oh, let him go on out and drink himself to death! He makes me sick to my stomach! (*She flings her coat against him and exits to bedroom*)

WALTER (*Violently flinging the coat after her*): And you turn mine too, baby! (*The door slams behind her*) That was my biggest mistake—

MAMA (*Still quietly*): Walter, what is the matter with you?

WALTER: Matter with me? Ain't nothing the matter with *me*!

MAMA: Yes there is. Something eating you up like a crazy man. Something more than me not giving you this money. The past few years I been watching it happen to you. You get all nervous acting and kind of wild in the eyes—(*Walter jumps up impatiently at her words*) I said sit there now, I'm talking to you!

WALTER: Mama—I don't need no nagging at me today.

MAMA: Seem like you getting to a place where you always tied up in some kind of knot about something. But if anybody ask you 'bout it you just yell at 'em and bust out the house and go out and drink somewheres. Walter Lee, people can't live with that. Ruth's a good, patient girl in her way—but you getting to be too much. Boy, don't make the mistake of driving that girl away from you.

WALTER: Why—what she do for me?

MAMA: She loves you.

WALTER: Mama—I'm going out. I want to go off somewhere and be by myself for a while.

MAMA: I'm sorry 'bout your liquor store, son. It just wasn't the thing for us to do. That's what I want to tell you about—

WALTER: I got to go out, Mama—

(*He rises*)

MAMA: It's dangerous, son.

WALTER: What's dangerous?

MAMA: When a man goes outside his home to look for peace.

WALTER (*Beseechingly*): Then why can't there never be no peace in this house then?

MAMA: You done found it in some other house?

WALTER: No—there ain't no woman! Why do women always think there's a woman somewhere when a man gets restless. (*Picks up the check*) Do you know what this money means to me? Do you know what this money can do for us? (*Puts it back*) Mama—Mama—I want so many things . . .

MAMA: Yes, son—

WALTER: I want so many things that they are driving me kind of crazy . . . Mama—look at me.

MAMA: I'm looking at you. You a good-looking boy. You got a job, a nice wife, a fine boy and—

Dreams

WALTER: A job. (*Looks at her*) Mama, a job? I open and close car doors all day long. I drive a man around in his limousine and I say, "Yes, sir; no, sir; very good, sir; shall I take the Drive,° sir?" Mama, that ain't no kind of job . . . that ain't nothing at all. (*Very quietly*) Mama, I don't know if I can make you understand.

MAMA: Understand what, baby?

WALTER (*Quietly*): Sometimes it's like I can see the future stretched out in front of me—just plain as day. The future, Mama. Hanging over there at the edge of my days. Just waiting for me—a big, looming blank space—full of *nothing*. Just waiting for *me*. But it don't have to be. (*Pause. Kneeling beside her chair*) Mama—sometimes when I'm downtown and I pass them cool, quiet-looking restaurants where them white boys are sitting back and talking 'bout things . . . sitting there turning deals worth millions of dollars . . . sometimes I see guys don't look much older than me—

MAMA: Son—how come you talk so much 'bout money?

WALTER (*With immense passion*): Because it is life, Mama!

MAMA (*Quietly*): Oh—(*Very quietly*) So now it's life. Money is life. Once upon a time freedom used to be life—now it's money. I guess the world really do change . . .

WALTER: No—it was always money, Mama. We just didn't know about it.

MAMA: No . . . something has changed. (*She looks at him*) You something new, boy. In my time we was worried about not being lynched and getting to the North if we could and how to stay alive and still have a pinch of dignity too . . . Now here come you and Beneatha—talking 'bout things we ain't never even thought about hardly, me and your daddy. You ain't satisfied or proud of nothing we done. I mean that you had a home; that we kept you out of trouble till you was grown; that you don't have to ride to work on the back of nobody's streetcar—You my children—but how different we done become.

WALTER (*A long beat. He pats her hand and gets up*): You just don't understand, Mama, you just don't understand.

MAMA: Son—do you know your wife is expecting another baby? (*Walter stands, stunned, and absorbs what his mother has said*) That's what she wanted to talk to you about. (*Walter sinks down into a chair*) This ain't for me to be telling—but you ought to know. (*She waits*) I think Ruth is thinking 'bout getting rid of that child.

WALTER (*Slowly understanding*): No—no—Ruth wouldn't do that.

MAMA: When the world gets ugly enough—a woman will do anything for her family. *The part that's already living.*

---

the Drive: Lake Shore Drive is an expressway in Chicago, lined with upscale high-rise apartments, condominiums, and hotels.

WALTER: You don't know Ruth, Mama, if you think she would do that.

(*Ruth opens the bedroom door and stands there a little limp*)

RUTH (*Beaten*): Yes I would too, Walter. (*Pause*) I gave her a five-dollar down payment.

(*There is total silence as the man stares at his wife and the mother stares at her son*)

MAMA (*Presently*): Well—(*Tightly*) Well—son, I'm waiting to hear you say something . . . (*She waits*) I'm waiting to hear how you be your father's son. Be the man he was . . . (*Pause. The silence shouts*) Your wife say she going to destroy your child. And I'm waiting to hear you talk like him and say we a people who give children life, not who destroys them— (*She rises*) I'm waiting to see you stand up and look like your daddy and say we done give up one baby to poverty and that we ain't going to give up nary another one . . . I'm waiting.

WALTER: Ruth—(*He can say nothing*)

MAMA: If you a son of mine, tell her! (*Walter picks up his keys and his coat and walks out. She continues, bitterly*) You . . . you are a disgrace to your father's memory. Somebody get me my hat!

ACT II *Scene 1*

(*Time: Later the same day.*)

(*At rise: Ruth is ironing again. She has the radio going. Presently Beneatha's bedroom door opens and Ruth's mouth falls and she puts down the iron in fascination.*)

RUTH: What have we got on tonight!

BENEATHA (*Emerging grandly from the doorway so that we can see her thoroughly robed in the costume Asagai brought*): You are looking at what a well-dressed Nigerian woman wears—(*She parades for Ruth, her hair completely hidden by the headdress; she is coquettishly fanning herself with an ornate oriental fan, mistakenly more like Butterfly° than any Nigerian that ever was*) Isn't it beautiful? (*She promenades to the radio and, with an arrogant flourish, turns off the good loud blues that is playing*) Enough of this assimilationist junk! (*Ruth follows her with her eyes as she goes to the phonograph and puts on a record and turns and waits ceremoniously for the music to come up. Then, with a shout—*) OCOMOGOSIAY!

(*Ruth jumps. The music comes up, a lovely Nigerian melody. Beneatha listens, enraptured, her eyes far away— "back to the past." She begins to dance. Ruth is dumbfounded*)

Butterfly: A character in Puccini's 1904 opera *Madame Butterfly*, set in Japan.

RUTH: What kind of dance is that?

BENEATHA: A folk dance.

RUTH (*Pearl Bailey°*): What kind of folks do that, honey?

BENEATHA: It's from Nigeria. It's a dance of welcome.

RUTH: Who you welcoming?

BENEATHA: The men back to the village.

RUTH: Where they been?

BENEATHA: How should I know—out hunting or something. Anyway, they are coming back now . . .

RUTH: Well, that's good.

BENEATHA (*With the record*):

> Alundi, alundi
> Alundi alunya
> Jop pu a jeepua
> Ang gu soooooooooo

> Ai yai yae . . .
> Ayehaye—alundi . . .

(*Walter comes in during this performance; he has obviously been drinking. He leans against the door heavily and watches his sister, at first with distaste. Then his eyes look off—"back to the past"—as he lifts both his fists to the roof, screaming*)

WALTER: YEAH . . . AND ETHIOPIA STRETCH FORTH HER HANDS AGAIN! . . .

RUTH (*Drily, looking at him*): Yes—and Africa sure is claiming her own tonight. (*She gives them both up and starts ironing again*)

WALTER (*All in a drunken, dramatic shout*): Shut up! . . . I'm digging them drums . . . them drums move me! . . . (*He makes his weaving way to his wife's face and leans in close to her*) In my *heart of hearts* —(*He thumps his chest*)—I am much warrior!

RUTH (*Without even looking up*): In your heart of hearts you are much drunkard.

WALTER (*Coming away from her and starting to wander around the room, shouting*): Me and Jomo° . . . (*Intently, in his sister's face. She has stopped dancing to watch him in this unknown mood*) That's my man, Kenyatta. (*Shouting and thumping his chest*) FLAMING SPEAR! HOT DAMN! (*He is suddenly in possession of an imaginary spear and actively spearing enemies all over the room*) OCOMOGOSIAY . . .

BENEATHA (*To encourage Walter, thoroughly caught up with this side of him*): OCOMOGOSIAY, FLAMING SPEAR!

Pearl Bailey: A popular African American actor and singer (1918–1990), known for sly jokes as a part of her routine.   **Jomo:** Jomo Kenyatta (1893?–1978), African anticolonialist activist and later first president of an independent Kenya (1964–1978).

WALTER: THE LION IS WAKING . . . OWIMOWEH!

(*He pulls his shirt open and leaps up on the table and gestures with his spear*)

BENEATHA: OWIMOWEH!

WALTER (*On the table, very far gone, his eyes pure glass sheets. He sees what we cannot, that he is a leader of his people, a great chief, a descendant of Chaka,° and that the hour to march has come*): Listen, my black brothers—

BENEATHA: OCOMOGOSIAY!

WALTER: —Do you hear the waters rushing against the shores of the coastlands—

BENEATHA: OCOMOGOSIAY!

WALTER: —Do you hear the screeching of the cocks in yonder hills beyond where the chiefs meet in council for the coming of the mighty war—

BENEATHA: OCOMOGOSIAY!

(*And now the lighting shifts subtly to suggest the world of Walter's imagination, and the mood shifts from pure comedy. It is the inner Walter speaking: the South-side chauffeur has assumed an unexpected majesty*)

WALTER: —Do you hear the beating of the wings of the birds flying low over the mountains and the low places of our land—

BENEATHA: OCOMOGOSIAY!

WALTER: —Do you hear the singing of the women, singing the war songs of our fathers to the babies in the great houses? Singing the sweet war songs! (*The doorbell rings*) OH, DO YOU HEAR, MY BLACK BROTHERS!

BENEATHA (*Completely gone*): We hear you, Flaming Spear—

(*Ruth shuts off the phonograph and opens the door. George Murchison enters*)

WALTER: Telling us to prepare for the GREATNESS OF THE TIME! (*Lights back to normal. He turns and sees George*) Black Brother!

(*He extends his hand for the fraternal clasp*)

GEORGE: Black Brother, hell!

RUTH (*Having had enough, and embarrassed for the family*): Beneatha, you got company—what's the matter with you? Walter Lee Younger, get down off that table and stop acting like a fool . . .

(*Walter comes down off the table suddenly and makes a quick exit to the bathroom*)

RUTH: He's had a little to drink . . . I don't know what her excuse is.

GEORGE (*To Beneatha*): Look honey, we're going *to* the theatre—we're not going to be *in* it . . . so go change, huh?

Chaka: Shaka kaSenzangakhona (c. 1787–1828), also known as Shaka Zulu and sometimes spelled Chaka, was the most influential leader of the African Zulu Kingdom.

(*Beneatha looks at him and slowly, ceremoniously, lifts her hands and pulls off the headdress. Her hair is close-cropped and unstraightened. George freezes midsentence and Ruth's eyes all but fall out of her head*)

GEORGE: What in the name of—

RUTH (*Touching Beneatha's hair*): Girl, you done lost your natural mind!? Look at your head!

GEORGE: What have you done to your head—I mean your hair!

BENEATHA: Nothing—except cut it off.

RUTH: Now that's the truth—it's what ain't been done to it! You expect this boy to go out with you with your head all nappy like that?

BENEATHA (*Looking at George*): That's up to George. If he's ashamed of his heritage—

GEORGE: Oh, don't be so proud of yourself, Bennie—just because you look eccentric.

BENEATHA: How can something that's natural be eccentric?

GEORGE: That's what being eccentric means—being natural. Get dressed.

BENEATHA: I don't like that, George.

RUTH: Why must you and your brother make an argument out of everything people say?

BENEATHA: Because I hate assimilationist Negroes!

RUTH: Will somebody please tell me what assimila-whoever means!

GEORGE: Oh, it's just a college girl's way of calling people Uncle Toms— but that isn't what it means at all.

RUTH: Well, what does it mean?

BENEATHA (*Cutting George off and staring at him as she replies to Ruth*): It means someone who is willing to give up his own culture and submerge himself completely in the dominant, and in this case *oppressive* culture!

GEORGE: Oh, dear, dear, dear! Here we go! A lecture on the African past! On our Great West African Heritage! In one second we will hear all about the great Ashanti empires;° the great Songhay civilizations;° and the great sculpture of Bénin°—and then some poetry in the Bantu°— and the whole monologue will end with the word *heritage*! (*Nastily*) Let's face it, baby, your heritage is nothing but a bunch of raggedy-assed spirituals and some grass huts!

BENEATHA: GRASS HUTS! (*Ruth crosses to her and forcibly pushes her toward the bedroom*) See there . . . you are standing there in your splendid ignorance

---

Ashanti empires: A precolonial West African empire in the eighteenth and nineteenth centuries in what is now Ghana.   **Songhay civilizations:** One of the largest and greatest West African empires, from the early fifteenth to the late sixteenth century.   **sculpture of Bénin:** A collection of more than a thousand brass plaques, dating from the fifteenth and sixteenth centuries, in the Kingdom of Dahomey, renamed Benin in 1975.   **Bantu:** The predominant language spoken in central, eastern, and southern Africa.

talking about people who were the first to smelt iron on the face of the earth! (*Ruth is pushing her through the door*) The Ashanti were performing surgical operations when the English—(*Ruth pulls the door to, with Beneatha on the other side, and smiles graciously at George. Beneatha opens the door and shouts the end of the sentence defiantly at George*)—were still tattooing themselves with blue dragons! (*She goes back inside*)

RUTH: Have a seat, George (*They both sit. Ruth folds her hands rather primly on her lap, determined to demonstrate the civilization of the family*) Warm, ain't it? I mean for September. (*Pause*) Just like they always say about Chicago weather: If it's too hot or cold for you, just wait a minute and it'll change. (*She smiles happily at this cliché of clichés*) Everybody say it's got to do with them bombs and things they keep setting off. (*Pause*) Would you like a nice cold beer?

GEORGE: No, thank you. I don't care for beer. (*He looks at his watch*) I hope she hurries up.

RUTH: What time is the show?

GEORGE: It's an eight-thirty curtain. That's just Chicago, though. In New York standard curtain time is eight forty.

(*He is rather proud of this knowledge*)

RUTH (*Properly appreciating it*): You get to New York a lot?

GEORGE (*Offhand*): Few times a year.

RUTH: Oh—that's nice. I've never been to New York.

(*Walter enters. We feel he has relieved himself, but the edge of unreality is still with him*)

WALTER: New York ain't got nothing Chicago ain't. Just a bunch of hustling people all squeezed up together—being "Eastern."

(*He turns his face into a screw of displeasure*)

GEORGE: Oh—you've been?

WALTER: *Plenty* of times.

RUTH (*Shocked at the lie*): Walter Lee Younger!

WALTER (*Staring her down*): Plenty! (*Pause*) What we got to drink in this house? Why don't you offer this man some refreshment. (*To George*) They don't know how to entertain people in this house, man.

GEORGE: Thank you—I don't really care for anything.

WALTER (*Feeling his head; sobriety coming*): Where's Mama?

RUTH: She ain't come back yet.

WALTER (*Looking Murchison over from head to toe, scrutinizing his carefully casual tweed sports jacket over cashmere V-neck sweater over soft eyelet shirt and tie, and soft slacks, finished off with white buckskin shoes*): Why all you college boys wear them faggoty-looking white shoes?

RUTH: Walter Lee!

(*George Murchison ignores the remark*)

WALTER (*To Ruth*): Well, they look crazy as hell—white shoes, cold as it is.

RUTH (*Crushed*): You have to excuse him—

WALTER: No he don't! Excuse me for what? What you always excusing me for! I'll excuse myself when I needs to be excused! (*A pause*) They look as funny as them black knee socks Beneatha wears out of here all the time.

RUTH: It's the college *style*, Walter.

WALTER: Style, hell. She looks like she got burnt legs or something!

RUTH: Oh, Walter—

WALTER (*An irritable mimic*): Oh, Walter! Oh, Walter! (*To Murchison*) How's your old man making out? I understand you all going to buy that big hotel on the Drive? (*He finds a beer in the refrigerator, wanders over to Murchison, sipping and wiping his lips with the back of his hand, and straddling a chair backwards to talk to the other man*) Shrewd move. Your old man is all right, man. (*Tapping his head and half winking for emphasis*) I mean he knows how to operate. I mean he thinks *big*, you know what I mean, I mean for a *home*, you know? But I think he's kind of running out of ideas now. I'd like to talk to him. Listen, man, I got some plans that could turn this city upside down. I mean think like he does. *Big*. Invest big, gamble big, hell, lose *big* if you have to, you know what I mean. It's hard to find a man on this whole Southside who understands my kind of thinking— you dig? (*He scrutinizes Murchison again, drinks his beer, squints his eyes and leans in close, confidential, man to man*) Me and you ought to sit down and talk sometimes, man. Man, I got me some ideas . . .

GEORGE (*With boredom*): Yeah—sometimes we'll have to do that, Walter.

WALTER (*Understanding the indifference, and offended*): Yeah—well, when you get the time, man. I know you a busy little boy.

RUTH: Walter, please—

WALTER (*Bitterly, hurt*): I know ain't nothing in this world as busy as you colored college boys with your fraternity pins and white shoes . . .

RUTH (*Covering her face with humiliation*): Oh, Walter Lee—

WALTER: I see you all all the time—with the books tucked under your arms—going to your (*British A—a mimic*) "clahsses." And for what! What the hell you learning over there? Filling up your heads—(*Counting off on his fingers*)—with the sociology and the psychology—but they teaching you how to be a man? How to take over and run the world? They teaching you how to run a rubber plantation or a steel mill? Naw—just to talk proper and read books and wear them faggoty-looking white shoes . . .

GEORGE (*Looking at him with distaste, a little above it all*): You're all wacked up with bitterness, man.

WALTER (*Intently, almost quietly, between the teeth, glaring at the boy*): And you—ain't you bitter, man? Ain't you just about had it yet? Don't you see no stars gleaming that you can't reach out and grab? You happy?—You contented son-of-a-bitch—you happy? You got it made? Bitter? Man, I'm a volcano. Bitter? Here I am a giant—surrounded by ants! Ants who can't even understand what it is the giant is talking about.

RUTH (*Passionately and suddenly*): Oh, Walter—ain't you with nobody!

WALTER (*Violently*): No! 'Cause ain't nobody with me! Not even my own mother!

RUTH: Walter, that's a terrible thing to say!

(*Beneatha enters, dressed for the evening in a cocktail dress and earrings, hair natural*)

GEORGE: Well—hey—(*Crosses to Beneatha; thoughtful, with emphasis, since this is a reversal*) You look great!

WALTER (*Seeing his sister's hair for the first time*): What's the matter with your head?

BENEATHA (*Tired of the jokes now*): I cut it off, Brother.

WALTER (*Coming close to inspect it and walking around her*): Well, I'll be damned. So that's what they mean by the African bush . . .

BENEATHA: Ha ha. Let's go, George.

GEORGE (*Looking at her*): You know something? I like it. It's sharp. I mean it really is. (*Helps her into her wrap*)

RUTH: Yes—I think so, too. (*She goes to the mirror and starts to clutch at her hair*)

WALTER: Oh no! You leave yours alone, baby. You might turn out to have a pin-shaped head or something!

BENEATHA: See you all later.

RUTH: Have a nice time.

GEORGE: Thanks. Good night. (*Half out the door, he reopens it. To Walter*) Good night, Prometheus!°

(*Beneatha and George exit*)

WALTER (*To Ruth*): Who is Prometheus?

RUTH: I don't know. Don't worry about it.

WALTER (*In fury, pointing after George*): See there—they get to a point where they can't insult you man to man—they got to go talk about something ain't nobody never heard of!

RUTH: How do you know it was an insult? (*To humor him*) Maybe Prometheus is a nice fellow.

Prometheus: A Greek god, one of the Titans, known for his crafty counsel (his name means "forethought"). The creator and benefactor of mankind, he bestowed on humans a number of gifts, including fire.

WALTER: Prometheus! I bet there ain't even no such thing! I bet that simple-minded clown—
RUTH: Walter—

(*She stops what she is doing and looks at him*)

WALTER (*Yelling*): Don't start!
RUTH: Start what?
WALTER: Your nagging! Where was I? Who was I with? How much money did I spend?
RUTH (*Plaintively*): Walter Lee—why don't we just try to talk about it . . .
WALTER (*Not listening*): I been out talking with people who understand me. People who care about the things I got on my mind.
RUTH (*Wearily*): I guess that means people like Willy Harris.
WALTER: Yes, people like Willy Harris.
RUTH (*With a sudden flash of impatience*): Why don't you all just hurry up and go into the banking business and stop talking about it!
WALTER: Why? You want to know why? 'Cause we all tied up in a race of people that don't know how to do nothing but moan, pray and have babies!

(*The line is too bitter even for him and he looks at her and sits down*)

RUTH: Oh, Walter . . . (*Softly*) Honey, why can't you stop fighting me?
WALTER (*Without thinking*): Who's fighting you? Who even cares about you?

(*This line begins the retardation of his mood*)

RUTH: Well—(*She waits a long time, and then with resignation starts to put away her things*) I guess I might as well go on to bed . . . (*More or less to herself*) I don't know where we lost it . . . but we have . . . (*Then, to him*) I—I'm sorry about this new baby, Walter. I guess maybe I better go on and do what I started . . . I guess I just didn't realize how bad things was with us . . . I guess I just didn't really realize—(*She starts out to the bedroom and stops*) You want some hot milk?
WALTER: Hot milk?
RUTH: Yes—hot milk.
WALTER: Why hot milk?
RUTH: 'Cause after all that liquor you come home with you ought to have something hot in your stomach.
WALTER: I don't want no milk.
RUTH: You want some coffee then?
WALTER: No, I don't want no coffee. I don't want nothing hot to drink. (*Almost plaintively*) Why you always trying to give me something to eat?
RUTH (*Standing and looking at him helplessly*): What else can I give you, Walter Lee Younger?

(*She stands and looks at him and presently turns to go out again. He lifts his head and watches her going away from him in a new mood which began to emerge when he asked her "Who cares about you?"*)

WALTER: It's been rough, ain't it, baby? (*She hears and stops but does not turn around and he continues to her back*) I guess between two people there ain't never as much understood as folks generally thinks there is. I mean like between me and you—(*She turns to face him*) How we gets to the place where we scared to talk softness to each other. (*He waits, thinking hard himself*) Why you think it got to be like that? (*He is thoughtful, almost as a child would be*) Ruth, what is it gets into people ought to be close?

RUTH: I don't know, honey. I think about it a lot.

WALTER: On account of you and me, you mean? The way things are with us. The way something done come down between us.

RUTH: There ain't so much between us, Walter . . . Not when you come to me and try to talk to me. Try to be with me . . . a little even.

WALTER (*Total honesty*): Sometimes . . . sometimes . . . I don't even know how to try.

RUTH: Walter—

WALTER: Yes?

RUTH (*Coming to him, gently and with misgiving, but coming to him*): Honey . . . life don't have to be like this. I mean sometimes people can do things so that things are better . . . You remember how we used to talk when Travis was born . . . about the way we were going to live . . . the kind of house . . . (*She is stroking his head*) Well, it's all starting to slip away from us . . .

(*He turns her to him and they look at each other and kiss, tenderly and hungrily. The door opens and Mama enters—Walter breaks away and jumps up. A beat*)

WALTER: Mama, where have you been?

MAMA: My—them steps is longer than they used to be. Whew! (*She sits down and ignores him*) How you feeling this evening, Ruth?

(*Ruth shrugs, disturbed at having been interrupted and watching her husband knowingly*)

WALTER: Mama, where have you been all day?

MAMA (*Still ignoring him and leaning on the table and changing to more comfortable shoes*): Where's Travis?

RUTH: I let him go out earlier and he ain't come back yet. Boy, is he going to get it!

WALTER: Mama!

MAMA (*As if she has heard him for the first time*): Yes, son?

WALTER: Where did you go this afternoon?

MAMA: I went downtown to tend to some business that I had to tend to.

WALTER: What kind of business?

MAMA: You know better than to question me like a child, Brother.

WALTER (*Rising and bending over the table*): Where were you, Mama? (*Bringing his fists down and shouting*) Mama, you didn't go do something with that insurance money, something crazy?

(*The front door opens slowly, interrupting him, and Travis peeks his head in, less than hopefully*)

TRAVIS (*To his mother*): Mama, I—

RUTH: "Mama I" nothing! You're going to get it, boy! Get on in that bedroom and get yourself ready!

TRAVIS: But I—

MAMA: Why don't you all never let the child explain hisself.

RUTH: Keep out of it now, Lena.

(*Mama clamps her lips together, and Ruth advances toward her son menacingly*)

RUTH: A thousand times I have told you not to go off like that—

MAMA (*Holding out her arms to her grandson*): Well—at least let me tell him something. I want him to be the first one to hear . . . Come here, Travis. (*The boy obeys, gladly*) Travis—(*She takes him by the shoulder and looks into his face*)—you know that money we got in the mail this morning?

TRAVIS: Yes'm—

MAMA: Well—what you think your grandmama gone and done with that money?

TRAVIS: I don't know, Grandmama.

MAMA (*Putting her finger on his nose for emphasis*): <u>She went out and she bought you a house!</u> (*The explosion comes from Walter at the end of the revelation and he jumps up and turns away from all of them in a fury. Mama continues, to Travis*) You glad about the house? It's going to be yours when you get to be a man.

TRAVIS: Yeah—I always wanted to live in a house.

MAMA: All right, gimme some sugar then—(*Travis puts his arms around her neck as she watches her son over the boy's shoulder. Then, to Travis, after the embrace*) Now when you say your prayers tonight, you thank God and your grandfather—'cause it was him who give you the house—in his way.

RUTH (*Taking the boy from Mama and pushing him toward the bedroom*): Now you get out of here and get ready for your beating.

TRAVIS: Aw, Mama—

RUTH: Get on in there—(*Closing the door behind him and turning radiantly to her mother-in-law*) So you went and did it!

MAMA (*Quietly, looking at her son with pain*): Yes, I did.

RUTH (*Raising both arms classically*): PRAISE GOD! (*Looks at Walter a moment, who says nothing. She crosses rapidly to her husband*) Please, honey—let me be glad . . . you be glad too. (*She has laid her hands on his shoulders, but he shakes himself free of her roughly, without turning to face her*) Oh Walter . . . a home . . . *a home.* (*She comes back to Mama*) Well—where is it? How big is it? How much it going to cost?

MAMA: Well—

RUTH: When we moving?

MAMA (*Smiling at her*): First of the month.

RUTH (*Throwing back her head with jubilance*): Praise God!

MAMA (*Tentatively, still looking at her son's back turned against her and Ruth*): It's—it's a nice house too . . . (*She cannot help speaking directly to him. An imploring quality in her voice, her manner, makes her almost like a girl now*) Three bedrooms—nice big one for you and Ruth . . . Me and Beneatha still have to share our room, but Travis have one of his own—and (*With difficulty*) I figure if the—new baby—is a boy, we could get one of them double-decker outfits . . . And there's a yard with a little patch of dirt where I could maybe get to grow me a few flowers . . . And a nice big basement . . .

RUTH: Walter honey, be glad—

MAMA (*Still to his back, fingering things on the table*): 'Course I don't want to make it sound fancier than it is . . . It's just a plain little old house—but it's made good and solid—and it will be *ours.* Walter Lee—it makes a difference in a man when he can walk on floors that belong to *him* . . .

RUTH: Where is it?

MAMA (*Frightened at this telling*): Well—well—it's out there in Clybourne Park—

(*Ruth's radiance fades abruptly, and Walter finally turns slowly to face his mother with incredulity and hostility*)

RUTH: Where?

MAMA (*Matter-of-factly*): Four o six Clybourne Street, Clybourne Park.

RUTH: Clybourne Park? Mama, there ain't no colored people living in Clybourne Park.

MAMA (*Almost idiotically*): Well, I guess there's going to be some now.

WALTER (*Bitterly*): So that's the peace and comfort you went out and bought for us today!

MAMA (*Raising her eyes to meet his finally*): Son—I just tried to find the nicest place for the least amount of money for my family.

RUTH (*Trying to recover from the shock*): Well—well—'course I ain't one never been 'fraid of no crackers,° mind you—but—well, wasn't there no other houses nowhere?

MAMA: Them houses they put up for colored in them areas way out all seem to cost twice as much as other houses. I did the best I could.

crackers: A disparaging term for lower-class white southerners.

RUTH (*Struck senseless with the news, in its various degrees of goodness and trouble, she sits a moment, her fists propping her chin in thought, and then she starts to rise, bringing her fists down with vigor, the radiance spreading from cheek to cheek again*): Well—well!—All I can say is—if this is my time in life—MY TIME—to say good-bye—(*And she builds with momentum as she starts to circle the room with an exuberant, almost tearfully happy release*)—to these goddamned cracking walls!—(*She pounds the walls*)— and these marching roaches!—(*She wipes at an imaginary army of marching roaches*)—and this cramped little closet which ain't now or never was no kitchen! . . . then I say it loud and good, HALLELUJAH! AND GOOD-BYE MISERY . . . I DON'T NEVER WANT TO SEE YOUR UGLY FACE AGAIN! (*She laughs joyously, having practically destroyed the apartment, and flings her arms up and lets them come down happily, slowly, reflectively, over her abdomen, aware for the first time perhaps that the life therein pulses with happiness and not despair*) Lena?

MAMA (*Moved, watching her happiness*): Yes, honey?

RUTH (*Looking off*): Is there—is there a whole lot of sunlight?

MAMA (*Understanding*): Yes, child, there's a whole lot of sunlight.

(*Long pause*)

RUTH (*Collecting herself and going to the door of the room Travis is in*): Well— I guess I better see 'bout Travis. (*To Mama*) Lord, I sure don't feel like whipping nobody today!

(*She exits*)

MAMA (*The mother and son are left alone now and the mother waits a long time, considering deeply, before she speaks*): Son—you—you understand what I done, don't you? (*Walter is silent and sullen*) I—I just seen my family falling apart today . . . just falling to pieces in front of my eyes . . . We couldn't of gone on like we was today. We was going backwards 'stead of forwards—talking 'bout killing babies and wishing each other was dead . . . When it gets like that in life—you just got to do something different, push on out and do something bigger . . . (*She waits*) I wish you say something, son . . . I wish you'd say how deep inside you you think I done the right thing—

WALTER (*Crossing slowly to his bedroom door and finally turning there and speaking measuredly*): What you need me to say you done right for? *You* the head of this family. You run our lives like you want to. It was your money and you did what you wanted with it. So what you need for me to say it was all right for? (*Bitterly, to hurt her as deeply as he knows is possible*) So you butchered up a dream of mine—you—who always talking 'bout your children's dreams . . .

MAMA: Walter Lee—

(*He just closes the door behind him. Mama sits alone, thinking heavily*)

Scene 2

(*Time: Friday night. A few weeks later.*)

(*At rise: Packing crates mark the intention of the family to move. Beneatha and George come in, presumably from an evening out again.*)

GEORGE: O.K. . . . O.K., whatever you say . . . (*They both sit on the couch. He tries to kiss her. She moves away*) Look, we've had a nice evening; let's not spoil it, huh? . . .

(*He again turns her head and tries to nuzzle in and she turns away from him, not with distaste but with momentary lack of interest; in a mood to pursue what they were talking about*)

BENEATHA: I'm *trying* to talk to you.

GEORGE: We always talk.

BENEATHA: Yes—and I love to talk.

GEORGE (*Exasperated; rising*): I know it and I don't mind it sometimes . . . I want you to cut it out, see—The moody stuff, I mean. I don't like it. You're a nice-looking girl . . . all over. That's all you need, honey, forget the atmosphere. Guys aren't going to go for the atmosphere—they're going to go for what they see. Be glad for that. Drop the Garbo° routine. It doesn't go with you. As for myself, I want a nice—(*Groping*)—simple (*Thoughtfully*)—sophisticated girl . . . not a poet—O.K.?

(*He starts to kiss her, she rebuffs him again and he jumps up*)

BENEATHA: Why are you angry, George?

GEORGE: Because this is stupid! I don't go out with you to discuss the nature of "quiet desperation" or to hear all about your thoughts—because the world will go on thinking what it thinks regardless—

BENEATHA: Then why read books? Why go to school?

GEORGE (*With artificial patience, counting on his fingers*): It's simple. You read books—to learn facts—to get grades—to pass the course—to get a degree. That's all—it has nothing to do with thoughts.

(*A long pause*)

BENEATHA: I see. (*He starts to sit*) Good night, George.

(*George looks at her a little oddly, and starts to exit. He meets Mama coming in*)

GEORGE: Oh—hello, Mrs. Younger.

MAMA: Hello, George, how you feeling?

GEORGE: Fine—fine, how are you?

Garbo: Greta Garbo (1905–1990), Swedish-born actor known for her air of remote sophistication.

MAMA: Oh, a little tired. You know them steps can get you after a day's work. You all have a nice time tonight?

GEORGE: Yes—a fine time. A fine time.

MAMA: Well, good night.

GEORGE: Good night. (*He exits. Mama closes the door behind her*) Hello, honey. What you sitting like that for?

BENEATHA: I'm just sitting.

MAMA: Didn't you have a nice time?

BENEATHA: No.

MAMA: No? What's the matter?

BENEATHA: Mama, George is a fool—honest. (*She rises*)

MAMA (*Hustling around unloading the packages she has entered with. She stops*): Is he, baby?

BENEATHA: Yes.

(*Beneatha makes up Travis's bed as she talks*)

MAMA: You sure?

BENEATHA: Yes.

MAMA: Well—I guess you better not waste your time with no fools.

(*Beneatha looks up at her mother, watching her put groceries in the refrigerator. Finally she gathers up her things and starts into the bedroom. At the door she stops and looks back at her mother*)

BENEATHA: Mama—

MAMA: Yes, baby—

BENEATHA: Thank you.

MAMA: For what?

BENEATHA: For understanding me this time.

(*She exits quickly and the mother stands, smiling a little, looking at the place where Beneatha just stood. Ruth enters*)

RUTH: Now don't you fool with any of this stuff, Lena—

MAMA: Oh, I just thought I'd sort a few things out. Is Brother here?

RUTH: Yes.

MAMA (*With concern*): Is he—

RUTH (*Reading her eyes*): Yes.

(*Mama is silent and someone knocks on the door. Mama and Ruth exchange weary and knowing glances and Ruth opens it to admit the neighbor, Mrs. Johnson,° who is a rather squeaky wide-eyed lady of no particular age, with a newspaper under her arm*)

Mrs. Johnson: This character and the scene of her visit were cut from the original production and early editions of the play.

MAMA (*Changing her expression to acute delight and a ringing cheerful greeting*): Oh—hello there, Johnson.

JOHNSON (*This is a woman who decided long ago to be enthusiastic about* EVERYTHING *in life and she is inclined to wave her wrist vigorously at the height of her exclamatory comments*): Hello there, yourself! H'you this evening, Ruth?

RUTH (*Not much of a deceptive type*): Fine, Mis' Johnson, h'you?

JOHNSON: Fine. (*Reaching out quickly, playfully, and patting Ruth's stomach*) Ain't you starting to poke out none yet! (*She mugs with delight at the overfamiliar remark and her eyes dart around looking at the crates and packing preparation; Mama's face is a cold sheet of endurance*) Oh, ain't we getting ready 'round here, though! Yessir! Lookathere! I'm telling you the Youngers is really getting ready to "move on up a little higher!"—Bless God!

MAMA (*A little drily, doubting the total sincerity of the Blesser*): Bless God.

JOHNSON: He's good, ain't He?

MAMA (*The same*): Oh yes, He's good.

JOHNSON: I mean sometimes He works in mysterious ways. . . but He works, don't He!

MAMA (*The same*): Yes, He does.

JOHNSON: I'm just soooooo happy for y'all. And this here child—(*About Ruth*) looks like she could just pop open with happiness, don't she. Where's all the rest of the family?

MAMA: Bennie's gone to bed—

JOHNSON: Ain't no . . . (*The implication is pregnancy*) sickness done hit you—I hope . . . ?

MAMA: No—she just tired. She was out this evening.

JOHNSON (*All is a coo, an emphatic coo*): Aw—ain't that lovely. She still going out with the little Murchison boy?

MAMA (*Drily*): Ummmm huh.

JOHNSON: That's lovely. You sure got lovely children, Younger. Me and Isaiah talks all the time 'bout what fine children you was blessed with. We sure do.

MAMA: Ruth, give Mis' Johnson a piece of sweet potato pie and some milk.

JOHNSON: Oh honey, I can't stay hardly a minute—I just dropped in to see if there was anything I could do. (*Accepting the food easily*) I guess y'all seen the news what's all over the colored paper this week . . .

MAMA: No—didn't get mine yet this week.

JOHNSON (*Lifting her head and blinking with the spirit of catastrophe*): You mean you ain't read 'bout them colored people that was bombed out their place out there?

(*Ruth straightens with concern and takes the paper and reads it. Johnson notices her and feeds commentary*)

JOHNSON: Ain't it something how bad these here white folks is getting here in Chicago! Lord, getting so you think you right down in Mississippi! (*With a tremendous and rather insincere sense of melodrama*) 'Course I thinks it's wonderful how our folks keeps on pushing out. You hear some of these Negroes 'round here talking 'bout how they don't go where they ain't wanted and all that—but not me, honey! (*This is a lie*) Wilhemenia Othella Johnson goes anywhere, any time she feels like it! (*With head movement for emphasis*) Yes I do! Why if we left it up to these here crackers, the poor niggers wouldn't have nothing—(*She clasps her hand over her mouth*) Oh, I always forgets you don't 'low that word in your house.

MAMA (*Quietly, looking at her*): No—I don't 'low it.

JOHNSON (*Vigorously again*): Me neither! I was just telling Isaiah yesterday when he come using it in front of me—I said, "Isaiah, it's just like Mis' Younger says all the time—"

MAMA: Don't you want some more pie?

JOHNSON: No—no thank you; this was lovely. I got to get on over home and have my midnight coffee. I hear some people say it don't let them sleep but I finds I can't close my eyes right lessen I done had that laaaast cup of coffee . . . (*She waits. A beat. Undaunted*) My Goodnight coffee, I calls it!

MAMA (*With much eye-rolling and communication between herself and Ruth*): Ruth, why don't you give Mis' Johnson some coffee.

(*Ruth gives Mama an unpleasant look for her kindness*)

JOHNSON (*Accepting the coffee*): Where's Brother tonight?

MAMA: He's lying down.

JOHNSON: Mmmmmm, he sure gets his beauty rest, don't he? Good-looking man. Sure is a good-looking man! (*Reaching out to pat Ruth's stomach again*) I guess that's how come we keep on having babies around here. (*She winks at Mama*) One thing 'bout Brother, he always know how to have a *good* time. And soooooo ambitious! I bet it was his idea y'all moving out to Clybourne Park. Lord—I bet this time next month y'all's names will have been in the papers plenty—(*Holding up her hands to mark off each word of the headline she can see in front of her*) "NEGROES INVADE CLYBOURNE PARK—BOMBED!"

MAMA (*She and Ruth look at the woman in amazement*): We ain't exactly moving out there to get bombed.

JOHNSON: Oh, honey—you know I'm praying to God every day that don't nothing like that happen! But you have to think of life like it is—and these here Chicago peckerwoods is some baaaad peckerwoods.

MAMA (*Wearily*): We done thought about all that Mis' Johnson.

(*Beneatha comes out of the bedroom in her robe and passes through to the bathroom. Mrs. Johnson turns*)

JOHNSON: Hello there, Bennie!

BENEATHA (*Crisply*): Hello, Mrs. Johnson.

JOHNSON: How is school?

BENEATHA (*Crisply*): Fine, thank you. (*She goes out*)

JOHNSON (*Insulted*): Getting so she don't have much to say to nobody.

MAMA: The child was on her way to the bathroom.

JOHNSON: I know—but sometimes she act like ain't got time to pass the time of day with nobody ain't been to college. Oh—I ain't criticizing her none. It's just—you know how some of our young people gets when they get a little education. (*Mama and Ruth say nothing, just look at her*) Yes—well. Well, I guess I better get on home. (*Unmoving*) 'Course I can understand how she must be proud and everything—being the only one in the family to make something of herself. I know just being a chauffeur ain't never satisfied Brother none. He shouldn't feel like that, though. Ain't nothing wrong with being a chauffeur.

MAMA: There's plenty wrong with it.

JOHNSON: What?

MAMA: Plenty. My husband always said being any kind of a servant wasn't a fit thing for a man to have to be. He always said a man's hands was made to make things, or to turn the earth with—not to drive nobody's car for 'em—or—(*She looks at her own hands*) carry they slop jars. And my boy is just like him—he wasn't meant to wait on nobody.

JOHNSON (*Rising, somewhat offended*): Mmmmmmmmm. The Youngers is too much for me! (*She looks around*) You sure one proud-acting bunch of colored folks. Well—I always thinks like Booker T. Washington° said that time—"Education has spoiled many a good plow hand"—

MAMA: Is that what old Booker T. said?

JOHNSON: He sure did.

MAMA: Well, it sounds just like him. The fool.

JOHNSON (*Indignantly*): Well—he was one of our great men.

MAMA: Who said so?

JOHNSON (*Nonplussed*): You know, me and you ain't never agreed about some things, Lena Younger. I guess I better be going—

RUTH (*Quickly*): Good night.

JOHNSON: Good night. Oh—(*Thrusting it at her*) You can keep the paper! (*With a trill*) 'Night.

MAMA: Good night, Mis' Johnson.

Booker T. Washington: Booker Taliaferro Washington (1856–1915) was an influential African American educator and political leader, but controversial because of his willingness to cooperate with supportive whites instead of actively confronting segregation policies.

(*Mrs. Johnson exits*)

RUTH: If ignorance was gold . . .

MAMA: Shush. Don't talk about folks behind their backs.

RUTH: You do.

MAMA: I'm old and corrupted. (*Beneatha enters*) You was rude to Mis' Johnson, Beneatha, and I don't like it at all.

BENEATHA (*At her door*): Mama, if there are two things we, as a people, have got to overcome, one is the Ku Klux Klan—and the other is Mrs. Johnson. (*She exits*)

MAMA: Smart aleck.

(*The phone rings*)

RUTH: I'll get it.

MAMA: Lord, ain't this a popular place tonight.

RUTH (*At the phone*): Hello—Just a minute. (*Goes to door*) Walter, it's Mrs. Arnold. (*Waits. Goes back to the phone. Tense*) Hello. Yes, this is his wife speaking . . . He's lying down now. Yes . . . well, he'll be in tomorrow. He's been very sick. Yes—I know we should have called, but we were so sure he'd be able to come in today. Yes—yes, I'm very sorry. Yes . . . Thank you very much. (*She hangs up. Walter is standing in the doorway of the bedroom behind her*) That was Mrs. Arnold.

WALTER (*Indifferently*): Was it?

RUTH: She said if you don't come in tomorrow that they are getting a new man . . .

WALTER: Ain't that sad—ain't that crying sad.

RUTH: She said Mr. Arnold has had to take a cab for three days . . . Walter, you ain't been to work for three days! (*This is a revelation to her*) Where you been, Walter Lee Younger? (*Walter looks at her and starts to laugh*) You're going to lose your job.

WALTER: That's right . . . (*He turns on the radio*)

RUTH: Oh, Walter, and with your mother working like a dog every day—

(*A steamy, deep blues pours into the room*)

WALTER: That's sad too—Everything is sad.

MAMA: What you been doing for these three days, son?

WALTER: Mama—you don't know all the things a man what got leisure can find to do in this city . . . What's this—Friday night? Well—Wednesday I borrowed Willy Harris's car and I went for a drive . . . just me and my-self and I drove and drove . . . Way out . . . way past South Chicago, and I parked the car and I sat and looked at the steel mills all day long. I just sat in the car and looked at them big black chimneys for hours. Then I drove back and I went to the Green Hat. (*Pause*) And Thursday—Thursday I borrowed the car again and I got in it and I pointed it the other way and I drove the other way—for hours—way, way up to Wisconsin, and I looked at the farms. I just drove and looked at the farms. Then I drove back and I went to the Green Hat. (*Pause*) And today— today I didn't get the car. Today I just walked. All over the Southside. And I looked at the Negroes and they looked at me and finally I just sat down on the curb at Thirty-ninth and South Parkway and I just sat there and watched the Negroes go by. And then I went to the Green Hat. You all sad? You all depressed? And you know where I am going right now—

(*Ruth goes out quietly*)

MAMA: Oh, Big Walter, is this the harvest of our days?

WALTER: You know what I like about the Green Hat? I like this little cat they got there who blows a sax . . . He blows. He talks to me. He ain't but 'bout five feet tall and he's got a conked° head and his eyes is always closed and he's all music—

MAMA (*Rising and getting some papers out of her handbag*): Walter—

WALTER: And there's this other guy who plays the piano . . . and they got a sound. I mean they can work on some music . . . They got the best little combo in the world in the Green Hat . . . You can just sit there and drink and listen to them three men play and you realize that don't nothing matter worth a damn, but just being there—

MAMA: I've helped do it to you, haven't I, son? Walter I been wrong.

WALTER: Naw—you ain't never been wrong about nothing, Mama.

MAMA: Listen to me, now. I say I been wrong, son. That I been doing to you what the rest of the world been doing to you. (*She turns off the radio*) Walter—(*She stops and he looks up slowly at her and she meets his eyes pleadingly*) What you ain't never understood is that I ain't got nothing, don't own nothing, ain't never really wanted nothing that wasn't for you. There ain't nothing as precious to me . . . There ain't nothing worth holding on to, money, dreams, nothing else—if it means—if it means it's going to destroy my boy. (*She takes an envelope out of her handbag and puts it in front of him and he watches her without speaking or moving*) I paid the man thirty-five hundred dollars down on the house. That leaves sixty-five hundred dollars. Monday morning I want you to take this money and take three thousand dollars and put it in a savings account for Beneatha's medical schooling. The rest you put in a checking account—with your name on it. And from now on any penny that come out of it or that go in it is for you to look after. For you to decide. (*She drops her hands a little helplessly*) It ain't much, but it's all I got in the world and I'm putting it in your hands. I'm telling you to be the head of this family from now on like you supposed to be.

---

conked: A hairstyle in which the hair is straightened and flattened down or lightly waved.

WALTER (*Stares at the money*): You trust me like that, Mama?
MAMA: I ain't never stop trusting you. Like I ain't never stop loving you.

(*She goes out, and Walter sits looking at the money on the table. Finally, in a decisive gesture, he gets up, and, in mingled joy and desperation, picks up the money. At the same moment, Travis enters for bed*)

TRAVIS: What's the matter, Daddy? You drunk?
WALTER (*Sweetly, more sweetly than we have ever known him*): No, Daddy ain't drunk. Daddy ain't going to never be drunk again. . . .
TRAVIS: Well, good night, Daddy.

(*The father has come from behind the couch and leans over, embracing his son*)

WALTER: Son, I feel like talking to you tonight.
TRAVIS: About what?
WALTER: Oh, about a lot of things. About you and what kind of man you going to be when you grow up. . . . Son—son, what do you want to be when you grow up?
TRAVIS: A bus driver.
WALTER (*Laughing a little*): A what? Man, that ain't nothing to want to be!
TRAVIS: Why not?
WALTER: 'Cause, man—it ain't big enough—you know what I mean.
TRAVIS: I don't know then. I can't make up my mind. Sometimes Mama asks me that too. And sometimes when I tell her I just want to be like you—she says she don't want me to be like that and sometimes she says she does. . . .
WALTER (*Gathering him up in his arms*): You know what, Travis? In seven years you going to be seventeen years old. And things is going to be very different with us in seven years, Travis. . . . One day when you are seventeen I'll come home—home from my office downtown some-where—
TRAVIS: You don't work in no office, Daddy.
WALTER: No—but after tonight. After what your daddy gonna do tonight, there's going to be offices—a whole lot of offices. . . .
TRAVIS: What you gonna do tonight, Daddy?
WALTER: You wouldn't understand yet, son, but your daddy's gonna make a transaction . . . a business transaction that's going to change our lives. . . . That's how come one day when you 'bout seventeen years old I'll come home and I'll be pretty tired, you know what I mean, after a day of conferences and secretaries getting things wrong the way they do . . . 'cause an executive's life is hell, man—(*The more he talks the farther away he gets*) And I'll pull the car up on the driveway . . . just a plain black Chrysler, I think, with white walls—no—black tires. More elegant. Rich people don't have to be flashy . . . though I'll have to get something a little sportier for Ruth—maybe a Cadillac convertible to

do her shopping in. . . . And I'll come up the steps to the house and the gardener will be clipping away at the hedges and he'll say, "Good evening, Mr. Younger." And I'll say, "Hello, Jefferson, how are you this evening?" And I'll go inside and Ruth will come downstairs and meet me at the door and we'll kiss each other and she'll take my arm and we'll go up to your room to see you sitting on the floor with the catalogues of all the great schools in America around you . . . All the great schools in the world! And—and I'll say, all right son—it's your seventeenth birthday, what is it you've decided? . . . Just tell me where you want to go to school and you'll *go*. Just tell me, what it is you want to be—and you'll *be* it. . . . Whatever you want to be—Yessir! (*He holds his arms open for Travis*) You just name it, son . . . (*Travis leaps into them*) and I hand you the world!

(*Walter's voice has risen in pitch and hysterical promise and on the last line he lifts Travis high*)

Scene 3

(*Time: Saturday, moving day, one week later.*)

(*Before the curtain rises, Ruth's voice, a strident, dramatic church alto, cuts through the silence.*)

(*It is, in the darkness, a triumphant surge, a penetrating statement of expectation: "Oh, Lord, I don't feel no ways tired! Children, oh, glory hallelujah!"*)

(*As the curtain rises we see that Ruth is alone in the living room, finishing up the family's packing. It is moving day. She is nailing crates and tying cartons, Beneatha enters, carrying a guitar case, and watches her exuberant sister-in-law.*)

RUTH: Hey!

BENEATHA (*Putting away the case*): Hi.

RUTH (*Pointing at a package*): Honey—look in that package there and see what I found on sale this morning at the South Center. (*Ruth gets up and moves to the package and draws out some curtains*) Lookahere—hand-turned hems!

BENEATHA: How do you know the window size out there?

RUTH (*Who hadn't thought of that*): Oh—Well, they bound to fit something in the whole house. Anyhow, they was too good a bargain to pass up. (*Ruth slaps her head, suddenly remembering something*) Oh, Bennie—I meant to put a special note on that carton over there. That's your mama's good china and she wants 'em to be very careful with it.

BENEATHA: I'll do it.

(*Beneatha finds a piece of paper and starts to draw large letters on it*)

RUTH: You know what I'm going to do soon as I get in that new house?

BENEATHA: What?

RUTH: Honey—I'm going to run me a tub of water up to here . . . (*with her fingers practically up to her nostrils*) And I'm going to get in it—and I am going to sit . . . and sit . . . and sit in that hot water and the first person who knocks to tell me to hurry up and come out—

BENEATHA: Gets shot at sunrise.

RUTH (*Laughing happily*): You said it, sister! (*Noticing how large Beneatha is absent-mindedly making the note*) Honey, they ain't going to read that from no airplane.

BENEATHA (*Laughing herself*): I guess I always think things have more emphasis if they are big, somehow.

RUTH (*Looking up at her and smiling*): You and your brother seem to have that as a philosophy of life. Lord, that man—done changed so 'round here. You know—you know what we did last night? Me and Walter Lee?

BENEATHA: What?

RUTH (*Smiling to herself*): We went to the movies. (*Looking at Beneatha to see if she understands*) We went to the movies. You know the last time me and Walter went to the movies together?

BENEATHA: No.

RUTH: Me neither. That's how long it been. (*Smiling again*) But we went last night. The picture wasn't much good, but that didn't seem to matter. We went—and we held hands.

BENEATHA: Oh, Lord!

RUTH: We held hands—and you know what?

BENEATHA: What?

RUTH: When we come out of the show it was late and dark and all the stores and things was closed up . . . and it was kind of chilly and there wasn't many people on the streets . . . and we was still holding hands, me and Walter.

BENEATHA: You're killing me.

(*Walter enters with a large package. His happiness is deep in him; he cannot keep still with his newfound exuberance. He is singing and wiggling and snapping his fingers. He puts his package in a corner and puts a phonograph record, which he has brought in with him, on the record player. As the music, soulful and sensuous, comes up he dances over to Ruth and tries to get her to dance with him. She gives in at last to his raunchiness and in a fit of giggling allows herself to be drawn into his mood. They dip and she melts into his arms in a classic, body-melding "slow drag"*)

BENEATHA (*Regarding them a long time as they dance, then drawing in her breath for a deeply exaggerated comment which she does not particularly mean*): Talk about—olddddddddddd-fashioneddddddddd—Negroes!

WALTER (*Stopping momentarily*): What kind of Negroes? (*He says this in fun. He is not angry with her today, nor with anyone. He starts to dance with his wife again*)

BENEATHA: Old-fashioned.

WALTER (*As he dances with Ruth*): You know, when these New Negroes have their convention—(*Pointing at his sister*)—that is going to be the chairman of the Committee on Unending Agitation. (*He goes on dancing, then stops*) Race, race, race! . . . Girl, I do believe you are the first person in the history of the entire human race to successfully brainwash yourself. (*Beneatha breaks up and he goes on dancing. He stops again, enjoying his tease*) Damn, even the N double A C P takes a holiday sometimes! (*Beneatha and Ruth laugh. He dances with Ruth some more and starts to laugh and stops and pantomimes someone over an operating table*) I can just see that chick someday looking down at some poor cat on an operating table and before she starts to slice him, she says . . . (*Pulling his sleeves back maliciously*) "By the way, what are your views on civil rights down there? . . ."

(*He laughs at her again and starts to dance happily. The bell sounds*)

BENEATHA: Sticks and stones may break my bones but . . . words will never hurt me!

(*Beneatha goes to the door and opens it as Walter and Ruth go on with the clowning. Beneatha is somewhat surprised to see a quiet-looking middle-aged white man in a business suit holding his hat and a briefcase in his hand and consulting a small piece of paper*)

MAN: Uh—how do you do, miss. I am looking for a Mrs.—(*He looks at the slip of paper*) Mrs. Lena Younger? (*He stops short, struck dumb at the sight of the oblivious Walter and Ruth*)

BENEATHA (*Smoothing her hair with slight embarrassment*): Oh—yes, that's my mother. Excuse me (*She closes the door and turns to quiet the other two*) Ruth! Brother! (*Enunciating precisely but soundlessly: "There's a white man at the door!" They stop dancing, Ruth cuts off the phonograph, Beneatha opens the door. The man casts a curious quick glance at all of them*) Uh—come in please.

MAN (*Coming in*): Thank you.

BENEATHA: My mother isn't here just now. Is it business?

MAN: Yes. . . well, of a sort.

WALTER (*Freely, the Man of the House*): Have a seat. I'm Mrs. Younger's son. I look after most of her business matters.

(*Ruth and Beneatha exchange amused glances*)

MAN (*Regarding Walter, and sitting*): Well—My name is Karl Lindner . . .

WALTER (*Stretching out his hand*): Walter Younger. This is my wife—(*Ruth nods politely*)—and my sister.

LINDNER: How do you do.

WALTER (*Amiably, as he sits himself easily on a chair, leaning forward on his knees with interest and looking expectantly into the newcomer's face*): What can we do for you, Mr. Lindner!

LINDNER (*Some minor shuffling of the hat and briefcase on his knees*): Well—I am a representative of the Clybourne Park Improvement Association—

WALTER (*Pointing*): Why don't you sit your things on the floor?

LINDNER: Oh—yes. Thank you. (*He slides the briefcase and hat under the chair*) And as I was saying—I am from the Clybourne Park Improvement Association and we have had it brought to our attention at the last meeting that you people—or at least your mother—has bought a piece of residential property at—(*He digs for the slip of paper again*)—four o six Clybourne Street . . .

WALTER: That's right. Care for something to drink? Ruth, get Mr. Lindner a beer.

LINDNER (*Upset for some reason*): Oh—no, really. I mean thank you very much, but no thank you.

RUTH (*Innocently*): Some coffee?

LINDNER: Thank you, nothing at all.

(*Beneatha is watching the man carefully*)

LINDNER: Well, I don't know how much you folks know about our organization. (*He is a gentle man; thoughtful and somewhat labored in his manner*) It is one of these community organizations set up to look after— oh, you know, things like block upkeep and special projects and we also have what we call our New Neighbors Orientation Committee . . .

BENEATHA (*Drily*): Yes—and what do they do?

LINDNER (*Turning a little to her and then returning the main force to Walter*): Well—it's what you might call a sort of welcoming committee, I guess. I mean they, we—I'm the chairman of the committee—go around and see the new people who move into the neighborhood and sort of give them the lowdown on the way we do things out in Clybourne Park.

BENEATHA (*With appreciation of the two meanings, which escape Ruth and Walter*): Un-huh.

LINDNER: And we also have the category of what the association calls— (*He looks elsewhere*)—uh—special community problems . . .

BENEATHA: Yes—and what are some of those?

WALTER: Girl, let the man talk.

LINDNER (*With understated relief*): Thank you. I would sort of like to explain this thing in my own way. I mean I want to explain to you in a certain way.

WALTER: Go ahead.

LINDNER: Yes. Well. I'm going to try to get right to the point. I'm sure we'll all appreciate that in the long run.

BENEATHA: Yes.

WALTER: Be still now!

LINDNER: Well—

RUTH (*Still innocently*): Would you like another chair—you don't look comfortable.

LINDNER (*More frustrated than annoyed*): No, thank you very much. Please. Well—to get right to the point I—(*A great breath, and he is off at last*) I am sure you people must be aware of some of the incidents which have happened in various parts of the city when colored people have moved into certain areas—(*Beneatha exhales heavily and starts tossing a piece of fruit up and down in the air*) Well—because we have what I think is going to be a unique type of organization in American community life—not only do we deplore that kind of thing—but we are trying to do something about it. (*Beneatha stops tossing and turns with a new and quizzical interest to the man*) We feel—(*gaining confidence in his mission because of the interest in the faces of the people he is talking to*)—we feel that most of the trouble in this world, when you come right down to it—(*He hits his knee for emphasis*)—most of the trouble exists because people just don't sit down and talk to each other.

RUTH (*Nodding as she might in church, pleased with the remark*): You can say that again, mister.

LINDNER (*More encouraged by such affirmation*): That we don't try hard enough in this world to understand the other fellow's problem. The other guy's point of view.

RUTH: Now that's right.

(*Beneatha and Walter merely watch and listen with genuine interest*)

LINDNER: Yes—that's the way we feel out in Clybourne Park. And that's why I was elected to come here this afternoon and talk to you people. Friendly like, you know, the way people should talk to each other and see if we couldn't find some way to work this thing out. As I say, the whole business is a matter of *caring* about the other fellow. Anybody can see that you are a nice family of folks, hard working and honest I'm sure. (*Beneatha frowns slightly, quizzically, her head tilted regarding him*) Today everybody knows what it means to be on the outside of *something*. And of course, there is always somebody who is out to take advantage of people who don't always understand.

WALTER: What do you mean?

LINDNER: Well—you see our community is made up of people who've worked hard as the dickens for years to build up that little community. They're not rich and fancy people; just hard-working, honest people who don't really have much but those little homes and a dream of the kind of community they want to raise their children in. Now, I don't say we are perfect and there is a lot wrong in some of the things they want. But you've got to admit that a man, right or wrong, has the right to want to have the neighborhood he lives in a certain kind of way. And at the moment the overwhelming majority of our people out there feel that people get along better, take more of a common interest in the life of the community, when they share a common background. I want you to believe me when I tell you that race prejudice simply doesn't enter into it. It is a matter of the people of Clybourne Park believing, rightly or wrongly, as I say, that for the happiness of all concerned that our Negro families are happier when they live in their *own* communities.

BENEATHA (*With a grand and bitter gesture*): This, friends, is the Welcoming Committee!

WALTER (*Dumbfounded, looking at Lindner*): Is this what you came marching all the way over here to tell us?

LINDNER: Well, now we've been having a fine conversation. I hope you'll hear me all the way through.

WALTER (*Tightly*): Go ahead, man.

LINDNER: You see—in the face of all the things I have said, we are prepared to make your family a very generous offer . . .

BENEATHA: Thirty pieces and not a coin less!

WALTER: Yeah?

LINDNER (*Putting on his glasses and drawing a form out of the briefcase*): Our association is prepared, through the collective effort of our people, to buy the house from you at a financial gain to your family.

RUTH: Lord have mercy, ain't this the living gall!

WALTER: All right, you through?

LINDNER: Well, I want to give you the exact terms of the financial arrangement—

WALTER: We don't want to hear no exact terms of no arrangements. I want to know if you got any more to tell us 'bout getting together?

LINDNER (*Taking off his glasses*): Well—I don't suppose that you feel . . .

WALTER: Never mind how I feel—you got any more to say 'bout how people ought to sit down and talk to each other? . . . Get out of my house, man.

(*He turns his back and walks to the door*)

LINDNER (*Looking around at the hostile faces and reaching and assembling his hat and briefcase*): Well—I don't understand why you people are reacting this way. What do you think you are going to gain by moving into a neighborhood where you just aren't wanted and where some elements— well—people can get awful worked up when they feel that their whole way of life and everything they've ever worked for is threatened.

WALTER: Get out.

LINDNER (*At the door, holding a small card*): Well—I'm sorry it went like this.
WALTER: Get out.
LINDNER (*Almost sadly regarding Walter*): You just can't force people to change their hearts, son.

(*He turns and puts his card on a table and exits. Walter pushes the door to with stinging hatred, and stands looking at it. Ruth just sits and Beneatha just stands. They say nothing. Mama and Travis enter*)

MAMA: Well—this all the packing got done since I left out of here this morning. I testify before God that my children got all the energy of the *dead*! What time the moving men due?
BENEATHA: Four o'clock. You had a caller, Mama.

(*She is smiling, teasingly*)

MAMA: Sure enough—who?
BENEATHA (*Her arms folded saucily*): The Welcoming Committee.

(*Walter and Ruth giggle*)

MAMA (*Innocently*): Who?
BENEATHA: The Welcoming Committee. They said they're sure going to be glad to see you when you get there.
WALTER (*Devilishly*): Yeah, they said they can't hardly wait to see your face.

(*Laughter*)

MAMA (*Sensing their facetiousness*): What's the matter with you all?
WALTER: Ain't nothing the matter with us. We just telling you 'bout the gentleman who came to see you this afternoon. From the Clybourne Park Improvement Association.
MAMA: What he want?
RUTH (*In the same mood as Beneatha and Walter*): To welcome you, honey.
WALTER: He said they can't hardly wait. He said the one thing they don't have, that they just *dying* to have out there is a fine family of fine colored people! (*To Ruth and Beneatha*) Ain't that right!
RUTH (*Mockingly*): Yeah! He left his card—
BENEATHA (*Handing card to Mama*): In case.

(*Mama reads and throws it on the floor—understanding and looking off as she draws her chair up to the table on which she has put her plant and some sticks and some cord*)

MAMA: Father, give us strength. (*Knowingly—and without fun*) Did he threaten us?
BENEATHA: Oh—Mama—they don't do it like that any more. He talked Brotherhood. He said everybody ought to learn how to sit down and hate each other with good Christian fellowship.

(*She and Walter shake hands to ridicule the remark*)

MAMA (*Sadly*): Lord, protect us . . .

RUTH: You should hear the money those folks raised to buy the house from us. All we paid and then some.

BENEATHA: What they think we going to do—eat 'em?

RUTH: No, honey, marry 'em.

MAMA (*Shaking her head*): Lord, Lord, Lord . . .

RUTH: Well—that's the way the crackers crumble. (*A beat*) Joke.

BENEATHA (*Laughingly noticing what her mother is doing*): Mama, what are you doing?

MAMA: Fixing my plant so it won't get hurt none on the way . . .

BENEATHA: Mama, you going to take *that* to the new house?

MAMA: Un-huh—

BENEATHA: That raggedy-looking old thing?

MAMA (*Stopping and looking at her*): It expresses ME!

RUTH (*With delight, to Beneatha*): So there, Miss Thing!

(*Walter comes to Mama suddenly and bends down behind her and squeezes her in his arms with all his strength. She is overwhelmed by the suddenness of it and, though delighted, her manner is like that of Ruth and Travis*)

MAMA: Look out now, boy! You make me mess up my thing here!

WALTER (*His face lit, he slips down on his knees beside her, his arms still about her*): Mama . . . you know what it means to climb up in the chariot?

MAMA (*Gruffly, very happy*): Get on away from me now . . .

RUTH (*Near the gift-wrapped package, trying to catch Walter's eye*): Psst—

WALTER: What the old song say, Mama . . .

RUTH: Walter—Now?

(*She is pointing at the package*)

WALTER (*Speaking the lines, sweetly, playfully, in his mother's face*):
> I got wings . . . you got wings . . .
> All God's children got wings . . .

MAMA: Boy—get out of my face and do some work . . .

WALTER:
> When I get to heaven gonna put on my wings,
> Gonna fly all over God's heaven . . .

BENEATHA (*Teasingly, from across the room*): Everybody talking 'bout heaven ain't going there!

WALTER (*To Ruth, who is carrying the box across to them*): I don't know, you think we ought to give her that . . . Seems to me she ain't been very appreciative around here.

MAMA (*Eyeing the box, which is obviously a gift*): What is that?

WALTER (*Taking it from Ruth and putting it on the table in front of Mama*):
Well—what you all think? Should we give it to her?

RUTH: Oh—she was pretty good today.

MAMA: I'll good you—

(*She turns her eyes to the box again*)

BENEATHA: Open it, Mama.

(*She stands up, looks at it, turns and looks at all of them, and then presses her hands together and does not open the package*)

WALTER (*Sweetly*): Open it, Mama. It's for you. (*Mama looks in his eyes. It is the first present in her life without its being Christmas. Slowly she opens her package and lifts out, one by one, a brand-new sparkling set of gardening tools. Walter continues, prodding*) Ruth made up the note—read it . . .

MAMA (*Picking up the card and adjusting her glasses*): "To our own Mrs. Miniver°—Love from Brother, Ruth and Beneatha." Ain't that lovely . . .

TRAVIS (*Tugging at his father's sleeve*): Daddy, can I give her mine now?

WALTER: All right, son. (*Travis flies to get his gift*)

MAMA: Now I don't have to use my knives and forks no more . . .

WALTER: Travis didn't want to go in with the rest of us, Mama. He got his own. (*Somewhat amused*) We don't know what it is . . .

TRAVIS (*Racing back in the room with a large hatbox and putting it in front of his grandmother*): Here!

MAMA: Lord have mercy, baby. You done gone and bought your grandmother a hat?

TRAVIS (*very proud*): Open it!

(*She does and lifts out an elaborate, but very elaborate, wide gardening hat, and all the adults break up at the sight of it*)

RUTH: Travis, honey, what is that?

TRAVIS (*Who thinks it is beautiful and appropriate*): It's a gardening hat! Like the ladies always have on in the magazines when they work in their gardens.

BENEATHA (*Giggling fiercely*): Travis—we were trying to make Mama Mrs. Miniver—not Scarlett O'Hara!°

MAMA (*Indignantly*): What's the matter with you all! This here is a beautiful hat! (*Absurdly*) I always wanted me one just like it!

(*She pops it on her head to prove it to her grandson, and the hat is ludicrous and considerably oversized*)

Mrs. Miniver: A character in the 1942 film *Mrs. Miniver*, a suburban British housewife who loves gardening.   **Scarlett O'Hara:** The strong, pragmatic, survivalist heroine in Margaret Mitchell's 1936 novel *Gone with the Wind*.

RUTH: Hot dog! Go, Mama!

WALTER (*Doubled over with laughter*): I'm sorry, Mama—but you look like you ready to go out and chop you some cotton sure enough!

(*They all laugh except Mama, out of deference to Travis's feelings*)

MAMA (*Gathering the boy up to her*): Bless your heart—this is the prettiest hat I ever owned—(*Walter, Ruth and Beneatha chime in—noisily, festively and insincerely congratulating Travis on his gift*) What are we all standing around here for? We ain't finished packin' yet. Bennie, you ain't packed one book.

(*The bell rings*)

BENEATHA: That couldn't be the movers . . . it's not hardly two good yet—

(*Beneatha goes into her room, Mama starts for door*)

WALTER (*Turning, stiffening*): Wait—wait—I'll get it.

(*He stands and looks at the door*)

MAMA: You expecting company, son?

WALTER (*Just looking at the door*): Yeah—yeah . . .

(*Mama looks at Ruth, and they exchange innocent and unfrightened glances*)

MAMA (*Not understanding*): Well, let them in, son.

BENEATHA (*From her room*): We need some more string.

MAMA: Travis—you run to the hardware and get me some string cord.

(*Mama goes out and Walter turns and looks at Ruth. Travis goes to a dish for money*)

RUTH: Why don't you answer the door, man?

WALTER (*Suddenly bounding across the floor to embrace her*): 'Cause sometimes it hard to let the future begin! (*Stooping down in her face*)
   I got wings! You got wings!
   All God's children got wings!

(*He crosses to the door and throws it open. Standing there is a very slight little man in a not too prosperous business suit and with haunted frightened eyes and a hat pulled down tightly, brim up, around his forehead. Travis passes between the men and exits. Walter leans deep in the man's face, still in his jubilance*)

   When I get to heaven gonna put on my wings,
   Gonna fly all over God's heaven . . .

(*The little man just stares at him*)

   Heaven—

(*Suddenly he stops and looks past the little man into the empty hallway*)
Where's Willy, man?

BOBO: He ain't with me.

WALTER (*Not disturbed*): Oh—come on in. You know my wife.

BOBO (*Dumbly, taking off his hat*): Yes—h'you, Miss Ruth.

RUTH (*Quietly, a mood apart from her husband already, seeing Bobo*): Hello,
Bobo.

WALTER: You right on time today . . . Right on time. That's the way! (*He
slaps Bobo on his back*) Sit down . . . lemme hear.

(*Ruth stands stiffly and quietly in back of them, as though somehow she senses
death, her eyes fixed on her husband*)

BOBO (*His frightened eyes on the floor, his hat in his hands*): Could I please get
a drink of water, before I tell you about it, Walter Lee?

(*Walter does not take his eyes off the man. Ruth goes blindly to the tap and gets a
glass of water and brings it to Bobo*)

WALTER: There ain't nothing wrong, is there?

BOBO: Lemme tell you—

WALTER: Man—didn't nothing go wrong?

BOBO: Lemme tell you—Walter Lee. (*Looking at Ruth and talking to her
more than to Walter*) You know how it was. I got to tell you how it was.
I mean first I got to tell you how it was all the way . . . I mean about the
money I put in, Walter Lee . . .

WALTER (*With taut agitation now*): What about the money you put in?

BOBO: Well—it wasn't much as we told you—me and Willy—(*He stops*)
I'm sorry, Walter. I got a bad feeling about it. I got a real bad feeling
about it . . .

WALTER: Man, what you telling me about all this for? . . . Tell me what
happened in Springfield . . .

BOBO: Springfield.

RUTH (*Like a dead woman*): What was supposed to happen in Springfield?

BOBO (*To her*): This deal that me and Walter went into with Willy—Me
and Willy was going to go down to Springfield and spread some money
'round so's we wouldn't have to wait so long for the liquor license . . .
That's what we were going to do. Everybody said that was the way you
had to do, you understand, Miss Ruth?

WALTER: Man—what happened down there?

BOBO (*A pitiful man, near tears*): I'm trying to tell you, Walter.

WALTER (*Screaming at him suddenly*): THEN TELL ME, GODDAMMIT . . . WHAT'S
THE MATTER WITH YOU?

BOBO: Man . . . I didn't go to no Springfield, yesterday.

WALTER (*Halted, life hanging in the moment*): Why not?

BOBO (*The long way, the hard way to tell*): 'Cause I didn't have no reasons to . . .

WALTER: Man, what are you talking about!

BOBO: I'm talking about the fact that when I got to the train station yesterday morning—eight o'clock like we planned . . . Man—*Willy didn't never show up.*

WALTER: Why . . . where was he . . . where is he?

BOBO: That's what I'm trying to tell you . . . I don't know . . . I waited six hours . . . I called his house . . . and I waited . . . six hours . . . I waited in that train station six hours . . . (*Breaking into tears*) That was all the extra money I had in the world . . . (*Looking up at Walter with the tears running down his face*) Man, Willy is gone.

WALTER: Gone, what you mean Willy is gone? Gone where? You mean he went by himself. You mean he went off to Springfield by himself—to take care of getting the license—(*Turns and looks anxiously at Ruth*) You mean maybe he didn't want too many people in on the business down there? (*Looks to Ruth again, as before*) You know Willy got his own ways. (*Looks back to Bobo*) Maybe you was late yesterday and he just went on down there without you. Maybe—maybe—he's been callin' you at home tryin' to tell you what happened or something. Maybe—maybe—he just got sick. He's somewhere—he's got to be somewhere. We just got to find him—me and you got to find him. (*Grabs Bobo senselessly by the collar and starts to shake him*) We got to!

BOBO (*In sudden angry, frightened agony*): What's the matter with you, Walter! *When a cat take off with your money he don't leave you no road maps!*

WALTER (*Turning madly, as though he is looking for Willy in the very room*): Willy! . . . Willy . . . don't do it . . . Please don't do it . . . Man, not with that money . . . Man, please, not with that money . . . Oh, God . . . Don't let it be true . . . (*He is wandering around, crying out for Willy and looking for him or perhaps for help from God*) Man . . . I trusted you . . . Man, I put my life in your hands . . . (*He starts to crumple down on the floor as Ruth just covers her face in horror. Mama opens the door and comes into the room, with Beneatha behind her*) Man . . . (*He starts to pound the floor with his fists, sobbing wildly*) THAT MONEY IS MADE OUT OF MY FATHER'S FLESH—

BOBO (*Standing over him helplessly*): I'm sorry, Walter . . . (*Only Walter's sobs reply. Bobo puts on his hat*) I had my life staked on this deal, too . . .

(*He exits*)

MAMA (*To Walter*): Son—(*She goes to him, bends down to him, talks to his bent head*) Son . . . Is it gone? Son, I gave you sixty-five hundred dollars. Is it gone? All of it? Beneatha's money too?

WALTER (*Lifting his head slowly*): Mama . . . I never . . . went to the bank at all . . .

MAMA (*Not wanting to believe him*): You mean . . . your sister's school money . . . you used that too . . . Walter? . . .

WALTER: Yessss! All of it . . . It's all gone . . .

(*There is total silence. Ruth stands with her face covered with her hands; Beneatha leans forlornly against a wall, fingering a piece of red ribbon from the mother's gift. Mama stops and looks at her son without recognition and then, quite without thinking about it, starts to beat him senselessly in the face. Beneatha goes to them and stops it*)

BENEATHA: Mama!

(*Mama stops and looks at both of her children and rises slowly and wanders vaguely, aimlessly away from them*)

MAMA: I seen . . . him . . . night after night . . . come in . . . and look at that rug . . . and then look at me . . . the red showing in his eyes . . . the veins moving in his head . . . I seen him grow thin and old before he was forty . . . working and working and working like somebody's old horse . . . killing himself . . . and you—you give it all away in a day—(*She raises her arms to strike him again*)

BENEATHA: Mama—

MAMA: Oh, God . . . (*She looks up to Him*) Look down here—and show me the strength.

BENEATHA: Mama—

MAMA (*Folding over*): Strength . . .

BENEATHA (*Plaintively*): Mama . . .

MAMA: Strength!

ACT III

(*An hour later.*)

(*At curtain, there is a sullen light of gloom in the living room, gray light not unlike that which began the first scene of Act One. At left we can see Walter within his room, alone with himself. He is stretched out on the bed, his shirt out and open, his arms under his head. He does not smoke, he does not cry out, he merely lies there, looking up at the ceiling, much as if he were alone in the world.*)

(*In the living room Beneatha sits at the table, still surrounded by the now almost ominous packing crates. She sits looking off. We feel that this is a mood struck perhaps an hour before, and it lingers now, full of the empty sound of profound disappointment. We see on a line from her brother's bedroom the sameness of their attitudes. Presently the bell rings and Beneatha rises without ambition or interest in answering. It is Asagai, smiling broadly, striding into the room with energy and happy expectation and conversation.*)

ASAGAI: I came over . . . I had some free time. I thought I might help with
the packing. Ah, I like the look of packing crates! A household in preparation for a journey! It depresses some people . . . but for me . . . it is
another feeling. Something full of the flow of life, do you understand?
Movement, progress . . . It makes me think of Africa.

BENEATHA: Africa!

ASAGAI: What kind of a mood is this? Have I told you how deeply you
move me?

BENEATHA: He gave away the money, Asagai . . .

ASAGAI: Who gave away what money?

BENEATHA: The insurance money. My brother gave it away.

ASAGAI: Gave it away?

BENEATHA: He made an investment! With a man even Travis wouldn't
have trusted with his most worn-out marbles.

ASAGAI: And it's gone?

BENEATHA: Gone!

ASAGAI: I'm very sorry . . . And you, now?

BENEATHA: Me? . . . Me? . . . Me, I'm nothing . . . Me. When I was very
small . . . we used to take our sleds out in the wintertime and the only
hills we had were the ice-covered stone steps of some houses down the
street. And we used to fill them in with snow and make them smooth
and slide down them all day . . . and it was very dangerous, you know . . .
far too steep . . . and sure enough one day a kid named Rufus came
down too fast and hit the sidewalk and we saw his face just split open
right there in front of us . . . And I remember standing there looking at
his bloody open face thinking that was the end of Rufus. But the ambulance came and they took him to the hospital and they fixed the
broken bones and they sewed it all up . . . and the next time I saw Rufus
he just had a little line down the middle of his face . . . I never got over
that . . .

ASAGAI: What?

BENEATHA: That that was what one person could do for another, fix him
up—sew up the problem, make him all right again. That was the most
marvelous thing in the world . . . I wanted to do that. I always thought
it was the one concrete thing in the world that a human being could
do. Fix up the sick, you know—and make them whole again. This was
truly being God . . .

ASAGAI: You wanted to be God?

BENEATHA: No—I wanted to cure. It used to be so important to me. I
wanted to cure. It used to matter. I used to care. I mean about people
and how their bodies hurt . . .

ASAGAI: And you've stopped caring?

BENEATHA: Yes—I think so.

ASAGAI: Why?

BENEATHA (*Bitterly*): Because it doesn't seem deep enough, close enough to what ails mankind! It was a child's way of seeing things—or an idealist's.

ASAGAI: Children see things very well sometimes—and idealists even better.

BENEATHA: I know that's what you think. Because you are still where I left off. You with all your talk and dreams about Africa! You still think you can patch up the world. Cure the Great Sore of Colonialism—(*Loftily, mocking it*) with the Penicillin of Independence—!

ASAGAI: Yes!

BENEATHA: Independence *and then what*? What about all the crooks and thieves and just plain idiots who will come into power and steal and plunder the same as before—only now they will be black and do it in the name of the new Independence—WHAT ABOUT THEM?!

ASAGAI: That will be the problem for another time. First we must get there.

BENEATHA: And where does it end?

ASAGAI: End? Who even spoke of an end? To life? To living?

BENEATHA: An end to misery! To stupidity! Don't you see there isn't any real progress, Asagai, there is only one large circle that we march in, around and around, each of us with our own little picture in front of us—our own little mirage that we think is the future.

ASAGAI: That is the mistake.

BENEATHA: What?

ASAGAI: What you just said about the circle. It isn't a circle—it is simply a long line—as in geometry, you know, one that reaches into infinity. And because we cannot see the end—we also cannot see how it changes. And it is very odd but those who see the changes—who dream, who will not give up—are called idealists . . . and those who see only the circle we call *them* the "realists"!

BENEATHA: Asagai, while I was sleeping in that bed in there, people went out and took the future right out of my hands! And nobody asked me, nobody consulted me—they just went out and changed my life!

ASAGAI: Was it your money?

BENEATHA: What?

ASAGAI: Was it your money he gave away?

BENEATHA: It belonged to all of us.

ASAGAI: But did you earn it? Would you have had it at all if your father had not died?

BENEATHA: No.

ASAGAI: Then isn't there something wrong in a house—in a world—where all dreams, good or bad, must depend on the death of a man? I never thought to see *you* like this, Alaiyo. You! Your brother made a mistake and you are grateful to him so that now you can give up the ailing human race on account of it! You talk about what good is struggle, what good is anything! Where are we all going and why are we bothering!

BENEATHA: AND YOU CANNOT ANSWER IT!

ASAGAI (*Shouting over her*): *I LIVE THE ANSWER!* (*Pause*) In my village at home it is the exceptional man who can even read a newspaper . . . or who ever sees a book at all. I will go home and much of what I will have to say will seem strange to the people of my village. But I will teach and work and things will happen, slowly and swiftly. At times it will seem that nothing changes at all . . . and then again the sudden dramatic events which make history leap into the future. And then quiet again. Retrogression even. Guns, murder, revolution. And I even will have moments when I wonder if the quiet was not better than all that death and hatred. But I will look about my village at the illiteracy and disease and ignorance and I will not wonder long. And perhaps . . . perhaps I will be a great man . . . I mean perhaps I will hold on to the substance of truth and find my way always with the right course . . . and perhaps for it I will be butchered in my bed some night by the servants of empire . . .

BENEATHA: *The martyr!*

ASAGAI (*He smiles*): . . . or perhaps I shall live to be a very old man, respected and esteemed in my new nation . . . And perhaps I shall hold office and this is what I'm trying to tell you, Alaiyo: Perhaps the things I believe now for my country will be wrong and outmoded, and I will not understand and do terrible things to have things my way or merely to keep my power. Don't you see that there will be young men and women—not British soldiers then, but my own black countrymen—to step out of the shadows some evening and slit my then useless throat? Don't you see they have always been there . . . that they always will be. And that such a thing as my own death will be an advance? They who might kill me even . . . actually replenish all that I was.

BENEATHA: Oh, Asagai, I know all that.

ASAGAI: Good! Then stop moaning and groaning and tell me what you plan to do.

BENEATHA: Do?

ASAGAI: I have a bit of a suggestion.

BENEATHA: What?

ASAGAI (*Rather quietly for him*): That when it is all over—that you come home with me—

BENEATHA (*Staring at him and crossing away with exasperation*): Oh— Asagai—at this moment you decide to be romantic!

ASAGAI (*Quickly understanding the misunderstanding*): My dear, young creature of the New World—I do not mean across the city—I mean across the ocean: home—to Africa.

BENEATHA (*Slowly understanding and turning to him with murmured amazement*): To Africa?

ASAGAI: Yes! . . . (*Smiling and lifting his arms playfully*) Three hundred years later the African Prince rose up out of the seas and swept the maiden back across the middle passage over which her ancestors had come—

BENEATHA (*Unable to play*): To—to Nigeria?

ASAGAI: Nigeria. Home. (*Coming to her with genuine romantic flippancy*) I will show you our mountains and our stars; and give you cool drinks from gourds and teach you the old songs and the ways of our people—and, in time, we will pretend that—(*Very softly*)—you have only been away for a day. Say that you'll come (*He swings her around and takes her full in his arms in a kiss which proceeds to passion*)

BENEATHA (*Pulling away suddenly*): You're getting me all mixed up—

ASAGAI: Why?

BENEATHA: Too many things—too many things have happened today. I must sit down and think. I don't know what I feel about anything right this minute.

(*She promptly sits down and props her chin on her fist*)

ASAGAI (*Charmed*): All right, I shall leave you. No—don't get up. (*Touching her, gently, sweetly*) Just sit awhile and think . . Never be afraid to sit awhile and think. (*He goes to door and looks at her*) How often I have looked at you and said, "Ah—so this is what the New World hath finally wrought . . ."

(*He exits. Beneatha sits on alone. Presently Walter enters from his room and starts to rummage through things, feverishly looking for something. She looks up and turns in her seat*)

BENEATHA (*Hissingly*): Yes—just look at what the New World hath wrought! . . . Just look! (*She gestures with bitter disgust*) There he is! *Monsieur le petit bourgeois noir*°—himself! There he is—Symbol of a Rising Class! Entrepreneur! Titan of the system! (*Walter ignores her completely and continues frantically and destructively looking for something and hurling things to floor and tearing things out of their place in his search. Beneatha ignores the eccentricity of his actions and goes on with the monologue of insult*) Did you dream of yachts on Lake Michigan, Brother? Did you see yourself on that Great Day sitting down at the Conference Table, surrounded by all the mighty bald-headed men in America? All

Monsieur . . . noir: Mr. black middle class (French).

halted, waiting, breathless, waiting for your pronouncements on industry? Waiting for you—Chairman of the Board! (*Walter finds what he is looking for—a small piece of white paper—and pushes it in his pocket and puts on his coat and rushes out without ever having looked at her. She shouts after him*) I look at you and I see the final triumph of stupidity in the world!

(*The door slams and she returns to just sitting again. Ruth comes quickly out of Mama's room*)

RUTH: Who was that?

BENEATHA: Your husband.

RUTH: Where did he go?

BENEATHA: Who knows—maybe he has an appointment at U.S. Steel.

RUTH (*Anxiously, with frightened eyes*): You didn't say nothing bad to him, did you?

BENEATHA: Bad? Say anything bad to him? No—I told him he was a sweet boy and full of dreams and everything is strictly peachy keen, as the ofay° kids say!

(*Mama enters from her bedroom. She is lost, vague, trying to catch hold, to make some sense of her former command of the world, but it still eludes her. A sense of waste overwhelms her gait; a measure of apology rides on her shoulders. She goes to her plant, which has remained on the table, looks at it, picks it up and takes it to the windowsill and sits it outside, and she stands and looks at it a long moment. Then she closes the window, straightens her body with effort and turns around to her children*)

MAMA: Well—ain't it a mess in here, though? (*A false cheerfulness, a beginning of something*) I guess we all better stop moping around and get some work done. All this unpacking and everything we got to do. (*Ruth raises her head slowly in response to the sense of the line; and Beneatha in similar manner turns very slowly to look at her mother*) One of you all better call the moving people and tell 'em not to come.

RUTH: Tell 'em not to come?

MAMA: Of course, baby. Ain't no need in 'em coming all the way here and having to go back. They charges for that too. (*She sits down, fingers to her brow, thinking*) Lord, ever since I was a little girl, I always remembers people saying, "Lena—Lena Eggleston, you aims too high all the time. You needs to slow down and see life a little more like it is. Just slow down some." That's what they always used to say down home—"Lord, that Lena Eggleston is a high-minded thing. She'll get her due one day!"

RUTH: No, Lena . . .

ofay: White (slang).

MAMA: Me and Big Walter just didn't never learn right.

RUTH: Lena, no! We gotta go. Bennie—tell her . . . (*She rises and crosses to Beneatha with her arms outstretched. Beneatha doesn't respond*) Tell her we can still move . . . the notes ain't but a hundred and twenty-five a month. We got four grown people in this house—we can work . . .

MAMA (*To herself*): Just aimed too high all the time—

RUTH (*Turning and going to Mama fast—the words pouring out with urgency and desperation*): Lena—I'll work . . . I'll work twenty hours a day in all the kitchens in Chicago . . . I'll strap my baby on my back if I have to and scrub all the floors in America and wash all the sheets in America if I have to—but we got to MOVE! We got to get OUT OF HERE!!

(*Mama reaches out absently and pats Ruth's hand*)

MAMA: No—I sees things differently now. Been thinking 'bout some of the things we could do to fix this place up some. I seen a secondhand bureau over on Maxwell Street just the other day that could fit right there. (*She points to where the new furniture might go. Ruth wanders away from her*) Would need some new handles on it and then a little varnish and it look like something brand-new. And—we can put up them new curtains in the kitchen . . . Why this place be looking fine. Cheer us all up so that we forget trouble ever come . . . (*To Ruth*) And you could get some nice screens to put up in your room 'round the baby's bassinet . . . (*She looks at both of them, pleadingly*) Sometimes you just got to know when to give up some things . . . and hold on to what you got. . . .

(*Walter enters from the outside, looking spent and leaning against the door, his coat hanging from him*)

MAMA: Where you been, son?

WALTER (*Breathing hard*): Made a call.

MAMA: To who, son?

WALTER: To The Man. (*He heads for his room*)

MAMA: What man, baby?

WALTER (*Stops in the door*): The Man, Mama. Don't you know who The Man is?

RUTH: Walter Lee?

WALTER: The Man. Like the guys in the streets say—The Man. Captain Boss—Mistuh Charley . . . Old Cap' n Please Mr. Bossman . . .

BENEATHA (*Suddenly*): Lindner!

WALTER: That's right! That's good. I told him to come right over.

BENEATHA (*Fiercely, understanding*): For what? What do you want to see him for!

WALTER (*Looking at his sister*): We going to do business with him.

MAMA: What you talking 'bout, son?

WALTER: Talking 'bout life, Mama. You all always telling me to see life like it is. Well—I laid in there on my back today . . . and I figured it out. Life just like it is. Who gets and who don't get. (*He sits down with his coat on and laughs*) Mama, you know it's all divided up. Life is. Sure enough. Between the takers and the "tooken." (*He laughs*) I've figured it out finally. (*He looks around at them*) Yeah. Some of us always getting "tooken." (*He laughs*) People like Willy Harris, they don't never get "tooken." And you know why the rest of us do? 'Cause we all mixed up. Mixed up bad. We get to looking 'round for the right and the wrong; and we worry about it and cry about it and stay up nights trying to figure out 'bout the wrong and the right of things all the time . . . And all the time, man, them takers is out there operating, just taking and taking. Willy Harris? Shoot—Willy Harris don't even count. He don't even count in the big scheme of things. But I'll say one thing for old Willy Harris . . . he's taught me something. He's taught me to keep my eye on what counts in this world. Yeah—(*Shouting out a little*) Thanks, Willy!

RUTH: What did you call that man for, Walter Lee?

WALTER: Called him to tell him to come on over to the show. Gonna put on a show for the man. Just what he wants to see. You see, Mama, the man came here today and he told us that them people out there where you want us to move—well they so upset they willing to pay us *not* to move! (*He laughs again*) And—and oh, Mama you would of been proud of the way me and Ruth and Bennie acted. We told him to get out . . . Lord have mercy! We told the man to get out! Oh, we was some proud folks this afternoon, yeah. (*He lights a cigarette*) We were still full of that old-time stuff . . .

RUTH (*Coming toward him slowly*): You talking 'bout taking them people's money to keep us from moving in that house?

WALTER: I ain't just talking 'bout it, baby—I'm telling you that's what's going to happen!

BENEATHA: Oh, God! Where is the bottom! Where is the real honest-to-God bottom so he can't go any farther!

WALTER: See—that's the old stuff. You and that boy that was here today. You all want everybody to carry a flag and a spear and sing some marching songs, huh? You wanna spend your life looking into things and trying to find the right and the wrong part, huh? Yeah. You know what's going to happen to that boy someday—he'll find himself sitting in a dungeon, locked in forever—and the takers will have the key! Forget it, baby! There ain't no causes—there ain't nothing but taking in this world, and he who takes most is smartest—and it don't make a damn bit of difference *how*.

MAMA: You making something inside me cry, son. Some awful pain inside me.

WALTER: Don't cry, Mama. Understand. That white man is going to walk in that door able to write checks for more money than we ever had. It's important to him and I'm going to help him . . . I'm going to put on the show, Mama.

MAMA: Son—I come from five generations of people who was slaves and sharecroppers—but ain't nobody in my family never let nobody pay 'em no money that was a way of telling us we wasn't fit to walk the earth. We ain't never been that poor. (*Raising her eyes and looking at him*) We ain't never been that—dead inside.

BENEATHA: Well—we are dead now. All the talk about dreams and sunlight that goes on in this house. It's all dead now.

WALTER: What's the matter with you all! I didn't make this world! It was give to me this way! Hell, yes, I want me some yachts someday! Yes, I want to hang some real pearls 'round my wife's neck. Ain't she supposed to wear no pearls? Somebody tell me—tell me, who decides which women is suppose to wear pearls in this world. I tell you I am a *man*—and I think my wife should wear some pearls in this world!

(*This last line hangs a good while and Walter begins to move about the room. The word "Man" has penetrated his consciousness; he mumbles it to himself repeatedly between strange agitated pauses as he moves about*)

MAMA: Baby, how you going to feel on the inside?

WALTER: Fine! . . . Going to feel fine . . . a man . . .

MAMA: You won't have nothing left then, Walter Lee.

WALTER (*Coming to her*): I'm going to feel fine, Mama. I'm going to look that son-of-a-bitch in the eyes and say—(*He falters*)—and say, "All right, Mr. Lindner—(*He falters even more*)—that's *your* neighborhood out there! You got the right to keep it like you want! You got the right to have it like you want! Just write the check and—the house is yours." And—and I am going to say—(*His voice almost breaks*) "And you—you people just put the money in my hand and you won't have to live next to this bunch of stinking niggers! . . ." (*He straightens up and moves away from his mother, walking around the room*) And maybe—maybe I'll just get down on my black knees . . . (*He does so; Ruth and Bennie and Mama watch him in frozen horror*) "Captain, Mistuh, Bossman—(*Groveling and grinning and wringing his hands in profoundly anguished imitation of the slow-witted movie stereotype*) A-hee-hee-hee! Oh, yassuh boss! Yasssssuh! Great white—(*Voice breaking, he forces himself to go on*)—Father, just gi' ussen de money, fo' God's sake, and we's—we's ain't gwine come out deh and dirty up yo' white folks neighborhood . . ." (*He breaks down completely*) And I'll feel fine! Fine! FINE! (*He gets up and goes into the bedroom*)

BENEATHA: That is not a man. That is nothing but a toothless rat.

MAMA: Yes—death done come in this here house. (*She is nodding, slowly, reflectively*) Done come walking in my house on the lips of my children.

You what supposed to be my beginning again. You—what supposed to be my harvest. (*To Beneatha*) You—you mourning your brother?

BENEATHA: He's no brother of mine.

MAMA: What you say?

BENEATHA: I said that that individual in that room is no brother of mine.

MAMA: That's what I thought you said. You feeling like you better than he is today? (*Beneatha does not answer*) Yes? What you tell him a minute ago? That he wasn't a man? Yes? You give him up for me? You done wrote his epitaph too—like the rest of the world? Well, who give you the privilege?

BENEATHA: Be on my side for once! You saw what he just did, Mama! You saw him—down on his knees. Wasn't it you who taught me to despise any man who would do that? Do what he's going to do?

MAMA: Yes—I taught you that. Me and your daddy. But I thought I taught you something else too . . . I thought I taught you to love him.

BENEATHA: Love him? There is nothing left to love.

MAMA: There is *always* something left to love. And if you ain't learned that, you ain't learned nothing. (*Looking at her*) Have you cried for that boy today? I don't mean for yourself and for the family 'cause we lost the money. I mean for him: what he been through and what it done to him. Child, when do you think is the time to love somebody the most? When they done good and made things easy for everybody? Well then, you ain't through learning—because that ain't the time at all. It's when he's at his lowest and can't believe in hisself 'cause the world done whipped him so! When you starts measuring somebody, measure him right, child, measure him right. Make sure you done taken into account what hills and valleys he come through before he got to wherever he is.

(*Travis bursts into the room at the end of the speech, leaving the door open*)

TRAVIS: Grandmama—the moving men are downstairs! The truck just pulled up.

MAMA (*Turning and looking at him*): Are they, baby? They downstairs?

(*She sighs and sits. Lindner appears in the doorway. He peers in and knocks lightly, to gain attention, and comes in. All turn to look at him*)

LINDNER (*Hat and briefcase in hand*): Uh—hello . . .

(*Ruth crosses mechanically to the bedroom door and opens it and lets it swing open freely and slowly as the lights come up on Walter within, still in his coat, sitting at the far corner of the room. He looks up and out through the room to Lindner*)

RUTH: He's here.

(*A long minute passes and Walter slowly gets up*)

LINDNER (*Coming to the table with efficiency, putting his briefcase on the table and starting to unfold papers and unscrew fountain pens*): Well, I certainly was glad to hear from you people. (*Walter has begun the trek out of the room, slowly and awkwardly, rather like a small boy, passing the back of his sleeve across his mouth from time to time*) Life can really be so much simpler than people let it be most of the time. Well—with whom do I negotiate? You, Mrs. Younger, or your son here? (*Mama sits with her hands folded on her lap and her eyes closed as Walter advances. Travis goes closer to Lindner and looks at the papers curiously*) Just some official papers, sonny.

RUTH: Travis, you go downstairs—

MAMA (*Opening her eyes and looking into Walter's*): No. Travis, you stay right here. And you make him understand what you doing, Walter Lee. You teach him good. Like Willy Harris taught you. You show where our five generations done come to. (*Walter looks from her to the boy, who grins at him innocently*) Go ahead, son—(*She folds her hands and closes her eyes*) Go ahead.

[handwritten margin notes: "Betray yourself in front of your son" and "If you are so proud, show your son"]

WALTER (*At last crosses to Lindner, who is reviewing the contract*): Well, Mr. Lindner. (*Beneatha turns away*) We called you—(*There is a profound, simple groping quality in his speech*)—because, well, me and my family (*He looks around and shifts from one foot to the other*) Well—we are very plain people . . .

LINDNER: Yes—

WALTER: I mean—I have worked as a chauffeur most of my life—and my wife here, she does domestic work in people's kitchens. So does my mother. I mean—we are plain people . . .

LINDNER: Yes, Mr. Younger—

WALTER (*Really like a small boy, looking down at his shoes and then up at the man*): And—uh—well, my father, well, he was a laborer most of his life. . . .

LINDNER (*Absolutely confused*): Uh, yes—yes, I understand. (*He turns back to the contract*)

[handwritten margin note: "Never going to understand them"]

WALTER (*A beat; staring at him*): And my father—(*With sudden intensity*) My father almost *beat a man to death* once because this man called him a bad name or something, you know what I mean?

LINDNER (*Looking up, frozen*): No, no, I'm afraid I don't—

WALTER (*A beat. The tension hangs; then Walter steps back from it*): Yeah. Well—what I mean is that we come from people who had a lot of *pride*. I mean—we are very proud people. And that's my sister over there and she's going to be a doctor—and we are very proud— *[handwritten margin note: "first time proud of sister"]*

LINDNER: Well—I am sure that is very nice, but—

WALTER: What I am telling you is that we called you over here to tell you that we are very proud and that this—(*Signaling to Travis*) Travis, come here. (*Travis crosses and Walter draws him before him facing the man*) This is

my son, and he makes the sixth generation our family in this country.
And we have all thought about your offer—

LINDNER: Well, good . . . good—

WALTER: And we have decided to move into our house because my
father—my father—he earned it for us brick by brick. (*Mama has her
eyes closed and is rocking back and forth as though she were in church, with
her head nodding the Amen yes*) We don't want to make no trouble for
nobody or fight no causes, and we will try to be good neighbors. And
that's *all* we got to say about that. (*He looks the man absolutely in the eyes*)
We don't want your money. (*He turns and walks away*)

LINDNER (*Looking around at all of them*): I take it then—that you have decided to occupy . . .

BENEATHA: That's what the man said.

LINDNER (*To Mama in her reverie*): Then I would like to appeal to you, Mrs.
Younger. You are older and wiser and understand things better I am
sure . . .

MAMA: I am afraid you don't understand. My son said we was going to
move and there ain't nothing left for me to say. (*Briskly*) You know how
these young folks is nowadays, mister. Can't do a thing with 'em! (*As he
opens his mouth, she rises*) Good-bye.

LINDNER (*Folding up his materials*): Well—if you are that final about it . . .
there is nothing left for me to say. (*He finishes, almost ignored by the family,
who are concentrating on Walter Lee. At the door Lindner halts and looks
around*) I sure hope you people know what you're getting into.

(*He shakes his head and exits*)

RUTH (*Looking around and coming to life*): Well, for God's sake—if the
moving men are here—LET'S GET THE HELL OUT OF HERE!

MAMA (*Into action*): Ain't it the truth! Look at all this here mess. Ruth, put
Travis's good jacket on him . . . Walter Lee, fix your tie and tuck your
shirt in, you look like somebody's hoodlum! Lord have mercy, where is
my plant? (*She flies to get it amid the general bustling of the family, who are
deliberately trying to ignore the nobility of the past moment*) You all start on
down . . . Travis child, don't go empty-handed . . . Ruth, where did I put
that box with my skillets in it? I want to be in charge of it myself . . . I'm
going to make us the biggest dinner we ever ate tonight . . . Beneatha,
what's the matter with them stockings? Pull them things up, girl . . .

(*The family starts to file out as two moving men appear and begin to carry out the
heavier pieces of furniture, bumping into the family as they move about*)

BENEATHA: Mama, Asagai asked me to marry him today and go to Africa—

MAMA (*In the middle of her getting-ready activity*): He did? You ain't old
enough to marry nobody—(*Seeing the moving men lifting one of her*

chairs precariously) Darling, that ain't no bale of cotton, please handle it so we can sit in it again! I had that chair twenty-five years . . .

(*The movers sigh with exasperation and go on with their work*)

BENEATHA (*Girlishly and unreasonably trying to pursue the conversation*): To go to Africa, Mama—be a doctor in Africa . . .

MAMA (*Distracted*): Yes, baby—

WALTER: *Africa!* What he want you to go to Africa for?

BENEATHA: To practice there . . .

WALTER: Girl, if you don't get all them silly ideas out your head! You better marry yourself a man with some loot . . .

BENEATHA (*Angrily, precisely as in the first scene of the play*): What have you got to do with who I marry!

WALTER: Plenty. Now I think George Murchison—

BENEATHA: *George Murchison!* I wouldn't marry him if he was Adam and I was Eve!

(*Walter and Beneatha go out yelling at each other vigorously and the anger is loud and real till their voices diminish. Ruth stands at the door and turns to Mama and smiles knowingly*)

MAMA (*Fixing her hat at last*): Yeah—they something all right, my children . . .

RUTH: Yeah—they're something. Let's go, Lena.

MAMA (*Stalling, starting to look around at the house*): Yes—I'm coming. Ruth—

RUTH: Yes?

MAMA (*Quietly, woman to woman*): He finally come into his manhood today, didn't he? Kind of like a rainbow after the rain . . .

RUTH (*Biting her lip lest her own pride explode in front of Mama*): Yes, Lena.

(*Walter's voice calls for them raucously*)

WALTER (*Off stage*): Y'all come on! These people charges by the hour, you know!

MAMA (*Waving Ruth out vaguely*): All right, honey—go on down. I be down directly.

(*Ruth hesitates, then exits. Mama stands, at last alone in the living room, her plant on the table before her as the lights start to come down. She looks around at all the walls and ceilings and suddenly, despite herself, while the children call below, a great heaving thing rises in her and she puts her fist to her mouth to stifle it, takes a final desperate look, pulls her coat about her, pats her hat and goes out. The lights dim down. The door opens and she comes back in, grabs her plant, and goes out for the last time*)

[1959]

AUGUST WILSON [1945–2005]

Fences

Characters

TROY MAXSON
JIM BONO, *Troy's friend*
ROSE, *Troy's wife*
LYONS, *Troy's oldest son by previous marriage*
GABRIEL, *Troy's brother*
CORY, *Troy and Rose's son*
RAYNELL, *Troy's daughter*

Setting: *The setting is the yard which fronts the only entrance to the Maxson household, an ancient two-story brick house set back off a small alley in a big-city neighborhood. The entrance to the house is gained by two or three steps leading to a wooden porch badly in need of paint.*

A relatively recent addition to the house and running its full width, the porch lacks congruence. It is a sturdy porch with a flat roof. One or two chairs of dubious value sit at one end where the kitchen window opens onto the porch. An old-fashioned icebox stands silent guard at the opposite end.

The yard is a small dirt yard, partially fenced, except for the last scene, with a wooden sawhorse, a pile of lumber, and other fence-building equipment set off to the side. Opposite is a tree from which hangs a ball made of rags. A baseball bat leans against the tree. Two oil drums serve as garbage receptacles and sit near the house at right to complete the setting.

The Play: Near the turn of the century, the destitute of Europe sprang on the city with tenacious claws and an honest and solid dream. The city devoured them. They swelled its belly until it burst into a thousand furnaces and sewing machines, a thousand butcher shops and bakers' ovens, a thousand churches and hospitals and funeral parlors and money-lenders. The city grew. It nourished itself and offered each man a partnership limited only by his talent, his guile, and his willingness and capacity for hard work. For the immigrants of Europe, a dream dared and won true.

The descendants of African slaves were offered no such welcome or participation. They came from places called the Carolinas and the Virginias, Georgia, Alabama, Mississippi, and Tennessee. They came strong, eager, searching. The city rejected them and they fled and settled along the riverbanks and under bridges in shallow, ramshackle houses made of sticks and tarpaper. They collected rags and wood. They sold the use of their muscles and their bodies. They cleaned houses and washed clothes, they shined shoes, and in quiet desperation and vengeful pride, they stole, and lived in pursuit of their own dream. That they could breathe free, finally, and stand to meet life with the force of dignity and whatever eloquence the heart could call upon.

By 1957, the hard-won victories of the European immigrants had solidified the industrial might of America. War had been confronted and won with new energies that used loyalty and patriotism as its fuel. Life was rich, full, and flourishing. The Milwaukee Braves won the World Series, and the hot winds of change that would make the sixties a turbulent, racing, dangerous, and provocative decade had not yet begun to blow full.

ACT I

Scene I

(*It is 1957. Troy and Bono enter the yard, engaged in conversation. Troy is fifty-three years old, a large man with thick, heavy hands; it is this largeness that he strives to fill out and make an accommodation with. Together with his blackness, his largeness informs his sensibilities and the choices he has made in his life.*)

(*Of the two men, Bono is obviously the follower. His commitment to their friendship of thirty-odd years is rooted in his admiration of Troy's honesty, capacity for hard work, and his strength, which Bono seeks to emulate.*)

(*It is Friday night, payday, and the one night of the week the two men engage in a ritual of talk and drink. Troy is usually the most talkative and at times he can be crude and almost vulgar, though he is capable of rising to profound heights of expression. The men carry lunch buckets and wear or carry burlap aprons and are dressed in clothes suitable to their jobs as garbage collectors.*)

BONO: Troy, you ought to stop that lying!

TROY: I ain't lying! The nigger had a watermelon this big.

(*He indicates with his hands.*)

Talking about . . . "What watermelon, Mr. Rand?" I liked to fell out! "What watermelon, Mr. Rand?" . . . And it sitting there big as life.

BONO: What did Mr. Rand say?

TROY: Ain't said nothing. Figure if the nigger too dumb to know he carrying a watermelon, he wasn't gonna get much sense out of him. Trying to hide that great big old watermelon under his coat. Afraid to let the white man see him carry it home.

BONO: I'm like you . . . I ain't got no time for them kind of people.

TROY: Now what he look like getting mad cause he see the man from the union talking to Mr. Rand?

BONO: He come to me talking about . . . "Maxson gonna get us fired." I told him to get away from me with that. He walked away from me calling you a troublemaker. What Mr. Rand say?

TROY: Ain't said nothing. He told me to go down the Commissioner's office next Friday. They called me down there to see them.

BONO: Well, as long as you got your complaint filed, they can't fire you. That's what one of them white fellows tell me.

TROY: I ain't worried about them firing me. They gonna fire me cause I asked a question? That's all I did. I went to Mr. Rand and asked him, "Why? Why you got the white mens driving and the colored lifting?" Told him, "what's the matter, don't I count? You think only white fellows got sense enough to drive a truck. That ain't no paper job! Hell, anybody can drive a truck. How come you got all whites driving and the colored lifting?" He told me "take it to the union." Well, hell, that's what I done! Now they wanna come up with this pack of lies.

BONO: I told Brownie if the man come and ask him any questions . . . just tell the truth! It ain't nothing but something they done trumped up on you cause you filed a complaint on them.

TROY: Brownie don't understand nothing. All I want them to do is change the job description. Give everybody a chance to drive the truck. Brownie can't see that. He ain't got that much sense.

BONO: How you figure he be making out with that gal be up at Taylors' all the time . . . that Alberta gal?

TROY: Same as you and me. Getting just as much as we is. Which is to say nothing.

BONO: It is, huh? I figure you doing a little better than me . . . and I ain't saying what I'm doing.

TROY: Aw, nigger, look here . . . I know you. If you had got anywhere near that gal, twenty minutes later you be looking to tell somebody. And the first one you gonna tell . . . that you gonna want to brag to . . . is gonna be me.

BONO: I ain't saying that. I see where you be eyeing her.

TROY: I eye all the women. I don't miss nothing. Don't never let nobody tell you Troy Maxson don't eye the women.

BONO: You been doing more than eyeing her. You done bought her a drink or two.

TROY: Hell yeah, I bought her a drink! What that mean? I bought you one, too. What that mean cause I buy her a drink? I'm just being polite.

BONO: It's all right to buy her one drink. That's what you call being polite. But when you wanna be buying two or three . . . that's what you call eyeing her.

TROY: Look here, as long as you known me . . . you ever known me to chase after women?

BONO: Hell yeah! Long as I done known you. You forgetting I knew you when.

TROY: Naw, I'm talking about since I been married to Rose?

BONO: Oh, not since you been married to Rose. Now, that's the truth, there. I can say that.

TROY: All right then! Case closed.

BONO: I see you be walking up around Alberta's house. You supposed to be at Taylors' and you be walking up around there.

TROY: What you watching where I'm walking for? I ain't watching after you.

BONO: I seen you walking around there more than once.

TROY: Hell, you liable to see me walking anywhere! That don't mean nothing cause you see me walking around there.

BONO: Where she come from anyway? She just kinda showed up one day.

TROY: Tallahassee. You can look at her and tell she one of them Florida gals. They got some big healthy women down there. Grow them right up out the ground. Got a little bit of Indian in her. Most of them niggers down in Florida got some Indian in them.

BONO: I don't know about that Indian part. But she damn sure big and healthy. Woman wear some big stockings. Got them great big old legs and hips as wide as the Mississippi River.

TROY: Legs don't mean nothing. You don't do nothing but push them out of the way. But them hips cushion the ride!

BONO: Troy, you ain't got no sense.

TROY: It's the truth! Like you riding on Goodyears!

(*Rose enters from the house. She is ten years younger than Troy, her devotion to him stems from her recognition of the possibilities of her life without him: a succession of abusive men and their babies, a life of partying and running the streets, the Church, or aloneness with its attendant pain and frustration. She recognizes Troy's spirit as a fine and illuminating one and she either ignores or forgives his faults, only some of which she recognizes. Though she doesn't drink, her presence is an integral part of the Friday night rituals. She alternates between the porch and the kitchen, where supper preparations are under way.*)

ROSE: What you all out here getting into?

TROY: What you worried about what we getting into for? This is men talk, woman.

ROSE: What I care what you all talking about? Bono, you gonna stay for supper?

BONO: No, I thank you, Rose. But Lucille say she cooking up a pot of pigfeet.

TROY: Pigfeet! Hell, I'm going home with you! Might even stay the night if you got some pigfeet. You got something in there to top them pigfeet, Rose?

ROSE: I'm cooking up some chicken. I got some chicken and collard greens.

TROY: Well, go on back in the house and let me and Bono finish what we was talking about. This is men talk. I got some talk for you later. You know what kind of talk I mean. You go on and powder it up.

ROSE: Troy Maxson, don't you start that now!

TROY (*puts his arm around her*): Aw, woman . . . come here. Look here, Bono . . . when I met this woman . . . I got out that place, say, "Hitch up my pony, saddle up my mare . . . there's a woman out there for me somewhere. I looked here. Looked there. Saw Rose and latched on to her." I latched on to her and told her—I'm gonna tell you the truth—I told her, "Baby, I don't wanna marry, I just wanna be your man." Rose told me . . . tell him what you told me, Rose.

ROSE: I told him if he wasn't the marrying kind, then move out the way so the marrying kind could find me.

TROY: That's what she told me. "Nigger, you in my way. You blocking the view! Move out the way so I can find me a husband." I thought it over two or three days. Come back—

ROSE: Ain't no two or three days nothing. You was back the same night.

TROY: Come back, told her . . . "Okay, baby . . . but I'm gonna buy me a banty rooster and put him out there in the backyard . . . and when he see a stranger come, he'll flap his wings and crow . . ." Look here, Bono, I could watch the front door by myself . . . it was that back door I was worried about.

ROSE: Troy, you ought not talk like that. Troy ain't doing nothing but telling a lie.

TROY: Only thing is . . . when we first got married . . . forget the rooster . . . we ain't had no yard!

BONO: I hear you tell it. Me and Lucille was staying down there on Logan Street. Had two rooms with the outhouse in the back. I ain't mind the outhouse none. But when that goddamn wind blow through there in the winter . . . that's what I'm talking about! To this day I wonder why in the hell I ever stayed down there for six long years. But see, I didn't know I could do no better. I thought only white folks had inside toilets and things.

ROSE: There's a lot of people don't know they can do no better than they doing now. That's just something you got to learn. A lot of folks still shop at Bella's.

TROY: Ain't nothing wrong with shopping at Bella's. She got fresh food.

ROSE: I ain't said nothing about if she got fresh food. I'm talking about what she charge. She charge ten cents more than the A&P.

TROY: The A&P ain't never done nothing for me. I spends my money where I'm treated right. I go down to Bella, say, "I need a loaf of bread,

I'll pay you Friday." She give it to me. What sense that make when I got money to go and spend it somewhere else and ignore the person who done right by me? That ain't in the Bible.

ROSE: We ain't talking about what's in the Bible. What sense it make to shop there when she overcharge?

TROY: You shop where you want to. I'll do my shopping where the people been good to me.

ROSE: Well, I don't think it's right for her to overcharge. That's all I was saying.

BONO: Look here . . . I got to get on. Lucille going be raising all kind of hell.

TROY: Where you going, nigger? We ain't finished this pint. Come here, finish this pint.

BONO: Well, hell, I am . . . if you ever turn the bottle loose.

TROY (hands him the bottle): The only thing I say about the A&P is I'm glad Cory got that job down there. Help him take care of his school clothes and things. Gabe done moved out and things getting tight around here. He got that job. . . . He can start to look out for himself.

ROSE: Cory done went and got recruited by a college football team.

TROY: I told that boy about that football stuff. The white man ain't gonna let him get nowhere with that football. I told him when he first come to me with it. Now you come telling me he done went and got more tied up in it. He ought to go and get recruited in how to fix cars or something where he can make a living.

ROSE: He ain't talking about making no living playing football. It's just something the boys in school do. They gonna send a recruiter by to talk to you. He'll tell you he ain't talking about making no living playing football. It's a honor to be recruited.

TROY: It ain't gonna get him nowhere. Bono'll tell you that.

BONO: If he be like you in the sports . . . he's gonna be all right. Ain't but two men ever played baseball as good as you. That's Babe Ruth and Josh Gibson.° Them's the only two men ever hit more home runs than you.

TROY: What it ever get me? Ain't got a pot to piss in or a window to throw it out of.

ROSE: Times have changed since you was playing baseball, Troy. That was before the war. Times have changed a lot since then.

TROY: How in hell they done changed?

ROSE: They got lots of colored boys playing ball now. Baseball and football.

BONO: You right about that, Rose. Times have changed, Troy. You just come along too early.

Josh Gibson: (1911–1947), notable 1930s baseball player, considered the Babe Ruth of the Negro leagues.

TROY: There ought not never have been no time called too early! Now you take that fellow . . . what's that fellow they had playing right field for the Yankees back then? You know who I'm talking about, Bono. Used to play right field for the Yankees.

ROSE: Selkirk?

TROY: Selkirk! That's it! Man batting .269, understand? .269. What kind of sense that make? I was hitting .432 with thirty-seven home runs! Man batting .269 and playing right field for the Yankees! I saw Josh Gibson's daughter yesterday. She walking around with raggedy shoes on her feet. Now I bet you Selkirk's daughter ain't walking around with raggedy shoes on her feet! I bet you that!

ROSE: They got a lot of colored baseball players now. Jackie Robinson was the first. Folks had to wait for Jackie Robinson.

TROY: I done seen a hundred niggers play baseball better than Jackie Robinson. Hell, I know some teams Jackie Robinson couldn't even make! What you talking about Jackie Robinson. Jackie Robinson wasn't nobody. I'm talking about if you could play ball then they ought to have let you play. Don't care what color you were. Come telling me I come along too early. If you could play . . . then they ought to have let you play.

(Troy takes a long drink from the bottle.)

ROSE: You gonna drink yourself to death. You don't need to be drinking like that.

TROY: Death ain't nothing. I done seen him. Done wrassled with him. You can't tell me nothing about death. Death ain't nothing but a fastball on the outside corner. And you know what I'll do to that! Lookee here, Bono . . . am I lying? You get one of them fastballs, about waist high, over the outside corner of the plate where you can get the meat of the bat on it . . . and good god! You can kiss it goodbye. Now, am I lying?

BONO: Naw, you telling the truth there. I seen you do it.

TROY: If I'm lying . . . that 450 feet worth of lying!

(Pause.)

That's all death is to me. A fastball on the outside corner.

ROSE: I don't know why you want to get on talking about death.

TROY: Ain't nothing wrong with talking about death. That's part of life. Everybody gonna die. You gonna die, I'm gonna die. Bono's gonna die. Hell, we all gonna die.

ROSE: But you ain't got to talk about it. I don't like to talk about it.

TROY: You the one brought it up. Me and Bono was talking about baseball . . . you tell me I'm gonna drink myself to death. Ain't that right, Bono? You know I don't drink this but one night out of the week. That's

Friday night. I'm gonna drink just enough to where I can handle it. Then I cuts it loose. I leave it alone. So don't you worry about me drinking myself to death. 'Cause I ain't worried about Death. I done seen him. I done wrestled with him.

Look here, Bono . . . I looked up one day and Death was marching straight at me. Like Soldiers on Parade! The Army of Death was marching straight at me. The middle of July, 1941. It got real cold just like it be winter. It seem like Death himself reached out and touched me on the shoulder. He touch me just like I touch you. I got cold as ice and Death standing there grinning at me.

ROSE: Troy, why don't you hush that talk.

TROY: I say . . . What you want, Mr. Death? You be wanting me? You done brought your army to be getting me? I looked him dead in the eye. I wasn't fearing nothing. I was ready to tangle. Just like I'm ready to tangle now. The Bible say be ever vigilant. That's why I don't get but so drunk. I got to keep watch.

ROSE: Troy was right down there in Mercy Hospital. You remember he had pneumonia? Laying there with a fever talking plumb out of his head.

TROY: Death standing there staring at me . . . carrying that sickle in his hand. Finally he say, "You want bound over for another year?" See, just like that . . . "You want bound over for another year?" I told him, "Bound over hell! Let's settle this now!"

It seem like he kinda fell back when I said that, and all the cold went out of me. I reached down and grabbed that sickle and threw it just as far as I could throw it . . . and me and him commenced to wrestling.

We wrestled for three days and three nights. I can't say where I found the strength from. Every time it seemed like he was gonna get the best of me, I'd reach way down deep inside myself and find the strength to do him one better.

ROSE: Every time Troy tell that story he find different ways to tell it. Different things to make up about it.

TROY: I ain't making up nothing. I'm telling you the facts of what happened. I wrestled with Death for three days and three nights and I'm standing here to tell you about it.

(*Pause.*)

All right. At the end of the third night we done weakened each other to where we can't hardly move. Death stood up, throwed on his robe . . . had him a white robe with a hood on it. He throwed on that robe and went off to look for his sickle. Say, "I'll be back." Just like that. "I'll be back." I told him, say, "Yeah, but . . . you gonna have to find me!" I wasn't no fool. I wasn't going looking for him. Death ain't nothing to play with. And I know he's gonna get me. I know I got to join his army . . . his camp followers. But as long as I keep my strength and see him coming . . . as long as I keep up my vigilance . . . he's gonna have to fight to get me. I ain't going easy.

BONO: Well, look here, since you got to keep up your vigilance . . . let me have the bottle.

TROY: Aw hell, I shouldn't have told you that part. I should have left out that part.

ROSE: Troy be talking that stuff and half the time don't even know what he be talking about.

TROY: Bono know me better than that.

BONO: That's right. I know you. I know you got some Uncle Remus° in your blood. You got more stories than the devil got sinners.

TROY: Aw hell, I done seen him too! Done talked with the devil.

ROSE: Troy, don't nobody wanna be hearing all that stuff.

(Lyons enters the yard from the street. Thirty-four years old, Troy's son by a previous marriage, he sports a neatly trimmed goatee, sport coat, white shirt, tieless and buttoned at the collar. Though he fancies himself a musician, he is more caught up in the rituals and "idea" of being a musician than in the actual practice of the music. He has come to borrow money from Troy, and while he knows he will be successful, he is uncertain as to what extent his lifestyle will be held up to scrutiny and ridicule.)

LYONS: Hey, Pop.

TROY: What you come "Hey, Popping" me for?

LYONS: How you doing, Rose?

(He kisses her.)

Mr. Bono. How you doing?

BONO: Hey, Lyons . . . how you been?

TROY: He must have been doing all right. I ain't seen him around here last week.

ROSE: Troy, leave your boy alone. He come by to see you and you wanna start all that nonsense.

TROY: I ain't bothering Lyons.

(Offers him the bottle.)

Here . . . get you a drink. We got an understanding. I know why he come by to see me and he know I know.

LYONS: Come on, Pop . . . I just stopped by to say hi . . . see how you was doing.

TROY: You ain't stopped by yesterday.

Uncle Remus: Fictional black narrator in the collection of black folktales adapted by Joel Chandler Harris.

Rose: You gonna stay for supper, Lyons? I got some chicken cooking in the oven.

Lyons: No, Rose . . . thanks. I was just in the neighborhood and thought I'd stop by for a minute.

Troy: You was in the neighborhood all right, nigger. You telling the truth there. You was in the neighborhood cause it's my payday.

Lyons: Well, hell, since you mentioned it . . . let me have ten dollars.

Troy: I'll be damned! I'll die and go to hell and play blackjack with the devil before I give you ten dollars.

Bono: That's what I wanna know about . . . that devil you done seen.

Lyons: What . . . Pop done seen the devil? You too much, Pops.

Troy: Yeah, I done seen him. Talked to him too!

Rose: You ain't seen no devil. I done told you that man ain't had nothing to do with the devil. Anything you can't understand, you want to call it the devil.

Troy: Look here, Bono . . . I went down to see Hertzberger about some furniture. Got three rooms for two-ninety-eight. That what it say on the radio. "Three rooms . . . two-ninety-eight." Even made up a little song about it. Go down there . . . man tell me I can't get no credit. I'm working every day and can't get no credit. What to do? I got an empty house with some raggedy furniture in it. Cory ain't got no bed. He's sleeping on a pile of rags on the floor. Working every day and can't get no credit. Come back here—Rose'll tell you—madder than hell. Sit down . . . try to figure what I'm gonna do. Come a knock on the door. Ain't been living here but three days. Who know I'm here? Open the door . . . devil standing there bigger than life. White fellow . . . got on good clothes and everything. Standing there with a clipboard in his hand. I ain't had to say nothing. First words come out of his mouth was . . . "I understand you need some furniture and can't get no credit." I liked to fell over. He say, "I'll give you all the credit you want, but you got to pay the interest on it." I told him, "Give me three rooms worth and charge whatever you want." Next day a truck pulled up here and two men unloaded them three rooms. Man what drove the truck give me a book. Say send ten dollars, first of every month to the address in the book and everything will be all right. Say if I miss a payment the devil was coming back and it'll be hell to pay. That was fifteen years ago. To this day . . . the first of the month I send my ten dollars, Rose'll tell you.

Rose: Troy lying.

Troy: I ain't never seen that man since. Now you tell me who else that could have been but the devil? I ain't sold my soul or nothing like that, you understand. Naw, I wouldn't have truck with the devil about nothing like that. I got my furniture and pays my ten dollars the first of the month just like clockwork.

BONO: How long you say you been paying this ten dollars a month?

TROY: Fifteen years!

BONO: Hell, ain't you finished paying for it yet? How much the man done charged you?

TROY: Ah hell, I done paid for it. I done paid for it ten times over! The fact is I'm scared to stop paying it.

ROSE: Troy lying. We got that furniture from Mr. Glickman. He ain't paying no ten dollars a month to nobody.

TROY: Aw hell, woman. Bono know I ain't that big a fool.

LYONS: I was just getting ready to say . . . I know where there's a bridge for sale.

TROY: Look here, I'll tell you this . . . it don't matter to me if he was the devil. It don't matter if the devil give credit. Somebody has got to give it.

ROSE: It ought to matter. You going around talking about having truck with the devil . . . God's the one you gonna have to answer to. He's the one gonna be at the Judgment.

LYONS: Yeah, well, look here, Pop . . . let me have that ten dollars. I'll give it back to you. Bonnie got a job working at the hospital.

TROY: What I tell you, Bono? The only time I see this nigger is when he wants something. That's the only time I see him.

LYONS: Come on, Pop, Mr. Bono don't want to hear all that. Let me have the ten dollars. I told you Bonnie working.

TROY: What that mean to me? "Bonnie working." I don't care if she working. Go ask her for the ten dollars if she working. Talking about "Bonnie working." Why ain't you working?

LYONS: Aw, Pop, you know I can't find no decent job. Where am I gonna get a job at? You know I can't get no job.

TROY: I told you I know some people down there. I can get you on the rubbish if you want to work. I told you that the last time you came by here asking me for something.

LYONS: Naw, Pop . . . thanks. That ain't for me. I don't wanna be carrying nobody's rubbish. I don't wanna be punching nobody's time clock.

TROY: What's the matter, you too good to carry people's rubbish? Where you think that ten dollars you talking about come from? I'm just supposed to haul people's rubbish and give my money to you cause you too lazy to work. You too lazy to work and wanna know why you ain't got what I got.

ROSE: What hospital Bonnie working at? Mercy?

LYONS: She's down at Passavant working in the laundry.

TROY: I ain't got nothing as it is. I give you that ten dollars and I got to eat beans the rest of the week. Naw . . . you ain't getting no ten dollars here.

LYONS: You ain't got to be eating no beans. I don't know why you wanna say that.

TROY: I ain't got no extra money. Gabe done moved over to Miss Pearl's paying her the rent and things done got tight around here. I can't afford to be giving you every payday.

LYONS: I ain't asked you to give me nothing. I asked you to loan me ten dollars. I know you got ten dollars.

TROY: Yeah, I got it. You know why I got it? Cause I don't throw my money away out there in the streets. You living the fast life . . . wanna be a musician . . . running around in them clubs and things . . . then, you learn to take care of yourself. You ain't gonna find me going and asking nobody for nothing. I done spent too many years without.

LYONS: You and me is two different people, Pop.

TROY: I done learned my mistake and learned to do what's right by it. You still trying to get something for nothing. Life don't owe you nothing. You owe it to yourself. Ask Bono. He'll tell you I'm right.

LYONS: You got your way of dealing with the world . . . I got mine. The only thing that matters to me is the music.

TROY: Yeah, I can see that! It don't matter how you gonna eat . . . where your next dollar is coming from. You telling the truth there.

LYONS: I know I got to eat. But I got to live too. I need something that gonna help me to get out of the bed in the morning. Make me feel like I belong in the world. I don't bother nobody. I just stay with my music cause that's the only way I can find to live in the world. Otherwise there ain't no telling what I might do. Now I don't come criticizing you and how you live. I just come by to ask you for ten dollars. I don't wanna hear all that about how I live.

TROY: Boy, your mamma did a hell of a job raising you.

LYONS: You can't change me, Pop. I'm thirty-four years old. If you wanted to change me, you should have been there when I was growing up. I come by to see you . . . ask for ten dollars and you want to talk about how I was raised. You don't know nothing about how I was raised.

ROSE: Let the boy have ten dollars, Troy.

TROY (to Lyons): What the hell you looking at me for? I ain't got no ten dollars. You know what I do with my money.

(To Rose.)

Give him ten dollars if you want him to have it.

ROSE: I will. Just as soon as you turn it loose.

TROY (handing Rose the money): There it is. Seventy-six dollars and forty-two cents. You see this, Bono? Now, I ain't gonna get but six of that back.

ROSE: You ought to stop telling that lie. Here, Lyons. (*She hands him the money.*)

LYONS: Thanks, Rose. Look . . . I got to run . . . I'll see you later.

TROY: Wait a minute. You gonna say, "thanks, Rose" and ain't gonna look to see where she got that ten dollars from? See how they do me, Bono?

LYONS: I know she got it from you, Pop. Thanks. I'll give it back to you.

TROY: There he go telling another lie. Time I see that ten dollars . . . he'll be owing me thirty more.

LYONS: See you, Mr. Bono.

BONO: Take care, Lyons!

LYONS: Thanks, Pop. I'll see you again.

(*Lyons exits the yard.*)

TROY: I don't know why he don't go and get him a decent job and take care of that woman he got.

BONO: He'll be all right, Troy. The boy is still young.

TROY: The *boy* is thirty-four years old.

ROSE: Let's not get off into all that.

BONO: Look here . . . I got to be going. I got to be getting on. Lucille gonna be waiting.

TROY (*puts his arm around Rose*): See this woman, Bono? I love this woman. I love this woman so much it hurts. I love her so much . . . I done run out of ways of loving her. So I got to go back to basics. Don't you come by my house Monday morning talking about time to go to work . . . 'cause I'm still gonna be stroking!

ROSE: Troy! Stop it now!

BONO: I ain't paying him no mind, Rose. That ain't nothing but gin-talk. Go on, Troy. I'll see you Monday.

TROY: Don't you come by my house, nigger! I done told you what I'm gonna be doing.

(*The lights go down to black.*)

Scene II

(*The lights come up on Rose hanging up clothes. She hums and sings softly to herself. It is the following morning.*)

ROSE (*sings*): Jesus, be a fence all around me every day
    Jesus, I want you to protect me as I travel on my way.
    Jesus, be a fence all around me every day.

(*Troy enters from the house.*)

Jesus, I want you to protect me
As I travel on my way.
(*To Troy.*) 'Morning. You ready for breakfast? I can fix it soon as I finish hanging up these clothes.

TROY: I got the coffee on. That'll be all right. I'll just drink some of that this morning.

ROSE: That 651 hit yesterday. That's the second time this month. Miss Pearl hit for a dollar . . . seem like those that need the least always get lucky. Poor folks can't get nothing.

TROY: Them numbers don't know nobody. I don't know why you fool with them. You and Lyons both.

ROSE: It's something to do.

TROY: You ain't doing nothing but throwing your money away.

ROSE: Troy, you know I don't play foolishly. I just play a nickel here and a nickel there.

TROY: That's two nickels you done thrown away.

ROSE: Now I hit sometimes . . . that makes up for it. It always comes in handy when I do hit. I don't hear you complaining then.

TROY: I ain't complaining now. I just say it's foolish. Trying to guess out of six hundred ways which way the number gonna come. If I had all the money niggers, these Negroes, throw away on numbers for one week—just one week—I'd be a rich man.

ROSE: Well, you wishing and calling it foolish ain't gonna stop folks from playing numbers. That's one thing for sure. Besides . . . some good things come from playing numbers. Look where Pope done bought him that restaurant off of numbers.

TROY: I can't stand niggers like that. Man ain't had two dimes to rub together. He walking around with his shoes all run over bumming money for cigarettes. All right. Got lucky there and hit the numbers . . .

ROSE: Troy, I know all about it.

TROY: Had good sense, I'll say that for him. He ain't throwed his money away. I seen niggers hit the numbers and go through two thousand dollars in four days. Man bought him that restaurant down there . . . fixed it up real nice . . . and then didn't want nobody to come in it! A Negro go in there and can't get no kind of service. I seen a white fellow come in there and order a bowl of stew. Pope picked all the meat out the pot for him. Man ain't had nothing but a bowl of meat! Negro come behind him and ain't got nothing but the potatoes and carrots. Talking about what numbers do for people, you picked a wrong example. Ain't done nothing but make a worser fool out of him than he was before.

ROSE: Troy, you ought to stop worrying about what happened at work yesterday.

TROY: I ain't worried. Just told me to be down there at the Commissioner's office on Friday. Everybody think they gonna fire me. I ain't worried about them firing me. You ain't got to worry about that.

(*Pause.*)

Where's Cory? Cory in the house? (*Calls.*) Cory?

ROSE: He gone out.

TROY: Out, huh? He gone out 'cause he know I want him to help me with
this fence. I know how he is. That boy scared of work.

(*Gabriel enters. He comes halfway down the alley and, hearing Troy's voice, stops.*)

TROY (*continues*): He ain't done a lick of work in his life.

ROSE: He had to go to football practice. Coach wanted them to get in a
little extra practice before the season start.

TROY: I got his practice . . . running out of here before he get his chores
done.

ROSE: Troy, what is wrong with you this morning? Don't nothing set right
with you. Go on back in there and go to bed . . . get up on the other side.

TROY: Why something got to be wrong with me? I ain't said nothing
wrong with me.

ROSE: You got something to say about everything. First it's the numbers . . . then it's the way the man runs his restaurant . . . then you
done got on Cory. What's it gonna be next? Take a look up there and see
if the weather suits you . . . or is it gonna be how you gonna put up the
fence with the clothes hanging in the yard.

TROY: You hit the nail on the head then.

ROSE: I know you like I know the back of my hand. Go on in there and
get you some coffee . . . see if that straighten you up. 'Cause you ain't
right this morning.

(*Troy starts into the house and sees Gabriel. Gabriel starts singing. Troy's
brother, he is seven years younger than Troy. Injured in World War II, he has a
metal plate in his head. He carries an old trumpet tied around his waist and
believes with every fiber of his being that he is the Archangel Gabriel. He carries
a chipped basket with an assortment of discarded fruits and vegetables he has
picked up in the strip district and which he attempts to sell.*)

GABRIEL (*singing*): Yes, ma'am, I got plums
You ask me how I sell them
Oh ten cents apiece
Three for a quarter
Come and buy now
'Cause I'm here today
And tomorrow I'll be gone

(*Gabriel enters.*)

Hey, Rose!

ROSE: How you doing, Gabe?

GABRIEL: There's Troy . . . Hey, Troy!

TROY: Hey, Gabe.

(*Exit into kitchen.*)

ROSE (*to Gabriel*): What you got there?

GABRIEL: You know what I got, Rose. I got fruits and vegetables.

ROSE (*looking in basket*): Where's all these plums you talking about?

GABRIEL: I ain't got no plums today, Rose. I was just singing that. Have some tomorrow. Put me in a big order for plums. Have enough plums tomorrow for St. Peter and everybody.

(*Troy reenters from kitchen, crosses to steps.*)
(*To Rose.*)

Troy's mad at me.

TROY: I ain't mad at you. What I got to be mad at you about? You ain't done nothing to me.

GABRIEL: I just moved over to Miss Pearl's to keep out from in your way. I ain't mean no harm by it.

TROY: Who said anything about that? I ain't said anything about that.

GABRIEL: You ain't mad at me, is you?

TROY: Naw . . . I ain't mad at you, Gabe. If I was mad at you I'd tell you about it.

GABRIEL: Got me two rooms. In the basement. Got my own door too. Wanna see my key?

(*He holds up a key.*)

That's my own key! Ain't nobody else got a key like that. That's my key! My two rooms!

TROY: Well, that's good, Gabe. You got your own key . . . that's good.

ROSE: You hungry, Gabe? I was just fixing to cook Troy his breakfast.

GABRIEL: I'll take some biscuits. You got some biscuits? Did you know when I was in heaven . . . every morning me and St. Peter would sit down by the gate and eat some big fat biscuits? Oh, yeah! We had us a good time. We'd sit there and eat us them biscuits and then St. Peter would go off to sleep and tell me to wake him up when it's time to open the gates for the judgment.

ROSE: Well, come on . . . I'll make up a batch of biscuits.

(*Rose exits into the house.*)

GABRIEL: Troy . . . St. Peter got your name in the book. I seen it. It say . . . Troy Maxson. I say . . . I know him! He got the same name like what I got. That's my brother!

TROY: How many times you gonna tell me that, Gabe?

GABRIEL: Ain't got my name in the book. Don't have to have my name. I done died and went to heaven. He got your name though. One morning St. Peter was looking at his book . . . marking it up for the judgment . . . and he let me see your name. Got it in there under M. Got Rose's name . . . I ain't seen it like I seen yours . . . but I know it's in there. He got a great big book. Got everybody's name what was ever been born. That's what he told me. But I seen your name. Seen it with my own eyes.

TROY: Go on in the house there. Rose going to fix you something to eat.

GABRIEL: Oh, I ain't hungry. I done had breakfast with Aunt Jemimah. She come by and cooked me up a whole mess of flapjacks. Remember how we used to eat them flapjacks?

TROY: Go on in the house and get you something to eat now.

GABRIEL: I got to go sell my plums. I done sold some tomatoes. Got me two quarters. Wanna see?

(*He shows Troy his quarters.*)

I'm gonna save them and buy me a new horn so St. Peter can hear me when it's time to open the gates.

(*Gabriel stops suddenly. Listens.*)

Hear that? That's the hellhounds. I got to chase them out of here. Go on get out of here! Get out!

(*Gabriel exits singing.*)

Better get ready for the judgment
Better get ready for the judgment
My Lord is coming down

(*Rose enters from the house.*)

TROY: He gone off somewhere.

GABRIEL (*offstage*): Better get ready for the judgment
Better get ready for the judgment morning
Better get ready for the judgment
My God is coming down

ROSE: He ain't eating right. Miss Pearl say she can't get him to eat nothing.

TROY: What you want me to do about it, Rose? I done did everything I can for the man. I can't make him get well. Man got half his head blown away . . . what you expect?

ROSE: Seem like something ought to be done to help him.

TROY: Man don't bother nobody. He just mixed up from that metal plate he got in his head. Ain't no sense for him to go back into the hospital.

ROSE: Least he be eating right. They can help him take care of himself.

TROY: Don't nobody wanna be locked up, Rose. What you wanna lock him up for? Man go over there and fight the war . . . messin' around with them Japs, get half his head blown off . . . and they give him a lousy three thousand dollars. And I had to swoop down on that.

ROSE: Is you fixing to go into that again?

TROY: That's the only way I got a roof over my head . . . cause of that metal plate.

ROSE: Ain't no sense you blaming yourself for nothing. Gabe wasn't in no condition to manage that money. You done what was right by him. Can't nobody say you ain't done what was right by him. Look how long you took care of him . . . till he wanted to have his own place and moved over there with Miss Pearl.

TROY: That ain't what I'm saying, woman! I'm just stating the facts. If my brother didn't have that metal plate in his head . . . I wouldn't have a pot to piss in or a window to throw it out of. And I'm fifty-three years old. Now see if you can understand that!

(*Troy gets up from the porch and starts to exit the yard.*)

ROSE: Where you going off to? You been running out of here every Saturday for weeks. I thought you was gonna work on this fence?

TROY: I'm gonna walk down to Taylors'. Listen to the ball game. I'll be back in a bit. I'll work on it when I get back.

(*He exits the yard. The lights go to black.*)

Scene III

(*The lights come up on the yard. It is four hours later. Rose is taking down the clothes from the line. Cory enters carrying his football equipment.*)

ROSE: Your daddy like to had a fit with you running out of here this morning without doing your chores.

CORY: I told you I had to go to practice.

ROSE: He say you were supposed to help him with this fence.

CORY: He been saying that the last four or five Saturdays, and then he don't never do nothing but go down to Taylors'. Did you tell him about the recruiter?

ROSE: Yeah, I told him.

CORY: What he say?

ROSE: He ain't said nothing too much. You get in there and get started on your chores before he gets back. Go on and scrub down them steps before he gets back here hollering and carrying on.

CORY: I'm hungry. What you got to eat, Mama?

ROSE: Go on and get started on your chores. I got some meat loaf in there. Go on and make you a sandwich . . . and don't leave no mess in there.

(*Cory exits into the house. Rose continues to take down the clothes. Troy enters the yard and sneaks up and grabs her from behind.*)

Troy! Go on, now. You liked to scared me to death. What was the score of the game? Lucille had me on the phone and I couldn't keep up with it.

TROY: What I care about the game? Come here, woman. (*He tries to kiss her.*)

ROSE: I thought you went down Taylors' to listen to the game. Go on, Troy! You supposed to be putting up this fence.

TROY (*attempting to kiss her again*): I'll put it up when I finish with what is at hand.

ROSE: Go on, Troy. I ain't studying you.

TROY (*chasing after her*): I'm studying you . . . fixing to do my homework!

ROSE: Troy, you better leave me alone.

TROY: Where's Cory? That boy brought his butt home yet?

ROSE: He's in the house doing his chores.

TROY (*calling*): Cory! Get your butt out here, boy!

(*Rose exits into the house with the laundry. Troy goes over to the pile of wood, picks up a board, and starts sawing. Cory enters from the house.*)

TROY: You just now coming in here from leaving this morning?

CORY: Yeah, I had to go to football practice.

TROY: Yeah, what?

CORY: Yessir.

TROY: I ain't but two seconds off you noway. The garbage sitting in there overflowing . . . you ain't done none of your chores . . . and you come in here talking about "Yeah."

CORY: I was just getting ready to do my chores now, Pop . . .

TROY: Your first chore is to help me with this fence on Saturday. Everything else come after that. Now get that saw and cut them boards.

(*Cory takes the saw and begins cutting the boards. Troy continues working. There is a long pause.*)

CORY: Hey, Pop . . . why don't you buy a TV?

TROY: What I want with a TV? What I want one of them for?

CORY: Everybody got one. Earl, Ba Bra . . . Jesse!

TROY: I ain't asked you who had one. I say what I want with one?

CORY: So you can watch it. They got lots of things on TV. Baseball games and everything. We could watch the World Series.

TROY: Yeah . . . and how much this TV cost?

CORY: I don't know. They got them on sale for around two hundred dollars.

TROY: Two hundred dollars, huh?

CORY: That ain't that much, Pop.

TROY: Naw, it's just two hundred dollars. See that roof you got over your head at night? Let me tell you something about that roof. It's been over ten years since that roof was last tarred. See now . . . the snow come this winter and sit up there on that roof like it is . . . and it's gonna seep inside. It's just gonna be a little bit . . . ain't gonna hardly notice it. Then the next thing you know, it's gonna be leaking all over the house. Then the wood rot from all that water and you gonna need a whole new roof. Now, how much you think it cost to get that roof tarred?

CORY: I don't know.

TROY: Two hundred and sixty-four dollars . . . cash money. While you thinking about a TV, I got to be thinking about the roof . . . and whatever else go wrong around here. Now if you had two hundred dollars, what would you do . . . fix the roof or buy a TV?

CORY: I'd buy a TV. Then when the roof started to leak . . . when it needed fixing . . . I'd fix it.

TROY: Where you gonna get the money from? You done spent it for a TV. You gonna sit up and watch the water run all over your brand new TV.

CORY: Aw, Pop. You got money. I know you do.

TROY: Where I got it at, huh?

CORY: You got it in the bank.

TROY: You wanna see my bankbook? You wanna see that seventy-three dollars and twenty-two cents I got sitting up in there.

CORY: You ain't got to pay for it all at one time. You can put a down payment on it and carry it on home with you.

TROY: Not me. I ain't gonna owe nobody nothing if I can help it. Miss a payment and they come and snatch it right out your house. Then what you got? Now, soon as I get two hundred dollars clear, then I'll buy a TV. Right now, as soon as I get two hundred and sixty-four dollars, I'm gonna have this roof tarred.

CORY: Aw . . . Pop!

TROY: You go on and get you two hundred dollars and buy one if ya want it. I got better things to do with my money.

CORY: I can't get no two hundred dollars. I ain't never seen two hundred dollars.

TROY: I'll tell you what . . . you get you a hundred dollars and I'll put the other hundred with it.

CORY: All right, I'm gonna show you.

TROY: You gonna show me how you can cut them boards right now.

(*Cory begins to cut the boards. There is a long pause.*)

CORY: The Pirates won today. That makes five in a row.

TROY: I ain't thinking about the Pirates. Got an all-white team. Got that boy . . . that Puerto Rican boy . . . Clemente. Don't even half-play him. That boy could be something if they give him a chance. Play him one day and sit him on the bench the next.

CORY: He gets a lot of chances to play.

TROY: I'm talking about playing regular. Playing every day so you can get your timing. That's what I'm talking about.

CORY: They got some white guys on the team that don't play every day. You can't play everybody at the same time.

TROY: If they got a white fellow sitting on the bench . . . you can bet your last dollar he can't play! The colored guy got to be twice as good before he get on the team. That's why I don't want you to get all tied up in them sports. Man on the team and what it get him? They got colored on the team and don't use them. Same as not having them. All them teams the same.

CORY: The Braves got Hank Aaron and Wes Covington. Hank Aaron hit two home runs today. That makes forty-three.

TROY: Hank Aaron ain't nobody. That's what you supposed to do. That's how you supposed to play the game. Ain't nothing to it. It's just a matter of timing . . . getting the right follow-through. Hell, I can hit forty-three home runs right now!

CORY: Not off no major-league pitching, you couldn't.

TROY: We had better pitching in the Negro leagues. I hit seven home runs off of Satchel Paige.° You can't get no better than that!

CORY: Sandy Koufax. He's leading the league in strikeouts.

TROY: I ain't thinking of no Sandy Koufax.

CORY: You got Warren Spahn and Lew Burdette. I bet you couldn't hit no home runs off of Warren Spahn.

TROY: I'm through with it now. You go on and cut them boards.

(*Pause.*)

Your mama tell me you done got recruited by a college football team? Is that right?

CORY: Yeah. Coach Zellman say the recruiter gonna be coming by to talk to you. Get you to sign the permission papers.

Satchel Paige: (1906?–1982), renowned black pitcher in the Negro leagues and Major League Baseball.

TROY: I thought you supposed to be working down there at the A&P. Ain't you suppose to be working down there after school?

CORY: Mr. Stawicki say he gonna hold my job for me until after the football season. Say starting next week I can work weekends.

TROY: I thought we had an understanding about this football stuff? You suppose to keep up with your chores and hold that job down at the A&P. Ain't been around here all day on a Saturday. Ain't none of your chores done . . . and now you telling me you done quit your job.

CORY: I'm gonna be working weekends.

TROY: You damn right you are! And ain't no need for nobody coming around here to talk to me about signing nothing.

CORY: Hey, Pop . . . you can't do that. He's coming all the way from North Carolina.

TROY: I don't care where he coming from. The white man ain't gonna let you get nowhere with that football noway. You go on and get your book-learning so you can work yourself up in that A&P or learn how to fix cars or build houses or something, get you a trade. That way you have something can't nobody take away from you. You go on and learn how to put your hands to some good use. Besides hauling people's garbage.

CORY: I get good grades, Pop. That's why the recruiter wants to talk with you. You got to keep up your grades to get recruited. This way I'll be going to college. I'll get a chance . . .

TROY: First you gonna get your butt down there to the A&P and get your job back.

CORY: Mr. Stawicki done already hired somebody else 'cause I told him I was playing football.

TROY: You a bigger fool than I thought . . . to let somebody take away your job so you can play some football. Where you gonna get your money to take out your girlfriend and whatnot? What kind of foolishness is that to let somebody take away your job?

CORY: I'm still gonna be working weekends.

TROY: Naw . . . naw. You getting your butt out of here and finding you another job.

CORY: Come on, Pop! I got to practice. I can't work after school and play football too. The team needs me. That's what Coach Zellman say . . .

TROY: I don't care what nobody else say. I'm the boss . . . you understand? I'm the boss around here. I do the only saying what counts.

CORY: Come on, Pop!

TROY: I asked you . . . did you understand?

CORY: Yeah . . .

TROY: What?!

CORY: Yessir.

TROY: You go on down there to that A&P and see if you can get your job back. If you can't do both . . . then you quit the football team. You've got to take the crookeds with the straights.

CORY: Yessir.

(*Pause.*)

Can I ask you a question?

TROY: What the hell you wanna ask me? Mr. Stawicki the one you got the questions for.

CORY: How come you ain't never liked me?

TROY: Liked you? Who the hell say I got to like you? What law is there say I got to like you? Wanna stand up in my face and ask a damn fool-ass question like that. Talking about liking somebody. Come here, boy, when I talk to you.

(*Cory comes over to where Troy is working. He stands slouched over and Troy shoves him on his shoulder.*)

Straighten up, goddammit! I asked you a question . . . what law is there say I got to like you?

CORY: None.

TROY: Well, all right then! Don't you eat every day?

(*Pause.*)

Answer me when I talk to you! Don't you eat every day?

CORY: Yeah.

TROY: Nigger, as long as you in my house, you put that sir on the end of it when you talk to me!

CORY: Yes . . . sir.

TROY: You eat every day.

CORY: Yessir!

TROY: Got a roof over your head.

CORY: Yessir!

TROY: Got clothes on your back.

CORY: Yessir.

TROY: Why you think that is?

CORY: Cause of you.

TROY: Ah, hell I know it's 'cause of me . . . but why do you think that is?

CORY (*hesitant*): Cause you like me.

TROY: Like you? I go out of here every morning . . . bust my butt . . . putting up with them crackers° every day . . . cause I like you? You about the biggest fool I ever saw.

crackers: Reference to white people, often used to belittle underprivileged whites.

(*Pause.*)

It's my job. It's my responsibility! You understand that? A man got to take care of his family. You live in my house . . . sleep you behind on my bedclothes . . . fill you belly up with my food . . . cause you my son. You my flesh and blood. Not cause I like you! Cause it's my duty to take care of you. I owe a responsibility to you! Let's get this straight right here . . . before it go along any further . . . I ain't got to like you. Mr. Rand don't give me my money come payday cause he likes me. He gives me cause he owe me. I done give you everything I had to give you. I gave you your life! Me and your mama worked that out between us. And liking your black ass wasn't part of the bargain. Don't you try and go through life worrying about if somebody like you or not. You best be making sure they doing right by you. You understand what I'm saying, boy?

CORY: Yessir.

TROY: Then get the hell out of my face, and get on down to that A&P.

(*Rose has been standing behind the screen door for much of the scene. She enters as Cory exits.*)

ROSE: Why don't you let the boy go ahead and play football, Troy? Ain't no harm in that. He's just trying to be like you with the sports.

TROY: I don't want him to be like me! I want him to move as far away from my life as he can get. You the only decent thing that ever happened to me. I wish him that. But I don't wish him a thing else from my life. I decided seventeen years ago that boy wasn't getting involved in no sports. Not after what they did to me in the sports.

ROSE: Troy, why don't you admit you was too old to play in the major leagues? For once . . . why don't you admit that?

TROY: What do you mean too old? Don't come telling me I was too old. I just wasn't the right color. Hell, I'm fifty-three years old and can do better than Selkirk's .269 right now!

ROSE: How's was you gonna play ball when you were over forty? Sometimes I can't get no sense out of you.

TROY: I got good sense, woman. I got sense enough not to let my boy get hurt over playing no sports. You been mothering that boy too much. Worried about if people like him.

ROSE: Everything that boy do . . . he do for you. He wants you to say "Good job, son." That's all.

TROY: Rose, I ain't got time for that. He's alive. He's healthy. He's got to make his own way. I made mine. Ain't nobody gonna hold his hand when he get out there in that world.

ROSE: Times have changed from when you was young, Troy. People change. The world's changing around you and you can't even see it.

TROY (*slow, methodical*): Woman . . . I do the best I can do. I come in here every Friday. I carry a sack of potatoes and a bucket of lard. You all line up at the door with your hands out. I give you the lint from my pockets. I give you my sweat and my blood. I ain't got no tears. I done spent them. We go upstairs in that room at night . . . and I fall down on you and try to blast a hole into forever. I get up Monday morning . . . find my lunch on the table. I go out. Make my way. Find my strength to carry me through to the next Friday.

(*Pause.*)

That's all I got, Rose. That's all I got to give. I can't give nothing else.

(*Troy exits into the house. The lights go down to black.*)

Scene IV

(*It is Friday. Two weeks later. Cory starts out of the house with his football equipment. The phone rings.*)

CORY (*calling*): I got it!

(*He answers the phone and stands in the screen door talking.*)

Hello? Hey, Jesse. Naw . . . I was just getting ready to leave now.
ROSE (*calling*): Cory!
CORY: I told you, man, them spikes is all tore up. You can use them if you want, but they ain't no good. Earl got some spikes.
ROSE (*calling*): Cory!
CORY (*calling to Rose*): Mam? I'm talking to Jesse.

(*Into phone.*)

When she say that? (*Pause.*) Aw, you lying, man. I'm gonna tell her you said that.
ROSE (*calling*): Cory, don't you go nowhere!
CORY: I got to go to the game, Ma!

(*Into the phone.*)

Yeah, hey, look, I'll talk to you later. Yeah, I'll meet you over Earl's house. Later. Bye, Ma.

(*Cory exits the house and starts out the yard.*)

ROSE: Cory, where you going off to? You got that stuff all pulled out and thrown all over your room.
CORY (*in the yard*): I was looking for my spikes. Jesse wanted to borrow my spikes.

ROSE: Get up there and get that cleaned up before your daddy get back in here.

CORY: I got to go to the game! I'll clean it up *when I get back*.

(*Cory exits.*)

ROSE: That's all he need to do is see that room all messed up.

(*Rose exits into the house. Troy and Bono enter the yard. Troy is dressed in clothes other than his work clothes.*)

BONO: He told him the same thing he told you. Take it to the union.

TROY: Brownie ain't got that much sense. Man wasn't thinking about nothing. He wait until I confront them on it . . . then he wanna come crying seniority.

(*Calls.*)

Hey, Rose!

BONO: I wish I could have seen Mr. Rand's face when he told you.

TROY: He couldn't get it out of his mouth! Liked to bit his tongue! When they called me down there to the Commissioner's office . . . he thought they was gonna fire me. Like everybody else.

BONO: I didn't think they was gonna fire you. I thought they was gonna put you on the warning paper.

TROY: Hey, Rose!

(*To Bono.*)

Yeah, Mr. Rand like to bit his tongue.

(*Troy breaks the seal on the bottle, takes a drink, and hands it to Bono.*)

BONO: I see you run right down to Taylors' and told that Alberta gal.

TROY (*calling*): Hey, Rose! (*To Bono.*) I told everybody. Hey, Rose! I went down there to cash my check.

ROSE (*entering from the house*): Hush all that hollering, man! I know you out here. What they say down there at the Commissioner's office?

TROY: You supposed to come when I call you, woman. Bono'll tell you that.

(*To Bono.*)

Don't Lucille come when you call her?

ROSE: Man, hush your mouth. I ain't no dog . . . talk about "come when you call me."

TROY (*puts his arm around Rose*): You hear this Bono? I had me an old dog used to get uppity like that. You say, "C'mere, Blue!" . . . and he just lay

there and look at you. End up getting a stick and chasing him away
trying to make him come.

ROSE: I ain't studying you and your dog. I remember you used to sing
that old song.

TROY (*he sings*): Hear it ring! Hear it ring! I had a dog his name was Blue.

ROSE: Don't nobody wanna hear you sing that old song.

TROY (*sings*): You know Blue was mighty true.

ROSE: Used to have Cory running around here singing that song.

BONO: Hell, I remember that song myself.

TROY (*sings*): You know Blue was a good old dog.
    Blue treed a possum in a hollow log.
    That was my daddy's song. My daddy made up that song.

ROSE: I don't care who made it up. Don't nobody wanna hear you sing it.

TROY (*makes a song like calling a dog*): Come here, woman.

ROSE: You come in here carrying on, I reckon they ain't fired you. What
they say down there at the Commissioner's office?

TROY: Look here, Rose . . . Mr. Rand called me into his office today when
I got back from talking to them people down there . . . it come from up
top . . . he called me in and told me they was making me a driver.

ROSE: Troy, you kidding!

TROY: No I ain't. Ask Bono.

ROSE: Well, that's great, Troy. Now you don't have to hassle them people
no more.

(*Lyons enters from the street.*)

TROY: Aw hell, I wasn't looking to see you today. I thought you was in jail.
Got it all over the front page of the *Courier* about them raiding Sefus'
place . . . where you be hanging out with all them thugs.

LYONS: Hey, Pop . . . that ain't got nothing to do with me. I don't go down
there gambling. I go down there to sit in with the band. I ain't got nothing to do with the gambling part. They got some good music down there.

TROY: They got some rogues . . . is what they got.

LYONS: How you been, Mr. Bono? Hi, Rose.

BONO: I see where you playing down at the Crawford Grill tonight.

ROSE: How come you ain't brought Bonnie like I told you. You should
have brought Bonnie with you, she ain't been over in a month of
Sundays.

LYONS: I was just in the neighborhood . . . thought I'd stop by.

TROY: Here he come . . .

BONO: Your daddy got a promotion on the rubbish. He's gonna be the
first colored driver. Ain't got to do nothing but sit up there and read the
paper like them white fellows.

LYONS: Hey, Pop . . . if you knew how to read you'd be all right.

BONO: Naw . . . naw . . . you mean if the nigger knew how to drive he'd be all right. Been fighting with them people about driving and ain't even got a license. Mr. Rand know you ain't got no driver's license?

TROY: Driving ain't nothing. All you do is point the truck where you want it to go. Driving ain't nothing.

BONO: Do Mr. Rand know you ain't got no driver's license? That's what I'm talking about. I ain't asked if driving was easy. I asked if Mr. Rand know you ain't got no driver's license.

TROY: He ain't got to know. The man ain't got to know my business. Time he find out, I have two or three driver's licenses.

LYONS (going into his pocket): Say, look here, Pop . . .

TROY: I knew it was coming. Didn't I tell you, Bono? I know what kind of "Look here, Pop" that was. The nigger fixing to ask me for some money. It's Friday night. It's my payday. All them rogues down there on the avenue . . . the ones that ain't in jail . . . and Lyons is hopping in his shoes to get down there with them.

LYONS: See, Pop . . . if you give somebody else a chance to talk sometime, you'd see that I was fixing to pay you back your ten dollars like I told you. Here . . . I told you I'd pay you when Bonnie got paid.

TROY: Naw . . . you go ahead and keep that ten dollars. Put it in the bank. The next time you feel like you wanna come by here and ask me for something . . . you go on down there and get that.

LYONS: Here's your ten dollars, Pop. I told you I don't want you to give me nothing. I just wanted to borrow ten dollars.

TROY: Naw . . . you go on and keep that for the next time you want to ask me.

LYONS: Come on, Pop . . . here go your ten dollars.

ROSE: Why don't you go on and let the boy pay you back, Troy?

LYONS: Here you go, Rose. If you don't take it I'm gonna have to hear about it for the next six months.

(He hands her the money.)

ROSE: You can hand yours over here too, Troy.

TROY: You see this, Bono. You see how they do me.

BONO: Yeah, Lucille do me the same way.

(Gabriel is heard singing offstage. He enters.)

GABRIEL: Better get ready for the Judgment! Better get ready for . . . Hey! . . . Hey! . . . There's Troy's boy!

LYONS: How are you doing, Uncle Gabe?

GABRIEL: Lyons . . . The King of the Jungle! Rose . . . hey, Rose. Got a flower for you.

(*He takes a rose from his pocket.*)

Picked it myself. That's the same rose like you is!

ROSE: That's right nice of you, Gabe.

LYONS: What you been doing, Uncle Gabe?

GABRIEL: Oh, I been chasing hellhounds and waiting on the time to tell St. Peter to open the gates.

LYONS: You been chasing hellhounds, huh? Well . . . you doing the right thing, Uncle Gabe. Somebody got to chase them.

GABRIEL: Oh, yeah . . . I know it. The devil's strong. The devil ain't no pushover. Hellhounds snipping at everybody's heels. But I got my trumpet waiting on the judgment time.

LYONS: Waiting on the Battle of Armageddon, huh?

GABRIEL: Ain't gonna be too much of a battle when God get to waving that Judgment sword. But the people's gonna have a hell of a time trying to get into heaven if them gates ain't open.

LYONS (*putting his arm around Gabriel*): You hear this, Pop. Uncle Gabe, you all right!

GABRIEL (*laughing with Lyons*): Lyons! King of the Jungle.

ROSE: You gonna stay for supper, Gabe. Want me to fix you a plate?

GABRIEL: I'll take a sandwich, Rose. Don't want no plate. Just wanna eat with my hands. I'll take a sandwich.

ROSE: How about you, Lyons? You staying? Got some short ribs cooking.

LYONS: Naw, I won't eat nothing till after we finished playing.

(*Pause.*)

You ought to come down and listen to me play, Pop.

TROY: I don't like that Chinese music. All that noise.

ROSE: Go on in the house and wash up, Gabe . . . I'll fix you a sandwich.

GABRIEL (*to Lyons, as he exits*): Troy's mad at me.

LYONS: What you mad at Uncle Gabe for, Pop.

ROSE: He thinks Troy's mad at him cause he moved over to Miss Pearl's.

TROY: I ain't mad at the man. He can live where he want to live at.

LYONS: What he move over there for? Miss Pearl don't like nobody.

ROSE: She don't mind him none. She treats him real nice. She just don't allow all that singing.

TROY: She don't mind that rent he be paying . . . that's what she don't mind.

ROSE: Troy, I ain't going through that with you no more. He's over there cause he want to have his own place. He can come and go as he please.

TROY: Hell, he could come and go as he please here. I wasn't stopping him. I ain't put no rules on him.

ROSE: It ain't the same thing, Troy. And you know it.

(*Gabriel comes to the door.*)

Now, that's the last I wanna hear about that. I don't wanna hear nothing else about Gabe and Miss Pearl. And next week . . .

GABRIEL: I'm ready for my sandwich, Rose.

ROSE: And next week . . . when that recruiter come from that school . . . I want you to sign that paper and go on and let Cory play football. Then that'll be the last I have to hear about that.

TROY (*to Rose as she exits into the house*): I ain't thinking about Cory nothing.

LYONS: What . . . Cory got recruited? What school he going to?

TROY: That boy walking around here smelling his piss . . . thinking he's grown. Thinking he's gonna do what he want, irrespective of what I say. Look here, Bono . . . I left the Commissioner's office and went down to the A&P . . . that boy ain't working down there. He lying to me. Telling me he got his job back . . . telling me he working weekends . . . telling me he working after school . . . Mr. Stawicki tell me he ain't working down there at all!

LYONS: Cory just growing up. He's just busting at the seams trying to fill out your shoes.

TROY: I don't care what he's doing. When he get to the point where he wanna disobey me . . . then it's time for him to move on. Bono'll tell you that. I bet he ain't never disobeyed his daddy without paying the consequences.

BONO: I ain't never had a chance. My daddy came on through . . . but I ain't never knew him to see him . . . or what he had on his mind or where he went. Just moving on through. Searching out the New Land. That's what the old folks used to call it. See a fellow moving around from place to place . . . woman to woman . . . called it searching out the New Land. I can't say if he ever found it. I come along, didn't want no kids. Didn't know if I was gonna be in one place long enough to fix on them right as their daddy. I figured I was going searching too. As it turned out I been hooked up with Lucille near about as long as your daddy been with Rose. Going on sixteen years.

TROY: Sometimes I wish I hadn't known my daddy. He ain't cared nothing about no kids. A kid to him wasn't nothing. All he wanted was for you to learn how to walk so he could start you to working. When it come time for eating . . . he ate first. If there was anything left over, that's what you got. Man would sit down and eat two chickens and give you the wing.

LYONS: You ought to stop that, Pop. Everybody feed their kids. No matter how hard times is . . . everybody care about their kids. Make sure they have something to eat.

TROY: The only thing my daddy cared about was getting them bales of cotton in to Mr. Lubin. That's the only thing that mattered to him.

Sometimes I used to wonder why he was living. Wonder why the devil hadn't come and got him. "Get them bales of cotton in to Mr. Lubin" and find out he owe him money . . .

LYONS: He should have just went on and left when he saw he couldn't get nowhere. That's what I would have done.

TROY: How he gonna leave with eleven kids? And where he gonna go? He ain't knew how to do nothing but farm. No, he was trapped and I think he knew it. But I'll say this for him . . . he felt a responsibility toward us. Maybe he ain't treated us the way I felt he should have . . . but without that responsibility he could have walked off and left us . . . made his own way.

BONO: A lot of them did. Back in those days what you talking about . . . they walk out their front door and just take on down one road or another and keep on walking.

LYONS: There you go! That's what I'm talking about.

BONO: Just keep on walking till you come to something else. Ain't you never heard of nobody having the walking blues? Well, that's what you call it when you just take off like that.

TROY: My daddy ain't had them walking blues! What you talking about? He stayed right there with his family. But he was just as evil as he could be. My mama couldn't stand him. Couldn't stand that evilness. She run off when I was about eight. She sneaked off one night after he had gone to sleep. Told me she was coming back for me. I ain't never seen her no more. All his women run off and left him. He wasn't good for nobody.

When my turn come to head out, I was fourteen and got to sniffing around Joe Canewell's daughter. Had us an old mule we called Greyboy. My daddy sent me out to do some plowing and I tied up Greyboy and went to fooling around with Joe Canewell's daughter. We done found us a nice little spot, got real cozy with each other. She about thirteen and we done figured we was grown anyway . . . so we down there enjoying ourselves . . . ain't thinking about nothing. We didn't know Greyboy had got loose and wandered back to the house and my daddy was looking for me. We down there by the creek enjoying ourselves when my daddy come up on us. Surprised us. He had them leather straps off the mule and commenced to whupping me like there was no tomorrow. I jumped up, mad and embarrassed. I was scared of my daddy. When he commenced to whupping on me . . . quite naturally I run to get out of the way.

(*Pause.*)

Now I thought he was mad cause I ain't done my work. But I see where he was chasing me off so he could have the gal for himself. When I see what the matter of it was, I lost all fear of my daddy. Right there is where I become a man . . . at fourteen years of age.

(*Pause.*)

Now it was my turn to run him off. I picked up them same reins that he had used on me. I picked up them reins and commenced to whupping on him. The gal jumped up and run off . . . and when my daddy turned to face me, I could see why the devil had never come to get him . . . cause he was the devil himself. I don't know what happened. When I woke up, I was laying right there by the creek, and Blue . . . this old dog we had . . . was licking my face. I thought I was blind. I couldn't see nothing. Both my eyes were swollen shut. I layed there and cried. I didn't know what I was gonna do. The only thing I knew was the time had come for me to leave my daddy's house. And right there the world suddenly got big. And it was a long time before I could cut it down to where I could handle it.

Part of that cutting down was when I got to the place where I could feel him kicking in my blood and knew that the only thing that separated us was the matter of a few years.

(*Gabriel enters from the house with a sandwich.*)

LYONS: What you got there, Uncle Gabe?

GABRIEL: Got me a ham sandwich. Rose gave me a ham sandwich.

TROY: I don't know what happened to him. I done lost touch with everybody except Gabriel. But I hope he's dead. I hope he found some peace.

LYONS: That's a heavy story, Pop. I didn't know you left home when you was fourteen.

TROY: And didn't know nothing. The only part of the world I knew was the forty-two acres of Mr. Lubin's land. That's all I knew about life.

LYONS: Fourteen's kinda young to be out on your own. (*Phone rings.*) I don't even think I was ready to be out on my own at fourteen. I don't know what I would have done.

TROY: I got up from the creek and walked on down to Mobile. I was through with farming. Figured I could do better in the city. So I walked the two hundred miles to Mobile.

LYONS: Wait a minute . . . you ain't walked no two hundred miles, Pop. Ain't nobody gonna walk no two hundred miles. You talking about some walking there.

BONO: That's the only way you got anywhere back in them days.

LYONS: Shhh. Damn if I wouldn't have hitched a ride with somebody!

TROY: Who you gonna hitch it with? They ain't had no cars and things like they got now. We talking about 1918.

ROSE (*entering*): What you all out here getting into?

TROY (*to Rose*): I'm telling Lyons how good he got it. He don't know nothing about this I'm talking.

ROSE: Lyons, that was Bonnie on the phone. She say you supposed to
pick her up.

LYONS: Yeah, okay, Rose.

TROY: I walked on down to Mobile and hitched up with some of them
fellows that was heading this way. Got up here and found out . . . not
only couldn't you get a job . . . you couldn't find no place to live. I
thought I was in freedom. Shhh. Colored folks living down there on
the riverbanks in whatever kind of shelter they could find for themselves. Right down there under the Brady Street Bridge. Living in
shacks made of sticks and tarpaper. Messed around there and went
from bad to worse. Started stealing. First it was food. Then I figured,
hell, if I steal money I can buy me some food. Buy me some shoes too!
One thing led to another. Met your mama. I was young and anxious to
be a man. Met your mama and had you. What I do that for? Now I got
to worry about feeding you and her. Got to steal three times as much.
Went out one day looking for somebody to rob . . . that's what I was, a
robber. I'll tell you the truth. I'm ashamed of it today. But it's the truth.
Went to rob this fellow . . . pulled out my knife . . . and he pulled out a
gun. Shot me in the chest. It felt just like somebody had taken a hot
branding iron and laid it on me. When he shot me I jumped at him
with my knife. They told me I killed him and they put me in the penitentiary and locked me up for fifteen years. That's where I met Bono.
That's where I learned how to play baseball. Got out that place and
your mama had taken you and went on to make life without me. Fifteen years was a long time for her to wait. But that fifteen years cured
me of that robbing stuff. Rose'll tell you. She asked me when I met her
if I had gotten all that foolishness out of my system. And I told her,
"Baby, it's you and baseball all what count with me." You hear me,
Bono? I meant it too. She say, "Which one comes first?" I told her,
"Baby, ain't no doubt it's baseball . . . but you stick and get old with me
and we'll both outlive this baseball." Am I right, Rose? And it's true.

ROSE: Man, hush your mouth. You ain't said no such thing. Talking
about, "Baby, you know you'll always be number one with me." That's
what you was talking.

TROY: You hear that, Bono. That's why I love her.

BONO: Rose'll keep you straight. You get off the track, she'll straighten
you up.

ROSE: Lyons, you better get on up and get Bonnie. She waiting on you.

LYONS (*gets up to go*): Hey, Pop, why don't you come on down to the Grill
and hear me play?

TROY: I ain't going down there. I'm too old to be sitting around in them clubs.

BONO: You got to be good to play down at the Grill.

LYONS: Come on, Pop . . .

TROY: I got to get up in the morning.

LYONS: You ain't got to stay long.

TROY: Naw, I'm gonna get my supper and go on to bed.

LYONS: Well, I got to go. I'll see you again.

TROY: Don't you come around my house on my payday.

ROSE: Pick up the phone and let somebody know you coming. And bring Bonnie with you. You know I'm always glad to see her.

LYONS: Yeah, I'll do that, Rose. You take care now. See you, Pop. See you, Mr. Bono. See you, Uncle Gabe.

GABRIEL: Lyons! King of the Jungle!

(*Lyons exits.*)

TROY: Is supper ready, woman? Me and you got some business to take care of. I'm gonna tear it up too.

ROSE: Troy, I done told you now!

TROY (*puts his arm around Bono*): Aw hell, woman . . . this is Bono. Bono like family. I done known this nigger since . . . how long I done know you?

BONO: It's been a long time.

TROY: I done known this nigger since Skippy was a pup. Me and him done been through some times.

BONO: You sure right about that.

TROY: Hell, I done know him longer than I known you. And we still standing shoulder to shoulder. Hey, look here, Bono . . . a man can't ask for no more than that.

(*Drinks to him.*)

I love you, nigger.

BONO: Hell, I love you too . . . but I got to get home see my woman. You got yours in hand. I got to go get mine.

(*Bono starts to exit as Cory enters the yard, dressed in his football uniform. He gives Troy a hard, uncompromising look.*)

CORY: What you do that for, Pop?

(*He throws his helmet down in the direction of Troy.*)

ROSE: What's the matter? Cory . . . what's the matter?

CORY: Papa done went up to the school and told Coach Zellman I can't play football no more. Wouldn't even let me play the game. Told him to tell the recruiter not to come.

ROSE: Troy . . .

TROY: What you Troying me for. Yeah, I did it. And the boy know why I
did it.

CORY: Why you wanna do that to me? That was the one chance I had.

ROSE: Ain't nothing wrong with Cory playing football, Troy.

TROY: The boy lied to me. I told the nigger if he wanna play football . . . to
keep up his chores and hold down that job at the A&P. That was the
conditions. Stopped down there to see Mr. Stawicki . . .

CORY: I can't work after school during the football season, Pop! I tried to
tell you that Mr. Stawicki's holding my job for me. You don't never
want to listen to nobody. And then you wanna go and do this to me!

TROY: I ain't done nothing to you. You done it to yourself.

CORY: Just cause you didn't have a chance! You just scared I'm gonna be
better than you, that's all.

TROY: Come here.

ROSE: Troy . . .

(Cory reluctantly crosses over to Troy.)

TROY: All right! See. You done made a mistake.

CORY: I didn't even do nothing!

TROY: I'm gonna tell you what your mistake was. See . . . you swung
at the ball and didn't hit it. That's strike one. See, you in the batter's
box now. You swung and you missed. That's strike one. Don't you
strike out!

(Lights fade to black.)

ACT II

Scene I

*(The following morning. Cory is at the tree hitting the ball with the bat. He tries
to mimic Troy, but his swing is awkward, less sure. Rose enters from the house.)*

ROSE: Cory, I want you to help me with this cupboard.

CORY: I ain't quitting the team. I don't care what Poppa say.

ROSE: I'll talk to him when he gets back. He had to go see about your
Uncle Gabe. The police done arrested him. Say he was disturbing the
peace. He'll be back directly. Come on in here and help me clean out
the top of this cupboard.

(Cory exits into the house. Rose sees Troy and Bono coming down the alley.)

Troy . . . what they say down there?

TROY: Ain't said nothing. I give them fifty dollars and they let him go. I'll talk to you about it. Where's Cory?

ROSE: He's in there helping me clean out these cupboards.

TROY: Tell him to get his butt out here.

(Troy and Bono go over to the pile of wood. Bono picks up the saw and begins sawing.)

TROY *(to Bono)*: All they want is the money. That makes six or seven times I done went down there and got him. See me coming they stick out their hands.

BONO: Yeah. I know what you mean. That's all they care about . . . that money. They don't care about what's right.

(Pause.)

Nigger, why you got to go and get some hard wood? You ain't doing nothing but building a little old fence. Get you some soft pine wood. That's all you need.

TROY: I know what I'm doing. This is outside wood. You put pine wood inside the house. Pine wood is inside wood. This here is outside wood. Now you tell me where the fence is gonna be?

BONO: You don't need this wood. You can put it up with pine wood and it'll stand as long as you gonna be here looking at it.

TROY: How you know how long I'm gonna be here, nigger? Hell, I might just live forever. Live longer than old man Horsely.

BONO: That's what Magee used to say.

TROY: Magee's a damn fool. Now you tell me who you ever heard of gonna pull their own teeth with a pair of rusty pliers.

BONO: The old folks . . . my granddaddy used to pull his teeth with pliers. They ain't had no dentists for the colored folks back then.

TROY: Get clean pliers! You understand? Clean pliers! Sterilize them! Besides we ain't living back then. All Magee had to do was walk over to Doc Goldblum's.

BONO: I see where you and that Tallahassee gal . . . that Alberta . . . I see where you all done got tight.

TROY: What you mean "got tight"?

BONO: I see where you be laughing and joking with her all the time.

TROY: I laughs and jokes with all of them, Bono. You know me.

BONO: That ain't the kind of laughing and joking I'm talking about.

(Cory enters from the house.)

CORY: How you doing, Mr. Bono?

TROY: Cory? Get that saw from Bono and cut some wood. He talking about the wood's too hard to cut. Stand back there, Jim, and let that young boy show you how it's done.

BONO: He's sure welcome to it.

(*Cory takes the saw and begins to cut the wood.*)

Whew-e-e! Look at that. Big old strong boy. Look like Joe Louis. Hell, must be getting old the way I'm watching that boy whip through that wood.

CORY: I don't see why Mama want a fence around the yard noways.

TROY: Damn if I know either. What the hell she keeping out with it? She ain't got nothing nobody want.

BONO: Some people build fences to keep people out . . . and other people build fences to keep people in. Rose wants to hold on to you all. She loves you.

TROY: Hell, nigger, I don't need nobody to tell me my wife loves me. Cory . . . go on in the house and see if you can find that other saw.

CORY: Where's it at?

TROY: I said find it! Look for it till you find it!

(*Cory exits into the house.*)

What's that supposed to mean? Wanna keep us in?

BONO: Troy . . . I done known you seem like damn near my whole life. You and Rose both. I done know both of you all for a long time. I remember when you met Rose. When you was hitting them baseball out the park. A lot of them old gals was after you then. You had the pick of the litter. When you picked Rose, I was happy for you. That was the first time I knew you had any sense. I said . . . My man Troy knows what he's doing . . . I'm gonna follow this nigger . . . he might take me somewhere. I been following you too. I done learned a whole heap of things about life watching you. I done learned how to tell where the shit lies. How to tell it from the alfalfa. You done learned me a lot of things. You showed me how to not make the same mistakes . . . to take life as it comes along and keep putting one foot in front of the other.

(*Pause.*)

Rose a good woman, Troy.

TROY: Hell, nigger, I know she a good woman. I been married to her for eighteen years. What you got on your mind, Bono?

BONO: I just say she a good woman. Just like I say anything. I ain't got to have nothing on my mind.

TROY: You just gonna say she a good woman and leave it hanging out there like that? Why you telling me she a good woman?

BONO: She loves you, Troy. Rose loves you.

TROY: You saying I don't measure up. That's what you trying to say. I don't measure up cause I'm seeing this other gal. I know what you trying to say.

BONO: I know what Rose means to you, Troy. I'm just trying to say I don't want to see you mess up.

TROY: Yeah, I appreciate that, Bono. If you was messing around on Lucille I'd be telling you the same thing.

BONO: Well, that's all I got to say. I just say that because I love you both.

TROY: Hell, you know me . . . I wasn't out there looking for nothing. You can't find a better woman than Rose. I know that. But seems like this woman just stuck onto me where I can't shake her loose. I done wrestled with it, tried to throw her off me . . . but she just stuck on tighter. Now she's stuck on for good.

BONO: You's in control . . . that's what you tell me all the time. You responsible for what you do.

TROY: I ain't ducking the responsibility of it. As long as it sets right in my heart . . . then I'm okay. Cause that's all I listen to. It'll tell me right from wrong every time. And I ain't talking about doing Rose no bad turn. I love Rose. She done carried me a long ways and I love and respect her for that.

BONO: I know you do. That's why I don't want to see you hurt her. But what you gonna do when she find out? What you got then? If you try and juggle both of them . . . sooner or later you gonna drop one of them. That's common sense.

TROY: Yeah, I hear what you saying, Bono. I been trying to figure a way to work it out.

BONO: Work it out right, Troy. I don't want to be getting all up between you and Rose's business . . . but work it so it come out right.

TROY: Ah hell, I get all up between you and Lucille's business. When you gonna get that woman that refrigerator she been wanting? Don't tell me you ain't got no money now. I know who your banker is. Mellon don't need that money bad as Lucille want that refrigerator. I'll tell you that.

BONO: Tell you what I'll do . . . when you finish building this fence for Rose . . . I'll buy Lucille that refrigerator.

TROY: You done stuck your foot in your mouth now!

(*Troy grabs up a board and begins to saw. Bono starts to walk out the yard.*)

Hey, nigger . . . where you going?

BONO: I'm going home. I know you don't expect me to help you now. I'm protecting my money. I wanna see you put that fence up by yourself. That's what I want to see. You'll be here another six months without me.

TROY: Nigger, you ain't right.

BONO: When it comes to my money . . . I'm right as fireworks on the Fourth of July.

TROY: All right, we gonna see now. You better get out your bankbook.

(*Bono exits, and Troy continues to work. Rose enters from the house.*)

ROSE: What they say down there? What's happening with Gabe?

TROY: I went down there and got him out. Cost me fifty dollars. Say he was disturbing the peace. Judge set up a hearing for him in three weeks. Say to show cause why he shouldn't be recommitted.

ROSE: What was he doing that cause them to arrest him?

TROY: Some kids was teasing him and he run them off home. Say he was howling and carrying on. Some folks seen him and called the police. That's all it was.

ROSE: Well, what's you say? What'd you tell the judge?

TROY: Told him I'd look after him. It didn't make no sense to recommit the man. He stuck out his big greasy palm and told me to give him fifty dollars and take him on home.

ROSE: Where's he at now? Where'd he go off to?

TROY: He's gone on about his business. He don't need nobody to hold his hand.

ROSE: Well, I don't know. Seem like that would be the best place for him if they did put him into the hospital. I know what you're gonna say. But that's what I think would be best.

TROY: The man done had his life ruined fighting for what? And they wanna take and lock him up. Let him be free. He don't bother nobody.

ROSE: Well, everybody got their own way of looking at it I guess. Come on and get your lunch. I got a bowl of lima beans and some cornbread in the oven. Come on get something to eat. Ain't no sense you fretting over Gabe.

(*Rose turns to go into the house.*)

TROY: Rose . . . got something to tell you.

ROSE: Well, come on . . . wait till I get this food on the table.

TROY: Rose!

(*She stops and turns around.*)

I don't know how to say this.

(*Pause.*)

I can't explain it none. It just sort of grows on you till it gets out of hand. It starts out like a little bush . . . and the next thing you know it's a whole forest.

ROSE: Troy . . . what is you talking about?

TROY: I'm talking, woman, let me talk. I'm trying to find a way to tell you . . . I'm gonna be a daddy. I'm gonna be somebody's daddy.

ROSE: Troy . . . you're not telling me this? You're gonna be . . . what?
TROY: Rose . . . now . . . see . . .
ROSE: You telling me you gonna be somebody's daddy? You telling your wife this?

(*Gabriel enters from the street. He carries a rose in his hand.*)

GABRIEL: Hey, Troy! Hey, Rose!
ROSE: I have to wait eighteen years to hear something like this.
GABRIEL: Hey, Rose . . . I got a flower for you.

(*He hands it to her.*)

That's a rose. Same rose like you is.
ROSE: Thanks, Gabe.
GABRIEL: Troy, you ain't mad at me is you? Them bad mens come and put me away. You ain't mad at me is you?
TROY: Naw, Gabe, I ain't mad at you.
ROSE: Eighteen years and you wanna come with this.
GABRIEL (*takes a quarter out of his pocket*): See what I got? Got a brand new quarter.
TROY: Rose . . . it's just . . .
ROSE: Ain't nothing you can say, Troy. Ain't no way of explaining that.
GABRIEL: Fellow that give me this quarter had a whole mess of them. I'm gonna keep this quarter till it stop shining.
ROSE: Gabe, go on in the house there. I got some watermelon in the frigidaire. Go on and get you a piece.
GABRIEL: Say, Rose . . . you know I was chasing hellhounds and them bad mens come and get me and take me away. Troy helped me. He come down there and told them they better let me go before he beat them up. Yeah, he did!
ROSE: You go on and get you a piece of watermelon, Gabe. Them bad mens is gone now.
GABRIEL: Okay, Rose . . . gonna get me some watermelon. The kind with the stripes on it.

(*Gabriel exits into the house.*)

ROSE: Why, Troy? Why? After all these years to come dragging this in to me now. It don't make no sense at your age. I could have expected this ten or fifteen years ago, but not now.
TROY: Age ain't got nothing to do with it, Rose.
ROSE: I done tried to be everything a wife should be. Everything a wife could be. Been married eighteen years and I got to live to see the day you tell me you been seeing another woman and done fathered a child by her. And you know I ain't never wanted no half nothing in my

family. My whole family is half. Everybody got different fathers and mothers . . . my two sisters and my brother. Can't hardly tell who's who. Can't never sit down and talk about Papa and Mama. It's your papa and your mama and my papa and my mama . . .

TROY: Rose . . . stop it now.

ROSE: I ain't never wanted that for none of my children. And now you wanna drag your behind in here and tell me something like this.

TROY: You ought to know. It's time for you to know.

ROSE: Well, I don't want to know, goddamn it!

TROY: I can't just make it go away. It's done now. I can't wish the circumstance of the thing away.

ROSE: And you don't want to either. Maybe you want to wish me and my boy away. Maybe that's what you want? Well, you can't wish us away. I've got eighteen years of my life invested in you. You ought to have stayed upstairs in my bed where you belong.

TROY: Rose . . . now listen to me . . . we can get a handle on this thing. We can talk this out . . . come to an understanding.

ROSE: All of a sudden it's "we." Where was "we" at when you was down there rolling around with some godforsaken woman? "We" should have come to an understanding before you started making a damn fool of yourself. You're a day late and a dollar short when it comes to an understanding with me.

TROY: It's just . . . She gives me a different idea . . . a different understanding about myself. I can step out of this house and get away from the pressures and problems . . . be a different man. I ain't got to wonder how I'm gonna pay the bills or get the roof fixed. I can just be a part of myself that I ain't never been.

ROSE: What I want to know . . . is do you plan to continue seeing her. That's all you can say to me.

TROY: I can sit up in her house and laugh. Do you understand what I'm saying. I can laugh out loud . . . and it feels good. It reaches all the way down to the bottom of my shoes.

(*Pause.*)

Rose, I can't give that up.

ROSE: Maybe you ought to go on and stay down there with her . . . if she's a better woman than me.

TROY: It ain't about nobody being a better woman or nothing. Rose, you ain't the blame. A man couldn't ask for no woman to be a better wife than you've been. I'm responsible for it. I done locked myself into a pattern trying to take care of you all that I forgot about myself.

ROSE: What the hell was I there for? That was my job, not somebody else's.

TROY: Rose, I done tried all my life to live decent . . . to live a clean . . . hard . . . useful life. I tried to be a good husband to you. In every way I knew how. Maybe I come into the world backwards, I don't know. But . . . you born with two strikes on you before you come to the plate. You got to guard it closely . . . always looking for the curve ball on the inside corner. You can't afford to let none get past you. You can't afford a call strike. If you going down . . . you going down swinging. Everything lined up against you. What you gonna do. I fooled them, Rose. I bunted. When I found you and Cory and a halfway decent job . . . I was safe. Couldn't nothing touch me. I wasn't gonna strike out no more. I wasn't going back to the penitentiary. I wasn't gonna lay in the streets with a bottle of wine. I was safe. I had me a family. A job. I wasn't gonna get that last strike. I was on first looking for one of them boys to knock me in. To get me home.

ROSE: You should have stayed in my bed, Troy.

TROY: Then when I saw that gal . . . she firmed up my backbone. And I got to thinking that if I tried . . . I just might be able to steal second. Do you understand after eighteen years I wanted to steal second.

ROSE: You should have held me tight. You should have grabbed me and held on.

TROY: I stood on first base for eighteen years and I thought . . . well, goddamn it . . . go on for it!

ROSE: We're not talking about baseball! We're talking about you going off to lay in bed with another woman . . . and then bring it home to me. That's what we're talking about. We ain't talking about no baseball.

TROY: Rose, you're not listening to me. I'm trying the best I can to explain it to you. It's not easy for me to admit that I been standing in the same place for eighteen years.

ROSE: I been standing with you! I been right here with you, Troy. I got a life too. I gave eighteen years of my life to stand in the same spot with you. Don't you think I ever wanted other things? Don't you think I had dreams and hopes? What about my life? What about me. Don't you think it ever crossed my mind to want to know other men? That I wanted to lay up somewhere and forget about my responsibilities? That I wanted someone to make me laugh so I could feel good? You not the only one who's got wants and needs. But I held on to you, Troy. I took all my feelings, my wants and needs, my dreams . . . and I buried them inside you. I planted a seed and watched and prayed over it. I planted myself inside you and waited to bloom. And it didn't take me no eighteen years to find out the soil was hard and rocky and it wasn't never gonna bloom.

But I held on to you, Troy. I held you tighter. You was my husband. I owed you everything I had. Every part of me I could find to give you. And upstairs in that room . . . with the darkness falling in on me . . . I gave everything I had to try and erase the doubt that you wasn't the finest man in the world. And wherever you was going . . . I wanted to be there with you. Cause you was my husband. Cause that's the only way I was gonna survive as your wife. You always talking about what you give . . . and what you don't have to give. But you take too. You take . . . and don't even know nobody's giving!

(*Rose turns to exit into the house; Troy grabs her arm.*)

TROY: You say I take and don't give!

ROSE: Troy! You're hurting me!

TROY: You say I take and don't give.

ROSE: Troy . . . you're hurting my arm! Let go!

TROY: I done give you everything I got. Don't you tell that lie on me.

ROSE: Troy!

TROY: Don't you tell that lie on me!

(*Cory enters from the house.*)

CORY: Mama!

ROSE: Troy. You're hurting me.

TROY: Don't you tell me about no taking and giving.

(*Cory comes up behind Troy and grabs him. Troy, surprised, is thrown off balance just as Cory throws a glancing blow that catches him on the chest and knocks him down. Troy is stunned, as is Cory.*)

ROSE: Troy. Troy. No!

(*Troy gets to his feet and starts at Cory.*)

   Troy . . . no. Please! Troy!

(*Rose pulls on Troy to hold him back. Troy stops himself.*)

TROY (*to Cory*): All right. That's strike two. You stay away from around me, boy. Don't you strike out. You living with a full count. Don't you strike out.

(*Troy exits out the yard as the lights go down.*)

Scene II

(*It is six months later, early afternoon. Troy enters from the house and starts to exit the yard. Rose enters from the house.*)

ROSE: Troy, I want to talk to you.

TROY: All of a sudden, after all this time, you want to talk to me, huh? You ain't wanted to talk to me for months. You ain't wanted to talk to me last night. You ain't wanted no part of me then. What you wanna talk to me about now?

ROSE: Tomorrow's Friday.

TROY: I know what day tomorrow is. You think I don't know tomorrow's Friday? My whole life I ain't done nothing but look to see Friday coming and you got to tell me it's Friday.

ROSE: I want to know if you're coming home.

TROY: I always come home, Rose. You know that. There ain't never been a night I ain't come home.

ROSE: That ain't what I mean . . . and you know it. I want to know if you're coming straight home after work.

TROY: I figure I'd cash my check . . . hang out at Taylors' with the boys . . . maybe play a game of checkers . . .

ROSE: Troy, I can't live like this. I won't live like this. You livin' on borrowed time with me. It's been going on six months now you ain't been coming home.

TROY: I be here every night. Every night of the year. That's 365 days.

ROSE: I want you to come home tomorrow after work.

TROY: Rose . . . I don't mess up my pay. You know that now. I take my pay and I give it to you. I don't have no money but what you give me back. I just want to have a little time to myself . . . a little time to enjoy life.

ROSE: What about me? When's my time to enjoy life?

TROY: I don't know what to tell you, Rose. I'm doing the best I can.

ROSE: You ain't been home from work but time enough to change your clothes and run out . . . and you wanna call that the best you can do?

TROY: I'm going over to the hospital to see Alberta. She went into the hospital this afternoon. Look like she might have the baby early. I won't be gone long.

ROSE: Well, you ought to know. They went over to Miss Pearl's and got Gabe today. She said you told them to go ahead and lock him up.

TROY: I ain't said no such thing. Whoever told you that is telling a lie. Pearl ain't doing nothing but telling a big fat lie.

ROSE: She ain't had to tell me. I read it on the papers.

TROY: I ain't told them nothing of the kind.

ROSE: I saw it right there on the papers.

TROY: What it say, huh?

ROSE: It said you told them to take him.

TROY: Then they screwed that up, just the way they screw up everything. I ain't worried about what they got on the paper.

ROSE: Say the government send part of his check to the hospital and the other part to you.

TROY: I ain't got nothing to do with that if that's the way it works. I ain't made up the rules about how it work.

ROSE: You did Gabe just like you did Cory. You wouldn't sign the paper for Cory . . . but you signed for Gabe. You signed that paper.

(*The telephone is heard ringing inside the house.*)

TROY: I told you I ain't signed nothing, woman! The only thing I signed was the release form. Hell, I can't read, I don't know what they had on that paper! I ain't signed nothing about sending Gabe away.

ROSE: I said send him to the hospital . . . you said let him be free . . . now you done went down there and signed him to the hospital for half his money. You went back on yourself, Troy. You gonna have to answer for that.

TROY: See now . . . you been over there talking to Miss Pearl. She done got mad cause she ain't getting Gabe's rent money. That's all it is. She's liable to say anything.

ROSE: Troy, I seen where you signed the paper.

TROY: You ain't seen nothing I signed. What she doing got papers on my brother anyway? Miss Pearl telling a big fat lie. And I'm gonna tell her about it too! You ain't seen nothing I signed. Say . . . you ain't seen nothing I signed.

(*Rose exits into the house to answer the telephone. Presently she returns.*)

ROSE: Troy . . . that was the hospital. Alberta had the baby.

TROY: What she have? What is it?

ROSE: It's a girl.

TROY: I better get on down to the hospital to see her.

ROSE: Troy . . .

TROY: Rose . . . I got to go see her now. That's only right . . . what's the matter . . . the baby's all right, ain't it?

ROSE: Alberta died having the baby.

TROY: Died . . . you say she's dead? Alberta's dead?

ROSE: They said they done all they could. They couldn't do nothing for her.

TROY: The baby? How's the baby?

ROSE: They say it's healthy. I wonder who's gonna bury her.

TROY: She had family, Rose. She wasn't living in the world by herself.

ROSE: I know she wasn't living in the world by herself.

TROY: Next thing you gonna want to know if she had any insurance.

ROSE: Troy, you ain't got to talk like that.

TROY: That's the first thing that jumped out your mouth. "Who's gonna bury her?" Like I'm fixing to take on that task for myself.

ROSE: I am your wife. Don't push me away.

TROY: I ain't pushing nobody away. Just give me some space. That's all. Just give me some room to breathe.

(*Rose exits into the house. Troy walks about the yard.*)

TROY (*with a quiet rage that threatens to consume him*): All right . . . Mr.
Death. See now . . . I'm gonna tell you what I'm gonna do. I'm gonna
take and build me a fence around this yard. See? I'm gonna build me a
fence around what belongs to me. And then I want you to stay on the
other side. See? You stay over there until you're ready for me. Then
you come on. Bring your army. Bring your sickle. Bring your wrestling
clothes. I ain't gonna fall down on my vigilance this time. You ain't
gonna sneak up on me no more. When you ready for me . . . when
the top of your list say Troy Maxson . . . that's when you come around
here. You come up and knock on the front door. Ain't nobody else got
nothing to do with this. This is between you and me. Man to man. You
stay on the other side of that fence until you ready for me. Then you
come up and knock on the front door. Anytime you want. I'll be ready
for you.

(*The lights go down to black.*)

Scene III

(*The lights come up on the porch. It is late evening three days later. Rose sits
listening to the ball game waiting for Troy. The final out of the game is made and
Rose switches off the radio. Troy enters the yard carrying an infant wrapped in
blankets. He stands back from the house and calls.*)

(*Rose enters and stands on the porch. There is a long, awkward silence, the
weight of which grows heavier with each passing second.*)

TROY: Rose . . . I'm standing here with my daughter in my arms. She ain't
but a wee bittie little old thing. She don't know nothing about grownups' business. She innocent . . . and she ain't got no mama.
ROSE: What you telling me for, Troy?

(*She turns and exits into the house.*)

TROY: Well . . . I guess we'll just sit out here on the porch.

(*He sits down on the porch. There is an awkward indelicateness about the way
he handles the baby. His largeness engulfs and seems to swallow it. He speaks
loud enough for Rose to hear.*)

A man's got to do what's right for him. I ain't sorry for nothing I done.
It felt right in my heart.

(*To the baby.*)

What you smiling at? Your daddy's a big man. Got these great big old
hands. But sometimes he's scared. And right now your daddy's scared

cause we sitting out here and ain't got no home. Oh, I been homeless before. I ain't had no little baby with me. But I been homeless. You just be out on the road by your lonesome and you see one of them trains coming and you just kinda go like this . . .

(*He sings as a lullaby.*)

Please, Mr. Engineer let a man ride the line
Please, Mr. Engineer let a man ride the line
I ain't got no ticket please let me ride the blinds

(*Rose enters from the house. Troy hearing her steps behind him, stands and faces her.*)

She's my daughter, Rose. My own flesh and blood. I can't deny her no more than I can deny them boys.

(*Pause.*)

You and them boys is my family. You and them and this child is all I got in the world. So I guess what I'm saying is . . . I'd appreciate it if you'd help me take care of her.

ROSE: Okay, Troy . . . you're right. I'll take care of your baby for you . . . cause . . . like you say . . . she's innocent . . . and you can't visit the sins of the father upon the child. A motherless child has got a hard time.

(*She takes the baby from him.*)

From right now . . . this child got a mother. But you a womanless man.

(*Rose turns and exits into the house with the baby. Lights go down to black.*)

Scene IV

(*It is two months later. Lyons enters from the street. He knocks on the door and calls.*)

LYONS: Hey, Rose! (*Pause.*) Rose!

ROSE (*from inside the house*): Stop that yelling. You gonna wake up Raynell. I just got her to sleep.

LYONS: I just stopped by to pay Papa this twenty dollars I owe him. Where's Papa at?

ROSE: He should be here in a minute. I'm getting ready to go down to the church. Sit down and wait on him.

LYONS: I got to go pick up Bonnie over her mother's house.

ROSE: Well, sit it down there on the table. He'll get it.

LYONS (*enters the house and sets the money on the table*): Tell Papa I said thanks. I'll see you again.

ROSE: All right, Lyons. We'll see you.

(*Lyons starts to exit as Cory enters.*)

CORY: Hey, Lyons.

LYONS: What's happening, Cory. Say man, I'm sorry I missed your graduation. You know I had a gig and couldn't get away. Otherwise, I would have been there, man. So what you doing?

CORY: I'm trying to find a job.

LYONS: Yeah I know how that go, man. It's rough out here. Jobs are scarce.

CORY: Yeah, I know.

LYONS: Look here, I got to run. Talk to Papa . . . he know some people. He'll be able to help get you a job. Talk to him . . . see what he say.

CORY: Yeah . . . all right, Lyons.

LYONS: You take care. I'll talk to you soon. We'll find some time to talk.

(*Lyons exits the yard. Cory wanders over to the tree, picks up the bat, and assumes a batting stance. He studies an imaginary pitcher and swings. Dissatisfied with the result, he tries again. Troy enters. They eye each other for a beat. Cory puts the bat down and exits the yard. Troy starts into the house as Rose exits with Raynell. She is carrying a cake.*)

TROY: I'm coming in and everybody's going out.

ROSE: I'm taking this cake down to the church for the bake sale. Lyons was by to see you. He stopped by to pay you your twenty dollars. It's laying in there on the table.

TROY (*going into his pocket*): Well . . . here go this money.

ROSE: Put it in there on the table, Troy. I'll get it.

TROY: What time you coming back?

ROSE: Ain't no use in you studying me. It don't matter what time I come back.

TROY: I just asked you a question, woman. What's the matter . . . can't I ask you a question?

ROSE: Troy, I don't want to go into it. Your dinner's in there on the stove. All you got to do is heat it up. And don't you be eating the rest of them cakes in there. I'm coming back for them. We having a bake sale at the church tomorrow.

(*Rose exits the yard. Troy sits down on the steps, takes a pint bottle from his pocket, opens it, and drinks. He begins to sing.*)

TROY: Hear it ring! Hear it ring!
    Had an old dog his name was Blue
    You know Blue was mighty true
    You know Blue was a good old dog

Blue trees a possum in a hollow log
You know from that he was a good old dog

(*Bono enters the yard.*)

BONO: Hey, Troy.

TROY: Hey, what's happening, Bono?

BONO: I just thought I'd stop by to see you.

TROY: What you stop by and see me for? You ain't stopped by in a month of Sundays. Hell, I must owe you money or something.

BONO: Since you got your promotion I can't keep up with you. Used to see you every day. Now I don't even know what route you working.

TROY: They keep switching me around. Got me out in Greentree now . . . hauling white folks' garbage.

BONO: Greentree, huh? You lucky, at least you ain't got to be lifting them barrels. Damn if they ain't getting heavier. I'm gonna put in my two years and call it quits.

TROY: I'm thinking about retiring myself.

BONO: You got it easy. You can *drive* for another five years.

TROY: It ain't the same, Bono. It ain't like working the back of the truck. Ain't got nobody to talk to . . . feel like you working by yourself. Naw, I'm thinking about retiring. How's Lucille?

BONO: She all right. Her arthritis get to acting up on her sometime. Saw Rose on my way in. She going down to the church, huh?

TROY: Yeah, she took up going down there. All them preachers looking for somebody to fatten their pockets.

(*Pause.*)

Got some gin here.

BONO: Naw, thanks. I just stopped by to say hello.

TROY: Hell, nigger . . . you can take a drink. I ain't never known you to say no to a drink. You ain't got to work tomorrow.

BONO: I just stopped by. I'm fixing to go over to Skinner's. We got us a domino game going over his house every Friday.

TROY: Nigger, you can't play no dominoes. I used to whup you four games out of five.

BONO: Well, that learned me. I'm getting better.

TROY: Yeah? Well, that's all right.

BONO: Look here . . . I got to be getting on. Stop by sometime, huh?

TROY: Yeah, I'll do that, Bono. Lucille told Rose you bought her a new refrigerator.

BONO: Yeah, Rose told Lucille you had finally built your fence . . . so I figured we'd call it even.

TROY: I knew you would.

BONO: Yeah . . . okay. I'll be talking to you.
TROY: Yeah, take care, Bono. Good to see you. I'm gonna stop over.
BONO: Yeah. Okay, Troy.

(*Bono exits. Troy drinks from the bottle.*)

TROY: Old Blue died and I dig his grave
    Let him down with a golden chain
    Every night when I hear old Blue bark
    I know Blue treed a possum in Noah's Ark.
    Hear it ring! Hear it ring!

(*Cory enters the yard. They eye each other for a beat. Troy is sitting in the middle of the steps. Cory walks over.*)

CORY: I got to get by.
TROY: Say what? What's you say?
CORY: You in my way. I got to get by.
TROY: You got to get by where? This is my house. Bought and paid for. In full. Took me fifteen years. And if you wanna go in my house and I'm sitting on the steps . . . you say excuse me. Like your mama taught you.
CORY: Come on, Pop . . . I got to get by.

(*Cory starts to maneuver his way past Troy. Troy grabs his leg and shoves him back.*)

TROY: You just gonna walk over top of me?
CORY: I live here too!
TROY (*advancing toward him*): You just gonna walk over top of me in my own house?
CORY: I ain't scared of you.
TROY: I ain't asked if you was scared of me. I asked you if you was fixing to walk over top of me in my own house? That's the question. You ain't gonna say excuse me? You just gonna walk over top of me?
CORY: If you wanna put it like that.
TROY: How else am I gonna put it?
CORY: I was walking by you to go into the house cause you sitting on the steps drunk, singing to yourself. You can put it like that.
TROY: Without saying excuse me???

(*Cory doesn't respond.*)

   I asked you a question. Without saying excuse me???
CORY: I ain't got to say excuse me to you. You don't count around here no more.
TROY: Oh, I see . . . I don't count around here no more. You ain't got to say excuse me to your daddy. All of a sudden you done got so grown

that your daddy don't count around here no more . . . Around here in his own house and yard that he done paid for with the sweat of his brow. You done got so grown to where you gonna take over. You gonna take over my house. Is that right? You gonna wear my pants. You gonna go in there and stretch out on my bed. You ain't got to say excuse me cause I don't count around here no more. Is that right?

CORY: That's right. You always talking this dumb stuff. Now, why don't you just get out my way.

TROY: I guess you got someplace to sleep and something to put in your belly. You got that, huh? You got that? That's what you need. You got that, huh?

CORY: You don't know what I got. You ain't got to worry about what I got.

TROY: You right! You one hundred percent right! I done spent the last seventeen years worrying about what you got. Now it's your turn, see? I'll tell you what to do. You grown . . . we done established that. You a man. Now, let's see you act like one. Turn your behind around and walk out this yard. And when you get out there in the alley . . . you can forget about this house. See? 'Cause this is my house. You go on and be a man and get your own house. You can forget about this. Cause this is mine. You go on and get yours 'cause I'm through with doing for you.

CORY: You talking about what you did for me . . . what'd you ever give me?

TROY: Them feet and bones! That pumping heart, nigger! I give you more than anybody else is ever gonna give you.

CORY: You ain't never gave me nothing! You ain't never done nothing but hold me back. Afraid I was gonna be better than you. All you ever did was try and make me scared of you. I used to tremble every time you called my name. Every time I heard your footsteps in the house. Wondering all the time . . . what's Papa gonna say if I do this? . . . What's he gonna say if I do that? . . . What's Papa gonna say if I turn on the radio? And Mama, too . . . she tries . . . but she's scared of you.

TROY: You leave your mama out of this. She ain't got nothing to do with this.

CORY: I don't know how she stand you . . . after what you did to her.

TROY: I told you to leave your mama out of this!

(*He advances toward Cory.*)

CORY: What you gonna do . . . give me a whupping? You can't whup me no more. You're too old. You just an old man.

TROY (*shoves him on his shoulder*): Nigger! That's what you are. You just another nigger on the street to me!

CORY: You crazy! You know that?

TROY: Go on now! You got the devil in you. Get on away from me!

CORY: You just a crazy old man . . . talking about I got the devil in me.

TROY: Yeah, I'm crazy! If you don't get on the other side of that yard . . . I'm gonna show you how crazy I am! Go on . . . get the hell out of my yard.

CORY: It ain't your yard. You took Uncle Gabe's money he got from the army to buy this house and then you put him out.

TROY (*Troy advances on Cory*): Get your black ass out of my yard!

(*Troy's advance backs Cory up against the tree. Cory grabs up the bat.*)

CORY: I ain't going nowhere! Come on . . . put me out! I ain't scared of you.

TROY: That's my bat!

CORY: Come on!

TROY: Put my bat down!

CORY: Come on, put me out.

(*Cory swings at Troy, who backs across the yard.*)

What's the matter? You so bad . . . put me out!

(*Troy advances toward Cory.*)

Cory (*backing up*): Come on! Come on!

TROY: You're gonna have to use it! You wanna draw that bat back on me . . . you're gonna have to use it.

CORY: Come on! . . . Come on!

(*Cory swings the bat at Troy a second time. He misses. Troy continues to advance toward him.*)

TROY: You're gonna have to kill me! You wanna draw that bat back on me. You're gonna have to kill me.

(*Cory, backed up against the tree, can go no farther. Troy taunts him. He sticks out his head and offers him a target.*)

Come on! Come on!

(*Cory is unable to swing the bat. Troy grabs it.*)

TROY: Then I'll show you.

(*Cory and Troy struggle over the bat. The struggle is fierce and fully engaged. Troy ultimately is the stronger and takes the bat from Cory and stands over him ready to swing. He stops himself.*)

Go on and get away from around my house.

(*Cory, stung by his defeat, picks himself up, walks slowly out of the yard and up the alley.*)

CORY: Tell Mama I'll be back for my things.

TROY: They'll be on the other side of that fence.

(*Cory exits.*)

TROY: I can't taste nothing. Helluljah! I can't taste nothing no more. (*Troy assumes a batting posture and begins to taunt Death, the fastball on the outside corner.*) Come on! It's between you and me now! Come on! Anytime you want! Come on! I be ready for you . . . but I ain't gonna be easy.

(*The lights go down on the scene.*)

Scene V

(*The time is 1965. The lights come up in the yard. It is the morning of Troy's funeral. A funeral plaque with a light hangs beside the door. There is a small garden plot off to the side. There is noise and activity in the house as Rose, Gabriel, and Bono have gathered. The door opens and Raynell, seven years old, enters dressed in a flannel nightgown. She crosses to the garden and pokes around with a stick. Rose calls from the house.*)

ROSE: Raynell!
RAYNELL: Mam?
ROSE: What you doing out there?
RAYNELL: Nothing.

(*Rose comes to the door.*)

ROSE: Girl, get in here and get dressed. What you doing?
RAYNELL: Seeing if my garden growed.
ROSE: I told you it ain't gonna grow overnight. You got to wait.
RAYNELL: It don't look like it never gonna grow. Dag!
ROSE: I told you a watched pot never boils. Get in here and get dressed.
RAYNELL: This ain't even no pot, Mama.
ROSE: You just have to give it a chance. It'll grow. Now you come on and do what I told you. We got to be getting ready. This ain't no morning to be playing around. You hear me?
RAYNELL: Yes, mam.

(*Rose exits into the house. Raynell continues to poke at her garden with a stick. Cory enters. He is dressed in a Marine corporal's uniform, and carries a duffel bag. His posture is that of a military man, and his speech has a clipped sternness.*)

CORY (*to Raynell*): Hi.

(*Pause.*)

I bet your name is Raynell.
RAYNELL: Uh huh.

CORY: Is your mama home?

(*Raynell runs up on the porch and calls through the screen door.*)

RAYNELL: Mama . . . there's some man out here. Mama?

(*Rose comes to the door.*)

ROSE: Cory? Lord have mercy! Look here, you all!

(*Rose and Cory embrace in a tearful reunion as Bono and Lyons enter from the house dressed in funeral clothes.*)

BONO: Aw, looka here . . .

ROSE: Done got all grown up!

CORY: Don't cry, Mama. What you crying about?

ROSE: I'm just so glad you made it.

CORY: Hey Lyons. How you doing, Mr. Bono.

(*Lyons goes to embrace Cory.*)

LYONS: Look at you, man. Look at you. Don't he look good, Rose. Got them Corporal stripes.

ROSE: What took you so long.

CORY: You know how the Marines are, Mama. They got to get all their paperwork straight before they let you do anything.

ROSE: Well, I'm sure glad you made it. They let Lyons come. Your Uncle Gabe's still in the hospital. They don't know if they gonna let him out or not. I just talked to them a little while ago.

LYONS: A Corporal in the United States Marines.

BONO: Your daddy knew you had it in you. He used to tell me all the time.

LYONS: Don't he look good, Mr. Bono?

BONO: Yeah, he remind me of Troy when I first met him.

(*Pause.*)

Say, Rose, Lucille's down at the church with the choir. I'm gonna go down and get the pallbearers lined up. I'll be back to get you all.

ROSE: Thanks, Jim.

CORY: See you, Mr. Bono.

LYONS (*with his arm around Raynell*): Cory . . . look at Raynell. Ain't she precious? She gonna break a whole lot of hearts.

ROSE: Raynell, come and say hello to your brother. This is your brother Cory. You remember Cory.

RAYNELL: No, Mam.

CORY: She don't remember me, Mama.

ROSE: Well, we talk about you. She heard us talk about you. (*To Raynell.*) This is your brother Cory. Come on and say hello.

RAYNELL: Hi.

CORY: Hi. So you're Raynell. Mama told me a lot about you.

ROSE: You all come on into the house and let me fix you some breakfast. Keep up your strength.

CORY: I ain't hungry, Mama.

LYONS: You can fix me something, Rose. I'll be in there in a minute.

ROSE: Cory, you sure you don't want nothing. I know they ain't feeding you right.

CORY: No, Mama . . . thanks. I don't feel like eating. I'll get something later.

ROSE: Raynell . . . get on upstairs and get that dress on like I told you.

(*Rose and Raynell exit into the house.*)

LYONS: So . . . I hear you thinking about getting married.

CORY: Yeah, I done found the right one, Lyons. It's about time.

LYONS: Me and Bonnie been split up about four years now. About the time Papa retired. I guess she just got tired of all them changes I was putting her through.

(*Pause.*)

I always knew you was gonna make something out yourself. Your head was always in the right direction. So . . . you gonna stay in . . . make it a career . . . put in your twenty years?

CORY: I don't know. I got six already, I think that's enough.

LYONS: Stick with Uncle Sam and retire early. Ain't nothing out here. I guess Rose told you what happened with me. They got me down the workhouse. I thought I was being slick cashing other people's checks.

CORY: How much time you doing?

LYONS: They give me three years. I got that beat now. I ain't got but nine more months. It ain't so bad. You learn to deal with it like anything else. You got to take the crookeds with the straights. That's what Papa used to say. He used to say that when he struck out. I seen him strike out three times in a row . . . and the next time up he hit the ball over the grandstand. Right out there in Homestead Field. He wasn't satisfied hitting in the seats . . . he want to hit it over everything! After the game he had two hundred people standing around waiting to shake his hand. You got to take the crookeds with the straights. Yeah, Papa was something else.

CORY: You still playing?

LYONS: Cory . . . you know I'm gonna do that. There's some fellows down there we got us a band . . . we gonna try and stay together when we get out . . . but yeah, I'm still playing. It still helps me to get out of bed in the morning. As long as it do that I'm gonna be right there playing and trying to make some sense out of it.

ROSE (*calling*): Lyons, I got these eggs in the pan.

LYONS: Let me go on and get these eggs, man. Get ready to go bury Papa.

(*Pause.*)

How you doing? You doing all right?

(*Cory nods. Lyons touches him on the shoulder and they share a moment of silent grief. Lyons exits into the house. Cory wanders about the yard. Raynell enters.*)

RAYNELL: Hi.

CORY: Hi.

RAYNELL: Did you used to sleep in my room?

CORY: Yeah . . . that used to be my room.

RAYNELL: That's what Papa call it. "Cory's room." It got your football in the closet.

(*Rose comes to the door.*)

ROSE: Raynell, get in there and get them good shoes on.

RAYNELL: Mama, can't I wear these. Them other one hurt my feet.

ROSE: Well, they just gonna have to hurt your feet for a while. You ain't said they hurt your feet when you went down to the store and got them.

RAYNELL: They didn't hurt then. My feet done got bigger.

ROSE: Don't you give me no backtalk now. You get in there and get them shoes on.

(*Raynell exits into the house.*)

Ain't too much changed. He still got that piece of rag tied to that tree. He was out here swinging that bat. I was just ready to go back in the house. He swung that bat and then he just fell over. Seem like he swung it and stood there with this grin on his face . . . and then he just fell over. They carried him on down to the hospital, but I knew there wasn't no need . . . why don't you come on in the house?

CORY: Mama . . . I got something to tell you. I don't know how to tell you this . . . but I've got to tell you . . . I'm not going to Papa's funeral.

ROSE: Boy, hush your mouth. That's your daddy you talking about. I don't want hear that kind of talk this morning. I done raised you to come to this? You standing there all healthy and grown talking about you ain't going to your daddy's funeral?

CORY: Mama . . . listen . . .

ROSE: I don't want to hear it, Cory. You just get that thought out of your head.

CORY: I can't drag Papa with me everywhere I go. I've got to say no to him. One time in my life I've got to say no.

ROSE: Don't nobody have to listen to nothing like that. I know you and your daddy ain't seen eye to eye, but I ain't got to listen to that kind of talk this morning. Whatever was between you and your daddy . . . the time has come to put it aside. Just take it and set it over there on the shelf and forget about it. Disrespecting your daddy ain't gonna make you a man, Cory. You got to find a way to come to that on your own. Not going to your daddy's funeral ain't gonna make you a man.

CORY: The whole time I was growing up . . . living in his house . . . Papa was like a shadow that followed you everywhere. It weighed on you and sunk into your flesh. It would wrap around you and lay there until you couldn't tell which one was you anymore. That shadow digging in your flesh. Trying to crawl in. Trying to live through you. Everywhere I looked, Troy Maxson was staring back at me . . . hiding under the bed . . . in the closet. I'm just saying I've got to find a way to get rid of that shadow, Mama.

ROSE: You just like him. You got him in you good.

CORY: Don't tell me that, Mama.

ROSE: You Troy Maxson all over again.

CORY: I don't want to be Troy Maxson. I want to be me.

ROSE: You can't be nobody but who you are, Cory. That shadow wasn't nothing but you growing into yourself. You either got to grow into it or cut it down to fit you. But that's all you got to make life with. That's all you got to measure yourself against that world out there. Your daddy wanted you to be everything he wasn't . . . and at the same time he tried to make you into everything he was. I don't know if he was right or wrong . . . but I do know he meant to do more good than he meant to do harm. He wasn't always right. Sometimes when he touched he bruised. And sometimes when he took me in his arms he cut.

When I first met your daddy I thought . . . Here is a man I can lay down with and make a baby. That's the first thing I thought when I seen him. I was thirty years old and had done seen my share of men. But when he walked up to me and said, "I can dance a waltz that'll make you dizzy," I thought, Rose Lee, here is a man that you can open yourself up to and be filled to bursting. Here is a man that can fill all them empty spaces you been tipping around the edges of. One of them empty spaces was being somebody's mother.

I married your daddy and settled down to cooking his supper and keeping clean sheets on the bed. When your daddy walked through the house he was so big he filled it up. That was my first mistake. Not to make him leave some room for me. For my part in the matter. But at that time I wanted that. I wanted a house that I could sing in. And that's what your daddy gave me. I didn't know to keep up his strength I had to give up little pieces of mine. I did that. I took on his life as mine and mixed up the pieces so that you couldn't hardly tell which was which anymore. It was my choice. It was my life and I didn't have to live it like that. But that's what life offered me in the way of being a woman and I took it. I grabbed hold of it with both hands.

By the time Raynell came into the house, me and your daddy had done lost touch with one another. I didn't want to make my blessing off of nobody's misfortune . . . but I took on to Raynell like she was all them babies I had wanted and never had.

(*The phone rings.*)

Like I'd been blessed to relive a part of my life. And if the Lord see fit to keep up my strength . . . I'm gonna do her just like your daddy did you . . . I'm gonna give her the best of what's in me.

RAYNELL (*entering, still with her old shoes*): Mama . . . Reverend Tollivier on the phone.

(*Rose exits into the house.*)

RAYNELL: Hi.

CORY: Hi.

RAYNELL: You in the Army or the Marines?

CORY: Marines.

RAYNELL: Papa said it was the Army. Did you know Blue?

CORY: Blue? Who's Blue?

RAYNELL: Papa's dog what he sing about all the time.

CORY (*singing*): Hear it ring! Hear it ring!
I had a dog his name was Blue
You know Blue was mighty true
You know Blue was a good old dog
Blue treed a possum in a hollow log
You know from that he was a good old dog.
Hear it ring! Hear it ring!

(*Raynell joins in singing.*)

CORY AND RAYNELL: Blue treed a possum out on a limb
Blue looked at me and I looked at him
Grabbed that possum and put him in a sack
Blue stayed there till I came back
Old Blue's feets was big and round
Never allowed a possum to touch the ground.

Old Blue died and I dug his grave
I dug his grave with a silver spade
Let him down with a golden chain
And every night I call his name
Go on Blue, you good dog you
Go on Blue, you good dog you

RAYNELL: Blue laid down and died like a man
Blue laid down and died . . .

BOTH: Blue laid down and died like a man
   Now he's treeing possums in the Promised Land
   I'm gonna tell you this to let you know
   Blue's gone where the good dogs go
   When I hear old Blue bark
   When I hear old Blue bark
   Blue treed a possum in Noah's Ark
   Blue treed a possum in Noah's Ark.

(*Rose comes to the screen door.*)

ROSE: Cory, we gonna be ready to go in a minute.
CORY (*to Raynell*): You go on in the house and change them shoes like
   Mama told you so we can go to Papa's funeral.
RAYNELL: Okay, I'll be back.

(*Raynell exits into the house. Cory gets up and crosses over to the tree. Rose
stands in the screen door watching him. Gabriel enters from the alley.*)

GABRIEL (*calling*): Hey, Rose!
ROSE: Gabe?
GABRIEL: I'm here, Rose. Hey Rose, I'm here!

(*Rose enters from the house.*)

ROSE: Lord . . . Look here, Lyons!
LYONS: See, I told you, Rose . . . I told you they'd let him come.
CORY: How you doing, Uncle Gabe?
LYONS: How you doing, Uncle Gabe?
GABRIEL: Hey, Rose. It's time. It's time to tell St. Peter to open the gates.
   Troy, you ready? You ready, Troy. I'm gonna tell St. Peter to open the
   gates. You get ready now.

(*Gabriel, with great fanfare, braces himself to blow. The trumpet is without a
mouthpiece. He puts the end of it into his mouth and blows with great force,
like a man who has been waiting some twenty-odd years for this single moment.
No sound comes out of the trumpet. He braces himself and blows again with
the same result. A third time he blows. There is a weight of impossible description that falls away and leaves him bare and exposed to a frightful realization.
It is a trauma that a sane and normal mind would be unable to withstand. He
begins to dance. A slow, strange dance, eerie and life-giving. A dance of atavistic
signature and ritual. Lyons attempts to embrace him. Gabriel pushes Lyons
away. He begins to howl in what is an attempt at song, or perhaps a song turning back into itself in an attempt at speech. He finishes his dance and the gates
of heaven stand open as wide as God's closet.*)

   That's the way that go!

   [1987]

DAVID IVES [b. 1950]

Sure Thing

Characters

BILL AND BETTY, *both in their late twenties*

Setting: *A café table, with a couple of chairs*
Betty, reading at the table. An empty chair opposite her. Bill enters.

BILL: Excuse me. Is this chair taken?

BETTY: Excuse me?

BILL: Is this taken?

BETTY: Yes it is.

BILL: Oh. Sorry.

BETTY: Sure thing. (*A bell rings softly.*)

BILL: Excuse me. Is this chair taken?

BETTY: Excuse me?

BILL: Is this taken?

BETTY: No, but I'm expecting somebody in a minute.

BILL: Oh. Thanks anyway.

BETTY: Sure thing. (*A bell rings softly.*)

BILL: Excuse me. Is this chair taken?

BETTY: No, but I'm expecting somebody very shortly.

BILL: Would you mind if I sit here till he or she or it comes?

BETTY (*glances at her watch*): They seem to be pretty late. . . .

BILL: You never know who you might be turning down.

BETTY: Sorry. Nice try, though.

BILL: Sure thing. (*Bell.*) Is this seat taken?

BETTY: No it's not.

BILL: Would you mind if I sit here?

BETTY: Yes I would.

BILL: Oh. (*Bell.*) Is this chair taken?

BETTY: No it's not.

BILL: Would you mind if I sit here?

BETTY: No. Go ahead.

BILL: Thanks. (*He sits. She continues reading.*) Everyplace else seems to be taken.

BETTY: Mm-hm.

1112

BILL: Great place.

BETTY: Mm-hm.

BILL: What's the book?

BETTY: I just wanted to read in quiet, if you don't mind.

BILL: No. Sure thing. (*Bell.*)

BILL: Everyplace else seems to be taken.

BETTY: Mm-hm.

BILL: Great place for reading.

BETTY: Yes, I like it.

BILL: What's the book?

BETTY: *The Sound and the Fury.*

BILL: Oh. Hemingway. (*Bell.*) What's the book?

BETTY: *The Sound and the Fury.*

BILL: Oh. Faulkner.

BETTY: Have you read it?

BILL: Not . . . actually. I've sure read *about* . . . it, though. It's supposed to be great.

BETTY: It is great.

BILL: I hear it's great. (*Small pause.*) Waiter? (*Bell.*) What's the book?

BETTY: *The Sound and the Fury.*

BILL: Oh. Faulkner.

BETTY: Have you read it?

BILL: I'm a Mets fan, myself. (*Bell.*)

BETTY: Have you read it?

BILL: Yeah, I read it in college.

BETTY: Where was college?

BILL: I went to Oral Roberts University. (*Bell.*)

BETTY: Where was college?

BILL: I was lying. I never really went to college. I just like to party. (*Bell.*)

BETTY: Where was college?

BILL: Harvard.

BETTY: Do you like Faulkner?

BILL: I love Faulkner. I spent a whole winter reading him once.

BETTY: I've just started.

BILL: I was so excited after ten pages that I went out and bought everything else he wrote. One of the greatest reading experiences of my life. I mean, all that incredible psychological understanding. Page after page of gorgeous prose. His profound grasp of the mystery of time and human existence. The smells of the earth . . . What do you think?

BETTY: I think it's pretty boring. (*Bell.*)

BILL: What's the book?

BETTY: *The Sound and the Fury.*

BILL: Oh! Faulkner!

BETTY: Do you like Faulkner?

BILL: I love Faulkner.

BETTY: He's incredible.

BILL: I spent a whole winter reading him once.

BETTY: I was so excited after ten pages that I went out and bought everything else he wrote.

BILL: All that incredible psychological understanding.

BETTY: And the prose is so gorgeous.

BILL: And the way he's grasped the mystery of time—

BETTY: —and human existence. I can't believe I've waited this long to read him.

BILL: You never know. You might not have liked him before.

BETTY: That's true.

BILL: You might not have been ready for him. You have to hit these things at the right moment or it's no good.

BETTY: That's happening to me.

BILL: It's all in the timing. (*Small pause.*) My name's Bill, by the way.

BETTY: I'm Betty.

BILL: Hi.

BETTY: Hi. (*Small pause.*)

BILL: Yes I thought reading Faulkner was . . . a great experience.

BETTY: Yes. (*Small pause.*)

BILL: *The Sound and the Fury* . . . (*Another small pause.*)

BETTY: Well. Onwards and upwards. (*She goes back to her book.*)

BILL: Waiter—? (*Bell.*) You have to hit these things at the right moment or it's no good.

BETTY: That's happened to me.

BILL: It's all in the timing. My name's Bill, by the way.

BETTY: I'm Betty.

BILL: Hi.

BETTY: Hi.

BILL: Do you come in here a lot?

BETTY: Actually I'm just in town for two days from Pakistan.

BILL: Oh. Pakistan. (*Bell.*) My name's Bill, by the way.

BETTY: I'm Betty.

BILL: Hi.

BETTY: Hi.

BILL: Do you come here a lot?

BETTY: Every once in a while. Do you?

BILL: Not much anymore. Not as much as I used to. Before my nervous breakdown. (*Bell.*) Do you come in here a lot?

BETTY: Why are you asking?

BILL: Just interested.

BETTY: Are you really interested, or do you just want to pick me up?

BILL: No, I'm really interested.

BETTY: Why would you be interested in whether I come in here a lot?

BILL: Just . . . getting acquainted.

BETTY: Maybe you're only interested for the sake of making small talk long enough to ask me back to your place to listen to some music, or because you've just rented some great tape for your VCR, or because you've got some terrific unknown Django Reinhardt record, only all you'll really want to do is fuck—which you won't do very well—after which you'll go into the bathroom and pee very loudly, then pad into the kitchen and get yourself a beer from the refrigerator without asking me whether I'd like anything, and then you'll proceed to lie back down beside me and confess that you've got a girlfriend named Stephanie who's away at medical school in Belgium for a year, and that you've been involved with her—*off and on*—in what you'll call a very "intricate" relationship, for about *seven YEARS*. None of which *interests* me, mister!

BILL: Okay. (*Bell.*) Do you come in here a lot?

BETTY: Every other day, I think.

BILL: I come in here quite a lot and I don't remember seeing you.

BETTY: I guess we must be on different schedules.

BILL: Missed connections.

BETTY: Yes. Different time zones.

BILL: Amazing how you can live right next door to somebody in this town and never even know it.

BETTY: I know.

BILL: City life.

BETTY: It's crazy.

BILL: We probably pass each other in the street every day. Right in front of this place, probably.

BETTY: Yep.

BILL (*looks around*): Well, the waiters here sure seem to be in some different time zone. I can't seem to locate one anywhere . . . Waiter! (*He looks back.*) So what do you—(*He sees that she's gone back to her book.*)

BETTY: I beg pardon?

BILL: Nothing. Sorry. (*Bell.*)

BETTY: I guess we must be on different schedules.

BILL: Missed connections.

BETTY: Yes. Different time zones.

BILL: Amazing how you can live right next door to somebody in this town and never even know it.

BETTY: I know.

BILL: City life.

BETTY: It's crazy.

BILL: You weren't waiting for somebody when I came in, were you?

BETTY: Actually, I was.

BILL: Oh. Boyfriend?

BETTY: Sort of.

BILL: What's a sort-of boyfriend?

BETTY: My husband. ✗

BILL: Ah-ha. (*Bell.*) You weren't waiting for somebody when I came in, were you?

BETTY: Actually I was.

BILL: Oh. Boyfriend?

BETTY: Sort of.

BILL: What's a sort-of boyfriend?

BETTY: We were meeting here to break up.

BILL: Mm-hm . . . (*Bell.*) What's a sort-of boyfriend?

BETTY: My lover. Here she comes right now! (*Bell.*)

BILL: You weren't waiting for somebody when I came in, were you?

✗ BETTY: No, just reading.

BILL: Sort of a sad occupation for a Friday night, isn't it? Reading here, all by yourself?

BETTY: Do you think so?

BILL: Well sure. I mean, what's a good-looking woman like you doing out alone on a Friday night?

BETTY: Trying to keep away from lines like that.

BILL: No, listen—(*Bell.*) You weren't waiting for somebody when I came in, were you?

BETTY: No, just reading.

BILL: Sort of a sad occupation for a Friday night, isn't it? Reading here all by yourself?

BETTY: I guess it is, in a way.

BILL: What's a good-looking woman like you doing out alone on a Friday night anyway? No offense, but . . .

BETTY: I'm out alone on a Friday night for the first time in a very long time.

BILL: Oh.

BETTY: You see, I just recently ended a relationship.

BILL: Oh.

BETTY: Of rather long standing.

BILL: I'm sorry. (*Small pause.*) Well listen, since reading by yourself is such a sad occupation for a Friday night, would you like to go elsewhere?

BETTY: No . . .

BILL: Do something else?

BETTY: No thanks.

BILL: I was headed out to the movies in a while anyway.

BETTY: I don't think so.

BILL: Big chance to let Faulkner catch his breath. All those long sentences get him pretty tired.

BETTY: Thanks anyway.

BILL: Okay.

BETTY: I appreciate the invitation.

BILL: Sure thing. (*Bell.*) You weren't waiting for somebody when I came in, were you?

BETTY: No, just reading.

BILL: Sort of a sad occupation for a Friday night, isn't it? Reading here all by yourself?

BETTY: I guess I was trying to think of it as existentially romantic. You know—cappuccino, great literature, rainy night . . .

BILL: That only works in Paris. We *could* hop the late plane to Paris. Get on a Concorde. Find a café . . .

BETTY: I'm a little short on plane fare tonight.

BILL: Darn it, so am I.

BETTY: To tell you the truth, I was headed to the movies after I finished this section. Would you like to come along? Since you can't locate a waiter?

BILL: That's a very nice offer, but . . .

BETTY: Uh-huh. Girlfriend?

BILL: Two, actually. One of them's pregnant, and Stephanie— (*Bell.*)

BETTY: Girlfriend?

BILL: No, I don't have a girlfriend. Not if you mean the castrating bitch I dumped last night. (*Bell.*)

BETTY: Girlfriend?

BILL: Sort of. Sort of.

BETTY: What's a sort-of girlfriend?

BILL: My mother. (*Bell.*) I just ended a relationship, actually.

BETTY: Oh.

BILL: Of rather long standing.

BETTY: I'm sorry to hear it.

BILL: This is my first night out alone in a long time. I feel a little bit at sea, to tell you the truth.

BETTY: So you didn't stop to talk because you're a Moonie, or you have some weird political affiliation—?

BILL: Nope. Straight-down-the-ticket Republican. (*Bell.*) Straight-down-the-ticket Democrat. (*Bell.*) Can I tell you something about politics? (*Bell.*) I like to think of myself as a citizen of the universe. (*Bell.*) I'm unaffiliated.

BETTY: That's a relief. So am I.

BILL: I vote my beliefs.

BETTY: Labels are not important.

BILL: Labels are not important, exactly. Like me, for example. I mean, what does it matter if I had a two-point at—(*bell*)—three-point at (*bell*)—four-point at college, or if I did come from Pittsburgh— (*bell*)—Cleveland—(*bell*)—Westchester County?

BETTY: Sure.

BILL: I believe that a man is what he is. (*Bell.*) A person is what he is. (*Bell.*) A person is . . . what they are.

BETTY: I think so too.

BILL: So what if I admire Trotsky? (*Bell.*) So what if I once had a total-body liposuction? (*Bell.*) So what if I don't have a penis? (*Bell.*) So what if I once spent a year in the Peace Corps? I was acting on my convictions.

BETTY: Sure.

BILL: You can't just hang a sign on a person.

BETTY: Absolutely. I'll bet you're a Scorpio. (*Many bells ring.*) Listen, I was headed to the movies after I finished this section. Would you like to come along?

BILL: That sounds like fun. What's playing?

BETTY: A couple of the really early Woody Allen movies.

BILL: Oh.

BETTY: Don't you like Woody Allen?

BILL: Sure. I like Woody Allen.

BETTY: But you're not crazy about Woody Allen.

BILL: Those early ones kind of get on my nerves.

BETTY: Uh-huh. (*Bell.*)

| BILL: Y'know I was | —(*simultaneously*)— | BETTY: I was thinking |
| headed to the— | | about— |

BILL: I'm sorry.

BETTY: No, go ahead.

BILL: I was going to say that I was headed to the movies in a little while, and . . .

BETTY: So was I.

BILL: The Woody Allen festival?

BETTY: Just up the street.

BILL: Do you like the early ones?

BETTY: I think anybody who doesn't ought to be run off the planet.

BILL: How many times have you seen *Bananas*?

BETTY: Eight times.

BILL: Twelve. So are you still interested? (*Long pause.*)

BETTY: Do you like Entenmann's crumb cake . . . ?

BILL: Last night I went out at two in the morning to get one. (*Small pause.*) Did you have an Etch-a-Sketch as a child?

BETTY: Yes! And do you like Brussels sprouts? (*Small pause.*)

BILL: I think they're gross.

BETTY: They *are* gross!

BILL: Do you still believe in marriage in spite of current sentiments against it?

BETTY: Yes.

BILL: And children?

BETTY: Three of them.

BILL: Two girls and a boy.

BETTY: Harvard, Vassar, and Brown.

BILL: And will you love me?

BETTY: Yes.

BILL: And cherish me forever?

BETTY: Yes.

BILL: Do you still want to go to the movies?

BETTY: Sure thing.

BILL AND BETTY (*together*): *Waiter!*

(*Blackout.*)

[1988]

LYNN NOTTAGE   [b. 1964]

POOF!

Production History: *POOF!* premiered at Actors Theatre of Louisville (Jon Jory, Producing Director; Alexander Speer, Executive Director) on March 20, 1993, as part of the Humana Festival of New American Plays under the direction of Seret Scott. The set design was by Paul Owen, the lights by Karl E. Haas and the costumes by Kevin R. McLeod. The stage manager was Julie A. Richardson and the production dramaturg was Michael Bigelow Dixon. The cast was as follows:

LOUREEN: Elain Graham
FLORENCE: Yvette Hawkins

Characters
SAMUEL, *Loureen's husband*
LOUREEN, *a demure housewife, early thirties*
FLORENCE, *Loureen's best friend, early thirties*

Time: *The present*
Place: *Kitchen*

A Note: Nearly half the women on death row in the United States were convicted of killing abusive husbands. Spontaneous combustion is not recognized as a capital crime.

(*Darkness.*)

SAMUEL (*In the darkness*): WHEN I COUNT TO TEN I DON' WANT TO SEE YA! I DON' WANT TO HEAR YA! ONE, TWO, THREE, FOUR—
LOUREEN (*In the darkness*): DAMN YOU TO HELL, SAMUEL!

(*A bright flash.*)
   (*Lights rise. A huge pile of smoking ashes rests in the middle of the kitchen. Loureen, a demure housewife in her early thirties, stares down at the ashes incredulously. She bends and lifts a pair of spectacles from the remains. She ever so slowly backs away.*)

Samuel? Uh! (*Places the spectacles on the kitchen table*) Uh! . . . Samuel! (*Looks around*) Don't fool with me now. I'm not in the mood. (*Whispers*) Samuel? I didn't mean it really. I'll be good if you come back . . . Come on now, dinner's waiting. (*Chuckles, then stops abruptly*) Now stop your foolishness . . . And let's sit down. (*Examines the spectacles*) Uh! (*Softly*) Don't be cross with me. Sure I forgot to pick up your shirt for tomorrow. I can wash another, I'll do it right now. Right now! Sam? . . . (*Cautiously*) You hear me! (*Awaits a response*) Maybe I didn't ever intend to wash your shirt. (*Pulls back as though about to receive a blow; a moment*) Uh! (*Sits down and dials the telephone*) Florence, honey, could you come on down for a moment. There's been a . . . little . . . accident . . . Quickly please. Uh!

(*Loureen hangs up the phone. She gets a broom and a dust pan. She hesitantly approaches the pile of ashes. She gets down on her hands and knees and takes a closer look. A fatuous grin spreads across her face. She is startled by a sudden knock on the door. She slowly walks across the room like a possessed child. Loureen lets in Florence, her best friend and upstairs neighbor. Florence, also a housewife in her early thirties, wears a floral housecoat and a pair of oversized slippers. Without acknowledgment Loureen proceeds to saunter back across the room.*)

FLORENCE: HEY!

LOUREEN (*Pointing at the ashes*): Uh! . . . (*She struggles to formulate words, which press at the inside of her mouth, not quite realized*) Uh! . . .

FLORENCE: You all right? What happened? (*Sniffs the air*) Smells like you burned something? (*Stares at the huge pile of ashes*) What the devil is that?

LOUREEN (*Hushed*): Samuel . . . It's Samuel, I think.

FLORENCE: What's he done now?

LOUREEN: It's him. It's him. (*Nods her head repeatedly*)

FLORENCE: Chile, what's wrong with you? Did he finally drive you out your mind? I knew something was going to happen sooner or later.

LOUREEN: Dial 911, Florence!

FLORENCE: Why? You're scaring me!

LOUREEN: Dial 911!

(*Florence picks up the telephone and quickly dials.*)

I think I killed him.

(*Florence hangs up the telephone.*)

FLORENCE: What?

LOUREEN (*Whimpers*): I killed him! I killed Samuel!

FLORENCE: Come again? . . . He's dead dead?

(*Loureen wrings her hands and nods her head twice, mouthing "dead dead." Florence backs away.*)

No, stop it, I don't have time for this. I'm going back upstairs. You know how Samuel hates to find me here when he gets home. You're not going to get me this time. (*Louder*) Y'all can have your little joke, I'm not part of it! (*A moment. She takes a hard look into Loureen's eyes; she squints*) Did you really do it this time?

LOUREEN (*Hushed*): I don't know how or why it happened, it just did.

FLORENCE: Why are you whispering?

LOUREEN: I don't want to talk too loud—something else is liable to disappear.

FLORENCE: Where's his body?

LOUREEN (*Points to the pile of ashes*): There! . . .

FLORENCE: You burned him?

LOUREEN: I DON'T KNOW! (*Covers her mouth as if to muffle her words; hushed*) I think so.

FLORENCE: Either you did or you didn't, what you mean you don't know? We're talking murder, Loureen, not oven settings.

LOUREEN: You think I'm playing?

FLORENCE: How many times have I heard you talk about being rid of him. How many times have we sat at this very table and laughed about the many ways we could do it and how many times have you done it? None.

LOUREEN (*Lifting the spectacles*): A pair of cheap spectacles, that's all that's left. And you know how much I hate these. You ever seen him without them, no! . . . He counted to four and disappeared. I swear to God!

FLORENCE: Don't bring the Lord into this just yet! Sit down now . . . What you got to sip on?

LOUREEN: I don't know whether to have a stiff shot of scotch or a glass of champagne.

(*Florence takes a bottle of sherry out of the cupboard and pours them each a glass. Loureen downs hers, then holds out her glass for more.*)

He was . . .

FLORENCE: Take your time.

LOUREEN: Standing there.

FLORENCE: And?

LOUREEN: He exploded.

FLORENCE: Did that muthafucka hit you again?

LOUREEN: No . . . he exploded. Boom! Right in front of me. He was shouting like he does, being all colored, then he raised up that big crusty hand to hit me, and poof, he was gone . . . I barely got words out and I'm looking down at a pile of ash.

(*Florence belts back her sherry. She wipes her forehead and pours them both another.*)

FLORENCE: Chile, I'll give you this, in terms of color you've matched my husband Edgar, the story king. He came in at six Sunday morning, talking about he'd hit someone with his car, and had spent all night trying to outrun the police. I felt sorry for him. It turns out he was playing poker with his paycheck no less. You don't want to know how I found out . . . But I did.

LOUREEN: You think I'm lying?

FLORENCE: I certainly hope so, Loureen. For your sake and my heart's.

LOUREEN: Samuel always said if I raised my voice something horrible would happen. And it did. I'm a witch . . . the devil spawn!

FLORENCE: You've been watching too much television.

LOUREEN: Never seen anything like this on television. Wish I had, then I'd know what to do . . . There's no question, I'm a witch. (*Looks at her hands with disgust*)

FLORENCE: Chile, don't tell me you've been messing with them mojo women again? What did I tell ya.

(*Loureen, agitated, stands and sits back down.*)

LOUREEN: He's not coming back. Oh no, how could he? It would be a miracle! Two in one day . . . I could be canonized. Worse yet, he could be . . . All that needs to happen now is for my palms to bleed and I'll be eternally remembered as Saint Loureen, the patron of battered wives. Women from across the country will make pilgrimages to me, laying pies and pot roast at my feet and asking the good saint to make their husbands turn to dust. How often does a man like Samuel get damned to hell, and go?

(*She breaks down. Florence moves to console her friend, then realizes that Loureen is actually laughing hysterically.*)

FLORENCE: You smoking crack?

LOUREEN: Do I look like I am?

FLORENCE: Hell, I've seen old biddies creeping out of crack houses, talking about they were doing church work.

LOUREEN: Florence, please be helpful, I'm very close to the edge! . . . I don't know what to do next! Do I sweep him up? Do I call the police? Do I . . .

(*The phone rings.*)

Oh God.

FLORENCE: You gonna let it ring?

(*Loureen reaches for the telephone slowly.*)

LOUREEN: NO! (*Holds the receiver without picking it up, paralyzed*) What if it's his mother? . . . She knows!

(*The phone continues to ring. They sit until it stops. They both breathe a sigh of relief.*)

I should be mourning, I should be praying, I should be thinking of the burial, but all that keeps popping into my mind is what will I wear on television when I share my horrible and wonderful story with a studio audience . . . (*Whimpers*) He's made me a killer, Florence, and you remember what a gentle child I was. (*Whispers*) I'm a killer, I'm a killer, I'm a killer.

FLORENCE: I wouldn't throw that word about too lightly even in jest. Talk like that gets around.

LOUREEN: You think they'll lock me up? A few misplaced words and I'll probably get the death penalty, isn't that what they do with women like me, murderesses?

FLORENCE: Folks have done time for less.

LOUREEN: Thank you, just what I needed to hear!

FLORENCE: What did you expect, that I was going to throw up my arms and congratulate you? Why'd you have to go and lose your mind at this time of day, while I got a pot of rice on the stove and Edgar's about to walk in the door and wonder where his goddamn food is. (*Losing her cool*) And he's going to start in on me about all the nothing I've been doing during the day and why I can't work and then he'll mention how clean you keep your home. And I don't know how I'm going to look him in the eye without . . .

LOUREEN: I'm sorry, Florence. Really. It's out of my hands now.

(*She takes Florence's hand and squeezes it.*)

FLORENCE (*Regaining her composure*): You swear on your right tit?

LOUREEN (*Clutching both breasts*): I swear on both of them!

FLORENCE: Both your breasts, Loureen! You know what will happen if you're lying. (*Loureen nods; hushed*) Both your breasts Loureen?

LOUREEN: Yeah!

FLORENCE (*Examines the pile of ashes, then shakes her head*): Oh sweet, sweet Jesus. He must have done something truly terrible.

LOUREEN: No more than usual. I just couldn't take being hit one more time.

FLORENCE: You've taken a thousand blows from that man, couldn't you've turned the cheek and waited? I'd have helped you pack. Like we talked about.

(*A moment.*)

LOUREEN: Uh! . . . I could blow on him and he'd disappear across the linoleum. (*Snaps her fingers*) Just like that. Should I be feeling remorse or regret or some other "R" word? I'm strangely jubilant, like on prom night when Samuel and I first made love. That's the feeling! (*The women lock eyes*) Uh!

FLORENCE: Is it . . .

LOUREEN: Like a ton of bricks been lifted from my shoulders, yeah.

FLORENCE: Really?

LOUREEN: Yeah!

(*Florence walks to the other side of the room.*)

FLORENCE: You bitch!

LOUREEN: What?

FLORENCE: We made a pact.

LOUREEN: I know.

FLORENCE: You've broken it . . . We agreed that when things got real bad for both of us we'd . . . you know . . . together . . . Do I have to go back upstairs to that? . . . What next?

LOUREEN: I thought you'd tell me! . . . I don't know!

FLORENCE: I don't know!

LOUREEN: I don't know!

(*Florence begins to walk around the room, nervously touching objects. Loureen sits, wringing her hands and mumbling softly to herself.*)

FLORENCE: Now you got me, Loureen, I'm truly at a loss for words.

LOUREEN: Everybody always told me, "Keep your place, Loureen." My place, the silent spot on the couch with a wine cooler in my hand and a pleasant smile that warmed the heart. All this time I didn't know why he was so afraid for me to say anything, to speak up. Poof! . . . I've never been by myself, except for them two weeks when he won the office pool and went to Reno with his cousin Mitchell. He wouldn't tell me where he was going until I got that postcard with the cowboy smoking a hundred cigarettes . . . Didn't Sonny Larkin look good last week at Caroline's? He looked good, didn't he . . .

(*Florence nods. She nervously picks up Samuel's jacket, which is hanging on the back of the chair. She clutches it unconsciously.*)

NO! No! Don't wrinkle that, that's his favorite jacket. He'll kill me. Put it back!

(*Florence returns the jacket to its perch. Loureen begins to quiver.*)

I'm sorry. (*She grabs the jacket and wrinkles it up*) There! (*She then digs into the coat pockets and pulls out his wallet and a movie stub*) Look at that, he said he didn't go to the movies last night. Working late. (*Frantically thumbs through his wallet*) Picture of his motorcycle, Social Security card, driver's license, and look at that from our wedding. (*Smiling*) I looked good, didn't I? (*She puts the pictures back in the wallet and holds the jacket up to her face*) There were some good things. (*She then sweeps her hand over the jacket to remove the wrinkles, and folds it ever so carefully, and finally throws it in the garbage*) And out of my mouth those words made him disappear. All these years and just words, Florence. That's all they were.

FLORENCE: I'm afraid I won't ever get those words out. I'll start resenting you, honey. I'm afraid won't anything change for me.

LOUREEN: I been to that place.

FLORENCE: Yeah? But now I wish I could relax these old lines (*Touches her forehead*) for a minute maybe. Edgar has never done me the way Samuel did you, but he sure did take the better part of my life.

LOUREEN: Not yet, Florence.

FLORENCE (*Nods*): I have the children to think of . . . right?

LOUREEN: You can think up a hundred things before . . .

FLORENCE: Then come upstairs with me . . . we'll wait together for Edgar and then you can spit out your words and . . .

LOUREEN: I can't do that.

FLORENCE: Yes you can. Come on now.

(*Loureen shakes her head no.*)

Well, I guess my mornings are not going to be any different.

LOUREEN: If you can say for certain, then I guess they won't be. I couldn't say that.

FLORENCE: But you got a broom and a dust pan, you don't need anything more than that . . . He was a bastard and nobody will care that he's gone.

LOUREEN: Phone's gonna start ringing soon, people are gonna start asking soon, and they'll care.

FLORENCE: What's your crime? Speaking your mind?

LOUREEN: Maybe I should mail him to his mother. I owe her that. I feel bad for her, she didn't understand how it was. I can't just throw him away and pretend like it didn't happen. Can I?

FLORENCE: I didn't see anything but a pile of ash. As far as I know you got a little careless and burned a chicken.

LOUREEN: He was always threatening not to come back.

FLORENCE: I heard him.

LOUREEN: It would've been me eventually.

FLORENCE: Yes.

LOUREEN: I should call the police, or someone.

FLORENCE: Why? What are you gonna tell them? About all those times they refused to help, about all those nights you slept in my bed 'cause you were afraid to stay down here? About the time he nearly took out your eye 'cause you flipped the television channel?

LOUREEN: No.

FLORENCE: You've got it, girl!

LOUREEN: Good-bye to the fatty meats and the salty food. Good-bye to the bourbon and the bologna sandwiches. Good-bye to the smell of his feet, his breath and his bowel movements . . . (*A moment. She closes her eyes and, reliving a horrible memory, she shudders*) Good-bye. (*Walks over to the pile of ashes*) Samuel? . . . Just checking.

FLORENCE: Good-bye Samuel.

(*They both smile.*)

LOUREEN: I'll let the police know that he's missing tomorrow . . .

FLORENCE: Why not the next day?

LOUREEN: Chicken's warming in the oven, you're welcome to stay.

FLORENCE: Chile, I got a pot of rice on the stove, kids are probably acting out . . . and Edgar, well . . . Listen, I'll stop in tomorrow.

LOUREEN: For dinner?

FLORENCE: Edgar wouldn't stand for that. Cards maybe.

LOUREEN: Cards.

(*The women hug for a long moment. Florence exits. Loureen stands over the ashes for a few moments contemplating what to do. She finally decides to sweep them under the carpet, and then proceeds to set the table and sit down to eat her dinner.*)

[1993]

PART FOUR

Reading and Writing about Literature

CHAPTER 1

Introduction to Reading and Writing about Literature

"Nobody reads anymore."

"People don't know how to write."

"We're becoming a nation of illiterates."

Maybe you've heard laments like these. They have sounded through our culture for several years now, indeed for at least several decades. Proclamations on the sad lack of literacy in modern life have been widely reported, as in January 2008, when Apple Computer cofounder Steve Jobs predicted that Amazon's Kindle e-book reader was doomed to failure because "people don't read anymore." (Perhaps ironically, he said this in a room full of reporters and must have known that these writers were going to quote these words in print and that millions of people would read them.) If we take these warnings seriously, it would seem that modern culture and modern education are in big trouble.

But news of the death of literacy is premature. In fact, one can make a good case that reading and writing occupy a more central place in our day-to-day life than they have at any other point in history. We are bombarded all day long with written messages. Billboards, product packaging, Web sites, blogs, flyers, wikis, advertisements, restaurant menus, e-mails, text messages, social media updates—the list goes on and on. Even while watching TV, arguably the least literary of media, we are often given a reading task: think of the "crawl" of updates that appears at the bottom of the screen during newscasts, the captions that identify interview subjects, even the station logos in the corner of the screen. The average North American in the early twenty-first century encounters literally hundreds of written messages every day, and most of us have no particular problem reading these messages. Often we don't even notice that we are doing so.

In a similar vein, most of us spend more time writing than people have at any earlier point in history. The vast majority of jobs these days require some amount of writing. Sometimes this requirement is extensive, as when engineers write sophisticated reports on their projects, while some work-related writing is as simple as a daily e-mail to communicate with others on the job. Students, of course, take notes, complete home-work assignments, and write papers. Even in our leisure time, we are likely to update our social media, comment on a friend's blog post, send a text message, or write a note to a family member or friend.

If you were to keep a list of every single thing you read and wrote in a day (a list that would, of course, have to include an entry for the list you were writing), you might be surprised at how extensive that list was by the end of the day.

So, if literacy is alive and well in the modern world, why is a book like this one necessary? Why do colleges and universities offer, or even re-quire, literature classes? Don't we already know enough about reading and writing? Do we really need to learn how to read and write about lit-erature? The answer as to why people *do* need to learn these skills is that imaginative literature is different from most of the other writing we read every day, and reading and writing about literature requires, and builds, a very different set of skills than those we bring to a Wikipedia article or a Facebook posting.

WHY READ LITERATURE?

Let's take a moment to reflect on why we read literature. Of course, there is no single or simple answer. People read to be informed, to be enter-tained, to be exposed to new ideas, or to have familiar concepts re-inforced. Often, people read just to enjoy a good story or to get a glimpse of how other people think and feel. But literature does much more than give us a compelling plot or a look into an author's thoughts and emo-tions—although at its best it does these things as well. Literature ex-plores the larger world and the ways in which people interact with that world and with one another. So even when what we read is entirely fic-tional, we nevertheless learn about real life. And, indeed, by affecting our thoughts and feelings, literature can indirectly affect our actions as well. Thus literature not only reflects but even helps to shape our world.

Literature, then, is not merely informational, like so much of the read-ing we do in our everyday lives. It does not stand up well to haste, dis-tractions, or multitasking. It is not meant to be browsed, skimmed, or linked away from as we search for particular facts or knowledge as effi-ciently as possible. Instead, it is designed for sustained reading, meaning that to do it justice we need to read it from beginning to end and pay it our full attention for all that time. What is most important in literature is rarely highlighted for us. Rather, we must use our intelligence to figure out the significance the literature holds for us, and we must realize that this significance may be different for a different reader. Because of this, reading literature helps us develop the skills of introspection, sustained attention, and deep analysis, skills that can help us in other areas of our lives as well.

WHY WRITE ABOUT LITERATURE?

Even students who enjoy reading poems, stories, or plays do not always enjoy writing about them. Some claim that having to analyze literature kills the fun they find in a good story. For others, the task of writing about literature can seem intimidating, frustrating, or just plain dull. If you share any of these prejudices, try to put them aside while we consider the value of writing about literature.

Writing about literature requires a special set of knowledge and skills. When you write about a story, a poem, or a play, you need to be particularly attentive to language, the medium of literature. This hones both analytical ability and creativity. In this sort of writing, you also need to pay close attention to your own use of language—just as you must pay attention to the language of the story, poem, or play—and doing so may have ripple effects that improve all your writing. Writing about literature, then, can help make you more thoughtful and articulate, better able to make yourself heard and understood, and obviously those are qualities that can improve your life well beyond the bounds of your literature classroom. And, far from killing the enjoyment of reading, writing about literature can increase that enjoyment and provide a sense of accomplishment as you look at the well-crafted paper you've written.

Writing about literature also has real-world usefulness. By forcing us to organize our thoughts and state clearly what we think, writing an essay helps us clarify what we know and believe. It gives us a chance to affect the thinking of our readers. Even more important, we actually learn as we write. In the process of writing, we often make new discoveries and forge new connections between ideas. We find and work through contradictions in our thinking, and we create whole new lines of thought as we work to make linear sense out of an often chaotic jumble of impressions. So, while *reading* literature can teach us much about the world, *writing* about literature often teaches us about ourselves.

WHAT TO EXPECT IN A LITERATURE CLASS

Every classroom, like every group of people in any setting, is its own unique world, with its own set of expectations and social interactions. However, there are certain features common to most literature classes, what might be considered the culture of a college or university literature class.

Unlike some other classes on campus, a literature class is not the sort of class where attendance is optional as long as you master the material and are able to pass the tests. Though your class may have a lecture component, it will almost certainly have a large discussion component as well, a give-and-take between students and instructor regarding the stories, poems, and plays you have read. In some ways, these discussions are the most important part of a literature class, and no amount of extra study on your own or sharing notes with a classmate can make up for having missed class. To follow these discussions, let alone to participate, you obviously will have to complete the reading. Whether or not your class has a stated attendance policy, to do well you need to be there and to be caught up with all reading and writing assignments. Participation is important.

Discussions in literature classes are usually interesting, because no two people come away from a particular literary text with exactly the same impressions. You may dislike a particular story and be surprised to discover that most of your fellow students loved it. A poem may leave you smiling while it makes one of your classmates cry. A character's motivation might seem obvious to you but baffle someone else. These differences arise because each reader is distinctive. Because you have lived a unique life, you have a knowledge of the world that is slightly different from any other reader's. You bring this personal history and knowledge to your reading, along with your own mind and temperament, your own likes and dislikes, and even all the knowledge gained from your past reading. Differing opinions are valid in literature classes, and each reader is in a position to enrich the conversation by speaking up in class.

Just as speaking up is part of participating, so too is attentive listening. While it is fair to regard your take on a piece of literature as valid, that doesn't mean you need only consider your own opinions. Listening to what your instructor and classmates have to say is equally important, especially when they disagree with you. If your position has value, so do theirs. Perhaps they have seen something you missed, or perhaps they consider crucial something that you had dismissed as unimportant. You may find your first impressions shifting during these discussions, or you may find them solidifying. Either of these outcomes is a good sign that you're learning. The most important thing you bring to a literary discussion is a willingness to share your own perspectives while remaining open to the possibility of learning from others.

Attentive listeners tend to make the best note takers, and having good class notes will prove incredibly helpful when you sit down to write your papers. This important skill will be covered in the next chapter.

LITERATURE AND ENJOYMENT

You may have noticed that little has been said so far about the idea that reading and writing about literature can also be fun. Some students really enjoy reading imaginative literature and writing papers about it. If you're in that group, you're lucky; your literature class will be fun and interesting for you, and—not incidentally—you'll probably do good work in the course. If you've never been fond of reading and writing about literature, though, you might spend a little time thinking about why some of your classmates enjoy this sort of work as well as what you might do to increase your own enjoyment of literature and investment in the writing process. You'll be happier and write better papers if you can put aside any previous negative experiences with literature and writing you may have had and approach your task with a positive mind-set. As you are introduced to new authors, new characters and settings, and new ideas, your literature class may surprise you. It could even end up being a favorite.

CHAPTER 2

The Role of Good Reading

Writing about literature begins, of course, with reading, so it stands to reason that good reading is the first step toward successful writing. But what exactly is "good reading"? Good reading is, generally speaking, not fast reading. In fact, often the best advice a student can receive about reading is to *slow down*. Reading well is all about paying attention, and you can't pay attention if you're text-messaging a friend as you read or racing to get through an assignment and move on to "more important" things. If you make a point of giving yourself plenty of time and minimizing your distractions, you'll get more out of your reading and probably enjoy it more as well.

THE VALUE OF REREADING

The best reading is often rereading, and the best readers are those who are willing to go back and reread a piece of literature again and again. It is not uncommon for professional literary critics—who are, after all, some of the most skilled readers—to read a particular poem, story, or play literally dozens of times before they feel equipped to write about it. And well-written literature rewards this willingness to reread, allowing readers to continue seeing new things with each reading. If you have a favorite book you return to over and over, or a favorite song you like to listen to again and again, you intuitively understand this truth. Realistically, of course, you will not have the time to read every assigned piece many times before discussing it in class or preparing to write about it, but you should not give up or feel frustrated if you fail to "get" a piece of literature on the first reading. Be prepared to go back and reread key sections, or even a whole work, if doing so could help with your understanding.

CRITICAL READING

The sort of reading that works best with imaginative literature—or any other complex writing—is sometimes called "active reading" or "critical reading," though *critical* here implies not fault-finding but rather thoughtful consideration. Much of the reading we do in everyday life is passive and noncritical. We glance at street signs to see where we are; we check a sports Web site to find out how our favorite team is doing; we read packages for information about the products we use. And in general, we take in all this information passively, without questioning it or looking for deeper meaning. For many kinds of reading, this is perfectly appropriate. It would hardly make sense to ask, "*Why* is this Pine Street?" or "What do they *mean* when they say there are twelve ounces of soda in this can?" There is, however, another type of reading, one that involves asking critical questions and probing more deeply into the meaning of what we read, and this is the kind of reading most appropriate to imaginative literature (especially if we intend to discuss or write about that literature later).

THE MYTH OF "HIDDEN MEANING"

There is a persistent myth in literature classes that the purpose of reading is to scour a text for "hidden meaning." Do not be taken in by this myth. In fact, many instructors dislike the phrase *hidden meaning*, which has unpleasant and inaccurate connotations. First, it suggests a sort of willful subterfuge on the part of the author, a deliberate attempt to make his or her work difficult to understand or to exclude the reader. Second, it makes the process of reading sound like digging for buried treasure rather than a systematic intellectual process. Finally, the phrase implies that a text has a single, true meaning and that communication and understanding move in one direction only: from the crafty author to the searching reader.

In truth, the meanings in literary texts are not hidden, and your job as a reader is not to root around for them. Rather, if a text is not immediately accessible to you, it is because you need to read more actively, and meaning will then emerge in a collaborative effort as you work *with* the text to create a consistent interpretation. (This is the basis of reader-response criticism, which is explained on pages 1275–76.) Obviously, active reading requires effort. If you find this sort of reading hard, take that as a good sign. It means you're paying the sort of attention that a well-crafted poem, story, or play requires of a reader. You also should not assume that English teachers have a key that allows them to unlock the one secret truth of a text. If, as is often the case, your instructor sees more or different meanings in a piece of literature than you do, this is because he or she is trained to read actively and has probably spent much more time than you have with literature in general and more time with the particular text assigned to you.

ACTIVE READING

Annotating

If the first suggestions for active reading are to slow down and to know that a second (or even a third) reading is in order, the next suggestion is to read with a pen or pencil in hand in order to annotate your text and take notes. If you look inside a literature textbook belonging to your instructor or to an advanced literature student, chances are you'll see something of a mess—words and passages circled or underlined, comments and questions scrawled in the margins (technically called *marginalia*) or even between the lines (called *interlinear* notes), and unexplained punctuation marks or other symbols decorating the pages. You should not interpret this as disrespect for the text or author or as a sign of a disordered mind. Indeed, it is quite the opposite of both these things. It is simply textual annotation, and it means that someone has been engaged in active reading. Perhaps an extreme example is the poet and critic Samuel Taylor Coleridge, who was famous for annotating not only his own books but also those he borrowed from friends—a habit unlikely to secure a friendship—and his marginalia actually make up one entire volume of his collected works.

If you are not accustomed to textual annotation, it may be hard to know where to begin. There is no single, widely used system of annotation, and you will almost certainly begin to develop your own techniques as you practice active reading. Here, however, are a few tips to get you started:

- **Underline, circle, or otherwise highlight passages that strike you as particularly important.** These may be anything from single words to whole paragraphs—but stick to those points in the text that really stand out, the briefer and more specific, the better. Don't worry that you need to find *the* most crucial parts of a poem, play, or story. Everyone sees things a little differently, so just note what makes an impression on *you*.

- **Make notes in the margins as to *why* certain points strike you.** Don't just underline; jot down at least a word or two in the margin to remind yourself what you were thinking when you chose to highlight a particular point. It may seem obvious to you at the moment, but when you return to the text in two weeks to write your paper, you may not remember.

- **Ask questions of the text.** Perhaps the most important aspect of active reading is the practice of asking critical questions of a text. Nobody—not even the most experienced literary critic—understands everything about a literary text immediately, and noting where you are confused or doubtful is an important first step toward resolving any confusion. Types of questions are discussed a little later in this chapter, but for now just remember that any point of confusion is fair game, from character **motivation** (*"Why would she do that?"*), to cultural or historical references (*"Where is Xanadu?"*), to the definitions of individual words (*"Meaning?"*). Most likely, you will eventually want to propose some possible answers, but on a first reading of the text it's enough to note that you have questions.

- **Talk back to the text.** Occasionally, something in a literary text may strike you as suspicious, offensive, or just plain wrong. Just because a story, poem, or play appears in a textbook does not make its author above criticism. Try to keep an open mind and realize that there may be an explanation that would satisfy your criticism, but if you think an author has made a misstep, don't be afraid to make note of your opinion.

- **Look for unusual features of language.** In creating a mood and making a point, literary works rely much more heavily than do purely informational texts on features of language such as **style** and **imagery**. As a reader of literature, then, you need to heighten your awareness of style. Look for patterns of images, repeated words or phrases, and any other unusual stylistic features—right down to idiosyncratic grammar or punctuation—and make note of them in your marginalia.

- **Develop your own system of shorthand.** Annotating a text, while it obviously takes time, shouldn't become a burden or slow your reading too much, so keep your notes and questions short and to the point. Sometimes all you need is an exclamation point to indicate an important passage. An underlined term combined with a question mark in the margin can remind you that you didn't immediately understand what a word meant. Be creative, but try also to be consistent, so you'll know later what you meant by a particular symbol or comment.

Student Jarrad Nunes was assigned to read Emily Dickinson's poem "Because I could not stop for Death." Here are some of the annotations he made as he read the poem:

EMILY DICKINSON [1830–1886]

Because I could not stop for Death

Because I could not stop for Death—   *Death personifie*
He kindly stopped for me—   *kind; not the grim reap*
The Carriage held but just Ourselves—
And Immortality.

We slowly drove—He knew no haste   *Strange punctuatic*
And I had put away   *esp. all the dashes.*
My labor and my leisure too,
For His Civility—

We passed the School, where Children strove   *Most nouns capitalized. Wh*
At Recess—in the Ring—
We passed the Fields of Gazing Grain—   *How does grain "gaze*
We passed the Setting Sun—

Or rather—He passed Us—   *Who is "he"? The Su*
The Dews drew quivering and chill—   *Repeated sounds—dew*
For only Gossamer, my Gown—   *drew, etc.*
My Tippet—only Tulle—

We paused before a House that seemed
A Swelling of the Ground—   *This "house" seems like a grav*
The Roof was scarcely visible—
The Cornice—in the Ground—   *cornice = horizontal projectic*
     from a wall (Dictionary.com)

Since then—'tis Centuries—and yet
Feels shorter than the Day
I first surmised the Horses' Heads   *Eternity and Immortality, bu*
Were toward Eternity—   *no reference to God or religio*
     Ends with a dash, not a period. Not a final endin

[c. 1863; 1890]

Jarrad's annotations cover everything from major points of content, like the personification of the character Death and the absence of overt religiosity, to small notations on style. He asks lots of questions and sometimes provides tentative answers. Having annotated the poem in this way, he was ready to participate in discussions both in the classroom and online, and later he had some good starting notes when he decided to write a paper on the poem.

Note Taking

It's a good idea, especially if you are reading a difficult text or one about which you expect to be writing, to keep a notebook handy as you read, a place to make notes that would be too long or complex to fit in the margins. What should these notes contain? Essentially, they should be more extensive versions of your marginalia. Note any unusual repetitions or juxtapositions, as well as anything that surprises you or frustrates your expectations as you read. Note passages that seem particularly crucial, or particularly confusing (using page numbers, and perhaps placing an asterisk or other symbol in the margins), and write a few sentences explaining why these stood out for you. Ask plenty of questions, as explained later in this chapter.

You might want to use the same notebook that you keep with you in class so that you can make reference to your class notes while reading at home and bring the insights from your reading to your class discussions. In class, write down any information your instructor writes on the board or projects using PowerPoint or other presentation software. If he or she thought it was important enough to write down, you probably should too. Your class notes should include new terminology or vocabulary, as well as any point the instructor repeats more than once or twice. Also take note of comments by your classmates that seem especially salient to your evolving understanding of the literature, particularly points you disagree with or would not have thought of on your own. Just be sure to distinguish which ideas in your notes are yours and which you read or heard from someone else. It may be obvious to you now, but can you guarantee that a month from now, when you're writing a paper, you'll remember who produced that gem of insight?

Remember that the best note takers are not necessarily those who have amassed the most pages of notes at the end of the term. Good notes need not be well-reasoned paragraphs or even complete sentences. In fact, they seldom are. The key to taking good notes is to take them quickly, with minimal interruption to your reading or participation in a discussion. As with annotating texts, try to develop your own shorthand for note taking. Just be sure that you write enough to jog your memory when you return to the notes days, weeks, or even months later. Try to be consistent in what and how you abbreviate. One specific piece of advice, though: it's a good idea to jot down page numbers in your notes, referring to the specific lines or passages under discussion. That way, you'll have no problem matching up the notes with the texts to which they refer.

Journal Keeping

You may be assigned to keep a reading journal for your class. Of course, you should follow your instructor's guidelines, but if you aren't sure what to write in a reading journal, think of it as a place to go a step further than you do in your annotations and notes. Try out possible answers, preferably several different ones, to the questions you have raised. Expand your ideas from single phrases and sentences into entire paragraphs, and see how they hold up under this deeper probing. Although a reading journal is substantially different from a personal journal or diary, it can at times contain reflections on any connections you make between a piece of literature and your own life and ideas. Some instructors ask students to respond to their readings with Web resources, including discussion boards, e-mail messages, or blog entries. These platforms allow you to build an archive of your responses so that you can easily return to them when you begin writing a draft of your paper; in addition, you can respond to other students as they develop their ideas. Here is an example of a Blackboard discussion board response to "Because I could not stop for Death":

Forum: Because I could not stop for Death
Date: Mon 10 Feb 2010 22:15
Author: Nunes, Jarrad
Subject: Hymn Meter

We read some Emily Dickinson poems in high school, and I remember my teacher saying that Emily Dickinson wrote all her poems in "hymnal stanzas," which are the typical meter used in hymns. My teacher used "Amazing Grace" as an example of a hymn in this style. "Because I could not stop for Death" follows this meter exactly, except in the first two lines of stanza 4, which reverses the scheme. According to Britannica Online, Dickinson was raised in a religious family, but she herself had a lot of questions and doubts about Christianity. It's notable that in this poem she never mentions God or associates death with heaven the way you might expect from a Christian. Is

> this maybe a sign of her religious doubts? She must have grown up singing
> hymns and associating that particular rhythm with church. I wonder why
> someone who was skeptical about religion would write her poems in a form
> that is so strongly associated with the church.

In this brief response, the student explores questions about both form and content. He connects his reading of the poem with insights gleaned from both previous experience in high school and some online research.

This kind of response will serve Jarrad well when it's time to generate a thesis for his paper on the subject. Even if your instructor doesn't require online forum participation or a journal for your class, many students find keeping a journal a useful tool for getting more out of their reading, not to mention a wealth of material to draw from when they sit down to write a paper.

Using Reference Materials

Many students are reluctant to use the dictionary or encyclopedia while reading, thinking they should be able to figure out the meanings of words from their context and not wanting to interrupt their reading. But the simple truth is that not all words are definable from context alone, and you'll get much more out of your reading if you are willing to make the small effort involved in looking up unfamiliar words. If you are reading John Donne's "A Valediction: Forbidding Mourning" (p. 455) and you don't know what the word *valediction* means, you obviously start at a big disadvantage. A quick look in a dictionary would tell you that a valediction is a speech given at a time of parting (like the one a *valedictorian* gives at a graduation ceremony). Armed with that simple piece of information, you begin your reading of Donne's poem already knowing that it is about leaving someone or something, and understanding the poem becomes much simpler. Notice that the annotations for the Dickinson poem earlier in the chapter include a definition of *cornice*.

An encyclopedia like *Britannica Online* (an online subscription service available at most university libraries) can also be a useful tool. If, as you're reading Dickinson's poem, you want to read her biography, *Britannica Online* can provide biographical and cultural context for her life and work. Or, if you want to learn more about the meter of the poem, you could look up "hymnal stanza" to develop an understanding of its use, or "personification" to understand how the poet makes characters out of Death and Immortality. *Britannica Online* often provides a bibliography for further reading, so it can be a good place to start your research.

ASKING CRITICAL QUESTIONS OF LITERATURE

As mentioned, one important part of active, critical reading is asking questions. If you are reading well, your textual annotations and notes will probably be full of questions. Some of these might be simple inquiries of fact, the sort of thing that can be answered by asking your instructor or by doing some quick research. But ideally, many of your questions will be more complex and meaty than that, the sort of probing queries that may have multiple, complex, or even contradictory answers. These are the questions that will provoke you and your classmates to think still more critically about the literature you read. You need not worry—at least not at first—about finding answers to all of your questions. As you work more with the text, discussing it with your instructor and classmates, writing about it, and reading other related stories, poems, and plays, you will begin to respond to the most important of the issues you've raised. And even if you never form a satisfactory answer to some questions, they will have served their purpose if they have made you think.

Questions about literature fall into one of four categories—questions about the text, about the author, about the cultural context of the work, and about the reader. We'll discuss each of these in the next few pages.

Questions about the Text

Questions about a text focus on issues such as **genre**, **structure**, language, and style. Queries regarding the text can sometimes, though not always, be answered with a deeper examination of the story, poem, or play at hand. You might ask about the presence of certain images—or about their absence, if you have reason to expect them and find that they are not there. Sometimes authors juxtapose images or language in startling or unexpected ways, and you might ask about the purpose and effect of such **juxtaposition**. You might wonder about the meanings of specific words in the context of the work. (This is especially true with older works of literature, as meanings evolve and change over time, and a word you know today might have had a very different definition in the past.) When looking at a poem, you might inquire about the purpose and effect of sound, rhythm, rhyme, and so forth.

Your previous experiences are a big help here, including both your experiences of reading literature and your experiences in everyday life. You know from personal experience how you expect people to think and act in certain situations, and you can compare these expectations to the literature. What might motivate the characters or persons to think and act as they do? Your previous reading has likewise set up expectations for you. How does the text fulfill or frustrate these expectations? What other literature does this remind you of? What images seem arresting or unexpected? Where do the words seem particularly powerful, strange, or otherwise noteworthy?

Notice some of the questions one reader asked in his annotations upon first reading Ben Jonson's "On My First Son."

BEN JONSON   [1572–1637]

On My First Son

Farewell, thou child of my right hand, and joy;
My sin was too much hope of thee, loved boy:
Seven years thou' wert lent to me, and I thee pay,
Exacted by thy fate, on the just day.
O could I lose all father now! for why
Will man lament the state he should envy,
To have so soon 'scaped world's and flesh's rage,
And, if no other misery, yet age?
Rest in soft peace, and asked, say, "Here doth lie
Ben Jonson his best piece of poetry."
For whose sake henceforth all his vows be such
As what he loves may never like too much.

Why is hope for his child a "sin"?

The rhyme in ll. 1–2 aligns "joy" with "boy."

Why does the speaker treat the son like a bank transaction?

The word just has two meanings: exact and fair. Which does the poet mean?

What does he mean by this line? (confusing)

Here the poem works as a kind of epitaph on a tombstone. Is it actually the boy's epitaph?

The questions the student asks of the poem are, for the most part, substantial and difficult, and they will require a good deal of thinking and interpretation to get to an answer. These are the sorts of questions that prompt good discussions and good writing.

Questions about the Author

When thinking about the connection between authors and the works they produce, two contradictory impulses come into play. One is the desire to ignore the biography of the author entirely and focus solely on the work at hand, and the other is to look closely at an author's life to see what might have led him or her to write a particular poem, story, or play. It is easy to understand the first impulse. After all, we are not likely to be able to ask an author what is meant by a certain line in a play or whether an image in a story is supposed to be read symbolically. The work of literature is what we have before us, and it should stand or fall on its own merits. This was, in fact, one of the principal tenets of **New Criticism**, a method of interpretation that dominated literary criticism for much of the twentieth century and is discussed on pages 1268–69.

We cannot deny, however, that a writer's life does affect that writer's expression. An author's age, gender, religious beliefs, family structure, and many other factors have an impact on everything from topic choice to word choice. Therefore, it is sometimes appropriate to ask questions about an author as we try to come to a better understanding of a piece of literature. It is crucial, however, that we remember that not everything an author writes is to be taken at surface value. For instance, if the narrator or principal character of a story is beaten or neglected by his parents, we should not jump to the conclusion that the author was an abused child. And if this character then goes on to justify his own actions by pointing to the abuse, we should also not assume that the author endorses this justification. In other words, we must distinguish between narrative voice and the actual author as well as between what is written and what is meant.

This separation of biography and narrative is relatively easy with stories and plays that we know to be fiction; just because a character says something doesn't necessarily mean the author believes it. Poetry is a little trickier, though, because it has the reputation of being straight from the heart. Not all poetry, however, is an accurate representation of the author's thoughts or beliefs. To give just two examples, T. S. Eliot's "The Love Song of J. Alfred Prufrock" (pages 1214–18) voices the thoughts of the fictional Prufrock, not of Eliot himself, and many of the poems of Robert Browning are "dramatic monologues," delivered by speakers very different from Browning himself, including murderous noblemen and corrupt clergy. (An example of such a monologue is "My Last Duchess" on pages 503–04.)

Questions about the Cultural Context

We are all creatures of a particular time and place, and nobody, no matter how unique and iconoclastic, is immune to the subtle and pervasive force of social history. Many appropriate questions about literature, then, involve the **cultural context** of the work. What was going on in history at the time a piece of literature was written? Were there wars or other forms of social disruption? What was the standard of living for most people in the author's society? What was day-to-day life like? What were the typical religious beliefs and traditions? How was society organized in terms of power relations, work expectations, and educational possibilities? How about typical family structure? Did extended families live together? What were the expected gender roles inside (and outside) the family? All of these issues, and many more besides, have an impact on how authors see the world and how they respond to it in their writing.

As you read and ask questions of literature, you have another cultural context to be concerned with: your own. How does being a resident of twenty-first-century America affect your reading and understanding? We are every bit as influenced by issues of history, culture, and lifestyle as were authors and readers of the past, but it is harder for us to see this, since the dominant way of living tends to seem "natural" or even "universal." Indeed, one of the great benefits of reading literature is that it teaches us about history and helps us understand and appreciate diverse cultures, not the least of which is our own.

In asking and answering the following questions about Ben Jonson's culture (seventeenth-century England), an attentive reader of "On My First Son" will also note features of our own present-day society, in which childhood death is relatively rare, family roles may be different, and religious attitudes and beliefs are considerably more diverse.

- How common was childhood death in the seventeenth century? What was the life expectancy?
- Typically, how involved were fathers in young children's lives at the time?
- Is the quotation in the poem (lines 9–10) the boy's epitaph?
- How difficult was life then? What exactly does Jonson mean by the "world's and flesh's rage"?
- How common was poetry on this topic? How "original" was Jonson's poem?
- What attitudes about God and heaven were common then? What was the conception of sin?

Questions about the Reader

Except in the case of private diaries, all writing is intended to be read by somebody, and an intended audience can have a big influence on the composition of the writing in question. Think about the differences in tone and structure between a text message you send to a friend and a paper you write for a course, and you'll get some idea of the impact of intended audience on a piece of writing. It is therefore worth considering a work's originally intended readers as you seek to understand a piece more fully. Who were these intended readers? Were they actually the people who read the literature when it was first published? How are readers' expectations fulfilled or disappointed by the structure and content of the literature? How did the original readers react? Was the work widely popular, or did only certain readers enjoy it? Did it have detractors as well? Was there any controversy over the work?

Of course, in addition to the original readers of any work of literature, there are also contemporary readers, including yourself. It is often said that great literature stands the test of time and can cross cultures to speak to many different sorts of people, but your reaction to a work may be very different from that of its original audience, especially if you are far removed from the work by time or culture. In earlier centuries in Europe and America, nearly all educated people were very familiar with the Bible and with stories and myths from Greek and Roman antiquity. Writers, therefore, could assume such knowledge on the part of their readers and make liberal reference in their work to stories and characters from these sources. Today many readers are less familiar with these sources, and we often need the help of footnotes or other study aids to understand such references. So what might have been enjoyable and enlightening for the original readers of a work might sometimes be tedious or frustrating for later readers. If we are to read a work critically, we must keep both past and present audiences in mind.

The first three of the following questions deal with the original audience of "On My First Son," while the final two compare this audience and a contemporary one.

- If childhood death was common in the seventeenth century, how would Jonson's readers have related to the subject of his poem?
- Did Jonson write this for wide circulation, or was it meant just for family and friends?
- Where was the poem first published, and who was likely to read it?
- Do readers with children of their own read the poem differently? Would I?
- Now that childhood death is fairly uncommon, do we take this poem more seriously than past readers? Or less seriously?

Looking over these questions about Jonson's poem—about the text, the author, the cultural context, and the reader—you will note that there are many differences among them. Some can be answered with a simple yes or no (*Is the quotation the boy's epitaph?*), while others require much more complex responses (*What was the conception of sin in Jonson's time?*). Others are matters of conjecture, opinion, or interpretation (*Do contemporary readers take this poem more seriously?*). Some can be answered simply by rereading and considering (*How can a child's death ever be considered fair?*), while others require discussion (*Do readers with children respond to the poem differently?*) or research (*Where was the poem first published?*).

For some inquiries, you may have tentative answers, as did the reader who asked these questions when she proposed both God and fate as potential candidates for who "lent" the child to the father. Others you won't be able to answer at first. If you are genuinely curious about any of them, do a little informal research to begin formulating answers. Some basic information can be found in the brief biographies or notes about authors that appear in most textbooks. There you could learn, for instance, the dates of Jonson's birth and death and some basic facts about his life and family. A quick look at a reputable reference work or Web site could provide still more valuable background information, like the fact that Jonson also lost his first daughter and that he wrote a poem about her death as well.

CHECKLIST FOR GOOD READING

Questions to ask as you read and think about literary texts:

☐ Have you *slowed down* and *reread* complex passages several times?

☐ Are you *looking up difficult words* in the dictionary to see if they have secondary meanings?

☐ Are you *annotating* the text by *underlining* key phrases? Writing questions or concerns in the *margins*?

☐ Are you taking your reading to the next level by asking *how* or *why* these passages are compelling to you?

☐ Are you marking those places in the text that make you feel uncomfortable, or present a worldview that feels strange to you?

☐ After you read, are you *taking notes* so that you can keep track of your ideas?

☐ Have you identified the genre of the text? Have you described its style and **tone**?

☐ Have you checked *Britannica Online* or other reference sources to learn more about the author and his or her cultural context?

☐ Have you reflected on your perspective as a twenty-first-century *reader*, and how that might affect your interpretation of literature from another time period?

Having simply formulated some questions, you've already gone a long way toward understanding and interpreting a poem or other work of literature. If you bring such a list of questions with you to class, you will be more than ready to contribute to the discussion, and when the time comes to write an essay, you will have a rich mine of source material from which to draw.

CHAPTER 3

The Writing Process

Experts often divide the writing process into three major components: prewriting, drafting, and revision (which includes editing). Bear in mind, though, that the process for most people is not as linear as this suggests, and the three components don't always happen in a straightforward fashion. For instance, you might begin revising a partial draft before completing the drafting process. Or you may find yourself stuck at a fairly late point in the draft and decide to revisit your prewriting. Don't think that these three steps need to be completed one at a time. Different projects will likely call for different strategies, and you'll enjoy the process more if you allow yourself to go back and forth between the steps according to the needs of the particular assignment you're trying to complete.

PREWRITING

Prewriting is everything that you do before beginning an actual draft of your paper. It includes annotating and questioning texts, taking notes and participating in class, and discussing the assignment with your instructor and/or classmates. It also includes specific topics covered in this chapter: choosing a topic, developing an argument and a thesis, gathering support, and proposing an organizational strategy for the paper.

Choosing a Topic

Obviously, your choice of a topic for your paper is of key importance, since everything else follows from that first decision. Your instructor may assign a specific topic, or the choice may be left to you. The most important piece of advice for choosing a topic is to write about something that genuinely interests you. If your instructor gives your class a choice, chances are that he or she really wants to see a variety of topics and approaches and expects you to find a topic that works for *you*. You'll write a better paper if your topic is something of genuine interest to you. A bored or uncertain writer usually writes a boring or unconvincing paper. On the other hand, if you care about your topic, your enthusiasm will show in the writing, and the paper will be far more successful.

Even if your instructor assigns a fairly specific topic, you still need to spend a little time thinking about and working with it. You want your paper to stand out from the rest, and you should do whatever you can to make the assignment your own. When you receive an assignment, give some thought as to how it might relate to your own interests and how you might call upon your background and knowledge to approach the topic in fresh and interesting ways.

Finally, if you've put in some thought and effort but still don't know what to write about, remember that you do not need to go it alone. Seek out guidance and help. Talk with other students in your class and see what they have decided to write about; although of course you don't want simply to copy someone else's topic, hearing what others think can often spark a fresh idea. And don't forget your instructor. Most teachers are more than happy to spend a little time helping you come up with a topic and an approach that will help you write a good paper.

Developing an Argument

With the possible exception of a *summary* (a brief recap of a text's most important points), all writing about literature is to some degree a form of argument. Before proceeding, though, let's dispel some of the negative connotations of the word *argument*. In everyday usage, this term can connote a heated verbal fight, and it suggests two (or more) people growing angry and, often, becoming less articulate and more abusive as time passes. It suggests combat and implies that the other party in the process is an opponent. In this sort of argument, there are winners and losers.

Clearly this is not what we have in mind when we say you will be writing argumentatively about literature. Used in a different, more traditional sense, argument refers to a writer's or speaker's attempt to establish the validity of a given position. In other words, when you write a paper, you work to convince your reader that what you are saying is valid and persuasive. The reader is not the enemy, not someone whose ideas are to be crushed and refuted, but rather a person whose thoughts and feelings you have a chance to affect. You are not arguing *against* your reader; rather, you are using your argumentative abilities to *help* your reader see the logic and value of your position.

The Thesis

To begin writing a literary argument, then, you must take a position and have a point to make. This principal point will be the *thesis* of your paper. It is important to distinguish between a topic and a thesis: your topic is the issue or area upon which you will focus your attention, and your thesis is a statement *about* this topic.

Here is an example of a topic for Emily Dickinson's "Because I could not stop for Death" from a student journal:

> Topic: I am interested in how Dickinson portrays the character of Death.

Here is an example of a thesis statement for a paper on this topic:

> Thesis: "Because I could not stop for Death" challenges preconceptions that Dickinson's contemporaries had about death, and in doing so it makes us challenge ours as well.

It might help to phrase your thesis as a complete sentence in which the topic is the subject, followed by a predicate that makes a firm statement or claim regarding your topic. This is your **thesis statement**, and it will probably appear toward the beginning of your paper. The foremost purpose of a paper, then, is to explain, defend, and ultimately prove the truth of its thesis.

Keep the following guidelines in mind as you think about a tentative thesis for your paper:

- **Your thesis should be both clear and specific.** The purpose of a thesis is to serve as a guide to both the reader and the writer, so it needs to be understandable and to point clearly to the specific aspects of the literature that you will discuss. This does not mean it will stand alone or need no further development or explanation—after all, that's what the rest of the paper is for. But a reader who is familiar with the story, poem, or play you are writing about (and it is fair to assume a basic familiarity) should have a good sense of what your thesis means and how it relates to the literature.

- **Your thesis should be relevant.** The claim you make should not only interest you as a writer but also give your reader a reason to keep reading by sparking his or her interest and desire to know more. Not every paper is going to change lives or minds, of course, but you should at least state your thesis in such a way that your reader won't have the most dreaded of responses: "Who cares?"

- **Your thesis should be debatable.** Since the purpose of an argumentative paper is to convince a reader that your thesis is correct (or at least that it has merit), it cannot simply be an irrefutable fact. A good thesis will be something that a reasonable person, having read the literature, might disagree with or might not have considered at all. It should give you something to prove.

- **Your thesis should be original.** Again, originality does not imply that every thesis you write must be a brilliant gem that nobody but you could have discovered. But it should be something you have thought about independently, and it should avoid clichés, contain something of you, and do more than parrot back something said in your class or written in your textbook.

- **You should be able to state your thesis as a complete sentence.** This sentence, generally referred to as the *thesis statement*, should first identify your topic and then make a claim about it. (Occasionally, especially for longer papers with more complex ideas behind them, you will need more than one sentence to state your thesis clearly. Even in these cases, though, the complete thesis must both identify the topic and make a claim about it.)

- **Your thesis should be stated in strong, unambiguous language.** Avoid thesis statements that begin, "In this paper, I will prove. . . ." If you have a point to prove, just prove it. Keep the reader's attention on the topic, not on your paper. For similar reasons, avoid phrases like "in my opinion . . ." or "I think. . . ." It is assumed that the paper is made up of your thoughts and opinions, and language like this turns the reader's focus to your thought process rather than the topic at hand.

- **Your thesis should be appropriate to the assignment.** This may seem obvious, but as we work with literature, taking notes, asking questions, and beginning to think about topics and theses, it is possible to lose sight of the assignment as it was presented. After you have come up with a tentative thesis, it's a good idea to go back and review the assignment as your instructor gave it, making sure your paper will fulfill its requirements.

Let us take a look at how two students arrived at strong, workable theses for their papers. Jarrad Nunes knew that he wanted to write about how Emily Dickinson dealt with the theme of death in her poetry. His first attempt at a thesis, however, was far too weak and general:

Emily Dickinson's poems about death are some of the most interesting ever written.

This is not so much a thesis statement as an assertion of personal preference and opinion. All we know from reading it is that Jarrad likes

Dickinson's death poems. He needs a thesis that is both more specific and more controversial:

> Dickinson's poems look at death in unconventional ways.

This version is better because it makes an assertion that can be defended, but it is still far too general. Here is the final version of Jarrad's thesis:

> "Because I could not stop for Death" challenges preconceptions that Dickinson's contemporaries had about death, and in doing so it makes us challenge ours as well.

Here we have a much stronger thesis. It limits the paper's scope by focusing on a single poem, it makes an assertion to defend (that Dickinson challenged nineteenth-century preconceptions about death), and it shows why this point is significant to a reader (because we too might have our preconceptions challenged).

Here is one more example of the process of refining and developing a thesis. When she first decided to write about the male characters in two nineteenth-century stories, Melanie Smith came up with the following:

> The husbands in the stories "The Yellow Wallpaper" by Charlotte Perkins Gilman and "The Story of an Hour" by Kate Chopin are very controlling of their wives.

This is not an adequate thesis because it is simply a statement of fact, something that will be immediately obvious to anyone who has read the stories. It left Melanie with nothing to defend, no point to prove, so she gave it a little more thought and refined her tentative thesis:

> Though the husbands in "The Yellow Wallpaper" and "The Story of an Hour" are controlling, they are not really as bad as they first appear.

At this point, the writer is definitely moving in the right direction. This version shows that she has a particular interpretation and a point to make, one that is not necessarily shared by everyone who reads the stories. However, it still doesn't give a reader much guidance about what to expect in the paper. In the end, Melanie needed two sentences to get her thesis right:

> By modern standards, the husbands of the two protagonists, particularly John in "The Yellow Wallpaper," seem almost unbearably controlling of their wives. From the vantage point of the late nineteenth century, however, their behavior looks quite different.

This version is much clearer and more precise. After reading this thesis, we are much more focused and have a good sense of what to expect in the paper as a whole.

You will note that in this discussion the phrase *tentative thesis* has come up several times. The word *tentative* is important. As you start to gather support and to write your paper, your thesis will help you focus clearly on your task and sort out which of your ideas, observations, and questions are relevant to the project at hand. But you should keep an open mind as well, realizing that your thesis is likely to evolve as you write. You are likely to change the focus in subtle or not so subtle ways, and you might even change your mind completely as you write and therefore need to create a new thesis from scratch. If this happens, don't regard it as a failure. On the contrary, it means you have succeeded in learning something genuine from the experience of writing, and that is what a literature class is all about.

Gathering Support for Your Thesis

Once you have crafted a tentative thesis, it is time to think about the evidence or support you will need to convince your reader of the claim's validity. But what exactly counts as support? What can you include in your paper as evidence that your thesis is true? Essentially, all support comes from one of three sources:

- **The text itself is the most obvious source of support.** It is not enough to *say* that a certain piece of literature says or means a certain thing. You will need to *show* this by summarizing, paraphrasing, or quoting the literature itself.

- **Other people's ideas are a good source of support.** Chances are you will find a lot of useful material for your paper if you pay attention to easily available sources of ideas from other readers. These include the notes and biographical information in your textbooks, research conducted online or in the library, lectures and discussions in class, and even informal conversations about the literature with your friends and classmates.

- **Your own thoughts are your most important source of support.** Remember that although you may want to integrate ideas and information from a variety of sources, your paper is yours and as such should reflect *your* thinking. The most indispensable source of material for your paper is your own mind; your own thoughts and words should always carry the heaviest weight in any paper you write.

One of the best ways to gather supporting ideas for your paper is **brainstorming**. You can brainstorm—alone or with classmates—even before settling on your topic and thesis, to explore the many possible threads that you could follow in your writing. When brainstorming to gather evidence, the idea is to write down, very quickly, every idea that comes to you, every possible idea that might be included in the draft of your paper. Don't censor yourself during this process. Allow yourself to write down everything that interests, puzzles, or delights you. Later you will have ample opportunity to prune your list of repetitions, tangents, or weaker ideas. For the time being, just let the ideas flow, and get as many as you can down on a piece of paper or a word processing document.

At this stage, use every resource available to you to find support for your thesis. What lines in the poem, short story, or play reinforce your claims? Have you looked up words in the dictionary? Have you checked difficult concepts in a respectable encyclopedia or other reference? Have you asked your teacher for further reading suggestions? Have you read articles or book chapters that are appropriate to your topic, and are you formulating your responses to them? Treat ideas from outside sources much as you would your own brainstorming: don't censor too soon. When the time comes to organize and draft your paper, it's far better to have too many ideas and have to eliminate some than to have too few and have to root around for more.

Organizing Your Paper

Once you've determined what evidence to use, it is time to begin sorting and organizing it. The organizing principle for any paper is the sequence of paragraphs, so at this stage you should be thinking at the level of paragraph content. Remember that each paragraph should contain one main idea and sufficient evidence and explanation to support that idea. When added together, these paragraph-level ideas lead a reader to your paper's ultimate point—your thesis. So the first stage of organizing the content of your essay is to cluster together similar ideas in order to begin shaping the substance of individual paragraphs. The second stage is to determine the order in which these paragraphs will appear.

As you write and revise your paper, you may have different ideas about how to structure it. You may want to put the topic sentence somewhere other than at the beginning of a paragraph, or perhaps the topic is so clear that no specific topic sentence is even needed. You may devise a more interesting way to structure your introduction or conclusion. (Some additional, more specific thoughts for those tricky introductory and concluding paragraphs follow.) Unless your instructor has specified the form in which your paper is to be organized, you should feel free to experiment a bit.

1158   READING AND WRITING ABOUT LITERATURE

For most writers, creating some version of an outline is the best way to approach the task of organizing evidence into a logical sequence for a paper. In the past, you may have been asked to write a formal outline, complete with Roman numerals and capital letters. If this technique has been helpful in organizing your thoughts, by all means continue to use it. For many writers, however, an informal outline works just as well and is less cumbersome. To construct an informal outline, simply jot down a heading that summarizes the topic of each paragraph you intend to write. Then cluster your gathered evidence—quotations or paraphrases from the literature, ideas for analysis, and so on—into groups under the headings.

The following is an example of an informal outline for a paper on Shakespeare's Sonnet 116. (The full paper appears on pages 1220–22.) In this outline, the student focuses on the positive and negative language in the poem and how it results in a more interesting definition of love than he had seen in other love poems.

Introduction
    Two kinds of typical love poems: happy and sad
    Sonnet 116 is more complex and interesting
    Tentative thesis: By including both negative and positive images and
        language, this sonnet gives a complex and realistic definition of
        love.

Vivid images in poem
    Positive/expected: "star," "ever-fixèd mark," "rosy lips and cheeks"
    Negative/unexpected: "sickle" (deathlike), "wandering bark" (lost
        boat), "tempests"

Negative language
    Words/phrases: "Let me not," "Love is not," "never," "nor," "no," etc.
    Abstractions: "alteration," "impediments," "error"

Conclusion
    Love never changes
    Shakespeare's definition still works some 400 years later

Obviously, this is not a formal outline. It does, however, group similar items and ideas together, and it gives the writer a basic structure to follow as he moves on to drafting, the next stage of the composing process.

DRAFTING THE PAPER

You have a topic. You have a tentative thesis. You have gathered evidence. You have an outline or tentative structure in mind for this evidence. It is time to begin writing your first draft. Every writer has his or her own slightly different process for getting the words down on paper. Some begin at the beginning of the paper and work straight through to the end in a clear, organized fashion. Others begin with the first body paragraph and save the introduction for later. Still others write bits and pieces of the paper out of order and allow the overall structure to emerge at a later time.

Some writers claim that they work better at the last minute and focus better under the pressure of a looming deadline. This, however, is almost always a justification for sloppy work habits, and procrastination rarely if ever results in a superior paper. When habitual procrastinators change their working methods and give themselves more time on a project, they are frequently surprised to discover that the process is more enjoyable and the final product of their efforts better than what they have produced in the past. Start early and work steadily—it will prove more than worth it.

Try to write your first draft fairly quickly. You don't need to get every sentence just right—that's what the revision phase of writing is for. What you want now is just to get as much good raw material as possible into the mix and see what works. Don't worry too much yet about style, transitions, grammar, and so forth. In fact, you don't even need to start at the beginning or work right through to the end. If you get stuck on one part, move on. You can always come back and fill in the gaps later. Introductions can be especially tricky, particularly since you haven't yet finished the essay and don't really know what it is you're introducing. Some writers find it easier to start with the body of the essay, or to write a short, sloppy introduction as a placeholder. You can go back and work on the real introduction when the draft is complete.

Introductions, Conclusions, and Transitions

Ideally, of course, all of the parts of your paper will be equally compelling and polished, but there are certain points in a paper that most often cause trouble for writers and readers, and these points may require a little additional attention on your part. The most typical trouble spots are introductory and concluding paragraphs and the transitional sentences that connect paragraphs. Although there is no one formula to help you navigate these waters, as each writing situation and each paper are different, we offer some general guidelines that can help you think through the problems that might arise in these areas.

Introductions

Essentially, an introduction accomplishes two things. First, it gives a sense of both your topic and your approach to that topic, which is why it is common to make your thesis statement a part of the introduction. Second, an introduction compels your readers' interest and makes them want to read on and find out what your paper has to say. Some common strategies used in effective introductions are to begin with a probing rhetorical question, a vivid description, or an intriguing quotation. Weak introductions tend to speak in generalities or in philosophical ideas that are only tangentially related to the real topic of your paper. Don't spin your wheels: get specific and get to the point right away.

Consider this introduction from a student essay on Susan Glaspell's *Trifles*:

> What is the relationship between legality and morality? Susan Glaspell's short play *Trifles* asks us to ponder this question, but it provides no clear answers. Part murder mystery, part battle of the sexes, the play makes its readers confront and question many issues about laws, morals, and human relationships. In the person of Mrs. Peters, a sheriff's wife, the play chronicles one woman's moral journey from a certain, unambiguous belief in the law to a more situational view of ethics. Before it is over, this once legally minded woman is even willing to cover up the truth and let someone get away with murder.

The student poses a philosophical question at the very beginning of the paper and then offers a tentative answer. (This paper appears in its entirety on pages 1228–30.)

Conclusions

Your conclusion should give your reader something new to think about, a reason not to forget your essay as soon as the reading is done. Some writers like to use the conclusion to return to an idea, a quotation, or an image first raised in the introduction, creating a satisfying feeling of completeness and self-containment.

In this example from the same student paper, note how the student offers a tentative answer in her conclusion to the question that began the essay:

In the end, Mrs. Peters gives in to what she believes to be emotionally right rather than what is legally permissible. She collaborates with Mrs. Hale to cover up evidence of the motive and hide the dead canary. Though very little time has gone by, she has undergone a major transformation. She may be, as the county attorney says, "married to the law," but she is also divorced from her old ideals. When she tries to cover up the evidence, a stage direction says she "goes to pieces," and Mrs. Hale has to help her. By the time she pulls herself together, the new woman she is will be a very different person from the old one. She, along with the reader, is now in a world where the relationship between legality and morality is far more complex than she had ever suspected.

Some writers use the conclusion to show the implications of their claims or the connections between the literature and real life. This is your chance to make a good final impression, so don't waste it with simple summary and restatement.

Transitions

Each paragraph is built around a different idea, and the job of the transitions is to show how these separate ideas are related to one another, to make the juxtaposition of two paragraphs seem as logical to a reader as it is to the writer. When you think a transition isn't working effectively, the first question you should ask yourself is, *why* does one paragraph follow another in this particular order? Would it make more sense to change the placement of some paragraphs, or is this really the best organizational strategy for this portion of the paper? Once you know why your paper is structured as it is, transitions become much easier to write, simply making apparent to your audience the connections you already know to be there. As you begin each new paragraph, give some consideration to the links between it and the previous paragraph, and try to make those links explicit in the opening sentence.

As with any other aspect of your writing, if you've had trouble in the past with introductions, conclusions, or transitions, one of your best sources of help is to be an attentive reader of others' writing. Pay special attention to these potential trouble spots in the writing you admire, whether by a classmate or a professional author, and see how he or she navigates them. Don't stick with the writing methods that have caused you headaches in the past. Be willing to try out different strategies, seeing which ones work best for you. In time you'll find you have a whole array of ways to approach these trouble spots, and you'll be able to find a successful response to each particular writing situation.

REVISING AND EDITING

Once you have a complete, or near-complete, draft, it's time to begin thinking about revision. Try to avoid the common pitfall of thinking of revision as locating and fixing mistakes. Revision is far more than this. Looking at the parts of the word, you can see that *re-vision* means "seeing again," and indeed the revision stage of the writing process is your chance to see your draft anew and make real and substantial improvements to every facet of it, from its organization to its tone to your word choices. Most successful writers will tell you that it is in the revision stage that the real work gets done, where the writing takes shape and begins to emerge in its final form. Most professional writers spend much more time revising than they do writing the first draft. Don't skimp on this part of the process or try to race through it.

It is a good idea not to start a major revision the minute a draft is complete. Take a break. Exercise, have a meal, do something completely different to clear your mind. If possible, put the draft aside for at least a day, so that when you return to it you'll have a fresh perspective and can begin truly re-seeing it. Print out your draft. Attempting serious revision on-screen is generally a bad idea—we see differently, and we usually see more, when we read off a printed page. Read with a pen in your hand and annotate your text just the way you would a piece of literature, looking for the strengths and weaknesses of your argument. The process laid out here consists of three phases: *global revisions*, or large-scale revisions; *local revisions*, or small-scale revisions; and a final *editing and proofreading*. If you haven't done so before, revising your paper three times may seem like a lot of work, but bear in mind that most professional writers revise their work many more times than that. Revision is the real key to writing the best paper you can.

Global Revision

On a first pass at revision—the large-scale, global part of the process—don't worry too much about details like word choice, punctuation, and so forth. Too many students focus so much on these issues that they miss the big picture. The details are important, but you will deal with them in depth later. You wouldn't want to spend your time getting the wording of a sentence just right only to decide later that the paragraph it is in weakens your argument and needs to be deleted. So at first, look at the overall picture—the argument, organization, and tone of the paper as a whole. While there's nothing wrong with making a few small improvements as you read, nothing smaller than a paragraph should concern you at this point. Here are some possibilities for how you might revise your paper globally.

GLOBAL REVISION CHECKLIST

Further develop your focus and thesis.

☐ Can your reader immediately identify what the topic of the essay will be—that is, which text(s), and which aspect of the text (for example, character development or the use of particular language features), you will analyze?

☐ Have you narrowed the scope of the thesis for your reader? How could it be further narrowed? Remember, it's not enough to say "Women are portrayed differently in X and Y." What do you mean by "differently"? Get as specific as possible.

☐ Does your thesis clearly identify a claim that is debatable but valid?

☐ Has your thinking about the issues evolved as you have written? If so, how will you change the thesis statement?

☐ Have you answered the larger "So what?" question? Do you get your reader thinking beyond your paper to the question of why this argument is important?

Reorganize your paper, if necessary.

☐ Does the order of the ideas and paragraphs make immediate sense to you, or does some alternate structure suggest itself?

☐ Experiment with different organizing principles, using the cut-and-paste feature of your word processor (or even old-fashioned paper and scissors). You can always put things back if your original organization worked better.

Expand your paper with new paragraphs or with new evidence within existing paragraphs.

☐ What textual evidence have you used? Is it sufficiently provocative and persuasive? Or does it veer off into another direction?

☐ Have you successfully integrated quotations, summaries, or paraphrases into your own writing, while at the same time acknowledging your source?

GLOBAL REVISION CHECKLIST (*continued*)

Eliminate any unnecessary, contradictory, or distracting passages.

☐ Does every piece of evidence, every sentence, and every paragraph contribute to the validity of your argument? If not, eliminate extraneous discussions and save them for another project.

Clarify difficult passages with more specific explanations or evidence.

☐ Have you worked to convey why you are citing a particular passage? What *particular* details in it provide evidence that supports your interpretation? Make sure the reasons for the presence of particular evidence are explicit in your writing. Don't assume a summary or a quotation speaks for itself.

Once you have completed your first, large-scale revision, chances are you will feel more confident about the content and structure of your paper. The thesis and focus are strong, the evidence is lined up, and the major points are clear. Print out the new version, take another break if you can, and prepare to move on to the second phase of revision, the one that takes place at the local level of words, phrases, and sentences.

Local Revision

The focus here is on style and clarity. The types of changes you will make in this stage are, essentially, small-scale versions of the changes you made in the first round of revision: adding, cutting, reorganizing, and clarifying. Are you sure about the meanings of any difficult or unusual words you have used? Is there enough variety in sentence style to keep your writing interesting? Do the same words or phrases appear again and again? Are the images vivid? Are the verbs strong? One way to assess the effectiveness of a paper's style is to read it aloud and hear how it sounds. You may feel a little foolish doing this, but many people find it very helpful.

LOCAL REVISION CHECKLIST

Consider your sentences.

☐ Do you keep the writing interesting by using a variety of sentence types and sentences of different lengths?

☐ Have you perhaps used an occasional rhetorical question to get your readers thinking? (This strategy should be used in moderation. Too many questions in a paper become distracting.)

☐ Does each sentence clearly follow from the last one? Or do you need to reorganize the sentences within a particular paragraph to provide clearer transitions between sentences?

☐ Look at the first and last sentences in each paragraph. Do they provide sufficient transitions from one paragraph to the next?

Consider your word choice.

☐ Do you use the same words and phrases again and again? If so, could you vary your word choice a bit?

☐ If you use any special literary terms or other jargon, are you absolutely certain that you are using these terms correctly?

☐ Take a look at the verbs. Are many of them strong and active, or do most sentences rely on dull linking verbs like *is* or *seems*?

Final Editing and Proofreading

Once you have revised your essay a second time and achieved both content and a style that please you, it's time for final editing. This is where you make it "correct."

FINAL EDITING CHECKLIST

Check your spelling.

☐ Have you spelled everything correctly? (Should it be *their* or *there*? *It's* or *its*?)

☐ Do not rely on your computer's spell-check function. This only tells you if the word you typed is a word, not if it's the correct word. When in doubt, look it up.

Check your punctuation.

☐ Look for things that have caused you trouble in the past. Should you use a comma or a semicolon? Again, when in doubt, look it up.

☐ Pay special attention to quotations. Does the question mark go inside or outside of the quotation marks? Have you used both opening and closing quotation marks for each quotation?

Check your formatting.

☐ Is your manuscript format correct? Unless your instructor has provided other instructions, follow the format described on pages 1179–80.

☐ Have you italicized or underlined titles of plays and novels (*Othello* or *The Woman Warrior*) and put the titles of short stories and poems in quotation marks ("Love in L.A.," "The Fish")?

☐ Does your works cited list follow MLA format, and do you properly cite your quotations in the body of the text? Nobody expects you to know all the rules on your own, but you should know where to look for them.

☐ If you have questions about citation and formatting, look them up in this book or in a good dictionary, grammar handbook, or other reference. A good online source is Diana Hacker's *Research and Documentation Online*: http://www.dianahacker.com/resdoc/.

Here is a paragraph ready for final editing from a student essay on *Hamlet*. Notice the kinds of corrections that the student will have to make before the paragraph is done.

The supernatural relm affects the revenge tragedy in other ways than the appearance and presence of ghosts. In Hamlet, the religious concern with final absolution both inflames Hamlet's desire for revenge and causes him to hesitate in carrying out revenge. Not only has Hamlet's father been murdered, but he was also Cut off even in the blossoms of [his] sin, / Unhousled, disappointed, unanel'd, / No reck'ning made, but sent to [his] account / With all [his] imperfections on [his] head (1.5.77-80). For Hamlet's father, being murdered is doubly disastrous; not only is his life cut short. But he must burn away "the foul crimes done in [his] days of nature" in purgatory before he can be granted access to heaven (1.5.13). A normal death would have afforded him final absolution, and thus a direct route to heaven. The same concern that makes Hamlet's father's death even more terrible also causes Hamlet to pass on a perfect opportunity to exact revenge on his father's murderer. Hamlet finds Claudius praying, alone. To kill a man in prayer means to kill a man who has had all his sins absolved. Hamlet observes Claudius and reasons: "A villain kills my father, and for that, / I, his sole son, do this same villain send / to heaven." (3.3.76-78) Hamlet's concern for the supernatural afterlife affects his carrying out revenge.

Spelling: "realm"
Italicize "Hamlet."

Remember to add quotation marks around the direct quotation.

This should be a comma joining two sentence fragments.

This period belongs outside the parentheses, after the act, scene, and line number.

One final word of advice as you revise your paper: ask for help. Doing so is neither cheating nor an admission of defeat. In fact, professional writers do it all the time. Despite the persistent image of writers toiling in isolation, most successful writers seek advice at various stages. More important, they are willing to listen to that advice and to rethink what they have written if it seems not to be communicating what they had intended.

PEER EDITING AND WORKSHOPS

Some instructors give class time for draft workshops, sometimes called peer editing, in which you work with your fellow students, trying to help one another improve your work-in-progress. Such workshops can benefit you in two ways. First, your classmates can offer you critiques and advice on what you might have missed in your own rereading. Second, reading and discussing papers other than your own will help you grow as a writer, showing you a variety of ways in which a topic can be approached. If you really like something about a peer's paper—say, a vivid introduction or the effective use of humor—make note of how it works within the paper and consider integrating something similar into a future paper of your own. We are not, of course, advocating copying your classmates; rather, we are pointing out that you can learn a lot from other people's writing.

Some students are uncomfortable with such workshops. They may feel they don't know enough about writing to give valid advice to others, or they may doubt whether advice from their peers is particularly valuable. But you don't need to be a great literary critic, much less an expert on style or grammar, to give genuinely useful advice to a fellow writer. Whatever your skills or limitations as a writer, you have something invaluable to give: the thoughts and impressions of a real reader working through a paper. It is only when we see how a reader responds to what we've written that we know if a paper is communicating its intended message. If you are given an opportunity to engage in peer workshops, make the most of them.

Your instructor may give you guidelines regarding what to look for in others' drafts, or you may be left more or less on your own. In either case, keep these general guidelines in mind:

- **Be respectful of one another's work.** You should, of course, treat your peers' work with the same respect and seriousness that you would want for your own. Keep your criticism constructive and avoid personal attacks, even if you disagree strongly with an opinion. You can help your fellow writers by expressing a contrary opinion in a civilized and thoughtful manner.

- **Be honest.** This means giving real, constructive criticism when it is due. Don't try to spare your workshop partner's feelings by saying "That's great" or "It's fine," when it really isn't. When asked what went badly in a peer workshop, students most commonly respond *not* that their peers were too harsh on their work but that they were not harsh enough. Wouldn't you rather hear about a problem with your work from a peer in a draft workshop than from your professor after you have already handed in the final draft? So would your classmates.

- **Look for the good as well as the bad in a draft.** No paper, no matter how rough or problematic, is completely without merit. And no paper, no matter how clever or well written, couldn't be improved. By pointing out both what works and what doesn't, you will help your classmates grow as writers.

- **Keep an eye on the time.** It's easy to get wrapped up in a discussion of an interesting paper and not allow adequate time for another paper. Say you're given half an hour to work with your draft and that of one classmate. When you reach the fifteen-minute mark, move on, no matter how interesting your discussion is. Fair is fair. On the other hand, don't stop short of the allotted time. If you are reading carefully and thinking hard about one another's drafts, it should be impossible to finish early.

- **Take notes on your draft itself or on a separate sheet.** You may be certain that you will remember what was said in a workshop, but you would be amazed how often people forget the good advice they heard and intended to follow. Better safe than sorry—take careful notes.

- **Ask questions.** Asking questions about portions of a draft you don't understand or find problematic can help its writer see what needs to be clarified, expanded, or reworked. Useful questions can range from the large scale (*What is the purpose of this paragraph?*) to the small (*Is this a quote? Who said it?*).

- **Don't assume that explaining yourself to your workshop partner can replace revision.** Sometimes your workshop partners will ask a question, and when you answer it for them, they will say, "Oh, right, that makes sense," leaving you with the impression that everything is clear now. But remember, your classmates didn't understand it from the writing alone, and you won't be there to explain it to your instructor.

- **Be specific in your comments.** Vague comments like "The introduction is good" or "It's sort of confusing here" are not much help. Aim for something more like "The introduction was funny and really made me want to read on" or "This paragraph confused me because it seems to contradict what you said in the previous one." With comments like these, a writer will have a much better sense of where to focus his or her revision energies.

- **Try to focus on the big picture.** When you are reading a draft, it's tempting to zero in on distracting little mistakes in spelling, punctuation, or word choice. While it's generally fine to point out or circle such surface matters as you go along, a draft workshop is not about correcting mistakes. It's about helping one another to re-see and rethink your papers on a global scale.

- **Push your partners to help you more.** If your workshop partners seem shy or reluctant to criticize, prompt them to say more by letting them know that you really want advice and that you are able to take criticism. Point out to them what you perceive as the trouble spots in the essay, and ask if they have any ideas to help you out. It feels good, of course, to hear that someone likes your paper and cannot imagine how to improve it. But in the long run it is even better to get real, useful advice that will lead to a better paper. If your classmates are not helping you enough, it's your responsibility to ask for more criticism.

Even if your class does not include workshop time, you can still use the many resources available to you on campus. Find one or two other members of your class and conduct your own peer workshop, reading and critiquing one another's drafts. Be sure to arrange such a meeting far enough in advance of the due date so that you will have ample time to implement any good revision advice you receive. Many campuses also have writing or tutoring centers, and the workers in these centers, often advanced students who are skilled writers, can offer a good deal of help. Remember, again, that you should make an appointment to see a tutor well in advance of the paper's due date, and you should *not* expect a tutor or mentor to revise or "fix" your paper for you. That is, ultimately, your job. And, of course, you can also approach your instructor at any phase of the writing process and ask for advice and help.

But remember, no matter where you turn for advice, the final responsibility for your paper is yours. Any advice and help you receive from classmates, tutors, friends—or even your instructor—is just that: advice and help. It is *your* paper, and *you* must be the one to make the decisions about which advice to follow and which to ignore, and how to implement changes to improve your paper. The key is to keep an open mind, seek help from all available sources, and give yourself plenty of time to turn your first draft into a final paper that makes you truly proud.

TIPS FOR WRITING ABOUT LITERATURE

Each genre of literature—fiction, poetry, and drama—poses its own, slightly different set of assumptions, opportunities, and problems for writers, which are covered in more detail in the sections that follow.

However, the following general principles can help you as you write about any form of literature:

- **Don't assume that your readers will remember (or consider important) the same ideas or incidents in the literature that you do.** You should assume that your readers have *read* the literature but not necessarily that they have reacted to it the same way you have. Therefore, whenever possible, use specific examples and evidence in the form of quotations and summaries to back up your claims.

- **Do not retell the plot or text at length.** Some writers are tempted to begin with a plot summary or even to include the text of a short poem at the beginning of a paper. However, this strategy can backfire by delaying the real substance of your paper. Be discriminating when you summarize—keep quotations short and get to the point you want to make as quickly as possible.

- **Do not assume that quotations or summaries are self-sufficient and prove your point automatically.** Summaries and quotations are a starting point; you need to analyze them thoroughly in your own words, explaining why they are important. As a general rule, each quotation or summary should be followed by at least several sentences of analysis.

- **It is customary to use the present tense when writing about literature**, even if the events discussed take place in the distant past. Example:

  When she sees that Romeo is dead, Juliet kills herself with his knife.

- **The first time you mention an author, use his or her full name.** For subsequent references, the last name is sufficient. (Do not use first names only; it sounds as if you know an author personally.)

- **Titles of poems, short stories, and essays should be put in quotation marks. Titles of books, plays, and periodicals (magazines, newspapers, etc.) should be italicized or underlined.** In titles and in all quotations, follow spelling, capitalization, and punctuation exactly as it occurs in the work itself.

- **Give your paper a title.** A title doesn't need to be elaborate or super clever, but it should give some clue as to what the paper is about and begin setting up expectations for your reader. Simply restating the assignment, such as "Essay #2" or "Comparison and Contrast Paper," is of little help to a reader and might even suggest intellectual laziness on the part of the writer. For the same reason, avoid giving your paper the same title as the work of literature you are writing about; unless you're Shakespeare or Hemingway, don't title your paper *Hamlet* or "A Clean, Well-Lighted Place."

- **Above all, use common sense and *be consistent*.**

USING QUOTATIONS EFFECTIVELY

At some point, you will want to quote the literature you are writing about, and you might also want to quote some secondary research sources as well. Quotations ground your paper in the literature you are discussing and prevent your argument from being overly abstract. They also allow the author of the literature a chance to shine through in his or her own words, showing that you respect and appreciate the author's work. Quotations bring emphasis, variety, and specificity to your writing. Be selective, though, in your use of quotations so that the dominant voice of the paper is your own, not a patchwork of the words of others. Here is general advice to help you integrate quotations effectively into your essays.

Try to avoid floating quotations. Sometimes writers simply lift a sentence out of the original, put quotation marks around it, and identify the source (if at all) in a subsequent sentence.

"I met a traveler from an antique land." This is how Shelley's poem "Ozymandias" begins.

Doing so can create confusion for a reader, who is momentarily left to ponder where the quotation comes from and why have you quoted it. In addition to potentially causing confusion, such quoting can read as awkward and choppy, as there is no transition between another writer's words and yours.

Use at least an attributed quotation; that is, one that names the source *within* the sentence containing the quotation, usually in a lead-in phrase.

Shelley begins his poem "Ozymandias" with the words "I met a traveler from an antique land."

This way the reader knows right away who originally wrote or said the quoted material and knows (or at least expects) that your commentary will follow. It also provides a smoother transition between your words and the quotation.

Whenever possible, use an integrated quotation. To do this, you make the quotation a part of your own sentence.

When the narrator of "Ozymandias" begins by saying that he "met a traveler from an antique land," we are immediately thrust into a mysterious world.

This is the hardest sort of quoting to do since it requires that you make the quoted material fit in grammatically with your own sentence, but the payoff in clarity and sharp prose is usually well worth the extra time spent on sentence revision.

Adding to or Altering a Quotation

Sometimes, especially when you are using integrated quotations effectively, you will find that you need to slightly alter the words you are quoting. You should, of course, keep quotations exact whenever possible, but occasionally the disparity between the tense, point of view, or grammar of your sentence and that of the quoted material will necessitate some alterations. Other difficulties can arise when you quote a passage that already contains a quotation or when you need to combine quotation marks with other punctuation marks. When any of these situations arise, the following guidelines should prove useful. The examples of quoted text that follow are all drawn from this original passage from *Hamlet*, in which Hamlet and his friend Horatio are watching a gravedigger unearth old skulls in a cemetery:

> HAMLET: That skull had a tongue in it, and could sing once. How the knave jowls it to the ground, as if 'twere Cain's jaw-bone, that did the first murder! This might be the pate of a politician, which this ass now o'erreaches, one that would circumvent God, might it not?
>
> HORATIO: It might, my lord.
>
> HAMLET: Or of a courtier, which could say "Good morrow, sweet lord! How dost thou, sweet lord?" This might be my Lord Such-a-one, that prais'd my Lord Such-a-one's horse when 'a meant to beg it, might it not?

If you ever alter anything in a quotation or add words to it in order to make it clear and grammatically consistent with your own writing, you need to signal to your readers what you have added or changed. This is done by enclosing your words within square brackets in order to distinguish them from those in the source. If, for instance, you feel Hamlet's reference to the gravedigger as "this ass" is unclear, you could clarify it either by substituting your own words, as in the first example here, or by adding the identifying phrase to the original quote, as in the second example:

> Hamlet wonders if it is "the pate of a politician, which [the gravedigger] now o'erreaches."

> Hamlet wonders if it is "the pate of a politician, which this ass [the gravedigger] now o'erreaches."

Omitting Words from a Quotation

To keep a quotation focused and to the point, you will sometimes want to omit words, phrases, or even whole sentences that do not contribute to your point. Any omission is signaled by ellipses, or three spaced periods, with square brackets around them. (The brackets are required to distinguish your own ellipses from any that might occur in the original source.)

> Hamlet wonders if the skull "might be the pate of a politician [. . .] that would circumvent God."

It is usually not necessary to use ellipses at the beginning of a quotation, since a reader assumes you are quoting only a relevant portion of text, but MLA style recommends using ellipses at the end of a quotation if words are dropped at the end of the final quoted sentence.

Quotations within Quotations

If you are quoting material that itself contains a quotation, the internal quotation is set off with single quotation marks rather than the standard double quotation marks that will enclose the entire quotation.

> Hamlet wonders if he might be looking at the skull "of a courtier, which could say 'Good morrow, sweet lord! How dost thou, sweet lord?'"

When the text you're quoting contains *only* material already in quotation marks in the original, the standard double quotation marks are all you need.

> Hamlet wonders if the courtier once said "Good morrow, sweet lord! How dost thou, sweet lord?"

Quotation Marks with Other Punctuation

When a period or a comma comes at the end of a quotation, it should always be placed inside the closing quotation marks, whether or not this punctuation was in the original source. In the first example that follows, note that the period following "horse" is within the quotation marks, even though there is no period there in the original. In the second example, the comma following "once" is also within the quotation marks, even though in Shakespeare's original "once" is followed by a period.

> Hamlet muses that the skull might have belonged to "my Lord Such-a-one, that prais'd my Lord Such-a-one's horse."

> "That skull had a tongue in it, and could sing once," muses Hamlet.

Question marks and exclamation points are placed inside quotation marks if they are part of the original quotation and outside of the marks if they are part of your own sentence but not part of the passage you are quoting. In the first example, the question is Hamlet's, and so the question mark must be placed within the quotation marks; in the second example, the question is the essay writer's, and so the question mark is placed outside of the quotation marks.

> Hamlet asks Horatio if the skull "might be my Lord Such-a-one, that prais'd my Lord Such-a-one's horse when 'a meant to beg it, might it not?"

> Why is Hamlet so disturbed that this skull "might be the pate of a politician"?

These sorts of punctuation details are notoriously hard to remember, so you should not feel discouraged if you begin forgetting such highly specialized rules moments after reading them. At least know where you can look them up, and do so when you proofread your paper. A willingness to attend to detail is what distinguishes serious students and gives writing a polished, professional appearance. Also, the more you work with quotations, the easier it will be to remember the rules.

Quoting from Stories

The guidelines that follow should be used not only when you quote from stories but also when you quote from any prose work, be it fiction or nonfiction.

Short Quotations

For short quotations of four lines or fewer, run the quotation in with your own text, using quotation marks to signal the beginning and end of the quotation.

> Young Goodman Brown notices that the branches touched by his companion "became strangely withered and dried up, as with a week's sunshine."

Long Quotations

When a quotation is longer than four lines in your text, set it off from
your essay by beginning a new line and indenting it one inch from the
left margin only, as shown here. This is called a block quotation.

> Young Goodman Brown then notices something strange about his companion:

> As they went, he plucked a branch of maple to serve for a walking stick,
> and began to strip it of the twigs and little boughs, which were wet
> with evening dew. The moment his fingers touched them they became
> strangely withered and dried up, as with a week's sunshine. Thus the
> pair proceeded, . . . , until suddenly, . . . Goodman Brown sat himself
> down on the stump of a tree and refused to go any further.

Note that no quotation marks are used with block quotations. The indentation is sufficient to signal to your readers that this is a quotation.

Quoting from Poems

Short Quotations

For quotations of up to three lines, run the text right into your own, using quotation marks just as you would with a prose quotation. However,
since the placement of line endings can be significant in a poem, you
need to indicate where they occur. This is done by including a slash
mark, with a single space on each side, where the line breaks occur.
(Some students find this awkward-looking at first, but you will quickly
get used to it. Your instructor will expect you to honor the poet's choices
regarding line breaks.)

> In "Sailing to Byzantium," Yeats describes an old man as "a paltry thing, / A
> tattered coat upon a stick."

Long Quotations

For quotations of four lines or more, "block" the material, setting it off
one inch from the left margin, duplicating all line breaks of the original.
Do not use quotation marks with block quotations.

> In "Sailing to Byzantium," Yeats describes both the ravages of age and the
> possibility of renewal in the poem's second stanza:

An aged man is but a paltry thing,
A tattered coat upon a stick, unless
Soul clap its hands and sing, and louder sing
For every tatter in its mortal dress,
Nor is there singing school but studying
Monuments of its own magnificence.

Quoting from Plays

Short Single-Speaker Passages

When you quote a short passage of drama with a single speaker, treat the quoted text just as you would prose fiction:

Nora's first words in *A Doll House* are "Hide the tree well, Helene. The children mustn't get a glimpse of it till this evening, after it's trimmed."

Longer or More Complex Passages

For a longer quotation, or a quotation of any length involving more than one character, you will need to block off the quotation. Begin each separate piece of dialogue indented one inch from the left margin with the character's name, typed in all capital letters, followed by a period. Subsequent lines of the character's speech should be indented an additional one-quarter inch. (Your word processor's "hanging indent" function is useful for achieving this effect without having to indent each separate line.) As with fiction or poetry, do not use quotation marks for block quotations.

We see the tension between Nora and her husband in their very first confrontation:

NORA. Oh, but Torvald, this year we really should let ourselves go a bit.
    It's the first Christmas we haven't had to economize.
HELMER. But you know we can't go squandering.
NORA. Oh yes, Torvald, we can squander a little now. Can't we?

Verse Drama

Many older plays, including classical Greek drama and much of the work of Shakespeare and his contemporaries, are written at least partly in poetic verse. When you quote a verse drama, you must respect the line endings, just as you do in quoting poetry. The first example here shows a short quotation with slash marks that indicate line endings; the second shows a longer, block quotation in verse form.

> Hamlet's most famous soliloquy begins, "To be, or not to be, that is the question: / Whether 'tis nobler in the mind to suffer / The slings and arrows of outrageous fortune."

> Hamlet then begins his most famous soliloquy:
> > To be, or not to be, that is the question:
> > Whether 'tis nobler in the mind to suffer
> > The slings and arrows of outrageous fortune,
> > Or to take arms against a sea of troubles,
> > And by opposing end them.

Tips for Quoting

- **Double-check the wording, spelling, and punctuation of every quotation you use.** Even if something seems "wrong" in the original source—a nonstandard spelling, a strange mark of punctuation, or even a factual error—resist the urge to correct it. When you put quotation marks around something, you indicate that you are reproducing it exactly as it first appeared. If you feel the need to clarify that an error or inconsistency is not yours, you may follow it by the word *sic* (Latin for *thus*), not italicized, in square brackets. Example: The mother in the anonymous poem "Lord Randal" asks her son "wha [sic] met ye there?"

- **Use the shortest quotation you can while still making your point.** Remember, the focus should always be on your own ideas, and the dominant voice should be yours. Don't quote a paragraph from a source when a single sentence contains the heart of what you need. Don't quote a whole sentence when you can simply integrate a few words into one of your own sentences.

- **Never assume a quotation is self-explanatory.** Each time you include a quotation, analyze it and explain why you have quoted it. Remember that your reader may have a different reaction to the quotation than you did.

- **If you are quoting a *character* in a story, play, or poem, be sure to distinguish that character from the *author*.** Hamlet says "To be or not to be," not Shakespeare, and you should make that distinction clear.

- **Take care not to distort the meaning of a quotation.** It is intellectually dishonest to quote an author or a speaker out of context or to use ellipses or additions in such a way as to change the meaning or integrity of source material. Treat your sources with the same respect you would want if you were to be quoted in a newspaper or magazine.

MANUSCRIPT FORM

If your instructor gives you directions about what your paper should look like, follow them exactly. If not, the following basic guidelines on manuscript form, recommended by the Modern Language Association of America (MLA), will work well in most instances. The most comprehensive guide to MLA style is *MLA Handbook for Writers of Research Papers*, 7th edition (New York: MLA, 2009). For an online guide to MLA style, see Diana Hacker's *Research and Documentation Online*: http://www.dianahacker.com/resdoc/. The guiding principle here is readability—you want the look of your paper to distract as little as possible from the content.

- **Use plain white paper, black ink, and a standard, easy-to-read font.** To make your paper stand out from the masses, it might seem like a nice touch to use visual design elements like colored or decorated paper, fancy fonts, and so forth. However, your instructor has a lot of reading to do, and anything that distracts or slows down that reading is a minus, not a plus, for your paper. For the same reason, avoid illustrations, pictures of authors, and so forth, unless they are needed to clarify a point. Distinguish your paper through content and style, not flashy design.

- **No separate cover page is needed.** Also, don't waste your time and money on report covers or folders unless asked to do so by your instructor. Many instructors, in fact, find covers cumbersome and distracting.

- **Include vital information in the upper left corner of your first page.** This information usually consists of your name, the name of your instructor, the course number of the class, and the date you submit the paper.

- **Center your paper's title.** The title should appear in upper- and lowercase letters, and in the same font as the rest of your paper—not italicized, boldface, or set within quotation marks.

- **Page numbers should appear in the upper right corner of each page.** Do not include the word *page* or the abbreviation *p.* with the page numbers. Use your word processing program's "header" or "running head" feature to include your last name before the page numbers.

See the sample student papers in this book for examples of correct MLA-style formatting. These basic guidelines should carry you through most situations, but if you have any questions regarding format, ask your instructor for his or her preferences.

CHAPTER 4
Common Writing Assignments

Chances are you will encounter a variety of writing assignments in your literature class, possibly ranging from a brief personal response to an extended literary research paper. Each assignment offers you two opportunities. First, writing about a particular piece (or multiple pieces) of literature forces you to think more closely than a simple reading does, so you will end up learning more about the story, poem, or play. Second, writing is your best opportunity to share your thoughts with your instructor, and possibly your classmates, so you can have an impact on someone else's thinking as well. Generally, the assignments in such a class build cumulatively on one another, so that explication and analysis, for instance, are useful techniques in a research paper, and writing a comparison and contrast paper might give you tools to help you answer a question on an essay exam. Each time you get a new assignment, ask yourself, "What did I learn from the last assignment that I might apply to this one?" This chapter outlines some of the assignments you might be given (summary, response, explication, analysis, comparison and contrast, and essay exams), provides examples of each, and demonstrates how each skill might build on the previous skill.

SUMMARY

A **summary** is a brief recap of the most important points—plot, character, and so on—in a work of literature. To demonstrate that you have understood a story or play, for instance, you may be asked to summarize its plot as homework before class discussions. A summary of Nathaniel Hawthorne's "Young Goodman Brown" (page 3) follows:

> Set in seventeenth-century Salem, Massachusetts, Nathaniel Hawthorne's "Young Goodman Brown" follows the fortunes of the title character when he leaves his young wife, Faith, for a mysterious rendezvous in a forest at night. The character he meets in the forbidding woods is unnamed, but Hawthorne hints that he may be the Devil himself. As they proceed deeper into the forest on their unspecified but presumably unholy errand, Goodman

Brown's misgivings increase, especially when they encounter his fellow townsfolk—people Goodman Brown thought were good Christians—en route to the same meeting. But when they are joined by Faith, Brown recklessly resolves to participate. At the ceremony, the new converts are called forth, but as he and Faith step forward to be anointed in blood, he rebels and urges Faith to resist. Instantly he finds himself alone in the forest, and when he returns to town the next morning, uncertain whether it was all a dream, he finds himself suspicious and wary of his neighbors and his wife. His "Faith" has been corrupted, and to the end of his days he remains a bitter and untrusting man: "his dying hour was gloom."

A summary can be longer or shorter than this example, depending on your purpose. Notice that interpretation is kept to a minimum ("His 'Faith' has been corrupted") and the summary is recounted in the present tense ("he returns to town," "he remains a bitter and untrusting man").

It is rare for a full essay assignment to be based on summary alone. Keep in mind that for most of the papers you write, your readers—your teacher and possibly your classmates—are probably familiar with the literary work you are writing about, and do not need a recap of the entire work. Generally, they need only to be reminded of key points about the text that are most relevant to the argument you are making about it.

While a *summary* is not a kind of writing assignment that you will likely have to produce often in a literature course, *summarizing* is a skill you will need to develop. It is useful to be able to focus on the most important parts of a text, knowing what is most vital. Short summaries, either of a work (or part of a work) of literature or of critical essays about literature, are commonly used as part of the supporting evidence in more complex papers. When you are using secondary sources in a paper about a literary work—as when you write a literary research paper—chances are that your audience has not read the critical essays you have read. Therefore, you may need to summarize for your readers the arguments of those critical essays.

Often such summaries are only a few sentences in length and restate the author's thesis, possibly with a few examples of the kind of evidence the author uses to support the thesis. Just as often, you may want to summarize only part of a critical essay, a part that is pertinent to your paper. For example, if you have read an essay about Hawthorne's use of imagery in "Young Goodman Brown," for the purposes of your paper you may need to summarize only the section that deals with the imagery of light and darkness in the story. Ask yourself, "What do my readers need to know to follow my argument, and what evidence do I need to provide to convince them of my point of view?" Summarize accordingly.

RESPONSE

Though you may state or imply whether or not you liked the literary selection in question when you write a response paper, the main purpose is not to provide a review or a rating. Rather, the goal of such a paper is twofold: to describe your personal response to a particular reading assignment and to explain why you had this reaction. Of course, our reactions to literature are often multiple and complex, so you need to be selective in what you write. Don't try to explain every response and every thought you had while reading. Rather, choose one significant thought you had while reading and explore that in depth.

Response papers in general are somewhat informal and do not necessarily follow the thesis-and-support model common in other types of literature papers. Response papers are often fairly brief, and since you are writing about your personal responses, it's generally okay to use the first-person pronoun I. Remember, though, that this is not simply a personal essay in which you explore your own life and thoughts. Keep the literature as the main focus, and if you call on your own experiences, do so in order to explain and analyze some facet of the story, poem, or play. Since there are no hard-and-fast rules about response papers, be sure to read your instructor's directions carefully and follow them closely. If you have any questions, ask.

After reading Jamaica Kincaid's very short story "Girl" (page 380), take a moment to consider your own response to it and where that response comes from. Then read and consider the student response paper that follows.

Tom Lyons
Professor Tritle
English 112
17 October 2011

A Boy's View of "Girl"

It may sound peculiar for a young man to say this, but I could really relate to the character in Jamaica Kincaid's story "Girl." My father is a very old-fashioned, conservative man, and all through my childhood he constantly instructed my brother and me about proper behavior for a boy. His instructions and corrections were meant to be for our own good, but they put a lot of pressure on us from a very young age. This is similar to the experience of the young girl in Kincaid's story.

I assume the speaker in the story is the girl's mother, or at least some older female relative. She keeps saying "this is how" you do things, as though there is only one right way for everything. It's as if the girl can't figure out anything for herself, not even how to smile at someone she likes. I notice that the girl doesn't even have a name, and she has almost no chance to speak for herself. It seems that the mother doesn't particularly care who the girl is as an individual; what matters is just the fact that she is a girl. The mother also makes huge assumptions about what the girl is like. She thinks that the girl sings inappropriate songs in Sunday school and that she is trying to become a "slut." The poor girl never gets a chance to defend herself against these accusations.

Of course, my father was not worried about me becoming a slut, but he was very concerned that my brother and I should grow up to be strong, masculine men. The mother in the story emphasizes the girl's domestic duties like cooking, cleaning, and sewing. My father always said that men should be good providers and that a man's work was very important. Men should also be responsible for protecting the family. I remember he went on a business trip when I was about twelve years old, and he said, "You need to take care of your mother while I'm gone." That's a big responsibility for a kid. My father thinks that our culture is too permissive and that

Tom's introduction makes clear his focus: the similarities between his own experience and that of the girl in Kincaid's story.

Tom points out particular features of the story that struck him, all related to the way the girl's mother forces her will on the girl.

Tom uses specifics from the story to demonstrate his point.

When Tom turns to his own childhood experience, he makes direct comparison to "Girl," so the focus is always on the story.

Lyons 2

any boys are not raised to be responsible men. This is similar to
the mother in the story, who seems to think the daughter needs to
be told constantly how to be a proper woman.

This story hit home for me. It really shows how parents and
elders can pass on expectations about gender roles to future
generations. Young boys and girls do need advice and strong role
models, but parents can sometimes go too far in imposing their
own values on the next generation. I hope that as time goes by,
both boys and girls are subjected to less of this sort of pressure so
that they are free to develop their own unique personalities as
people, not just as gender stereotypes.

Tom ends his response paper by explaining the thoughts and feelings the story provoked in him.

EXPLICATION

One common assignment is to perform an **explication** or a close-reading
of a poem or short prose passage. As the word implies, an *explication*
takes what is implicit or subtle in a work of literature and makes it explicit and clear. Literary language tends to be densely packed with meaning, and your job as you explicate it is to unfold that meaning and lay
it out for your reader. The principal technique of explication is close-
reading; indeed, explication and close-reading are so closely related that
many writers use the words virtually interchangeably. When you write
this sort of paper, you will examine a piece of literature very closely, paying special attention to such elements of the language as sentence structure, **style**, **imagery**, **figurative language** (such as **similes** and **metaphors**), word choice, and perhaps even grammar and punctuation. The
job of an explication is twofold: to point out particular, salient elements
of style and to explain the purpose and effect of these elements within
the text.

When assigned an explication or a close-reading, you might be tempted
to simply walk through a text line by line, pointing out interesting features of style as they occur. A paper written in this way, though, can de-
volve into little more than summary or restatement of the literature in
more prosaic language. A better idea is to isolate the various features of
the literature on which you will focus and then deal separately with the
specifics and implications of each.

The paper that follows is an example of a student essay that provides
an explication of a literary text. First, take a look at Robert Herrick's
"Upon Julia's Clothes," and then read the student's paper.

ROBERT HERRICK   [1591–1674]

Upon Julia's Clothes

Whenas in silks my Julia goes,
Then, then (methinks) how sweetly flows
That liquefaction of her clothes.

Next, when I cast mine eyes, and see
That brave vibration each way free,
O how that glittering taketh me!

[1648]

Jessica Barnes

Professor White

English 108

3 March 2008

Poetry in Motion: Herrick's "Upon Julia's Clothes"

In its brief six lines, Robert Herrick's "Upon Julia's Clothes" is celebration of the physical sensuousness of the speaker's object desire. The poem is structured like a seashell with two parts. In the first stanza, the speaker makes a seemingly simple observation: when Julia walks past, her silken clothes seem to flow as if they're liquid. In the second stanza, though, he provides a second observation: when Julia's body is "each way free" of the clothing, the speaker is completely overtaken by the beauty of Julia's "brave vibration."

Jessica's introduction lays out clearly the focus and structure of her paper.

Herrick provides several inversions of syntax to place emphasis on certain images. For example, in line 1, Herrick inverts my Julia goes" with "in silks" to emphasize the importance of silks" to Julia's sensuality. He creates another inversion in lines 3. The sense of the lines is as follows: "Then, then (methinks) that liquefaction of her clothes flows sweetly." Herrick rearranges the sentence to emphasize the sweetness of the flowing and to place the emphasis on "flows" and "clothes" at the ends of the lines.

In this paragraph, Jessica focuses on a specific language feature, syntax, and provides several examples from Herrick's poem.

Herrick also provides several changes in the iambic tetrameter meter to create varied lines within the poem's strict form. In line he repeats "then" two times. In doing so, he forces the reader pause deeply between each "then" and encourages the reader to meditate on the poet's decision to repeat the word in the first place. In line 6, too, Herrick alternately accelerates and decelerates the tempo of the line. The exclamatory "O" at the beginning the line suggests that the speaker has been utterly charmed by Julia's beauty. It is a long sound that slows the reader down at the beginning of the line; in addition, it provides a stress on the first syllable of the line, instead of an unstressed syllable followed by a

This paragraph examines a different language feature, poetic meter.

Barnes 2

stressed one (see, for example, "That **brave** vi**bra**tion" in line 5). "Glittering" also disrupts the strict tetrameter of the line. Its three syllables are compressed into two brief syllables ("**glitt**ring") so that the next accent can fall on "**tak**eth me," which emphasizes the fact that the speaker is totally overwhelmed by Julia's naked body.

Jessica begins to tie up her observations about specific language features with some preliminary analysis.

Ultimately, the poem reveals that Julia's beauty is beyond words. We cannot know whether Julia has actually taken her clothes off, or whether she has done so in the imagination of the speaker. Either way, the poem provides many sounds that mirror the "O" of line 6. The end rhyme for all of the lines in the first stanza rhyme with the "O": *goes, flows, clothes.* Each of these words reinforces the importance of Julia's shimmering beauty, and the power of her movements. The "ee" rhymes at the ends of the lines in stanza 2 — *see, free, me* — reinforce the idea that Julia's freedom in her nakedness also frees the poet's pleasure in imagining, or seeing, the "brave vibration" of her body.

The final language feature the paper examines is the repetition of vowel sound.

ANALYSIS

To analyze, by definition, is to take something apart and examine how the individual parts relate to one another and function within the whole. Engineers frequently analyze complex machinery, looking for ways to improve efficiency or performance. In a similar way, you can take apart a piece of literature to study how a particular part of it functions and what that part contributes to the whole. Typical candidates for literary analysis include **plot development**, **characterization**, **tone**, **irony**, and **symbols**.

Here is an example of a student essay that provides an analysis. First, take a look at Robert Browning's "My Last Duchess" (page 503); then read the student's paper.

Walker 1

dam Walker

rofessor Blitefield

nglish 203

2 February 2008

Possessed by the Need for Possession:

Browning's "My Last Duchess"

In "My Last Duchess," Robert Browning's duke reveals his

elings of jealousy and betrayal as he discusses the duchess's

ortrait. In his dramatic monologue, the duke's public persona as

n aristocratic gentleman is shattered by the revelations of his

ctual feelings about his dead duchess. The duke reveals what

osets him most: his late wife's liberal smiles and attentions to

thers besides himself. With this focus on the duchess's attentions,

rowning creates a compelling portrait of a gentleman who could

ot exert complete control over his former wife, and may fail to

ontrol his future wife as well.

The introduction names the poem to be analyzed and clearly explains that the focus of the paper will be the duke's jealous nature.

The duke repeatedly calls attention to what he sees as the

uchess's misinterpretations. The duke imagines the duchess as she

at for Fra Pandolf: "such stuff / Was courtesy, she thought, and

ause enough / For calling up that spot of joy" (lines 19-21).

ccording to the duke, the duchess mistook the painter's atten-

ons as courtesies. Her blush, or "spot of joy" (21) on her cheeks,

as too indiscriminate for the duke. The duke admits that the

uchess blushed at his own advances, but she also blushed at the

ainter, the "dropping of the daylight in the West" (26), a bough

f cherries, and a white mule. The duchess's gaze is an indiscrimi-

ate one: she appreciates whatever pleases her, whether it be

uman, animal, or organic. This infuriates the duke, who thinks

at his "nine-hundred-years-old name" (33) ought to make him

ore valuable in the eyes of the duchess.

Adam quotes specific lines from the poem in order to demonstrate his point. In each case, he integrates the quotation cleanly into his own prose.

Eventually, the duke restricts the duchess's blushes with

ommands: "This grew; I gave commands; / Then all smiles

topped together. There she stands / As if alive" (45-47). These

nes are concise and quick compared with the rhetoric of the other

The quotation is immediately followed by an explanation of its purpose in the paper.

Walker 2

lines in the poem. Even so, they are in some ways the most
important. What made the smiles stop? Was the duchess silenced
in life? Or was it her death that stopped the smiling? And why
does the duke need this portrait that resembles the duchess when
she was alive?

Adam uses rhetorical question to provide stylistic variety and to get the reader thinking.

Ultimately, the showing of the portrait is a way for the duke
to show his possessions — and his command of his possessions — to the envoy of the Count. As the duke invites the envoy
to come downstairs, he already characterizes his future bride as a
kind of possession:

> I repeat,
> The Count your master's known munificence
> Is ample warrant that no just pretence
> Of mine for dowry will be disallowed;
> Though his fair daughter's self, as I avowed
> At starting, is my object. (48-53)

Note that the long quotation is blocked (indented from the left margin) and does not use quotation marks.

After alluding to the generous dowry that he will receive, the duke
checks himself by saying that it is "his [the Count's] fair daughter's self" that he has found so compelling. Even so, the duke has
started to limit and control the status of his future bride, suggesting that he will exert the same controls on her that he exerted on
his late wife. In the end, she runs the same risk of becoming a sea
horse that requires Neptune's taming.

Adam's concluding sentence alludes to the final lines of the poem.

COMPARISON AND CONTRAST

Another common paper assignment is the **comparison and contrast** essay. You might be asked to draw comparisons and contrasts within a
single work of literature — say, between two characters in a story or play.
Even more common is an assignment that asks you to compare and contrast a particular element — characters, setting, style, tone, and so on — in
two or more stories, poems, or plays. A *comparison* emphasizes the similarities between two or more items, while a *contrast* highlights their
differences. Though some papers do both, it is typical for an essay to
emphasize one or the other.

If you are allowed to choose the works of literature for a comparison and contrast paper, take care to select works that have enough in common to make such a comparison interesting and valid. Even if Henrik Ibsen's *A Doll House* and Shirley Jackson's "The Lottery" are your favorites, it is difficult to imagine a well-focused paper comparing these two, as they share virtually nothing in terms of authorship, history, theme, or style, having been written in different genres, in different centuries, and on different continents. It would make far more sense to select two seventeenth-century poems or two love stories.

The paper that follows compares Robert Browning's "My Last Duchess" (page 503) and Christina Rossetti's "After Death." First, read Rossetti's poem; then read the student paper.

CHRISTINA ROSSETTI   [1830–1894]

After Death

The curtains were half drawn, the floor was swept
  And strewn with rushes, rosemary and may°
Lay thick upon the bed on which I lay,
Where through the lattice ivy-shadows crept.
He leaned above me, thinking that I slept
  And could not hear him; but I heard him say,
  "Poor child, poor child": and as he turned away
Came a deep silence, and I knew he wept.
He did not touch the shroud, or raise the fold
  That hid my face, or take my hand in his,
    Or ruffle the smooth pillows for my head:
    He did not love me living; but once dead
  He pitied me; and very sweet it is
To know he still is warm though I am cold.

[1849]

May: green or flowering branches used for May Day celebrations.

Todd Bowen
Professor Harrison
English 215
12 May 2008

Speakers for the Dead:
Narrators in "My Last Duchess"
and "After Death"

In "My Last Duchess," Robert Browning creates a duke whose tight control over his wife — and his preoccupation with his own noble rank — reveal a misogynistic character. Browning's dramatic monologue stands in stark contrast to Christina Rossetti's "After Death," a sonnet in which the speaker comes back from the dead to reveal what she observes about her lover. When paired together, these poems speak to each other in a time period that seemed to have a gothic obsession with the death of young women.

In the poems' style and structure, Browning and Rossetti create completely different portraits of women after death. In "My Last Duchess," the duke uses the actual portrait of his dead wife to create a portrait in words of a woman who smiled too liberally at men who fawned over her. The duke says, "She had / A heart — how shall I say? — too soon made glad, / Too easily impressed; she liked whate'er / She looked on, and her looks went everywhere" (lines 21-24). Throughout his long dramatic monologue, the duke meditates on several moments when the duchess betrays him by smiling at others; however, we as readers never get to hear the duchess's side of the story.

In Rossetti's "After Death," however, the tables are turned: the dead woman gets to speak back to the man who performs his grief over her death. In doing so, she carefully observes the behavior of her lover, who thinks that she is merely a lifeless corpse. In each line of the small sonnet, the speaker observes the man as he leans above her, says "Poor child, poor child" (7), and then turns away without actually touching her body. Even so, the woman suggests that this is an improvement from when she was

Todd's concise introduction names the authors and poems that will be the subject of his comparison as well as the paper's focus on certain shared features of the poems.

The first two body paragraphs each focus on one of the poems, providing a combination of specific evidence — mostly in the form of quotations — and analysis of this evidence.

Bowen 2

ive: "He did not love me living; but once dead / He pitied me"
l. 12-13). The speaker's final couplet is especially chilling: "and
ery sweet it is / To know he still is warm though I am cold"
3-14). The speaker says that it is "sweet" to know that the man
as outlived her. She doesn't explain this sweetness, but perhaps it
because she can observe his emotion in a way that she never
uld have while she was alive.

Note that Todd distinguishes between the poet Rossetti and the speaker of the poem.

When read together, Rossetti's "After Death" and Browning's
My Last Duchess" function as companion pieces, each speaking to
e other in a kind of call-and-response. Browning's duke shuts
wn any speech beyond his own, talking at length in the silence
the portrait and the visitor who looks at it. His story is the only
ory that he wants to present, even if his speech reveals his own
ortcomings. Rossetti's woman provides an alternative perspective
death and mourning as the woman speaks from the dead to
veal the shortcomings of the man who mourns her. Both poems
ovide chilling perspectives on death, mourning, and marriage in
e Victorian period.

The concluding paragraph contains the heart of the actual comparison of the poems.

ESSAY EXAMS

The key to getting through the potentially stressful situation of an essay
exam is to be prepared and to know what will be expected of you.

Preparation takes two forms: knowing the material and anticipating
the questions. Knowing the material starts with keeping up with all reading and homework assignments throughout the term. You can't possibly
read several weeks' or months' worth of material the night before the test
and hope to remember it all. The days before the test should be used not
for catching up but for review—revisiting the readings, skimming or
rereading key passages, and studying your class notes. It's best to break
up study sessions into manageable blocks if possible. Reviewing for two
hours a night for three nights before the exam will be far more effective
than a single six-hour cram session on the eve of the test.

Anticipating the questions that might be on the exam is a bit trickier,
but it can be done. What themes and issues have come up again and
again in class lectures or discussions? What patterns do you see in your

class notes? What points did your instructor stress? These are the topics most likely to appear on the exam. Despite what you might think, it is very rare that an instructor poses intentionally obscure exam questions in an attempt to trip up students or expose their ignorance. Most often, the instructor is providing you with an opportunity to demonstrate what you know, and you should be ready to take that opportunity. You can't, of course, second-guess your instructor perfectly and know for sure what will be on the test, but you can spend some time in advance thinking about what sorts of questions you are likely to encounter and how you would answer them.

Your exam may be open-book or closed-book; find out in advance which it will be, so that you can plan and study accordingly. In an *open-book* test, you are allowed to use your textbook during the exam. This is a big advantage, obviously, as it allows you access to specific evidence, including quotations, to support your points. If you know the exam is going to be open-book, you might also jot down any important notes in the book itself, where you can find them readily if you need them. Use your textbook sparingly, though—just enough to find the evidence you know to be there. Don't waste time browsing the literature hoping to find inspiration or ideas. For a *closed-book* exam, you have to rely on your memory alone. But you should still try to be as specific as possible in your references to the literature, using character names, recalling plot elements, and so forth.

When you sit down to take the exam, you may have the urge to start writing right away, since your time is limited. Suppress that urge and read through the entire exam first, paying special attention to the instruction portion. Often the exam will offer you choices, such as "Answer two of the following three questions" or "Select a single poem as the basis of your answer." If you miss such cues, you may find yourself racing to write three essays and running out of time or discussing several poems shallowly instead of one in depth. Once you are certain what is expected of you, take a few more minutes to plan your answers before you start writing. A few jotted notes or an informal outline may take a moment, but it will likely save you time as you write. If you will be writing more than one essay, take care not to repeat yourself or to write more than one essay about any one piece of literature. The idea is to show your instructor your mastery of the course material, and to do so effectively you should demonstrate breadth of knowledge.

When you do begin writing, bear in mind that instructors have different expectations for exam answers than they do for essays written outside of class. They know that in timed exams you have no time for research or extensive revisions. Clarity and concision are the keys; elegant prose style is not expected (though, of course, it will come as a pleasant surprise if you can manage it). Effective essay answers are often more formulaic than other sorts of effective writing, relying on the schematic of a straightforward introduction, simple body paragraphs, and a brief conclusion.

Your introduction should be simple and to the point. A couple of sentences is generally all that is needed, and these should avoid rhetorical flourishes or digressions. Often the best strategy is to parrot back the instructions as an opening statement. Body paragraphs for essay answers should also be simple and will often, though not always, be briefer than they would be in an essay you worked on at home. They should still be as specific as possible, making reference to and perhaps even quoting the literature to illustrate your points. Just as in a more fully developed essay, try to avoid dwelling in generalities; use specific examples and evidence. Conclusions for essay exams are usually brief, often just a sentence or two of summary.

Finally, take a watch with you on exam day and keep a close eye on the time. Use all the time you are given and budget it carefully. If you have an hour to write two answers, don't spend forty-five minutes on the first. Even though you will likely be pressed for time, save a few minutes at the end to proofread your answers. Make any corrections as neatly and legibly as possible. Watch the time, but try not to watch your classmates' progress. Keep focused on your own process. Just because someone else is using his or her book a lot, you shouldn't feel you need to do the same. If someone finishes early and leaves, don't take this as a sign that you are running behind or that you are less efficient or less smart than that person. Students who don't make full use of the exam time are often underprepared; they tend to write vague and underdeveloped answers and should not be your role models.

An open-book essay exam on poetry gave students several options, including "Select two poems by different poets, each of which deals with the theme of time, and compare how the authors present this theme." A student chose William Shakespeare's Sonnet 73 (page 454) and Robert Herrick's "To the Virgins, to Make Much of Time" (page 459). Read the two poems and then the student's essay exam answer.

Midterm Essay: Option #2

Shakespeare's Sonnet 73 ("That time of year thou mayest in me behold") and Herrick's "To the Virgins, to Make Much of Time" both deal with the theme of time, and particularly the effect that time has on love. Though there are important differences in their focus and style, both poems urge their readers to love well and make the most of the time they have left.

Both poems make their points about time through a series of metaphors, and in fact they use some of the same metaphors. Herrick begins with the image of rosebuds, which bloom and then die quickly. Shakespeare's first metaphor is also drawn from the natural world of plants, in this case a tree losing its leaves in the autumn. In the sonnet, the natural world is even connected to the spiritual world of church when the poet refers to the branches of the tree as "choirs." Both poems also compare life to a single day, with the setting sun symbolizing death. Toward the end of his sonnet, Shakespeare writes of life as a fire that burns brightly in youth and then cools as a person nears death. While Herrick does not refer to fire specifically, he follows a similar line of reasoning when he mentions a time "When youth and blood are warmer" (line 10).

The most significant difference between the two poems lies in the characters of the speaker and the implied listener. Herrick offers his advice about the nature of time and its effect on love to "the Virgins" generally. He tells them to "go marry," but he offers no specifics about whom they should be marrying or how they might choose these mates. Shakespeare's poem, on the other hand, seems to be addressed to a single "you" who is in some sort of relationship with the speaker, the "me" who narrates the poem. When he urges the listener "To love that well which thou must leave ere long" (line 14), he is referring to himself as the object of love.

In the end, the differences end up overshadowing the superficial similarities of theme and purpose. Herrick's poem, with its relative lack of specificity, comes across as the sort of kindly advice an older person, perhaps an uncle, might give to any young man or woman. Shakespeare's is a more intimate, and ultimately somewhat darker, poem.

The introductory paragraph is brief and restates the assignment, adding in specifics to begin focusing the essay.

The two body paragraphs are also fairly brief, but they give lots of specific examples from the poems rather than relying on generalizations.

Because this was an open-book exam, the student was even able to incorporate brief quotations in her answer.

The organization is clear and straightforward, with one body paragraph comparing similarities between the poems and one contrasting a key difference.

The conclusion is also simple in form and purpose; it restates the main points of the body paragraphs in new language and makes the contrast more explicit.

CHAPTER 5

Writing about Stories

Fiction has long been broken down and discussed in terms of specific elements common to all stories, and chances are you will be focusing on one or more of these when you write an essay about a story.

ELEMENTS OF FICTION

The **elements of fiction** most commonly identified are **plot**, **character**, **point of view**, **setting**, **theme**, **symbolism**, and **style**. If you find yourself wondering what to write about a story, a good place to begin is isolating these elements and seeing how they work on a reader and how they combine to create the unique artifact that is a particular story.

Plot

While on some level we all read stories to find out what happens next, in truth plot is usually the least interesting of the elements of fiction. Students who have little experience writing about fiction tend to spend too much time retelling the plot. You can avoid this by bearing in mind that your readers will also have read the literature in question and don't need a thorough replay of what happened. In general, readers just need small reminders of the key points of plot about which you will write, and these should not be self-standing but rather should serve as springboards into analysis and discussion. Still, writing about the plot sometimes makes sense, especially when the plot surprises your expectations by, for instance, rearranging the chronology of events or otherwise presenting things in nonrealistic ways. When this happens in a story, the plot may indeed prove fertile ground for analysis and may be the basis of an interesting paper.

Character

Many interesting essays analyze the actions, motivations, and development of individual characters. How does the author reveal a character to the reader? How does a character grow and develop over the course of a story? Readers have to carefully examine what insights the text provides about a character, but sometimes readers have to consider what's left out. What does the reader have to infer about the character that isn't explicitly written? What does the character refrain from saying? What secrets do characters keep from others, or from themselves? These questions can be fertile ground for analysis. Although the most obvious character to write about is usually the **protagonist**, don't let your imagination stop there. Often the **antagonist** or even a minor character can be an interesting object of study. Keep in mind, too, that characters can start out as antagonistic figures and experience a transformation in the eyes of the narrator or other characters, or in the eyes of the reader. Your job in writing a paper is to consider these transformations and try to understand why a text explores these complex character developments. Usually not a lot has been said and written about less prominent characters, so you will be more free to create your own interpretations. (Playwright Tom Stoppard wrote a very successful full-length play entitled *Rosencrantz and Guildenstern Are Dead* about two of the least developed characters in *Hamlet*.)

Point of View

Related to character is the issue of point of view. The perspective from which a story is told can make a big difference in how we perceive it. Sometimes a story is told in the *first person*, from the point of view of one of the characters. Whether this is a major or a minor character, we must always remember that **first-person narrators** can be unreliable, as they do not have access to all vital information, and their own agendas can often skew the way they see events. The **narrator** of Edgar Allan Poe's "The Cask of Amontillado" (page 14) seeks to gain sympathy for a hideous act of revenge, giving us a glimpse into a deeply disturbed mind. A **third-person narrator** may be **omniscient**, knowing everything pertinent to a story; or limited, knowing, for instance, the thoughts and motives of the protagonist but not of any of the other characters. As you read a story, ask yourself what the point of view contributes and why the author may have chosen to present the story from a particular perspective.

Setting

Sometimes a setting is merely the backdrop for a story, but often place plays an important role in our understanding of a work. John Updike chooses a small, conservative New England town as the setting of his story "A & P" (page 294). It is the perfect milieu for an exploration of values and class interaction, and the story would have a very different feel and meaning if it had been set, say, in New York City. As you read, ask yourself how significant a setting is and what it adds to the meaning of a story. Remember that setting refers to time as well as place. "A & P" is about three young women walking into a small-town grocery store wearing only bathing suits, an action more shocking when the story was written in 1961 than it would be now (although it would doubtless still raise eyebrows in many places).

Theme

All **short stories** have at least one theme—an abstract concept such as *love, war, friendship, revenge,* or *art*—brought to life and made real through the plot, characters, and so on. Identifying a theme or themes is one of the first keys to understanding a story, but it is not the end point. Pay some attention to how the theme is developed. Is it blatant or subtle? What actions, events, or symbols make the theme apparent to you? Generally, the driving force of a story is the author's desire to convey something *about* a particular theme, to make readers think and feel in a certain way. First ask yourself what the author seems to be saying about love or war or whatever themes you have noted; second, whether you agree with the author's perceptions; and finally, why or why not.

Symbolism

Some students get frustrated when their instructors or their classmates begin to talk about **symbolism.** How do we know that an author intended a symbolic reading? Maybe that flower is just a real flower, not a stand-in for youth or for life and regeneration as some readers insist. And even if it is a symbol, how do we know we are reading it correctly? While it's true that plenty of flowers *are* simply flowers, and while students should identify symbols with caution, the more prominent an image in a story, the more likely it is meant to be read symbolically. Careful writers choose their words and images for maximum impact, filling them with as much meaning as possible and inviting their readers to interpret them. When John Steinbeck entitles his story "The Chrysanthemums," we would do well to ask if the flowers are really just plants or if we are being asked to look for a greater significance.

Style

The final element of fiction isolated here is style, sometimes spoken of under the heading of tone or language. A text may strike you as sad or lighthearted, formal or casual. It may make you feel nostalgic, or it may make your heart race with excitement. Somewhat more difficult, though, is isolating the elements of language that contribute to a particular tone or effect. Look for characteristic stylistic elements that create these effects. Is the diction elevated and difficult, or ordinary and simple? Are the sentences long and complex, or short and to the point? Is there dialogue? If so, how do the characters who speak this dialogue come across? Does the style stay consistent throughout the story, or does it change? What does the author leave out? Paying close attention to linguistic matters like these will take you far in your understanding of how a particular story achieves its effect.

STORIES FOR ANALYSIS

Read Charlotte Perkins Gilman's story "The Yellow Wallpaper" (page 76) and Kate Chopin's "The Story of an Hour," which we have annotated below. Both stories explore issues of women's identity and freedom. The questions following the annotated story ask you to analyze how the elements of fiction work in these two stories.

KATE CHOPIN   [1851–1904]

The Story of an Hour

Knowing that Mrs. Mallard was afflicted with a heart trouble, great care was taken to break to her as gently as possible the news of her husband's death.

It was her sister Josephine who told her, in broken sentences; veiled hints that revealed in half concealing. Her husband's friend Richards was there, too, near her. It was he who had been in the newspaper office when intelligence of the railroad disaster was received, with Brently Mallard's name leading the list of "killed." He had only taken the time to assure himself of its truth by a second telegram, and had hastened to forestall any less careful, less tender friend in bearing the sad message.

Her family a
friends seem
think she's c

She did not hear the story as many women have heard the same, with a paralyzed inability to accept its significance.

She wept at once, with sudden, wild abandonment, in her sister's arms. When the storm of grief had spent itself she went away to her room alone. She would have no one follow her.

There stood, facing the open window, a comfortable, roomy armchair. Into this she sank, pressed down by a physical exhaustion that haunted her body and seemed to reach into her soul.

She could see in the open square before her house the tops of trees that were all aquiver with the new spring life. The delicious breath of rain was in the air. In the street below a peddler was crying his wares. The notes of a distant song which some one was singing reached her faintly, and countless sparrows were twittering in the eaves.

A beautiful day. Why does Chopin take the time to describe it in such a short story, especially one about a death?

There were patches of blue sky showing here and there through the clouds that had met and piled one above the other in the west facing her window.

She sat with her head thrown back upon the cushion of the chair, quite motionless, except when a sob came up into her throat and shook her, as a child who had cried itself to sleep continues to sob in its dreams.

She was young, with a fair, calm face, whose lines bespoke repression and even a certain strength. But now there was a dull stare in her eyes, whose gaze was fixed away off yonder on one of those patches of blue sky. It was not a glance of reflection, but rather indicated a suspension of intelligent thought.

There was something coming to her and she was waiting for it, fearfully. What was it? She did not know; it was too subtle and elusive to name. But she felt it, creeping out of the sky, reaching toward her through the sounds, the scents, the color that filled the air.

Ominous. What could be coming? Something physical or emotional?

Now her bosom rose and fell tumultuously. She was beginning to recognize this thing that was approaching to possess her, and she was striving to beat it back with her will—as powerless as her two white slender hands would have been.

When she abandoned herself a little whispered word escaped her slightly parted lips. She said it over and over under her breath: "free, free, free!" The vacant stare and the look of terror that had followed it went from her eyes. They stayed keen and bright. Her pulses beat fast, and the coursing blood warmed and relaxed every inch of her body.

She did not stop to ask if it were or were not a monstrous joy that held her. A clear and exalted perception enabled her to dismiss the suggestion as trivial.

She knew that she would weep again when she saw the kind, tender hands folded in death; the face that had never looked save with love upon her, fixed and gray and dead. But she saw beyond that bitter moment a long procession of years to come that would belong to her absolutely. And she opened and spread her arms out to them in welcome.

There would be no one to live for her during those coming years: she would live for herself. There would be no powerful will bending hers in that blind persistence with which men and women believe they have a right to impose a private will upon a fellow-creature. A kind intention or a cruel intention made the act seem no less a crime as she looked upon it in that brief moment of illumination.

And yet she had loved him—sometimes. Often she had not. What did it matter! What could love, the unsolved mystery, count for in face of this possession of self-assertion which she suddenly recognized as the strongest impulse of her being!

"Free! Body and soul free!" she kept whispering.

Josephine was kneeling before the closed door with her lips to the keyhole, imploring for admission. "Louise, open the door! I beg; open the door—you will make yourself ill. What are you doing, Louise? For heaven's sake open the door."

"Go away. I am not making myself ill." No; she was drinking in a very elixir of life through that open window.

Her fancy was running riot along those days ahead of her. Spring days, and summer days, and all sorts of days that would be her own. She breathed a quick prayer that life might be long. It was only yesterday she had thought with a shudder that life might be long.

She arose at length and opened the door to her sister's importunities. There was a feverish triumph in her eyes, and she carried herself unwittingly like a goddess of Victory. She clasped her sister's waist, and together they descended the stairs. Richards stood waiting for them at the bottom.

Some one was opening the front door with a latchkey. It was Brently Mallard who entered, a little travel-stained, composedly carrying his gripsack and umbrella. He had been far from the scene of accident, and did not even know there

How could it b[e]
Her emotions
quick to chang[e]
hard to keep u[p]
even for her.

Was their mar[riage]
unhappy? Wou[ld]
friends and fa[mily]
think so? Wou[ld]
husband have [thought]
so?

Has she becom[e]
assertive? St[...]

had been one. He stood amazed at Josephine's piercing cry; at Richards' quick motion to screen him from the view of his wife.

But Richards was too late.

When the doctors came they said she had died of heart disease—of joy that kills.

Surprising, ironic ending.

[1894]

QUESTIONS ON THE STORIES

☐ How would you summarize the plot of each story? What, if anything, makes it difficult to do so?

☐ Who, in your opinion, are the most sympathetic characters? Who are the most antagonistic? What kinds of information do we learn about the emotional lives of these characters?

☐ What is the point of view of each story? How would you compare the effects of these choices? What are the advantages and disadvantages of each choice?

☐ How would you describe the setting of each story? What details of setting contribute to the tone or atmosphere of the story?

☐ How would you describe the style of writing in each story? Is the prose formal? Archaic? Conversational? Melodramatic? Be as specific as possible, and note examples that bolster your claims.

☐ What kinds of symbols recur in each story? Are they fanciful? Ordinary? Conventional? Surprising? How do they move the narrative forward?

SAMPLE PAPER: AN ESSAY THAT COMPARES AND CONTRASTS

Melanie Smith was given the assignment to compare and contrast an element of her choosing in Kate Chopin's "The Story of an Hour" and Charlotte Perkins Gilman's "The Yellow Wallpaper" and to draw some conclusions about life in the nineteenth century. Rather than examining the female protagonists, Melanie chose to focus on the minor male

characters in the stories. She wrote a point-by-point comparison designed to demonstrate that these men, despite the opinions of them that
she heard expressed in class, were not bad people. Rather, they were led
by their social training to behave in ways that were perfectly acceptable
in their day, even if they now strike readers as oppressive.

Smith 1

elanie Smith
rofessor Hallet
aglish 109
3 May 2008

Good Husbands in Bad Marriages

When twenty-first-century readers first encounter literature of
arlier times, it is easy for us to apply our own standards of
anduct to the characters and situations. Kate Chopin's "The Story
an Hour" and Charlotte Perkins Gilman's "The Yellow Wallpaper"
'fer two good examples of this. Both written by American women
the last decade of the nineteenth century, the stories give us a
ok into the lives, and especially the marriages, of middle-class
amen of the time. By modern standards, the husbands of the two
otagonists, particularly John in "The Yellow Wallpaper," seem
most unbearably controlling of their wives. From the vantage
aint of the late nineteenth century, however, their behavior looks
aite different. Both men are essentially well-meaning and try to
a good husbands. Their only real crime is that they adhere too
osely to the conventional Victorian wisdom about women and
arriage.

To begin with, both men are well respected in their communi-
as. John in "The Yellow Wallpaper" is described as "a physician of
gh standing" who has "an intense horror of superstition, and he
offs openly at any talk of things not to be felt and seen and put
awn in figures." These are just the qualities that we might expect
find in a respectable doctor, even today. It is less clear what
ently Mallard in "The Story of an Hour" does for a living. (In
ct, Chopin's story is so short that we learn fairly little about
ay of the characters.) But he and his wife seem to live in a com-
artable house, and they are surrounded by family and friends,
ggesting a secure, well-connected lifestyle. In the nineteenth
ntury, a man's most important job was to take care of his wife
ad family, and both men in these stories seem to be performing
is job very well.

Melanie signals that she will focus on these two stories and makes a claim about them that she will go on to support.

Melanie's first observation about what the male characters have in common.

In addition to providing a comfortable life for them, it also seems that both men love their wives. When she believes her husband has died, Mrs. Mallard thinks of his "kind, tender hands folded in death; the face that had never looked save with love upon her." Her own love for him is less certain, which may be why she feels "free" when he dies, but his love for her seems genuine. The case of John in "The Yellow Wallpaper" is a bit more complicated. To a modern reader, it seems that he treats his wife more like a child than a grown woman. He puts serious restraints on her actions, and at one point he even calls her "little girl." But he also calls her "my darling" and "dear," and she does admit, "He loves me very dearly." When he has to leave her alone, he even has his sister come to look after her, which is a kind gesture, even if it seems a bit like he doesn't trust his wife. If the narrator, who is in a position to know, doesn't doubt her husband's love, what gives us the right to judge it?

A smooth transition into the next point.

To a certain extent, we must admit that both husbands do oppress their wives by being overprotective. Part of the point of both stories is to show how even acceptable, supposedly good marriages of the day could be overly confining to women. This is especially obvious when we see how much John restricts his wife — forbidding her even to visit her cousins or to write letters — and how everyone expects her to submit to his demands. Though Mrs. Mallard isn't literally confined to a house or a room the way the narrator of "The Yellow Wallpaper" is, she stays inside the house and is looking out the window longingly when she realizes she wants to be free. But it is important for a reader not to blame the husbands, because they really don't intend to be oppressive.

Melanie establishes a similarity between the husbands.

In fact, it is true that both of the wives are in somewhat frail health. Mrs. Mallard is "afflicted with a heart trouble," and the narrator of "The Yellow Wallpaper" seems to have many physical and mental problems, so it is not surprising that their husbands worry about them. It is not evil intent that leads the men to act

A point of similarity between the wives.

Smith 3

, they do; it is simply ignorance. John seems less innocent than rently because he is so patronizing and he puts such restrictions n his wife's behavior and movement, but that kind of attitude was ormal for the day, and as a doctor, John seems to be doing what e really thinks is best.

All the other characters in the stories see both men as good d loving husbands, which suggests that society would have pproved of their behavior. Even the wives themselves, who are the ctims of these oppressive marriages, don't blame the men at all. e narrator of "The Yellow Wallpaper" even thinks she is "un-ateful" for not appreciating John's loving care more. Once we derstand this, readers should not be too quick to blame the men ther. The real blame falls to the society that gave these men the ea that women are frail and need protection from the world. The en may be the immediate cause of the women's suffering, but the al cause is much deeper and has to do with cultural attitudes and w the men were brought up to protect and provide for women.

Melanie returns to her original claim.

Most people who live in a society don't see the flaws in that ociety's conventional ways of thinking and living. We now know at women are capable and independent and that protecting them ; if they were children ultimately does more harm than good. But the late Victorian era, such an idea would have seemed either lly or dangerously radical to most people, men and women alike. ories like these, however, could have helped their original aders begin to think about how confining these supposedly good arriages were. Fortunately, authors such as Chopin and Gilman me along from time to time and show us the problems in our nventional thinking, so society can move forward and we can gin to see how even the most well-meaning actions should metimes be questioned.

Melanie's con-clusion argues for the idea that literature is capable of chal-lenging the status quo.

CHAPTER 6

Writing about Poems

Poetry may be divided into several major subgenres and types. A **narrative poem**, for instance, tells a story. An **epic**, a subgenre of narrative, is a long poem that narrates heroic events. A **lyric poem** expresses the personal thoughts and feelings of a particular poet or speaker. And many other types of poems have venerable histories.

As with stories, you should be aware of certain elements as you prepare to write about poetry. Sometimes these elements are the same as for fiction. A narrative poem, for instance, will have a **plot**, **setting**, and **characters**, and all poems speak from a particular **point of view**. To the extent that any of the elements of fiction help you understand a poem, by all means use them in your analysis. Poetry, however, does present a special set of concerns for a reader, and elements of poetry frequently provide rich ground for analysis.

ELEMENTS OF POETRY

The Speaker

First, consider the speaker of the poem. Imagine that someone is saying the words of this poem aloud. Who is speaking, where is this **speaker**, and what is his or her state of mind? Sometimes the voice is that of the poet, but frequently a poem speaks from a different perspective, just as a short story might be from a point of view very different from the author's. It's not always apparent when this is the case, but some poets will signal who the speaker is in a title, such as "The Passionate Shepherd to His Love" (page 452) and "The Love Song of J. Alfred Prufrock" (page 1214). Be alert to signals that will help you recognize the speaker, and remember that some poems have more than one speaker.

The Listener

Be attentive also to any other persons in the poem, particularly an implied listener. Is there a "you" to whom the poem is addressed? If the poem is being spoken aloud, who is supposed to hear it? When, early in his poem "Dover Beach" (page 518), Matthew Arnold writes, "Come to the window, sweet is the night-air!" he gives us an important clue as to how to read the poem. We should imagine both the speaker and the implied listener together in a room, with a window open to the night. As we read on, we can look for further clues as to who these two people are and why they are together on this night. Many poems create a relationship between the "I" of the speaker and the "you" of the listener; however, that is not always the case. Sometimes the speaker does not address a "you" and instead provides a more philosophical meditation that isn't explicitly addressed to a listener. Consider the effect: Do they feel more abstract? More detached from the material conditions of time and place? Do they provide certainty, or resolution? The questions about the speaker and the listener are crucial to your analysis of poetry.

Imagery

Just as you should be open to the idea that there are frequently symbols in stories, you should pay special attention to the **images** in poems. Although poems are often about such grand themes as love or death, they rarely dwell long in these abstractions. Rather, the best poetry seeks to make the abstraction concrete by creating vivid images appealing directly to the senses. A well-written poem will provide the mind of an attentive reader with sights, sounds, tastes, scents, and sensations. Since poems tend to be short and densely packed with meaning, every word and image is there for a reason. Isolate these images and give some thought to what they make you think and how they make you feel. Are they typical or unexpected?

Consider these lines from John Donne's "The Good Morrow":

> My face in thine eye, thine in mine appears,
> And true plain hearts do in the faces rest;
> Where can we find two better hemispheres,
> Without sharp north, without declining west? (lines 15–18)

Here, Donne celebrates the love between the speaker and his object of desire, comparing the faces of the lovers to two "hemispheres" on globes. Elsewhere in the poem, Donne uses imagery that is borrowed from the world of navigation and mapping; here, he suggests that the lovers' faces are an improvement upon whatever instruments explorers and learned men use to understand the world. By examining the images in a poem, their placement, juxtaposition, and effect, you will have gone a long way toward understanding the poem as a whole.

Sound and Sense

Of all the genres, poetry is the one that most self-consciously highlights language, so it is necessary to pay special attention to the sounds of a poem. In fact, it is always a good idea to read a poem aloud several times, giving yourself the opportunity to experience the role that sound plays in the poem's meaning.

Rhyme

Much of the poetry written in English before the twentieth century was written in some form of **rhyme**, and contemporary poets continue to experiment with its effects. Rhymes may seem stilted or old-fashioned to our twenty-first-century ears, but keep in mind that rhymes have powerful social meanings in the cultural context in which they're written. And even today rhyme remains a viable and significant convention in popular songs, which are, after all, a form of poetry. As you read poems, ask yourself how rhymes work. Do they create **juxtapositions**? Alignments of meaning? And what is the effect of that relationship as the poem progresses?

Assonance and Consonance

While it is important to look at the end of a line to see how the poet uses sounds, it is also important to look inside the line. Poets use **assonance**, or repeated vowel sounds, to create an aural effect. Consider these opening lines from Gerard Manley Hopkins's "Pied Beauty" (page 526):

> Glory be to God for dappled things—
>   For skies of couple-colour as a brinded cow;
>   For rose-moles all in stipple upon trout that swim;
> Fresh-firecoal chestnut-falls; finches' wings;
>   Landscape plotted and pieced—fold, fallow, and plough;
>   And all trades, their gear and tackle and trim. (lines 1–6)

Throughout these lines, Hopkins pays special attention to "uh" and "ow" sounds. Notice "couple-colour" and "cow" in line 2, "upon" and "trout" in line 3, "fallow" and "plough" in line 5. As you read through each line, ask yourself: Why does the poet align these sounds? Do these sounds speed up the tempo of the line, or slow it down? What do these sounds—and words—reveal about the poet's praise of "dappled things"?

Poets also use **consonance**, repeated consonant sounds, to create alignments and juxtapositions among consonants. Consider these first lines from Christopher Marlowe's "The Passionate Shepherd to His Love" (page 452):

> Come live with me and be my love,
> And we will all the pleasures prove (lines 1–2)

In line 1, Marlowe aligns "live" with "love" to suggest that there is an equation between cohabitation and romance. In line 2, he aligns the "p" sound in "pleasures prove"; in addition, though, the **slant rhyme** of "love" and "prove" also creates meaning between the lines. What "proof" is there in love? Is love what will make the speaker feel most alive?

Meter

Poetry written in English is both **accentual** and **syllabic**. That is, poets count the number of accents as well as the number of syllables as they create each line of poetry. Patterns of syllable and accent have names like "iambic pentameter" and "dactylic tetrameter," and each meter has its own unique properties and effects. Your literature instructor may help you learn about the specifics of meter, or you can find several sites online that explain the art—called **scansion**—of determining the meter of a poem. Whether or not you have a clear understanding of the many meters of poetry in English, when you read a poem, listen to each line to find out how many accents and syllables it contains. If you can determine what that meter is, consider how the poet uses—and subverts—that formula as part of a strategy for the poem.

Form

Poets writing in English use dozens of traditional forms from a variety of traditions. Some of the most common of these forms are the **sonnet**, the **villanelle**, and the **ballad**, but there are too many to name here. As you read a poem in a traditional form, think of the form as a kind of template in which poets arrange and explore challenging emotional and intellectual material. A sonnet, for example, has a concise fourteen-line structure that allows the poet to address a religious, romantic, or philosophical argument in a very compressed space. As you read a sonnet, you might ask yourself: What does its form accomplish that is different from a looser, more extended form like a ballad? The two sample poems later in this chapter provide a good opportunity to compare a short, highly conventional form with a longer, more loosely structured one.

Note, too, that many contemporary poets write in **free verse**, which means that they don't necessarily use a strict traditional form or meter for their poems. That doesn't mean that the free verse poet is writing without rules; it just means that the poet is creating his or her own system for the unique needs of each poem.

Stanzas

A **stanza** is any grouping of lines of poetry into a unit. The term *stanza* comes from the Italian word for "room." As you read poetry, imagine each stanza as a room with its own correspondences and relationships, and consider how that stanza creates a singular effect. Sometimes a stanza can be one line long; sometimes the poet creates a block of lines with no stanza breaks. All of these choices create distinct effects for readers of poetry.

Lineation

Lineation—or how a poet uses the line breaks in the poem—is a crucial component of poetry. Sometimes poets use punctuation at the end of every line, but more often they mix end-stopped lines with enjambed lines. **Enjambment** occurs when the line is not end-stopped with a comma, dash, or period. Its meaning spills over onto the next line, creating the effect of acceleration and intensity. Poets also use **caesuras** in the middle of lines to create variety in the pattern of the line. A caesura is a deep pause created by a comma, colon, semicolon, dash, period, or white space.

Poetry written in English can have many kinds of rhyme schemes, forms, and meters. For more information, see the "Elements of Poetry" online tutorial at http://bcs.bedfordstmartins.com/virtualit/poetry/rhyme_def.html.

TWO POEMS FOR ANALYSIS

Take a few minutes to read William Shakespeare's Sonnet 116 and T. S. Eliot's "The Love Song of J. Alfred Prufrock" and consider the student annotations and the questions that follow the poems. Both of these poems are complex, though in very different ways. What elements of poetry do you notice in these poems? What insights do you have in addition to those suggested by the annotations and questions?

WILLIAM SHAKESPEARE   [1564–1616]

Sonnet 116

Let me not to the marriage of true minds   *Consonance: marriage/minds.*
Admit impediments. Love is not love
Which alters when it alteration finds,   *Repetition: love/love, alters/alteration,*
Or bends with the remover to remove.   *remover/remove.*
O, no, it is an ever-fixèd mark   5
That looks on tempests and is never shaken;   *Abstract ideas become specific*
It is the star to every wandering bark,°   *images: tempests, ships.*
Whose worth's unknown, although his height be taken.°
Love's not time's fool, though rosy lips and cheeks   *Rosy lips and cheeks: clas-*
Within his bending sickle's compass come;   *sic love poem images.*   10
Love alters not with his brief hours and weeks,
But bears it out even to the edge of doom.°   *Sickle is a death image, unusual*
    If this be error and upon me proved,   *for a love poem.*
    I never writ, nor no man ever loved.

                                       Final rhyme is slant rhyme.

                      [1609]

7. **bark:** ship
8. **taken:** is measured
12. **doom:** Judgment Day

The student who annotated noticed both structural features of the poem (such as the move from abstract to concrete language) and small-scale language features, such as consonance and repetitions of individual words. This provides a good beginning to understanding the poem; answering the questions that follow will deepen that understanding, making it easier to write a paper about the poem.

QUESTIONS ON THE POEM

☐ What images are most striking in this poem? Do they seem conventional? Surprising? Experimental? Why?

☐ A sonnet often reveals its own logic in order to argue for a point of view. What is the argument of this poem? Do you find it persuasive? If so, why? If not, why not?

☐ What is the rhyme structure of this sonnet? What words are aligned as a result of this scheme?

☐ How does Shakespeare use enjambment and caesura to manage the tempo of the poem? What effects does this create?

T. S. ELIOT   [1888–1965]

The Love Song of J. Alfred Prufrock

S'io credesse che mia risposta fosse
A persona che mai tornasse al mondo,
Questa fiamma staria senza piu scosse.
Ma perciocche giammai di questo fondo
Non torno vivo alcun, s'i'odo il vero,
Senza tema d'infamia ti rispondo.

Footnote say
from Dante's
The speaker is
Why start a "
song" with he

Let us go then, you and I,
When the evening is spread out against the sky
Like a patient etherised upon a table;

Who is this "you"? Where are the

Epigraph: "If I thought that my answer were being made to someone who would ever return to earth, this flame would remain without further movement; but since no one has ever returned alive from this depth, if what I hear is true, I answer you without fear of infamy" (Dante, *Inferno* 27.61–66). Dante encounters Guido de Montefeltro in the eighth circle of hell, where souls are trapped within flames (tongues of fire) as punishment for giving evil counsel. Guido tells Dante details about his evil life only because he assumes that Dante is on his way to an even deeper circle in hell and will never return to earth and be able to repeat what he has heard.

Let us go, through certain half-deserted streets,
The muttering retreats   5
Of restless nights in one-night cheap hotels
And sawdust restaurants with oyster-shells: *Setting grubby and seedy. Depressing.*
Streets that follow like a tedious argument
Of insidious intent
To lead you to an overwhelming question . . .   10
Oh, do not ask, "What is it?"
Let us go and make our visit.   *Who are they visiting? Why?*
    In the room the women come and go   *New setting, in a room. Visiting "the women"?*
Talking of Michelangelo.

    The yellow fog that rubs its back upon the window-panes,   15
    The yellow smoke that rubs its muzzle on the window-panes
    Licked its tongue into the corners of the evening,   *Fog like an animal, almost*
    Lingered upon the pools that stand in drains,   *a character.*
    Let fall upon its back the soot that falls from chimneys,
    Slipped by the terrace, made a sudden leap,   20
    And seeing that it was a soft October night,
    Curled once about the house, and fell asleep.   *Uses rhyme in irregular pattern.*

    And indeed there will be time
For the yellow smoke that slides along the street,
Rubbing its back upon the window-panes;   25
There will be time, there will be time   *Lots of repetition here, as*
To prepare a face to meet the faces that you meet;   *if he's fixated on these ideas*
There will be time to murder and create,   *and can't let go.*
And time for all the works and days of hands
That lift and drop a question on your plate;   30
Time for you and time for me,   *He seems obsessed with time*
And time yet for a hundred indecisions,   *and how much of it there is.*
And for a hundred visions and revisions,
Before the taking of a toast and tea.

    In the room the women come and go   *Another repetition. Same women?*   35
Talking of Michelangelo.   *Same room?*

    And indeed there will be time
To wonder, "Do I dare?" and, "Do I dare?"
Time to turn back and descend the stair,
With a bald spot in the middle of my hair—   40
(They will say: "How his hair is growing thin!")   *Physical description: aging,*
My morning coat, my collar mounting firmly to the chin,   *thin, well dressed.*
My necktie rich and modest, but asserted by a simple pin— *Insecure.*
                                                            Indecisive.

(They will say: "But how his arms and legs are thin!")
Do I dare
Disturb the universe?

How could he "disturb t universe"?

In a minute there is time
For decisions and revisions which a minute will reverse.

For I have known them all already, known them all:—
Have known the evenings, mornings, afternoons,
I have measured out my life with coffee spoons;
I know the voices dying with a dying fall
Beneath the music from a farther room.
    So how should I presume?

He seems bore with his life. Maybe depressed?

And I have known the eyes already, known them all—
The eyes that fix you in a formulated phrase,
And when I am formulated, sprawling on a pin,
When I am pinned and wriggling on the wall,

Like a bug. More insecurit

Then how should I begin
To spit out all the butt-ends of my days and ways?
    And how should I presume?

And I have known the arms already, known them all—
Arms that are braceleted and white and bare
(But in the lamplight, downed with light brown hair!)
Is it perfume from a dress
That makes me so digress?
Arms that lie along a table, or wrap about a shawl.
    And should I then presume?
    And how should I begin?

He asks many questions in this section. Maybe unsure of self. Women seem to make him insecur

.   .   .

Shall I say, I have gone at dusk through narrow streets
And watched the smoke that rises from the pipes
Of lonely men in shirt-sleeves, leaning out of windows? . . .

    I should have been a pair of ragged claws
Scuttling across the floors of silent seas.

Earlier he was like a bug, now like crab.

.   .   .

And the afternoon, the evening, sleeps so peacefully!
Smoothed by long fingers,
Asleep . . . tired . . . or it malingers,
Stretched on the floor, here beside you and me.
Should I, after tea and cakes and ices,

Have the strength to force the moment to its crisis?   80
But though I have wept and fasted, wept and prayed,
Though I have seen my head (grown slightly bald) brought in upon a
       platter,   *Lots of disconnected body parts: eyes, arms, claws, head!*
I am no prophet—and here's no great matter;
I have seen the moment of my greatness flicker,
And I have seen the eternal Footman hold my coat, and snicker,   85
And in short, I was afraid.

Eternal Footman = Death?

   And would it have been worth it, after all,   *Again, he thinks someone is laughing at him.*
After the cups, the marmalade, the tea,
Among the porcelain, among some talk of you and me,
Would it have been worth while,   90
To have bitten off the matter with a smile,
To have squeezed the universe into a ball
To roll it toward some overwhelming question,
To say: "I am Lazarus, come from the dead,   *More about death. Who is dead here? Prufrock himself?*
Come back to tell you all, I shall tell you all"—   95
If one, settling a pillow by her head,
    Should say: "That is not what I meant at all.   *Sunsets and teacups seem so much nicer, sweeter than the grim cityscape earlier. Another new setting? How do they connect?*
    That is not it, at all."

   And would it have been worth it, after all,
Would it have been worth while,   100
After the sunsets and the dooryards and the sprinkled streets,
After the novels, after the teacups, after the skirts that trail along the
       floor—
And this, and so much more?—
It is impossible to say just what I mean!
But as if a magic lantern threw the nerves in patterns on a screen: 105
Would it have been worth while
If one, settling a pillow or throwing off a shawl,
And turning toward the window, should say: *Who is repeating this? "That is not what I meant" = misunderstanding.*
    "That is not it at all,
    That is not what I meant, at all."   110

      •   •   •

No! I am not Prince Hamlet, nor was meant to be;   *Why compare self to Hamlet? He's not a prince? Not famous?*
Am an attendant lord, one that will do
To swell a progress, start a scene or two,
Advise the prince; no doubt, an easy tool,
Deferential, glad to be of use,   115
Politic, cautious, and meticulous;

Full of high sentence, but a bit obtuse;
At times, indeed, almost ridiculous—
Almost, at times, the Fool.

I grow old . . . I grow old . . .   *Worry about aging. How old is he?*   1
I shall wear the bottoms of my trousers rolled.

Shall I part my hair behind? Do I dare to eat a peach?   *A peach? How*
I shall wear white flannel trousers, and walk upon the beach.   *that darin*
I have heard the mermaids singing, each to each.

I do not think that they will sing to me.   1

I have seen them riding seaward on the waves   *Setting changes aga*
Combing the white hair of the waves blown back   *now a beach.*
When the wind blows the water white and black.

We have lingered in the chambers of the sea   *Underwater (like the cr*
By sea-girls wreathed with seaweed red and brown   *earlier).*   1
Till human voices wake us, and we drown.   *Wake us? Is this all a dream?*
                                              nightmare?

[1915]

On a first reading, the student was baffled by the complexities of this poem and felt certain that it was over her head. After annotating it on a second read-through, however, she realized that she had gotten far more out of it than she originally believed and that she had begun to develop some interesting ideas about the speaker and the setting. When her class discussed the poem, she had insightful comments to add to the discussion. The following questions build on and deepen these insights.

QUESTIONS ON THE POEM

☐ What images are most striking in this poem? What makes them striking or memorable?

☐ How do the stanza breaks work in this poem? Why do you suppose Eliot chose these particular places for breaks?

☐ The rhyme and meter of the poem are highly irregular, but it's not quite free verse. Why use rhyme and meter at all? Why not make the rhyme and meter more regular?

☐ What are the various settings of the poem? How does each contribute to your understanding of the poem?

☐ What specific words would you use to sum up the character of Prufrock?

SAMPLE PAPER: AN EXPLICATION

Patrick McCorkle, the author of the paper that follows, was given the assignment to perform a close-reading of one of the poems his class had studied. He needed first to pick a poem and then to choose specific features of its language to isolate and analyze. He chose Shakespeare's Sonnet 116 (page 1213) because it seemed to him to offer an interesting and balanced definition of love. After rereading the poem, he became interested in several unexpectedly negative, even unsettling images that seemed out of place in a poem about the positive emotion of love. This was a good start, and it allowed him to write a draft of the paper. When he was finished, however, the essay was a little shorter and less complex than he had hoped it would be. During a peer workshop in class, he discussed the sonnet and his draft with two classmates, and together they noticed how many positive words and images appeared in the poem as well. That was the insight Patrick needed to fill out his essay and feel satisfied with the results.

Patrick McCorkle
Professor Bobrick
English 102
10 January 2008

Shakespeare Defines Love

From the earliest written rhymes to the latest radio hit, love is among the eternal themes for poetry. Most love poetry seems to fall into one of two categories. Either the poet sings the praises of the beloved and the unending joys of love in overly exaggerated terms, or the poet laments the loss of love with such bitterness and distress that it seems like the end of life. Anyone who has been in love, though, can tell you that both of these views are limited and incomplete and that real love is neither entirely joyous nor entirely sad. In Sonnet 116, "Let me not to the marriage of true minds," Shakespeare creates a more realistic image of love. By balancing negative with positive images and language, this sonnet does a far better job than thousands of songs and poems before and since, defining love in all its complexities and contradictions.

Patrick identifies his topic and states his thesis

Like many poems, Sonnet 116 relies on a series of visual images to paint vivid pictures for the reader, but not all of these images are what we might expect in a poem celebrating the pleasures of lasting love. A reader can easily picture "an ever-fixèd mark," a "tempest," a "star," a "wandering bark" (a boat lost at sea), "rosy lips and cheeks," and a "bending sickle." Some of these, like stars and rosy lips, are just the sort of sunny, positive images we typically find in love poems of the joyous variety. Others, though, are more unexpected. Flowers and images of springtime, for instance, are standard issue in happy love poetry, but a sickle is associated with autumn and the death of the year, and metaphorically with death itself in the form of the grim reaper. Likewise, a boat tossed in a raging tempest is not exactly the typical poetic depiction of happy love.

Patrick introduces the poem's contradictory imagery.

Such pictures would hardly seem to provide an upbeat image of what love is all about, and in fact they might be more at home

Patrick explains the effect of this imagery.

McCorkle 2

one of the sad poems about the loss of love. But these tempests
d sickles are more realistic than the hearts and flowers of so
any lesser love poems. In fact, they show that the poet recog-
zes the bad times that occur in all relationships, even those
rong enough to inspire love sonnets. And the negative images
e tempered because of the contexts in which they occur. The
andering bark," for instance, might represent trouble and loss,
t love itself is seen as the star that will lead the boat safely
ck to calm waters. Meanwhile, the beloved's "rosy lips and
eeks" may fade, but real love outlives even the stroke of death's
kle, lasting "to the edge of doom."

Just as positive and negative images are juxtaposed, so are
sitive and negative language. The first four lines of Sonnet 116
e made up of two sentences, both negatives, beginning with the
rds "Let me not" and "Love is not." The negatives of the first few
es continue in phrases like "Whose worth's unknown" and "Love's
t time's fool." From here, the poem goes on to dwell in abstract
eas such as "alteration," "impediments," and "error." None of this
what readers of love poems have been led to expect in their
evious reading, and we might even wonder if the poet finds this
ve thing worth the trouble. This strange and unexpected language
ntinues on through the last line of the poem, which contains no
wer than three negative words: "never," "nor," and "no."

*Patrick inte-
grates direct
quotations from
the poem into his
close-reading.*

Where, a reader might ask, are the expected positive de-
riptions of love? Where are the summer skies, the smiles and
ughter? Clearly, Shakespeare doesn't mean to sweep his readers
 in rosy images of a lover's bliss. Ultimately, though, even with
e preponderance of negative images and words, the poem strikes
 hopeful tone. The hedging about what love isn't and what it
n't do are balanced with positive words and phrases, saying
early what love is: "it is an ever-fixèd mark" and "it is the star."
ve, it would seem, does not make our lives perfect, but it gives
 the strength, stability, and direction to survive the bad times.

Though more than four hundred years have passed since

McCorkle 3

Shakespeare wrote his sonnets, some things never change, and among these is the nature of complex human emotions. In a mere fourteen lines, Shakespeare succeeds where many others have failed through the years, providing a much more satisfying definition of love than one normally sees in one-dimensional, strictly happy or sad poetry. The love he describes is the sort that not everyone is lucky enough to find — a "marriage of true minds" — complicated, unsettling, and very real.

In his conclusion, Patrick suggests that the poem is successful because of the juxtapositions he has discussed.

CHAPTER 7

Writing about Plays

Perhaps the earliest literary critic in the Western tradition was Aristotle, who, in the fifth century B.C.E., set about explaining the power of the genre of **tragedy** by identifying the six **elements of drama** and analyzing the contribution each of these elements makes to the functioning of a play as a whole. The elements Aristotle identified as common to all dramas were plot, characterization, theme, diction, melody, and spectacle. Some of these are the same as or very similar to the basic components of prose fiction and poetry, but others are either unique to drama or expressed differently in dramatic texts.

ELEMENTS OF DRAMA

Plot, Character, and Theme

The words *plot*, *character*, and *theme* mean basically the same thing in drama as they do in fiction, though there is a difference in how they are presented. A story *tells* you about a series of events, whereas a play *shows* you these events happening in real time. The information that might be conveyed in descriptive passages in prose fiction must be conveyed in a play through **dialogue** (and to a lesser extent through **stage directions** and the **set** and character descriptions that sometimes occur at the start of a play). The "How to Read a Play" section later in this chapter gives suggestions and advice for understanding these special features of drama.

Diction

When Aristotle speaks of **diction**, he means the specific words that a playwright chooses to put into the mouth of a character. In a well-written play, different characters will have different ways of speaking, and these will tell us a good deal about their character and personality. Does one character sound very formal and well educated? Does another speak in slang or dialect? Does someone hesitate or speak in fits and starts, perhaps indicating distraction or nervousness? Practice paying attention to these nuances. And keep in mind that just because a character says something, that doesn't make it true. As in real life, some characters might be mistaken in what they say, or they may be hiding the truth or even telling outright lies.

Melody and Spectacle

When Aristotle writes of **melody**, he is referring to the fact that Greek drama was written in verse and was chanted or sung onstage. The role of melody varies substantially with the work created in different cultures and time periods. In the English Renaissance, Shakespeare and his contemporaries used iambic pentameter and occasional end-rhymes to create dramas in verse, and staged productions have often used some kind of music, whether it be instrumental, vocal, or a mix of both. Melody is much less significant in drama today, though some plays do contain songs, of course. In musical theater, and even more in opera, songs carry much of the meaning of the play. Even in a play with no overt musical component, though, the rhythm of spoken words is important, just as it is in a poem. Even an actor's tone of voice can be considered a part of melody in the Aristotelian sense.

Spectacle refers to what we actually see onstage when we go to a play—the costumes, the actors' movements, the sets, the lights, and so forth. All of these details make a difference in how we understand and interpret a play's message. Hamlet's famous "To be or not to be" soliloquy will resonate differently with an audience if the actor playing Hamlet is wearing ripped jeans and a T-shirt, or a modern military uniform, rather than the conventional Renaissance doublet and hose. In reading a play, it is important to remember that it was not written to be read only, but rather so that it would be seen onstage in the communal setting of a theater. Reading with this in mind and trying to imagine the spectacle of a real production will increase your enjoyment of plays immensely. Specific suggestions for this sort of reading can be found in the "How to Read a Play" section of this chapter.

Setting

Setting, which Aristotle ignores completely, is just as important in drama as it is in fiction. But again, in drama it must be either displayed onstage or alluded to through the characters' words rather than being described as it might be in a story or a poem. The texts of modern plays often (though not always) begin with elaborate descriptions of the stage, furniture, major props, and so forth, which can be very useful in helping you picture a production. These tend to be absent in older plays, so in some cases you will have to use your imagination to fill in these gaps. In Act 4 of *Hamlet*, the characters are in a castle one moment and on a windswept plain the next. The only way a reader can be aware of this shift, though, is by paying close attention to the words and actions that characters use to signal a change of locale.

HOW TO READ A PLAY

Very few of us read plays for pleasure in the same way that we might take a novel with us to the beach. This isn't surprising: most playwrights, in fact, never intend for their plays to be read in this way. Drama is a living art, and if you read the play text on the page, you are getting only one part of what has made drama so important to all cultures across many time periods. Plays are written for the stage and are meant to be experienced primarily in live performance. This means that as a reader you must be especially attentive to nuances of language in a play, which often means imagining what might be happening onstage during a particular passage of speech. Using your imagination in this way—in effect, staging the play in your mind—will help you with some of the difficulties inherent in reading plays.

If you have access to film versions of the play that you are examining, be sure to watch them. Do bear in mind, though, that play scripts usually undergo substantial rewriting to adapt them for film, so you will still need to read the play in its original form, perhaps making comparisons between the stage and film versions. If you are reading a Shakespeare play, you can usually choose from several film versions, many of which might be in your library's collection. Live drama, of course, is different from film. Check the listings of local theaters to see what they are staging; you might find that a theater company is performing the play that you have to read for your class.

Some of the most skilled readers of plays are theater directors. These professionals have developed the ability to read a play and instantly see and hear in their minds the many possibilities for how the play might look and sound onstage. Directors understand that a play script is just one piece of a large, collaborative process involving playwright, director, designers, actors, backstage crew, and audience. Every new production of a play is different—sometimes vastly different—from the productions that have gone before, and every play script yields nearly endless possibilities for creative staging. By altering the look and feel of a play, a director puts his or her individual stamp on it, connecting with the audience in a unique way and helping that audience understand the playwright's and the director's messages. The questions that follow are the sort that a director would consider when reading a play. As you read plays for your literature class, these questions can help you formulate a consistent and strong interpretation.

DIRECTOR'S QUESTIONS FOR PLAY ANALYSIS

☐ What is the main message or theme of the play? What thoughts and/or feelings could be stirred up in an audience during a performance?

☐ In what kind of theater would you like to stage this play? A large, high-tech space with room to accommodate a huge audience? Or something more intimate?

☐ What sort of audience would you hope to attract to a production of this play? Older people? Young adults? Kids? Urban or rural? A mix? Who would get the most from the play's messages and themes?

☐ What sort of actors would you cast in the lead roles? Think about the sort of people you want for the various roles in terms of age, physical description, and so on. What should their voices sound like? Loud and commanding? Soft and timid?

☐ What kind of physical movement, blocking, or choreography would you want to see onstage? What are the most dramatic moments in the script? The most quiet or subtle?

☐ What would the set design look like? Would it change between acts and scenes or remain the same for the duration of the play?

☐ How would the characters be costumed? Period clothes? Modern dress? Something totally different? How could costuming contribute to character development?

☐ How much spectacle do you want? Would there be vivid sound and lighting effects? Or are you looking for a more naturalistic feel? How would this help portray the play's message?

SAMPLE PAPER: AN ANALYSIS

Sarah Johnson was free to choose the topic and focus of her paper. In the same semester as her literature class, she was enrolled in a philosophy course on ethics where she was introduced to the idea of situational ethics, the notion that exterior pressures often cause people to act in ways they might normally deem unethical, often to prevent or allay a worse evil. This philosophical concept was on Sarah's mind when she read Susan Glaspell's play *Trifles* (page 909). She noticed that the character of Mrs. Peters does indeed end up behaving in a way she would probably never have imagined for herself. This seemed an interesting concept to pursue, so Sarah decided to trace the development of Mrs. Peters' journey away from her original moral certainty.

Johnson 1

Sarah Johnson

Professor Riley

English 253

24 October 2007

Moral Ambiguity and Character Development

in *Trifles*

What is the relationship between legality and morality? Susan
Glaspell's short play *Trifles* asks us to ponder this question, but it
provides no clear answers. Part murder mystery, part battle of the
sexes, the play makes its readers confront and question many
issues about laws, morals, and human relationships. In the person
of Mrs. Peters, a sheriff's wife, the play chronicles one woman's
moral journey from a certain, unambiguous belief in the law to a
more situational view of ethics. Before it is over, this once legally
minded woman is even willing to cover up the truth and let someone get away with murder.

*Sarah focuses c
Mrs. Peters righ
away.*

At the beginning of the play, Mrs. Peters believes that law,
truth, and morality are one and the same. Though never unkind
about the accused, Mrs. Wright, Mrs. Peters is at first firm in her
belief that the men will find the truth and that the crime will be
punished as it should be. Mrs. Hale feels the men are "kind of
sneaking" as they look about Mrs. Wright's abandoned house for
evidence against her, but Mrs. Peters assures her that "the law is
the law." It is not that Mrs. Peters is less sympathetic toward
women than her companion, but she is even more sympathetic
toward the lawmen, because her version of morality is so absolute.
When the men deride the women's interest in so-called trifles, like
sewing and housework, Mrs. Hale takes offense. But Mrs. Peters,
convinced that the law must prevail, defends them, saying, "It's
no more than their duty," and later, "They've got awful important
things on their minds."

*Sarah uses dire
quotations from
the play text as
backup for her
claims.*

As she attempts to comply with the requirements of the law,
Mrs. Peters is described in a stage direction as "businesslike," and
she tries to maintain a skeptical attitude as she waits for the truth

emerge. Asked if she thinks Mrs. Wright killed her husband, she
[sa]ys, "Oh, I don't know." She seems to be trying to convince
[he]rself that the accused is innocent until proven guilty, though
[sh]e admits that her husband thinks it "looks bad for her." She
[se]ems to have absorbed her husband's attitudes and values and
[to] be keeping a sort of legalistic distance from her feelings about
[th]e case.

Mrs. Hale is less convinced of the rightness of the men or the
[la]w. Even before the two women discover a possible motive for the
[mu]rder, Mrs. Hale is already tampering with evidence, tearing out
[th]e erratic sewing stitches that suggest Mrs. Wright was agitated.
[Mr]s. Peters says, "I don't think we ought to touch things," but she
[do]esn't make any stronger move to stop Mrs. Hale, who continues
[to] fix the sewing. At this point, we see her first beginning to
[wa]ver from her previously firm stance on right and wrong.

It is not that Mrs. Peters is unsympathetic to the hard life
[th]at Mrs. Wright has led. She worries with Mrs. Hale about the
[ac]cused woman's frozen jars of preserves, her half-done bread, and
[he]r unfinished quilt. But she tries to think, like the men, that
[th]ese things are "trifles" and that what matters is the legal truth.
[Bu]t when she sees a bird with a wrung neck, things begin to
[ch]ange in a major way. She remembers the boy who killed her
[ki]tten when she was a child, and the sympathy she has felt for
[Mr]s. Wright begins to turn to empathy. The empathy is enough to
[pr]ompt her first lie to the men. When the county attorney spies
[th]e empty birdcage, she corroborates Mrs. Hale's story about a cat
[ge]tting the bird, even though she knows there was no cat in the
[ho]use.

In this paragraph, Sarah analyzes a turning point in the play text: a moment in which Mrs. Peters experiences a transformation.

Even after she has reached that point of empathy, Mrs. Peters
[tri]es hard to maintain her old way of thinking and of being. Alone
[ag]ain with Mrs. Hale, she says firmly, "We don't know who killed
[th]e bird," even though convincing evidence points to John Wright.
[Mo]re important, she says of Wright himself, "We don't know who
[ki]lled him. We don't *know*." But her repetition and her "rising

voice," described in a stage direction, show how agitated she has become. As a believer in the law, she should feel certain that everyone is innocent until proven guilty, but she thinks she knows the truth, and, perhaps for the first time in her life, legal truth does not square with moral truth. Her empathy deepens further still when she thinks about the stillness of the house in which Mrs. Wright was forced to live after the death of her beloved pet, which brought song to an otherwise grim life. She knows Mrs. Wright is childless, and she now remembers not just the death of her childhood kitten but also the terrible quiet in her own house after her first child died. She reaches a moment of crisis between her two ways of thinking when she says, "I know what stillness is. (*Pulling herself back.*) The law has got to punish crimes, Mrs. Hale." This is perhaps the most important line in the chronicle of her growth as a character. First she expresses her newfound empathy with the woman she believes to be a murderer; then, as the stage directions say, she tries to pull herself back and return to the comfortable moral certainty that she felt just a short time before. It is too late for that, though.

Here and else-where, Sarah relies on stage directions as evidence for her claims about Mrs. Peters.

In the end, Mrs. Peters gives in to what she believes to be emotionally right rather than what is legally permissible. She collaborates with Mrs. Hale to cover up evidence of the motive and hide the dead canary. Though very little time has gone by, she has undergone a major transformation. She may be, as the county attorney says, "married to the law," but she is also divorced from her old ideals. When she tries to cover up the evidence, a stage direction says she "goes to pieces," and Mrs. Hale has to help her. By the time she pulls herself together, the new woman she is will be a very different person from the old one. She, along with the reader, is now in a world where the relationship between legality and morality is far more complex than she had ever suspected.

Sarah isolates this passage to emphasize the complexity of Mrs. Peters.

CHAPTER 8

Writing a Literary Research Paper

Writing a literary research paper draws on the same set of skills as writing any other paper—choosing a topic, developing a thesis, gathering and organizing support, and so on. The main difference between research writing and other sorts of writing lies in the number and types of sources from which one's support comes. All writing about literature begins with a **primary source**—the poem, story, or play on which the writing is based. Research papers also incorporate **secondary sources**, such as biographical, historical, and critical essays.

As you begin the process of research writing, the most important thing to remember is that you are writing a critical argument. Your paper should not end up reading like a book report or a catalog of what others have said about the literature. Rather, it should begin and end by making an original point based on your own ideas, and like any other paper, it needs a clear, sharply focused thesis. The sources, both primary and secondary, are there to support your thesis, not to take over the paper.

The method laid out below seems very linear and straightforward: find and evaluate sources for your paper, read them and take notes, and then write a paper integrating material from these sources. In reality, the process is rarely, if ever, this neat. As you read and write, you will discover gaps in your knowledge, or you will ask yourself new questions that will demand more research. Be flexible. Keep in mind that the process of research is recursive, requiring a writer to move back and forth between various stages. Naturally, this means that for research writing, even more than for other kinds of writing, you should start early and give yourself plenty of time to complete the project.

FINDING SOURCES

For many students, research is more or less synonymous with the Internet. It may be easy to think that all the information anybody could ever want is available online, readily and easily accessible to the public. But when it comes to literary research, this is not the case at all. True, there are plenty of Web sites and newsgroups devoted to literary figures, but the type of information available on these sites tends to be limited to a narrow range—basic biographies of authors, plot summaries, and so forth—and the quality of information is highly variable. Though serious literary scholarship does exist on the Web, proprietary online databases (available through a library portal) and print books and journals are still the better sources for you in most cases.

Online Indexes

You can begin to locate sources for your research paper by using the online indexes and databases available through your college or university library. These services sort and index journal and magazine articles to help researchers find what they are looking for. Although using these indexes is somewhat similar to using an Internet search engine, the two should not be confused. The Internet links to an array of documents— some of very high quality, some worse than useless—that are available for free to the public. By contrast, college, university, and many public libraries pay a fee to allow their users access to the more specialized and highly vetted sources found in various indexes and databases. When you use these services, you are assured that any articles you locate have been published by reliable, respected sources.

Your library probably subscribes to dozens of databases covering many fields of knowledge. These are some of the most useful ones for literary research:

- *Academic OneFile* and *Expanded Academic ASAP* (both from InfoTrac) index a combination of scholarly journals and popular magazines and provide a good starting point for articles of general interest.
- *Literary Reference Center* (EBSCO) provides full-text articles from specialized encyclopedias and reference works, including author biographies, synopses of major literary works, and articles on literary history and criticism.
- *MLA International Bibliography* (EBSCO) indexes scholarly books and articles on modern languages, literature, folklore, and linguistics; many have full-text links.
- *Humanities Index* (H. W. Wilson) indexes periodicals in the humanities, including scholarly journals and lesser-known specialized magazines; many have full-text links.
- *JSTOR* provides searchable, full-text articles digitized from more than a thousand academic journals, some dating back to the nineteenth century.

The indexes listed on the facing page are just a sampling of those most generally applicable to literary research. Depending on your particular topic or interests, you may find yourself drawn to one of the many more specialized indexes, such as *GenderWatch* (for topics related to feminism and other gender issues), *GreenFile* (for environmental topics), and *Hispanic American Periodicals Index*, to name just a few.

If you do not know how to access or use these sources, ask the reference librarian on duty at your college library. Helping students find what they need is this person's principal job, and you will likely learn a lot from him or her. Both your librarian and your instructor can also suggest additional indexes to point you toward good secondary sources. One of the great advantages of databases and indexes is that results can be filtered and sorted according to a wide array of criteria. You can find articles written in a particular year or in a particular language; you can choose to look only at articles that have been peer-reviewed (the process that assures scholarly legitimacy); or you can select any of a number of other filters to help you find exactly what you need.

When you begin searching, use fairly specific search terms to help the database focus on what you really need and to filter out irrelevant material. Let's say you are researching the nature of love in Shakespeare's sonnets. If you perform a search on the keyword or topic *Shakespeare*, you will get many thousands of hits, many of them about topics unrelated to yours. Searching on both *Shakespeare* and *sonnet*, however, will get you closer to what you want, while searching on *Shakespeare*, *sonnet*, and *love* will yield far fewer and far better, more targeted results. If your search nets you fewer results than you expected, try again with different terms (substitute *romance* for *love*, for example). Be patient, and don't be afraid to ask your instructor or librarian for help if you are experiencing difficulty.

Once you have a screen full of results, you will be able to access a **text**, an abstract, or a citation. Some results will give you a link to the complete text of an article; just click on the link, and you can read the article on-screen, print it out, or e-mail it to yourself. Frequently, a link is provided to an abstract, a brief summary (generally just a few sentences) of the content of the full article. Reading an abstract is a good way of finding out whether it is worth tracking down the whole article for your paper. A citation gives only the most basic information about an article — its title, its author, the date of publication, and its page numbers — and it is up to you to then find and read the whole article.

It may be tempting to settle on only those articles available immediately in full-text versions. Don't fall into this trap. Even in this electronic age, scholars and specialists still write books, as well as articles for academic journals that are not always available in electronic versions. Many of the best sources of literary research are available only in print, and the only way to obtain these is to follow the citation's lead and locate the book or journal in the library stacks. If a title or an abstract looks promising, go and retrieve the article. If you think getting up and tracking down a journal is frustrating or time-consuming, imagine how frustrating and time-consuming it will be to attempt to write a research paper without great sources.

Periodicals

At this point, you should be aware of the distinction between two types of periodicals that your search may lead to: magazines, which are directed at a general readership, and scholarly journals, which are written by and for specialists in various academic fields. *Scientific American*, for instance, is a well-respected magazine available on newsstands, whereas *The Journal of Physical Chemistry* is a scholarly journal, generally available only by subscription and read mainly by chemists and chemistry students. In the field of literary studies, there are hundreds of journals, ranging from publications covering a general period or topic (*American Literary Realism*, *Modern Drama*) to those devoted to specific authors (*Walt Whitman Review*, *Melville Society Extracts*).

While magazines like *Time* and *Newsweek* are sometimes appropriate research sources, and you certainly should not rule them out, the highest-quality and most sophisticated literary criticism tends to appear in journals. If you are uncertain whether you are looking at a scholarly journal, look for the following typical characteristics:

- Scholarly journal articles tend to be *longer* than magazine articles, ranging anywhere from five to more than fifty pages.
- Journal articles are *written by specialists* for researchers, professors, and college students. The author's professional credentials and institutional affiliation are often listed.
- Journal articles tend to be written in a given profession's *special language* and can be difficult for nonspecialists to understand. Articles in literary journals use the specialized language of literary theory and criticism.
- Journal articles are usually *peer-reviewed* or refereed, meaning that other specialists have read them and determined that they make a significant contribution to the field. Peer referees are often listed as an editorial board on the journal's masthead page.
- Journal articles usually include *footnotes or endnotes* and an often substantial references, *bibliography*, or works cited section.

Books

As mentioned earlier, many scholars still publish their most important work in print books, and the place to look for these is in your college or university library's catalog. (Public libraries, no matter how well run, seldom carry the sorts of specialized sources needed for college-level research.) Start by looking for one or two good books on your topic. Books tend to be more general in their scope than journal articles, and they can be useful at the early stages of your research to help you focus and refine your thinking. If you have given yourself sufficient time for the process, take a book or two home and skim them to determine which parts would be most useful for you. When you return to the library to perform more research, you will have a clearer sense of what you are looking for and therefore will be more efficient at completing the rest of your search.

Interlibrary Loan

If you find a promising lead but discover that your library doesn't have a particular book or has no subscription to the needed periodical, you still may be in luck. Nearly all libraries offer interlibrary loan services, which can track down books and articles from a large network of other libraries and send them to your home institution, generally free of charge. Of course, this process takes time—usually, a couple of days to a couple of weeks—and this is yet another reason to get started as early as possible on your research.

The Internet

Lastly, if your quest for books and periodicals has not yielded all the results you want, search the World Wide Web. As with a search of a specialized index, you will do better and filter out a lot of low-quality sources if you come up with some well-focused search terms in advance. Be sure to ask your instructor or reference librarian about authoritative Web sites. Your librarian may have already created a special page on the library's Web site that provides links to the best Web sites for students of English. If you use the Web for your research, look especially for scholarly sites, written by professors or researchers and maintained by colleges and universities. For example, if you want to research the poetry and artwork of William Blake, you might check The Blake Archive, an online project sponsored by the Library of Congress and the University of North Carolina, Chapel Hill: http://www.blakearchive.org/blake/. If you are interested in learning more about Walt Whitman's life and work, check The Walt Whitman Archive, a project developed and edited by Ed Folsom and Kenneth M. Price, both of whom are eminent Whitman scholars: http://www.whitmanarchive.org/. If you want to read the 1603 printing of *Hamlet*, check the British Library's Web site: http://www.bl.uk/treasures/ shakespeare/homepage.html. Also potentially useful are the online equivalents of scholarly journals, as well as discussion groups or newsgroups dedicated to particular authors, literary schools, or periods.

How do you know when you have enough sources? Many instructors specify a minimum number of sources for research papers, and many students find exactly that number of sources and then look no further. Your best bet is to stop looking for sources when you think you have enough material to write a top-quality paper. Indeed, it is far better to gather up too many sources and end up not using them all than to get too few and find yourself wanting more information as you write. And remember that any "extra" research beyond what you actually cite in your paper isn't really wasted effort—every piece of information you read contributes to your background knowledge and overall understanding of your topic, making your final paper sound smarter and better informed.

EVALUATING SOURCES

As you locate research sources, you should engage in a continual process of evaluation to determine both the reliability of the potential source and its appropriateness to your particular topic and needs. Keep the following questions in mind to help you evaluate both print and electronic sources:

- **Who is the author, and what are his or her credentials?** If this information is not readily available, you might ask yourself why not. Is the author or publisher trying to hide something?
- **What is the medium of publication?** Books, journals, magazines, newspapers, and electronic publications all have something to offer a researcher, but they do not all offer the same thing. A good researcher will usually seek out a variety of sources.
- **How respectable is the publisher?** Not all publishers are created equal, and some have a much better reputation than others for reliability. Just because something is published, that doesn't make it accurate—think of all those supermarket tabloids publishing articles about alien autopsies. In general, your best sources are books from university presses and major, well-established publishers; scholarly journal articles; and articles from well-regarded magazines and newspapers such as the *Atlantic Monthly* or the *New York Times*.

If you are not sure how respectable or reliable a particular publisher or source might be, ask your instructor or librarian.

- **If it's an online publication, who is hosting the site?** Though commercial sites (whose Web addresses end in *.com*) should not be ruled out, keep in mind that these sites are often driven by profit as much as a desire to educate the public. Sites hosted by educational institutions, nonprofit organizations, or the government (*.edu*, *.org*, and *.gov*, respectively) tend to be more purely educational, though they likely won't be free of an agenda either.

- **How recent is the publication?** While older publications can often be appropriate—you may be doing historical research, or you may want to refer to a classic in a certain field—newer ones are preferable, all other things being equal. Newer publications take advantage of more recent ideas and theories, and they often summarize or incorporate older sources.

- **How appropriate is the source to your specific project?** Even the highest-quality scholarly journal or a book by the top expert in a given field will be appropriate for only a very limited number of research projects. Let your topic, your tentative thesis, and your common sense be your guides.

WORKING WITH SOURCES

You now have a stack of articles and printouts of electronic sources, and perhaps a book or two as well. How do you work through these to get the support you need for your paper?

- *First*, sort the various sources by expected relevance, with those you think will be most informative and useful to you on the top of the list.

- *Next*, skim or read through everything quickly, highlighting or making note of the parts that seem most directly applicable to your paper. (Obviously, you should not mark up or otherwise deface library materials—take notes on a separate piece of paper.)

- *Then*, slow down and reread the important passages again, this time taking careful notes.

- *When taking notes*, keep yourself scrupulously well organized, making sure that you always know which of your notes refers to which source.

If you are taking notes by hand, it's a good idea to start a separate page for each source. If you are using a computer to take notes, start a separate file or section for each new source you read.

Notes will generally fall into one of four categories: quotations, paraphrases, summaries, and commentaries.

Quotations

While quotations are useful, and you will almost certainly incorporate several into your paper, resist the urge to transcribe large portions of text from your sources. Papers that rely too heavily on quotations can be unpleasant reading, with a cluttered or choppy style that results from moving back and forth between your prose and that of the various authors you quote. Reserve direct quoting for those passages that are especially relevant and that you simply can't imagine phrasing as clearly or elegantly yourself. When you do make note of a quotation, be sure also to note the pages on which it appears in the source material so that later you will be able to cite it accurately.

Paraphrases and Summaries

Most often, you should take notes in the form of **paraphrase** or summary. To paraphrase, simply put an idea or opinion drawn from a source into your own words. Generally, a paraphrase will be about equal in length to the passage being paraphrased, while a summary will be much shorter, capturing the overall point of a passage while leaving out supporting details. Here is a brief passage from *Britannica Online*'s biography of Emily Dickinson, followed by a paraphrase and a summary:

> She began writing in the 1850s; by 1860 she was boldly experimenting with language and prosody, striving for vivid, exact words and epigrammatic concision while adhering to the basic quatrains and metres of the Protestant hymn. The subjects of her deceptively simple lyrics, whose depth and intensity contrast with the apparent quiet of her life, include love, death, and nature. Her numerous letters are sometimes equal in artistry to her poems.

Paraphrase

> Dickinson began writing poetry in the 1850s, and within ten years she had begun experimenting with poetic styles and forms. She used meters that were familiar to her from church hymns, but her words were chosen to be especially concise and vivid. She wrote about love, death, and nature in ways that seem simple but contain a great deal of emotional depth and intensity. She was also an avid letter-writer, and her letters show the same care and artistry as her poems.

Summary

> In both her poems and her many letters, Dickinson used formal experimentation and precision to get to the heart of the themes of love, death, and nature.

Paraphrasing and summarizing are usually superior to quoting for two reasons. First, if you can summarize or paraphrase with confidence, then you know you have really understood what you have read. Second, a summary or paraphrase will be more easily transferred from your notes to your paper and will fit in well with your individual prose style. (For more on the use of summary, see pages 1185–86.) Just as with quotations, make a note of the page numbers in the source material from which your summaries and paraphrases are drawn.

Commentaries

Finally, some of your notes can be written as commentaries. When something you read strikes you as interesting, you can record your reaction to it. Do you agree or disagree strongly? Why? What exactly is the connection between the source material and your topic or tentative thesis? Making copious commentaries will help you keep your own ideas in the forefront and will keep your paper from devolving into a shopping list of other writers' priorities. Be sure to note carefully when you are commenting rather than summarizing or paraphrasing. When you are drafting your paper, you will want to distinguish carefully between which ideas are your own and which are borrowed from others.

Keeping Track of Your Sources

As you take notes on the substance of your reading, it is also essential that you record the source's author, title, and publication information for later use in compiling your works cited list, or bibliography. Nothing is more frustrating than having to retrace your research steps on a computer, or even to return to the library, just to get a page reference or the full title of a source. Most accomplished researchers actually put together their works cited list as they go along rather than waiting until the essay is drafted. Such a strategy will ensure that you have all the information you need, and it will save you from the painstaking (and potentially tedious) task of having to create the list all at once at the end of your process.

WRITING THE PAPER

After what may seem like a long time spent gathering and working with your sources, you are now ready to begin the actual writing of your paper.

Refine Your Thesis

Start by looking again at your tentative thesis. Now that you have read a lot and know much more about your topic, does your proposed thesis still seem compelling and appropriate? Is it a little too obvious, something that other writers have already said or have taken for granted? Do you perhaps need to refine or modify it in order to take into account the information you have learned and opinions you have encountered? If necessary—and it usually is—refine or revise your tentative thesis so that it can help you stay focused as you write. (For advice on what makes a good thesis, see pages 1153–56.)

Organize Your Evidence

Just as with any other essay, you will need to organize the evidence in support of your thesis. Follow whatever process for organization you have used successfully in writing other papers, while bearing in mind that this time you will probably have more, and more complex, evidence to deal with. You will likely need an outline—formal or informal—to help you put your materials in a coherent and sensible order. But, once again, flexibility is the key here. If, as you begin to work your way through the outline, some different organizational strategy begins to make sense to you, revise your outline rather than forcing your ideas into a preconceived format.

Start Your Draft

The actual drafting of the research paper is probably the part you will find most similar to writing other papers. Try to write fairly quickly and fluently, knowing you can and will add examples, fill in explanations, eliminate redundancies, and work on style during the revision phase. As with your other papers, you may want to write straight through from beginning to end, or you may want to save difficult passages like the introduction for last. Interestingly, many writers find that the process of drafting a research paper actually goes a bit more quickly than does drafting other papers, largely because their considerable research work has left them so well versed in the topic that they have a wealth of ideas for writing.

What might slow you down as you draft your research papers are the citations, which you provide so that a reader knows which ideas are your own and which come from outside sources. Before you begin drafting, familiarize yourself with the conventions for MLA in-text citations (see pages 1247–50). Each time you incorporate a quotation, paraphrase, or summary into your essay, you will need to cite the author's name and the relevant page numbers (if available) from the source material. Do not, however, get hung up at this stage trying to remember how to format and punctuate citations. There will be time to hammer out these details later, and it is important as you write to keep your focus on the big picture.

Revise

As you go through the revision process, you should do so with an eye toward full integration of your source material. Are all connections between quotations, paraphrases, or summaries and your thesis clear? Do you include sufficient commentary explaining the inclusion of all source material? Is it absolutely clear which ideas come from which research source? Most important, is the paper still a well-focused argument, meant to convince an audience of the validity of your original thesis? Bearing these questions in mind, you will be ready to make the same sorts of global revision decisions that you would for any other paper—what to add, what to cut, how to reorganize, and so forth. (See pages 1163–64 for a reminder of what to look for.)

Edit and Proofread

During the final editing and proofreading stage, include one editorial pass just for checking quotations and documentation format. Make sure each quotation is accurate and exact. Ensure that each reference to a source has an appropriate in-text citation and that your list of works cited (bibliography) is complete and correct. Double-check manuscript format and punctuation issues with the guidelines included in this book or with another appropriate resource. After putting so much time and effort into researching and writing your paper, it would be a shame to have its effectiveness diminished by small inaccuracies or errors.

UNDERSTANDING AND AVOIDING PLAGIARISM

Everyone knows that **plagiarism** is wrong. Buying or borrowing someone else's work, downloading all or part of a paper from the Web, and similar practices are beyond reprehensible. Most colleges and universities

have codes of academic honesty forbidding such practices and imposing severe penalties—including expulsion from the institution in some
cases—on students who are caught breaking them. Many educators feel
these penalties are, if anything, not severe enough. Instructors tend to be
not only angered but also baffled by students who plagiarize. In addition
to the obvious wrongs of cheating and lying (nobody likes being lied to),
students who plagiarize are losing out on a learning opportunity, a waste
of the student's time as well as the instructor's.

Not everyone, though, is altogether clear on what plagiarism entails,
and a good deal of plagiarism can actually be unintentional on the part
of the student. A working definition of plagiarism will help to clarify
what plagiarism is:

- presenting someone else's ideas as your own
- using information from any print or electronic source without fully
  citing the source
- buying or "borrowing" a paper from any source
- submitting work that someone else has written, in whole or in part
- having your work edited to the point that it is no longer your work
- submitting the same paper for more than one class without the express permission of the instructors involved

Some of this is obvious. You know it is cheating to have a friend do
your homework or to download a paper from the Web and submit it as
your own. But the first and last items on the list are not as clear-cut or
self-explanatory. What exactly does it mean to present someone else's
ideas as your own? Many students believe that as long as they rephrase
an idea into their own words, they have done their part to avoid plagiarism; however, they are mistaken. Readers assume, and reasonably so,
that everything in your paper is a product of your own thinking, not just
your own phrasing, unless you share credit with another by documenting your source. No matter how it is phrased, an original idea belongs to
the person who first thought of it and wrote it down; in fact, the notion
of possession in this context is so strong that the term applied to such
ownership is *intellectual property*.

As an analogy, imagine you invented a revolutionary product, patented
it, and put it up for sale. The next week, you find that your neighbor has
produced the same product, painted it a different color, changed the
name, and is doing a booming business selling the product. Is your
neighbor any less guilty of stealing your idea just because he or she is
using a new name and color for the product? Of course not. Your intellectual property, the idea behind the product, has been stolen. And you
are no less guilty of plagiarism if you glean a piece of information, an

opinion, or even an abstract concept from another person, put it into your own words, and "sell" it in your paper without giving proper credit.

Let us say, for example, that you find this passage about William Butler Yeats:

> Religious by temperament but unable to accept orthodox Christianity, Yeats throughout his life explored esoteric philosophies in search of a tradition that would substitute for a lost religion. He became a member of the Theosophical Society and the Order of the Golden Dawn, two groups interested in Eastern occultism, and later developed a private system of symbols and mystical ideas.

Drawing from this passage, you write:

> Yeats rejected the Christianity of his native Ireland, but he became interested in occultism and Eastern philosophy. From these sources, he developed his own system of mystical symbols that he used in his poetry.

Clearly the words of this new passage are your own, and some elements of the original have been streamlined while other information has been added. However, the essential line of reasoning and the central point of both passages are largely the same. If this second passage appears in your paper without an acknowledgment of the original source, *this is plagiarism*.

Finally, let's look at the last item on the list: submitting the same paper for more than one class without the express permission of the instructors involved. Sometimes, you will find substantial overlap in the subject matter of two or more of your classes. A literature class, for instance, has elements of history, psychology, sociology, and other disciplines, and once in a while you might find yourself working on writing projects in courses that share common features. You might be tempted to let your research and writing in such a case do double duty, and there is not necessarily anything wrong with that. However, if you wish to write a paper on a single topic for more than one class, clear these plans with both instructors first. And, of course, even if you use the same research sources for both assignments, you will almost certainly need to write two separate essays, tailoring each to meet the specifications of individual classes and disciplines.

WHAT TO DOCUMENT AND WHAT *NOT* TO DOCUMENT

Everything borrowed from another source needs to be documented. Obviously, you should document every direct quotation of any length from primary or secondary sources. Equally important is the documentation of all your paraphrases and summaries of ideas, information, and opinions, citing authors and page numbers. The rule of thumb is that if you didn't make it up yourself, you should probably document it.

The word *probably* in the previous sentence suggests that there are exceptions, and indeed there are. You do not need to document proverbial sayings ("Live and let live") or very familiar quotations ("I have a dream"), though in the case of the latter you may want to allude to the speaker in your text. You also do not need to document any information that can be considered **common knowledge**. Common knowledge here refers not only to information that you would expect nearly every adult to know immediately (that Shakespeare wrote *Hamlet*, for instance, or that George Washington was the first president of the United States). Common knowledge also encompasses undisputed information that you could look up in a general or specialized reference work. The average person on the street probably couldn't tell you that T. S. Eliot was born in 1888, but you don't need to say where that piece of information comes from, as it is widely available to anyone who wishes to find it.

Use both your common sense and your sense of fairness to make any necessary decisions about whether or not to document something. When in doubt, ask your instructor, and remember, it's better to document something unnecessarily than to be guilty of plagiarism.

DOCUMENTING SOURCES: MLA FORMAT

This section includes information on how to document the following:

Some students seem to believe that English teachers find footnotes and bibliographies and textual citations fun and interesting. In truth, few people know better than those who have to teach it how tedious format and documentation can be for a writer. Chances are your instructor will insist that you document your sources. There are at least three reasons for requiring documentation. First, a sense of fair play demands that we give proper credit to those whose ideas benefit us. Second, by documenting your sources, you make it possible for your readers to find the sources themselves and follow up if they become interested in something in your paper. Third, documenting your sources, and doing it accurately, enhances your credibility as a writer by highlighting your professionalism and thoroughness.

As you read the following pages, and as you work on documenting sources in your own papers, don't say that you don't understand it or that you can't learn this. If you learned the difficult and abstract skills of reading and writing, you can certainly learn something as concrete as documentation. Actually, documentation is the easy part of research writing, since there is only one right way to do it. The hard part is the creative work of discovering and presenting your original ideas and integrating them fluently with the work of others. And, of course, you don't need to actually memorize the specifics of format. Nobody does. When you need to know how to cite an anonymous newspaper article or what to include in a bibliographic entry for a radio broadcast, for instance, you can look it up. That's what professional writers do all the time.

There are many different forms and formulas for documenting sources—the APA (American Psychological Association) format commonly used in the social sciences, the CBE (Council of Biology Editors) format used in the life sciences, the *Chicago* (*Chicago Manual of Style*) format used in history, and so on. Each system highlights the type of information most relevant to experts in a particular field. If you have received contradictory instructions about documentation format for research projects in the past—include dates in your in-text references or don't; use footnotes or use endnotes—chances are you were working in different documentation systems. The format most often used in the humanities is MLA, the system developed by the Modern Language Association.

MLA format breaks down into two main elements: in-text citations and a works cited list (bibliography). In-text citations are parenthetical references that follow each quotation, paraphrase, or summary and give the briefest possible information about the source, usually the author's last name and a page number. The works cited list, which comes at the end of the paper, gives more detailed information about all sources used. The idea is that a reader coming across a parenthetical reference in your text can easily turn to the works cited list and get full details about the type of publication from which the material comes, the date of publication, and so on. (Some writers use a third element of MLA style, content endnotes, which come between the end of the paper and the works cited list and contain extra information not readily integrated into the paper. Although you may use endnotes if you wish, they are not necessary.)

The following pages describe the major types of sources you are likely to encounter and how to reference those sources both in the text of your research paper and in your works cited list. The information here, however, is not exhaustive. If you want to cite a source not covered here, or if you would like more information about MLA style and citation format, turn to:

MLA Handbook for Writers of Research Papers. 7th ed. New York: MLA, 2009. Print.

In-Text Citations

The purpose of an in-text citation is to give a very brief acknowledgment of a source within the body of your essay. In MLA format, in-text citations take the form of brief parenthetical interruptions directly following each quotation, paraphrase, or summary. Some students find these interruptions a bit distracting at first, but you will quickly find that you grow accustomed to them and that soon they will not slow your reading or comprehension. The following explanations and examples of in-text citations should cover most instances you will encounter.

Citing Author and Page Number in Parentheses

Typically, a citation will contain the last name of the author being cited and a page number. The first example here shows a direct quotation, the second a paraphrase.

> One reviewer referred to Top Girls as, "among other things, a critique of bourgeois feminism" (Munk 33).

> When English wool was in demand, the fens were rich, but for many years now they have been among the poorest regions in England (Chamberlain 13).

Coming across these references in your text, your readers will know that they can turn to your works cited list and find out the full names of Munk and Chamberlain; the titles of what they have written; and where, when, and in what medium the works were published.

Please note:

- **In-text references contain no extraneous words or punctuation.** There is no comma between the name and the page number. Neither the word *page* nor the abbreviation *p.* precede the number. There are no extra spaces, just the name and the number.

- **Quotation marks close *before* the citation.** The in-text citation is not part of a direct quotation, so it does not belong inside the quotation marks.

- **The period that ends the sentence is placed *after* the citation.** Probably the most common error students make in MLA in-text citation is to put the period (or other closing punctuation mark) at the end of the quotation or paraphrase and then give the reference in parentheses. Doing so, however, makes the citation the beginning of the next sentence rather than the end of the one being cited.

Citing the Author in Body Text and Only the Page Number in Parentheses

If you have already named the author in your own text, for instance in a lead-in phrase, you do not need to repeat the name in parentheses, as your reader will already know which author to look for in your works cited. In this case, the parenthetical reference need only contain the page number. The two examples already given could be rewritten as follows:

Reviewer Erika Munk referred to *Top Girls* as, "among other things, a critique of bourgeois feminism" (33).

Martha Chamberlain writes that when English wool was in demand, the fens were rich, but for many years now they have been among the poorest regions in England (13).

Citing Multiple Pages in a Source

You may find yourself wanting to make a brief summary of an extended passage, in which case you might need to cite the inclusive pages of the summarized material.

John McGrath's Scottish theater company was destroyed by the end of government subsidies, as Elizabeth MacLennan chronicles in *The Moon Belongs to Everyone* (137-99).

Citing a Source without Page Numbers

Many electronic publications do not have page numbers. If you are citing one of these sources, simply give the author's last name either in parentheses or in a signal phrase before the quotation or summary.

> Critics have noted that "Dickinson declined to make the public confession of faith that would admit her to the church" (Yezzi).

or

> David Yezzi writes that "Dickinson declined to make the public confession of faith that would admit her to the church."

Citing Multiple Sources at Once

Sometimes several different sources say roughly the same thing, or at least there is substantial overlap in the parts you want to cite. Following are two ways of handling this situation; use whichever one best suits your needs.

> This particular passage in the play has been the source of much critical speculation, especially by Freudian critics (Anders 19; Olsen 116; Smith 83-84; Watson 412).

> A number of Freudian critics have commented on this passage, including Anders (19), Olsen (116), Smith (83-84), and Watson (412).

Citing Two or More Sources by the Same Author

It is common for one author to write multiple books or articles on the same general topic, and you might want to use more than one of them in your paper. In this case, a shortened version of the title must appear in the parenthetical reference, to show which work by the author is being quoted or cited. In citations for an article and a book about playwright Caryl Churchill, both by the author Geraldine Cousin, one would give the first word of the work's title (other than *the* or *a*, etc.). As seen here, *Common* and *Churchill* are the first words in the title of the article and the book, respectively.

> Churchill claims that this sentiment was expressed to her by one of the gangmasters she encountered in the fens (Cousin, "Common" 6).

> Churchill's notebooks from her visit to the fens record her seeing baby prams parked around the fields in which the women worked (Cousin, *Churchill* 47).

Note the comma between the author's name and the title. Note that these shortened titles are formatted (with italics or quotation marks) just as they would be in the works cited list or elsewhere in your writing, in quotation marks for an article and in italics (or underscored) for a book.

If the author is named in a signal phrase, only the shortened title and page number are needed in the parenthetical reference.

> "Violence," says Ruby Cohn, "is the only recourse in these brutalized lives on the Fen" (*Retreats* 139).

Citing a Quotation or Source within a Source

On page 58 of his book about Margaret Thatcher, Charles Moser writes:

> In a speech to Parliament in June of 1983, Thatcher said, "A return to Victorian values will encourage personal responsibility, personal initiative, self-respect, and respect for others and their property."

Let us say you do not have the text of Thatcher's original speech and that Moser doesn't make reference to a primary source that you can track down. But Moser is a reliable author, so you believe the Thatcher quotation is accurate and want to use a portion of it in your paper. This is done by giving the original speaker's name (in this case Margaret Thatcher) in your text and using the abbreviation *qtd. in* and the author from whom you got the quote (in this case Charles Moser) in the parenthetical citation.

> These "Victorian values," Thatcher claimed, would "encourage personal responsibility, personal initiative, self-respect, and respect for others" (qtd. in Moser 58).

Preparing Your Works Cited List

It is a good idea to begin preparing your list of works cited during the research process, adding new entries each time you find a source that might be useful to you. That way, when the time comes to finalize your paper, you can just edit the list you already have, making sure it contains all the necessary entries and no extraneous ones, and checking each for accuracy and format. If you wait until the end to create your works cited list, you will have to compile the whole list from scratch at a time when you are most tired and therefore least able to focus your attention on this necessary, detailed work.

A number of online resources exist to help you compose and format your works cited. Two of the best respected are *easybib.com* and *citationmachine.net*. These sites allow you to select the type of source from a menu and then enter information about author names, titles, and so on in a form. Once all the information is entered, the software formats and punctuates it appropriately, and you can then save it to your document. You can choose from MLA, APA, or other popular formats. Most instructors do not mind you using these services (ask if you are unsure how your instructor feels about this), but a word of caution is needed. These services can format and punctuate, but they cannot proofread. They will use the information exactly as you enter it, so you must double-check for accuracy before submitting the information for formatting. Many word processing programs also have bibliography generators, but these are usually not adequate for specialized, scholarly sources and are therefore not recommended.

General Guidelines

- **Begin your list of works cited on a new page.** Continue paginating as you have throughout the paper, with your last name and the page number appearing in the upper right corner.

- **Center the heading Works Cited at the top of the page** in capital and lowercase letters; do not use italics, boldface print, or quotation marks.

- **Arrange the sources alphabetically, by the last name of the source's author** (or by title, in the case of anonymous works), regardless of the order in which the sources are cited in your paper.

- **Begin each entry flush with the left margin.** When an entry takes up more than one line, all lines after the first are indented one-half inch. (For an example, see the works cited list in the research paper by Jarrad Nunes, on page 1262.) This is called a hanging indent, and all major word processing programs can be set to format your entries this way.

- **Double-space the entire list.**

- **Do not put extra line spaces between entries.**

- **As always, carefully follow any additional or contrary instructions provided by your instructor.**

Citing Books

To list books in your works cited, include as much of the following information as is available and appropriate, in the following order and format. Each bulleted element here should be separated by a period. If no other formatting (quotation marks, italics, etc.) is specified, then none should be added.

- **The name of the author or editor**, last name first for the first author or editor listed. Names of additional authors or others listed, anywhere in the entry, should appear in the regular order (first name first). (Multiple authors or editors should be listed in the order in which they appear on the book's title page. Use initials or middle names, just as they appear. You need not include titles, affiliations, and any academic degrees that precede or follow names.)

- **Title of a part of the book**, in quotation marks. Needed only if you cite a chapter, an introduction, or other part of a book written by someone other than the principal author or editor listed on the title page. See "A work in an anthology or compilation," "An article in a reference work," or "An introduction, preface, foreword, or afterword" on the following pages.

- **The title of the book**, italicized. If there is a subtitle, put a colon after the main title, and follow this with the full subtitle. This is the standard format for a works cited entry, even if no colon appears on the book's title page. (If the main title ends in a question mark, an exclamation point, or a dash, however, do not add a colon between the main title and the subtitle.)

- **Name of the editor** (for books with both an author and an editor), **translator**, or **compiler**, if different from the primary author(s), with the abbreviation *Ed.*, *Trans.*, or *Comp.*, as appropriate.

- **Edition used**, if other than the first.

- **Volume used**, if a multivolume work.

- **City or place of publication**, followed by a colon (if more than one city is listed on the title page, use only the first one); **name of the publisher**, followed by a comma; **year of publication** (if multiple copyright dates are listed, use the most recent one).

- **Page numbers.** Needed only if you cite a chapter, an introduction, or other part of a book written by someone other than the principal author or editor listed on the title page. See "A work in an anthology or compilation," "An article in a reference work," or "An introduction, preface, foreword, or afterword" on the following pages.

- **Medium of publication**, such as Print, Web, CD, DVD, Film, Lecture, Performance, Radio, Television, or E-mail.
- **Series name**, if the book is part of a series.

Copy your entries directly from the book's title page, which provides more complete and accurate information than does a cover or another bibliography. The following examples cover most of the sorts of books you are likely to encounter.

A book by a single author. The simplest entry is a single-volume book by a single author, not part of a series, and without additional editors, translators, or compilers.

> Alexie, Sherman. *The Absolutely True Diary of a Part-Time Indian*. New York: Little, 2007. Print.

If a book has an editor, a translator, or a compiler in addition to an author, identify this person by role and by name, between the book's title and the place of publication.

> Sebald, W. G. *The Rings of Saturn*. Trans. Michael Hulse. New York: New Directions, 1998. Print.

The following example cites a third-edition book by a single author.

> Richter, David H. *The Critical Tradition: Classic Texts and Contemporary Trends*. 3rd ed. Boston: Bedford, 2007. Print.

A book by two or three authors. Note that in the following example only the first author's name appears in reverse order. UP (with no periods) is the abbreviation for University Press. Note also the series title, Oxford Shakespeare Topics, is included when citing a book in a series.

> Gurr, Andrew, and Mariko Ichikawa. *Staging in Shakespeare's Theaters*. Oxford: Oxford UP, 2000. Print. Oxford Shakespeare Topics.

A book by four or more authors. If four or more authors or editors are listed on a book's title page, you can list all names or give only the name of the first, followed by *et al.* (Latin for "and others").

> Gardner, Janet E., et al., eds. *Literature: A Portable Anthology*. 2nd ed. Boston: Bedford, 2009. Print.

A book by an unknown or anonymous author. Simply include all the other information, beginning with the title.

> *Gilgamesh: A New English Version.* Trans. Stephen Mitchell. New York: Free,
>   2006. Print.

A book by a corporate author. Corporate authorship refers to a book that lists an organization rather than an individual as its author. This is especially common with publications from government and nonprofit organizations. GPO stands for the Government Printing Office, which publishes most U.S. federal documents.

> Bureau of the Census. *Historical Statistics of the United States, 1789-1945: A*
>   *Supplement to the Statistical Abstract of the United States.* Washington:
>   GPO, 1945. Print.

Two or more books by the same author. If you cite more than one work by a single author, alphabetize the entries by title. For the second and all subsequent entries by the same author, replace the author's name with three hyphens.

> Bloom, Harold. *Hamlet: Poem Unlimited.* New York: Riverhead-Penguin, 2003.
>   Print.

> ---. *Shakespeare's Poems and Sonnets.* Broomall: Chelsea, 1999. Print.
>   Bloom's Major Poets.

A work in an anthology or compilation. The first example that follows is a citation from a literature anthology; the second is from a scholarly work in which each chapter is written by a different author. The title of the work or chapter being cited is usually enclosed in quotation marks. However, if the piece is a play or novel, you should italicize its title instead.

> Baldwin, James. "Sonny's Blues." *Literature: A Portable Anthology.* Ed. Janet
>   E. Gardner et al. 2nd ed. Boston: Bedford, 2009. 250-76. Print.

> Keyishian, Harry. "Shakespeare and the Movie Genre: The Case of *Hamlet.*"
>   *The Cambridge Companion to Shakespeare on Film.* Ed. Russell Jackson.
>   Cambridge: Cambridge UP, 2000. 72-81. Print.

Two or more works in a single anthology or compilation. If you cite two or more works from a single anthology or collection, you can create a cross-reference, citing the full publication information for the collection as a whole and cross-referencing the individual pieces using only the name of the editor and page numbers of the particular work within the anthology or compilation.

Chopin, Kate. "The Story of an Hour." Gardner et al. 66-68.

Gardner, Janet E., et al., eds. *Literature: A Portable Anthology*. 2nd ed.
Boston: Bedford, 2009. Print.

Gilman, Charlotte Perkins. "The Yellow Wallpaper." Gardner et al. 70-83.

An article in a reference work. The format for citing material from dictionaries, encyclopedias, or other specialized reference works is similar to that for a work in an anthology, but the name of the reference work's editor is omitted. Often, such reference articles are anonymous anyway. The first example is for a signed article in a print book, the second for an anonymous entry in an electronic encyclopedia.

Brown, Andrew. "Sophocles." *The Cambridge Guide to Theatre*. Cambridge:
Cambridge UP, 1988. 899-900. Print.

"Browning, Elizabeth Barrett." *Encyclopaedia Britannica Online*. Encyclopaedia Britannica, 2008. Web. 4 Feb. 2008.

An introduction, preface, foreword, or afterword. After the author's name, give the name of the part of the book being cited, capitalized but neither italicized nor in quotation marks, followed by the title of the book and all relevant publication information.

Bode, Carl. Introduction. *The Portable Thoreau*. By Henry David Thoreau. Ed.
Bode. Revised ed. Harmondsworth, Eng.: Penguin, 1977. 1-27. Print.
Viking Portable Library.

Citing Periodicals

An article in a scholarly journal. Most scholarly journals publish several issues in each annual volume and paginate continuously throughout the entire volume. (In other words, if one issue ends on page 230, the next will begin with page 231.) Your works cited entry should list the author, article title, journal title, volume number (in arabic numerals, even if it appears in roman numeral form on the journal cover), issue number, year (in parentheses), page numbers, and medium. Follow the punctuation shown here exactly.

Miller, Greg. "The Bottom of Desire in Suzan-Lori Parks's *Venus.*" *Modern Drama* 45.1 (2002): 125-37. Print.

An article in a magazine. For an article in a magazine, omit the volume and issue numbers (if given) and include the date of publication. The first example here shows the format for a monthly, bimonthly, or quarterly magazine; the second, which includes the date as well as the month, is appropriate for weekly and biweekly magazines.

McChesney, Robert W., and John Nichols. "Holding the Line at the FCC." *Progressive* Apr. 2003: 26-29. Print.

Welch, Jilly. "Campaign Spells Out Concern for Literacy." *People Management* 18 Apr. 1996: 6-7. Print.

An article in a newspaper. When a newspaper is separated into sections, note the letter or number designating the section as a part of the page reference. Newspapers and some magazines frequently place articles on nonconsecutive pages. When this happens, give the number of the first page only, followed by the plus sign (+). For locally published newspapers, state the city of the publication if not included in the paper's name. Do this by adding the city in square brackets after the newspaper's name: *Argus Leader* [Sioux Falls]. If the masthead notes a specific edition, add a comma after the date and list the edition (for example, *natl. ed., late ed.*). Different editions of the same issue of a newspaper contain different material, so it's important to note which edition you are using.

Mahren, Elizabeth. "University's 'Leap of Faith' Becomes Lesson in Community." *Los Angeles Times* 16 Mar. 2003: A1+. Print.

A review. To cite a review, you must include the title and author of the work being reviewed between the review title and the periodical title. The first entry that follows is for a book review in a magazine. The second is an untitled review in a scholarly journal that includes the name of an adaptor as well as the place and date of the play's production.

Ilan Stavans. "Familia Faces." Rev. of *Caramelo*, by Sandra Cisneros. *Nation* 10 Feb. 2003: 30-34. Print.

Sofer, Andrew. Rev. of *Lysistrata*, by Aristophanes. Adapt. Robert Brustein. Amer. Repertory Theatre, Cambridge, 28 May 2002. *Theater Journal* 55.1 (2003): 137-38. Print.

Citing Electronic Sources

Sometimes online sources do not list all the information required for a complete citation. They are, for instance, frequently anonymous, and they do not always record the dates when they were written or updated. Give as much of the information as you can find, using the formats that follow. Note that entries for online sources generally contain two dates. The first is the date when the document was posted or updated; the second is the date the researcher accessed the document.

An article from an online subscription database or index. When you access an article through an online index or database (*MLA International Bibliography*, *JSTOR*, etc.), treat it as you would a print source, with the addition of the title of the database (italicized), the medium of publication, and the date you accessed the material.

> Farland, Maria Magdalena. "'That Tritest/Brightest Truth': Emily Dickinson's
> Anti-Sentimentality." *Nineteenth-Century Literature* 53.3 (1998): 364-
> 89. *JSTOR*. Web. 21 Mar. 2010.

> Shaw, Mary Neff. "Dickinson's 'Because I could not stop for Death.'" *Explicator*
> 50.1 (1991): 20-21. *MLA International Bibliography*. Web. 20 Mar. 2010.

A CD-ROM. An entry for a CD-ROM resembles a book entry, with the addition of the acronym *CD-ROM* inserted at the end as the medium of publication.

> *Shakespeare: His Life, Times, Works, and Sources*. Princeton: Films for the
> Humanities and Sciences, 1995. CD-ROM.

An online scholarly project or database. A full entry for an online scholarly project or database includes the editor's name; the title of the project, italicized; the name of the sponsoring organization or institution; the date of the project's most recent update; the medium; and the date that you accessed the project.

> Folsom, Ed, and Kenneth M. Price, eds. *The Walt Whitman Archive*. Walt
> Whitman Archive, 2009. Web. 1 Apr. 2009.

An online journal or magazine. The first entry that follows is from an online scholarly journal that does not have issue numbers or page numbers; the second is from the online version of a popular magazine.

> Fukuda, Tatsuaki. "Faulknerian Topography." *The Faulkner Journal of Japan* 4
> (2002): n. pag. Web. 20 Mar. 2003.

Keegan, Rebecca Winters. "Redeeming Roman Polanski." *Time*. Time Inc., 24
Jan. 2008. Web. 4 Feb. 2008.

A professional or personal Web page. Include as much of the following
information as appropriate and available: the author of the document or
site; the document title, in quotation marks (if the site is divided into
separate documents); the name of the site, italicized; the sponsoring organization or institution; the date of creation or most recent update; the
medium; and your date of access. If the site has no official title, provide
a brief identifying phrase, neither italicized nor in quotation marks, as in
the second example below.

Werner, Liz. "A Brief History of the Dickinson Homestead." *The Dickinson
Homestead: Home of Emily Dickinson*. Amherst Coll., 2001. Web. 12 June
2003.

Korista, Kirk. Home page. Western Michigan U, 3 June 2008. Web. 20 Oct.
2008.

A page on a Web site. For an individual page on a Web site, list the author (if given), followed by the rest of the information for the entire Web
site, as above.

Arthur, Luke. "Financial Advice for Young Adults." *eHow.com*. eHow, 31 May
2011. Web. 10 Aug. 2011.

A blog. An entry for a blog citation includes the blogger's name (or online handle), the title of the posting, blog title, date of posting, medium,
and date of access.

Curran, Kevin. "The Newspaper and the Culture of Print in the Early American
Republic." *Textual Studies, 1500-1800*, Blogger, 7 Jan. 2008. Web. 14
Jan. 2008.

A wiki. An entry for a wiki citation begins with the title of the wiki page,
followed by the wiki title (italicized), sponsor or publisher, date of posting, medium, and date of access.

"Cornelius Eady." *Wikipedia*. Wikimedia Foundation, 7 Apr. 2009. Web. 20
Apr. 2009.

An e-book. Treat e-books as you would print books, changing only the
medium.

Enterline, Lynn. *The Rhetoric of the Body from Ovid to Shakespeare*. Cambridge: Cambridge UP, 2000. *Northwestern University Ebrary*. Web. 30
Nov. 2007.

A posting to a discussion list or newsgroup. Give the author's name, the
title of the posting (in quotation marks) taken from the subject line, the
title of the site on which the forum is found (italicized), the sponsor of
the site, the date of posting, the medium, and your date of access. If the
posting has no title, use the identifying phrase *Online posting*.

Arnove, Anthony. "Query Regarding Arthur Miller." *Campaign against Sanc-
tions on Iraq*. Iraq Analysis Group, 28 Jan. 2000. Web. 20 Apr. 2003.

Citing Other Miscellaneous Sources

A television or radio program. Begin with the name of the author or
another individual (director, narrator, etc.), only if you refer primarily to
the work of a particular individual. Otherwise, begin with the title of a
segment or episode (if appropriate), in quotation marks; the title of the
program, italicized; the title of the series (if applicable), italicized; the
name of the network; the call letters and city of the local station (if applicable); the date of broadcast; and the medium. The first entry that
follows is a citation of a segment of a radio broadcast. The second is a
citation of an episode of a television program.

Alison, Jay. "For Sale." *This American Life*. Public Radio Intl. WCAI, Woods
Hole, MA, 11 Oct. 2002. Radio.

"The Undertaking." *Frontline*. PBS. WGBH, Boston, 30 Oct. 2007. Television.

A film, video, or DVD. Film citations begin with the film title (italicized),
followed by *Dir.* and the director's name, the year the film was originally
released, the distributor, the year of release, and the medium (Videocas-
sette, DVD, etc.).

Hamlet. Dir. Laurence Olivier. 1948. Home Vision Entertainment, 2000. DVD.

An interview. Begin with the name of the person interviewed. For a published interview, give the title, if any, in quotation marks (if there is no
title, simply use the designation *Interview*, neither in quotation marks
nor italicized), followed by the name of the interviewer, publication information, and medium. The first example that follows is for an interview published in a magazine. The second example is for an interview

conducted personally by the author of the research paper and gives the name of the person interviewed.

> Shields, David. "The Only Way Out Is Deeper In." Interview by Andrew C.
> Gottlieb. *Poets & Writers* July/Aug. 2002: 27-31. Print.

> Smith, Stephen. Personal interview. 20 Mar. 2002.

A lecture or speech. To cite a speech or lecture that you've attended, use the following format, listing the speaker's name; the title of the presentation, in quotation marks (if announced or published); the sponsoring organization; the location; the date; and a descriptive label such as *Address* or *Lecture*. The first example given here is for a speech with an announced title. The second is for an untitled address.

> Cohen, Amy R. "Sharing the Orchestra: How Modern Productions Reveal
> Ancient Conventions." Sixth Natl. Symposium on Theater in Academe.
> Washington and Lee U, Lexington, VA. 15 Mar. 2003. Speech.

> Nader, Ralph. U of Massachusetts Dartmouth, North Dartmouth. 24 Mar.
> 2003. Address.

To cite a lecture, speech, or address you've seen in a film or TV broadcast or heard on the radio, use the appropriate format for the medium of transmission. Generally speaking, you do not need to cite a class lecture; to quote or otherwise refer to something an instructor says in class, you may do so simply by crediting the instructor in the text of your essay.

A letter or e-mail. There are three kinds of letters: published, unpublished (in archives), and personal. A published letter includes the writer's name, the recipient's name (in quotation marks), the date of the letter, the number of the letter (if assigned by the editor), and publication information for the book or periodical in which it appears.

> Thomas, Dylan. "To Donald Taylor." 28 Oct. 1944. *Dylan Thomas: The Col-
> lected Letters*. Ed. Paul Ferris. New York: Macmillan, 1985. 529-30. Print.

In citing an unpublished letter, give the writer's name, the title or a description of the material (for example, *Letter to Havelock Ellis*), the date, the medium (*MS* for a handwritten letter, *TS* for a letter composed on a machine), and any identifying number assigned to it. Include the name and location of the library or institution housing the material.

Sanger, Margaret. Letter to Havelock Ellis. 14 July 1924. MS. Margaret Sanger
Papers. Sophia Smith Collection, Smith Coll., Northampton, MA.

To cite a letter you received personally, include the author, the designation *Letter to the author*, the date posted, and the medium (*MS* for a handwritten letter, *TS* for a letter composed on a machine). To cite an e-mail you received personally, include the author, the designation *Message to the author*, the date of the message, and the designation *E-mail*.

Green, Barclay. Letter to the author. 1 Sept. 2008. TS.

Kapadia, Parmita. Message to the author. 12 Mar. 2010. E-mail.

A work of visual art. Give the artist's name, the title of the artwork (in italics), the date of composition, the medium of composition, and, if you saw the original artwork in person, the name and location of the institution that houses the artwork. If you used a reproduction of the artwork in a print or electronic source, provide appropriate bibliographic information for that source.

Goya, Francisco. *The Family of Charles IV*. 1800. Oil on canvas. Museo del
Prado, Madrid.

Evans, Walker. *Bud Fields and His Family*. Photograph. 1935. "A Photo Essay
on the Great Depression." *Modern American Poetry*. U of Illinois, 2011.
Web. 5 Aug. 2011.

SAMPLE RESEARCH PAPER

When choosing a research paper topic, Jarrad Nunes recalled how interesting he had found Emily Dickinson's poem "Because I could not stop for Death" (page 1140), which seemed to defy his expectations of literature about death and dying. Jarrad decided to see what professional literary critics had to say on the subject and how closely their ideas matched his own. His paper, which follows, is a type of **reader-response criticism**, because it attends to reader expectations and how Dickinson manipulates these, and it combines a close-reading of the primary literary text with research from a variety of secondary sources.

Jarrad S. Nunes
Professor Gardner
English 204
2 April 2010

Emily Dickinson's "Because I
could not stop for Death":
Challenging Readers' Expectations

With a keen eye for detail and a well-known conciseness and
compression, Emily Dickinson's poetry records the abstractions
of human life so matter-of-factly that her readers often take her
technical skill for granted. Take, for example, the six-stanza poem
"Because I could not stop for Death" — a detached, but never
completely dispassionate, recollection of a human's journey to its
final conclusion. The verse is crafted so succinctly and with such
precision that its complex and vivid images are made even more
extraordinary and meaningful. At least one critic has pointed out
how Dickinson employs "rhetorical strategies that resist and
contest dominant cultural conceptions of death and immortality"
(Farland 370). We might expect literature on the theme of death
to invoke religious imagery, stillness, and a sense of dread or
foreboding, but none of this is the case. Instead, the poem
challenges the preconceptions Dickinson's contemporaries had
about death, and in doing so it makes us challenge ours as well.

Jarrad focuses in on one Dickinson poem.

From the start, Dickinson infuses this often-grim topic with a
palpable humanity, beginning with her personification of death as
the courteous, careful carriage driver bearing the speaker's body
to rest. Literary critic Harold Bloom asserts, "The image here
of a woman and her escort, Death, meditating on the prospect
of eternity, is neither one of despair nor loss nor outrage, but of
resignation" (37). This "resignation," though, does not come
across as the predictable acceptance of God's will. In fact, any
mention of God or the soul is remarkably absent from this poem
about death and eternity. This suggests the uneasy relationship
Dickinson had with the strict religious beliefs of her society and

Because he mentions Bloom at the beginning of the sentence, Jarrad does not have to include Bloom's name in the in-text citation.

Nunes 2

r family. "Raised during the period of New England Revivalism,"
ites David Yezzi, "Dickinson declined to make the public con-
ssion of faith that would admit her to the church (her father
ade his twice) and by the age of thirty she left off attending
rvices altogether." Clearly at odds with familial and social
pectations, Dickinson nonetheless fearlessly expresses her
igious "doubt, which her poems later absorbed as ambiguity and
ntradiction" (Yezzi).

Jarrad integrates Yezzi's quotation with his own writing in order to provide some cultural context.

Dickinson's narrator does not fear death, perhaps because
ath is associated here not so much with endings or divine
dgment but instead with a very human journey. The driver seems
fable, "kindly stopp[ing]" and driving slowly. In stanza 2, the
rrator puts her work away to observe the driver calmly. It may
em unlikely that she would be trusting of so ominous a charac-
r, but as critic Betsy Erikkila explains it, "Death himself comes
urting as an aristocratic gentleman with horses and a carriage"
). David Baker carries this one step further, noting "[h]ow
mely and comfortable is this ride" and comparing it to "a mild
th-century date." Indeed, the fact that the carriage driver has
opped for the narrator on a day when she was too busy to do the
me emphasizes his courtesy and thoughtfulness as a character.
is is an original and deeply humanistic perception of death, in
ich the personified entity is neither a black-cloaked grim reaper
r a stern servant of God.

Along with its deep humanity, Dickinson's image of Death has
fluidity and graceful movement that is, at first, juxtaposed
ainst our more frightening preconceptions of the idea. This
ngible sense of motion is perhaps best illustrated in the poem's
rfectly constructed third stanza. Here, a series of images
etaphorically re-creates a natural progression — childish play
ves way to growing grain and, eventually, to the setting of the
n (lines 9-12). One critic has demonstrated how these three
ages might represent childhood, maturity, and old age (Shaw
). The very fact that the narrator views these scenes from a

Jarrad para-phrases Shaw's point in his own words and then provides an appropriate in-text citation.

slowly rolling carriage lends the passage a clear sense of movement and an unexpected vitality. The absurdity of this meandering vessel passing "the Setting Sun" perhaps suggests a sense of quickening as death draws near, or it may even signal the dissolution of temporal reality altogether. Regardless, the steady progression of this section is undeniable.

The strong sense of motion is continued in the fourth stanza, though with some differences. Here, the movement is less concrete, as the narrator herself moves from a life marked by careful self-control into a position in which she all but succumbs to outside forces. As "[t]he Dews drew quivering and chill" (14), the narrator has lost the ability to keep herself warm. Her earthly garments do not provide adequate protection. From her philosophical viewpoint, however, these difficulties, like death itself, are to be calmly accepted rather than feared. Indeed, before this point, there is not a single truly fearful image in this remarkable poem about death, and even here any sense of foreboding is muted.

Jarrad's smooth transition provides a link between his analyses of two stanzas.

As the poem moves into its fifth stanza, the momentum is halted temporarily, and a more traditional death image is finally introduced with the lines "We paused before a House that seemed / A Swelling of the Ground" (17–18). At this point, the character of Death seems to bid his passenger a rather unceremonial good-bye at the foot of her earthen grave. As the resting place is described, he retreats, returning to the world of the living to repeat his duty with another passenger. While the sparse but vivid description of the grave should invoke a paralyzing loneliness, Dickinson again thwarts our expectations, tempering the reader's fear by having her narrator merely pause at the sight, as if staying for a short while at a hotel or a friend's house. Once again, a usual symbol of finality is given a transitive purpose.

Jarrad consistently chooses important quotations from the poem as evidence for his claims.

The final stanza brings the narrator to a new place, Eternity. However, as one critic explains it, "Eternity, for Dickinson, is not a place at which one arrives. It is rather a journey-towards, a continual evolving" (Baker). Once again Dickinson has thwarted

ders' expectations. While this should certainly be the logical
d of her journey, Dickinson's exquisite use of language suggests
at the entire account may simply be a daydream — a mental
ess rehearsal for the real death to come. Consider this account of
e poem's final stanza:

> All of this poetically elapsed time "Feels shorter than the
> Day," the day of death brought to an end by the setting sun
> of the third stanza. . . . "Surmised," carefully placed near the
> conclusion, is all the warranty one needs for reading this jour-
> ney as one that has taken place entirely in her mind . . . the
> poem returns to the very day, even the same instant, when it
> started. (Anderson 245)

*Jarrad indents
this long quo-
tation to set it
apart from his
own prose.*

us even the most basic facts about death — its finality and
rmanence — are brought into question.

Finally, "Because I could not stop for Death" indicates both
ckinson's precise and vivid style and her unwillingness to settle
the ordinary interpretation. Death no longer conforms to the
aders' preconceptions, as religion, stillness, and finality give
y to humanist philosophy, motion, and continuity. The poet
serves, experiences, and recounts her perceptions in metaphor.
e opens up many questions about the nature of death, yet she
ovides no easy answers to her readers. Instead, we are provided
th an account of death that weaves in and out of time, finally
ping back on its own structure to provide a stunningly dramatic
nclusion. In six short stanzas, Dickinson cleverly exposes what
e saw as fundamental flaws in the traditional conception of
ath, burial, and the eternal afterlife, and in doing so, she opens
new pathways of thought for us all.

*In his conclu-
sion, Jarrad
reinforces his
claim: that the
poem challenges
nineteenth-
century notions
of death.*

Works Cited

Anderson, Charles R. *Emily Dickinson's Poetry: Stairway of Surprise.* *A print book.*
New York: Holt, 1960. Print.

Baker, David. "Elegy and Eros." *Virginia Quarterly Review* 81.2
(2005): 207-20. *MLA International Bibliography.* Web. 20 Mar.
2010.

Bloom, Harold. *Emily Dickinson.* New York: Chelsea, 1999. Print. *Book in a serie*
Bloom's Major Poets.

Dickinson, Emily. "Because I could not stop for Death." *Literature:* *A poem reprint*
A Portable Anthology. Ed. Janet E. Gardner et al. 2nd ed. *in an antholog*
Boston: Bedford, 2009. 537. Print.

Erikkila, Betsy. "Emily Dickinson and Class." *American Literary* *Articles accesse*
History 4.1 (1992): 1-27. *JSTOR.* Web. 21 Mar. 2010. *through online*
database servi

Farland, Maria Magdalena. "'That Tritest/Brightest Truth': Emily
Dickinson's Anti-Sentimentality." *Nineteenth-Century Literature*
53.3 (1998): 364-89. *JSTOR.* Web. 21 Mar. 2010.

Shaw, Mary Neff. "Dickinson's 'Because I could not stop for Death.'"
Explicator 50.1 (1991): 20-21. *MLA International Bibliography.*
Web. 20 Mar. 2010.

Yezzi, David. "Straying Close to Home." *Commonweal.* Commonweal *An online ver-*
Foundation, 9 Oct. 1998. Web. 20 May 2009. *sion of a maga*
zine article.

CHAPTER 9

Literary Criticism and Literary Theory

Anytime you sit down to write about literature, or even to discuss a story, play, or poem with classmates, you are acting as a literary critic. The word *criticism* is often interpreted as negative and faultfinding. But literary criticism is a discipline and includes everything from a glowing review to a scathing attack to a thoughtful and balanced interpretation. Criticism can be broken down into two broad categories: evaluative and interpretive. Evaluative criticism seeks to determine how accomplished a work is and what place it should hold in the evolving story of literary history. Book reviews are the most common form of evaluative criticism. Interpretive criticism comprises all writing that seeks to explain, analyze, clarify, or question the meaning and significance of literature. Although you may engage in a certain amount of evaluative criticism in your literature class, and while your attitude about the value of literature will likely be apparent in your writing, the criticism you write for class will consist largely of interpretation.

All literary critics, including you, begin with some form of literary theory. Just as you may not have thought of yourself as a literary critic, you probably haven't thought of yourself as using literary theory. But you are doing so every time you write about literature, and it is a good idea to become familiar with some of the most prevalent types of theory. This familiarity will help you understand why so many respected literary critics seem to disagree with one another and why they write such different analyses of the same work of literature. It may also help to explain why you might disagree with your classmates, or even your instructor, in your interpretation of a particular story, poem, or play. Perhaps you are simply starting from a different theoretical base. You will be able to explain your thinking more eloquently if you understand that base.

Literary theory has the reputation of being incredibly dense and difficult. Indeed, the theories—sometimes called *schools* of criticism—discussed in the following pages are all complex, but here they are presented in their most basic, stripped-down forms. As such, these explanations are necessarily incomplete and selective. You should not feel you need to master the complexities of literary theory right now. You need only be aware of the existence of these various schools and watch for them as you read and write. Doing so will give you a better sense of what you're reading and hearing about the literature you explore, and it will make your writing more informed and articulate. There are many other schools and subschools in addition to those described here, but these are the most significant—the ones you are most likely to encounter as you continue to explore literature.

Focusing on Jamaica Kincaid's "Girl" (page 380) and T. S. Eliot's "The Love Song of J. Alfred Prufrock" (page 1214), the last paragraph of each entry offers a few directions one might take in a critical reading, with the specific critical theory applied to the analysis. While these notes are by no means exhaustive, they might help spark ideas for a paper, or at least grant greater insight into the literature and theory discussed.

FORMALISM AND NEW CRITICISM

For a large part of the twentieth century, literary criticism was dominated by various types of theory that can broadly be defined as **formalism** and **New Criticism**. (New Criticism is no longer new, having begun to fall out of prominence in the 1970s, but its name lives on.) Formalist critics focus their attention on the formal elements of a literary text—things like **structure**, **tone**, **characters**, **setting**, **symbols**, and linguistic features. Explication and close-reading (explained on page 1185) are techniques of formalist criticism. While poetry, which is quite self-consciously formal in its structure, lends itself most obviously to formalist types of criticism, prose fiction and drama are also frequently viewed through this lens.

Perhaps the most distinguishing feature of formalism and New Criticism is that they focus on the text itself and not on extratextual factors. Formalist critics are interested in how parts of a text relate to one another and to the whole, and they seek to create meaning by unfolding and examining these relationships. Excluded from consideration are questions about the author, the reader, history or culture, and the relationship of the literary text to other texts or artwork. Chances are you have written some formalist criticism yourself, either in high school or in college. If you have ever written a paper on **symbolism**, character development, or the relationship between sound patterns and sense in a poem, you have been a formalist critic.

A formalist critic of Jamaica Kincaid's story "Girl" might choose to focus on how the language used by the speaker of this monologue illuminates her character, while a formalist critic of T. S. Eliot's "The Love

Song of J. Alfred Prufrock" might focus on Eliot's irregular use of rhyme and meter in the poem.

FEMINIST AND GENDER CRITICISM

Have you ever had a classroom discussion of a piece of literature in which the focus was on the roles of women in the literature or the culture, or on the relationships between men and women? If so, you have engaged in **feminist criticism**. Some version of feminist criticism has been around for as long as readers have been interested in gender roles, but the school rose to prominence in the 1970s at the same time the modern feminist movement was gaining steam. Most feminist criticism from this time was clearly tied to raising consciousness about the patriarchy in which many women felt trapped. Some feminist critics sought to reveal how literary texts demonstrated the repression and powerlessness of women in different periods and cultures. Others had a nearly opposite agenda, showing how female literary characters could overcome the sexist power structures that surround them and exercise power in their worlds. Still others looked to literary history and sought to rediscover and promote writing by women whose works had been far less likely than men's to be regarded as "great" literature.

Before long, however, some critics began to point out that women were not alone in feeling social pressure to conform to gender roles. Over the years, men have usually been expected to be good providers, to be strong (both physically and emotionally), and to keep their problems and feelings more or less to themselves. Though the expectations are different, men are socialized no less than women to think and behave in certain ways, and these social expectations are also displayed in works of literature. Feminist criticism has expanded in recent years to become **gender criticism**. Any literary criticism that highlights gender roles or relationships between the sexes can be a type of gender criticism, whether or not it is driven by an overt feminist agenda.

The story "Girl" would be an obvious choice for a feminist critic, since it focuses on how a young girl is socialized into the domestic roles expected of women in her society. A gender critic might also be interested in "Prufrock" and in the ways that the poem's aging speaker feels his masculinity called into question.

QUEER THEORY

Queer theory is one of the more recent and more challenging critical schools to emerge out of critical interest in gender. It came into prominence in the 1990s, when some gay and lesbian literary critics perceived a need for a critical school that reflected their own particular circumstances and viewpoints. Some queer theorists insist that sexuality—or even the binary male/female division of gender itself—is culturally constructed rather than determined by physical characteristics present at birth. Many of these critics and theorists seek to destabilize the cultural norm that suggests that certain sexual preferences, marriage and family customs, and so forth are "normal" or "natural" while others are "deviant."

Queer theorists, like all literary critics, differ substantially in their focus. Some are interested in studying literary texts written by authors known or suspected to be gays, lesbians, bisexual, or transgender, particularly if these authors have been devalued in the past because of their sexual identity. Other queer theorists are interested in portrayals of gay or lesbian characters in literature by either gay or straight authors. Still others seek a "queer subtext" in canonical works of literature that have long been considered hetero-normative. (Included in this latter category are the many critics who have asked whether Shakespeare's Hamlet had something more than a traditional heterosexual friendship with his close confidante Horatio.)

At first glance, Jamaica Kincaid's "Girl" might not look like a promising candidate for examination by queer theory. But a queer theorist might, in fact, be interested in how the very possibility of homosexuality is erased by the narrator, the way the young girl is assumed to have an interest in "wharf-rat boys" and a need to know "how to love a man," though she never expresses these heterosexual urges.

MARXIST CRITICISM

Just as feminist criticism and queer theory came into their own because of the political agenda of certain critics, so too did **Marxist criticism**, which originally sought to use literature and criticism to forward a socialist political program. Early Marxist critics began with Karl Marx's (1818–1883) insistence that human interactions are economically driven and that the basic model of human progress is based on a struggle for power between different social classes. For Marxist critics, then, literature was just another battleground, another venue for the ongoing quest for individual material gain. Literary characters could be divided into powerful oppressors and their powerless victims, and literary plots and themes could be examined to uncover the economic forces that drove them. According to this model, the very acts of writing and reading literature can be characterized as production and consumption, and some Marxist critics have studied the external forces that drive education, publication, and literary tastes.

The sort of Marxist criticism that ignores all forces but socioeconomic ones is sometimes referred to as *vulgar* Marxism because, in its single-mindedness, it ignores certain complexities of individual thought and action. Its sole purpose is to expose the inequalities that underlie all societies and to thus raise the consciousness of readers and move society closer to a socialist state. Such Marxist criticism tends to be full of the language of Marxist political analysis—references to *class struggle*, to the economic *base* and *superstructure*, to the *means of production*, to worker *alienation* and *reification* (the process whereby oppressed workers lose their sense of individual humanity), and so forth.

But just as feminist criticism soon opened up into the broader and more complex school of gender criticism, so too did most Marxist criticism break free of a single-minded political agenda. You no longer have to be a committed Marxist to engage in Marxist criticism; all you need to do is acknowledge that socioeconomic forces do, in fact, affect people's lives. If you notice inequalities in power between characters in a work of literature, if you question how the class or educational background of an author affects his or her work, or if you believe that a certain type of literature—a Shakespearean sonnet, say, or a pulp western novel— appeals more to readers of a particular social background, then you are, at least in part, engaging in Marxist criticism.

Social class roles, one of the primary interests of Marxist critics, are visible in the apparently modest circumstances of the characters in "Girl" (where class and gender have a clear overlap) as well as in the more bourgeois world of porcelain teacups and perfumed dresses on display in "Prufrock."

CULTURAL STUDIES

Cultural studies is the general name given to a wide variety of critical practices, some of which might seem on the surface to have little in common with one another. Perhaps the best way to understand cultural studies is to begin with the notion that certain texts are privileged in our society while others are dismissed or derided. Privileged texts are the so-called great works of literature commonly found in anthologies and on course syllabi. Indeed, when we hear the word *literature*, these are probably the works we imagine. All other writing—from pulp romance novels to the slogans on bumper stickers—belongs to a second category of texts, those generally overlooked by traditional literary critics.

One major trend in cultural studies is the attempt to broaden the **canon**—those texts read and taught again and again and held up as examples of the finest expressions of the human experience. Critics have pointed out that canonical authors—Shakespeare, Milton, Keats, Steinbeck—tend (with obvious exceptions) to be from a fairly narrow segment of society: they are usually middle to upper-middle class, well educated, heterosexual white males. Some cultural critics, therefore, have sought out and celebrated the writing of historically disadvantaged groups such as African Americans or gay and lesbian authors. Other proponents of cultural studies turn their attention to the works of various social "outsiders," like prisoners, schoolchildren, or mental patients. This attempt at broadening the canon is designed to provide students and scholars alike with a more inclusive definition of what art and literature are all about.

Cultural critics seek to blur or erase the line separating "high" art from "low" art in the minds of the literary establishment. Some cultural critics believe that all texts are to some extent artistic expressions of a culture and that any text can therefore give us vital insights into the human experience. Rather than traditional literary objects, then, a cultural critic might choose to study such things as movies and television shows, advertisements, religious tracts, graffiti, and comic books. These texts—and virtually any other visual or verbal works you can imagine—are submitted to the same rigorous scrutiny as a sonnet or a classic novel. Some cultural critics suggest that English departments should become departments of cultural studies, in which a course on hip-hop culture would be valued as much as a course on Victorian poetry.

The poems of T. S. Eliot, including "The Love Song of J. Alfred Prufrock," occupy an important place in the early-twentieth-century literary canon. A cultural critic might seek to explain how and why Eliot came to be so firmly associated with high culture.

POSTCOLONIAL CRITICISM

One very active branch of cultural studies is **postcolonial criticism**, which focuses on writing from former British (and other, mostly European) colonies around the world. Postcolonial criticism is most strongly associated with the Indian subcontinent (India, Pakistan, and Bangladesh), large portions of Africa and the Middle East, parts of Asia (such as Singapore and Vietnam), the Caribbean, and Latin America. In such places, indigenous authors often possess attitudes, tastes, and literary traditions very different from those of their former colonial masters. Postcolonial criticism seeks to discover these attitudes and tastes, to recover literary history that was ignored or suppressed during the colonial period, and to celebrate indigenous cultures of storytelling, drama, and poetry. At the same time, it attempts to understand how occupation by a more powerful colonizing nation disrupted and changed the course of history in a particular place.

In a colonial setting, members of the ruling group tend to see as natural and ordinary attitudes that might be better understood as racist, classist, and/or religiously intolerant, such as assuming that indigenous traditions are "superstitious" or "primitive" compared to the more "civilized" culture of the imperialists. Postcolonial theorists demand that indigenous attitudes and customs be treated with full respect and understanding. Postcolonial literary theory is situated within a larger move to comprehend the effect of colonial culture on history, art, architecture, politics, law, philosophy, sociology, sex and race relations, and daily life.

A postcolonial critic reading "Girl" would likely focus his or her attention on the details of language and culture—*benna* music, for instance, or the belief that blackbirds might really be spirits—that locate the story in a particular postcolonial Caribbean setting.

HISTORICAL CRITICISM AND NEW HISTORICISM

If you have ever written a research paper that involved some background reading about the life and times of an author, you have already engaged in a form of **historical criticism**. Literary scholars have long read history books and various sorts of historical documents—from newspaper articles to personal letters—to gain insights into the composition and significance of a given work. The explanatory footnotes that often appear in literary reprints and anthologies are one obvious manifestation of this type of sleuthing. Indeed, some works of literature would be virtually inexplicable if we did not understand something of the times in which they were written and first read. If you did not know that Walt Whitman's "When Lilacs Last in the Dooryard Bloom'd" was an elegy written upon the assassination of Abraham Lincoln, it would be difficult to make any sense at all of the poem, since neither the president's name nor the cause of his death actually appear in the poem.

Likewise, historians have long turned to literary works and the visual arts in order to gain insights into the periods they study. While archives and contemporary documents can teach us a lot about the broad sweep of history—wars, leaders, the controversies of the day—it is often difficult to see from these documents what life was like for ordinary people, whose interior lives were not often documented. We may be able to learn from parish burial records, for example, how common childhood mortality was at a particular time in English history, but only when we read Ben Jonson's poem "On My First Son" (page 1145) do we begin to understand how this mortality may have affected the parents who lost their children. Likewise, the few pages of James Joyce's story "Araby" (page 107) may tell us more about how adolescent boys lived and thought in early-twentieth-century Dublin than would several volumes of social history.

One school of historical criticism, known as **New Historicism**, takes account of both what history has to teach us about literature *and* what literature has to teach us about history. (New Historicism has been around since the 1960s, and as with New Criticism, the name of the school is no longer as accurate as it once was.) New Historicists are sometimes said to read literary and nonliterary texts *in parallel*, attempting to see how each illuminates the other. Typically, New Historicists examine many different types of documents—government records, periodicals, private diaries, bills of sale—in order to re-create, as much as possible, the rich cultural context that surrounded both an author and that author's original audience. In doing so, they seek to give modern audiences a reading experience as rich and informed as the original readers of a literary work.

A historical critic of "Prufrock" might be able to untangle the meaning of certain lines or images that have little meaning for contemporary readers. These would include, for instance, what Prufrock means when he describes his "necktie rich and modest, but asserted by a simple pin" (line 43) or says, "I shall wear the bottoms of my trousers rolled" (121).

PSYCHOLOGICAL THEORIES

Early in the twenty-first century, it is easy to underestimate the enormous influence that the theories of the psychoanalyst Sigmund Freud (1856–1939) have had on our understanding of human behavior and motivation. For many modern readers, Freud seems to have little to say; his work is too focused on sex and too thoroughly bound by the norms of the bourgeois Viennese society in which he lived. But if you have ever wondered what the buried significance of a dream was or whether someone had a subconscious motivation for an action, you have been affected by Freudian thinking. Freud popularized the notions that the mind can be divided into conscious and unconscious components and that we are often motivated most strongly by the unconscious. He taught us to think in terms of overt and covert desires (often referred to in Freudian language as *manifest* and *latent*) as the basis of human actions.

Like many intellectual movements of the twentieth century, psychology, and specifically Freudian psychology, has had a major influence on literary criticism. The most typical **psychological literary criticism** examines the internal mental states, the desires, and the motivations of literary characters. (In fact, Freud himself used Shakespeare's Hamlet as an example of a man whose life was ruled by what the psychoanalyst called an Oedipal complex—man's unhealthy, but not uncommon, interest in his mother's sexuality.) Another subject of psychological criticism can be the author. A critic may examine the possible unconscious urges that drove an author to write a particular story or poem. Finally, a critic might examine the psychology of readers, trying to determine what draws us to or repels us from certain literary themes or forms. If any of these aspects of literature have ever interested you, you have engaged in psychological literary criticism.

Psychological critics often interpret literature as a psychologist might interpret a dream or a wish. Special attention is often paid to symbols as the manifest representation of a deeper, less obvious meaning. Attention is also focused on the unstated motives and unconscious states of mind of characters, authors, or readers. Freud is not the only psychological theorist whose ideas are frequently used in literary analysis. Other important figures include Carl Jung (1875–1961), who gave us the notion of the collective unconscious and the influence of **archetypes** on our thinking, and Jacques Lacan (1901–1981), who had a special interest in the unconscious and the nature of language. However, you don't need to be well versed in the intricacies of psychoanalytic theory in order to be interested in the inner workings of the human mind or the ways in which they manifest themselves in literature.

The narrator of "Prufrock" is an excellent candidate for psychological study, displaying many signs of social anxiety, depression, and other recognizable psychological conditions. Or a Jungian critic of this poem might focus on archetypal symbols such as the animalistic fog early in the poem or the mermaids that appear near the end.

READER-RESPONSE THEORIES

You no doubt have heard the old question: If a tree falls in the forest and nobody hears it, did the tree make a sound? Let us rephrase that question: If a book sits on a shelf and nobody reads it, is it still a book? If you use **reader-response criticism**, your answer to that question will be a resounding *no*. Of course, the book exists as a physical object, a sheaf of paper bound in a cover and printed with symbols. But, say reader-response critics, as a work of art or a conduit for meaning, no text exists without a reader.

A text, according to the various theories of reader-response criticism, is not a container filled with meaning by its author but rather an interaction between an author and a reader, and it can never be complete unless readers bring to it their own unique insights. These insights come from a number of sources, including the reader's life experience, as well as his or her beliefs, values, state of mind at the time of the reading, and, of course, previous reading experience. Reading is not a passive attempt to understand what lies within a text but an act of creation, no less so than the writing itself. Reader-response critics try to understand the process by which we make meaning out of words on a page. If you have ever wondered why a classmate or friend saw something entirely different than you did in a story or poem, then you have been a reader-response critic.

Two key terms associated with reader-response criticism are *gaps* and *process*. Gaps are those things that a text doesn't tell us, that we need to fill in and work out for ourselves. Let us say, for instance, that you read a story told from the perspective of a child, but the author never explicitly mentions the child's age. How, then, do you imagine the narrator as you read? You pay attention to his or her actions and thoughts, and you compare this to your experience of real children you have known and others whose stories you have read. In doing so, you fill in a *gap* in the text and help solidify the text's meaning. Imagine, though, that as the story continues, new clues emerge and you need to adjust your assumptions about the child's age. This highlights the idea that reading is a *process*, that the meaning of the text is not fixed and complete but rather evolving as the text unfolds in the time it takes to read.

Some reader-response critics focus on the ways that meanings of a text change over time. To illustrate this idea, let us look at a specific example. Contemporary readers of Kate Chopin's short novel *The Awakening*, first published in 1899, tend to find the book's treatment of the heroine's sexuality subtle or even invisible. Such readers are often shocked or amused to learn that the book was widely condemned at the time of its publication as tasteless and overly explicit. Expectations and tastes change over time and place, and we can tell a lot about a society by examining how it responds to works of art. Reader-response critics, therefore, sometimes ask us to look at our own reactions to literature and to ask how, if at all, they match up with those of earlier readers. When we look at reactions to *The Awakening* at the end of the nineteenth century and then at the beginning of the twenty-first, we learn not only about Chopin's culture but also about our own.

The response paper written by Tom Lyons (pages 1184–85) shows how a student with no formal background in literary theory might still approach "Girl" in a way that gives credence to the core reader-response tenet that readers bring their own meanings to literary texts.

STRUCTURALISM

Structuralism, as the name implies, is concerned with the structures that help us understand and interpret literary texts. This may sound like a return to formalism, which, as we saw earlier, examines the formal and linguistic elements of a text. But the elements scrutinized by structuralist critics are of a different order entirely—namely, the structures that order our thinking rather than the interior architecture of poems, stories, and plays. Structuralist criticism actually derives from the work of anthropologists, linguists, and philosophers of the mid-twentieth century who sought to understand how humans think and communicate. The basic insight at the heart of the movement is the realization that we understand nothing in isolation but rather that every piece of our knowledge is part of a network of associations. Take, for instance, the question "Is Jim a good father?" In order to form a simple yes or no answer to this question, we must consider, among other things, the spectrum of "good" and "bad," the expectations our culture holds for fathers, and all we know of Jim's relationship with his children.

For a structuralist literary critic, questions about literature are answered with the same sort of attention to context. Two different types of context are especially salient—the cultural and the literary. Cultural context refers to an understanding of all aspects of an author's (and a reader's) culture, such as the organizing structures of history, politics, religion, education, work, and family. Literary context refers to all related texts, literary and nonliterary, that affect our ability to interpret a text. What had the author read that might have affected the creation of the text? What have we read that might affect our interpretation? What are the norms of the textual genre, and how does this piece of literature conform to or break from those norms?

According to structuralist critics, then, we can understand a text only by placing it within the broader contexts of culture (that of both the reader and the author) and other texts (literary and nonliterary). To fully understand one of Shakespeare's love sonnets to the mysterious "dark lady," for example, we would need to understand the conventions of romantic love, the conceptions of dark versus fair women in culturally accepted standards of beauty, and the acceptable interactions between men and women in Shakespeare's England. We would also need to relate the sonnet to the history of love poems generally, to the development of the sonnet form specifically, and to the other works in Shakespeare's cycle of 154 sonnets.

A structuralist reading of "Prufrock," then, would be likely to consider, among other things, the types of poetry that were in vogue in 1915, when the poem was first published, as well as the specific poems and poets that Eliot, who wrote literary criticism as well as poetry, most admired.

POSTSTRUCTURALISM AND DECONSTRUCTION

Poststructuralism, it will come as no surprise, begins with the insights of structuralism but carries them one step further. If, as the structuralists insist, we can understand things only in terms of other things, then perhaps there is no center point of understanding but only an endlessly interconnected web of ideas leading to other ideas leading to still other ideas. This is the starting point of poststructuralist criticism, which posits that no text has a fixed or real meaning because no meaning exists outside of the network of other meanings to which it is connected. Meaning, then, including literary meaning, is forever shifting and altering as our understanding of the world changes. The best-known version of poststructuralism is **deconstruction**, a school of philosophy and literary criticism that first gained prominence in France and that seeks to overturn the very basis of Western philosophy by undermining the notion that reality has any stable existence.

At its worst, of course, this school of thought leads to the most slippery sort of relativism. What does it matter what I think of this poem or this play? I think what I want, you think what you want. Perhaps next week I will think something different. Who cares? Every interpretation is of equal value, and none has any real value at all. At its best, though, poststructuralist criticism can lead toward truly valuable insights into literature. It reminds us that meaning within a text is contingent on all sorts of exterior understandings; it allows for several interpretations, even contradictory interpretations, to exist simultaneously; and, by insisting that no text and no meaning are absolute, it allows for a playful approach to even the most "serious" of literary objects. Indeed, one of the recurrent themes of deconstructionist criticism is the French term *jouissance*, often translated as *bliss*, which refers to a free-spirited, almost sexual enjoyment of literary language.

Having thus briefly described deconstruction, we would do well to dispel a common misconception about the word. In recent years, many people, both within and outside of academia, have begun to use *deconstruct* as a synonym for *analyze*. You might hear, for instance, "We completely deconstructed that poem in class—I understand it much better now," or "The defense attorney deconstructed the prosecutor's argument." In both these cases, what the speaker likely means has little if anything to do with the literary critical practice of deconstruction. When we take apart a text or an argument and closely examine the parts, we are engaging not in deconstruction but in analysis.

A deconstructionist reading of "Girl" might call into question the very basis for our belief in gender divisions, class structure, or the need for the socialization of young people by their elders.

These are only some of the many varieties of literary theory and criticism. In addition, you might encounter eco-criticism, which focuses on the environment and human beings' relationship with the rest of nature; religious (for example, Christian, Muslim, or Buddhist) criticism; comparative literature, which compares related works from different languages and/or cultures; various schools of critical inquiry based on race and ethnicity; and many, many more. There are even literary critics who perform textual analysis using sophisticated computer programs.

By now you may be wondering what sort of literary critic you are. You may feel that you have been a formalist one day and a psychological critic the next. This is not surprising, and it should cause you no worry, as virtually none of these schools are mutually exclusive. Indeed, most professional critics mix and match the various schools in whatever way best suits their immediate needs. The close-reading techniques of the New Critics, for instance, are frequently adopted by those who would fervently reject the New Critical stance that social and political context be excluded from consideration. If you wished to write about the social decline of Mme. Loisel in Guy de Maupassant's story "The Necklace," you might well find yourself in the position of a Marxist–feminist–New Historicist critic. That's fine. Writing with the knowledge that you are drawing from Marxism, feminism, and New Historicism, you will almost certainly write a better-organized, better-informed, and more thorough paper than you would have had you begun with no conscious basis in literary theory.

Take a look at the annotations and notes you have made on literary works, the notes you have taken in class, and any exams or papers you have written. Are there particular themes and issues to which you keep returning, particular genres or literary features that continue to attract or interest you? If so, you may have the beginning of an answer to the question: *What sort of literary critic am I?*

Biographical Notes on the Authors
[Arranged Alphabetically]

Born the fifth of six children to Igbo parents in Nigeria, **Chimamanda Ngozi Adichie** (b. 1977) grew up in the former house of fellow Nigerian writer Chinua Achebe. She came to the United States at the age of nineteen and completed a B.A. at Eastern Connecticut State University and an M.A. in creative writing from the Writing Seminars at Johns Hopkins University. She published her first novel, *Purple Hibiscus*, in 2003 and her second novel, *Half of a Yellow Sun*, in 2006. After serving as a Hodder Fellow at Princeton University and completing an M.A. in African studies at Yale University, she published her short-story collection *The Thing around Your Neck* in 2009. She splits her time between the United States and Nigeria and was awarded a fellowship by Radcliffe Institute for Advanced Study, Harvard University, for 2011–2012.

Self-described as one-half Japanese, one-eighth Choctaw, one-fourth black, and one-sixteenth Irish, **Ai** (1947–2010) was born Florence Anthony in Albany, Texas, and grew up in Tucson, Arizona. She legally changed her name to "Ai," which means "love" in Japanese. She received a B.A. in Japanese from the University of Arizona and an M.F.A. from the University of California at Irvine. She was the author of nine volumes of poetry, among them *Vice* (1999), which won the National Book Award for Poetry. She taught at Wayne State University, George Mason University, the University of Kentucky, and Oklahoma State University. Her last book was *No Surrender* (2010).

Of Spokane/Coeur d'Alene Native American descent, **Sherman Alexie** (b. 1966) was born on the Spokane Indian Reservation in Wellpinit, Washington. He earned his B.A. from Washington State University in Pullman. He has published eleven books of poetry, most recently *Face* (2009); three novels, of which *Flight* (2007) is the latest; and four collections of short fiction, including *The Lone Ranger and Tonto Fistfight in Heaven* (1993), *Ten Little Indians* (2003), and *War Dances* (2009). His first novel for young adults, *The Absolutely True Diary of a Part-Time Indian*, received the 2007 National Book Award for Young People's Literature.

Agha Shahid Ali (1949–2001) was born in New Delhi and grew up Muslim in Kashmir. He was educated at the University of Kashmir, Srinagar, and at the University of Delhi. He earned a Ph.D. from Pennsylvania State University in 1984 and an M.F.A. from the University of Arizona in 1985. He was a poet (author of eight books of poetry), critic (author of *T. S. Eliot as Editor* [1986]), translator (*The Rebel's Silhouette: Selected Poems* by Faiz Ahmed Faiz [1992]), and editor (*Ravishing Disunities: Real Ghazals in English*

1281

[2000]). He held teaching positions at the University of Delhi and at several colleges and universities in the United States. "I Dream It Is Afternoon When I Return to Delhi" (p. 658) shows Ali's use of Western formal cultural principles in work that focuses on his own cultural background.

Julia Alvarez (b. 1950) was born in New York City, lived in the Dominican Republic until she was ten, and returned to New York when her father had to flee because he was involved in a plot to overthrow the dictator Rafael Trujillo. Thus she needed to adjust to a new culture and a new language. Since childhood she says she has loved stories — hearing them and telling them — so it was natural for her to decide to become a writer. She graduated from Middlebury College in Vermont and earned an M.A. in creative writing from Syracuse University. Since 1998 she has been writer-in-residence at Middlebury. Alvarez has published five novels, many short stories, numerous books for young readers, four volumes of poetry, and a book of essays about herself and her writing life, *Something to Declare* (1998).

Matthew Arnold (1822–1888) was born in the small English village of Laleham and raised at Rugby School, where his father was headmaster. He attended Oxford University and, in 1857, was elected professor of poetry at Oxford, a position he held for ten years, writing mostly literary criticism. He also worked for thirty-five years as an inspector of schools and made two lecture tours of the United States.

Margaret Atwood (b. 1939) was born in Ottawa and grew up in northern Ontario, Quebec, and Toronto. She began writing while attending high school in Toronto. She received her undergraduate degree from Victoria College at the University of Toronto and her master's degree from Radcliffe College. She won the E. J. Pratt Medal for her privately printed book of poems, *Double Persephone* (1961), and has published sixteen more collections of poetry. She is perhaps best known for her thirteen novels, which include *The Handmaid's Tale* (1983), *The Robber Bride* (1994), and *The Blind Assassin* (2000; winner of the Booker Prize). She has also published ten collections of short stories, six children's books, and six books of nonfiction and edited several anthologies. Her work has been translated into more than thirty languages, including Farsi, Japanese, Turkish, Finnish, Korean, Icelandic, and Estonian.

W. H. [Wystan Hugh] Auden (1907–1973) was born in York, England. He attended private school and later Oxford University, where he began to write poetry. He supported himself by teaching and publishing, writing books based on his travels to Iceland, Spain, and China. He also wrote (with Chester Kallman) several librettos, including the one in Igor Stravinsky's *The Rake's Progress* (1951). He lived in the United States from 1939 until his death, having become a U.S. citizen in 1946. His work combines lively intelligence, quick wit, careful craftsmanship, and social concern.

Jimmy Santiago Baca (b. 1952) was born in Sante Fe, New Mexico, of Chicano and Apache heritage. Abandoned by his parents at the age of two, he lived with one of his grandparents for several years before being placed in an orphanage. He lived on the streets as a youth and was imprisoned for six years for drug possession. In prison, he taught himself to read and write and began to compose poetry. A fellow inmate convinced him to submit some of his poems for publication. He has since published a dozen books of poetry, a memoir, a collection of stories and essays, a play, a screenplay, and a novel. He lives outside Albuquerque in a hundred-year-old adobe house.

Born in New York City, the son of a revivalist minister, **James Baldwin** (1924–1987) was raised in poverty in Harlem, where, at the age of fourteen, he became a preacher in the Fireside Pentecostal Church. After completing high school, he decided to become a writer and, with the help of the black American expatriate writer Richard Wright, won a grant that enabled him to move to Paris, where he lived for most of his remaining years. There he wrote the critically acclaimed *Go Tell It on the Mountain* (1953), a novel about the religious awakening of a fourteen-year-old black youth. Subsequent works, focusing on the intellectual and spiritual trials of black men in a white, racist society, included the novels *Giovanni's Room* (1956), *Another Country* (1962)—both famous at the time for their homosexual themes— *Tell Me How Long the Train's Been Gone* (1968), *If Beale Street Could Talk* (1974), *Just Above My Head* (1979), and *Harlem Quartet* (1987); the play *Blues for Mister Charlie* (1964); and the powerful nonfiction commentaries *Notes of a Native Son* (1955), *Nobody Knows My Name* (1961), and *The Fire Next Time* (1963). Baldwin's short stories are collected in *Going to Meet the Man* (1965).

Born in New York City and raised in Harlem, **Toni Cade Bambara** (1939–1995) attended Queens College, where she wrote stories, poems, scripts, and other works and was part of the staff of the literary magazine. She continued writing stories as she studied for an M.A. at City College. After her story collection *Gorilla, My Love* (1972) was published, her sense of herself as a black writer gradually clarified and deepened. Her other story collections include *The Black Woman* (1970), *Tales and Stories for Black Folks* (1971), and *The Sea Birds Are Still Alive* (1977). Her two novels are *The Salt Eaters* (1980) and *If Blessing Comes* (1987). *Deep Sightings and Rescue Missions*, a collection of fiction and nonfiction, appeared posthumously, in 1996.

Jim Barnes (b. 1933), born in Oklahoma of Choctaw and Welsh heritage, worked for ten years as a lumberjack. He studied at Southeastern Oklahoma State University and received his M.A. and Ph.D. from the University of Arkansas. He has published many books of poetry, most recently *Visiting Picasso* (2006); several books of translations and criticism; and over five hundred poems in more than a hundred journals, including *Chicago Review*, *American Scholar*, *Prairie Schooner*, and *Georgia Review*. He is the founding editor of the Chariton Review Press and editor of *Chariton Review*. He taught at Truman State University from 1970 to 2003, then at Brigham Young University, and presently lives in Santa Fe.

Wendell Berry (b. 1934) was born in Henry County, Kentucky, the first of four children born to Virginia and John Berry, a lawyer and tobacco farmer. His families have farmed in Henry County for five generations. He attended Millersburg Military Institute, earned his B.A. and M.A. from the University of Kentucky, and was a Wallace Stegner

Fellow at Stanford University. A prolific author of poetry, essays, short stories, and novels, he is also recognized for his academic, cultural, environmental, and economic criticism. Since 1965 he has farmed his 125-acre homestead, Lane's Landing. His work focuses on the life that he deeply values, one that includes sustainable agriculture, community, a connection to place, local economics, good work, and the interconnectedness of all life. He most recently published *What Matters? Economics for a Renewed Commonwealth* (2010), in which he argues for agricultural policy reform, and *The Poetry of William Carlos Williams of Rutherford* (2011), a reflection on one of his major influences.

Born in Worcester, Massachusetts, **Elizabeth Bishop** (1911–1979) was raised in Nova Scotia by her grandparents after her father died and her mother was committed to an asylum. She attended Vassar College intending to study medicine but was encouraged by MARIANNE MOORE to be a poet. From 1935 to 1937, she traveled in France, Spain, northern Africa, Ireland, and Italy. She settled in Key West, Florida, for four years and then in Rio de Janeiro for almost twenty years. She wrote slowly and carefully, producing a small body of technically sophisticated, formally varied, witty, and thoughtful poetry, revealing in precise, true-to-life images her impressions of the physical world. She served as Consultant in Poetry at the Library of Congress from 1949 to 1950.[1]

[1]The first appointment of a Consultant in Poetry at the Library of Congress was made in 1937. The title was changed to Poet Laureate Consultant in Poetry in 1986. Appointments are made for one year, beginning in September, and sometimes have been renewed for a second year.

William Blake (1757–1827) was born and raised in London. His only formal schooling was in art—he studied for a year at the Royal Academy and was apprenticed to an engraver. He later worked as a professional engraver, doing commissions and illustrations, assisted by his wife, Catherine Boucher. Blake, who had started writing poetry at the age of eleven, later engraved and handprinted his own poems, in very small batches, with his own illustrations. His early work was possessed of a strong social conscience, and his mature work turned increasingly mythic and prophetic.

Eavan Boland (b. 1944) was born in Dublin and educated there as well as in London and New York. She has taught at Trinity College and University College, Dublin; Bowdoin College; and the University of Iowa. She is currently the Bella Mabury and Eloise Mabury Knapp Professor in Humanities and the Melvin and Bill Lane Professor and Director of the Creative Writing Program at Stanford University. An influential figure in Irish poetry, Boland has published a dozen volumes of poetry, including *The Journey and Other Poems* (1987), *Night Feed* (1994), *The Lost Land* (1998), *Code* (2001), *New Collected Poems* (2005), and *Domestic Violence* (2007), and has edited several other books, including *Three Irish Poets: An Anthology* (2003) and *Irish Writers on Writing* (2007). Her poems and essays have appeared in magazines such as *The New Yorker*, *The Atlantic*, *Kenyon Review*, and *American Poetry Review*. A collection of essays, *A Journey with Two Maps: Becoming a Woman Poet*, was published in 2011. She is a regular reviewer for the *Irish Times*.

Born into a working-class family in New York State, **T. Coraghessan Boyle**

(b. 1948) earned a bachelor's degree from the State University of New York at Potsdam before completing his M.F.A. at the University of Iowa Writers' Workshop. His writing is often satirical and employs irony and surrealist imagery contrasted against the more mundane aspects of the baby boomer generation he usually chronicles. He has published thirteen novels and eight short-story collections. His work regularly appears in *Harper's*, *The New Yorker*, and *The Atlantic*, among other magazines, and has received numerous awards. He joined the faculty at the University of Southern California in 1978 and serves as Distinguished Professor of English there.

Born in Northampton, England, **Anne Bradstreet** (1612–1672) was educated by tutors, reading chiefly religious writings and the Bible. In 1628 she married Simon Bradstreet, a brilliant young Puritan educated at Cambridge. They were among the earliest settlers of the Massachusetts Bay Colony, in 1630, and her father and husband were leading figures in its governance. She wrote regularly in both prose and verse throughout her busy and difficult years in Massachusetts.

Born in Topeka, Kansas, **Gwendolyn Brooks** (1917–2000) was raised in Chicago and wrote her first poems at age seven. She began studying poetry at the Southside Community Art Center. Her second collection of poems, *Annie Allen* (1949), earned the first Pulitzer Prize given to an African American poet. She served as Consultant in Poetry at the Library of Congress from 1985 to 1986 and worked in community programs and poetry workshops in Chicago to encourage young African American writers.

Olga Broumas (b. 1949) was born in Hermoupolis, Greece, and immigrated to the United States in 1967. She studied at the University of Pennsylvania and the University of Oregon and has taught at the University of Oregon, the University of Idaho, and Boston University. She was the first non-native speaker of English to be selected for the Yale Younger Poets Series when Stanley Kunitz chose her in 1977. Her poetry, often containing echoes of Greek mythology, deals openly with homosexuality and eroticism. Broumas founded Freehand, Inc., a community for female artists located on Cape Cod, where she spends her summers. Since 1995 she has served as poet-in-residence and Director of Creative Writing at Brandeis University.

Born in Durham, England, **Elizabeth Barrett Browning** (1806–1861) studied with her brother's tutor. Her first book of poetry was published when she was thirteen, and she soon became the most famous female poet up until that time in English history. A riding accident at the age of sixteen left her a semi-invalid in the home of her possessive father, who forbade any of his eleven children to marry. At age thirty-nine, Elizabeth eloped with ROBERT BROWNING; the couple lived in Florence, Italy, where Elizabeth died fifteen years later. Her best-known book of poems is *Sonnets from the Portuguese*, a sequence of forty-four sonnets recording the growth of her love for her husband.

Robert Browning (1812–1889) was the son of a bank clerk in Camberwell, then a suburb of London. As an aspiring poet in 1844, Browning admired ELIZABETH BARRETT's poetry and began a correspondence with her that led to one of the world's most famous romances. His and Elizabeth's courtship lasted until 1846, when they secretly wed and ran off to Italy, where they lived until Elizabeth's death in 1861. The years in Florence were among the happiest for both of them. To her he dedicated *Men and Women* (1855), which contains his best poetry. Although she was the more popular poet during their time together, his reputation grew upon his return to London, after her death, assisted somewhat by public sympathy for him. The late 1860s were the peak of his career: he and TENNYSON were mentioned together as the foremost poets of the age.

Robert Burns (1759–1796) was born in Ayrshire in southwestern Scotland, the son of a poor farming family. His formal education lasted only to about his ninth year, when he was needed to work on the farm, but he read widely and voraciously whenever he could find time. His first book of poems, published in 1785, sold out within a month. Despite living in poverty, Burns poured out a flood of his finest poems in the early 1790s. He is regarded as Scotland's national bard for his ability to depict with loving accuracy the life of his fellow rural Scots. His use of dialect brought a stimulating, much-needed freshness and raciness into English poetry, but his greatness extends beyond the limits of dialect: his poems are written about Scots, but in tune with the rising humanitarianism of his day, they apply to a multitude of universal problems.

Byron—see George Gordon, Lord Byron.

Born in Clatskanie, Oregon, **Raymond Carver** (1938–1988) lived in Port Angeles, Washington, until his death. Among the honors accorded this short-story writer and poet during his lifetime were a 1979 Guggenheim fellowship, two grants from the National Endowment for the Arts, and election to the American Academy of Arts and Letters. Carver's writing, known for its spare, stark depiction of contemporary existence, has been translated into more than twenty languages. His story collections are *Will You Please Be Quiet, Please?* (1976), nominated for a National Book Award; *Furious Seasons* (1977); *What We Talk About When We Talk About Love* (1981); *Cathedral* (1983), nominated for the Pulitzer Prize; and *Where I'm Calling From* (1988).

Born near Winchester, Virginia, **Willa Cather** (1873–1947), as a child, moved with her family to a ranch outside Red Cloud, Nebraska, a prairie frontier town. After attending high school there, she studied classics at the University of Nebraska. She then moved east; worked on a Pittsburgh newspaper; taught school in Allegheny, Pennsylvania; worked at the magazine *McClure's*, first on the staff, then as managing editor; and wrote poetry and fiction. After a volume of poetry, she wrote *The Troll Garden* (1905), a collection of stories, and *Alexander's Bridge* (1912), her first novel. Thereafter, Cather wrote full-time, often returning to western communities and landscapes for her subject; with them she felt she could plumb her own experience and examine the frontier spirit. Among the many works that followed are stories, story collections, and novels including *O Pioneers!* (1913), *Song of the Lark* (1915), *My Ántonia* (1918), *One of Ours* (Pulitzer Prize, 1923), and *Death Comes for the Archbishop* (1927). Among her many honors is a gold medal from the National Institute of Arts and Letters (1944).

Lorna Dee Cervantes (b. 1954) was born in San Francisco and grew up in San Jose. There she studied at San Jose City College and San Jose State University. She is the author of two volumes of poetry, *Emplumada* (1981), which won an American Book Award, and *From the Cables of Genocide: Poems on Love and Hunger* (1991). She is also coeditor of *Red Dirt*, a cross-cultural poetry journal, and her work has been included in many anthologies. Cervantes, who considers herself "a Chicana writer, a feminist writer, a political writer," lives in Colorado and was a professor at the University of Colorado at Boulder.

Born the son of a grocer and the grandson of a serf in Taganrog, a seacoast town in southern Russia, **Anton Chekhov** (1860–1904) began writing humorous tales to support himself while studying medicine at Moscow University. In 1884 he received his medical degree and published his first collection of short stories, *Tales of Melpomene*. Other early collections are *Motley Tales* (1886), *At Twilight* (1887), and *Stones* (1888). Besides being a masterful writer of short stories, Chekhov is probably Russia's most esteemed playwright. In 1898 the Moscow Art Theatre produced his play *The Seagull*, followed by *Uncle Vanya* in 1899, *The Three Sisters* in 1901, and *The Cherry Orchard* in 1904. Chekhov, known for his sad and subtle exploration of people's inability to communicate as well as for his humanitarian activities, died at age forty-four of tuberculosis, which he contracted in his student days.

A first-generation Chinese American, **Marilyn Chin** (b. 1955) was born in Hong Kong and raised in Portland, Oregon. She is the author of three volumes of poetry, *Dwarf Bamboo* (1987), *The Phoenix Gone, The Terrace Empty* (1994), and *Rhapsody in Plain Yellow* (2002); and a novel, *Revenge of the Mooncake Vixen* (2009). She also is a coeditor of *Dissident Song: A Contemporary Asian American Anthology* (1991) and has translated poems by the modern Chinese poet Ai Qing and cotranslated poems by the Japanese poet Gozo Yoshimasu. She has received numerous awards for her poetry, including a Stegner fellowship, the PEN/Josephine Miles Award, and four Pushcart Prizes. She is codirector of the M.F.A. program at San Diego State University.

Born Katherine O'Flaherty, the daughter of a French Creole mother and a prosperous St. Louis businessman who died when she was four, **Kate Chopin** (1851–1904) was raised by her mother and a great-grandmother who sent her to Catholic school and trained her for a place in St. Louis society. At the age of eighteen, she married Oscar Chopin and accompanied him to New Orleans, where he became a cotton broker. When her husband's business failed, the family moved to a plantation in northern Louisiana and opened a general store, which Kate managed for a year after her husband's death in 1883. She then returned to St. Louis with her six children and began a career as a writer of realistic fiction. Among her works are the story collections *Bayou Folk* (1894) and *A Night in Acadie* (1897) as well as the novel *The Awakening* (1899), shocking in its time for its frank portrayal of adultery but widely praised today for its sensitive portrayal of a woman's need for independence and sensual fulfillment.

Born in a Hispanic neighborhood in Chicago, **Sandra Cisneros** (b. 1954) spoke Spanish at home with her Mexican father, Chicana mother, and six brothers. At ten she began writing poetry, and soon experimented with other forms. In 1977, when she was studying in the M.F.A. program at the University of Iowa Writers' Workshop, she came to see herself as a Chicana writer. Cisneros has published three books of poems; a book of interrelated narratives, *The House on Mango Street* (1983); a fiction collection, *Woman Hollering Creek and Other Stories* (1991); and a novel, *Carmelo* (2002).

Lucille Clifton (1936–2010) was born in Depew, New York, and studied at Howard University. She published many books of poetry, including *Blessing the Boats: New and Selected Poems, 1988–2000* (2000), which won the National Book Award. She also published a memoir and more than twenty books for children. She taught at several colleges, worked in the Office of Education in Washington, D.C., served as poet laureate for the state of Maryland, and was Distinguished Professor of Humanities at St. Mary's College of Maryland. Her poems typically reflect her ethnic pride, womanist principles, and race and gender consciousness.

Judith Ortiz Cofer (b. 1952) was born in Hormigueros, Puerto Rico. Her family moved to Paterson, New Jersey, in 1955. For the next decade, she grew up moving between those two very different worlds. She graduated from Augusta College in Georgia, married and had a daughter, completed a graduate degree, and began teaching En-

glish. But, she says, something was missing from her life: she realized that she needed to write. Her first book of poetry, *Reaching for the Mainland* (1987), was followed by several others, including, most recently, *A Love Story Beginning in Spanish: Poems* (2006). She has also published novels for adults; a memoir, *Silent Dancing: A Partial Remembrance of a Puerto Rican Childhood* (1990); and a book about writing, *Woman in Front of the Sun: On Becoming a Writer* (2000). She has written several award-winning books for young adults, including *An Island Like You: Stories of the Barrio* (1996). She is Regents' and Franklin Professor of English and Creative Writing at the University of Georgia and lives with her husband on the family farm near Louisville, Georgia.

Samuel Taylor Coleridge (1772–1834) was born in Devonshire and sent to school in London after his father's death. He went to Jesus College, Cambridge, in 1791 and dropped out twice without a degree. In 1798 Coleridge and WILLIAM WORDSWORTH published *Lyrical Ballads*, which initiated the Romantic movement in English poetry and established both poets' reputations. After 1802 Coleridge became addicted to opium, which he used to treat physical discomfort and seizures. He and his wife separated, his friendship with Wordsworth ended, and he stopped producing poetry. From 1816 until his death, Coleridge lived under constant medical supervision and yet still published a journal and wrote several plays, pieces of criticism, and philosophical and religious treatises.

Born and raised in New York City, **Billy Collins** (b. 1941) is the author of several collections of poems. Perhaps no poet since ROBERT FROST has managed to combine high critical acclaim with such broad popular appeal. The typical Collins poem opens on a clear and hospitable note but soon takes an unexpected turn; poems that begin in irony may end in a moment of lyric surprise. Collins sees his poetry as "a form of travel writing" and considers humor "a door into the serious." Collins is the author of numerous books of poetry, most recently *She Was Just Seventeen* (2006) and *Ballistics* (2008). In 2009 he edited, with illustrator David Sibley, *Bright Wings: An Illustrated Anthology of Poems about Birds*. He served as Poet Laureate Consultant in Poetry at the Library of Congress from 2001 to 2003 and as New York State Poet Laureate from 2004 to 2006. He has taught at Columbia University, Sarah Lawrence College, and Lehman College, City University of New York.

Countee Cullen (1903–1946) was born either in Louisville, Kentucky; Baltimore, Maryland; or, as he himself claimed, New York City. He was adopted by the Reverend Frederick A. Cullen and his wife and grew up, as he put it, "in the conservative atmosphere of a Methodist parsonage." He studied at New York University and Harvard University. A forerunner of the Harlem Renaissance movement, he was, in the 1920s, the most popular black literary figure in America. From the 1930s until his death, he wrote less while working as a junior high school French teacher. For many years, Cullen's reputation was eclipsed by that of other Harlem Renaissance writers, particularly LANGSTON HUGHES and ZORA NEALE HURSTON; recently, however, there has been a resurgence of interest in Cullen's life and work.

E. E. Cummings (1894–1962) was born in Cambridge, Massachusetts, where his father was a Unitarian minister and a sociology lecturer at Harvard University. He graduated from Harvard and then served as an ambulance driver during World War I. *The Enormous Room* (1922) is an account of his confinement in a French prison camp during the war. After the war, he lived in rural Connecticut and Greenwich Village, with frequent visits to Paris. In his work, Cummings experimented radically with form, punctuation, spelling, and syntax, abandoning traditional techniques and structures to create a new, highly idiosyncratic means of poetic expression. At the time of his death in 1962, he was the second most widely read poet in the United States after ROBERT FROST.

Born and raised in Detroit, **Toi Derricotte** (b. 1941) earned a B.A. in special education from Wayne State University and an M.A. in English literature from New York University. She is the author of several collections of poetry as well as a memoir, *The Black Notebooks* (1997). With poet CORNELIUS EADY, she cofounded Cave Canem, which offers workshops and retreats for African American poets. Among the many honors she has received is the Distinguished Pioneering of the Arts Award from United Black Artists. Derricotte teaches creative writing at the University of Pittsburgh.

Junot Díaz (b. 1968) immigrated to the United States from the Dominican Republic at the age of six. He worked his way through Rutgers University by pumping gas, washing dishes, and performing a variety of other odd jobs. He later received an M.F.A. from Cornell University. He published his first story collection, *Drown*, in 1996, and several years later *The New Yorker* named him one of the top twenty writers of the twenty-first century. His debut novel, *The Brief Wondrous Life of Oscar Wao*, was published in 1997 to critical acclaim and won the Pulitzer Prize. Díaz's writing often deals with the tensions of the immigrant experience and the two cultures he has had to negotiate. He currently teaches creative writing at MIT and is the fiction editor for *The Boston Review*.

Emily Dickinson (1830–1886) was born in Amherst, Massachusetts, and lived there her entire life, leaving only rarely. She briefly attended a woman's seminary but became homesick and left before a year was out. Dickinson never married and became reclusive later in life, forgoing even the village routines and revelries she once had enjoyed. She published very few of the more than 1,700 poems she wrote; most were written for herself or for inclusion in her many letters. It was not until 1955 that a complete edition of the verses, attempting to present them as they were originally written, appeared.

Born in London to a prosperous Catholic family (through his mother he was related to statesman and author Sir Thomas More and the playwright John Heywood), **John Donne** (1572–1631) studied at Oxford University for several years but did not take a degree. He fought with Sir Walter Raleigh in two naval strikes against Spain. In 1601 Donne's promising political career was permanently derailed by his precipitate marriage to Anne More without her father's consent. He was briefly imprisoned, lost a very promising position with Sir Thomas Egerton, and spent years seeking political employment before finally being persuaded by King James I in 1615 to become a priest of the Church of England. His life was described by Isaac Walton later in the century as having been divided into two parts. In phase one, he was "Jack Donne" of Lincoln's Inn: when young, Donne employed a sophisticated urban wit that lent a sort of jaded tone to his earlier poetry. "A Valediction: Forbidding Mourning" presumably appeared during this stage of his life and is a typical metaphysical poem. In phase two, he was John Donne, dean of St. Paul's: after Donne took holy orders in 1615, his poetry became markedly less amorous and more religious in tone. His Holy Sonnets, of which "Death, be not proud" is one, are as dense and complex as his earlier work but directed toward an exploration of his relationship with God.

Mark Doty (b. 1953) is the author of twelve collections of poetry and three memoirs—*Heaven's Coast* (1996), about the loss of his partner, Wally Roberts; *Firebird* (1999), a gay coming-of-age story that chronicles the gradual process of finding in art a place of personal belonging; and *Dog Years* (2007), about the relationships between humans and the dogs they love. He has taught at Brandeis University, Sarah Lawrence College, Vermont College, and the University of Iowa Writers' Workshop. He now divides his time between New York City and Fire Island, New York, and he teaches at Rutgers University.

Rita Dove (b. 1952) was born in Akron, Ohio; her father was the first research chemist to break the race barrier in the tire industry. She graduated from Miami University in Oxford, Ohio, with a degree in English; after a year at

Tübingen University in Germany on a Fulbright fellowship, she enrolled in the University of Iowa Writers' Workshop, where she earned her M.F.A. in 1977. She has taught at Tuskegee Institute and Arizona State University and now is on the faculty of the University of Virginia. In 1993 she was appointed Poet Laureate Consultant in Poetry at the Library of Congress, making her the youngest person—and the first African American woman—to receive this highest official honor in American letters. She is the author of numerous collections of poetry, including *Thomas and Beulah* (1986), a book-length sequence loosely based on the lives of her grandparents, which was awarded the Pulitzer Prize in 1987.

Paul Laurence Dunbar (1872–1906) was the first African American to gain national eminence as a poet. Born and raised in Dayton, Ohio, the son of former slaves, he was an outstanding student. The only African American in his class, he was both class president and class poet. Although he lived to be only thirty-three years old, Dunbar was prolific, writing short stories, novels, librettos, plays, songs, and essays as well as the poetry for which he became well known. Popular with both black and white readers of his day, Dunbar's style encompasses two distinct voices—the standard English of the classical poet and the evocative dialect of the turn-of-the-twentieth-century black community in America.

Born in Oakland, California, **Robert Duncan** (1919–1988) was raised by adoptive parents who were devout theosophists and who instilled in him a lifelong interest in occult spirituality. He entered the University of California at Berkeley in 1936 and was drawn to leftist politics and a bohemian lifestyle. Drafted in 1941, he was discharged after declaring his homosexuality. His 1944 essay "The Homosexual in Society" compared the situation faced by homosexuals in modern society to that of blacks and Jews. Influenced by a variety of poets, Duncan credited his long correspondence with DENISE LEVERTOV with helping him find a new poetics—a magical, mystical blend of the experimental and the traditional. His first book, *Heavenly City, Earthly City*, was published in 1947, the same year he met Charles Olson, whose literary theories helped shape Duncan's "grand collage" concept of verse. He returned to San Francisco in 1948, becoming part of the San Francisco Renaissance and cultivating the role of a guru, discoursing on literature, spiritualism, and sexual diversity. He became affiliated with Olson's Black Mountain movement and taught at Black Mountain College in 1956. His reputation as a poet was established by three major collections: *The Opening of the Field* (1960), *Roots and Branches* (1964), and *Bending the Bow* (1968). He was awarded the Harriet Monroe Memorial Prize in 1961, a Guggenheim fellowship in 1963, the Levinson Prize in 1964, and the National Poetry Award in 1985.

Born and raised in Rochester, New York, **Cornelius Eady** (b. 1954) attended Monroe Community College and Empire State College. He began writing as a teenager. His poems are his biography, their subjects ranging from blues musicians to Eady's witnessing his father's death. He has published six volumes of poetry. With poet TOI DERRICOTTE, he cofounded Cave Canem, which offers workshops and retreats for African American poets, and with composer Diedre Murray he has collaborated on two highly acclaimed music-dramas. Formerly the director of the Poetry Center at the State University of New York, Stony Brook, he is currently Associate Professor of English and Director of the Creative Writing Program at the University of Notre Dame.

Born and raised in St. Louis, **T. S. [Thomas Stearns] Eliot** (1888–1965) went to prep school in Massachusetts and then to Harvard University, where he earned an M.A. in philosophy in 1910 and started his doctoral dissertation. He studied at the Sorbonne, in Paris, and then in Marburg, Germany, in 1914, when the war forced him to leave. Relocating to Oxford, he abandoned philosophy for poetry, and he married. After teaching and working in a bank, he became an editor at Faber and Faber and editor of the journal *Criterion* and was the dominant force in English poetry for several decades. He became a British citizen and a member of the Church of England in 1927. He won the Nobel Prize in Literature in 1948. He also wrote plays and essays as well as a series of poems on cats that became the basis of a musical by Andrew Lloyd Weber. The Eliot poems included in this anthology show the poet's use of collage techniques to relate the fragmentation he saw in the culture and individual psyches of his day.

Ralph Ellison (1914–1994) was born in Oklahoma City. His father, an ice and coal vendor, died when Ralph was three; his mother supported herself and her son with domestic work. After studying music at the Tuskegee Institute, in 1936 Ellison went to New York City, where, encouraged by the novelist Richard Wright, he became associated with the Federal Writers' Project. His first novel, *Invisible Man* (1952), received a 1953 National Book Award and became a classic in American fiction. Ellison taught literature and writing at Bard College, the University of Chicago, Rutgers University, and New York University. His other works include the collections of essays *Shadow and Act* (1964) and *Going to the Territory* (1986), and three posthumous works prepared by John F. Callahan: *The Collected Essays of Ralph Ellison* (1995); *Flying Home and Other Stories* (1996), a short-story collection; and *Juneteenth* (1999), a novel shaped and edited by Callahan from manuscripts left unfinished when Ellison died.

Born in Long Beach, California, of Yaqui and European ancestry, **Anita Endrezze** (b. 1952) earned her M.A. from Eastern Washington University. She is a poet, writer, storyteller, teacher, and painter (in watercolor and acrylics) who also works in fiber and creates handmade books. She is a member of Atlatl, a Native American arts service organization. In addition to four volumes of poetry, she has published a children's novel, short stories, and nonfiction. She lives in Everett, Washington, where she is a storyteller, teacher, and writer.

Born in Brooklyn, New York, **Martín Espada** (b. 1957) has an eclectic résumé: radio journalist in Nicaragua, welfare-rights paralegal, advocate for the mentally ill, night desk clerk in a transient hotel, attendant in a primate nursery, groundskeeper at a minor league ballpark, bindery worker in a printing plant, bouncer in a bar, and practicing lawyer in Chelsea, Massachusetts. He is the author of eight books of poetry, most recently *The Republic of Poetry* (2006). His earlier book, *Alabanza: New and Selected Poems, 1982–2002* (2003), received the Paterson Award for Sustained Literary Achievement and was named an American Library Association Notable Book of the Year. He is an essayist, editor, and translator as well as a poet. He presently teaches at the University of Massachusetts, Amherst.

Born in New Albany, Mississippi, **William Faulkner** (1897–1962) moved as a young boy to Oxford, Mississippi, the place he was to call home for the rest of his life. He completed two years of high school and a little more than one year at the University of Mississippi. After a brief stint in the Royal Air Force in Canada during World War I, he worked at various jobs before becoming a writer. His first book, *The Marble Faun* (1924), was a collection of poems. Encouraged by the writer Sherwood Anderson, whom he met in New Orleans in 1925, Faulkner wrote his first novel, *Soldier's Pay* (1926), a work that was favorably reviewed. His third novel, *Sartoris* (1929), was the first set in Yoknapatawpha County, a fictional re-creation of the area around Oxford whose setting appeared throughout his later fiction. Over three decades Faulkner published nineteen novels, more than eighty short stories, and collections of poems and essays; he also wrote several film scripts to supplement his income. Collections of his short fiction include *Go Down, Moses* (1942); *Collected Stones* (1950), which won a National Book Award; and *Big Woods* (1955). Among his best-known novels are *The Sound and the Fury* (1929), *As I Lay Dying* (1930), *Sanctuary* (1931), *Light in August* (1932), and *Absalom, Absalom!* (1936). Faulkner

was awarded the Nobel Prize in Literature in 1949; *A Fable* (1954) and *The Reivers* (1962) each won the Pulitzer Prize for fiction.

Born on September 24, 1896, in St. Paul, Minnesota, **F. Scott Fitzgerald** (1896–1940) was a spoiled, undisciplined child and a failure at school. He began writing at an early age and while attending the Newman School had one of his plays produced in an amateur performance. At Princeton University, he worked on musical productions for the Triangle Club and wrote stories and poems, some of which were published by his friend and collaborator Edmund Wilson in the *Nassau Literary Magazine*, which Wilson edited. At the beginning of his senior year, he left Princeton to report for officer's training at Fort Leavenworth, Kansas. After basic training, he was stationed at Camp Sheridan, Alabama, and there met and fell in love with the southern belle Zelda Sayre. In 1920 his first novel, *This Side of Paradise*, was published; it brought Fitzgerald fame and financial success. As a result of his newfound wealth, he and Zelda were able to marry and lead a glamorous, extravagant life, traveling back and forth between New York and Europe. *The Great Gatsby*, published in 1925 to critical acclaim, was probably his greatest novel, but it was a financial disappointment. His life at this time was in disorder: he was plagued by increasing alcoholism and Zelda's deterioration into madness, as well as by severe financial difficulties. After 1930 Zelda was intermittently institutionalized. In 1932 she published *Save Me the Waltz*, a novel describing the Fitzgeralds' life together as seen through her eyes. Fitzgerald's final years were spent in Hollywood trying to support himself by writing film scripts. There he met and had a love affair with the English journalist and columnist Sheilah Graham. He died in her apartment of a heart attack on December 21, 1940. His other novels include *Tender Is the Night* (1934) and *The Last Tycoon*, unfinished at the time of his death but edited by his friend Edmund Wilson and published posthumously in 1941. In addition, several collections of his short stories have been published.

Born in Detroit, **Carolyn Forché** (b. 1950) attended Michigan State University and earned an M.F.A. from Bowling Green State University. She achieved immediate success as a writer, winning the Yale Younger Poets prize in 1976. Her work underwent a remarkable change following a year spent in El Salvador on a Guggenheim fellowship, when she worked with human rights activist Archbishop Oscar Humberto Romero and with Amnesty International. After seeing countless atrocities committed in Central America, Forché began writing what she calls "poetry of witness." The volume *The Country between Us* (1981) stirred immediate controversy because of its overtly political topics and themes. "The Colonel," a prose poem in which the speaker conveys a horrific story with chilling flatness, is probably the most disturbing and memorable poem in the collection. She is the author of four books of poetry, most recently *Blue Hour* (2004), and the editor of *Against Forgetting: Twentieth-Century Poetry of Witness* (1993). She has also translated several books of poetry. She is a faculty member at George Mason University, in Virginia.

Robert Francis (1901–1987) lived most of his life in a one-room house just outside Amherst, Massachusetts, that he named "Fort Juniper." The University of Massachusetts Press later named its poetry award the Juniper Prize in his honor. He spent his childhood in Pennsylvania before attending Harvard University. He later served as Phi Beta Kappa poet both at Harvard and at Tufts University. He was an avid traveler who visited Europe frequently and taught for a period of time at the American University in Beirut, Lebanon. Besides several volumes of poetry, Francis wrote an autobiography, *The Trouble with Francis* (1971); a novel; and criticism.

Robert Frost (1874–1963) was born in San Francisco and lived there until he was eleven. When his father died, the family moved to Massachusetts, where Robert did well in school, especially in the classics, but later dropped out of both Dartmouth College and Harvard University. He went unrecognized as a poet until 1913, when he was first published in England, where he had moved with his wife and four children. Upon returning to the States, Frost quickly achieved success with more publications and became the most celebrated poet in mid-twentieth-century America. He held a teaching position at Amherst College and received many honorary degrees as well as an invitation to recite a poem at John F. Kennedy's inauguration. Although his work is principally associated with the life and landscape of New England, and although he was a poet of traditional verse forms and meters, he is also considered a quintessentially modern poet for his adherence to language as it is actually spoken, the psychological complexity of his portraits, and the degree to which his work is infused with layers of ambiguity and irony.

Richard Garcia (b. 1941) was born in San Francisco, a first-generation American (his mother was from Mexico, his father from Puerto Rico). While still in high school, Garcia had a poem published by City Lights in a Beat anthology. After publishing his first collection in 1972, however, he did not write poetry again for twelve years, until an unsolicited letter from Octavio Paz inspired him to resume. Since then Garcia's work has appeared widely in such literary magazines as the *Kenyon Review, Parnassus,* and the *Gettysburg Review,* as well as in three later collections, *The Flying Garcias* (1991), *Rancho Notorious* (2001), and *The Persistence of Objects* (2006). He is also the author of the bilingual children's book *My Aunt Otilia's Spirits* (1987). For twelve years he was the poet-in-residence at Children's Hospital Los Angeles, where he conducted poetry and art workshops for hospitalized children. He teaches creative writing in the Antioch University Los Angeles M.F.A. program and at the College of Charleston.

Gabriel García Márquez (b. 1928) was born one of twelve children into a poor family in Aracataca, a small village in Colombia, and attended the University of Bogotá. He gave up studying law to pursue a career as a writer, working as a journalist and film critic for *El Espectador,* a Colombian newspaper. His first short novel, *La Hojarasca* (1955; translated as *Leaf Storm* in 1972) was followed by *One Hundred Years of Solitude* (1967), his most famous work. *The Autumn of the Patriarch* (1975) and *Love in the Time of Cholera* (1988) are other novels. A political activist, García Márquez moved to Mexico in 1954, to Barcelona, Spain, in 1973, and back to Mexico in the late 1970s. He was awarded the Nobel Prize in Literature in 1982. The award cited him for novels and short stories "in which the fantastic and the realistic are combined in a richly composed world of imagination, reflecting a continent's life and conflicts." His most recent book is *Memories of My Melancholy Whores* (2005).

Shortly after **Charlotte Perkins Gilman** (1860–1935) was born in Hartford, Connecticut, her father left his family and provided only a small amount of support thereafter. Gilman studied at the Rhode Island School of Design and worked briefly as a commercial artist and teacher. This great-niece of Harriet Beecher Stowe became concerned at quite a young age with issues of social inequality and the circumscribed role of women. In 1884 she married Charles Stetson but left him and moved to California four years later after the birth of a child and a severe depression. Divorced, she married George Gilman, with whom she lived for thirty-five years. In 1935, afflicted by cancer, she took her own life. Charlotte Gilman wrote many influential books and articles about social problems, including *Women and Economics* (1898). From 1909 to 1917, she published her own journal. "The Yellow Wallpaper," written about 1890, draws on her experience with mental illness and has been praised for its insight and boldness.

Born in Newark, New Jersey, **Allen Ginsberg** (1926–1997) graduated from Columbia University, after a number of suspensions, in 1948. Several years later, he left for San Francisco to join other poets of the Beat movement. His poem "Howl," the most famous poem of the movement, was published in 1956 by Lawrence Ferlinghetti's City

Lights Books; the publicity of the ensuing censorship trial brought the Beats to national attention. Ginsberg was co-founder with Anne Waldman of the Jack Kerouac School of Disembodied Poetics at the Naropa Institute in Boulder, Colorado. In his later years, he became a distinguished professor at Brooklyn College.

Born, raised, and educated in Iowa, **Susan Glaspell** (1882–1948) came to be associated with Massachusetts, where she and her husband, George Cram Cook, founded the Provincetown Players on Cape Cod. This small theater company was influential in giving a start to several serious playwrights, most notably Eugene O'Neill, and promoting realist dramas at a time when sentimental comedy and melodrama still dominated the stage. Glaspell began her writing career publishing short stories and novels, including the critically acclaimed *Fidelity* (1915). Glaspell's first several plays, including *Trifles* (1916), were one acts, and with them she began her lifelong interest in writing about the lives and special circumstances of women. She went on to write and produce a number of full-length plays as well, among the best known being *The Inheritors* (1921) and *Alison's House* (1930), which was based loosely on the life of Emily Dickinson and won a Pulitzer Prize. Though some of Glaspell's work was lighthearted, much of it dealt with serious issues of the day. Respected in its own time, Glaspell's writing fell out of fashion until it was "rediscovered" by feminist scholars and critics in the 1960s.

Ray González (b. 1952) received his M.F.A. in creative writing from Southwest Texas State University. He has published ten books of poetry, including *The Heat of Arrivals* (winner of the 1997 Josephine Miles Book Award) and *The Hawk Temple at Tierra Grande*, winner of a 2003 Minnesota Book Award in Poetry. The editor of twelve anthologies, González is also the author of three books of nonfiction—*Memory Fever* (1999); *The Underground Heart* (2002), which received the 2003 Carr P. Collins/Texas Institute of Letters Award for Best Book of Nonfiction; and *Renaming the Earth* (2008)—and two collections of short stories—*The Ghost of John Wayne* (2001) and *Circling the Tortilla Dragon* (2002). He has served as poetry editor for *The Bloomsbury Review* since 1980. He teaches creative writing at the University of Minnesota.

One of the great Romantic poets, **George Gordon, Lord Byron** (1788–1824) is best known for his lighthearted and humorous verse, such as *Don Juan*. Born in London and raised in Scotland, he studied at Harrow and at Trinity College, Cambridge. He inherited the title of sixth baron Byron (with estate) at age ten. The last few years of his life were spent in Italy, but he died in Greece after joining the Greek forces in their war for independence.

Thomas Gray (1716–1771) was born in London and educated at Eton and at Cambridge University, where he studied literature and history. When in November 1741 his father died, Gray moved with his mother and aunt to the village of Stoke Poges, in Buckinghamshire, where he wrote his first important English poems, "Ode on the Spring," "Ode on a Distant Prospect of Eton College," and "Hymn to Adversity," and began his masterpiece, "Elegy Written in a Country Churchyard," called the most famous and diversified of all graveyard poems. These poems solidified his reputation as one of the most important poets of the eighteenth century. In 1757 he was named poet laureate but refused the position. In 1762 he was rejected for the Regius Professorship of Modern History at Cambridge but was given the position in 1768 when the successful candidate was killed. A painfully shy and private person, he never delivered any lectures as a professor.

Born in New York City, **Marilyn Hacker** (b. 1942) is the author of nine books of poetry, including *Presentation Piece* (1974), the Lamont Poetry Selection of the Academy of American Poets and a National Book Award winner, and *Selected Poems, 1965–1990* (1994), which received the Poets' Prize. Her most recent collection is *Essays on Departure: New and Selected Poems* (2006). She was editor of the *Kenyon Review* from 1990 to 1994 and has received numerous honors and awards, including the PEN/Voelcker Award for Poetry in 2010. She lives in New York City and Paris. Often labeled a neo-formalist, Hacker often handles traditional forms in fresh ways, as "Villanelle" illustrates.

Kimiko Hahn (b. 1955) was born in Mt. Kisco, New York, to two artists, a Japanese American mother from Hawaii and a German American father from Wisconsin. She majored in English and East Asian studies at the University of Iowa and received an M.A. in Japanese literature from Columbia University. She is the author of nine volumes of poetry, including *The Unbearable Heart* (1996), which received an American Book Award; *The Narrow Road to the Interior* (2006); and *Toxic Flora: Poems* (2010). In 1995 she wrote ten portraits of women for a two-hour

HBO special titled *Ain't Nuthin' but a She-Thing*. She has taught at Parsons School of Design, the Poetry Project at St. Mark's Church, and Yale University. She lives in New York and is a Distinguished Professor in the English department at Queens College/CUNY.

Lorraine Hansberry (1930–1965) was born in Chicago, the daughter of parents who were intellectuals and activists, her father winning an antisegregation case before the Illinois Supreme Court on which the events in *A Raisin in the Sun* are loosely based. When she was eight, her parents bought a house in a white neighborhood and were subjected to racist attacks. The legal struggle over their move led to a landmark Supreme Court case, *Hansberry v. Lee*. The family home is now a designated landmark in Chicago. Her parents sent her to public schools rather than private ones as a protest against segregation. She studied art at the University of Wisconsin and in Mexico. In 1950 she dropped out of college, moved to New York, and took classes in writing at the New School. She worked on the staff of the black newspaper *Freedom* under the direction of Paul Robeson, with W. E. B. DuBois, whose office was in the same building, and as a waitress and cashier, while writing in any spare time she could find. During this time, she completed *A Raisin in the Sun* (1959), the first play written by an African American woman to be produced on Broadway. At twenty-nine she became the youngest American playwright to receive the New York Drama Critics Circle Award for Best Play. Her premature death from pancreatic cancer cut short her promising career.

Thomas Hardy (1840–1928) was born in a cottage in Higher Bockhampton,

Dorset, near the regional market town of Dorchester in southwestern England. Apprenticed at age sixteen to an architect, he spent most of the next twenty years restoring old churches. Having always had an interest in literature, he started writing novels in his thirties, publishing more than a dozen, including *Tess of the D'Urbervilles* (1891) and *Jude the Obscure* (1895). In 1896 Hardy gave up prose and turned to poetry, writing verse until his death at age eighty-eight. He had a consistently bleak, even pessimistic, outlook on life. Many of his works stress the dark effects of "hap" (happenstance, coincidence) in the world, a central motif in "The Convergence of the Twain."

Born in Tulsa, Oklahoma, to a mother of Cherokee-French descent and a Creek father, **Joy Harjo** (b. 1951) moved to the Southwest and began writing poetry in her early twenties. She earned her B.A. from the University of New Mexico and her M.F.A. from the University of Iowa Writers' Workshop. Harjo has published numerous volumes of poetry, including *In Mad Love and War* (1990), which received an American Book Award and the Delmore Schwartz Memorial Award. She performs her poetry and plays saxophone with her band, Poetic Justice. She is professor of English at the University of New Mexico, Albuquerque. Of "She Had Some Horses" Harjo has said, "This is the poem I'm asked most about and the one I have the least to say about. I don't know where it came from."

Michael S. Harper (b. 1938) was born in Brooklyn and grew up surrounded by jazz. When his family moved to Los Angeles, he worked in several sectors ranging from the U.S. Postal Service to professional football. He attended the City College of Los Angeles; California State University, Los Angeles; and the University of Iowa Writers' Workshop. He has written more than ten books of poetry, most recently *Selected Poems* (2002), and edited or coedited several collections of African American poetry. He is University Professor and professor of English at Brown University, where he has taught since 1970. He lives in Barrington, Rhode Island.

Robert Hass (b. 1941) was born in San Francisco and grew up in nearby San Rafael. He completed his education at St. Mary's College in Moraga, California, and at Stanford University, and his West Coast upbringing and mind-set are reflected heavily in his poetry. He was also profoundly influenced by Beat poets such as ALLEN GINSBERG, GARY SNYDER, and Lew Welch. In addition to publishing several books of his own poems, he has published a book of essays, has collaborated with Czeslaw Milosz on a translation of his poems, and has published a volume of translations of and commentary on haiku. Hass was appointed Poet Laureate Consultant in Poetry at the Library of Congress for 1995–1996. He has been awarded a MacArthur "Genius" Fellowship and has twice won the National Book Critics' Circle Award. He currently teaches in the English department at the University of California, Berkeley.

Born in Salem, Massachusetts, into a family descended from the New England Puritans, **Nathaniel Hawthorne** (1804–1864) graduated from Bowdoin College, Maine, in 1825. For the next twelve years, he lived in Salem in relative seclusion, reading, observing the New England landscape and people, and writing his first novel, *Fanshawe* (published anonymously in 1828), and the first series of *Twice-Told Tales* (1837). (The second series, published in 1842, was reviewed by EDGAR ALLAN POE and won some notice.) To support himself, Hawthorne took a job in the Boston Custom House, resigning in 1841 to live at Brook Farm, a utopian community. The following year he left Brook Farm, married Sophia Peabody, and moved to Concord, Massachusetts, where his neighbors included Ralph Waldo Emerson and Henry David Thoreau. There he wrote the stories collected in *Mosses from an Old Manse* (1846). Returning to Salem, he took a position as a customs inspector and began full-time work on what was to become his most celebrated novel, *The Scarlet Letter* (1850). The novels *The House of the Seven Gables* (1851) and *The Blithedale Romance* (1852), based on his Brook Farm experience, quickly followed. Also in 1852, he wrote a campaign biography of Franklin Pierce, a former college friend who, on becoming president, appointed Hawthorne U.S. consul at Liverpool. Hawthorne's subsequent travels in Europe contributed to the novel *The Marble Faun* (1860), his last major work.

Raised in a poor neighborhood in Detroit, **Robert Hayden** (1913–1980) had an emotionally tumultuous childhood. Because of impaired vision, he was unable to participate in sports and spent his time reading instead. He graduated from high school in 1932 and attended Detroit City College (later Wayne State University). His first book of poems, *Heart-Shape in the Dust*, was published in 1940. After working for newspapers and on other projects, he studied under W. H. AUDEN in the graduate creative writing program at the University of Michigan, later teaching at Fisk University and the University of Michigan. His poetry gained international recognition in the 1960s; he was awarded the grand prize for poetry at the First World Festival of Negro Arts in Dakar, Senegal, in 1966 for his book *Ballad of Remembrance*. In 1976 he became the first black American to be appointed as Consultant in Poetry to the Library of Congress.

Terrance Hayes (b. 1971) was born in Columbia, South Carolina. In addition to being a writer, he is an accomplished artist and athlete. After receiving a B.A. from Coker College, where he was named an Academic All-American for his athletic and academic accomplishments, he earned an M.F.A. from the University of Pittsburgh. His first book of poetry, *Muscular Music* (1999), won both the Whiting Writers Award and the Kate Tufts Discovery Award. His next collection, *Hip Logic* (2002), won the National Poetry Series award. His most recent book, *Lighthead*, won the National Book Award in Poetry for 2010. After teaching at Xavier University, he returned to Pittsburgh, where he is professor of creative writing at Carnegie Mellon University.

Of Lebanese and Syrian heritage, **Samuel Hazo** (b. 1928) is a highly influential Arab American writer of verse, educator, and advocate on behalf of poetry. He is the author of numerous collections of poetry, fiction, and essays. He is founder, director, and president of the International Poetry Forum in Pittsburgh and McAnulty Distinguished Professor of English Emeritus at Duquesne University. A recipient of the 1986 Hazlett Memorial Award for Excellence in the Arts, Hazo was chosen in 1993 to be the first state poet of the Commonwealth of Pennsylvania, a position he still holds.

Raised on a small farm near Castledawson, County Derry, Northern Ireland, **Seamus Heaney** (b. 1939) was educated at St. Columb's College, a Catholic boarding school situated in the city of Derry, and then at Queen's University, Belfast. As a young English teacher in Belfast in the early 1960s, he joined a poetry workshop and began writing verse, subsequently becoming a major force in contemporary Irish literature. The author of many volumes of poetry, translations, and essays as well as two plays, he is well known at present for his best-selling verse translation of *Beowulf* (2000). He held the chair of professor of poetry at Oxford University from 1989 to 1994. He was awarded the Nobel Prize in Literature in 1995.

Born in Oak Park, Illinois, **Ernest Hemingway** (1899–1961) led an active, vigorous life from childhood, summering in the wilds of northern Michigan with his physician father and boxing and playing football at school. His first job as a writer was as a reporter for the Kansas City *Star*. During World War I, he served as an ambulance driver in Italy; severely wounded before he had turned nineteen, he was decorated by the Italian government. Later, while working in Paris as a correspondent for the Toronto *Star*, he met Gertrude Stein, Ezra Pound, F. Scott Fitzgerald, and other artists and writers who had a significant influence on his work. Hemingway's first book, *Three Stories and Ten Poems* (1923), was followed by the well-known story collection *In Our Time* (1924; rev. and enl. ed., 1925). His novel *The Sun Also Rises* (1926) brought acclaim as well as recognition

of Hemingway as the spokesman for the "lost generation." *A Farewell to Arms* (1929), based on his wartime experiences in Italy, and *For Whom the Bell Tolls* (1940), drawn from his time as a correspondent during the civil war in Spain, established his enduring reputation. In World War II, he served as a correspondent and received a Bronze Star. His frequent travels took him to Spain for the bullfights, on fishing trips to the Caribbean, and on big-game expeditions to the American West and to Africa. In his later years, he suffered from declining physical health and severe depression, which led to his suicide at his home in Ketcham, Idaho. The fullest collection of his short stories, the Finca-Vigía edition, came out in 1991. Hemingway was awarded the Nobel Prize in Literature in 1954.

The fifth son of an ancient and wealthy Welsh family, **George Herbert** (1593–1633) studied at Cambridge, graduating with honors, and was elected public orator of the university. He served in Parliament for two years, but after falling out of political favor he became rector of Bemerton, near Salisbury. Herbert was a model Anglican priest and an inspiring preacher. All his poetry, religious in nature, was published posthumously in 1633. "Easter-wings" is among the earliest of his concrete poems (see the Glossary).

Born in Aguas Buenas, Puerto Rico, **Victor Hernández Cruz** (b. 1949) moved to New York City with his family at the age of five. His first book of poetry was published when he was seventeen. A year later, he moved to California's Bay Area and published his second book. In 1971, Hernández Cruz visited Puerto Rico and reconnected with his ancestral heritage; eighteen years later, he returned to Puerto Rico to live. He now divides his time between Puerto Rico and New York. He is the author of five collections of poetry, including *Maraca: New and Selected Poems, 1965–2000* (2001). He is a co-founder of the East Harlem Gut Theatre in New York and the Before Columbus Foundation and has taught at the University of California at Berkeley and San Diego, San Francisco State College, and the University of Michigan. Much of his work explores the relation between the English language and his native Spanish, playing with grammatical and syntactical conventions within both languages to create his own bilingual idiom.

The son of a well-to-do London goldsmith, **Robert Herrick** (1591–1674) was apprenticed to his uncle (also a goldsmith), studied at Cambridge University, then lived for nine years in London, where he hobnobbed with a group of poets that included BEN JONSON. Under familial pressure to do something more "worthwhile," Herrick became an Anglican priest. He was given the parish of Dean Prior, Devonshire—a rural area that he hated at first—and there he quietly wrote poems about imagined mistresses and pagan rites (as in his well-known "Corinna's Going A-Maying") and deft but devout religious verse. When he returned to London in 1648, having been ejected from his pulpit by the Puritan revolution, he published his poetry in a volume with two titles, *Hesperides* for the secular poems and *Noble Numbers* for those with sacred subjects. Probably his most famous poem is "To the Virgins, to Make Much of Time," a short lyric on the traditional *carpe diem* theme (see the Glossary).

Bob Hicok (b. 1960), in addition to writing poetry, spent years as an automotive die designer and computer systems administrator in Ann Arbor, Michigan. His first collection of poetry, *The Legend of Light* (1995), won the Felix Pollack Prize in Poetry and was named an ALA Booklist Notable Book of the Year. He has published five more books: *Plus Shipping* (1998); *Animal Soul* (2001), a finalist for the National Book Critics Circle Award; *Insomnia Diary* (2004); *This Clumsy Living* (2007); and *Words for Empty and Words for Full* (2010). He currently teaches in the M.F.A. program at Virginia Tech University.

Raised in Michigan, **Conrad Hilberry** (b. 1928) earned his B.A. at Oberlin College and his M.A. and Ph.D. at the University of Wisconsin. He taught at Kalamazoo College until his retirement. Hilberry has published nine collections of poetry, most recently *The Fingernail of Luck* (2005), and has been poetry editor of *Passages North* and of the anthology *Poems from the Third Coast* (1976). He has been praised for his mastery of tone, through which he achieves subtleties of implication, as is evidenced in "Player Piano."

Jane Hirshfield (b. 1953) is the author of nine books of poetry, editor and co-translator of three anthologies of poetry by women, and author of the collection of essays *Nine Gates: Entering the Mind of Poetry* (1997). A graduate of Princeton University, she studied Soto Zen from 1974 to 1982, including three years of monastic practice, the influence of which is apparent in her work. "For me, poetry, like Zen practice, is a path toward deeper and more life. There are ways to wake up into the actual texture of one's own existence, to widen it, to deepen and broaden it, and poetry is one of the things that does that." Hirshfield teaches at Bennington College and lives in the San Francisco Bay area.

Tony Hoagland (b. 1953) was born in Fort Bragg, North Carolina, the son of an army doctor. He grew up on military bases throughout the South. He was educated at Williams College, the University of Iowa, and the University of Arizona. He currently teaches at the University of Houston and Warren Wilson College. His collection *What Narcissism Means to Me* (2003) was a finalist for the National Book Critics Circle Award. His most recent book is *Unincorporated Persons in the Late Honda Dynasty* (2010). In 2002 he received the Academy Award in Literature from the American Academy of Arts and Letters, and in 2005 he was the recipient of the Poetry Foundation's Mark Twain Award in recognition of his contribution to humor in American poetry.

Born in Denver, **Linda Hogan** (b. 1947) is a poet, novelist, essayist, playwright, and activist widely considered to be one of the most influential and provocative Native American figures in the contemporary American literary landscape. Because her father, who was from the Chicksaw Nation, was in the army and was transferred frequently during Hogan's childhood, she lived in various locations while she was growing up, but she considers Oklahoma to be her true home. In her late twenties, while working with children with orthopedic disabilities, she began writing during her lunch hours, though she had no previous experience as a writer and little experience reading literature. She pursued her writing by commuting to the University of Colorado, Colorado

Springs, for her undergraduate degree and earning an M.A. in English and creative writing at the University of Colorado, Boulder, in 1978. She has published more than a dozen books—poetry, novels, and nonfiction—and received numerous awards for her work. She is a professor emeritus in the University of Colorado English department.

Born in Volcano, Hawaii, **Garrett Kaoru Hongo** (b. 1951) grew up on Oahu and in Los Angeles and did graduate work in Japanese language and literature at the University of Michigan. Hongo has published two books of poetry, including *The River of Heaven* (1988), the Lamont Poetry Selection of the Academy of American Poets and a finalist for the Pulitzer Prize. He has also written *Volcano: A Memoir of Hawai'i* (1995) and edited collections of Asian American verse. He teaches at the University of Oregon, Eugene, where he directed the creative writing program from 1989 to 1993. His work often comments through rich textures and sensuous detail on conditions endured by Japanese Americans during World War II and thereafter.

Born in London, **Gerard Manley Hopkins** (1844–1889) was the eldest of eight children. His father was a ship insurer who also wrote a book of poetry. Hopkins studied at Balliol College, Oxford, and, after converting to Catholicism, taught in a school in Birmingham. In 1868 he became a Jesuit and burned all of his early poetry, considering it "secular" and worthless. He worked as a priest and teacher in working-class London, Glasgow, and Merseyside and later as a professor of classics at University College, Dublin. Hopkins went on to write many poems on spiritual themes but published little during his lifetime. His poems, which convey a spiritual sensuality, celebrating the wonder of nature both in their language and in their rhythms, which Hopkins called "sprung rhythm" (see **accentual meter** in the Glossary), were not widely known until they were published by his friend Robert Bridges in 1918.

A. E. Housman (1859–1936) was born in Fockbury, Worcestershire. A promising student at Oxford University, he failed his final exams (because of emotional turmoil, possibly caused by his suppressed homosexual love for a fellow student) and spent the next ten years feverishly studying and writing scholarly articles while working as a clerk at the patent office. Housman was rewarded with the chair of Latin at University College, London, and later at Cambridge University. His poetry, like his scholarship, was meticulous, impersonal in tone, and limited in output, consisting of two slender volumes—*A Shropshire Lad* (1896) and *Last Poems* (1922)—published during his lifetime and a small book titled *More Poems* (1936) that appeared after his death. His poems often take up the theme of doomed youths acting out their brief lives in the context of agricultural communities and activities, especially the English countryside and traditions that the poet loved.

Born in Joplin, Missouri, **Langston Hughes** (1902–1967) grew up in Lincoln, Illinois, and Cleveland, Ohio. He began writing poetry during his high school years. After attending Columbia University for one year, he held odd jobs as an assistant cook, a launderer, and a busboy and traveled to Africa and Europe working as a seaman. In

1924 he moved to Harlem. Hughes's first book of poetry, *The Weary Blues*, was published in 1926. He finished his college education at Lincoln University in Pennsylvania three years later. He wrote novels, short stories, plays, songs, children's books, essays, memoirs, and poetry, and is also known for his engagement with the world of jazz and the influence it had on his writing. His life and work were enormously important in shaping the artistic contributions of the Harlem Renaissance of the 1920s.

Zora Neale Hurston (1891–1960) was born to a family of sharecroppers in Notasula, Alabama, but grew up in Eatonville, Florida, a town founded by African Americans. After her mother's death in 1904, Hurston lived with various relatives. She never finished grade school. At sixteen she joined a traveling theater group and later did domestic work for a white household. The woman for whom she worked arranged for her to attend high school at Morgan Academy (now known as Morgan State University) in Baltimore. In her twenties, she attended Howard University, where she published her first stories in student publications and later in newspapers and magazines. In 1925 she moved to New York City and became active in the Harlem Renaissance. She collaborated with LANGSTON HUGHES in a folk comedy, *Mule Bone* (1931). Her first book, *The Eatonville Anthology* (1927), gained her national attention. At Barnard College, she took courses in anthropology and studied traditional folklore in Alabama and native culture in the Caribbean. During the 1930s and early 1940s, she completed graduate work at Columbia University and published four novels and an autobiography. Hurston published more books than any other African American woman writer of her time—novels, collections of stories, nonfiction, an autobiography—but she earned very little from her writing and spent her final years in near poverty. In the mid-1970s, her work was rediscovered, and she is now recognized as an important American author.

Henrik Ibsen (1828–1906) was born and raised in Skien, Norway, and he is still principally associated with that country, though he also lived for an extended period in Italy, where he did much of his writing. His earliest literary successes were the poetic plays *Brand* (1865) and *Peer Gynt* (1867), which were intended as closet dramas, though both eventually were performed onstage. His real breakthrough, though, came in the late 1870s, when he began to write realistic dramas that are sometimes called *problem plays* because they explore social issues and problems. Some of the problems Ibsen chose to depict, however, were too controversial for the theater of his day—the subjugation of women in marriage in *A Doll House* (1879), venereal disease and incest in *Ghosts* (1881), and the will of an individual against social and political pressure in *An Enemy of the People* (1882). Their subject matter led some critics in Norway and elsewhere to protest against public performances of these works. But despite their controversial nature, or perhaps because of it, these plays secured Ibsen's reputation as one of the most influential playwrights of the late nineteenth century. Important later works by Ibsen include *The Wild Duck* (1884), *Hedda Gabler* (1890), and *The Master Builder* (1892). Although many of his dramas resemble the tightly structured, plot-driven theatrical entity known as the **well-made play** (see the Glossary), Ibsen's work contains subtleties of characterization and theme that raise it above commonplace theatrical experience.

David Ives (b. 1950) was born in Chicago and attended Northwestern University. After graduating, he moved to New York and worked as an editor for *Foreign Affairs*, in addition to writing plays. He enrolled in the Yale School of Drama in 1981 and earned his M.F.A. degree. Many of his plays, often described as "wacky one-act comedies," have been staged at the Manhattan Punch Line's Festival of One-Act Comedies. His full-length comedy *Don Juan in Chicago* (1994) received the Outer Critics Circle's John Gassner Playwriting Award from Young Playwrights Inc. He has published many plays and collections of short plays, as well as three novellas for children or young adults: *Monsieur Eek* (2001), *Scribe* (2005), and *Voss* (2008).

Born in San Francisco, California, and raised in Rochester, New York, **Shirley Jackson** (1919–1965) was educated at the University of Rochester and Syracuse University, where she founded and edited the campus literary magazine. After graduation she married the author and literary critic Stanley Edgar Hyman and settled in North Bennington, Vermont. She is best known for her stories and novels of gothic horror and the occult. Among her novels are *Hangsaman* (1949), *The Bird's Nest* (1954), *The Haunting of Hill House* (1959), and *We Have Always Lived in the Castle* (1962). Her short stories are collected in *The Lottery* (1949), *The Magic of Shirley Jackson* (1966), and *Come Along with Me* (1968). In 1997 *Just an Ordinary Day: The Uncollected*

Stories of Shirley Jackson was published.

Born in Nashville, Tennessee, **Randall Jarrell** (1914–1965) earned his B.A. and M.A. at Vanderbilt University. From 1937 to 1939, he taught at Kenyon College, where he met JOHN CROWE RANSOM and ROBERT LOWELL, and afterward taught at the University of Texas. He served in the air force during World War II. Jarrell's reputation as a poet was established in 1945 with the publication of his second book, *Little Friend, Little Friend*, which documents the intense fears and moral struggles of young soldiers. Other volumes followed, all characterized by great technical skill, empathy, and deep sensitivity. Following the war, Jarrell began teaching at the University of North Carolina, Greensboro, and remained there, except for occasional leaves of absence to teach elsewhere, until his death. Besides poetry, he wrote a satirical novel, several children's books, numerous poetry reviews—collected in *Poetry and the Age* (1953)—and a translation of Goethe's *Faust*.

Honorée Fanonne Jeffers (b. 1967) has published fiction in addition to three books of poetry, *The Gospel of Barbecue* (2000), which won the 1999 Stan and Tom Wick Prize for Poetry and was the finalist for the 2001 Paterson Poetry Prize; *Outlandish Blues* (2003); and *Red Clay Suite* (2007). She has won the 2002 Julia Peterkin Award for Poetry and awards from the Barbara Deming Memorial Fund and the Rona Jaffe Foundation. Her poetry has been published in the anthologies *At Our Core: Women Writing about Power*, *Dark Eros*, and *Identity Lessons* and in many journals, including *Callaloo*, the *Kenyon Review*, and *Prairie Schooner*.

She teaches at the University of Oklahoma.

Sarah Orne Jewett (1849–1909) was born in South Berwick, Maine, to an old-stock New England family. After publishing a story in the *Atlantic Monthly* at the age of nineteen, she quickly sealed her reputation as a regional writer known for stories depicting life along the Maine coast and in rural New England. Among her major successes were the novel *A Country Doctor* (1884) and her short-story collection *A White Heron* (1886). She also published a poetry collection, *Verses*, in 1916, along with three children's books and numerous other novels, novellas, and stories. She became the first woman to receive an honorary degree from Bowdoin College when the Maine school awarded her a Litt.D. in 1901.

Ha Jin (b. 1956), whose birth name was Xuefei Jin, was born to a military family in Liaoning, China, just before the Cultural Revolution. Schools were closed in 1966. At seventeen he joined the army and served on the border with the Soviet Union for five years and decided that he wanted an education. When his term was finished, he took a job as a telegrapher in a railroad station and studied English from a radio course. After the colleges and universities reopened in 1977, Jin earned a B.A. in English from Heilongjiang University, Harbin, in 1981 and an M.A. in American literature from Shandong University in 1984. In 1985 he entered the doctoral program at Brandeis University in the United States. He expected to return to China to teach English and do translation, but the violent events at Tiananmen Square in 1989 persuaded him, his wife, and son to remain in the United States. By 1993 he completed his doctorate and wrote poetry and fiction seriously. His first publication was *Between Silences* (1990), a book of poems. He continued writing and, because he could not find a job teaching Chinese literature, worked for a while as a busboy and waiter to support his family. Jin is now a professor of creative writing at Boston University. From the start, Ha Jin's writing received high praise. His first story collection, *Ocean of Words* (1996), won a PEN/Hemingway Award, and his second collection, *Under the Red Flag* (1997), received a Flannery O'Connor Award for Short Fiction. His novella, *In the Pond* (1998), was chosen by the *Chicago Tribune* as the best work of fiction for that year. His stories have appeared twice in *Best American Short Stories* and three times in *Pushcart Prize* anthologies. His novel *Waiting* (2000) won the 1999 National Book Award for Fiction and the 2001 PEN/Faulkner Award. More recent novels are *War Trash* (2004); *The Crazed* (2005); and *A Free Life* (2007), his first novel set in the United States.

Richard Jones (b. 1953) was born in London, where his father was serving in the U.S. Air Force, and studied at the University of Virginia. Jones is the author of several books of poems, including *The Blessing: New and Selected Poems*, which received the Midland Authors Award for Poetry for 2000. His most recent volume is *The Correct Spelling and Exact Meaning* (2010). He has also published two critical anthologies and has been the editor of the literary journal *Poetry East* since 1979. He has taught at Piedmont College and the University of Virginia and currently is professor of English and director of the creative writing program at DePaul University in Chicago.

Born in London, **Ben Jonson** (1572–1637) was the stepson of a bricklayer (his father died before he was born). He attended Westminster School and then joined the army. Jonson later worked as an actor and was the author of such comedies as *Everyman in His Humor* (in which SHAKESPEARE acted the lead), *Volpone*, and *The Alchemist*. He wrote clear, elegant, "classical" poetry that contrasted with the intricate, subtle, **metaphysical poetry** (see the Glossary) of his contemporaries JOHN DONNE and GEORGE HERBERT. He was named poet laureate and was the idol of a generation of English writers, who dubbed themselves the Sons of Ben.

A. Van Jordan (b. 1965) was born and raised in Akron, Ohio. He is a graduate of the M.F.A. Program for Writers at Warren Wilson College, where he taught in the undergraduate writing program and served as the 1999–2000 and 2000–2001 Joan Beebe Graduate Teaching Fellow. In 1995 he was awarded a D.C. Commission on the Arts and Humanities Literary Award. He was also a semifinalist for the 1999 "Discovery"/The Nation Award. He is the author of three collections of poetry, most recently *Quantum Lyrics: Poems* (2007). He teaches in the M.F.A. program at the University of North Carolina, Greensboro.

Born in London to Caribbean parents, **Allison Joseph** (b. 1967) grew up in Toronto and the Bronx. She earned her B.A. from Kenyon College and her M.F.A. from Indiana University. She is the author of seven collections of poetry. Her most recent volume is *My Father's Kites: Poems* (2010). Her poems are often attuned to the experiences of women and minorities. She holds the Judge William Holmes Cook Endowed

Professorship and directs the M.F.A. Program in Creative Writing at Southern Illinois University, Carbondale, and is editor of the *Crab Orchard Review*.

Born in Dublin, Ireland, **James Joyce** (1882–1941) was educated at Jesuit schools in preparation for the priesthood. But at an early age he abandoned Catholicism and in 1904 left Dublin for what he felt would be the broader horizons of continental Europe. Living in Paris, Zurich, and Trieste over the next twenty-five years, he tried to support himself and his family by teaching languages and singing. In 1912 he returned to Dublin briefly to arrange for the publication of his short stories. Because of the printers' fear of censorship or libel suits, the edition was burned, and *Dubliners* did not appear until 1914 in England. During World War I, Joyce lived in Zurich, where he wrote *Portrait of the Artist as a Young Man* (1916), a partly autobiographical account of his adolescent years that introduced some of the experimental techniques found in his later novels. About this time Joyce fell victim to glaucoma; for the rest of his life he suffered periods of intense pain and near blindness. His masterpiece, the novel *Ulysses* (1922), known for its "stream of consciousness" style, was written and published in periodicals between 1914 and 1921. Book publication was delayed because of obscenity charges. *Ulysses* finally was issued by Shakespeare & Company, a Paris bookstore owned and operated by Sylvia Beach, an American expatriate; U.S. publication was banned until 1933. *Finnegans Wake* (1939), an equally experimental novel, took seventeen years to write. Because of the controversy surrounding his work, Joyce earned little in royalties and often had to rely on friends

for support. He died after surgery for a perforated ulcer in Zurich.

Born in Prague and raised in Bohemia, **Franz Kafka** (1883–1924), the son of middle-class German Jewish parents, studied law at the German University of Prague. After winning his degree in 1906, he was employed in the workmen's compensation division of the Austrian government. Because he wrote very slowly, he could not earn a living as a writer. At the time of his death, he had published little and asked his friend Max Brod to burn his incomplete manuscripts. Brod ignored this request and arranged posthumous publication of Kafka's major long works, *The Trial* (1925), *The Castle* (1926), and *Amerika* (1927), as well as a large number of his stories. Important stories published during his lifetime include "The Judgment" (1913), "The Metamorphosis" (1915), and "A Hunger Artist" (1924). Kafka's fiction is known for its gripping portrayals of individual helplessness before political, judicial, and paternal authority and power.

John Keats (1795–1821) was born in London. His father, a worker at a livery stable who married his employer's daughter and inherited the business, was killed by a fall from a horse when Keats was eight. When his mother died of tuberculosis six years later, Keats and his siblings were entrusted to the care of a guardian, a practical-minded man who took Keats out of school at fifteen and apprenticed him to a doctor. But as soon as he qualified for medical practice, in 1815, Keats abandoned medicine for poetry, which he had begun writing two years earlier. In 1818, the year he himself contracted tuberculosis, he also fell madly in love with a pretty, vivacious young woman named Fanny Brawne whom he could not marry because of his poverty, illness, and devotion to poetry. In the midst of such stress and emotional turmoil, his masterpieces poured out, between January and September 1819: the great odes, a number of sonnets, and several longer lyric poems. In February 1820, his health failed rapidly; he went to Italy in the autumn, in the hope that the warmer climate would improve his health, and died there on February 23, 1821. His poems are rich with sensuous, lyrical beauty and emotional resonance, reflecting both his delight in life as well as his awareness of life's brevity and difficulty.

Jane Kenyon (1947–1995) was born in Ann Arbor, Michigan, and grew up in the Midwest. She earned her B.A. and M.A. from the University of Michigan. She was married to poet Donald Hall from 1972 until her death from leukemia in 1995. During her lifetime, she published four books of poetry — *Constance* (1993), *Let Evening Come* (1990), *The Boat of Quiet Hours* (1986), and *From Room to Room* (1978) — and a book of translation, *Twenty Poems of Anna Akhmatova* (1985). Two additional volumes were published after her death: *Otherwise: New and Selected Poems* (1996) and *A Hundred White Daffodils: Essays, Interviews, the Akhmatova Translations, Newspaper Columns, and One Poem* (1999). At the time of her death, she was New Hampshire's poet laureate.

Born in St. John's, Antigua, and raised by devoted parents, **Jamaica Kincaid** (b. 1949) entered college in the United States but withdrew to write. After her stories appeared in notable publications, she took a staff position on *The New Yorker*. Her first book, a story collection titled *At the Bottom of the River* (1984), won a major award from the American Academy and Institute of Arts and Letters. *Annie John* (1985), an interrelated collection, further explored life in the British West Indies as experienced by a young girl. Kincaid now lives in the United States and continues to write about her homeland in works including *A Small Place* (1988), *Lucy* (1990), *Autobiography of My Mother* (1996), *My Brother* (1997), *Talk Stories* (2002), *Mr. Potter* (2003), and *Jupiter* (2004).

Born in Providence, Rhode Island, **Galway Kinnell** (b. 1927) attended Princeton University and the University of Rochester. He served in the U.S. Navy and then visited Paris on a Fulbright fellowship. Returning to the United States, he worked for the Congress on Racial Equality and then traveled widely in the Middle East and Europe. He has taught in France, Australia, and Iran as well as at numerous colleges and universities in the United States. He has published many books of poetry, including *Selected Poems* (1980), for which he received both the Pulitzer Prize and the National Book Award. He has also published translations of works by Yves Bonnefoy, Yvanne Goll, François Villon, and Rainer Maria Rilke. He was the Erich Maria Remarque Professor of Creative Writing at New York University. He is now retired and lives in Vermont.

Etheridge Knight (1931–1991) was born in Corinth, Mississippi. He dropped out of school at age sixteen and served in the U.S. Army in Korea from 1947 to 1951, returning with a shrapnel wound that caused him to fall deeper into a drug addiction that had begun during his service. In 1960 he was arrested for robbery and sentenced to eight years in an Indiana state prison. During this time, he began writing poetry. His first book, *Poems from Prison* (1968), was published one year before his release. The book was a success, and Knight joined other poets in what came to be called the Black Arts Movement, the aesthetic and spiritual sister of the Black Power concept. He went on to write several more books of poetry and receive many prestigious honors and awards. In 1990 he earned a B.A. in American poetry and criminal justice from Martin Center University in Indianapolis.

Born and raised in Bogalusa, Louisiana, **Yusef Komunyakaa** (b. 1947) earned degrees at the University of Colorado, Colorado State University, and the University of California, Irvine. His numerous books of poems include *Neon Vernacular: New and Selected Poems, 1977–1989* (1994), for which he received the Pulitzer Prize and the Kingsley Tufts Poetry Award, and *Thieves of Paradise* (1998), which was a finalist for the National Book Critics Circle Award. His most recent collection is *The Chameleon Couch* (2011). Other publications include *Blues Notes: Essays, Interviews & Commentaries* (2000), *The Jazz Poetry Anthology* (co-edited with J. A. Sascha Feinstein, 1991), and *The Insomnia of Fire* by Nguyen Quang Thieu (cotranslated with Martha Collins, 1995). He has taught at the University of New Orleans, Indiana University, and Princeton University.

Ted Kooser (b. 1939) was born in Ames, Iowa. He received his B.A. from Iowa State University and his M.A. in English from the University of Nebraska, Lincoln. He is the author of

eleven collections of poetry, including *Sure Signs* (1980), *One World at a Time* (1985), *Weather Central* (1994), *Winter Morning Walks: One Hundred Postcards to Jim Harrison* (2000, winner of the 2001 Nebraska Book Award for poetry), and *Valentines* (2008). His fiction and nonfiction books include *Local Wonders: Seasons in the Bohemian Alps* (2002, winner of the 2003 Nebraska Book Award for nonfiction) and *Braided Creek: A Conversation in Poetry* (2003), written with fellow poet and longtime friend Jim Harrison. His honors include two NEA fellowships in poetry, a Pushcart Prize, the Stanley Kunitz Prize, and a Merit Award from the Nebraska Arts Council. He served as the United States Poet Laureate Consultant in Poetry to the Library of Congress from 2004 to 2006. He lives on acreage near the village of Garland, Nebraska, and is a visiting professor in the English department of the University of Nebraska, Lincoln.

Born in Philadelphia, **Maxine Kumin** (b. 1925) received her B.A. and M.A. from Radcliffe College. She has published eleven books of poetry, including *Up Country: Poems of New England* (1972), for which she received the Pulitzer Prize. She is also the author of a memoir, *Inside the Halo and Beyond: The Anatomy of a Recovery* (2000); five novels; a collection of short stories; more than twenty children's books; and four books of essays. Her most recent collection is *Where I Live: New and Selected Poems, 1990–2010* (2010). She has taught at the University of Massachusetts, Columbia University, Brandeis University, and Princeton University and has served as Consultant in Poetry to the Library of Congress and as poet laureate of New Hampshire, where she lives.

Stanley Kunitz (b. 1905–2006) was born in Worcester, Massachusetts, and earned his B.A. and M.A. at Harvard University. His first two books of poetry attracted little attention, but after service in World War II he continued to write and taught at various places, including Bennington College and Columbia University. His third book *Selected Poems: 1928–1958* received the Pulitzer Prize for Poetry in 1959. Kunitz served as Consultant in Poetry to the Library of Congress twice from 1974 to 1976 then again in 2000 and founded both the Fine Arts Work Center in Provincetown, Massachusetts, and Poets House in New York City.

Jhumpa Lahiri (b. 1967) was born in London but grew up in Rhode Island. As a child, she wrote stories in her school notebooks. She received her B.A. from Barnard College, and, rejected by creative writing programs, she continued to write stories while working at an office job. She was then accepted to the graduate program at Boston University and earned an M.A. in English, an M.A. in creative writing, and a Ph.D. in Renaissance studies. The daughter of parents born in India who frequently took her there as a child, she has been influenced by the culture of India and the United States. Her first collection of short fiction, *Interpreter of Maladies* (1999), won the Pulitzer Prize for fiction in 2000, in addition to a number of other prestigious awards. Her first novel, *The Namesake*, was published in 2003 and made into a motion picture (2007). She published her second short-story collection, *Unaccustomed Earth*, in 2008. The *New York Times Book Review* selected the title as the best book of the year. She has taught creative writing at Boston University and the Rhode Island School of Design and has been a vice president of the PEN American Center since 2005.

Born David Herbert Lawrence in Nottinghamshire, England, the son of a coal miner and a mother who had high ambitions for her son, **D. H. Lawrence** (1885–1930) spent his early years in poverty. After graduating from University College in Nottingham, he worked as a schoolmaster in a London suburb and wrote fiction and poetry that introduced the themes of nature and the unconscious that pervaded his later work. His short stories began to be published in 1909. After his first novel, *The White Peacock* (1911), was published with the help of the writer Ford Madox Ford, Lawrence was forced by illness to return to Nottingham, where he fell in love with Frieda von Richthofen Weekley, the German wife of a professor at the college. The two eloped to continental Europe and subsequently married. They then spent the years of World War I in England, where, because of Frieda's German origins and opposition to the war, they were suspected of being spies. They traveled widely and lived in Ceylon, Australia, the United States, Italy, Tahiti, Mexico, and France. In London in 1929, police raided an exhibition of Lawrence's paintings; pronouncing them obscene, authorities confiscated many of them. Three of Lawrence's novels were also suppressed. The most famous of these was *Lady Chatterley's Lover* (1928), privately printed in Italy and banned, because of its explicit depiction of loving sexuality, until 1959 in the United States and until 1960 in England. A victim of tuberculosis for many years, Lawrence succumbed to that disease at the age of forty-four. Among his other well-known novels are *Sons and Lovers* (1913), *The Rainbow* (1915), and *Women in Love* (1921). Lawrence is also widely acclaimed for his short stories, poetry, travel writing, and literary commentary.

Li-Young Lee (b. 1957) was born in Jakarta, Indonesia, to Chinese parents. His father, who had been personal physician to Mao Zedung, relocated his family to Indonesia, where he helped found Gamaliel University. But in 1959 the Lee family fled that country to escape anti-Chinese sentiment, settling in the United States in 1964. Lee studied at the University of Pittsburgh, the University of Arizona, and the Brockport campus of the State University of New York. He has taught at several universities, including Northwestern University and the University of Iowa. He is the author of four collections of poetry—*Rose* (1986), which won the Delmore Schwartz Memorial Poetry Award; *The City in Which I Love You* (1991), the 1990 Lamont Poetry selection; *Book of My Nights* (2001); and *Behind My Eyes* (2008)—and a memoir, *The Winged Seed: A Remembrance* (1995), which received an American Book Award from the Before Columbus Foundation. In his poems one often senses a profound sense of exile, the influence of his father's presence, and a rich, spiritual sensuality.

Denise Levertov (1923–1997) was born in Ilford, England. Her mother was Welsh, and her father was a Russian Jew who had become an Anglican priest. Educated at home, Levertov said she decided to become a writer at the age of five. Her first book, *The Double Image* (1946), brought her recognition as one of a group of poets dubbed the "New Romantics"—her poems often blend objective observation with the sensibility of a spiritual searcher. Having moved to the United States after marrying the American writer Mitchell Goodman, she turned to free-verse

poetry and with her first American book, *Here and Now* (1956), became an important voice in the American avant-garde. In the 1960s, she became involved in the movement protesting the Vietnam War. Levertov went on to publish more than twenty collections of poetry, four books of prose, and three volumes of poetry in translation. From 1982 to 1993, she taught at Stanford University. She spent the last decade of her life in Seattle.

Born in Detroit, **Philip Levine** (b. 1928) received his degrees from Wayne State University and the University of Iowa. He is the author of sixteen books of poetry, including *The Simple Truth* (1994), which won the Pulitzer Prize. He has also published a collection of essays, *The Bread of Time: Toward an Autobiography* (1994), edited *The Essential Keats* (1987), and coedited and translated two books of poetry by the Spanish poet Gloria Fuertes and the Mexican poet Jamie Sabines. He divides his time between Fresno, California, and New York City, where he taught at New York University.

Larry Levis (1946–1996) grew up on a farm near Fresno, California. He earned his B.A. from Fresno State College (now California State University), an M.A. from Syracuse University, and a Ph.D. from the University of Iowa. He published six collections of poetry—several of them receiving major awards—and a collection of short fiction. He taught at the University of Missouri, the University of Utah, and Virginia Commonwealth University. He died of a heart attack at the age of forty-nine. PHILIP LEVINE wrote that he had years earlier recognized Levis as "the most gifted and determined young poet I have ever had the good fortune to have in one of my classes. . . . His early death is a staggering loss for our poetry, but what he left is a major achievement that will enrich our lives."

Born in New York City to West Indian parents, **Audre Lorde** (1934–1992) grew up in Manhattan and attended Roman Catholic schools. While she was still in high school, her first poem appeared in *Seventeen* magazine. She earned her B.A. from Hunter College in New York City and her M.A. in library science from Columbia University. In 1968 she left her job as head librarian at Town School Library in New York City to become a lecturer and creative writer. She accepted a poet-in-residence position at Tougaloo College in Mississippi, where she discovered a love of teaching; published her first volume of poetry, *The First Cities* (1968); and met her long-term partner, Frances Clayton. Many volumes of poetry followed, several winning major awards. She also published four volumes of prose, among them *The Cancer Journals* (1980), which chronicled her struggles with cancer, and *A Burst of Light* (1988), which won a National Book Award. In the 1980s, Lorde and writer Barbara Smith founded Kitchen Table: Women of Color Press. She was also a founding member of Sisters in Support of Sisters in South Africa, an organization that worked to raise awareness about women under apartheid. She was the poet laureate of New York from 1991 to 1992.

Born into a prominent family in Kent, England, **Richard Lovelace** (1618–1658) went to Oxford, where his dashing appearance and wit made him a social and literary favorite. He fought in the English civil war on the Royalist side and was imprisoned and then exiled. Later he fought in France against the Spanish and was again imprisoned on his return to England. After his release, he spent ten years in poverty and isolation before his death. He was a leader of the "Cavalier poets," followers of King Charles I who were soldiers and courtiers but who also wrote well-crafted, lighthearted lyric poetry. "To Lucasta, Going to the Wars" is an excellent example of this type.

Born in Boston into a prominent New England family, **Robert Lowell** (1917–1977) attended Harvard University and then Kenyon College, where he studied under JOHN CROWE RANSOM. At Louisiana State University, he studied with Robert Penn Warren and Cleanth Brooks as well as Allen Tate. He was always politically active—a conscientious objector during World War II and a Vietnam War protestor—and suffered from manic depression. Lowell's reputation was established early: his second book, *Lord Weary's Castle*, was awarded the Pulitzer Prize for poetry in 1947. In the mid-1950s, he began to write more directly from personal experience and loosened his adherence to traditional meter and form. The result was a watershed collection of the "confessional" school, *Life Studies* (1959), which changed the landscape of modern poetry, much as T. S. Eliot's *The Waste Land* had done three decades earlier. He died suddenly from a heart attack at age sixty.

Katherine Mansfield (1888–1923) was raised in New Zealand but relocated to Great Britain to go to university. There she met many of the modernist writers who would come to influence her, including D. H. LAWRENCE and Virginia Woolf. After traveling continental Europe, Mansfield returned to New Zealand, where she began her writing career. Best known for her short stories, Mansfield would eventually be regarded as one of the leading writers of the modernist period. She contracted tuberculosis during World War I, and the disease eventually led to her premature death at the age of thirty-four. She published five short-story collections over the course of her brief career.

Christopher Marlowe (1564–1593) was born in Canterbury the same year as WILLIAM SHAKESPEARE. The son of a shoemaker, he needed the help of scholarships to attend King's School, Canterbury, and Corpus Christi College, Cambridge. He was involved in secret political missions for the government. He was one of the most brilliant writers of his generation in narrative poetry, lyric poetry, and drama (his best-known play is *Doctor Faustus*). He died after being stabbed in a bar fight, reportedly over his bill, at the age of twenty-nine. "The Passionate Shepherd to His Love" is among the most famous of Elizabethan songs.

Born in Hull, Yorkshire, **Andrew Marvell** (1621–1678) was educated at Trinity College, Cambridge. After traveling in Europe, he worked as a tutor and in a government office (as assistant to JOHN MILTON) and later became a member of Parliament for Hull. Marvell was known in his lifetime as a writer of rough satires in verse and prose. His "serious" poetry, like "To His Coy Mistress," a famous exploration of the *carpe diem* theme (see the Glossary), was not published until after his death.

Heather McHugh (b. 1948) was born to Canadian parents in San Diego and grew up in Virginia. She is a graduate of Radcliffe College and the University of Denver. McHugh has published numerous books of poetry, including *Hinge & Sign: Poems, 1968–1993* (1994), which won both the *Boston Book Review*'s Bingham Poetry Prize and the Pollack-*Harvard Review* Prize, was a finalist for the National Book Award, and was named a "Notable Book of the Year" by the *New York Times Book Review* and *Upgraded to Serious* (2009). She has also published a book of prose, *Broken English: Poetry and Partiality* (1993), and two books of translations. She was awarded a MacArthur Foundation grant in 2009. She teaches as a core faculty member in the M.F.A. Program for Writers at Warren Wilson College and as Milliman Writer-in-Residence at the University of Washington, Seattle.

The son of poor farmworkers, **Claude McKay** (1890–1948) was born in Sunny Ville, Jamaica. He was educated by his older brother, who possessed a library of English novels, poetry, and scientific texts. At age twenty, McKay published a book of verse called *Songs of Jamaica*, recording his impressions of black life in Jamaica in dialect. In 1912 he traveled to the United States to attend Tuskegee Institute. He soon left to study agriculture at Kansas State University. In 1914 he moved to Harlem and became an influential member of the Harlem Renaissance. After committing himself to communism and traveling to Moscow in 1922, he lived for some time in Europe and Morocco, writing fiction. McKay later repudiated communism, converted to Roman Catholicism, and returned to the United States. He published several books of poetry as well as an autobiography, *A Long Way from Home* (1937). He wrote a number of sonnets protesting the injustices of black life in the United States, "America" among them, which are of interest for the way they use the most Anglo of forms to contain and intensify what the poem's language is saying.

Born in New York City, the second son of well-established, affluent parents, **Herman Melville** (1819–1891) lived comfortably until he was eleven, when his father went bankrupt and moved the family to Albany. After his father's death in 1832, Melville left school to work. In 1839 he sailed as a merchant seaman to Liverpool, and in 1841 as a whaleman to the South Pacific. On his return to the United States in 1844, he immediately began to write about his sea adventures. He wrote at an extraordinary pace, producing seven novels in six years, beginning with *Typee* (1846) and *Omoo* (1847), about the South Seas, and including *Moby-Dick* (1851) and *Pierre* (1852). The early novels were well received, but *Moby-Dick*, now recognized as a masterpiece, was misunderstood, and *Pierre* was considered a total failure. During this period, Melville had married Elizabeth Shaw, daughter of the chief justice of Massachusetts; in 1850 the couple bought a farm near Pittsfield, Massachusetts, where the writer became close friends with NATHANIEL HAWTHORNE. Despite serious financial problems and a slight nervous breakdown, Melville published stories and sketches in magazines—several of the best, including "Bartleby, the Scrivener" and "Benito Cereno," were collected in *The Piazza Tales* (1856)—as well as the novels *Israel Potter* (1855) and *The Confidence Man* (1857) before turning almost exclusively to poetry for thirty years. Needing money, he sold the farm and worked as a customs inspector in New York City for twenty years; when his wife received a small inheritance, he

was able to retire. In his final years, he wrote the novella *Billy Budd*, which was not published until 1924, thirty-three years after he died in poverty and obscurity. Many of his unpublished stories and journals were also published posthumously.

The son of a well-off London businessman, **John Milton** (1608–1674) was educated at St. Paul's School and at home with private tutors. After graduating with an M.A. from Christ's College, Cambridge, he spent the next six years reading at home. Having written verse since his university days, Milton began to write prose tracts in favor of Oliver Cromwell, in whose government he was later employed as head of a department. The strain of long hours of reading and writing for the revolutionary cause aggravated a genetic weakness and resulted in his total blindness around 1651. He wrote his most famous works—*Paradise Lost* (1667), *Paradise Regained* (1671), and *Samson Agonistes* (1671)—by dictating them to his daughter and other amanuenses.

Marianne Moore (1887–1972) was born near St. Louis and grew up in Carlisle, Pennsylvania. After studying at Bryn Mawr College and Carlisle Commercial College, she taught at a government Native American school in Carlisle. She moved to Brooklyn, where she became an assistant at the New York Public Library. She loved baseball and spent a good deal of time watching her beloved Brooklyn Dodgers. She began to write Imagist poetry and to contribute to *The Dial*, a prestigious literary magazine. From 1925 to 1929, she served as acting editor of *The Dial* and then as editor for four years. Moore was widely recognized for her work, receiving among other honors the Bollingen Prize, the National Book Award, and the Pulitzer Prize.

Born in Cleveland, Ohio, **Thylias Moss** (b. 1954) attended Syracuse University and received her B.A. from Oberlin College and M.F.A. from the University of New Hampshire. She is the author of numerous books of poetry, most recently *Tokyo Butter* (2006); a memoir, *Tale of a Sky-Blue Dress* (1998); two children's books; and two plays, *Talking to Myself* (1984) and *The Dolls in the Basement* (1984). Among her awards are a Guggenheim fellowship and a MacArthur Foundation fellowship. She lives in Ann Arbor, where she is a professor of English at the University of Michigan.

Marilyn Nelson (b. 1946) was born in Cleveland, Ohio, and grew up on numerous military bases. Her father was a U.S. serviceman in the air force, one of the last Tuskegee airmen, and her mother was a teacher. While still in elementary school, she started writing. She earned her B.A. from the University of California, Davis, her M.A. from the University of Pennsylvania, and her Ph.D. from the University of Minnesota. *The Homeplace* (1990), *The Fields of Praise: New and Selected Poems* (1997), and *Carver: A Life in Poems* (2001) were all finalists for the National Book Award. In addition to many collections of her own poetry for adults and for children, she has translated from Danish Halfdan Rasmussen's *Hundreds of Hens and Other Poems*. She is founder and director of Soul Mountain Retreat, a writer's colony that encourages and supports poets who belong to underrepresented racial or cultural groups. She is professor emerita of English at the University of Con-

necticut and was poet laureate of Connecticut from 2001 to 2006.

Lorine Niedecker (1903–1970) was born and died in Fort Atkinson, Wisconsin. She lived much of her life in a small cabin on Black Hawk Island on Lake Koshkonong. Though celebrated by many of the most acclaimed experimental/modernist/objectivist writers of the twentieth century, among them WILLIAM CARLOS WILLIAMS and Louis Zukofsky, she chose to remain apart from the poetry world, living an all but isolated life. Niedecker said that she spent her childhood outdoors and from that developed her keen eye and strong sense of place. In 1931 she discovered "Objectivist" poetry, which called for sincerity and objectification, values that fit well with her own vision and influenced her poems from that time on. While living on Black Hawk Island, she worked in a local hospital cleaning the kitchen and scrubbing floors. Her books included *New Goose* (1946), *North Central* (1968), *My Life by Water* (published the year of her death), and *Blue Chicory* (published posthumously in 1976). Her selected poems, compiled in *The Granite Pail*, were not published until 1985.

Born in Muskegon, Michigan, **John Frederick Nims** (1913–1999) studied at DePaul University, the University of Notre Dame, and the University of Chicago, where he received his Ph.D. in 1945. By that time, he had already distinguished himself as a poet and critic. He went on to teach at numerous colleges and universities, including Harvard University, the University of Florence, the University of Toronto, the Bread Loaf School of English, Williams College, and the University of Missouri. Editor of *Poetry* magazine from 1978 to 1984, Nims was the author of many books of poetry and translations as well as several critical works and a widely used textbook, *Western Wind: An Introduction to Poetry*.

Lynn Nottage (b. 1964) was born to a schoolteacher and a child psychologist in Brooklyn. She wrote her first play while attending New York's High School of Music and Art and went on to attend Brown University and the Yale School of Drama. Her plays often deal with African Americans and women and have been performed off-Broadway and regionally. Her play *Intimate Apparel* won the majority of major theater awards for the 2003–2004 theater season, and *Ruined*, first performed in 2007, won the Pulitzer Prize. She has been awarded numerous playwriting fellowships and continues to reside in Brooklyn.

Born in St. Louis of a Palestinian father and an American mother, **Naomi Shihab Nye** (b. 1952) grew up in both the United States and Jerusalem. She received her B.A. from Trinity University in San Antonio, Texas, where she still resides with her family. She is the author of many books of poems, most recently *You and Yours* (2005), which received the Isabella Gardner Poetry Award. She has also written short stories and books for children and has edited anthologies, several of which focus on the lives of children and represent work from around the world. She is a singer-songwriter and on several occasions has traveled to the Middle East and Asia for the U.S. Information Agency, promoting international goodwill through the arts. Nye's work often attests to a universal sense of exile—from place, home, love, and oneself—and looks at the ways the human spirit confronts it.

Joyce Carol Oates (b. 1938) was born in Lockport, New York. She began storytelling in early childhood, composing picture stories even before she could write. Only after earning a B.A. from Syracuse University and an M.A. from the University of Wisconsin did she focus on writing as a career. Her first book was a collection of stories, *By the North Gate* (1963). Since then she has gone on to become one of the most versatile, prolific, and important American writers of her time, publishing more than one hundred books—novels, story collections, poetry, plays, children's books, and literary criticism. She has been nominated for the Nobel Prize for Literature three times. She is the Roger S. Berlind Distinguished Professor of Humanities at Princeton University.

Born in Austin, Minnesota, **Tim O'Brien** (b. 1946) studied at Macalester College and Harvard University. During the Vietnam War, he was drafted into the army, promoted to the rank of sergeant, and decorated with a Purple Heart. Many of his novels and stories draw on his experiences during the war. His novels are *If I Die in a Combat Zone, Box Me Up and Ship Me Home* (1973); *Northern Lights* (1975); *Going after Cacciato* (1978), winner of the National Book Award; *The Nuclear Age* (1985); *In the Lake of the Woods* (1994); and *July, July* (2002). His short-story collection is entitled *The Things They Carried* (1990). He lives in Texas and teaches alternate years in the creative writing program at Texas State University, San Marcos.

Born in Savannah, Georgia, and raised on a farm in Milledgeville, Georgia, **Flannery O'Connor** (1925–1964) graduated from Georgia State College for

Women in 1945 and attended the Writers' Workshop at the University of Iowa, from which she received a master's degree in 1947. From Iowa she moved to New York City to begin her writing career but, after little more than two years, was forced by illness to return to her mother's Georgia farm. Confined as an invalid by the degenerative disease lupus, O'Connor spent her remaining fourteen years raising peacocks and writing fiction set in rural Georgia. Her works are distinguished by irreverent humor, often grotesque characters, and intense, almost mystical affirmation of the challenges of religious belief. Her work includes two novels, *Wise Blood* (1952) and *The Violent Bear It Away* (1960), and two short-story collections, *A Good Man Is Hard to Find* (1955) and *Everything That Rises Must Converge* (1965). After her death at the age of thirty-nine, a selection of occasional prose, *Mystery and Manners* (1969), was edited by her friends Sally and Robert Fitzgerald, and a collection of letters, *The Habit of Being* (1979), was edited by Sally Fitzgerald. *The Complete Stories* (1971) received the National Book Award.

Born in Baltimore and raised in Massachusetts, **Frank [Francis Russell] O'Hara** (1926–1966) studied piano at the New England Conservatory in Boston from 1941 to 1944 and served in the South Pacific and Japan during World War II. He majored in English at Harvard and received his M.A. in English at the University of Michigan in 1951. He moved to New York, where he worked at the Museum of Modern Art and began writing poetry seriously as well as composing essays and reviews on painting and sculpture. His first volume of poems, *A City in Winter*, thirteen poems with two drawings by the artist Larry Rivers, was published in 1952. Other collaborations with artists followed. His first major collection of poetry was *Meditations in an Emergency* (1957). His poetry is often casual, relaxed in diction, and full of specific detail, seeking to convey the immediacy of life. He described his work as "I do this I do that" poetry because his poems often read like entries in a diary, as in the opening lines of "The Day Lady Died." He was killed at forty when he was struck by a sand buggy while vacationing on Fire Island, New York.

Sharon Olds (b. 1942) was born in San Francisco and educated at Stanford and Columbia universities. She has written nine books of poetry—most recently *One Secret Thing* (2008)—and received numerous important prizes and awards. In the words of Elizabeth Frank, "[Olds] and her work are about nothing less than the joy of making—of making love, making babies, making poems, making sense of love, memory, death, the feel—the actual bodily texture, of life." She held the position of New York State Poet from 1998 until 2000. She teaches poetry workshops in New York University's graduate creative writing program along with workshops at Goldwater Hospital in New York, a public facility for physically disabled persons.

Mary Oliver (b. 1935) was born in Cleveland and educated at Ohio State University and Vassar College. She is the author of some twenty volumes of poetry, including *American Primitive* (1983), for which she won the Pulitzer Prize, and four books of prose. Her most recent book is *Swan: Poems and Prose Poems* (2010). She held the Catharine Osgood Foster Chair for Distinguished Teaching at Bennington

College until 2001 and now lives in Provincetown, Massachusetts. Oliver is one of the most respected of poets concerned with the natural world.

Tillie Olsen (1913–2007) was born Tillie Lerner in Omaha, Nebraska, in 1912 or 1913; the author isn't sure which is her birth date because her birth was unrecorded. The daughter of refugees from Tsarist Russia after the Revolution of 1905, she grew up in a poor, hard-working family. Her father worked as a farmer, a house-painter, and a packer; her mother in a factory; and she at odd jobs as a sixteen-year-old high school dropout during the Depression. She started her first novel, *Yonnondio*, when she was nineteen, and completed four chapters in four years; at the same time, she married, had a child, and was left by her husband. In 1934 *Partisan Review* published a part of the first chapter of *Yonnondio*, but Olsen put the manuscript aside in 1937. One year earlier she had married Jack Olsen, raised three more children, and worked in a factory, as a secretary, and for political causes. In 1953, when her youngest daughter started school, Olsen began writing again. That same year, at the age of forty, she took a fiction writing course at San Francisco State College, and in 1955 and 1956 won creative writing fellowships from Stanford University. *Tell Me a Riddle*, a collection of stories written in the 1950s, came out as a paperback in 1961 and received acclaim. Two years later, assisted by more grants and fellowships, she published the unfinished *Yonnondio*. An essay collection titled *Silences*, about writers' experiences when language fails and writing becomes impossible, appeared in 1978. In 1994, Olsen won an Era Award for the Short Story, given to a living American writer for "a significant contribution to the short story as an art form."

Simon J. Ortiz (b. 1941) was born and raised in the Acoma Pueblo Community in Albuquerque, New Mexico. He received his early education from the Bureau of Indian Affairs school on the Acoma reservation, later attending the University of New Mexico and completing his M.F.A. at the University of Iowa, where he was a part of the International Writing Program. Unlike most contemporary Native American writers, Ortiz is a full-blooded Native American, and his first language is Keresan. By learning English, he found a way to communicate with those outside his immediate culture. His poetry explores the significance of individual origins and journeys, which he sees as forming a vital link in the continuity of life. His many writing accomplishments include poems, short stories, essays, and children's books. Ortiz has taught Native American literature and creative writing at San Diego State University, Navajo Community College, Marin College, the Institute for the Arts of the American Indian, the University of New Mexico, and most recently at the University of Toronto.

Born in Oswestry, Shropshire, **Wilfred Owen** (1893–1918) attended Birkenhead Institute and Shrewsbury Technical School. When forced to withdraw from London University for financial reasons, Owen became a vicar's assistant in Dunsden, Oxfordshire. There he grew disaffected with the church and left to teach in France. He enlisted in 1915 and six months later was hospitalized in Edinburgh, where he met Siegfried Sassoon, whose war poems had just been published. Sent back to the front, Owen was killed one week before the armistice. He is the most widely recognized of the "war poets," a group of World War I writers who brought the realism of war to poetry.

Linda Pastan (b. 1932) was born in New York City, graduated from Radcliffe College, and earned an M.A. from Brandeis University. She has published many books of poetry, including *Traveling Light* (2011), and received numerous awards for them, including a Dylan Thomas Award. Her deeply emotional poetry often has grief at its center. She is known for writing short poems that address topics like family life, domesticity, motherhood, the female experience, aging, death, loss and the fear of loss, and the fragility of life and relationships. She served as poet laureate of Maryland from 1991 to 1994 and was a staff member at the Breadloaf Writers Conference for twenty years. She lives in Potomac, Maryland.

Born in working-class Detroit, **Marge Piercy** (b. 1936) studied at the University of Michigan and Northwestern University. She has published many books of poetry and novels, as well as a collection of essays on poetry, *Parti-Colored Blocks for a Quilt* (1982), and a memoir, *Sleeping with Cats* (2002). She has been deeply involved in many of the major progressive political battles of the past fifty years, including anti–Vietnam War activities, the women's movement, and most recently resistance to the war in Iraq.

Robert Pinsky (b. 1940) was born in Long Branch, New Jersey. He is the author of many books of poetry, including *The Figured Wheel: New and Collected Poems, 1966–1996* (1996), which won the 1997 Lenore Marshall Poetry

Prize and was a Pulitzer Prize nominee. He has also published several books of criticism, two books of translation, a biography—*The Life of David* (2005)—several books on reading poetry, and *Mindwheel* (1984), an electronic novel that functions as an interactive computer game. In 1999 he coedited with Maggie Dietz *Americans' Favorite Poems: The Favorite Poem Project Anthology*. He is currently poetry editor of the weekly Internet magazine *Slate*. He teaches in the graduate writing program at Boston University, and in 1997 he was named Poet Laureate Consultant in Poetry to the Library of Congress.

Raised in a middle-class family in Boston, **Sylvia Plath** (1932–1963) showed early promise as a writer, having stories and poems published in magazines such as *Seventeen* while she was in high school. As a student at Smith College, she was selected for an internship at *Mademoiselle* magazine and spent a month working in New York in the summer of 1953. Upon her return home, she suffered a serious breakdown, attempted suicide, and was institutionalized. She returned to Smith College for her senior year in 1954 and received a Fulbright fellowship to study at Cambridge University in England, where she met the poet Ted Hughes. They were married in 1956. They lived in the United States as well as in England, and Plath studied under ROBERT LOWELL at Boston University. Her marriage broke up in 1962, and from her letters and poems it appears that she was approaching another breakdown at that time. On February 11, 1963, she committed suicide. Four books of poetry appeared during her lifetime, and her *Selected Poems* was published in 1985. The powerful, psychologically intense poetry for which she is best known (including "Daddy") was written after 1960, influenced by the "confessional" style of Lowell (see **confessional poetry** in the Glossary).

Born in Boston, Massachusetts, **Edgar Allan Poe** (1809–1849), the son of itinerant actors, was abandoned at one year of age by his father; his mother died soon after. The baby became the ward of John Allan of Richmond, Virginia, whose surname became Poe's middle name. When the family fortunes declined, the Allans moved to England. Poe was educated there and at the new University of Virginia upon his return to Richmond. Although an excellent student, Poe drank and gambled heavily, causing Allan to withdraw him from the university after one year. Poe made his way to Boston, enlisted in the army, and eventually, with Allan's help, took an appointment at West Point. After further dissipation ended his military career, Poe set out to support himself by writing. Three volumes of poetry brought in little money, and in 1835 Poe took a position as an assistant editor of the *Southern Literary Messenger*, the first of many positions he lost because of drinking. He began to publish short stories. In 1836 he married his thirteen-year-old cousin, Virginia Clemm, and took on the support of her mother as well, increasing his financial difficulties. They went to New York City, where Poe published *The Narrative of Arthur Gordon Pym* (1838) and assembled the best stories he had published in magazines in *Tales of the Grotesque and Arabesque* (1840), his first story collection. At that time he also began to write detective stories, virtually inventing the genre. Already respected as a critic, Poe won fame as a poet with *The Raven and Other Poems*

(1845). In 1847, after the death of his wife, Poe became engaged to the poet Sarah Helen Whitman, a wealthy widow six years his senior, who ultimately resisted marriage because of Poe's drinking problem. In 1849 Poe met a childhood sweetheart, Elmira Royster Shelton, now a widow, who agreed to marry him. After celebrating his apparent reversal of fortune with friends in Baltimore, he was found unconscious in the street and died shortly thereafter. Always admired in Europe, Poe's major stories of horror and detection, his major poems, and his major critical pieces on the craft of writing are considered American classics.

Born in London to a successful textile merchant, **Alexander Pope** (1688–1744) spent his childhood in the country, stunted by tuberculosis of the spine (his height never exceeded four and a half feet). Pope was also limited by his Catholicism, which prevented him from going to a university, voting, or holding public office. He turned to writing and gained considerable fame for his satire *The Rape of the Lock* and for his translations of Homer. Fame also brought ridicule and vehement attacks from critics holding different political views, and Pope struck back with nasty satires of his detractors. Later in his career, he wrote a good deal of ethical and philosophical verse.

Ezra Pound (1885–1972) was born in Idaho but grew up outside Philadelphia; he attended the University of Pennsylvania for two years and graduated from Hamilton College. He taught for two years at Wabash College, then left for Europe, living for the next few years in London, where he edited *The Little Review* and founded several literary movements — including the Imagists and the Vorticists. After moving to Italy, he began his major work, the *Cantos*, and became involved in fascist politics. During World War II, he did radio broadcasts from Italy in support of Mussolini, for which he was indicted for treason in the United States. Judged mentally unfit for trial, he remained in an asylum in Washington, D.C., until 1958, when the charges were dropped. Pound spent his last years in Italy. He is generally considered the poet most responsible for defining and promoting a modernist aesthetic in poetry.

Dudley Randall (1914–2002) was born in Washington, D.C., and lived most of his life in Detroit. His first published poem appeared in the *Detroit Free Press* when he was thirteen. He worked for Ford Motor Company and then for the U.S. Postal Service and served in the South Pacific during World War II. He graduated from Wayne State University in 1949 and then from the library school at the University of Michigan. In 1965 Randall established the Broadside Press, one of the most important publishers of modern black poetry. "Ballad of Birmingham," written in response to the 1963 bombing of a church in which four girls were killed, has been set to music and recorded. It became an anthem for many in the civil rights movement.

Born in Pulaski, Tennessee, **John Crowe Ransom** (1888–1974) was the son of a preacher. He studied at Vanderbilt University and then at Christ Church College, Oxford, on a Rhodes scholarship. After service in World War I, he taught first at Vanderbilt and later at Kenyon College, where he edited the *Kenyon Review*. He published three volumes of highly acclaimed poetry but after 1927 devoted himself principally to critical writing. He was a guiding member of the Fugitives, a group of writers who sought to preserve a traditional aesthetic ideal that was firmly rooted in classical values and forms. As a critic, he promulgated the highly influential **New Criticism** (see the Glossary), which focused attention on texts as self-sufficient entities to be analyzed through rigorous methodologies intended to reveal their depth, subtleties, and intricacies of technique and theme.

Adrienne Rich (1929–2012) was born in Baltimore, Maryland. She published over sixteen volumes of poetry and five volumes of critical prose, including *Tonight No Poetry Will Serve: Poems 2007–2010* (2010), *Telephone Ringing in the Labyrinth: Poems 2004–2006* (2007), and *A Human Eye: Essays on Art in Society* (2009). She also edited Muriel Rukeyser's *Selected Poems* for the Library of America. Among numerous other recognitions, she was the 2006 recipient of the National Book Foundation's Medal for Distinguished Contribution to American Letters. Her poetry and essays have been widely translated and published internationally.

Alberto Ríos (b. 1952) was born to a Guatemalan father and an English mother in Nogales, Arizona, on the Mexican border. He earned a B.A. in English, a B.A. in psychology, and an M.F.A. at the University of Arizona. In addition to ten books of poetry, he has published three collections of short stories and a memoir, *Capirotada: A Nogales Memoir* (1999). His work often fuses realism, surrealism, and magical realism. Since 1994 he has been Regents Professor of English at Arizona

State University, where he has taught since 1982.

Born in Head Tide, Maine, **Edwin Arlington Robinson** (1869–1935) grew up in the equally provincial Maine town of Gardiner, the setting for much of his poetry. He was forced to leave Harvard University after two years because of his family's financial difficulties. He published his first two books of poetry in 1896 and 1897 ("Richard Cory" appeared in the latter). For the next quarter century, Robinson chose to live in poverty and write his poetry, relying on temporary jobs and charity from friends. President Theodore Roosevelt, at the urging of his son Kermit, used his influence to get Robinson a sinecure job in the New York Custom House in 1905, giving him time to write. He published numerous books of mediocre poetry in the next decade. The tide turned for him with *The Man against the Sky* (1916); the numerous volumes that followed received high praise and sold well. He was awarded three Pulitzer Prizes: for *Collected Poems* in 1921, *The Man Who Died Twice* in 1924, and *Tristram* in 1927. Robinson was the first major American poet of the twentieth century, unique in that he devoted his life to poetry and willingly paid the price in poverty and obscurity.

Theodore Roethke (1908–1963) was the son of a commercial greenhouse operator in Saginaw, Michigan. As a child, he spent much time in greenhouses, and the impressions of nature he formed there later influenced the subjects and imagery of his verse. Roethke graduated from the University of Michigan and studied at Harvard University. His eight books of poetry were held in high regard by critics, some of whom considered Roethke among the best poets of his generation. *The Waking* was awarded the Pulitzer Prize in 1954; *Words for the Wind* (1958) received the Bollingen Prize and the National Book Award. He taught at many colleges and universities, his career interrupted several times by serious mental breakdowns, and gained a reputation as an exceptional teacher of poetry writing.

Mary Ruefle (b. 1952) was born near Pittsburgh but spent her early life moving around the United States and Europe as the daughter of a military officer. She graduated from Bennington College with a literature major. She has published ten books of poetry, including *Memling's Veil* (1982), *The Adamant* (1989; winner of the 1988 Iowa Poetry Prize), *A Little White Shadow* (2006), and *Selected Poems* (2010). She published her first collection of short stories, *The Most of It*, in 2008. Among awards she has received are a Guggenheim fellowship, an American Academy of Arts and Letters Award in Literature, and a Whiting Foundation Writer's Award. She lives in Vermont, where she is a professor in the Vermont College M.F.A. program.

Born in Newton, Massachusetts, **Anne Sexton** (1928–1974) dropped out of Garland Junior College to get married. After suffering nervous breakdowns following the births of her two children, she was encouraged to enroll in a writing program. Studying under ROBERT LOWELL at Boston University, she was a fellow student with SYLVIA PLATH. Like the work of other "confessional" poets, Sexton's poetry is an intimate view of her life and emotions. She made the experience of being a woman a central issue in her poetry, bringing to it such subjects as menstruation and abortion as well as drug addiction. She published at least a dozen books of poetry—*Live or Die* was awarded the Pulitzer Prize for poetry in 1966—as well as four children's books coauthored with MAXINE KUMIN. Sexton's emotional problems continued, along with a growing addiction to alcohol and sedatives, and she committed suicide in 1974.

William Shakespeare (1564–1616) was born in Stratford-upon-Avon, England, where his father was a glovemaker and bailiff, and he presumably went to grammar school there. He married Anne Hathaway in 1582 and sometime before 1592 left for London to work as a playwright and actor. Shakespeare joined the Lord Chamberlain's Men (later the King's Men), an acting company for which he wrote thirty-seven plays—comedies, tragedies, histories, and romances—upon which his reputation as the finest dramatist in the English language is based. He was also arguably the finest lyric poet of his day, as exemplified by songs scattered throughout his plays, two early nondramatic poems (*Venus and Adonis* and *The Rape of Lucrece*), and the sonnet sequence expected of all noteworthy writers in the Elizabethan age. Shakespeare's sonnets were probably written in the 1590s, although they were not published until 1609. Shakespeare retired to Stratford around 1612, and by the time he died at the age of fifty-two, he was acknowledged as a leading light of the Elizabethan stage and had become successful enough to have purchased a coat of arms for his family home.

Born into a wealthy aristocratic family in Sussex County, England, **Percy Bysshe Shelley** (1792–1822) was educated at Eton and then went on to Oxford University, where he was expelled after six months for writing a defense of atheism, the first price he would pay for his nonconformity and radical (for his time) commitment to social justice. The following year he eloped with Harriet Westbrook, daughter of a tavern keeper, despite his belief that marriage was a tyrannical and degrading social institution (she was sixteen, he eighteen). He became a disciple of the radical social philosopher William Godwin; fell in love with Godwin's daughter, Mary Wollstonecraft Godwin (the author, later, of *Frankenstein*); and went to live with her in France. Two years later, after Harriet had committed suicide, the two married and moved to Italy, where they shifted about restlessly and Shelley was generally short on money and in poor health. In such trying circumstances, he wrote his greatest works. He died at age thirty, when the boat he was in was overturned by a sudden storm.

Born in Albuquerque of mixed Pueblo, Mexican, and white ancestry, **Leslie Marmon Silko** (b. 1948) grew up on the Laguna Pueblo reservation in New Mexico. She earned her B.A. (with honors) from the University of New Mexico. In a long and productive writing career (she was already writing stories in elementary school), Silko has published poetry, novels, short stories, essays, letters, and film scripts. She taught creative writing first at the University of New Mexico and later at the University of Arizona. She has been named a Living Cultural Treasure by the New Mexico Humanities Council and has received the Native Writers' Circle of the Americas Lifetime Achievement Award. Her work is a graphic telling of the life of native peoples, maintaining its rich spiritual heritage while exposing the terrible consequences of European domination.

Charles Simic (b. 1938) was born in Belgrade, Yugoslavia. In 1953 he, his mother, and his brother joined his father in Chicago, where Charles continued to live until 1958. His first poems were published when he was twenty-one. In 1961 he was drafted into the U.S. Army, and in 1966 he earned his B.A. from New York University. His first book of poems, *What the Grass Says*, was published in 1967. Since then he has published more than sixty books of poetry, translations, and essays, including *The World Doesn't End: Prose Poems* (1990), for which he received the Pulitzer Prize for poetry. Since 1973 he has lived in New Hampshire, where he is a professor of English at the University of New Hampshire. In 2007 he was named Poet Laureate Consultant in Poetry to the Library of Congress.

Gary Snyder (b. 1930) was born in San Francisco and grew up in Oregon and Washington. He studied anthropology at Reed College and Asian languages at the University of California, Berkeley, where he became associated with the Beat movement; however, his poetry often deals with nature rather than the urban interests more typical of Beat poetry. He has published sixteen books of poetry and prose, including *Turtle Island* (1974), which won the Pulitzer Prize for poetry. Snyder is active in the environmental movement and spent a number of years in Japan practicing Zen Buddhism. He taught for many years at the University of California, Davis.

Cathy Song (b. 1955) was born in Hawaii of Korean and Chinese ancestry and grew up in the small town of Wahiawa on Oahu. She was encouraged to write during her childhood. She left Hawaii for the East Coast, earning a B.A. in English from Wellesley College and an M.A. in creative writing from Boston University. In 1987 she returned to Honolulu, where she continues to write and teaches creative writing. Her first book, *Picture Bride*, was chosen by Richard Hugo for the Yale Series of Younger Poets in 1982. Since then she has published four other books of poetry. With island poet Juliet S. Kono, she coedited and contributed poetry and prose to *Sister Stew* (1991). Her writing has earned the Hawaii Award for Literature and a Shelley Memorial Award.

Sophocles (c. 496–c. 406 BCE) was not the first important voice to emerge in drama, but as a representative of classical Greek tragedy, it is hard to imagine a more important figure. Indeed, his works were considered such models of the craft that Aristotle based much of his *Poetics* on an analysis of *Oedipus Rex*. Sophocles was born to a wealthy Athenian family and became active in many aspects of civic life as a soldier, a priest, and a statesman. Today, however, he is remembered principally for his achievements as a playwright. During a long and distinguished career, he won first prize in Greek drama competitions more often than any other writer. Though there is evidence that he wrote more than 120 plays, only seven have survived in their entirety, along with fragments of many others. In his plays, Sophocles wrestled with some of the most important issues of his time and indeed of all time—the conflict between fate and free will;

between public and private morality; and between duty to one's family, the state, and the gods—giving his work enduring appeal. *Oedipus Rex* (*Oedipus the King*, first performed in 430 BCE) is one of Sophocles' three Theban plays, the others being *Antigone* (441 BCE) and *Oedipus at Colonus* (401 BCE, first performed posthumously).

Raised in Fresno, California, **Gary Soto** (b. 1952) earned his B.A. from California State University, Fresno, and an M.F.A. from the University of California, Irvine. He worked his way through college doing such jobs as picking grapes and chopping beets. Much of his poetry comes out of and reflects his working background, that of migrant workers and tenant farmers in the fields of southern California, and provides glimpses into the lives of families in the barrio. Soto's language comes from gritty, raw, everyday American speech. His first book, *The Elements of San Joaquin*, won the 1976 United States Award from the International Poetry Forum. He has published eleven collections of poetry, eight novels, four essay collections, and numerous young adult and children's books and has edited four anthologies. He lives in Berkeley and Fresno, California.

A contemporary of WILLIAM SHAKESPEARE, **Edmund Spenser** (1552–1599) was the greatest English nondramatic poet of his time. Best known for his romantic and national epic *The Faerie Queene*, Spenser wrote poems of a number of other types as well and was important as an innovator in meter and form (as in his development of the special form of sonnet that bears his name—the **Spenserian sonnet** [see the Glossary]).

Born in Hutchinson, Kansas, **William Stafford** (1914–1995) studied at the University of Kansas and then at the University of Iowa Writers' Workshop. In between, he was a conscientious objector during World War II and worked in labor camps. In 1948 Stafford moved to Oregon, where he taught at Lewis and Clark College until he retired in 1980. His first major collection of poems, *Traveling through the Dark*, was published when Stafford was forty-eight. It won the National Book Award in 1963. He went on to publish more than sixty-five volumes of poetry and prose and came to be known as a very influential teacher of poetry. From 1970 to 1971, he was Consultant in Poetry to the Library of Congress.

Gerald Stern (b. 1925) was born in Pittsburgh and studied at the University of Pittsburgh and Columbia University. Stern came late to poetry: he was forty-six when he published his first book. Since then he has published more than fifteen collections of poems, most recently *Save the Last Dance: Poems* (2008) and *Early Collected Poems, 1965–1992* (2010), and received many prestigious awards, including the 1998 National Book Award for Poetry for his book *This Time: New and Selected Poems*. Stern has often been compared to WALT WHITMAN and JOHN KEATS for his exploration of the self and the sometimes ecstatic exuberance of his verse. Until his retirement in 1995, he taught at many universities, including Columbia University, New York University, Sarah Lawrence College, and the University of Pittsburgh, and for many years at the University of Iowa Writers' Workshop. He is currently serving as distinguished poet-in-residence at Drew University's low-residency M.F.A. Program in Poetry.

Born in Reading, Pennsylvania, **Wallace Stevens** (1879–1955) attended Harvard University for three years. He tried journalism and then attended New York University Law School, after which he worked as a legal consultant. He spent most of his life working as an executive for the Hartford Accident and Indemnity Company, spending his evenings writing some of the most imaginative and influential poetry of his time. Although now considered one of the major American poets of the twentieth century, he did not receive widespread recognition until the publication of his *Collected Poems* just a year before his death.

Mark Strand (b. 1934) was born on Prince Edward Island, Canada, and studied at Antioch College, Yale University, the University of Florence, and the University of Iowa. He is the author of numerous collections of poetry, including *Reasons for Moving* (1968); *The Story of Our Lives* (1973); *Selected Poems* (1980); *The Continuous Life* (1990); *Blizzard of One* (1998), which won the Pulitzer Prize for poetry; *Dark Harbor* (1993); and *Man and Camel* (2006). He has also published two books of prose, several volumes of translation (of works by Rafael Alberti and Carlos Drummond de Andrade, among others), several monographs on contemporary artists, and three books for children. He served as Poet Laureate Consultant in Poetry to the Library of Congress from 1990 to 1991 and is a former chancellor of the Academy of American Poets. He teaches English and comparative literature at Columbia University in New York.

Born in Havana, Cuba, **Virgil Suárez** (b. 1962) was eight years old when he left with his parents for Spain, where they lived until they came to the United States in 1974. He is the author of eight collections of poetry, five novels, and a volume of short stories and is the editor of several best-selling anthologies. His work often reflects the impact of the diaspora on the everyday life of Cuban and other exiles. He is professor of creative writing at Florida State University.

Sekou Sundiata (1948–2007) was born and raised in Harlem. His work was deeply influenced by the music, poetry, and oral traditions of African American culture. A self-proclaimed radical in the 1970s, for the next several decades he used poetry to comment on the life and times of our culture. His work, which encompasses print, performance, music, and theater, is praised for its fusion of soul, jazz, and hip-hop grooves with political insight, humor, and rhythmic speech. He regularly recorded and performed on tour with artists such as Craig Harris and Vernon Reid.

Born in Ireland of English parents, **Jonathan Swift** (1667–1745) was educated at Kilkenny College and Trinity College, Dublin. He worked in England for a decade as a private secretary and for four years as a political writer but spent the rest of his life in Ireland, as dean of St. Patrick's Cathedral in Dublin. Although he is best known for his satires in prose (such as *Gulliver's Travels* and "A Modest Proposal"), Swift's original ambition was to be a poet, and he wrote occasional verse throughout his life.

Born in Oakland, California, and raised to become a neurosurgeon and a concert pianist by parents who had emigrated from China to the United States two and a half years before her birth, **Amy Tan** (b. 1952) became first a consultant to programs for disabled children and then a professional writer. In 1987 she visited China for the first time and found it just as her mother had described it: "As soon as my feet touched China, I became Chinese," she has said. Her widely acclaimed novel *The Joy Luck Club* (1989) contrasts the lives of four women in pre-1949 China with those of their American-born daughters in California. Her other work includes *The Kitchen God's Wife* (1991); a children's book, *The Moon Lady* (1992); *The Hundred Secret Senses* (1995); *The Bonesetter's Daughter* (2001); and *The Valley of Amazement* (2011).

A native of Kansas City, Missouri, **James Tate** (b. 1943) studied at the University of Missouri and Kansas State College during his undergraduate years. He then earned his M.F.A. at the University of Iowa Writers' Workshop in 1967, the same year his first poetry collection, *The Lost Pilot*, was published (selected by Dudley Fitts for the Yale Series of Younger Poets). Tate is the author of numerous books of poetry, including *Selected Poems* (1991), which won the Pulitzer Prize and the William Carlos Williams Award. Tate's poems often include highly unusual juxtapositions of imagery, tone, and context, as is evident in "The Wheelchair Butterfly." Tate has taught at the University of Iowa, the University of California, Berkeley, and Columbia University and now teaches at the University of Massachusetts, Amherst.

Born in Somersby, Lincolnshire, **Alfred, Lord Tennyson** (1809–1892), grew up in the tense atmosphere of his unhappy father's rectory. He went to Trinity College, Cambridge, but when he was forced to leave because of family and financial problems, he returned home to study and practice the craft of poetry. His early volumes, published in 1830 and 1832, received bad reviews, but his *In Memoriam* (1850), an elegy on his close friend Arthur Hallam, who died of a brain seizure, won acclaim. He was unquestionably the most popular poet of his time (the "poet of the people") and arguably the greatest of the Victorian poets. He succeeded WILLIAM WORDSWORTH as poet laureate, a position he held from 1850 until his death.

Dylan Thomas (1914–1953) was born in Swansea, Wales, and after grammar school became a journalist. He worked as a writer for the rest of his life. His first book of poetry, *Eighteen Poems*, appeared in 1934 and was followed by *Twenty-Five Poems* (1936), *Deaths and Entrances* (1946), and *Collected Poems* (1952). His poems are often rich in textured rhythms and images. He also wrote prose, chiefly short stories collectively appearing as *Portrait of the Artist as a Young Dog* (1940), and a number of film scripts and radio plays. His most famous work, *Under Milk Wood*, written as a play for voices, was first performed in New York on May 14, 1953. Thomas's radio broadcasts and his lecture tours and poetry readings in the United States brought him fame and popularity. Alcoholism contributed to his early death in 1953.

Jean Toomer (1894–1967) was born in Washington, D.C., of mixed French, Dutch, Welsh, Negro, German, Jewish, and Indian blood (according to him). Although he passed for white during certain periods of his life, he was raised in a predominantly black community and attended black high schools. He began college at the University of Wisconsin but transferred to the College of the City of New York. He spent several years publishing poems and stories in small magazines. In 1921 he took a teaching job in Georgia and remained there for only four months; the experience inspired *Cane* (1923), a book of prose poetry describing the Georgian people and landscape that became a central work of the Harlem Renaissance. He later experimented in communal living and both studied and tried to promulgate the ideas of Quakerism and the Russian mystic George Gurdjieff. From 1950 on, he published very little, writing mostly for himself.

Natasha Trethewey (b. 1966) was born in Gulfport, Mississippi. She has degrees from the University of Georgia, Hollins University, and the University of Massachusetts. She has won many awards for her poetry, including the inaugural Cave Canem Poetry Prize for her first collection, *Domestic Work* (2000). Her second collection, *Bellocq's Ophelia* (2002), received the 2003 Mississippi Institute of Arts and Letters Book Prize and was a finalist for both the Academy of American Poets' James Laughlin and Lenore Marshall prizes. In 2007 her collection *Native Guard* received the Pulitzer Prize. She has taught at Auburn University, the University of North Carolina, and Duke University. From 2009 to 2010 she was the James Weldon Johnson Fellow in African American Studies at Yale University's Beinecke Rare Books and Manuscript Library. She presently teaches at Emory University, as holder of the Phillis Wheatley Distinguished Chair in Poetry. Her book of creative nonfiction, *Beyond Katrina: A Meditation on the Mississippi Gulf*, was published in 2010.

Quincy Troupe (b. 1943) was born in New York City and grew up in St. Louis, Missouri. He is the author of sixteen books, including eight volumes of poetry, most recently *The Architecture of Language* (2006). He is the recipient of two American Book Awards, for his collection of poetry *Snake-Back Solos* (1980) and his nonfiction book *Miles: The Autobiography* (1989). In 1991 he received the prestigious Peabody Award for writing and coproducing the seven-part "Miles Davis Radio Project" aired on National Public Radio in 1990. *Transcircularities: New and Selected Poems* (2002) received the Milt Kessler Award for 2003 and was a finalist for the Paterson Poetry Prize. Troupe has taught at UCLA, Ohio University, the College of Staten Island (CUNY), Columbia University (in the graduate writing program), and the University of California, San Diego. He is now professor emeritus of creative writing and American and Caribbean literature at UCSD. He is the founding editorial director for *Code* magazine and former artistic director of "Arts on the Cutting Edge," a reading and performance series at the Museum of Contemporary Art, San Diego. He was the first official poet laureate of the state of California, appointed to the post in 2002 by Governor Gray Davis.

Born an only child in Shillington, Pennsylvania, to a mother who was a writer and a father who taught high school, **John Updike** (1932–2009) studied at Harvard University and the Ruskin School of Drawing and Fine Art at Oxford, England. On his return to the United States, he joined the staff of *The New Yorker*, where he worked from 1955 to 1957. From 1957 until his death, he lived and worked near Ipswich, Massachusetts. In addition to numerous volumes of poetry, books of essays and speeches, and a play, Updike published some twenty novels and some ten collections of short fiction noteworthy for their incisive presentation of the quandaries of contemporary personal and social life. Among his novels are *Rabbit, Run* (1960), *The Centaur* (1963; National Book Award), *Couples* (1968), *Rabbit Redux* (1971), *Rabbit Is Rich* (1981; Pulitzer Prize), *The Witches of Eastwick* (1984), *Rabbit at Rest* (1990; Pulitzer Prize), *In the Beauty of the Lilies* (1996), *Toward the End of Time* (1997), *Bech at Bay* (1998), *Villages* (2004), and *Terrorist* (2006). His story collections include *The Same Door* (1959), *Pigeon Feathers* (1962), *Olinger Stories* (1964), *The Music School* (1966), *Museums and Women* (1972), *Too Far to Go: The Maples Stories* (1979), *Bech Is Back* (1982), *Trust Me* (1987), and *The Afterlife and Other Stories* (1994).

Alice Walker (b. 1944) was born in Eatonton, Georgia. Her parents were sharecropper farmers. When she was eight, she lost sight in one eye when one of her older brothers accidentally shot her with a BB gun. She was valedictorian of her high school class. Encouraged by her teachers and her mother to go to college, she attended Spelman College in Atlanta, a school for black women, for two years and graduated from Sarah Lawrence College. From the mid-1960s to the mid-1970s, she lived in Tougaloo, Mississippi. She was active in the civil rights movement of the 1960s and remains an involved activist today. Her first book was a collection of poetry, *Once* (1968). She is a prolific writer, having gone on to publish more than thirty books of poetry, novels, short stories, and nonfiction. Her best-known novel, *The Color Purple* (1982), won the American Book Award and the Pulitzer Prize for fiction and was made into a motion picture directed by Steven Spielberg.

James Welch (1940–2003) was born in Browning, Montana. His father was a member of the Blackfoot tribe, his mother of the Gros Ventre tribe. He attended schools on the Blackfoot and Fort Belknap reservations and took a degree from the University of Montana, where he studied under Richard Hugo. Welch published many books of poetry, fiction, and nonfiction. His hard, spare poems often evoke the bleakest side of contemporary Native American life. He received a Lifetime Achievement Award for literature from the Native Writers' Circle in 1997.

Eudora Welty (1909–2001) was born in Jackson, Mississippi, and graduated from the University of Wisconsin. She is admired for her fine photographic studies of people—*One Time, One Place* (1972) collects her photos of Mississippi in the 1930s—as well as for her fiction, which also depicts the inhabitants of rural Mississippi. Among her seven volumes of short stories, which explore the mysteries of individuals' "separateness," are *A Curtain of Green* (1941), *The Wide Net* (1943), *The Golden Apples* (1949), *The Bride of Innisfallen* (1955), and *The Collected Stories* (1980). Her novels include *Delta Wedding* (1946), *The Ponder Heart* (1954), and *The Optimist's Daughter* (1972), which won the Pulitzer Prize. Welty also wrote many reviews, articles, and books of literary criticism.

Born in rural Long Island, **Walt Whitman** (1819–1892) was the son of a farmer and carpenter. He attended grammar school in Brooklyn and took his first job as a printer's devil for the *Long Island Patriot*. Attending the opera, dabbling in politics, participating in street life, and gaining experience as a student, printer, reporter, writer, carpenter, farmer, seashore observer, and a teacher provided the bedrock for his future poetic vision of an ideal society based on the realization of self. Although Whitman liked to portray himself as uncultured, he read widely in the King James Bible as well as SHAKESPEARE, Homer, Dante, Aeschylus, and SOPHOCLES. He worked for many years in the newspaper business and began writing poetry only in 1847. In 1855, at his own expense, he published the first edition of *Leaves of Grass*, a thin volume of twelve long untitled poems. Written in a highly original and innovative **free verse** (see the Glossary), influenced significantly by music, and with a wide-ranging subject matter, the work seemed strange to most of the poet's contemporaries— although some did recognize its value: Ralph Waldo Emerson wrote to the poet shortly after Whitman sent him a copy, saying, "I greet you at the beginning of a great career." He spent much of the remainder of his life revising and expanding this book. Today *Leaves of Grass* is considered a masterpiece of world literature, marking the beginning of modern American poetry, and Whitman is widely regarded as America's national poet.

Richard Wilbur (b. 1921) was born in New York City and grew up in rural New Jersey. He attended Amherst College and began writing poetry during World War II while fighting in Italy and France. After the war, he studied at Harvard University and then taught there and at Wellesley College, Wesleyan University, and Smith College.

He has published many books of poetry, including *Things of This World* (1956), for which he received the Pulitzer Prize for poetry and the National Book Award, and *New and Collected Poems* (1988), which also won the Pulitzer Prize. He has always been respected as a master of formal constraints, comparing them to the bottle that contains the genie, a restraint that stimulates the imagination to achieve results unlikely to be reached without it. Wilbur has also published numerous translations of French plays, two books for children, a collection of prose pieces, and editions of WILLIAM SHAKESPEARE and EDGAR ALLAN POE. In 1987 he was appointed Poet Laureate Consultant in Poetry to the Library of Congress.

Raised in Ann Arbor, Michigan, **Nancy Willard** (b. 1936) was educated at the University of Michigan and Stanford University. She is a noted writer of books for children. *A Visit to William Blake's Inn: Poems for Innocent and Experienced Travelers* (1981) was the first book of poetry to win the prestigious Newbery Medal, which recognizes the most distinguished American children's book published in a given year. Willard is also an excellent essayist and novelist. Her work in all genres frequently leads to a most uncommon experience of the common. She teaches at Vassar College and lives in Poughkeepsie, New York.

Born Thomas Lanier Williams in Columbia, Mississippi, as a child **Tennessee Williams** (1911–1983) moved with his family to St. Louis. His childhood was not easy: his parents were ill-matched, the family had little money, and both he and his beloved sister, Rose, suffered from depression and medical problems. It took Williams three attempts at college before he finished, finally earning a degree in playwriting from the University of Iowa at the age of twenty-four. His earliest efforts at writing were unsuccessful, but in 1944 *The Glass Menagerie* opened in Chicago and later began a very successful run in New York, winning the prestigious Drama Critics Circle Award. Other successes followed, including *A Streetcar Named Desire* (1947), which won the Pulitzer Prize and helped launch the career of its young star, Marlon Brando; *Cat on a Hot Tin Roof* (1955); and *Suddenly Last Summer* (1958). The American stage in the 1940s and 1950s was not yet ready to accept overt homosexuality, so Williams transformed his own tortured searching for sexual and emotional fulfillment into plays with remarkably frank heterosexual themes. This frankness and dreamy, poetic language are key elements of his style. In his later years, Williams suffered from drug and alcohol problems and was occasionally institutionalized for these and the crippling depressions that continued to plague him. Though his later work never achieved the popular success of his early plays, Williams's reputation in the American theater is secure.

William Carlos Williams (1883–1963) was born in Rutherford, New Jersey; his father was an English emigrant and his mother was of mixed Basque descent from Puerto Rico. He decided to be both a writer and a doctor while in high school in New York City. He graduated from the medical school at the University of Pennsylvania, where he was a friend of EZRA POUND and Hilda Doolittle. After completing an internship in New York, writing poems between seeing patients, Williams practiced general medicine in Rutherford

(he was ALLEN GINSBERG's pediatrician). His first book of poems was published in 1909, and he subsequently published poems, novels, short stories, plays, criticism, and essays. Initially one of the principal poets of the Imagist movement, Williams later sought to invent an entirely fresh—and distinctly American—poetic whose subject matter was centered on the everyday circumstances of life and the lives of common people. Williams, like WALLACE STEVENS, became one of the major poets of the twentieth century and exerted great influence upon poets of his own and later generations.

Born and raised in the Hill District, an African American section of Pittsburgh that provides the backdrop to many of his plays, **August Wilson** (1945–2005) has come to be seen as one of the most important voices on the contemporary American stage. The son of a mixed-race marriage, his white father was not in the household when he was growing up. He dropped out of high school but continued to read widely, beginning his serious writing with poetry, the rhythms of which can be heard in his plays. In the 1960s, he became involved in the Black Power movement and also began to turn his writing talents to the stage. His best-known work is his cycle of historical plays, known as "The Pittsburgh Cycle," which examines important elements of African American experience and consists of one play for each decade of the twentieth century. Among these are *Ma Rainey's Black Bottom* (1985), *Fences* (1987), *Joe Turner's Come and Gone* (1988), *The Piano Lesson* (1990), and *Seven Guitars* (1996). Each of these plays won the New York Drama Critics Circle Award, and the final play in the cycle, *Radio Golf* (2005), received a Tony Award nomination. *Fences* and *The Piano Lesson* each also earned Wilson the Pulitzer Prize.

William Wordsworth (1770–1850) was born and raised in the Lake District of England. Both his parents died by the time he was thirteen. He studied at Cambridge, toured Europe on foot, and lived in France for a year during the first part of the French Revolution. He returned to England, leaving behind a lover, Annette Vallon, and their daughter, Caroline, from whom he was soon cut off by war between England and France. He met SAMUEL TAYLOR COLERIDGE, and in 1798 they published *Lyrical Ballads*, the first great work of the English Romantic movement. He changed poetry forever by his decision to use common language in his poetry instead of heightened **poetic diction** (see the Glossary). In 1799 he and his sister Dorothy moved to Grasmere, in the Lake District, where he married Mary Hutchinson, a childhood friend. His greatest works were produced between 1797 and 1808. He continued to write for the next forty years, but his work never regained the heights of his earlier verse. In 1843 he was named poet laureate, a position he held until his death in 1850.

Charles Wright (b. 1935) was born in Pickwick Dam, Tennessee, and grew up in Tennessee and North Carolina. He studied at Davidson College, served a four-year stint in Italy as a captain in the U.S. Army Intelligence Corps, and then continued his education at the University of Iowa Writers' Workshop and at the University of Rome on a Fulbright fellowship. He has published many books of poetry—including *Black Zodiac*, which won the Pulitzer Prize for poetry in 1997—two volumes of criticism, and a translation of Eugenio Montale's poetry. His most recent collection is *Outtakes* (2010). Wright's poems have been labeled impressionistic, combining images from the natural world, Catholicism, and the rural South. He taught at the University of California, Irvine, for almost twenty years and now is Souder Family Professor of English at the University of Virginia.

Raised in Martin's Ferry, Ohio, **James Wright** (1927–1980) attended Kenyon College, where the influence of JOHN CROWE RANSOM sent his early poetry in a formalist direction. After spending a year in Austria on a Fulbright fellowship, he returned to the United States and earned an M.A. and a Ph.D. at the University of Washington, studying under THEODORE ROETHKE and STANLEY KUNITZ. He went on to teach at the University of Minnesota, Macalester College, and Hunter College. His working-class background and the poverty that he witnessed during the Depression stirred in him a sympathy for the poor and for "outsiders" of various sorts that shaped the tone and content of his poetry. He published numerous books of poetry; his *Collected Poems* received the Pulitzer Prize in 1972.

The niece of Sir Philip Sidney and Mary Sidney Herbert, **Lady Mary Wroth** (1587?–1651?) was one of the best and most prolific women writers of the English Renaissance and an important literary patron. Her husband's early death left her deeply in debt. She wrote *Pamphilia to Amphilanthus*, the only known English sonnet sequence on love themes by a woman; seventy-four poems that appeared in *Urania* (the first full-length work of prose fiction by a woman); and several other pieces. BEN JONSON said that reading her sonnets had made him "a better lover and a much better poet."

Born in Kent, **Sir Thomas Wyatt** (1503–1542) was educated at St. John's College, Cambridge. He spent most of his life as a courtier and diplomat, serving King Henry VIII as ambassador to Spain and as a member of several missions to Italy and France. In his travels, Wyatt discovered the Italian writers of the High Renaissance, whose work he translated, thus introducing the sonnet form into English. He was arrested twice and charged with treason, sent to the Tower of London, and acquitted in 1541. Aristocratic poets at the time rarely published their poems themselves: works circulated in manuscript and in published collections ("miscellanies") gathered by printers. The most important of these is a volume published by Richard Tottel in 1557 titled *Songs and Sonnets*, but more commonly known as *Tottel's Miscellany*, which includes ninety-seven of Wyatt's sonnets and delightful lyrics.

William Butler Yeats (1865–1939) was born in Sandymount, Dublin, to an Anglo-Irish family. On leaving high school in 1883, he decided to be an artist, like his father, and attended art school but soon gave it up to concentrate on poetry. His first poems were published in 1885 in the *Dublin University Review*. Religious by temperament but unable to accept orthodox Christianity, Yeats throughout his life explored esoteric philosophies in search of a tradition that would substitute for a lost religion. He became a member of the Theosophical Society and the Order of the Golden Dawn, two groups interested in Eastern occultism, and later developed a private system of symbols and mystical ideas. Through the influence of Lady Gregory, a writer and promoter of literature, he became interested in Irish nationalist art, helping to found the Irish National Theatre and the famous Abbey Theatre. He was actively involved in Irish politics, especially after the Easter Rising of 1916. He continued to write and to revise earlier poems, leaving behind a body of verse that, in its variety and power, placed him among the greatest twentieth-century poets of the English language. He was awarded the Nobel Prize for Literature in 1923.

Born in Ocean Springs, Mississippi, **Al Young** (b. 1939) lived for a decade in the South and then moved to Detroit. He attended the University of Michigan and the University of California, Berkeley. Young has been a professional guitarist and singer, a disk jockey, a medical photographer, and a warehouseman; he has written eight books of poetry, most recently *Something about the Blues: An Unlikely Collection of Poetry* (2008); five novels; memoirs; essays; and film scripts. He also has edited a number of books, including *Yardbird Lives!* (1978) and *African American Literature: A Brief Introduction and Anthology* (1995). He has taught literature and creative writing at numerous college and universities. In the 1970s and 1980s, Young cofounded the journals *Yardbird Reader* and *Quilt* with poet-novelist Ishmael Reed. From 2005 to 2007, he served as California's poet laureate.

Ray A. Young Bear (b. 1950) was born and raised in the Mesquakie Tribal Settlement near Tama, Iowa. His poetry has been influenced by his maternal grandmother, Ada Kapayou Old Bear, and his wife, Stella L. Young Bear. He attended Pomona College in

California as well as Grinnell College, the University of Iowa, Iowa State University, and Northern Iowa University. He has taught creative writing and Native American literature at the Institute of American Indian Art, Eastern Washington University, the University of Iowa, and Iowa State University. Young Bear and his wife cofounded the Woodland Song and Dance Troupe of Arts Midwest in 1983. Young Bear's group has performed traditional Mesquakie music in the United States and the Netherlands. Author of four books of poetry, a collection of short stories, and a novel, he has contributed to contemporary Native American poetry and the study of it for three decades.

Paul Zimmer (b. 1934) was born in Canton, Ohio, and educated at Kent State University. He is the author of fifteen poetry collections, including *The Great Bird of Love*, which was selected for the National Poetry Series in 1998, and *Crossing to Sunlight Revisited: New and Selected Poems* (2007). His latest collection, *The Importance of Being Zimmer* (2010), brings together a selection from his more than 130 poems in the voice of the persona "Zimmer," a tragicomic everyman. He has also published several collections of personal essays. Zimmer directed the university presses at the University of Pittsburgh, the University of Georgia, and the University of Iowa, where he was responsible for the discovery and first publication of many of the finest contemporary poets. He currently lives with his wife in a small house on 117 acres of forest and meadows in Wisconsin.

Glossary of Critical and Literary Terms

This glossary provides definitions for important literary terms used in this anthology. Words and phrases highlighted in **boldface** in individual entries are defined elsewhere in the glossary.

Abstract language Any language that employs intangible, nonspecific concepts. *Love*, *truth*, and *beauty* are abstractions. Abstract language is the opposite of **concrete language**. Both types have different effects and are important features of an author's style.

Absurd, theater of the Theatrical style prominent in the mid-twentieth century that seeks to dramatize the absurdity of modern life. **Conventions** of the style include disjointed or elliptical plot lines, disaffected characters, non-**naturalistic** dialogue, and, often, **black comedy**. Proponents include Eugene Ionesco and Samuel Beckett.

Accent The stress, or greater emphasis, given to some syllables of words relative to that received by adjacent syllables.

Accentual meter A metrical system in which the number of accented, or stressed, syllables per line is regular— all lines have the same number, or the corresponding lines of different stanzas have the same number—while the number of unstressed syllables in lines varies randomly. Accentual meter consisting of two accented syllables in each half line linked by a system of alliteration was the hallmark of Old English poetry (up to the eleventh century),

and some modern poets, such as W. H. Auden, have sought to revive it. Gerard Manley Hopkins developed a unique variety of accentual verse he called *sprung rhythm* (see pp. 526–527).

Accentual-syllabic verse Verse whose meter takes into account both the number of syllables per line and the pattern of accented and unaccented syllables. The great majority of metrical poems in English are accentual-syllabic. Cf. **quantitative verse**.

Act One of the principal divisions of a full-length play. Plays of the Renaissance are commonly divided into five acts. Although four acts enjoyed a brief period of popularity in the nineteenth century, two or three acts are more typical of modern and contemporary dramas.

Agon The central conflict in a play. In Greek drama, the agon is a formal structural component, often a debate between two characters or parts of the **chorus**.

Alexandrine A poetic line with six iambic feet (iambic hexameter).

Allegory (1) An extended **metaphor** in which characters, events, objects, settings, and actions stand not only for themselves but also for abstract concepts, such as death or knowledge. Allegorical plays, often religious, were popular in medieval times; a famous example is *Everyman*. (2) A form or manner, usually narrative, in which objects, persons, and actions make coherent sense on a literal level but also are equated in a sustained and obvious way with (usually) abstract meanings that lie outside the story. A classic example in prose is John Bunyan's *The Pilgrim's Progress*; in narrative poetry, Edmund Spenser's *The Faerie Queene*.

Alliteration The repetition of identical consonant sounds in the stressed syllables of words relatively near to each other (in the same line or adjacent lines, usually). Alliteration is most common at the beginnings of words ("as the *g*rass was *g*reen") but can involve consonants within words ("*g*reen and care*f*ree, *f*amous among the barns"). Alliteration applies to sounds, not spelling: "And honoured among *f*oxes and *ph*easants" is an example. (The examples are from Dylan Thomas's "Fern Hill," p. 575.) Cf. **consonance**.

Allusion A figure of speech that echoes or makes brief reference to a literary or artistic work or a historical figure, event, or object, as, for example, the references to Lazarus and Hamlet in "The Love Song of J. Alfred Prufrock" (p. 547). It is usually a way of placing one's poem within or alongside a context that is evoked in a very economical fashion. See also **intertextuality**.

Alternative theater Any theater— most often political or experimental— that sets itself up in opposition to the **conventions** of the mainstream theater of its time.

Ambiguity In expository prose, an undesirable doubtfulness or uncertainty of meaning or intention resulting from imprecision in the use of one's words or the construction of one's sentences. In poetry, the desirable condition of admitting more than one possible meaning resulting from the capacity of language to function on levels other than the literal. Related terms sometimes employed are *ambivalence* and *polysemy*.

Anagnorisis A significant recognition or discovery by a character, usually the **protagonist**, that moves the **plot** forward by changing the circumstances of a play.

Anapest A metrical **foot** consisting of three syllables, with two unaccented syllables followed by an accented one (˘˘´). In *anapestic meter*, anapests are the predominant foot in a line or poem. The following line from William Cowper's "The Poplar Field" is in anapestic meter: "And the whis | pering sound | of the cool | colŏnnáde."

Anaphora Repetition of the same word or words at the beginning of two or more lines, clauses, or sentences. Walt Whitman employs anaphora extensively in "Song of Myself" (p. 505).

Antagonist The character (or, less often, the force) that opposes the **protagonist**.

Anticlimax In drama, a disappointingly trivial occurrence where a **climax** would usually happen. An anticlimax can achieve comic effect or disrupt audience expectations of dramatic structure. In poetry, an anticlimax is an arrangement of details such that one of lesser importance follows one or ones of greater importance, where something of greater significance is expected. A well-known example is "Not louder shrieks to pitying heaven are cast, / When husbands die, or when lapdogs breathe their last" (Alexander Pope, *The Rape of the Lock*).

Antihero, antiheroine A character playing a hero's part but lacking the grandeur typically associated with a **hero**. Such a character may be comic or may exist to force the audience to reconsider its notions of heroism.

Antistrophe The second part of a choral **ode** in Greek drama. The antistrophe was traditionally sung as the **chorus** moved from **stage left** to **stage right**.

Antithesis A figure of speech in which contrasting words, sentences, or ideas are expressed in balanced, parallel grammatical structures. "She had some horses she loved. / She had some horses she hated," from Joy Harjo's "She Had Some Horses" (p. 664), illustrates antithesis.

Apostrophe A figure of speech in which an absent person, an abstract quality, or a nonhuman entity is addressed as though present. It is a particular type of personification. See, for example, Ben Jonson's "On My First Son" (p. 457) and Allen Ginsberg's "A Supermarket in California" (p. 588).

Approximate rhyme See **slant rhyme**.

Archetype An image, symbol, character type, or plot line that occurs frequently enough in literature, religion, myths, folktales, and fairy tales to be recognizable as an element of universal experience and that evokes a deep emotional response. In "Spring and Fall" (p. 527), Gerard Manley Hopkins develops the archetypes in his title, those of spring (archetype for birth and youth) and fall (archetype for old age and the approach of death).

Aside A brief bit of dialogue spoken by a character to the audience or to him- or herself and assumed to be unheard by other characters onstage.

Assonance The repetition of identical or similar vowel sounds in words relatively near to one another (usually within a line or in adjacent lines) whose consonant sounds differ. It can be initial ("*a*pple . . . *a*nd h*a*ppy *a*s") or, more commonly, internal ("gr*ee*n and car*e*fr*ee*," "T*i*me held m*e* gr*ee*n and d*y*ing"). (Examples taken from Dylan Thomas's "Fern Hill," p. 575).

Aubade A dawn song, ordinarily expressing two lovers' regret that day has come and they must separate.

Ballad A poem that tells a story and was meant to be recited or sung; originally, a folk art transmitted orally, from person to person and from generation to generation. Many of the popular ballads were not written down and published until the eighteenth century, though their origins may have been centuries earlier. "Lord Randal" (p. 449) is a popular Scottish ballad.

Ballad stanza A **quatrain** in iambic meter rhyming *abcb* with (usually) four feet in the first and third lines, three in the second and fourth. See, for example, Robert Burns's "A Red, Red Rose" (p. 475).

Black comedy A type of comedy in which the traditional material of tragedy (that is, suffering, or even death) is staged to provoke laughter.

Blank verse Lines of unrhymed **iambic pentameter**. Blank verse is the most widely used verse form of poetry in English because it is closest to the natural rhythms of English speech. Shakespeare's plays, as well as Milton's *Paradise Lost* and *Paradise Regained*, and countless other long poems were composed in blank verse because it is well suited to narrative, dialogue, and reflection. Robert Frost's "Birches" (p. 537) starts out as regular blank verse and then moves to a modified, less regular adaptation of blank verse.

Blocking The process of determining the stage positions, movement, and groupings of actors. Blocking generally is proposed in rehearsal by the director and may be negotiated and reworked by the actors themselves.

Brainstorming An information-gathering process in which a group or an individual writes down any and all ideas that come to mind regarding the topic of a given paper or project. The list is later fine-tuned during the organizing stage of the project.

Cacophony A harsh or unpleasant combination of sounds, as in lines 368–369 in Alexander Pope's "An Essay on Criticism": "But when loud surges lash the sounding shore, / The hoarse, rough verse should like the torrent roar" (p. 468). Cf. **euphony**.

Caesura A pause or break within a line of verse, usually signaled by a mark of punctuation.

Canon The group of literary works that form the backbone of a cultural tradition.

Carpe diem A Latin phrase from an ode by Horace meaning "seize the day." It became the label for a theme common in literature, especially in sixteenth- and seventeenth-century English love poetry, that life is short and fleeting and that therefore one must make the most of present pleasures. See Robert Herrick's "To the Virgins, to Make Much of Time" (p. 459) and Andrew Marvell's "To His Coy Mistress" (p. 464).

Catastrophe The final movement of a **tragedy**, which brings about the fall or death of the **protagonist**. In plays other than classical tragedy, a **denouement** takes the place of a catastrophe.

Catharsis A purging of the emotions of pity and fear. Aristotle argued in *Poetics* that catharsis is the natural, and beneficial, outcome of viewing a **tragedy**.

Characters, characterization Broadly speaking, characters are usually the people of a work of literature—although characters may be animals or some other beings. In fiction, characterization means the development of a character or characters throughout a story. Characterization includes the narrator's description of what characters look like and what they think, say, and do (these are sometimes very dissimilar). Their own actions and views of themselves, and other characters' views of and behavior toward them, are also means of characterization. Characters may be minor, like Goody Cloyse, or major, like Goodman Brown, both of Hawthorne's "Young Goodman Brown" (p. 3). Depending on the depth of characterization, a character may be simple or complex, flat or round. Character is one of the six **elements of drama** identified by Aristotle, and characterization is the process by which writers and actors make a character distinct and believable to an audience.

Chaucerian stanza A seven-line iambic stanza rhyming *ababbcc*, sometimes having an **alexandrine** (hexameter) closing line. See, for example, Sir Thomas Wyatt's "They flee from me" (p. 451).

Chorus In classical Greek theater, a group of actors who perform in the **orchestra** and whose functions might include providing **exposition**, confronting or questioning the **protagonist**, and commenting on the action of the play. Much of the **spectacle** of Greek drama lay in the chorus's singing and dancing. In theater of other times and places, particularly that of the Renaissance, the functions of the Greek chorus are sometimes given to a single character identified as "Chorus."

Climax In drama, the turning point at which a play switches from **rising action** to **falling action**. In fiction, the moment of greatest intensity and conflict in the action of a story. In Nathaniel Hawthorne's "Young Goodman Brown" (p. 3), events reach their climax when Brown and his wife stand together in the forest, at the point of conversion.

Closed form Any structural pattern or repetition of meter, rhyme, or stanza. Cf. **open form**.

Closet drama A play intended to be read rather than performed.

Comedy Originally, any play that ended with the characters in a better condition than when the play began, though the term is now used more frequently to describe a play intended to be funny. Traditional comedy is generally distinguished by low or ordinary characters (as opposed to the great men and women of tragedy), a humble style, a series of events or role reversals that create chaos and upheaval, and a conclusion or **denouement** that marks a return to normalcy and often a reintegration into society (such as with a wedding or other formal celebration).

Comic relief A funny scene or character appearing in an otherwise serious play, intended to provide the audience with a momentary break from the heavier themes of tragedy.

Commedia dell'arte Semi-improvised comedy relying heavily on **stock characters** and **stage business**, performed originally by traveling Italian players in the sixteenth and seventeenth centuries.

Complication One of the traditional elements of **plot**. Complication occurs when someone or something opposes the **protagonist**.

Compression The dropping of a syllable to make a line fit the meter, sometimes marked with an apostrophe (e.g., William Shakespeare, Sonnet 73 [p. 454], line 13: "This thou perceiv'st"). Another common device is elision, the dropping of a vowel at the beginning or end of a word (e.g., in lines 7 and 28 of John Donne's "A Valediction: Forbidding Mourning" [p. 455]: "'Twere profanation of our joys" and "To move, but doth, if th' other do").

Conceit A figure of speech that establishes a striking or far-fetched analogy between seemingly very dissimilar things, either the exaggerated, unrealistic comparisons found in love poems (such as in Shakespeare's Sonnet 18 [p. 453] or the complex analogies of metaphysical wit (as in John Donne's "A Valediction: Forbidding Mourning" [p. 455]).

Concrete language Any specific, physical language that appeals to one or more of the senses—sight, hearing, taste, smell, or touch. *Stones, chairs,* and *hands* are concrete words. Concrete language is the opposite of **abstract language**. Both types are important features of an author's style.

Concrete poem A poem shaped in the form of the object the poem describes or discusses. See, for example, George Herbert's "Easter-wings" (p. 460).

Confessional poetry Poetry about personal, private issues in which a poet usually speaks directly, without the use of a **persona**. See, for example, Robert Lowell's "Skunk Hour" (p. 579) and Sylvia Plath's "Daddy" (p. 609).

Confidant A character, major or minor, to whom another character confides secrets so that the audience can "overhear" the transaction and be apprised of unseen events.

Conflict Antagonism between characters, ideas, or lines of action; between a character and the outside world; or between different aspects of a character's nature. Conflict is essential in a traditional plot, as in the conflict between Montresor and Fortunato in Edgar Allan Poe's "The Cask of Amontillado" (p. 14). Shakespeare's Hamlet is in conflict both with his stepfather Claudius for killing his father and with himself as he tries to decide a course of action.

Connotation The range of emotional implications and associations a word may carry outside of its dictionary definitions. Cf. **denotation**.

Consonance The repetition of consonant sounds in words whose vowels are different. In perfect consonance, all consonants are the same—*live, love; chitter, chatter; reader, rider;* words in which all consonants following the main vowels are identical also are considered consonant—*dive, love; swatter, chitter; sound, bond; gate, mat; set, pit.*

Convention An unstated rule, code, practice, or characteristic established by usage. In drama, tacit acceptance of theatrical conventions prevents the audience from being distracted by unrealistic features that are necessarily part of any theater experience. Greek audiences, for instance, accepted the convention of the **chorus**, while today's audiences readily accept the convention of the **fourth wall** in realistic drama and of songs in musical comedy.

Couplet Two consecutive lines of poetry with the same **end-rhyme**. English (Shakespearean) **sonnets** end with a couplet; for an entire poem in tetrameter couplets, see Andrew Marvell's "To His Coy Mistress" (p. 464). See also **heroic couplets**.

Cruelty, theater of Term coined by Antonin Artaud in the early twentieth century to describe a type of theater using light, sound, **spectacle**, and other primarily nonverbal forms of communication to create images of cruelty and destruction intended to shock audiences out of complacency.

Cultural context The milieu that gives rise to a work of literature.

Cultural studies A general name given to a wide variety of critical practices that examine and challenge why certain texts are privileged in our society while others are dismissed or derided. Rather than focusing on traditional literary objects, cultural studies critics might choose to study movies, television shows, advertisements, graffiti, or comic books, often in conjunction with **canonical** works of literature.

Dactyl A metrical **foot** consisting of three syllables, an accented one followed by two unaccented ones (‿‿‿). In "dactylic meter," dactyls are the predominant foot of a line or poem. The following lines from Thomas Hardy's "The Voice" are in dactylic meter: "Wómăn mŭch | mĭśsed, hŏw yŏu | cáll tŏ mĕ, | cáll tŏ mĕ, / Sáyĭng thăt | nów yŏu aře | nót ăs yŏu | wére."

Deconstruction A variety of **poststructuralism**, deconstruction derives from the efforts of Jacques Derrida to undermine the foundations of Western philosophy, but as a literary critical practice it often emerges as a kind of close-reading that reveals irreconcilable linguistic contradictions in a text that prevents the text from having a single stable meaning or message.

Denotation The basic meaning of a word; its dictionary definition(s).

Denouement Literally, "unknotting." The end of a play or other literary work, in which all elements of the **plot** are brought to their conclusion.

Description Language that presents specific features of a character, object, or setting; or the details of an action or event. The first paragraph of Franz Kafka's "The Metamorphosis" (p. 112) describes Gregor's startling new appearance.

Deus ex machina Literally, "god out of the machine," referring to the mechanized system used to lower an actor playing a god onto the stage in classical Greek drama. Today the term is generally used disparagingly to indicate careless plotting and an unbelievable **resolution** in a play.

Dialogue Words spoken by characters, often in the form of a conversation between two or more characters. In stories and other forms of prose, dialogue is commonly enclosed between quotation marks. Dialogue is an important element in **characterization** and **plot**: much of the characterization and action in Ernest Hemingway's "Hills Like White Elephants" (p. 212) is presented through its characters' dialogue.

Diction A writer's selection of words; the kind of words, phrases, and figurative language used to make up a work of literature. In fiction, particular patterns or arrangements of words in sentences and paragraphs constitute prose style. Hemingway's diction is said to be precise, concrete, and economical. Aristotle identified diction as one of the six **elements of drama**. See also **poetic diction**.

Dimeter A line of verse consisting of two metrical feet.

Double rhyme A rhyme in which an accented, rhyming syllable is followed by one or more identical, unstressed syllables: *thrilling* and *killing*, *marry* and *tarry*. Formerly known as "feminine rhyme."

Downstage   The part of the stage closest to the audience.

Dramatic irony   A situation in which a reader or an audience knows more than the speakers or characters, about either the outcome of events or a discrepancy between a meaning intended by a speaker or character and that recognized by the reader or audience.

Dramatic monologue   A poem with only one speaker, overheard in a dramatic moment (usually addressing another character or characters who do not speak), whose words reveal what is going on in the scene and expose significant depths of the speaker's temperament, attitudes, and values. See Robert Browning's "My Last Duchess" (p. 503) and T. S. Eliot's "The Love Song of J. Alfred Prufrock" (p. 547).

Elegy   In Greek and Roman literature, a serious, meditative poem written in "elegiac meter" (alternating hexameter and pentameter lines); since the 1600s, a sustained and formal poem lamenting the death of a particular person, usually ending with a consolation, or one setting forth meditations on death or another solemn theme. See Thomas Gray's "Elegy Written in a Country Churchyard" (p. 469). The adjective *elegiac* is also used to describe a general tone of sadness or a worldview that emphasizes suffering and loss. It is most often applied to Anglo-Saxon poems like *Beowulf* or *The Seafarer* but can also be used for modern poems, such as A. E. Housman's in *A Shropshire Lad*.

Elements of drama   The six features identified by Aristotle in *Poetics* as descriptive of and necessary to drama. They are, in order of the importance assigned to them by Aristotle, **plot, characterization, theme, diction, melody,** and **spectacle.**

Elements of fiction   Major elements of fiction are **plot, characters, setting, point of view, style,** and **theme.** Skillful employment of these entities is essential in effective novels and stories. From beginning to end, each element is active and relates to the others dynamically.

Elements of poetry   Verbal, aural, and structural features of poetry, including **diction, tone, images, figures of speech, symbols, rhythm, rhyme,** and poetic **form,** which are combined to create poems.

Elision   See **compression.**

Empathy   The ability of the audience to relate to, even experience, the emotions of characters onstage or in a text.

End-rhyme   Rhyme occurring at the ends of lines in a poem.

End-stopped line   A line of poetry whose grammatical structure and thought reach completion by its end. Cf. **run-on line.**

English sonnet   A sonnet consisting of three quatrains (three four-line units, typically rhyming *abab cdcd efef*) and a couplet (two rhyming lines). Usually, the subject is introduced in the first quatrain, expanded in the second, and expanded still further in the third; the couplet adds a logical, pithy conclusion or introduces a surprising twist. Also called the Shakespearean sonnet. Cf. **Spenserian sonnet**.

Enjambment   See **run-on line**.

Epic   A long narrative poem that celebrates the achievements of great heroes and heroines, often determining the fate of a tribe or nation, written in formal language and an elevated style. Examples include Homer's *Iliad* and *Odyssey*, Virgil's *Aeneid*, and John Milton's *Paradise Lost*.

Epic theater   The name given by Bertolt Brecht to a theatrical style emphasizing the relationship between form and ideology. It is characterized by brief scenes, narrative breaks, political and historical themes, an analytical (rather than emotional) tone, and characters with whom it is difficult to feel empathy. Though considered **alternative theater** when it was new, many of its **conventions** have since been adopted by mainstream dramatists.

Epigram   Originally, an inscription, especially an epitaph; in modern usage, a short poem, usually polished and witty with a surprising twist at the end. (Its other dictionary definition, "any terse, witty, pointed statement," generally does not apply in poetry.)

Epigraph   In literature, a quotation at the beginning of a poem or on the title page or the beginning of a chapter in a book. See the epigraph from Dante's *Inferno* at the beginning of T. S. Eliot's "The Love Song of J. Alfred Prufrock" (p. 547).

Epilogue   A final speech or scene occurring after the main action of the play has ended. An epilogue generally sums up or comments on the meaning of the play.

Epiphany   An appearance or manifestation, especially of a divine being; in literature, since James Joyce adapted the term to secular use in 1944, a sudden sense of radiance and revelation one may feel while perceiving a commonplace object; a moment or event in which the essential nature of a person, a situation, or an object is suddenly perceived, as at the end of Joyce's "Araby" (p. 107).

Episode   In Greek drama, the scenes of dialogue that occur between the choral **odes**. Now the term is used to mean any small unit of drama that has its own completeness and internal unity.

Euphony   Language that strikes the ear as smooth, musical, and agreeable. An example can be found in Alexander Pope's "An Essay on Criticism," lines 366–67: "Soft is the strain when Zephyr gently blows, / And the smooth stream in smoother numbers flows" (p. 468). Cf. **cacophony**.

Exact rhyme   Rhyme in which all sounds following the vowel sound are the same: *spite* and *night*, *art* and *heart*, *ache* and *fake*, *card* and *barred*.

Exaggeration   See **hyperbole**.

Explication   The process of making clear that which is implicit or subtle in a work of literature. This is achieved by performing a close-reading—reading a piece of literature with an eye toward such sentence-level elements as sentence structure, style, imagery, word choice, and figurative language—and then explaining the larger purpose and effect of those elements.

Exposition A means of filling in the audience on events that occurred off-stage or before the play's beginning. Clumsily handled exposition, in which characters talk at length about things they normally would not, is characteristic of much bad drama.

Expressionism Nonrealistic play-making style using exaggerated or otherwise unreal gestures, light, and sound. Expressionistic techniques are often used to convey a sense of memory, dream, or fantasy.

Extension Pronunciation that adds a syllable for the sake of the meter. See, for example, the third line of the fifth stanza in John Donne's "A Valediction: Forbidding Mourning" (p. 455): "Inter-assurèd of the mind."

Falling action The action after the **climax** in a traditionally structured play whereby the tension lessens and the play moves toward the **catastrophe** or **denouement**.

Falling meter Meter using a **foot** (usually a trochee or a dactyl) in which the first syllable is accented and those that follow are unaccented, giving a sense of stepping down. Cf. **rising meter**.

Farce Comedy that relies on exaggerated characters, extreme situations, fast and accelerating pacing, and, often, sexual innuendo.

Feminine rhyme See **double rhyme**.

Feminist criticism A school of literary criticism that examines the roles of women in literature and culture as well as the relationships between men

and women. Contemporary feminist criticism rose to prominence in the 1970s, when the modern feminist movement began to explore the patriarchal structures in which many women felt trapped. Some feminist critics seek to show the ways in which literary texts demonstrate the repression and powerlessness of women — or, alternately, to show how female literary characters could overcome sexist power structures. Still others seek to rediscover and promote writing by women whose works have been excluded from the mostly male **canon** of "great" literature.

Feminist theater Any play or theater whose primary object is to shine light on the issues of women's rights and sexism.

Fiction Generally speaking, any imaginative, usually prose, work of literature. More narrowly, narratives — **short stories**, **novellas**, or **novels** — whose plots, characters, and settings are constructions of its writer's imagination, which draws on the writer's experiences and reflections.

Figurative language Uses of language — employing **metaphor** or **simile** or other figures of speech — that depart from standard or literal usage in order to achieve a special effect or meaning. Figurative language is often employed in poetry; although less often seen in plays and stories, it can be used powerfully in those forms. Alice Walker's "Everyday Use" (p. 336) opens with a figurative description of the family's yard.

First-person narrator In a story told by one person, the "I" who tells the story. Sometimes the first-person narrator is purely an observer; more often he or she is directly or indirectly involved in the action of the story. Montresor is the first-person narrator of, and one of two characters in, Edgar Allan Poe's "The Cask of Amontillado" (p. 14). As a first-person narrator, he reveals much about his own emotions and motivations.

Fixed form Poetry written in definite, repeating patterns of line, rhyme scheme, or stanza.

Flashback A writer's way of introducing important earlier material. As a narrator tells a story, he or she may stop the flow of events and direct the reader to an earlier time. Sometimes the narrator may return to the present, sometimes remain in the past. The narrator in William Faulkner's "A Rose for Emily" (p. 204) uses flashbacks to depict the events leading up to Emily Grierson's death.

Foil A character who exists chiefly to set off or display, usually by opposition, the important character traits of the **protagonist** or another important person.

Foot The basic unit in metrical verse, comprising (usually) one stressed syllable and one or more unstressed syllables. See also **anapest**, **dactyl**, **iamb**, **spondee**, and **trochee**.

Foreshadowing Words, gestures, or other actions that suggest future events or outcomes. The opening of Nathaniel Hawthorne's "Young Goodman Brown" (p. 3) foreshadows serious trouble ahead when Faith, Brown's wife, begs him to stay home with her "this night, dear husband, of all nights in the year."

Form (1) Genre or literary type (e.g., the lyric form); (2) patterns of meter, lines, and rhymes (stanzaic form); (3) the organization of the parts of a literary work in relation to its total effect (e.g., "The form [structure] of this poem is very effective").

Formalism A broad term for the various types of literary theory that advocate focusing attention on the text itself and not on extratextual factors. Formalist critics are interested in the formal elements of a literary text— structure, tone, characters, setting, symbols, linguistic features—and seek to create meaning by examining the relationships between these different parts of a text.

Fourth wall The theatrical convention, dating from the nineteenth century, whereby an audience seems to be looking and listening through an invisible fourth wall, usually into a room in a private residence. The fourth wall is primarily associated with **realism** and domestic dramas.

Free verse See **open form**.

Gender criticism A broad term for literary criticism that highlights gender roles or relationships between the sexes. In this expansive sense, **feminist criticism** is a kind of gender criticism, although the latter term is most often applied to gay and lesbian approaches to literature that explore the construction of sexual identity.

Genre A type or form of literature. While the major literary genres are **fiction**, **drama**, **poetry**, and **exposition**, many other subcategories of genres are recognized, including **comedy**, **tragedy**, **tragicomedy**, **romance**, **melodrama**, epic, lyric, pastoral, novel, short story, and so on.

Haiku A lyric form, originating in Japan, of seventeen syllables in three lines, the first and third having five syllables and the second seven, presenting an image of a natural object or scene that expresses a distinct emotion or spiritual insight. Gary Snyder incorporates haiku into "Hitch Haiku" (p. 604).

Half rhyme See **slant rhyme**.

Hamartia Sometimes translated as "tragic flaw" but more properly understood as an error or general character trait that leads to the downfall of a character in **tragedy**.

Heptameter A poetic line with seven metrical feet.

Hero, heroine Sometimes used to refer to any **protagonist**, the term more properly applies only to a great figure from legend or history or to a character who performs in a remarkably honorable and selfless manner.

Heroic couplets Couplets in **iambic pentameter** that usually end in a period. See Alexander Pope's "An Essay on Criticism" (p. 467). Also called *closed couplets*.

Hexameter A poetic line with six metrical feet. See also **alexandrine**.

Historical criticism A kind of literary criticism based on the notion that history and literature are often interrelated. For example, literary critics might read history books and various sorts of historical documents in order to gain insights into the composition and significance of a literary work.

Hubris An arrogance or inflated sense of self that can lead to a character's downfall. The **protagonists** of **tragedy** often suffer from hubris.

Hyperbole Exaggeration; a figure of speech in which something is stated more strongly than is logically warranted. Hyperbole is often used to make a point emphatically, as when Hamlet protests that he loves Ophelia much more than her brother does: "Forty thousand brothers / Could not with all their quantity of love / Make up my sum" (5.1.239–41). See also Robert Burns's "A Red, Red Rose" (p. 475).

Iamb A metrical **foot** consisting of two syllables, an unaccented one followed by an accented one (˘ ´). In iambic meter (the most widely used of English metrical forms), iambs are the predominant foot in a line or poem. The following line from Thomas Gray's "Elegy Written in a Country Churchyard" (p. 469) is in **iambic pentameter**: "Thĕ cúr | fĕw tólls | thĕ knéll | ŏf párt | ĭng dáy." See **pentameter**.

Image (1) Sometimes called a "word-picture," an image is a word or group of words that refers to a sensory experience or to an object that can be known by one or more of the senses. **Imagery** signifies all such language in a poem or other literary work collectively and can involve any of the senses; see, for example, the first two stanzas of T. S. Eliot's "Preludes" (p. 552) or the narrator's description of the girl he loves in James Joyce's "Araby" (p. 107): "The light from the lamp opposite our door caught the white curve of her neck, lit up her hair that rested there and, falling, lit up the hand upon the railing." See also **synesthesia**. (2) A metaphor or other comparison. **Imagery** in this sense refers to the characteristic that several images in a poem may have in common, as for example, the Christian imagery in William Blake's "The Lamb" (p. 473).

Imitation Since Aristotle, drama has been differentiated from fiction because it is said to rely on an imitation (in Greek, *mimesis*) of human actions rather than on a narration of them.

Implied metaphor Metaphor in which the *to be* verb is omitted and one aspect of the comparison is implied rather than stated directly. Whereas "a car thief is a dirty dog" is a direct metaphor, "some dirty dog stole my car" contains an implied metaphor. Examples from John Frederick Nims's "Love Poem" (p. 571) include "whose hands *shipwreck* vases," "A *wrench* in clocks and the solar system," and "In *traffic* of wit expertly maneuver."

Interlude A brief, usually comic, performance inserted between the **acts** of a play or between courses at a formal banquet. Interludes were most popular during the Renaissance.

Internal rhyme Rhyme that occurs with words within a line, words within lines near each other, or a word within a line and one at the end of the same or a nearby line. Edgar Allan Poe's "Annabel Lee" (p. 494) offers many examples: "chilling / And killing," "Can ever dissever," "And the stars never rise but I see the bright eyes."

Intertextuality The implied presence of previous texts within a literary work or as context, usually conveyed through allusion or choice of genre. An intertextual approach assumes that interpretation of a text is incomplete until the relation of the work to its predecessors—response, opposition, and development—has been considered.

Irony A feeling, tone, mood, or attitude arising from the awareness that what *is* (reality) is opposite from, and usually worse than, what *seems* to be (appearance). What a person says may be ironic (see **verbal irony**), and a discrepancy between what a character knows or means and what a reader or an audience knows can be ironic (see **dramatic irony**). A general situation also can be seen as ironic (see **situational irony**). Irony should not be confused with mere coincidence. See also **Socratic irony**.

Italian sonnet Generally speaking, a sonnet composed of an octave (an eight-line unit), rhyming *abbaabba*, and a sestet (a six-line unit), often rhyming *cdecde* or *cdcdcd*. The octave usually develops an idea, question, or problem; then the poem pauses, or "turns," and the sestet completes the idea, answers the question, or resolves the difficulty. Sometimes called a Petrarchan sonnet. See Gerard Manley Hopkins's "God's Grandeur" (p. 526).

Juxtaposition Placement of things side by side or close together for comparison or contrast, or to create something new from the union. See Alexander Pope's "An Essay on Criticism" (p. 467): "Now his fierce eyes with sparking fury glow, / Now sighs steal out, and tears begin to flow" (lines 378–379).

Line A sequence of words printed as a separate entity on a page; the basic structural unit in poetry (except in **prose poems**).

Lineation The arrangement of lines in a poem.

Literal   In accordance with the primary or strict meaning of a word or words; not figurative or metaphorical.

Litotes   See **understatement**.

Lyric   Originally, a poem sung to the accompaniment of a lyre; now a short poem expressing the personal emotion and ideas of a single speaker.

Marxist criticism   Deriving from Karl Marx's theories of economics and class struggle, Marxist criticism sees literature as a material product of work, one that reflects or contests the ideologies that generated its production and consumption.

Masculine rhyme   See **single rhyme**.

Melodrama   A type of play employing broadly drawn heroes and villains, suspenseful plots, music, and a triumph of good over evil. Melodrama thrived throughout the nineteenth century and remained popular into the twentieth.

Melody   One of the six **elements of drama** identified by Aristotle. Since the Greek **chorus** communicated through song and dance, melody was an important part of even the most serious play, though it is now largely confined to musical comedy.

Metaphor   A figure of speech in which two things usually thought to be dissimilar are treated as if they were alike and have characteristics in common: "Whose *palms are bulls* in china" (John Frederick Nims's "Love Poem," p. 571). See also **implied metaphor**.

Metaphysical poetry   The work of a number of seventeenth-century poets that was characterized by philosophi-

cal subtlety and intellectual rigor; subtle, often outrageous logic; an imitation of actual speech sometimes resulting in a "rough" meter and style; and far-fetched analogies. John Donne's "A Valediction: Forbidding Mourning" (p. 455) exemplifies the type. See also **conceit**.

Meter   A steady beat, or measured pulse, created by a repeating pattern of accents or syllables, or both.

Metonymy   A figure of speech in which the name of one thing is substituted for something closely associated with it, as in "The *White House* announced today . . . ," a phrase in which the name of a building is substituted for the president or the staff members who issued the announcement; "He's got *a Constable* on his wall"; "The *trains* are on strike"; or "*Wall Street* is in a panic." In the last line of John Frederick Nims's "Love Poem" (p. 571), "All the toys of the world would break," *toys* is substituted for "things that give happiness" (as toys do to a child). See also **synecdoche**.

Mock epic   A literary form that imitates the grand style and conventions of the epic genre — the opening statement of a theme, an address to the muse, long formal speeches, and epic similes — but applies them to a subject unworthy of such exalted treatment. Also called "mock heroic." See also **epic**.

Monometer   A poetic line with one metrical **foot**.

Motivation   What drives a character to act in a particular way. To be convincing to an audience, an actor must understand and make clear to the audience the character's motivation.

Narrative   A story in prose or verse; an account of events involving characters and a sequence of events told by a storyteller (narrator). A poem such as John Keats's "La Belle Dame sans Merci" (p. 491) tells a story and is thus a **narrative poem**. Usually, the characters can be analyzed and generally understood; the events unfold in a cause-and-effect sequence; and some unity can be found among the characters, plot, point of view, style, and theme. Novels as well as stories are most often narratives, and journalism commonly employs narrative form.

Narrative poem   See **narrative**.

Narrator   The storyteller, usually an observer who is narrating from a third-person point of view or a participant in the story's action speaking in the first person. Style and tone are important clues to the nature of a narrator and the validity and objectivity of the story he or she is telling. Montresor, the narrator of Edgar Allan Poe's "The Cask of Amontillado" (p. 14), creates his own self-portrait as he relates what has happened.

Naturalism, naturalistic   A style of writing or acting meant to mimic closely the patterns of ordinary life.

Near rhyme   See **slant rhyme**.

New comedy   An ancient form of comedy that told of initially forbidden but ultimately successful love and that employed **stock characters**. New comedy is particularly associated with the Greek playwright Menander (342–292 B.C.E.).

New Criticism   A kind of **formalism** that dominated Anglo-American literary criticism in the middle decades of the twentieth century. It emphasized close-reading, particularly of poetry, to discover how a work of literature functioned as a self-contained, self-referential aesthetic object.

New Historicism   A school of **historical criticism** that takes account of both what history has to teach us about literature *and* what literature has to teach us about history. New Historicists examine many different types of texts—government records, periodicals, private diaries, bills of sale—in order to re-create, as much as possible, the rich cultural context that surrounded both an author and that author's original audience.

Novel   An extended prose narrative or work of prose fiction, usually published alone. Nathaniel Hawthorne's *The Scarlet Letter* is a fairly short novel, Herman Melville's *Moby-Dick, or, The Whale* a very long one. The length of a novel enables its author to develop characters, plot, and settings in greater detail than a short-story writer can. Ralph Ellison's story "Battle Royal" (p. 230) is taken from his novel *Invisible Man* (1948), Amy Tan's story "Two Kinds" (p. 382) from her novel *The Joy Luck Club* (1989).

Novella   Between the short story and the novel in size and complexity. Like them, the novella is a work of prose fiction. Sometimes it is called a long short story. Herman Melville's "Bartleby, the Scrivener" (p. 20) and Franz Kafka's "The Metamorphosis" (p. 112) are novellas.

Octameter   A poetic line with eight metrical feet.

Octave   The first eight lines of an **Italian sonnet**.

Ode (1) A multipart song sung by the **chorus** of Greek drama. A classical ode consists of a **strophe** followed by an **antistrophe** and sometimes by a final section called the *epode*. (2) A long **lyric** poem, serious (often intellectual) in tone, elevated and dignified in style, dealing with a single theme. The ode is generally more complicated in form than other lyric poems. Some odes retain a formal division into strophe, antistrophe, and epode, which reflects the form's origins in Greek tragedy. See William Wordsworth's "Ode: Intimations of Immortality" (p. 477).

Old comedy   **Comedy**, such as that of Aristophanes, employing raucous (sometimes coarse) humor, elements of **satire** and **farce**, and often a critique of contemporary persons or political and social norms.

Omniscient narrator   A **narrator** who seems to know everything about a story's events and characters, even their inner feelings. Usually, an omniscient narrator maintains emotional distance from the characters. The narrator of Sarah Orne Jewett's "A White Heron" (p. 51) is omniscient.

One act   A short play that is complete in one **act**.

Onomatopoeia   The use of words whose sounds supposedly resemble the sounds they denote (such as *thump*, *rattle*, *growl*, *hiss*), or a group of words whose sounds help to convey what is being described; for example, Emily Dickinson's "I heard a Fly buzz — when I died" (p. 522).

Open form   A form free of any predetermined metrical and stanzaic patterns. Cf. **closed form**.

Orchestra   In Greek theater, the area in front of the stage proper where the chorus performed its songs and dances. Later, a pit for musicians in front of the stage.

Organic form   The idea, grounded in Plato and strong since the nineteenth century, that subject, **theme**, and **form** are essentially one, that a work "grows" from a central concept. A contrary idea, that literary works are unstable and irregular because of changes in linguistic meanings and literary conventions, has led to a critical approach called **deconstruction**.

Ottava rima   An eight-line stanza in **iambic pentameter** rhyming *abababcc*.

Overstatement   See **hyperbole**.

Oxymoron   A figure of speech combining in one phrase (usually an adjective and a noun) two seemingly contradictory elements, such as "loving hate" or "feather of lead, bright smoke, cold fire, sick health" (from Shakespeare's *Romeo and Juliet*, 1.1.176–80). Oxymoron is a type of **paradox**.

Pantoum   A poem composed of **quatrains** rhyming *abab* in which the second and fourth lines of each stanza serve as the first and third lines of the next, continuing through the last stanza, which repeats the first and third lines of the first stanza in reverse order.

Paradox   A figure of speech in which a statement initially seeming self-contradictory or absurd turns out, seen in another light, to make good sense. The closing line of John Donne's sonnet "Death, be not proud" (p. 457) contains a paradox: "Death, thou shalt die." See also **oxymoron.**

Parallelism (1) A verbal arrangement in which elements of equal weight within phrases, sentences, or paragraphs are expressed in a similar grammatical order and structure. It can appear within a line or pair of lines ("And he was always quietly arrayed, / And he was always human when he talked"—Edwin Arlington Robinson, "Richard Cory" [p. 543]) or, more noticeably, as a series of parallel items, as found in Langston Hughes's "Harlem" (p. 560). (2) A principle of poetic structure in which consecutive lines in **open form** are related by a line's repeating, expanding on, or contrasting with the idea of the line or lines before it, as in the poems of Walt Whitman (pp. 505–507).

Paraphrase: To restate a passage of literature or criticism in your own words, particularly useful as a method for taking research notes, or for interpreting a text. Generally, a paraphrase will be about equal in length to the passage being paraphrased, while a **summary** will be much shorter.

Parody   Now, a humorous or satirical imitation of a serious piece of literature or writing. In the sixteenth and seventeenth centuries, poets such as George Herbert practiced "sacred parody" by adapting secular lyrics to devotional themes.

Partial rhyme   See **slant rhyme.**

Pastoral   A poem (also called an *eclogue,* a *bucolic,* or an *idyll*) that expresses a city poet's nostalgic image of the simple, peaceful life of shepherds and other country folk in an idealized natural setting. Christopher Marlowe's "The Passionate Shepherd to His Love" (p. 452) uses some pastoral conventions, as do certain elegies.

Pause   See **caesura.**

Pentameter   A poetic line with five metrical feet.

Performance art   Loose term for a variety of performances that defy traditional categories of play, monologue, musical act, and so on. The term arose in the late twentieth century as a catch-all to name the growing number of nontraditional performances, many of which addressed controversial subjects and themes.

Peripeteia   A reversal or change of fortune for a character, for better or worse.

Persona   Literally, the mask through which actors spoke in Greek plays. In some critical approaches of recent decades, *persona* refers to the "character" projected by an author, the "I" of a narrative poem or novel, or the speaker whose voice is heard in a lyric poem. In this view, a poem is an artificial construct distanced from a poet's autobiographical self. Cf. **voice.**

Personification   A figure of speech in which something nonhuman is treated as if it had human characteristics or performed human actions. Sometimes it involves abstractions, as in Thomas Gray's phrase "Fair Science frowned" ("Elegy Written in a Country Churchyard," p. 469); science cannot literally frown. In other cases, concrete things are given human characteristics, as in the phrase "Wearing white for Eastertide" from A. E. Housman's

"Loveliest of trees, the cherry now" (p. 528). Cherry trees do not actually wear clothes—but here they are being given, briefly, a human attribute. Difficulty can arise when personification is incorrectly defined as treating something nonhuman in terms of anything alive rather than what is specifically human; "the mouth of time," for instance, in Nancy Willard's "Questions My Son Asked Me, Answers I Never Gave Him" (p. 622) is metaphor, not personification, since animals as well as humans have mouths. See also **apostrophe**.

Petrarchan sonnet See **Italian sonnet**.

Plagiarism The act of closely imitating or outright adopting the language or ideas of another author and presenting them as one's own work without giving credit to the original author. This includes copying and pasting from any web source. Most colleges and universities have codes of academic honesty forbidding such practices and imposing severe penalties—including expulsion from the institution in some cases—on students who are caught breaking them.

Plot (1) The sequence of major events in a story, usually related by cause and effect. **Plot development** refers to how the sequence evolves or is shaped. Plot and character are intimately related, since characters carry out the plot's action. Plots may be described as simple or complex, depending on their degree of complication. "Traditional" writers, such as Edgar Allan Poe and Guy de Maupassant, usually plot their stories tightly; modernist writers such as James Joyce employ looser, often ambiguous plots.

(2) The action that takes place within the play. Of the six **elements of drama**, Aristotle considered plot to be the most important. Typical elements of plot include a **prologue** or **exposition**, **rising action**, **complication**, **climax**, **falling action**, and **catastrophe** or **denouement**.

Plot development See plot.

Poem A term whose meaning exceeds all attempts at definition. Here is a slightly modified version of the definition of William Harmon and C. Hugh Holman in *A Handbook to Literature* (1996): A poem is a literary composition, written or oral, typically characterized by imagination, emotion, sense impressions, and concrete language that invites attention to its own physical features, such as sound or appearance on the page.

Poetic diction In general, specialized language used in or considered appropriate to poetry. In the late seventeenth and the eighteenth centuries, a refined use of language that excluded "common" speech from poetry as indecorous and substituted elevated circumlocutions, archaic synonyms, or such forms as *ope* and *e'er*.

Point of view One of the elements of fiction, point of view is the perspective, or angle of vision, from which a narrator presents a story. Point of view tells us about the **narrator** as well as about the characters, setting, and theme of a story. Two common points of view are *first-person narration* and *third-person narration*. If a narrator speaks of himself or herself as "I," the narration is in the first person; if the narrator's self is not apparent and the story is told about others from some distance, using "he," "she," "it," and "they," then third-person narration is likely in force. The point of view may be omniscient (all-knowing) or limited, objective or subjective. When determining a story's point of view, it is helpful to decide whether the narrator is reporting events as they are happening or as they happened in the past; is observing or participating in the action; and is or is not emotionally involved. Eudora Welty's "A Worn Path" (p. 216) is told from the third-person objective point of view, since its narrator observes what the character is doing, thinking, and feeling, yet seems emotionally distant. Edgar Allan Poe's "The Cask of Amontillado" (p. 14) and James Joyce's "Araby" (p. 107) are told in the first-person subjective and limited point of view, since their narrators are very much involved in the action. In Kate Chopin's "The Story of an Hour" (p. 59), shifting points of view enable us to see Mrs. Mallard from the outside, as her family does (third-person objective); learn about her most private emotional responses and secrets (third-person subjective); and hear her thoughts directly as if we were inside her mind (first-person subjective).

Postcolonial criticism   A branch of cultural studies that focuses on writing from former British (and other, mostly European) colonies around the world. Postcolonial criticism seeks to recover literary history that was ignored or suppressed during the colonial period, and to celebrate indigenous cultures of storytelling, drama, and poetry. At the same time, it attempts to understand how occupation by a more powerful colonizing nation disrupted and changed the course of history in a particular place.

Poststructuralism   Positing that no text can have a fixed or real meaning because no meaning can exist outside the network of other meanings to which it is connected, poststructuralism carries the insights of **structuralism** one step further. If, as structuralists claim, we can understand things only in terms of other things, then perhaps there is no center point of understanding, but only an endlessly interconnected web of ideas leading to other ideas leading to still other ideas. Meaning, then, is forever shifting and altering as our understanding of the world changes.

Primary source   Term used in writing about literature to refer to the literature itself—the poem, story, or play on which the writing is based. Cf. **secondary source**.

Prologue   A speech or scene that occurs before the beginning of the **plot** proper.

Properties, props   Any movable objects, beyond scenery and costumes, used in the performance of a play. Early drama was performed with few props, but as theater moved toward **realism**, props took on greater importance.

Proscenium arch   An arch across the front of a stage, sometimes with a curtain. The proscenium frames the action and provides a degree of separation between the actors and the audience.

Prose poem   A poem printed as prose, with lines wrapping at the right margin rather than being divided through predetermined line breaks. See Carolyn Forché's "The Colonel" (p. 662).

Prosody The principles of versification, especially of meter, rhythm, rhyme, and stanza forms.

Protagonist The lead character of a play, though not necessarily a **hero** in the classic sense.

Psychological literary criticism A broad term for the various types of literary theory that focus on the inner workings of the human psyche and the ways in which they manifest themselves in literature. Psychological critics often interpret literature as a psychologist might interpret a dream or a wish, often paying special attention to unstated motives and to the unconscious states of mind in characters, authors, or readers.

Pun A play on words based on the similarity in sound between two words having very different meanings. Also called *paronomasia*. See the puns on "heart" and "kindly" in Sir Thomas Wyatt's "They flee from me" (p. 451).

Quantitative verse Verse whose meter is based on the length of syllables. (Phonetic length was a distinguishing feature of ancient Greek and Latin, whereas English is an accentual language.) Classical poetry exhibits a great variety of meters, and some English poets in the late 1500s attempted to fashion English verse on this principle. In *Evangeline*, Henry Wadsworth Longfellow used dactylic hexameter in imitation of Virgil's *Aeneid*, but defined it by accent, not quantity. Cf. **accentual-syllabic verse**.

Quatrain A **stanza** of four lines or other four-line unit within a larger form, such as a **sonnet**.

Queer theory One of the more recent and more challenging critical schools to emerge out of critical interest in gender. Queer theorists, like all literary critics, differ substantially in their focus: Some queer theorists are interested in studying literary texts written by authors known or suspected to be gay, lesbian, bisexual, or transgender. Other queer theorists are interested in portrayals of gay or lesbian characters in literature. Still others seek a "queer subtext" in canonical works of literature that have long been considered heteronormative.

Reader-response criticism The various theories of reader-response criticism hold that a text is an interaction between author and reader, and a text can never be complete unless readers bring to it their own unique insights. Reading, then, is not a passive attempt to understand a text but is itself an act of creation, no less than writing.

Realism Any drama (or other art) that seeks to closely mimic real life. Realism more specifically refers to a sort of drama that rose in opposition to **melodrama** in the late-nineteenth and early-twentieth centuries and that attempted to avoid some of the more artificial **conventions** of theater and present the problems of ordinary people living their everyday lives.

Recognition See **anagnorisis**.

Refrain One or more identical or deliberately similar lines repeated throughout a poem, such as the final line of a stanza or a block of lines between stanzas or sections.

Resolution A satisfying outcome that effectively ends the conflict of a play.

Rhyme The repetition of the accented vowel sound of a word and all succeeding consonant sounds. See also **exact rhyme; slant rhyme**.

Rhyme royal An alternative term for **Chaucerian stanza** coined by King James I of Scotland in his poem *The Kingis Quair* ("The King's Book"), written about 1424.

Rhyme scheme The pattern of end-rhymes in a poem or stanza usually represented by a letter assigned to each word-sound, the same word-sounds having the same letter (e.g., a **quatrain's** rhyme scheme might be described as *abcb*).

Rhythm The patterned "movement" of language created by the choice of words and their arrangement, usually described through such metaphors as fast or slow, smooth or halting, graceful or rough, deliberate or frenzied, syncopated or disjointed. Rhythm in poetry is affected by, in addition to meter, such factors as line length; line endings; pauses (or lack of them) within lines; spaces within, at the beginning or end of, or between lines; word choice; and combinations of sounds.

Rising action The increasingly tense and complicated action leading up to the **climax** in a traditionally structured play.

Rising meter A **foot** (usually an iamb or an anapest) in which the final, accented syllable is preceded by one or two unaccented syllables, thus giving a sense of stepping up. Cf. **falling meter**.

Romance A play neither wholly comic nor wholly tragic, often containing elements of the supernatural. The best-known examples are Shakespeare's late plays, such as *The Winter's Tale* and *The Tempest*, which have a generally comic structure but are more ruminative in theme and spirit than traditional **comedy**.

Run-on line A line whose sense and grammatical structure continue into the next line. In the following lines by William Stafford ("Traveling through the Dark," p. 574), the first line is run-on, the second end-stopped: "Traveling through the dark I found a deer / dead on the edge of the Wilson River road." Also called *enjambment*. Cf. **end-stopped line**.

Sarcasm A harsh and cutting form of **verbal irony**, often involving apparent praise that is obviously not meant: "Oh, no, these are fine. I *prefer* my eggs thoroughly charred."

Satire A work, or manner within a work, employing **comedy** and **irony** to mock a particular human characteristic or social institution. Generally, a satirist wants the audience not only to laugh but also to change its opinions or actions. See, for example, Margaret Atwood's "Happy Endings" (p. 326).

Scansion The division of metrical verse into feet in order to determine and label its meter. Scanning a poem involves marking its stressed syllables with an accent mark (´) and its unstressed syllables with a curved line (˘), and using a vertical line to indicate the way a line divides into feet, then describing (or labeling) the type of foot used most often and the line length—that is, the number of feet in each line. See also **foot** and **line**.

Scene   One of the secondary divisions within an **act** of a play.

Secondary source   Outside source used in writing about literature: biographical, historical, or critical writing that discusses the literature but is not the literature itself. (The literature itself is considered a **primary source**.)

Sestet   The last six lines of an **Italian sonnet**.

Sestina   A lyric poem consisting of six six-line **stanzas** and a three-line concluding stanza (or "envoy"). The last words of the lines of the first stanza must be used as the last words of the lines of the other five stanzas in a specified pattern (the first line ends with the last word of the last line of the previous stanza, the second line with that of the first line of the previous stanza, the third line with that of the previous fifth line, the fourth line with that of the previous second line, the fifth line with that of the previous fourth line, the sixth line with that of the previous third line). The three-line envoy must use the end-words of lines 5, 3, and 1 from the first stanza, in that order, as its last words and must include the first stanza's other three end-words within its lines.

Set   The stage dressing for a play, consisting of backdrops, furniture, and similar large items.

Setting   One of the elements of fiction, setting is the context for the action: the time, place, culture, and atmosphere in which it occurs. A work may have several settings; the relation among them may be significant to the meaning of the work. In Nathaniel Hawthorne's "Young Goodman Brown" (p. 3), for example, the larger setting is seventeenth-century Puritan Salem, Massachusetts, but Brown's mysterious journey is set in a forest, and its prelude and melancholy aftermath are set in the village.

Shakespearean sonnet   See **English sonnet**.

Shaped poem   See **concrete poem**.

Short story   A short work of narrative fiction whose plot, characters, settings, point of view, style, and theme reinforce one another, often in subtle ways, creating an overall unity.

Simile   Expression of a direct similarity, using such words as *like*, *as*, or *than*, between two things usually regarded as dissimilar, as in "Shrinking from far *headlights pale as a dime*" (John Frederick Nims's "Love Poem," p. 571). It is important to distinguish *simile* from *comparison*, in which the two things joined by "like" or "as" are *not* dissimilar.

Single rhyme   A rhyme in which the stressed, rhyming syllable is the final syllable: *west* and *vest*, *away* and *today*. Formerly called "masculine rhyme."

Situational irony   The mood evoked when an action intended to have a certain effect turns out to have a different and more sinister effect. See Thomas Hardy's "The Convergence of the Twain" (p. 524).

Slant rhyme Consonance at the ends of lines; for example, *Room* and *Storm*, *firm* and *Room*, and *be* and *Fly* in Emily Dickinson's "I heard a Fly buzz—when I died" (p. 522). It can also be internal, if repeated enough to form a discernible pattern.

Socratic irony A pose of self-deprecation, or of belittling oneself, in order to tease the reader into deeper insight.

Soliloquy A speech delivered by a character who is alone onstage or otherwise out of hearing of the other characters. Since the character is effectively speaking to himself or herself, a soliloquy often serves as a window into the character's mind and heart.

Sonnet A fourteen-line poem usually written in **iambic pentameter**; originally lyrical love poems, sonnets came to be used also for meditations on religious themes, death, and nature and are now open to all subjects. Some variations in form have been tried: Sir Philip Sidney's "Loving in truth, and fain in verse my love to show" (1591) is written in hexameters; George Meredith wrote sixteen-line sonnets; John Milton's "On the New Forcers of Conscience under the Long Parliament," written around 1646, is a "caudate" (tailed) sonnet with a six-line coda appended; and Gerard Manley Hopkins designed "Pied Beauty" (p. 526) as a "curtal" (abbreviated) sonnet (six lines in place of the octave, then four lines, and a half-line ending in place of a sestet). See **English sonnet** and **Italian sonnet**.

Sonnet sequence A group of sonnets arranged so as to imply a narrative progression in the speaker's experience or attitudes; used especially in the sixteenth century. Also called a sonnet cycle.

Speaker The persona(e) voicing the poem. The speaker is sometimes the poet, though other times a poem may speak from a different perspective.

Spectacle The purely visual elements of a play, including the **sets**, costumes, **props**, lighting, and special effects. Of the six **elements of drama** he identified, Aristotle considered spectacle to be the least important.

Spenserian sonnet A variation of the **English sonnet** that employs the structure of three quatrains followed by a couplet but joins the quatrains by linking rhymes: *abab bcbc cdcd ee*.

Spenserian stanza A stanza of nine iambic lines, the first eight in pentameter and the ninth in hexameter, rhyming *ababbcbcc*. They are used in Edmund Spenser's *The Faerie Queene* (1590, 1596) and in such romantic narrative poems as John Keats's *The Eve of St. Agnes* (1820) and Percy Bysshe Shelley's *Adonais* (1824).

Spondee A metrical **foot** made up of two stressed syllables (ˊˊ), with no unstressed syllables. Spondees could not, of course, be the predominant foot in a poem; they are usually substituted for iambic or trochaic feet as a way of increasing emphasis, as in this line from John Donne's "Batter my heart, three-personed God" (1633): "As yet | but knock, | breathe, shine, | and seek | to mend."

Sprung rhythm See **accentual meter**.

1358 GLOSSARY OF CRITICAL AND LITERARY TERMS

Stage business Minor physical activity performed by actors on stage, often involving **props**, intended to strengthen **characterization** or modulate tension in a play.

Stage directions Written instructions in the script telling actors how to move on the stage or how to deliver a particular line. To facilitate the reading of scripts and to distinguish them from simple dialogue, stage directions are interspersed throughout the text, typically placed in parentheses and set in italics.

Stage left, stage right Areas of the stage seen from the point of view of an actor facing an audience. Stage left, therefore, is on the audience's right-hand side, and vice versa.

Stanza A grouping of poetic lines into a section, either according to form—each section having the same number of lines and the same prosody (see Sir Thomas Wyatt's "They flee from me," p. 451)—or according to thought, creating irregular units comparable to paragraphs in prose (see William Wordsworth's "Ode: Intimations of Immortality," p. 477).

Stichomythia Short lines of dialogue quickly alternating between two characters.

Stock character Any of a number of traditional characters easily identified by a single, stereotypical characteristic. Stock characters include innocent young women, rakish young men, clever servants, and so forth.

Stress See **accent**.

Strophe The first part of a choral **ode** in Greek drama. The strophe was traditionally sung as the **chorus** moved from **stage right** to **stage left**.

Structuralism Based on the work of anthropologists, linguists, and philosophers of the mid-twentieth century who sought to understand how humans think and communicate, structuralism is concerned with the cognitive and cultural structures that help us understand and interpret literary texts. The basic insight at the heart of the movement is the realization that we understand nothing in isolation, but rather that every piece of knowledge is part of a network of associations.

Structure (1) The framework—the general plan, outline, or organizational pattern—of a literary work; (2) narrower patterns within the overall framework. Cf. **form**.

Style One of the elements of fiction, style refers to the diction (choice of words), syntax (arrangement of words), and other linguistic features of a literary work. Just as no two people have identical fingerprints or voices, so no two writers use words in exactly the same way. Style distinguishes one writer's language from another's. William Faulkner and Ernest Hemingway, two major modern writers, had very different styles.

Subplot A secondary **plot** that exists in addition to the main plot and involves the minor characters. In **tragedy**, particularly, a subplot might provide **comic relief**.

Substitution The use of a different kind of foot in place of the one normally demanded by the predominant meter of a poem, as a way of adding variety, emphasizing the dominant foot by deviating from it, speeding up or slowing down the pace, or signaling a switch in meaning.

Subtext   The unspoken meaning, sense, or **motivation** of a scene or character.

Summary   A brief recap of the most important points in a work of literature, such as plot, character, setting, etc.

Surrealism   An artistic movement that attempted to portray or interpret the workings of the unconscious mind, especially as realized in dreams, by an irrational, noncontextual choice and arrangement of images or objects. Now more often used to refer to anything defying the normal sense of reality.

Syllabic verse   A metrical pattern in which all lines in a poem have the same number of **syllables** (as in Sylvia Plath's "Metaphors," p. 608) or all the first lines of its stanzas have the same number, all second lines the same, and so on (see Dylan Thomas's "Fern Hill," p. 575)—while the stressed syllables are random in number and placement.

Syllable   A unit of language consisting of one uninterrupted sound. "Ferry" (feh/ree) has two syllables, for example.

Symbol   Something that is itself and also stands for something else; a literary symbol is a prominent or repeated image or action that is present in a story, poem, or play and can be seen, touched, smelled, heard, tasted, or experienced imaginatively, but also conveys a cluster of abstract meanings beyond itself. Most critics agree that the wallpaper in Charlotte Perkins Gilman's "The Yellow Wallpaper" (p. 76), the tiger in William Blake's "The Tyger"

(p. 474), and the glass animals in Tennessee Williams's *The Glass Menagerie* (p. 921), for example, carry symbolic meaning. See also **archetype**.

Symbolism   The use of objects or events to suggest meaning beyond their immediate, physical presence. Symbolism exists in all genres of literature, but in drama it might include visual or sound elements as well as language.

Synecdoche   A special kind of **metonymy** in which a part of a thing is substituted for the whole, as in the commonly used phrases "give me a hand," "lend me your ears," or "many mouths to feed." See, for example, "whose *hands* shipwreck vases" and "For should your *hands* drop white and empty" (John Frederick Nims's "Love Poem," p. 571).

Synesthesia   Description of one kind of sense experience in relation to another, such as attribution of color to sounds ("blue notes") and vice versa ("a loud tie") or of taste to sounds ("sweet music"). See, for example, "With Blue—uncertain stumbling Buzz—" (Emily Dickinson's "I heard a Fly buzz—when I died," p. 522).

Tercet   A stanza of three lines, each usually ending with the same rhyme; but see **terza rima**. Cf. **triplet**.

Terza rima   A poetic form consisting of three-line **stanzas** (**tercets**) with interlinked rhymes, *aba bcb cdc ded efe*, and so on, made famous by Dante's use of it in *The Divine Comedy*.

Tetrameter   A poetic line with four metrical feet. Robert Frost's line "The woods are lovely, dark, and deep" ("Stopping by Woods on a Snowy

Evening," p. 540) is an example of iambic tetrameter.

Text Traditionally, a piece of writing. In recent **reader-response criticism**, "text" has come to mean the words with which the reader interacts; in this view, a story, poem, or play is not an object, not a shape on the page or a spoken performance, but what is apprehended and completed in the reader's mind.

Theater in the round A circular stage completely surrounded by seating for the audience.

Theater of the absurd/of cruelty See **Absurd, theater of the; Cruelty, theater of.**

Theme The central idea embodied by or explored in a literary work; the general concept, explicit or implied, that the work incorporates and makes persuasive to the reader. Other literary elements, including characters, plot, settings, point of view, figurative language, symbols, and style, contribute to a theme's development.

Thesis statement A few sentences, usually located toward the beginning of a paper, declaring the position the author plans to take on the proposed topic.

Third-person narrator The type of narration being used if a storyteller is not identified, does not speak of himself or herself with the pronoun *I*, asserts no connection between the narrator and the characters in the story, and tells the story with some objectivity and distance, using the pronouns *he, she, it,* and *they* — but not *I*. Eudora Welty chose third-person narration to

tell the moving story of Old Phoenix in "A Worn Path" (p. 216), because as a writer she wanted distance.

Title The name attached to a work of literature. For poetry, a title in some cases is an integral part of a poem and needs to be considered in interpreting it; see, for example, George Herbert's "The Collar" (p. 461). In other cases, a title has been added as a means of identifying a poem and is not integral to its interpretation. Sometimes a poem is untitled and the first line is used as a convenient way of referring to it, but should not be thought of as a title and does not follow the capitalization rules for titles.

Tone The implied attitude, or "stance," toward the subject and toward the reader or audience in a literary work; the "tone of voice" it seems to project (serious or playful; exaggerated or understated; formal or informal; ironic or straightforward; or a complex mixture of more than one of these). For example, the tone of Toni Cade Bambara's "The Lesson" (p. 330) is streetwise and tough, the voice of its first-person narrator.

Tragedy A play in which the **plot** moves from relative stability to death or other serious sorrow for the **protagonist**. A traditional tragedy is written in a grand style and shows a **hero** of high social stature brought down by **peripeteia** or by events beyond his or her control.

Tragicomedy A play in which **tragedy** and **comedy** are mingled in roughly equal proportion.

Transferred epithet A figure of speech in which a modifier that ought, strictly, to apply to one word is transferred to another word that it does not strictly fit. In "The drunk clambering on his undulant floor" (in John Frederick Nims's "Love Poem," p. 571), the drunk's perception, not the floor, is undulating.

Trimeter A poetic line with three metrical feet.

Triolet A verse form of eight lines with only two rhymes, rhyming *abaaabab*. The first two lines repeat in the last two lines, with the fourth line the same as the first line.

Triplet A group of three consecutive lines with the same rhyme, often used for variation in a long sequence of couplets. Cf. **tercet**.

Trochee A metrical **foot** consisting of two syllables, an accented one followed by an unaccented one (ˊ ˘). In trochaic meter, trochees are the predominant foot in a line or poem. The following lines from William Blake's introduction to *Songs of Innocence* (1789) are in trochaic meter (each line lacking the final unaccented syllable): "Píping | dówn thĕ | válleys | wíld, / Píping | Sóngs ŏf | pléasănt | glée, / Ŏn ă | clóud Ĭ | sáw ă | chíld, / Ańd hĕ | laúghing | sáid tŏ | me."

Understatement A figure of speech expressing something in an unexpectedly restrained way. Paradoxically, understatement can be a way of emphasizing something, of making people think "there must be more to it than that." When Mercutio in Shakespeare's *Romeo and Juliet*, after being stabbed by Tybalt, calls his wound "a scratch, a scratch" (3.1.92), he is understating, for the wound is serious—he calls for a

doctor in the next line, and he dies a few minutes later.

Unities The elements of a play that help an audience understand the play as a unified whole. Aristotle commented on the unities of time (the action of a play usually takes place within approximately one day) and action (the play should have a single, principal plot line). Renaissance critics added a third unity—unity of place (the play has only one main setting). Though Aristotle intended these merely as observations about the most successful dramas he had seen, some later playwrights took them as inflexible laws of drama.

Unity The oneness of a short story. Generally, each of a story's elements has a unity of its own, and all reinforce one another to create an overall unity. Although a story's unity may be evident on first reading, more often discovering the unity requires rereading, reflection, and analysis. Readers who engage in these actions experience the pleasure of seeing a story come to life.

Upstage As a noun or an adjective, the part of the stage farthest from the audience, at the back of the playing area. As a verb, to draw the audience's attention away from another actor onstage.

Verbal irony A figure of speech in which what is said is nearly the opposite of what is meant (such as saying "Lovely day out" when the weather actually is miserable). The name *Arnold Friend*, in Joyce Carol Oates's "Where Are You Going, Where Have You Been?" (p. 312), is an example, for Arnold is anything but a friend to Connie.

Villanelle A nineteen-line lyric poem divided into five **tercets** and a final four-line stanza, rhyming *aba aba aba aba aba abaa*. Line 1 is repeated to form lines 6, 12, and 18; line 3 is repeated to form lines 9, 15, and 19. See Elizabeth Bishop's "One Art" (p. 570) and Dylan Thomas's "Do not go gentle into that good night" (p. 576).

Voice The supposed authorial presence in poems that do not obviously employ **persona** as a distancing device.

Well-made play A type of play that rose to prominence in the nineteenth century and that relied for its effect on clever, causal plotting and a series of startling discoveries or revelations rather than on subtleties of character or language.

Lorna Dee Cervantes. "Freeway 280." From *Latin American Literary Review* 5, 10. Copyright © 1977. Reprinted by permission of the publisher, Latin American Literary Review.

Marilyn Chin. "How I Got That Name." From *The Phoenix Gone, the Terrace Empty* (Minneapolis: Milkweed Editions). Copyright © 1994 by Marilyn Chin. Reprinted by permission of Milkweed Editions.

Sandra Cisneros. From *The House on Mango Street*. Copyright © 1984 by Sandra Cisneros. Published by Vintage Books, a division of Random House, Inc. and in hardcover by Alfred A. Knopf in 1994. By permission of Susan Bergholz Literary Services, New York, NY, and Lamy, NM. All rights reserved.

Lucille Clifton. "at the cemetery, walnut grove plantation, south carolina, 1989." From *Quilting: Poems, 1987–1990*. Copyright © 1991 by Lucille Clifton. Reprinted with the permission of The Permissions Company, Inc. on behalf of BOA Editions, Ltd., www.boaeditions.org.

Judith Ortiz Cofer. "Cold as Heaven." From *Reaching for the Mainland and Selected New Poems* by Judith Ortiz Cofer. Copyright © 1995 by Bilingual Press/Editorial Bilingue. Reprinted by permission of the publisher.

Billy Collins. "I Chop Some Parsley While Listening to Art Blakey's Version of 'Three Blind Mice.'" From *Picnic, Lightning* by Billy Collins. Copyright © 1998. Reprinted by permission of the University of Pittsburgh Press.

Countee Cullen. "Incident." From *Color*. Copyright © 1925 Harper Bros., New York, NY. Renewed 1952 by Ida Cullen. Copyrights held by Amistad Research Center, Tulane University. Administered by Thompson and Thompson, Brooklyn, NY.

E. E. Cummings. "in Just-." Copyright 1923, 1951, © 1991 by the Trustees for the E. E. Cummings Trust and copyright © 1976 by George James Firmage. "next to of course god america i." Copyright 1926, 1954, © 1991 by the Trustees for the E. E. Cummings Trust and copyright © 1985 by George James Firmage, from *Complete Poems: 1904–1962* by E. E. Cummings, edited by George J. Firmage. Used by permission of Liveright Publishing Corporation.

Toi Derricotte. "A Note on My Son's Face." From *Captivity* by Toi Derricotte. Copyright © 1989. Reprinted by permission of the University of Pittsburgh Press.

Junot Diaz. From *Drown*. Copyright © 1996 by Junot Diaz. Used by permission of Riverhead Books, an imprint of Penguin Group (USA) Inc.

Emily Dickinson. "Wild nights—Wild nights!," "I like to see it lap the Miles," "It sifts from Leaden Sieves," "Much Madness is divinest Sense," "I heard a Fly buzz—when I died," and "Because I could not stop for Death" are reprinted by permission of the publishers and the Trustees of Amherst College from *The Poems of Emily Dickinson*, edited by Thomas H. Johnson, Cambridge, Mass.: The Belknap Press of Harvard University Press. Copyright © 1951, 1955, 1979, 1983 by the President and Fellows of Harvard College.

Mark Doty. "Tiara." From *Bethlehem in Broad Daylight* by Mark Doty. Reprinted by permission of David R. Godine, Publisher, Inc. Copyright © 1991 by Mark Doty.

Rita Dove. "Fifth Grade Autobiography." From *Grace Notes* by Rita Dove. Copyright © 1989 by Rita Dove. Used by permission of the author and W. W. Norton & Company, Inc.

Robert Duncan. "The Torso, Passages 18." From *Bending the Bow*. Copyright © 1968 by Robert Duncan. Reprinted by permission of New Directions Publishing Corp.

Cornelius Eady. "My Mother, If She Had Won Free Dance Lessons." From *Victims of the Latest Dance Craze*. Copyright © 1985 by Cornelius Eady. Reprinted by permission of the author.

T. S. Eliot. "The Love Song of J. Alfred Prufrock" and "Preludes." From *The Complete Poems and Plays, 1909–1950*. Reprinted with the permission of Faber & Faber Ltd.

Ralph Ellison. "Battle Royal." From *Invisible Man* by Ralph Ellison. Copyright © 1948 and renewed 1976 by Ralph Ellison. Used by permission of Random House, Inc.

Anita Endrezze. "The Girl Who Loved the Sky." From *At the Helm of Twilight* (Broken Moon Press). Copyright © 1992. Reprinted by permission of the author.

Martín Espada. "Latin Night at the Pawnshop." From *Alabanza* by Martín Espada. Copyright © 1990 by Martín Espada. Used by permission of the author and W. W. Norton & Company, Inc.

the Estate of Jane Kenyon. Reprinted with the permission of The Permissions Company, Inc. on behalf of Graywolf Press, Minneapolis, Minnesota, www.graywolfpress.org.

Jamaica Kincaid. "Girl." From *At the Bottom of the River* by Jamaica Kincaid. Copyright © 1983 by Jamaica Kincaid. Reprinted with permission by Farrar, Straus and Giroux, LLC.

Galway Kinnell. "The Bear." From *Body Rags*. Copyright © 1965, 1966, 1967 by Galway Kinnell. Reprinted by permission of Houghton Mifflin Harcourt Company. All rights reserved.

Etheridge Knight. "Hard Rock Returns to Prison from Hospital for the Criminal Insane." From *The Essential Etheridge Knight* by Etheridge Knight. Copyright © 1986.

Yusef Komunyakaa. "Facing It." From *Neon Vernacular*. Copyright © 1993 by Yusef Komunyakaa. Reprinted by permission of Wesleyan University Press.

Ted Kooser. "Student." From *Delights & Shadows*. Copyright © 2004 by Ted Kooser. Reprinted with the permission of The Permissions Company, Inc. on behalf of Copper Canyon Press, www.coppercanyonpress.org.

Maxine Kumin. "The Sound of Night." From *Halfway* by Maxine Kumin. Reprinted by permission of The Anderson Literary Agency Inc.

Stanley Kunitz. "The War against the Trees." From *The Collected Poems* by Stanley Kunitz. Copyright © 1957 by Stanley Kunitz.. Used by permission of the author and W. W. Norton & Company, Inc.

Jhumpa Lahiri. "Interpreter of Maladies." From *Interpreter of Maladies*. Copyright © 1999 by Jhumpa Lahiri. Reprinted by permission of Houghton Mifflin Harcourt Publishing Company. All rights reserved.

D. H. Lawrence. "The Rocking Horse Winner." From *Complete Short Stories of D. H. Lawrence* by D. H. Lawrence. Copyright © 1933 by the Estate of D. H. Lawrence, renewed © 1961 by Angelo Ravagli and C. M. Weekley, Executors of the Estate of Frieda Lawrence. Used by permission of Viking Penguin, a division of Penguin Group (USA) Inc.

Li-Young Lee. "Eating Alone" and "Visions and Interpretations." From *Rose*. Copyright © 1986 by Li-Young Lee. Reprinted with the permission of The Permissions Company, Inc. on behalf of BOA Editions, Ltd., www.boaeditions.org.

Denise Levertov. "Talking to Grief." From *Poems, 1972–1982*. Copyright © 1978 by Denise Levertov. Reprinted by permission of New Directions Publishing Corp.

Philip Levine. "What Work Is." From *What Work Is* by Philip Levine. Copyright © 1992 by Philip Levine. Used by permission of Alfred A. Knopf, a division of Random House, Inc.

Larry Levis. "The Poem You Asked For." From *Wrecking Crew* by Larry Levis. Copyright © 1972. Reprinted by permission of the University of Pittsburgh Press.

Audre Lorde. "Coal." From *Undersong: Chosen Poems Old and New*. Copyright © 1973, 1970, 1968 by Audre Lorde. Used by permission of W. W. Norton and Company, Inc.

Robert Lowell. "Skunk Hour." From *Selected Poems* by Robert Lowell. Copyright © 1976 by Robert Lowell. Reprinted by permission of Farrar, Straus and Giroux, LLC.

Heather McHugh. "What He Thought." From *Hinge & Sign* by Heather McHugh. Copyright © 1994 by Heather McHugh. Reprinted by permission of Wesleyan University Press.

Thylias Moss. "The Lynching." From *Rainbow Remnants in Rock Bottom Ghetto Sky* by Thylias Moss. Copyright © 1991 by Thylias Moss. Reprinted by permission of Persea Books, Inc., New York.

Marilyn Nelson. "Minor Miracle." From *The Fields of Praise: New and Selected Poems* is reprinted by permission of Louisiana State University Press. Copyright © 1997 by Marilyn Nelson.

Lorine Niedecker. "My Life by Water" in *The Granite Pail*. Copyright 1985 by Lorine Niedecker. Reprinted by permission of Bob Arnold for the Estate of Lorine Niedecker.

John Frederick Nims. "Love Poem." From *Selected Poems*. Copyright © 1982 by the University of Chicago Press. Reprinted by permission of the University of Chicago Press.

Lynn Nottage. "Poof!" From *Crumbs from the Table of Joy and Other Plays* by Lynn Nottage. Copyright © 1993, 2004 by Lynn Nottage. Published by Theatre Communications Group. Used by permission of Theatre Communications Group.

Mary Ruefle. "Barbarians." From *Life without Speaking* by Mary Ruefle (University of Alabama Press, 1987) is reprinted by permission of the author.

Anne Sexton. "Cinderella." From *Transformations*. Copyright © 1971 by Anne Sexton. Reprinted with the permission of Houghton Mifflin Harcourt Company. All rights reserved.

William Shakespeare. Notes to "Othello, the Moor of Venice" from *The Complete Works of Shakespeare*, 3rd ed., by David Bevington. Copyright © 1980 by Scott, Foresman and Company. Reprinted by permission of Pearson Education, Inc., Upper Saddle River, NJ.

Leslie Marmon Silko. "The Man to Send Rain Clouds." From *Storyteller* by Leslie Marmon Silko. Copyright © 1969, 1981 by Leslie Marmon Silko. "Prayer to the Pacific" from *Storyteller*. Copyright © 1981 by Leslie Marmon Silko. Used by permission of The Wylie Agency LLC.

Charles Simic. "Begotten of the Spleen." From *Selected Early Poems* by Charles Simic (New York: George Braziller, 1999). Copyright © 1999 by Charles Simic. Reprinted by permission of George Braziller, Inc.

Gary Snyder. "Hitch Haiku." From *The Back Country*. Copyright © 1968 by Gary Snyder. Reprinted by permission of New Directions Publishing Corp.

Cathy Song. "Heaven." From *Frameless Windows, Squares of Light: Poems* by Cathy Song. Copyright © 1988 by Cathy Song. Used by permission of W. W. Norton & Company, Inc.

Sophocles. *Oedipus Rex of Sophocles: An English Version* by Dudley Fitts and Robert Fitzgerald. Copyright © 1949 by Harcourt, Inc. and renewed 1977 by Cornelia Fitts and Robert Fitzgerald. Reprinted by permission of Houghton Mifflin Harcourt Publishing Company. Caution: All rights, including professional, amateur, motion picture, recitation, lecturing, performance, public reading, radio broadcasting, and television, are strictly reserved. Inquiries on all rights should be addressed to Harcourt, Inc., Permissions Dept., Orlando, FL 32887-6777.

Gary Soto. "Moving Away." From *New and Selected Poems*. Copyright © 1995 by Gary Soto. Used with permission of Chronicle Books LLC, San Francisco. Visit ChronicleBooks.com.

William Stafford. "Traveling through the Dark." From *The Way It Is: New and Selected Poems*. Copyright © 1972, 1998 by William Stafford and the Estate of William Stafford. Reprinted with the permission of The Permissions Company, Inc. on behalf of Graywolf Press, Minneapolis, Minnesota, www.graywolfpress.org.

Gerald Stern. "The Dog." From *Leaving Another Kingdom: Selected Poems* by Gerald Stern. Copyright © 1990 by Gerald Stern. Reprinted by permission of the author.

Wallace Stevens. "The Anecdote of the Jar" and "The Emperor of Ice-Cream." From *The Collected Poems of Wallace Stevens*. Copyright © 1954 by Wallace Stevens and renewed 1982 by Holly Stevens. Used by permission of Alfred A. Knopf, a division of Random House, Inc.

Mark Strand. "Eating Poetry." From *Selected Poems* by Mark Strand. Copyright © 1979, 1980 by Mark Strand. Used by permission of Alfred A. Knopf, a division of Random House, Inc.

Virgil Suárez. "Tea Leaves, Caracoles, Coffee Beans." From *90 Miles: Selected and New Poems* by Virgil Suárez. Copyright © 2005. Reprinted by permission of the University of Pittsburgh Press.

Sekou Sundiata. "Blink Your Eyes." Copyright © 1995 by Sekou Sundiata. Reprinted with permission.

Amy Tan. "Two Kinds." From *The Joy Luck Club* by Amy Tan. Copyright © 1989 by Amy Tan. Used by permission of G. P. Putnam's Sons, a division of Penguin Group (USA) Inc.

James Tate. "The Wheelchair Butterfly." From *Selected Poems*. Copyright © 1991 by James Tate. Reprinted by permission of the author.

Dylan Thomas. "Fern Hill," copyright © 1945 by The Trustees for the Copyrights of Dylan Thomas. "Do Not Go Gentle into That Good Night," copyright © 1952 by Dylan Thomas, from *The Poems of Dylan Thomas*. Reprinted by permission of New Directions Publishing Corp.

Jean Toomer. "Face." From *Cane* by Jean Toomer. Copyright © 1923 by Boni & Liveright and renewed 1951 by Jean Toomer. Used by permission of Liveright Publishing Corporation.

Natasha Trethewey. "History Lesson." From *Domestic Work*. Copyright © 1994, 2000 by

Natasha Trethewey. Reprinted with the permission of The Permissions Company, Inc. on behalf of Graywolf Press, www.graywolfpress.org.

Quincy Troupe. "A Poem for 'Magic.'" From *Avalanche*. Copyright © 1996 by Quincy Troupe. Reprinted with the permission of The Permissions Company, Inc. on behalf of Coffee House Press, www.coffeehousepress.org.

John Updike. "A & P." From *Pigeon Feathers and Other Stories* by John Updike. Copyright © 1962 and renewed 1990 by John Updike. Used by permission of Alfred A. Knopf, a division of Random House, Inc.

Alice Walker. "Everyday Use." From *In Love and Trouble: Stories of Black Women* by Alice Walker. Copyright © 1973 by Alice Walker. Reprinted by permission of Houghton Mifflin Harcourt Publishing Company.

James Welch. "Christmas Comes to Moccasin Flat." From *Riding the Earthboy 40* by James Welch. Copyright © 1971 by James Welch. Reprinted by permission of Markson Thoma Literary Agency.

Eudora Welty. "The Worn Path." From *A Curtain of Green and Other Stories* by Eudora Welty. Copyright © 1941 and renewed 1969 by Eudora Welty. Reprinted by permission of Houghton Mifflin Harcourt Publishing Company.

Richard Wilbur. "Love Calls Us to the Things of the World." From *Things of the World*. Copyright © 1956 and renewed 1984 by Richard Wilbur. Reprinted by permission of Houghton Mifflin Harcourt Publishing Company.

Nancy Willard. "Questions My Son Asked Me, Answers I Never Gave Him." From *Household Tales of Moon and Water*. Copyright © 1978 by Nancy Willard. Reprinted by permission of Houghton Mifflin Harcourt Publishing Company.

Tennessee Williams. "The Glass Menagerie." Copyright © 1945 and renewed 1973 by The University of The South. Reprinted by permission of Georges Borchardt, Inc. for the Estate of Tennessee Williams.

William Carlos Williams. "The Red Wheelbarrow," "This Is Just to Say," and "Spring and All." From *Collected Poems: 1909–1939*, Volume I. Copyright © 1938 by New Directions Publishing Corp. Reprinted by permission of New Directions Publishing Corp.

August Wilson. *Fences* by August Wilson. Copyright © 1986 by August Wilson. Used by permission of Dutton Signet, a division of Penguin Group (USA) Inc.

Charles Wright. "March Journal." From *The World of Ten Thousand Things: Poems, 1980–1990*. Copyright © 1990 by Charles Wright. Reprinted by permission of Farrar, Straus and Giroux, LLC.

James Wright. "A Blessing." From *The Branch Will Not Break* by James Wright. Copyright © 1963 by James Wright. Reprinted by permission of Wesleyan University Press.

W. B. Yeats. "Leda and the Swan" and "Sailing to Byzantium." From *The Collected Works of W. B. Yeats, Volume One: The Poems*, revised by W. B. Yeats, edited by Richard J. Finneran. Copyright © 1928 by The Macmillan Company and renewed 1956 by Georgie Yeats. All rights reserved. Reprinted with the permission of Scribner, a Division of Simon & Schuster, Inc.

Al Young. "A Dance for Ma Rainey." Copyright © 1969, 1972 by Al Young. Reprinted by permission of the author.

Ray A. Young Bear. "From the Spotted Night." From *The Invisible Musician*. Copyright © 1990 by Ray A. Young Bear. Reprinted with the permission of The Permissions Company, Inc. on behalf of Holy Cow! Press, www.holycowpress.org.

Paul Zimmer. "The Poet's Strike" by Paul Zimmer from *Crossing to Sunlight: Selected Poems* (1996). Copyright © 1989 by Paul Zimmer. Used by permission of Paul Zimmer.

Art Credit:

"Landscape with the Fall of Icarus," c.1555 (oil on canvas). Bruegel, Pieter the Elder (c.1525–69) / Musées Royaux des Beaux-Arts de Belgique, Brussels, Belgium / Giraudon / The Bridgeman Art Library.

Index of Authors, Titles,
and First Lines